Gun Digest

37th Anniversary

1983 Deluxe Edition

EDITED BY KEN WARNER

DBI BOOKS, INC., NORTHFIELD, ILL.

OUR COVER GUNS

FRONT COVER

Weaver broke into stainless in time to harmonize their new handgun scope with the many new stainless steel handguns currently entering the marketplace. This, the latest offering from Weaver, will undoubtedly appeal to hunters and shooters who are looking for a rugged, moisture-resistant, steel-bodied scope. Naturally, the Weaver rings and base are finished to match. For more details, see Scopes and Mounts Review, page 174.

INSIDE COVERS

Front: It was with the Standard Automatic that Ruger success began, so when time came to phase that splendid design out to make room for an improved model, a certain Ruger flair was applied: the last 5,000 will be stainless, and signed like this. For those who remember—the wood box is what Ruger Standard Autos were first shipped in.

Back: The future has a 12-gauge Red Label Ruger in it, and a scaled-up 20-gauge, which is what this gun is, feels pretty good. The geometric curves, the flat planes—they are Ruger, too. There are no 20-gauges safer or stouter than the Red Label; that will be true in 12-gauge, too.

KW

GUN DIGEST STAFF

EDITOR-IN-CHIEF
Ken Warner
ASSISTANT TO THE EDITOR
Lilo Anderson
SENIOR STAFF EDITOR
Harold A. Murtz
ASSOCIATE EDITOR
Robert S. L. Anderson
PRODUCTION MANAGER
Pamela J. Johnson
CONTRIBUTING EDITORS
Bob Bell
Dean A. Grennell
Rick Hacker
Edward A. Matunas
Layne Simpson
Larry S. Sterett
Hal Swiggett
J.B. Wood
EUROPEAN CORRESPONDENT
Raymond Caranta
EDITOR EMERITUS
John T. Amber
PUBLISHER
Sheldon L. Factor

DBI BOOKS INC.

PRESIDENT
Charles T. Hartigan
VICE PRESIDENT & PUBLISHER
Sheldon L. Factor
VICE PRESIDENT — SALES
John G. Strauss
TREASURER
Frank R. Serpone

ISBN 0-910676-43-7   **Library of Congress Catalog #44-3588**

Stuart Otteson Wins $1,000 John T. Amber Award

The John T. Amber Literary Award for excellent writing in the 1982 GUN DIGEST was presented to Stuart Otteson for his design story of the Remington 721-722 rifles. The award was based on the judgment of a panel of firearms publication editors who rated ten articles nominated by Editor-in-Chief Ken Warner.

"We're happy to see our judgment confirmed by others," said Chuck Hartigan, DBI Books president, on announcing the award, "since Otteson's article opened the 1982 book, and we're even happier at the caliber of writing represented in the whole list of candidates."

Announced in the 1982 GUN DIGEST, this competition is named for Editor Emeritus John T. Am-

Writers like recognition and money and here in this picture Stuart Otteson (left) gets both from Editor Ken Warner—that paper is the $1,000 check for the John T. Amber Literary Award.

ber, who guided the DIGEST for nearly 30 years. The payment of $1,000 is in addition to the regular author's fee, paid on acceptance.

GUN DIGEST is one of the few firearms and outdoors publications to have a tradition of literary prizes and cash awards unrelated to subscriptions. Editor Amber instituted the Townsend Whelen Memorial Award in 1967 and it has been awarded each year since, though it was not awarded for 1982.

For writers, GUN DIGEST is an ideal forum in which to compete. It offers something like 200 pages of freelanced material each issue, all of it filtered professionally to reach the best possible mix of current events, technical news, scholarship and history, advice and counsel, and, sometimes, sheer entertainment in firearms.

The other nine candidates for excellence in the 1982 GUN DIGEST included, in alphabetical order:

Bill Davidson: Raising Kids with Guns
Dan L. Flores: Whitetails: North America's Challenge
Rick Hacker: As Authentic As A Hawken
Bob Hagel: Modern Cartridge Failure and Success
Ashley Halsey, Jr.: Long Rifles With Smooth Bores
Wallace Labisky: Shotgun Choke/Its History and Mystery
John W. Sanders: Swivel Guns Of Southeast Asia
Donald M. Simmons: Single-Action Safety
Layne Simpson: A Fresh Look At The Old Standards.

The competition continues. There will be another $1,000 John T. Amber Award made to a writer whose work appears in this edition.

Don't Shoot Hot Load

Two editions ago, in an article by Nick Sisley (1981 GUN DIGEST, No. 35, pages 59-61), a load of Hercules Red Dot that simply should not be fired in a shotgun was mentioned. The load was 18 grains of Red Dot with 1⅜ths ounce of shot. If you have been using it in the mistaken idea it was OK, stop forthwith. If it is in your plans, cancel them.

How this or any other inadvertence occurs is not germane, but one is bound to speculate. It could be here that a typing error no one caught gave 1⅜ instead of 1⅛. Maybe the wrong powder slipped in.

The purpose of the whole exercise was to give upland shooters wider patterns. That is why the author was discussing so heavy a load as 1⅜ ounces in the first place. They were to be, of course, 1⅜ ounces at standard velocities. The given load of Red Dot is simply far too hot; don't use it. Some ballisticians tell us it could blow up your gun with the first shot.

Please turn to page 92.

CONTENTS

FEATURES

Six Working Guns
by Robert K. Sherwood 6

How Choke Works
by Arvid B. Pedersen 12

Make That Big Trip Now
by Stuart Williams.. 18

The Holes In Stopping Power Theory
by Leon Day.. 24

Crumpler!!
by Jeff Cooper.. 29

GUN DIGEST Discussion No. 2:
The Shape of Stocks
by Norm Nelson 34
by Dave Petzal.. 35

Elko Arms Double Rifle
by John T. Amber.. 40

Troublesome Cartridges
by Edward A. Matunas.. 46

Computers Look At Accuracy For You
by David Leestma.. 54

Black Powder Review
by Rick Hacker 60

The Maligned .410 Bore
by Marshall R. Williams.. 67

Early 22 Auto Pistols
by Charles E. Petty.. 72

Sixty Million Guns
by L. R. Wallack 80

How It Was In The Medium Good Old Days
by Roy Dunlap.. 89

Handguns Today: Sixguns and Others
by Hal Swiggett.. 94

Handguns Today: Autoloaders
by J. B. Wood 103

Long Guns In Review
by Layne Simpson 116

Delightful Doubles
by Don Zutz.. 126

Great Guns and Accessories in full color 129

The Pneumo-Nimrod At Work
by J. I. Galan.. 153

Handloading To Date
by Dean A. Grennell.. 159

A New Slice of Zeiss
by Harold A. Murtz 164

The Ultimate Turkey-Shoot Pistol
by Ashley Halsey, Jr. 168

Scopes and Mounts
by Bob Bell.. 174

Great Arc of the Wild Sheep Guides
by James L. Carkhuff 183

Small Game Takes A Small Bore
        by Toby Bridges 190

Murata Types 13 and 18
        by Charles S. Small 196

The One That Never Was
        by Tom Turpin.. 200

The Sauer 38H Story
        by Donald M. Simmons 204

Sporting Arms of the World
        by Larry S. Sterett.. 216

One Magnum That Works
        by Norman Rowcliff 222

Is An Ounce Of Shot Enough?
        by Dave Duffey 227

Especially Good Books 232

TESTFIRE:
    Three Short Shotguns 236
    FIE's Super Titan II... 238
    Short 1100 Magnum... 239
    The Beeman/Webley Vulcan 240
    Mayflower Drawtube Scope 241
    Sanftl Schuetzen Rifle 242
    Rossi's 62 SAC 243
    Interdynamics KG-9 244

Lenard M. Brownell (1922-1982) 245

The Hunter Specials
        by Lowell Manley 246

Custom Guns 248

Custom Revolvers: A Special Look
        by Ken Warner 250

Seminars 1981:
    Remington 252
    Winchester... 253
    Colt's New Mark V 254
    Sturm, Ruger, Inc. 256

Art of the Engraver 258

The Shows of Europe:
    IWA '82 / Hunfishow '82
        by Raymond Caranta 260
    World Hunting Exposition
        by Sidney Du Broff 262

O.K. Corral Commemorative Gun
        by Don Shumar 263

Shooter's Showcase 264

Ammunition, Ballistics, and Components
        by Edward A. Matunas.................................... 266

Ammunition Tables 275

DEPARTMENTS

The Complete Compact Catalog	279	Chokes and Brakes	427
Handguns—U.S. and Imported	280	Metallic Sights	428
Rifles—U.S. and Imported	317	Scopes and Mounts	431
Shotguns—U.S. and Imported	362	Arms Associations	438
Black Powder Guns	392	Arms Library	440
Air Guns	411	Directory of the Arms Trade	453

SIX WORKING GUNS

by ROBERT K. SHERWOOD

Sherwood spends a lot of time on the sage flats and if he has no rifle, he has this handgun. Since his draggle-tail holster works, he doesn't need another one.

YOU COULD say I am a gun person. Guns have been a part, and a large one at that, of both my personal and professional life, and there haven't been too many days in the last 30-odd years that I haven't carried or worn one.

I have a lot of guns, some I've needed and some I haven't really, and there isn't anything fancy about any of them, except for accuracy in a few cases. In fact they are so plain-Jane I never considered them of much interest, until Ken Warner looked over my pile of utilitarian iron and remarked:

ish off, there were occasional specimen collection jobs, and there were a few depredations that could only be handled by a Speer tranquilizer. There was even the then-remote possibility that some non-intellectual might try to put the bash on a hapless minion in the Thin Green Line.

The rough and tumble treatment accorded a horse and jeep gun dictated a highly durable rifle or carbine with well-protected non-fragile iron sights. It had to be cheap; you could get it stolen or lose it when the boat turned over. It had to have sufficient power; assaulting even a crippled elk with a

There were a lot of times when my filling my own deer or bear tag did not interfere with my duties, and I took both with the 303. It was an ideal saddle gun for horse and snow-machine work.

It grouped at 100 yards at something around three inches; perhaps some will sneer at that, but I never did. I could put a 150- or 180-grain bullet ahead of an animal's diaphragm out to about 300 yards, and that was all I needed. The best group you can get has just one hit—between the tank and the whistle.

Of course, I loaded for it, working

No one has taken files and emery paper to dress up this old 357 Blackhawk. It has come to look this tough naturally, grinding away the years since 1958, putting in hard time.

. . . they lose their pretty, but they don't lose their good if they were good to start with . . .

"You have a story in six of those, if you care to write it."

So I picked six working guns to tell you about:

Some of the hardest and most copious work has been the lot of a British 303, the relative of the SMLE better known as the Jungle Carbine; it has but an 18.5″ barrel and was designed for jungle warfare. I got it back when Conservation Officers were still servicing dinosaur depredation complaints and I had gone to work for the Idaho Fish and Game Department.

An officer or biologist needed a rifle in his pickup or saddle scabbard. There were wounded animals to fin-

30-cal. Army carbine is something like purifying stockyard wastes with Pine-Sol. It is nice to have a big magazine, which puts a day's (or more) shells in the gun.

A $16.00 303 has just been described.

So I had a lifetime utility gun for hard odd jobs; and it has done a lot of those. I took a renegade bull buffalo with it, up on the Cave Falls road; I shot crippled and almost lost deer, elk, antelope and moose for hapless tyro hunters; and I shot coyotes, foxes, badgers and bobcats with it, sometimes for pesticide sampling and sometimes for their salable hides.

up a good one or two with each bullet weight to be used. The best for the 150-grain Speer spitzer was a bit over 40 grains of 4064, and I propelled Speer's 180-grain and Hornady's 174-grain round-noses with measured 4350, or maybe all the 4831 I could get in the case comfortably.

The rifle has survived horse wrecks, truck turnovers and shipboard disasters losing no accuracy and gaining only a few more dents than those inflicted on it by the original British custodian. It is now the extra rifle kept in the deer camps in case some dude has a nasty and wrecks a fragile scoped sporter.

It has always worked and still will. The day is past when one can readily pick up a cast-off military for a utility gun; most are worn out or rusting away in idleness. It might be well for some major manufacturer to produce a work-horse carbine like the Jungle Carbine, a working gun for working men.

Back when colleges handed out stone diplomas, I got one and bought myself a graduation present, a 357 Ruger Blackhawk, serial #4653, with a 4⅝-inch barrel. That was the only length I could get in 1958.

Author would rather have had almost any other gun along when he had to kill this bobcat, but the 357 Ruger got it done.

Then I took the job with Idaho F&G. I needed a sidearm now and then, and they didn't issue them; having neither a police-approved double action nor the money to buy one, I just walked along beside the Blackhawk and behind the badge for 20 years. I wasn't an entirely approved policeman anyway, just a working cowboy gone wrong and went to college.

For that brand of law enforcement the single action was adequate. It even had a few advantages over the ratchet-blasters, namely durability. It has fewer moving parts and is less likely to malfunction. The Blackhawk has a lot of weight in the front end and will substitute for a sap better than any double action in cases of extreme uproar. There is no difference in accuracy potential. Obviously, a double-action revolver loads and unloads a lot faster than the thumb-buster; most shoot-outs take place over ranges of

seven yards or less and are likely to finish in the first five rounds.

Some practice will have the officer unshucking and reloading his single action in nearly unbelievable time. After the Department got into such niceties as revolver issue and qualification, I and another Ruger fan qualified over the standard double action course several times with our Blackhawks. I continued to carry it for a duty arm and still would today.

Through the years I'd frequently take vacation time and work for a Montana outfitter or two as a guide. I usually took the Ruger along. If a guide is carrying a rifle, or has one on his saddle, then the best handgun for him is a 22. If he is carrying a revolver and nothing else, then it had better be a big one. I wore the Blackhawk a lot when pulling pack-string; I killed two deer, a bear and several coyotes with it. It did the job, although poorly on one deer. That was due to the combination of a hard bullet and an underload of powder.

I didn't care much for the factory ammunition results; I had trouble getting bullet expansion with them too. I had a few hundred Norma half-jackets with very soft cores that did much better than anything else. They weighed 160 grains and I launched them with enough 2400. The effect of this load on a deer was about the equivalent of a 32-40 carbine I once carried. Normas don't seem to be that common any more, but Speer makes

an excellent 160-grain half-jacket and my tests on wet paper and jugs of stock molasses indicate that it should be a good game bullet, too.

You can lose a rifle in an avalanche or impromptu rodeo; if you are wearing a good sixgun in protective leather you are always armed all the way through the aftershock. It goes where you go. So I still carry the Blackhawk, as I have for thousands of trail miles. It has worked for me; it will until I die. Then it will work for my son, has he need of it. They don't wear out, even if they do lose their pretty.

Multitudes are no doubt now wondering if I have any cannon in the battery for any purpose other than absolute utility. While it has served utilitarian purposes, my best-beloved sporter (BBS) is and has been used primarily in sport. It might even not be best beloved; it has some competition from some of the harem sisters; but it is not pure utility.

Said BBS is a Husqvarna Crown Grade, chambered for the 6.5mm Swedish military round. I talked it out of Tradewinds back in the '60s with some of the most adept linguistics I ever performed.

We don't hear much of Husqvarna lately; the brand name and the mildly adulterated 98 Mauser design have faded without much logical explanation. They were very handsome and durable arms, featuring fine workmanship and excellent materials. They were usually lighter and more graceful than their American counterparts. And they would shoot better than anyone could hold them.

At least mine did. Twice I took antelope at 400-plus yards with it, and once I anesthetized a coyote at a measured 346 yards, him stepping high and far at the time. Once, to satisfy conventional curiosity and ego gratification, I even benched it, using sandbags and armrests and a concrete chair, and shot 10 rounds into a half-inch, measured across centers.

Most of the ballistics published on the 6.5x55 were taken using the Swedish 94 Mauser carbine with its 17.7-inch barrel. The 23.75-inch sleeve of the Crown Grade gave substantially better velocities. I obtained the following figures with an Oehler 33 chronograph:

Bullet/grs.	Velocity, (fps)	Best group 5 rounds
Nosler 125	2894	1.2″
Speer 120	2933	.5″
Speer 100	3000	1.0″
Sierra 140	2735	.9″
Norma 160	2554	1.1″

I am not currently looking for better velocities, trajectory or groups.

I carried the Crown Grade for much of my personal hunting, killing deer, antelope, goats, elk, bears and a moose with it. It required one (1) chest section hit to flop any of these where the bullet hit him. I concluded that since dead was all they could be, any further power would merely go out the other side of the animal. The 6.5x55 was and is all the rifle I need for Western big game hunting.

I carried the CG while guiding elk hunters and it did the work I had for it. The most important shooting a guide does is to finish a badly-shot animal some dude has bobbled. The guide has almost no time to make it good, and good it had better be. He wants to blow blood and bone meal all over the hillside behind when he sees a bull hump from a gut shot or run on three while flopping one. He wants a fast-handling rifle with tack-smacking accuracy. That is my 6.5; it comes up fast and throws as good as I hold it, and that is the upper limit of things you can say about a rifle for that work.

Every battery should feature a luxury gun or two, those that you could do without but would feel very deprived. I bought my Savage Model 99-A 250-3000 because I didn't need it. I had excellent scoped sporters, saddle guns and truck rifles, but I have always had a failing for fast-handling lever guns and am emotional about accuracy. Most lever guns don't scope well and a lot of them have pie-plate accuracy, but the Savage 99 is a lovely exception. I found I had both a fine long range sporter and a good saddle gun in one with it. In it, the right loads will go under an inch and a half.

I didn't get my 99 for work, but luck and confusion found me guiding mule deer hunters last fall with the 250 in my saddle scabbard. When the season was over I wished I'd carried it for work in other years. It was all the deer-guide rifle anyone would need; I have never carried a better one. The weight, length, balance and accuracy were right for the job.

The 250 has a paper credit of something like 30-30 power and 250 yards range limit; perhaps it can't read. I have shot deer and antelope a little past 300 yards with it and had them collapse like a blown balloon. I have had a very high percentage of down-

No change in twenty more years, except more lumps and less metal finish for this No. 5 Rifle. The ballistics have been adequate, the precision sufficient, and the durability remarkable.

This buffalo needed killing and Sherwood in his civilian clothes was sent to do the job and between him and his 303 it got done.

This Crown Grade Husqvarna in 6.5x55mm is Sherwood's Best Beloved Sporter, has proven remarkably accurate and able on a wide variety of shots over the years.

A relative newcomer to the Sherwood stable is this Savage 99A in 250 Savage. The recoil pad was there when the gun arrived; also inherent was the capacity to be a working gun out West.

It doesn't look right, but it does very well, this Fox Model B once rearranged for a woman and now operated by six-foot Sherwood. It hits, so relatively open chokes and a gauge of 16 don't hurt.

Here it is, the one and only 22 rifle Sherwood has ever associated with longer than a day, but he's been with this one 40-odd years and still trusts it.

right-now kills with it; my experience with the 30-30 featured a lot of tracking of well-hit animals, not always very far, but it did not often knock the props out from under them on impact. The 250 shows considerable advantage in practical terms.

You get a lot from a 250, and you get it without much uproar. Muzzle blast is negligible and recoil is the least you can get short of none. Mine came with a kick pad on it, which is kind of like having a roll bar on a tricycle.

I have found that powders of medium burning rate give the best accuracy, especially when combined with the lighter bullets, those weighing 100 grains or less. My pet load for it puts Norma 203 behind a 100-grain Speer; it is accurate and a good killer.

Sometimes it is well to spoil one luxury with another. I figure my wife, the Famous Charlotte, must be a luxury; good wives are scarce and dear. I gave her the 250 and she goes about mashing meat deer with no unpleasant side effects. This is a further example of gainful use of a good working gun.

Sometimes some of the best working guns are not expected to be that at all. My Fox Model B is a prime example. I bought it back before the Wheel for a wife who shortly became an ex-wife. Because of her short arms, I had the stock shortened a full 1¾-inch and even with the kick pad, its back end looks like a pistol gone wrong. The gauge is 16, which more and more shooters are calling a bastard round.

After some divorce and much disaster, I found myself with one shotgun to my name and it was this economy grade lady gun. I had been shooting a full choke Winchester Model 12 pump and it was with grave apprehension that I faced a shooting season with nothing but a butchered double, bored improved and modified, with barrels only 26 inches long.

After the season was over and the house was full of feathers, I never considered serious use of another shotgun. It wasn't supposed to fit me but I found my snap-shooting hits on rising birds were far more frequent than with any other scatterblaster I had ever carried. I could pass-shoot creditably with it; I took a lot of ducks and geese that year.

I soon ceased to lament the late pump gun, although I couldn't understand why I didn't miss more high birds with it than with the pump. Then an old Conservation Officer pointed out the Roberts grain elevator to me and asked me how much higher than that did I try for a bird? I said I

never tried for one that high, and he told me the elevator was 47 yards tall. I apparently would not shoot at a bird more than 35 yards from the muzzle of any shotgun—so the modified choke was fine, giving me more birds with its bigger pattern. The bedsheet-sized spreads from the improved cylinder were boosting my birds-rounds ratio markedly. As for geese, if you wait until they get inside 25 yards, you can kill them with about anything that will hit them. If they are out beyond 30 yards you can have a crippling loss with anything you can stand behind. With my shotgun range limits, the 16 was a helluva goose gun; it hit them.

The Famous Charlotte, her Famous Grin, the Famous 250, and a regular eating buck, all loaded and en route to the freezer without fuss.

I liked the double triggers and the instant choice of choke. You can say it wasn't engineered for a six-footer that buys 35-inch shirtsleeves, but it kills more birds with fewer shells than shotguns that supposedly fit me. If I ever come down with a fancier shotgun it will be bored, stagged and stocked like my Fox 16-gauge. It works for me.

You have to start somewhere, as Columbus said to the codfish, and I started, as did many, with a Winchester 22. At the aspiring age of 9 I swapped a foolish lady out of a Model 62-A pump gun. It was the first, last and only 22 rifle I have owned; I'm not sure I'll ever want another.

Takedowns are said to lack accuracy, especially those with one sight on the front end and the other on the back end. Those who say that are theorizing more than practicing. I

shot the 62-A for 10 years because it was the only 22 I had and then I shot it for the next 30 years because it was the only 22 I wanted. It got all the use a ranch gun usually gets. With it, I beheaded chickens for the pot and market, shot ground squirrels, skunks and marmots for sport, chicken hawks supposedly to protect the chickens and a vast assortment of small game to eat. If I didn't hit with it, it was because I didn't hold that well. It was and is quite accurate.

I shot jackrabbits for the market in later years, and it often earned a place in elk-camp cook tents, as a grouse and rabbit gun for the idle to use. I cannot compute the number of species I have taken with it, let alone the number of creatures. I collected birds and animals for mercury analysis and for PCB determinations after the Teton Flood, in my Department work.

Most important, I taught both myself and my children to shoot with it. It gave us a pass through the gate to the shooting world. Whenever we fire whatever we fire during our multi-varied shooting lives, we'll be using what we first learned with that fine, battered Winchester Model 62-A.

And after puncturing all those birds, beasts, and beer cans, it still shoots well. Winchester should make more like it.

Thus are six working guns of mine own use. Others might have equalled their performance; few could have bettered it. The job done or meat on the table is what counts. ●

HOW CHOKE WORKS

by ARVID B. PEDERSEN

This is simple, so simple it deceives: you have never read it before.

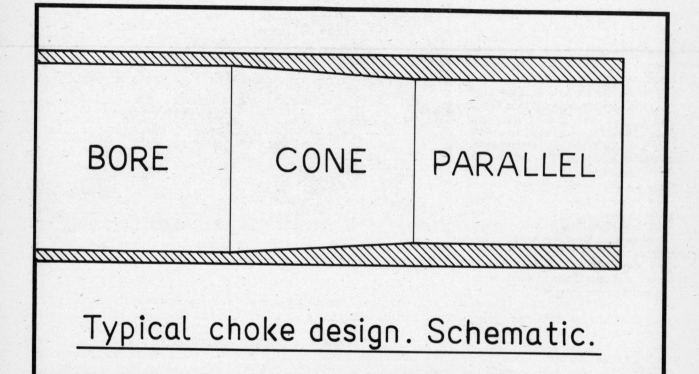

BORE   CONE   PARALLEL

Typical choke design. Schematic.

THE ART OF shooting by virtue of a multiple pellet charge may not have been long established before ever-complaining mankind noticed the reduced range when compared to the single bullet. Now the ideal became the shot barrel delivering its charge most bullet-like, and every possible—and impossible—way of boring was tried out for the purpose.

Late in the 18th century there appear to have been a few individual successes in increasing the range of shotgunning by some sort of choke, but choke boring as a regular feature did not evolve until 100 years later with W. W. Greener in the center of the final development. After him, only minor deviations have appeared and, in fact, no definite improvement can be claimed.

How the choke actually managed to control the pellets remained obscure. It was accepted without much reasoning that constriction of the muzzle meant constriction of the flow of pellets all the way, as it is even today. At the end of the 19th century, however, when the great French authority General Journée advanced into the problems of shotgunning, he was just not the man to relax on practical proof of choke function.

The Journée Theory

After circling the problem theoretically and by numerous experiments, he ventured a conclusion shown in our drawing, which is faithfully redrawn from his celebrated treatise *"Tir des fusils de chasse."*

His accompanying text is not very

specific, but apparently he attributes the concentrating effect to the inward-acting impulses on the pellets striking the sloping wall of the choke cone. The force directs the pellets toward the axis of the bore, and this concentrating effect is supposed to remain effective at shooting range. He himself acknowledged that the drawing was schematic to a degree making it misleading, and doubt probably made him refrain from a detailed verbal description.

Despite this vagueness but on the weight of his authority, the Journée theory has greatly influenced later views on choke function. Even in our day the spell of the old Frenchman is still unmistakeable. And a spell it must be, as the weaknesses of the concept are grave indeed.

deflecting forces. He also states that the dispersal shown in his drawing was grossly exaggerated, and from an adjacent simplified calculation estimates pellet layers to be separated little more than .01″ ($\frac{1}{100}$th-inch) when the column has just passed the choke's cone. This separation, however, does not provide the free lateral movement essential to the theory. Thus, if his calculation holds, the principle expressed in his drawing does not.

Now, the probability of pellets jumping during the choke passage may be settled by calculations of unquestionable validity. Let us consider a modest jump carrying a No. 7 pellet half a diameter ahead during the time when the column itself has moved one pellet diameter. The reality of this jump is that our froggy pellet must

can be no free lateral movement.

Furthermore, the Journée theory has no role for the parallel. Only the cone is acting and directing the pellets. Yet, numerous experiments had already proved that the parallel did a job in concentrating the pattern. If the charge was directed only by the cone, a distorted pattern should be expected if the parallel was set askew, making the charge rub onesidedly against its wall. Journée had himself tested eccentrically bored choke barrels made by M. Breuil, a barrelmaker of St. Etienne, and he found no abnormality of pattern, even when the displacement made one side of the parallel flush with the bore.

Both the acknowledgement of the shot column to be fairly compact following the choke passage and the per-

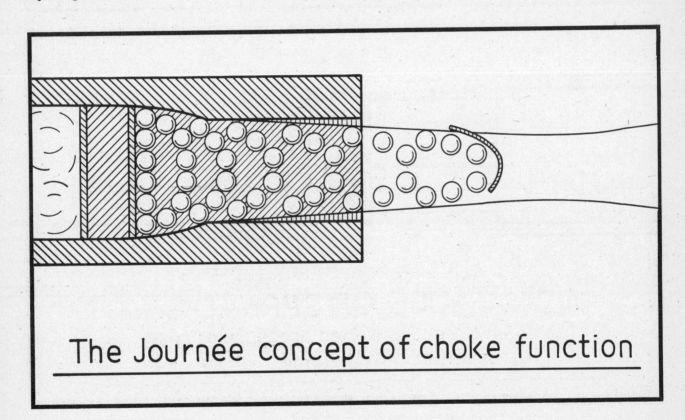

The Journée concept of choke function

Failure of the Journée Theory

To respond to the inward-acting force, the pellets need freedom of movement laterally, otherwise, the radial forces acting from all sides on a compact shot column would largely cancel each other, and no general movement toward the pattern center could prevail.

Journée implies the central pellets in the squeezed column jump ahead creating freedom of movement allowing the outer pellets to respond to the

gain 50% in velocity and more than double its kinetic energy in about six millionths of a second! The achievement requires an accelerating force on this single pellet amounting to 900 pounds.

The example shows the futility of thinking in "sudden jumps" when the pellets are already travelling at 1300 fps. Even the front pellets are not all moving freely in that sense, and they are much more readily deformed than separated noticeably from the column. Without jumping pellets, there

formance of the eccentric choke points to the charge being guided by the parallel and not by the cone. We have to leave the Journée concept behind as a gallant try, but indeed a blind alley.

Starting Afresh

While Journée authority decidedly has been a block on the road to a workable choke theory, another obstacle has been the general approach to the problem. We ask quite naturally why the choke works, as that is our question to be answered, but this is in

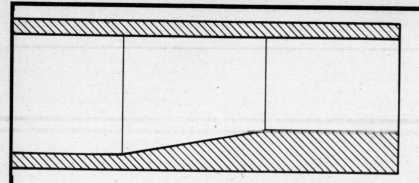
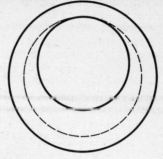

ECCENTRIC CHOKE
Pattern performance equals that of similar concentric choke

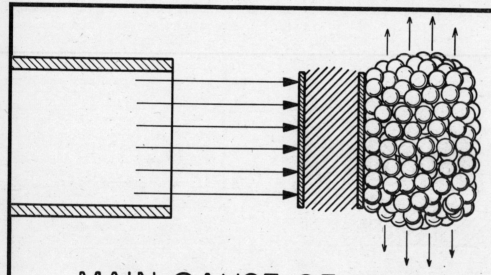

MAIN CAUSE OF SPREAD by the cylinder bore: Sustained pressure at rear of the emerged shot column.

fact a bad start almost bound to lead us astray. It makes us look for "inward-acting impulses," and in the end we cannot much better Journée.

The key to success is to recognize that our ignorance does not start at the choke. Let us forget for the moment why the choke provides a dense pattern and ask why the cylinder throws an open one. Why does the shot charge not just travel along in the neat column formed by the cylindric barrel?

Or: Why does the shot charge spread?

When we inspect the pattern from a cylinder-bored barrel, spread may be related to the following causes:

1. The emerged shot column is not stable to the pressure still acting at the rear. A push starting at more than 200 pounds results in a collapse and the pellets start moving outward, bulging the column to disc shape. Once such a radial velocity component has been imparted, the pellet formation is bound to open up along the route.

2. Pellet deformation may cause erratic flight.

3. Differing air resistance due to differences in size and sphericity make some pellets fly faster than others. Collisions between the faster and the slower moving pellets may cause diversions.

4. Pellet spin may alter the course.

5. The blast from the outstreaming powder gases behind the charge may create an outward suction, when they are diverted around the charge at a much higher

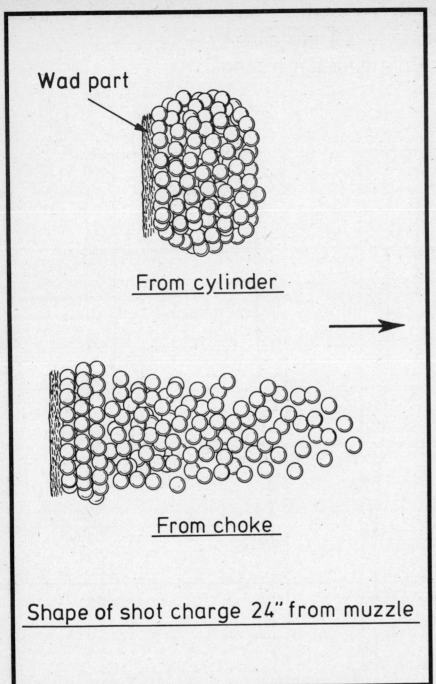

Wad part

From cylinder

→

From choke

Shape of shot charge 24" from muzzle

its emergence from the muzzle.

And this is the indispensable ballast allowing us to proceed to the main theme:

What Happens In the Choke?

An obvious result of constricting the muzzle is the stretching of the shot column to accommodate the volume in the smaller section of the parallel. In practice, a full choke constriction may demand a $\frac{1}{10}$th inch (.1″) elongation of the column. Then, the foremost pellets have gained the $\frac{1}{10}$th inch (.1″) over the rearmost pellets during the choke passage.

This may look insignificant until it is realized that the transition has taken place in $\frac{1}{10,000}$ of a second. The $\frac{1}{10}$th inch (.1″) change of position in this short time equals a difference in velocity of roundly 80 feet per second. So, following the choke passage, the front pellets must travel at 80 fps higher speed than the rearmost pellets to form the new elongated column.

Now, over the assumed 1½″ length of the choke passage, the remaining barrel pressure is adding little to the speed of the charge. A 1½″ difference in barrel length means a difference in muzzle velocity of approximately 10 fps only, and furthermore the turmoil in the choke absorbs a substantial amount of energy. Journée states a 1% loss in muzzle energy from this cause.

So, the differing velocities in the column are obtained by transfer of kinetic energy from the rear to the front of the column. In other words, the rear part of the column forces the front part to a higher speed through the constriction and is itself retarded in the process. Journée experimented with abnormally heavy chokes, where the rear part of the charge stuck in the choke as a solid mass, while the front part emerged at 1300 fps.

Likewise the indefatigable Journée fired solid cylindrical lead bullets in heavily choked barrels and found them likely to separate due to the difference in speed attained by the front and the rear part during the choke passage. In the normal full choke we may expect a grading of the total velocity spread of 80 fps from plus-40 fps in front of the column to minus-40 fps at rear, while the speed remains constant at the center.

When we pursue the progressing velocity differentiation during the choke passage more carefully by calculation, we find a surplus acceleration in the cone causing higher velocities than necessary to accommodate

speed than the charge itself.

6. Air resistance may force the pellets at the rim at the front of the column outwards.

7. If a top wad is present, it causes some spread when colliding with pellets taking over the lead.

That looks rather confusing but more consideration shortens the list. Calculations indicate Numbers 3, 4, 5 and 6 to be of minor importance, and Number 7 is eliminated entirely in modern crimped cartridges.

That leaves us with Numbers 1 and

2. Number 2 is of some consequence, as we know "fliers" form the outskirt of the pattern, and deliberately deformed pellets are utilized in scatter loads. But we may say for certain that deformation as a cause of spread is a secondary factor in the performance of ordinary loads. This is proved by the denser pattern thrown by the choke, even though the choke definitely adds to pellet deformity.

So, we end at the simple conclusion—the spread of the shot charge is principally caused by the pressure still exerted on the column following

THE O & T PROBLEM —
Role of friction in cone

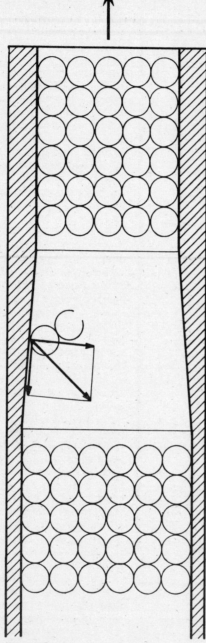

Left: Friction breaks up original column, thereby helping in restacking a new elongated column implying the velocity differentiation basic to choke effect.

Right: In the absence of friction the charge may adjust to the smaller section of the Parallel by deformation of the pellets, and velocity remains uniform throughout the charge. Then the barrel does perform almost like a cylinder bore but spreading even more due to pellet deformation.

In reality both restacking and deformation may be expected at a balance determined by the amount of friction.

the charge in the parallel. The result is a separation of the column lengthwise. Each layer of pellets is disconnected at the entrance to the parallel and, although the separation is very slight, this allows the differing velocities that are to disperse the column lengthwise still more throughout its flight.

When the complete shot charge has passed into the parallel, the calculated separation between adjacent pellet layers is approximately .004″. That is not much, but the column is in fact disconnected, and we may realize our main cause of spread to be eliminated. Pressure acting through the wad just outside the muzzle cannot affect the longer unconnected column as it can the compact one from the cylinder bore. Only a few pellet layers are caught by the wad due to last-stage acceleration by the gas pressure in the parallel and just outside the muzzle, and they form a shorter and more stable column. Also, the spread from the Number 3 and 6 causes in our list is reduced, though they are of little consequence.

So: **the paramount feature of the choke is the disconnection of the shot column relieving the emerged charge of the spreading influence from the gas pressure.** The degree of choke determines the length of the compact rear part comprising the layers caught by the wad at the last stage of acceleration. The longer the compact part, the less stability and the more bulging and spread.

The theory here described accords perfectly with electronic flash photographs showing emerged shot charges. The collapsing column from the cylinder bore expands to form a discoid, while the longitudinally dispersed column from the choke is unaffected by pressure from behind improving the chance of the pellets to end in the pattern center.

Role of the Parallel

Contrary to the Journée theory, we have no use for lasting radial movements of the pellets. They are most likely to give spread. And while the radial forces from the cone wall are largely balancing each other when acting on the near-compact column, the symmetry is not perfect as this would imply a non-existing perfectly symmetrical stack of pellets. Some unbalance and tendency to "turbulence" must be expected. The disturbance shall live to give spread unless it is suppressed in the parallel, and the "laminar" flow is restored. But as the wad is catching up in the parallel

due to continued accelerating gas pressure, the choke effect is suffering, and a happy compromise in length of the parallel must be chosen.

Choke Designation

To specify a choke by stating the amount of constriction is not satisfactory as the choke effect is dependent on the length of the cone as well.

The deciding figure is theoretically **the rate of relative change in the sectional area of the bore.**

This quantity could be represented by a figure reasonably nominated as "Choke Power."

$$\text{Choke Power} \; = \; \frac{1 - (D_2/D_1)^2}{L}$$

L is length of cone, and D_1 and D_2 are the diameters of bore and parallel respectively.

Choke Power should enable us to compare choke-effect of different bores at different lengths of cones, but there is still a factor which in some cases may obscure Choke Power as a reliable measure of choke-effect:

The Stacking Problem

The process of column elongation demands a restacking of the pellets and we cannot expect a very short cone to behave like the more common lengths during the transition. Furthermore, the problem of stacking efficiency enters.

In the densest stack, spheres occupy $^{74}/_{100}$ths of the volume. This is not realizable in a bore, and if the perfect stack represents 100% stacking efficiency, we may as example find a stacking efficiency in the bore of 85%. The stacking efficiency is obviously dependent on the relation between pellet diameter and bore diameter. The smaller the bore, relatively, the less is the chance of arranging the pellets in a near-perfect stack.

But the stacking efficiency is not continuously dependent on the bore-diameter relation. It is a matter of *fit*, too. If the pellets are stacking more efficiently in the parallel than in the bore, then the column does not elongate to the degree expected from the Choke Power figure, and choke-effect is reduced, perhaps even to the verge of disappearance. On the other hand a slight choke that happens to reduce the stacking efficiency materially may result in a denser pattern than expected.

Role of Friction in the Cone

A fine surface finish of the cone wall has been observed by Oberfell

and Thompson to detract from choke-effect, as related in their book *The Mysteries Of Shotgun Patterns.* Likewise, it has been the experience, especially in trapshooting, that the first shot from an oily barrel made a more open pattern. These phenomena are easily explained by the present theory.

Imagine a column of men marching in ranks along a road narrowing into an entrance, under orders to keep the formation as far as possible. The entrance hardly accommodates the original width of the column but as the gateway is flanked by smooth marble walls, the ranks are kept, though somewhat jammed, and no elongation of the column takes place! But if the flanking walls are rough and do not allow the men on the outside to slide along? Then friction forces them back, breaking up the formation, reforming it into a longer column.

And so with pellets. The purely radial forces from the friction-free cone wall are just deforming the pellets and not breaking up the layers. The result is a much reduced column elongation and choke-effect. Moreover, the deformation is a source of spread in itself.

(Here at last is a practical gain from the lesson: If you are shooting an open bore, there is no need to remove a reasonable oil protection from the barrels before shooting. There will be no practical difference in pattern of the first and succeeding shots, and frequently I have observed a higher quality pattern from the oily bore. And the oil protects as long as it stays.)

Epilogue

While the idea of the choke not acting directly was revolutionary to me when it first grew out of the considerations, it was not new to mankind. Credit should be given to W. Borland of the British EC Powder Company, whose analysis of early spark photographs was published in "The Field" in 1908. Unfortunately, his work attracted little attention, though he was quoted by W. W. Greener in the 1910 edition of *The Gun and its Development.* Borland acknowledged the function of the choke as a prevention of spread due to delaying the wad. Unlike Journée, he did not grasp the delaying mechanism, and attributed the delay to friction.

If these two good men had joined their efforts, they could hardly have failed in settling the matter well over 70 years ago. ●

IN THE PAST decade, the hunter's world has suffered an alarming contraction. Parts of the world that for years have been taken for granted have been walled off by revolution and political turmoil, the spread of Communism, xenophobia, misguided protectionism, and political quarantine. There are other forces at work which do not close hunting areas outright, but have much the same effect: prohibitively high costs and very restrictive quota, drawing, or permit systems. Moreover, in many areas hunter success ratios and trophy quality are declining.

The message thus becomes quite clear: if you are at all serious about a certain hunting trip or trips, the time to go is now.

The receding boundaries of the hunter's world have been more or less coterminous with the receding boundaries of Western domination or influence. When the Shah fled from Iran, chaos reigned supreme, and within months the wildlife riches of a great hunting land had been utterly annihilated. When the Russians invaded Afghanistan, all opportunity to hunt Marco Polo sheep was lost. When the Portuguese abandoned Mozambique and Angola, those countries declared independence and were quickly closed to all tourism. Under that xenophobic buffoon, "Big Daddy" Amin, Uganda was closed to safaris, and has not reopened despite his fall from power. Other—temporary—losses were Ethiopia and Tanzania, but safaris are not of the quality they once were.

Of course, some areas have opened up, but when losses are weighed against gains, the former will surely predominate.

To get a balanced perspective, we must consider the bright side of the picture as well. Let us look at the few gains in the international hunting world:

Foremost has probably been the opening up of the vast rich gamelands of the Soviet Union to foreign sport hunters. The USSR has the greatest wildlife riches in the world. At the World Hunting Congress in 1971 the USSR had the largest pavilion. I was very much impressed by the variety and the quality of the trophies displayed in the pavilion. In fact, the USSR has over 300 huntable species. They include six species of stag; two species of roedeer; three species of antelope; four species of wild sheep (including Marco Polo and argali); three species of wildcats; two species each of leopards, ibex, and tur; four species of

bear; moose, wild boar, wolf, and so in indefinitely. There is also a great wealth of winged game. Here there are "treasures untold" for the hunter.

So far, however, most of it is off limits to the foreign hunter. He may enter only seven small enclaves, primarily in the Caucasus Mountains and the Crimea, where he will have access to Daghestan tur, Russian brown bear, roedeer, maral stag, wild boar, and chamois in varying combinations. Moreoever, the seasons in some of these hunting reserves are quite short, i.e., 2-4 weeks, and organization is not up to standard. These opportunities represent mere crumbs in contrast to what could be a banquet. Let us hope

and wild boar. The Spanish Grand Slam—a 16-day hunt for all the species of Spanish big game—has become quite popular among well-traveled American hunters.

Very fine duck and goose shooting, and driven red-legged partridge shooting—perhaps the most exciting wing shooting in the world—are also available. However, the most authentically Spanish hunt, and the most exciting hunt that Spain has to offer, is the *monteria*. On this huge-scale hunt 20-40 shooters are placed in a circle that surrounds an area of 500-2000 acres. Others are placed on lines that traverse the area. Then packs of dogs—totaling 300-500 or more—are

no matter where it takes you . . .
make that BIG TRIP NOW!
by STUART WILLIAMS

that the Russians will in future see fit to give much greater access to their hunting riches.

Spain has been another big gain for the international hunting world. Until recently Spain was off limits to all but a few foreign hunters with well-placed contacts. Now, however, a new outfitting company—Cazatur, Ltda.—under the competent aegis of Ricardo Medem, (Apartado de Correos 50. 57T, Madrid) has for the very first time opened the vast hunting riches of Spain to foreign hunters. Game available includes the much-sought after and prestigious Spanish ibex; record-quality western red stag; moufflon; fallow deer; two species of chamois;

released to drive the area. The game to be shot is typically wild boar and red stag, although on some preserves an occasional roedeer, fox, or wolf may also be killed. The size of the bag will vary according to the density of game populations and the skill of the shooters, and can go up to as many as 60 head in a day.

The tab for all this wonderful hunting is pretty heady, but the experience is rich and rare. I don't believe it is overpriced.

Most of the important additions in recent years have been in bird shooting, whereas most of the important losses have been in big game hunting. The trend is almost certain to continue. Mike Fitzgerald, president of Fish and Game Frontiers, of Wexford, Pa., explains that for that very reason his firm has come to book high-quality bird shoots almost exclusively. He says that the really important additions to the international hunting map over the past half-dozen years have been the extraordinary duck, dove, and quail shooting in Colombia, which is perhaps the number one wing-shooting country in the world; the wonderful duck shooting in Egypt and Peru; the superb dove shooting in Morocco; the beautifully managed estate shoots for mallards and pheasants in Denmark; and the great mixed-bag shooting—ducks, geese, doves, pi-

Logistics are poor, and malaria, bilharzia, sleeping sickness, and dysentery are widespread.

There have been recurring reports from returning hunters of serious shortages of food and gasoline on safaris, resulting in considerable discomfort and wasted hunting time at $600 and up a day. It seems that the Portuguese professional hunters are particularly culpable. Moreoever, the game department is reported beset with graft and corruption. And, Sudan is coming under heavy hunting pressure displaced there by the closure of other African gamelands. Four Seattle-area hunters, returning recently from an absolutely disastrous

Empire, where political turmoil has sealed off the borders; Uganda, which Amin closed to all tourism, and which has not reopened since his fall from power; Ethiopia, which has become essentially a Soviet vassal-state since the coup d'état and elimination of Haile Selassie; and Angola, likewise a Soviet fiefdom that closed the gates to hunting safaris upon gaining independence from Portugal. Of course, Somalia has been forbidden ground for political reasons for a number of years, and it has been pretty well shot over anyway.

The future of safaris in Zimbabwe is a big question mark. Now that the U.S. has recognized the Mugabe government, anybody can hunt there without perjuring himself to get his trophies back into the U.S. Zimbabwe has exceptionally good hunting, and it is just about the cheapest in Africa. One can get good kudu, sable, elephant, lion, and cape buffalo in *14* days—the only place in Africa where that is possible. The only problem is that nobody knows what is going to happen under Mugabe. He has shown himself to be unusually restrained and rational so far—and not at all the white-hating Marxist tyrant that many observers had expected. But who can say what kind of government will be ruling Zimbabwe in two years or three?

Of course, Iran and Afghanistan are two of the greatest losses to the international hunting community. Iran was one of the greatest hunting lands on earth, and was an especially great sheep-hunting country. Under the aegis of Prince Abdorreza Pahlavi, brother to the Shah, the Iranian Department of Conservation had in the past score years built up very abundant populations of urial, ibex, maral stag, roedeer, wild boar, gazelle, Armenian sheep, red sheep, Shiraz sheep, and Laristan sheep. There was also excellent shooting for ducks and woodcock along the Caspian littoral. All of that is gone, probably forever.

Author with a Spanish ibex and, obviously, some of the glamour hunting in the world. Williams knows this subject very well.

geons, and jungle fowl—of India.

In big game, Sudan offers another gain for the international sport hunter. Many professional hunters, forced out of business in Angola, Mozambique, and Kenya, have set up operations there. In fact, Sudan has promise of becoming the outstanding safari destination on the African continent. It is producing some very big elephants and a high rate of success on bongo and giant eland. However, according to Mike Fitzgerald and Jack Jonas, both eminently knowledgeable booking agents, safaris in Sudan have a long way to go before they can come up to the level of comfort and organization of former East African safaris.

safari in Sudan, report strong and widespread anti-American sentiment there. Potentially, and I lay stress on that word, Sudan could be listed among the Happy Hunting Grounds of the earth, but it has many problems to overcome.

The most favorable hunting conditions in Africa today exist in South Africa, Southwest Africa, Zambia, and Botswana. At this writing, peaceful conditions and stable governments prevail, excellent safari companies operate, and game abounds.

On the loss side of the tally sheet in Africa are Kenya, where misguided protectionism shut down hunting safaris in May, 1977; Central African

Numerically, the loss of Marco Polo sheep hunting in Afghanistan was not very significant, because only a few permits were issued each year. However, it was a great loss in that the expedition for Marco Polo sheep was certainly the last and greatest *hunting adventure* left on earth. The trip into the Wakhan Corridor of the Pamir Mountains required many days of riding in jeeps on virtually non-existent roads, of riding horseback, and finally yak-back to elevations up to 19,000 feet. That was an adventure that demanded iron resolve and the utmost in physical conditioning. It even demanded at least one hunter's life—he died of pulmonary edema. The hunter's world is a poorer place for the loss of Marco Polo sheep hunting in Afghanistan.

There are a lot of rumors flying around about booking agents negotiating with the Chinese to open up Marco Polo sheep hunting in China. At this stage there is nothing really substantial to report, but I would not be at all surprised to see China open up to foreign sport hunters. Since the recent rapprochement with the U.S.,

the '50s. Settlers had in the early years of the century imported Himalayan tahr from India; chamois from Austria; red stag from Scotland and Germany; whitetail deer from the U.S.; moose from Canada; rusa deer from Java; and Sika deer from Japan. With a moderate climate, plenty of foodstuffs, no predators, and total protection from hunters, most of these species thrived in their new home. However, greed and ignorance conspired to destroy the great game herds of yesteryear, so that New Zealand is essentially a wasteland for the sport

"In fact, today most of the guides have been forced out of business as they just cannot find enough game.

"I worked on a chopper in 1969 as a shooter to get a grub stake. We were killing 100-200 deer a day and if we got less we were fired. The effort was worth approximately $9000 a day, so you can see how chopper owners have become millionaires . . .

"Most guides have gone bush building live game traps, and most farmers won't let a sportsman within miles of his place or within five miles of a deer trap . . .

Dramatic milieus, startling scenes and important hunts are not all overseas. There is a lot in North America, as here in the Yukon.

China has been very cooperative about permitting travel by Americans.

(The latest is that the People's Republic of China has officially opened hunting, but no one has yet gone to hunt. Among the stumbling blocks: At first blush, the Chinese won't permit personal guns and plan to issue guns. What guns? Who knows?)

Another very grievous loss for hunters to bewail is New Zealand. With proper game management, New Zealand might have become one of the greatest gamelands of them all, as it had fair promise of becoming back in

hunter today. Rex Forrester, Hunting and Fishing Officer for the New Zealand government, wrote a very revealing—and saddening—letter to a Montana sportsman contemplating a hunt in New Zealand. It is worthwhile to print a few excerpts here.

" . . . professionals . . . have found lucrative markets in Germany for venison and in the East for by-products such as velvet antlers. It's now a multi-million dollar export industry, and over 60 helicopters are employed full-time as gun ships or capture ships . . .

"Poaching is rife, and chopper companies even have spies dropped off in the hills with a radio behind farmers' houses to radio the day the farmer goes to town, whereupon the chopper arrives and guns down all his handy deer which disappear over the range suspended on a sling under the chopper.

"No place is remote anymore and the poor old sportsmen just have no place left to hunt . . .

"My advice . . . is not to come; you will be bitterly disappointed. . . . Sports hunting here is a thing of the past."

What hunting remains in New Zealand today is the tattered and frayed relic of what was once a magnificent garment.

One possible exception is professional hunter Gary Joll's concession, Lilybank Lodge near Lake Teckapo in the South Island. Joll says he still produces old-style hunts on this ground never shot over commercially. Recent—1981—clients of his I talked to back him up.

Alaska is another of the great hunting lands that is fast becoming a thing of the past. Escalating trophy fees and the requirement that hunters pay trophy fees *before* they go afield rather than after they have actually killed their game have reduced the number of non-resident hunters to the point where Alaska now receives fewer non-resident hunters than any other state in the union. From a high of 11,659 in 1972 the numbers of non-resident hunters dropped to 8800 in 1973 to a 15-year low of 4459 in 1977. Furthermore, the end is not in sight. It appears that hunters wishing to visit Alaska may be in for even rougher treatment.

In what is a transparent move to reduce non-resident hunting and eventually to eliminate it altogether, British Columbia has greatly increased trophy fees and license fees for non-resident hunters and has required that they be paid before going afield, not after the game has been taken. As a result the number of non-resident hunters visiting British Columbia is now less than half of what it was in the early 70's, and will certainly decline even further.

The same desire to eliminate the non-resident hunter is very strong in Alberta. Most importantly, the Alberta fish and game department has drastically reduced the number of non-resident sheep permits in recent years. Whereas it formerly issued 15 such permits, it now issues only *4*.

Severely restrictive quotas and drawings and permit systems are also excluding hunters from many hunting opportunities. The Yukon Territory is now limiting hunters to one grizzly bear in a lifetime, and the other great gamelands of the North will inevitably follow suit. Moreover, I look for the practice to spread to other game animals and to the lower 48 states. Elk will almost certainly be so restricted. Already Wyoming has a very restrictive drawing for elk permits. Colorado is even more restrictive in those areas that require drawing for elk. Glynn Fraser, former president of the Colorado Outfitters Professional Society,

reported that he lost one third of his hunters in the 1978 season because they failed to draw. Other outfitters, however, lost all their hunters and were wiped out. New Mexico now permits non-resident hunters to buy elk and antelope licenses only every other year, but there is serious talk of restricting sales of elk and antelope licenses to every *third* year.

The factor eroding hunting opportunities worldwide faster and far more than all the other factors combined is wildly increasing cost. Caused by the death of the dollar, confiscatory worldwide inflation, an imbalance of supply of quality hunting opportunities and demand for them, extortionate trophy fees, and just plain greed, cost levels keep rising.

A fully outfitted African safari, based on one hunting client with one professional hunter, will cost an average $550-$700 per day. Thus a 21-day safari—the minimum acceptable booking in countries such as Zambia and Botswana—will cost, including licenses, concession fee, air fare, and freight, an absolute minimum of $20,000! At the time of closure, hunting in Iran cost on average $500 per day, but hunting for certain less available species cost closer to $600 per day. An Alaskan brown bear hunt will cost on average $7,000; a quality 21-day mixed bag hunt in British Columbia, $12,000; and a Stone sheep hunt, $9,000. This last figure has been brought about by a simple matter of demand vastly exceeding supply. The desire to fill out a Grand Slam on North American sheep has made all North American sheep very coveted and prestigious trophies; at the same time the British Columbia Department of Fish and Game has severely limited the quota of Stone sheep allowed to any outfitter in any given area. The resulting situation is that the outfitter must generate his dollar volume from far fewer hunters. The anticipated quotas on goat and grizzly bear in British Columbia will almost certainly have the same effect on hunting those species.

The World's Number One Ripoff must certainly be hunting for argali sheep in the Upper Altai mountains of Mongolia. Up until the 1978 season the cost for a 10-day hunt was $10,000, but as of the 1978 season it was raised to $16,500! (Despite all their strident denunciations of the profit motive, nobody is more greedy than the Communists or socks it to visiting hunters harder.) As a result, only six hunters booked in 1978. Now, for $16,500 one

would expect a hunt so luxurious that it would be worthy of Genghis Khan himself. Such, however, was far from the case. The outfitting standards actually deteriorated badly. The food was garbage, and the general level of efficiency and organization was low. Yet all this apparently did not discourage German hunters, who seem to have been infected with sheep madness by their North American counterparts. A German booking agent reserved two of the three high Altai camps for 1979. German hunters seemed to have little reluctance to pay that $16,500 because the dollar had depreciated so much in relation to the mark since that price was set that the hunt was actually cheaper for them than when it cost $10,000!

Of course, outfitting costs are just one component of the total cost of a hunting trip, and in many cases they are not even the major component. On many hunts, once a hunter has left the bush and returned to his jumping-off point, he can expect to be rocked and rolled by trophy fees so huge they are almost obscene. Let's start with North America, where the trophy fees are the world's most modest. Even so, a caribou or moose will cost you $200 in Alaska, and a Dall sheep $250. Should you shoot a grizzly bear in the Yukon that brief caress of the trigger will make you just half a thousand dollars poorer. Moreover, there is serious talk about increasing that fee.

By comparison with trophy fees in other parts of the world, however, those here in North America are mere tuppenny-halfpenny matters, hardly worthy of mention. In the Central African Empire (where hunted) a bongo or hippopotamus cost $628; an elephant with ivory weighing (total) less than 100 pounds, $1000; and an elephant with total ivory weight over 100 pounds, $1500. You must, in fact, reckon with spending at least $5000 in trophy fees to take a good representative bag. In Zambia a black rhino will cost $2900.

If you had shot a gold medal red stag in Iran, you would have been socked a trophy fee of $857; a gold medal brown bear would have set you back $1500; and a gold-medal leopard would have cost you $2571. Record-class trophies of these animals cost, respectively, $1071, $1714, and $3000! That's hardly for the welfare and foodstamp crowd.

These trophy fees, in turn, are mere bagatelles, so puny as to scarcely merit mention, in comparison to the absolutely ruinous fees levied by some of the Communist bloc countries.

In the Soviet Union a good red stag will cost about $2500, but a gold medal stag about $5000! During a hunt in Austria several years ago I met a plutocratic German hunter who was absolutely determined to shoot a world record red stag. In this endeavor he annually shot 4-6 outstanding red stags in Yugoslavia. The average trophy fee per head? About $14,000!! Consider that that was in 1973, and that trophy fees have escalated wildly since then. In fact, a hunter shot a near world-record stag in Yugoslavia in the fall of 1978 that set him back over $58,000!!

Quality hunting for European hunters means that you are willing to pay an escalating amount of trophy surcharge if the scoring of your trophy goes up. It is a more sophisticated system with trophies classified in these categories: bronze, silver and gold medals.

Sometimes the so-called quality surcharge is higher than the trophy fee itself and maybe even the entire trip, but it is fair to say that with this system you pay for what quality of trophy you actually get. American hunters should be well versed in the quality surcharge before they pull the trigger in front of a "monster."

All this brings up another point: that European hunters are willing—in general—to pay much higher fees for quality hunting than American hunters, and that increasingly American hunters will have to compete with European hunters for quality hunting, whether it be in Africa, Asia, or North America. European hunters long ago accepted the reality that quality hunting is a very, very scarce commodity on this earth, and that therefore it is a sport and passion reserved for "the few and the very few," as Benjamin Disraeli said long ago in another context.

(At press-time, East Bloc hunts and fees were being heavily discounted to encourage Continental hunters. Soft economies have slowed the rush for trophies, I'm told.)

Many American hunters are still suffering from the delusion that hunting is a right rather than a privilege; that they should be able to enjoy quality hunting just for paying their license fees; and that there are still lots of wide-open spaces in North America where game abounds just for the taking. European hunters, however, have long been accustomed to the hunting preserve system. Such preserves are usually offered to let at public auction, and the bidding drives the prices stratospherically high. Con-

sequently more and more European hunters are seeking quality hunting opportunities abroad.

For example, in Italy there is a joke going around that Italy's biggest export is hunters. On a hunting trip in the Yukon last fall I spent several days in Whitehorse on the way into and out of the hunting area. I would guess that at least half the non-resident hunters I encountered were Europeans. Those I spoke with thought that hunting costs in the Yukon—about $300 per day on average at that time—were quite reasonable. Undoubtedly they were, compared with costs back in Europe. Moreover, they were paying that $300 per diem in much stronger currencies —Swiss francs, Austrian schillings, and German marks—so that that rate seemed doubly a bargain.

ing phenomenon—is the purchase of some of the very finest guiding areas in British Columbia by wealthy German interests. One such area recently sold for one million dollars! It hardly needs saying that American hunters will no longer have access to such areas.

Let us briefly consider the hunting situation closer to home, specifically, hunting for whitetail deer and mule deer. These two species are our most abundant—and most sought after— big-game species, so any discussion of the future of big-game hunting in this country must begin and end with these species.

Whitetail deer herds, if not at an all-time high, still continue to thrive throughout many parts of the U.S. Yet there is a very disconcerting tendency

This nice standard six-point Wyoming bull elk is a grand trophy by any standards, anywhere, and would dwarf most of the world's deer.

Increasingly, then, European hunters will be competing for the best hunting in Yukon, British Columbia, and Alaska—areas that were once virtually private American hunting preserves. I predict that that competition will—sooner rather than later— drive outfitting costs in those areas up to the level of outfitting costs in Africa.

There is some indication that it is already doing so. I keep hearing persistent reports of a double pricing system being used by some British Columbia outfitters—one price for American hunters and a much higher price for European hunters. This, of course, gives the Europeans preferential booking for dates and areas, and could eventually eliminate all American hunters wishing to book with the best outfitters.

Another related—and very disturb-

of forests in some of the most productive whitetail states—Minnesota, Michigan, Maine, Pennyslvania, and West Virginia, among others—to reach cathedral-like maturity. That may be great for turkeys and squirrels, but it's death for deer. There has been some serious discussion of control-burning and more intensive logging in these states, but neither is yet practiced on a wide scale for the specific purpose of improving deer habitat.

On the other hand is a very encouraging phenomenon, game-ranching in Texas, which has by far the biggest whitetail herd in the nation. As with hunting for many other species, the ultimate salvation of whitetail deer hunting will probably be the free-enterprise system. There are at least two-dozen game ranches in

Texas that can offer virtually guaranteed success on good whitetail bucks—at a price. However, the cost in many cases is so exorbitant—up to $2000 for a trophy buck—that the hunting that is given by the right hand of opportunity is taken away by the left hand of high cost.

Moreover, the trophy quality of whitetail bucks nationally is considerably compromised by the very large numbers of them that game departments are under pressure to produce. The terrific hunting pressures exerted on these same deer in the major whitetail "factory" states—Michigan, Wisconsin, Pennsylvania—further militate against the development of trophy animals. The average buck shot in those states is a yearling spike or forkhorn.

It might cost a Continental sportsman $15,000 as a trophy fee to shoot this most unusual red deer and he'd think it worth the money.

Two encouraging characteristics of the whitetail deer are its adaptability and its ability to thrive and even increase in proximity to man. A recently released study done by the West Virginia Department of Natural Resources concludes that whitetail deer populations increase in any given area as human populations increase. It states, further, that whereas hunter success in West Virginia was one in ten ten years ago, and is about one in seven now, it will be about one in five within five years—even though the numbers of hunters will have increased.

Another quality of the whitetail deer that is a mixed blessing is its aggressiveness. Whitetails are gradually taking over much habitat in western states that used to be the exclusive domain of mule deer. They have pushed mule deer out of large areas in Montana, Wyoming, and Washington. Moreover, some of those areas are now producing very impressive whitetail trophies.

If the whitetail picture in general looks encouraging, the mule deer picture is just the opposite. Hunting pressures on mule deer have increased tremendously in the past ten years. Hunters are more mobile than ever, and can gain ready access to more and more areas. Besides, some of the best mule deer states—Wyoming, Colorado, Arizona, and Nevada—have experienced alarming growth in human populations over the past decade, and there is no sign that this rate of growth is going to slow down. Mule deer are just not as tolerant of the encroachment of man as whitetails.

Major ecological disruptions—stripmining for coal and drilling for oil and gas—will continue to expand in some of the major mule deer states—Colorado, Montana, Wyoming, and Utah—as the search for further sources of energy intensifies.

Bill Huey, former director of the New Mexico Game Department, named Game Management Professional of the Year for 1980, is very pessimistic about the future of mule deer hunting. He says that a big part of the problem is that the so-called science of mule deer management is not a science at all—yet. It is what he calls an art, and is still in a rather primitive stage. He says that there are an awful lot of questions, but few or no really satisfactory answers. He says that mule deer are much more difficult to manage than most other species that western game departments have to deal with.

Hunting for trophy mule deer—as we knew them from the mid-50's to the mid-60's—seems to be a pleasure that is sliding irrevocably into the past. Recently Jack Jonas—big-game hunter extraordinaire and booking agent par excellence—told me that if a prospective client wished to book a hunt for trophy mule deer, he would have to tell him honestly that he couldn't help him. He says flatly that there are no more of these "trophy hotspots" that the outdoor press used to boost so breathlessly.

Of course, one does read ads by mule deer outfitters offering hunts for "trophy bucks." When one telephones them and asks what they consider a trophy buck, most of them are quite evasive. If one really presses them hard, they might say that their idea of a trophy rack is a typical four-pointer with a 22"-26" spread. That, by the standards of 1955-65, is a good buck, but certainly not a trophy, then or now.

The antelope hunting picture is not much brighter. The two states that have large antelope populations—Montana and Wyoming—require drawing for a permit. In some permit areas in Wyoming the percentage of drawing success is high, but in some other areas it is low. According to Bill Huey, things can only get worse. All the available antelope habitat in New Mexico is already being used, yet at the same time the demand for permits increases. Moreover, Bill anticipates that some of the ecological disturbances that will degrade mule deer hunting—strip mining, oil and gas drilling, pasture sheepherding, and the erection of net-wire fences—will also tend to degrade antelope hunting.

What does all this mean to you as a hunter? It means that now—not next year or the year after or when you have gotten ahead of the game financially, or when you have retired, but now—is the time to make that hunting trip that has been the substance of your dreams for so long. Costs will never be lower, you will never be younger, your powers of enjoyment will never be greater. What did William Wordsworth write?

The world is too much with us; late and soon,
Getting and spending, we lay waste our powers.
Little we see in Nature that is ours.

So, do it now! A way of life is passing that will not come again. •

the HOLES in

by **LEON DAY**

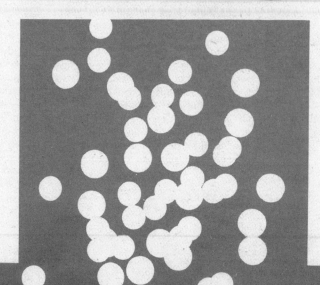

STOPPING POWER THEORY

No one who already knows he knows the truth should read this.

FROM HUNTERS talking about stopping power, you get simple and direct ideas derived from their experiences. They will tell you that the movement of the game after it is hit depends strictly on the damage done to relevant parts of the critter's anatomy. No hunter of any experience will pretend for a second that a deer shot through the guts or the left hind leg will fall down in a swoon and wait for a second shot—rather, they think it will try to run off.

This is not the attitude you find in policemen and soldiers. Many of them think that their human targets are very different, and that certain calibers or bullet weights or bullet constructions or velocities will produce nervous collapse and prostration even if nothing essential to fighting or fleeing is damaged. I used to think so, myself.

Everybody who has reflected on it realizes that bullets—especially handgun bullets—don't have any knock-down power. Our projectiles are fine for punching holes in things, but lousy for pushing them around. The impact of a bullet is of too short a duration to overcome the inertia of anything heavy. The momentum of the bullet and that of the recoiling weapon are roughly the same, so any firearm that could knock down your attacker would certainly floor you at the same moment. Finally, the experience of men wearing body armor shows that so long as the bullet doesn't penetrate the skin most men can run, shoot, and do anything else needed in a fight.

If an animal moves violently when shot, that's the animal moving, not the slug moving the animal. I noticed this with the first rabbit I shot. The critter turned a backward somersault that any gymnast would be proud of and wound up pointed south instead of north. Since I had shot from the east, it was plain that my bullet hadn't *pushed* the beast through this gyration. I soon found that I could depend on this dramatic display whenever I hit a rabbit just behind the head. But if I shot at a dead rabbit, or a sandbag of the same weight, my 22 wouldn't produce more than a twitch. This was a novelty to a 12-year-old, because shooting at tin cans had led me to expect that things shot would bounce around some.

While few people believe in "knock-down," quite a few brilliant men have believed in "stopping power" or "shocking power." The best of these in recent times is Carroll E. Peters, author of *Defensive Handgun Effectiveness*. Peters' work is a mathematical elaboration of the formulas of Julian S. Hatcher. Hatcher's work, in turn, is designed to agree with the experimental test firings of Major Louis Anatole LaGarde and Captain John T. Thompson, who tried some of the weapons available in 1904 against live steers.

All these authorities deserve more than a casual salute. Thompson was the developer of the Thompson submachine gun; LaGarde wrote *Gunshot Injuries,* which remained the primary medical text on the subject until well beyond WW II; and Col. (later Major General) Hatcher brought ballistic science to millions of practical shooters in a series of interesting and well-written works.

Popular articles on handgun stopping power are easy to find, but a serious student really needs Hatcher's *Textbook of Pistols and Revolvers,* where his theory of stopping power is presented in detail. Since it is long out of print, we should review the theory briefly.

Hatcher's first effort at a stopping power theory was presented in 1927 in his book *Pistols and Revolvers and Their Use.* Hatcher ranked pistol cartridges by multiplying their cross-sectional area by their muzzle energy by a shape factor accounting for the form of the bullet. This produced an evaluation of pistol ammo that in general, substantiated the common experience that bigger is better, but the exceptions were bothersome. Hatcher had two accounts of the Thompson-LaGarde tests, one from LaGarde's *Gunshot Injuries,* another from an article by Stephen Trask in the magazine *Arms and the Man.* Neither gave good marks to 30 Luger and 30 Mauser, but by the energy formula those rounds ranked above 38 S&W and nearly equaled 38 Long Colt. Further, 9mm Luger came in ahead of *all* contemporary 38-cal. revolver loads. This worried Hatcher more than somewhat.

So, in 1935 in *Textbook of Pistols and Revolvers,* Hatcher published a revised formula—cross-sectional area times *momentum* times shape factor. This put all those foreign cartridges in their place. In spite of its flat point, 9mm Luger was now slightly below 38 Super Auto. In spite of their high energy, 30 Luger and 30 Mauser were now ranked barely superior to 380 ACP. The theory was now in line with conventional wisdom.

No additions were made to stopping power theory for 17 years. In 1952, the Medical Corps produced a volume of theoretical and experimental studies titled *Wound Ballistics.* By animal tests, cadaver tests, and gelatin studies the GI doctors established that the actual damage done to an animal was proportional to the energy lost by any projectile in its impact with the body.

Basing himself on these findings, medical examiner Vincent J. DiMaio published in *FBI Law Enforcement Bulletin,* Dec., 1974, "A Comparison of Wounding Effects of Commercially Available Ammunition Suitable for Police Use." This study by the Southwest Institute of Forensic Science was simple and straightforward. The medics shot at 6-inch blocks of flesh-simulating gelatin. The speed of the bullet was measured going in, and measured going out again, and the difference in energy was taken as a figure of wounding effectiveness. Simple.

This study provoked some controversy. By 1974, jacketed hollow-points were popular in all calibers, and many cops probably supposed that some 38-cal. loadings were as good as some 45 loadings. But few uniformed or civilian shooters were prepared to believe that a 22 revolver could do as much actual damage as a 44 Special with the standard round-nose bullet. Many marksmen were plainly dismayed by the idea that from now on a ruler would be insufficient for making a choice of weapons. Slide rules and calculators were beating on the doors of people who were uncomfortable with even the basic mathematics of Hatcher's Relative Stopping Power formula.

Less than a year later, the Department of Justice released its study *An Evaluation of Police Handgun Ammunition.* This document brought a new wave of shocks and surprises to everyone who thought they understood bullets. The humble 38-cal. wadcutter loads, intended for nothing more hostile than a piece of paper, ranked about halfway up the list of 142 tested loadings. They were fully three times as effective in wounding power as the 38 158-grain lead round-nose loads that most police departments still carried on duty. The paper-punchers also dumped nearly twice the energy in a 6-inch gelatin block as the much-honored 45 ACP. The tests also revealed that many expanding bullets never did, and the ammo manufacturers consistently fibbed about how fast their slugs would go.

Many denounced the new tests, but others, more scientifically inclined, screened the results with great interest. Those who had really studied Hatcher's Formula had long realized

MORE ON NUMBERS

BULLET/grs. Round-Nose Hardball 45-cal.	VELOCITY feet-per-second	ENERGY foot-lbs.	HATCHER SCORE	PETER'S IMPULSE
500	391	169	62.5	.692
400	488.75	212.2	"	.774
300	651.6	282.9	"	.894
230	850	369	"	1.02
180	1086.1	471	"	1.15
140	1394.4	606	"	1.31
60	3258.3	1414	"	2.0

Here are seven loads, some real, some only possible. They all have the same Hatcher score—62.5—though they vary from sedate to frantic in velocity and energy. Few would believe they had the *same* stopping power, but Hatcher's formula says they do.

Hatcher disregarded energy entirely, although that is hard to tell in the welter of calibers, point forms and momentums. And something else: Hatcher said "stopping power" doesn't apply to very scared or angry men, which seems to mean that it disappears at the moment of need. Peters' rankings show a steady progression and is a description of relationships that might be useful.

Leon Day

that its weakest point was the form factors assigned to different bullet shapes. The new data seemed to them an opportunity to discover *actual,* not approximate, figures. The best of these researchers was Carroll E. Peters.

Peters' book, *Defensive Handgun Effectiveness,* is an inspiring *individual* achievement. With no government grants, and no impressive equipment except his mind, he has made it practical for a shooter to know in advance the momentum loss in any thickness of flesh, the energy loss, the penetration in soft wood, and the recoil of nearly any bullet at common velocities. Any shooter can sit down with the book and a hand calculator and learn nearly as much about the combat utility or any current or hypothetical load as the Justice Department discovered in 1975 with a million dollar laboratory.

Because Peters' book lets us figure out how our slugs will act in flesh, it will be extremely useful even if Hatcher's Theory is *wrong.* Hatcher thought that stopping power was proportional to the momentum the bullet lost in the human body. He did no tests himself on live animals which could either verify that there was any such phenomenon as stopping power, or that momentum was the key to it. Rather, he constructed his theory to agree with what he knew had been established by the Thompson-LaGarde handgun tests of 1904. He believed those firings against live steers to be extensive and definitive, and saw no purpose in repeating them.

Thanks to the Old Army Branch of the National Archives, I now have a copy of the original Thompson-LaGarde Report. Of the 13 cattle shot,

not one collapsed from anything resembling our modern conception of "stopping power." Nor did the live animal firings justify that board's recommendation that any new service pistol should be at least 45 caliber. *(Editor's Note: That's right. The hoopla of 75 years has been based on 13 dead beef animals. Why, I have shot nearly that many myself. KW)*

Hatcher apparently never had this document. In his book, he refers only to a chapter in LaGarde's *Gunshot Injuries* and a description of the tests in *Arms and the Man* by Stephen Trask. When I saw that there were discrepancies between the two accounts, I decided that I needed the original and set the Archives searching.

My suspicions about stopping power and shock effect were also aroused by Hatcher's extensive use of what doctors call "anecdotal material." We all like to hear stories about gunfights, and there are enough in *Textbook of Pistols and Revolvers* to please anybody. But if a 45 failed to stop its target, some excuse was always made for the cartridge. None were offered for 32s and 38s. In fact, at one point it is suggested that anybody who drops from a non-lethal hit with a small caliber must be a sissy quitter, or must have been totally surprised. Thus the reader was encouraged to discount any incident in his knowledge when a small caliber was successful. In the following paragraphs, it was explained that people who were excited or desperate wouldn't be stopped by anything less than a hit to heart, brain, or spine. Any failure of a fat slug was thus discounted at once.

So we got a bunch of entertaining war stories, but we were not encour-

aged to sort them out in any way that contradicted the approved theory.

I'll now describe and summarize the tests themselves. First, a word about the cartridges, many of which are now justly obscure. The 476 Eley did not throw a 48-caliber bullet. Rather, .476″ is the diameter of the case body. The *bullet* is very like a 455. This is important because both Hatcher and Peters assume in their calculations that .476″ is the diameter of the slug, assigning it a larger cross-sectional area. The four large-caliber bullets in the Thompson-LaGarde tests don't differ appreciably in diameter, only in weight, speed, shape, and energy.

Of the 13 animals shot, a total of eight were attacked with the four 45-cal. cartridges. The 30 Luger was used on two critters, and 38 ACP, 38 Long Colt, and 9mm Luger got to show their stuff on one beast apiece. Of the 45s, two types had bullets designed to expand. Both expanded in the testing. Of the smaller calibers, none were constructed to expand without striking bone, and none did.

On the first day, eight animals were shot. The scene was the killing floor of the Nelson Morris Co. Union Stockyards, Chicago. Range was 3 feet. Every effort was made to shoot cattle in non-vital areas, so as to measure stopping power instead of wounding effect. In these summaries, we have rearranged the firings according to caliber, and eliminated unnecessary detail in the autopsies.

(Editor's Note: From the official report, what follows is what happened in 1904. It's middling ugly. There doesn't seem to be an honest way around publishing it. KW)

● **476 Eley**

288-grain lead round-nose, 729 fps, 340 ft. lbs.

1st animal: Stag, 4 years old, 1200-1300 lbs. (A stag is a critter castrated after maturity.)

Two shots were fired through the lungs, left to right. The impacts were 4 inches apart. Did not fall for 4 minutes, was dead at 5 minutes.

4th animal: Stag, 1300 lbs.

Shot through the intestines, once. After 2 minutes, shot through intestines again.

After 70 seconds, (3 minutes and 10 seconds from first shot), shot through intestines again.

Still standing at 6 minutes and 10 seconds, the beast was shot twice in the head.

Standing at 7 minutes and 15 seconds, shot in the ear.

Standing at 8 minutes and 15 seconds, shot behind the ear.

With no effect noted, the animal was killed with four blows of a sledgehammer to the head. Autopsy showed that no slug had reached the brain.

● **455 Man-Stopper**
lead cylinder, hollow point, hollow base, 218.5 grains, 801 fps, 312 ft. lbs.

8th animal: Stag, 1250 lbs.

Shot once through lungs left to right.

After 1 minute, shot again through lungs.

At 2 minutes and 10 seconds, shot through intestines

At 3 minutes and 15 seconds, shot through intestines.

At 4 minutes and 15 seconds, showing "no particular manifestation of pain or shock" animal was killed with hammer. The bullets recovered from the abdomen, where no bone was struck, were uniformly expanded.

● **45 Colt**
220-grain hollow point, 700 fps, 239 ft. lbs.

6th animal: Cow, 1000 lbs.

One shot through lungs.

At 1 minute, shot through lungs again.

At 2 minutes, began to fall and was shot through the abdomen twice.

Both bullets shot through the lungs struck ribs and expanded. Only one bullet was recovered from the abdomen, and it was undeformed.

● **45 Colt**
250-grain lead bullet with small flat on point, 720 fps, 288 ft. lbs.

7th animal: Bull, 10 years old, 1300 lbs.

Shot through lungs.

At 1 minute, shot again through lungs.

At 2 minutes, shot again.

At 2 minutes 35 seconds, shot through abdomen and fell.

At 2 minutes 45 seconds, shot again through abdomen, *got up,* then fell again—tried to regain his feet for 70 seconds—and was killed with the hammer.

● **38 ACP**
130-grain round-nose full metal jacket, 1107 fps, 354 ft. lbs.

5th animal: Steer, 1100 lbs. (A steer is a bovine castrated before having any fun at all.)

Shot through lungs.

At 1 minute, shot through lungs again.

At 1 minute 35 seconds, shot again, same way.

The animal fell only after four blows with the hammer. The two bullets recovered had struck ribs and were slightly flattened. The last struck no rib and was lost.

● **38 Long Colt**
148-grain round-nose lead, 723 fps, 191 ft. lbs.

3rd animal: Stag, 1200 lbs.

Shot through lungs, scampered about.

Two minutes, 30 seconds; shot through lungs again, jumped around.

Three minutes, 20 seconds; shot again, staggered for 30 seconds and fell.

This critter had a 16″x18″ tumor of the right lung. Further, it was discovered that the last shot had punched through the aorta.

● **30 Luger**
92.5-grain full-jacket flat point, 1420 fps, 415 ft. lbs.

2nd animal: Stag, 1200-1300 lbs.

Shot through lungs left to right; dropped 30 seconds later.

Autopsy showed that bullet cut posterior aorta, left body and was lost. Contusion surrounding the wound track described as "not quite so extensive as with 476 revolver."

At the end of the first day's tests, Thompson and LaGarde could not have been very happy. They had shown that bullets through the aorta led to prompt collapse from bleeding, that shots through the lungs led to *eventual* collapse by suffocation, and that shots through the intestines might fell the foe the next day through peritonitis and hemorrhage. Nothing like Stopping Power or Shock Effect had happened. Sometimes the animals had showed fright; sometimes blood flowed from mouth and nose as a result of bleeding in the lungs, but on the first day no critter fell promptly with any non-lethal wound. Not only did these shootings fail to show the superiority of the 45s, they did not demonstrate that "stopping power" existed at all.

So, on the second day, a new procedure was adopted. Animals were now to be shot as fast as possible, until they fell, or until they had been hit 10 times. It was hoped that the shock to the nervous system was additive, and that the number of shots needed to floor an animal would reveal the relative merit of the cartridges being tested.

On the second day five cattle were shot.

● **476**
12th animal: Bull, 1100-1150 lbs.

Dropped after sixth shot. All shots through lungs.

● **455 Man-Stopper**
13th animal: Bull, 1150 lbs.

Five shots through lungs.

After 30 seconds, three more shots through lungs.

After one more minute, two more shots through lungs, animal began to fall and two more shots were fired through abdomen.

Abdominal shots mushroomed to .70; all others were deformed to some extent.

● **45 Colt**
flat point

9th animal: Cow, 950 lbs.

Shot through lungs, fell at the sixth shot.

Free hemorrhage from one exit wound; four bullets recovered, considerably deformed.

● **9mm Luger**
FMJ, flat point, 123.5 grains, 1048 fps, 301 ft. lbs.

11th Animal: Cow 1100 lbs.

Shot twice through lungs.

After 1 minute, (there was a jam) shot six more times through lungs.

After reloading break, shot twice through abdomen and twice through lungs.

Killed with hammer.

● **30 Luger**
10th animal: Cow, 950 lbs.

Shot through lungs, three times.

After 1 minute, (to clear jam) shot five times.

After reloading break, shot twice; then killed with hammer.

On the second day, two of the five animals fell promptly. The bull hit with 455 Man-Stopper had stood for a minute and a half, taking 10 lung hits before collapse. The two Luger rounds couldn't be fairly compared to the revolver loads, for their jams had given the targets a considerable intermission for recovery. And if the felled steers had dropped from shock effect, why not from wounding effect? Shock effect is hypothetically cumulative, but wounding effect is certainly cumulative. The lesser calibers were not given a fair test, and *still* the 45s didn't look very good.

In their report to the Ordnance Department, Thompson and LaGarde recommended that any new service pistol be at least 45 caliber. They maintained that *caliber* was important, not velocity or energy. But they hedged their conclusions thusly:

"...the Board is of the opinion that soldiers armed with pistols or revolvers should be drilled unremittingly in the accuracy of fire, and that the vital parts of the body, their location and distribution in the organism, should be intelligently explained. Based upon the distribution of the vital parts, and parts of the body which when hit insure sudden stopping of an adversary, the Board hopes, in its complete report, to furnish a target of a shape to include the more essential points to be hit in the body ... The Board has been prompted to refer to this point because of the prime importance of decisive shooting at close quarters, and of the large amount of the target area of the human body which *offers no hope of stopping an adversary by shock or other immediate results when hit.*"

You may think a 45 slug through the abdomen or the muscles of the arm will make you fall down in a swoon. Maybe it will, especially since you *think* it should, but Thompson and LaGarde did not believe it. They wanted soldiers trained to make head, heart, and spine shots.

Neither Col. LaGarde nor Stephen Trask remembered the tests rightly in later years. Trask says of the quick-firing test:

"...the steers shot with 38 ACP and 38 Long Colt dropped after six or seven shots ..."

But, as we have seen, neither of these cartridges was used in the quick-firing.

"With the 45 Colt revolver the steers dropped after the fourth or fifth shot ..."

But as we have seen, no critter dropped before six hits.

"With the 455 and the 476, they dropped after the third or fourth shot ..."

Which didn't happen.

Harder to understand is the way Col. LaGarde misquotes himself in *Gunshot Injuries:*

"The animals invariably dropped to the ground when shot from three to five times with the larger caliber Colt's revolver bullets ..."

But in truth, both 476 and 45 Colt needed all six. And 455 needed 10.

The remarks for 45 Colt—"free hemorrhage from one exit wound"—suggest an artery hit. But this was not investigated.

You can't prove anything about

stopping power from the Thompson-LaGarde live animal tests. Maybe it exists, but not at handgun energy levels. Maybe it exists in people, but not in animals. And maybe it doesn't exist at all, and every combat shooter should use his handgun as deliberately as a surgeon wields a knife.

A modern experimenter would do things very differently. He would shoot more critters—say, 10 for each load. He would take pains to have all of them about the same age, weight, sex, and glandular condition. He would assign the same number of beasts to each cartridge. He would test a wider variety of cartridges, and make sure that expanding bullets were available in each caliber. All these things Thompson and LaGarde could have done, but they neglected them. They did not get Man-Stopper slugs for 38 Long Colt, or hollow-points for 30 Luger, 9mm, and 38 ACP. They did, however get 476 Eley from Britain and have a Colt New Service chambered for it. And 32-20, 38-40, and 44-40 were available at the corner store, but they were not tested.

So the work of Hatcher—and to some degree the work of Peters—is based on a false understanding of both the quality and the results of the live animal tests of 1904. If anyone wishes to claim that stopping power is some phenomenon independent of wound effect, he will have to prove it some other way.

In the cadaver testing there was much better uniformity among the targets: All were dead. These human bodies were hung by the head and shot with various loads at various ranges—3 feet, 37.5 yards, and 75 yards. The amount the corpses swayed when hit permitted the board to estimate (they did not measure) the momentum imparted to the target.

A little anatomy: Between the joints, human bones are hard, strong, and brittle; sort of like glass tubes. At the joint ends, the bones become much thicker to provide a large bearing area, and though the hard outer layer—the cortex—is thinner, it is backed up by a thick layer of spongy honeycomb. So we should expect a bullet to have different effects in different parts of the same bone.

When flesh alone was hit, only the hollow-points—45 Colt HP and 455 Man-Stopper—produced any sway at all. When the joint ends of bone were hit, all loads made a pretty similar twitch, though 455 and 476 seemed somewhat better.

When the hard shafts of bones were fired on, there was enough difference

in the amount of sway for the researchers to put numbers on it. However, you must remember that these are not *measurements,* but subjective impressions.

38 Long Colt lead round-nose	50
30 Luger, flat point FMJ	60
38 ACP, round nose FMJ	60
30 Luger FP FMJ, *tip filed*	60
38 ACP soft-point	70
38 ACP RN FMJ, *filed*	70
9mm Luger FP-FMJ	80
45 Colt, lead small flat	80
45 Colt, lead hollow-point	85
455 Man-Stopper	87
476 (really 455) lead round-nose	100

The impressions don't line up according to caliber. The 30 Luger FMJ flat-point did better than 38 Long Colt, and equaled 38 ACP RN-FMJ. 9mm Luger FP-FMJ matched 45 Colt lead flat-point.

In wounding effect against the bones, all these rounds were *tactically* equal. All could easily produce a compound fracture of shin or thigh bone, making it impossible for a man to run, and difficult for him even to stand.

Directed at the softer joint ends, all but one round punched simple holes that would not always be prompt handicaps. The 455 Man-Stopper would fracture joint-ends at 3 feet, but failed even to penetrate them at a distance.

LaGarde did observe that the revolver fractures were more complex, and would take longer to heal. This isn't relevant to gun-fighting. The break may knit in 6 weeks, or it may take 10—gunfights don't last that long. Six weeks after the fight, the survivors are sitting around the fire telling lies—oops, *anecdotes*—and the losers are rarely present to correct exaggerations or offer their own.

The live animal testing provided no sound basis for any estimate of stopping power. The cadaver testing proved you could have fine wound effect with the 9mm flat-point, or 38 ACP with a similar bullet. In neither test series did the results justify or support the Board's conclusion that *caliber,* rather than energy or bullet form, was the important factor.

Why did LaGarde make recommendations that his tests would not sustain?

I don't know. It is interesting that the flat-point 9mm recently adopted by the U.S. Air Force is very like the one tested in 1904. We have taken 76 years to come full circle in the design of 9mm military ammo. Louis Anatole LaGarde had a lot to do with that delay. ●

by JEFF COOPER

Long Ago and far away—in the great days of hunting before the rot set in—there existed an association of gentlemen known as the Five Seven Seven Club. A member in good standing never ventured out of doors without a cartridge in his pocket, a 577 Nitro Express cartridge suitably engraved with his name. Upon meeting with fellow members, he who could not produce his badge of membership was honor bound to buy the drinks.

The 577 Nitro Express was quite something and it still is. It is a "super heavy," one of two hunting rifles in that category, the other being the 600 Nitro. The 577 fires a bullet that weighs 750 grains at an initial velocity of 2050 feet per second (fps). It is not the most powerful hunting rifle ever built, but it was certainly the most popular, and probably the most effective, piece of this kind. It outshone the 600 during the era of big ivory by a considerable margin, probably due to its reputation for superior penetration.

The super heavies are very specialized instruments. They are not just "elephant guns;" they are useful only to the tradesman, not the sportsman. The sportsman who hunts elephant does not need such devastating power, since he hunts in the company of a competent professional who is also powerfully armed, he chooses his one bull with care, and he avoids any single-handed confrontations with an enraged herd. On the other hand the tradesman—the money hunter—hunted by himself, and his objective was all the ivory he could gather in one session. He went right in among them and he worked like a tight-end amid 12,000-pound line-backers. His shot had to work—every time—or he was squashed like a bug. Often shooting from the hip at ranges of a few steps, he needed all the power he could hold. Hence the super heavies.

An elephant's skull is made of spongy bone much like styrofoam, with the brain—the size of a football—situated deep inside that huge mass. Shooting at the head and hoping to hit the brain is like shooting at

One carries a really big gun when one needs a . . .

CRUMPLER!!

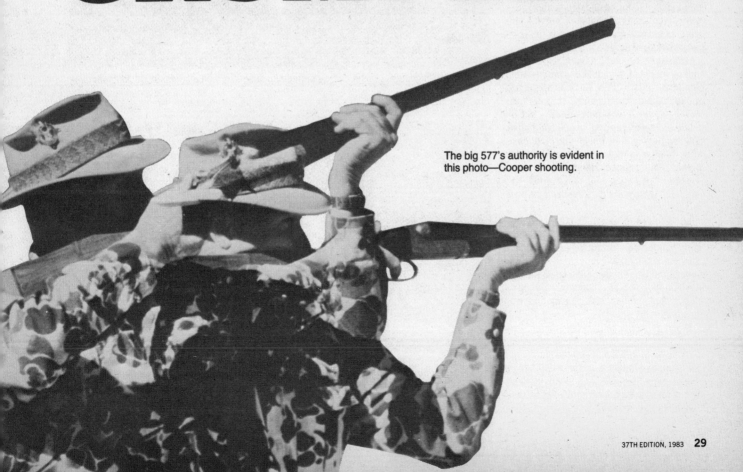

The big 577's authority is evident in this photo—Cooper shooting.

the Pentagon and hoping to hit the gymnasium. A brain shot with any gun will stop any elephant, *but the head shot with a super heavy will knock an elephant out.* With a super heavy all you had to do was hit the head, solidly. And you may have had to do that just as the trunk was reaching out to seize you. That is why you squandered a year's profits on a pair of rifles only a duke could afford.

Jim Wilkinson, the renowned hunter from Prescott, Arizona, recently acquired a magnificent "Best Grade" Westley-Richards 577, and when he showed it to me I all but lost my composure. Here was a true work of art—from the zenith of the machine age—manifesting man's ultimate genius in steel. The concept is Euclidean, the design is Archimedean, and the execution is worthy of Benvenuto Cellini. Everything has been foreseen, nothing has been sacrificed to economy, and the workmanship is such as we will never see again. The action rolls open and shut with soft, silent precision and the seams, when closed, can scarcely be seen without a magnifying glass.

Such artifacts have never been cheap, and today they are very costly. Jim's rifle is worth about four times what I paid for my first Porsche (in 1953) and now you might buy its sister for half what a new, top-of-the-line, street Porsche costs. In the Twenties, when this rifle was made, one of its cartridges was worth the price of a first-class dinner in a first-class restaurant. It still is today.

Despite the intimidating cost of such a piece, it was not conceived as a rich man's toy. While the very rich might buy it for display, it is a completely serious weapon. Such gold as it bears is not placed there for show, but rather to assure by bright contrast that a vital message will be unmistakably transmitted. "Safe" and "Bolted" glow on the tang, and "L" and "R" below denote which barrel will fire first.

The lockwork is instantly detachable, without tools, and the fitting of these parts can only be appreciated under glass. This is no mere affectation, for this rifle was intended for use months beyond the help of any gunsmith. It had to work. Your life depended on it.

Jim's example is fitted with a selective single trigger and automatic ejectors, both of which features were optional and debatable in the brave days of old. Barrel selection is an advantage if one lock has broken, but it does make for complexity—a thing to be

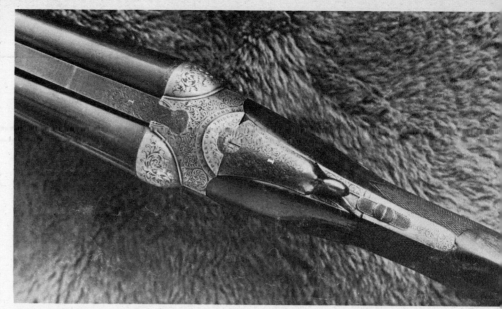

Fitting—metal to metal, wood to metal—in the 1920's Westley Richards rifle brings joy to writer's heart.

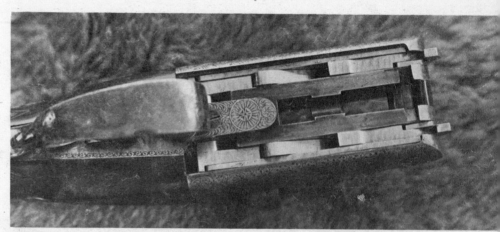

Expensive? Of course, but the money brought such sensibilities as dropping locks, even prefitted spares.

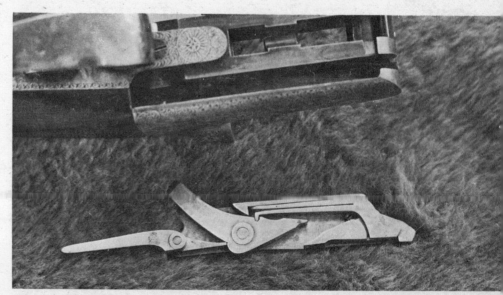

This bit of lockwork is easy to get at, even in the field, which means maintenance isn't slacked.

avoided. Automatic ejection is fast but noisy, and it tends to lose brass in tall grass. The noise of ejection always seemed irrelevant to me, in view of the immediately preceeding blast, until it was explained that the beasts are not alert before the shot but are very much so immediately thereafter. The *bang* comes as a bolt from the blue, but any *clink* that follows is a dead giveaway. We American hunters tend to forget that the hunting of really dangerous game is usually an arm's-length business.

The power of the super heavies is enormous, just on the edge of controllability. "Pondoro," the famous John Taylor, states that they are really practical only for men of "quite exceptional physique." Such values are subjective. After shooting Jim's 577 at some length I feel that anyone who could play first-rate high school football—as a lineman, line backer, or blocking back—could manage it with confidence, after a bit of conditioning. It kicks, you may be sure, but not so much that a strong man cannot control it. (I cannot resist the jibe that any lady who can shoot it well is no lady.)

At the front end, the 577 "literally crumples elephant"—John Taylor speaking again. Its striking energy exceeds 7000 foot pounds, but kinetic energy is a misleading measure of striking power. Momentum is better. If we use the "M" factor now in force in I.P.S.C. rifle competition a sampling looks like this:

Caliber	"M"
308	42
375	75
458	100
460 Weatherby	135
577	144
600	171

But momentum disregards impact area, which is not to be disregarded. The cross-sectional area of a 46-caliber bullet is 1.6 square inches. That of a 58 is 2.6. Thus on Pondoro's "knock-out" scale we see this:

Caliber	"KO" Rating
7×57	15.6
318	27.25
375	40.1
404	49
470	71.3
505 Gibbs	86.25
577	126.7
600	150.4

If John Taylor is accepted, the super heavies are simply not comparable to the lesser calibers—not even to

Wilkinson holds his pride with pleasure. He likes to shoot his double rifles.

Strong hands are needed to manipulate a really good and really big rifle.

such old reliables as the 470. I do not interpolate more recent developments such as the 458, the 460 G&A Special, and the 460 Weatherby, all of which fire the same 500-grain, 46-caliber bullet; but we can estimate the 458 at something between the 404 and the 470, and the Weatherby at about 95.

Ammunition for the 577 is scarce. The original English Kynoch is long out of print and thus a rather choice scalper's item. New brass may be had from B.E.L.L. (if you can get their attention) but the bullets must be hand-made unless you wish to order a thousand or so. Jim does not have any shooting ammunition for his prize but I was able to impose on Ross Seyfried, who also owns a crumpler, to let us have 15 test rounds. Fifteen is enough. After half-a-dozen I began to notice a certain lack of delicacy creeping into my trigger squeeze. All that is needed is a short breather, however, and the touch comes back.

Shooting Jim Wilkinson's marvelous rifle was a rare delight. I was admittedly a little intimidated by all this talk of unmanageable power, so it was a nice surprise to discover that the 577 is really not all that bad. The "Number One" Westley-Richards weighs 13½ pounds—no more than one of these heavy-barrel M1A's, scoped and loaded, and it is neither so heavy as to feel clumsy nor so light as to break your bones. And it is *short,* a characteristic of doubles that makes for fine balance and easy mounting.

The trigger is quite good enough for clean control, and there is no problem in hitting an apple-size target from offhand at elephant range. We found that we could keep our shots in the black if we concentrated on it—a three-inch bull at thirty-five paces. The requisite concentration did become more difficult as the experiment progressed, but then one does not shoot a 577 in long strings. Among other things, only an Arab could afford to.

I noticed that it is wise to keep the thumb over on the right when hip shooting, since if the butt is not supported against the shoulder the locking lever may be driven back into the web of the hand. Held waist high, the rifle pointed very well for me, and it was apparent that this technique could prove very useful in various close encounters of the terminal kind.

Another thing that became obvious was that very strong hands are required to load and unload the piece. The moving parts fit so perfectly that they seem to glue together, and both opening and closing the breech takes force.

Cooper found the hip-shooting potential of the 13½-pound rifle just fine for the requirements—a 55-gal. drum at five or ten yards.

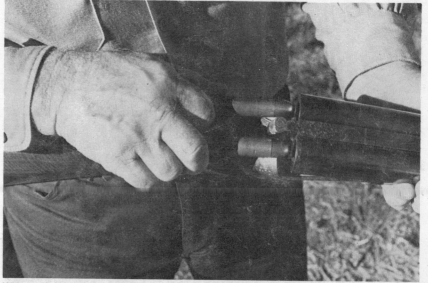

With multiple targets sometimes on the menu, the professional 577 shooter learned quick-loading technique.

As a reward for unspecified merits and services, an official once furnished GUN DIGEST with honorary membership in the .577 Club of Rhodesia, but made no mention of engraved cartridges or rounds of drinks. One wonders if there is a .577 Club of Zimbabwe and who belongs?

.577 CLUB OF RHODESIA

.577 NITRO KYNOCH

GUN DIGEST MAGAZINE of Illinois in the United States of America.

28th. October. 1980.

This is to certify that Gun Digest has been made an Honarary Member of the .577. Club of Rhodesia and is entitled to all the priveliges of membership.

Dennis CASTELL.

President.

Stock fit is an individual matter, but the stock of Jim's rifle suited me very well. The day after shooting I felt no tenderness at all on cheek or shoulder, and only a trace of discoloration on the biceps due to one bad mount in which I dropped my right elbow. There was no abuse of the second finger, such as is common on bolt-action heavies with vertical trigger-guard backs.

Various commentators have held that the super heavies, while undeniably perfect as "back-up guns," are too cumbersome to pack around all day. On this subject it is unwise for one man to speak for another. What bothers Smith may not bother Jones. My own opinion is that exhaustion is exhaustion, and two or three pounds of rifle have little effect upon it. What is a "practical weight" is a matter of dispute among practical rifle contest organizers, but it would seem wiser to put up with 13½ pounds of 577 than to quibble about the questionable advantages of a 14½-pound 308. The two problems are not the same, of course, but I cannot credit the notion that a heavy rifle, at 11½ pounds, is appreciably handier than a super heavy at 13½.

The prewar British gunmakers were justly proud of their work. They combined theory with practice in a way that can no longer be justified economically, even if the necessary skills still exist. Artistry in steel is strictly a function of free enterprise and does not fit into the catalogs of the welfare state. Jim, who deals in fine guns, is of the opinion that certain Italian shops might be able to make rifles of this quality, assuming they had a guide to show them what they were trying to achieve. I suppose there are people in Liége and Ferlach who might be able to do the same. But since there no longer is a demand there is clearly no need to meet it.

A thing of beauty is a joy forever, indeed. And if that thing is a perfect instrument for a demanding task the joy is greater. And if that task is a matter of immediate life and death, the effect is inspirational.

Sinfully, I covet my neighbor's rifle. Not only sinfully but foolishly, for I have no earthly use for it. Even in the grand old safari days I would never have needed it, for the ivory trade is properly left to ivory traders. Wanting to possess what one cannot use is wicked, yet, being mortal, most of us have an occasional wicked thought. If I could find a really good use for a Westley-Richards "Best Grade" double 577, I'd keep having one. ●

The Monte Carlo Is Functional

by NORM NELSON

I SUBMIT THERE are, next to teenagers, no more trendy, fad-conscious peer-conforming groups than gun nuts. The best current proof is the Great Classic Stock Craze.

Teenagers show they're really with it by going slack-jawed and catatonic in the presence of highly repetitive and totally inane rock music. Gun nuts and gun writers show almost identical symptoms when exposed to today's shooting world theme songs which go, in punk rock style, something like: "Classic stocks are the Alpha and Omega, than which there is none whicher."

The contrapuntal melody is that the humpbacked or Monte Carlo type of assuredly non-classic stock with cheekpiece is a horrid thing, utterly demeaning.

Recently a shooting buddy and I browsed the second-hand rack of a large gun store. A nice-looking 375 H&H caught his eye.

"Look—it has a Classic Stock!" he murmured in an excited but reverentially low tone. You could hear the religious capitalizations.

If we loosely define the outstanding features of today's so-called "classic stock" as witless recidivism, he was right. This moderately light big magnum had a narrow, low comb betraying its Old Europe design inspiration, from whence we also received the Curse of Dracula. If the comb had been any narrower, it would have served to flesh coyote pelts. That is not the type of contact I want my face exposed to, particularly when 30-plus foot-pounds of recoil is the initial bonding agent.

That obvious *caveat* was lost on my friend. He stood there, mouth agape and eyes glazing, for all the world like John Steinbeck's halfwit Lonnie stroking a dead rodent. He fondled—there is no other word for it—this lovely example of how not to fashion a rifle stock.

Since first I found them, my favorite folk heroes have been the urchins who loudly and rudely announced that the passing emperor wore no clothes. So I couldn't resist snatching that 375 from my friend's hands before he broke out in glossolalia or other manifestations of religious ecstacy.

"Very nice," I jeered. "This lovely classic stock with all that heel-drop and skinny comb will beat you to death with recoil. I bet the owner consigned it for sale to help pay for the dental repairs this torture stick made necessary."

My chum first looked as if he were passing a kidney stone. Then the storm broke. Couldn't I see the great, classic lines of this stock? Unmarred, that is, by any damned Monte Carlo or droopy cheekpiece?

All I could see was a well-made, nicely figured stock that was both pleasing to the eye and almost hilariously in error from a functional standpoint.

To argue was apples-and-oranges pointlessness. He was talking aesthetics or beauty in the eye of the beholder. I was talking functionalism or how the thing works in use. Interestingly, he never tried to rebut me about the fairly vicious facial recoil problem that this good example of the classic stock promised along with other inherent design problems. His argument in this case would have been not with me but with Isaac Newton.

That's typical of the Classic Cult. Their worship of the classic stock and ridicule of the Monte Carlo-cheekpiece school are invariably on esthetic grounds. I think that's a tacit admission that the Monte Carlo cannot be logically assailed on functional grounds. The hard, philistinian truth is that a well-designed, properly dimensioned Monte Carlo stock with cheekpiece is superior for scope-sighted rifles. It's the common-sense stock.

Continued on page 36.

Classic stocks are fine on rifles meant for look-pretty wall hanging, Nelson says, but for serious hunting he picks a decent Monte Carlo.

EDITOR'S NOTE

The two writers involved in this GUN DIGEST Discussion were only last year represented in a discussion of shotguns in *Field & Stream*. On that occasion, Petzal took up typewriter on behalf of the double gun; Nelson, as you might imagine, bespoke the pump gun.

I didn't know that was going to happen, but I think it's neat. When, in one of his customarily acid letters, Norm fussed and fretted over the "witless recidivism" of the straight-comb stock, this whole thing came into blinding focus. I had recently broken bread with Dave and observed his gold Rolex watch and J. Press

The Monte Carlo Kicks And It's Ugly

by DAVE PETZAL

Only Filson gear truly suits a man who shoots a left-handed Model 98 by P. O. Ackley, stocked by Joe Balickie—this is Petzal prepared for elk.

suit, so I knew he was the natural-born other half of the piece.

In case the photos don't show it, Nelson and Petzal are the same height. Petzal is a fitness freak and regularly presses something like 300 pounds and has a big chest and shoulders and stuff. The last time Nelson pressed 300 pounds was when he cashed a big check in London—he's more the lean and enduring Scandinavian sort of fellow. I think those circumstances affect their attitudes, but I don't know how.

Myself, I favor the classic German *schweinrücken* form of buttstock. It combines the best shooting features of both styles and is better looking than either.   *Ken Warner*

IT WOULD BE easy to start off an article like this with a cultural comparison of riflemen who prefer classic stocks and them as favors stocks with Monte Carlo combs.

We could say that the classic-stock shooter spends his evenings by the fireplace in the library, listening to Beethoven's *Eroica*, and sipping from a snifter of rare brandy.

The gent who prefers the hunchback stock would start his evening thrown out of a bar called "Bill Bob's Bucket of Blood," and finish in his pickup drinking beer and listening to Johnny Paycheck tapes. He would greet the sunrise by throwing up on his $25 imitation lizard cowboy boots.

But this is neither true nor is it good journalism. We must not dwell on the failings of one group of people or another, but instead evaluate the Monte Carlo and the classic from two viewpoints: Which works better, and which looks better?

The classic stock is an idea that has been evolving since the early 1920s when the first Springfield sporters were made. Over the ensuing 60 years it has undergone only a few real changes. The comb is much straighter, the cheekpiece is likely to be the Schuetzen type rather than the Whelen. The detailing is far superior, and the finish may be synthetic. Otherwise, the two are quite similar.

Therefore, when I read that my counterpart in this debate blamed the late Jack O'Connor for " . . .this witless recidivism. . ." (the classic stock) I went to the dictionary, and found that recidivism means "a tendency to lapse into a previous condition or mode of behavior."

The late, great Jack was no recidivist. He was merely using what worked, as are the thousands of riflemen who have refused to go along with the idea that because something is new and weird, it is good.

We have seen that the classic stock

goes back a long way, and that it has been subject to constant, if subtle, improvement. Now, let's look at the pedigree of the Monte Carlo.

Monte Carlo stocks came to their height of popularity during the 1950s and 1960s, an era which produced two major developments in sporting rifles. The first was a proliferation of new cartridges, and the second was the ascendance of the California stock.

To understand this golden era, you must recall that then people actually had money to spend on frivolous objects. Yep, honest to recidivism, in those dear, departed days you could buy a house with a single-digit mortgage, or get a car every two years, or buy a new rifle if something revolutionary was announced.

The 1950s and 1960s saw the introduction of such highly useful cartridges as the 458 and 338 Winchester Magnums, the 280 Remington and the 7mm Remington Magnum. Those years also saw the arrival of such questionable rounds as the Winchester Magnum 264, the 256, the 221 Fireball and the 6.5 Remington Magnum. Hand in hand with these developments came a new style of rifle stock. It had a Monte Carlo comb, rosewood fore-end tip, whiteline spacers, a shiny finish, and, often, skipline checkering. Pistol grips were exaggerated, and fore-ends assumed strange cross-sectional shapes, such as square or trapezoidal.

Now there's nothing wrong with all this. Shooting is a hobby, and therefore for fun. God is not going to get you if you like California stocks. (I don't know what He thinks about recidivism.)

But remember, we're talking about function, and about that hump atop the stock. Well, it sure was different. After years of straight combs, there was this thing rising up like a wave out of the sea, and sometimes it even

Continued on page 38.

For all its art-for-art's-sake charm, the classic rifle stock became as obsolescent as the biplane fighter when good low-priced scopes killed iron sights in the hunting field.

Never mind the non-sequitur, peripheral arguments in behalf of the classic stock. True, today's classic stock is notably free of wild scrimshaw and over-ornamentation. That's beside the point, since a Monte Carlo job can also be left unembellished and many are. The classic classic has a usefully slender forearm profile in contrast to the semi-varminter clubbiness of too many custom stocks in the post-World War II Golden Age of Godawful Gunsmithery. But a practical stock's front end can be graceful, too, so no score either way.

Classic stockmakers today tend toward sweptback pistol grips. I know not if they're inspired by esthetics or functionalism here, but that's the best grip for fast handling, as shotgunners have known all along. Again, a Monte Carlo stock can be made this way.

The classic stock's key problem is the travesty of good shooting design executed in the low and lovely, big-heel-drop, often slender-combed, buttstock. This simply robs the shooter of cheek support when he's trying to center his eye in a scope mounted at least 1¼ to 1½ inches above the rifle. This problem becomes more acute with varmint scopes and the big-optic variables, all of which require even higher mounting. Unless you have the facial dimensions of a Grand Canyon jackass, you wind up cheeking your classic stock comb not up against your cheek for maximum stability but precariously down along your jaw line.

Not only is that low, classic comb less steady, but it's very unpleasant with today's powerful cartridge recoil. As the rifle kicks back, the high-in-front comb jacknifes itself up against your cheekbone. If recoil is potent, this wedging action is violent enough to induce flinching.

By contrast, what I think of as the neo-classic, the Monte Carlo with cheekpiece, has a comb line that can and should be shaped to slope down toward the front. It looks non-traditional, and thus has a near-laxative effect on pseudo-classicists, but in recoil, this front-sloping comb slides below your cheekbone. It does not leverage you a mean sock in the sinuses.

It's a common-sense design.

Does it make a difference? You bet. Your cheekbone area is one of the more sensitive parts of the body. As you read this, try giving yourself a sharp little jab under the cheekbone. It doesn't take much impact to cross the discomfort/pain threshold. Furthermore, that impact leaves a surprising after-ache. It could last a whole day if obtained from a classic stock comb propelled by reasonably stout recoil.

Even striplings can take lots of shoulder recoil. That's a somewhat insensitive area or no one could stand to play football. Anyone, however, who says he doesn't mind taking big-cartridge recoil in the face is either prevaricating wildly or had better check medically to see if a little case of leprosy has killed his facial nerve endings.

Case in point: I have a very light 35 Whelen Mauser. This is one hard-kicking rifle, naturally, but I crafted

Above and right—Nelson says suitable Monte Carlo cheekpieces are simply more practical in the field for the near-universal use of scopes, East and West.

Below—Nelson's personally-stocked 257 Roberts G33-40 here shows the best of the Common Sense school of stocking: a Monte Carlo cheekpiece to assure fast, solid cheeking with a scoped rifle, slender forearm flattened on the bottom for rest shots, and a moderately sweptback pistol grip without awkward flaring to hamper the hand.

THE SHAPE OF STOCKS

the Monte Carlo comb line to slope down evenly toward the front. When a combination of 250-gr. bullets and near-max powder charge drives this light sporter back violently, that comb slides back hard and fast, all right, but departs from the cheekbone area en route. Result: it's less tough in facial recoil than some sharply dropping, thin-combed and elderly Winchester 94s, even though the Whelen is generating three times or more the recoil energy.

Of course, the Monte Carlo and cheekpiece must have suitable dimensions, and those may vary with the individual shooter. Last fall, I blew a now-or-never snapshot at an elderly, heavy-beamed whitetail due to too thick a cheekpiece of my own making. The tick of time it took to cant my face a tad right blew my chance at a buck already airborne toward thick balsams. With better fitting Monte Carlo stocks, I've killed a fair number of bounding whitetails, muleys and blacktails that required all the celerity of snapshooting flushed grouse. Those shots leave no time for rubbernecking from a too-low comb, believe me. Here the curse of the classic stock is that a quick attempt to snapshoot too often finds you looking not through the scope but somewhere underneath it until you correct your cheeking. There is no time for that when a spooked buck is kicking gravel.

Well, then, if the classic stock is not logically the superior gun handle that a decently made Monte Carlo version is, why today's near-worship of the classic lines? Why do most gun nuts today upon handling a classic stock manifest the body twitching and eye-whites exposure seen at Rolling Stones concerts?

For one thing, the classic stock is a natural backswing from the gaudiness of the so-called California or Hundred Dollar Whorehouse school of stock design. Navaho Thunderbird inlays, patriotically red, white and blue spacer plates, and inletted Plexiglas renditions of Venus de Milo with a compass in her navel deserved their present oblivion.

Then, I suspect that a real hidden factor in the hard-sell of the classic stock by stockmakers is that a Monte Carlo is a hell of a lot more work to make, narrows the choice of blanks available, and reduces the profit margin. Thus stockmakers would naturally much rather talk you into a classic stock.

Third reason for the classic stock cult, dear hearts and gentle shooters, is that we were most enjoyably brainwashed into it. The cult's latterday founder and most articulate high priest was the late, lamented Jack O'Connor who had more influence on gun nuts and gun writers in the last four decades than anyone else even approached. Jack was easily the most readable, entertaining gun writer of our age and had a huge magazine and book audience.

Jack was also an extremely conservative chap in all outlooks, including tastes in firearms. He was firmly wedded to the classic stock. His early bolt action sporters were classic, no-cheekpiece jobs, simply because that was still the age of iron sights. With those, the Monte Carlo's higher comb line is not needed and may in fact be a literal pain in the neck. So Jack approached the flowering of his career with classic stocks. And what Jack was comfortable with in his early years, he was self-confessedly reluctant to depart from with the passage of mere time. His wit about the esthetic shortcomings of Monte Carlo combs and cheekpieces was always humorously sardonic. Interestingly, these criticisms, as I recall them from four decades as an avid reader of O'Connor, were always on purely esthetic, not functional, grounds.

There you have it. If your admiration of classic stock rifles overwhelms both common sense and your grasp of Newtonian laws of motion, fine. Of course, they're still useable hunting rifles—the kerosene lamp is still useable illumination, too. Classic rifles do look lovely on the wall; no argument there. And thanks to the great snow job that has blown from all compass quarters, they will arouse envy and approval from your fellow poseurs.

If they, true to form, slaver a bit and make the approving, soulful grunts reminiscent of a pig farm at feeding time, my advice is to quickly name some inflated selling figures and unload your classic-stocked musketry before the bubble bursts. The modern revival of the classic stock, with its foot-stomping, hallelujah overtones of a camp meeting, is one of the Great Nostalgia throwbacks of our times,

but no fad lasts forever.

However, if you are a shooter, not just an armchair firearms voyeur, you want—nay, you need—the greater steadiness fore and aft and the less-felt impact in the kisser that a Monte Carlo cheekpiece of the Common Sense school of rational gunstock design offers. This includes a somewhat flattened forearm—it can still be slender, mind—in contrast to the fulsomely round cross-section of the true classic rifle stock. Reason? The rounded classic forearm is much more prone to tip or cant when you're trying that tough cross-canyon rest shot from a rolled-up jacket or daypack, the shot that can make or break your whole hunt.

The Common Sense stock, like the classic, avoids the hideously flared and severely arched pistol grip that is a hallmark of the California school. These recurving grips, looks aside, commit the unpardonable sin of leaving you precariously clinging to the grip with only your thumb and little finger in firm contact. Meanwhile, common sense more than esthetics warns that ultra-glossy stock finishes can heliograph an alert to sharp-eyed game like antelope, elk and sheep at long distance on a sunny day.

Just remember that the great gospel of the classic stock herd boils down to emotional pitchmanship on personal ethics. You like brunettes; I like blondes; we're both right, right?

When it comes to personal hangups about firearms esthetics, I consider even the best checkering on finely figured gunstocks to be as much an act of barbarism as painting a mustache on the Mona Lisa. Meanwhile, yea or nay quibbling about forearm tips is fun, but puts no bullets in X-rings or horns on the wall.

In the final crunch, the prime function of the woodwork on a working rifle—contrasted with a wall-hanging rifle meant to please the eye and perhaps excite the prostate gland—is to—guess what—improve the shooting. The Monte Carlo approach does this better than the classic stock if you're using a scope—and who doesn't these days? If the classic stock cognoscenti sniff at your humped cheekpiece, be charitable. It may just be their recoil-battered sinuses acting up again. . . .

●

had a rollover on it which, to quote the late, recidivist Mr. O'Connor, was as useful as mammary glands on a male of the genus *Sus scrofa*.

Advocates of the Monte Carlo claim it is necessary to get your eye into line with a scope. For the most part, this is plain untrue. Griffin & Howe, for example, which has been building custom stocks for longer than most of us have been alive, will build a Monte Carlo comb for a shooter, but only if the person has an extremely long neck. Otherwise, they say, it just isn't needed. With a straight modern comb (i.e., one that has just enough drop at the nose to clear the bolt, and no drop at the heel) and a low-mounted scope, it just isn't required. Possibly, a person of normal build could require one if they were using one of the absurd tunnel mounts that are so popular among the greenhorns and the pilgrims these days, but for a person who does not

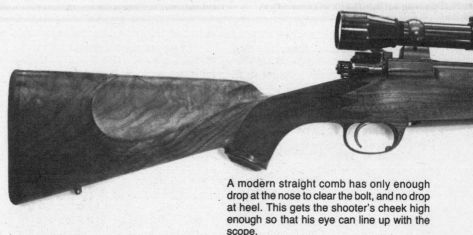

A modern straight comb has only enough drop at the nose to clear the bolt, and no drop at heel. This gets the shooter's cheek high enough so that his eye can line up with the scope.

modate the limp-wrists who now wear the uniform, went to an ineffective, if kickless, cartridge, and an absolutely straight stock. The M-16 may not be worth a damn as a military arm, but it does not kick, either.

A Monte Carlo stock has exactly the

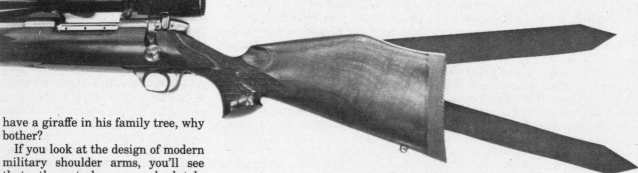
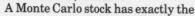

have a giraffe in his family tree, why bother?

If you look at the design of modern military shoulder arms, you'll see that the stocks are absolutely straight, and that the iron sights are quite high above the comb. Nevertheless, these guns, which are designed to fit all sorts of weird physiognomies, do fit, and without a hump.

The reason military stocks are so

Above and below—The amount of punishment delivered depends largely on the angle between the line of the comb and the centerline of the stock. With all else equal, the extreme Monte Carlo comb (above) will hurt more, since more of its force will be directed upward into the head. The smaller the angle between the arrows, the better. (Note: Arrows are correctly aligned; camera angle makes them look low.)

straight brings us to our second, and greater condemnation of the Monte Carlo—recoil. It is no secret that one

Petzal demonstrates that when he shoulders a straight-comb stock with head nearly erect, only a very slight movement is required to line up the eye with the sight; the head had to come down only an inch or two. That is, he says, provided the scope is mounted low, and you don't have a neck like a greater kudu, or Norm Nelson.

reverse effect. In the 21st GUN DIGEST, W. John Farquharson wrote an article entitled "Handsome Rifles," in which he examined stock types in detail, and explained that the high-comb Monte Carlo stock accentuated recoil, while the straight-comb classic minimized it. The key element, said Farquharson, is the angle between the line of recoil and the centerline of the buttplate. A stock with a pronounced Monte Carlo comb has a buttplate centerline which angles sharply downward, while the recoil thrust is straight back. The net effect of this is that when you pull the trigger, the comb is driven into your face, rather than the butt into your shoulder, exactly as on those old rifles with lots of drop at comb and heel.

A straight comb has far less of an angle between the buttplate centerline and the line of recoil. This design allows the stock to come straight back, and keeps the pain in the shoulder where it belongs. It will not make much difference to your shoulder which type of stock you prefer, but prolonged use of a high Monte Carlo with a hard-kicking rifle will leave you thinking that you are Louis XIV, *Le Roi Recidivist.*

But, says the Monte Carloist, what about the fact that the sharply downsloping comb of the M.C. lets your face slide along it, and away from the recoil? Well, in theory that's nice, but what really happens when you fire a rifle is that your head doesn't move at all in the case of a light-kicking gun, and is flung away from the stock, backward, in the case of a heavy kicker. That forward-sliding business does not occur.

About looks. If you like shiny stocks, huge, flaring pistol grips, rollover combs and great humped cheekpieces, who am I to tell you that you have less taste than the beasts of the field? After all, is not art subjective?

Well, yes, but the fact remains that there are certain immutable laws of design. Objects that exhibit economy and purpose of line, that are under-rather than overstated, are generally held to be handsome. As an illustration, let us contemplate the 1959 Cadillac, the one with the tail fins that could be used to slice salami, punch holes in beer cans or impale unsuspecting pedestrians. At the time it appeared, it was hot stuff, and Cadillac sold a lot of them. Today, it is grotesque; huge, garish and ill-proportioned, with those monstrous, non-functional fins overshadowing the whole dismal profile.

If you look at a Rolls-Royce of the same year, you will perceive that it is a dated design, certainly, but there is a dignity to it which says that this was the best of its time. It is a car that you would not be embarrassed to drive in 1982. That is because the Rolls designers employed only those forms that were functional, stayed with the minimum, and relied on understatement to achieve their effect.

To extend this principle to another field, let us take the designs of Bob Loveless, the man who revolutionized custom knives. The Loveless Dropped Hunter is, above all, subtle. There are no humps or knobs, no great swooping curves or other exaggerated lines. It is a very plain knife—unless you have experience using a knife on game. Then you can see that it is a work of genius. Every line is there for a reason, and every line is reduced to its absolute minimum. Bo Randall, who was the Main Man before Loveless, had that same gift for simplicity and grace of line.

So that is why today, when a knowledgeable shooter takes $3,000 to $5,000 to a first-class stockmaker, the odds are that the end result will be a conservative, classic stock with a straight comb. The more experienced the shooter and the more talented the stockmaker, the more inevitable will be this type of stock.

It was the classic gun buffs who, while we were deluged with weird new cartridges, kept having guns made up in 257 Roberts, 7x57, 280 Remington and 250 Savage. Oddly enough, all these once "outmoded" loads are enjoying a renaissance. Could them pesky recidivists have known something all along?

As for myself, I own two Monte Carlo stocks. One is on an o/u trap gun. The other is a Weatherby that was made up in the Southgate custom shop in the early 1960s. It is a very handsome piece of California claro which I have no intention of discarding. Everything else of mine is humpless.

That's what's in my heart. I hope you agree with me. After all, I'm right. Now, if you'll excuse me, I have to throw a log on the fire and put on the Beethoven. ●

THERE ARE FEW wildcatters among shooters or hunters in Europe, and fewer still among gunmakers. But Doctor Lauren Kortz is one such, and he's been a designer of powerful non-standard cartridges for some years. His prime favorite at this time is the 459 Elsa K, a rimmed-case round with impressive size and matching performance.

Dr. Kortz' career—in medicine and gunmaking—has had its difficult and dangerous periods. He obtained his degree in chemistry from Oxford and not long after was a member of the British armed forces, fighting in Burma. Captured there, he spent four years in a Japanese prisoner-of-war camp, lucky indeed to have survived its rigors without serious physical damage.

As a native of Austria, Dr. Kortz had hunted over much of his country, mainly in the mountainous Tyrol area. Living in Austria after the war, he looked forward to hunting in Africa and India, trips he'd planned during his long confinement. At that point, he's told me, he could find no big game cartridge that satisfied his desires—the big British calibers were disappearing fast. He set about investigating the making of his own designs, not that his big 459 Elsa K appeared just then.

Kortz, with characteristic determination and dedication, decided he'd become a gunmaker. That was about 35 years ago, and he has long been a member of the Ferlach *Genossenschaft*—the gunmakers of Ferlach in association. That's where his guns are made, though his practice and official residence is now in Brussels, Belgium.

As is the general practice at Ferlach, Elko Arms can—and has—supplied rifles, shotguns and combination guns in any configuration desired. That covers boxlocks and true sidelocks, side-by-side and over-unders, single-barrel break-open rifles—well, you name it. Kortz specializes in the exotic styles. He's made the various forms of three-barrel guns (drillings), including those with all shot barrels or all rifle barrels. He has also made *vierlings*, that is, four-barrel guns. He is working now on an improved four-barrel shotgun/rifle, having patented a simplified single trigger for it.

I've known the energetic Doctor for many years, and his knowledge of gun design and construction is vast. I don't know how he finds time for his industrial clients! For about the same lengthy period, I'd been thinking about having a *Bergstutzen* made, one to fit me and made to my ideas and dimensions.

The term means "mountain rifle," one of light weight which combines two calibers in an over-under rifle of rather different form than usual, about which more later. These rifles are chambered for a big game caliber and a *schonzeit* (off season) small caliber. My choice in calibers was the 375 H&H belted magnum and the 22 Hornet, the latter still a popular load in much of Europe. Certainly not the Alpha-Omega of disparate cartridges available to a custom gunmaker/wildcatter—or customer—but ample performance differences, yes?

Matter of fact, I'd asked Dr. Kortz for his big rimmed 375 at first, but reamers were not ready for his "im-

ELKO ARMS DOUBLE RIFLE

by **John T. Amber**

Muzzle view of John Amber's double rifle, an over-under chambered for the 375 H&H Magnum and 22 Hornet. Note flattened sides of top barrel.

The Editor Emeritus selects yet another very special gun

proved" version so we settled on the justly famed and time-tried old workhorse. I was never much of a wildcatter, so it's doubtful if I'll have my new *Bergstutzen* converted to his 375 Elsa K rimmed case.

As usual these days, I didn't get my Elko Arms rifle in a minimum of time. Some 34 months have passed since Kortz and I got our heads together at a London gun show. But the wait has been well worth it.

The handsome over-under double rifle now here exemplifies the traditional *Bergstutzen* in its adherence to the elements of style that distinguish the type. First, it is a light firearm at 7 pounds, meant for easy carrying in the steep places of the world. Next, the sides of the top barrel are flattened from muzzle to forend tip, giving a sort of octagon-barrel appearance; some *Bergstutzen* have both barrels flat-sided. Last, the forend—a three-piece affair—rises to all-but-cover the top barrel. In this rifle the top edges of the rounded-section forend stop at the sides of the quarter-rib.

This quarter-rib, its matted top

about 9mm wide, holds a shallow-V rear sight, its rear surface matted to reduce glare. Just ahead of the rear sight this integral rib drops down a bit, narrows to about ⅛-inch, and runs out to the front sight base, also integral with the barrel and well matted. The front sight is a 1/16-inch gold bead.

The barrels are 25 inches long. The top barrel, measured across the opposing flats, is 0.374-inch; the 375 H&H runs 0.535-inch, both muzzle measurements. Side ribs connect the barrels, these slightly concave in form. The barrels and ribs are well and fully polished, no signs of ripples or waviness marring their satin luster.

The action is stongly bolted. Besides two underlug bits, there is a third fastener a la Merkel, this a bolt entering a cut in the rear face of the rear locking lug. In addition, double Kersten-type rear lugs project from the barrel-breech faces at top, these round-holed to accept the top-lever-actuated crossbolt.

This Elko Arms double rifle is not a true sidelock, though a hasty first look would so indicate. The plates are

The Elko Arms over-under rifle has only one firing pin bushed, that for the 375 H&H Magnum barrel.

An unusual aspect of Bergstutzens (mountain rifles) is a 3-piece forend, the upper sides curving over the top barrel to abut against the raised rib. Non-functional, to be sure—a long-observed fashion or custom.

Center of interest here are the twin Kersten-bolt barrel extensions and the plain extractor, a one-piece affair. (Donna Coss photo)

Amber's light mountain rifle shows trim clean lines, a first in classic form for Elko Arms. The 25-inch barrels are unlike in caliber—375 H&H Magnum (lower barrel) and 22 Hornet, the latter for off-season or varmint shooting. (Donna Coss, Hillside Studio, photo)

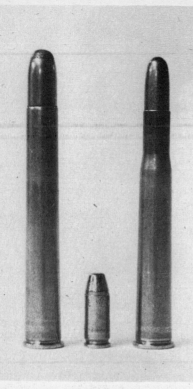

Maximum cartridge dimensions of the 459 ELSA K Super Magnum. The desired 3.5-inch length was not feasible using B.E.L.L. Lab. brass, hence the 3.3-inch length shown. The 375 EK case has the same dimensions except for mouth diameter.

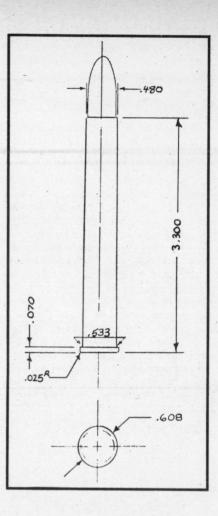

Headstamp of the 459 ELSA K MAGNUM.

The Elsa K 459 (left) compares with the same cartridge in 375 caliber. The 9mm Luger cartridge is included (center) for scale comparison.

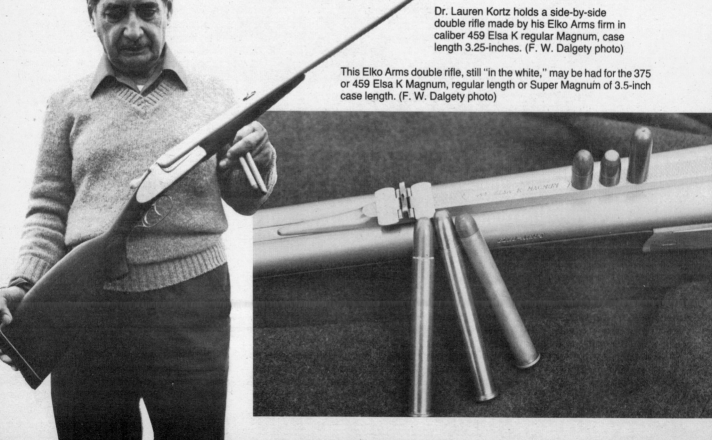

Dr. Lauren Kortz holds a side-by-side double rifle made by his Elko Arms firm in caliber 459 Elsa K regular Magnum, case length 3.25-inches. (F. W. Dalgety photo)

This Elko Arms double rifle, still "in the white," may be had for the 375 or 459 Elsa K Magnum, regular length or Super Magnum of 3.5-inch case length. (F. W. Dalgety photo)

dummies, though they do carry cocking indicators on each side. The action is, in fact, a trigger-plate system, long known in Germanic gunmaking circles as the Blitz action, and best known in Great Britain as the action form used by John Dickson on his round-action guns. Today, it's also used on some Perazzi shotguns, among other makers.

The bar of the action is reinforced by integral extensions of the fences, these tapering forward. Most of this added steel lies at the foot of and behind the standing breech. The firing pin for the top barrel is not bushed for ready removal; the lower 375 firing pin is set in a bushing.

Two triggers are fitted, either of which can be used normally or pushed forward to act as a set trigger. Both are well rounded and smoothly polished.

Another traditional part of Austrian and German gunmaking is the trigger guard made of Indian buffalo horn, which this over-under has. However, mine is not as bulky as were many in the past, and there's room within the guard for a gloved finger.

The safety, blued and checkered, lies in the top tang, locking the triggers. The safety operates smoothly and silently, but some effort is needed to move it. It is not likely to be moved inadvertently.

The stock wood was furnished by me, as were the grip cap and recoil pad. The American walnut blank I'd had for over 20 years, so it had ample time to air dry. Dr. Kortz was also able to get the forend out of it, and the result is pleasing—the crotch-feather grain looks much like the fancy figured wood that Winchester used for many years on their high grade guns. The blank was originally properly cut, too, for the pattern of the grain is virtually identical on both sides. The color is a warm, reddish hue, moderately dark yet still revealing the grain.

The buttstock form is pure classic, I'm glad to say, but I would not have been greatly surprised if it were not. It took a bit of arm twisting to get it done this way, but Dr. K. came through nobly, once he learned what was wanted, via talks with him and some photographs I'd furnished.

The top line of the comb is straight, as is the heel-to-guard line, and there is no cheekpiece. The comb is fairly full, as is the body of the stock, and the comb-nose fluting is done to perfection. There is an old relief-engraved silver grip cap, with a gold initial A, one I got years ago from Bill

A different Elko Arms drilling. The rifled tubes may be ordered alike or differing, as shown; the smooth bore barrel can be had in any standard gauge.

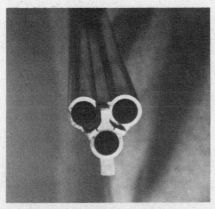

Breech-end view of an Elko Arms all-smooth bore drilling, here in 20 gauge.

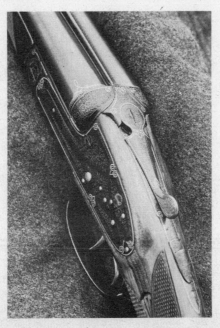

A true sidelock double gun made by Elko Arms in de luxe grade. Inlaid gold lines and fine scroll engraving embellish the frame and lockplates. (F. W. Dalgety photo)

Dyer; the dark brown recoil pad is a Pachmayr Old English, without white spacer or vents.

The pistol grip has a fillet behind it, the sort of style touch Tom Shelhamer liked. The grip is a bit too closely curled at a guess; my second finger pushes against the rear of the horn guard, especially when the front (375 H&H) trigger is engaged. So there may be some bruising—I'll know better once I've shot it.

The checkering, cut to a multi-diamond pattern, covers most of the forend, sides and bottom—9 inches overall. The pistol grip panels are broad and full length. The checkering is very well done, considering its fineness; the pattern is bordered, so no runouts show, but some diamonds are flat topped along the borders. My old hunk of walnut took the checkering well, but at 30 lines per inch it is too fine; I've already found a couple of broken areas in the forend, but when or where this happened I can't say. What I can mention is that the gun was held by U.S. Customs in New York and Chicago for some 10 days.

The engraving is very nice, done in the Austrian style—a combination of acanthus leaves, scroll and game scenes, all showing well against the

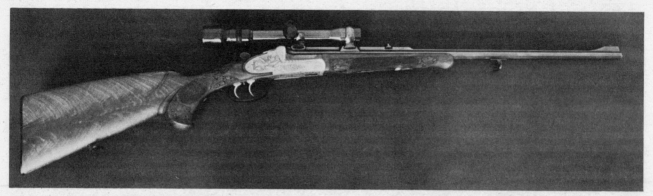

A single barrel break-open rifle produced by Elko Arms of Brussels, Belgium. (F. W. Dalgety photo)

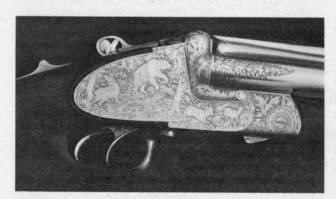 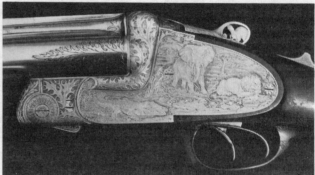

Customer's choice. This 4-barrel may be had with all barrels rifled or with rifled and smooth bore tubes. Here the owner asked for and got an extra quartet of barrels. (F. W. Dalgety photos)

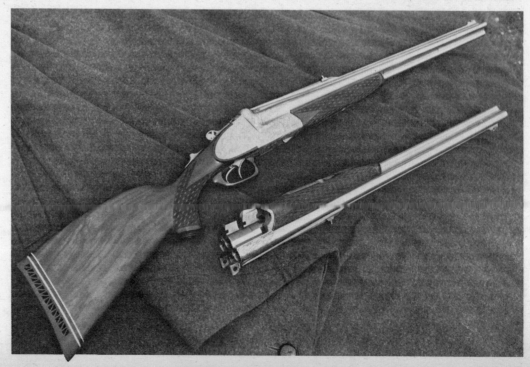

grayed sideplates and the receiver bottom. On the last is an *Auerhahn*, tail fanned and booming its mating call. On one side are two European moose, a bull and a cow; the opposite plate shows a pair of moufflon

The DB rifle fits me well. I gave Dr. K. my dimensions, and I got 'em—14⅜" pull to front trigger, 2¼" drop at comb nose and 2½" at heel. That is with open sights, to be sure. Whether

I'll add a scope and mounts, I don't know at the moment. If I can get a low-lying mount, perhaps using the ¼-rib for a base, I'll probably have a glass mounted. Otherwise, I don't want to spoil the clean, smooth lines of this delectable rifle.

As always, I'm anxious to get out and shoot this new rifle. Well, maybe not all that eager to touch off a 375 H&H 300-gr. bullet in a near-7 lb. ri-

fle. As many of you know, I'm a pretty old party now, and I'm probably pretty fragile, too. I don't want to bust a collarbone. Rather than shoot from a bench, I'll try a ladder I've rigged up for shotgun patterning. That—and a sissy bag—should help. We'll see.

Dr. Kortz is firmly convinced that rimmed cases are the best by far for break-open rifles—and I fully agree. He gives compelling reasons for his preference: Because the drop-down gun accepts long-length cases without the problems a bolt-action rifle would have, cartridge cases as long as 3.3 inches are available; his rimmed magnums are 3.25 inches long, his super magnums 3.3 inches. Both are made from Jim Bell's latest case, big enough to let existing 375 H&H and 458 Winchester rifles be converted to the Kortz design.

A. F. "Tony" Sailer of C-H has long worked with Dr. Kortz on these new case designs, and it is he who will eventually supply handloaded ammo, according to present plans.

Further benefits of the rimmed case lie in its much simpler, more reliable and positive extraction ability. Because extraction/ejection systems for break-open guns are complicated and hard to regulate, Dr. Kortz warns prospective buyers that he cannot guarantee trouble-free extraction of rifles made for rimless cartridges.

Regardless of their form, Kortz makes amazing claims for his rifles' grouping ability at 50 or 60 meters range. He guarantees that left-and-right or top-and-bottom barrel groups won't exceed three inches. Even more surprisingly, he maintains that such grouping, which is fully acceptable, will result whatever the bullet weight loaded! Frankly, I find that hard to believe, and I'd want a field demonstration as proof. It is usually difficult enough to regulate double-barreled rifles, much less multi-barrel types.

Bottom line! What do the Kortz magnums provide that factory loads don't? Tony Sailer says worthwhile muzzle velocity increases for both, hence better energy figures, of course. How much? Some 200 or more foot seconds for both, with pressures *normal*. Either case holds 100 grains of powder.

The 375 EK will retain more of the gain at its useful ranges of 100-200 yards. The 459 EK, used at its ideal ranges, 50 to 80 yards, won't shed much MV or ME. A 600-gr. bullet load will be available from Sailer, too, projected to produce 2200 fps or more, and should lose very little velocity at 50 yards-plus. •

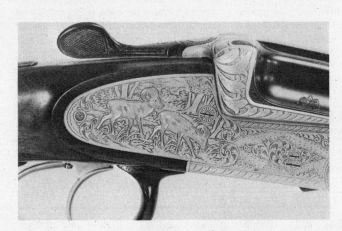

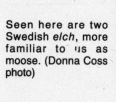

The animal depicted here is the European moufflon, a favorite nowadays with Continental engravers. (Donna Coss photo)

Seen here are two Swedish *elch*, more familiar to us as moose. (Donna Coss photo)

This sterling silver-gold grip cap was furnished by Bill Dyer. The high-relief scroll is cast in. (Donna Coss photo)

The underside of the Bergstutzen shows an Auerhahn male in the mating season, the background cut to scroll and forest scenes.

For the most part, I cannot imagine any consumer product as reliable and trouble-free as most of the ammunition produced by the major ammunition manufacturers in the United States. There are over a billion rounds of factory shotshells produced each year and the factory centerfire rounds total nearly as many. The number of rounds of rimfire ammunition produced is no less than staggering. These cartridges as a whole produce very, very few problems, but there are a few cartridges which one can justifiably call troublesome. Some are troublesome in factory form while others become troublesome only when one attempts to reload them. A few are troublesome both as factory rounds and as reloads. Being well-informed about these cartridges can help you avoid the potential problems, or perhaps you may choose to avoid the cartridges completely.

Troublesome, in the context of this discussion, goes well beyond the potential hazard created by sticking the wrong shell in an inappropriate chamber. The problems that can be caused by the misuse of ammunition under such conditions have been discussed on a number of occasions and in a number of different publications. However, to my knowledge, no one has previously addressed the problems caused by the very nature of a few specific cartridges. To keep the suspense at a minimum, let me state that the cartridges I consider troublesome include the following: 22 Remington Jet, 225 Winchester, 220 Swift, 256 Winchester, 30-30 Winchester, 303 British, 38 Super, 358 Winchester, and finally, the 444 Marlin.

If you were on a hunt and lost your opportunity at a trophy due to the fact that your gun misfired, you might be inclined to blame a bad primer rather than the cartridge itself. Such things as revolver malfunctions, poor accuracy, a blown-up gun, shells that won't chamber, pierced primers and misfires can be caused by a great many different problems. In some cases like these, the problem may well be the choice of cartridge you made when selecting your firearm. Some problem cartridges can be used successfully if one is fully aware of the precautions that should be taken. There are only nine calibers involved amongst almost 100 different offerings currently available to the American consumer, so it is easy to deal with them on an individual basis:

22 Remington Jet

Many owners of the fine Smith & Wesson revolvers chambered for the

TROUBLESOME

by EDWARD A. MATUNAS

These eight cartridges and the 256 Winchester make trouble. The problems with the 22 Jet, the 38 Super and the 225 are correctable by the shooter.

22 Remington Jet cartridge have complained of extreme difficulty encountered with cylinder rotation in the use of their handgun. Some have reported that the cylinder would simply not rotate in either the single-action or double action mode. A number of these shooters have felt that their guns had excessive headspace, thus creating the problems. Others have blamed the ammunition producer for loading shells that produced excessive chamber pressures. Few, if any, have laid the fault at the doorstep of the cartridge designer. And it is at his doorstep that the fault lies.

When the folks at Smith & Wesson decided that a high velocity centerfire 22-caliber handgun cartridge would be beneficial to their line of handguns, the task was put to the cartridge designer. It was decided that the 38 Special case would be used as the basis of the new cartridge. Un-

but I can still remember the hopeless binding of the cylinder. It was impossible to fire the gun after the first few shots. I began my inspection by opening the cylinder and removing the cases. What could possibly be wrong? The cases ejected from the cylinder without any undue effort and a physical examination showed no signs of excessive pressure. A careful scrutiny of the gun revealed no possible reason for the gun malfunction, so I retired the gun to the pistol box and finished my shooting using several other guns.

Back at my bench, I sat down to try to isolate the problem. When I placed the fired shells into the revolver and attempted to close the cylinder, a fair amount of resistance was encountered. I was also unable to make the cylinder rotate once it was closed. It was obvious that the cases had stretched. But why? Recalling similar experiences in long guns I found the

tates is minimal.

The 22 Jet cartridge is best described as triangular in longitudinal section. As extensive examination has proved, the Jet is borderline with respect to its ability to cling to chamber walls. When this cartridge is fired with even the slighest trace of lubricant in the chambers or on the case, the thrust against its base is such that the case cannot cling to the chamber walls, and is forced rearward while it expands.

Repeated tests and investigation soon revealed to me that if the chambers of the revolver were completely free of any lubricant, normal operation of the revolver was possible. But even the slightest trace of lubricant in the chamber or on a cartridge, would result in a useless revolver.

I found that by cleaning the cylinder with carbon tetrachloride I could remove any trace of lubricant. I simi-

CARTRIDGES

doubtedly there was at least a favorable leaning to this decision due to the excellent reputation of the 38 Special.

The 22 Jet is, in effect, a necked-down 38 Special case. It was the style of "necking-down" which caused the problem. Instead of using a rather straight body with an abrupt shoulder to neck the case from 38 to 22 caliber, the designer instead used a very heavy body taper and a long tapered shoulder. Past cartridges of this type should have been a clue to the potential problem. However, for whatever reason, the cartridge was brought to its final commercial form with its excessively tapered body and shoulder.

The initial interest in the cartridge was quite high. Even I was compelled to try one of the then-new S&W revolvers chambered for the 22 Jet. Some of my fascination was, no doubt, in part due to special adapters that came with the revolver which allowed the use of standard 22 rimfire ammunition. I first fired my new Jet with the 22 rimfire ammunition. When I switched to firing with the centerfire 22 Jet loads my problems began. And my problem was identical to that of every other user of the Jet cartridge.

It has been quite a number of years,

obvious connection—that heavy case taper and very long shoulder section. Obviously the thrust created on the relatively large head area of this cartridge due to the heavy body taper and poorly designed shoulder was causing the case to back out of the chamber firmly against the recoil shield during firing. The case was being held in this position while the case body expanded to fill the chamber under the pressure generated by the cartridge.

When, with most cartridges, the cylinder rotates in a revolver, the case is simply pushed back into the chamber. With the very heavy taper and shoulder design of the Jet cartridge, this is impossible. Cocking the gun simply does not offer sufficient mechanical leverage to "resize" the cartridge by forcing it back into the cylinder. Normally, a revolver is matched with a cylindrical cartridge with fairly straight walls. Upon firing, there is usually enough tension created between the cylinder and straight case walls to keep the case from backing out of the cylinder. Also, should a cylindrical case back out of the cylinder slightly, the amount of effort required to force it forward as the cylinder ro-

larly cleaned reloaded cases. After any rimfire shooting session, the cylinder had to be completely cleaned and given the carbon-tet treatment in order to remove the waxy deposits left by this type of ammunition.

I do *not* recommend the use of carbon-tet as a cylinder or case cleaning agent. The hazards to health are simply not worth it. Undoubtedly, other cleaning agents are useful for the purpose. Cases and cylinders must be almost clinically clean and dry, before shooting Jet cartridges.

This demanding care proved more than too much to bear and I rapidly lost interest in the 22 Remington Jet. Apparently, so did most shooters. Smith & Wesson discontinued chambering for this cartridge in 1974. However, they did get to suggesting a "clean and dry system" to their customers before discontinuing the gun. In time, the cartridge will pass into complete obsolescence. Until it does, it would pay to remember that the 22 Jet is one of the troublesome cartridges.

225 Winchester

This cartridge was intended to be

the replacement for the 220 Swift as far as the marketing people at Winchester were concerned. It fell flat on its face with respect to Winchester's hopes. Accuracy in the 225 quickly proved to be very "iffy." Some shooters reported accuracy at a very high level and others claimed accuracy was non-existent. As time progressed many shooters found they were experiencing a yo-yo of accuracy—up one day, down the next.

My first clue to the problem occurred when I was doing the data for the *Lyman #45—Handbook for Metallic Cartridge Reloading*. I quickly discovered it was the most erratic cartridge I had ever worked with. I simply could not reproduce my test results from one day to the next.

After about a week of frustrating results I called the lab of one of the major data producers to ask what experience had shown them with respect to the 225 Winchester cartridge. I was told the 225 had proven so erratic in their testing they had almost decided not to list it. They indicated their data was at best an approximation of what a reloader could expect.

Further investigations revealed that others had had similar experiences. From where I sit, any cartridge that performs erratically or in an unpredictable manner is, at best, a very poor cartridge. And so it is with the 225 Winchester. To my knowledge there are no firearms being chambered for the 225 at this time. The cartridge is rapidly becoming obsolete.

The 225 Winchester is one troublesome cartridge with respect to ballistic uniformity and accuracy which will not be missed by this writer and based on ammunition sales records, it will not be missed by many other shooters. Its erratic accuracy is the kind of problem few shooters will tolerate.

220 Swift

This cartridge ranks as one of the all-time greats as a long range varmint round. Its accuracy is superb and trajectory as flat as a stretched string. Yet is is available as a loaded round only in Hornady's Frontier line, despite the fact that one can purchase new rifles chambered for it. Imported Norma ammunition is also available.

In viewing the problem, one should be aware that more than one worker in Winchester ammunition has been heard to condemn the 220 Swift as the cause of more problems and lawsuits than all other cartridges combined. Or as others from Winchester have put it: "We'll never manufacture an-

other round of that 'blankety-blank' cartridge regardless of how high the demand may be."

During my tenure at Winchester, I was able to get the 220 Swift brass case back into the normal trade channels. But I am convinced that, regardless of the demand, the cartridge will never again be available from Winchester. It was without a doubt a very serious liability for Winchester when in production and a return to production would bring back all the problems. Why? Let me trace the problem for you:

When introduced in the mid-1930s, the 220 Swift was almost a miracle cartridge. It was the flattest, fastest shooting cartridge ever to see the light of day. The muzzle velocity of over 4100 feet per second with its 48-grain bullet was almost unbelievable. But this ultra high velocity did not come about without a very high price tag. The price paid was extremely short barrel life. Even the advent of more modern and tougher steel alloys could not prevent the very rapid barrel erosion that occurred with the 220 Swift.

But so what? Shooters wanted the Swift and it became very popular with varmint hunters. Slowly the problem began to surface—a blown-up gun here and there. The frequency of blown-up guns became such a problem that Winchester finally stopped producing both rifles and cartridges for the 220 Swift. So long as anyone remains in the employ of the Winchester ammunition firm who can remember the severity of the problem, I doubt you will ever see production of this cartridge reinstated.

What caused all those blow-ups is no secret, in my opinion. The problem came about from two causes. One was that barrels eroded very quickly. The other was that users of the 220 Swift were, for the most part, reloaders. Unfortunately, during the period of difficulties, no one chose to educate the user-reloader about the hazards of this multifaceted problem.

Due to the very high pressure levels generated by maximum 220 Swift loads, the Swift case tends to stretch very rapidly. The stretching quickly thickens the neck area of the case. Normally, one can reload cartridges quite a few times between the necessary case trimmings, and, naturally, after a case has been trimmed a number of times, it should be discarded. The number of trimmings to which I limit myself with any case is four. When a case needs its fifth trimming, I discard it. I do this for safety's sake.

After a case has been trimmed four times, one can assume it has stretched to the point where a noticeable weakening of the case has occurred. The brass removed in trimming flowed from the case body, leaving the case thinner and weaker. If you doubt this, you need only section a case that has been properly trimmed four times. The thinned area of the brass wall ahead of the case head will be obvious. Trimming, when required, usually means discarding a case after 16 to 20 loadings.

With the 220 Swift and maximum loads it is necessary to trim every shot or, at best, every second shot. It therefore becomes essential to discard cases somewhere between the fourth and twelfth firing, with the average at about eight firings. Users have shown their reluctance to discard 220 Swift cases that had not been used at least 10 or 15 times. A good number of the blown-up Swifts were wrecked by weakened brass cases that were kept in service for too long.

This problem is compounded by the fact that as the brass flows forward making case trimming necessary, it also thickens the case neck. The neck will rapidly thicken so that the case neck bears firmly against the chamber walls. When the cartridge is fired, there is no room for the case neck to expand to release the bullet. This raises pressure notably. Combine this increased pressure with a weakened case and you will find even more explanation for the large number of blown-up Swifts.

Extensive neck thickening can occur well before a fifth trimming. A prudent handloader should carefully measure the neck diameter of his loaded case before the first firing. This diameter should be checked after each loading. When it has increased by .002″, the case should be discarded without further firing. Some turn the neck down to relieve this problem. This procedure does not take into consideration the fact that a case which has thickened in the neck has had a weakening material flow from the case body.

The Swift's problems were undoubtedly aggravated by reloaders who put together loads which developed pressures exceeding the maximum 53,000 pounds per square inch. Actually, if one wants more than just a few loadings from a case, pressures should be held to a maximum of 50,000 pounds. I personally do not think that loads over 48,000 psi should be used in cases that are to be used for more than a half-dozen firings. The literature of the past shows that many of the suggested 220 Swift loads did indeed produce very high pressures. Combine a weakened case with a too-thick neck and too much pressure, and it is easy to understand why so many 220 Swifts were blown up.

There is yet another problem which contributed to the number of wrecked Swift rifles—barrel erosion. The Swift eroded barrels very rapidly due to hot chamber temperatures and very high velocity. Eroded barrels may not look very rough to the shooter examining his bore from the muzzle or chamber end of the barrel. However, a cross-sectioned area of an eroded barrel greatly magnified presents a surface that is extremely rough. My first inspection of such surfaces came as a real shock. The coefficient of friction of a bullet passing through such a bore would be raised many times over the normal level. The greatly increased friction level will increase internal pressures notably, thereby increasing the risk of a blown gun.

During the period of the Swift's greatest popularity there was a misconception amongst handloaders that as a barrel wore, it resulted in a loss of velocity *and chamber pressure*. Obviously, chamber pressures will actually increase as a barrel erodes. Velocities may go up or down depending upon the amount of erosion and the extent of increase in pressure. However, the uninformed reloader of this period was in the habit of increasing his powder charge as his Swift barrel (or any other) started to wear (read erode). Hence, he compounded the already complex problem. The results were still more blown-up or wrecked Swifts. Needless to say, Winchester had good reason to stop the manufacture of 220 Swift rifles and cartridges.

Today Winchester manufactures only the brass case for the Swift. This relieves them of any liability due to an uninformed reloader's reckless actions. Because of all the past experiences with the Swift, it will probably never become a very popular cartridge again. After all, how many good shooters can be depended upon to use their brass for no more than six firings, to keep pressure at a modest level, and finally, to rebarrel their rifles every 3,000 to 5,000 rounds?

I believe you can now see why the Swift was at best an extremely troublesome cartridge. And why even today it is a cartridge for only the most careful and meticulous handloader, one who is willing to throw away brass cases that still "look good" and who is willing to tolerate frequent re-

barreling. Today's shooter desiring a very flat-shooting 22-caliber cartridge can turn to the 22-250. With only a modest decrease in the Swift's velocity the 22-250, loaded between 48,000 to 50,000 psi, can offer a very pleasing alternative.

256 Winchester

The 256 Winchester presents no problems to the user of factory ammunition. It performs as it should in its original loaded form. It's when the reloader attempts to assemble ammunition from fired cases that the trouble starts.

The chambers of most 256 rifles, such as the Marlin "Levermatic," are substantially larger with respect to length than factory cartridges. The case shoulder therefore moves forward—quite a bit forward—when the cartridge is fired. It the cartridge is full length-resized, the shoulder is then pushed back quite a bit. The firing and loading cycle thus results in a large amount of brass working.

The original—that is, the first—firing and case stretch results in substantial weakening of the case. To repeat the process over and over leads to very early case failure. The ideal pro-

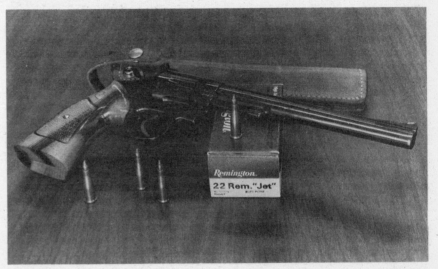

The author's 22 Jet is seldom used because of the difficulties described. "Clean and dry" is the only way it works.

This custom built (by Winchester) single shot Model 70 in 225 Winchester never lived up to expectations. The erratic performance showed up even in this fine rifle.

cedure would be to neck size only, but most rifles chambered for the 256 will not accept cases that have been only neck-sized. The problem for many firearms is not solvable.

My experience has shown that in the Thompson-Center Contender single shot handgun this problem may or may not exist. Since this is the only gun now readily available for the cartridge the problem has become a very "iffy" situation. Despite the merits of the 256 as a handgun varmint round, the reloading problem and resulting short case life makes this troublesome cartridge a very poor choice. Brass cases will seldom stand more than a few reloadings due to the stretch-shrink-stretch routine.

If one would care to have a custom set of dies made to match his chamber

the problem would be greatly reduced, but the case would still be subjected to undue stretch on the first firing. This would weaken them enough to shorten case life noticeably.

30-30 Winchester

As loaded by the factory this cartridge presents no problem. It is only the handloader who will discover the difficulty, a difficulty which may even go unnoticed by many handloaders. The problem manifests itself as a confusion. If one were to start to analyze the available data for the 30-30 an appreciation for the problem would come about quickly. For instance, for a given bullet weight, look in our charts at the extreme variety of data that exists with just a few of the powder selections:

BULLET WEIGHT — 150 Grains
(30-30 Winchester)

Source	Powder Charge (grains)	Velocity (FPS)	Pressure (LUP)
Dupont	35.5/IMR3031	2370	37,700
Lyman	29.5/IMR 3031	2274	39,400
Speer	Not recommended		
Dupont	37.5/LIMR4064	2350	37,800
Lyman	32.0/IMR4064	2313	39,400
Speer	Not recommended		
Dupont	38.5/IMR4350	2080	29,600
Lyman	36.0/IMR4350	2218	38,100
Speer	36.0/IMR4350	2225	MAX (not over 38,000)

BULLET WEIGHT — 170 Grains
(30-30 Winchester)

Source	Powder Charge (grains)	Velocity (FPS)	Pressure (LUP)
Dupont	32.0/IMR3031	2120	37,700
Lyman	28.5/IMR3031	2110	38,600
Speer	29.5/IMR3031	1979	MAX (not over 38,000)
Dupont	34.0/IMR4064	2130	38,000
Lyman	30.5/IMR4064	2150	38,100
Speer	31.0/IMR4064	2056	MAX (not over 38,000)
Dupont	36.5/IMR4350	1935	30,200
Lyman	34.5/IMR4350	2104	38,000
Speer	34.5/IMR4350	2095	MAX (not over 38,000)

Keep in mind that the Dupont and Speer data are for a 20" barrel and the Lyman data is for a 26" barrel. The Dupont data was obtained using Hornady 150-grain bullets and Remington 170-grain bullets, and in both cases new factory-primed Remington cases were used. Lyman used Remington 150-grain bullets and Winchester 170-grain bullets in Winchester cases with Winchester component primers. Speer used (of course) Speer bullets and CCI primers in Winchester cases. Obviously these differences can cause notable changes in the data.

A powder charge change of 10 percent would not be an unheard-of requirement to accommodate a change in components. However, in the 150-grain bullet weight, the Dupont charge is over *20 percent heavier* than the Lyman charge and produces *5 percent less* pressure when IMR3031 is used. With the same bullet weight, Dupont's IMR4064 recommendation is for a 17 percent heavier powder charge than Lyman with a 4 percent lower pressure level. With IMR4350 the charge weights are within reason, being only 7 percent apart. However, with a 7 percent heavier powder charge, Dupont obtained approximately 23 percent less pressures. These differences are more than my experience would indicate possible for the component changes involved.

With the 170-grain bullet weight the maximum powder charge difference is approximately 12 percent. However, the maximum pressure difference is almost 21 percent. The fact that Lyman and Speer closely agree in their powder charge weights does not make Dupont wrong. I am sure that Dupont's numbers are a very accurate reflection of their testing. So what is the reloader to think? Which data does he follow?

The deeper one gets into this confusion of conflicting data, the worse the problem becomes. Of course, it's not unusual for different data sources to present slightly different recommendations. However, the spreads on 30-30 data become far too great to attribute to different lab equipment, techniques and component variations.

I have a theory to explain why data for this cartridge appears to be so erratic, but it doesn't make data selection any easier, not even if I'm right. I suspect the Remington factory primed 30-30 cases that Dupont used contained a primer unlike any available to the reloader. See—it doesn't help even if it might explain.

The reloader simply must be very prudent if he wishes to avoid potential problems with the 30-30 and start with the lowest load shown from a collection of at least three different sources and then work up loads very carefully. There should not be visible signs of pressure in the load you finally select: There should be no signs of primer cratering; cases should extract virtually effortlessly; and they should rechamber easily after firing; there should be no expansion of the solid portion of the case head when the cartridge is fired. If you detect any negative indications in this area, immediately reduce your load to a safer level, and hope that the industry can get together a more uniform approach to developing data for the 30-30. This cartridge should be free of any trouble even if it is only a difficulty in selection of data. It has been with us for almost 90 years and it is supposed to operate at modest pressures.

303 British

This one is a born loser. Perhaps there have not been as many damaged 303s as there have been 220 Swifts, but this is due to lack of popularity more than any other single factor, I think.

Let me tell you about a story that appeared in a trade journal a number of years ago: Harry Shooters was sueing Joe Gun Dealer. It seems a 303 surplus mililtary rifle Harry purchased blew up when he fired one of his reloads. It obviously wasn't the reload's fault since the load was taken from a well-known and respected reloading manual. And it was a light cast bullet load to boot. The gun was obviously defective or it would not have blown up with such a light load, or so the plaintiff's lawyer contended.

Defective rifle? I guess that depends on how you view the situation. The problems with the 303 British cartridge occur frequently enough that at least two data sources have refused to list the cartridge. For a cartridge which served the British empire for so long this seems to be a highly unlikely fate, but nevertheless it is a deserved fate.

The problem starts with the original military ammunition loaded for this cartridge, and some sporting ammunition loaded overseas is also at fault. The 303 British was, in the offending ammunition, loaded with cordite powder. Combined with the primers used, these cordite loads proved to be extremely corrosive. Barrels that were subjected to any notable use with cordite loads soon became severely corroded. The corrosion was so bad in many cases that the bullet friction in passing through the bore became many times higher than normal. The actions of most 303 British rifles do not leave a large margin of safety, so when high internal friction produces excessive pressure it does not take very many rounds to take its toll. Eventually, this toll can lead to a burst gun.

The shooter of any 303 British rifle should take extreme precautions to insure that his barrel is smooth and free of corrosion. If the barrel is rough and corroded the gun simply should not be used.

The problem of corrosion is not limited to surplus military rifles. A good number of 303 British Winchester 95s I have examined have shown extensive corrosion. Obviously the extensive availability of British military surplus 303 ammunition (after World War II) in this country has had its toll on some fine sporting rifles. So this cartridge has become troublesome due to the poor condition of a great many barrels caused by the use of highly corrosive ammunition.

The moral here is if you have any doubts about the condition of any bore in a 303 British rifle, don't use the gun. And of course, should you encounter any bargain ammunition, avoid it like the plague. Finally, slug your barrel. Some 303s have groove diameters as small as .308″ and others as large as .318″. Obviously this can cause problems with bullets that are nominally .311″ in diameter.

This pair of deadly cartridges can raise havoc with more than game. The pictured 220 Swift and 303 British have ruined many a fine rifle.

38 Super Automatic

This cartridge is often cited for its

excellent ballistics. Many an author has expounded on its virtues and then in the next paragraph wondered why the cartridge wasn't more popular.

I'm sure that part of the lack of popularity was caused by the fact that only one basic model handgun was ever readily available in this caliber. The other part of the reason for its low popularity is attributed to its troublesome habit: Pierced primers, or blanked primers, as they are more properly called in this instance, are a relatively common occurrence with this cartridge. This occurrence is most unnerving to any shooter who is concerned with safety. Blanked primers occur as frequently with factory loads

changed in order to develop higher velocity and hence higher pressures.

In the Colt automatic, an inertia-type firing pin is used. This type of firing pin offers some unique firearm safety aspects, but by design, the firing pin is immediately withdrawn from the primer when the gun is fired. This leaves a portion of the primer in front of the firing pin hole unsupported. With the higher pressures in the 38 Super, a blanking of the primer is inevitable. The pressures simply push out a small disc of metal into the firing pin hole. This metal disc *usually* falls free of all the working parts of the handgun. However, it can sometimes tie up a gun. If this happens at

the 38 Super is and will remain a very troublesome cartridge indeed.

358 Winchester

The 358 Winchester cartridge has never become very popular despite its excellence as a medium range big game cartridge. Part of the problem may well be attributable to its only modest level of accuracy. Even when used in a good bolt action rifle such as a Winchester Model 70 Featherweight, accuracy is seldom better than 2″ for 5 shots at 100 yards. Also, the hefty recoil of this cartridge has kept popularity down. However, perhaps the true reason which kept the 358 from making it was its trouble-

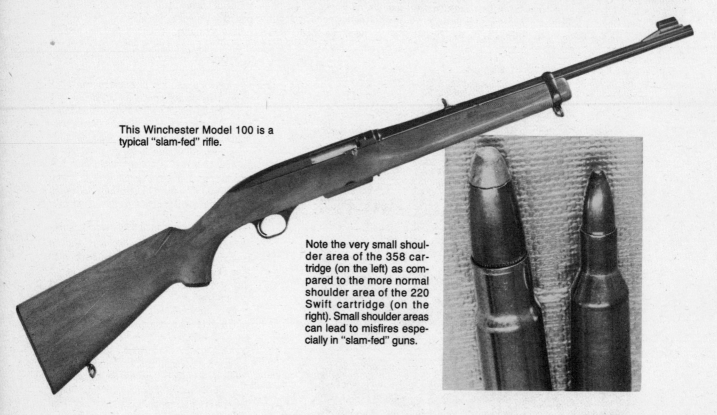

This Winchester Model 100 is a typical "slam-fed" rifle.

Note the very small shoulder area of the 358 cartridge (on the left) as compared to the more normal shoulder area of the 220 Swift cartridge (on the right). Small shoulder areas can lead to misfires especially in "slam-fed" guns.

as they do with reloads in the 38 Super.

No such problems were encountered with the original parent cartridge, the 38 Automatic. When Colt decided to chamber their 1911 model automatic pistol for the cartridge, it was felt a beefed up version of the 38 Automatic could be used since the 1911 was basically a strong handgun. So the 38 Super Auto came to be. A 38 Super Auto cartridge is, in every way, simply a 38 Automatic cartridge loaded to substantially higher pressures. The same case, bullet and primer were used. The powder charge was

the wrong moment, an irate shooter is the best you can hope for. Obviously, depending upon the exact circumstances, a varying amount of gas can be dumped into the pistol action. None of the foregoing are desirable characteristics.

Had the 38 Super been put into a firearm that offered adequate support to the primer by means of a small firing pin hole with a close-fitting firing pin that was held securely against the fired primer, then perhaps the 38 Super would not have earned its reputation as a troublesome cartridge. However, in its present choice of firearms,

some habit of cartridge misfires.

The 358 is no worse an offender in the area of misfires than any other cartridge that has a relatively small shoulder area and which headspaces off the shoulder, but in some of the guns that were chambered for it the problem was magnified considerably.

The very small shoulder area of this cartridge must hold the case back against the bolt so that the primer is crushed fast enough to insure ignition under the fall of the firing pin. Under most circumstances the small shoulder area of this case can get the job done to complete satisfaction. However, there is a problem that many industry people refer to as "a cushioned firing pin blow" which causes the 358 (and often other similar small-shouldered cases) to misfire. This problem can be caused by many factors, but it all boils down to moisture on the case neck in cold weather.

Let's say a case accumulates some moisture on the neck due to being dropped in the snow or being exposed to any environment which would leave moisture on or cause moisture to condense on the case neck. The cartridge, upon exposure to cold temperatures, allows the moisture to freeze, leaving small deposits of ice and/or frost—not water—on the neck of the case. The case shoulder, due to its small surface area, is now unable to hold the case firmly against the firing pin blow because part of the force of the firing pin is used in pushing the case forward in the chamber against the cushion of ice and/or frost. Under such conditions the cartridge can be forced forward into the chamber to an abnormal depth. The cartridge then simply does not go off when the firing pin strikes it.

When inspecting a cartridge after such an occurrence, one would find a full firing pin indent. After all, the firing pin fall was not impaired; it simply was cushioned. The total depth of firing pin indent will be the same as normal. The primer will not ignite, however, because it needs a rapidly applied blow to crush the pellet in a fashion suitable for positive ignition. Upon discovering a good indent, most shooters would blame the primer. In such case as this, however, the primer is not at fault. The cartridge design which leaves such a small area of shoulder for support should be blamed. If the 358 had a belt or rim to headspace on, then the small shoulder area would present no problem as the rim or belt would offer sufficient support for positive ignition. Even if the case is covered with ice or snow, etc., a flat rim or belt area against a similarly flat chamber area would prevent the case from being squeezed forward. The small slope of a tiny shoulder doesn't provide this insurance.

Of course, the problem would be accented in any gun in which the cartridge was "slam-fed" into the chamber as opposed to a "soft feed." By slam-fed, I mean a cartridge rapidly forced into a chamber without the support of an extractor to hold it back against the bolt. A semiautomatic Winchester 100 is a slam-fed gun. The cartridge is driven forward into the chamber at great speed by a bolt which is under heavy spring compression. The extractor does not snap over the rim of the shell until the cartridge has gone as far forward into the chamber of the gun as it can.

An old style Model 70 with its Mauser extractor would pick up a cartridge from the magazine as the bolt was pushed forward. The cartridge rim would slip under the lip of the bolt's extractor long before the bolt reached its maximum forward speed. The extractor would then hold the cartridge more or less against the bolt face. Such a bolt action rifle with a Mauser-type extractor is what I call "soft-fed." A bolt action rifle without a Mauser-type extractor would fit somewhere on a line between the two extreme types of feed. On the end of the line called "soft-fed," misfires caused by cushioned firing pin blows do not occur. On the other end called "slam-fed," cushioned firing pin blows are not at all uncommon.

The amount of trouble with a given gun will depend upon how closely it comes to being a "slam-fed" gun. The Winchester lever action Model 88, while not as violently fed as the Model 100 semiauto, surely qualifies as a "slam-fed" gun. Users of cartridges such as the 358 can avoid misfires caused by cushioned firing pin blows by making certain that their cartridges *and* chambers are kept dry at all times. To do less, especially with the 358 Winchester, will soon convince you that the 358 is indeed a troublesome cartridge.

444 Marlin

The 444 Marlin is a troublesome cartridge only to reloaders. The exclusive use of factory ammunition will not cause any cartridge-related problems. However, the uninformed reader will ruin quite a few fired cases unless he is aware of the peculiarities of loading the 444 (and similar straight walled cases). The problem comes when the reloader attempts to seat and crimp his bullets into the case. Frequently 444 cases will buckle and collapse during this reloading procedure. However, certain steps can be taken to avoid this occurrence.

Success comes from employing the maximum in handloading quality control:

● Cases must be kept to a uniform length by trimming. If the case mouth does not exactly align with the center of the crimping groove in the bullet then a collapsed case will sooner or later occur when crimping bullets.

● Before the first loading of any 444 case and after each trimming you must place a good chamfer on the inside of the case mouth. A Wilson deburring tool or any similar tool will do this. Forget to chamfer and you're going to crush some cases.

● Dies for bullet seating must be precisely adjusted to insure that the center of the bullet cannelure aligns with the center of the case mouth. Crimping dies must make the crimp appropriate for the amount of cannelure on the chosen bullets. It is best to seat bullets in one operation and then crimp in another separate operation. Therefore the 444 Marlin is an ideal candidate for the convenience of loading with a 4-die set. One can use just one bullet seating/crimping die if the die is adjusted to perform only one operation at a time.

Improperly approached, reloading the 444 Marlin can be very troublesome. The expense of ruined cases, however, can be avoided by making sure that all cases are of uniform length, well chamfered on the inside of the neck, and loaded with careful adjustments of the dies.

Conclusion

The troubles encountered with the 22 Jet, 225 Winchester, 256 Winchester and the 38 Super are not readily overcome by the shooter and reloader. It would therefore be my advice that these four cartridges be avoided completely. The problems with the 220 Swift, 30-30 Winchester, 303 British, 358 Winchester and 444 Marlin can be overcome if the shooter is willing to approach these troublesome cartridges in an educated manner. Therefore these five troublesome cartridges can be used by those who are willing to take the necessary precautions. However, there are more than sufficient alternative cartridges available to satisfy the needs of a shooter who wants to avoid unnecessary and troublesome difficulties.

In this light the 22-250 makes a fine substitute for the 220 Swift. A reloader could avoid confusion in 30-30 data by electing to use a 300 Savage or other suitable cartridge. Those who like the 303 British cartridge can elect to use the 30-40 Krag or a similar round. The 358 is nicely bested by the 350 Remington Magnum whose belt will prevent any cushioned firing pin blows. The 444 Marlin is nicely replaced by any good short to medium range cartridge ranging from the 300 Savage to the 350 Remington Magnum.

I have chosen to avoid the troublesome cartridges completely. You make up your own mind. ●

COMPUTERS LOOK AT RIFLE ACCURACY FOR YOU

by DAVID LEESTMA

As simple as can be, you can figure your hitting chances with just a bunch of groups and a ruler — if you're willing to be honest.

OFF AND ON over the years I had given some thought to rifle accuracy and what it meant. After a good bit of thought I decided that the ability to answer the following five questions would indicate I really had a handle on accuracy.

The Questions

1. What does it really mean to say you have a minute-of-angle (MOA) rifle?
2. Knowing the average extreme spread for a 5-shot group with a given rifle and load, how do you calculate the probability of hitting the kill-zone of a game animal?
3. How do holding errors such as those resulting from an inaccurate estimation of range to the target or to neglecting a crosswind affect the probability of hitting a game animal?
4. How do you go about getting a valid average 5-shot group?
5. What effect does the inherent (benchrest) accuracy of a rifle have on group sizes shot from field positions such as kneeling or prone?

Let me tell you the answers to these questions as I found them, applying the methods and tools I use in my work:

The Minute-of-Angle Rifle

Many shooters talk as if a 1 MOA rifle is capable of putting all its shots within a 1 MOA diameter circle about the aim point. This would be approximately true if a rifle was called 1 MOA because several 50 or 100-shot groups never went outside a 1″ diameter circle about the aim point at 100 yards.

When most shooters say they have a minute-of-angle rifle, they mean that the average of several 5-shot

Editor's Note

There are not so many *Docteurs Troisieme Cycle* about that we can ignore one who comes by. Having earned just such a degree at the University of Paris in theoretical physics, David Leestma became, of course, a woodchuck shooter who thinks about it. He calls Virginia's groundhogs woodchucks because he's from Michigan and he think-tanks for a living. Think-tanking is a major industry in Northern Virginia. *K.W.*

groups was 1 MOA. What does this imply about the ability to hit a 1 MOA target? Suppose your varmint rifle has an average 5-shot group of 3″ at 300 yards when shot from benchrest. Furthermore you know exactly where your rifle is zeroed in at 300 yards. Now you put up a 3″ diameter piece of paper at 300 yards and aim at the center of it. Shooting from the same benchrest, what do you think is the chance of hitting that 3″ circle? It is 0.675 or about 7 out of 10. (Obviously the same results hold for a 1″ target at 100 yards or a 2″ target at 200 yards.)

Why is this? Two reasons, principally: First, an average of 1 MOA for a 5-shot group implies there were some 5-shot groups larger than 1 MOA and some smaller. So there is a chance that any given shot will be outside the 1 MOA circle. Second, if the rifle is aimed at the same point on a target and two or more 5-shot groups are fired, the center of each 5-shot group will be in a slightly different position from any other 5-shot group. It is because of these two reasons, for example, that the average 10-shot group from a given rifle is about 1.3 times the average 5-shot group.

As a matter of interest, to have a 0.95 (95 out of 100) chance of putting any given shot within a 1 MOA circle, the average 5-shot group for the rifle would have to be 0.61 MOA. That's why your 1 MOA rifle (based on an average 5-shot group) doesn't keep them all within the 1″ circle when you shoot in a Hunter's Benchrest Match.

Probability of Hitting the Kill-Zone

What does this mean to the varmint or big game hunter? In investigating accuracy I came across a very simple way for any shooter to determine the probability of hitting the kill-zone of a particular game animal target once he knows his rifle's average 5-shot group with a given load and from a given firing position. It is based on the fact that the average 5-shot extreme spread (center-to-center of the farthest hole) is three times as large as a quantity that statisticians call the *standard deviation* of the rifle's dispersion.

This relationship is based upon a computer simulation of a large number of 5-shot groups. Reference 1 gives the relationship for simulations run in 1961. I recently reran the simulation by generating 10,000 5-shot groups and again verified this relationship.

To determine the probability of hitting the kill-zone, proceed as follows:

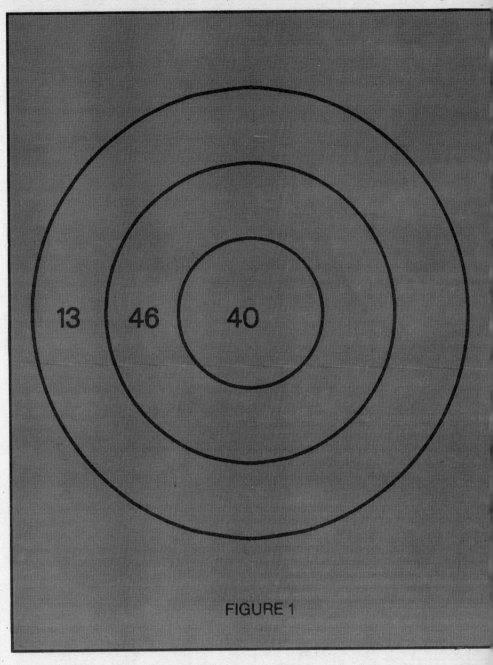

FIGURE 1

1. DETERMINE YOUR AVERAGE 5-SHOT GROUP AT THE DESIRED RANGE.

Suppose you are interested in knowing the chances of hitting the kill-zone of a woodchuck at 300 yards. You have already shot several 5-shot groups at 100 yards (how many groups are necessary will be discussed below) and found the average to be 1″ or 1 MOA. This means that your average group at 300 yards is 3″.

2. DIVIDE THE AVERAGE 5-SHOT GROUP SIZE *AT THE DESIRED RANGE* BY 3.

The resulting number is called the *standard deviation* of the rifle's dis-

persion. *(Note: Dividing by 3 is valid only for 5-shot average groups. For 10-shot average groups the number would be 3.8.)* In the above example the standard deviation is 3″ ÷ 3 = 1″.

3. DRAW THREE CONCENTRIC CIRCLES WITH A RADIUS OF ONE, TWO AND THREE STANDARD DEVIATIONS RESPECTIVELY.

This is illustrated in Figure 1. For the example the circles would have radii of 1″, 2″ and 3″. Statistics tell us something very important about these circles. They say that 40 percent of all shots fired will fall within the circle whose radius is one standard

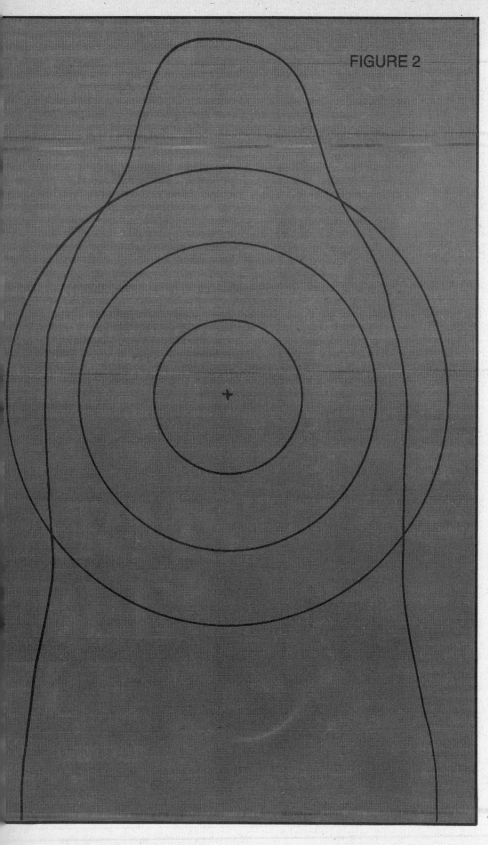

FIGURE 2

OUTLINE OF THE ANIMAL'S KILL-ZONE ON THESE CIRCLES.

This is shown in Figure 2 for a woodchuck. The woodchuck kill-zone I chose is 5″ wide at its widest part and 10″ high. Since I would be aiming to put the center of the group at the center of the woodchuck's chest, I drew the outline in relation to the circles as shown in Figure 2.

5. ESTIMATE THE FRACTION OF THE CENTRAL CIRCLE AND THE MIDDLE AND OUTER RINGS WHICH ARE WITHIN THE KILL-ZONE. MULTIPLY THE FRACTION OF THE CENTRAL CIRCLE WITHIN THE KILL-ZONE BY 40, THE FRACTION OF THE MIDDLE RING WITHIN THE KILL-ZONE BY 46 AND THE FRACTION OF THE OUTER RING WITHIN THE KILL-ZONE BY 13.

As seen for the example in Figure 2, the entire central circle and middle ring are within the kill-zone. Only three-fourths of the outer ring is within the kill-zone. Thus we get

$$1 \times 40 = 40$$
$$1 \times 46 = 46$$
$$3/4 \times 13 = 10 \text{ approximately}$$

6. ADD THESE THREE NUMBERS AND YOU HAVE THE PROBABILITY OF HITTING THE KILL-ZONE.

For the example we have 40 + 46 + 10 = 96. Thus there is a 96 out of 100 chance of hitting the kill-zone.

What does 96 out of 100 chances mean? Well, if you fired a very large number of shots under identical conditions 96 percent of them would be within the kill-zone. However, having a probability of 96 out of 100 doesn't guarantee that for every 100 tries exactly 96 shots would hit the kill-zone. The possibility—although remote—does exist that the first 400 shots would miss the kill-zone while the next 9600 would hit it. *Probabilities don't guarantee an event will happen on a given try; they only indicate what can be expected to happen on the average.*

It is prior to firing a bullet from the rifle in the above example that you have a 96 out of 100 chance of hitting the kill-zone. Once fired the bullet will either be in the kill-zone or outside it.

Table 1 gives the probability of hitting the kill-zone of a woodchuck at several ranges for various average 5-shot extreme spreads. If you really want to score out to 300 yards, it is fairly evident that you need a rifle which groups 1 MOA or less *from the position it will be fired in the field.* (If you will fire from prone in the field,

deviation, 86 percent of all shots fired will fall within the circle whose radius is two standard deviations, and 99 percent of all shots within the circle with radius of three standard deviations. Thus as is shown in figure 1,

40 percent fall in the central circle, 46 precent *(86−40=46)* fall in the middle ring and 13 percent *(99−86=13)* fall into the outer ring.

4   SKETCH *TO ACTUAL SIZE* THE

use the prone position to obtain the average 5-shot extreme spread.) Table 1 also shows that if your big game rifle groups about 3 MOA you still have about 7 out of 10 chances of hitting a chuck out to 200 yards. So, if you want to sharpen up your big game shooting by potting a few woodchucks off-season, don't get discouraged if you can only get 3 MOA groups. You still should connect with a respectable number of woodchucks.

So the big game hunter won't feel neglected, let's say a few words about hitting the kill-zone of a mule deer. The kill-zone can be approximated by a 10″ diameter circle. Suppose from a kneeling position you average an 8″ 5-shot group at 200 yards (4 MOA). If you know exactly where your rifle is shooting at various ranges and haven't made any error in judging the distance to the deer, your chances of hitting the kill-zone at 100 yards is better than 99 out of 100. At 200 yards it is about 83 out of 100 and at 300 yards it has dropped to 55 out of 100. If shooting from prone will cut your group down to 3 MOA, your chances of putting a shot into the 10″ circle at 100, 200 and 300 yards are 99, 96 and 76 out of 100 respectively. A fairly small improvement in group size has had a significant impact on the chances of hitting the deer at 300 yards. That's why it's always desirable to get into your best position for long-range shooting even if your second best position is also pretty good.

Holding Errors

In obtaining Table 1, it was assumed that you know exactly where your rifle is shooting at a given range and that you aimed so as to impact at the center of the woodchuck's chest. For example, if your rifle and load shoot 2½″ low at 300 yards it is assumed that you held the cross-hairs 2½″ above the desired impact point. It was also assumed that there was no wind. What happens if there is a wind you don't compensate for or if you misjudged the range and held too high?

Let's consider the case of a mild (1.6 mph) cross-wind and see how it affects the probability of hitting the kill-zone. Suppose you are shooting a 55-grain 22-250 bullet at a muzzle velocity of 3600 feet per second. At 300 yards it will have been deflected 2″ by the 1.6 mph wind (Ingall's calculation). To observe and gauge the effect, all you have to do is shift the woodchuck outline 2″ horizontally as indicated in Figure 3 and repeat steps 5 and 6 above.

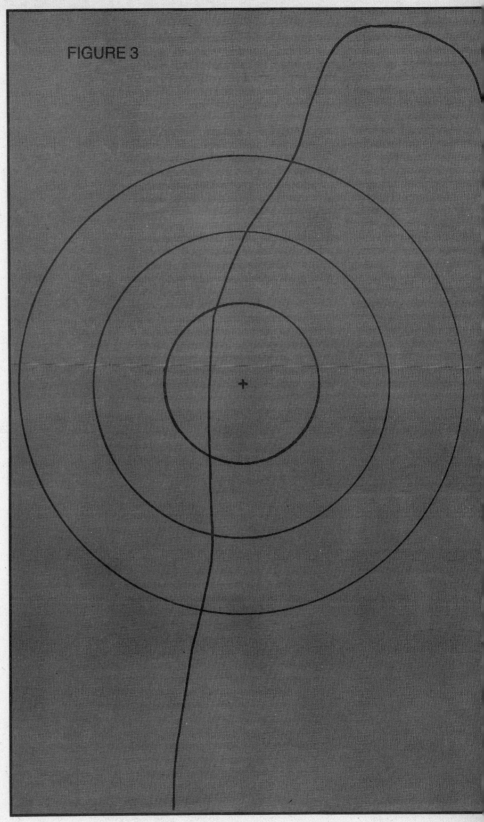

FIGURE 3

Table 2 shows the result. By comparing it with Table 1, you can see that even a relatively mild wind can have significant effect on the chances of hitting a woodchuck's kill-zone. It really pays to develop some skill in estimating winds and knowing how they deflect your particular bullet. Remember, if you had known there was a 1.6 mph wind and compensated for it, your probabilities would be the higher ones in Table 1 instead of those in Table 2.

As for errors due to holding too high or too low, proceed in a similar fashion. For example, if you held 4″ too high, redraw your circles so that their center is 4″ above the center of the woodchuck's chest and go through steps 5 and 6 again. I'll let you do the calculations this time.

You are now in the position to play all sorts of interesting games in investigating how various constant errors affect the probability of kill on different types of game animals.

Determining an Average Group

In everything discussed up to this point we have taken for granted that you know your average 5-shot group size. It's now time to say a few words about how to obtain it. The immediate concern is how many 5-shot groups should be fired. Some shooters fire a bunch of groups, pick the best one and call it the average. Obviously the only value to such a selection is to make the shooter feel good. It certainly doesn't give a true average.

To get an average 5-shot group size you add the sizes of all the 5-shot groups fired and divide the answer by the number of groups fired. The more groups, the closer you get to the true average for your rifle and load fired from a given position. However, a small number of groups can tell an awful lot. For instance, there is a very good chance (95 percent confidence, as the statisticians say) that the true average is less than 1.2 times the average you get by firing only five 5-shot groups. Of course, the true average could be less than, or equal to, the average obtained from only five groups. It is just that it is very unlikely to be bigger than 1.2 times that average. There was an excellent article in the NRA *Handloader's Guide* which discusses how close the true average is approximated by firing different numbers of groups. *(Reference 2).*

I personally fire five 5-shot groups to determine my average and use that value for all calculations. To see if I goof too badly by doing that, I perform what systems analysts call a *worst case sensitivity analysis*. It sounds impressive but really only means that I redo the calculation using the worst value of standard deviation which can reasonably be expected. Since the largest true average that can be reasonably expected is 1.2 times the five group average, the largest reasonable value of the standard deviation is 1.2 times that obtained in step 2 above. To do the calculation proceed exactly as before except in step 3 draw circles with radii equal to 1.2, 2.4 and 3.6 times the standard deviation calculated in step 2. The result of such a sensitivity analysis is shown in Table 3. Comparing it to Table 1 it is evident that appreciable differences for this worst case only start showing up for averages of 2 MOA or greater when shooting at woodchucks. So if my groups are 2 MOA or larger I can expect probabilities somewhere between the results of Table 3 and Table 1.

Knowing the true average is enough for the benchrest shooter but the hunter must also know exactly *where* his rifle is shooting. It is best to make use of all 25 shots from the five 5-shot groups in determining the rifle's zero. Take a piece of paper and mark a small X on it. Place this X over the point on the target at which the cross-hairs were centered. Then trace the five bullet holes on the paper. Repeat this with the same piece of paper on each of the other four 5-shot groups. What results is a 25-shot group identical to what would have been obtained if all 25 shots were fired at the same target.

To the left of the 25 shots draw a vertical line. Measure the horizontal distance straight out (perpendicular) from the vertical line to each of the bullet holes. Add these distances and divide by 25. Draw a dotted vertical line parallel to the first vertical line and at a distance to the right of it equal to the number just calculated. If you have done everything right, this dotted line should go right through the center of the 25-shot group.

Now draw a horizontal line beneath the 25-shot group. Measure the distance straight up (vertical) from the horizontal line to each bullet hole. Add these numbers and divide by 25. Now draw a dotted horizontal line parallel to the first horizontal line and at a distance above it equal to the number just calculated. The point where the two dotted lines cross is the center of the group. If you are shooting ½″ groups the shots are so close to-

	TABLE 1		
Average 5-Shot Group	Probability of Hitting Woodchuck Kill-zone at Distance Indicated		
	100 yards	200 yards	300 yards
½ MOA	99	99	99
1 MOA	99	99	96
2 MOA	99	87	67
3 MOA	96	67	45

	TABLE 2		
Average 5-Shot Group	Probability of Hitting Woodchuck Kill-zone at Distance Indicated in the Case of a 2″ Horizontal Shift in Center of Impact		
	100 yards	200 yards	300 yards
½ MOA	98	85	81
1 MOA	85	69	62
2 MOA	69	57	48
3 MOA	62	48	35

	TABLE 3		
Average 5-Shot Group	Probability of Hitting Woodchuck Kill-zone at Distance Indicated For Case 1.2 Times the Average 5-Shot Group		
	100 yards	200 yards	300 yards
½ MOA	99	99	99
1 MOA	99	99	92
2 MOA	99	78	57
3 MOA	92	57	34

gether that you can't use this procedure. For such small groups just make an estimate of where the center is. With ½ MOA groups, that gives more than acceptable results.

Benchrest and Field Accuracy

Suppose you know that with a very accurate rifle (½MOA) you can shoot 3″ groups at 100 yards from a kneeling position. What do you suppose your group size would be if you used a rifle which averages 3 MOA from a benchrest instead of ½MOA? The average group would be 4.2″, not 6″ as many people assume!

Why is this? For the dispersion patterns encountered with good rifles and good shooters the average group size for a given shooter's holding ability and his rifle's benchrest group is determined from the equation:

$$G_{total} = \sqrt{G^2_{shooter} + G^2_{Benchrest}}$$

In words this says that the average group size is equal to the square root of the sum of the squares of the average group the shooter would get by firing a perfect (one-holer) rifle from that position and the average benchrest group for the rifle he actually uses.

Table 4 shows some very interesting results obtained from this equation. For example, if from offhand position with a perfect rifle you could get an average 6″ group at 100 yards, the group would only grow to 6.7″ if you started using a rifle capable of only 3 MOA from benchrest!

For you benchrest shooters, Table 5 shows how holding errors combine with the rifle's machine-rest accuracy to give the benchrest groups. If your holding error is ½ MOA or less, Table 5 shows that in benchrest testing rifles that can do no better than 1 MOA you are for all practical purposes as good as a machine rest. (If you can average ⅝″ groups at 100 yards with a rifle which was tested at the factory to give ⅜″ groups, then your holding error is ½ MOA.)

As a matter of interest if you know the average benchrest group of your rifle and the average group size you get when shooting from a field position, it is easy to determine the average group size you would shoot from that position with a perfect rifle. Just use the equation:

$$G_{shooter} = \sqrt{G^2_{total} - G^2_{Benchrest}}$$

Think back to the mathematics you learned in high school and you should be able to do this calculation easily.

There are some general conclusions about rifle accuracy which can be drawn from this examination:

First, if you are a bad shot from a field position, having an accurate rifle won't help you. Second, if you are an average shot who rarely practices and have no real ambition to improve your shooting, a 3 to 5 MOA rifle is about all you need. Third, if you really enjoy shooting and keep trying to improve, get the most accurate rifle you can afford. With it, you will be able to call your shots with confidence and correct any bad holding habits. Eventually, you should be shooting as well as your rifle.

A Few Words in Closing

Throughout this article, it has tacitly been assumed that both the dispersion due to the rifle and that due to the shooter closely follow what statisticians call a circular Gaussian distribution. For very good rifles and very good shooters, this is a valid approximation. It implies that the 25-shot group will be roughly circular in shape and have 40, 86 and 99 percent of the shots within circles with radii equal to one, two and three times the standard deviation calculated in step 2. If you find your groups are stringing out, then the assumption of a circular Gaussian distribution is no longer valid and the results given in this article will give only a rough approximation to what you actually obtain.

(Groups string out for many reasons, but principal among them are action and bedding faults, physical holding variations, visual hold variations and variation in the ammunition. If a shooter known to be a good benchrest shot shows improvement—less stringing—with the same equipment, then you need more practice. If he can't substantially improve the shape of the groups, then there are mechanical variations. Techniques for correcting these are well known: EDITOR.)

Some people function superbly under pressure. That's why some shoot much better under the pressure of bagging game than they do on the range. If you are one of these, you should do better than the probabilities indicated in this article. On the other hand there are some people who suffer from buck fever. If you are one of these, all I can do is wish you lots of luck. •

REFERENCES:
1. Frank Grubbs, "Statistical Measures of Accuracy for Rifleman and Missile Engineers" privately published in 1964. Available through NRA Reader Service.
2. William C. Davis, "Determining Rifle Accuracy", NRA Handloader's Guide, 1969 edition, pages 136-39.

TABLE 4

Average Group Shooter Would Obtain Using Perfect Rifle	Average Group Size Using Rifle Having Accuracy as Indicated (In M.O.A.) Average Benchrest Group			
	½ MOA	1 MOA	2 MOA	3 MOA
1 MOA	1.12	1.4	2.2	3.2
3 MOA	3.04	3.2	3.6	4.2
6 MOA	6.02	6.1	6.3	6.7
9 MOA	9.01	9.1	9.2	9.5

TABLE 5

Average Group From Benchrest Using Perfect Rifle	Average Benchrest Group Using Rifle with Machine Rest Accuracy as Indicated Average Machine Rest Group				
	¼ MOA	½ MOA	1 MOA	2 MOA	3 MOA
1/10 MOA	0.27	0.51	1.00	2.00	3.00
1/4 MOA	0.35	0.56	1.03	2.02	3.01
1/3 MOA	0.42	0.60	1.05	2.03	3.02
1/2 MOA	0.56	0.71	1.12	2.06	3.04
3/4 MOA	0.79	0.90	1.25	2.14	3.09

BLACK POWDER REVIEW

by RICK HACKER

YEARS AGO, before "replica" became standard nomenclature in the black powder shooter's vocabulary, practically every front-stuffer in America's gun stores was made in this country. However, that situation has been completely reversed and the list of factories in the U.S. making black powder arms has shrunk to a very small coterie, whose members include Thompson/Center, Mowrey, Shiloh Sharps, some of the Navy Arms products, and Sturm, Ruger.

In the black powder world of today, the majority of new-made muzzle-loaders are manufactured in Italy, with those guns imported by Lyman, Euroarms, Allen Fire Arms, and some Navy Arms products the most obvious examples. However, American black powder marketing is truly international, for CVA's guns come from Spain while Dixie Gun Works' Tennessee Mountain and Squirrel rifles are made in Japan. If it were not for the excellent manufacturing abilities of these foreign countries, coupled with the design guidelines of their U.S.-based importers, we would have very few black powder guns from which to choose.

COLT

There's bad news and good news from the only present-day maker of cap and ball revolvers who can truly call them "re-issues." Let's start with the bad news: This company, generally credited with perfecting the cap and ball revolver in 1836, has announced it is again discontinuing those revolvers. The 11 black powder models that Colt currently catalogs will be phased out throughout 1982-83, until all the parts have been used up, thereby ending a brief but notable resurrection of a famous gun company's past history.

As part of Colt's farewell to black powder arms, they will be producing a limited number of *stainless steel* cap and ball revolvers. That's right: The first stainless revolver ever to be offered by Colt will be a black powder handgun. To make these polished jewels even more attractive, only 1,500 of each gun will be produced, starting with the 1860 Army, then going to the '51 Navy, the '61 Navy and finally the

1862 Pocket Police and the '62 Pocket Navy.

In keeping with the precedent they have already set for their guns, prices for these limited edition (although they don't call them that) stainless steel Colts won't be cheap. The 1860 Army will list for $484.50, the '51 and '61 Navies will cost $472.50 each and the diminutive Pocket Models will retail for $437.50 apiece. The Army should be about ready to come out as you read this, with its four brothers not far behind. The Walker and Dragoons will not be offered in stainless.

ALLEN FIRE ARMS

To set the matter straight, this is the firm that until two years ago was known as Western Arms. A rather sobering letter was received by company owner Leonard Allen from an attorney for a firm which thought Western Arms might be confused with

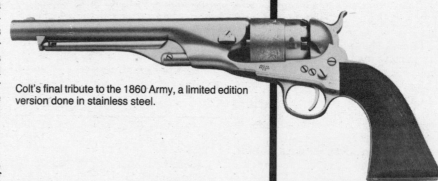

This faithful replica of an early over-under Beretta fowling piece is gotten up cased, with double triggers and cylinder chokes and 15 accessories and in limited quantity, to be the Beretta Model 1000 Tercentennial (that's 300 years) Commemorative.

Colt's final tribute to the 1860 Army, a limited edition version done in stainless steel.

the name of a well-known cartridge-making corporation. Leonard decided to avoid any such future conflict by changing the name of his company to Allen Fire Arms, which is what they now roll-stamp on the barrels of their Italian-made guns. Most of Leonard's black powder products are manufactured to his specifications by Aldo Uberti in Italy.

No new models have been added this year, but the massive 4½-pound 44 Colt Walker and the tiny 31 Colt 1849, Wells Fargo and square-backed Baby Dragoon pocket pistols announced last year are ready for shipment.

The Walker was held up because Leonard did not like the contours of the first hammer spurs and the 31s just got lost in production, probably because they were so small. Prices are $244.80 for the Walker and $184.80 for any of the 31 pockets, which come in barrel lengths of 3, 4, and 5 inches.

The big news is that all Allen Fire Arms Colt-style revolvers are finished with the original, 19th Century style of charcoal bluing, a process and color substantially different from the deep-blued finishes found on most modern replicas. The charcoal bluing is slightly lighter in color and, when oiled, has a misty undertone to it like finishes on the unfired old Colts I have seen in some of the country's better collections.

THOMPSON/CENTER

Warren Center has decided to take a select number of T/C Hawkens to make presentation muzzleloaders. Two things will make the Hawken Cougar unique; first, all major metal furniture—including double-set triggers, lock and ramrod thimbles—is to be stainless steel. The buttplate is cast brass, plated with hard chrome and brushed to match the stainless steel. Only the barrel and sight assembly remains blued. The second special feature is hand-selected premium grade walnut.

The fancy grain on my test model does not run through the entire length of the halfstock, but it is rather pronounced in the buttstock portion and lends an elegant touch to what many have considered to be a functional rifle. To my mind, the real value of the Cougar lies in the stainless steel fittings—less flashy than brass and good against corrosion as well, especially on the hammer and lockplate.

A nicely relief-cast cougar medallion is inset into the right side of the stock. The Cougar is available in 45 and 50 caliber and comes only in caplock. For those hunters wanting a larger caliber, Branch Meany of Green Mountain Rifle Barrel, makes a drop-in replacement barrel for the Hawken in 54 for round ball.

Production of the Cougar will be limited due to the scarcity of quality-grained walnut required to produce them, but at $350 each, and finished in stainless steel, they would seem to be guns to live up to T/C's Lifetime Warranty.

DIXIE GUN WORKS

The oldest firm in the black powder industry keeps on coming out with something new every year, and 1983 is no exception. Perhaps the most spectacular new rifle for match shooters to come along in years is Dixie's Sanftl Schuetzen percussion 45-caliber target rifle. The Sanftl with its precision German-made barrel and exquisite Paulo Bondini workman-

Moore & Patrick Dueling Pistol is a handsome English-styled flinter from Dixie, a firm also offering complete cased accessories for the gun.

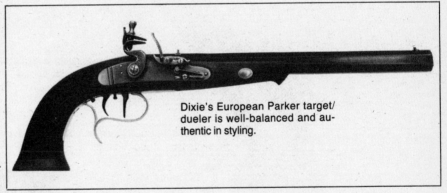

Dixie's European Parker target/dueler is well-balanced and authentic in styling.

The French-styled LePage dueler is being imported under the Dixie name this year.

ship is destined to set some new black powder recordbook scores. For the serious black powder target shooter, $595 does not seem too high a price to pay. For details, see Testfire, p. 242.

Dixie also imports Bondini's three new single shot dueling pistols. Of the three, the most attractive to my eye is the flintlock Moore & Patrick Dueler Stocked in dark European walnut, hand-checkered and exhibiting silver plated furniture and a single-set, adjustable trigger, this 45-caliber copy of one of England's nicest 19th century gentleman's pistols is a superb shooter for muzzle-loading gentlemen of today, especially if ordered in pairs. The London-marked Moore dueler sells for $225, and Dixie also stocks a complete range of cases and accessories, should you feel compelled to transport this fine flintlock to the field of honor in style.

Another London favorite, slightly earlier in styling, is Dixie's copy of the W. Parker flintlock, also in 45 caliber, with double-set, adjustable triggers and silverplating on the trigger guard and front sight. This flat-butt target pistol sells for $250. From across the Channel, Dixie's third Bondini dueler is a copy of the French LePage, also in 45 caliber, but with a percussion lock. The French-styled walnut stock is slightly larger than the other duelers, making the double set-triggered LePage ideal for shooters with larger hands. The gun sells for $155 and is a fine example of the single shot pistol so prevalent in Europe around the 1850s.

One other observation concerning Dixie that bears mentioning is that the price of their famous, phone-book-thick catalogue has now gone up to $3, the first price increase in over 10 years. Even at the newly inflated price, the Dixie book is still a bargain, and they ship it postpaid.

MOWREY GUN WORKS

For years, this Texas firm has been making guns based on the Ethan Allen action design of 1837. Some years back there were problems with quality, but since Neil McMullen took over, workmanship and service has been restored to where old E. Allen himself would be proud.

Mowrey has now created a hunter's version of their famous 50 and 54 Great Plains Rifle. This new hunter's rifle will still feature the simple Mowrey design with its premium quality curly maple, but will only be available in browned furniture, with a 28-inch barrel, thicker front sight, and

Dixie's Germanic Schuetzen is this year's ultimate muzzle-loading target rifle.

CVA's Hawken pistol is available in 50 caliber and is designed to be a companion piece to their Hawken-named rifle.

rifled for either conical or round ball. This lighter and easier to handle hunting rifle should be available by the time you read this. The price has not been established.

TRAIL GUNS ARMORY

Trail Guns Armory re-introduced the muzzle-loading double rifle to America. Now TGA has come out with their own Italian-made percussion long rifle. Christened the Alamo, this full-stocked rifle sports the Texas Star and the year 1836 stamped on its lockplate. The walnut stock has brass fittings and its fancy, open work patchbox is decorated with filigree, a portrait of the Alamo, two Texans resting beneath a tree, and the motto, "Liberty or Death, 1836." Aside from its fancy Lone Star State beauty, the gun also sports excellent set triggers and an optional adjustable Marble's sight. Available in either 38 (that's right—it takes a .375″ ball!), 45 or 50 caliber, the Alamo long rifle sells for $275 in percussion (the price includes a brass flashcap to protect the shooter from flying fragments of #11's) or $285 for a flintlock version.

TGA offers a Revolver Repair Kit, a prepackaged ensemble of six nipples, mainspring, trigger, hand and all major screws for the 1851 Navy, Colt Walker, Dragoon and pocket pistols. If you shoot a lot, or have a replica Colt black powder revolver that is not quite up to snuff, Trail Guns Armory's Repair Kit might be useful.

HOPKINS & ALLEN

Hank Goodman, new owner of the H&A firm recently showed me a new variation of his standard Boot Pistol, bored to a smaller 36 caliber. With only three moving parts in the action, this new smallbore, which sells for $78.15, might be worth considering for the target shooter or squirrel hunter who wants a sidearm to match his rifle.

RICHLAND ARMS

Richland Arms has shown some ingenuity this year by coming out with a 12-inch barrel version of the 1858 Remington 44 revolver. Although such a gun never existed—up until now—its adjustable sights and extended radius hold some promise for the black powder small game hunter and impromptu silhouette shooter. The gun, dubbed the "Remington Buffalo," sells for $150 readymade, or $95 in kit form.

EUROARMS

Known for its fine quality black powder replicas, this firm has added an elegant new touch to a revolver that has already been in their line for the past three years. Their Rogers & Spencer 44 Army, which has been accepted by the North-South Skirmish Association, is now available engraved and furnished with a "burnished brush satin finish" that resembles (but is not) stainless steel. At

$225, it would seem to be just the sidearm to grace an officer's uniform during Great Rebellion celebrations, even though the originals of these guns never saw battle, but were relegated to storage until after the turn of the century.

NAVY ARMS

A pioneer firm in the black powder field, Navy has introduced a rather unique double-barreled percussion 12-gauge shotgun for those of you who like to do your scattergunning up close, or who merely want a formidable black powder defense gun. Dubbed the Terry Texas Ranger, this side-by-side sports sawed-off 14-inch tubes! Not to worry; it's perfectly legal for muzzleloaders under the 1968 Federal guidelines. This shotgun allegedly had its historical origin with a Southern cavalry group who used them along the Texas borders. Nowadays, its chief advantage is to serve as a light (5½ pounds) black powder scattergun for backpackers, or people who want to command a lot of attention at the shooting range. At $325, it is guaranteed to do just that!

Improving on an already good thing seems to be Val Forgett's style, so it comes as no surprise to learn that his well-made Ithaca Hawken Rifle, in 50 or 54 calibers, now comes with a stainless steel liner in the bolster and breech, those areas that are not always reached with a patch during cleaning. There is no increase in the

The Jennings rifle, made in this country by Hawken Armory, is a well-made hunting rifle designed for the black powder sportsman of today.

Thompson/Center's new Cougar is in reality their best-selling Hawken, outfitted in stainless steel and fancy wood.

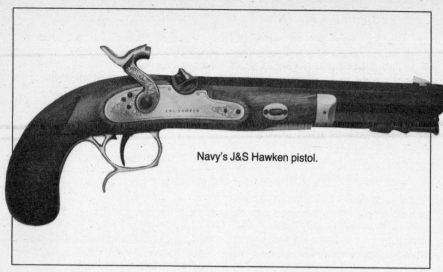

Navy's J&S Hawken pistol.

Ithaca Hawken's $395 pricetag.

Pistols seem to be the coming trend in the black powder world. (And why not? Most of the well known black powder rifles have already been reproduced.) Navy is helping to establish the trend by bringing out an Italian-made replica of the J&S Hawken percussion pistol. It sells for $200 in either 50 or 54, and a 45-caliber French Rochatte percussion dueler, which lists at $250.

CONNECTICUT VALLEY ARMS

CVA is now one of the largest producers of muzzle-loading arms in the country, second only to Thompson/Center. Their new muzzleloader this year is the 50-caliber Hawken Pistol, designed as a companion piece to CVA's Hawken Rifle, introduced in 1981. Like the rifle, the Hawken pistol has no relationship (other than in name) to the original J&S Hawken guns, but it is a good shooter nonetheless. I found it to be a mite on the heavy side, just a tad under four

pounds, most of which was in the barrel. This extra weight, however, was helpful in soaking up recoil with loads of 40 grains of FFg.

The Hawken Pistol has the same post and bead front and rear adjustable sights as found on the rifle, which makes it easy for a shooter of one to go directly to the other. My only adverse comments are that I wish CVA would put a heavier spring in the trigger to keep it from rattling, and change it from "early style brass" to early style steel as on their rifles to make it feel more firm when firing. The Hawken pistol price is $106.95 in percussion and $116.95 in flintlock, with kits going for about $35 less.

Also introduced by CVA this year, and so new it is not even catalogued, is their 50-caliber Pennsylvania Long

Alamo's brass patchbox exhibits Texas-themed motif.

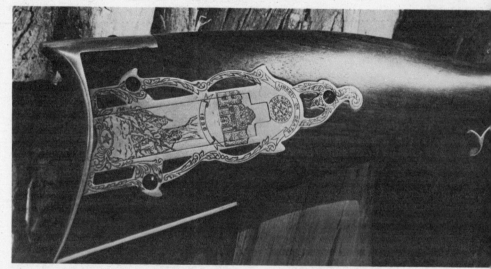

Rifle, a graceful shoulder arm highlighted with double set triggers, brass patchbox, walnut stock and fixed sights. As of this writing a price has not been set, but it should be somewhere in the neighborhood of $250.

HAWKEN ARMORY

Relatively low-key until this past year, the upsurge in activity at the Hawken Armory has been due to the enthusiasm of its new owner, Ted Jennings. Ted's firm makes an excellent copy of the J&S Hawken and a Cattaraugus County Squirrel Rifle, but his newest offering is called, appropriately enough, the Jennings Rifle.

Named after his gunsmithing grandfather, this halfstock plains rifle is a Dimmick-styled hunting gun, available in either flintlock or percus-

The French Rochatte dueler is an elegant new addition imported from Italy by Navy Arms.

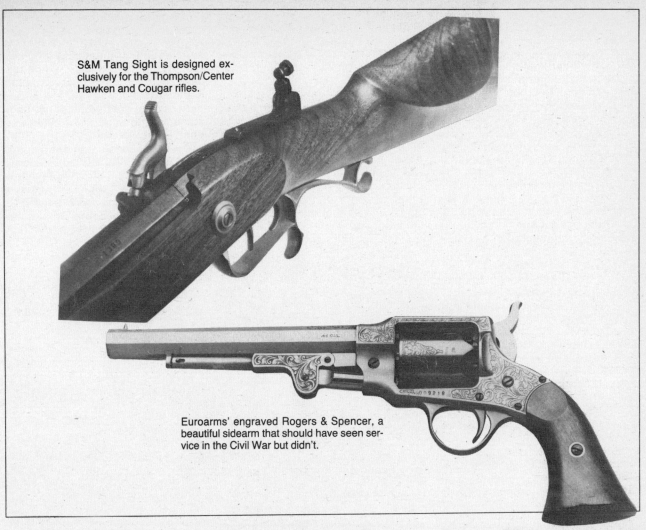

S&M Tang Sight is designed exclusively for the Thompson/Center Hawken and Cougar rifles.

Euroarms' engraved Rogers & Spencer, a beautiful sidearm that should have seen service in the Civil War but didn't.

sion and comes in calibers 45, 50 and 54. Sights are fixed and dovetailed into the excellent Montana Rifle Works barrels rifled for round ball. Double set triggers, and poured pewter nosecap top off this new beauty. Price for the finished rifle is $289 for percussion, $309 for flintlock or $50 less for either in kit form. The Jennings is a well made rifle.

LYMAN

Although no new muzzleloaders were introduced this year, an interesting option now available on their Great Plains Rifles and Trade Rifles is the shooter's choice of either (but not both) fixed or adjustable sights. Formerly, only fixed sights were available on the Trade Rifle and the Great Plains Rifle only came with adjustable buckhorn. Now you gits yer choice.

ACCESSORIES

Black powder shooters require an infinite amount of paraphernalia to keep their smokepoles functioning, and here are some of the newest prod-

ucts I've uncovered this year that actually *work*:

Winchester Sutler has created a Minie ball lube called 300-Plus, so named because you can theoretically fire 300 shots without cleaning. I somewhat doubted Tom Hunger when he told me this, but after firing 18 shots out of a Euroarms Musketoon without swabbing the bore, I figure that was good enough for any day on the range, and about 13 more shots than I can get with most conventional lubes. The green stuff is similar to the old Springfield Armory formula and I understand that mice love it. An 8-oz. container sells for $5 plus a $1 for shipping.

Owners of Thompson/Center Hawkens and Renegades desiring to fine tune their shooting ability will be interested in an extremely well-made peep sight produced by **S&M Tang Sights.** The adjustable sight is all-steel, fits on the tang of the rifle, can be easily installed by the owner in just a few minutes, and sells for $29.95 plus $1.50 for shipping.

Blue & Gray Products has a cata-

log that is well worth having, but their most unique new products are the totally unbreakable Super Shaft cleaning rod, ramrod and short-starter, made from a non-abrasive synthetic material, and a unique Powder Can Nozzle that screws onto a black powder can and sports a tapered nozzle for no-spill pouring into horn or flask.

Uncle Mike's (Michael's of Oregon) has come out with a replacement touchhole liner for T/C and CVA flintlocks, designed to produce a hotter flash in the pan (working on the same principle as their Hot Shot nipples).

Another firm that is making waves in the black powder accessory business is **Mountain States Muzzleloading Supplies,** whose 108-page catalogue, which sells for $1, is well worth having. They sell everything from raccoon tails to long rifles, but their two newest products which caught my eye were 2-oz. containers of boiled linseed oil and high-quality handsawn flints. Ironically, both of these items were once common, but now are occasionally hard to find. ●

THE MOST maligned shotgun gauge is the .410 bore. Every expert on shotguns declaims it as a poor choice, suitable only for poachers, experts, cripplers, taxidermists and so on down the line. Experts notwithstanding, I find it to be effective and useful within its limitations.

My first gun was a .410 bolt action Mossberg with interchangeable choke tubes, and a very good little gun it was for the grand sum of $24.95. The hardware store owner threw in a silicone wiping cloth and, I think, a box of three-inch shells, which cost $2.15.

My father suggested we pattern it and we went out to a vacant lot in the country and did just that on shirt cardboards at an estimated 30 yards. We discovered two things: the patterns were dense enough to kill small game and the modified choke tube shot a slightly more open pattern than the full choke tube. I rightly concluded the full choke tube would kill farther than the modified tube. I wrongly concluded the full choke was a more desirable choke and used it exclusively for some years.

This was the only shotgun in our household for some time and with it we killed rabbits, quail, doves, crows, buzzards, squirrels, skunks, possums, chipmunks, raccoons, one catfish, and goodness knows what else. Eventually, I grew up, joined the U.S. Air Force and learned to shoot Skeet using this gun.

Of course, all of this happened while I was yet naive about shotguns and, more or less, a boy. My father had somehow imbued me with the notion that a .410 bore shot its pellets just as far and just as hard as a 12 bore did and the fact that there were fewer pellets didn't matter at short range. This is more or less true.

Eventually I outgrew the little Mossberg and gave it to the children of a friend who had a son and daughter who were young enough to use it. They promised when they outgrew it that it would get passed on to another kid. I've lost track of the friends and the gun but I hope somebody somewhere is still using it and I hope that person is a beginner.

When I outgrew the Mossberg .410, I got a 12-gauge Remington Model 870 pump Skeet gun and a Remington 11-48 Automatic .410 with full choke. I also borrowed a Winchester Model 42 Skeet gun with Cutts Compensator. I used all three guns to shoot Skeet and frequently did better with the .410's than with the 12.

"This Turkey has got to be kidding,"

some Skeet shooter may mutter. Nevertheless it's true. One day in particular stands out in my memory. I broke 15 out of 25 of the 12 and followed it up with a 23 out of 25 with the .410.

Here I learned something new. The 12-gauge gun kicked and roared and I was recoil and noise-shy. The .410 punched and popped and I wasn't afraid of it. Consequently, I concentrated on the fundamentals of Skeet and ignored the gun. Additionally, of course, I had learned to shoot with the .410 and had confidence in it. I had only been shooting the 12 for a couple of months.

Since those halcyon days, I have owned a large number of shotguns and many of them were .410's. There have been several Remington 11-48's, several Winchester Model 42's in different configurations, a Remington 1100, a Remington 870, a High Standard pump, and probably others I don't now remember. Most of these were Skeet guns but some were choked differently. I have made it a point to shoot as many other .410's as I could talk their owners into letting me use, and have shot and used Browning, Winchester, Daly, SKB over and unders and Fox, L. C. Smith, Iver Johnson, Ithaca, and one fabulous Winchester Model 21 in

A good combination for close-rising grouse—a late season, a .410 Remington 870 Skeet and a fair grouse dog.

side-by-side doubles. All of these guns were delightful to shoot and play with. Some of them I shot well and some not so well.

I patterned as many as it was convenient to pattern. I occasionally break 25 at Skeet with them and once did so with frequency. I believe I have now learned a little about these guns and understand why they get short shrift from shooters less familiar with them.

There have been a number of things going against the .410 over the years. Not the least of them was, and is, the general unavailability of good quality, well-constructed working guns. The only repeaters available now are the

Remington Model 1100 Automatic and the same company's Model 870 pump and Mossberg's Model 500 pump. If you can afford the price, you can get over and unders in .410 from Browning, Winchester, and SKB. If you fancy a double, the Fox Model B and Stevens 311 are available but only with one barrel length and choke combination. I believe the Mossberg bolt action is still available and of course the various single barrel guns. However, the average gun store will probably not stock .410 bore guns except in the cheap single barrel models. Thus, while .410's can be had, they are more trouble to obtain and frequently require special ordering. It isn't nearly as simple as getting a 12 gauge.

Another problem, and perhaps the biggest overall, is the general unavailability of any choke except full choke in the more common .410's or the choice of full choke when more open choking is available. While there is some apparent logic behind such a choice, I think it fails under critical examination. The logic runs thus: the .410 is a small bore with a small shot charge; therefore, in order to kill cleanly at maximum range, we want a tight pattern. While that logic is unassailable, who would pick a .410 for a long range gun? My observations lead me to believe that the tightest choked .410 can't be an effective 40-yard gun, but an improved cylinder or Skeet bored .410 will do nicely to 30 yards.

The use of the full choke in the .410 may account for some of the claims that the .410 is a crippler. It is a well known and frequently observed phenomenon that choking causes the center of patterns to be denser than the fringes. The tighter the choke is, the denser the center. The smaller the bore is for a degree of choke, the denser the center. Therefore, the pattern of a full choke .410 will have the densest center and sparsest fringes. I remember a particular gun, a Remington Model 11-48 with full choke, I used for hunting blue quail in South Texas many years ago and which seemed to be extremely particular about whether the birds were centered or not. Those birds which were centered came down like stones. Those which weren't centered came down flapping. They did come down, though, and I did collect them. Of course, I had to wring their little necks. I have seen the same thing in larger gauge guns which were tightly choked. With them it happens at longer range.

An interesting sequel to this occurred a couple of years ago. I had an identical gun which I frequently used to shoot Skeet. With my Skeet reloads I generally did as well as with any of my .410 Skeet guns but when I used factory Skeet shells I shot Skeet poorly. I patterned the gun with both types of shells and discovered the cause. My reloads, which were made up using cheap soft lead shot, gave wide, round, well-distributed patterns practically identical to a good Skeet gun. The factory shells, loaded with best quality hard shot gave very tight patterns.

The .410 cartridges deserve some discussion. I think the .410 bore dates back to around the turn of the century

THE MALIGNED .410 BORE

. . . has been a lot better than its publicity for the last 40 years.

by MARSHALL R. WILLIAMS

There's quite a range of .410 bore loads. From left: slug, ⅕ oz. at 1830 fps; Skeet load, ½ oz. of 9s at 1200 fps; field load, ¹¹⁄₁₆ oz. of 7½s at 1135 fps; another field load—¾ oz. of 7½s at 1135 fps.

In close cover like this, a .410 makes a more than satisfactory game gun. There are no long shots here, so everything is in range.

possibly a little earlier. I can't find any definitive date for it but it may well stem from the practice of putting up shot loads in .44 brass cases similar to the 44-40 case. Early shells were shorter than present being 1¾ or 2 inches rather than 2½ and 3 inches. The older load for the 2½-inch shell was ⁵⁄₁₆ or ⅜ oz. rather than the present ½ oz.

The 3-inch shell with ¾ of an ounce of shot was introduced by Winchester about 1934 along with their delightful little Model 42 pump gun. Some 3-inch shells are loaded with ⅝ oz. of shot. This includes most English and European brands. The present 3-inch American shells are marked ¹¹⁄₁₆ oz.; older ones are marked ¾ oz.

For comparison, I weighed the shot charges from some ¹¹⁄₁₆ oz. shells and from some old shells marked ¾ oz. Not too much to my surprise, both shot charges averaged identical weights of .71 ounces or about midway between. When I reload 3-inch shells, which is not too often, I use the same ¾-oz. measure I use for my 28-gauge shells.

Some older writers no doubt considered the older .410 shells having the small shot charges when condemning the .410 as inadequate. Some of them didn't notice when things improved. W.H. Foster, in his book *New England Grouse Shooting,* (Charles Scribner's Sons, New York, 1942), dismissed the .410 as a "plaything" while saying 28 gauge is adequate and even calls the ⅝ oz. load "spiteful." This was some seven years after the 3-inch .410 with its ¾ oz. load was introduced, a load at least the equal of the ⅝ oz. 28-gauge load. Mr. Foster is also remembered as the inventor of the game of Skeet.

Another problem area is shot size. I once listened to a sales person, whom I knew to be a good groundhog hunter and relatively knowledgeable about guns in general, advise a customer who wanted some .410 shells for shooting starlings to use number five shot in the 2½-inch shell. That was a poor recommendation; the only worse would have been 4's or slugs. There are only about 85 pellets in that shot charge. Starlings are small birds. Assuming an evenly distributed 30-inch pattern at 30 yards, there would be only one pellet per 8.3 square inches of coverage. Such a pattern would not assure regular hits on small birds. Number 9 would provide more than 290 pellets in the pattern, or one pellet for each 2.4 square inches. A pattern this dense would assure several hits on each bird. Using 3-in. shells with Number 9 shot would result in more than 400 pellets in the pattern; one pellet for each 1.75 square inches.

Small shot may be objected to on the grounds that it lacks killing power. Like the full choke argument there is some logic to this contention. Clearly a Number 5 will have more energy and momentum than a Number 9, more than three times as much, but the same load of 9's will have more than three times as many pellets. There are two other considerations to be taken into account: The .410 should be used at short range, where energy is still high in the small pellet; and the denser pattern of the small shot is much more likely to result in multiple hits which have a cumulative knock down effect and increase the likelihood of hits in vital areas.

American factory shells in both lengths are available in shot sizes 4, 5, 6, 7½, and 9. I think that shells loaded with 8's or 8½'s would make the .410 a better bird gun than either 7½'s or 9's. I generally use 9's on doves and quail and 7½'s if I expect to see a rabbit or two. If I were shooting rabbits or squirrels only, I might consider 6's. I don't think I would ever use anything larger because I consider the .410 a relatively close-range gun and the smaller shot penetrates well at close ranges, while the larger shot thins out the pattern too much for reliable hits. I use 3-inch shells for nearly all of my hunting but I have successfully used the 2½-inch shell with 9's for doves. I try to limit my shots to 25 yards when I use the shorter shell.

One of the benefits of the .410 bore used to be that the shells were cheaper than other shells. This is still true comparing express loads and Skeet loads. However, the big three brands all offer field loads in 12, 16, and 20 gauges which are cheaper than standard .410 shells. For the reloader, however, the biggest savings of reloads over factory shells are in the .410 bore.

The .410 bore shells were the last of the common gauges to receive the benefits of plastic shells and plastic shot protectors. Remington offered the first plastic shells in .410. Federal offered the first plastic shell in .410 with the plastic shot cup wads. I think this was in 1969 but I might be off a year or two. Prior to that, the National Skeet Shooting Association (N.S.S.A.) had sort of a Hall of Fame listing the shooters who had shot 100 straight with the .410 in N.S.S.A. Competition. Before the introduction of the plastic shell and shot cup wads there had only been a handful, about seven or eight. That year there were five 100

A good group of .410's: From left—Ithaca SKB .410 Skeet, 2½-inch chambers; Winchester 101 Skeet, 2½-inch chambers (part of a three-gauge Skeet set); Remington 11-48 Skeet, with Cutts Compensator, a grand old Skeet and quail shooter; Remington 1100 Skeet, 2½-inch chamber, a super Skeet gun; Remington 870 Skeet, 3-inch chamber, a nearly ideal .410 bore gun for small game.

A genteel approach to doves: Two neckties, a Remington 11-48 .410 with Cutts, Remington .410 870 Skeet and a Brittany spaniel.

straights in the National Championships. Since then they have become more or less common. The proper Skeet load in the .410 bore is the 2½-inch shell with a maximum load of ½ oz. of shot.

I have persisted throughout this article in calling the .410 a bore and the other shotgun sizes gauges. The .410 bore, usually written with a decimal point before the number, is the actual bore diameter in inches. The other shotgun gauges are according to the number of bore-diameter pure lead balls in a pound of lead. Thus a 12-gauge gun has a bore diameter of .729 inches which is the diameter of a lead ball weighing one-twelfth of a pound. The English gauges originally stopped at 50 gauge which is about .453 inches. Under the English system the .410 would be a 67.4 gauge. I try not to be pedantic about the distinction and if anyone prefers to call it the four hundred and ten gauge, it suits me. I have seen the .410 bore designated a 12 millimeter in some older references. This must refer to the case diameter, if it refers to anything at all, because the .410 bore is about 10.4 millimeters.

Many fans of 28-gauge guns claim that the 28's will outperform the 3-inch .410. The argument is that in the .410 the shot charge is long and thin and shot scrubs on the barrel and flattens out ruining the pattern, while the 28 gauge, which has a bore diameter of .55 inches, has a shorter shot charge and handles the charge better. I buy this argument to a limited extent but only a very limited one. I feel the 28s pattern better but only slightly and part of this is due to having about 5% more shot. Using shot of identical quality and quantity and plastic wads to protect the shot, and guns of equal quality and degree of choke, I doubt you will find much significant difference.

I am a fan of the 28 gauge as well as the .410 and one thing I've noticed is that most older 28 gauge guns are high quality guns such as the Remington 11-48, the Winchester Model 12 and the various doubles by Parker, Ithaca, Iver Johnson (which company once made good quality doubles) and Greener of Birmingham, England. I have never seen or heard of any A. H. Fox doubles in 28 gauge, but I have seen a photograph of what is purportedly the one and only L. C. Smith 28-gauge gun. These guns were well made and no doubt had some attention paid to proper choking. If one is going to compare one of these guns with a .410, it would only be reasonable to compare it with a gun of similar quality. I doubt there could be a valid comparison between a Parker or Greener 28-gauge gun and a Stevens or a H. & R. single barrel gun. The latter are good, well designed guns, but they are made to be sold for a small fraction of the cost of the former and they simply cannot have the attention paid to choking that the former could.

There was once a different standard for choking .410's than was used in the larger gauges. The chokes were determined by patterning the guns in a 20-inch circle at thirty yards rather than in a 30-inch circle at forty yards. It has been a long time since I saw a reference on this and I don't remember whether the required percentages (i.e. 70% for full choke) were the same. I think they were slightly lower, like 65% in a 20-inch circle at thirty yards for full choke guns. I do not know if this standard is still adhered to in the industry.

I suppose a reasonable person might ask what good is a gun which only kills reliably out to thirty yards. My response would have to be that it is good enough for all but two shots at game that I have taken in recent years. Most quail I have shot have been taken around 20 yards. Doves might go five yards farther, rabbits and squirrels probably less. The largest game I ever took with a .410 were large jackrabbits and within my modest ranges they were killed as quickly and cleanly as cottontails. I have an acquaintance who killed two big Virginia turkeys with a .410 and Number 8 shot. The kills came while he was hunting grouse and scared up the big birds. According to him both were one-shot kills. The range was stated to be about 20 yards. I wouldn't choose a .410 for a turkey gun but within its limitations it should be adequate. I have never shot geese or ducks but unless I could do it inside 25 yards I wouldn't choose a .410 for it.

If the .410 can in fact be so effective, why do some very good shooters scoff at it and say it's not suitable for anyone but experts or those who are unconcerned about crippling game? I think I have observed enough Skeet shooters trying out .410's for the first time to get an idea about it. Most shotgunners start out with big bore guns. The 12 gauge is made in greater numbers than all other gauges combined. Most of them weigh more than seven and a half pounds and, contrary to the advertising, most probably go eight pounds. Those made for Skeet have very open chokes and usually ventilated ribs. This results in a gun with considerable weight out front. It's muzzle heavy. It has sufficient inertia when it is moving that it is hard to stop and consequently the shooter using, say, a Remington Model 1100 Skeet gun in 12 gauge, doesn't have to concentrate on follow through as much as when he shoots a lighter gun.

In contrast, most .410 bore guns will weigh much less and because of the slimmer barrel may be very muzzle light. Some people would say whippy. Such a gun doesn't follow through nearly as well as a muzzle-heavy gun. This failure to follow through causes frequent misses and then human nature takes over. The shooter may be used to breaking 24's or 25's at Skeet. If he breaks a 17 or 15 with the .410 he must conclude it is a poor gun for the job and have no confidence in it. To assuage his pride he may go back to his big bores with never a backward glance and condemn .410's forever. On the other hand, he may try it a few more times and eventually get used to the differences. Once this happens, his scores will come up, he will get some confidence and probably discover that he averages only a little worse with the .410 than with the bigger guns. I have seen one case where a fairly ordinary shooter broke his highest Skeet score ever when I loaned him my .410 Skeet gun. It was his first experience with the .410 and he broke a 22.

When my wife and I were courting, I started her on Skeet shooting with a Winchester Model 42 Skeet gun with a Cutts Compensator on it. She had never shot and I didn't want to have to teach her the fundamentals of lead and follow through using a gun whose kick and roar would make her flinch. In order to be intellectually honest with you, when I bought her a gun of her own, I chose a lightweight Remington 1100 in 20 gauge with improved cylinder choke. But this, mind you, was after she had learned to shoot. When our little girls are old enough to begin shooting, I will start them with a .410.

There is a rifled slug load for the 2½-inch shell. The slug is advertised as weighing ⅕ oz. This works out to 87.5 grains and the advertised velocity is 1830 feet per second. The resulting muzzle energy is 650 foot pounds. This is about the same muzzle energy as a .357 Magnum revolver with a six-inch barrel. It is also nearly identical in performance to a 40-caliber muzzle-loading rifle using a .39-inch diameter pure lead round ball at the same velocity. Each of these latter would be regarded as at least marginally adequate for deer.

The .410 is a challenging gun and load for Skeet, but rewarding when you succeed, or so it seems at first. Later, you realize the .410 is not a *big* handicap.

Breaking hand-thrown clay targets with the .410 is good practice. Practice builds confidence; and confidence builds success. It's corny, but it works.

surely place the little slug in his heart-lung area, I would not hesitate to try it. Incidentally, this is one area where the .410 has the advantage over the 28 gauge. No slugs are presently available in American 28-gauge shells. They once were, but were discontinued about the time of World War II.

My old Lyman Reloading Manual #44 shows a load using a heavy slug made out of Lyman Number 2 Alloy, an alloy much harder than the pure lead recommended for other slugs. The slug weight shown is 238 grains and the highest velocity shown is 1565 feet per second. The resulting muzzle energy of this load is 1294 foot pounds. This should be nearly as effective as the factory 20-gauge slug load. Lyman no longer catalogs the .410 slug mould, though.

Most .410 bore guns have the advantages of lightness and compactness. They are easy to carry in the field and are quick to shoulder when game appears. Noise and recoil are the lightest of any shotgun gauge. In doubles, the barrels are not so wide as the larger gauges. Additionally, the shells are lighter and more compact than any larger gauge. This can be viewed two ways. You can carry more of them than a larger gauge or carry the same number and have room and weight for something else.

Does all of this mean the .410 bore is the ideal all around gun? Not quite. However, if you are willing to limit yourself to game that can be killed inside of about thirty yards with shot sizes on the order of 7½ to 9's, it will prove quite good. If you are afraid of recoil your shooting might even improve.

A .410 would not be my first choice if I were going to shoot deer, turkey, waterfowl or anything requiring shots beyond about thirty yards or shot sizes larger than 6's. However, within these limitations the .410 is effective.

What does this leave you with? Well, I live in central Virginia. Small game here consists of rabbits, squirrels, bobwhite quail, ruffed grouse, doves, and woodcock. I have taken all of them except grouse with the .410 and have found it entirely adequate. In fact, in dense cover I have shot quail and woodcock as close as 10 to 15 yards. At ranges this short even the 3-inch .410 and the 28 gauge amount to overkill.

I have concluded that a .410 bore gun with an open choke and small shot is a very effective little gun. But then I reached that conclusion a long time before I used bigger guns.　●

I have never known of anyone endorsing the .410 slug as adequate for anything but small animals and I have never shot any game with these little slugs. When I was a kid I shot one into an old excelsior-filled hassock to see how deep it would penetrate. It penetrated entirely through the hassock, which was about 18″ thick, and took a thumb-size chunk out of a cinder block in the wall behind it. My father, were he still alive to read this, would now know what caused the funny hole in the basement wall at our house. Of course, were he alive to read this, I would not write this paragraph because he would beat the hell out of me for it. Justifiably, I might add.

When I hunt small game with the .410 during deer season, I carry a couple of these slugs with me. Were I to see a deer at close enough range to

WHEN ONE CONSIDERS the historical development of 22 automatic pistols in this country the names of John Browning and Colt seem to appear first. Browning and Colt enjoyed a uniquely symbiotic relationship that began in the late 1890s and flourished for decades. It brought wealth and prosperity to both.

Browning's genius was such that he would retire to his shop and make a model for a new design. He rarely made drawings, and left to others the task of transferring his work to paper. When a model was completed he would travel to Colt and sell them the design. For this he was paid a reported $10,000 per gun plus a substantial royalty on each gun sold.

It has been estimated that the royalty was around five percent, and it was paid for the entire 17-year life of the patent, and renewed if the patented features were improved or used on another model. The payment for the patent was, in fact, a mere token compared to the worth of the royalties which may have amounted to millions considering Browning's prolific output and Colt's success with his guns.

In the very early days of automatic pistols, the 22 cartridge was ignored, and thought to be impractical due to its relatively low recoil. In early 1911, Browning began a series of letters with the officers of Colt in which he discussed a proposed new pistol in 22 caliber. For a short time Colt considered placing the new gun into production in 1911, and the gun was originally called the Model 1911 by some of the Colt management. Introduction was delayed due to a combination of circumstances: first, economic conditions were poor in 1911-12, and later an epidemic of hoof and mouth disease caused hunting seasons to be closed in 1913-14.

It was a surprise to me to discover, in an old Colt memo, that hunting was a deciding factor in the production of a gun most would consider a plinking or target pistol. The memo found the climate to be "fairly optimistic" for 1915 and although there was some concern due to passage of laws requiring permits to purchase handguns, the decision was made to go ahead with production in 1915. The first guns were shipped in April, and production reached a modest level by the end of the year.

Browning's original design was adapted for production by Colt engineers F.C. Chadwick and G.H. Tansley. For their work, they received U.S. Patent 1,277,379 and added a bit of color to Colt's history. Collectors will note that most Woodsman models have three patent dates. The first, December 22, 1903, is for a Browning patent for the safety lock used on the pocket models, and adapted for use on the Woodsman. The date August 27, 1918, is Browning's patent on the gun, and September 3, 1918, is Chadwick and Tansley's. Both applications were

There is the Woodsman, and the rest. This is about the rest.

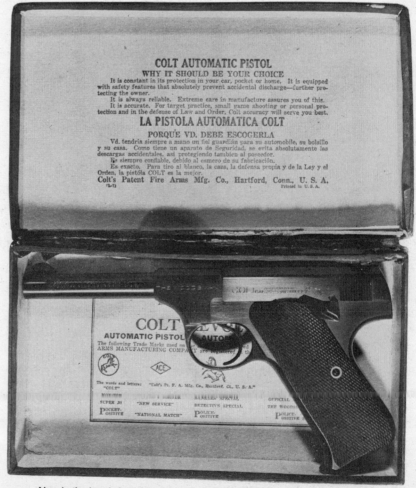

New in the box is how people now want Colt's Woodsman. They collect it.

filed March 30, 1917, and Colt received notice that both would be issued on August 27, 1918. Colt president C.J. Ebbets wanted to have two different patent dates, so he delayed payment of the final patent fee for Chadwick and Tansley's patent and directed the secretary, A.L. Ulrich, to mail the second check August 2. In a letter to the Commissioner of Patents he explained that his tactic was intended to obtain two different dates with which to mark the gun.

Colt's initial designation for the gun was "Caliber 22 Target Model," and the Woodsman name was not used until 1927. Still, it is by this name that the gun is almost universally known and I have used it throughout. But for economics and hoof and mouth disease, I wonder what we might have called the 45?

Eugene C. Reising was a contemporary of John Browning, and worked at Colt during the years when Browning was a frequent visitor. In March,

1914, Reising filed a patent application for a 22-caliber automatic pistol. In this sense he can be said to have been first, but it is more likely that he and Browning pursued their projects simultaneously. The Reising pistol did not reach production until 1920, primarily delayed by World War I. The gun boasted a 12-shot magazine (compared to 10 for the Woodsman) and a magazine disconnector which was certainly novel for the time.

Perhaps the most notable feature was the tip-up barrel which was highly touted since it permitted easy cleaning. The design mounted a recoil spring low in the frame which engaged a cross member at the front of the slide. The slide is a frail thing with most of the weight at the rear, and the energy of recoil is absorbed by the cross member and the thin slide rails. This led to cracks in the thin slide rails, and several pieces have been seen that show little evidence of use but are nevertheless cracked.

The Reising also had the dubious distinction of being the most expensive 22 which, combined with the weakness of the design, may have contributed to its rapid demise. Today, the Reising pistol is sought by collectors and is becoming rather scarce. Production covered only about five years, and during that time there were several variations.

Early models are marked "The Reising Arms Co., Hartford, Conn. U.S.A." and carry the patent date May 16, 1916. Later Reising moved his offices to New York and guns from this period are marked "The Reising Mfg. Corp., New York, N.Y., U.S.A." and have an additional patent date of Oct. 25, 1921. No detailed record of production is known, but observed serial numbers offer some clues. Hartford-marked guns appear to begin with serial number 1000 and continue to around 2500. New York-marked guns seem to have begun at 10,000 and continue to around 12,000.

First Issue High Standard Model B is exactly the same as Hartford Arms—an early collectible.

Early 22 Auto Pistols

by CHARLES E. PETTY

Reising: note the bear trademark in the grips with the legend, "It's A Bear."

New York-marked Reising pistol. The slide is cracked just above the barrel latch, which happened a lot to Reisings.

Although his handgun was not too successful, Reising continued to be involved in the gun business and is known for his World War II submachine gun and the 22 rifles he designed while working for Harrington and Richardson.

A less well-known contemporary of Browning and Reising was Lucius N. Diehm. He is believed to have begun work in the firearms industry as a young man and worked at Colt and Winchester. In 1915, he was granted his first patent for an automatic pistol that looks something like a cross between a Clement and a Savage, but it was apparently not produced. In 1917, he became associated with Middletown Firearms and Specialty Co. of Middletown, Connecticut, and it was there that he created most of his designs.

Beginning in 1919 Diehm was granted a series of patents for 22-caliber pistols. First was a manually operated repeating pistol in 1919, followed by a single shot in 1920, and two automatic pistols in 1921 and 1925. All his patents were partially assigned to Berkley C. Stone of Middletown who is thought to have been involved with Middletown Firearms and Specialty, although none of Diehm's guns were produced by that

firm, and the company involvement in the firearms field is obscure. Diehm was employed there until 1925, and was also engaged in the antique business.

At 39 Grant St. in New Haven there was a contract machine shop operated by J.E. Schall, and it was here that the first of Diehm's guns was produced. How the association came about is unknown, but Diehm, Schall and Major Anthony Fiala began production of Diehm's repeating pistol. Fiala was an explorer and adventurer of some fame who had been involved in Arctic exploration with Peary. Fiala had an idea for a combination rifle/pistol to be used as a survival and utility gun. It seems most probable that Fiala's ideas were incorporated into the existing Diehm repeater.

Fiala's gun was to have interchangeable barrels and was offered with 3″, 7½″ and 20″ barrels as well as a detachable shoulder stock which made a compact rifle when used with the long barrel. I have often speculated as to why Fiala chose to use a manual repeater when the automatic was available and could have been made with this feature just as easily. Perhaps, since Fiala intended for his gun to be used in the Arctic—he used a po-

lar bear for a trademark—he felt that the manual operation would be more reliable in the extreme cold.

The Fiala Arms and Equipment Co. began advertising the Fiala Repeating Target Pistol, Model 1920, as "three guns in one." It is interesting to note that Fiala's address was 39 Grant St, the same address as Schall, and it has been said that Fiala's office consisted of a desk in the corner of Schall's shop. Undoubtedly, Schall did the manufacturing and Fiala the marketing; both hoping to capitalize on Fiala's substantial fame for his Arctic adventures.

The gun could be purchased in almost any combination the customer wanted, a fixed 7½″ barrel or any assortment of barrels. A complete set was offered with three barrels, stock, and a choice of three different cases. The simplest was a canvas roll-up type, and hard cases were available in leatherette or genuine leather. A smoothbore 7½″ barrel was cataloged, as was a silencer.

Barrels were usually serial numbered to the gun, and some stocks are; although most aren't. Serial numbering began with 1 and apparently ran consecutively. Before his death, Maj. Fiala is reported to have said that Schall produced 4044 guns for him.

Early Fiala Arms and Equipment Co. pistol with fixed barrel. Note the polar bear trademark above the trigger.

Fiala Arms and Equipment Co. Model 1920. This is a fixed barrel version, without provision for shoulder stock.

Fiala's compact rifle looks like this, ready to shoot. The rear sight is upright, the buttstock securely fastened. The barrel is 20 inches long.

Observed serial numbers go considerably higher to around 5600.

In 1922, Maj. Fiala moved his office to 342 Madison Ave., New York, and later guns are marked "Fiala Outfitters, New York." Fiala also produced a small number of guns for other companies, and these are the rarest of the Fiala variations. It is beyond coincidence that the Columbia Rifle Company had offices at 342 Madison Ave., and a small number of guns are marked "Columbia." Even more unusual are guns marked Botwinick Bros. for the Botwinick Bros. Hardware.

Fiala's outfitting business was not successful, and he was forced to suspend operations in 1923. Schall continued production and we are left with another mystery. If Fiala's reported statement of production is correct, then there must have been a substantial number of guns in inventory that were sold by Schall, The "Schall & Co." marking does not appear until around serial number 5700 and continues to around 7500.

Schall dropped the combination gun concept and produced only fixed 7½" barrels without shoulder stocks. It is doubtful that precise data on the production of the Fiala and Schall guns can be found, and it is conjecture

at best that the serial numbers ran consecutively. The late Frank E. Williams of Salina, Kansas, had made the study of these guns his lifetime hobby, and he was never able to locate any records. He had a remarkable fund of other knowledge though, and he was kind enough to share it with me before his death.

In 1925, the Hartford Arms and Equipment Co. was founded to produce guns designed by Lucius Diehm. Located at 618 Capitol Ave. in Hartford, just a stone's throw from the Colt factory, they began production of their Single Shot Target Pistol and the Model 1925 automatic. It has long been reported that Hartford also offered a repeating pistol, manually operated, and this may be so, but Frank Williams was fond of saying he'd been looking for 40 years and hadn't seen one yet. If they did, it would have surely been like the Fiala or Schall.

All three of Diehm's guns are remarkably similar in appearance, although each operates differently. The single shot and repeater are quite alike mechanically, with the obvious difference of a magazine for the repeater. Operation is strictly two-handed for both. When the slide is closed, the firing pin engages a sear which protrudes through the top of

the frame. After firing, the shooter must push the slide release located on the left side of the frame, and manually draw back the slide to eject the spent round. A fresh round is stripped from the magazine by pushing the slide closed to repeat the process.

The single shot pistol was apparently not a big seller. Serial numbers began with S-1, which is known to have been Diehm's personal gun, and continued to a little over S-400. Again, precise records are not available, and some sources report that Hartford's records were lost in a flood.

The automatic was much more successful. There is a physical similarity to the Woodsman, but it is mechanically different. Designers familiar with both guns speculate that Diehm was attempting to improve on the Woodsman, particularly in the takedown. Production began at serial number 1, and continued to around 4700.

Hartford was a small company, but was able to capture a fair portion of the market during the short time it was in business. As the economy began to tremble and tumble in 1929-30, there was little chance and it quickly fell victim to the Great Depression. Although the company was listed in the Hartford City Directory until

1933, the actual closing probably took place in 1931.

Little is known of the Hartford employees except for Diehm who had been shop foreman, and a young man named George Wilson who was a beginner in the gun business and friend of Diehm. When Hartford failed, Diehm retreated to his antique shop called The Olde Curiosity Shop on Asylum St. in Hartford. He gave George Wilson whatever work he could, usually refinishing furniture. Diehm apparently never returned to the gun business, and became successful in the antique shop. George Wilson Jr. recalls going there with his father and it must have been a marvelous place for the younger Wilson's memories are vivid. He recalls particularly the large number of clocks that filled the shop with their chimes, and a gift of some stamps from Diehm. The elder Wilson was not unemployed for long; he was soon hired by Winchester and placed in charge of barrel-making for their Model 52.

Shortly after Hartford Arms was formed in 1925, another company, the High Standard Manufacturing Co., was founded by Carl Gustave (Gus) Swebelius. High Standard manufactured equipment for the firearms industry, particularly deep hole drills. Swebelius, a Swedish immigrant, had been involved with guns since he came to this country, most notably at Marlin. There he had advanced from sweeping floors to designer. He is credited with the first American development of a synchronizer which permitted firing a machinegun through the blades of an aircraft propeller. High Standard was only a part-time effort for Swebelius as he was also employed at Winchester.

When Swebelius learned of the Hartford closing he attempted to buy some of their machinery for his young business. The story is told that Swebelius traveled to Hartford to examine the machinery, and returned with the surprise announcement that he had bought the whole company, and High Standard was in the gun business. It was surely a bold venture, in the worst of the depression, to consider expansion, and times were not easy for High Standard.

Swebelius moved the machinery and a substantial number of unfinished single shots to his small plant at 169 East St. in New Haven and hired George Wilson as foreman. The single shot which had not been successful for Hartford became the salvation of High Standard. Some 800 frames, and most of the other parts were included

Fiala set, with 7½-, 3- and 20-inch barrels and shoulder stock. Note that the 3-inch barrel is knurled and does not have a front sight. These are seen either plain or knurled but most have a front sight.

Fiala with 3-inch barrel in place.

Schall & Co. repeating pistol which came along after Fiala's efforts ceased. Again—this is a repeater, not an autoloader.

Schall & Co., repeating target pistol was identical to the Fiala except that the barrel was shortened to 6¾ inches.

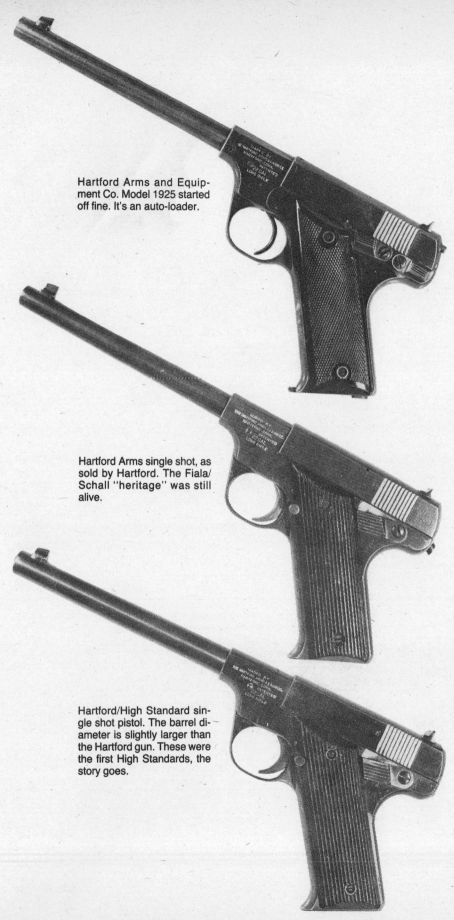

Hartford Arms and Equipment Co. Model 1925 started off fine. It's an auto-loader.

Hartford Arms single shot, as sold by Hartford. The Fiala/Schall "heritage" was still alive.

Hartford/High Standard single shot pistol. The barrel diameter is slightly larger than the Hartford gun. These were the first High Standards, the story goes.

in the purchase, and High Standard immediately began completing them. Each Friday the output for the week was taken to New York, by car, where they were sold to J.L. Galef for a reported $3 cash. This was enough to meet the payroll and eventually turn a small profit. Rumor, which has acquired the ring of truth over the years, has it that Swebelius paid $800 for the entire Hartford Arms business.

Since the single shot frames were already marked, the collector has had difficulty in identifying which company actually sold the gun. Two clues are available though: first, High Standard dropped the "S" prefix to the serial number and almost all the guns sold by High Standard will be found in the serial number range of 800 to 1626. Secondly, the barrel of the High Standard gun is somewhat heavier although side by side comparison or measurement is necessary.

The sale of the single shots gave High Standard time to prepare for production of the automatic which became the High Standard Model B. Sales of the Model B began in November, 1932, and the first guns were produced exactly as Diehm had designed them. Swebelius continued to work at Winchester, and George Wilson was the main force at High Standard. In talking with a number of people who knew Swebelius, I find that he is most regarded as a manager with an ability to choose the right people. Wilson was such a person, and he was responsible for all the changes and improvements High Standard made in the basic Diehm design.

Through a gradual series of steps the gun was improved and modified, leaving a great variety for the collector to sort out. The first major variation was the Model C which was simply a 22 Short version. There is evidence that Hartford Arms had also worked on this, for one Hartford automatic chambered for the 22 Short is located in the Imperial War Museum in London. It is serial number 36, and how it got there is anybody's guess. D.J. Penn, keeper of the department of firearms and exhibits, feels that it was among the thousands of guns sent from this country to arm England's Home Guard during the early years of World War II.

The gun shows all the customary British proofs along with the caliber designation "SHORT." According to Mr. Penn, the original caliber markings appear to have been removed and overstamped. The existence of serial number 1 of this variation is also

Before World War II, High Standard had a full line of autoloaders. Tops was the finely finished Model E.

High Standard Model USA-HD. The military version of the original H-D, which was modified after the war to become the H-D Military. Note U.S. Property marking, and ordnance acceptance stamp. The U.S. Property marking is also found on top of the barrel. The USA-HD is seen with both blued and parkerized finish.

High Standard's famous H-D Military. Some 150,000 HDMs were sold between 1946 and 1951, every one an offspring of the company's war-time model.

known, leading to the conclusion that there are probably others. If so, they are surely the rarest of the Hartfords.

High Standard's production of both models was rather small until 1938 when several major changes were made. First, Swebelius left Winchester to devote full time to his company, and George Wilson began a major redesign of the gun. An improved takedown was introduced in February of 1938 followed by three new models, the A, D and E, in April and May. All had larger frames in response to complaints that the Model B (and the Woodsman) frame was too small for most hands. Wilson's solution was simply to lengthen the frame, and his first model guns have an extension silver-soldered to the bottom of a regular Model B frame.

The three models were essentially alike except for barrel diameter. The A had a slim barrel, the D a heavier one, and the E very heavy "bull" barrel. All were available in both 4½" and 6¾" lengths, as had been the B and C. All used High Standard's new adjustable sight. The Model E was the most expensive, was better finished, and was furnished with hand-checkered walnut grips.

In August, 1939, the takedown was further improved, and sales really began to take off. From 1932 to 1939, High Standard had sold 40,000 guns, mostly Model Bs. In the following year, sales were around 50,000 guns. This was a major accomplishment by any standard, but even more impressive when one considers that an output of 20 guns a week was the goal for an assembler, the key man in production. George Wilson Jr., who joined his father in 1935, recalls his days as an assembler as frustrating. Swebelius was a fanatic on quality, and his inspectors took seriously his mandate for perfection, and living up to the company name. The younger Wilson relates that it was a cause for celebration when a gun passed inspection on the first try.

By late 1939, the effect of the growing war in Europe was felt in this country. Although the United States was officially neutral, it was apparent in Washington that the United States could ill afford to allow England to fall to Germany. In a celebrated series of letters, President Roosevelt and Winston Churchill communicated their concerns. Roosevelt initiated the correspondence soon after Churchill was appointed First Lord of the Admiralty, and continued after Churchill became Prime Minister. Through these letters and personal meetings Churchill was able to obtain Roosevelt's support. The Neutrality Act of 1938 was amended to allow "cash and carry" sales of strategic material to belligerent nations.

In 1940, the British Purchasing Commission opened offices in Washington and New York for the purchase of needed items. In those early days of the war, England had substantial dollar reserves and was able to stimulate wartime production in this country with cash. An example of this was a contract between High Standard and the British Purchasing Commission for 12,000 Browning 50-caliber machineguns. Swebelius was experienced in machinegun production from his World War I duties at Marlin, and the contract was signed in November, 1940, with completion scheduled for a year.

This was another of Swebelius's bold ventures, for he had virtually nothing suitable for this type of manufacturing, no plant and no machinery. A cash advance of $6,000,000, and the leverage of a multimillion dollar contract was enough. Under a lease-purchase agreement with the Defense Plant Corporation, a government agency, the plant at 1817 Dixwell Ave. in Hamden was erected, equipped, and deliveries begun on schedule. When the United States entered the war in 1941, they were prepared to continue production.

Two of High Standard's handguns were adopted for training use by the military. The Model B-US was a slightly changed version of the Model B which was sold to the War Department from 1942 to 1943. Then the USA-HD, an adaptation of the Model H-D, was sold from 1943 to 1945. In addition, the company had special contracts for other weapons and parts. Of these the best known are the silenced versions of the USA-HD which were made for the OSS. When the war ended High Standard was among the first of the gun companies to resume sales to the civilian market by adapting the USA-HD into the famous HD-Military.

It is not always possible to measure the influence of a great man, for his influence may be no more than the spark of an idea for another. The competition generated by Browning's followers deeply affected the gun business. There has always been speculation that Diehm copied the Woodsman, and the two are remarkably similar. Others feel Diehm's work was an effort to improve Browning's design.

I have been unable to locate any proof that Diehm and Browning even knew each other, and it is certain that Diehm didn't study at the feet of the master. Since both are long dead it is purely academic anyhow. Whether Diehm copied or improved, he must have been profoundly influenced by the Woodsman for the magazines are interchangeable. Without Diehm's guns, of course, there would have been no Hartford Arms and Equipment Co. to go bankrupt for Swebelius to buy.

A more direct, and far greater, influence of Browning on High Standard is found in the wartime production of the Browning 50-caliber machinegun, long after Browning's death in 1928. Almost overnight the company was changed from a relatively small operation with around 150 employees to a major corporation with over 3000 workers. The royalties paid by High Standard to Colt as holder of the patent, amounted to $738,900 on the British contract alone. Of this sum, $337,500 was paid to Browning's estate by Colt.

The meanderings of fate are strange indeed. Each man who played a part in this story (with the exception of Browning) moved from company to company, frequently to work for the competition of his last employer. In so doing, they learned, were influenced, and moved on. Without Reising, Fiala, Schall and Hartford Arms, the progression we accept as history might well not have happened, and had it not been for the efforts of Lucius Diehm, we might still be shooting the Woodsman, not collecting it. ●

References

1. Petty, Charles E., *High Standard Automatic Pistols 1932-1950*, American Ordnance Publications, 1976
2. Penn, D.J., Personal communication
3. Schrang, O.B., Personal communication
4. Sutherland, R.Q. and Wilson, R.L., *The Book of Colt Firearms*, Robert Q. Sutherland, 1971
5. Walker, Charles W., "It's a Bear," GUNS ILLUSTRATED, 1978
6. Williams, Frank E., Personal communication
7. Wilson, George Jr., Personal communication

Acknowledgements

The author would like to thank Ralph Kennedy of Colt for his invaluable assistance.

SIXTY MILLION GUNS

The U.S. is the only place it happens, where millions of just one sporting firearm can be sold. Here are 23 guns that have done it.

by L. R. WALLACK

A REVOLUTION in the gun business began during the 1960s when sales vaulted to unprecedented volume. There appear to be many reasons behind this unparalleled escalation but first let's discuss some other factors that had an indirect bearing.

One of the most striking was what Winchester did to its product line in 1964. Shortly, the whole gun world began to hear about "pre-64" Winchesters and their desirability compared to what came after. The "1964 massacre" of the Model 70 put Remington's 700 into soaring orbit; the Model 12 gave way to Remington's 870; and the Model 94 bowed to Marlin's 336.

There was more:

Savage's market-wise president Joe Falcon retired, and the new president was less market-savvy, allowing Marlin to move into the 22 rifle business in a major way. Harrington & Richardson almost simultaneously took over the single barrel shotgun market from Savage. These takeovers happened so fast that Savage has reeled ever since.

Remington, Marlin, Ruger and H&R retained a competitive edge by modernizing plants and equipment, stealing a march on companies that maintained a status quo. This alone would have meant major changes.

None of it would have meant anything if the market had not been there in the first place. Why have so many guns been sold since 1960?

I asked Remington's Dick Dietz and his answers were along these lines: There is a larger market; that is the population has increased. There is more disposable income, especially among blue collar Americans, and there is more available time. There also have been many added calibers and options, which have increased the market significantly. These are all logical and predictable reasons.

I also asked Snow Smart, now retired, who was Marlin's sales director and vice president for many years. Smart suggests that after every war there has always been an es-

---

Winchester In Its Halcyon Days

Any discussion of guns made and sold in volume has to include some guns now obsolete turned out during the period ending in 1964 by the mammoth Winchester plant in New Haven. For examples: More than a million Model 1897 shotguns were made before that gun was dropped in 1957; more than a million Model 1892 rifles were made before 1941 when that model was removed from the line; and over two million Model 12 shotguns were finished prior to 1963 when that model was dropped (though briefly reborn at much higher cost). Add the unsung Model 37 single barrel shotgun, 1936 to 1963, which sold more than a million units. And the Model 70 sold approximately a million units before the 1964 massacre.

Many other old Winchester models achieved significant sales volume, especially when compared with competitors. Yet these years were not all roses for Winchester for the company expanded into other areas which didn't pan out. These moves led to the purchase by Western Cartridge (now Olin) in 1931. Western and Olin proved excellent managers for nearly 50 years

when Olin sold the gun making facility in New Haven to newly organized U.S. Repeating Arms Co. in 1981.

Despite the 1964 massacre, some models continued in solid volume. The company unveiled Models 1200, a new pump gun, and 1400, a new auto shotgun, in 1964. Both exceed the million mark today.

Will Winchester ever recapture its old market position of dominance?

That's hard to say. Today, the industry wonders if USRAC will make it. They are licensed by Olin to make and market Winchester brand firearms, except the Japanese shotguns made by Olin-Kodensha, and they face a formidable task. DuPont-owned Remington is in the driver's seat today and shows no signs of slowing down. Other companies like Marlin and Sturm, Ruger are vital forces now. Marlin was weak from WW I until post-WW II and Ruger wasn't even in business until 1949. Harrington & Richardson is also a vital factor in its own market niche. USRAC's biggest need now is a modern plant and peace with its labor force—the former is planned and the latter hoped for.

---

calation. This was true following WW II, Korea and Vietnam. The rise in discount stores and their rapid expansion—K-Mart probably sells more guns than any other single source—is important, although Smart feels traditional dealers are now becoming more of a factor. And, says Snow Smart, the 1968 law boosted sales by calling attention to firearms.

Let's look at some of those really big sellers, always bearing in mind that in some cases early records are non-existent or unreliable. Further, prior to the 1968 law there was no requirement to serialize long guns, so most of the cheaper guns were never numbered. The quantities I have listed are responsible estimates, the sources in all cases are the companies themselves.

high power rifles

This is Remington country—pump, autoloading and bolt action. The only system Remington has ignored is the lever rifle which is Marlin country these days.

Since early in the century Remington has furnished pump and auto rifles and they were very popular. After WW II, when the company redesigned and retooled, improved models sold better than ever. Today there is virtually no competition in pump actions and Ruger is the leading competitor in auto high power rifles, though Rugers don't compete directly with Remington's 30-06 class rifles.

Remington's bolt rifles were an insignificant market force until after WW II, but today the Model 700 dominates. Bolt rifles, as a matter of fact, were not themselves a big factor in the hunting market until relatively recently. With total sales of more than three million (Remington and Winchester alone) since WW II, this market has increased substantially, and it can be expected to continue to do so. Remington will continue to dominate bolt, auto and pump guns; Marlin in lever actions.

Winchester Model 94: More than 6 million

What everyone thinks of as "the 30-30" is the all-time leader in *rifle* sales though the total number is eclipsed by single barrel shotgun sales. This total of six million includes about a million commemoratives and around 100,000 Model 64s and 55s.

Winchester made the first million mark in 1932, almost 40 years after the 94's introduction. Fifty years later, they've added five million more. In the 1930s, Winchester was the lion in the gun market, Remington was way behind and Savage was a much bigger market factor than it is today. Nobody else came close.

What makes the 94 the all-time leader in rifle sales? I don't know. The gun is not readily scoped and is chambered only for the 30-30 (the new 375 is not a volume seller), yet it survived the 1964 massacre and if the company can continue to find reasons for additional commemoratives it seems likely the numbers will continue for some time to come. Much will depend upon how well U.S. Repeating Arms Co. can do in today's market. We'll have to wait and see.

Marlin Model 336: More than 3.5 million.

Marlin's 336 started in 1893 as the Model 1893. It was John Marlin's major triumph although I suspect he didn't know it at the time. Marlin anticipated the popularity of smokeless powder and designed the 1893 with it in mind. In 1895 it came out in 30-30.

Through a succession of minor changes the model became simply "93," then "36" and, finally 336 in 1948 when the old square bolt was changed to round, vastly increasing the action's strength.

The Marlins were always "second banana" to Winchester's 1894. In 1964 when Winchester re-engineered its

line, the 94 fell upon hard times, and hunters and dealers looked hard at the 336. It was still "made like the old ones" and sales took off in the '60s and the company has made sales records every year since. Years ago the Winchester 94 was the only high power lever rifle hunters thought about. Today it's a different story.

From my vantage point it appears that Marlin's 336 is outselling the Winchester 94 now and has for some time. Winchester's forte now seems to lie with commemoratives which they turn out in vast numbers. Nobody can out-commemorative Winchester.

Remington Model 700: More than 2 million.

The total includes Models 721, 722 and 725, all of which have the same basic action. From 1921 through 1941, Remington produced the Model 30 and 720 bolt rifles using 1917 Enfield parts left over from WW I. Up against the superior Winchester 54 and 70 they never sold well—about 1,000 a year for a grand total of about 25,000. In 1948 Models 721 and 722 (a short action) were introduced and first year sales were 42,000! It was Remington's first modern success.

The Model 725 was announced to stem the tide of falling sales since the 721-2 were plain, unckeckered models and had begun to slip. But 725 only sold about 10,000 copies

and was replaced in 1962 by the present Model 700. The 700 took off with a substantial assist from Winchester and their 1964 product massacre. In its usual fashion, Remington smothered the market with options so that one can find what he wants in a Remington 700 from ground squirrels to elephants.

There have been new cartridges introduced for this series of rifles, some of them phenomenal successes, like the 222 Remington and the 22-250. Styling and finish kept up with the times. And then, of course, the whole 700 series shot very well indeed. That, coupled with competitive pricing, told the story.

Winchester Model 70: More than 1 million.

Winchester's great Model 70 bolt action rifle was introduced in 1936 and instantly became the "standard by which others were judged." However, that mantle was lost in 1964 when the company re-engineered its whole line. Critics are still crying that the rifle was ruined. That 1964 rifle was pretty ugly and its action changes were not well received, but it has been altered significantly since and is now much better received than it once was. In 1981 the company reintroduced the Featherweight model with a classic stock that has great appeal.

Included in the total are model variations 670, 770 and 70A although there are well over a million 70s. Model 70 rifles of the pre-'64 vintage (and there are a lot of them) are

now mostly collector's items; those still with factory cartons bring a premium price especially if they are unfired. Even battered pre-'64 70s bring fancy prices for the action which is favored by many experienced riflemen for custom rifle building.

Credit Winchester, and its current manufacturer U.S. Repeating Arms, for bringing the 70 back closer to its glory days. It will probably never be as appealing to many older riflemen but it's a great deal closer than it was in those wilderness years of '64-'68. Experts then and now cited technical improvements over the pre-'64 product, but the market never acknowledged them.

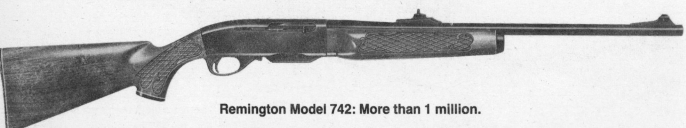

Remington Model 742: More than 1 million.

From 1906 till World War II one of the more popular woods rifles was the Remington autoloader known as Model 8, called the 81 after 1936. This was based on a Browning patent, long recoil operated and chambered for more or less moderate cartridges up to and including 300 Savage. It was a good rifle and established Remington as the only U.S. maker of a high power auto rifle in America.

But Model 81 was eclipsed in 1955 when Model 740 was produced in 30-06 caliber. Gas operated with non-moving barrel and a rotary locking bolt, the 740 was a significant design. Creating a sporting-weight rifle in high power chamberings was a very difficult achievement. The Model

740 was replaced in 1961 by the Model 742—slight alterations necessitated a new designation. By this time, the rifle was available in a rather long list of chamberings still headed by the 30-06.

Auto rifles have never been very popular among writers, which is one reason why you never read much about them. They are popular among hunters which is evidenced by the fact that more than a million 740-742s have been made to date. Remington has just spent seven years re-engineering the 742 which resulted in the Model Four (and 7400, a less fancy version) announced in 1981 to replace it.

Savage Model 99: More than 1.5 million.

The flag of the Savage line, the Model 99 has long been a famous rifle. Developed in the 1890s and first issued as Model 1895, it was slightly revised in 1899. Arthur Savage was a promotional genius and he pushed his rifle hard in the early days. He also designed well, for today's action only differs from those made early in the metals used. This is a 19th century action that very nicely handles such modern cartridges as 243 and 308. Hunters who prefer lever rifles find the Savage possesses more power and range than either Marlin's 336 or Winchester's 94.

Model 99 rifle bearing serial number 1,000,000 was presented to the NRA in 1960. It's a bit of a surprise that the following 20-plus years have only seen another half million which would seem to be added testimony that Savage has been on a downslide. However, new owners took control in mid-1981 and we'll have to see what happens.

There has not, over the years, been much variety in the 99. Takedown versions were popular before WW II, and a clip-loading variety was tried. Several popular cartridges, early on, were created just for the 99—the 22 Savage Hi-Power, the 250-3000 and the 300 Savage, for instance.

shotguns

The big numbers continue to be in single barrels, pumps and autoloaders. Remington dominates the latter, H&R the singles. I see little reason to expect any upsetting of those places in the foreseeable future. Savage and Winchester once had large shares of the single barrels but H&R now dominates and appears well entrenched. Autoloaders have been a Remington market for so many years it's difficult to expect any change.

Remington also owns the pump gun market and, while challenged on occasion, is unlikely to be disturbed. The only double gun selling in volume today is the Stevens/Fox. It should continue although Savage has recently been sold and it is difficult to assess the direction that company will take. There is room in the market for a competitive double, either side by side or over-under. The Remington 3200 is strictly a target gun although it sells well, but target guns are not big volume. For a large number of hunters to enjoy doubles we need a good double at a good price.

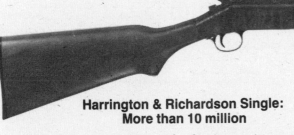

Harrington & Richardson Single: More than 10 million

That is a staggering number but it was given me by company president C. Edward Rowe, Jr. The basic action has been made since about 1900; the guns have been made in high volume for over 80 years except during war time. Most in earlier days were made with no serial numbers and there are no accurate records, but Mr. Rowe opines that ten million is a "safe" figure. There have been no major changes in the action over the years.

Single barrels have always been a big export item, many finding their ways to virtually all corners of the globe. They have been popular on the farm and ranch and vast numbers of youngsters have begun their hunting experiences with a single. H&R today makes more of this type gun than anybody, though in years gone by Savage and Winchester were also major factors.

Unfortunately for arms historians, very little has ever been written about this gun so exact quantities will never be known. They have always been inexpensive; they have been private branded for hundreds of firms; and the actions have, especially by H&R, been used for rifles as well as shotguns. They have been made in all gauges—indeed, the H&R line includes 410, 28, 20, 16, 12 and 10 gauge magnum today.

Stevens Model 94 Single: More than 4.5 million.

This gun was introduced in 1926, was made in high volume for many years and has long been popular. When you add the ten million H&R single barrels, and Winchester's million-plus Model 37 you have the staggering total of approximately 15 million single barrel shotguns made since 1900.

Single barrel guns have been made in many variations, with many cosmetic changes, and under many brand names over the years. Basically they are all pretty much alike regardless of brand or manufacture. Many of these guns, indeed possibly most of them, have been export guns shipped to all parts of the world.

Variations in Savage-Stevens single gun actions exist in many forms, many of them tried lately as designers fought the cost squeeze. The classic 94 Stevens has a top snap lever; a variation called the 9478 has the opening catch built into the trigger guard. Normally, the single gun is full-choked, but latterly the Youth (shortened) models have modified boring, and slug or deer specials have cylinder bores.

Remington Model 870: More than 3 million.

Those three million model 870s have been made since the introduction as late as 1955. Remington pump guns have been popular since 1907, when Model 10 was first manufactured under Pedersen patents. Model 10 featured bottom ejection: it was followed in 1931 by Model 31 which featured side ejection; the 870 came much later.

As with the later Model 1100, Remington's market clout gave the 870 its initial success. Winchester's 1964 product line engineering changes abandoned the great old Model 12 pump gun and virtually handed the market to Remington, although the 870 already had made great inroads.

Remington was quick to sense the kill and thereafter moved in with so many model variations that the market was covered like a blanket. Moreover, the 870, like the 1100, is an excellent gun which deserves to be the leader that it is. Some of its particular design features, such as double action bars, have come to set standards for pump guns and new models from other makers follow suit.

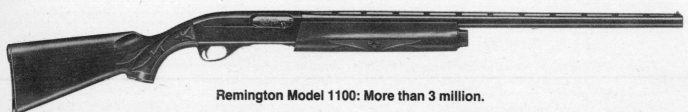

Remington Model 1100: More than 3 million.

This is the big one in terms of total dollars because those more than three million guns since its introduction in 1965 were all big tickets. The 1100 has never been a cheap gun. There are numerous reasons for its ascendency. Remington has the longest product line in the field which gives it substantial market clout in terms of distribution, meaning that nearly every dealer carries Remington. The 1100's brilliant designer, Wayne Leek, produced an action system that significantly reduces recoil. And finally, Remington has the capability of producing this gun in so many variations that it boggles the mind.

Remington has long been known as a "shotgun company" and its semiauto guns go back to 1905 when the old Model 11 was produced under Browning patents. That was the first successful auto shotgun produced in America and it stayed in the line until 1948.

Since the 1100's introduction and sales success, it has been copied widely here and abroad. Most of the copies very frankly owe their ancestry to this Remington which has pioneered a new form of successful auto gun.

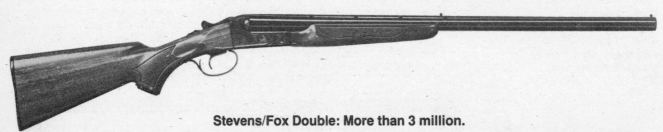

Stevens/Fox Double: More than 3 million.

This is a complicated story. The Stevens firm has been making double shotguns since as early as 1876 and the present gun, now marketed under both Stevens and Fox brand names, originated in 1926. Savage Arms bought Stevens in 1920 and, later, bought Fox. There is a clear difference between genuine Fox guns (made by Fox in Philadelphia and made later by Savage) and the Stevens gun. Genuine Fox guns were among the highest grade guns made in the U.S. The Stevens gun was always meant for low-cost high-volume sales.

Someplace along the line, after Savage discontinued manufacture of the old Fox, it was decided to market the Stevens double under the Fox label. There can be no quarrel with that; Savage owned all the brand names and could do as they pleased. But understand that today when you talk about a Fox double, it's really a Stevens.

The Fox/Stevens of today is a low-cost gun made in several models. Basically these are single trigger ejector guns or double trigger models without ejectors at lower cost. They are serviceable guns, though at times were made with certain manufacturing shortcuts. The interesting thing this gun has done is to make double guns available to many hunters who are unable or unwilling to pay the price of higher grade guns. There is no way to know exactly how many of these guns have been made for records are incomplete. What is certain however is that this is the biggest-selling double gun ever made.

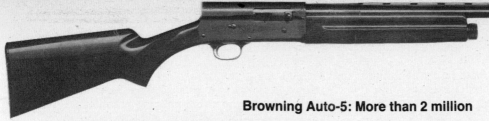

Browning Auto-5: More than 2 million

Browning Arms still makes the old autoloading gun invented by John M. Browning for which U.S. patent was awarded in 1900. This was the first successful autoloader and Browning himself called it his best achievement. It was that indeed for in those times there was a multitude of shotgun shells the modern hunter can't imagine! And the gun had to work with them all. It did, and it still does nearly a century later.

The two-million figure does not include guns made by other manufacturers on the same Browning patents. Remington made the Model 11 for nearly 40 years; Savage also made such a gun, as did Franchi and others in Europe and elsewhere, so the total guns of this type are much higher than two million.

When it was designed, John Browning was working with Winchester. Recognizing the value of this gun he asked for a royalty arrangement. Winchester refused. Browning went to Remington but that company's president had just died and the company was reorganizing. Browning then went to the great Liege, Belgium, manufacturer Fabrique Nationale (FN) where the guns were made until recently. A Browning source indicates 1,400,000 guns were made at FN until 1961. Browning today states "more than two million." I suspect the number may be higher. Like many Brownings, the A-5 today is made in Japan.

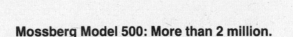

Mossberg Model 500: More than 2 million.

Mossberg's Model 500 pump gun was introduced in 1962, just in time to get entrenched before Winchester abandoned the Model 12 in 1963. Remington's 870 was already available but the Mossberg came in at a lower price point—about $75—and secured its own market niche. The rest is history.

This is a fine gun made in many options including a unique trap model which has proved popular. While there have been a number of cosmetic changes over the 20 years of Model 500's existence, the basic gun remains unchanged. It is something of a surprise that this company, which for so many years was known for its low-cost 22 rifles has succeeded better with a shotgun.

From the first, the 500 had a top tang safety, interchangeable barrels and optional magnum chambering, so perhaps its success could have been better predicted. There were even C-Lect-Choke barrels.

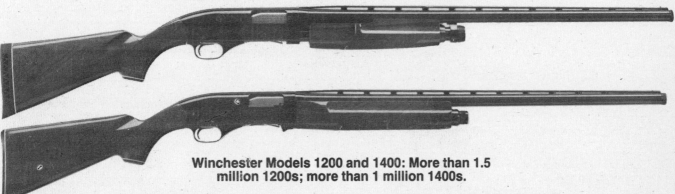

Winchester Models 1200 and 1400: More than 1.5 million 1200s; more than 1 million 1400s.

Models 1200 pump and 1400 semi-auto shotguns were introduced in 1964, the year that Winchester massacred its product line. The guns are essentially alike in all respects except that the operational system differs. Both have similar 4-lug bolts which rotate into a barrel extension.

The Model 1200 replaced the lamented Model 12 which could no longer be manufactured competitively. The new guns were meant to insure streamlined production and help Winchester regain its place in the market. They have succeeded to a remarkable degree even though Remington's competitive models 870 and 1100 have outsold the Winchesters by a three to one margin.

In 1969 Winchester added Winchoke, a screw-in muzzle attachment which offers inexpensive choke changes in the same barrel. In 1978, the model designation was changed to 1300 for the pump and 1500 for the auto variations along with a general upgrading in appearance, branded XTR. Today, Model 1200 still exists for law enforcement models and a low cost pump gun named Ranger has been added. These are all the same basic guns.

rimfire rifles

This market is dominated by Marlin; the company makes one third of all the 22 rifles made in America. How did Marlin take over a market once held largely by Savage and Winchester? Marlin held two big aces in its hand. One was the Model 99 action which was the right rifle at the right price at the right time. The other was Sales Director Snow Smart who reorganized the sales force and boosted volume distribution.

As a shooter for more than 50 years, it disturbs me that today's market is dominated by autoloaders. Since the early 1960s, there have been ten million 22 autoloaders made and sold. Today's kids and/or their parents apparently prefer "nineteen shots as fast as you can pull the trigger" to the old traditional "make each aimed shot count" via a single shot, bolt action 22.

There was a need a few years ago for a good bolt action 22, a need which has now been satisfied by the Kimber 82, Remington 541S, a new Anschutz and the H&R 5200, all high grade sporters. Now there is a need, a desperate need, for solid, dependable single shot bolt 22s with good sights, safeties and trigger pulls. Some things change but learning how to shoot hasn't and youngsters ought to be trained to make each shot count. That calls for single shot rifles.

The market at the moment, however, does not. It likes autoloaders.

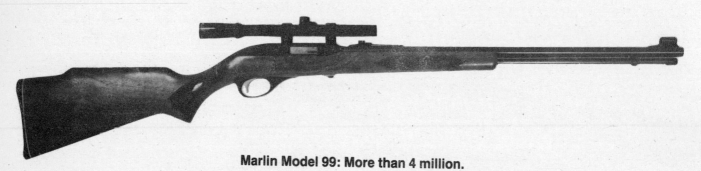

Marlin Model 99: More than 4 million.

Introduced in 1960 as the Model 99, this little rifle designed by the late Ewald Nichol has been sold in more than 35 variations, some of them private brands. The fastest seller among the variations is known as the Glenfield Model 60; Glenfield is Marlin's promotional brand and more than two million have been sold in this brand alone.

The Model 99 turned into the fastest-selling sporting rifle ever made. It's interesting to speculate why. In the 1960 GUN DIGEST I reviewed "U.S. Rifles" and I used three pages and several pictures to illustrate the Nylon 66 by Remington. I never even mentioned the Marlin! This was fairly typical for I have noticed many other articles covering this subject which do not mention it either. The press has never paid that much attention to Marlin.

What happened in the early '60s is roughly this: Marlin's 336 came into big demand after 1964 when the Winchester 94 was "re-engineered." The Marlin sales effort was simply stated—if you want 336s you'll take Glenfield 60s . . . by the truckload. Coupled to this was the fact that Savage president Joe Falcon had retired. Savage had had the lion's share of rimfire sales, but now allowed a highly aggressive Marlin sales force to move in.

The millions of sales wouldn't have happened had not this been a thoroughly reliable rifle. The public wanted auto 22s and Marlin proceeded to fill that demand in a big way.

Stevens Falling Block Singles: More than 3.5 million.

It isn't well known today but Stevens made some great single shot falling block rifles during the 1880-1920 period, fully the equals of such more famous rifles as the Ballard and Winchester. The rifle made today is a direct descendant of other and cheaper old favorites known as "Crackshot," "Little Scout," "Marksman," "Favorite" and other brand names—millions of cheap, sound rifles before there were bolt actions. Some of these rifles were made in the great and now obsolete cartridge, the 25 Stevens rimfire.

Stevens is credited with development of the 22 Long Rifle cartridge in the 1880s to put in an action similar to the present one. Today's rifle is still called Crackshot Model 72 and retains a bit of nostalgia with its octagon barrel. It is meant for the beginner's market, but there's no doubt kids never see a lot of those sold.

Stevens Single Shot
Bolt Action: More than 2.5 million.

Introduced in 1929, the Stevens single shot bolt 22 has appeared in many variations and model numbers. For many years, Savage (Savage bought Stevens in 1920) produced more guns than any other manufacturer and most of them were in low-cost brackets. This gun is still in the line and still being sold in volume.

It is in fact one of the few remaining single shot bolt rifles still made and it is encouraging to see that at least one manufacturer has been successful with the type of rifle with which every youngster should start his shooting.

Remington Nylon 66: More than 1 million.

In 1959, Remington pretty much stood the gun world on its ear by introducing a 22 auto rifle made of structural Nylon. The barrel, breech bolt and other operating parts are made of the usual steel; but the stock-receiver is a single unit of molded Zytel Nylon, a DuPont product. To date more than a million of these rifles have been made as the Remington Nylon 66 and in the Mohawk brand, Remington's "promotional" label.

Weighing a scant four pounds, the rifles are available in brown or black; the action is covered by a sheet metal steel shroud. Interestingly, when the company announced this radical rifle they publicized the exhaustive tests made to show that the firing of hundreds of thousands of cartridges produced no measurable wear on the Nylon. Even though the steel breech bolt rides back and forth on Nylon, there was measurable wear of the steel!

The light weight and rugged dependability of this little rifle, coupled with the market clout of Remington and the popularity of 22 auto rifles, plus good press notices, produced great sales for this remarkable little rifle.

Marlin Model 39A: More than 1 million

The oldest design continuously manufactured, the Marlin 39 began its life in 1891 as Model 1891. In 1892 it became Model 1892; today's system of front-end tubular loading was substituted for the loading through the receiver, difficult with small 22 cartridges. In 1897, it was made a takedown, becoming Model 1897, later just 97. In 1921, it became Model 39 and the 39A in 1937. There is relatively little difference between today's 39A and the original 1891 in terms of the actions. The one million total includes all variations from 1891, although the bulk of these rifles have been made since the 1950s.

For many years Marlin was known as a one gun company for its famous lever action 22. Over the years these rifles have been preferred and used by many of the top exhibition shooters. Until recently in fact, this Marlin was the only lever 22 on the market. It was the first to work with all the popular cartridges interchangeably (shorts, longs and long rifles). It was the first to use today's common system of loading a tubular magazine from the muzzle end via an inner tube. And, today, it's the oldest sporting firearm in manufacture, its production having been interrupted by two wars, but otherwise undisturbed.

Winchester Models 290 and 190: More than 2 million.

The relatively short-lived Winchester auto rifles Models 290 and 190 were only made from 1963 until 1980 but production exceeded 2.2 million units. These models were introduced at about the time the company was experimenting, for the most part disastrously, with its product line. The Model 190 was a less expensive copy of the 290.

There were pump and lever action variations of this "family" of 22s. A deluxe version was added later for a brief time. Interestingly these rifles were originally chambered for 22 Short, Long and Long Rifle although the Short was dropped in 1970 from both rifles.

The 290/190 rifles were big sellers during their lifetime and were heavily discounted—as are most guns today—by the mass merchandisers.

Stevens Model 87: More than 1 million.

A 1938 introduction that has appeared under many model numbers, including private brands, this likely would have sold several million units had Marlin not been so aggressive. It is a good, dependable rifle still in the Savage/Stevens line.

As the Savage Model 6—the one with the "bird cage" cut into the left side of the receiver—it was a standard article of trade. With only minor cosmetic changes the same gun was sold by Sears and others at prices $5 and $10 cheaper than the Savage model.

Savage Model 24: More than 1 million.

This model is unique; it has had some minor competition over the years but none seriously; and the best known combination is this Savage Model 24 which was introduced in 1939. The upper barrel is for rifle cartridges, in a rather wide variety of calibers, among which today are both 22 Long Rifle and WMR, 222, 223, 22 Hornet, 30-30 and 357 Magnum; the lower shot barrel is either 20 gauge or 410. There have been other cartridge variations over the years.

The combination gun has always been hard to classify. It's not just a rifle and not just a shotgun. Its major use would seem to be for turkey hunters when sometimes a rifle barrel is more useful than a charge of shot, but the gun also is favored by many varmint and small game hunters. It's a good camp gun and a good barn gun.

There have been walnut and Tenite plastic and walnut-finished hardwood stocks. There have been several types of barrel selecting systems. There have been several modes of barrel fitting. All have been Model 24s, and all sold well. ●

EDITOR'S NOTE

We all ride our favorite horses. For writers and editors, that means opinions. Certainly you know the old story of the guy with his mind made up who doesn't want it confused with the facts.

This article is, I am happy to say a severe dose of facts to confuse almost any set of recently published opinions about firearms. Naturally, there is bound to be a little ambiguity, some gray area, in any such attack on such a subject. Not to put too fine a point on it: Some fellows prevaricate and other fellows just don't know.

You're entitled to believe, therefore, and as your opinion, that there are an awful lot of Ruger Model 77s and Mini-14s being sold, that Ithaca has sold a lot of Model 37s, that some one or other of Mossberg's 22 rifles has reached a million mark, that High Standard made an awful lot of shotguns, while it was making shotguns. Any or all of those possibilities may well be so, but nobody in a position to know would say so.

So, among long guns, these are the best sellers, surprise or not. It's worth noting that, bar the odd several million collectables, something like 50 million of these are probably still working. KW

How It Was in the
Medium Good Old Days

The '30s weren't much, but they were all we had.

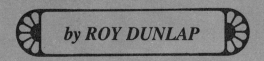

by ROY DUNLAP

LONG AGO I swore I'd never become one of these tiresome self-appointed old timers, and I haven't—until I was asked to write this, to tell a present generation how the gun world was in the 1930's, the years when the sporting arms and cartridges of today were being developed.

We of low income in the Depression years could afford little, but we tried. The Smith & Wesson 357 Magnum came into our lives, the most expensive handgun made, at $60.00 list. Cheap? You are laughing? Don't. At the time, my salary was $15.00 per week.

Foreign handguns were available—Walther, ($36 for a PP!) Mauser, Webley and Spanish makes. Colt made autos in six calibers, eight or so models of revolvers in assorted calibers: Smith & Wesson had about a dozen models; H&R and Stevens made fine 22 single-shot pistols. And, lads, ALL were available all the time. If your dealer didn't have the one you wanted in stock, it might take him a week to get it.

Almost every town had a smallbore and pistol range, and an indoor gallery for winter shooting. People were not so uptight about shooting. The Chicago Rifle Club's indoor range was in the basement of the Austin Town Hall, on the west edge of Chicago. A public building. No rent! *(Editorial note: I was almost 12 in 1940 and learned to shoot—to a degree—in that Austin Town Hall myself. KW.)*

However, if you could scrape up a few bucks you could obtain choice shooting stuff—single-shot rifles: I used to buy Ballards and Winchesters by mail at $5 each, from A.W. Peterson in Denver. Cleaned-up actions sold in Chicago for $10.00. He had lots of Colt "singleactions" (used as one word, then) at $5 to $12, but I had no market for them. New ones could be had for $30, any caliber, 32-20 on up. Good used guns went from $10 to $30, all sorts, from 45 ACP to Pennsylvania long rifles.

Ammunition? Well, 30-30's cost about a buck and a quarter a box at the high-priced stores, 38 Specials about a dime more. I shot quite a few 38 wadcutters at a buck a box. DuPont powders listed at $1.70 a pound. Laflin & Rand black powder was $9.00 for a 25-lb. keg.

Bullets were cheap. Cast lead bullets could be bought from Lyman, if you wanted to try different numbers before ordering moulds. Skilled, responsible individuals like Guy Loverin and J. Bushnell Smith could furnish custom bullets, custom wildcat cases, loaded ammunition, at fair prices.

A lot of wild-catting of rifle cartridges was going on. Today's wide range of factory cases may not be exactly the same in all respects, but for the 22-3000 or R-2 Lovell and the 224 Lindahl Chucker we have the 222 and 223 cartridges having almost identical ballistics. Lots of 310 cases then; now we have the 243 & 6mm. A 25-06? Sukalle or Niedner or Griffin & Howe would gladly make you one. The 7mm Remington Magnum was then the 276 DuBiel. I think Vernor Gipson had a 276 on the belted magnum case also.

Gipson and the Wasp

Gipson was a master machinist and rifle enthusiast. He originated the 22 Wasp, which Donaldson publicized and got his own name attached to. Vernor didn't care—he liked bigger cartridges. He once necked a 50 Browning MG down to 30 and made a barrel and rifle for it, but was prevailed upon to bolt the outfit to a stump for testing. That first shot tore the stump up. He decided not to shoot any more, as the cartridge did not seem entirely practical for a long-range varmint rifle. Gip was a lousy shot and someone else always had to shoot his test groups. Even a benchrest didn't help him.

No one had much money so for most men gunsmithing was too expensive for anything but barrel jobs or other work demanding machine tools. We did our own as far as possible, learning the hard way. There were no gunsmithing schools, no shop could pay trainees, or gunsmith feed an apprentice. August Pachmayr sent Frank to his brother in Germany to learn, not an easy life for a boy. Frank said once his uncle was not patient: one slip when holding tools to forge set-triggers or such, and he dropped everything, ran two steps, ducked to let the forging hammer pass over his head, then continued on out of range.

In the Midwest, the Niedner Rifle Corporation of Dowagiac, Michigan, a few miles north of South Bend, Indiana, was the holy font of barrels, workmanship, and knowledge. The company was owned not by Niedner, but by the man who owned the Heddon and South Bend Fishing tackle companies. It was philanthropy, for they never made any money. A. O. Niedner was the tool-maker and general machinist, known to everybody as simply "The Old Man." The barrelmaker was Carl Bierman, whose interest and hobby was the making

of fancy harnesses for show horses. He could slug a barrel and feel a ten-thousandths mike very well indeed. They had a Pratt & Whitney sine-bar universal rifling machine that could produce any twist desired and long barrels if wanted. The old man being interested in muzzle-loading shooting, they made barrels up to 48" long. There was one general workman whose name I do not remember.

The manager of Niedner was also the custom metal man, for altering bolt handles, guards and such, handling their superb cold-rust blueing and stock-making, as well as letter-writing, test-firing, making 22 jacketed bullets. That was Thomas Shelhamer. His salary was $25.00 a week. Most of us assorted riflemen in the area considered him to be the best stockmaker working. A genuine perfectionist, he was very proud of his matchless inletting, more so than of the flawless checkering and oil finish. He tolerated me through the years as I also was never really satisfied with

Shelhamer's Judgement

Early in the depression, Alvin Linden, famed Wisconsin stockmaker, hit hard times and asked for a job. The overworked Shelhamer hired him, then fired him three days later. Linden was a witty, intelligent man, very skilled at making a stock to fit a man, good with checkering and finish, but poor at inletting by top standards.

About 30 years later, when I was probably the best-known gunsmith in America and had made hundreds of rifles and stocks, I visited Tom in Dowagiac and he insisted on seeing some stocks out of the truck-load of stuff I was taking to Camp Perry to sell. He studied the shaping and the inletting, muttered, "It'll do, it'll do." I felt then I had learned how.

A Niedner barrel cost $30.00; the custom Shelhamer stock, in fine European walnut, $60.00. A new nickel-steel 1903 Springfield action was $25; M70 Winchester $45; commercial

genuine Mauser, $80. Tom really loved the British-made Farquharson single-shot action above all. He said they made the most accurate single shots.

Vernor Gipson and Ray Langguth of Chicago bought the Niedner Rifle Corporation in 1938, retired the old man and gave Tom a little more money and less work. Gip got tired of the small town in a few months and sold out his share. Ray was a skilled machinist and top shop man, but like the old man, proved not to be lucky in business. In WWII, he made front sights for M1-carbines, more and cheaper than anyone else. He put all the money into machine tools and shop improvements. The end of war saw him get renegotiated—meaning the government wanted a lot of money back. He didn't have it, and he lost the business, and the Niedner Rifle Corporation went under.

Bill Sukalle, the western barrel-maker, was happy with his men making some small part during the war. When he got a request to bid on

. . . a new nickel-steel 1903

any job, and didn't ask stupid questions.

another, and didn't want the job, he figured his price, multiplied by six to make sure he'd be high bidder and lose. Wrong. He got the contract, made a fortune, and was never renegotiated.

Hunting rifle scopes were German and expensive, though Bill Weaver was quietly making little, low-cost scopes and educating the populace. In California, Noske designed scopes and mounts for western hunting. Few of the gun writers pushed scope use.

Achieving The Classics

Townsend Whelen sort of held up sporting rifle progress for about 20 years. He was a very large, very strong man in his prime, and could handle a ten-pound rifle like a fly rod. He did most of his hunting in Canada just north of the Great Lakes in swamp and brush country where you couldn't see 20 yards with an X-ray machine, so he saw no justification for light rifles, high velocity calibers, or scope sights. Nothing less than 9½ lbs. could shoot well, and if you must have a scope, a 2x for antelope might be considered.

There was no general demand for, or factory production of, light rifles. In the late 1930's, Jack O'Connor started writing about western hunting with the 270 Winchester and 30-06 aided by 4x telescopic sights, and we began to see custom light rifles also.

I never knew Whelen except by mail, by the way. We had a bit of correspondence in his later years. After WW II, I lived next door to Jack for a year or so and we did quite a bit of varmint hunting together.

In the '30's the handgun people had a few things going—the 357, and if you wanted more, Pop Eimer used large Colt or Smith frames to build a super-whooper using cut-off 405 Winchester cases. Also, a few 44 Specials got loaded up very warm.

The Springfield was the most popular centerfire rifle of the time. Beginning around 1920, Bob Owen and Tom Shelhamer developed the American sporter stock for bolt action rifles, now known as the "Classic" styling. The 1903 Springfield barrelled action was the basis of most of the early sporters,

Springfield action was $25 . . .

could not do very well. He just laughed and said I'd have to be apprenticed to an English cabinetmaker when ten years old to really learn it, and, besides, oil was better. As I agreed, we left it there.

Fixing Up Springfields

At any rate, the Springfield was even made in sporter form by Springfield Armory until early 1930's, with polished, blued barrel and action, well-shaped stock and Lyman 48 receiver sight. NRA members could buy all parts at low cost to assemble rifles for target or hunting. And believe me, there are some strange 1903's around! And others.

Some dyed-in-wool high-power competitors (high power competition meant you shot a 1903 as issued!) even bought the 22 Long Rifle 1922 M2 Springfields and put Type C NM stocks and hardware on them to use as practice arms. Most kept the Lyman 48, as the service peep drift-slide out on barrel was very rough to see in gallery, where the rifles were mostly

wanted to be busy, you could shoot all three. Every evening you got your squadding tickets for next day at a little square building just north of messhall, two windows on a side. You found the proper window for your category, gave your name and got the tickets. You would be so scheduled as to be able to make it from one range to next firing point in time. The sergeant and his ten privates in the shack did a better job than the computers did in the '60's, and handled three times as many competitors. Remember, each state, territory, ROTC, National Guard of each state, etc., had a minimum of fourteen team members—ten firing, two alternates, captain and coach. The services—Marines, Navy, CG, Reserves, Infantry, Cavalry and Engineers—might have as many as 50 men on a squad. Add the pistol and smallbore shooters and the unattached civilians and there were a hell of a lot of people at Perry.

The messhall was run by the Army: prices cheap, food good. I have gone to Perry for two weeks with $30, bought stuff, gone out nights, had big time. Plenty of practice every day if you wanted to shoot. There was free ammunition in high power.

You met all the people in the shooting world then. I spent a rainy afternoon once in the Springfield Armory shop with Phil Sharpe picking at Al Woodworth's brain. Teams were on line alphabetically. When I was on the Illinois team, I met a coming writer, a scrawny, scarred character pretty good at 1000 yards prone, but weak on rapid fire named Keith. Most of those men are gone now: Sharpe, Con Schmitt, Hatcher, Hession, Owen and Shelhamer and Linden and the many others whose names now are just words in the out-of-print books.

The Era ended slowly. Russia began WWII, really, by attacking Finland in 1939. One Finnish shooter swore he was going to break the world 300-meter record, and he did. I don't think he cut notches in his stock every time, but he scored over 1100. As he may still be alive, I don't think I'll mention his name.

Hitler got the "cold war" going and for a year we waited for action. By Camp Perry time in 1940, shooting was training, not a sport. We fired the M1 Garands in general familiarization, but not for record. In 1941, only the smallbore and pistol matches were held at Perry. The military was too busy for competition.

Three months later there was Pearl Harbor and I stored my stuff and enlisted.

●

testified to by the pictures of beautiful Owen sporters shown in the old gun books.

Bob was born in England and came to U.S. as a young man. He was driving freight wagons in Arizona before WWI, though he was a skilled cabinet-maker by trade. Interested in rifles, he got into stock work after WW I. He made many fine stocks in the 20's, but by 1930 had to take a job with Winchester to make a living. The Depression, remember?

He ran their custom stock setup until his retirement after WWII, and used to come West and visit me a couple days every year. Self-taught, he and Shelhamer worked entirely differently to produce the same sort of fine rifle stock. Bob was fast, said he could inlet and rough out (shape from blank) a stock in eight hours, finish a stock in two days. Tom would spend thirty hours inletting, thirty more on the outside, and keep on for 3 or 4 months getting his finish to suit him.

I asked Bob once how he got a decent finish with French polish, which I

used. A few fellows did turn the 22 barrel down and install the 1903 rear sight, with regular service handguard. Except for bolt and caliber, these were identical to the 30 NM Springfields and drive present-day collectors wild trying to find out why such rifles are not listed anywhere in the records.

A new Match Springfield cost either $42 or $46, I forget which, but most of us picked up used actions and put our own rifles together. Ammunition was so cheap we only handloaded a little for long-range special matches. We used M1 (173-gr. boattail service) or National Match, which we could pick up for two or three cents a round. At Camp Perry you had to use the Springfield as issued in all but two matches—the Wimbledon and the Member's, which was then a 600-yard any-rifle match. Perry lasted three weeks . . . one week individual matches, one week team matches, and final week, the Nationals—Individual, Team, Infantry, etc.

High power, pistol and smallbore all went on at same time, and if you

x

x

Continued from page 3.

This 20-gauge Parker A-1 Special, possibly one of only eight ever built, set an auction record, we are told, when it brought $95,000. Its provenance and owner were unannounced.

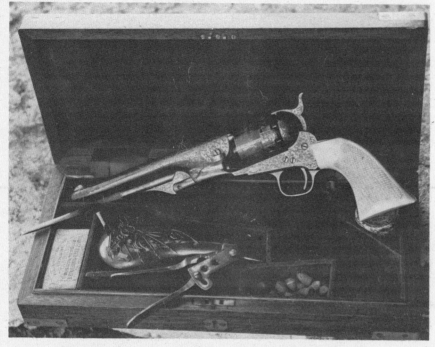

This is the "Cox Navy" presented by Colt's long ago to a New York banker and now sold from the collection of Jerry Berger, who showed his guns at many places, most notably perhaps being the 1980 NRA Meeting in Kansas City. This gun brought $75,000 at auction.

This pair of Manton pistols owned by John T. Amber brought $7,500 in the famous Christie's/Colt auction and present even the unpracticed eye with unmistakable elegance.

Manhattan Auction Sets Many Records

Those who keep score of such things tell us the famous Colt-Christie's auction held in October, 1981, on Park Avenue set many records. In the nature of such things, some are more interesting than others.

A Parker gun brought $95,000, which is a new high for a modern American gun. A single Colt revolver—percussion, of course—brought $75,000. And there now exists a $50,000 Kentucky rifle. Indeed, there are now, thanks to this auction, such things in the world as $17,000 Detective Specials, $6,000 Model 1911s, $7,500 Colt 25 Autos and, going back a ways, even a $14,000 Roots model.

In all, from highly engraved and finished 18th and 19th Century pieces to Ernest Hemingway's own 22 Colt automatic—the pre-Woodsman model—the total ran to $900,000, which is respectable indeed, considering that what was happening was these fellows were selling guns on Park Avenue, right out in public. A lot of guns are sold each day in New York, of course, but very few in public.

That indeed, apart from the money, was the idea of the Colt and Christie entrepreneurs who got the whole thing going. Getting firearms treated as *objets d'art* in New York is a fair public relations ploy. And the money wasn't bad.

Somewhat unusually, we are told, the chap who wielded the hammer was David Bathurst, president of Christie's in America. The firm collected a 10% surcharge from the buyers. Larry (R. L.) Wilson is the cataloguer and he was very happy with the sale of 6,000 catalogs at mostly $25 each. The money really wasn't so bad.

And it was a grand occasion all around, according to John T. Amber who was there and had some items on the block—successfully. Selling successfully is always nice. And the money wasn't bad.

Milestones

● Its statistics may bore you after a while, but the Fourth Annual SHOT Show was yet again onwards and upwards. It was battered by the winter storm of the century in Atlanta, but emerged alive. The Fifth Show was set for San Francisco, but then the legal climate got uncertain—there are all manner of strange legislative machinations about firearms out there—and business prudence dictat-

From 22 Hornet to 416 Rigby, Griffin & Howe calculates this six-rifle battery will cover most hunters' needs. They're all Model 70s (pre-64, they say) and they're all in the white because the buyer gets to specify the engraving which, considering the $60,000 price tag, seems only fair.

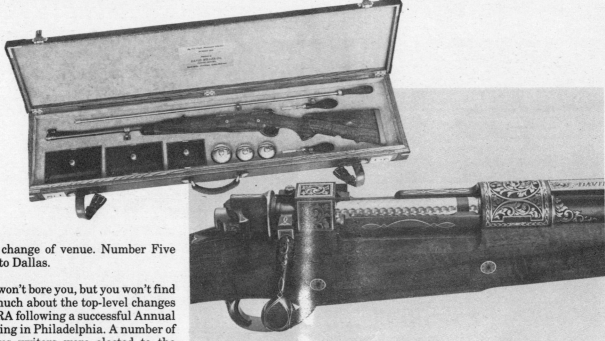

ed a change of venue. Number Five goes to Dallas.

● It won't bore you, but you won't find out much about the top-level changes at NRA following a successful Annual Meeting in Philadelphia. A number of famous writers were elected to the Board and one famous writer—Neal Knox—some time subsequently left NRA's employ. As he was in charge of ILA at the time, there has been a great deal of speculation, but no hard facts whatever.

If you never thought you'd see a $41,000 elephant rifle, you were wrong because here it is. Assembled by the David Miller Co., with Lynton McKenzie engraving, this 458 is the first a Big Five series of elaborate creations from Safari Club International. John ... paid $41,000 for it at auction during SCI's 1982 Banquet.

HANDGUNS TODAY:

SIXGUNS AND OTHERS

by HAL SWIGGETT

FOR A YEAR that started off rather slow—many of the handguns announced earlier had trouble—it changed course mid-stream and ended up on the high side. Nothing radically new showed up, yet innovations were added here and there. And there was the opportunity to try some of the models announced last year.

A complete change for this correspondent came in the form of an interest in mini-revolvers. At first I felt I should wash my mind with soap when those thoughts started creeping in, but now that they have been tried I found out I had been wrong again.

Yes—1982 was a good year.

Trying to figure some way to report on all this without the usual A to Z arrangement I finally hit on something different—this year we are going to start at the other end. Here it is—from Z (how about W) to A:

Dan Wesson 44 Magnum with 8-inch barrel assembly.

T/C's Recoil Proof 2.5x scope.

Sheila Link, president of the Outdoor Writers of America, with a javelina and the Remington XP-100 chambered for 6mm TM.

The rear sight is a Sterling design. The button on the side unlatches the action. The transfer bar can be seen against the hammer.

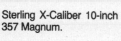

Sterling X-Caliber 10-inch 357 Magnum.

Dan Wesson

Dan Wesson's mighty 44 Magnum. That's the way their ads tout it. According to those I have talked to who have shot it, the ad is correct. It is delivered with 4, 6, 8 or 10-inch barrel in plain configuration or with eight small holes drilled around the circumference of the barrel three-quarters of an inch short of the muzzle. This porting is called Power Control.

Factory recommendations specifically state "jacketed bullets only" for Power Control barrels. Word of mouth has it there are problems. I've been told the barrel and shroud have to be cleaned every couple hundred shots, even with jacketed bullets. The revolver is a good one, no doubt about it. Where there is heavy smoke, there has to be some fire so buyers might do well to stick to plain barrels.

Dan Wesson 44's are delivered in a Pistol Pac with 6- and 8-inch barrels. The 4- and 10-inch versions are ordered separate. The Pistol Pac includes extra sight inserts, an extra grip, a belt buckle, emblem and of course the tools necessary for changing barrels.

United Sporting Arms

This is another of the small companies that makes a good solid single action six-gun but seems to ride hand-in-hand with hard times. The Seville is made in 45 Winchester Magnum, 45 Colt, 44 Magnum, 41 Magnum, 9mm Winchester Magnum and 357 Magnum. It wears barrel lengths of 4⅝, 5½, 6½ and 7½ inches.

Sights are good, the rear is fully adjustable. The front is a red insert ramp. A transfer bar makes it possible to carry the Seville fully loaded with six rounds safely.

Last year we tested a convertible barrel/cylinder combination using one frame for both 44 Magnum and 45 Colt. I see no indication it ever got off the ground but I do know at least a few were made. If you run into one, grab it; the test combo worked fine.

Trapper Gun

Lin "Trapper" Alexiou and well-known gun writer Bob Milek put their heads together and decided a better 24- or 25-caliber pistol could be made out of the XP-100 Remington. So they did it. Using 223 brass, the neck is expanded to take the bigger bullet. That's all.

I've been shooting the 6mm TM with a 12-inch barrel and a 2x Leupold scope. Sierra's 60-grain hollow point loaded over a good load of H322 does disastrous things to jackrabbits. It doesn't do coyotes any good either.

While sighting in the pistol in my usual manner, across the hood of a pickup with a hat for a rest, rocks of grapefruit size were exploded shot after shot at 136 steps. There was a low mound at that distance. A dozen rocks were put in a row. All were shattered. It did take 13 shots however. Holding on the first put the bullet right over the top. From then on those rocks rested on the crosshair and it was all down hill.

There must be a reason for the 6mm TM and the 25 TM if for no other than there wasn't one before. Long-range varmint hunters can have a ball with either. So can hunters of medium sized game.

Thompson/Center

Still chambered for 17 calibers, the Thompson/Center Contender single shot pistol is the one all others are compared against. Barrels are currently made in four configurations; the original octagon, bull, vent rib/internal choke in 10-inch and the Super "14" which gets its name from its length.

Many subtle changes have been made since the first Contender hit dealers' shelves, quietly worked into production and on out to shooters. This year there is to be new lockwork designed to do away with some of the fitting problems. The frame—it will be called the Mach IV—will be a bit different in appearance but all barrels now in use will fit. The action will open a bit differently and trigger adjustments will be possible from the outside.

Whether your druthers are hunting, plinking, silhouette, or all three, there is a T/C caliber made in a barrel that will fit your purpose almost as if you had designed it yourself.

Sterling

Last year we announced the X-Caliber. It finally made the scene for a brief test this year. It's made in 22 LR, 22 WMR, 357 Magnum and 44 Magnum. Our test X-Caliber came with a 357 barrel installed and an extra 22 LR barrel with its own forend. Both

THE TENTH MAN
Just 10 of these handsome bronzes were cast over a decade ago to be presented to those chosen as Outstanding American Handgunners and the 10th was awarded Hal Swiggett at the Philadelphia NRA meetings in 1982. And here he is—what better place to announce it than right here where he works?

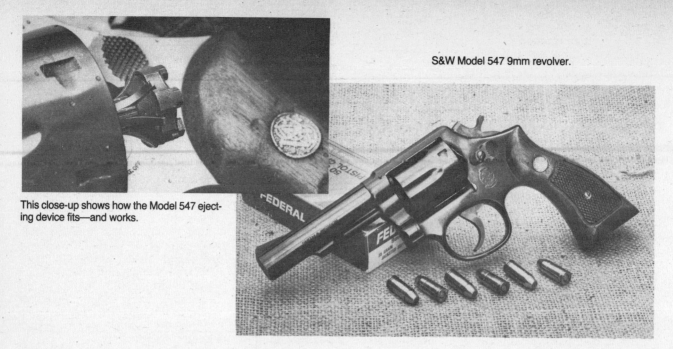

S&W Model 547 9mm revolver.

This close-up shows how the Model 547 ejecting device fits—and works.

barrels are 10 inches though 8-inch barrels are also available in each of the four calibers.

With the 357 barrel, the X-Caliber pushed my scale to 59.5 ounces. The trigger pull was too hefty for my RCBS Trigger Gauge. Another scale put it at 7.5 pounds. Both sights are Sterling's own design. The rear is fully click adjustable. The front is a narrow blade, obviously made that way so as to not cover the target. It does not, for this shooter at least, fit the rear notch. It is possible I have looked at so many ⅛-inch front sights that this one seems unduly slender by comparison. Could also be that practice will prove its worth.

Metal work is good. The polish and blueing are first order. The hammer spur is very wide, ½-inch, and very long, 1¾-inches. It is grooved for no-slip thumbing.

The stock is one-piece, finger-grooved, and massive in appearance but fits my hand perfectly.

The action is easily opened via a thumb button high on the left side, just in front of the hammer. It is relatively easy to reach with the right thumb, for right-handed shooters, but it seemed easier for me to hold the pistol in the shooting hand and open it with the opposite thumb.

Nothing was proven on the range— good, bad or indifferent. The exceptionally heavy trigger pull at 7.5 pounds coupled with enough creep to remind one of a military rifle made it mighty near impossible to see what the barrels would do. I have a hunch they will shoot rather well. John Leak let me see one of the first production guns and I have no doubt triggers will be considerably better before many leave the factory, so chances are you won't get to see one like this yourself.

SSK Industries

If holes through barrels aren't big and cases long, J.D. Jones hasn't much use for them. That's how his JDJ "Hand Cannons" came to be. Manufactured by his SSK Industries,

J. D. Jones says, "Even the ladies with the right mental attitude don't have problems shooting JDJ Hand Cannons." Jane (Jones) seems to agree.

the custom barrels are for Thompson/Center Contender pistols in most instances but sometimes they are made up in XP-100's.

They come in four sizes: 411 JDJ, 430 JDJ. 45-70 and 50-70. I guess the 375 JDJ qualifies here, too, since Jones considers anything over 35 caliber "Hand Cannon" material.

I'm not sure what case the 375 is made from, but the 411 and 430 call the 444 Marlin "daddy." Not only are the "Hand Cannons" big cases they also emphasize big—heavier than usually considered normal for the caliber—bullets.

I've shot the 375 JDJ and didn't find it to be a bit punishing. I regularly shoot a 45-70 on a T/C. It has become a fun gun of the highest order. So far it has taken critters from seven or so pounds (jackrabbits) to near 500 pounds (oryx) without a hitch along with a good many rather vicious rocks at assorted lengthy distances.

The "Hand Cannons" are punishing enough, however, that J.D. had to design a scope base to handle their recoil. He calls it the T'SOB. Three Bushnell rings are used. None of his "big boomers" as they are sometimes called has knocked one off or even shook it loose.

SSK also markets bullet moulds for the JDJ designs. Two of his most popular are a 315 grain and a 350-grain for his 430 JDJ. They both serve 44 Magnum shooters well too.

Smith & Wesson

Nothing new from Springfield, Massachusetts this year so let's review one that was announced last year but

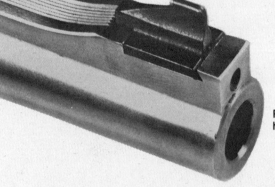

Colored accessory front sights for the Ruger Redhawk. Colors are white, fluorescent red, yellow and sky blue. The dark one with the insert is original equipment.

North America's 1⅝-inch 22 WMR 5-shot mini revolver. Swiggett has found this to be a handy little carry gun. So much so he had it dressed for formal wear by engraver Jim Riggs.

Ruger's new accessory gold bead sight for the Redhawk and the rear sight to match.

didn't make it in time to see any use:

The "K" frame Model 547 9mm Luger 6-shot double action revolver with the 4⅛-inch barrel weighed 34 ounces on my postal scale, same as their tech sheet said, which doesn't seem to happen often to me. Double action trigger pull is an even 12 pounds. Single action is crisp, no creep, and one ounce under four pounds.

The front sight is ⅛-inch ramp serrated and the rear ⅛-inch square notch. The 4⅛-inch version is square butt with checkered Magna Service stocks. The shorter 3-inch edition is round butt wearing checkered target stocks with speed loader cutaway.

The Model 547 started out as a Model 13 and was modified to answer the needs of French police. Since 9mm ammo is rimless, the extractor had to be redone or the half-moon clips employed. Redo was the decision. As a result, the extractor head is beryllium copper, hardened to the same level as the steel part it replaces. It is also smaller than those normally found on S&W revolvers.

The extractor system is unusual.

There is nothing to catch the case until the extractor is pushed to eject those cases. When this is done, out pops a tiny "tongue"—or whatever—and lifts the empty up, out and away. It seems to work. At least it has on this particular revolver through 150 rounds. There have been a few foul-ups, but I leaned towards watching it perform more often than I should have.

The gun is easy to handle and it shoots well but one expects S&Ws to handle and shoot. I have been accused of having 45-caliber veins, but I'm a 9mm funatic. That's why I had to try this Model 547.

But I'm still not convinced. S&W folks say those little "pop outs" are as strong as the rim of a 9mm shell. Could be. I have nothing against the French police, but if push came to shove, I'd rather see them using this Model 547 than my hometown officers.

Ruger

Old Model Ruger single actions were and are perfectly safe when used the way the design was intended to be used or, lacking that knowledge, used

with plain ordinary everyday common sense. Ruger honchos have now gone all out to make their guns safe as humanly possible. The New Model had done just that, but Ruger has added a conversion service—free—to make Old Models safer. Read about it on page 257.

The Redhawk, Ruger's big double action 44 Magnum, has only one fault—there hasn't been enough of them. Dealers in my part of the country are getting $500 and up for this $350 (suggested price) revolver. It has been accused of being the strongest double action revolver manufactured. It comes by that honor by reason of having cylinder walls 25 percent thicker than competitive models, even thicker than the New Model Super Blackhawk.

Now there are accessory sight kits for the Redhawk. There is a steel front sight with a gold bead and matching "V" notch rear sight with a white centerline. Should colored front sights be your thing, there is a set of four molded Delrin sights in white, yellow, fluorescent red, and sky blue. All the front sights interchange; $5.50 for the color, $7.50 for the gold bead.

The Abilene by Mossberg. This one is a 6-inch 45 Colt. Swiggett has used it on several hunts.

Mitchel Arms 18-inch barrel single action with shoulder stock. This stock is legal only for the 18-inch barrel revolver.

North American Arms

Mini-revolvers did little for me for a long time. Somehow it was hard to think of them as real guns. Looking over a North American 5-shot mini 22 Magnum at one of the SHOT shows made me think maybe a good thing had been passed up.

I got one and tried it and now I know a good thing had been passed up.

The North American mini-revolver is made in several models from 1⅛-inch-barreled 22 Short to 1⅝-inch-barreled 22 Magnum. I selected the latter for test purposes.

Never really tried for accuracy, the little 5½-ounce 5-shot revolver has still hit a lot of tin cans of soft drink size at three or four steps. An FBI agent friend tried it at seven steps, hit a can with his first shot, then suddenly thought of something else he had to do.

Nothing but CCI hollow points have gone through mine. The fourth box is nearly gone which means it's been fired almost 200 times. It goes lots of places in my shirt pocket behind a notebook that's always there. Visiting a South Texas ranch one day it was brought out to show off. The rancher reached in his right jacket pocket, pulled out an identical gun and said, "Sure are nice, aren't they."

All stainless steel, it is obvious these little mini's have a use. That South Texas rancher used to be a sheriff, Texas Highway Patrolman and a Deputy U.S. Marshal. He had one in his pocket. I know three San Antonio police officers who carry mini-revolvers as back-ups for their back-up handguns.

Mine has become such a part of my everyday life it has been dressed for the occasion by Jim Riggs. Both sideplates, all five surfaces between the cylinder chambers, full length both sides of the barrel and the backstrap: full dress. All it needs is a bow tie.

Mossberg

There is nothing new about the Abilene other than it has proven every bit as good as I thought it was last year. Since then a 6-inch in 45 Colt has lived with me nearly nine months. It has devoured several hundred rounds of Federal 225-grain hollow points and my own concoction of a 255-grain hard-cast bullet over a healthy dose of powder.

The Abilene's anvil safety is unique and not easily described. Rather than the usual transfer bar between the hammer and firing pin the anvil pivots on the hammer. There is a transfer bar of sorts, but its duty is to activate the anvil. It is different and it does work.

Mitchell Arms

Faithful to the original design, these six-guns are made with the very latest technology, materials and expertise that just weren't available a century ago. Calibers are 357, 44 Magnum and 45 Colt, and barrels come in 5½-inch, 6-inch, 7½-inch, 10-, 12- and 18-inch lengths. There is a shorter 4¾-inch version in dual cylinder models, which come in 22 LR-22 Magnum and 44 Magnum-44-40. There are both fixed sight and adjustable sight versions.

Then there is that long one—the 18-inch—for which a shoulder stock is available. Some day I'm going to try one of these. I have the feeling we might be amazed at the accuracy possible with a shoulder stock on a long-barreled six-gun chambered for that fine oldie, the 45 Colt.

Llama

The Llama Super Comanche 44 Magnum is a fine piece of machinery. I have been shooting a 6-inch version several weeks. A new 8½-incher will be available this year aimed at silhouette shooters (please forgive). Stoeger imports them.

The Super Comanche is easy to like. It weighs 50.5 ounces and it feels like a big gun. The ventilated rib with a ramp front sight on one end and a ful-

High Standard 6-inch Camp Gun.

Llama Super Comanche 44 Magnum.

High Standard Sentinel Mk IV 22 WMR.

Freedom Arms 5-shot 22 LR mini-revolver. With the 1-inch barrel it weighs 4 ounces.

ly adjustable rear sight on the other doesn't hurt either. The wood grips on mine fit perfectly, something a few American gunmakers seem to have a problem with. The checkering is on a raised side panel bringing it in direct contact with the hand.

The safety is unique, at least to this reviewer. The hammer of the Super Comanche is on an eccentric cam. With the trigger fully back as in firing, the hammer hits the firing pin. Releasing the trigger causes the hammer to raise above the firing pin. There is no way possible the gun can be made to fire without pulling the trigger. Ingenious. Unique. Whatever, it is very nice.

The barrel has to be the slickest I've ever seen. Though no lead bullets have gone through this test revolver it would appear near leading-free unless awfully hot loads were set off. The hammer is wide and deeply grooved; the trigger wide and smoothly polished. Single-action trigger pull is 4.5 pounds and double-action goes a bit

over 11 pounds.

This Super Comanche 44 will outshoot all but a selected few and I'm not sure about them.

For 1982, there is a new Super Comanche. It's the same revolver, near as I can tell, but chambered for 357 Magnum. It should make the 357 feel like a popgun.

There's another Llama 357 Magnum. This is the standard-frame Comanche, but with most of the Super Comanche features incorporated, including the eccentric cam safety mechanism.

Move over and make room fellows. These Spanish-made revolvers are here to stay.

Interarms

All sorts of goodies in this line:

The Virginian Dragoon now has a stainless steel silhouette model, a fixed sight "Deputy" in either blue or stainless, and for that individual wanting "something extra" there is the hand-engraved Virginian presen-

tation grade. This one is 44 Magnum only with either 6-inch or 7½-inch barrels. The others are 357 Magnum, 44 Magnum, and 45 Colt. Barrels run from five to 12 inches, not all lengths in all models.

Then there is the new Virginian 22 convertible. It comes with both cylinders, of course, and in either blue or stainless steel.

The Rossi M88 is a new stainless steel version of the 3-inch 38 Special that's been imported for 15 years or so.

High Standard

High Standard has reintroduced another derringer, another double action revolver and a new finish.

The H-S derringer is now again to be had in 22 LR. This caliber had been dropped during their interlude. It's available in blue with black grips or in electroless nickel (both external and internal surfaces) with walnut grips.

The Sharpshooter 22 semi-auto pistol is now offered as a Survival Pack with a canvas case and an extra magazine. The finish is electroless nickel—inside and out. J. B. Wood will doubtless tell all, starting on page 103.

Both the Sentinel and Camp Gun 22 rimfire revolvers are back. The Sentinel comes with fixed sights and a 2-inch barrel, or adjustable sights on a 4-inch barrel. The Camp Gun is six inches of barrel with adjustable sights. All three come with dual cylinders, and all are finished in blue.

There is no mention yet of the Crusader. Maybe next year.

Harrington & Richardson

At H&R, long known for inexpensive good guns, there are several additions this year:

Freedom Arms Boot Gun, top, has a 3-inch barrel and oversize grips. The regular model with 1¾-inch barrel is compared for size. Both are convertible 22 LR-22 WMR.

Colt's scaled down 22 New Frontier single action has been reintroduced.

A 10-inch barrel is now available in the Model 686, for the silhouette shooter.

The Model 830 and 833 3-inch swing outs (22 LR and 32 S&W Long) are finished in Hard-Guard electroless matte nickel.

There are new accessory walnut wrap-around grips for models 733-WG, 930-WG, 732-WG and 929-WG. These are 2½-inch barreled 22's and 32's.

H&R also offers a 3x Hunter/Silhouette 1-inch scope with ¼-minute clicks with an eye relief of 20 inches and a 13½-foot field at 100 yards.

Charter Arms Undercover 38 Special in all stainless steel.

One-inch rings are available that fit the rib on their model 903, 603, 904, 905 and 604 Swing-Out revolvers.

Freedom Arms

I'm hooked on mini-revolvers, as I said earlier. It took a while but now it's happened.

Freedom Arms is making five models. Three are here by the Smith-Corona as I write about them. All are stainless steel.

There is to be a 1-inch barrel, 4-ounce 22 S/LR; a 1¾-inch 22 S/LR; a 1-inch 22 Magnum; and a 1¾-inch 22 Magnum. The fifth model is so brand new I have, here on the desk, the one showed at the SHOT show. It is a 3-Inch Boot Gun with oversized grips and available in both 22 LR or 22 Magnum—it's a convertible.

At least one of the others also goes as a convertible. Instructions were definite, too: Do not mix them up because each cylinder is fitted to each frame. Since I was sent two guns with pairs of cylinders, Bradley Woodbury

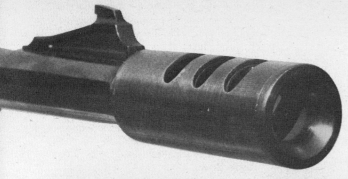

Cellini's Muzzle Brake and Recoil Reducer is barely 2½ inches long and weighs just 3.5 ounces yet it controls the recoil of the 44 Magnums. This one is on a T/C 10-inch 44 Magnum.

Vito Cellini with his personal S&W 357 Magnum

was positive in telling me to "keep them separate."

I have, Brad. Honest I have.

The 1-inch 22 LR has white grips. I have dubbed it the Dian since that name is on the backstrap. It is 5-shot, as are all their 22 LR revolvers. This will be a personal purse gun I feel certain. It weighs four ounces.

Another of the three has a 1¾-inch barrel. It is 22 Magnum, hence a 4-shot, and with it is a 22 LR 4-shot cylinder. It weighs five ounces; the extra cylinder weighs 1¾-ounces.

The third of our test guns is the Boot Gun. It wears three inches of barrel, oversize black grips and weighs 5.5 ounces. The longer barrel and bigger grip cause an entirely different look. Still a mini, it sort of graduates though to a magna-mini, and almost gains the appearance of a real honest-to-goodness handgun. Velocity and accuracy are sure to be increased. Could be the added punch will make it a hot item where hideout

guns are needed. On the other hand, it is out of the shirt pocket class. Good looking as it is, I tend towards the original size.

Freedom Arms' minis are Dick Casull designs. He has been around the industry many years. My first connection came with a black powder rifle that started a round ball in the chamber but shot out a 22 bullet. The black powder was set off with a cap from a toy pistol, and it worked. He also had the 454 Casull, a behemoth of a 45 starting off with a triplex load. Now the minis. He has hit one this time that's good. I'm happy for him.

Colt

The big news from Colt this year is the new MK V. Actually there are several things but let's start with their new 357 Magnum double action revolver. These are totally re-engineered versions of the famous MK III Trooper and Lawman. Basically a new mainspring and sear release de-

sign gives a lighter, faster, double action trigger pull. You can read a detailed review on page 254.

Colt will produce the famous Python revolver with the Royal Coltguard finish. Coltguard is an electroless plating that provides protection against adverse weather conditions.

The second end of an era has come: Approximately 1500 black powder revolvers will be made in stainless steel; the 1860 Army, 1851 and 1861 Navy models, and the 1862 Pocket Police and Pocket Navy. These will be produced by the end of 1982 and will end Colt's 20th century black powder program—so far.

A new beginning for another: Colt's popular scaled-down 22 New Frontier single action Army has been reintroduced. Featuring an adjustable rear sight, ramp front sight, original style black composition rubber grips, and the famous Colt color case-hardened frame, the New Frontier 22 has a crossbolt safety and will be available in three barrel lengths: 4¾-, 6- and 7½-inch.

Charter Arms

These fellows sure stay busy. Four guns for this year are so new they don't even have photos. Actually it's two new guns offered a pair of ways each

There is a new Law Enforcement 2-inch 38 Special with a spurless hammer, making it snag-free, but with serrations on what there is so it can be cocked for single action. It has a new neoprene grip, with finger grooves to take the "shock" out of firing and relieved for all speed loaders.

There is a full-length ramp front sight and the usual square-notch rear. This little dude is offered in chrome moly steel with their service blue finish or all stainless steel for corrosion resistance.

The new Law Enforcement 3-inch Bulldog 44 Special is the same story, second chapter, as above. Same sights, same grip, same finishes—chrome moly service blue or all-stainless steel.

I have shot neither of the above but have carried Charter revolvers since shortly after they hit the market in 22 LR, 38 Special and 44 Special. My newest acquisition came last spring: One of the first all-stainless steel 38 Specials. It has received a rather thorough workout. Right now it is barely elbow distance away. Most all types of 38 Special factory ammo has been put through it—158-grain, 140-grain, 125-grain, 110-grain and 90-grain loads along with about three one-

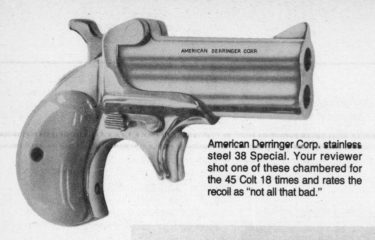

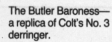

American Derringer Corp. stainless steel 38 Special. Your reviewer shot one of these chambered for the 45 Colt 18 times and rates the recoil as "not all that bad."

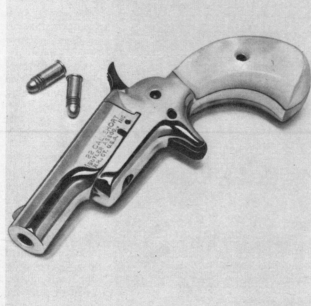

The Butler Baroness— a replica of Colt's No. 3 derringer.

pound coffee cans full of cast 148-grain wadcutters.

It has the slickest trigger I've encountered on any over-the-counter pocket gun, except one, come to think of it. I'm also blessed with a Charter 22 Magnum which has to have the best trigger I've ever seen on a factory gun.

They do, in talking of their all-stainless steel, list it as corrosion resistant. I'm glad. My little 38 developed a bad case of rash on the front sight but probably this came from its installation. My wife had a emery board handy which, along with a soaking application of Break Free, took care of the situation. This was several months ago and no more problem.

Cellini

I stumbled onto the Cellini Muzzle Brake and Recoil Reducer quite by accident. The range manager where I do much of my shooting told me about it.

Vito Cellini showed me a videotape of the device in action. I saw, among others, a 2½-inch Dan Wesson 357 barely jump as it fired full factory 158-grain loads, so I got interested.

Cellini then took me to the range where I fired all the guns I'd seen on tape. I do not hold handguns tight at all, so in my hands these did raise a little, but no more than a few inches. Cellini holds them to no jump at all.

Since then I've shot a 41 Magnum S&W 4-inch rigged with one of the devices rather extensively. Several of my shooting friends have seen it in action and done it themselves, but they still don't believe it.

Cellini has his muzzle brake/recoil reducer patented and will install one for you for $150. It works.

Butler

Long years back I owned a Colt No. 3 derringer. A close friend of many years duck hunting association grew fonder and fonder of it and eventually acquired it as a birthday present.

Butler is reproducing the No. 3 in

four styles in 22 Short. There is the Baron with gold frame, black barrel, walnut grip; the Baroness with gold frame, gold barrel, pearl grip; the Countess has a nickel frame, nickel barrel and pearl grip; the Count has black frame, black barrel, walnut grip.

Presentation cases are made for individual guns, a pair or even the quartette, and 31-caliber black powder models are also available, the brochure says.

American Derringer Corp.

These little guns were mentioned last year and I said nothing bigger than 38 Special did much for me. I have relented.

These stainless steel twin-holders are made in 38 Special in bunches. Special order calibers include 22 LR, 22 WRM, 22 Jet, 223 Remington, 30-30, 380 Auto, 38 Super, 9mm Luger, 357 Magnum, 41 Magnum, 44-40, 44 Special, 44 Magnum, 45 Auto and 45 Colt.

The 38 Special weighs 15.5 ounces, and the 45 Colt 15 ounces, and I say that for a reason. All of these "special order" calibers from 38 Super on up wear the label, "WARNING: SEVERE RECOIL IN THIS CALIBER" also for a reason—it's the truth.

Bob Saunders of ADC is a likeable chap even when he doesn't have what's necessarily good for me in mind. He proved it by showing up with one of his 45 Colt derringers to suggest I shoot it. So I did: six times with W-W factory loads, six times with Federal's newer 225-grain load, and six times with my own 45 Colt 255-grain loads about 150 fps hotter than factory.

It wasn't all that bad. In fact, the four-barreled 357 COP tested last year kicked harder. That's it, Bob. Don't come back at me with a 44 Magnum. I ain't going to do it.

We're Not Alone

Used to be magnum calibers belonged to us six-gun and single shooters nearly exclusively. Not anymore. At the Atlanta SHOT show I saw three autoloaders crowding our territory. Make that four. A big 357 Magnum self-loader from Israel called the Eagle; another 357 Magnum autoloader from Coonan Arms; the N.A.M. 45 Winchester Magnum + chambering both the 45 and 9mm Winchester Magnums (different guns of course) and Will Moore claims his big Wildey 45 will be out for sure this year.

They are crowding us.   ●

HANDGUNS TODAY:

AUTOLOADERS

by J.B. WOOD

The 9mm Omni really impresses with innovations inside and smooth functioning outside plus big magazine capacity.

The Coonan 357 autoloader is still heralded, was shown at SHOT Show, will provide Browning-type lock for 357 Magnum cartridge.

(Above and Left) Israelis are to make the Eagle, another 357 Magnum selfloader, this one with lugged bolt, interchangeable barrels, and real heft.

JUST A COUPLE of years ago, a handgun in 357 Magnum almost had to be a revolver or a single shot or a derringer or a four-shooter. Now, there are to be *two* autoloaders for this rimmed cartridge, one made in Israel, the other in the United States. The Israeli entry is called the "Eagle," and it is imported by Magnum Research, Incorporated. THe U.S.-made gun is by Coonan Arms, and these two guns are entirely different mechanically. The Eagle is gas operated, and the Coonan uses the traditional Browning falling-barrel pattern.

The Joint Services testing program in search of a 9mm U.S. military pistol is on "hold." I've heard that service branches may still continue testing, but procurement of a chosen gun would have to be by the separate services. By the time you read this, the entire picture may have changed, so I'll make no predictions. So far, the only sure things to come out of the tests were some new models now available, and several interesting prototypes that may or may not be made.

In the marketplace, prices have continued to spiral upward, and the inflationary trend of our national economy is only a part of this. When the guns are imports, the relative value of our dollar and foreign monetary units is a big factor. In some cases, this has resulted in importation of certain guns in very limited numbers. Still, even though prices are generally high, the upper level usually reflects quality that matches the price.

Our old-line companies didn't produce much autoloading news for this year. Colt discontinued the Woodsman; High Standard has a 22 semi-auto for survivalists; Charter jazzed up its survivalist entry. Smith just kept making guns.

This year's new designs have gone in several directions. In the mainstream, the trend is still toward stainless steel, double action, or large capacity magazines, and sometimes a combination of these features. Some, though, have ignored this trend and concentrated on guns that are specifically made for competition, or on new cartridge applications. In alphabetical order, then, let's see what's new:

Action Arms, Ltd.

Already well-known for their marketing of the Uzi semi-auto carbine, Action Arms is now doing a big favor for the serious target shooters. They're importing the excellent Britarms 2000 Mark II from England. As with most guns of this type, it is expensive (around $1000), but its design is virtually 22 rimfire state-of-the-art. After it's in the hands of more shooters, I predict we'll hear of it winning some matches. The bore centerline is very low to the hand, the trigger position is fully adjustable, and the anatomic-style grip is by Wilhelm Hofman of Germany. It's a nice package for serious competition.

AMT, Incorporated

Now those who own the fine little 380 Back-Up can purchase its 22 counterpart and practice for pennies. The 22 Long Rifle version is practically identical, the only visible differences being the breechblock and right-side extractor and the smaller hole at the muzzle. The construction is still entirely stainless steel. The 22 magazine holds eight rounds, three more than an unaltered 380. Aside from its personal protection possibilities, the 22 Back-Up should be a perfect minimum gun for backpackers, survivalists, campers, and fishermen. I've been trying one out in recent weeks, and it has functioned flawlessly with all brands of high-velocity ammo.

Arminex, Ltd.

This new Arizona-based company is producing a pistol that at first glance might appear to be a slightly-modified version of the U.S. service auto. On closer inspection, this is definitely not the case. The most notable features are a slide-mounted firing-pin-block safety and a solid, one-piece backstrap with an absolutely perfect shape. The rear sight is fully adjustable, and the front sight blade is double-pinned and easily replaceable. The slide stop lever is extended just the right distance into the top of the left grip panel, and the extractor and ejector are both pivoted for positive contact. Finally, with a change of barrel and magazine, the pistol can be used with 45 Auto, 38 Super, or 9mm Parabellum. This last feature gives it its name: "Trifire." I have shot the prototypes, and they perform beautifully. Initial production is scheduled for the summer of 1982.

Beretta

For police and military customers only, Beretta has a new modification of the basic Model 92 design, with a muzzle brake, forward hand grip, detachable stock, and extended 20-round magazine. The firing system is modified to give three-shot full-auto bursts, and the pistol has been designated Model 93R. Of much more interest to the average shooter is the new reduced-size version of the Model 92SB, now becoming available in quantity. The Model 92SB Compact is only 7¾ inches long, 5 inches in height. It has the reversible push-button magazine release of the full-sized Model 92SB, and the slide-mounted firing-pin-block safety is ambidextrous. There is an automatic internal safety that blocks the firing pin until the final fraction of trigger movement. The quality is what you'd expect from Beretta, and I've put several hundred assorted rounds through my 92SB Compact so far, with absolutely no problems.

Browning

The big news here is the bull-barrel 22 Challenger III pistol. The other features of the gun are the same well-liked arrangement as the Challenger II, but the 5½-inch barrel of the new gun gives it slightly less over-all length. While the Challenger III is four ounces lighter, the gun has the forward weight distribution that is favored by many target shooters. New versions of the centerfire autos are also offered. The 9mm Hi-Power is available in "silver chrome," and has a Pachmayr rubber wrap-around grip as standard equipment. The excellent BDA 380 is now offered in nickel finish, and this, too, will be good news for those who carry these guns in humid conditions. The DA and SA versions of the Hi-Power, developed for the U.S. government tests, are still only prototypes, and we don't know if they'll be produced commercially.

The Arminex Trifire offers 1911-like look but considerable difference—safety on slide, grip shape improved, and three-caliber potential.

Beretta's 92SB Compact is not three-shot burst style as the Model 93R is, but it is a neat version for us average folks.

AMT's 22 Backup is a sure lookalike and feelalike for its 380 brother, except for the 22's right-side extractor assembly.

CB Arms, Inc.

The little 22 "Double Deuce," an all-steel double action which externally resembles the Walther TPH, was scheduled for production start in May of 1982. Original plans were for late 1981, but this was held up by the spectre that looms over all new gun production—castings. The Double Deuce will be offered in regular blued steel and in stainless, with prices around $250 and $290, respectively. I have handled only prototypes of the gun, and haven't yet fired one, but the basic design is, from where I sit, excellent.

Charter Arms

This excellent revolver-oriented firm is specializing its Explorer II 22 pistol for the survivalist trade. New metal finishes look like stainless steel and serve to dress up the gun mightily.

Coonan Arms

One of the two new autos in 357 Magnum chambering, the Coonan is only slightly heavier than a standard 45 Auto at 40.4 ounces. The Coonan 357 shares several operational features with the service auto, and many of the parts will actually interchange. The material is stainless steel, and the grips are smooth oil-finished walnut. The first 500 guns were scheduled to begin production in April, 1982, with general availability expected around July or August. The prototype guns I've seen are handsome and well-made pieces. The locking system is the tried-and-true Browning-pattern, with the linked barrel falling before the breech opens. The system has been modified, of course, to handle the higher pressures.

Detonics

Close on the heels of their new

Browning Challenger III offers a bull barrel, is shorter over-all and lighter, but puts more weight up forward for good feel.

Here's a Hi-Power dressed from the factory the way the custom guys have been doing them—"silver chrome" and Pachmayr grips standard.

Browning's Beretta-made BDA is also fitted out with shiny nickel, which is good news if you carry it in a hot damp climate.

The loaded round is a standard 45ACP; the empty is the case for the 451 Detonics which the firm says makes a remarkable hideaway gun.

sightless and thinner Mark VII pistol, Detonics has announced another new model, the 451 Detonics Magnum. The pistol comes in its own aluminum carrying case, containing the gun, 50 rounds of 451DM brass, and a Forster tool to use in converting 30-06 or 308 cases to 451DM. Complete instructions and a cleaning kit are also included. The 451DM case is slightly longer than a standard 45 Auto, and an average velocity of 1240 fps is claimed. After using a regular Mark V for some time, I have a lot of respect for Detonics quality and workmanship, and I'm sure the new 451DM will perform well. No loaded rounds were available at the time this was written, but I assume that a lighter bullet will be used, to get that level of velocity from the short Detonics barrel.

Dornaus & Dixon

If there is to be a Bren Ten, the first 2000 will be sold in a Jeff Cooper Commemorative edition, elegantly cased in wood with the raven motif and Jeff's signature on the lid. The pistol will have a stainless frame, blued slide, and detailing in 22k gold plate. On the burgundy velvet inside the case, along with the gun, will be 12 inert rounds of the new 10mm cartridge, also plated in gold. The price is substantial—$2000. Presumably, when the commemorative run is finished and sold the gun will go into regular production, since 2,000 times $2,000 is $2,000,000. The average shooter can then think about owning one and it should be a fine-looking gun, sort of a cross between the Czech 75 and the SIG P-210, but with special features beyond both. The ballistics of the 10mm cartridge are impressive.

Firearms Import/Export, Inc.

Those of you who have wanted to own and shoot the almost legendary Czech 75, be patient. Your wish is about to be granted . . . almost . F.I.E. is bringing in a close copy of this pistol from Italy, to be called the TCZ-75. Exact specifications and price are not available at the time this is written, but I'm told it will sell in the $350 to $375 area—maybe late in 1982. In the meantime, the first production of the Interdynamic KG-9, the nicely-made semi-auto with a machine-pistol look, practically sold out in record time. By now, it should be available again. My own KG-9 performs flawlessly. I've also been testing the recently introduced Super Titan II in both the 32 and 380 versions, and found these to be quality guns at reasonable prices.

Both guns are all-steel, with stagger-type magazines that hold 11 rounds in 380, 12 in 32 caliber. For more details on the Super Titan and the KG-9, see Testfire, page 238 and page 244.

Heckler & Koch

No startling official word from the folks at H&K this year, but there are some interesting rumors and possibilities. It's no secret that a P7 pistol with an increased-capacity magazine was prepared for the Joint Services Program tests. Whether this version will eventually be offered commercially is a big question mark. Meanwhile, the standard 9mm P7, the P9S in both chamberings, and the VP70Z continue to perform perfectly. I have great respect for things that *work*.

High Standard

Plenty of new revolvers did not distract this firm from its duty to produce something new to replace the Sport King. It's the Sharpshooter, with military style frame borrowed from the best-selling target autoloaders, and done up with electroless nickel and a spare magazine in a canvas satchel. It's survival time again.

Interarms

The fine 9mm Astra A-80 is now widely available, well-liked for all-steel construction and ultra-smooth double action. The 38 Super and 45 Auto versions should be available soon. Another excellent 9mm double action from Spain being imported by Interarms is the Star Model 28, which made its first appearance here as an entry in the U.S. government tests. The Model 28 has an ambidextrous firing-pin-block safety, and the entire firing system is contained in a subframe, easily lifted out for cleaning.

The well-known SIG/Sauer pistols, the P220, P225, and P230 have also been added to the Interarms catalogue, along with the new 15-shot version of the Mauser HSc in 32 and 380. It's now called the Mauser HSc Super, and it's made by Renato Gamba in Italy. There is a new choice of barrel lengths in the 22 Bersa pistol, and a 380 version has been added. My own standard 22 Bersa has seen a lot of use, and is still working perfectly. It's a good quality gun at a reasonable price.

Iver Johnson

Introduced just last year, the neat little Erma-designed double action 25 Auto is now offered in a 22 Long Rifle version, and the internal mechanism has had an addition—the automatic trigger-activated firing pin block of the larger Erma 22 pistol (Excam's RX-22) is being incorporated into the small Iver Johnson versions. I've been trying one of the 25 pistols in recent months, and its performance is excellent, especially with the new Winchester steel-ball load. The new 22 version should have even wider applications than the 25, and practice with it will be more economical.

Magnum Research, Inc.

The Eagle pistol, to be made by IMI in Israel for Magnum Research, Incorporated, has several interesting features, not the least of which is its cartridge, the 357 Magnum. The gun has a rotating six-lug bolt within a conventional-appearing slide, and interchangeable barrels will be offered in 6-, 8-, 10-, and 14-inch lengths. The latter option will be of particular interest to handgun hunters and silhouette shooters. A slide-mounted ambidextrous safety blocks the firing pin, and the Eagle has combat-style configuration in the trigger, trigger guard, and adjustable rear sight. It's a large pistol—10¼ inches in length with the six-inch barrel—but it has good balance in the hand. I examined both the prototype and an early production piece at the 1982 SHOT Show in Atlanta, and I was favorably impressed by its all-machined-steel construction and obvious good quality.

M&N Distributors

Early in its history, the elegant little 25 stainless-steel TP-70 pistol was made in 22 Long Rifle chambering, but there were a few operational problems. When M&N decided to offer a small, double action stainless steel 22, they opted for a very slightly larger 10-shot gun of entirely different design, designated the TP-80. It's only $2/10$ of an inch longer than the TP-70, and at 16 ounces it's four ounces heavier. I've handled the prototype of the TP-80, and it sits well in the hand. First availability is expected around September of 1982. Meanwhile, I've been trying a 25 TP-70 for the first time. It's a pocket pistol with the features of a large-caliber gun, including an external slide latch and a firing-pin-block safety. Now in its third manufacturing try, Mr. Budischowsky's design is still a good one.

North American Manufacturing Corp.

Externally, the new N.A.M. pistol has the appearance of a U.S. service auto with a heavier, sculptured slide and a tangent-type adjustable rear sight. The real difference, though, lies in its two chamberings—45 Winchester Magnum and 9mm Winchester Magnum. With conversion units, the same gun can be used with either cartridge. The action is traditional Browning-pattern falling-barrel, with the locking system suitably strengthened for these two powerful rounds. Regular production pieces are scheduled to be available by around September of 1982. I haven't had an opportunity to examine this one, but the concept is interesting, and it's good to see yet another gun chambered for these two high-performance rounds.

M-S Safari Arms

I've known for several years about the extensive line of accessories offered by M-S Safari Arms, but I hadn't really paid attention to the fact that they also make finished semi-custom guns which feature most of the accessories in their line. The full-sized version is called the MatchMaster, while the "Commander-sized" version is the Enforcer. Both feature the deep finger recesses in the frontstrap and the wide beavertail grip safety extension that have become trademarks of the Safari line, as well as many other exclusive features.

I had seen statements to the effect that the frame configuration and the grip safety extension reduced muzzle whip and felt recoil, and wondered whether this was really true. Well, I've been shooting an Enforcer model in recent weeks, and it's definitely a fact. Other options from M-S Safari include a Model 81 Match gun, with heavy slide and six-inch barrel with top rib, in 45 or 38 Special, and guns designed specifically for Bowling Pin shoots and National Match use, the latter conforming to the NRA rules.

L.W. Seecamp Company

Known for their excellent double action conversions of the large-frame autos, Seecamp has now produced its first complete gun, and it's a little jewel. In 25 ACP, it's all stainless, with a double-action-*only* trigger system. For those who are not familiar with this terminology, this means that the hammer is never cocked by the slide movement, and each pull of the trigger is a full double action stroke. There is no manual safety, and no need for one, as the gun can only be fired intentionally. There are no sights. The magazine holds seven rounds, and the gun is a back-up and personal defense piece *par excellence*. The quality and performance are outstanding, and the price is quite reasonable. Inside, the pistol is a masterpiece of good engineering. I've fired my own Seecamp 25 DA exten-

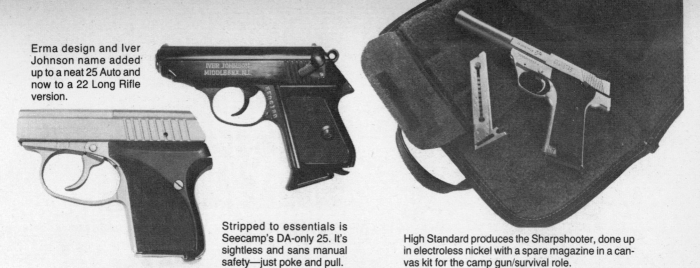

Erma design and Iver Johnson name added up to a neat 25 Auto and now to a 22 Long Rifle version.

Stripped to essentials is Seecamp's DA-only 25. It's sightless and sans manual safety—just poke and pull.

High Standard produces the Sharpshooter, done up in electroless nickel with a spare magazine in a canvas kit for the camp gun/survival role.

sively with the new Winchester steel-ball load—it makes a fine combination.

Steyr

Steyr Daimler Puch of America is importing two new guns of special note. One is their own 9mm GB80 pistol, a large gas-locked gun with a double action trigger and an 18-round magazine. Those who keep close track of autos will note its resemblance to the now-dead Rogak P-18, but don't be misled. This is the original gun on which the P-18 was loosely based, and it's precision-made in Austria as only Steyr could do it. The other pistol is the Helwan, a commercial version of the Egyptian military pistol, a variation of the Beretta Model 951. This gun is available now, while the GB80 is expected in quantity late in 1982.

Stoeger

Last year, at a range in New Jersey, I fired the first production samples of the new Llama Omni, and to say that the impression was favorable would be an understatement. A co-operative effort of designer Gary Wilhelm and engineers at Gabilondo y Compania, the Omni has a long list of interesting and innovative features. These include a ball-bearing hammer spring system, separate trigger bars for single and double action, a ball-joint two-piece firing pin, and a buttressed locking system, among several others. The 9mm Omni has a unique 13-round stagger-type magazine which narrows to single-line feed about 1/3 of its length from the top, and feeding is flawless. The 9mm is scheduled for first availability, in the spring of 1982, with the 45 version to follow soon after. The Omni pistols that I have fired had the smoothest double action trigger pulls I have ever experienced in an auto, right out of the box. This is one case where the hyperbole of the ads is close to fact. It's an amazing gun.

Sturm, Ruger & Company

After a final production run of a stainless commemorative edition, the old Ruger Standard 22 Auto pistol went into the collector's realm. To replace it, there is the new Mark II, with several nice design improvements. Among these are an external bolt latch, which holds the bolt open after the last shot in the new 10-round magazine has been fired. The bolt can now be cycled with the safety in "on safe" position. The rear edges of the receiver are scooped in front of the bolt wings for easier grasping. These remain roughly the same models—short and long-barreled utility guns and long and bull-barreled target pistols.

Wilkinson Arms

In the as-yet-unnamed category of large semi-auto pistols that have an SMG look, Ray Wilkinson offers the Linda in 9mm chambering. The gun is generally similar to the Wilkinson Terry carbine, and the 31-round magazine will interchange, but otherwise it's very different. The receiver is much shorter, and it's domed rather than square-section. The gun weighs just under five pounds, and is 13 inches long, so a two-handled hold is necessary. For those who want to carry it slung in Uzi or Ingram fashion, a sling and swivels are available. The Linda comes with a fully-adjustable Williams aperture sight, but there is also a full-length scope rail on top, and I recently added the special mount and scope to my own Linda pistol, with excellent range results. As with all of Ray's guns, the Linda is a quality piece.

Weapons System, Inc.

The third gun in the unnamed category—the category which includes the Interdynamic KG-9 and the Wilkinson Linda—is the 9mm Viking, produced by Weapons System, Incorporated. In design, the Viking has an Uzi-ish look, with a 36-round magazine which enters through the hand-grip. A carrying sling is standard equipment. The grip safety is unusual, being mounted in the *front* of the hand-grip and pivoted at the lower edge. In handling a sample gun last January, I found that this arrangement is actually less bothersome than the rear-of-grip type. A manual safety is also provided. The gun is 14 inches long, and weighs about 5½ pounds. I haven't fired a Viking yet, but I'm looking forward to trying one. The sample I examined was well-made.

Footnote:

Three years ago in this space, I wrote a little "requiem" that noted the passing from the scene of two guns—the Thomas 45 and the Indian Arms 380 stainless. Well, it seems I spoke too soon. Manufacturing rights for the Thomas have been purchased by a gentleman in California, frame castings are already being produced, and a well-known designer/manufacturer was slated to begin production of the gun in mid-1982. Similarly, the rights to the Indian Arms 380 are now owned by Michigan Armament, Incorporated, and the gun will be made as their Model 3800 "Guardian." ●

Added Note

Just before this edition went to press, I received word that the excellent French 9mm MAB PA-15 is being imported by Howco Distributing. A relatively small quantity came into the U.S. in the early 70's, and have brought increasingly higher prices. Those who are unfamiliar with the gun should know it is a large, nicely-made single action auto, with a turning-barrel locking system and a 15-round magazine capacity. Late in 1982, Howco says, a 45 ACP 9- or 10-round version will be available.

GENERAL JOHN JACOB
and his
ECCENTRIC RIFLE

by **GARRY JAMES**

This gallant brigadier apparently never let a fact change his mind, once he was sure.

A soldier of Jacob's Rifles as envisaged by their founder. It is highly unlikely that the unit was issued the double rifles that were ordered for it from England.

Brigadier-General John Jacob, commandant of the Scinde Ir-regular Horse and inventor of the double-barreled rifle that bears his name.

ON THE OUTSKIRTS of Jacoboabad on India's Northwest Frontier in the 1850's Brigadier-General John Jacob, Commandant of the Scinde Irregular Horse, erected an elaborate range at which he tested a new rifle and explosive bullet. Barrels of gunpowder were set at distances in excess of 1000 yards and the indefatiguable Jacob went through the process of blowing them up with his percussion "shells," which, with characteristic overstatement, he termed "the most formidable missile ever invented by man."

Jacob, known chiefly today to historians as the man who tamed and kept order in the turbulent Scinde region in the years just before the Indi-

Upon graduation two years later, he was granted a second lieutenancy in the Bombay Artillery. During the First Afghan War (1841) he was attached to the Scinde Irregular Horse, where his riding ability, natural leadership qualities and easy manner with the native troopers under his command drew the attention of authority. Thus, in late 1841, Jacob was recommended to command the regiment, a post he accepted with alacrity.

The Scinde Irregular Horse was what was termed a *sillidar* regiment. This meant that the native Indian cavalrymen or *sowars* received a greater rate of pay than did their counterparts in regular units and were required to supply and maintain their own equipment and horses. The

his renown spread throughout Northern India. He greatly improved the living conditions of the people in the area in which he was stationed and in recognition of this the town of Khangur was officially renamed Jacobabad in 1851.

Even while on campaign, Jacob worked on ways to improve the military service rifles of the period. From 1837 until 1851, rifle units of the East India Company and those of Crown troops, were issued the Brunswick rifle, one of the most controversial arms of the period. The Brunswick system involved a bore cut with two deep spiraled grooves into which a mechanically fitting .704 caliber "belted" ball was loaded. The girdle on the bullet corresponded to the width and depth

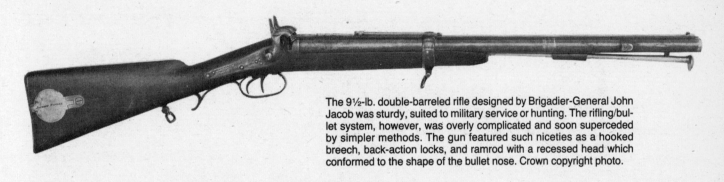

The 9½-lb. double-barreled rifle designed by Brigadier-General John Jacob was sturdy, suited to military service or hunting. The rifling/bullet system, however, was overly complicated and soon superceded by simpler methods. The gun featured such niceties as a hooked breech, back-action locks, and ramrod with a recessed head which conformed to the shape of the bullet nose. Crown copyright photo.

an Mutiny of 1857, was typical of that breed of adventurer who expanded Britain's frontiers during the 19th century. Called by Major-General Sir Charles Napier "the Siedlitz of the Scinde Army," Jacob could be at once charming, opinionated, bellicose, and boorish. A stammer which made him appear somewhat shy in no way affected his self-image. He was one of India's most able administrators and military leaders.

He was considered absolutely fearless on the battlefield, and he was addicted to romantic poetry. Firearms had interested him from an early age, and though his practical knowledge of ballistics was somewhat indifferent, his skill as a mechanic and outright enthusiasm for the subject, coupled with a substantial income, allowed him to carry on the experiments which are the subject of this article.

Jacob was born in 1812, the son of a Wiltshire vicar. At 14, he enrolled in the Honourable East India Company's training school at Addiscombe where he noted that the entrance examination involved nothing more than to perform "an easy sum in vulgar and decimal fractions and to construe a few lines of Caesar."

East India Company provided only ammunition and firearms. Everything else, including rations, fodder and medical care, was the responsibility of the trooper.

Upon enlistment the soldier normally paid an *assami* for a horse and uniform. When he left the regiment this was returned to him. His pay was subject to levies which allowed him to build up an account to replace his mount and equipment when necessary. Should a horse be killed on active duty, it was replaced using money from a regimental fund, subscribed to by the men.

Naturally, the lack of encumbrance inherent in such a system, allowed the unit to travel lightly and swiftly, attributes which suited Jacob's mercuric temperament ideally. He felt that military units should "be able to move far and fast at a moment's notice, and to be as self-contained and independant of the 'regular' transport as possible."

His men figured heavily in the conquest of the Scinde in 1843, and throughout the middle years of the 19th century they were constantly involved in skirmishes with border tribesmen. Jacob's star ascended and

of the grooves, and when the gun was fired, a spin was imparted to the projectile. Brunswicks could keep most of their shots in a two-foot circle at 200 yards.

The arm was damned by most of those who had to use it, one officer commenting, "The loading of this rifle is so difficult that it is wonderful how rifle regiments can have continued to use it so long. The force required to ram down the ball being so great as to render a man's hand much too unsteady for accurate shooting."

Jacob had seen the gun in use in India and was also unimpressed. While he felt no particular animosity toward the concept of a mechanically fitting projectile, he correctly surmised that the irregularity of the Brunswick bullet was not conducive to superior accuracy.

He proceeded to design a barrel which increased the Brunswick's two grooves to four. This allowed him to fire a symmetrical ball, cast with a pair of crossing belts.

The rifle was extensively tested by Jacob, according to Lieutenant Hans Busk, first lieutenant of the Victoria Rifles, in his book *"The Rifle and How to Use It."* Jacob's range was a level

The Brunswick rifle was one of the most hated arms ever issued to the British Army. Jacob's four-studded conical projectile was an attempt to improve on the Brunswick's belted ball. Crown copyright photo.

The Pattern 1853 Enfield rifle-musket was acknowledged to be the finest military muzzleloader of the period. Although the Minié system employed in this arm proved very successful, General Jacob rejected it in favor of his own design.

Like the Jacob rifle, the Whitworth employed a mechanically fitting bullet. The Whitworth, however, was found to be more accurate at greater distances and enjoyed great favor with target shooters.

plain "studded with numerous targets and stretching far away into the sandy desert in front of the lines of the Scinde Irregular Horse, near Jacobabad."

Busk further described the "practice ground" as having massive "targets, thirteen in number, costing many hundred pounds in their construction . . .of sun dried brick almost as hard as stone, and placed at various distances from the shooting shed, so as to afford ranges varying from 100 up to 2000 yards. . . .the surface of each target is whitewashed, and marked with circular bull's eyes, increasing one inch in radius and raised one foot from the ground for each hundred yards of increased range."

Experiments were so encouraging that Jacob offered his improved rifle

to the East India Company, who flatly rejected him stating "the two-grooved rifle, which is thought good enough for the Royal Army, is good enough for the soldier in India."

Undaunted, Jacob continued his experiments. He next tried a conical bullet with a pointed nose, round base, and four studs to engage the rifling. Accuracy was markedly superior to that of his belted ball and he claimed he was able to hit targets regularly out to 000 yards. Jacob also noticed that the heavy conical bullet required less powder to do the same job the round ball did.

About this time (1851) the French-designed Minié rifle, using hollow-based bullets which were expanded into the riflings by the main charge, was adopted by the British govern-

ment. Early Minié bullets employed iron cups in their bases to aid in the expansion, although because very often these cups were blown through the bullet, they were eventually replaced by boxwood plugs.

As events later proved, the Minié rifle was one of the soundest, most accurate muzzle-loading rifles ever issued to the common soldier, but Jacob, after what he claimed to be exhaustive testing, rejected it outright, and proceeded to design his own, a severely pointed projectile *sans* expansive cup (in this he was in advance of the authorities) and with the addition of four studs to engage the rifling in the manner of his previous design.

The results were impressive, Jacob said, with good accuracy attained out

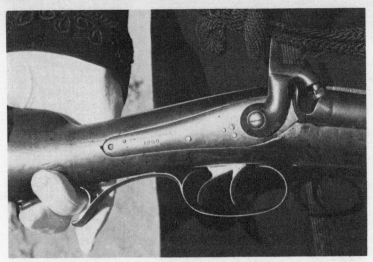

The back-action lock on our test Jacob rifle was stamped with the maker's name, Swinburn & Son, and the date 1860. Specimens of this gun have been found dated from 1859-1861.

The butt boxes of Jacob's rifles were engraved with the name of the unit for which they were intended.

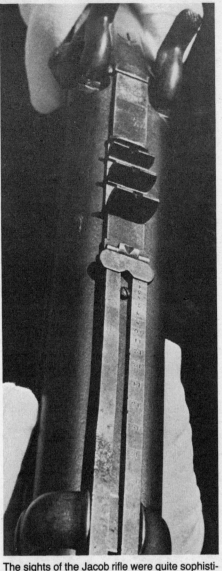

The sights of the Jacob rifle were quite sophisticated for a military arm, consisting of express sights to 300 yards and a 5-inch high "ladder" graduated to 2000 yards.

to 1200 yards. The bullet was further "refined" by elongating it to 2½ diameters and eliminating the hollow base. Jacob was still locked into the concept of a mechanically fitting projectile. As the projectile was developed, so was the rifle. Specimens reflecting Jacob's changing concepts were ordered from England from the best makers, which included Witton and Daw, John Manton, and Swinburn & Son.

During his trials, Jacob became infatuated as well with the concept of the double rifle and turned his attentions toward its further development, and to the perfection of the explosive bullet.

The "rifle shell" was not original to Jacob, having been thought up by Captain Norton of the 34th Regiment

of Foot. Both Norton and Jacob recognized the value of a bullet which could be used to explode enemy artillery caissons at great distances, although as noted by Busk, "a solid acorn-shaped shot fired from a common rifle will expand for half its length, but will not carry its point foremost during the whole of its flight, unless the centre of gravity be in the fore part of the shot." It was imperative that the point of the bullet, containing the explosive compound, strike the target first.

To this end Jacob designed his "perfected" bullet with the dimensions noted earlier. It was available in two forms, solid and "shell." The General also conceived his own explosive devices which consisted of pointed percussion tubes, "made of copper, and

The bayonet for the Jacob rifle was a basket-hilted sword with 30-inch blade. A figure "8" ring in the hilt slipped over the gun's twin barrels. Crown copyright photo.

which fit into the fore part of the shell. Each tube, about the thickness of a quill, and three quarters of an inch long, is closed at one end, terminating in a cone that contains the fulminating powder; the rest of the tube is filled with fine gunpowder, stopped with a cork or plug varnished over."

All the while the "ideal" rifle was being perfected. Finally, Jacob felt confident enough in its design to describe it:

"Double—32-gauge—4-grooved—DEEP grooves, of breadth equal to that of LANDS, to take four-fifths of a turn in the length of the barrel—barrels the best that can be made, twenty-four (24) inches long, weight of pair of barrels alone about six pounds, NOT LESS: the ends of the lands to be rounded off at the muzzle—patent breech—no side vents—first sight EXACTLY PARALLEL to the bore—the muzzle sight being raised if necessary for this purpose—four points to be inserted inside the barrel near the breech for tearing open a blank cartridge when rammed down whole—full stock, well bent, of the best heart walnut wood, attached to barrel by bands—best plain case-hardened mountings—folding sights attached to the barrel twenty inches from the muzzle, five (5) inches long, secured by spring below, protected by projecting wings when lying flat on the barrel, the slide of this sight to be well secured by springs at its back, so as never to work loose—the slide to come down quite low on the sight, the top of the sight, etc., to be strongly made and nicely finished, marked and engraved for distances, say up to 1500 or 2000 yards—leaf sights folding flush for 100 and 200 yards—muzzle sight to be fine. Best locks, strong mainsprings, and heavy cocks. Half cock half an inch above nipple (not less). Triggers easy to pull, plenty of play in the cocks, external vents in nipples to be small—six spare nipples of each size to fit Eley's No. 13 and No. 26 caps—one mould for balls and two for Jacob's shells, flat ended, two-and-a-half (2½) diameters long—moulds to be made of good steel, to open in the middle of one pair of bands—the balls and their bands of size and depth to fit the barrel nicely but easily with a patch, exact diameter of the bore in thousandths of an inch .529—of shell or ball .524—plugs of shell moulds to fit Jacob's shell tubes ('long 16-gauge,' as made by Eley) —plugs or cores of shell moulds to have wooden cross-handles."

Apparently experimental versions of this rifle were manufactured for Jacob by George H. Daw, who later advertised sporting models of the piece. A writer of the period described shooting a gun made on this pattern:

"The recoil is by no means pleasant. The gauge is 32. This rifle does not seem to have any advantages at sporting ranges; but for military purposes it has been strongly recommended, especially in reference to the explosive shells which are used with it. In 1856, a report on General Jacob's rifle was

Due to the weight of the gun (9½ lbs.) recoil was not prohibitive. Accuracy, while adequate for a military rifle, was not phenomenal, and regulation proved to be something of a problem.

made to the Indian Government, which states that at ranges from 300 to 1200 yards the flight of the shell (used with this rifle) was always point foremost, and the elevation at the extreme range inconsiderable. The shell which struck the butt invariably burst with full effect; and practice was made by the many officers who attended, at distances which could not have been attained with any other missile. The shells alluded to in the report require a short stout barrel, and cannot be used with a long thin one, like the Enfield. For killing large animals, like the elephant or rhinoceros, they are particularly qualified; and I should strongly recommend elephant hunters to examine the merits of this rifle, as made by Mr. Daw, of Threadneedle-Street London."

Lieutenant Busk, a strong supporter of the Jacob system did have some reservations about the efficiency of a double rifle, however. He recognized the expense and difficulty of manufacture as well as the problems of regulation. Loads had to be carefully measured and bullets cast perfectly to insure that both barrels would strike in the same place at a given distance.

"General Jacob states that 'the double rifle is found to perform better than the single'," wrote Busk. "This I confess myself at a loss to understand. Speaking from personal experience, the result of many thousands of experiments, I certainly had arrived at an opposite conclusion. Nor was I surprised at the circumstance because every pair of rifle barrels, in order that one sight should serve for both, must converge; consequently at some point, however remote, the lines of trajectory of the two barrels must inevitably cross."

By this time Sir Joseph Whitworth's hexagonally-bored rifle, using "smallbore" (.451) bullets of great sectional density, was receiving considerable acclaim as a long-range target gun. Granted, Jacob has never intended his short-barrelled double to have pinpoint accuracy, however now even his claims of superior range were being challenged.

Although Jacob was not directly involved in the Indian Mutiny—his command belonged to the Bombay Army and it was primarily the Bengal Army that revolted—there are oblique references to one of his single barrel rifles and explosive shells being used by an officer to blow up an Indian artillery caisson at a distance of over 1000 yards.

Despite being an outspoken critic of the rebellion, Jacob was realistic enough to be aware that, "to attempt to keep the natives of India or the soldier of the Indian Army in darkness and ignorance, in the hope of increasing power over them will be as contemptible and base as it would be unwise and useless."

Perhaps bearing this in mind, he decided in 1858, while the Mutiny was still raging, to raise a battalion of native riflemen to be armed with his double gun. The men were also to be issued an unusual sword bayonet which Jacob described as "Best double-edged straight sword with blade thirty inches long, to attach to rifle by

The Jacob projectile, as pictured in Lieutenant Hans Busk's treatise, *The Rifle and How to Use it*. Note the cavity in the nose of the shell for the explosive percussion tube.

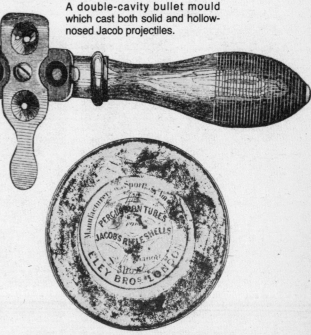

A double-cavity bullet mould which cast both solid and hollow-nosed Jacob projectiles.

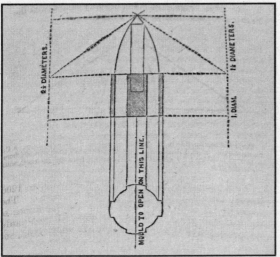

The Jacob bullet (second from left) and its competitors (left-right) 577 Enfield "Pritchett" Minié bullet, hexagonal Whitworth "bolt," and Brunswick belted ball.

A tin of percussion tubes produced by Eley for Jacob's explosive shells. The projectile found favor with hunters for use against big game.

To fire the Jacob rifle at extreme ranges, the butt must be held against the shooter's chest for proper sighting.

As per original specifications, the test Jacob rifle was charged with 2½ drams (68 grains) of FFg black powder.

Test bullets cast from an original mould were lubricated with a beeswax/tallow mixture. While they slid easily down the bore, there was no room for a patch.

ring around the muzzle of both barrels, as well as by spring socket, with scabbard and belt complete (scabbard of strong wood covered with leather, case-hardened mountings riveted on. . . . The sword to be made with good steel, or case-hardened iron. Half basket hilt."

Jacob's Rifles, as the unit was to be called, was to be organized on the sillidar system, like the Scinde Irregular Horse, and would number about 1000 officers and men, over 900 of whom would have to be armed with very expensive and complicated rifles.

It is at this point that the history of the Jacob rifle becomes hazy. Jacob died of "exhaustion" on December 5, 1858, but apparently not before he was able to place an order with Swinburn & Son for the requisite number of guns. These arms, along with their swords, were produced, for a number of examples of both still exist. They follow Jacob's descriptions very closely, with the exception that it was apparently felt prudent to dispense with the cartridge-breaking studs in the chambers. Each gun had the date of manufacture (varying from 1859-1861) engraved on the back action locks and the legend "Jacob's Rifles" emblazoned on the cover of a round iron butt box on the right side of the stock.

The unit, redesignated the 3rd Baluchi Rifles in 1861, and later the 30th Bombay Native Infantry, had a long and distinguished career; however, there is no indication they were ever issued their originator's weapons. The most probable reason for this was that following the Mutiny, the Peel Commission decreed that native soldiers were not to be armed with weapons as up-to-date as those carried by Crown troops. To this end there was even a pattern of smoothbore longarm authorized for sepoys which had the external appearance of the P-53 Enfield Rifle-Musket.

The General's years of insistence upon the marked superiority of his weapon apparently had been taken to heart in some quarters, and without his strong advocacy the authorities felt it wise not to equip native troops with such a "sophisticated" weapon. The men were more than likely given old Brunswicks until the adoption of the Snider breechloader in 1866, after which they received muzzle-loading Enfield rifles.

It is curious however that, although the decision to rearm the Indians with inferior weapons was made quite early, Swinburn & Son continued to produce Jacob rifles until at least 1861.

Perhaps official vacillation kept the makers hoping the guns would, in fact, finally be accepted.

Concurrently with the production of the rifle, Swinburn was also manufacturing a double-barreled smoothbore carbine (with a marked resemblance to the rifle) and a double-barreled pistol, both for the Scinde Irregular Horse. These arms *were* issued and continued to be carried by the *sowars* for a good number of years.

Swinburn must eventually have accepted the inevitable and overstocked with a number of costly double rifles, offered them to sportsmen or militia units. In any event, the number of Jacob rifles that have turned up in England indicate that few ever left the island, except perhaps for hunting expeditions. In fact, Daw had already had some success marketing single and double-barreled Jacob rifles for such purposes. At any rate, his explosive shell experienced considerable vogue amongst hunters for use against large, thick-skinned game.

Though currently Jacob rifles are scarce and desirable collectors' pieces, we managed to locate a specimen in good shooting condition, along with a number of bullets cast from an original mould. Our rifle followed Jacob's description, with the exception that there were no cartridge tearers in the breech, and the nipples were of the standard Enfield variety to accept large musket caps.

The gun was carefully cleaned and the tubes found to be about perfect. A preliminary fitting of bullet to bore showed very little windage, certainly not enough to accept the "patch" noted in *The Rifle and How to Use it*. The chosen charge was, as per Hans Busk, 2½ drams (68 grains) of FFg black powder. Bullets were lubricated with a period mixture of 40 percent tallow and 60 percent beeswax. The rifle was carefully loaded, insuring that the bullets, while firmly seated atop the powder, were not deformed in any way.

Our first pair of shots, fired at 100 yards, were disappointing, with hits six inches either side of the target. The gun was then loaded and fired again with even more distressing results, as the bullets expanded their error by about two feet each. A fifth round produced our first hit on the target, but alas, it had keyholed.

The bores were now scrupulously cleaned and gun fired again with the first pair of shots duplicating the premier experience. Again the gun was scrubbed and fired with similar results.

Our sights were now raised to 200 yards and the rifle aimed at a 2½-foot diameter gong at that distance, both rounds elicited a satisfying reverberation as the 600-grain bullets unerringly found their mark. This feat was repeated a number of times, although it was necessary to brush and swab the tubes after each discharge. About 75% of the shots struck the target, with the right barrel being the most accurate. The vent on the right barrel's nipple was quite eroded, indicating that it had been used more frequently than the left.

Long range firing (out to 500 yards) produced groups similar to those achieved by Busk in the late 1850s. Thirty rounds were loosed at a 6-foot by 3-foot white cardbooard target. All but six projectiles hit, with the majority of them grouping in about 3-feet on the lower left of the rectangle. A half dozen bullets, however, had the temerity to dot the target at distances approaching five feet from one another. It was necessary to set the sight slide at 700 yards to strike the board.

Unfortunately no appropriate ranges were available to try the gun at anything over 500 yards. Based upon our experience, however, 2000-yard shots would be extremely optimistic. In fact, when the arm is to be fired at this extreme distance, it is necessary to rest the butt on one's chest in order that it be properly sighted.

Although a number of charges were tried during several separate outings, 2½ drams was found to produce the most consistent results. Because of the weight of the arm, recoil was not prohibitive.

The Jacob rifle and its creator remain enigmas. While the gun performed well enough under carefully controlled conditions, it was in no way markedly superior to the standard P–53/58 Enfield service rifle. Granted, a rifle that could find its target at the long distances encountered in India's Northwest Frontier, was an attractive proposition. However, the time-consuming care that had to be taken to insure the Jacob rifle's proper functioning far offset any advantages it might have had.

As has been noted by a number of his critics, General John Jacob's tenacity on the battlefield was only matched by his narrow-mindedness in other matters. He was the sort of person who, though an innovator, could become enamored with his product to the exclusion of all else. A considerable private fortune was spent to promote the Jacob rifle to no avail. Time and technology simply overtook the concept. ●

The author wishes to thank Dave Cumberland, The Old West Gun Room; John Fabb, A.R. Fabb Bros., Ltd; and Val Forgett, Navy Arms Co., for their assistance in the preparation of this article.

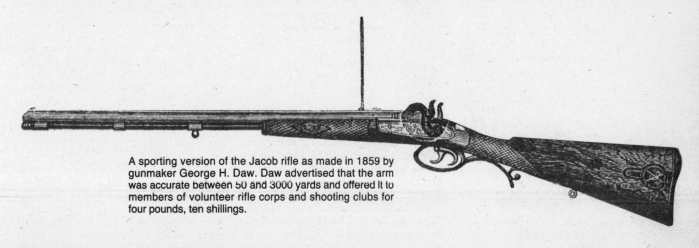

A sporting version of the Jacob rifle as made in 1859 by gunmaker George H. Daw. Daw advertised that the arm was accurate between 50 and 3000 yards and offered it to members of volunteer rifle corps and shooting clubs for four pounds, ten shillings.

LONG GUNS

by LAYNE SIMPSON

Probably THE biggest long gun question has been, "What's with Winchester, now that a company called U.S. Repeating Arms has entered the picture?"

Speculation has run amuck, with a new rumor born about every other day. In a nutshell, USRAC reports it is a privately held company with approximately 85 percent of its stock owned by former employees of Olin and Winchester, several of whom had been with these firms for two and three decades.

USRAC now owns the New Haven manufacturing facility formerly owned by Olin, as well as the right to produce and sell Winchester firearms that had been manufactured in the United States. According to Charles Rhodes of USRAC their rights to the Winchester name as related to firearms are, with a couple of exceptions, exclusive and perpetual.

Apart from all that, I suppose it's fair to say that as compared to some years that I remember, all is relatively quiet on the 1982 gun making front. We've suffered a few casualties, one sure to be mourned by single shot rifle buffs, two others bid a tearful farewell by woods hunters.

Unfortunately, the trend in prices continues upward at an alarming pace. A gloomy situation, no doubt, but you might try prorating the cost by the number of years service in a gun. For example, a Model 70 that I bought in 1960 is now down to a $6.19 per year investment. If you buy a new Model 70 today and use it for twenty years, it will average out at just over $20 per year.

Limited edition rifles and shotguns are pouring out of several factories and interchangeable choke tube systems are now the thing to offer. One shotgun and a pocketful of chokes is definitely a good idea—one that is here to stay, I might add. Riot guns with fancy, modern names are hot numbers, no doubt spooked out of the bushes by the so-called assault rifle and survival gun craze. For grownups we now have a fantastic 22 rim-

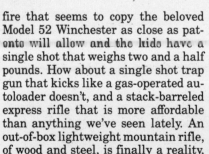

The remarkable little Chipmunk, 30 inches long and 2½ lbs. over-all, makes grown men chuckle. Kids may like it, also.

fire that seems to copy the beloved Model 52 Winchester as close as patents will allow and the kids have a single shot that weighs two and a half pounds. How about a single shot trap gun that kicks like a gas-operated autoloader doesn't, and a stack-barreled express rifle that is more affordable than anything we've seen lately. An out-of-box lightweight mountain rifle, of wood and steel, is finally a reality, as are bolt-on fiberglass stocks that the budget-minded rifleman can install with nothing more complex than a screwdriver.

Stainless steel invades the muzzleloader and shotgun market and also makes the old M-1 carbine even more indestructible. No, one of our favorite bolt action rifle variations is not being discontinued as rumor has it, and yes, the other rumor is true—there is a short-barreled rifle with Mannlicher-type stock. There is a new look to one of the world's most popular rifles, one that in less than twenty years has undergone more facelifts than a former Hollywood starlet.

As rifle chamberings go, the sweet little 22 Hornet has found a new home, the prettiest one yet, and back from the grave is a necked-down 30 carbine wildcat called the 224 Spitfire. The famed 22-250 is now available in a lever-action rifle, and Ned Roberts, I hope you can see what keeps happening with your 257 cartridge.

Alpha Arms

First written up in detail by Larry Sterett in Gun Digest 35, Homer Koon's much awaited Alpha I rifle is now in full production. The stock has been slightly modified (an improvement), making this one the finest out-of-box mountain rifles available—at a price that I still can't believe. Quality

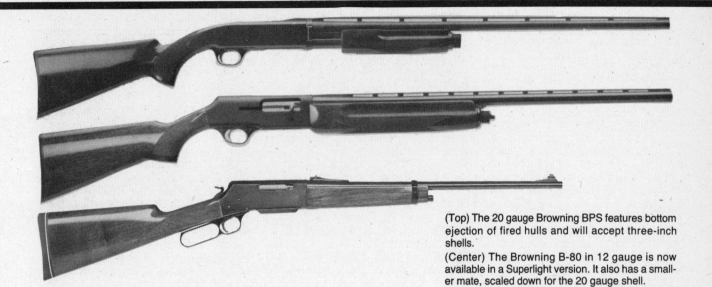

(Top) The 20 gauge Browning BPS features bottom ejection of fired hulls and will accept three-inch shells.

(Center) The Browning B-80 in 12 gauge is now available in a Superlight version. It also has a smaller mate, scaled down for the 20 gauge shell.

(Bottom) The Browning BLR now sports a semiflush magazine box, longer wrist and new chambering, the 22-250 Remington. It is also available in 243, 308 and 358 Winchester.

and workmanship on the two specimens that I examined are up to snuff and I really want to put one through its paces. Chamberings will eventually include most of the short cartridges—7mm-08 Remington, 243 Winchester, 308 Winchester, etc.

Brown Precision

Sure to prove popular with the more budget-minded is Chet Brown's completely finished replacement stock for the Model 700 Remington. Constructed of fiberglass, this stock requires no fitting and reduces gun weight by about a pound, not to mention its inherent stability and ruggedness. To come later are replacement stocks for Model 70s, Model '98 Mausers, Sakos and other popular actions. All you have to do with this one is drop a barreled action into it and you're ready to scamper amongst the craggy peaks where sheep and goat like to hang out.

Browning

No doubt about it, Browning can honestly boast of the fattest press kit handed out to gun writers in 1982. Counting bows, knives, hunting clothing, fishing rods and reels, gun cases, boots, handguns, and of course long guns, the news releases number a whopping eighty-two. More important to this opus is that nine pertain to long guns.

They revamped their BLR and its almost-flush, four-round magazine box makes it a much better carrying rifle than the old BLR. A shortened comb serves to lengthen the wrist, more in keeping with the saddle gun look. Its chamberings are: 243, 308 and 358, with the 22-250 added for 1982.

Browning now calls the BBR the Lightning Bolt. Its stock is lighter, slimmer, trimmer, and the pistol grip angle has been reduced which looks and feels better. Barrel lengths are 24-inch in 25-06, 7mm Remington Magnum and 300 Winchester Magnum, 22-inch in 270 and 30-06 calibers.

Commemorative guns are hot this year and Browning has a production run of 600 BARs they call the Deer Issue Collectors Edition. Mule deer scamper about the receiver's left side while whitetails romp and play on the right. Each rifle is signed by its engraver, and close-up will flat knock your eyeballs out.

The B-92 lever-action carbine is a popular woods rifle in my neck of the woods in 44 Magnum. Now it has a smaller-bored companion in 357 Magnum. And a straight-grip stock and rounded forend tip identify Browning's revisions to the BAR-22 autoloader, as does a urethane buffer to cushion the bolt during cycling. Otherwise, the BAR-22 is the same.

Considerable activity in the smoothbore line goes out in Utah: The sleek 12-gauge B-80 autoloader now comes in a Superlight version with six barrel options; 26-inch improved cylinder or Skeet; 28-inch full or modified and 30-inch full. A Buck Special tube with adjustable sights is also offered.

The B-80 in 20 gauge is not a 12 gauge frame modified to accept 20-gauge barrels—it is scaled down to proportions compatible to the smaller shell. The Browning Pump Shotgun (BPS) hasn't been overlooked by R&D either and it, too, is now available in 20-bore. This is one slick bird gun and my handloads like the bottom ejection.

A straight grip stock, schnabel forearm and 26-inch barrels puts the Superlight Citori in a nutshell. Available in 12 and 20 gauges at rated weights of 6 pounds, nine ounces and 5 pounds, twelve ounces, respectively, I like this one.

Last year there was the American Mallard commemorative; this year it's Browning's Pintail Edition. It is limited to 500 Superposed guns, each signed by its engraver. Engraving and gold inlay cover the trigger and receiver, surrounding a scene depicting gold pintails in flight, all in a velvet-lined walnut case.

In case you haven't noticed, the B-78 single shot rifle is now defunct. In their inventory, Browning shows a few round-barrel models in 22-250 and 25-06 and when these are gone the B-78 will be history. I'm glad I have two of these fine rifles.

Chipmunk Manufacturing Co.

Chipmunks are cute little critters, no doubt about it. I recently handled a couple that, unlike most of their kind, don't store away nuts for winter, dig holes in the ground or sing at Christmas. They do eat 22 rimfire cartridges—one at a time. Built for kids, I'll bet most of this chipmunk's time will be spent with dad, though I'm not at all sure what he'll do with it, except maybe take it out of the case when in need of a chuckle or two.

It's 30 inches long, which includes just over 16 inches of barrel. Its stock pulls 11½ inches and it weighs two and a half pounds. A rebounding firing pin combined with manual cocking serves as the Chipmunk's safety. A sillier little single shot, bolt action rifle you'll never see and no grown man

stock with a full-length accessory rail.

H&R now offers what they call the ultimate slug gun. It's a 10-ga. Model 176 single barrel with open sights, set up for Federal's new 10-ga. slug. The barrel measures 28 inches while its forend and padded buttstock offer sling swivels. A lot of punch at an economy price is the aim.

A metal finish called Hard-Guard is described by H&R as a nickel process with matted surface. The Model 099 Deluxe in 12, 16, 20 and 410 has it, as does the Model 258 Handy Gun II. The Model 258 is a combination gun in 20 gauge with 22-inch rifle barrels available in 22 Hornet, 30-30 WCF, 357 Magnum and 44 Magnum.

And last but by no means least, fans of the pleasingly classic Model 340 bolt action will be happy to hear that more chamberings are now available—243 Winchester, 308 Winchester, 270 Winchester and 7x57 Mauser. Counting the 30-06 and 7mm Remington Magnum, that adds up to six possibilities.

Want an entire shotgun battery that handles the 10-gauge shell? Then take a look at what Ithaca calls their gooseturkeyduckdeer gun. It's a Mag-10 with 32-inch barrel for geese; 26-inch or 28-inch for turkey or ducks over decoys and a 22-inch Deerslayer barrel for Federal's new slug load. Two metal finishes are available on this big boomer, high gloss blue and vapor-blasted matte. The latter comes with dull, oil-finished wood.

Yep, Ithaca has commemoratives too—200 Model 37s and a like number of Model 51s and Mag-10s. Known as the Presentation Series, they are available individually or in three-gun sets, replete with matching serial numbers and hard, leather-lined case. For those who listen to a lower-priced drummer, Ithaca offers the 2500 Series, with etched receiver.

Called the Slimgrip Shortstock option, Ithaca now offers their Model 37 pump gun with 12½-inch or 13-inch pulls. Both have a smaller grip circumference for smaller than average

H&R's 5200 is an unabashed attack on the market identified by the Model 52 Winchester Sporter made possible by the fact that used original Model 52s now sell for as high as $1,500.

would dare buy one for himself. I just bought two for the kids.

Harrington & Richardson

Those who yearn for the looks, feel and quality of the beloved Winchester Model 52 sporter, yet can't see their way clear to spend $1500 for a used 22 rimfire, should take a look at H&R's latest pride and joy, the 5200 Sporter. Fact is, you can buy three or four of these for the going price of a good Model 52. The 5200 is a slick little 6½ pound rifle, from its twin extractors and classic stock to its shapely 24-inch barrel. Sights are a Lyman 66 on the receiver with a hooded ramp out front. It's drilled and tapped for scope mounts too. Also available is a match version, called the 5200 Match. It has a heavy 28-inch barrel, adjustable match-grade trigger and target

Ithaca Gun

I'm a quail hunter from way back and spend a shameful number of hours digging singles out of thick places. Such an activity calls for a light 20 gauge that jumps to shoulder, pointing exactly where those little feathered bombs are about to be. Ithaca now has what appears to be just the proper recipe. Called the Model 37 English Ultra, it's a spin-off from their Ultrafeatherlight. How about cut checkering, straight grip stock and a weight of 4¾ pounds? Ithaca bills it as America's lightest 20 gauge and I'm not about to dispute them. Absent is a buttplate. Instead, horizontal grooves provide purchase between butt and shoulder. I'll soon find out how such an arrangement holds up under the rigors of briar-busting.

hands, such as those operated by most youngsters.

Iver Johnson

My very first smoothbore was a single barrel hammer gun with an owl's head molded into its buttplate. Iver Johnson no longer makes scatterguns or revolvers, but in additon to the X300 and PP22 autoloading handguns, they do turn out M-1 carbines at a steady pace. According to I.J. literature, theirs is the only such arm being built to original government designs. Several models are available including the standard; a 224 Spitfire and the "paratrooper" configuration with collapsing, wire stock. I expect their stainless steel version to become quite popular with boat owners. I.J. also offers bayonets, flash hiders, muzzle breaks, clips and oil-finished walnut stocks, all compatible with the thousands of DCM carbines still kicking around.

Kimber

Just as Kimber said, their slick little Model 82 Classic is now available in one of my favorite cartridges—the 22 Hornet. Other than a longer ejection port centerfire firing pin, and modified magazine (both to handle the longer cartridge), this one is identical to its rimfire mate. It will be rifled with a 14-inch twist. It's a real sweetie pie and you can safely bet lunch money that when I get my hands on one in mid-'82 it will go in the keeper rack.

There will be just 500 of Kimber's Limited Edition Supergrade Model 82. Called the "S" Series, it's one of the most attractive bolt action 22 rimfires ever turned out by U.S. manufacturers. It has a classic stock with European cheekpiece; Niedner-type checkered steel buttplate; ebony forearm tip and express rear sight. Also available upon special request is a plain barrel, sans open sights. My gosh, it's a pretty thing.

Kimber has also jumped into the growing smallbore metallic silhouette market with their Model 82 MS. The stock form is designed in compliance with NRA rules; and with free-floated barrel, adjustable target-type trigger, and a few other goodies, it should be murder on those tiny steel animals.

The one I examined had a Leupold 6.5x20 scope attached. Speaking of scopes, Kimber now has its own line of compacts, built by Leupold.

Mossberg

Now with its interchangeable choke tube system, the best-selling Model 500 pump gun is chock-full of versatility. It's called Accu-Choke and is standard on the field gun as well as the Hi-Rib trap version. Also standard are a tang safety, cut checkering and free-floating vent rib. For those who prefer it and don't mind its presence, the old reliable C-Lect-Choke is still available. I count eighteen barrel options in 12 gauge alone, not to mention the 20 and 410 bores. This includes 18½-inch and 24-inch slug barrels, replete with ramped front and adjustable rear sights.

Mossberg also offers "security" shotguns in 12, 20 and 410, with three metal finishes—blue, nickel and parkerized. The six-shot version has an 18½-inch barrel, the eight-shooter is 1½-inch longer.

Still no definitive word on the RM-7 bolt action rifle that peek-a-booed a couple of years back. This one might have withered on the vine.

Remington

Remington's quick-handling pump and autoloading carbines are dead. Darn it.

Now for the good stuff.

I'll start by squelching a nasty rumor. The Model 700 Classic that we all love, cherish and asked for will not be discontinued says Dick Dietz. Remington's jaw is still agape over how fast their short run of 7x57mm Classics was scooped up, with demand far exceeding production. They promise that such won't happen with the 257 Roberts version, scheduled for delivery in mid-1982.

Those old enough to do so and still able to read this fine print might recall that Ned Roberts and F.J. Sage developed the father of this cartridge back in the late 1920s. In 1934 Remington modified its case a bit and introduced the 257 commercially in their Model 30. Later, during the '50s and '60s this fine cartridge appeared in their Model 722 and 725 rifles but short magazines choked a good hundred feet per second out of the poor thing. This time around the old/new chambering will be available in a long Model 700 action which is a grand idea if there's a long magazine and chamber throat as well.

The 222 Remington is back in the Model 788, and with a 24-inch barrel that squeezes out the full potential of this fine little fun cartridge. Otherwise, the 788 is unchanged—accurate and rugged as a blacksmith's anvil—all at a price that still allows new shoes for the kiddies.

In 1906 Remington first made their Model 8, the first American autoload-

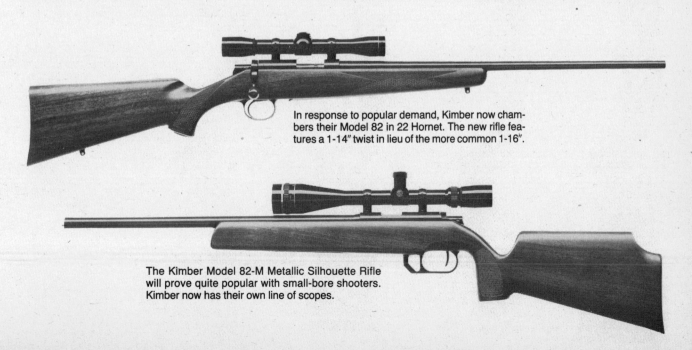

In response to popular demand, Kimber now chambers their Model 82 in 22 Hornet. The new rifle features a 1-14″ twist in lieu of the more common 1-16″.

The Kimber Model 82-M Metallic Silhouette Rifle will prove quite popular with small-bore shooters. Kimber now has their own line of scopes.

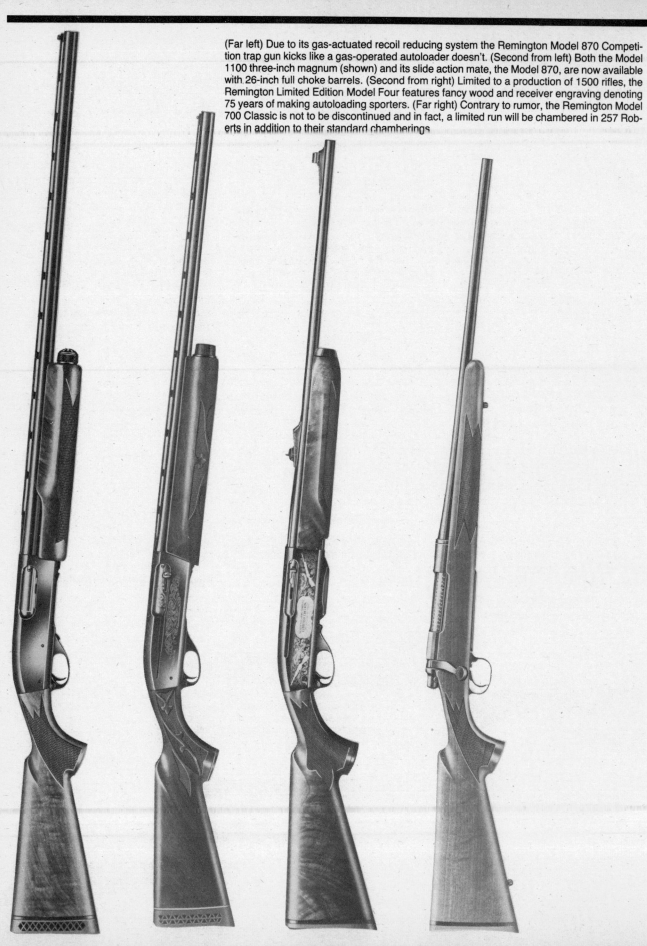

(Far left) Due to its gas-actuated recoil reducing system the Remington Model 870 Competition trap gun kicks like a gas-operated autoloader doesn't. (Second from left) Both the Model 1100 three-inch magnum (shown) and its slide action mate, the Model 870, are now available with 26-inch full choke barrels. (Second from right) Limited to a production of 1500 rifles, the Remington Limited Edition Model Four features fancy wood and receiver engraving denoting 75 years of making autoloading sporters. (Far right) Contrary to rumor, the Remington Model 700 Classic is not to be discontinued and in fact, a limited run will be chambered in 257 Roberts in addition to their standard chamberings.

ing sporting rifle chambered for cartridges considered adequate for big game. Except for minor modifications in 1936, this dependable old woods rifle stayed around until 1950 when it was discontinued. In 1955 we saw its replacement, the Model 740 emerge, this one succeeded by the 742 in 1960, which in turn became the Model Four in 1981.

That adds up to 75 years of producing centerfire autoloaders for those who stalk around in thickety places. In commemoration of this Diamond Anniversary, 1982 will see the production of 1500 high grade Model Fours in 30-06 Springfield. Nicely figured, hand-finished wood, graced with cut checkering and a brown butt pad catch the eye quick enough but that receiver is what tells the story—a panel reading "REMINGTON ARMS COMPANY, LIMITED EDITION, ONE OF FIFTEEN HUNDRED" plus gold reproductions of a Model 8 and a Model Four, sitting in scrollwork, and a diamond anniversary motif and deer head, flanking two hunters in a canoe, confronting a watering bear, a reproduction from a painting by N.C. Wyeth. There's a special block of serial numbers, LE 81 0001 through LE 81 1500.

It doesn't take three feet of barrel to burn modern shotgun powders or to squeeze shot into a tight pattern, and to prove it, Remington now offers 26-inch full choke barrels for their 12-ga. Models 1100 and 870, standard and magnum. It's just the ticket for a cramped duck blind or to swing quickly on an old tom as he freezes at 30 paces and decides that you're not as sexy as your cedar box says.

Remington's latest Model 1100 commemorative is dedicated to the Atlantic flyway and to Ducks Unlimited. This special-edition 12 gauge has a 32-inch full-choke, vent-ribbed barrel chambered for three-inch shells. A portion of the retail price of each ATLANTIC will be donated to Ducks Unlimited.

Two or three years back, Remington introduced a special version of their Model 1100 LT-20 with a 12½-inch buttstock. The idea is to offer a relatively light shotgun, short enough to fit youngsters. The stock, of course, can be replaced by one of standard length once the young shooter grows up. Two 23-inch barrels are available, one modified, the other improved cylinder and both with vent ribs. The Model 1100 venture was so successful for Remington they now offer the same deal in their Model 870. Since these barrels fit the grownup size 1100 and 870, we've discovered another neat little trick. I installed one on my Tournament Grade LT-20 and that short 23-inch barrel makes it the handiest thing you ever saw for bird shooting in close places.

Back in 1980 Remington showed a prototype version of their Model 870 Competition and got trap shooters all excited. Now, after months of debugging and refinement, it's available. Its basic 870 look has been with us for over thirty years now and will be quite familiar to the clay pigeon crowd, but the new gun has a gas-assisted recoil absorbing system.

In operation, a small amount of gas, bled from the barrel, impinges on a spring-buffered inertia piston, housed in what was the magazine tube, the latter no longer used as this is a single shot. Remington claims a stronger receiver due to the deletion of shell latch cuts and a new step-up vent rib is there for improved pointing and getting on target fast. Its target-type trigger is crisp and that new choke might be worth an extra bird or two. Due to its integral gas system the Competition will not accept standard Model 870 barrels. Remington calls it their ultimate, out-of-the-box, ready-to-shoot trap gun. Time will tell.

Ruger

Shown in the Custom Guns section of GUN DIGEST 36, as a prototype rifle, the Model M-77 International is now for real. What it amounts to is a short-action Model 77 with 18¼-inch barrel and full-length, Mannlicher-type stock. This adds up to a 6¼-pound package. Available in 243 and 308 Winchester calibers, it costs about $100 more than the standard Model 77.

A modified version of the Mini-14, designated Mini-14/5-R, is now available with an integral scope mounting system. It utilizes Ruger rings to secure a compact scope as available from Burris, Leupold and Kimber. When the scope is removed a folding aperture sight at the rear comes into play.

Ruger has announced production, but not delivered, the long-awaited 12-gauge over-under.

Savage-Stevens

Not much activity at Westfield this year except for the Model 311-R double and Model 69-RXL slide action, which are 12 gauges with 18¼-inch barrels. Both are called guard guns.

I see the dandy little 250-3000 cartridge still thriving in Savage's Model 99-A. Buy one of these whether you need it or not, because we have to keep the 250-3000 alive. It works out pretty good in the long run, because after you try this cartridge, you'll discover that you really did need it in the first place.

Six Enterprises

Fiberglass stocks never win any beauty contests but for hunting in high and rugged places they are as practical as dirt, aside from being stable in sloppy weather and about a pound lighter than wood. You might look at it this way—a glass-stocked Model 700 with scope and mounts will weigh about the same as one with iron sights and the factory wood. They are relatively expensive, unless you decide on one of Lee Six's economy grade Timberliner rifles. In place of the painted finish of the standard Timberliner, this one has color pigment in the fiberglass. It ain't very pretty, but it's mighty practical. And it cuts the cost of one of these lightweights by $125.

Smith & Wesson

This Massachusetts handgun firm continues to invade the long gun market. Varmint shooters will be delighted to see another option in the Model 1500 bolt action—a 24-inch heavy barrel chambered in 222 Remington, 22-250 or 223 Remington. The 222, 223, and 308 Winchester are now available in their standard rifle with 22-inch barrel. This brings the total number of cartridge options offered with the Model 1500 to ten.

Probably the best seller in S&W's long gun line is their Model 1000 gas-powered shotgun. In 12 gauge, it's now offered with an interchangeable choke tube system called Multi-Choke. There is a 12-gauge, three-inch magnum with such features as a dull, oil-finished stock; parkerized metal, and detachable swivels holding an Uncle Mike's camouflage sling. It's called the Waterfowler but I'll bet it would drop a turkey as well.

And there are four Model 1000's

(Left) Smith & Wesson Model 1500 Deluxe Varmint rifle is offered in 222, 22-250 and 223 calibers.

(Right) Smith & Wesson Waterfowler Model 3000 Pump, with dull finish stock, Parkerized metal and padded camouflage sling.

rigged up for competition. The 12-gauge Skeet gun, in 12 and 20 gauges, has been around awhile, joined last year by the 12-gauge Super Skeet. Now there is a 20-gauge Super Skeet, replete with hand-tuned trigger; cast-off buttstock; recessed choke and muzzle brake—just like its 12-gauge mate. For trap shooting, S&W has unveiled their Model 1000 with padded, Monte Carlo stock; step-up rib and Bradley front sight. This one comes with a 30-inch Multi-Choke barrel.

Smith & Wesson's slide action Model 3000 sports some additions as well. There's a 12-gauge, three-inch magnum, with or without Multi-Choke, and a Waterfowler here too. A 20-gauge, three-inch field gun and three 12-gauge slug guns round out the Model 3000 changes. Slug gun options include: blued and parkerized metal finishes; 18-inch and 20-inch barrels; bead and adjustable sights and quick-detach sling swivels.

Texas Gun & Machine Co.

It would take a very long article to describe all the bolt action rifle variations turned out by this almost-obscure company, so I'll just list the myriad actions available and the cartridge lengths they will handle:

Action	Cartridges
1.750	50 Browning MG
1.360	25-06 thru 300 H&H
1.360 Magnum	378 Weatherby 510 Wells
1.360 Short	222 thru 7x57mm
1.360 Aluminum	25-06 thru 300 H&H
1.360 Alum. Short	222 thru 7x57mm
1.300	25-06 thru 300 H&H
1.300 Short	222 thru 7x57mm
1.150	25-06 thru 300 H&H
1.150 Short	222 thru 7x57mm
1.000	22 Hornet thru 222

The action number designates the receiver ring diameter and with the decimal point dropped, it becomes the model number in a completed rifle. For example, the receiver that takes the 50 Browning is 1.750-inches in diameter and when a rifle is built on this action it becomes a Model 1750. The word "aluminum" means the receiver is aluminum with a steel locking lug recess. The 1.750 action is available in single shot only; all others are offered as single shot or repeater. All are available with right- or

Smith & Wesson Multi-choke shotguns. Model 1000 Auto top and Model 3000 Pump bottom. Interchangeable choke tubes adapt the gun to different hunting challenges without changing the barrel, balance, swing or weight of the gun.

This 25-06 is but one of a myriad of rifles turned out by Texas Gun and Machine Co., in any caliber from 22 Hornet to 50 Browning.

S&W Multi-choke muzzle section cutaway shows how barrel wall thickness increases only at the end to accommodate the choke tube. Mating of barrel and tube bores eliminates the shoulder where residue can build up.

left-hand turn bolts and most can be had with round or octagon receivers.

All component parts are machined from solid bar stock—the receiver, bolt and barrel from 4140 steel. From the 22 Hornet to the 50 Browning, Texas Gun & Machine offers an action proportionate in size to any cartridge one might come up with. I'm especially intrigued with the little 1.000 action. It weighs about 22 ounces and compares in size with the old Winchester Model 43 action, yet this one has front locking lugs. They do nice things in Texas City, TX.

And to top it all off, Texas Gun offers actions, barreled actions and completed rifles. I'm absolutely amazed at the variety. In case you're interested, they say they build about 50 rifles per year chambered for the 50 Browning. As this is written I do not have a complete price list but a typical barreled action, in the white, will run around $500.

Weatherby

Gone are the Regency and Olympian over-unders, as are the Centurion autoloader and Patrician slide-action shotguns, but just take a gander at their successors:

Top of the Weatherby smoothbore line is the Athena, with a Greener crossbolt locking system, automatic selective ejectors and single trigger. The monobloc is jeweled and all internal parts are hand fitted and polished. The silver-gray receiver has floral engraving; the select claro walnut has hand-cut checkering. The 12-bore as a field, Skeet or trap gun, in four barrel lengths and five choke combinations. The 20 offers choice of field or Skeet, both with three-inch chambers. All Athena models have ventilated top and side ribs.

Next it's the Orion. Leave the quality and workmanship but take away the Athena's fancy and you have the Orion, except the field model has a solid rib. In both the Athena and Orion, an internal adjustment allows a choice of mechanical or recoil actuation or the single trigger.

After more than six years of development and testing, Weatherby says his Model Eighty-Two autoloader and Model Ninety-Two pump guns are in full production. Both have hand checkered, select claro walnut; fluted bolts; etched receivers and optional Multi-Choke interchangeable tubes. Built into the Eighty-Two is a self-aligning slide assembly that lets the gas piston float on the magazine tube,

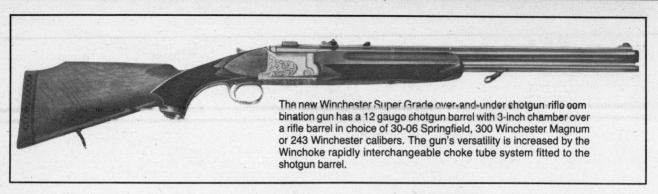

The new Winchester Super Grade over-and-under shotgun rifle combination gun has a 12 gauge shotgun barrel with 3-inch chamber over a rifle barrel in choice of 30-06 Springfield, 300 Winchester Magnum or 243 Winchester calibers. The gun's versatility is increased by the Winchoke rapidly interchangeable choke tube system fitted to the shotgun barrel.

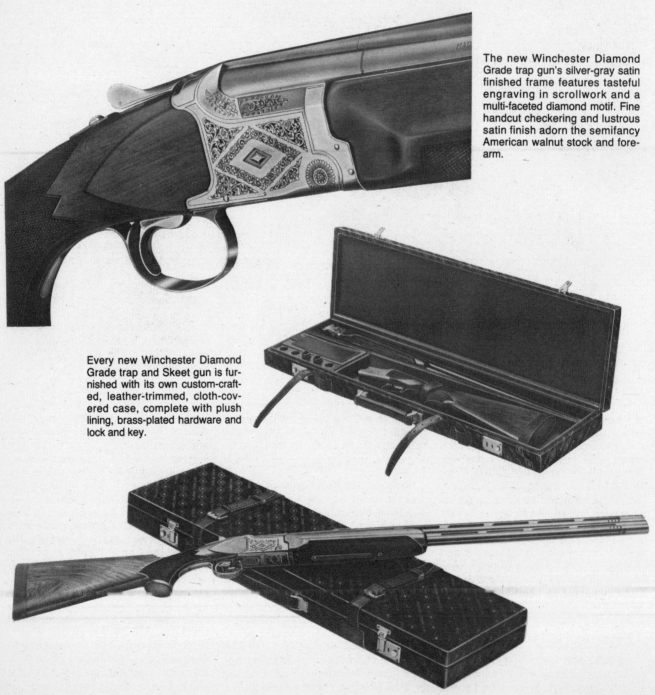

The new Winchester Diamond Grade trap gun's silver-gray satin finished frame features tasteful engraving in scrollwork and a multi-faceted diamond motif. Fine handcut checkering and lustrous satin finish adorn the semifancy American walnut stock and fore-arm.

Every new Winchester Diamond Grade trap and Skeet gun is furnished with its own custom-crafted, leather-trimmed, cloth-covered case, complete with plush lining, brass-plated hardware and lock and key.

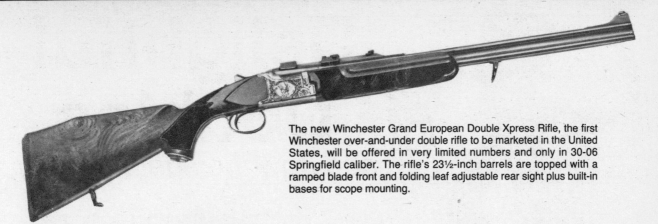

The new Winchester Grand European Double Xpress Rifle, the first Winchester over-and-under double rifle to be marketed in the United States, will be offered in very limited numbers and only in 30-06 Springfield caliber. The rifle's 23½-inch barrels are topped with a ramped blade front and folding leaf adjustable rear sight plus built-in bases for scope mounting.

independent of any other internal part. The Ninety-Two boasts the shortest stroke of any pump shotgun made and the handiest release lever in the business. Both shotguns are available in field, Skeet and trap models as well as a Buckmaster with adjustable sights.

Winchester/USRAC

Holy smoke, was the Model 70 Featherweight a good move. On the phone with a certain fellow, a short time back, I casually suggested another chambering be added and he used up half my nickel laughing. They can't meet demand for the six calibers presently cataloged. I finally latched on to one in 257 Roberts and it's a sweet-shooting bugger, but I wish the chamber throat were a bit longer.

And once again, almost the entire line of Model 70s take on a new look. What we now have are five basic Model 70s. The Westerner comes in 243, 270, 308, 30-06, 7mm Remington Magnum and 300 Winchester Magnum, 22-inch barrels for the standard cartridges and 24-inch for the magnums. Recoil lugs are hand-bedded in epoxy. American walnut is still there, finished in a XTR satin sheen and fancied up by cut checkering. Optionally available is a 4x scope which I guess to be by Weaver.

Next we have the Sporter Magnum, available in 264, 7mm, 300 and 338 calibers, all with 24-inch barrels. The Sporter Magnum has an undercut cheekpiece; cut checkering; epoxy-bedded recoil lug; satin finished wood and a recoil pad.

Take the Sporter Magnum model, mount its front sling swivel out on the barrel; reinforce its stock with two steel crossbolts; stamp 375 H&H or 458 Winchester on an appropriate barrel and you have the Model XTR Super Express Magnum. This one re-

places the old African model and it's very nice looking.

The Model 70 Varmint, in 222 Remington, 22-250 and 243 Winchester is still with us and is the only one that still has a high gloss finish in its wood. I surely like the new XTR satin finish.

Winchester has also hopped aboard the riot gun bandwagon with three shorties, built on the Model 1200 slide action. All are in 12 gauge with three-inch chambers and 18-inch barrels. The Security model resists corrosion with its stainless steel barrel and bright chrome-plated receiver. The chrome finish is triple-plated; first with copper for adherence; then with nickel for rust protection and finally with chrome for a hard finish. The Police model differs only with its satin chrome finish that diffuses light reflection. The Defender is an economy model, without stainless steel and chrome, designed for home security, so says Winchester.

Winchester/OLIN

Part of the excitement at Winchester Group comes in over-under form and is called the Grand European Double Xpress Rifle. Available only in 30-06 caliber, its frame is finished in silver-gray satin and embellished with big game scenes, surrounded by scroll engraving. A semifancy American walnut buttstock is hand-checkered and finished to a satin hue, its grip terminating in blued steel. A solid rifle pad adorns the butt. Quick detachable sling swivels are there, the front mounted out on the 23½-inch barrels. Sights consist of a ramped blade out front and an adjustable folding leaf at the rear. Bases are attached for scope mounting and rings are included. A whale of a timber rifle for the carriage trade is what this one is. I'd surely like to see a plain-Jane version.

A bit less expensive is the Super Grade Shotgun/Rifle Combination. Basically the same as the Xpress rifle except that a 12-gauge Winchoked barrel goes over a 300 Winchester Magnum, 30-06 or 243 Winchester tube. Barrel length is 25-inch and four choke tubes are included. The Super Grade has a single selective, mechanical-type trigger, combined with a combination tang safety and barrel selector. The shotgun barrel is equipped with a selective automatic ejector while the rifle barrel has a conventional extractor.

The Diamond Grade series is a premier line of competition smoothbores in over-under persuasion and in about any configuration one could possibly dream up. All feature highly polished, deeply blued barrels; silver-gray satin finished frames with scroll engraving and a multi-faceted diamond motif; top and side ventilated ribs; white front and middle beads and chromed bores. The semifancy American walnut is hand-checkered and satin finished. Two diamond-shaped inlays of ebony appear, one on the underside of the pistol grip, another near the top tang. Additional features include an inertia-type, single selective trigger and selective automatic ejectors. The trap gun series includes 30-inch and 32-inch barrels and straight or Monte Carlo stocks, as well as a single shot with 34-inch barrel, all with Winchoke. Also available is a combination set consisting of an over-under barrel set and a single tube. Diamond Grade Skeet guns are offered in 12, 20, 28 and 410 bores with 27-inch barrels choked Skeet #1 and Skeet #2.

All Double Xpress, Super Grade and Diamond Series guns are sold in plush-lined, cloth-covered, leather-trimmed cases with brass-plated hardware. They're beauties, one and all. ●

Delightful Doubles
and how they get that way

A harmony of balance and beauty reaches crescendo proportions in well designed side-by-sides and over-unders.

by DON ZUTZ

BEFORE GETTING to the meat and potatoes of this article I must point out that everything herein depends upon the term "well designed." For not all doubles are delightful. Some are mass-produced klunks, others are *el cheapo* imports. Poorly designed, imbalanced, ill-fitted, crudely adorned, and dubious performers at the patterning board, these lesser specimens have none of the desirable and dignifying features possessed by the better twin-tubed bird guns.

Nor do trap and Skeet model break-opens fit this discussion. Encumbered by massive fore-ends, long stocks, heavy trap barrels stretching 32 inches or more, and ventilated ribs wider than a 4-lane freeway, target model doubles must be regarded mainly as specialized smoothbores suited primarily to controlled games with clay targets; in general, their weight, balance, and proportions deny the possibility of optimum handling ease from a low-gun position.

Essentially, the "delightful doubles" upon which this piece pivots are those designed for effortless handling qualities and natural pointing accuracy afield. Simply stated, they are bird guns, not clay target or live pigeon ordnance. Moreover, they are the classical varieties, guns which tower above all cheaply-made specimens and muzzle-heavy clubs by virtue of excellent stocks and fore-ends and finely engineered balance, features which enable the hunter to get on a fast-flushing bird with ease and

The Weatherby Regency O-U bore axes run through the writer's leading hand, thus improving chances for an accurate point when the hands naturally swing toward and through the target. The gun has good hand-to-barrel relationship, brings recoil back in nearly straight line.

accuracy. Yes, indeed, the double gun is a true delight when its design and construction harmonize with the requirements of wingshooting theory.

Unfortunately, the desirable qualities of a fine double are not widely known to very many Americans; they're oblivious to such refinements because they have been nurtured on grandpaw's Long Tom pumpgun. True, we can admire the mechanical features of a well-done trombone gun or autoloader, but somehow we have forgotten the concepts by which a classical double is judged.

Good D.B. Design

What, then, are the fine points of good double-gun design? Insofar as handling qualities are concerned, knowledgeable shotgunners are interested in a smoothbore's "responsiveness." To be judged acceptably responsive according to classical and traditional wing-gunning and gun-making concepts, any shotgun swept into action from a lowered position—such as a field carry or the hip-level hold used in International Skeet—should have a fit and feel that not only make minimal demands on a shooter's

With the bulk of its weight—what I call the half-weight—between the shooter's hands, a finely built side-by-side gets into action effortlessly ● American clay target games, which allow the shooter to mount his gun solidly and obtain alignment before the bird is re- leased, generally negate the need for a quick-handling, well-balanced, properly-fitted gun. Thus American Skeet and trap guns are poor measuring sticks for evaluating the finely built bird gun, which is at its best for instinctive use in the game fields.

energy, but also draw that energy equally from both hands. In other words, the delightful double will (a) swing into action effortlessly, (b) have a balance that contributes to fast handling, and (c) possess a quality perhaps best expressed as "pointability," so that accurate alignment is a certainty even under pressure.

The matter of balance is hardly new to any discussion of sporting equipment. It applies to fishing tackle, boats, tennis rackets, and experimental aircraft. The problem, however, is that the term has a different meaning as it applies to various items. Many outdoorsmen understand the need to match a flyline's weight with a particular rod's action to obtain a balanced outfit, but they often don't know the whys and wherefores of balancing a fine bird gun. Let's clarify the issue:

Balance and Liveliness

The word "balance" tends to imply an equal weight fore and aft of a certain fixed point. As applied to classical bird guns, though, that definition is far too simple and misleading. The balance of a lively, responsive double is more complex, involving the *distribution* of weight to attain a specific balance point *and* weight concentration for spirited and effortless handling.

To achieve this lively feel, master guncrafters have traditionally given the classical bird gun a "between-the-hands" balance, meaning that the gun's weight is concentrated betwixt the trigger hand and fore-end tip. The importance of between-the-hands balance and construction rests in the physical fact that a shotgun so designed will pivot easily about its approximate middle, there being relatively little inertia in butt and/or

muzzles to retard movement. The advantages of this kind of weight distribution are rapid and effortless manipulation of a gun's extremities for quick alignment on fast-flushing targets—and shoulders.

By contrast to such well-organized doubles, a long-barreled pump or autoloader with weight-forward bias will develop a hard-to-handle flywheel action when started after a fleeting mark, since a weighty muzzle, once moving, has considerable momentum. True, such a weight-forward condition is helpful for long-range waterfowling, but for upland birds and fast clays the classical double's centered point of balance and weight concentration helps one get on target faster and with minimal effort.

A pair of integral elements which, along with between-the-hands balance, give break-open scatterguns their vaunted "pointability" are (1) a hands-in-line factor and (2) a hands-to-barrel relationship. To appreciate these niceties, we must remember that shotguns are pointed, not aimed, and that, because the smoothbore is also pathetically short ranged, success will come consistently only to those who can point and swing quickly and accurately.

The secret of combining both speed and accuracy in handling the upland gun depends on coordination. Both hands must work together as the gun is thrust toward and through the bird in one smooth movement. Any need to jiggle, wiggle, fight, or squirm as the bird gun is mounted means it's poorly designed for field use or does not fit the user. (It could also mean that the shooter does not have proper form, but that's another story.) All that unnecessary squiggling to establish alignment slows or destroys that

which should be a naturally smooth and precise—almost instinctive—gun handling movement.

Optimum speed and accuracy with a bird gun will be realized when stock and fore-end designs place the hunter's hands on about the same plane relative to the axes of the bores. One's hands naturally work toward a common plane, and if we destroy that plane by forcing one hand significantly higher or lower than the other by means of bulky forearms or tightly-curved pistol grips, the natural coordination between the hands will be canceled out. If one hand is depressed by a fat fore-end, or if one hand is elevated by a too-slim pistol grip, the bird gun will invariably be tilted as the hands work back to their natural plane, thus reducing chances for a quick and accurate point.

Pointing Speed

The second factor, hand-to-barrel relationship, is the final major aspect related to pointing speed and accuracy. If we accept the theory that a shooter's hands go naturally toward the target—and master gunmakers do work on that assumption—it then follows that any bore axis which sits low in the shooter's palm will also travel faster and more precisely toward the mark. The bore axis, in effect, becomes an extension of the hunter's naturally extended leading hand. Consequently, prestigious over-unders derive at least part of their glory from low-profile receivers which allow trim forearms to keep the bores deep in the shooter's slightly cupped hand.

The man who is evaluating a twin-tubed bird gun according to classical and theoretical concepts, then, will be primarily interested in finding the

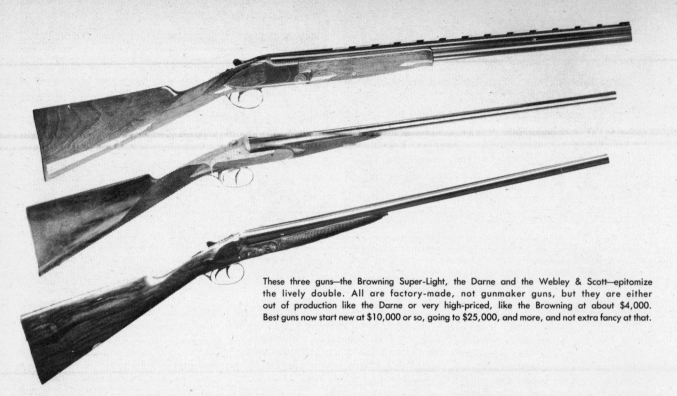

These three guns—the Browning Super-Light, the Darne and the Webley & Scott—epitomize the lively double. All are factory-made, not gunmaker guns, but they are either out of production like the Darne or very high-priced, like the Browning at about $4,000. Best guns now start new at $10,000 or so, going to $25,000, and more, and not extra fancy at that.

balance—the gun's half-weight or more—between his hands, the balance point within an inch or so of the knuckle pin. Moreover, the stock and fore-end should be designed to keep both hands on the same plane relative to the axes of the bores, and the barrel should run through the cupped leading hand rather than sitting high above it—as is the case with most pump guns and autoloaders.

But if repeaters do not possess these finer attributes of between-the-hands balance, hands-in-line factors, and hand-to-barrel relationship, why do American clay target competitors often post perfect scores with pumps and autoloaders? The answer is twofold. First, it must be noted that we are herein discussing the ultra-fine points of bird-gun design. No attempt has been made to declare other action types wholly ineffective. A good field shot will still hit more with a rusty bolt-action shotgun than a poor shot will with a custom-built Purdey. Indeed, this discussion is based on a matter of degrees, taste, intrinsic values, and an application of theory. When we access the finer points of wingshooting, when we consider the ultimate in harmonizing design with perfect form, timing, and handling theory, and when we view the quiet elegance, the dignity of simplicity, the stock dimensions and the proper balance for quick and accurate pointing afield—then the break-open doubles become prestige items capable of adding some-

thing extra to both pride and performance.

Second, American forms of Skeet and trap allow competitors to have their guns fully mounted and aligned *before* the target appears, thus eliminating the need for rapid gun mounting. The beautiful balance and pointing qualities of a well-designed and finely built double are wasted on domestic clay target games, for the qualities of a classical double are important mainly to rapid gun handling and alignment from a low-gun, field-carry position.

Over-Under Profiles

A final assessment of the over-under must involve mention of the receiver's profile, especially the 12-gauge guns. Over-unders having a "low profile," so-called, are desirable; those with a "high profile" are farther from perfection. Basically, a height of 2.50 inches through the standing breech is the dividing line for 12-gauge over-unders.

Low-receiver profiles are found on those designs using the "trunnion" or "bifurcated lump" system. The trunnion is a cylindrical extension machined onto the barrel assembly to duplicate the function of a knuckle pin by fitting into matching recesses in the receiver wall—or vice versa. The value of a trunnion design is that these "buttons" can be placed high, about on the centerline of the lower barrel, thereby eliminating the need to provide space between barrel-bottom assembly and receiver for a lug/lump

arrangement. Too, less strain is placed on the receiver and locks when trunnions are placed opposite the lower tube's axis, because recoil will be in a straighter line—and lessened thereby—than if the pivot point (hinge pin) is below the barrels.

A high profile is normally associated with over-unders using a full knuckle pin with under-lug locking arrangements. The under-bolting arrangement, jutting downward from the lower barrel, must be surrounded by the receiver, and this requires greater receiver depth than is desirable in a truly fine vertical double. A high profile implies a deep fore-end, meaning poor hand-to-barrel relationship, and the high-sitting tubes can, when fired, place greater radial strain on the receiver and bolting system.

Is it possible to obtain a break-open bird gun with all the refinements mentioned above? Sure. But it's expensive. Two thousand dollars is about rock bottom—or it was! There are some mass-produced doubles which, in the range of $1000-$2000, offer many fine features, but not always the full treatment.

If I were faced with a choice between buying a cheap twin-tubed gun this year or saving my coin for another year to finance a better grade double, I'd take the latter course, or borrow the money. For once a discriminating fellow hunts with a properly balanced field gun, he develops a genuine appreciation for its spirited and effortless handling qualities. ●

Ruger's New Mk II Rimfire Auto Pistols

Sturm, Ruger & Co. has revamped their Standard Auto line rimfire pistols. Now called the Mark II series, a number of internal and external modifications have been made. From left to right: The Standard Mark II with 4¾-inch barrel; the Mark II Target with 6⅞-inch barrel and the Mark II Target with 5½-inch heavy bull barrel.

H&K Models 300 & 270

H&K offers a pair of semiauto rimfire rifles—the H&K 300 (in 22 Mag.) and the H&K 270 (in 22 LR). Available with a 5-round magazine, the H&K 300 features polygonal rifling, and a European-styled walnut stock with Monte Carlo cheekpiece. H&K's Model 270 (right) is a slimmed-down 22 LR version of the 300.

H&K Models 770 & 630

Well known for their military-styled firearms, Heckler & Koch also offers a more traditionally styled series of sporting long guns. Shown here are a pair of those rifles. The H&K 770 is scoped, the H&K 630 is beneath the 770. The 630 is available in 223 Remington; the 770 comes in 308 Winchester. Both rifles are semiauto in design and feature hand checkered, walnut stocks.

Omark Industries

Omark's latest addition to their corporate lineup is Outers Labs, Inc., a well-established company known for its excellent cleaning gear. Featured to the left of Outers gear is a selection of Speer, CCI and RCBS products—all of which surround the new RCBS "Green Machine," a progressive reloading press that's designed for pistol calibers.

Dan Wesson

Dan Wesson revolvers have carved out a niche in the American handgunning scene. They are noted for their interchangeable front sight blades and quick-change barrels. From top to bottom: the Dan Wesson 22 LR; the Dan Wesson 44 Magnum; and the Dan Wesson 357 Magnum. Barrel assemblies are available in a variety of lengths and styles, depending upon caliber.

Krico

Krico rifles are available in a number of styles and calibers. The Krico 650 SS (left) is a bolt action, match-barreled rifle that's available in 222, 223, 243 and 308. The Krico 700 KE (center), is a bolt action centerfire sporter with hand checkered walnut stock and detachable 3-shot clip. On the right is Krico's 22 LR clip-fed 340 S rimfire Silhouette Match Sporter.

KRICO

Shown is a sampling of Brownells gunsmithing tools. No other gunsmith supply house comes close to offering the assortment of tools and accessories that Brownells does. Professional gunsmiths and hobbyists worldwide have acknowledged that fact for over 40 years, and you just couldn't find nicer people to do business with.

BROWNELLS, Inc.

H&K P7 & H&K 4 Semiauto Pistols

H&K's P7 (top) features polygonal rifling and is recoil operated. Adjustable sights and an 8-round magazine are standard. The H&K 4 double-action pistol (below) is available in 380 ACP, 32 ACP, 25 ACP or 22 LR. You can easily convert from one caliber to another by changing the barrel, and the magazine (the extractor, too, when converting to 22 LR).

H&K P 9S & VP 70Z Semiauto Pistols

The H&K P 9S (left) is available in 9mm Luger or 45 ACP and has a delayed roller-block system, polygonal rifling, a frame-mounted cocking lever and excellent sights. The VP 70Z (right) is a large semiauto that fires double-action only and features a staggered column, 18-round magazine. Amazingly, this large pistol has only four moving, operating parts.

Pacific Tool Company

Pacific Tool Company, a division of Hornady, introduced its O-7 press about two years ago. The O-7 was quickly followed by a larger unit of the same design—the OO-7—which is shown here. This large but lightweight O-frame reloading tool is easily described as a single-station progressive press because of its unique fully-automatic priming system.

Action Arms Ltd. UZI

Simply put, the UZI (manufactured by I.M.I.-Israel) is one of the most identifiable firearms in the world. Now available from Action Arms, Ltd., the 9mm Parabellum, semiauto civilian version of the UZI fires from a closed bolt and features a legal-length barrel and a collapsible stock. The UZI is notable for its compactness and reliable function.

H&K Models 91 A-2 & 91 A-3

The H&K 91 is a magazine fed, semi-auto sporting rifle that's chambered for the 7.62 NATO (308 Winchester) round. The "91" comes with retractable (A-3) or standard (A-2) stocks. Its reliability can be traced to the rifle's modern, simplified construction and roller-lock breech. This 9½-pound rifle is also available with an optional "Q.D." 1-inch scope mount as shown.

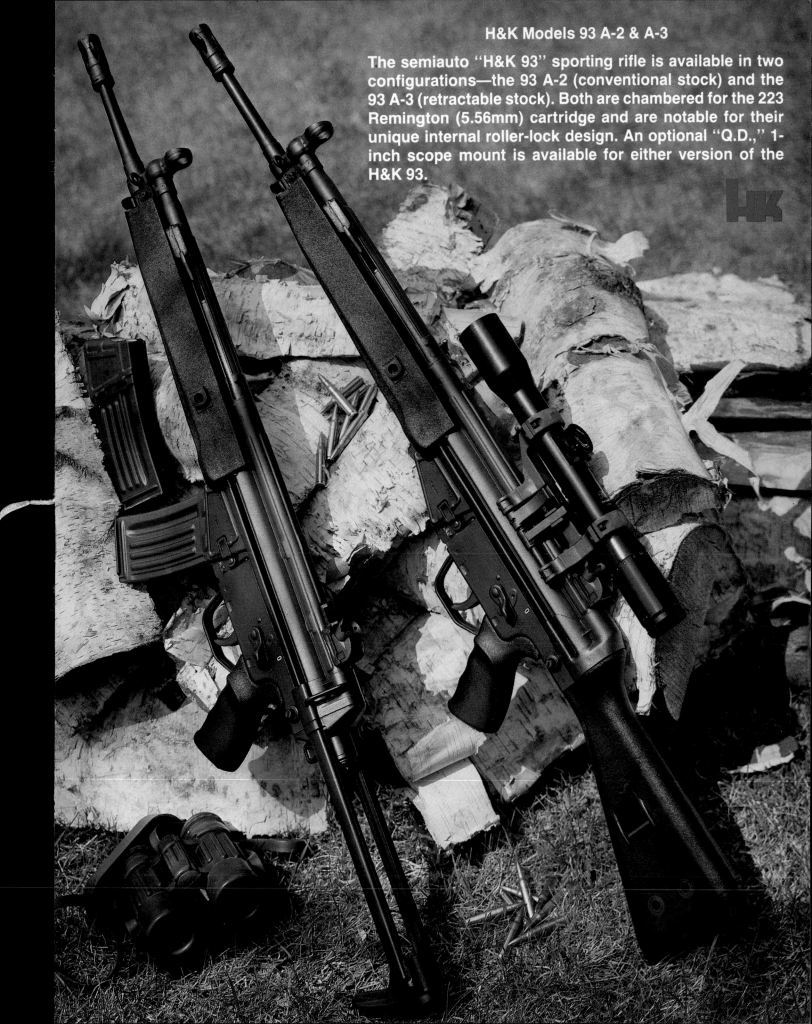

H&K Models 93 A-2 & A-3

The semiauto "H&K 93" sporting rifle is available in two configurations—the 93 A-2 (conventional stock) and the 93 A-3 (retractable stock). Both are chambered for the 223 Remington (5.56mm) cartridge and are notable for their unique internal roller-lock design. An optional "Q.D.," 1-inch scope mount is available for either version of the H&K 93.

Ruger Mini 14 Ranch Rifle

Ruger's semiauto Mini-14 Ranch Rifle features a hardwood stock that has a newly designed shotgun-type butt. Also new is the large, ventilated plastic handguard. The receiver has integral scope bases, an adjustable rear sight and a buffer system that minimizes shock to a mounted scope. The Ranch Rifle is chambered for the 223 Remington.

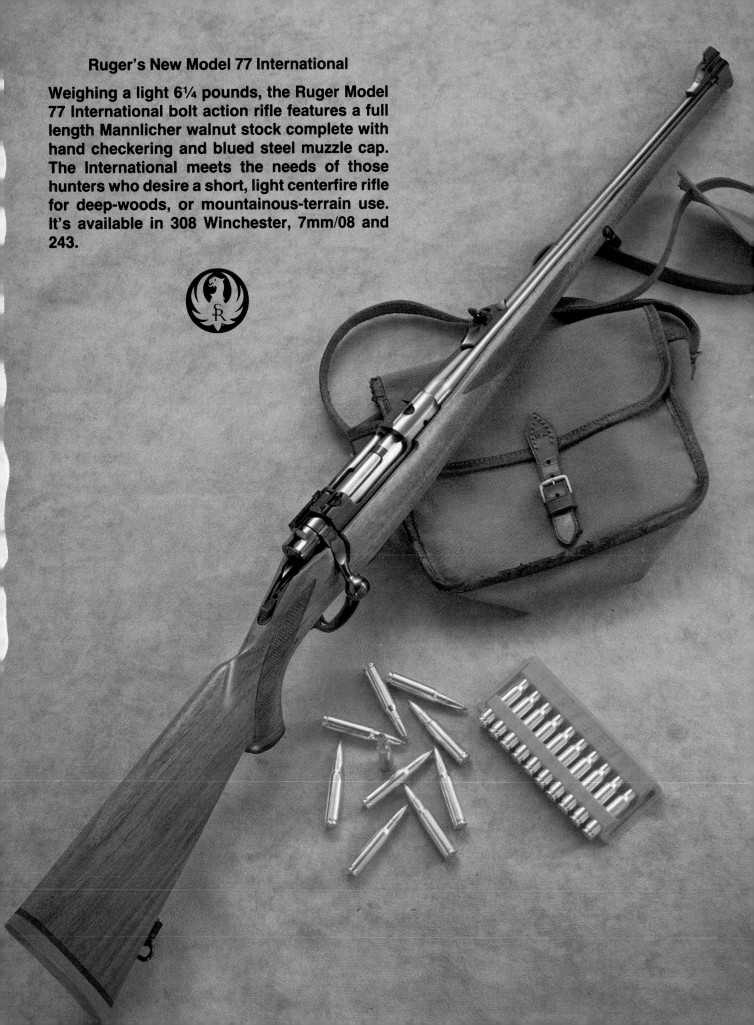

Ruger's New Model 77 International

Weighing a light 6¼ pounds, the Ruger Model 77 International bolt action rifle features a full length Mannlicher walnut stock complete with hand checkering and blued steel muzzle cap. The International meets the needs of those hunters who desire a short, light centerfire rifle for deep-woods, or mountainous-terrain use. It's available in 308 Winchester, 7mm/08 and 243.

Mag-na-port ®

Pro-port

Mag-Num
Sales Limited,
Inc.

Mag-Na-Port, Pro-Port,
Mag-Num Sales, Ltd., Inc.

Most shooters are familiar with Magna-Port-ing and its recoil-reduction characteristics. Center: a customized Thompson/Center single shot that has been Mag-Na-Ported. Left: a shotgun barrel that has been vented by Pro-Porting which also reduces recoil and muzzle jump on shotguns (only). Right: a Ruger Super Blackhawk 44 Magnum that's the first of the Big-Five African Series from Mag-Num Sales, Ltd., Inc.

RIG Products

In business for a half-century, this Mid-West firm recently moved its headquarters to Sparks, Nevada where they continue to manufacture their well known grease. From back to front: RIG Universal (rust inhibiting grease), RIG 3 (a degreaser), and RIG 2 (a light-oil lubricant). Also shown is a sheepskin RIG-RAG and a new product for handgunners, the collapsible, self contained, RIG-ROD.

Benelli Semiauto Shotguns

From left to right: Benelli Model Special Trap, Standard Model 121 and the SL 123V Deluxe. All of these Benelli autos feature hand-checkered walnut stocks, ventilated ribs and alloy receivers. Available in 12 or 20 gauge, the Benelli line of shotguns feature interchangeable barrels, in all popular chokes. (Benelli shotguns are imported by Heckler & Koch.)

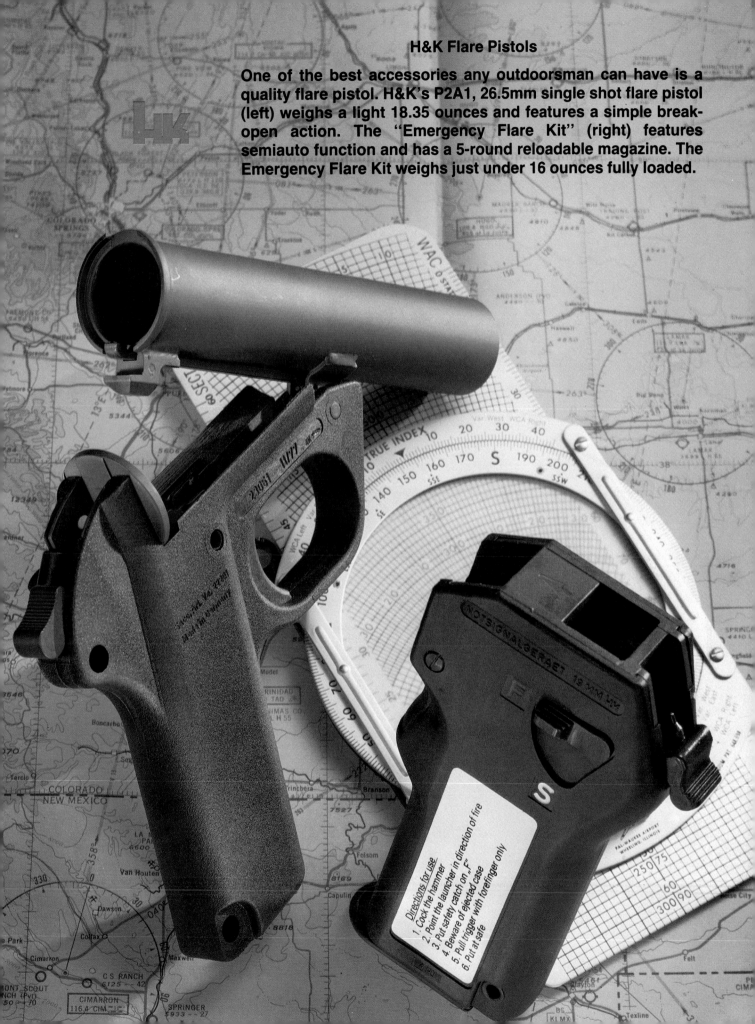

H&K Flare Pistols

One of the best accessories any outdoorsman can have is a quality flare pistol. H&K's P2A1, 26.5mm single shot flare pistol (left) weighs a light 18.35 ounces and features a simple break-open action. The "Emergency Flare Kit" (right) features semiauto function and has a 5-round reloadable magazine. The Emergency Flare Kit weighs just under 16 ounces fully loaded.

Directions for use
1. Cock the hammer
2. Point the launcher in direction of fire
3. Put safety catch on "F"
4. Beware of ejected case
5. Pull trigger with forefinger only
6. Put at safe

Crosman Airguns

Crosman is one of the acknowledged leaders in the exciting, fast growing airgun industry. Featured on this page are three top-notch Crosman products—the 1861 Shiloh .177-caliber revolver, the 2200 Magnum rifle in 22 caliber and the 766 American Classic, .177-caliber BB/pellet rifle. Also shown are Crosman Copperhead® pellets and Copperhead CO_2 Powerlets.

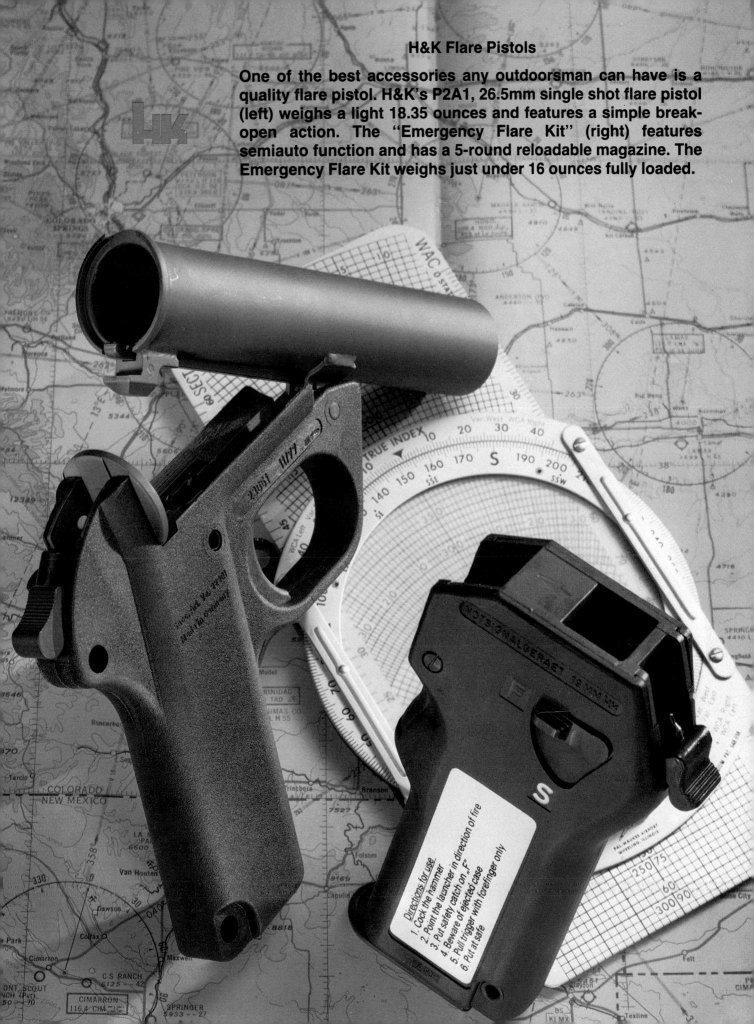

H&K Flare Pistols

One of the best accessories any outdoorsman can have is a quality flare pistol. H&K's P2A1, 26.5mm single shot flare pistol (left) weighs a light 18.35 ounces and features a simple break-open action. The "Emergency Flare Kit" (right) features semiauto function and has a 5-round reloadable magazine. The Emergency Flare Kit weighs just under 16 ounces fully loaded.

Directions for use
1. Cock the hammer
2. Point the launcher in direction of fire
3. Put safety catch on "F"
4. Beware of ejected case
5. Pull trigger with forefinger only
6. Put at safe

Crosman Airguns

Crosman is one of the acknowledged leaders in the exciting, fast growing airgun industry. Featured on this page are three top-notch Crosman products—the 1861 Shiloh .177-caliber revolver, the 2200 Magnum rifle in 22 caliber and the 766 American Classic, .177-caliber BB/pellet rifle. Also shown are Crosman Copperhead® pellets and Copperhead CO₂ Powerlets.

M-S Safari Arms

Safari Arms turns out a broad range of quality firearms. Featured here are three Safari autos based on the reliable 1911, 45 auto design. Upper left: an Armoloyed Safari Enforcer with shortened frame and slide. Center: the Safari Model 81L Deluxe (in 38 WC or 45ACP), a bullseye gun with long slide. To the right is a Safari Stainless Matchmaster.

Ruger's Single Action Conversion Kit

Ruger has announced a no-cost conversion service for "old model" Single-Six, Blackhawk and Super Blackhawk revolvers. Owners are requested to contact the factory for the fitting of a transfer-bar system which involves the installation of the parts shown nearby. Ruger will install those parts (without modifying the frame) and will return the "old model" parts to the owner. (Before returning your gun to the factory, contact Ruger for shipping instructions.)

Modern "magnum" airguns reclaim a modest
share of a rich and colorful history.
Once again, we can see . . .

The Bavaria-Wischo 55N is one of author's favorite field rifles. It is superbly accurate and
has a MV of 780 fps in 177 caliber.

THE PNEUMO-NIMROD AT WORK

by J. I. GALAN

ONE FAIRLY POPULAR misconception presents the air rifle as a wholly inadequate small-game taker. Such blindness is simply an unwillingness to accept the fact that the powerful, precision-engineered airgun of today is not a toy. Really, it is not surprising from those who grew up with that uniquely American shooting machine, the BB gun. Possessing relatively low power and chancy accuracy at best, the BB gun became synonymous with "airgun" in

the minds of generations of American shooters and hunters, most of whom went from a BB gun to a 22 rimfire or to a shotgun.

Although pellet air rifles have been available for decades, their accuracy and reliability were not always up to satisfactory levels, serving to reaffirm the widespread myth that airguns in general were mere toys. Those adventurous, pioneering souls who many years ago saw and understood the potential of the adult airgun as a small-

game hunting weapon were always a tiny minority. At best, they were tolerated as amusing weirdos; at worst, viewed with suspicion and objurgated for using an "inadequate" weapon.

Are airguns really wrong and out of place entirely as small-game hunting arms?

In a purely historical context, airguns have a long and well-documented tradition as hunting and—to some degree—poaching arms, dating back hundreds of years. Countless written and illustrated accounts of European royalty hunting stag and wild boar and smaller animals with airguns have survived. One such account in an old hunting journal kept in the Schlossmuseum at Darmstadt, West Germany illustrates a stag killed in 1749 by Landgrave Ludwig VIII at a range of 154 paces using a large caliber air rifle. In his classic and scholarly work, *Air Guns*, the late Eldon G. Wolff reported that numerous deer and wild boar fell to Ludwig's air rifle.

Since airguns were largely custommade by a handful of highly skilled gunsmiths in those long-gone days, their steep cost was one of the main reasons that the nobles and their wealthy cohorts were usually the only ones who could afford them. Poachers, however, were quick to realize the potential of the air rifle as the main tool of their trade. Lacking the vagaries of matchlock and flintlock ignition systems, while at the same time delivering a powerful and almost silent shot, the large bore air rifle was the ideal poaching weapon. It was nearly as quiet as the crossbow, an old favorite of the poacher, with the additional advantage that it left no incriminating bolts stuck in tree trunks.

Some poachers of the 18th and 19th Centuries may have used air rifles disguised as firearms of the period, to the extent that some surviving specimens even have flintlocks that really spark, though the pans are not connected to the barrels. Presumably, these spurious firearms could pass just about any casual inspection. Perhaps there is a more plausible reason for this deception, though. By the late 1700s, many European states and nations had severe restrictions against the use and possession of airguns. In some locales, airguns were considered to be the work of the devil and, as such, were totally banned. It is quite conceivable that, under such conditions, those who fancied airguns, especially for hunting purposes, would go to great lengths to conceal them.

Even the most powerful modern airguns are considerably weaker than the hunting airguns mentioned in the old journals and in historical literature on the subject. That, however, does not mean that they are incapable of killing small-game and other similar-size animals humanely.

There are many thoroughly valid points in favor of the modern adult air rifle in the role of a small-game hunting arm. Foremost on the list is the cost factor. You can purchase a tin of 500 good quality hunting pellets for little more than the cost of a box of 50 22-cal. rimfire cartridges. More and cheaper ammo means more shooting. Thus, it is possible to sharpen up one's markmanship to a fine edge with an air rifle, even at home. Since precise shot placement is quite important in this sport, the added shooting helps to take care of that.

Small game suitable for air rifles means mainly squirrels and rabbits. The latter are just about the upper limit for most air rifles at moderate distances, although larger animals can and have been taken by keen hunters under ideal field conditions, using the right rifle/pellet combination. Airgun literature of the past decade recounts at least one story, with photograph and all, of a hunter shooting—and killing—a full-grown bobcat with his high power pellet rifle. I personally cannot recommend the use of an air rifle to hunt bobcat, although I do not doubt for one second that a well-placed pellet in the head, from a magnum air rifle, is quite capable of killing such an animal.

Raccoon, possum, jackrabbit, and most small varmints can be hunted successfully with air rifles, if the hunter has the proper level of skill *and knows his weapon's limitations as well as his own.* On a few occasions I have killed rabbits at ranges of between 60 and 70 yards with a couple of my best spring-piston air rifles. Having said that, I must admit that field conditions were ideal, without even a hint of breeze, with the target fully exposed, my rifle highly tuned and precisely zeroed-in for the pellet type that I was using. Forty yards

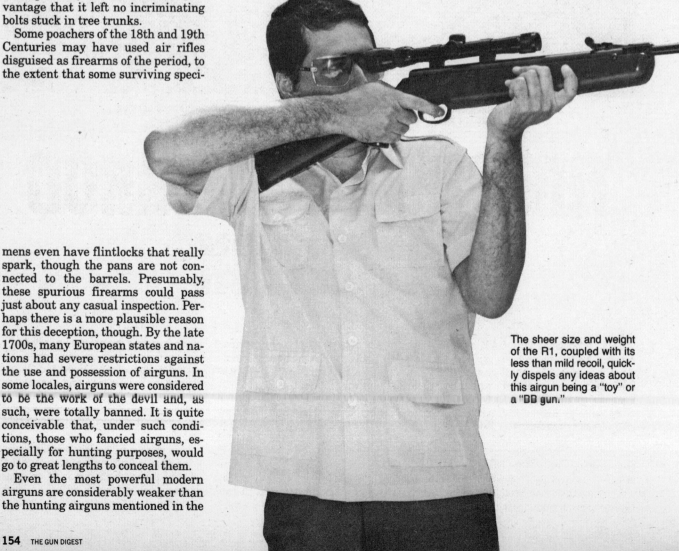

The sheer size and weight of the R1, coupled with its less than mild recoil, quickly dispels any ideas about this airgun being a "toy" or a "BB gun."

seems to be a more sensible *maximum* range under less than ideal field conditions.

Any arm that expels or throws a projectile has a practical range within which there is a high probability of inflicting lethal damage to living organisms, if hit in vital organs or kill zones. This principle applies to the bow-and-arrow, the slingshot and the elephant gun. As the range in a given case is stretched beyond practical limits, the probability of lethal damage diminishes until it becomes just a possibility. If the distance is extreme, this possibility is uncertain even with what normally would be considered a lethal hit.

In the case of air rifles, the principle applies. Modern magnum or high-power "adult" air rifles are being used with increasing frequency to bag small game, quietly and efficiently, at moderate ranges, and in areas where *any* firearm would be out of the question. This brings us to another point in favor of the air rifle in hunting as well as in many other sporting applications.

A few years ago, I used to hunt rabbits a good deal in a small wooded area flanked on two sides by private homes. The place teemed with cottontail as well as swamp rabbits which did much damage to the bean and vegetable crops bordering the wood along its southern side. The proximity of homes and people—about 100 yards from the edge of the wood to the first houses—ruled out the use of even 22 shorts. Yet, I could spend hours in the wood, *undisturbed and disturbing no one,* quietly popping bunnies, secure in the knowledge that there was no chance of a ricochet accidentally striking a house or a person.

There are three basic airgun calibers in widespread use for hunting today—the 177, 20, and 22. The 177 has

a much flatter trajectory than heavier 22 counterparts. The average 177 pellet weighs 8 grains, while the 22 caliber pellet weighs approximately 14 grains. Flatter trajectory means better long-range accuracy. It is often difficult to judge distance accurately afield, and the 22's more pronounced trajectory is not as easy to place in the kill zone of a rabbit or squirrel. That kill zone, incidentally, is about two inches in diameter for either head or chest shots on both animals. Most top-notch magnum European air rifles in 177 caliber are capable of grouping well within two inches at distances of 40 to 50 yards.

On the other hand, 22 air rifles can deliver up to 20% higher kinetic energy than 177's, although that difference is quickly reduced as the range increases. The 22 pellet has a higher ballistic coefficient than the 177 and decelerates at a slower rate than the 177, both in flight and on impact. Therein may be a hidden advantage of the 177—the faster deceleration means that energy is transferred quicker with the 177.

All of the above, and much more, is part of a raging debate among airgun hunters over which caliber is best for hunting purposes. Fans of the 177 bring out reams of data in support of their claims and 22 supporters will recount how their rifles bowl over rabbits more reliably than 177 counterparts.

A new and still relatively small group are the fans of the 20-caliber air

The R1 sports the clean, sleek lines that a top-quality hunting air rifle should have.

The makings of a fine meal, taken by a 22-caliber BSA Super Meteor, using a Silver Jet pointed pellet.

Surprised in the open, this bunny is about to jump.

rifle. The traditional Bantam 20-caliber pellet designed by Sheridan for their pneumatic rifles some 35 years ago has a much higher ballistic coefficient than most 177 and 22 pellets and is a proven game-getter. Until quite recently, however, the only rifles produced in this caliber were Sheridan's own pump up and CO_2 models. Excellent as those are, many hunters still shy away from pneumatic and CO_2 rifles. British and German airgun manufacturers are now becoming quite interested in developing their own line of 20-caliber rifles and we will probably see a proliferation of magnum models in this caliber, suitable for hunting, very shortly.

The level of kinetic energy imparted to the animal's body by the pellet is second only to accuracy regarding air rifles. We know that kinetic energy is a function of the mass of the projectile, times the square of its velocity. The latter value is the principal factor when it comes to the wound-producing ability of a projectile. Doubling the MV, for example, quadruples the muzzle energy; while doubling the weight of the pellet will only double its muzzle energy, assuming that the velocity stays the same.

Low as the muzzle velocities of even the "magnum" air rifles may seem, the pellets retain a high enough velocity at more than 60 yards to produce lethal wounds on squirrel, rabbit and, sometimes, even larger animals. Point of impact energy needed for a reliable kill on a rabbit-size animal is in the neighborhood of 4½ ft. lbs. In terms of pellet velocity, this means that an 8-grain 177 pellet must be traveling at 500 fps (feet per second) when it strikes the kill-zone of the animal. Based on that, a 177 rifle with a muzzle velocity of just 600 fps is quite capable of consistent kills on rabbits at 20 to 25 yards. The weight of the pellet is not nearly as important as impact velocity.

Pellet shape, on the other hand, is of great importance in determining the size and depth of the wound. Pointed pellets, like Silver Jet, RWS Super Point and Beeman Silver Sting, have much better penetration than either match pellets or round-head pellets. Because of this, the last two types should be used mostly on head shots to approximately 30 yards, while pointed pellets can be used for both head and chest shots at longer distances.

Pointed pellets produce superior penetration. They reach way in there, but do not expand much. I have recovered some from rabbits and found

These are some of the most powerful spring-piston rifles available today. From left to right: Beeman R1, HW 35, Beeman/FWB-124, BSA Airsporter S, Beeman/Webley "Vulcan," Dynamit-Nobel RWS 45, and Wischo 55N.

These are medium-power (650-730 fps) 177-cal. spring-piston rifles. From top to bottom: Sig-Hammerli 420, Lion (Chinese), Diana 50, Diana 35, HW 55T, and an older Hammerli side-lever rifle.

The importance of camouflage cannot be overestimated when hunting with air rifles. Every possible trick has to be used to full advantage. This rather rotund swamp bunny was bowled over at more than 20 yards by a 22-caliber pellet from a BSA Super Meteor. Telesight is a Weaver 4x20.

The lineup of current "magnum" pneumatic rifles available in the U.S. From left—Crosman 2200, Sharp "Innova," Benjamin 347, Sheridan "Blue Streak," Crosman Model 1, and Benjamin 3120.

they had bored right through tough muscle and sinew before reaching vital organs. I have also seen ribs and other bones smashed by those pellets in one-shot kills. Match pellets, on the other hand, deliver exceptional accuracy at short to moderate ranges (up to around 30 yards) and, because of their flat-faced wadcutter design, they transmit quite a bit of shock to the quarry. The traditional round-head pellet exhibits some mushrooming effect, coupled with satisfactory penetration. The Beeman Silver Bear pellet has a hollow-point configuration that ensures good expansion nearly every time.

What about the airguns themselves? The choices for the pneumonimrod are, fortunately, quite varied. For short to medium range work, say up to 25 yards, there are several spring-piston and pneumatic rifles. These guns are relatively inexpensive—most are under $150—reliable and provide enough power and accuracy to get the job done. At the upper end of the power-accuracy scale, there are excellent spring-piston models available in the U.S. Some, in addition to elevated muzzle velocities, are real tack-drivers. Their muzzle velocities usually are in excess of 750 fps in 177 caliber and at least 580 fps in 22 caliber. Fine workmanship inside and out is another common characteristic. Prices generally start at over $250.00 in this class.

Late in 1981, Beeman Precision Airguns, Inc., introduced a new air rifle made in West Germany, capable of delivering power hitherto unheard of in a modern production spring-piston rifle. The Beeman R1 produces a sizzling 900-940 fps in 177 and a smashing 700-770 fps in the 22 version. These figures translate into minimum muzzle energy levels of about 14 ft. lbs. and 15 ft. lbs. respectively. The R1, which is 45.2 inches long and weighs 8½ lbs., is an extremely accurate rifle besides. My own tests revealed that the R1 can group within 2½" at 60 yards with pointed pellets.

Despite its impressive accuracy, the R1 is simply not the kind of rifle you would choose to punch paper targets with. It commands a hefty 37 to 40 pounds of cocking effort and its recoil is definitely above average for a rifle of this type. It is doubtful many people would spend $289.50 to blast tin cans or other typical plinking targets with this gun.

Metallic silhouette shooters would find the R1 ideally suited to their sport, but there are spring-piston rifles of less power that are excellent silhouette guns. The R1 was created for something more—small-game hunting and pest control sure is beginning to get the attention of the adult airgun industry. This gun proves it.

Beside extreme power and superb accuracy, the R1 boasts a number of refinements. The trigger unit is match-grade, with a silky two-stage pull, adjustable for weight. There is an automatic trigger safety located on the left rear side of the receiver. The front sight is a tunnel that accepts different inserts, while the steel rear sight is fully adjustable for windage and elevation via micrometer dials.

The R1 sports one of the nicest, most elegant stocks I have ever seen on an air rifle. The standard stock is walnut-stained beech with a Monte Carlo style cheekpiece and cut checkering on the pistol grip. The rubber buttplate is set off by a thin white spacer, as is the pistol grip cap. Unlike the stocks of other break-barrel spring-piston rifles, the stock of the R1 extends all the way to the front of the breechblock, which is one of the reasons for this rifle's excellent balance and sleek profile. Beeman offers four different custom walnut stocks in addition to the standard version, for those who want the best and can afford the luxury.

The receiver of the R1 is grooved for a telesight mount. This is, of course, of vital importance in a hunting air ri-fle. A telesight will not make an air rifle more accurate; it will simply allow the hunter to utilize his rifle's inherent accuracy to the fullest, provided the scope is properly zeroed. Pellet placement is extremely important in air rifle hunting activity.

The introduction of the R1 could very well signal the beginning of another "race for power" among the leading European airgun manufacturers. The previous race began in the mid-1970s and gave us such high-power rifles as the Feinwerkbau 124/127, the Webley Vulcan, Diana Model 45, BSA Airsporter Super, and a couple of other spring-piston models generating over 800 fps in 177. Any of those models, by the way, packs enough oomph and accuracy to be used with confidence against small edible game, as well as against some varmints, at up to 40 or 50 yards.

Although the Beeman R1 comes quite close to the practical limits of the spring-piston powerplant, as far as the relationship of its physical size versus power output, there is still room for a bit more development. It may be possible to surpass 1,000 fps in 177 caliber in a *standard production* spring-piston rifle very soon; however, the pneumatic powerplant looms as the only viable solution to the development of air rifles with power levels unheard of in this century. Pioneering work in that direction is currently taking place in England, where a few individuals are producing custom-made pneumatic guns that exceed the power of the latest regular production pneumatic rifles by a wide margin. As far as regular production high-power pneumatic rifles go, the Japanese have the Sharp "Innova," which delivers over 900 fps in 177.

No doubt about it, the future of the airgun looks extremely bright. For hunting, it appears to be on the rise again, if only limited to small game. As more powerful models such as the R1 become available, the airgun carves its own secure niche in the sport of hunting. ●

Even a vintage air rifle in good working order, such as the 25-caliber Apache carried by author's brother, can easily dispatch small game efficiently, but the airgun hunter, regardless of his equipment, should let the game go if it gets the jump.

About the Author
This is that same J. I. Galan who has now written of air guns in three GUN DIGESTS *in a row, and that same Galan who last year revealed the new word "telesight" to* GUN DIGEST *readers, and who himself this year has produced the word "pneumo-Nimrod" and I can prove it.*

K.W.

HAND-LOADING TO DATE

by DEAN A. GRENNELL

O NE OF THE attractions of hand-loading is that it saves money or, perhaps, that it enables you to do a lot more shooting for the same amount of money. The potential savings have long favored the loader of the metallics—ammo for rifles and pistols—over the shotgunner who handloads. That is due to the fact that the center-fire brass case is a fairly expensive item to manufacture, coupled with the fact that many loaders of metallics manage to make their own bullets.

The shotgunner's empty hulls are comparatively inexpensive, and all of the rest of the components that go into the shotshell handload must be purchased. That might seem to leach away some of the motive for hand-loading shotshells, but it doesn't seem to do so, since shotshells continue to make up a substantial slice of the handloading market, as indicated by sale of such components as shotshell primers.

Sad to note, however, handloading is no longer quite the nickel-dime pursuit it used to be. Regard, if you will, the cost of the powder. About 20 years ago, several useful propellants could be purchased at retail for as little as a buck a pound, perhaps a bit less in the larger quantities. A shooters' emporium near my home at that time obtained large supplies of Hodgdon H4227 and dealt it out for one dollar the one-pound can. It was a good price, even by the inflationary standards of that era, and I've long been partial to that useful and versatile powder, so I bought heavily before the dealer's stock ran dry. This week, I opened my next-to-last can of H4227 with the old green and yellow label. Stopping at a nearby gun store a day later, I made note of the cost of a new can, and nearly dissolved in quivering shock. It was a bit over ten bucks.

Stop and think about it: How many things come to mind that have increased ten-fold in cost since, for example, 1962? Even the runaway flight of a first-class postage stamp is only five times what it was then; twenty cents against four cents.

My reason for visiting the store was

While not all powders have shown the same rate of inflation, all have gone up considerably. The can of H4227 at left sold for $1, about 1962, while the current packaging, at right, marked "Newly Manufactured," goes for a bit over $10. Many other reloading components have shown similar cost trends, suggesting that their purchase may be a good investment in terms of long-range appreciation.

that I needed some 7mm gas checks, for the first time in my handloading career, and none were on hand in the shop. The good news was the dealer had some. The jarring news was that a tin of one thousand cost $10.28, counting sales tax. It was cold consolation to reflect that, if the Fates are kind, I might consume the last of that batch around the year 2014 or so, by which time, we can extrapolate forty or fifty dollars to replace them. I base this on the fact that I've handloaded for thirty-two years or so without using or needing any 7mm gas checks, so a thousand of them should last and last and last.

The reason for this absurd but alarming state of affairs is that the price of copper, zinc, tin, lead, antimony and various other raw materials that go to make bullets, cartridges and gas checks have soared in a manner most berserk. The people who make and market such things are not getting rich in the lavish manner you might assume. Indeed, most of them are at least as concerned with the problem as you are, and as I am.

As if we need further worries, moves are under way to slap an 11 percent excise tax on reloading com-

ponents of every type. I suspect our views of that run remarkably parallel to each other.

Is there a message here? I think so. Look back, take note, and extrapolate. The trend is clearly apparent: Great yesterday, bad today, probably worse tomorrow. Instead of plowing all your surplus capital—brief pause, while the tumult subsides—into money market investments and the like, give thought to buying up reserve supplies of the reloading components you expect to need and want in the years ahead. Barring a major collapse of the economy—and, by no means, saying it couldn't happen—those cartons of primers, cans of powder, boxes of bullets, sacks of shot and so on are fairly apt to appreciate in value on a scale that will look good in contrast to most other investments available today. While you're at it, salt away a few cartons of rimfire ammo, too.

Last year, we noted that the Green Machine from **RCBS** was said to be nearing production and it turned out to be true. This is a progressive loader, with a pretty decent rate of output, once the reservoirs are filled and everything is working smoothly. Under those happy conditions, I can produce a 50-round box of 38 Specials in about six minutes. Production over the span of one hour would lag behind that, since you have to keep an eye on the magazine feed tubes, on the powder level in the measure, and on the primers in the feed tray, pausing to replenish the supplies from time to time.

The Green Machine produces a loaded round with each cycle of bringing the handle down and up to full stops at either end. On completing the up-stroke, you place a bullet in the port of the bullet seating die and that's the only manual operation, apart from pumping the handle. Currently retailing for about $500, the first models handle the 38 Special or, by suitable die adjustment, the 357 Magnum. By the spring of 1982, it's planned that case feed assemblies will be available for the 9mm Luger and, about early fall, for the 45 ACP.

The Ransom Grand Master is another progressive press recently introduced. Made by C'Arco, the firm that brought you the Ransom Rest, it retails for around $800, and can be had to handle just about any handgun cartridge apt to be reloaded in quantity, down to and including the 32 S&W Long. The Grand Master has a manually actuated case feed system, functioning by working a knob in a rectangular pattern. Cases are fed from a single plastic tube, topped by a hopper of ingenious design that somehow manages to direct all of the empty hulls into the tube, base-down.

Pacific, in the meantime, has brought forth a nice, no-nonsense reloading press, and it's a fine machine, called the OO7, or double-oh-seven. As with many others of today's presses, it features the compound toggle linkage, similar to Pacific's earlier Multi-Power C press. It has the convenient priming system of Pacific's Model O-7, and it allows the left hand to feed cases in, for removal by the right hand after the stroke. That is a feature that permits a conventional reloading press to be operated with gratifying speed and efficiency.

Lyman has a new press coming out. It's called the Orange Crusher and, in line with current trends, it features the useful compound toggle linkage, along with a working stroke of generous length to cope cheerfully with tall cartridges, such as the 8mm Remington Magnum. Speaking of Lyman, their long-awaited 46th edition of the *Lyman Reloading Handbook* is said to be in final boarding stage. It's been an extended hiatus, there, since the 45th edition appeared in late 1970.

Please turn to page 162

Turret Press

Is there a ray of sunshine in all this pall of thick and tenebrous gloom? As a matter of fact, there is, in the form of a brand-new loading press and a line of dies, new on the market since last year's edition appeared. In round numbers, the three-station turret press, with a powerful compound-toggle linkage, sells for $60; two-die sets for bottleneck calibers go for $20, and three-die sets for straight-sided handgun cartridges are $30 the set, including a tungsten carbide resizing die. All die sets are furnished with the appropriate shell holder, in a handsome and sturdy plastic storage cannister, along with a dipper-type powder measure and a card of data for its use with suitable powders.

Lee Precision is the source of these remarkable new items, directed by Richard J. Lee; my personal nomination as the Henry Ford of handloading. You'll perhaps recall his compact but competent little loading kits that sold for ten bucks in 1960 and gradually edged their way up to about twice that, today. The first of these were for handloading shotshells, with kits for metallic calibers following a few years later. The past few years have seen Lee Precision's venture into presses for shotshell handloading in the shape of the Load-All and Load-All Junior. The Lee Precision turret press rounds out this particular stage of the transition upward. As to what Dick Lee still has up his crafty sleeve for the handloaders of the world, I can only say you've not seen it all, yet.

In this vale of tears and sorrow, there is a perfectly natural tendency to be skeptical of the worth of anything priced substantially below typical figures. Thus, one is apt to wonder if a sixty-buck turret press is any good at all. With that in mind, I'll give you my first-hand impressions, for such value as you care to place upon them.

The operating handles of most of today's loading presses move through arcs of about ninety degrees. The Lee turret press goes closer to 180 degrees, but not quite. With the compound toggle linkage, that reduces the required effort for most handloading operations down to really ridicu-

Lee Precision turret press is lightweight, compact and powerful. Bolted to a piece of plank, as here, with the bolt heads countersunk flush with the lower plank surface, it can be C-clamped to any reasonably sturdy support, for field handloading, if desired. The handle of hard maple can be used, although leverage is more than enough to load most cartridges in easy comfort without the handle and the shortened stroke is a convenience.

lous levels. For example, as nearly as I can measure, the force required to resize a fired 30-06 case full-length in the Lee turret press runs somewhere between 12 and 14 pounds.

The stress upon the surface to which the press is mounted is proportional to that, which means that the Lee turret does not require a monolithically massive loading bench. Along the way, I've encountered some presses that did. Once, many years ago, I saved up and splurged for a new loading press that took my fancy. I bolted it to what I viewed as a decently sturdy surface and started to use it. About the second or third case through the new gizmo, the entire upper part of the bench self-destructed. On the second try, I concocted a mount that stood the gaff, but the press got swapped down the river before much

Spare turrets for the Lee Precision press are easily removable and can be left with dies installed and adjusted for rapid changes of caliber. The two-ended priming punch drops into the press base, neatly bypassing the plaguing problem of keeping track of one size when the other is in use.

(Right) Grennell built this mounting base for the Lee Precision turret press, with a discontinued Pacific powder measure added on. Weighing about 18 pounds, it can be taken to the range for on-site loading, and small items can be carried in the base.

longer, for the simple reason that it was easier than shoving the cases into the dies and pulling them out with your bare hands, but not a heck of a *lot* easier, if you follow? Understandably enough, that press is off the market, a long time since.

A further good feature of the Lee turret press is that the three-station turret snaps out of the top of the press, with extra turrets available at about ten dollars apiece. It uses dies with the conventional 7/8-14 threads, as well as the so-called universal shell holders. Thus, you can use it with loading dies you may have on hand from other makers, as well as with most shell holders. Some universal shell holders, I've ruefully noted, are more universal than others. The die locking rings supplied with the Lee die sets are rather small, six-sided, rather than knurled, with neoprene O-rings to hold them in place. Some die sets of other makes come with locking rings of girths so large that they won't fit the turret of the Lee press. I'm fairly sure that the smaller locking rings can be obtained from Lee Precision.

Meanwhile, for those calibers you load frequently, you can obtain spare turrets to fit the Lee press, install the dies, adjust them once and, as of that moment, the whole die set can be removed or replaced in scant seconds. Snap the appropriate shell holder in or out of the top of the ram and you have the capability to change calibers in less than one minute, with lots of time to spare.

Are you ready for one more unlikely feature? If you happen to be a southpaw by innate preference, you can convert the Lee turret press to left-hand mode by merely moving the handle from one side of the toggle block to the other, and by moving the front spacer brace from the right to the left side. No, if you were about to ask, Dick Lee is a northpaw, same as I am. The thing is, he's a *thoughtful* northpaw!

Given a press that's not only attractively priced but light in weight and modest in bulk, with the happy trait of needing no more than modest mounting rigidity, one speculates about loading at the shooting site. I've been conducting explorations into

these possibilities, with generally encouraging results. A packabout loading press has long been a wistful dream of mine, and feedback from readers suggests that many others share my interest. The Lee turret press is the most compatible machine along such lines that I've encountered to date.

My researches are still going on. So far, I've put together a reasonably neat little support base, capable of coping with the most stressful handloading operations. With the press, dies and everything installed, I can hold the whole shebang on the tips of two fingers. Try that with *your* loading bench! Ever the renegade, I included provisions to mount a tiny powder measure, once made by Pacific when they were in Lincoln, Nebraska. It is just a bit quicker and handier than dipping the charges, and sufficiently accurate that loads for the 45 ACP made up on it have grouped down around two inches at 50 yards off the machine rest.

But I do not regard even that as the irreducible minimum. I've another rig, in which the Lee turret press is just held to a small piece of two-inch plank, with the three mounting bolts countersunk from the underside, so that the plank can be attached to any handy surface with a pair of C-clamps. That rig can be installed on an unused portion of my portable shooting bench, and has been so used, with generally good results. I'm thinking of making up a zip-together mounting base for the plank-mounted press, as an alternative approach.

Likewise available from Lee Precision is a handsome and very durably made carrying case for the turret press, crafted of rock maple with impressive skill. This case can be drilled, and used to mount the press for routine use. By attaching three legs, you come up with a handy little mount that's well suited for handloading in the living room, while watching television, to suggest one possibility.

I nearly forgot to mention it, but the Lee turret press comes with a double priming arm, T-shaped, with punches for both small and large primer diameters. It drops into the base of the press for use, or plucks out, if you don't need it. When installed, it deflects nearly all of the expelled primers neatly into recesses in the press base for later disposal. I have always taken kindly to loading presses that do not litter the floor with spent primers.

Those who enjoy shooting the 25 ACP cartridge may wish to handload the wee round, particularly after pricing factory ammo for it. For quite a lot of years now, Lyman has made and continues to offer a pretty good bullet mould for the 25 auto, their No. 252435, at a nominal weight of 51 grains. Until this year, they've never made a lube-sizing die in the requisite .251-inch diameter, but it's available now. If you're partial to the Saeco lube-sizer, as I am, Saeco now offers dies in .251-inch, to handle the Lyman No. 252435, although Saeco does not plan to offer a mould suitable for that cartridge. For a few years along there, RCBS listed both moulds and dies for their lube-sizer in 25 ACP, but has deleted both in their current catalog.

Lyman continues to drop mould designs, with each annual catalog showing fewer and fewer. Bullet moulds are cut with a specialized and sophisticated reamer known as a cherry.

After some given number of mould cavities are cut with a cherry, honing it to fresh sharpness every so often, the cherry wears down and gets undersized, requiring replacement. If it is a design that has maintained good sales figures, they make up a new cherry; if not, the design is dropped. If you happen to own one or more moulds in some of those discontinued designs—as I do, I'm happy to report—you'd do well to maintain them lovingly, for the world will never see their like again, nor will you.

It has not been a year overly notable for the introduction of new bullet designs, in the area of factory-made projectiles. **Sierra** has four new ones: a 284/7mm spitzer boat tail weighing 140 grains in their Game King line; a 224/5.56mm spitzer with a thin jacket—which Sierra terms the Blitz—weighing 55 grains in their Varminter line, and two new handgun bullets in their Sports Master line. One is a 210-grain jacketed hollow cavity for the 44—neatly splitting the difference between their 180 and 240 entries. The other is a 140-grain JHC in .357-inch diameter, with a new feature Sierra terms the Power Jacket. This consists of longitudinally serrated jackets at the tip, to aid and encourage expansion. The PJ feature has also been added to three other models of their existing line: the 110-grain/.357-inch, and the 125-grain and 150-grain versions in the same diameter.

Quite recently, **Hornady** added a 90-grain swaged lead semi-wadcutter bullet for use in the 32 S&W Long cartridge, .314-inch diameter. As with other models introduced earlier, this has knurling around the base to carry the lubricant. Earlier, since last year's edition, they brought forth a remarkable new bullet for use in the 45 ACP. Designated the Combat/Target Match (C/T Match), it is a jacketed semi-wadcutter, roughly similar in general profile to the long-popular Hensley & Gibbs No. 68 bullet from their mould of that designation. The new 45 bullet, Index No. 4515, weighs 200 grains. A sheet of load data for its use, as well as another for the new 32 S&W Long bullet, is available on request from Hornady's Reloading Advisory Center, at their address given in the directory at the back of this

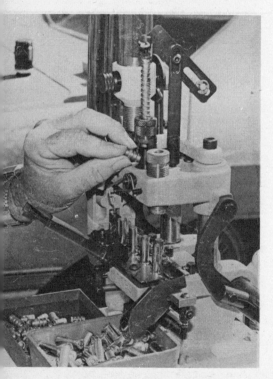

Apart from working the handle, the only manual operation on the RCBS Green Machine is insertion of the bullet in the side port of the seating die when the handle is at the upper end of its stroke.

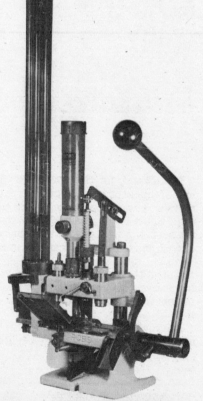

The RCBS Green Machine, a progressive loader, is now in full production for 38 Special and 357 Magnum, with 9mm Luger and 45 ACP versions to follow. Priced at $500, the Green Machine can turn out 50 rounds in six minutes without undue effort at achieving top speed. Accuracy of its output, in 38 Special with 2.7 grains of Bullseye and the 148-grain Speer HB wadcutter, is extremely impressive, comparing favorably with the better factory match loads in that caliber.

Expelled primers are neatly caught in this small plastic bottle, which must be removed and emptied occasionally.

year's edition. A recent updating of the third edition of the *Hornady Handbook* also carries a data listing for the new 45 bullet.

Speer has a new trio of Match bullets: a 145-grain 7mm boat-tail hollow point; and caliber 30 BT/HP designs weighing 168 and 190 grains. In addition, they have three more boat-tail spitzer points: a 100-grain 6mm/243; a 100-grain 257; and a 130-grain 7mm/284.

Midway Arms continues to bring forth Boxer-primed and eminently handloadable brass in persuasions that are pretty hard to put hands upon from any other source. The newest such entry is the 7.62x39mm case for use in the AK-47 assault rifle. Also fresh from the Midway oven is brass for the caliber 30 Broomhandle Mauser and its dietary contemporaries, such as the Tokarev. Midway also puts this forth in the form of loads, carrying an 86-grain full metal jacketed, round nose bullet.

The field of wildcat cartridges—the kind you have to make, because they're not marketed commercially—continues to teem briskly. J. D. Jones advises that the hot new parent cartridge is the 225 Winchester, for the sake of its rim and notably burly build. I'd tend to look askance at that one, because I've never owned either an empty case nor loaded round in 225 Winchester, which makes it a horse far deader, in my personal book, than even Winchester's tragically fated 256 Winchester Magnum. It's probably a great approach, as I'm inclined to take J.D.'s knowledgeable word on such matters—provided you can put hands upon the needed brass in suitable quantities.

For my part, I've been doing a lot of poking and probing at the 7mm T/CU; a wildcat based upon the 223 Remington case opened to .284-inch bullet diameter. Thompson/Center Arms offers barrels in the 7mm T/CU for their Contender single-shot pistol, in ten and 14-inch lengths and reports are that the barrels have been selling by the—well—by the barrel, and the bushel, hogshead, firkin, or what-have-you.

I can see why. I put a Redfield 4x pistol scope on my Super-14 barrel, in a set of Conetrol mounts, and have managed groups as clannish as .914-inch at 100 yards, firing off the bench. I own quite a number of rifles I'd be delighted to coax into grouping that well. The load was 32.0 grains of Hodgdon BL-C2 behind the 120-grain Sierra spitzer, but quite a number of other loads do nearly as well, and a load that approaches three inches at that distance is a rare thing.

As to powders and primers, the good news is that we still have—we hope—all the powders we had last year. The less-good news is that no new ones have appeared. Norma has changed distributors for their products, so it's anyone's guess as to what the availability of their powders will be in the months ahead. The lovely Alcan powders are gone from the market, and remaining supplies are tenderly hoarded, grudgingly expended.

The only new primer to report is the CCI No. 209 M. CCI says the M does not stand for Magnum. It does, however, carry a slightly larger charge of priming mix, and it needs to have charges listed for the CCI 209 reduced by ten percent. It's said to be more sensitive, producing superior ballistic uniformity. The latest listing of data from Du Pont carries a few loads for the CCI 209 M, and the new booklet from Hercules lists even more.

Most of the equipment formerly available, along with the components, can still be had, perhaps at greater cost. No one ever said it was supposed to be *simple!*

A jacketed semi-wadcutter bullet for the 45 ACP has been added to the line of Hornady bullets. Weighing 200 grains, it has shown exceptional accuracy and functioning reliability, making it a highly effective choice for Combat/Target Match applications. Load data for this new 45-cal. bullet has been included in recent reprints of the third edition of the Hornady Handbook.

The new CCI No. 209 M shotshell primers deliver improved sensitivity and more uniform ballistics. Carrying a larger cake of priming mix, they require reduction of the powder charges listed for CCI's No. 209 primers.

The 7mm T/CU cartridge, left, resembles a scaled-down 35 Brown-Whelen, right. Based upon the 223 Remington case, the 7mm wildcat handles bullets from 115 to 175 grains in weight, and is capable of holding 1-MOA groups off the bench in a scoped T/C Contender. Muzzle energies of nearly 1700 fpe can be obtained. The 7mm T/CU has won unusual popularity for a wildcat round, and a 6.5mm version, also designed by Wes Ugalde, is under consideration as a further offering in chambered T/C Contender barrels.

New from Lyman is their Orange Crusher loading press, here shown on their 1982 catalog, which is $2 per copy from the factory. Lyman also has a pair of new cartridge case tumblers of unique and nnovative design.

Midway Arms is now making Boxer-primed brass cases for the 7.62x39mm cartridge, as used in the AK-47 Russian assault rifle and other guns. The primer pocket accepts the large rifle diameter of primers, which makes it impractical to convert these cases into 22 or 6mm PPC wildcat benchrest brass.

The first Carl Zeiss prism riflescope in 1904 was mounted on a rod and the rod was attached to the receiver. The set-up did not quite permit sighting in the same position as with iron sights.

Pesky Americans would buy quality, but not 26mm tubes, so in Wetzlar they cut . . .

A New Slice of Zeiss

"IT STARTED IN 1846 with microscopes."

That's the way one of the Zeiss advertising brochures begins. From a comparatively simple but precision-oriented mechanical and optical workshop, Carl Zeiss, with the aid of his scientific partner, Prof. Ernst Abe, built a vast high-technology organization that is today a world leader in the optical and precision measurement industry.

However far removed you feel microscopes are from guns and shooting, it was through the experience gained in developing such optical systems that led to Zeiss' introducing their first riflescope in 1904. It was a prism design of only 2x magnification but it had two distinct advantages over the

other scopes of the period: the eyepiece was on the same level as the iron sights on the gun and it weighed only 14 ounces. Production of this design continued until about 1918.

Compact riflescopes as we know them today, more or less, didn't appear until 1920 when Zeiss developed multi-lens systems to allow higher magnification and greater light transmission. Standard offerings from Zeiss were 4x, 6x and 8x hunting

by HAROLD A. MURTZ

scopes. Variable-power scopes, thought by most American shooters to be a development of 1960's technology, were introduced in 1922—the world's first, and from Zeiss. These were regularly available in 1x-4x and 1x-6x models. It wasn't until 1936 that Zeiss brought out 4x and 6x "Featherweight" scopes with body tubes made of a non-corrosive, light metal alloy. They weighed 10 and 13 ozs., respectively.

Lens coatings, which can practically make or break an optical system, were developed by the Zeiss works in 1935. The anti-reflection coating process was first intended for industrial application, but was considered so important for military optics that the German government kept it secret for

Top view of the new line of Zeiss scopes, the C-Series, from left: Diavari-C 3-9x and Diatal-C fixed powers in 4x, 6x and 10x. All have rubber armored objective bells and rubber eyepiece ring.

carried their Z-Series one logical step further. In late 1981, Zeiss unveiled the C-Series line-up, designed *specifically* for American shooters. Four models are currently available: the straight-power Diatal-C 4x, 6x and 10x, and the Diavari-C in 3x-9x. These four scopes pretty well cover the bases for most any hunting needs.

In November, 1981, Carl Zeiss, Inc., invited a number of American gun writers to tour their West German facilities and use these new scopes on the target range as well as hunting in Spain.

In catering to American tastes in optics, Zeiss had to design four basic features: the tube diameter had to be 1-inch to conform to standard U.S. mounting systems; since only two reticle designs are really popular in this country they must be used—the "Z-Ple" (or duplex) and crosshair; in the variable model, the reticle must be non-magnifying; and whether it is necessary or not, the scope must be filled with dry nitrogen.

With those basic parameters set down, Zeiss engineers went to work to give us what *we* wanted, all at a price that wouldn't be too far out of line with American-made scopes. The bonuses the designers added made the package even more attractive:

The scope tubes are again a lightweight alloy of one-piece design. They are precision-drawn and have integral adjustment turrets to give one less place for possible leakage.

All of the gaskets used to seal the scope are precision fitted and are impervious to oil and grease and won't deteriorate with age.

Windage and elevation adjustments are stainless steel click-stop types with ¼-MOA intervals and precise repeatability.

All glass-to-air surfaces have Zeiss' "T-Star" multi-coating to give the best image brightness, contrast and color rendering possible. Zeiss claims that light transmission is over 90 percent with this coating.

Each of the four C-Series scopes has a rubber-armored objective bell and rubber-padded ocular lens cell. This makes good sense. The black rubber on the front of the scope not only protects the scope itself from dings and dents, it also helps prevent damage to other gear. Just as important, it serves, if you will, as a "silencer." Those shooters who have a tendency to "crawl" on the stock will appreciate the padded eyepiece and generous 3½" eye relief on all these scopes.

All the best intentions of the finest engineers in the world can be ruined,

5 years. Since that time, all Zeiss riflescopes have had coated lenses.

The World War II years brought an end to the commercial availability of Zeiss riflescopes and it took until 1964 before they were back on the international market. Hensoldt, a Zeiss subsidiary and well-known name in optics, did develop a sizable line of riflescopes and binoculars for international consumption between the war and the early '60s. Sixteen models with steel or light alloy tubes were offered in powers from 2.75 to 8, as well as two variable models.

The fourth generation of Zeiss riflescopes was introduced in 1975 with the "Z" series. This line of rifle optics incorporates all of the current-day lens technology, precision engineering and manufacturing expertise Zeiss can muster, but the designs are based on European tastes and needs. Standard features included constantly centered reticles and click-stop windage and elevation adjustments similar to that used on Zeiss microscopes.

The only drawback to this line of scopes is its European tradition: 26mm or 30mm tubes (different from our standard of 1″), extra large objective lenses, and reticles in variables that magnified as the power increased. Also, the Z-Series was prohibitively expensive for the average American shooter.

Realizing they just weren't reaching their intended, most-lucrative market—the shooters of the U.S.—Zeiss

however, if the actual manufacture of the product isn't carried out with equal attention to detail and precision. Many excellent designs and ideas have been rejected by the paying public because of shoddy workmanship.

The Zeiss company, dedicated to quality as it has always been, carries through their promise of superb engineering *and* manufacture. This was demonstrated to the writers on the Zeiss tour during the tours of each of the manufacturing facilities. The factories all looked as you'd imagine German plants to be—well organized, impeccably clean, and quality oriented.

One of the quality control tests *each* riflescope must pass is its ability to maintain zero despite rough handling and recoil. Each scope—not every third, fifth or tenth example—is clamped into a special jig and subjected to a force impact of 1000 G's, more force than that generated by 1000 rounds of 458 Winchester Magnum ammunition. The deviation of impact must be less than 0.7 MOA for Zeiss scopes. Those made by other optics firms showed a deviation of more than 3 MOA after the same test. (That's about 3 inches at 100 yards!)

Variable scopes have always been suspect of their ability to maintain a consistent point of impact (POI) throughout their power range. Once again, every Zeiss scope made and tested must provide a guaranteed shift in POI of *less* than 0.7 inches at 100 yards throughout the variable power range. That's about the diameter of a dime.

While few except silhouette shooters make a practice of running the windage and elevation adjustments up and down, the accuracy and repeatability of these adjustments are important. Zeiss's wear test of 100 click-stop changes is a tough one and the deviation of POI must not be more than 0.5 MOA. In comparison, the other makes so tested by Zeiss showed a deviation of up to 3.8 MOA.

Carl Zeiss engineers claim that riflescopes needn't be filled with the ubiquitous dry nitrogen gas *if* they are properly sealed. That's good reasoning and it's hard to fight. However, American shooters demand that their scopes be filled with this gas to prevent fogging so that's just what Zeiss is doing. After filling them with nitrogen, each scope is water-pressure tested to be sure there are no leaks.

Lens coatings, often a measure of optical quality of camera lenses, binoculars and riflescopes, are known by a number of names. Bluing, anti-re-

The writers in Europe got a really close look at two Zeiss factories, and processes for making all the various optical systems.

Zeiss Diatal-C 4x mounted on a Mauser Model 77 rifle in the excellent EAW mount.

All Zeiss riflescopes and binoculars have to pass a final quality control inspection. Here, a master inspector applies sophisticated bench optics to a finished scope.

flection coating, multi-coating and super-coating are just some of them. These coatings are ultra-thin layers of a low refracting fluoride that is applied under vacuum to all glass-to-air surfaces. Their purpose is to reduce light reflection and thus increase the amount of light passing through the lens system.

Zeiss began coating their optical systems in the mid-1930s. Their current process for binoculars and rifle-

scopes is called "T-Star" multi-layer coating. Depending on the type of glass, up to seven layers are applied to all glass-to-air surfaces to reduce reflections. Because of this, total light transmission has been increased to over 90 percent in Zeiss riflescopes and binoculars.

Just about any scope will give a clear, sharp and brilliant picture when you look at it in the bright lights of a gun shop. But, take one

This red stag helped Murtz prove the Zeiss system in the Toledo mountains of Spain. There were no complaints on optical quality.

Cut-away of a Diavari-C 3-9x shows the path of light and the 11 optical elements. All glass-to-air surfaces have the T-Star coating.

From left: Jon Sundra; Murtz; Rick Jamison; Jim Lagiss, (a Zeiss sales rep); and C. E. Harris. All managed to bag stags.

the excellent light-gathering qualities of the Zeiss optics. The Z-Plex reticles in our scopes made aiming quick and sure, even under the difficult conditions.

The new 7x42 binoculars we were issued for hunting were designed specifically for stalking, woods and mountain hunting. They provide a field-of-view greater than any other 7x42 binocular (160 yards) at a distance of 1100 yards. Those binoculars have crystal-clear sharpness from edge to edge of the viewing area, and they have the special B-eyepieces that allow eyeglass wearers to use them without removing the glasses, yet still get that same wide field of view.

These are the straight-barrel, roof-prism design with center and individual right-eye focus. The black rubber armoring, often copied on other makes, keeps the binoculars easy to handle in cold or warm weather. This soft cushioning also prevents damage to the binoculars as well as a gun or riflescope should they bang together during a hunt.

Personally, I've never used a finer pair of binoculars. Combined with the new Zeiss scope, a hunter should need or want nothing more in optical aids. With all of the quality and features built into these latest Zeiss offerings they will be tough to beat at any price. For the *serious* hunters these scopes could almost be considered "must-have" equipment on any hunting trip.

In the past, Zeiss products have been prohibitively expensive for the average hunter or shooting enthusiast, and some still are. The new C-Series scopes are not out of reach of most shooters, however.

Zeiss C-Series Riflescopes
Retail Prices, 1982

Diatal C 4x32	$295.00
Diatal C 6x32	$325.00
Diatal C 10x36	$375.00
Diavari 3-9x36	$495.00

Z-Plex or fine crosshair reticles only.

outside when the sun is almost down, or when there's a light fog, or in the early minutes of dawn or dusk, and that's when you'll see great differences in brands, and, that's when the Zeiss scopes really shine.

On the hunting phase of our trip to Spain, we had ample opportunity to use the Zeiss 4x32 scopes mounted on Mauser Model 77 rifles chambered for the 30-06 cartridge.

We were hunting European red stag

at Cazatur's main hunting area about 130 miles south of Madrid. This is low mountain country that is covered with thin fog and mist in the early morning hours. The stag were difficult to see with the naked eye, but once spotted with both the Zeiss scope and a pair of their new 7x42 rubber armored binoculars they stood out clearly, even in the poor light.

It was easy to choose a good trophy grazing in the high eucalyptus, due to

Would I buy one? Yes, because it just doesn't make much sense to short-change yourself on optics when you've already laid out big bucks for a fine rifle. Buying a Zeiss riflescope is like buying a piece of optical history and they've never been known to sell a second-rate piece of equipment. So I'd go that "extra yard" for the best scope you can buy, because from what I've seen that's pre-Zeiss-ly what you'll get.   •

If it's too big for one-hand use, and it's well-made and accurate and weighs six pounds, it's . . .

Preferred turkey-shoot position as described by oldtimers. Recoil toward face had to be watched, while holding close in an accuracy match.

The Ultimate Turkey-Shoot Pistol

by Ashley Halsey, Jr.

PHOTOS: CAROL BARKER

IMAGINE holding a six-pound weight 20 inches long at arm's length absolutely motionless.

Maybe you think it's easy, especially if you are a weight lifter or other form of muscle man.

All right, now imagine trying to sight through a small peep sight and hooded front sight mounted on that object.

You won't find it easy if you can do it at all.

What you'll be doing, if you do it at all, is shooting a monster percussion target pistol which represents perhaps the ultimate in turkey-shoot handguns of its time.

matches and the modern shotgun turkey shoots, however, there flourished another kind of target competition also called turkey shooting. It developed during the 1800s mostly in the backwoods of the eastern and midwestern United States. That locale lent it obscurity to this day.

These contests called for pistols, and what pistols! The huge handgun outlined at the start of this article was one of them, perhaps representing their maximum development. A few of these arms were flintlocks but most had percussion locks. That fact helps to date the heyday of the sport as the mid-1800s or later. Over the years, the pistols evolved into special target

This percussion weapon was regularly fitted and issued with a detachable shoulder stock. Yet, as a pistol without stock, it measured only 17¾ inches and weighed less than four pounds.

For those who like extra-big handguns or just statistics, the largest cartridge pistols now commercially produced weigh four to five pounds and measure little over 21 inches. All, by Remington, Weatherby, Wichita, are single-shot bolt action arms in rifle calibers.

Like today's huge hunting handguns, the big percussion match pistols required special techniques for their mastery. Fire them offhand with one

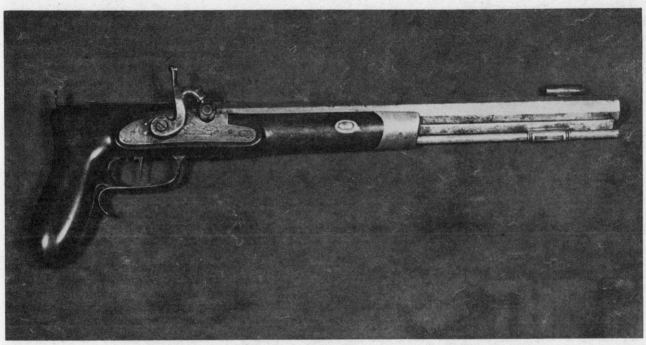

The "ultimate" form of turkey shoot pistol, 20 inches and six pounds. From rear peep to hooded post front sight, it offered an 18½-inch sighting plane—and also a challenge to shooters.

Today a turkey shoot means shotgunning, usually 12 gauge, on paper. Such matches are tremendously popular in many parts of the country. There are nine such regularly advertised in the mid-Virginia area where I live.

A century and more ago, turkey shoots were different. The contestants fired rifles, either offhand or from rest, at distances such as 15 rods or about 250 ft. The targets were live turkeys—hence the name of the matches—tethered or caged with their heads projecting. Inanimate targets like shingles with a charcoal center cross won preference later on.

Between the muzzleloader rifle

arms with characteristics of their own, notably double set triggers and sophisticated sights. The big six-pounder with its 14½-in. deeply rifled barrel typically has both double set triggers and target sights.

As many of the pistols originated with the same gunsmiths who made Pennsylvania or Kentucky long rifles, the early ones reveal such features as striped maple fullstocks, octagon barrels and rifle-style sights. Soon, however, they became more specialized and exceptionally—some might say excessively—large. Some surpassed in size the alltime mammoth of American single-shot military pistols, the Model 1855 U.S. pistol-carbine.

hand? Oh, it could be done, yes, but with competitive accuracy? Even if there were "giants in those days," one cannot help but have doubts. Certainly it was not a general practice. So how were they fired?

Fortunately, in my collecting and muzzleloader shooting more than a quarter-century ago, I came across an answer to the puzzle at about the same time that I acquired the big "ultimate" pistol itself.

The solution to the best way of holding and firing such oversized handguns was given me by Dr. Carl Drepperd, noted Pennsylvania Dutch historian and antiquarian. Carl descends from a long line of gunsmiths

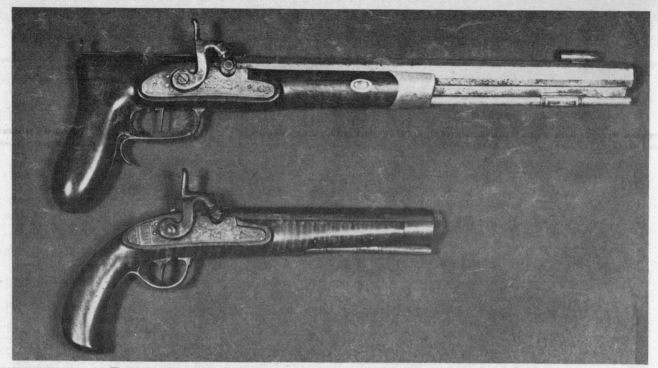

The big match pistol, perhaps the biggest of its kind, contrasted with an average size Kentucky pistol of the same period and caliber.

whose distinction included their "reversible" name: Read either front to back or back to front, it still spelled Drepperd. Carl told me he had seen the big pistols in action. He said, in sum:

The modern offhand position, using only one hand, was shunned even by the most ham-handed competitors.

The preferred stance called for bending the left arm, locking the left hand around the right elbow, nestling the long barrel in the crotch of the left arm, and firing from that solid position.

Alternatives, when permissible under match rules, included using the left forearm as a rest; supporting the long barrel in the left hand, rifle-style; employing a modern two-handed grip; or firing from atop a post or beside a tree.

The extreme muzzle-heaviness of most turkey-shoot pistols rendered a modern two-handed grip impractical for nearly all competitors even if permissible.

An impromptu jury of experts from the Pennsylvania Dutch country was unanimous recently in its verdict that the monster turkey shoot pistols demanded the use of both hands and both arms. Those voicing that opinion included Sam E. Dyke, of York, Pa., author of "Thoughts on the American Flintlock Pistol," essentially a summary of fine Kentucky or Pennsylvania handguns, and Vincent W. Nolt, proprietor of the Eagle Gun Museum

at Strasburg, Pa. Nolt's museum displays a late form of the pistol, 19½ inches overall with 14-inch barrel, weighing almost four pounds. It bears the signature of H. E. Leman, Lancaster, Pa., a noted late Kentucky maker, and has an under-hammer action. This places hammer and nipple beneath the barrel, thus keeping the shooter's vision clear of exploding cap and powder. The under-hammer was much used by New England gunsmiths. As for the Leman pistol, Nolt, an experienced muzzleloader marksman, comments:

"To hold this pistol without an arm rest, with any kind of accuracy, is next to impossible."

One of the earliest recorded examples of a handgun created for turkey-shoot matches evidently began life not long after 1800. In appearance it is simply an extra-long Kentucky or Pennsylvania pistol, fullstocked in the traditional striped maple. The lock, converted from flint to percussion, is stamped "A. Armstrong, Warranted." An Allen Armstrong is listed in a standard reference book as a Kentucky rifle and pistol maker in Philadelphia, Pa., "about 1800." This may well represent his craftsmanship.

Though only about two-thirds as heavy as the "ultimate" pistol we have described, the Armstrong is a whopper: 20 inches overall, 15-inch deeply rifled barrel in 34-caliber, and double set triggers, the strongest clue to its target identity.

By the time the turkey-shoot pistol reached its prime in the second half of the past century, targets of wood, paper or cardboard replaced live birds. The distance was most often 25 yards, subject to stretch upon demand. Hams were common prizes. The pistol matches were usually held in conjunction with weekend rifle events.

Characteristics of the big pistols varied by that time. Whatever their outward appearance, they usually shared some or all of the following:

1. Exceptionally large size, making them too big for traditional offhand shooting, duelling, or anything but the special matches for which they were designed.

2. Absence of shoulder stocks or provision for attaching them, thus setting them apart from pistol-carbines and target handguns which could be fired from the shoulder.

3. Some Kentucky-Pennsylvania pistol features such as octagon barrels and maple stocks, though walnut was much used.

4. Special target sights, especially on the later ones; early ones often had open rifle sights.

5. Double set triggers, a true rarity on muzzle-loading handguns in general but a distinctive feature of most turkey-shoot pistols.

The double set trigger consisted actually of two triggers. A pull on one set the other on hair edge. A flick could then fire the gun. Such mechanisms were widespread on rifles of the middle and late Kentucky-Pennsylvania period. Apparently they carried over to the turkey match pistols. They are not to be confused with the single set triggers found on fine muzzle-loading pistols, especially duellers.

Neither double set triggers nor large size, however, is sufficient to confirm that an early American single-shot handgun is a turkey-shoot piece.

A few Kentucky pistols with double set triggers must be regarded as duellers, not target arms. The duelling code called for smoothbores, though that was often ignored. A Kentucky flintlock pistol with double set triggers in the noted collection of the late William M. Locke almost certainly was meant for duelling, being a smoothbore. Also, duellers came in pairs. The brace of representative Kentucky pistols signed by maker "B. Bean", with 50-cal. octagon barrels and striped maple stocks, in the Tom Seymour collection, have double set triggers. But, being a pair, they no doubt were intended for duelling.

As for extra-large muzzle-loading pistols in general, few exceeded the size of those made by William Billinghurst, the Rochester, N.Y., gunmaker. When handgun match shooting was widespread in the 1850s, Billinghurst built target pistols with heavy octagon barrels 10½ inches to 16 inches long. Some were fitted with false muzzles and scopes in bench-rest rifle style; William Lawrence, Nicanor Kendall and others produced similar pistols in New England and upstate New York. All, however, came equipped with shoulder stocks so they could be fired rifle style, whereas the true turkey-shoot pistols were not.

The existence of enormous black-powder rifles for match shooting has long been recognized. Some of the bench-resters weighed 40 or 50 pounds or more. One of the grand old men of muzzleloader competition, the late Ned H. Roberts, traces this breed of rifle back before 1800. He terms them "turkey or match rifles"—but says nary a word about any companion pistols. His silence would seem to bear out the belief that the pistols represented a spinoff from Pennsylva-

A tree could be helpful, as was shooting from atop a fence post, but often these were not permissible positions under usual rules, however handy in the woods.

A forearm enabled the shooter to take a rifle-style hold if wished, but certainly did not make using the peep sight easy.

This alternative to the arm-crotch hold kept the pistol away from the face, but certainly did not make using the peep sight easy, either.

Patented peep sight by Van Kirk, dated 1860, adjusts for elevation by turning disc in front of it, but offers no adjustment for windage.

Double-set triggers like these are rare on a handgun. Engraved lock is signed "G. Goulcher," member of noted gunsmithing family coast to coast.

nia or Kentucky rifles and predominated in the Middle Atlantic-Ohio Valley area. Roberts, as it happens, was a New Englander.

The turkey-shoot pistol in any case represented calculated attempts over a period of time to create a special firearm for a special purpose. In final form, it embodied just the right elements for that purpose.

The big pistol that I regard as the ultimate in this evolution first "came out of the woods" many years ago near Philadelphia. It was in the hands of a bewildered little man. He resembled a cherub cradling a cannon. He had wanted to start collecting old guns, he

explained, and someone told him to begin by buying a Kentucky rifle. But was this, he asked, a Kentucky rifle? The artful rustic who had sold it to him assured him that it was—"See the octagon barrel, the brass trigger guard, them two triggers. . . ."

Several experienced collectors, sometimes a merciless breed, later laughed in his face and jeered that he had bought a monstrosity, a hybrid neither rifle nor pistol. His real dismay began when some wag warned him that his prize might violate a Federal law against machine guns and bazookas. Not being entirely innocent or stupid, he knew the piece

wasn't a machine gun. But a bazooka? By then they had him so confused that he was half ready to believe it.

At that point they piled on the menacing thought that the Federals, if they were out to get you or just to run up a string of arrests, sometimes stretched the definition of the law beyond all ordinary belief. Some quiet bystander who had been watching the fun moved forward about then. In the kindliest manner, he offered to relieve the little man of his embarrassment and his gigantic handgun. I acquired it several owners later from a local gun fancier who knew approximately what it was and indulged him-

Old Pistol 'Only One Legal'

COLUMBIA—Sol. B. O. Thomason Jr. of Greenville (left) and Ashley Halsey of Columbi eapons enthusiast, hold a 100-year-old oversized target pistol that they say is the only o eeting requirements of antiquated South Carolina laws. They spoke at a Tuesday legislati ommittee hearing in Columbia.—(AP Wirephoto)

The big pistol "testified" against an antiquated gun control law, since repealed.

self in gorgeously inflated ideas of what it was worth. The necessary deflation once accomplished, it became mine.

Once past the collector's love-at-first-sight, I submitted my acquisition to cold scrutiny. The big octagon barrel, 14½-inch by ⅞-inch across the muzzle, gauged 36 caliber on the lands and showed deep seven-groove rifling with a slow twist. Furniture or fittings consisted of a rather handsome pewter nosecap, a single forearm wedge put through German silver escutcheons, and a brass trigger guard with spur to steady the hold. The stock was American walnut. The engraved percussion lock bore the name "G. Goulcher" in a ribbon. Generations of Goulchers or Golchers, from Philadelphia in the 1770s to San Francisco in the 1880s, are identified with American firearms. In all likelihood, however, G. Goulcher furnished only the lock of this one.

Whoever manufactured the pistol blessed it with an 18½-inch sighting radius by mounting the rear sight at the very back of the piece. That sight, a peep, adjusted for elevation by means of a small brass disc with milled edge operating a vertical screw. The disc is lettered "Van Kirk & Co., Patent July 17, 1860," a date clearly indicating manufacture after 1860. The sight lacked windage adjustment. The front sight consisted of a pinhead post, hooded. As additional evidence that the pistol originated as a target arm, it was fitted with double set triggers. These and the lock proved to be in good working order.

Temptation soon stepped in. Finding the answer to "How does it shoot?" has converted innumerable collectors at least temporarily into shooters. Being already a shooter, I readily succumbed.

One spring day more than 25 years ago, Paul Nichols, of Jenkintown, Pa., and I took the big handgun out on the Bucks County (Pa.) Fish and Game Association range. We sortied for a minimum test, not an endurance performance. Paul, a human gun turret in his prime, fired the monster offhand with one hand. In doing so, he demonstrated that few could match his mighty arm or iron hand. I used the elbow crotch position recommended by Drepperd. We varied the load of 3F blackpowder: First 30-gr., then 20, then 18-gr. twice.

With three load variations and two shooters firing from different positions, we got off four shots at 25 yards. The "string," or shortest distance between the four centers, measured scarcely two inches. All factors considered, the old pistol really could deliver.

Not only did the big pistol respond with good accuracy as a firearm, it also earned the distinction of becoming a silent lobbyist againt gun controls. Without firing a round, it helped to strike down a silly state handgun law in 1965.

The state was my native state of South Carolina, which an eminent Charleston anti-secessionist, James L. Petigru, described before the Confederate War as "too small for a nation and too large for a madhouse." The objectionable law smacked of the madhouse. Enacted before the turn of the century, it flatly outlawed all handguns except those exceeding 18 inches and four pounds. To get it repealed, we trotted out the big turkey-shoot pistol and held it up before a legislative committee as "the only legal handgun in South Carolina." The pistol so entranced the committee that it paused in its deliberations to admire and handle it. The legislature later repealed the obnoxious law.

Like a winning racehorse put out to graze, the giant old target piece was thereupon "retired." It had proved twice over, on the range and in legislative halls, that it could hit the mark. ●

SCOPES AND MOUNTS

You aim with the reticle

by BOB BELL

EVERY TELESCOPE intended for use as a sighting device has within it an aiming unit. Without one, that expensive glass sight on the top deck of your whitetail walloper is just another terrestrial telescope, handy for examining a distant target, but of no use whatsoever for putting a bullet into it.

For a projectile to hit a pre-specified target, there has to be some way to make its path coincide, within acceptable error, with the shooter's line of sight. Since the bullet's path is invisible to the shooter and is controlled by forces which are largely beyond his control, to hit he must have a reliable reference point. This point must be moveable, so that it can be shifted into the desired relationship with the bullet's path (revealed during preparation for a hunt by impact holes in a target), yet once adjusted it must remain constant in relation to the telescope, so that the shooter can be confident of where the bullet will strike. Such an aiming unit nowadays is called a reticle*, and scope reticles are what this article is about.

As mentioned, the reticle is located within the scope tube, but it cannot be stuck in there just anywhere if you want to see it. The only place it will be perfectly visible is in the focal plane of some lens or lens system—a place where the light rays entering the scope are assembled into an image. In

a hunting scope, this means either the objective or ocular lens.

Admittedly, the reticle can be seen if the image does not strike *exactly* on it. Most times it doesn't in a low power hunting scope which is focused at a compromise distance of 100 or 150 yards. This lack of perfect focus results in what is called parallax—the apparent movement of the reticle when the head is moved while the rifle is motionless. Because the image falls slightly ahead of or behind the reticle, moving the head introduces an angle in the line of sight and the reticle seems to jump. In scopes which can be adjusted for range—the target models and the higher-power varmint designs, generally—lenses can be moved so that they focus precisely upon the reticle. This eliminates parallax at that one distance, but it is present, to some degree, at all others, as with the hunting models. If the shooter's face is always in the same position on the stock, and his eye in the same relation to the scope, parallax effects do not appear, of course.

Before variable scopes became common, the reticles of most hunting models were placed in the focal plane of the objective lens. This placement was continued in early variables. Because the lens shifting which altered magnification took place behind the reticle, the reticle's size varied directly with scope power; that is, if the power was switched from 4x to 8x, say, the reticle appeared twice as large. Actually, because the image grew at the same rate, the reticle did not subtend any more target at top power than at bottom, but it seemed to because it was twice as conspicuous to the shooter. This annoyed most users and many of them complained.

The reticle was later placed in the focal plane of the ocular, where it was unaffected by any shift in magnification. Now the apparent size varied inversely with magnification: as power went up and the target got larger, reticle subtension got less, and vice versa. This gave a coarse, conspicuous reticle at low power—ideal for fast use on big game in the woods—and a fine reticle at top power—as preferred for precise aiming on big game at long range or for varmint shooting.

Changing the reticle position has some drawbacks. As long as it was in the plane of the objective, the reticle and the target image remained in the same relationship to each other regardless of power switch. The moving lenses were behind them and therefore saw both reticle and target as a single image. However, when the reticle is behind the power changing unit, any imperfection as it is moved bends the target image away from the reticle, altering the zero of the rifle.

Since movement between adjacent surfaces requires some clearance, there must be *some* imperfection in any variable scope of this type. It can be found by firing successive groups at each power with the scope mounted on an accurate rifle, or by watching the crosshairs intersection against a collimator's grid with the rifle in a vise. Errors in some early inexpensive variables were horrifying, with the intersection sometimes following an S-track which could give an impact spread of 6-8 MOA. By comparison, errors in today's best quality variables often are so small they're hard to see in a collimator. It always pays to check, as they are not necessarily the same in successive scopes off the assembly line.

*A few decades back the common term in this country was "reticule," whereas in England "graticule" was preferred. Reticle and reticule both derive from the Latin *reticulum* (network), graticule from *craticula* (fine latticework), also Latin. The three are obviously synonymous, so the only advantage of reticle is that it saves a letter or two. This is important to some editors.

So now I suppose we agree that a reticle is necessary in a hunting scope and we have some idea of where they are placed and why. All of which brings us to a discussion of what they look like. For our purposes, these are the crosshair, crosshair and post, Duplex, center dot and minor variations of all of these. We won't deal here with the comparatively recent assortment of reticles seemingly engineered to serve first as rangefinders and second as aiming points.

I don't know which reticle type was installed in the earliest scopes. I'd guess it was the crosshair.* In Franklin Mann's *The Bullet's Flight,* written before World War I, he mentions a 16x Sidle scope fitted with fine crosshairs. There were earlier scopes, of

mately an inch at 100 yards—for big game hunting with a low power scope. In high power varmint and target scopes, crosshairs are often so fine you can hold on a 22-caliber bullet hole.

The address of the manufacturer might have something to do with crosshair diameter. Just after World War II, the crosshairs in some of Weaver's brilliant K-model scopes were so fine they were difficult to see in Pennsylvania's wet, gloomy deer woods, though they doubtless worked perfectly in the clear desert environment outside El Paso. I got the impression these were enlarged later, at least in the scopes delivered to my part of the country.

Though the simplicity of the crosshair could not be improved, some

variable if the 6-minute separation came at the top power—the setting which would normally be used for rangefinding—they put one into a V7 and sent it along. I used it for some years with perfect satisfaction before giving it to a friend.

Such a unit serves much the same as Keith's. However, instead of moving the bottom wire so the far zero comes at a specific range, you determine by shooting where bullet drop coincides with the lower intersection. This is done after zeroing conventionally with the top wire, of course—usually up 3 inches at 100 yards, which takes care of things up to 300 yards or so with most of today's hopped-up loads.

An interesting and useful variation

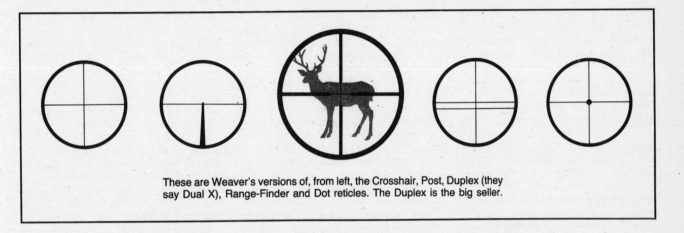

These are Weaver's versions of, from left, the Crosshair, Post, Duplex (they say Dual X), Range-Finder and Dot reticles. The Duplex is the big seller.

course, but I haven't found any earlier reference to a reticle. To me, the simplicity and efficiency of the crosshair would have made it a natural choice. As Warren Page once wrote, "Your Aunt Susie would automatically dab the intersection on the target, without the slightest instruction; but she must be told how to use the post."

One problem with crosshairs is getting them heavy enough to be conspicuous in poor light, yet not so thick that they blot out too much of the target at long range. The latter is rarely a problem on big game, but can be on varmints. The experience of countless riflemen suggests a diameter which subtends about one MOA—approxi-

hunters believed they could benefit from a variation—a second horizontal wire beneath the primary one. This would serve as a long range aiming point and, if the angle of subtension between the two wires were known, along with the approximate withers-to-brisket measurement of the game being hunted, it would be a basic sort of rangefinder.

In *Keith's Rifles for Large Game* (Standard Publications, Inc., 1946), Elmer mentions having double lateral wires in a Lyman Alaskan, one wire being adjustable by clicks, the other by screw. This permitted him to zero his 334 OKH at 300 yards with the top wire and at 500 with the bottom one. This gave two precise zeroes, and if checked out for separation could serve as a rangefinder.

For some years, Weaver offered their double-horizontal wire Rangefinder reticle in various straight-power scopes. These wires had a 6-minute separation and moved as a unit. When I mentioned in a GUN DIGEST article that this would also be useful on a

of the crosshair was the design introduced by Bausch & Lomb in the mid-'50s. It was a tapered crosshair, very fine at the intersection and enlarging toward the outer ends. This reticle was a metallic deposit on an optically plane lens.

In variables of small power range, such as B&L's earlier 2½-4x BALvar, conventional crosshairs had worked okay, but going from 2½x to 8x meant an apparent enlargement of over three times, a distinct annoyance. So the B&L designers came up with this tapered design, which worked very well, though their published claim that it didn't change in apparent size with a power switch just wasn't true. To my eyes, the intersection at 2½x was too fine, especially in dark woods, while it was just about right at 4x or 6x, and a bit heavy at 8x.

The field reduction at top power obliterated the heaviest portions of the reticle, and this helped maintain a similar view at all powers. The tapered lines, pointing at the intersection, helped rapid aiming. The same

*Neither do I know why these are called cross*hairs.* It's probably because their fineness suggests hairs to a new or casual user. Practically all so-called crosshairs are actually wires; some are etchings or metallic deposits on a plane lens. I have read that occasional riflemen experimented with individual hairs of lynx fur or whatever (sometimes with a knot tied to resemble a dot!), but this seems like doing things the hard way. No matter; for custom's sake, we'll go on calling them crosshairs in this article.

design was later used in the BALvar 6-24x, a big target job favored by many competitive shooters.

Another crosshair variation was Weaver's Multi-Range in the V8 scope. This had three vertical and three horizontal wires—conventional crosshairs bracketed by another pair—to give an assortment of aiming points and maybe some reference points for wind or lead or whatever. The whole thing had a transparent yet complicated look to it, and it didn't last too long.

Crosshairs are so satisfactory overall that it's hard for me to understand the popularity of the post, but for decades it was recommended by many American gunwriters. I've always thought this the military training of most of them—the post resembled the blade front sight of an '03 Springfield. (Or maybe medium-grade military brass have always seen things in a different way than most people.)

Anyway, a post is conspicuous in bad light or if the shooter's eyesight is poor. The sides of some are tapered, others parallel; the top can be blunt, pointed, flat, or some silly shape. I like the tapered flat top best, if I have to use a post, because it draws my gaze to the top and the flat surface there makes a consistent aiming point. The addition of a horizontal crosswire helps to prevent canting and makes a natural reference when swinging on running game.

One interesting variation was Bushnell's Command Post. This was primarily a crosshair, but flipping a tiny lever in the windage turret raised a post to cover the bottom half of the vertical wire. Interestingly, its

top came just level with the horizontal wire, rather than projecting above as most posts do. I liked that because it meant the aiming point was where the eye naturally expected to find it, instead of sticking up there by its lonesome as in most post-crosshair combinations. The only reason I can think of for having a post project above the lateral CII is that knowing the amount it extends can make it possible to use in estimating distance. Usually, though, this doesn't work too well because the post covers so much of an animal at long range, the primary disadvantage of this reticle in the first place.

When it came to posts, the Germans almost had a corner on the market, of course. They used lots of 'em—usually at least three, but the four-post unit also was common, with one entering the field from each of the cardinal compass points. Quite often each was pointed, the points sometimes snuggling into a neat little nest, at other times sitting back coyly, attached by crosshairs—doubtless the ancestors of today's Duplex reticle. Even that wasn't complicated enough for some designers, for occasionally the intersection was decorated with a center dot.

To give the Germans their due, though, we must admit that when they didn't get too carried away with things, those big ol' posts in 6x or 8x Zeiss, Hensoldt or Kahles scopes did the job for which they'd been designed. For their type of shooting— usually from man-built treestands, at slow-moving or motionless game at dawn or dusk—a conspicuous reticle was absolutely necessary and they

created a near-perfect unit for this. My first experience with one was during World War II when I acquired a 3-post 6x Zeiss Zielsechs. . . .did I ever mention that before?

Anyway, that brings us to the center dot reticle, for the first thing I did when I got that Zielsechs home in '46 was have Tackhole Lee replace those fenceposts with a 1¾-minute dot so I could use it on a 257 chuck rifle. Other companies installed center dots later on, but it was T.K. Lee who popularized them in this country and who is still the man who comes to mind when this design is discussed. He's gone now, but Dan Glenn continues to install Lee Dots in most any size and number you want.

The center dot is, if anything, even more natural to use than the crosshair. What else would anyone seeing one in a scope do except put it on the target? There it is in the center of the field—all you do is paste it on the target and touch the trigger. A dot of known size also serves as a rangefinder.

Lee Dots can be made to subtend almost any amount, from ⅛-minute in high power scopes to 12 minutes, perhaps more, in low power models. One of the most important things is choosing the best size for the job. It must be large enough for instant visibility under the poorest light conditions, yet not so big that it will obscure the aiming point at long range.

This isn't particularly difficult in a big game scope. A 3 MOA dot in one of today's bright 4x scopes is visible in wet, gloomy hemlock woods, yet covers only 12 inches at 400 yards, so doesn't even cover the chest depth of a whitetail or pronghorn at that distance. The same size at 4½x in a small variable grows to 9 minutes when set at 1½x, thus is immediately visible for fast, short-range shooting. I have that size in a Weaver V4.5 and it has worked perfectly for many years, as has a 6-minute dot in an old Norman-Ford 2½x Texan.

Some might think these are on the big side, but after 35 years of dot use, I've concluded that the commonest mistake is getting them too small in low power scopes. For instance a 2-minute dot in a 4x Lyman is sometimes difficult to find in the deer woods, as is a 4-minute dot in a K2.5.

Veteran 30-06 shooter Bob Wise deigns to try Zeiss scope though it's mounted on 7mm Magnum. A stock-crawler despite years behind a Springfield, Wise manages to get the full field in this rig.

Bob Bell's investigations take him thousands of miles, this time all the way to El Paso and the Weaver factory where he actually sits down and tries the test gear with Bill Schearfl's help.

Both would work perfectly in desert country, of course, so consider the environment when making a choice.

Anyone who hasn't considered the subject might think there is no significant difference between a 2-minute and a 3-minute dot, but there is. The 3-minute dot is not merely 50 percent larger, as it might seem. Areas of circles don't vary in proportion to their diameters, but as the square of their diameters, so the relationship here is as 4 to 9, which means the 3-incher has 225 percent as much area as the 2-incher.

Varmint and target scopes usually run 8x to 24x or so, and tend to be used on smaller aiming points and under better light conditions than big game scopes, so smaller dots are usable. The half-inch dot which would be nearly invisible in a 2½x is perfectly usable in a 12x, and a benchrester can use a quarter-inch or smaller dot with good results.

A second dot installed a given number of minutes beneath the center one can serve as a rangefinder as well as a long-range aiming point. In fact, Glenn can put in a series of dots for extreme range shooting if the user can specify the spacing. However, this

is not a cure-all for long-range hitting problems; bullet path changes with temperature, humidity and other conditions, and what you can see changes with ambient light, and the wind is always with us.

For those who want a dot that isn't a dot, the open or hollow style is occasionally offered. This is a small circle which permits aiming through it. It takes some getting used to and I was never comfortable holding over with it at long range, but it does let you see your aiming spot at normal range and it's fast.

Under the worst light conditions, a dot can be hard to see as it has much smaller total area than a post and no visible crosswires to show up in light portions of the field and guide your eye to the center. To solve this complaint, some years back Bushnell offered a 4x which could project a dot of light onto the crosshairs intersection, for early morning or late evening shooting. It was a bit unusual to see in the tube, but it worked. If you could see your target at all, you could aim at it. Would have been a useful rig on an '03-A4 back in '45.

And then there is the Duplex. From all indications, this is the most popu-

lar reticle currently made, and deservedly so. It combines the best qualities of the multiple post (in this case four of 'em) and crosshairs. Leupold introduced the design in the early '60s, and the advantages were immediately obvious to many shooters. In the Duplex, medium-width posts project into the scope's field from 12, 3, 6 and 9 o'clock. They don't meet; instead, they are connected by crosshairs. The posts, of course, are visible in any shooting light and direct one's gaze at the center. There, the crosshairs provide a precise aiming point which does not block out any significant part of the target at any range. The best of all possible worlds, as Voltaire would doubtless put it, were he alive today and a rifleman.

It's easy to trace the Duplex's ancestry to Middle Europe, but that's neither here nor there. The important thing is that Leupold saw the advantages of this type, improved it, made it available, publicized it and, we hope, is profiting by it. Others are, too, of course. I can't think of an American scope maker who doesn't offer a Duplex reticle. They call 'em by other names—Center Range, Plex, Multi-X, 4-Plex, Quadraplex, 30-30, Dual-X, Thick-N-Thin, and doubtless others— but they're all basically the same. And since Leupold started the whole thing off here, and they call theirs the Duplex, that's what I use as the generic term.

Despite their similarities, Duplex reticles from different manufacturers are not identical. Nor, in a sense, are even those from the same manufacturer, for the angular distance subtended by the crosshair section of different scope models is different. And of course it changes with every power switch of any variable power glass, according to how the field varies.

For instance, the space between opposing horizontal posts in Kahles scopes intended for use in Austria corresponds to a span of two feet at 50 yards—what they consider to be the length of a normal roebuck from breast to rump. It's been a long time since I shot a roebuck, but I remember them as being somewhat larger than this. Maybe they grow bigger in Germany. For non-Austrian use, this space in Kahles scopes is two feet at 100 yards.

A quick check of several American scope makers' literature indicates different ideas as to what this should be—or else they're just haphazard, with no intention that they be used as a rangefinder. The following specs are those given for assorted scopes; measurements are inches (rounded off) of subtension between opposing posts at 100 yards:

FIXED POWER

	2.7x	4x	6x	12x
Burris	22	18	11	6
Leupold	00*	10	9	5
Redfield	32	22	14	6

*Leupold 2.5x Compact

VARIABLE

	1.7-5x	2-7x	3-9x
Burris	39-14	27-9	237
Leupold	34-12	22-9	16-7
Redfield	42-16	33-11	27-8

What this suggests, and it would be even more obvious if we listed more scopes, is that anyone accustomed to using a Duplex as a rangefinder in his Burris can get into trouble if he switches to a Redfield and assumes the reticles are identical. Or vice versa.

Besides the differences in "thin section" measurements, another variation in the Duplex should be noted. This is a two-diameter version of the posts themselves, in which they step down to a thickness about midway between that of the outer portion of the posts and the crosshairs themselves. Personally, I find the jog in there more distracting than helpful, but some users like it.

Both the conventional Duplex and the stepped-down version provide long-range aiming points. It's obvious that once a bullet passes the conventional crosshair zero range—200 to 300 yards, depending upon the load—it will be falling below that line of sight. It's just as obvious that out yonder its path will coincide with the top of the 6 o'clock post, but just where depends mostly upon average velocity and the measurement between the crosshairs and post. Any calculated approach should be verified by shooting, but the "post top" range *can* be determined and it can be very useful as it will probably be at about the maximum distance anyone should ever shoot at game.

Knowing how many inches a reticle, or part of it, subtends at a given range, and the approximate size of some usually visible part of the game being hunted, such as body depth, can give a reasonable suggestion of shooting distance. Obviously, animals vary in size and there is imperfection in the visual comparison, but use of a reticle in this way can help a shooter avoid gross error in range estimation. This can be especially important when an

TWILIGHT TEST

A new Zeiss 4x scope arrived after our hunting season, so there was no chance of using it on game this year. I was interested in the high light transmission, so did some field comparisons with three other 4x scopes of similar size but having different reticles—a Lyman AA with 2-MOA Lee Dot, a Bausch & Lomb BALfor B with crosshairs, and a Schmidt & Bender with 3-post/crosshairs German reticle.

My typing desk faces a window overlooking the backyard. Beyond a lawn are dense clumps of hemlocks, pines and assorted other trees. It was a simple matter to place a blanket on the window sill and, as darkness approached, repeatedly look into the dark evergreens with each scope. There were still some patches of snow

on the ground at this time.

It quickly became obvious that the first limiting factor, insofar as shooting would have gone, was reticle design. Even when the Lyman had enough light-gathering ability to reveal considerable detail in the dark shadows—shadows which were just a gray-black area to the naked eye—I could not have aimed with it because that small dot had simply vanished. Next to disappear were the crosshairs of the B&L, though parts of them could still be seen against lighter areas after the intersection was absorbed in darkness.

At this stage, the Zeiss Z-Plex and S&B's posts were still conspicuous and the crosshair intersections still usable. About here, the 2-minute dot could not even be seen against a large

patch of snow some 35 yards away. Its area was just too small for use in such dim light—which admittedly was very dim, close to dark. I continued looking through the Zeiss and S&B until it was impossible to make out anything among the hemlocks. Everything was darkness except a grayish circle seen through the scopes.

Even now the posts of each reticle were visible, though the CH intersections could not be seen and it would have been literally impossible to make out any animal among those trees. In other words, these reticles apparently have more visibility than is actually usable, unless perhaps you are looking at a large animal in a meadow or field where its tone contrasts with the background. Personally, I think that's too late for shooting,

This is the Zeiss version of a Duplex reticle, somewhat heavier, and with more post and less crosshair than most American Duplexes.

except in a true emergency. Interestingly, the Zeiss Z-Plex was for all practical purposes as visible as the Schmidt & Bender's posts, though the latter are approximately twice as thick. This indicates a Duplex-type reticle is usable in any light where an animal can be seen in the scope, and thus the thicker German-type posts add no practical value in these circumstances.

Admittedly, such a test is informal and does not necessarily give results comparable to those obtained on an optical bench. Nevertheless, the conditions were similar to those which a hunter often encounters and might be more understandable than a report coming out of a laboratory. If nothing else, they illustrate the value of a Duplex-type reticle.

eastern woods hunter, used to a damp, dark, heavy atmosphere, makes his first trip to the high Rockies. There's often a feeling of complete inadequacy when first viewing an animal on the far side of an alpine meadow, and rightly so. What a Pennsylvania whitetail hunter thinks is 350 yards can well turn out to be 500 or 600 and that makes a difference in where to hold. Or whether to shoot at all.

In the end, it's obvious that with countless reticles of each type giving good service out there, in almost all cases any style will serve adequately if the shooter is completely familiar with it. That's more important than any theoretical advantage of a particular design, I feel. Commonsense dictates a coarse reticle for short range big game use and a fine one for longer shooting. For use with one of today's cartridges which can handle all types of shooting, the top reticle choice than is obviously the Duplex.

SCOPES AND MOUNTS

LINE BY LINE

B-Square's Uzi mount needs no gunsmithing. A see-under type, it goes on and off with a single knob. $69.95, complete with rings.

Armson O.E.G. (Occluded Eye Gunsight), manufactured in South Africa and distributed here by Leadership Keys, Inc., is primarily a day/night binocular combat gunsight, but it does have potential as a quick-into-action aiming device for short-range big game hunting. It must be used with both eyes open (thus the term "binocular"), for the off eye focuses on the target while the other sees a red dot which serves as an aiming point, similar to the Weaver Qwik-Point. The O.E.G. is 5¼ inches long, weighs about 5 oz., and will fit an assortment of rifles, shotguns and handguns. Price, $190-$240.

Armsport supplies a considerable line of centerfire rifle scopes, one for black powder rifles, a small handgun model and several for rimfires. They come in the usual powers—2½x, 4x and 6x in straight magnifications, 1½-5x, 2-7x and 3-9x in variables, and, in many cases, a choice of 32mm or 40mm objective. The larger objective can be helpful, particularly in the bigger variables, for it gives more light at top power. The big game Armsports are said to be waterproof, have extremely high light transmission, and locked eyepieces to prevent disassembly and protect the reticle.

Several samples were received for testing, but unfortunately came too late for use during the past hunting season. They are good looking scopes and we hope to have a fuller report on them in the next GD. Prices for the big game models run from $110-$250.

B-Square has a new Mono-Mount for Ruger 22 auto pistols. A single ring holds the scope, while a lower "U" portion clamps to the receiver ahead of the ejection port. The mount allows use of the iron sights, and comes in blue or stainless at $39.95.

Two military types can be scoped with new B-Square mounts. One is the near-legendary UZI, though why anyone would want to scope this little popper eludes me. It installs without gunsmithing, permits use of the irons—a pious thought on such an outfit—and provides easy access to the cocking knob. Complete with 1-inch rings, $69.95. The FN-LAR also can be scoped without gunsmithing, ruggedly enough to support a heavy sniper scope or night aiming device, they say. $149.95 with 1-inch rings.

Buehler has added a two-piece dovetail mount base to fit the short, medium and long Sako actions. These actions of course have integral male dovetail beams, wider at front than rear, so that if there is any movement at all due to recoil, it simply tightens things together. There is little likelihood of any such movement because, in addition to the closely machined bases, there are four set screws as backup. The new Buehler bases are designed and positioned to give about 4-inch centers for the rings.

Burris now provides precision click adjustments on all models. This can be a help when sighting in, for it often is difficult to make a final tiny correction with a friction-type adjustment. These Fullfield models are available in all conventional powers from 2½x to 6-18x, with several "Mini" models.

New this year is a 5x LER (Long Eye Relief) handgun scope, the highest power Burris offers for this use. It has a 22-inch eye relief, 8½-foot field, and weighs 9½ oz. Also new are Parallax Adjustable models on the 2x, 3x, 4x and 5x LER's. These have enlarged objective units which boost weight 5 oz. and permit parallax elimination at distances from 25 to 200 meters (which is infinity insofar as such scopes go). These LER-PA scopes also have target knobs with audible clicks. After sighting in, adjustment references can be set to zero—particularly useful for silhouette shooters. Standard 5x LER, $140.95; PA version, $158.95.

Not new this year but deserving mention are big game-type scope rings to fit the grooved receivers of many rimfires. Of anodized aluminum, they are made for both ¾- and 1-inch scopes. $12.95 per pair.

Bushnell is another company with a wide variety of scopes. New this year in their top of the line Scopechiefs are a 4-12x with 40mm objective, Bullet Drop Compensator ($209.95) and, if desired, Prismatic Range Finder ($234.95); a 3-9x Wide Angle (38mm) with PRF and BDC ($239.95); without PRF ($219.95); and a 4x (40mm) Wide Angle with BDC ($159.95).

There's one new Banner, a 6x with 40mm lens that lists for $109.95, and a pair of new Sportviews—a 4x ($66.95) and a 3-9x ($86.95). Both of these have 38mm objectives and are the Wide Angle design. For rimfire riflemen there's a new 3-7x Sportview with 20mm objective. It comes with tip-off mounts for grooved receivers.

Heckler & Koch furnishes an interesting quick-detachable mount for their semi-auto hunting rifles, and markets, among others, Schmidt & Bender scopes. I have a sample rifle, mount and 4x scope.

The scope is unequivocally a good scope; about the mount I am equivocal. It's sort of a Rube Goldberg rig and puts the scope too high for my taste. What really counts, of course, is whether or not it is rigid and whether or not it loses its zero when taken off.

Rube Goldberg or not, having shot it, I think the mount is a solid mount and it doesn't lose its zero. It's one of those cases where first impressions are misleading.

J.B. Holden has enlarged the See-Thru area of his Ironsighter mount significantly, making it over one-third wider to give a bigger field when aiming with the open sights. The revised version is called the 700 Series Wide Ironsighter. It's available for many centerfires and some shotguns, and in most cases will handle 40mm objective lens scopes.

Kahles of America (Del-Sports) continues to supply high-grade Helia-Super scopes. New this year—in fact, just coming out of the prototype stage—is a small 1.5x14 intended mainly for military use. About 7½ inches long with a 26mm tube, it will have mounts for the FN-FAL, H&K G3-91 and 93, and later for the M16A1 and AR15. Price is expected to be $250-$300.

Kwik-Site mounts have a new set of rings to fit Weaver bases. They are split for easy scope installation and come in low or high versions, the latter for scopes with objectives of over 32mm. Bottoms of these rings are designed to slide over the bases from either end, with recessed allen-head crossbolts to lock in the base grooves. For straight-tube scopes, this makes an extremely low mounting system.

Leupold continues to expand its scope options, this year offering a new 12x for silhouette matches, a redesigned 24x, a "silver"-finish version of the 2x Extended Eye Relief, and a Silhouette Model of the 4x EER with target style clicks for elevation adjustment.

The 12x Silhouette ($289.55) comes with two types of redesigned adjustment knobs. A more compact set has numerals every 3 minutes, while the optional set, which is easily substituted, has 1-minute numerals. Both have

quarter-minute visual/audible clicks and 15 minutes of adjustment per revolution.

The 24x ($358.55) is 1.6 inches shorter and 1.5 oz. lighter than the earlier Leupold of this power, now going only 13.6 inches and 14.5 oz. It has an adjustable objective unit and comes with a short sunshade. The 36x, incidentally, is only ⅒-inch longer than the 24x and 1 oz. heavier.

Last year we described the new 6.5-20x variable. It has been used considerably since on a couple of M700 varmint rifles, a 22-250 and a 25-06, and it's right at home on rigs like this. Our use suggested one change would be helpful—target type click adjustments. Up to 300 yards or so, trajectory is no problem with a typical varmint load, for a sliver of light above a chuck's back will drop a slug into it. However, at this distance 10x is plenty of power, we just don't need double that. Out at 400 to 600 yards, where the top power is helpful, it would help to add elevation via reliable clicks, rather than try to hold over some feet. So we suggested a change in adjusting methods and —surprisingly—sales manager Chub Eastman said it could be done with no particular problem. So anyone who has felt frustrated by the 6.5-20x's friction adjustments might get in touch with Chub.

Orchard Park Enterprise is the name of a new scope mount company headed up by mechanical engineer/sometime gunwriter Ralph Avery. Currently only one rig is produced, designed for only the Marlin 336 in 30-30 or 35 Remington. Called the Saddleproof Scope Mount, it accepts only 1-inch tubes with unenlarged objectives and round eyepieces, which means 2½x or 3x, but that's plenty for these woods outfits. The Saddleproof

This Saddleproof mount—for the 336 only as yet—is quite rugged. Fits straight tubes only.

provides a stream-lined tube to accept the front of the scope tube and engages the rear sight barrel notch with an integral dovetail. The tube is split partway along its bottom and snugs up with two screws. A rear unit straddles the action behind the ejection port and can be installed without drilling or tapping. Adaptations for other rifles are being designed, $46.50.

Redfield has been delivering the 3-9x Illuminator described here last year. It's available in either Traditional or Widefield versions and the Accu-Trac rangefinder reticle is offered in the latter.

Three new medium-price scopes are now among Redfield's extensive line. Called the Trackers, they come in 4x, 2-7x and 3-9x, with 4-Plex reticle. All are built on 1-inch tubes with enlarged objectives. Prices are $89.20, $133.85 and $151.70.

Also new in the optical line is an unusually small, light spotting scope which should be especially appealing to mountain hunters who want to examine a distant trophy once it's been located with binoculars. Using a catadioptric lens system has made it possible to produce a spotter only 7½ inches long 11½ oz. in weight,

Swarovski hunting set—binoculars, telescope, riflescope.

though it integrates a 60mm objective. Maximum outside tube diameter is 2½ inches. Magnification is 30x, field is 9½ feet at 100 yards, and eye-relief ½ inch. Price, $390.40.

S & K Mfg. Co. is in the process of adding an Insta Mount for the 1898 Krag. According to Sid Haight, this latest military rifle mount should be available about the time you read this. Projected price is $36 for the base, $18 for 1-inch rings. The Insta Mounts are solid units which require no drilling or tapping for attachment.

Swarovski Optik of Austria (Strieter Corp., importer), manufactures the high-grade Habicht (Hawk) scopes in 1.5x20, 4x32, and 6x42 versions. Centered reticles with internal adjustments may be had in cross-hairs, three posts with or without cross-hairs, or a Day and Night reticle—what we call a Duplex. All have steel tubes, 26mm diameter, except that the 4x is also available in light alloy. A spring-loaded, rubber-protected eye-piece compresses if struck, which reduces the chance of injury if it hits your eyebrow. Lenses are double Transmax coated, and factory tests indicate that alternate submersion in cold and 80-degree C. water will not cause fogging. Prices run from $435 to $625, varying somewhat with reticle as well as power, and for $66 more you can have a spirit level installed to eliminate canting.

Weaver has come up with some interesting variations on a number of rifle scopes this year, and has added a pistol scope, a series of no-drill, no-tap handgun mounts, and—surprisingly—two spotting scopes.

The K4, long said to be America's most popular hunting scope, is now offered with a tube swaged from solid stainless steel, which makes the surface pretty much immune to all weather conditions and most anything else. Called the K4S, at 13.3 oz. it's 1.3 oz. heavier than the K4 and, at $190, costs $66 more.

The fairly new but extremely popular T Models have been altered slightly for long-range hunters and are called the KT Varmint scopes. They come in the same powers—6x, 10x and 16x—with the same Micro-Trac adjustment system, but due to smaller knobs, capped against the elements, they are an ounce or so lighter. Each has a fast-focus objective that adapts from 15 yards to infinity in one turn, with ¼-minute clicks. KT6, $229, KT10, $247; KT16, $267.

New non-glare finish from Weaver. The K4M is bead blasted to create the tracker finish, a non-glare look that eliminates reflections that might give away a hunter's position. For additional versatility in a non-glare scope, Weaver also offers the 3-9 V9m variable.

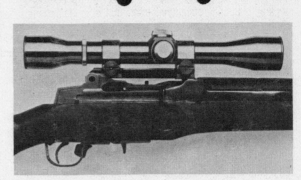

Weaver's new stainless-steel hunting scope. The K4S is pictured here atop a matching stainless-steel Mini-14.

New stainless-steel handgun scope from Weaver, mounted in matching stainless-steel finish mounts, is the P2S, a 2x with Dual-X reticle.

The V9M and K4M are non-glare versions of the older V9 and K4. Their bead-blasted matte finish is intended to eliminate reflections and is made available because a survey indicated that 51.6 percent of those questioned preferred such a finish. This is an interesting buyer's reaction against the super-shiny scopes so many makers have pushed for so long. Makes me a little less self-conscious about my flat spray painted approach.

Weaver's new handgun scope is the P2S, a 2x stainless steel unit which comes with Dual-X reticle only. It's 10 inches long, has a 14-foot field and eye relief of 10-24 inches. Adjustments are Micro-Trac, graduated in half-minutes. Price, $157.

An Integral 1-inch See-Thru mount

Two new spotting scopes from Weaver. The TS6 (top) and TS4 provide superior eye relief, bright optics, and rugged construction.

is new for rifles this year. It attaches directly to the action instead of to separate bases, using the factory holes. $13.30.

Nine no-drill, no-tap handgun mount base systems are now available from Weaver. They come in kit form and include everything needed to attach a scope to any of the following: Colt 357, Python, Trooper, Mark III Trooper, Officer's Model Match, Ruger Blackhawk, Super Blackhawk, Security Six, all Ruger 22 autoloading pistols, and most Smith & Wesson L, N, and K frame revolvers. $44.95; in stainless, $58.50.

A pair of spotting scopes round out Weaver's new optical equipment this year. The TS6 is a straight-eyepiece model useful to hunters as well as on the range, while the TS4 has the 45-degree eyepiece preferred by many competitive riflemen. Each is about 12.5 inches long and 37.4 oz., the TS6 having a 60mm objective, the TS4 a 50mm and a telescoping sunshade. Different power eyepieces are available and are sold separately from the body which costs $224 for the TS4, $280 for the TS6. TS4 eyepieces come in 12x, $65; 16x or 20x, $75; 32x, $80. TS6 eyepieces are 15x, 20x, 25x and 40x, at the same price graduations. Each body has a stainless steel tripod socket.

Eye distance ranges from about .9 to .2 inches, according to the eyepiece used, so should be okay for those who wear glasses, except possibly at highest magnification. Both scopes have micrometer focusing control.

I've several times mentioned an old V4.5 that's mounted on my 284 Mauser. Well, it came through again last fall—twice. In October, on a deer-boar hunt with Paul Wright, in South Carolina's Santee-Cooper country. I spotted a 5-point approaching my stand. He stopped at 76 paces, nervous about something, but by then I had the big Lee Dot on the neck-shoulder junction and that's just where my bullet hit. Then in December I caught a Pennsylvania 8-point angling across a wooded hillside just above me. With the scope again set at 1½x, I centered the dot on his neck and squeezed, and that was that. This one was 56 paces. In both cases, the 139-gr. Hornady kicked out by 50 grs. of 4895 gave instantaneous kills. With a chronographed velocity of 3000 fps, the results weren't unexpected. Still, it was nice.

Williams Gun Sight Co. has an unusual approach to advertising their rifle scopes. Their Twilight scopes are claimed to be "the highest quality scopes in the medium priced field." That's a refreshing statement, to say the least. There are four Twilights, a 2½x20, 4x32, 2-6x32, and 3-9x38, the second number of each being the unobstructed diameter of the objective lens. All have T-N-T (Thick-and-Thin or Duplex) reticles, and prices are, respectively, $104.75, $111.40, $151.50 and $159. As it happens, the Twilights are one of the few current lines I've never used, so I can't comment personally, but Williams has always had an excellent reputation and I'm sure their scopes are good values.

Williams has offered a large number of mounts for decades, adapting them to new rifles, and some handguns, as necessary. There are Quick

Convertible top and side mounts, Sight-Thru models for centerfires and rimfires, and Streamline units. The 2-piece Streamlines are particularly interesting because the bottom halves of the rings and the bases are machined in one solid unit. This eliminates the usual ringbase joint, and thus one area of possible movement. Also, the rings are offset fore-and-aft; this permits reversing either or both, front to rear, to accommodate for eye relief, unusual turret placement or whatever. $17.75; $24.20 with Sub Blocks for Thompson/Center Hawken and Renegade.

Zeiss scopes are once again available in the U.S. Four models with features American hunters have come to expect can now be had from this long-respected manufacturer. The new "C" series consists of the Diatal 4x, 6x, 10x and Diavari 3-9x.

Because it has been so long since Zeiss scopes were readily available here, we'll list some detailed specs. See the table.

The first good rifle scope I ever saw was a Zeiss, a 2½x Zielklein my cousin Dave Bell had on a M70 300 H&H Magnum. That was in the late '30s, and I shot that combination quite a bit before going into the Army in

1943. The first good scope I ever owned was a Zeiss, the 6x Zielsechs I've often mentioned in these Reviews.

At any rate, I can claim some experience with Zeiss scopes, and I've always been impressed. I never felt they (or any others) were perfect, and I was anxious to see one of the new C models, and selected the 4x to serve in place of the Zielvier I never owned.

It was shorter than I expected and felt lighter, with a chunky, definitely Germanic, look. Focused for my eyes and deducting the rubber shield's overhang, mine measures only 9¾ inches long. It has the Z-plex reticle.

I used a Redfield Jr. with low rings to mount it on a M700 Remington 7mm Magnum. This is a long action, which results in a 4-inch ring spacing, so there is little room for fore-and-aft scope positioning. With scope as far to the rear as the swell of the objective unit will permit, the eyepiece comes just behind the cocking piece. Anyone whose stock is a bit long might have trouble getting close enough to see a full field, and it diminishes rapidly as eye distance increases, or decreases, from the optimum 3½ inches. The Williams Streamline mount mentioned elsewhere would give more adaptability, as might some others. •

Zeiss Scope Specifics

	Diatal C			Diavari C	
Magnification	4x	6x	10x	3x — 9x	
Tube diameter (in.)	1	1	1	1	
Objective tube diameter (in.)	1.65	1.65	1.87	1.73	
Eyepiece diameter (in.)	1.67	1.67	1.67	1.67	
Length (in.)	10.6	10.6	12.7	11.2	
Weight (oz.)	11.3	11.3	14.1	15.2	
Objective lens diameter (mm)	32	32	36	36	
Exit pupil (mm)	8	5.3	3.6	9.8	4
Field at 100 yds. (ft.)	30	20	12	36	13
Maximum internal adj. (moa)	80	80	50		50

Retail prices on these are: 4x, $295; 6x, $325; 10x, $375; 3-9x, $495.

Zeiss Diatal-C 4x32 on M700 Remington, Redfield Jr. mount.

Great Arc of the Wild Sheep Guides

The trophy of trophies, Chadwick's ram, on rock-slide soon after the kill. Frank Golata is on left; Curley Cochrane is on the right. Golata is holding what appears to be L. S. Chadwick's Winchester Model 54 30-06 backup rifle. Chadwick used 404 Hoffman Magnum for the first shots at the ram.

The sheep were up there, and the dudes were down *there*. It was the guides and the outfitters that got them together.

by JAMES L. CARKHUFF

THERE IS A GROUP of sporting heroes, now in their own Hall of Fame, who plied their trade without fanfare far from public accolade, with spectators often only a pair of winded mountain horses and a lone trophy hunter, yet note of their field prowess has come down through the years. The lore wrapping them in legend is zealously maintained. Uniformed in wool shirts, suspendered breeches and rock-nicked mountain boots, they have passed into the annals of sport as master guides pre-eminent in pursuit of the hunter's grail—the heavy-horned mountain ram.

This anecdotal narrative describes the fabled few who, early on, comprised the Great Arc of the North American Sheep Guides. They lived and worked out of mountain-perimeter locations overlaying the Great Arc of the North American sheep.* From the north to south, this vanguard included:

---

*The Great Arc of the Wild Sheep, by James L. Clark, a treatise on the distribution and habitat of wild sheep. University of Oklahoma Press, Norman, OK. 1964.

- Eugene and Louis Jacquot of Burwash Landing, Yukon Territory—Dall sheep.
- Frank Golata, Dawson Creek, British Columbia—Stone sheep.
- Roy Hargreaves, Mt. Robson, British Columbia—Rocky Mountain bighorns and some Stone sheep.
- Bert Riggal, Pincher Creek, Alberta—Rocky Mountain bighorns.
- Ned Frost, Cody, Wyoming—Rocky Mountain bighorns.
- Charlie Ren, Sonoyta, Sonora—Desert sheep.

They were mountain men, sheep hunters, horsemen, logistics experts—giants indeed in their field. From the first pulsings of momentum and interest in sheep hunting generated by that great hunter and naturalist Charles Sheldon, in his books *Wilderness of the Upper Yukon* and *Wilderness of the Denali*, they nurtured and developed the infant outfitting business operating into the far sheep ranges.

There were no roads anywhere near most of the areas they hunted. Aerial transportation came only after years of doing it the hard way. Much of the hunting area was only sketchily mapped, if at all.

And even in the "rugged" first decades of this century, not every aspiring sheep hunter was a tuned athlete. The old days had their share of overweight people, much like many of those who can afford today's excursions. So they managed men as well as sheep.

From a work in progress, here are some facts about these great guides, their guns, their clients, their hunts:

Jean and Louis Jacquot

Pursuing Dall sheep in the rugged country around Kluane Lake and the heads of the Generc, the Donjek, and the White rivers from outfitting headquarters at Burwash Landing, provided a substantial living for several decades for two diminutive French chefs. In 1898 these brothers backpacked over the Chilkoot Pass, built a boat on Lake Bennett and floated down the Yukon to the Klondike during the great gold rush. They ultimately sold their Klondike claims in 1904 and moved south to another strike on Burwash Creek, draining into Kluane Lake. And while continuing to prospect, they began trading in furs, trapping supplies, food and dry goods.

They picked up their first big game outfitting and hunting experience through a local named Morley Bones, who outfitted an extended hunt in the fall of 1919 for a party from the States. You can read of it in the classic book, *Alaskan-Yukon Trophies Won and Lost* by G. O. Young.

By the 1930s, the Jacquot reputation was well-established. Their hunts were conducted primarily in the Donjek River basin, prime Dall habitat and fine grizzly country. Trophy aspirants in pursuit of the magnificent Dall rams included hunters from all walks of life and some notables, including General R. E. Woods, Nelson Rockefeller, Richard K. Mellon, and Jack O'Connor.

Capable afield themselves, the Jacquots were possibly the first to see the virtues of employing native guides. They happily watched guides Jimmie Copper Joe, Jimmie Johnson, Johnny Allen, and Jack O'Connor's field mentor, Field Johnson, garner word-of-mouth reputations in their own right.

The Jacquots provided abundant amenities of good camp life. In addition to good tentage, horses and abundant game, the famous quantity and quality of their grub stood on its own. Jacquot-outfitted hunts were gastronomically memorable.

The brothers' recommendation for an all-around mountain rifle centered on the 30-06 with a 180-grain bullet for sheep and a somewhat heavier bullet for grizzly. Such armament was more than adequate also when they wandered towards the White River for caribou and moose. Gene himself carried a 250-3000 and Louis a 30-06 Springfield.

Frank Golata

Frank Golata's present stature did not evolve, certainly, from his physical size but from a spectacular career as British Columbia's most famous sheep guide. Who can forget the classic photos of the 5-ft., 7-in. Golata, in those high laced boots and the distinctive high-crowned hat with its beaded hatband, binoculars raised?

Born in Dunkirk, New York, of Polish parentage, Golata was hung up in the old world custom of collective pooling of wages until *all* the children of the family were educated. After stints as a bellhop, a time clerk, and even a draftsman, his familial responsibilities were concluded in 1912 and he embarked on the long dreamed-of escape to Canada.

In Rolla, British Columbia, not far from Dawson Creek, Golata came under the tutelage of an old-time cowboy named Bill Conn. From him Golata gained an introduction to horses and learned much of his early bush-lore.

Golata acquired a pack string in the early 1920s and perfected his technique packing gear to trappers, and it was not until 1933 that he made his first commercial hunt with a gunsmith from Iowa named Harry Gibson. He liked the job.

On the advice of his trapper friends, in 1935 he made a solo trip into the Prophet River/Musqua River country for a two-month reconnoiter, and in 1936, a local Rolla compadre, Curley Cochrane, accompanied Golata and Roy Hargreaves on the now-famous L. S. Chadwick hunt, on which the world's record Stone sheep was killed.

On this trip, in addition to the record head, Chadwick also took a second ram measuring 39-in. on one horn and 38¼-in. on the other, after it broke 6 to 7-in. of horn off each side in a 250-yard skid down a rock slide. Hargreaves shot for himself a Stone ram

Roy Hargreaves, master outfitter, hunted a paradise for sheep, provided Jack O'Connor with the unforgettable trip of a lifetime, all while making a living.

L. S. Chadwick, Roy Hargreaves and Curley Cochrane with a wolf shot by Chadwick in 1936. Hargreaves is 6-feet tall; Chadwick much taller. The wolf is not small, either.

Mac McGuire with 43-inch Stone's ram taken by Joseph H. Shirk in 1948. It holds 8th place in current Boone & Crockett records. Massive bases measure 15⅝-inch. That's probably Shirk's rifle

Legendary Ned Frost of Cody, Wyoming, carried his old Model 95 carbine in 30-06 up to where they posed these rams as he carried it most other places.

Golata with a pair of Stone rams.

Two of Golata's own trophies and his own taxidermy.
His brand is G4.

Classic photo of Frank Golata, in
high-laced boots worn in early
years, glassing for rams at head
of Prophet, circa 1935.

measuring 41$\frac{1}{16}$-in. and 42-in.; and another, measuring 38-in. per side, in which he expressed disappointment. That made four trophy Stone sheep in nine days, with the monster 51$\frac{5}{8}$-in. head dominating them all.

It was 14 days by packtrain up Bear Creek to the Halfway River, then on to Deadman Lake to get into Frank's base camp at Redfern Lake. Once the Alaska Highway went through, Golata steadfastly refused to book anyone for a period shorter than 30 days. He felt anything less than 30 days in the mountains "shorted" the hunter.

It was as a jack-of-all-trades that Golata shone. He was a trapper and big-game guide supreme; a taxidermist of no mean accomplishment; an artist, working in oil; he did extraordinary bead work; he tanned hides for his own taxidermy work and for his own leather jackets. He made his own saddle and bridle and the distinctive curved pack boxes for sawbuck saddles were an early creation. So also was a special campstove that went into the mountains with him for 30 years.

As a rifleman, Frank was not so unsophisticated as he was unimpressed. To him, a rifle was a tool. In the early years he used a well-worn 30-30 Winchester carbine. Later, he replaced it with a 30-06 Winchester Model 70. His ammunition was off-the-shelf. He did treasure and swear by a pair of 7x50 Zeiss binoculars.

Hunters to the high country with Frank Golata took the world record Stone ram and another Stone sheep taken by Joseph Shirk that still holds eighth place in the Boone and Crockett record book with horn lengths of 43-in. and 43$\frac{4}{8}$-in. and incredibly heavy (for Stone sheep) bases of 15$\frac{6}{8}$-in. One Golata hunter took a gigantic 72-in. moose. Another, of reported timid personal traits, shot one of the largest of grizzlies, judging by the photograph, before he lapsed into hysteria.

Frank Golata did it all, in professional style, at a time when access into the Stone sheep country was measured not in hours but in trekking *days*.

Roy Hargreaves

Roy Hargreaves and his brothers, of Mt. Robson, British Columbia, operated in eastern B.C. and the fabulous Smoky River country of western Alberta. During much of Hargreaves' active tenure, that may have been the finest game country on earth.

In 1935, L. S. Chadwick, one year before taking the world record Stone sheep in British Columbia, hunted with Hargreaves on a classic. They covered over 800 miles on horseback and made 26 camps. In one day, Chadwick related that he saw 34 nice bighorn rams, 50 ewes and lambs, 25 goats, 7 black wolves and one silver fox.

Hargreaves, in those days, maintained both an Alberta and a British Columbia outfitter's license. In so doing, he harvested the finest trophies on both sides of the provincial border running down the spine of the Canadian Rockies. Locally, despite awesome success with bighorn sheep, Hargreaves came to be known as the Grizzly King because of an uncanny ability to find grizzly bears.

He was born in Gardner, Oregon, on February 17, 1918, but his family soon moved. They went to southern British Columbia, then during the winter of 1912-1913, they moved on to settle at Jasper, Alberta. Roy went to work as a hunting guide for Curley Phillips. In 1913, in Phillips' employ, he found the site of what would subsequently be his Mt. Robson ranch.

For World War I, Hargreaves went off to Europe. He spent 18 months in the hospital after being gassed on the battlefield, but Armistice Day found Roy and his father and brothers back at the spot, with the breath-taking view of Mt. Robson, he had discovered in 1913. The family team cut and hauled logs for the ranch buildings and by 1920 were established ranchers and outfitters.

It was his association with L. S. Chadwick in 1935 and again in 1936 that launched his major following. Incidentally, there is considerable credence to the story that Hargreaves himself actually trailed, caught up with and despatched the lightly wounded monster Stone ram. It may be Chadwick's 404 Hoffman had caused only a hip wound on the record sheep before Hargreaves put it down and into the records forever.

In his account of a hunt with Roy in 1943 down the Smoky River, Jack O'Connor related that it was one of "the great experiences and most successful hunts of a lifetime." On that trip, they saw 180 bighorn ewes and lambs, 35 mature rams, 33 grizzlies, thousands of goats, hundreds of caribou, and a dozen bull moose and about that many mule deer and black bear. It was eight years after Chadwick's account of the region's vast game resources. Sadly, today it is all but gone.

A utilitarian approach to rifles prompted Roy to carry an iron-sighted 30-06 that succeeded a lever action Winchester 30-30. In Alberta, however-

er, it was illegal for a guide to carry a rifle and that particular Model 70 spent a lot of time propped near the wood pile in camp.

Curley Cochrane, an early Hargreaves sidekick, who moved to the Peace River country in 1924 and from there all over the North hunting and trapping, used a 33 Winchester Model 1886 take-down. Cochrane, probably by necessity, loaded for his rifle but Hargreaves bought his ammunition over the counter.

Ned Frost

Ned Frost of Cody, Wyoming, guide to the likes of James L. Clark and Dr. Saxton Pope and Ralph Young, was larger-than-life and difficult to describe. His hunting career got off to a prodigious start when he killed his first grizzly at the age of 7 using a 45-90 Model 1886 Winchester.

Ned Ward Frost was born in 1881. His reputation as a sheep guide evolved through the years from about 1900. Do not confuse him with Nedward Mahlan Frost, or "Chew," his son. Chew was a tremendous sheep guide in his own right, running up a string of 83 sheep hunting clients and 83 successes, but he was Chew, not Ned.

Ned was extremely competent at one of the things which built his reputation—getting hunters to the game. However, his personality also encompassed the roles of rancouteur, public speaker, photographer, promoter and general businessman. He made many trips "back East" in the early days to show his black and white movie footage (shot in the old 32mm format) of the breathtaking scenery around Cody and of the myriad big game resources of the time.

Frost's life included a grizzly mauling while on a hunting trip with the colorful "Phonograph" Jones, and he guided and backed up Pope and Young when they collected, with vintage 1920 archery tackle, 3 grizzly bears in Yellowstone Park for a museum diorama. He also introduced James L. Clark to the world of mountain sheep.

Frost was not a horse fancier. He was a good and efficient packer, sat a horse with the aplomb and assurance of long-familiarity, could shoe and doctor his equine charges but he looked upon them only as a long-legged means to an end. He was more of a firearms enthusiast than most.

Frost used a variety of firearms over the years. The old 45-90 Model 1886 Winchester actually belonged to his father. Later, Ned drifted over to a Remington Model 8, in 35 Remington

(Below) Bert Riggal (R) with client at ease during early fall junket to the high country. Riggal's clients got the best of everything, including gun talk.

An early photograph depicting a hunter Riggal guided successfully to a truly trophy bighorn ram. Note massive horns, the muzzle protector on the rifle, and the walking stick.

A Riggal pack train moving out for a hunt in country north of Waterton Lakes National Park. Getting into untouched country was a matter of weeks on horses in the old days. Most felt that was a good part of the whole idea.

caliber. Finally, he acquired a Winchester Model 1895 carbine in 30-06.

Jessee Frost, Ned's youngest son and a most gracious source of information for this piece, once used the rifle to kill a buck antelope 100 yards away in a coulee. He was instructed to "draw a fine bead" on the antelope's front knee as the animal stood broadside. Jessee did, and the animal fell, shot through the heart. It becomes obvious Ned kept his sheep rifle sighted in for the longer distances.

After World War II, still not sold on bolt-action saddle arms, Frost acquired a slide action Remington 270, and retired the old Model 95. With the exception of the old 45-90 cartridge, Frost did not handload. He bought off the shelf, and stuck to the same bullet weight for which the rifle was sighted. None of his rifles, except for a 222 Sako acquired in the early '50s, ever wore a telescopic sight.

Frost considered himself somewhat of an anachronism. He was frequently heard to remark, "Damn it, I was born 100 years too late!"

Bert Riggal

Bert Riggal was the consummate professional hunter. Born in England, he emigrated to Canada about 1900 and took his first paying client into what is now Waterton Lakes National Park in 1907. He was a naturalist, a noted botanist, a photographer, a mountain climber, a rancher, a most sophisticated gun enthusiast and handloader. He was a student of the Greek classics and an original thinker.

Riggal, the author, was a long-time contributor to *Arms and the Man*, the predecessor of *The American Rifleman*. He occasionally wrote for *Outdoor Life*. And his mountain expertise and intellect, as applied to all phases of outfitting, made him the dean of the western Canada sheep guides. His clients took 66 bighorn rams over the years.

Riggal became perhaps as knowledgeable about sheep habits as any man alive. Andy Russell, Bert's son-in-law and a man who has risen to great heights himself as an outfitter, writer, and naturalist, remembered one uncanny occasion when Riggal, two clients and he were pinned down in a windy saddle most of one day by a band of rams on a rock slide above them. Bert finally announced after hours of studying the leader: "They'll be here at 4:00."

Sure enough, at 4:00 p.m. the band meandered out onto the low end of the saddle and grazed slowly towards the waiting hunters. One took his ram at 30 yards, the other at 50.

Of all the sheep guides, Riggal was far and away the most knowledgeable regarding firearms. Riggal once killed—with a 25 Niedner—a trotting coyote at 492 measured yards. Typically, this rifle was stocked by Griffin & Howe on a Springfield action. The rifle was a joint effort between the NRA and Townsend Whelen, who oversaw its make-up and then presented it to Riggal. Later, the rifle was fitted with a Lyman 5A telescopic sight with a Litschert attachment that converted it to an 8x.

Other rifles ran through the Riggal collection over the years. Among them was a 7x57 Mauser by Greener. The rifle is still around. I have handled it and it has that "live" feel. Riggal's favorite "big game" rifle—read grizzly, moose, and elk—was a 30-06 cut-down Mauser carbine. Originally stocked to the muzzle, Bert cut it back to a half-stock. There was a flat bolt handle and a Zeiss Zielklein telescopic sight. This Englishman-turned-outfitter did not have much use for the hard-kicking magnums, feeling that they were unnecessary.

Bert used interesting paraphernalia. In old photographs, one will see Riggal leaning on his ever-present walking stick; when shooting or glassing, he habitually dropped a pre-tied loop of sash cord around his knees for steadiness; and he also equipped many of his clients with handmade leather muzzle protectors for their rifles.

Charles Ren

Charlie Ren was a high-achieving master guide, but he is a bit of a mystery. Jack O'Connor, a Ren amigo, could doubtless have shed considerable light, but he has also passed on.

Ren was born in the 1870s in the Jackson Hole country of Wyoming. He worked as a market hunter during the Klondike gold rush. Frank Hibben tells me he remembers Ren working as a guide for Wes Brown on Bucking Horse Creek in northern British Columbia in the 1920s. Given that, we know Ren had experience with Dall rams and with Stone sheep during his association with Brown. It is not too improbable to speculate he knew Rocky Mountain bighorns around his own home stomping grounds near Jackson Hole.

Eventually, from a hunting lodge in Sonoyta, Sonora, Ren outfitted the likes of Jack O'Connor, Grancel Fitz, Elmer Keith, and Doctor Wilson DuComb, who turned up everywhere. As resident desert sheep impresario, Ren was acquainted with both Frank Hibben and George Parker. With the hunting passed, he disappeared.

Ren had a vast store of mountain sheep savvy, gained through years of chasing them, and imparted much of this treasure to one Jose del Rosario, a red-headed Mexican associate. By 1935, Charlie simply drove a specially-equipped open truck in and acted as straw boss, cook and general camp jack while the client and del Rosario hunted.

There is considerable question whether all Ren's hunting in Sonora was strictly "legal." If he *was* a peripheral outfitter, he nonetheless managed to keep his clients out of trouble. Several have written, however, how strange it was to go back across the border, sans sheep head, and then have it magically appear in their hotel room in Ajo, Arizona, soon before their departure.

Probably the most significant factor in Ren's success was his knowledge of the regions he hunted—the Pinacates, the Cubabais, and the San Franciscos. A further strength was his ability to deal with this harsh and arid environment. He took clients into it, hunted successfully and returned safely, withal a logistical and tactical effort not many were willing to tackle.

Charlie's tastes in rifles leaned to the traditional. He touted the 7x57 Mauser or his favorite 300 Savage Model 99 lever action. His weapons were always equipped with rubber recoil pads for rock gripping, as he always used them for alpenstocks.

Charlie operated professionally in a desolate, treacherous, physically and politically inhospitable environment without fanfare. In his life, he saw his footprints over all the continent's sheep ranges. ●

Acknowledgments

The author wishes to acknowledge with heartfelt thanks the cooperation of the following for access to family photo archives and for the kind reconstruction of family history during preparation of this article:

Josie Sais, daughter of Louis Jacquot
Mrs. Frank Golata
Martin Hunter
Murray Cochrane and family
Andy and Kaye Russell
Jessee Frost

For dredging up old memories, thanks also to:

Frank Hibben
and
George Parker.

After dumping one fox squirrel from a nearby hickory, Bridges eyes a second bushytail while he reloads a Hatfield small-bore rifle.

SMALL GAME TAKES A SMALL BORE

by **TOBY BRIDGES**

The muzzle-loading rifle for squirrels and other such "small deer" is with us once again.

Uᴎᴛɪʟ JUST A few years ago, a black powder shooter looking to buy a small bore muzzle-loading rifle simply didn't have many choices. Until the late 1970s, only several such reproduction rifles were available. The shooter who wanted authentic and traditional styling could either contract a custom riflemaker to build him an ideal small game rifle or he could gather up the necessary component parts and build the rifle himself.

Well, that's the way it used to be. Now, hunting with muzzle-loading guns has seen a tremendous increase. It is estimated that several million hunters are now using a frontloading rifle for at least some of their hunting.

The primary focus of most muzzle-loading arms makers and importers has been the new breed of black powder deer hunter and the occasional black powder shooter, so the 45 and 50-caliber rifles reigned. At the same time, the 45-caliber bore has been under attack as inadequate for deer-sized game. Unless loaded with a stiff powder charge and a conical projectile, many feel the 45 just doesn't carry enough wallop to drop even small deer cleanly. And all who have tried it will agree that the 45, even with light loads, is entirely too large for use on game as small as rabbit and squirrel.

Deer season in most states runs from 10 days to two weeks in length. Even with separate muzzle-loading seasons, the most time a deer hunter can expect to spend afield would be three weeks or so. Many recent converts, it seems, now show a rising interest in small game with frontloading rifles. Those seasons are generally longer than deer seasons. A number of importers and manufacturers are now offering small bore versions of some models.

The most popular of today's small bore frontloaders, and the front-runner, has to be the lightweight Seneca model offered by Thompson/Center. It's a slimmer, scaled down version of the firm's popular Hawken. T/C introduced the Seneca in 1974 as a lightweight deer hunting rifle in 45 caliber and for small game in 36 caliber.

The 36-caliber Seneca is a real delight to shoot and its 6½-pound weight makes for easy carrying. The 28-inch octagonal barrel is fitted with a fully adjustable rear sight and a square-topped, steel blade front sight. Rifling is eight lands and grooves of equal width, one turn in 48 inches.

One 36-caliber Seneca I've been shooting practically since this rifle was first put on the market does well for me with a variety of powder charges. With a 30-gr. charge of FFFg behind a 65-grain .305″ round ball, patched with .015″ pillow ticking, the rifle I've been shooting will punch one-hole five-shot groups at 25 yards when fired from a sandbag rest. At 50 yards I've found I can usually keep this load under two inches with most five-shot groups. Out of the 28-inch barrel of the Seneca halfstock this particular load develops right at 1500 fps (feet per second) muzzle velocity and produces just slightly over 300 ft. lbs. of muzzle energy, practically duplicating some of today's hot 22 Long Rifle cartridges.

While the light 30-gr. charge of FFFg is ideal for use on small game intended for tablefare, such as rabbit and squirrel, it should be considered just a little on the light side if woodchucks, foxes or coyotes are the intended targets. A heftier 40-gr. charge of FFFg and patched .350″ round balls have accounted for quite a few central Illinois chucks and several red foxes for me in the past couple of seasons. The extra 10 grains of powder ups muzzle velocity to around 1700 fps and increases muzzle energy to nearly 450 ft. lbs.

The Seneca's adjustable rear sight comes in handy when different powder charges are used with a slight lowering or raising of the elevation screw, the sights are quickly adjusted for heavier or lighter powder charges. This short American-made halfstock shoots as well as it looks. The double-phase double-set triggers allow the rifle to be fired with the triggers either set or unset.

Seneca lockwork incorporates a coil mainspring; the stock is turned from American walnut; all the stock furniture is highly polished brass. Steel thimbles and a machined underrib securely tote the rifle's ramrod. The Seneca is a slim, well-designed copy of what is usually referred to as a light New England-style hunting rifle. Suggested retail is currently $270.00.

Mowrey Gun Works, of Iowa Park, Texas, also offers a domestic percussion small bore rifle dubbed their "Squirrel Rifle" model. All Mowreys are copies of the rifles once produced by master armsmaker Ethan Allen during the 1850s at his Grafton, Massachusetts, or Norwich, Connecticut, plants. These rifles are readily identified by their metal frames. Up until 1979, Mowrey used brass for the frames and furniture; now the shooter can choose between the colorful yellow metal or a more authentic steel frame and steel furniture.

The Squirrel Rifle is now offered in 32, 36 and 45 caliber, the smaller two

Bridges uses a solid benchrest to test a Tennessee Valley Arms semi-custom small-bore rifle.

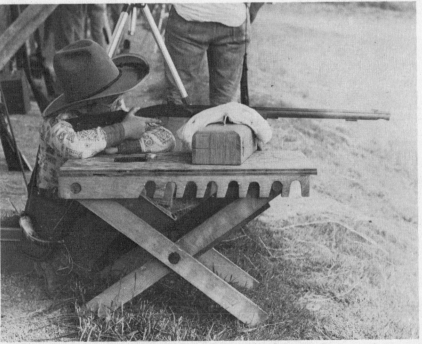

Young Warren Spradlin touches one off with his TVA Tennessee Rifle, scaled down to fit his nine-year-old frame.

bores being of most interest to the small game hunter. This rifle wasn't introduced until 1978, about the time hunting small game with a muzzle-loader started to gain in popularity. At that time the Squirrel Rifle was available in 36 and 45 caliber only.

According to Neil McMullen, president of Mowrey, the smaller 36-caliber rifle sold as well as the 45-caliber rifle for the first year or so, then more recently took a slight lead in sales. It was this apparent interest in small bore rifles that led to his decision to offer the light seven-pound rifle in 32 caliber in late 1981.

At 28 inches and $^{13}/_{16}$-inch across the flats, the barrel makes the Mowrey rifle an excellent pointing rifle. The maple buttstock is attached with a long bolt; the maple forearm is held to the barrel by a pair of tenons and a pair of pins.

I've found the 36-caliber Mowrey to perform very well with the same 40-gr. load I use in the T/C Seneca. Mowrey cuts its own barrels with eight lands and grooves and one turn in 60 inches. Depth of rifling is just a shade shy of .010". With the aforementioned load, accuracy at 25 yards is excellent with five shots generally printing into one ragged hole. At 50 yards groups normally open up to around 1½ inches across.

With the lighter 30-gr. charge of FFFg, groups with the Mowrey rifle open up slightly. At 25 yards most five-shot benchrest groups approach an inch across and at 50 yards groups commonly open up to around 2½ inches. The heftier 40-gr. charge could prove a little too powerful on small game for the table. Although my shooting has proven the 30-gr. charge a little less accurate in this rifle, I would personally go with it for my small game shooting.

Mowrey's new 32-caliber Squirrel Rifle should prove an excellent choice for small game. I have not used one on any game, but I have fired one enough to know I'll be using it a lot come next squirrel season. Loaded with a .315" ball weighing scarcely 47 grains, the rifle I've been shooting performs nicely with just 25 grains of FFFg. If I were to make an educated guess, I'd say this load is developing right at 1500 to 1600 fps in the Mowrey's 28-inch barrel. Average five-shot group spread with the 32 at 25 yards was well under an inch and I expect accuracy to improve as the barrel is broken in. Mowrey retails the Squirrel rifle for $299.00 with a choice of steel or brass frame and mountings.

Another new 32-caliber reproduction on the market, and one I have both shot and hunted with, is the small bore version of Dixie Gun Works' Tennessee Mountain Rifle. The 32 maintains the 41½-inch length of the 50-caliber model and utilizes the same lock. The barrel is just $^{13}/_{16}$-inch across the flats, and the one-piece cherry fullstock is trimmed to match the slender barrel.

Frank Boutwell and I checked several rifles from Dixie's first shipment. We found they weren't at all choosy,

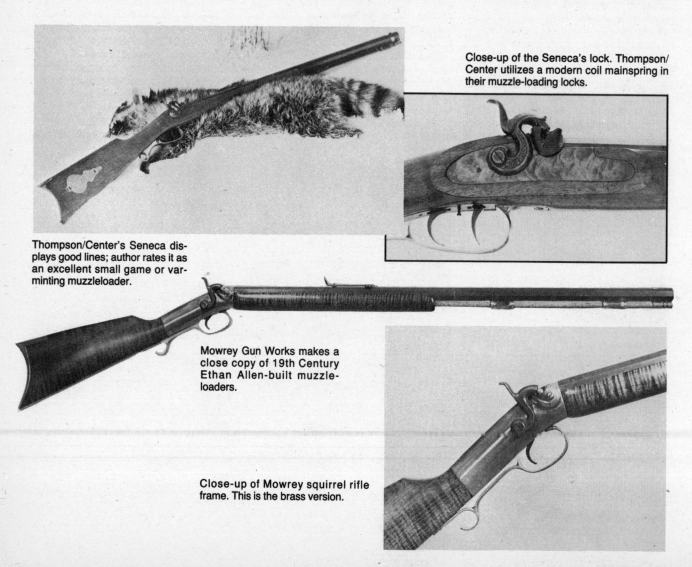

Close-up of the Seneca's lock. Thompson/Center utilizes a modern coil mainspring in their muzzle-loading locks.

Thompson/Center's Seneca displays good lines; author rates it as an excellent small game or varminting muzzleloader.

Mowrey Gun Works makes a close copy of 19th Century Ethan Allen-built muzzle-loaders.

Close-up of Mowrey squirrel rifle frame. This is the brass version.

but they seemed to perform best when loaded with 30 grains of FFFg behind a .010″ thick cotton patched .315″ round ball. At 25 yards we were both able to group most shots well inside an inch from a bench rest.

The light lead balls didn't fare too well at 50 yards with most groups opening to around 2½ inches. With heavier .015″ thick pillow ticking for patching we were able to shrink 50-yard groups to under 2 inches, but found loading difficult with such a tight patch and ball combination.

The thin ⁵⁄₁₆-inch ramrods necessary with such small bores just won't stand up under a lot of hard use and aren't recommended when loading ball and patch combinations as tight as the .315″ ball and .015″ patching we were using in the Dixie rifle. Stainless steel combination loading/cleaning rods are best with such loads instead of the wooden ramrod that comes with the rifle. For most hunting we were both content with the accuracy arrived at using the thinner and

easier loading .010″ thick cotton patching, and several limits of cottontails taken at 10 to 20 yards never realized that I wasn't shooting the most accurate load possible.

Made in Italy, Dixie's 32 is authentically styled, fitted with an exceptionally long barrel and very well balanced. Double set triggers are standard equipment. The late 1981 price was $295.00, flint or percussion.

A step above mass-produced reproduction rifles would be one of today's so-called "semi-custom" muzzleloaders. The fact that the basics are standard in each rifle produced is about the only factor that distinguishes a semi-custom rifle from a true custom rifle. In order to produce a stylish, authentic muzzle-loading rifle to a price, production demands a considerable amount of machine work. The result, however, can be a rifle with fine lines, excellent fit and beautiful finish at about half the cost of a true custom-built rifle.

The rifle offered by Tennessee Val-

ley Arms, of Union City, Tennessee, is about as close to custom a semi-custom rifle can come. The basic design is the steel-mounted southern mountain, or southern "poor boy." TVA sells a "basic" rifle built without full buttplate, lower entry thimble or nose cap, but offers these items as options. The heel of the butt has a horn plate and the toe a steel plate in the basic model. Interchangeable Siler flint and percussion locks are used on these rifles and North Star Enterprises' single-phase double-set triggers are standard. A piece of premium maple is machine-turned for the full-length stock.

TVA will build their rifle to just about any length of pull the shooter desires and has produced a few as short as 12 inches and as long as 15½ inches. Full-length 44-inch Green Mountain custom barrels are used unless a shorter length is specified by the buyer. The TVA Tennessee rifle is available in 32, 36, 40, 45, 50, 52, 54, 58 and 62 caliber, and the firm selects

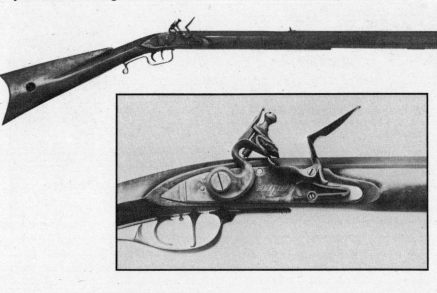

Dixie Gun Works offers this small-bore 32-caliber version of their long-barreled Tennessee Mountain Rifle.

Dixie Gun Works' big early-styled Ketland lock is used in the Hatfield semi-custom flinter. It's a little large for the rifle's over-all slim lines, author feels it still looks good.

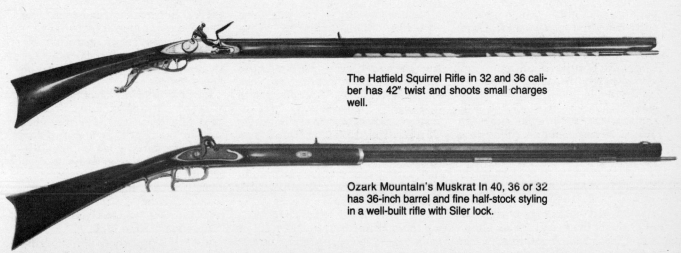

The Hatfield Squirrel Rifle in 32 and 36 caliber has 42″ twist and shoots small charges well.

Ozark Mountain's Muskrat In 40, 36 or 32 has 36-inch barrel and fine half-stock styling in a well-built rifle with Siler lock.

The author's 36-caliber TVA southern "poor boy" took this plump juvenile wild turkey gobbler.

This foursome of Illinois cottontails were taken with a 32-caliber rifle and light powder charges.

The author feels 36 and 40 caliber rifles are best for hard-to-down eastern woodchuck, but he had no problem taking this fat fall chuck with a 32-caliber Dixie.

Thompson/Center's Seneca put an end to this chicken coop raider.

the smallest diameter barrel they feel safe for the caliber rifle being built to maintain lines as sleek as possible.

Several years ago I had a TVA rifle built in 36 caliber using optional curly ash wood for the stock. Other than the wood, everything else on the rifle was standard. That rifle has remained a favorite small game gun ever since the first time I hunted with it. Green Mountain custom cuts its smaller caliber barrels—32, 36 and 40 calibers—one turn in 60 inches for TVA. Green Mountain's rifling runs right at .012" deep. With such deep grooves to fill with patching, I've found my 36 TVA rifle to shoot exceptionally well with a 30-gr. charge of FFFg behind a tight .015" pillow ticking patched .353" round ball, cast from one of the Lee Precision aluminum-blocked round ball moulds. The combination starts fairly hard, but

once started the smooth bore of the Green Mountain barrel lets the tight patch and ball be seated with the rifle's $^5/_{16}$" hickory ramrod.

Muzzle velocity with this load should be in the 1700 fps range, with muzzle energy right at 350 ft. lbs. Although this load is not much different from the load discussed earlier for the Thompson/Center Seneca 36, the longer barrel of the TVA rifle results in a slightly higher velocity. I get superb accuracy at both 25 and 50 yards. Off a good solid rest, it will consistently punch one hole groups at the shorter distance and occasionally will turn in five-shot groups at 50 yards that are barely more than one hole and measure around ¾-inch. The longer sight radius also aids in making those killing head shots on small game. A fat young juvenile turkey gobbler once made the mistake of

waltzing within 50 yards of the business end of this rifle, a mistake he'll never make again.

The basic TVA Tennessee rifle is $410.00 in percussion and $425.00 in flint. There is a long list of options, including several better grades of stock wood, sideplate, patchbox, nose cap and several others, all adding to the cost, of course.

Hatfield Rifle Works, of St. Joseph, Missouri, also offers a semi-custom long rifle that will rival the rifles built by many of today's skilled custom builders. Hatfield's "Squirrel Rifle" is not available in such variation as with the TVA rifle. Instead, it's a fairly plain but nicely executed copy of the rifles once produced by master riflesmith John Rupp of east-central Pennsylvania circa 1780.

Hatfield offers their rifle in 32, 36, 45 or 50, and here again we find the excellent Green Mountain barrels. Dixie Gun Works' reliable early-styled Ketland flint lock is used; though it's generally large for the over-all slim lines, the lock looks good on the early Pennsylvania styling.

Barrels for small bore Hatfield rifles are $^{13}/_{16}$-inch across the flats and cut one turn in 42 inches. This relatively fast twist allows a shooter to obtain reasonably fine accuracy while shooting light powder charges. The bore of a 36-caliber Hatfield I've been shooting for several seasons is like my TVA rifle except for the rate of twist. The 30-gr. charge of FFFg performs equally in the Hatfield, but I've also found absolutely no loss of accuracy by dropping the powder charge back to only 25 grains in the faster twist barrel. Muzzle velocity of the lighter charge from the 39-inch barrel runs right at 1400 fps, with muzzle energy slightly under 300 ft. lbs. This is one of the finest shooting 36-caliber squirrel hunting rifles I've ever had the pleasure to shoot.

An occasional hunting partner of mine was so impressed with the performance of the 36-caliber Hatfield rifle, he ordered one of the early styled flinters in 32 caliber. Last season he dumped quite a few treetop tricksters with his favorite squirrel hunting load comprised of only 20 grains of FFFg and a 44-gr. .311″ round ball, which he patches with .015″ thick pillow ticking. The light load is effective on 25 to 30-yard shots at small game, but really drops at longer 50-yard distances. Since most of his shots at game are taken well within the accuracy limits of his small bore rifle, ineffectiveness at longer ranges doesn't bother him.

Hatfield sells their rifle for $499.95, with the only options being choice of caliber and steel or brass mounts. Premium grade maple is used for the full length stock and high quality components, including a fine set of double-phase double-set triggers, are used in the construction of this semi-custom rifle.

Halfstock fans wanting a semi-custom rifle of traditional and authentic styling can turn to Ozark Mountain Arms, of Branson, Missouri. Ozark is best known for fine Hawken copies, but they also manufacture a superb little small bore muzzle-loading rifle they call the "Muskrat." Available in 32, 36 and 40 calibers, this little percussion rifle is reminiscent of the 19th century small game hunting rifles produced throughout Kentucky, southern Indiana and southern Ohio.

Like the TVA and Hatfield rifles, the Muskrat has a Green Mountain custom barrel, custom cut 36 inches long, with rifling depth at .012″, and one turn in 42 inches twist. Loads given for the 36 and 32-caliber Hatfield rifle should also work well in the Muskrat of the same caliber, the barrels all having the same rate of twist.

At one time, 40-caliber rifles were extremely popular. Quite a few original rifles, especially the late percussion halfstocks which the Muskrat closely copies, had 40-caliber bores. This size must be considered too small for use on deer and experience will soon dictate that it's just too large for satisfactory results on edible small game species. The 40 caliber's popularity was likely as an economical target shooting bore or for use hunting such species as woodchuck, foxes, coyotes and maybe turkey.

The fast rate of twist in the 40-caliber Muskrat allows the rifle to be shot with relatively light loads that could be used for taking squirrel and rabbit if the shooter were careful to try placing his hits in the head. Even a light loaded 92-gr. round ball would ruin edible meat if a shot caught a rabbit or squirrel through the front shoulders or rib cage. A 40-gr. charge of FFFg black powder behind a tightly patched .395″ ball would result in a muzzle velocity of around 1400 fps while developing approximately 400 ft. lbs. of energy in this rifle.

The Muskrat is well built, and would make an excellent small game hunting rifle. If rabbit and squirrel are a hunter's primary targets, then I would have to suggest either the 32 or 36 caliber. Larger game, including most varmints and turkey, could be taken with the little 32, but either the 36 or 40 caliber would be best suited. The 36 caliber would be the best all-round choice.

Ozark currently sells their Muskrat for $525.00 in finished form. A money-saving alternative is to purchase their completely assembled, but unfinished "semi-kit" at $395.00. This is the same rifle, assembled with Green Mountain barrel, premium maple stock, poured pewter nose cap, double-set triggers and completely brass mounted. It needs minor contouring around the lock and cheekpiece, final sanding and finishing, browning and polishing. This rifle has a Siler percussion lock, one of the finest on the market.

Although the selection of small bore muzzleloaders is far from mindboggling, the rifles described here should answer the needs of most hunters. Aside from being the best suited for taking small game for the freezer and table, the pea-sized bores of these rifles make them economical to shoot. A pound of FFFg black powder has 7,000 grains. An average powder charge for most 45 and 50-caliber rifles could be somewhere around 70 grains, or about 100 shots per pound. Even 35-gr. charges in a 36 caliber would double the number of shots in a can of powder. Think how many shots in a pound shooting just 20 gr. in a pipsqueak 32-caliber rifle. Shooters that cast their own balls will realize the same kind of savings in valuable lead.

A small bore rifle requires that a shooter either buy or put together a smaller diameter short starter. A starter that closely fits the bore of a 45 or 50-caliber rifle won't begin to go into the muzzle of a 32, 36 or 40-caliber barrel. Dixie Gun Works and the Log Cabin Shop, of Lodi, Ohio, offer starters for bores as small as 31 caliber. Also, a powder measure that adjusts from zero up is suggested. Some measures offered today start at 50 grains and aren't suitable for small bore charges of 20 to 40 grains.

Most small bore rifles I've shot seem to shoot best when the patches are lubed with saliva. As a rule, the smaller the bore, the quicker it fouls. A saliva-lubed patch helps to wipe some of the residue from the previous shot as the ball is seated. It's a good idea to install a good rod tip and cleaning jag on the end of the ramrod, pinning it through the rod tip and rod to make sure it doesn't pull off. When the bore shows signs of fouling, usually after just two or three shots, a saliva-dampened cleaning patch can be quickly run in and out of the barrel. The rifle will then load as easily as it did with the first shot.

Powder charges for smallbores need to be as precise as possible. With such a small projectile, a half-grain more or less of powder can result in as much as an inch variation in impact on even a 25-yard target. The smaller the bore the more variation in the powder charge affects accuracy. When shooting a 32-caliber rifle for best accuracy, I now weigh powder charges and carry individual charges in separate small containers. For most hunting, a good powder measure—sold by a number of muzzle-loading equipment suppliers—works well enough if care is taken to tap the measure slightly to settle powder the same each time. Getting one of the small bore muzzleloaders to deliver pinpoint accuracy at close range is part of the enjoyment of shooting them. ●

MURATA TYPES 13 and 18:

They founded an arsenal system, part of the beginnings of empire.

by CHARLES S. SMALL

The outside appearance of the Murata single shot rifle gives no clue to the unusual bolt construction—closed, left, or open, below.

LITTLE attention has been paid to the man who was responsible for creating Japan's small arms industry. Because there was no information available in the USA, I went to the logical source, the Diet Library at Tokyo. This library, the equivalent of our Library of Congress, contains a detailed biography.

Tsuneyoshi Murata was the man, born in 1832, who started his military career in the army of Lord Shimazu, one of the local daimyo, at Kagoshima in southern Japan. He ended his career by retirement as a General in 1890. Constantly striving to improve Japan's shoulder arms, as a Lt. Colonel in the Imperial Army, he convinced his superiors to let him visit Europe to review their arms development, their manufacturing methods, and their training methods.

The day that he left for Marseilles, January 18, 1875, the nine-year-old Imperial Army had a motley collection of secondhand European shoulder arms. For three hundred years they

The right side of the action showing the two-piece bolt construction. The groove and hole at the front end are part of the gas vent system. The inscription on the receiver is the design approval date Meiji 18 (1885).

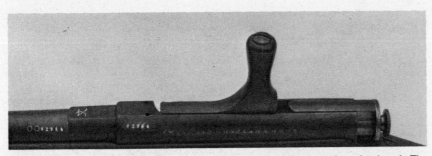

The two circles in front of the serial number on the barrel are the arsenal overhaul mark. The character indicates transfer to The Ministry of Education. The long inscription on the receiver translates: "Imperial Japan Murata Rifle Tokyo Ordnance Arsenal Small Arms Factory."

The top view of the Beaumont action. It has a three-piece bolt assembly, a non-rotating bolt head, and the bolt handle is split for easy removal of the V spring.

had used the matchlock. In the 1860s they got a batch of percussion muzzle-loading Enfields. Over the next ten years they acquired surplus obsolete arms from England, France and Belgium. They had Sniders, Braendlin-Albinis, the Tabitiere, Chassepot and probably others which have gone unrecorded.

Some of the troops had been trained by the British and others by the French. Murata realized, early in his career, that Japan required one standard shoulder arm and that it should be made at home. He dedicated himself to these two objectives.

Murata carried with him to France his design for the standard Japanese rifle. When he showed this design to the French officers they told him that it resembled the Dutch Beaumont.

When it came time, circa 1870, for the Dutch to develop a metallic cartridge musket their engineer, Beaumont, evidently decided that he wanted no part of the new-fangled coil spring. Gunsmiths in Europe had been making V springs for several centuries and the art was well understood. Beaumont's design for a single shot bolt action rifle contained two sturdy V springs, one which was tucked away in the bolt handle and which powered the striker, and another which was integral with the sear and served as the trigger spring.

How Murata got his hands on a Beaumont has not been recorded. One can understand why he liked this design. Japan had competent metalsmiths who made superb swords and who had had several centuries of experience turning out matchlocks which contained a V spring. In addition most of the surplus weapons imported had V springs.

Murata's design must have evolved in the years between 1871, when the Beaumont appeared, and his arrival in France early in 1875. One obvious solution would have been to purchase the Beaumont design and the machinery and gauges to make the rifles. In this case national honor would not have been served. Murata had to design his own rifle.

Murata has been credited with "inventing" his design. Others have called him a small arms genius. When you compare the Beaumont and Murata rifles it is obvious that there is no invention in the true sense of the word. Copying an obsolete design is not the hallmark of genius.

One must understand that the Japan of the 1870s was not an affluent country. Just out of the handicraft stage they had almost no industrial base. Machine tools were scarce and industrial design techniques unknown.

Murata spent the better part of a year touring the arsenals and military training camps in Europe. Both the British and Germans made excuses to keep him out of their arms manufacturing plants. It is apparent that he learned very little about rifle design during his tour. After he returned he spent the next four years working out the details of his design and persuading his superiors to go ahead with the project adopting the basic design he had taken to Europe in 1875.

The design was approved during Meiji 13, 1880 in our calendar, and

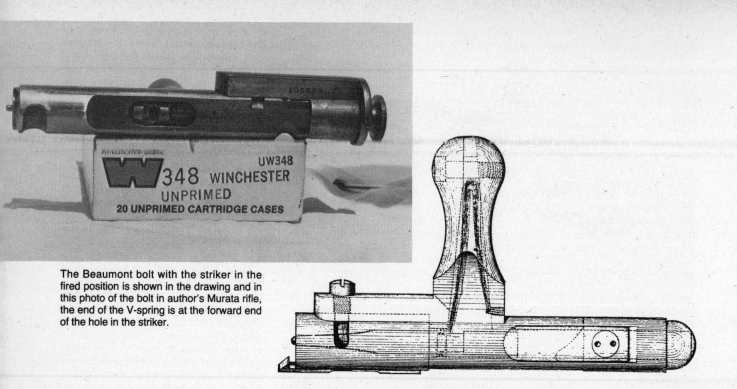

The Beaumont bolt with the striker in the fired position is shown in the drawing and in this photo of the bolt in author's Murata rifle, the end of the V-spring is at the forward end of the hole in the striker.

plans for actual production commenced. In effect the final design was a poor man's copy of the Beaumont. Murata and his assistants had redesigned the Beaumont to make it cheaper to manufacture.

The other influence on the design was the French Gras. Japan had a large number of old Chassepot rifles and had seen their conversion to metallic cartridge rifles. Minus a few thousands of an inch here and there, the 11mm Murata cartridge is a copy of the French Gras round of 1874. These few thousands of an inch made it enough different to serve national honor and win a place in the cartridge collectors lexicon with the 11x60R Murata cartridge.

One source says that the first Murata cartridge had a paper case and that the change to a metallic case was made during 1884. Tokyo Arsenal had hired a German technician in 1880 to teach them the art of drawing solid brass cases. Certainly paper cases were never made for the Type 13 service rounds.

The major design change which sets the Type 13 apart from the original Beaumont was the simplification of the bolt. The redesign was a retrograde step. It eliminated the features of the Dutch bolt which made this peculiar design successful.

The Beaumont has a conventional three-piece bolt assembly, nonrotating bolt head, bolt and handle, and a cocking piece. The bolt handle is split

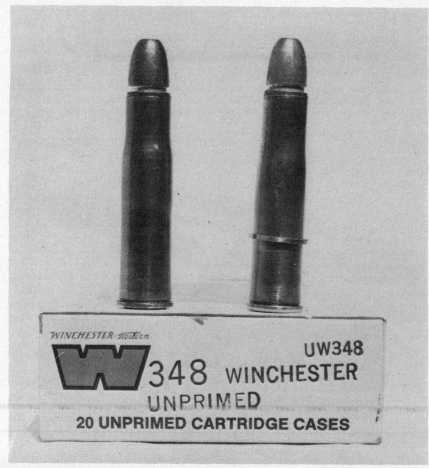

Both these cases were reformed from 348 Winchester brass. The one on the left fits the French Gras. On the right is a Murata case which is almost, but not quite indentical. On this case is the 0.055 brass ring—not in its final position—necessary to get the correct headspace.

and the V spring can be inserted in the cavity in the bolt handle when the front part of the handle is removed. The long end of the V spring has a curved notch which bears on a shoulder of the striker. The striker is pinned to the cocking piece and does not rotate.

The Murata has a two-piece bolt assembly. The bolt head, bolt body and handle are all in one piece. The V spring is contained in a recess in the bolt handle. With the striker removed the V spring is pushed up into the recess from the bottom. The striker is then inserted, the hole in the striker aligned with the front of the handle cavity, and then through a hole in the end of the bolt handle the spring is pushed down until the long arm of the spring goes through the hole of the striker. As a result of this construction when the bolt is rotated the striker is also rotated.

The Beaumont extractor is attached to the bolt head. The Murata extractor has a long leg which terminates in a lug which rides in a groove in the bolt. It is prevented from rotating by riding in a groove in the left wall of the receiver.

On both designs, the sear is integral with the sear/trigger spring. Neither has an ejector. The Murata has no safety. The Murata bolt stop is a pin in the left side of the receiver. The Gras has the same type of bolt stop only it is on the right side.

The disassembly of the Beaumont bolt only takes a few minutes. After removing the screw which holds the front part of the handle this piece comes off and the spring comes out easily. To get the Murata bolt apart you first remove the screw at the top of the bolt handle. Then turning the bolt upside down with a drift or brass punch you drive the long arm of the spring out of the hole in the striker. This permits the striker to be removed. To remove the spring from the cavity in the bolt handle you use the drift or punch again, this time through the hole in the end of the handle, and pound the spring out of its cavity.

Ammunition manufacturing for the Murata 13 began during 1881. While the Tokyo Arsenal was producing the Murata 13 they were also rebuilding the Chassepot to a cartridge rifle presumably with the Murata bolt. This accounts for the Murata 13 rifles with a barrel and bayonet lug which takes the French bayonet.

The principal difference between the first 1880 model and its successor, the Type 18 which was approved during 1885, was the provision in the lat-

ter for venting the gas in the event of a blown primer or a ruptured case. The 1885 design has an annular cut at the bottom of the receiver just to the rear of the chamber. This cut is in line with a hole in the bolt rib when the bolt is in the closed and locked position. In addition there are two holes in the receiver bridge for good measure. Murata did not believe in hiding his light under the proverbial bushel for on both versions Murata got his name stamped on the right side of the receiver.

The materials are not the best. The stocks are made of one piece of a relatively soft wood similar to Philippine mahogany. The steel is also relatively soft but adequate for the low black powder pressures. The worst feature is the soft metal of the sear which wears rapidly.

The standard instructions for making Type 13 or 18 ammunition start with a .348 Winchester case and building up the rim by sweating on a brass disc to the base. You then have to put a bushing in the primer hole. If you follow these instructions the resulting case will no longer fit the standard reloading press shell holder. I know of no way to alter the standard .348 shell holder with ordinary tools.

These two rifles were made with chambers approximating that of the French Gras which means that the rim thickness was that of the old folded head case. To make matters worse Murata added a Mauser Type A base. The result is a very thick rim dimension.

The .348 Winchester case has an 0.065 inch thick rim. My Murata has a distance from the face of the bolt to the bottom of the chamber rim recess of 0.12 inches. The use of an unaltered case would result in 0.055″ excess headspace.

There is a simple solution to this problem open to anyone posessing a lathe. Make a brass ring with outside diameter .640″ inches and inside diameter 0.550″. This ring is slipped over the neck of the case and rests against the front of the .348 rim. It is not soldered or fixed in any way. The ring thickness should be 0.055″. After firing the ring can be slipped off the case and the base fits the standard shell holder. The .348 Winchester case is thick enough just forward of the rim so that no expansion should take place with reasonable black powder or Pyrodex loads.

Regretfully I must admit that I have never fired a single shot. After having made the ring I loaded a .348 case for fire forming and found that the V spring in the bolt handle would not

impart sufficient velocity to the striker to fire a modern primer. Possibly the original Berdan primers had a thinner skin and were more sensitive. I did make one case by, after pulling the trigger and releasing the striker, hitting the end of the striker with a brass hammer which fired the primer and fire-formed the case. At this point, I quit.

The annular ring technique works very well with the Dutch Beaumont which has a really powerful spring in the bolt handle. It also works with a large number of other 1870-era rifles whose cartridges had thick rims. It has the added advantage, when cases are used with rim diameter less than the original, of being made to the larger rim diameter so that the extractor gets a firm grip. Soldered-on base shims are liable to be torn off, if larger than the diameter of the rim of the case being used, when extraction gets just a little sticky.

My rifle was evidently used in the 1894-5 China War for it was sent back to the Tokyo Arsenal for reconditioning. Just ahead of the serial number stamped on the barrel are two circles which is the designator for arsenal overhaul.

Over the chrysanthemum on the barrel is stamped a Japanese character which indicates that the rifle was taken out of Imperial Army service and transferred to the Ministry of Education. The Ministry of Education supplied obsolete rifles to the school system where the youth received their preliminary indoctrination, prior to Army service, in the art of dying for the Emperor.

I have some sympathy for Colonel, later General, Murata. When he designed his Beaumont copy Japan was only a few years out of their centuries of non-industrial feudal system. Only three years before his first rifle was approved the Imperial Army had to put down a revolt when the government forbade the samurai from carrying their swords in public. Murata was a patriot, a rifleman of great skill, and an extrovert. He had no technical education, no advantage of having been brought up in an environment current with the development of machine tools, firearms, or mass production. He did his best and while his national pride and lack of technical skill resulted in his taking an obsolete design and making it worse, he thought he was acting in his country's interests. Whatever we think of his designs, the arsenals that made them survived to serve. ●

The One That Never Was

by TOM TURPIN

Good design really *isn't* everything.

The Friedrich Wilhelm Heym Arms factory in Muennerstadt, West Germany.

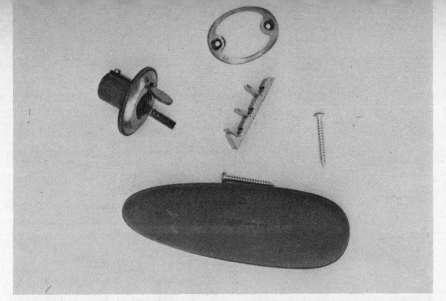

Some of the accessories used in the construction of the two prototypes. The skeleton grip cap was fitted on the 270, and the remainder of the items shown on the 375. Shown in the trap of the grip cap is a "night" sight front sight. It features a large ivory bead that can be flipped up in poor light conditions.

The Heym version of the Magnum Mauser alongside the Heym-Ruger. The latter is a Teutonic variation of the Ruger Number One.

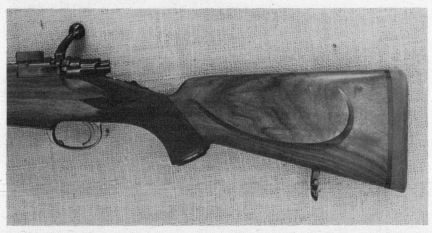

The buttstrock design of the rifle is pure classic. Please note the detachable sling swivels, the Pachmayr Old English recoil pad, and the tang safety.

E VERY confirmed gun-nut dreams of designing a factory-made firearm, of seeing his baby in all the gun shops around the country. Aside from a few well-known gun writers—Elmer Keith, the late Jack O'Connor and John T. Amber, for examples—gun fanciers have little, if any chance to exert the least bit of influence on firearms' design. One can have a custom firearm built to his own specifications, but that's about it.

Four years ago, however, one average gun-nut did have the opportunity to be heard by an arms manufacturer. As unlikely as it may seem, this arms manufacturer actually sought the advice of Mr. Average. I know the story to be true, as the nut whose advice was sought was me!

At the time, I was assigned with the U.S. Forces in Germany. A close friend, German master engraver Erich Boessler, had and has a close association with the arms factory of Friedrich Wilhelm Heym. I was familiar with Heym by reputation, but had never had first-hand experience with Heym arms.

In about 1973, Rolf Heym, the last of the Heym sons, passed away very suddenly and left the firm essentially "headless." For a short period, the quality of the Heym product slipped a bit, but after a couple of years the owner hired a management specialist as Managing Director. With a most appropriate name for the job, Peter Bang got Heym back on the track.

About a year after Bang had taken the job, I visited Erich Boessler in Muennerstadt, which is also the location of the Heym factory, and discovered Erich had arranged an appointment with Peter Bang.

It turned out Heym had attended the NSGA show in the United States that year, and Peter was trying to reintroduce the Heym line into the U.S. market. I received a complete tour of the factory, and spent the biggest part of the day in Peter's private office. He was most interested in getting my views on how to improve the line, and more particularly, on what could be done to the line to make it more palatable to American tastes.

Toward the end of the day, Peter mentioned that John T. Amber, longtime editor of GUN DIGEST, had suggested Heym produce a long-extractor Mauser-type bolt action rifle for the U.S. market. Heym had once manufactured just such a rifle, but in recent years had followed the trend and switched to the small hook extractor action. Peter solicited my views.

Naturally, I agreed with John Amber (to do otherwise would have been tantamount to blasphemy.) Out of the blue, and then and there, Peter asked me to design the rifle for him! I accepted faster than Ed McGivern drew a revolver.

I promised to assemble all the needed components, and get back with him. I was also asked to come back to the factory to oversee the final stages of construction and agreed to do so. I don't think a tank could have stopped me from doing so.

We were to build two prototypes, one in a standard caliber, and the other in a magnum. For calibers, the 270 Winchester and the 375 H&H, both longtime pets of mine, were chosen. Peter procured two commercially available long-extractor Mauser type actions, and barreled them with Heym hammer-forged barrels. I obtained a Pachmayr Old English recoil pad for the 375, and a Biesen skeleton steel buttplate and grip cap for the 270.

I also contacted my old shooting buddy "Bud" Miller who lives in Los Angeles, and he stopped by London Guns in Santa Monica where Phil Katsenes provided him with one of his trap grip caps, night sight front sight insert, and a three folding leaf express sight. These items were forwarded to me in Germany.

While awaiting receipt of all the "goodies," I bombarded Peter with sketches and drawings of how portions of the rifles were to be constructed. I requested quarter-ribs, barrel band sling swivel and front sight ramp, soft rust bluing, etc. If Peter tired of receiving my endless string of notes, letters, comments, and suggestions, he certainly kept it quiet. I suspect that toward the end of the project, he was probably wishing that he had never heard of this guy named Turpin.

When all the accessories had been received, I sent them to the factory with another mass of notes and suggestions. Peter notified me when the rifles were ready for the final stock shaping, and I took another leave and headed for Muennerstadt. There, I drove the factory's two master stockmakers absolutely bananas until the shaping of the stocks was finished. A few changes here and there were also made and the rifles were then ready for the rust blue jobs, and stock finishing and checkering. I had to leave, unfortunately, before this final stage of the rifles' construction was completed. The workers in the factory, on the other hand, were overjoyed with my departure.

Shortly thereafter, I departed Ger-

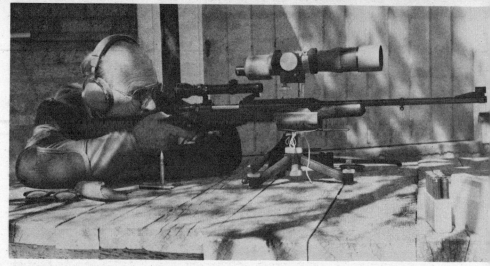

Jim Wilkinson, world big game hunter and owner/operator of the Rifle Ranch, Prescott, AZ puts the Heym prototype to the bench test.

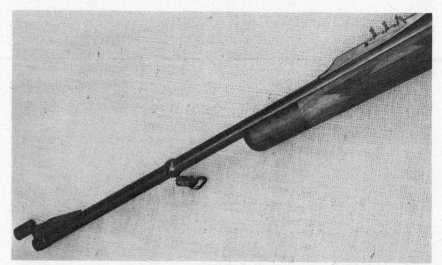

Some of the features of the Heym magnum include barrel band front sight ramp with night sight, barrel band front swivel, and quarter-rib with folding leaf express sights.

An ideal scope mount for the 375 is the EAW quick-detachable mount, also from Germany. These mounts are superb, and always return the scope to zero.

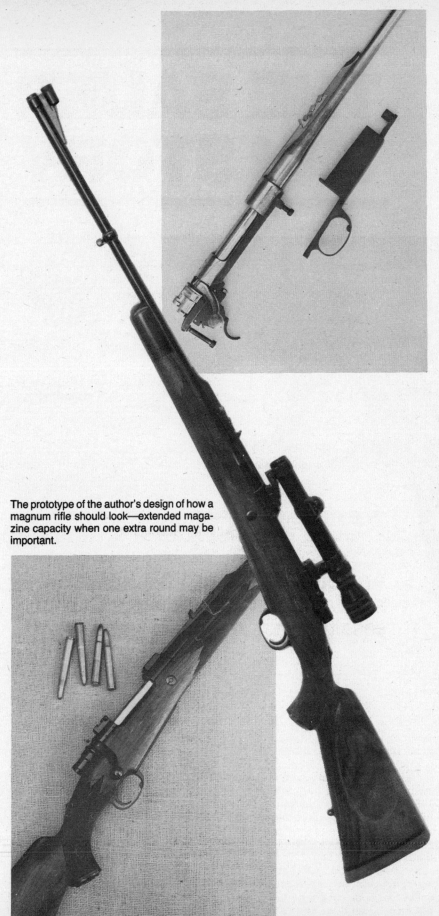

The early stages of construction of the 270 prototype on the reliable 98-style action. Notice the quarter rib and folding leaf express sights.

The prototype of the author's design of how a magnum rifle should look—extended magazine capacity when one extra round may be important.

many for a new assignment in the United States without seeing the finished products. Six months later, at the first Shooting, Hunting and Outdoors Trade Show (SHOT) in St. Louis, I finally saw the completed rifles. At the risk of sounding conceited, they were super.

The lines were exactly as I had envisioned them, and the workmanship was superb. The Heym gunmakers had followed my suggestions to the letter. Minor glitches needed correcting, but these rifles were prototypes and could be corrected.

I wish I could end this Cinderella story by saying that the rifles sold like hotcakes, and within a few months my creations were displayed in every gun shop from Bangor to Seattle. Alas, such is not the case. The guns did receive numerous compliments during the SHOT show, and subsequently at the HUNFI Show in Paris and the German Firearms Exposition in Nuernberg, they simply did not sell in enough numbers to warrant Heym going into production. Therefore, to date, a grand total of two have been built; the two prototypes.

At the 1980 SHOT Show in San Francisco, the magnum prototype was once again on display. The beautiful classic stock of European walnut glowed with a sheen that only a hand-rubbed oil finish can provide. That alone attracted many admirers. The quarter rib and folding leaf express sights, trap grip cap, and folding ivory bead "night sight" in the front ramp attracted others. By the end of the show, however, my design had attracted many admirers, but no buyers.

At show's end, Peter called me aside and presented me with the rifle. If there was ever a death knell for its production, that was it. Naturally, I was most grateful to receive this beautiful rifle, and will cherish it always. I would have been much happier however, had it gone into production.

As I write these lines in my little den, the rifle reposes in a rack ten feet away. My one chance as a designer of great rifles is now gone. I tried, but either my taste in rifles is out of touch with the buying public, or we picked a terrible time to introduce the design. Whichever, it is immaterial. The fact is that the rifle is now the one that never was! ●

THE SAUER 38H STORY

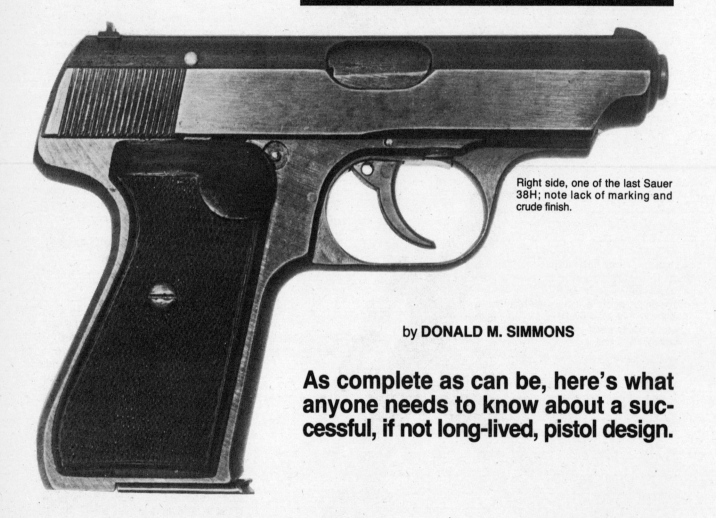

Right side, one of the last Sauer 38H; note lack of marking and crude finish.

by **DONALD M. SIMMONS**

As complete as can be, here's what anyone needs to know about a successful, if not long-lived, pistol design.

ASK ANYONE who is interested in guns, particularly semi-automatic pistols, what were the three great pocket automatic pistols to come out of Germany after World War II? You will usually get this answer, "The Walther PP and PPK, the Mauser HSc and that other double action auto." It is "that other auto" that this article is about—the Sauer 38H, possibly the most advanced pistol of the three.

What made the Sauer 38H so great? And why did it disappear? These ques-

tions and others will, I hope, be answered here.

J.P. Sauer & Son is an old and honored maker, having been founded in 1751. They then made smoothbore flintlocks at Suhl in Thuringia. Suhl was so important as an arms manufacturing center that a guild was located there as early as 1563.

By 1905, the firm was looking at the emerging semi-automatic pistol and about that time offered a unique low-powered locked breech automatic, the

Roth-Sauer. This first auto was not a great success although it was made up to the 1930's in Europe. The Roth-Sauer was the brainchild of George Roth who also designed the sound-a-like Roth-Steyr.

The Roth-Sauer took its own short 32-caliber round with even less punch than the 7.65mm Browning or 32 ACP (Automatic Colt Pistol). By 1913, Sauer produced a new pocket automatic, characterized by well rounded appearance with no sharp corners and excellent construction and finish. The first pistols were in 7.65mm Browning (32 ACP) but by 1920 a scaled down version, the 6.35mm Browning (25 ACP) was added. In the mid-1920's Sauer came out with an even smaller pistol—their W.T.M. (Westentaschen Model or Vest Pocket Model) in 6.35mm Browning, somewhat like a Baby Browning. Next, in the Sauer auto pistol line, was an upgrading of the original Model 1913 which was called either the Model 1930 or more often the "Behörden" Model ("Behörden" means authority in German). The Behörden, as one of its improvements, had a rounder and fuller grip than its predecessor and a loaded chamber indicator pin. The "Behörden" Model was, to my knowledge, made only in 7.65mm Browning.

All these pistols made by Sauer, from the earliest Roth-Sauer to the latest "Behörden" Model, had at least one characteristic in common—they were all striker-firing pistols. A striker-fired pistol has a spring-loaded striker or heavy firing pin which is cocked and locked rearward by the sear. When the trigger is pulled, the sear drops and the striker is driven forward by the striker spring. The strength of the spring and the weight of the striker determine its effectiveness in igniting the primer of the cartridge. For reliability in firing, many designers and users prefer the hammer-equipped pistol over the striker. The hammer, for instance, may be recocked in a second attempt to fire a misfire and clear the gun.

Sometime, as early as 1932, arms authority Dr. Mathews tells us that Sauer started work on a double-action hammered pistol to compete with their neighbor, Walther. The Sauer design team was led by Herr O. Zehner, it is believed. Starting with a modified "Behörden," they arrived by 1938 at an entirely new concept of a pistol. This new arm was named the Sauer 38H, the "38" standing for 1938, of course, and the "H" for hammer. I believe that in-house, the "H" became almost the model designation as we find most of the major parts of a Sauer 38H stamped with an "H."

Production of the Sauer 38H did not begin until late 1939 or early 1940. As early as 1934, the German Wehrmacht let the arms industry know it wanted a pistol to replace the P-08, which we call the Luger. One can be sure, with the possibility of an Army contract, Sauer devoted a large portion of their design time to larger military pistols.

Today, we know only that Sauer &

Roth-Sauer pistol, left side, caliber 7.65mm Roth-Sauer. This is Sauer's first type of self-loading pistol.

Sauer Model 1913, left side, caliber 7.65mm Browning ACP.

Sauer "Behörden" model, left side, caliber 7.65mm Browning 32 ACP.

Sohn did submit a prototype to the military in 1937, but so did Walther and several other firms and when the smoke cleared, it was Walther's HP which became the P-38. The Sauer submission is thought to have been a locked-breech enlarged 38H. In any case, by 1939 at the earliest, the Sauer 38H was beginning to appear on the German market. Samples we have of these early commercial pistols show outstanding workmanship and finish.

Most collectors are well aware of both the Walther PP and PPK and the Mauser HSc. This awareness is no doubt attributable in part to several excellent books on both pistols. Jim Rankin's Volume I and Volume II *Walther Models PP and PPK 1929-1945*, and the late Roy Pender's *Mauser Pocket Pistols 1910-1946* has a section on the HSc as did Walter Smith in his *Mauser Rifles and Pistols* and Jim Belford & Jack Dunlap who wrote *The Mauser Self-Loading Pistol*. Yet strangely, the Mauser HSc pistol appeared later on the German scene than the ignored Sauer 38H. The Mauser double-action pistol appeared first no earlier than April 1940 by which time Sauer had made and proofed at least 9000 pistols.

Walther, Mauser and Sauer all added their new double action pistols to their lines by just continuing where the older model's serial numbering stopped. Thus, Walther started the PP and the later PPK at serial number 750,000, Mauser began the HSc at serial number 700,000 and Sauer commenced at serial number 260,000.

The quantities made by each firm are also interesting, showing that during roughly the same time period, both Walther and Mauser outproduced Sauer.

Approximate Quantities Made

Walther PP & PPK

1929-1945
550000

April 1940 to 1945
269000

Mauser HSc

1940-1945
251000

Sauer 38H

1939-1945
253000

April 1940 to 1945
244000

I have always maintained that the Sauer 38H was a better pistol than either of its rivals. To judge this objectively, it is only fair to have an early example of each pistol.

All three have so many good features that an over-all comparison almost becomes a matter of personal preference. The PP's and PPK's and HSc's all stay open after firing their last round unlike the Sauer. However, this desirable feature is somewhat negated in the HSc because the slide goes forward automatically when a loaded magazine is inserted. This always makes me nervous. The Walther in most cases and the Sauer have side operating magazine catches like the Colt 45 Model 1911, while the Mauser HSc has a bottom operating catch; one which requires the non-shooting hand to operate it. The Sauer and the Walthers both had loaded chamber indicators, a strong safety feature. The Sauer 38H, because of its concealed hammer would seem to need a cocked indicator, but it has this feature in the cocking lever since one can feel if the hammer is back or not by lightly depressing that lever.

Field stripping any of the three pistols is very easy—my own preference is for the Sauer because no maintained pressure on the takedown latch is required and yet it is impossible to accidentally pull the trigger unless this latch is in the up or locked position. The Mauser HSc mostly used wooden grips which to my mind was the right way to go; oddly Walther used wood on their very late PP's, but Sauer, never to my knowledge, used wood which certainly would have added to the durability of their fragile grip pieces.

The Mauser HSc and the Sauer 38H each have a magazine safety disconnect. This device insures that should the magazine be removed from the pistol leaving a live round in the chamber, the piece will not fire unless the magazine is reinserted. This is an excellent safety, though some auto pistol users do not like it.

If one adds up all the safety features found on the three different pistols, the Sauer is ahead of its rivals.

A collector trying to weed out the variations and changes in a firearm's history is first required to look over as many samples as he can see, preferably owning some so that they can be completely disassembled. He can then ask fellow collectors to see their similar pistols and he can look for examples at gun shows and record these. This is about the limit that most collectors and writers can go; some do far less.

Detailed Description of a Very Early Pistol

V-1 The Sauer 38H has a left side slide legend or logo that is all in one line. This logo stamp reads as follows: "J.P. Sauer & Sohn (son), Suhl Cal. 7.65."

V-2 The right side of the slide reads "D.R.P." which translates to "German patent."

V-3 The pistol's magazine catch is retained in the frame by a pin.

V-4 The cocking/decocking lever is mounted on a large headed screw.

V-5 The pistol's barrel has six lands and grooves.

V-6 The Sauer is proof marked with a crown over a "U."

V-7 In order to improve night firing of the pistol, the sights are both painted with a luminous paint.

V-8 The pistol has no manual safety.

V-9 The trigger bar is thick and has a short riveted pin. It also has a bottom mounted wire spring.

V-10 The pistol's magazine has a well-finished machined floorplate with a pair of intertwined "S's" and a "U" all superimposed on each other at the forward end; at the rear is "Cal. 7.65."

V-11 The Sauer has a well polished exterior finish with a deep luster blue.

V-12 If one removes the slide from the frame, immediately under the barrel there is a rather large milled lightening cut. The axis of the milling cutter runs perpendicular to the barrel's axis.

V-13 The frame mounted magazine safety lever is machined and has a spring which has a special groove in the frame above the safety lever mounting stud. The lever is not attached permanently to the stud.

V-14 In order to reduce the weight of the frame and to allow easy disassembly of the hammer strut spring, there are a series of three lightening holes. These are located in the lower section of the rear grip strap. The larger and lower hole aids in disassembly and all three serve to lighten the frame of the pistol.

V-15 The body of the magazine has a small rivet on its right side toward the top. This rivet operates the magazine safety lever. The magazine has eight holes which serve as cartridge counting holes.

V-16 The trigger is made of machined steel.

V-17 The area immediately behind the trigger is covered with a steel machined plate pinned in place.

V-18 The pistol's six digit serial number is stamped on the frame at the right rear above that grip.

Right side, very early Sauer 38H; note the two square pins of the magazine catch.

AN EARLY PISTOL

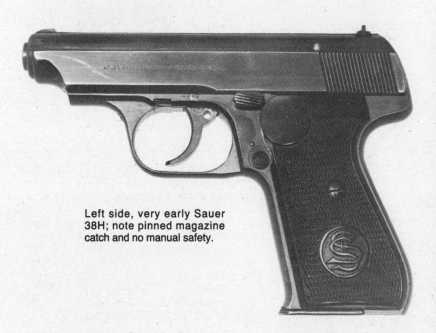

Left side, very early Sauer 38H; note pinned magazine catch and no manual safety.

V-19 There will be no serial number found on the magazine of this Sauer.

V-20 The button on the magazine catch has concentric grooves to improve the grip surface.

V-21 The pistol has no acceptance stamps to indicate military or police use. These early pistols are all commercial.

V-22 The Sauer 38H is in 7.65mm Browning caliber.

V-23 The pistol's barrel is fitted to a boss in the frame and is secured by a pin. It is $3^{13}/_{32}''$ long.

V-24 The grips of the Sauer are made of a dull black material which is quite durable.

In the case of the Sauer 38H, I am indebted to Leonard Hunter who over the years sent out questionnaires to all the Sauer 38H owners he could find. He basically used fellow members of the National Automatic Pistol Collectors Association (NAPCA), but he also received data from people at gun shows. Mr. Hunter, being also blessed as an expert in electronics, put all this incoming data on a Univac computer and thus the task of where each variation occurs is very simply extracted from the marvel of our age. More than 300 pistols were recorded, providing a broad base for this article.

You will note no attempt to call one set of variations Type I and the next Type II and so on. This type of breakdown is excellent if enough is known, but firearms manufacturers don't hold up production to launch a series of changes—they just work them into production when they can. As soon as some later expert says, "This is what Type I looks like," somebody will come up with an exception. To my mind, the best way to describe any pistol is to first give its name and Model, then its serial number and then anything which is unusual about it. These things which are unusual can be a feature not usually found in this serial range or some special marking or caliber.

With this in mind and thanking both Len Hunter, and the contributing members of NAPCA, here is the Sauer 38H story. In order to understand the variations, it is best to describe what a sample of the first hundred produced was like.

First, the catalogue description giving the vital statistics: Sauer 38H semi-automatic pistol (self-loading), 7.65mm Browning caliber (32 ACP), 8 rounds capacity magazine, over-all length= 160mm (6 $^5/_{16}''$), barrel length= 80mm (3 $^{13}/_{32}''$), weight loaded= 785 grams (27.7 ounces). Special features, double action, hammerless (concealed hammer), with a unique hammer cocking and decocking lever. (While I call the use of the cocking-decocking lever unique, it did appear at least once before in the little known Mannlicher Model 1903, also a concealed hammer pistol in 7.63mm Mannlicher caliber.) There is also a magazine safety disconnect, and a loaded chamber indicator.

Each variation will be dealt with in detail but in this description of an early pistol, the variation number will precede the brief description as it would appear on the earliest production automatic. Following this description, a more detailed variation section will be found which delves into all known variations and their serial number ranges. The Sauer 38H, although made for only a few years, has a wealth of variations, most due to the continual effort to reduce the manufacturing time as Germany began to feel the bite of the Allied war effort.

Field stripping the 38H is very simple. Be sure that the pistol's chamber is empty; then withdraw the magazine. Next, pull down the takedown latch in front of the trigger. Now, pull the slide back as far as it will go and lift it off by raising it. The recoil spring can now be removed; this completes the field stripping of the pistol. How do you do a full strip of the 38H? My best advice would be—*DON'T!*

In today's rapidly shifting market and our eroding inflation, the task of trying to give a value of a Sauer 38H is not easy. In looking over various sources, I would say that a run of the mill pistol in very good condition is bringing from $150 to $175. This is virtually the bottom of the pile from a collector's point of view. The top prices for rare variations is virtually unlimited, $3000 for a 22 variant and $6000 for a late 380-caliber 38H. Be sure if you enter the arena of rare Sauer's, that you get the most expert opinion of the authenticity of your prize before you commit your bucks.

Sauer 38H, shown with a Sauer marked holster. Marked on inside of holster is "Sauer H 7.65." From the Len Hunter collection.

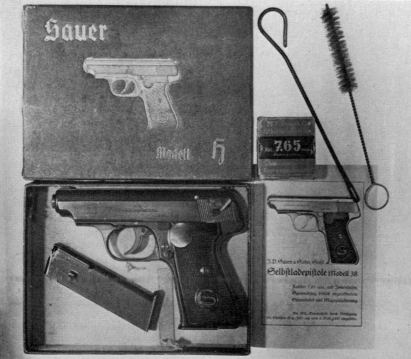

Sauer 38H in original box with extra magazine, ammo, cleaning rod and brush and manual. From the Len Hunter collection.

That is the story of the Sauer 38H, the littlest known of the German triumverate in pocket automatics. The Sauer's two rivals each appeared on the market after World War II. The Mauser HSc was made by the French when they took over the plant after World War II and then more recently, the Mauser has been made and imported here by Interarms of Virginia. The Walther plant fell into the Russian sector of Germany and we understand that it was dismantled by them. PP and PPK's however, were made in Mulhouse, France under license to Fritz Walther. These Manurhin were imported to America by Thalson of San Francisco. Later on, Walther set up his own plant in Ulm, Germany and produces today a complete line of firearms including the PP and PPK— these have been imported by Interarms, which now also makes a version called the PPK/S in their plant in Virginia.

(continued on page 214)

VARIATIONS

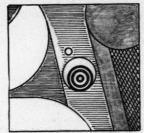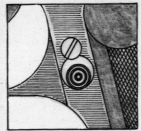

Magazine Catch. Left—pin retained magazine catch. Middle—screw retained. Right—special checkered magazine catch button found on "eagle C" police pistols.

V-1 Left Side Slide Logo

The very early Sauer 38H had a single line logo on the left-hand side of the slide. This inscription reads "J.P. Sauer & Sohn, Suhl Cal. 7.65." This one line logo started with s/n 260001 and lasted at least to s/n 260198. The logo was then changed to a two line pattern, "J.P. Sauer & Sohn, Suhl" over and to the left of "Cal. 7.65." The two line logo has been observed from s/n 260716 to s/n 408096. The two line logo gave way to the deletion of the company name leaving only "Cal. 7.65." This caliber only stamp has been recorded from s/n 411540 to s/n 510836. The caliber stamp was dropped and nothing was stamped on the left-hand side. This type was recorded from s/n 511601 to the highest s/n recorded 513349.

The left side of the slide of some special pistols have different stampings, among these are: The special caliber stampings of "Cal. 9K" and "Cal. 22 Kurz" and "Cal. 22L" all of which are found replacing the normal "Cal. 7.65." In addition some Nazi Party pistols are known. One is marked "Eigentum NSDAP" SA Gruppe Alpenland s/n 457618 and two others seen are marked "SA Gruppe Alpenland" s/n 465322 and s/n 465779. One special pistol has a German inscription which was awarded by H. Himmler, the head of the SS, to a marksman for special shooting ability. This rare pistol is s/n 474412.

V-2 Right Side Slide Logo

The early Sauer's 38H had slides with the right side legend of "D.R.P" which stands for "German Patent." This stamping was seen from s/n 260001 to s/n 260198. The next stamp to grace the right side was the single word "Patent." This was seen from s/n 260716 to s/n 409163. The next change in slide marking on the right side was to delete all stamps. These unmarked slides have been recorded from s/n 411540 to s/n 512478. The highest pistol recorded s/n 513349, has a special marking "Suhl, Ger. 1945" which seems to indicate it was made or assembled after the war with Germany was over, possibly for sale to the American G.I.'s.

V-3 Pinned Magazine Catch

The first type of magazine was pinned in place on the frame and had two square guide pins in the right side which kept it oriented in its hole—these square pins will protrude when the catch is depressed. These were seen from s/n 260001 to s/n 260716. Next, this complicated catch was replaced with a much more conventional one which was held in place by a screw head. This Sauer magazine catch doesn't protrude from the right side at all when depressed. The screw-held catch is recorded on pistols s/n 261113 to s/n 513349 which is the highest numbered pistol seen in this survey.

V-4 Cocking Lever Pivot Pin

The cocking/decocking lever in the earliest Sauer 38H is attached to a large headed screw pivot which must of course be unscrewed to remove the cocking lever. This type was seen from s/n 260001 to s/n 260716. The pivot was then changed to a headless screw which had an annular groove at its top to accept a lock ring. To remove the lever, the ring was now pried off and the entire assembly removed without unscrewing the pivot screw. The lock ring type was seen from s/n 267500 to s/n 513349.

V-5 Barrel Rifling

The Sauer 38H was, as has been stated, a modernized updating of the Sauer "Behörden" pistol, itself an improvement on the Sauer Model 1913. These two earlier pistols each had six-groove rifling so, as might be expected, did the earliest 38H's. The six groove barrels have been seen from s/n 260001 to s/n 261657. The Sauer firm somewhat later decided to go to four-groove rifling. Whether this was to improve the pistol or reduce tooling and machining is not known but the four-groove barrels are from around s/n 267500 to the final s/n 513349.

V-6 Proof Marks

The German proof mark which was established in May 1891 was a crown over "U." This nitro proof will be found on very early Sauer 38H's on the right hand side of the frame near the serial number. Also it will be found on the slide immediately above and finally on

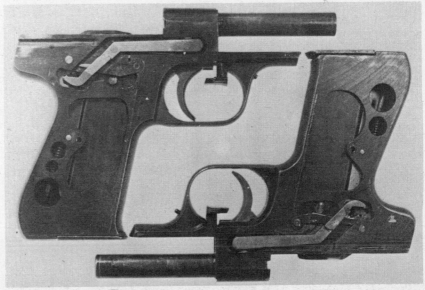

Trigger Bar and Magazine Safety Lever. Top—old type trigger bar and safety lever machined and pin mounted. Bottom—new type trigger bar and safety lever stamped and riveted.

Proof Marks. Left—"crown over N" up until April 1st, 1940. Right—"eagle over N" from April 1st, 1940 on.

the barrel of the pistol on the same right hand side just below the muzzle. Pistols bearing the "Crown U" stamp have been observed from s/n 260001 to s/n 268852. Since we know that the proof was changed on April 1, 1940, we can thus date approximately the first nine thousand as made before April 1940. This is about the only date we have in the entire Sauer 38H line.

On April 1, 1940, the nitro proof was changed to eagle over "N." These new proofs appeared in the same positions as the former proofs. They were found on pistols s/n 269466 up to at least s/n 506527. After the eagle "N" proof, the pistols at the very end of the war were not proofed at all. This may mean they were found in both the proof house and the Sauer factory by Allied troops and "liberated," or these pistols may have been assembled by our troops, also explaining the lack of proof marks. Knowing the thoroughness of the Germans, I doubt if any issued pistols to the Waffenamt (Army) were issued unproofed. There was one recorded pistol in the police F series that had no proofs but did have the police acceptance stamp. This was pistol s/n 510230. Pistols with no proof started with s/n 507065 and went to our highest s/n 513349.

V-7 Painted Sights

The Sauer in an effort to improve sighting in failing light, painted the visible surface of the front sight yellow, and the rear of the back sight red. The paint used had originally a phosphoresence which reduced with age. The paint used was often removed by the owner when it became chipped and unattractive. For this reason, one may find some pistols without painted sights, well within the range of the painted ones. Painted sights were seen from s/n 260001 to s/n 269944, starting with at least s/n 268852 some sights were no longer painted. Painted sights were never seen again by the high se-

rial s/n 513349. No military or police Sauers have been recorded with painted sights.

V-8 Manual Safety Lever

The earliest Sauer 38H had no manual safety. In the design of this pistol, the cocking lever makes a manual safety redundant. As designed, the pistol was to have a loaded magazine inserted and the slide then retracted and released, running a live round into the chamber of the barrel. If the pistol at this point was not to be fired, the cocking lever was depressed and the hammer lowered with complete safety on a loaded chamber. To fire the pistol, the trigger could be given a strong pull for a quick shot or the cocking lever could be depressed, cocking the hammer and allowing a more deliberate shot.

Probably due to the fact that Walther's PP's and PPK's have a slide mounted manual safety, Sauer added a safety to their already safe pistol. One feels that the military and/or the police may have asked for this feature, because no early pistols martially accepted have been seen without a manual safety. The earliest pistols without a manual safety have been observed from s/n 260001 to s/n 269954.

The safety was added but there was a period of overlap. The lowest pistol

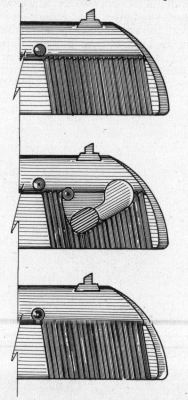

Manual Safety Lever. Top—no safety lever early. Middle—with safety lever. Bottom—no safety lever late.

seen that was equipped with a safety was s/n 263993 and the highest was s/n 511601. As the war progressed, the effort to reduce production time and material caused the manual safety to be dropped. These high numbered pistols without the safety run from s/n 472025 to s/n 513349. There is again a period of overlap.

The addition of the manual safety required a built up ridge on the top of the hammer so that when the safety was in the locked position the hammer could not move. The safety locked the hammer in either the cocked or uncocked position. Obviously, the modified hammers appeared at the same time as the pistols with a manual safety. However, when this safety was deleted toward the end of the war, the ridged hammers were still used for a while and then a non-ridged hammer was again used in production. For this reason, safetyless s/n 480778 had a ridged hammer while safetyless s/n 507557 did not. Stranger still, pistol s/n 511601 had both a safety and a ridged hammer.

V-9 Trigger Bar

The trigger bar, reaching from the trigger to the sear in early pistols, was thick and had a small straight wire spring mounted in its lower surface. There was also a small riveted stud behind the trigger pin. This type of trigger bar was observed from s/n 260001 to s/n 269954.

The later trigger bar had no spring on its bottom and got its tension from a leg of the trigger spring bearing on a much longer riveted stud. These new trigger bar pistols were seen from s/n 272251 to the terminal s/n 513349.

V-10 Magazine Floorplate

There is no part in most automatic pistols that is more subject to change than its magazine. Each Sauer pistol started life with two magazines. There is a pouch on all German holsters to carry this second magazine. When these pistols were captured by our troops, the magazines were sometimes swapped around. Because of this, any attempt to give the serial numbers where the various magazines will be seen, is very open to revision.

There seem to be seven types of magazine floorplates, a very high number for a five-year production time. The first floorplate is made of machined steel with the Sauer logo of the overlapping "S and S" on the forward edge and the caliber at the rear "Cal. 7.65," both read from the bottom. These are seen from s/n 260001 to s/n 272351. The next looks exactly like

a.   b.   c.   d.   e.   f.   g.

Magazine Floorplates. **a.**—machined steel "S,U,S" over upright small "CAL. 7.65." **b.**—machined steel "S,U,S" over upright large "CAL. 7.65." **c.**—machined steel "S,U,S" over large upside down "CAL. 7.65." **d.**—die cast "S,U,S" only. **e.**—machined steel upside down "CAL. 7.65" only. **f.**—machined steel, unmarked. **g.**—sheet metal steel with dimple, unmarked.

the first except the "Cal. 7.65" is much larger, seen from s/n 291473 to s/n 297955. The third floorplate has the words "Cal. 7.65" upside down. These were from s/n 337130 to s/n 352834. The fourth floorplate is a die casting, the "S and S" logo is still in place, but the caliber designation is completely deleted and seen from s/n 370038 to s/n 429432. Also, a die cast magazine floorplate was seen in a much higher number on s/n 478638, a possible replacement. The fifth type reverts back to machine steel with the logo deleted but the "Cal. 7.65." is back, still upside down. This magazine was seen in s/n 480778 and may well be a replacement. Type six is exactly like type five except there is no caliber designation. This was seen on s/n 329608, again this may be a replaced magazine. Type seven is a stamping and is characterized by a dimple in its forward edge. These were seen from s/n 457617 to terminal at s/n 513349.

These floorplates and the pistols so tied to them, are very tentative but if you find a late pistol with a type one or two floorplate, one can surely conclude that the magazine has been substituted somewhere along the line.

V-11 Pistol Finish

Early Sauer 38H's have as good a finish as any peacetime firearm. As the war progressed, the finish and the polishing of these pistols deteriorated. There must have been a general order to delete all polishing and this can be pinpointed fairly accurately. The high polish finish was seen from s/n 260001 to s/n 330432, from s/n 334649 we find polishing stopped. From there to s/n 513349, the finish becomes more and more crude, but the function and the safety of these late pistols is above reproach.

V-12 Lightening Cut In Frame Over The Trigger Guard

In early Sauer 38H's, the upper surface of the trigger guard under the

slide has a rather large milled lightening cut. The milling cutter that made this cut had its axis running perpendicular to the axis of the bore. These pistols were observed from s/n 260001 to s/n 337130. The cut was deleted from s/n 352834 to s/n 429432. At this point, the cut was restored but in a different form. The mill's axis is still at ninety degrees to the axis of the bore but the cut is much smaller. These small cuts were seen from s/n 439117 to s/n 513349.

While this cut is relatively unimportant, it and some other features are given to avoid swapping frames as pistols become more valuable and gun counterfeiters begin their nefarious work. If one comes across an allegedly early Sauer 38H but you find the late cut or none, take a very good look at the serial number on the frame.

V-13 Magazine Safety Lever

The magazine safety is an excellent feature found only in advanced automatic pistols. In the Sauer 38H there is a small machined lever mounted on a riveted stud under the right grip. In its earliest form, it was just resting on its stud and could be lost when and if the grip was removed. The operating spring had a small open notch above the stud in the frame. These notched frames found on s/n 260001 to s/n 337130. A headed rivet was added to the mounting stud to avoid accidental disassembly. This riveting of the safety started by at least s/n 267500 and continued until terminal s/n 513349. Later, the lever was changed to a sheet metal stamping, this simplified set-up was from s/n 352834 to terminal s/n 513349.

V-14 Lightening Holes In The Frame's Grip

In order to reduce large sections of steel in the grip and to reduce weight, lightening holes were drilled into the lower rear grip strap. The lowest hole also allows a wire to trap the hammer

spring. Above this hole are found two additional holes which serve only as lightening holes. These three hole frames are from s/n 260001 to s/n 370038. The upper two holes were replaced by one hole giving roughly the same metal removal with one less operation. The two hole frames were from s/n 383021 to s/n 513349.

V-15 Magazine Body Safety Stud

The original magazine body had a rivet on its right side to operate the magazine safety disconnect. In order to set this rivet from the left side, an extra hole was added to the cartridge counting holes. There are therefore eight hole magazine tubes, seen from s/n 260001 to s/n 383021. In later magazine tubes, the rivet was dropped and the metal of the tube itself was upset to form a stud-like protrusion. The punch which formed the protru-

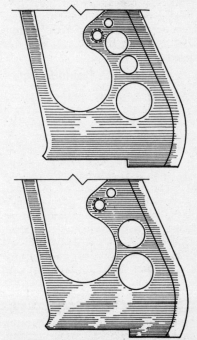

Lightening Holes in the Frame's Grip. Top—early three-hole type. Bottom—late two-hole type.

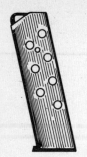

Magazine Body. Left—left and right sides of early magazine body, riveted stud type. Right—left and right sides of late magazine body, extruded stud type.

sion needed a larger clearance hole on the left side and so a bigger diameter hole was punched which did away completely with one of the counter holes, and these tubes are called the seven hole magazine. These were from s/n 405263 to terminal at s/n 513349. The integral protrusion magazine tubes began to appear with the die cast magazine floorplate. Thus, magazines with die cast floorplates will be found with either riveted or protruded magazine safety studs.

V-16 Trigger Material

The trigger in early Sauer 38H's was a forging that was then machined and polished and finally blued. These triggers were recorded on s/n 260001 to s/n 393629. As an attempt to save machining, the Germans later went to a die cast trigger; these were found on s/n 334950 to s/n 513349. They were left as cast with a grey appearance. There is obviously an overlap where one can find either type of trigger, by s/n 396446 the die cast trigger prevailed. Even to this, there are exceptions such as pistols s/n 457617 and s/n 511601 which had steel machined blue triggers.

V-17 Cover Plate Behind Trigger

Because the trigger of the Sauer requires a large cavity in the trigger guard, a large cutter milled in part behind the trigger, making an unattractive and dirt catching depression. In order to cover this, a sheet metal plate with a U-shaped piece of steel spot welded on the back was pinned in place in the frame. This cover plate was polished and blued and became almost invisible. Such plates were found on pistols s/n 260001 to s/n 405263. As an economy, a one-piece sheet metal cover with bilateral ears was made and pinned in place like the original cover. This piece required no polishing as it was already smooth. These covers with the integral ears are found on s/n 429432 to s/n 513349. There are many exceptions to the above, to list those seen in the survey: s/n 466576, 500066, 501777, 502459,

508171 and 511601 all had early covers.

One feels that the cover plate was mounted onto the frame before that part was serial numbered and then these partially finished frames were dumped into a bin. They were then drawn from stock as needed with obviously no attention given to what type cover plate was on the frame. This would lead to many exceptions in the high range of serial numbers. The steel or die cast triggers and the spot-welded or sheet metal with ears cover plates will be found in any combination.

V-18 Serial Number Location

On most Sauer 38H pistols, the serial number will be found on the right-hand side of the frame at the top of the grip. There will also be the last three digits of this number found on the slide on the underside of the muzzle which can only be seen with slide disassembled. There is also the last three numbers on the rear of the breech block assembly. This means that the three major pieces of the pistol are numbered. Pistols with the right-hand serial are s/n 260001 to s/n 478454. For some reason, it was decided to stamp the serial on the left side exactly opposite from the original placement of the number. There are again exceptions to the above and are found around the breakoff point. If a range is desired with no exceptions, then it would be from s/n 260001 to s/n 472025. Left-hand serialed pistols are from s/n 473043 to s/n 513349. The range without exceptions that have left-hand serials would be from s/n 478465 to s/n 513349. I think we can again see that frames which had been serialed in batches, were binned and drawn from as needed. The group from s/n 472025 to s/n 478465 may have either right or left serials. To illustrate, the following had a right serial—s/n's 472025, 474043, and 478454. The following had left serials—s/n's 473043, 474334, 474780, 475412, 475594, 475768, 476288, 477814, 477995, 478465 and from there on.

V-19 Serial Number On Pistol's Magazine

There are some pistols which are police-accepted which will have the pistol's serial number on the two magazines. These are quite rare and I believe the numbers on the magazines were added by the police and not done at the Sauer factory. They will be found in three different locations—on the side of the magazine tube, at the rear of the magazine tube, and on the floorplate of the magazine. The side of the tube has the full serial number plus a one or two indicating the first or second magazine. The back of the tube is much the same. The floorplate will usually have only the last three digits of the serial number.

My guess is that certain troops of police had a policy of having their magazines tied to their pistols. Different troops probably had different numbered positions on the magazine.

Examples with the serial number on the side of the magazine tube are s/n's 291473, 293396 and 305573.

Examples with the serial number on the rear of the tube are s/n's 289279, 311525 and 312214.

Examples with the serial number on the floorplate are s/n's 295043, 317283, and 320430.

All of the above examples are police accepted—eagle "C."

V-20 Magazine Catch Button

Another characteristic of the police-accepted Sauer 38H was to have a rather crudely done checkering on their magazine button. The regular pistol had a neat set of concentric grooves to form this non-slip surface. Some police groups specified checkering and I would guess that they checkered their own pistols in their police armory. We found these checkered magazine buttons only on police eagle "C" pistols, never on eagle "F," but they were not on all eagle "C" or even on all eagle "C" in the same serial number range. Checkered buttons were found on s/n's 270956, 274298, 276492, 279301, 288514, 288550, 291473, 297955, 308293, 311383, 314897, 315264, 317283, 326088, 337130, 343582, 346280, and 346607. The feature was certainly on most early eagle "C"s and by s/n 340007, it was dropped, never to reappear.

V-21 Acceptance Stamp

There were three primary markets for Sauer 38H pistols: Commercial, Army, and Police. Commercial pistols have no acceptance stamps on the left-

Acceptance Stamp. **a.**—commercial. **b.**—early military double "eagle over 37." **c.**—"eagle C"
police. **d.**—military "eagle over 37." **e.**—"eagle F" police.

hand forward edge of the trigger guard. Commercial pistols would probably also be any pistols used by officials of the Nazi party. Commercial pistols have been encountered from s/n 260001 to s/n 513349 or over the entire span of the pistol's numbers. The original Army procurement is characterized by having two eagle-over-37 stamps. These early Army pistols are relatively rare, this survey found the following pistols—s/n 271456, 272168, 272351, 272488, and 273082. As the Army continued to use Sauer 38H's, the stamp changed to a single eagle-over-37, such were seen from s/n 274047 to s/n 504527. The early police pistols will be characterized by having an eagle over a "C." These were seen from s/n 270956 to s/n 481013. The later police pistols were marked with an eagle over "F" and the survey turned up these from s/n 488246 to s/n 510230. I feel that eagle "C" and eagle "F" represent different police contracts in time and were probably issued to the same police troops. Other makes of pistols issued to police have been seen with eagle "K" and eagle "L." Before the survey, I felt that there were many more Army-issued Sauer 38H pistols than commercial or police. The actual percentage judging from 300 pistols examined, would be an even 33⅓ split.

V-22 Caliber

The Sauer to all intents and purposes was issued in only one caliber—7.65mm Browning. There were other calibers made but they are very rare. The odd caliber pistols are found in most cases in a special serial number range under the normal range of the 7.65mm Sauers. Added to this group is a small number of 22's in the regular run of pistols. The Sauer 38H in 9mm Kurz (380 ACP) is very rare; there were two found. One had a high polish and had the characteristics of an early pistol in the s/n 267000 range but not the earliest range, having neither the earliest logo nor the pinned magazine catch. Its s/n is 210034 showing, I think, that the range of 210000 was left in the "Behörden" series for experimental Sauer 38H's. The second 380 was unserial numbered and had a

greenish finish and late pistol characteristics.

There was a very small group of special 22's made in the regular serial numbered series of Sauer 38H. These are for the 22 Long cartridge and at least one had an extra long barrel giving it the looks of a Colt Woodsman. The recorded serials are s/n 269942, s/n 269944 and s/n 269954.

There is also a group of 22-caliber Sauers which use the 22 Short and may or may not have light aluminum frames and/or slides. These pistols are back in the special serial numbered series. The two recorded pistols are s/n 210027 and s/n 210028. All the above are very rare pistols and are highly desirable to any collector.

While on the subject of caliber variations in the Sauer 38H, there is one more caliber that allegedly was manufactured. This rumor started with W.H.B. Smith's book "Pistols & Revolvers" in which he said the Sauer was made in 6.35mm (25 ACP). This was also reinforced by Elmer Swanson in *Automatic Firearm Pistols* in which was shown a Sauer 38H drawing with "Cal. 6.35" on the slide. The survey failed to turn up such a pistol, also neither Smith nor Swanson mentioned the existence of 22-caliber Sauers. I certainly feel that a 25-caliber 38H never appeared in the normal serial number range.

V-23 Barrel Length

The regular Sauer has a barrel 86mm (3 $^{13}/_{32}$") long. The examination of many of these pistols turned up one pistol with an exceptionally longer barrel, much too much different than precise German tolerance would allow. This pistol, s/n 266676, had a 3 $^{15}/_{32}$" long barrel. The extra $^1/_{16}$" all protrudes from the slide at the muzzle and it has no threads at the muzzle for attaching a silencer or other device.

V-24 Grips

Grips are a subject calculated to raise the hackles of any Sauer collector. The early pistols were issued with dull black plastic grips which had a good life expectancy. Next, a new type of plastic was introduced and it broke if you even looked at it cross-eyed. For

this reason, many late Sauer 38H's will be found with Franzite replacement grips. These U.S.-made grips are only one step better than the fragile German ones. On the Franzite grips, if the grip screw is tightened, the grips curl at the top and bottom. These grips come in a black that is a reasonably good substitution, they are also offered in a white grip which had a pearl shade that looked like a dead fish's belly, and in a mottled brown finish.

The Sauer also will be found with cast aluminum grips with the S&S logo, but I believe these are German replacements. There also must have been a run of plastic grips made in the war that had a reddish color instead of black. Since grips are almost as easily substituted as magazines, it is hard to say when, what was used and for how long.

On the inside of early grips, we find an interwoven MHD with 431 over it and a series of different letters and numerals at the bottom. These letters are "S," "T-1" and "K" and there may be others. This entire logo is encircled and it is very possible that it represents the grip manufacturer's legend with a date code. Below the logo is "242/25L" or "242/25R" depending on whether the grip is right or left.

In a "Behörden" s/n 205712, the grips are marked with a different insignia RWS with three lines under the initials, while we still find the apparent Sauer code 242/23L and 242/23R. I think Sauer jobbed out their grips to various plastic fabricators, but their company number was 242 and their part number was 23 or 25 depending on the pistol's model. At a later date, grips are found marked just "Ia." These are the type which break so easily.

On examining one pistol's grips, we found extensive grinding on the inside but the letters "SS-38H" were left—this is the code number for a "Franzite" replacement grip. The normal "Franzite" grips are clearly marked with a logo which in this case had been deliberately ground off. There is no doubt that a pair of "Franzite" grips are better than no grips at all, but no attempt should be made to make them appear original.

Sauer 38H, caliber 22 Short, aluminum slide and not blued. From the Joe Buffer collection. (Andy Southard Jr. photo)

Sauer 38H, marked as belonging to the Nazi party group Alpenland. From the Len Hunter collection.

Sauer 38H special presentation pistol from H. Himmler to a winning marksman. From the Joe Buffer collection. (Andy Southard Jr. photo)

Sauer 38H "eagle C" police with matching magazine, number 1. From the Len Hunter collection.

(continued from page 208)

What happened to the Sauer 38H and why hasn't it reappeared? Well, first let's look at Sauer in the post-war days. The Sauer plant at Suhl was taken over by the Russians and has been renamed VEB-Ernst Thalmann works. Mr. Sauer's son, Rolf-Dieter Sauer being the only heir, reestablished the Sauer plant in Eckernförde, West Germany in 1951. At first, the new Sauer plant concentrated on hunting rifles and shotguns. These were followed by a modern copy of the Colt Single Action Army which is imported here by Hawes of Los Angeles. About 1974, Sauer announced the manufacture of the SIG-Sauer automatic pistol Model P-230. It is made in 380 ACP, 32 ACP, and a new caliber 9mm Police which is a more powerful 380 or a less powerful 9mm Luger depending on how you look at it. They also make the 230 in 22 Long Rifle. The line is imported here by Hawes. The Model 230 has some of the features of the 38H. The hammer decocking lever is present but now used only to lower the hammer since it is no longer concealed in the Model 200. The slide remains open after the last shot has been fired—a feature not found in the 38H. The new SIG-Sauer weighs only a little over a pound in the 380, 32, 22 form which makes it a lot lighter than the 38H. There simply was no need to revive the 38H, so it never happened. ●

Sauer 38H, very special length in caliber 22 Long Rifle. From the Len Hunter collection.

Sauer 38H, caliber 9mm Short or 38 ACP. From the Edward Macauley collection. (Nester Dick photo)

SIG-Sauer Model P-230 in 9mm Police caliber. (Photo from J. P. Sauer & Sohn GmbH, Eckernförde)

Acknowledgements

Special thanks to Leonard Hunter who made this article possible.

Thanks to D.C. Cole, and Don Andrews who undertook earlier efforts in cataloguing the variations of the Sauer 38H.

Thanks to all the members of the National Automatic Pistol Collectors Association for their help in the survey.

Thanks to Rich Lechman, Joe Buffer, Ed Macauley and Herr A. Krohm of J.P. Sauer & Sohn.

Bibliography

Firearms Identification Vol I, II, III, J. Howard Mathews. Charles C. Thomas, Springfield, IL.

Pistols, a Modern Encyclopedia, Henry M. Stebbins, et al. The Stackpole Co., Harrisburg, PA.

Walther Pistols, W.H.B. Smith. The Military-Service Publishing Co., Harrisburg, PA.

Automatic Firearm Pistols, Elmer Swanson. Wesmore Book Co., Weehawken, NJ.

German Pistols & Holsters 1934-1945, Robert Whittington. Taylor Publishing Co., Dallas, TX.

Mauser Rifles and Pistols, W.H.B. Smith. The Military Service Publishing Co., Harrisburg, PA.

The Mauser Self-Loading Pistol, James Belford, Jack Dunlap. Borden Publishing Co., Alhambra, CA.

Mauser Pocket Pistols 1910/1946, Roy G. Pender II. Collectors Press, Houston, TX.

NRA Illustrated Firearms Assembly Handbook. The NRA Office of Publications, Washington, DC.

GUN DIGEST 29th Edition, John T. Amber, Ed. Digest Books, Inc., Northfield, IL.

Small Arms Makers, Robert E. Gardener. Crown Publisher, Inc., New York, NY.

The World of Lugers–Proof Marks, Sam Costanzo. Privately Printed.

The Famous Automatic Pistols of Europe, Vol. I. John Olson, Ed. Jolex, Inc., Paramus, NJ.

Walther Models PP and PPK, Vol. I, II, James L. Rankin. Privately Printed.

The P-38 Pistol Vol. I, Warren H. Buxton. Privately Printed.

The Gun Digest Book of Exploded Firearms Drawings, Harold A. Murtz, Ed. Digest Books, Inc., Northfield, IL.

The NRA Book of Small Arms Vol. I Pistols & Revolvers, W.H.B. Smith. The Military Service Publishing Co., Harrisburg, PA.

SPORTING ARMS OF THE WORLD

by LARRY S. STERETT

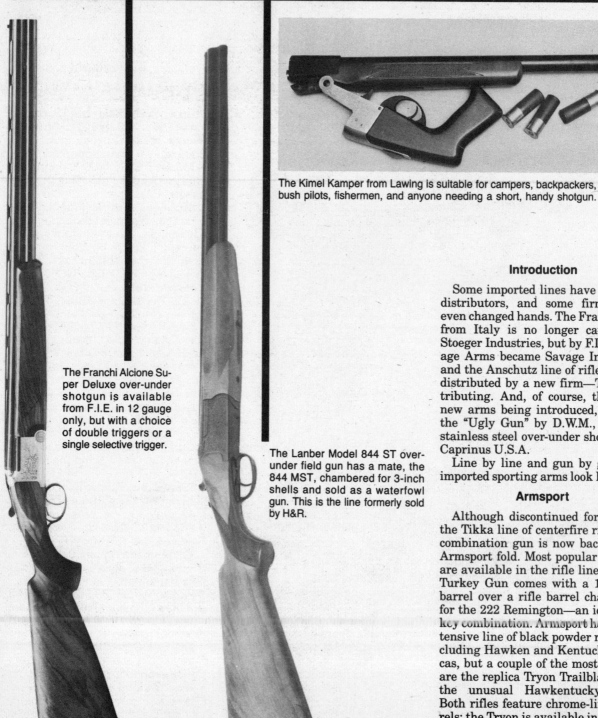

The Kimel Kamper from Lawing is suitable for campers, backpackers, bush pilots, fishermen, and anyone needing a short, handy shotgun.

The Franchi Alcione Super Deluxe over-under shotgun is available from F.I.E. in 12 gauge only, but with a choice of double triggers or a single selective trigger.

The Lanber Model 844 ST over-under field gun has a mate, the 844 MST, chambered for 3-inch shells and sold as a waterfowl gun. This is the line formerly sold by H&R.

Introduction

Some imported lines have changed distributors, and some firms have even changed hands. The Franchi line from Italy is no longer carried by Stoeger Industries, but by F.I.E., Savage Arms became Savage Industries and the Anschutz line of rifles is now distributed by a new firm—Talo Distributing. And, of course, there are new arms being introduced, such as the "Ugly Gun" by D.W.M., and the stainless steel over-under shotgun by Caprinus U.S.A.

Line by line and gun by gun, the imported sporting arms look like this:

Armsport

Although discontinued for awhile, the Tikka line of centerfire rifles and combination gun is now back in the Armsport fold. Most popular calibers are available in the rifle line and the Turkey Gun comes with a 12-gauge barrel over a rifle barrel chambered for the 222 Remington—an ideal turkey combination. Armsport has an extensive line of black powder rifles, including Hawken and Kentucky replicas, but a couple of the most popular are the replica Tryon Trailblazer and the unusual Hawkentucky rifles. Both rifles feature chrome-lined barrels; the Tryon is available in 50 or 54 caliber, and features a back action

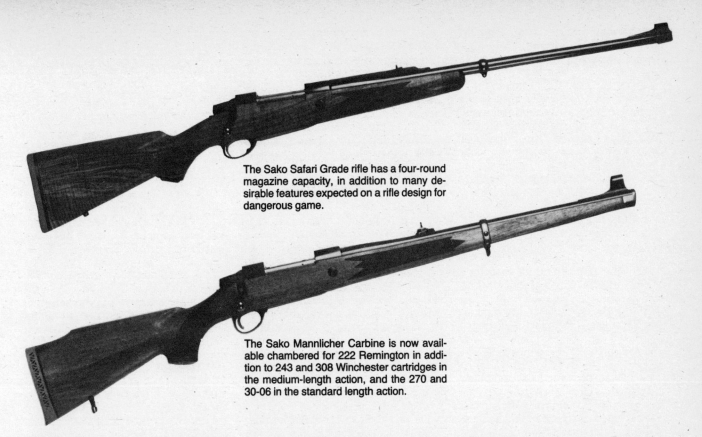

The Sako Safari Grade rifle has a four-round magazine capacity, in addition to many desirable features expected on a rifle design for dangerous game.

The Sako Mannlicher Carbine is now available chambered for 222 Remington in addition to 243 and 308 Winchester cartridges in the medium-length action, and the 270 and 30-06 in the standard length action.

percussion lock, while the Hawkentucky in a choice of 36 or 50 caliber, percussion or flintlock (50 caliber only) is a modern blend of the Hawken and Kentucky design to provide a rifle suitable for women and younger shooters of small stature. Both rifles represent exceptional values for black powder shooters.

Beretta U.S.A.

The entire line of A.301 autoloading 12-gauge shotguns has been discontinued, being replaced by the A.302 design, which can handle either standard or magnum barrels; all the A.301 autoloaders in 20 gauge are still available, in addition to the A.302 models in 20 gauge. In the Model 680 Trap line, a 32-inch over-under barrel assembly has been added, and the Combo sets can be had with this barrel length also, with either a 32-inch or 14-inch Mono barrel. The only other additions to the Beretta line include the Model 687EL in 20 gauge, with a choice of 26-inch barrels in improved cylinder/modified, or 28-inch barrels choked modified/full, standard length chambers only.

Caprinus U.S.A.

It's a new name to U.S. shooters, but one which should become well-known in the near future. Eventually "Caprinus Sweden" will consist of a shooting system of over-under shotgun barrels, shotgun-rifle barrels, and over-under rifle barrels, all manufactured of stainless steel, and all using a common action.

The action is "self-opening," and the coil spring-powered firing pins are set by operation of the top lever. In place of a conventional hinge pin/hook or trunnions/hooks, the "Caprinus Sweden" uses a circular receiver segment method of joining and pivoting the barrels. This arrangement allows a trim receiver depth, in addition to acting as a bolt and recoil absorbing surface, plus "lifting" the lower barrel upward to provide self-opening.

In 1982, only the 12-gauge over-under shotgun is available, in field, Skeet, and trap grades, all chambers standard. Barrel lengths of 28 or 30 inches are available, depending on the grade, and a choice of stocks includes pistol grip or English grip, with or without Monte Carlo. Deluxe walnut is standard, but Grand Luxe, Super Luxe, and Collector Grade walnut is also available at extra cost, in addition to special dimensions. Interchangeable choke tubes are standard on all but the Special Skeet grade, and six choke tubes are included with each shotgun, with special off-bored tubes available as options to adjust the shot patterns up, down, right or left. The tang safety is automatic, but is readily switched to manual operation if desired. There is also a patent-

ed safety interruptor which prevents accidental discharge if the loaded shotgun is dropped or subjected to a powerful impact.

As an example of the "Caprinus Sweden," the field grade gun might include 28-inch barrels, with six interchangeable choke tubes, gas-pressure activated automatic ejectors, an automatic safety, a barrel selector just forward of the trigger, an English-style stock with checkered grip, a slim forearm, a weight of under 7 pounds, and a fitted carrying case of Indian water buffalo. Although not low priced—from $5500 to just under $6000 in early 1982—the "Caprinus Sweden" over-under is unique in design and construction, and the shotguns examined were literally works of art.

F.I.E.

The Franchi line of field shotguns is now available from this Florida firm in over-under and autoloading models. The 48/AL Ultra-Lite autoloader is available in Standard and Hunter grades in a choice of 12 or 20 gauge versions chambered for standard length shells, plus a 12-gauge Magnum version chambered for 3-inch shells. The 48/AL is a recoil-operated design, with a tough, lightweight alloy receiver that has a full one-year warranty, and barrels are interchangeable between the Standard and Hunter grades within a gauge. Barrel length choices range from a 22-inch Slug model, with sights, to a 30-inch full choke. The Magnum comes only with 32-inch full choke barrel.

The three over-under models are available only in 12 gauge at present, with 28-inch modified/full choke barrels, in addition to 27-inch improved cylinder/improved modified choke barrels in the Alcione and Falconet models, all chambered for standard length shells. All models feature single selective triggers—inertia-set on the Diamond Grade, and mechanical on the other two models—selective automatic ejectors, and French walnut stocks and semi-beavertail forends. The Diamond Grade features a scroll-engraved silver-plated steel receiver, while the Falconet Super has a "Guaranteed-For-Life" lightweight alloy receiver, silver-plated and hand engraved, and weighs about 6 pounds 1 ounce with the 28-inch barrels. The Alcione Super Deluxe, with hand-engraved steel receiver, 24 kt. gold-plated trigger, and a 14 kt. gold inlay on the receiver bottom, in addition to a fitted, luggage-style carrying case, is the top of the line.

F.I.E. is planning to have, by the time you read this, the Franchi SPAS (Special Purpose Automatic Shotgun) 12, which can be used as a pump action or an automatic, with a wide range of 12-gauge ammunition. The SPAS 12 has a folding, removable stock, rifle sights, three safety systems, can be fired with one hand, weighs 8 pounds, and measures 37 inches over-all with a barrel length of 18½ inches.

Interarms

The Alexandria firm has discontinued much of its shotgun line, except for Rossi guns, but has added a new Falco over-under 410-bore. Featuring 24-inch full choke barrels, the Falco is priced under $300. The Mark X rifles, the Rossi pump 22s and lever-action carbines, and the Whitworth Express rifles remain high-volume items for Interarms.

La Paloma Marketing

The Japanese K.F.C. M-250 autoloading 12-gauge shotgun and their 12-gauge over-under shotgun in field, Skeet and trap versions are still available, and this Arizona firm now imports two Unique rimfire rifles from France. Manufactured by Manufacture des Pyrenees Francaises, the bolt action T-Dioptra is available chambered for either 22 Long Rifle or 22 WRM cartridges; it has a steel receiver, hand checkered French walnut stock, adjustable trigger, 5-round detachable box magazine, a barrel length of 23½ inches, and a weight of just under 6½ pounds.

The other rifle is the semi-automatic X-51, a design Firearms International imported a couple of decades back. Chambered for the 22 Long Rifle, the X-51 is a takedown model in which the barrel stays with the receiver; the detachable 5-round magazine is located ahead of the trigger guard. Cocking is via a rod in the forearm. The barrel length is 23½ inches, the wood is French walnut, and the weight is approximately 5¾ pounds.

One unusual feature of the X-51 is a stud on the right side which, if loosened, changes the rifle to an auto-ejecting repeating design; tightening the stud changes the rifle back to a conventional autoloader. Both rifles come without sights, but with the receivers grooved for tip-off scope mounts—each has a 2-year warranty.

Lanber Arms of America

The Spanish-manufactured Lanber 12-gauge over-under shotguns used to be imported by H&R, but an expanded Lanber line is now available from this Michigan-based firm. The Model 844 ST is a field gun chambered for standard length shells, while the 844 MST Waterfowl gun is chambered for 3-inch shells. In addition, there is a Model 844 Skeet gun and a Model 900 Trap gun, both with engraved receivers, single selective trigger, selective auto ejectors, and ventilated top and side ribs. The latest models have a 2 prefix, such as 2.844 MST, plus four upgraded models—the 2.004 Adventura II (field), 2.005 Aventura I (field), 2.008 Rival II (Skeet, pigeon, etc.), and 2.009 Rival I (trap)—all of which feature new screw-in Lanberchoke tubes, very similar to Winchoke tubes. The Rival I and II versions have no side ribs between the barrels, and the upper portion of the forearm is grooved longitudinally to reduce finger slippage. The Rival II trap gun has a Lanberchoke only in the under barrel, while the other three models have Lanberchokes in both barrels.

Morris Lawing

Folding shotguns are not new, but the version manufactured in Italy to Lawing's specifications is a bit differ-

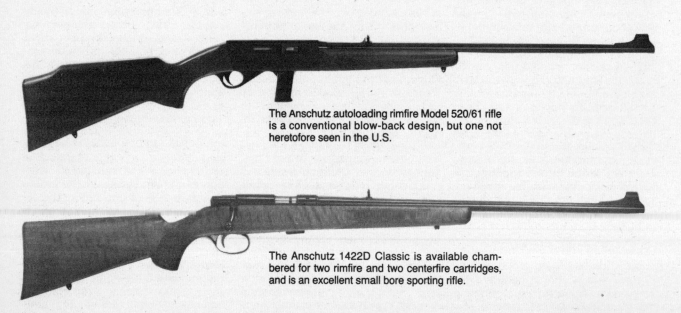

The Anschutz autoloading rimfire Model 520/61 rifle is a conventional blow-back design, but one not heretofore seen in the U.S.

The Anschutz 1422D Classic is available chambered for two rimfire and two centerfire cartridges, and is an excellent small bore sporting rifle.

The Super Match 1813 Anschutz was the 1413 Super Match 54, and is definitely the apex of the rimfire match rifles. And certainly looks it.

The Anschutz 1808ED Super is specially designed for International running target shooting.

The 1427B Biathlon rifle offers special spring hinge caps on the sights—here in the "down" position—as well as built-in magazine holders and other ski-shooters' niceties.

ent. Available in a choice of 410-bore, and 20- or 12-gauge sizes, the Kamper by Lawing features a 19-inch chrome-lined barrel, an over-all length of 27 inches in firing mode, and a weight of approximately 4 pounds. Folded, the Kamper measures approximately 4 inches by 19 inches, for easy storage or transport. The receiver of the hammerless action is nickel-plated, with a hardwood pistol grip stock and a sliding tang safety.

Leland Firearms

Hand-crafted to the customer's specifications by Union Armera in Spain, shotguns from Leland are basically English-style hammerless models of classic design. Four of the models are available from stock, if desired, while the 219E is available only on special order. The 204E is a boxlock hammerless of Anson & Deeley design with Purdey triple bolting, double triggers and a choice of 26-, 27- or 28-inch barrels in 12, 16, 20 or 28 gauge. The 209E, 210E, and 215E are sidelock models, with more engraving, and special selected walnut in the English-type stock and forearm. The same gauges and barrel lengths are

available, except for the 215E, which is not currently available in 16 gauge. The 219E features side clips, a Holland-type "Easy Opener" action, and extra special figured walnut; it represents the top of the Leland line, although many optional features are available at extra cost, such as a Churchill rib, single non-selective trigger, 30-inch barrels, 3-inch chambers, etc.

Puccinelli Company

Several grades of Italian-manufactured Bernardelli side-by-side shotguns are available, including a Puccinelli Gran Lusso boxlock with full scroll-engraved sideplates, a Gran Lusso Hammer gun with hand engraving in coil finish and gold inlaid lettering, and a Gran Lusso Sidelock with scroll engraving in relief-ribbon pattern, plus inlaid lettering and hand-detachable sidelocks. All three Gran Lusso models come with fitted leather luggage-style carrying cases, and all three are stocked to the customer's specifications in French walnut, with semi-beavertail forearm. Barrel lengths are to the customer's specifications, as are the chokes, and

gauges available include 12, 16, 20, and 28, except for the sidelock which is available only in 12 gauge at present.

Shotguns of Ulm/ H. Krieghoff

New is a lightweight K-80 Skeet gun. Featuring a receiver of Dural, a tough aircraft-grade aluminum alloy, the lightweight K-80 will weigh under 8 pounds in 12 gauge. The lightweight is also available in a K-80 Pigeon Gun grade, with a choice of 28-, 29-, or 30-inch barrels, specially choked and designed for pigeon shooting; the K-80 Pigeon is standard with a regular steel receiver. The K-80 Trap gun has been upgraded with a new tapered-step ventilated rib, aluminum rib on the Unsingle barrel, and screw-in choke tubes for the Unsingle barrel. All K-80 shotguns are available in five grades—Standard (I), Bavaria (II), Danube (III), Gold Target (IV), and Custom (V)—and all come in a special carrying case.

The sidelock Model U.L.M.-P over-under live pigeon gun with Kersten action is now available with a release trigger. The U.L.M.-P has hand-detachable sidelocks with coil springs and safety catch sears, plus a single non-selective trigger, 30-inch barrels, and selected fancy English walnut stock and forearm.

A H&H side-by-side shotgun—the KS-2—with sidelocks, is available in limited quantities on special order only. Also new are the Models Trumpf (boxlock) and Neptun (sidelock) drillings and over-under double rifles. Featuring 12-, 16- or 20-gauge side-by-side shotgun barrels and a wide choice of rifle calibers, from 22 Hornet to 9.3x74R, the drillings have 25-inch barrels, double triggers—front trigger is for the rifle barrel when properly activated—and come in a custom leather carrying case. The stocks are German-styled, but custom stocks are available.

Stoeger Industries

The excellent Sako line of rifles has two new chamberings—222 Remington and 308 Winchester—in the

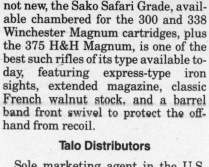

The Mauser 66 SP rifle is a precision match or silhouette rifle chambered for 308 Winchester. It features a thumbhole stock with spring-loaded cheekpiece and a Morgan adjustable recoil pad.

Mannlicher carbine line. Although not new, the Sako Safari Grade, available chambered for the 300 and 338 Winchester Magnum cartridges, plus the 375 H&H Magnum, is one of the best such rifles of its type available today, featuring express-type iron sights, extended magazine, classic French walnut stock, and a barrel band front swivel to protect the offhand from recoil.

Talo Distributors

Sole marketing agent in the U.S. for Anschutz rifles, previously sold through Savage dealers, Talo is headquartered in Westfield, Massachusetts. The entire line has been pretty well revamped with the introduction of some new models, and the relabeling of the older models.

The Models 164 and 164M have been replaced by the Models 1416D and 1516D, but the Model 64MS has been retained, and the 64-S is now the Model 1403D. The Mark 2000 is basically an improved version of the single shot Mark 12, with a 26-inch ¾-inch diameter barrel. The Model 1418D remains the same, but the Model 1411 Match 54 is now the 1810 Prone Match, while the Model 54-MS is now the 54.18MS, and the 1807 ISU has been upgraded from the 1407 Match 54 by the addition of a ventilated forearm and adjustable and removable cheekpiece.

The Model 1813 Super Match was the 1413 Super Match 54 which established five new world records and four new European records at Titograd, Yugoslavia, in September 1981. The new 5018 trigger on the 1813 has a lock time of 1.7 millisecond—that's 0.0017 second—making it the fastest in the world—another record. The Model 1810 Super Match II, available on special order only, is a more economical version, minus some of the features, such as the palm rest and hand rest. The Model 1808ED Super has the same basic action and lock time as the 1813 Super Match, but is stocked for running targets. Weight of the 1808ED, without sights, is 9¼ pounds, and it is available only on special order, as with many expensive Anschutz target rifles.

Small game hunters wanting a quality bolt action rifle in the $600 price range will like the new Models 1422E, 1522D, 1432D, and 1532D Classic design chambered for the 22 Long Rifle, 22 WRM, 22 Hornet, and 222 Remington cartridges respectively. Featuring the Match 54 action and barrel and a classic stock design of European walnut, this rifle averages

7½ pounds in weight, and has a magazine capacity of from 3 to 5 shots, depending on the cartridge. The same rifle, as the Custom, is available with a roll-over cheekpiece, Monte Carlo stock and schnabel forearm for $35 to $50 additional.

Among the really new rifles are the Model 520/61 autoloader and the two Biathlon rifles—the 1403B and 1327B. The 520 has a blowback action, barrel length of 24 inches, weight of 6½ pounds, a 10-round detachable box magazine, Monte Carlo stock and beavertail forearm, and a price tag of just under $250. The 1403 B rifle has a Model 64 action, a weight of approximately 8½ pounds with sights, an over-all length of 39¾ inches, and a barrel length of 21½ inches, and a barrel length of 21½

ly of the buttstock and the forearm. Weight of the 1427B is 9 pounds with sights, and the over-all length is 41½ inches. Special hinged cap sights to protect from snow are also available on special order.

All Anschutz barrel actions and stocks are interchangeable, which means a shooter can order these components separately and combine to produce a more or less custom rifle. It would no doubt be more expensive this way, but it is possible.

Valmet

The Shooting System has been around for over three years now, and it continues to grow. The latest additions to the over-under line include a 412 K Field version with extractors

sporting arms imported by this firm. The short action Mauser 66 is available in three grades—S, SM, and SL—plus a Silhouette version—the SP—and calibers range from 243 Winchester to the 458 Winchester Magnum, including the 5.6x61 vom Hofe, 9.3x64, 30-06, and 300 Weatherby Magnum, with barrel length in a choice of 21, 24, or 26 inches. Many feature double-set triggers—engraving is at additional cost.

The Model 77, a more conventional bolt action with detachable box magazine, is available in two grades—one with integral muzzle brake—and a variety of calibers ranging from the 243 Winchester to 375 H&H Magnum. Barrel lengths include 20, 24, or 26 inches, depending on the caliber.

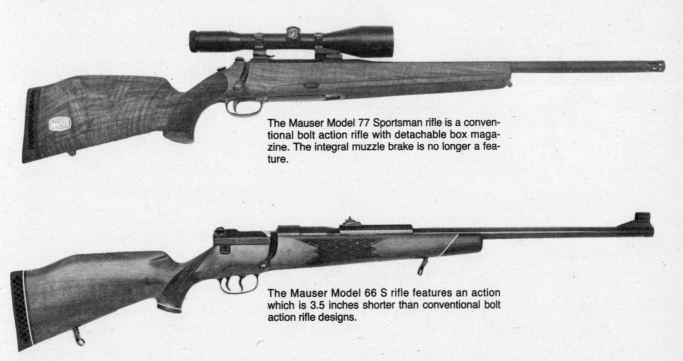

The Mauser Model 77 Sportsman rifle is a conventional bolt action rifle with detachable box magazine. The integral muzzle brake is no longer a feature.

The Mauser Model 66 S rifle features an action which is 3.5 inches shorter than conventional bolt action rifle designs.

inches. The two-stage trigger is adjustable, but is factory set at 1 pound 5 ounces.

The 1427B at just under $1000, is $300 more expensive than the 1403, but with additional features, plus the Match 54 action with the extra fast lock time. Both rifles have 5-round box magazines, adjustable wooden buttplate, stippled deep thumb rest fluted, extra full pistol grip stock, and Model 6723 sight sets, including the Anschutz Globe front and the 6707 rear peep. Other features of the 1427B, which can be obtained in a left-handed version, include an adjustable Biathlon-style removable hook, an oversize bolt knob for faster operation, and a stock which carries five extra 5-shot magazines in the bel-

only, chambered for 3-inch 12-gauge loads, choked full/full; a 412 KE double rifle with automatic ejectors, and 24-inch barrels in a choice of 375 Winchester or 9.3x74R calibers, either of which is suitable for North American big game; and a 412 K Shotgun/Rifle Combination gun with extractors. The Combination gun is available only with 24-inch barrels; the shotgun barrel is chambered for 3-inch 12-gauge shells and is choked improved modified, while the rifle barrel is available in a choice of 222, 223, 243, 308, or 30-06 chamberings.

Waidmanns Guns International

Two bolt action centerfire rifles, an over-under shotgun, and a side-by-side shotgun make up the Mauser

The Contest over-under shotgun is a conventional 12 gauge Browning design, with engraved false sideplates, a single selective trigger, and chrome-lined barrels chambered for standard length 12-gauge shells; field and trap grades are available. The Bristol side-by-side is a classic English sidelock, heavily engraved, with select walnut, straight grip stock, Churchill sighting rib, choice of 12 or 20 gauge, and a barrel length of 25 inches, choked improved cylinder/improved modified, or 27½ inches choked modified/full. A single trigger is available at an extra charge, and the shotgun can be obtained in matched pairs. The Bristol comes with a leather-covered wood-framed carrying case. ●

Because it is marginal in power and noise and range and because it is a non-reloadable rimfire, this writer believes the 22 WMR is . . .

ONE MAGNUM THAT WORKS

by **NORMAN ROWCLIFF**

THE FIRST true varmint rifle I owned was a Winchester Model 43 in 22 Hornet, bought in my senior year of high school, 1961, for $50. It was used and in excellent condition—a good buy.

The first disconcerting expense came when I paid out $6.40 for a box of ammunition. Now and again, it also came to my attention that not many stores carried 22 Hornet ammo.

I then decided a telescopic sight was the correct sighting gear, and since the Model 43 did not come drilled and tapped from the factory, I took it to my local gunsmith to see what his recommendation was. He did not want to do it himself, but was willing to send it to a custom gunsmith, so with shipping charges it would come to about $20. A high school student cuts lawns and the like to earn spending money, and this project seemed like it was going to cut into gas money for my car. Besides, I wanted to take out my first varmint rifle and do some shooting rather than have it tied up for weeks in a gunsmith's shop. What I did was send for a Williams aperture sight, which was no scope, but a considerable improvement over the original open sight.

In my hands several crows did fall to the 22 Hornet. To a young person using a first varmint rifle, it was fascinating to disintegrate half a crow and watch the cut-off feathers blow wildly across the snow. However, I soon found I just could not hit small targets like crows beyond 100 yards.

One of my neighbors shortly expressed an interest in the rifle, and then made me a reasonable offer. After thinking it over a bit, I sold it to him.

A lot of hunting seasons and shooting experiences passed before I tried another Hornet-type rifle-cartridge combination. This was a Winchester 9422M in 22 WMR (Winchester Rimfire). After owning a 9422M for four years, and comparing it to the 22 Hornet rifle I once owned, I find it somewhat like the development of the electric can opener or tubeless tire. The 22 Hornet may still have its fans among nostalgia buffs who don't mind inconvenience, but being of an everyday practical sort, I'll pick the 22 WMR for varmint shooting out to the 125-yard mark without exception.

When the Hornet took a nose dive in popularity during the early 1950's, it quickly became a money-losing proposition to manufacture rifles especially designed for it. The now obsolete Winchester Model 43 is an example of a compact bolt action built specifically for cartridges of 22 Hornet size.

A somewhat smaller package than the Hornet or Bee, the 22 WMR circumvented this problem. Manufacturers found it an easy matter to adapt bolt actions designed for the 22 Long Rifle to the 22 WMR. Before long Marlin, Mossberg, Savage, and Harrington & Richardson, even Colt, all had bolt action 22 WMR's on the market and with price tags only slightly higher than for standard 22's.

The current list of rifles available in 22 WMR is tempting indeed, and there should be one for anyone's requirements. Most come from the factory with grooved receivers so scope mounting is easy and convenient. I used a 1-inch scope meant for a centerfire rifle briefly on my own 22 WMR, but found it gave evidence of parallax on targets under 50 yards. I switched to the Redfield ¾-inch .22 scope, and it has since then served flawlessly. A good quality .22 scope like the Weaver or Redfield is all that's necessary to complement any of the current rifles, I feel.

The bolt actions range from economy models to the Ritz. A Mossberg 640K Chuckster currently retails for a little over $100. Add another $35 to $60 to that for a good quality scope, and for about $150, you are in chuck shooting business. The Savage 65-M, Marlin 782, and Western Field 832 also retail for near $100. The Savage/Anschutz 164-M currently retails at about $300 and there is a Mannlicher-stocked version, the Anschutz 1518. Based on the 54 Match action, the Savage/Anschutz 54-M Sporter features a French walnut stock with hand checkering, and should be the ultimate in a 22 WMR bolt action. Comparatively recent entries in the quality bolt action competition are the Sako P72 and the Kimber. You can get from $350 to $650 or so in this class of gun pretty easily.

One of the early entries in the 22 WRM competition was Winchester's 61-M slide-action, but it has long since disappeared from the Winchester line-up, and has become one of the most sought after of Winchester collectables commanding prices quite out of reach of the average shooter. There are once again 22 WMR pump rifles on the market, as Browning now chambers the BPR for 22 WMR and Interarms imports the Rossi Gallery rifle in the magnum chambering.

The Savage 24 combination rifle/shotgun sells in two models in 22 WMR and 20 gauge. This combination gun has made a reputation for having a wide application of uses and being one of the best of turkey shooting pieces.

Many hunters like semi-automatic rimfire rifles, and the Harrington & Richardson or the German-made Heckler & Koch 300 should do nicely, if one is inclined to a semi-automatic. Both come in plain standard grade and also in deluxe grades. The H&R 700 Deluxe comes factory equipped with a 4x scope.

The only widely available 22 WMR lever action repeater is Winchester's 9422M. This rifle has those touches that get favorable comment by gun writers and the general public. The 9422M was nice enough as introduced in 1973; it is now an XTR model with checkered stock, which is better.

If top-notch accuracy is a hunter's only serious consideration, a full-length bolt action will probably be the best bet, unless one wanted to match the handling characteristics of his big game rifle. Most 22 WMR's weigh about a pound more than the average 22 rimfire rifle, and this comes a bit closer to the weight of a big game rifle. The extra pound also makes for steadier holding.

My 9422M lever rifle sees pretty much year-round use, except when it is put aside in the fall and I take out my shotgun for the game bird seasons. The fox, raccoon, and coyote furs I have taken with the rifle amount to considerably more than its original purchase price, so this particular shooting piece has the distinction of having paid for itself, as well as being a pleasure to shoot.

To begin with I used the solid point loading in CCI brand with a 100-yard zero. Most 5-shot groups went right around the 2-inch mark. I tried this load on squirrel, but for my taste, it destroyed too much meat at average squirrel shooting yardages.

For shooting foxes and raccoons, the solid proved excellent both at killing well and at not harming pelts. On several occasions I have picked off dozing raccoons out of trees at midday during the fall. I do not trap, but see no reason why the solid point loading should not be excellent for trapline use.

My home is in the farm land of the far west Chicago suburbs. There is ample opportunity for varmint shooting—even, in recent years, coyote shooting. One overcast December day while using the CCI solid point, I was out in a wooded area still hunting for

---

(Facing page.) Coyote was taken with one shot at 50 yards using CCI 22 WMR solid.

whatever in the varmint line might happen to come along. From a vantage point on a hillside I could look down toward a swamp some 50 yards away. The snow cover was a bit thin for tracking, but there was enough present to give a good background as an aid to visibility.

After I waited there about ten minutes a coyote moved through the willows at the swamp edge. I pulled up and shot, and the coyote, while still on is feet, spun around completely once in nervous reaction to being hit. I chambered another round just in case, but the first shot had effectively done the job. The bullet hit him in the rear part of the lungs and exited out the opposite side.

The solid point bullet, despite its nonexpanding characteristic, killed well out to 75 yards on varmints. However, for serious varminting, the solid point is not in the same class as the hollow point. The hollow point loading will give effective results out to 125 yards.

In the '78-'79 winter, which set so many temperature and snowfall records, I took another coyote at about 80 yards, and a red fox at 100 yards. This time I was using the Winchester hollow point loading. Both animals required finishing shots, but neither moved out of their tracks after the first shot. The coyote had been hit through the lungs, and the fox's front shoulder had been broken.

For chuck and crow shooting the

125-yard range of the cartridge is very useful. Fenceline cover or wooded area where I live will give a person the chance to stalk within that range, but to get within the 75-yard effective range of the 22 Long Rifle can be difficult, and often just not possible.

On several occasions on days of relative calm, I have picked off crows out to the 150 yard mark. This is stretching things a bit and a wind will definitely rule such range stretching out. Before crops are up, when the ground is dry enough, a miss will kick up dust. This can be a real aid should you miss that first shot because of wind conditions and the critter is foolish enough to stay put so you can try a second shot.

What I originally had in mind for range sessions was to record shooting results under optimum conditions which would show the rifle and ammunition at its accurate best. Eventually I settled for three days in March with varying wind conditions. While this was not favorable to showing the rifle at its accurate best, they were pretty much the average type of day out in the field hunting, especially in the spring.

I have heard of hunters zeroing 22 WMR's at anywhere from 50 yards out to 125 yards. To date, I have used a 100-yard zero and very little or no allowance for bullet rise or drop is necessary at practical yardages.

Two 5-shot groups were fired at each of four distances to make up a trajectory table. The first two groups were fired at 100 yards to check zero, and they measured 1.7 inches and 1.3 inches, respectively. Wind was under 10 mph this first day.

The first 125-yard group measured 1.8 inches, the second 2.1 inches. Instead of changing targets, I had marked the bullet holes and then fired the second 5-shot string. Since I wanted to be absolutely sure on the drop figured, I decided to fire a third 5-shot group on the same target. When the string of 15 shots was measured as a single group it measured 2.68 inches. That kind of consistent accuracy should take varmints for any competent shooter. The Winchester 40-grain hollow point was used during this instance, but the following table should hold true for other 22 WMR loadings as well.

TWO DAYS AT THE BENCH
Groups (in.)

	smallest	largest	average	Drift*
CCI Solid	1.55	3.92	2.86	N.A.
CCI HP	1.09	4.00	2.93	3.1
Win. HP	1.36	3.91	2.91	2.2

*In 10-12 mph crosswind in inches.

The author benches his Winchester 9422M. From rest, most WMRs will shoot 2½-inch 5-shot groups at 100 yards, he feels. More accurate rifles will shoot into two inches or slightly less.

It might go well to mention that while the various factory loadings for the 22 WMR are loaded to the same 2000 fps muzzle velocity, this does not necessarily mean they will shoot to the same point of impact. On the occasions when I have switched from one loading to another while shooting at 100 yards, I have found changes in point of impact of up to 1¼ inches, with this movement being almost entirely vertical. Change of point of impact with different ammunition, like accuracy, is also partly a matter of differences in individual rifle barrels, and thus, it can vary with the particular rifle. If you do switch from one load type or ammunition brand to another, firing a group or two to check for a change in point of impact is recommended.

On a second morning, all was well except for a slight headwind from the east. Beginning with the CCI 40-grain solid point, the first group went 1.5 inches, the second and third groups about 2.7 inches each, and a fourth group 3.4 inches. The spread on the fourth group was almost entirely vertical; horizontally it spread only .4-inch. During my shooting, the wind had picked up considerably.

I will leave the physics to someone else, but let it be said a fairly stiff headwind or tailwind can do some strange things with rifle bullets. After the fifth group, the wind continued to pick up and I decided there was not much point in continuing. Though the CCI solid point was used during erratic headwind conditions, it showed equal accuracy to the other two loadings tested.

On the third day, there was a crosswind at 10-12 mph in the late afternoon, and the temperature was in the mid-30's. Beginning with the CCI brand ammunition, I fired a series of five 5-shot groups with both the CCI and Winchester 40-grain hollow point loadings. The tabulated results of the two days' shooting are nearby.

Measured Trajectories

50 yds.	75 yds.	100 yds.	125 yds.
+.6	+.9	0	−2.0

To me the last day's shooting was most significant. It shows what the shooter may expect under average early season wind conditions, just the type of days one is out hunting. As long as there is a fairly steady crosswind, making allowance for drift should not be that difficult and a high percentage of hits should be likely.

The 10-12 mph wind did materially enlarge groups, but even on the largest groups three of the five shots stayed within 2½ inches. The best 5-shot groups of 1.09 inches and 1.36 inches were surprising. Besides showing what the 22 Magnum will do under average wind conditions, maybe the lesson to be learned here is that range shooting on a fairly windy day can add useful knowledge to the varmint shooter's battery of skills.

The 22 WMR's 40-grain jacketed hollow-point bullet, as far as varminting purposes go, is the genuine article, similar to jacketed bullets used in 22 centerfire cartridges. The jacketed hollow-point bullet is a key point in the cartridge's design, and to me makes the 22 WMR the one 22-cal.

rimfire that goes first class.

Recent attempts to beef up the standard 22 rimfire, in the form of the CCI Stinger, Winchester Xpediter and Remington Yellow Jacket, do boost the 22 rimfire's energy figures and thus its killing power somewhat, and certainly no one will argue contrary than this is going to make for cleaner varmint kills. However, these beefed-up rounds do not really extend the 75-yard maximum range of the 22 Long Rifle, so, in short, the 22 WMR still offers more bullet weight, velocity, energy, and effective range.

As useful a hunting cartridge as the 22 WMR is, it is probably economy that keeps it popular. In rough figures factory 22 WMR ammunition retails

Rowcliff took this sizeable coyote with the 22 WMR solid, but took others with the hollow-point load and recommends it.

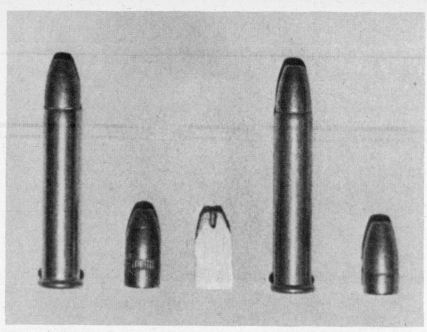

The cartridge at the left is the Winchester 40-grain hollow point 22 WMR. Next to it are a pulled bullet and a sectioned bullet. The cartridge at the right is the CCI 40-grain solid, and to its right is a pulled solid bullet.

at not quite one-third the cost of either 22 Hornet or 222 Remington ammunition. While the 22 Hornet and 222 are more powerful cartridges, the 22 Magnum's economy is obviously a factor to be considered. And some of us just don't handload.

Also in 1980, the retail cost of 22 Hornet ammunition has risen to 2.5 times what it was in 1960, for the 222 the rise in cost is 2.3 times, and for the 22 WMR, 1.7 times. The current price of the brass in the cartridge cases has a good deal to do with these rises in product cost, but rimfire ammunition is less costly to process than centerfire, and thus cheaper.

The weekends I've spent crow and chuck busting with the 22 WMR have been valuable skill-sharpening exercises and the fall deer hunt becomes that much more likely of ending successfully. So if a centerfire varminter is too expensive for you, or impractical for the hunting conditions in your area, the 22 WMR is the one 22 rimfire that goes first class. •

Both 100-yard groups were fired in a 10-12 mph crosswind. The group at the left measures 1.09 inches; the other opened to 3.84 inches when the wind became more gusty. Knowledge of the wind's effects can make the difference as to whether one's day of varmint hunting is a success or failure.

Hunters may want to hedge their bets with 1¼-ounce 12-gauge loads on spooky prairie grouse, but otherwise an ounce is OK in any uplands, Duffey believes. (Dave Johnson photo)

IS AN OUNCE OF SHOT ENOUGH?

If it weren't for psychology, Duffey thinks so, and his two really expert friends know it.

by DAVE DUFFEY

WHEN THE STAGING areas in England were loaded with American GIs preparing to land on the Normandy beachheads in 1944, their British hosts had this comment about their presence:

"The only things wrong with Yanks are they are over-sexed, over-fed, over-paid and over here."

We've a not wholly undeserved reputation for being profligate and excessive and this extremism includes the shotgun shells customarily used to bag North American upland game and waterfowl. Put plain and simply, the most popular U.S. shotshells—12 gauge with 3¾ drams equivalent of powder and 1¼ ounces of shot in a 2¾-inch case—are overloaded.

Having conceded that, however, it is fair to question whether "light" loads, particularly one ounce of shot in 12 gauge, are adequate.

With few exceptions, my own conclusion is that in most hunting situations an ounce will do the job. It took about 40 years of shotgunning to convince me and I still have some reservations that may be more psychological than physical. Accepting light loads is difficult for most of us because we're all wound up in the American syndrome that more of anything that's good has to be even better. If a glass of milk a day is good for you, gulping down a quart will make you even healthier . . . the bigger the better, the more the merrier, and so on.

Transposed to the upland covers and waterfowl marshes, that thinking comes up with "If I've got some extra pellets flying around out there they'll scratch down birds I'd miss otherwise." That premise has at least a grain of validity. But it also implies a reliance on chance rather than skillful gun swinging to bag birds and a disregard for the creed of making clean kills within reasonable range.

L. W. "Bill" Johnson, now 82 years old, is a retired Remington-Peters exhibition shooter living near Scandinavia, Wisconsin. He's field-tested arms and ammunition on all manner of game and from 1933 to 1960 gave shooting demonstrations nationwide. A hunter and shooting instructor as well as a showman, he retains an encyclopedic knowledge about both the theoretical and practical aspects of firearms and ammunition.

When asked what's good or bad about a one-ounce 12 gauge load, Bill Johnson responded:

"The only thing bad about it is that it isn't popular.

"It's an efficient load and comes pretty close to being in ballistic balance. Push that ounce with 3½ drams of powder and it makes an excellent duck load. If you go down to 3 drams, a one-ounce load of No. 6 will still give you a very good high velocity load, plenty of energy for upland birds or most anything you want to shoot.

"If more people would use it they'd find it's more comfortable to shoot. Its transmission of energy is very good; pellet velocity is high. It's a fast load that I've shot quite a bit and you get good penetration with it on game.

"I used to hunt down on the Illinois river bottoms with an old boy who shot a 12-gauge double barrel, two triggers, with an ounce of No. 4s in each tube for pass shooting. He'd pick out an old mallard coming across there, curl two fingers around the triggers, pull them both at once and just roll ducks like nothing out there at 75, 80, 85 yards."

Or listen up to what Vic Reinders has to say about one-ounce loads. Named to the All-American Trapshooting Team 21 times, Reinders, a retired chemistry professor is analytical and leaves nothing to chance. His average of 98.002% on the first 140,000 registered trap targets he shot has never been equalled. He's run some 608,000 shells through a Remington Model 31 trap gun he purchased second-hand in 1933.

"The one-ounce load is more comfortable to shoot, due to less recoil, and in clay target shooting there is no need for even the 1⅛-ounce load. Lately I have been using slightly under an ounce, 430 grains (an ounce is 437.5 grains) of shot, on both trap and skeet and do not feel at all handicapped by that load. Other shooters have shared that experience and the older ones, particularly, say their averages have gone up. I'm sure that's due to greater comfort from the lighter load which cuts down flinching.

"A few years back I decided to try light loads on ducks in Canada. What I wound up with was just over an ounce of 6s in front of 25 or 26 grains of Dupont PB powder. That loading produced spectacular results—so good that my hunting buddy, who has always been a No. 4 man, loaded up some for the next year and has used that load ever since.

"Those loads produce tighter patterns than the regular 1¼ ounce loads. The main part of the pattern at 35-40 yards is 4 to 5 inches narrower than that of heavy loads, so I have to point better. But I *don't* get cripples. In one two-day stretch I got 14 ducks

with 17 shells, missing two and using two shells on another."

But you're thinking, "Hold on! I'm not a crack shot like those guys. I need all the help I can get. That pattern fringe and those 50-odd extra pellets in the 1¼-ounce shell give me an edge."

No argument from me. I'm just a dog trainer who hunts a lot and happens to write about what I do. I'm not in the Johnson-Reinders class either and as noted earlier I have reservations about 100% endorsement of one-ounce loads, which we'll get to later along with the technical question of ballistic balance.

But their experiences serve to illustrate what one-ounce loads are *capable* of and can do in the hands of *good* gunners during actual field use. For, as Johnson summed it up, even if the ammo makers could come up with a super-shell, "It's still up to the shooter to go out there and do his job."

You may also be thinking, "All this may be well and good with No. 8 shot for quail or woodcock when the shooting is close and there's about 410 pellets in that one-ounce pattern and maybe even those 225 No. 6 pellets will do it. But what about coarser shot, like No. 4 which contains only 135 pellets per ounce? Didn't that old Illinois bottoms hunter have to touch off both barrels to get his ducks?"

He was, we are told, killing birds out to 85 yards, which is at least twice as far as you and I are capable of even hoping to intercept a passing bird with a killing pattern of shot.

Carrying his one-ounce experimentations even farther, Reinders said, "I even loaded some one-ouncers with BBs and No. 2s. One day a coyote made the mistake of appearing broadside about 30 yards away. I doubt if any of that ounce of BBs missed him. They went plumb through and he just

About The Author

Using light loads to shoot barn pigeons over dogs in training first got Dave Duffey interested in one-ounce loads. Duffey, hunting dogs editor of *Outdoor Life* magazine since 1959, has resumed public dog training and also offers a consultation service at his kennel and training grounds in central Wisconsin. His gun knowledge, he says, is modest compared to the practical and theoretical expertise of the two senior shooters emeritus, Bill Johnson and Vic Reinders, who collaborated with him here in taking a hard look at the efficacy of one-ounce 12-gauge loads.

died without a quiver. I also used those BBs and 2s on geese and had no complaints."

Johnson recommends an ounce of No. 4 shot on duck-size game because "Even though there aren't as many pellets you get use out of all of them because most stay in that 30-inch circle. And that's what you've got to visualize out there. There's enough No. 4s in the 30-inch pattern for a large bird and a duck that flies into it *will* come down. When you're figuring to get a duck with a 60-inch circle you might get him, but you probably won't."

If you argue that "Those guys and the guys they shoot with are not only crack shots but they reload their own special shells while I just buy mine off the shelf," you are onto a possible fly in the one-ounce ointment.

Consumer research done by ammo makers must show a public demand for "long range" shells crammed with excess powder and shot. The one-ounce shells they do turn out are mostly low price No. 6 and No. 8 loads which discount stores use as loss-leaders.

I've had few complaints about the cases of these less expensive commercial loads I've shot over the years. Shell costs are a factor when you train dogs and do a lot of hunting and informal clay bird practicing. Like most other hunters, if the shell goes "bang" I'm inclined to assume it's a good round. Furthermore, one year the only 25 straight I shot at a local trap club was scored with a box of 3 dram-1-ounce economy loads. So they do work.

Although conceding that in-range birds can be killed with them, Johnson and Reinders are unimpressed by the commercial one-ounce hunting or field loads. Referring to them as "rabbit" loads, Johnson said, "You get one shell that shoots a good pattern, the next one doesn't. It's not the amount of shot that's at fault. The quality of what goes into the shell has a lot to do with it. Generally those 3 dram-1-ounce loss-leaders are made as cheaply as possible with soft, not chilled, shot and the wad column is not as good as you'll find in No. 1 grade target loads. This means somewhat distorted patterns."

Hunters may, however, find quality one-ounce loads available since manufacturers are now producing them for clay target shooters who are demanding the lighter loads. Originally trap loads were a full 1¼ ounces of shot; they were dropped to the present official 1⅛ ounce; and Reinders is campaigning to drop the official weight to one-ounce.

"The hunting variety of one-ounce loads is nothing to brag about as a trap load, too much powder and soft shot," Reinders said. "But I got a chance to shoot one box of factory *trap* loads at the 1981 Grand American and broke a 25 with them."

Testing his own loads of approximately one-ounce (actually 460 grains) in handicap events, where better shooters are stationed as far back as 27 yards instead of 16 yards, Reinders said:

"I broke all I pointed correctly and my average for over 1,000 rounds was about two percentage points better with those loads than with the standard 1⅛ ounce loads. Used for the right things, I should point out that I have nothing against soft or even reclaimed shot. Both will open up patterns, which is an advantage in Skeet, and I now shoot reloads using reclaimed shot on Skeet. Reducing the official trap load to one-ounce may cut handicap scores a little bit, but that would be good."

If one-ounce loads become standard for trap and there is also a hunter demand for light loads, it's a safe bet that quality one-ounce loads will become readily available. But if hunters continue to be dazzled by the magnum complex you can also bet manufacturers will continue to roll out expensive, over-stuffed shotshells. And the heavy load trend has reached ridiculous extremes.

"We're now making 12 gauge shells with 1⅞ ounces of shot, three inch, of course, but that's a 10 gauge magnum load," Johnson observed. "We're into overloads that are uncomfortable to shoot because of heavy recoil and they don't throw good patterns by any stretch of the imagination. But that shot quantity out there does increase the chance of hitting a vital area and that means one for the bag. For some people, I guess getting one bird for many shots is fine success."

So how about Joe Average who's a mite surprised and very happy when he knocks down something with any load? Doesn't the standard high brass, 3¾ dram, 1¼-ounce load literally give him fringe benefits?

"With that one-quarter ounce more shot out there in the air, the wider fringe and strays might gain him a little, but that's getting back to this lucky shot business, not good shooting," Johnson contends.

Although it may be a Catch-22 situation, and despite being in virtual agreement with the experts regarding the efficacy of one-ounce loads, based on field experience I'm inclined to believe that the casual hunter who doesn't shoot too well may do better with heavier loads.

When taking over the guiding and management duties of a pheasant hunting club, I "inherited" several cases of one-ounce and 1⅛-ounce 12-gauge field loads. Shells were furnished for guests to shoot and these had been purchased by my predecessor, an English gamekeeper. In Great Britain, 1⅛-ounce is considered a heavy

L.W. "Bill" Johnson, shortly after his retirement as an exhibition shooter and field representative for Remington-Peters with a Labrador friend, a classic side-by-side and a brace of cock pheasant. (Duffey photo)

load. As the guests used up those shells, I didn't note any difference in the percentage of birds knocked down in relation to shots fired than I had observed during a previous stint at the club when we used 1¼-ounce loads. But I was guiding, handling my dogs and doing back-up gunning, not taking a statistical survey.

Eventually the light loads were replaced with 1¼-ounce shells and during the next shooting season an interesting situation occurred. We knocked down more birds with the heavy loads and my dogs delivered to hand a disproportionately high share of live birds, pheasants that hadn't been shot dead. A significant number *could* have run off and gone unrecovered but for the retrieving ability of the dogs.

I took that as an indication that many of those pheasants, though most were shot at reasonable range, were caught by the pattern fringes of sloppily pointed shotguns. A concomitant conclusion would be that the lighter loads out of poorly swung guns either missed entirely or connected with too few pellets to furnish the energy to drop a bird.

I continued using high brass shells. My guests got more birds with them. The retrieving ability of the dogs held the crippling loss to virtually nil. And for myself, because the back-up shooting required longer shots than I normally would take at upland game, I felt more confident with the heavier loads.

A possible high crippling loss should, however, be of concern to the hunter who hunts without a proficient retriever. Rather than suffer qualms of guilt about birds that were hit but not recovered, he might well subscribe to the precept of "kill clean or miss completely" and the light loads may help him do just that.

Hunters forced to take questionable shots at hard-to-find game if they are to shoot at all, if accompanied by a keen retriever may want to gamble on heavier loads scratching down a bird or two that would not be touched with one-ounce loads. The same thinking applies when long shots are necessary on waterfowl made wary by heavy hunting pressure.

self, it would seem the opposite to be true. Heavy loads are game cripplers, and I discussed this with Johnson.

He said, "Okay, let's just designate one-ounce as a medium range load and a 1¼-ounce as a long range load because at least theoretically it pushes the shot along faster and there are more pellets in the load. When you guide or have guests, you get the dirty end of the shooting stick. No set-up shots; you have to reach out. Sure you should try to adapt a load to the situation you are in and good shots

to that damn fringe on the pattern. For the sloppy shot, I guess you'd have to say the fringe isn't wasted. It *might* knock down a bird for him and that luck thing is what some shooters count on to bring something home."

If you're not a phenomenal shot but you hunt a lot and shoot pretty well, are there guidelines for when the light 12-gauge loads are sure to be adequate or times when their use might be questionable? Based on what I've worked out over the years here's something to go on, plus Bill Johnson's explanation of why it works.

On decoying ducks or for *any* shooting at *any* upland game bird that is pointed by a dog, heavy loads are a waste of shot, money and birds. Overkill usually means ruined meat. You'll do well and save money and meat, even with the cheap charges available over the counter.

Doubt it? Then consider how popular the 20 gauge gun is with quail, ruffed grouse and woodcock shooters. No one seriously contends that a one-ounce 20 gauge load is inadequate. In training both flushing and pointing dogs and while actually hunting I fire about ten 20-gauge shells for every 12-gauge load I use and I don't shoot the smaller gauge because I like to miss or cripple birds.

Most importantly, you'll get a better pattern when that ounce of shot is delivered by a 12-gauge than if you use a 20 bore. It's a matter of ballistic balance. The larger bore gun permits loading a shell with a *shorter shot column,* that stack of shot in the shell casing. It's not to be confused with the *shot string* that is flung out the muzzle, though the same pellets are involved.

A 12 gauge shot column is not as "tall" as a 20 gauge's and has a broader base. Instant pressure occurs when the load is ignited. That pressure will deform some of the pellets at the base of the column. The shorter the column height, the less pressure on the bottom pellets that causes deformity. True pellets fly straight. It's the deformed ones that freak out and make up the pattern fringes and flyers which no shooter can control. And as the shot is rammed through the barrel and through the choke restriction the larger bore is less likely to mangle pellets.

It's the tall shot column in the 410 bore's $^{11}/_{16}$-ounce loads that make the 410 notorious as a bad patterning smoothbore. High pressures in the "heavy" 410 load really put the squeeze on the bottom pellets; an-

Vic Reinders, holder of a slew of trap-shooting records since he began shooting in 1933, brings up the Remington pump gun he bought second-hand that year and through which he had run 608,275 shells by the end of 1981.

But the oddity is that the use of heavy loads is generally justified by the belief that they should cut crippling losses at reasonable ranges in addition to reaching out to score on long shots. Everyone, according to his or her abilities, is entitled to a personal interpretation of the terms reasonable and long range. To me, reasonable range is anything under 45 yards, long range anything over 50.

Hunters who want to kill clean have bought that bill of goods. But if there is validity to the field observations of Reinders, Johnson and my-

aren't likely to cripple more game at reasonable ranges because they are on their birds anyway. And if you have confidence in the load you'll do better on tough shots.

"But I still believe that if manufacturers put components of equal quality in their one-ounce loads they'd do the job just as well as the 1¼-ounce loads. Even with the cheap commercial light loads a good shot will knock down birds at reasonable ranges. It's all a matter of when you fail to point accurately you aren't doing your job as a gunner, which gets us right back other example of over-loading since the 410 was originally designed to handle ⅜-ounce of shot.

Conversely, another small-bore load, ¾-ounce in 28 gauge is, according to Johnson, "one of the finest ballistically balanced loads available to sportsmen today."

"It delivers excellent patterns and excellent energy to individual pellets," Johnson said. "You could even say the load is equal in efficiency to the 20 gauge one-ounce load. While it may not be a real concrete example,

Reduced recoil from light loads can help make a better shot of young hunters like Mike Duffey, shown at age 13 coming up on a woodcock with his 12-gauge Remington 1100. (Duffey photo)

it's significant that Skeet shooters in the national events are now shooting as good or better scores with 28s than they are with 20s, even though they're now running a full ounce of shot through their 20s, not the ⅞-ounce of the past."

The world's best ballistically balanced load? You'll never use it or even see it. It's one-ounce of shot out of a 6 gauge tube. According to Johnson, years back some of the world's top gunsmiths got together at St. Etienne in France to try to come up with a load that would shoot 100% patterns. Only with one-ounce of shot in a 6-bore single barrel were they able to shoot 100% patterns one after the other.

That shot column was very short.

While I wouldn't hesitate to use good one-ounce loads on duck if I had a marsh all to myself, I can't psyche myself into trying them on geese and all too often duck hunting today is a matter of competing with overly optimistic shooters for whom 80 yards look like 40.

If only because of the psychological factor you may do better at some waterfowling with 1¼-ounces of lead, or even the miserable patterning magnums. But with the advent of steel shot requirements in so many areas, the question of what load is best on waterfowl has become largely academic.

In any situation involving ruffed grouse, woodcock, quail, rail or snipe, one-ounce loads are adequate. On prairie grouse and Hungarian partridge, I'm tempted by heavy loads, particularly late in the season when wary birds flush wild or run out from under a dog's point or suck a flushing spaniel or retriever out to extreme range.

On a pheasant drive in cornfields, walking them up with a hunting partner or having to contend with a hard-to-manage spaniel or retriever who is

flushing out on the rim of reasonable range, there is cause for considering 1¼-ounce charges. However, British guns do right well with much lighter loads on the high passing shots that pheasants afford on their famed driven bird shoots when hundreds of birds are bagged in a day's shoot.

Were I a better shot, I'd swear by one-ounce loads for dove. They are small and fast and can be taken within reasonable range, but the way they jink around makes them the one game bird I'm satisfied to "fringe." I'm torn between light and heavy loads because there is less recoil with one-ouncers, a definite comfort and anti-flinch factor when you are firing a lot of shells while clad in light, warm-weather clothing. And I do no better or worse when shooting a 20 gauge with its one-ounce load at dove and frequently use cheap ⅞-ounce 20-gauge loads on barn pigeons, a tough bird to kill, when dog training.

It may all boil down to a matter of the pride you take in solid hits or settling for being content with scratching down a bird. But certainly out to 40 yards, beyond which few of us can claim any degree of shooting proficiency, the one-ounce load is satisfactory when the shotgun is properly swung.

Perhaps it's only serious shooters who really have little concern about such technicalities as ballistic balance because they can do pretty well with any load who now pay much attention to the debate over the adequacy of one-ounce 12-gauge loads. But all hunters ought to give thought to the futility and waste of overloading.

For today, perhaps the one-ounce load's time has come, like the small, economical automobile. With the emphasis on frugality and spending cutbacks during the current economic situation, the rabbit load of the Great Depression years may dovetail well with the pullback to conservatism; a swing of the pendulum following a shooting binge that played up the questionable qualities of long range and magnum loads as super shells that could compensate for the poor shooting form that causes most misses. ●

EDITOR'S NOTE: This article was commissioned several months before the new one-ounce 12-gauge loads were announced for 1982. Obviously, the author and his friends have made the case that if we give the new loads a fair trial, we'll probably be satisfied.

ESPECIALLY GOOD BOOKS

Of the crop in recent years, these are books you shouldn't miss. They are either virtually standard references, or particularly well-done.

Gunmarks

by David Byron

This quietly impressive little book compiles the tradenames, codemarks, and proofs from 1870 to the present for an exceedingly wide range of manufacturers. The jacket says it is the "most comprehensive and useful collection" and it might well be.

Perhaps the most interesting thing is that the marks are classified and arranged by their own structure without reference to what sort of gun they might have appeared on. Letters—whether they are initials or monograms or whatever—are found in one place; figural, geometric and animate marks are in another place. There are subdivisions according to the border shape—oval, square, diamond. And then there is a list of all the firearms manufacturers with cross references to their marks.

As some measure of the length to which such a book might go, it is worth knowing there are 34 different representations of lions used as gunmarks herein. There are about eight renditions of dogs, and 10 of horses.

Published by Crown Publisher, Inc., New York, at $10.00. 186 pages, 7x10 inch. 1979. At book stores.   K.W.

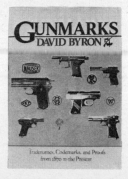

The Muzzle Loading Hunter

by Rick Hacker

Both his publisher and Mr. Hacker call this the "complete guide for the black powder sportsman" and perhaps it is. Certainly, the list of chapter titles, from "The Hunter's Heritage" to "A Cache of Lore For Hunting Success," covers the subject.

In graphic design, the book is an attempt to recapture the past. There is a little brown in the black ink, and the photographs resemble sepiatones. Engravings and woodcuts as well as photographs are used for illustration.

Published by Winchester Press, P.O. Box 1260, Tulsa, OK 74101, at $14.95. 224 pages, 6x9. 1981.   K.W.

Records of North American Big Game, 8th edition

Boone and Crockett Club

This is "the book"—the one North American trophy hunters try to achieve. It has editorial material—over 100 pages of it—and editors—William H. Nesbitt and Philip L. Wright—but what really counts are the over 200 pages of tabulations of statistics on those many and varied species which make up North American big game hunting, from black bear to Stone's sheep. This edition has, perhaps, more and better illustrations than earlier editions. In fact that is so, and this reviewer judges as one who was responsible for the production of the 7th edition of Records of North American Big Game.

Published at $29.50 by the Boone and Crockett Club, 205 S. Patrick St., Alexandria, VA 22314. Ca. 412 pages, 7½x10. 1981.   K.W.

Firearms In Colonial America

by M. L. Brown

The subtitle of this 510-page treatise is "The impact on history and technology, 1492-1792." Through its almost 400 photographs and maps, and its reliance on facts from firearms artifacts discovered at known historical sites, Firearms In Colonial America traces the spread of steel technology from origins in the weapons shops of Europe to frontier outposts and frontier artisans on the far reaches of North America.

Throughout, Brown insists on calling Indians "native Americans" and thus betrays a certain bias, but that bias does not affect the main trust of the book. It is handsomely mounted.

Published at $45 by the Smithsonian Institution Press, Washington, DC 20560, Ca. 510 pages, 8½x11 clothbound. 1980.   K.W.

The Colt Heritage
by R. L. Wilson

This is called the official history of Colt firearms from 1836 to the present, and that is what it is. There are well over 200 illustrations in full color by noted photographer Sid Latham. The book is simply gorgeous and is itself, of course, a Colt collectible.

Larry Wilson, the author, has made rather a career of being associated with lavishly presented books on Colts, but he has done other things, mostly prestigious associations with the world's museums, concentrating, of course, on those museums with fine arms collections. He is in fact Historical Consultant to the Colt Firearms Division today, and this is his 14th book on firearms.

Published by Simon & Schuster at $39.95, 368 pp., size 9x12 horizontal. At book stores. — K.W.

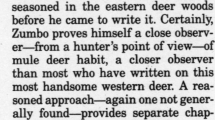

Hunting America's Mule Deer
by Jim Zumbo

It is this reviewer's personal opinion that Zumbo's book on mule deer is the better for his being thoroughly seasoned in the eastern deer woods before he came to write it. Certainly, Zumbo proves himself a close observer—from a hunter's point of view—of mule deer habit, a closer observer than most who have written on this most handsome western deer. A reasoned approach—again one not generally found—provides separate chapters on tactics in each habitat.

Published by Winchester Press, P.O. Box 1260, Tulsa, OK 74101, at $14.95. 272 pages, 6x9. 1981. — K.W.

The History of Winchester Firearms 1866 to 1980
by Duncan Barnes

This is the fifth edition of what we have long known as the Watrous book, and indeed, its title page says that it is by Duncan Barnes, George B. Watrous, J. C. Rikhoff, Thomas A. Hall, and Pete Kuhlhoff—all contributors to this book's publishing history.

As such, the book is more or less familiar to those who fancy gun books. This one is done up largely as its predecessors—handsomely printed and presented in its own case.

Each rendition has its own merit, as time goes on. In this one it is possible to learn of the Winchester Model 22 double side-by-side and the Model 91 Winchester over-under, which turn out to be Winchester-branded shotguns manufactured by Laurona in Spain for sale in international markets only.

Indeed, in contrast to previous Watrous books, this edition is signalized by its coverage of special models of all kinds from the cowboy commemorative of 1970 and earlier commemoratives and many later commemoratives—all of those have to be considered special models.

Published by Winchester Press, P.O. Box 1260, Tulsa, OK 74101. *Ca.* 238 pages, 8½x11. Price $24.95. 1980. — K.W.

The Game-Trophies Of The World
by Paul Parey

The International Council for Game and Wildlife Conservation presents this book, which for the first time in three languages makes available the general rules for evaluation of hunting trophies in Europe, Asia, Africa and South America and also the formulae used by the North American Big Game award program of the Boone & Crockett Club.

Outline drawings with descriptive text explain how each trophy is measured and provides methods for recording the trophies' measurements on tables acceptable to the various organizations involved. It was edited and compiled by G. Kenneth Whitehead in collaboration with the Working Group of the International Council, and published by Paul Parey, Scientific Publishers of Berlin and Hamburg. Suite 903, 461 Park Ave. South, NY, NY 10016.)

It has 215 pages, 146 illustrations and many tables. It is written in English, French and German. In soft cover, 6x9, it is $29.00. 1981. — K.W.

The Complete Black Powder Handbook
by Sam Fadala

As much as any book for muzzle-loading enthusiasts has, this effort by Fadala has excited and satisfied the black powder fancy. The aim of the book, its author says, is "to help smooth any bumps on the road for the newcomer and to offer up a hundred-and-one ideas for the oldtimer."

Fadala knows whereof he speaks, and what he didn't know, he went to discover experimentally. Along other things, which include 30 days on the trail by himself on at least one occasion, the author blew up—deliberately—several muzzle-loading guns experimentally.

The Black Powder Handbook isn't all guns. It includes optics and accessories and knives and games and organizations and a considerable directory and glossary.

Published at $9.95 by DBI Books, Inc., One Northfield Plaza, Northfield, IL 60093. 8½x11, 288 pages. 1979. — K.W.

Guns And Shooting, A Bibliography
by Ray Riling

This new re-issue of a classic reference work is a must in the library of anyone who intends to read of guns. It is published now in a memorial edition of just 500 numbered copies.

A revised and amended and extended edition must await another time. This is the book as completed in 1950 by Ray Riling. It has to be the foundation for all other firearms bibliographies for Americans. There are 2747 complete descriptions of individual works presented in chronological order from 1420 AD, a list of pseudonyms, an author index, a list of 22 other bibliographies, and a most interesting Introduction.

Republished by Ray Riling Arms Books, P.O. Box 135, Wyncote, PA 19095 at $75. 436 pages, 7x9. 1982. K.W.

American Engravers
by C. Roger Bleile

For many years, the art of the engraver has been displayed in the pages of GUN DIGEST. Here a writer who is himself an engraver displays, in color and in black and white, the work of 73 of the over-140 arms engravers he says are working in the United States today. There is a surprising variety of artistic endeavor shown. Naturally, some engravers are simply better engravers than other engravers, but that is not the big difference. Only in such a book as this, or in a wide experience of the guns themselves, can one get such a sense of the differences in attack among artisans.

At $29.95 from Roger Bleile, 5040 Ralph Ave., Cincinnati, OH 45238. 9½x12½ inches, 216 pp. 1980. K.W.

The Gun Digest Book of MODERN GUN VALUES, Third Edition
by Jack Lewis

In order to set a price on a modern firearm, one must first know with some precision which gun he has, and then needs guidance on its price. Nearly identical guns can have widely varying prices. *Modern Gun Values* succeeds in serving both these needs.

The magazine-format book is divided according to type of gun—handguns, rifles, shotguns—and then by maker, with dozens of factories represented in each type. The book distinguishes between one sort of latter-day production and another. For instance, the Model 70 African, vintage 1956-1963, is treated differently than the Model 70 African 1964-1971. And well it might, of course, since the one rifle is worth twice as much as the other.

Published at $9.95 by DBI Books, Inc., One Northfield Plaza, Northfield, IL 60093. 8½x11, 384 pages. 1981. K.W.

The Krag Rifle
by William S. Brophy

Bill Brophy has here parlayed a consuming interest in the Springfield Armory and a life-long association with firearms into a book to fill the gaps, intended to provide information necessary to understand the Krag.

The book is handsomely if not lavishly illustrated in black and white and printed on good paper. And Brophy brings his military eye to the selection of photographs, which include portraits of representative organizations on duty in Peking after its relief during the Boxer Rebellion, and an informal portrait of Company H, First Battalion, United States Marine Corps on duty in the Philippines in 1901. Close-ups of inspectors' cartouches, stacking swivel screws and receiver markings attack the problem of understanding the Krag from the purely mechanical point of view.

From William Brophy, Marlin Firearms, 100 Kenna Dr., North Haven, CT 06473, at $24.95. *Ca.* 260 pages, 9x11. 1980. K.W.

Plans and Specifications of the L. C. Smith Shotgun
by William S. Brophy

This is a collection of all the original factory blueprints and exploded view drawings, tables and charts and notes with dimensions and tolerances used to make L. C. Smith shotguns. It is all the drawings that have survived.

The working gunsmith, of course, can use actual factory blueprints to properly make and replace broken and missing parts. The book can also be used as a roadmap to find parts by scrounging them from other and equal models. And beyond that, one rarely can find 1679 dimensional engineering views and 624 reproductions of original blueprints bound to lie flat and admire.

Published by F. Brownell & Son, Montezuma, IA 50171 at $19.95. 247 pages, 8½x11 inches black and white. 1982. K.W.

The Commercial Mauser '98 Sporting Rifle
by Lester Womack

To a degree the title of this book is misleading, since it covers what the author calls custom Mauser rifles as well as original commercial models from Oberndorf. The author's reason for writing it is probably found in two facts: every one of his personal rifles is on a '98 action, and he has seen rifles built on the '98 action forgive all manner of stupidity in loading and practice.

Indeed, much of the allure of this relatively small book with its very fine black and white photography is the author's collection of anecdotes concerning the custom makers of Mauser sporting rifles from Hoffman to Halger.

Published by Womack Associates, 512 Westwood Drive, Prescott, AZ 86301. 70 pages, 8½x11. $20.00 post paid. 1980. K.W.

Trapdoor Springfield

by M. D. Waite and B. G. Ernst

One of the most tenacious investigators into modern arms history was at the same time Technical Editor of the *American Rifleman*—M. D. Waite, one of the authors of this book. The late Bud Waite's peculiar expertise shows in this investigation of the first breech-loading rifle of the United States Army. The book provides accurate information for the collector on the series of Allin-system firearms manufactured in the United States Armory in Springfield, Massachusetts from 1865 until 1893.

The authors properly describe the oft-found and nearly always suspect 20-gauge trapdoor "Forager Models" as well as some 30-caliber test rifles on the Allin system. Tables of dimensions and production information as well as sketches of production machinery and test devices all add to the story. The book is lavishly illustrated in black and white.

At $29.95 from Rutgers, 127 Raritan, Highland Park, NJ 08904. *Ca.* 220 pages, 9x11½. 1980　　K.W.

High Standard Automatic Pistols 1932-1950

by Charles E. Petty

The evolution of the 22 automatic pistol in the United States led author Petty into High Standards early and he has rarely deviated. He is genuinely an expert in the subject.

This book is the standard for collectors, of whom there are bound to be plenty according to the author, since BATF has seen fit to classify all but one of the early High Standard automatic pistols as curios and relics. The book discusses history, serial numbers, takedown types, barrel lengths, and boxes and cases as collectors need these things discussed.

There are some mysteries raised and some solved in this book. As for whether or not it goes into sufficient detail: It discusses and photographs the High Standard P-38, a 38 Special autoloader decorated with an outline of the twin-engine fighter of WWII.

Published by American Ordnance Publications,, P.O. Box 9494, Charlotte, NC 28204. *Ca.* 130 pages. $12.95. Size 6x9. 1976.　　K.W.

Pennsylvania Game News Treasury

edited by Bob Bell

Here are 528 pages of really good reading about hunting in Pennsylvania, put together from 50 years of *Pennsylvania Game News* magazine, a little magazine most dedicated hunters should read, regardless where they live.

It helps to be a regular reader of Pennsylvania Game News because that somehow improves the flavor and zest of the hunter's stew of yarn, anecdote and hard news that this treasury provides. At least, such is the conceit of this regular reader of Pennsylvania Game News.

From "The Pennsylvania Rifle," written by Norman Wilkinson of the Pennsylvania Museum and Historical Commission to "What I Should Have Done" by none other than Archibald Rutledge, to—well, there is 50 years of good reading here and there doesn't seem to be much bad reading.

Published by the Pennsylvania Game Commission, P.O. Box 1567, Harrisburg, PA 17120. Soft cover, $7.50, 6x9. 1979.　　K.W.

In The Gravest Extreme

by Massad F. Ayoob

In a world full of books about self-defense with firearms, Ayoob here strikes a genuinely different note in what he has chosen to subtitle "the role of the firearm in personal protection." The author's father killed the armed criminal who maimed him. Ayoob's interest in lawful violence accomplished with firearms came to him early.

A measure of the difference between this book and others might be found in some of the chapter titles. There is "The Dangerous Myth Of Citizens Arrest" and "Samaritans With Guns."

In brief, Ayoob warns his readers that there are dangers involved in the use of guns for self-defense not limited to a shooting affray itself. The legalities and illegalities of citizen action are all explored by Ayoob and anyone who contemplates defending himself in the United States with a firearm ought read the book.

Published by Gravest Extreme, P.O. Box 122, Concord, NH 03301 at $7.95. Paperbound, 5½x8—*Ca.* 136 pages. 1980.　　K.W.

The Bullet's Flight

by Franklin W. Mann

Wolfe Publishing did not simply reprint this basic American book on the ballistics of small arms, first published in 1909. Wolfe found great shooter and gunsmith Harry Pope's personal copy and has here reprinted that copy, including his pencilled notes and comments.

Possibly most interesting is that Pope originally sent his copy to the author, Dr. Mann, who read the notes and made his own notations—and all of those are here. This is the third reprint of the work—it was done once in 1942 by Standard Publishing Company, and again in 1965 by Ray Riling. A great deal of work was gone into to obtain the best reproduction and copies of the several editions were surveyed to find the best basis.

The result is to be described only as a suitably embellished classic work, bound as the original, in the same size—a meticulously prepared replica.

Published by Wolfe Publishing Co., Inc., Box 30-30, Prescott, AZ 86302, at $22.50. Cloth covers, 392 pages, 7x10. 1980.　　K.W.

Three Short Shotguns

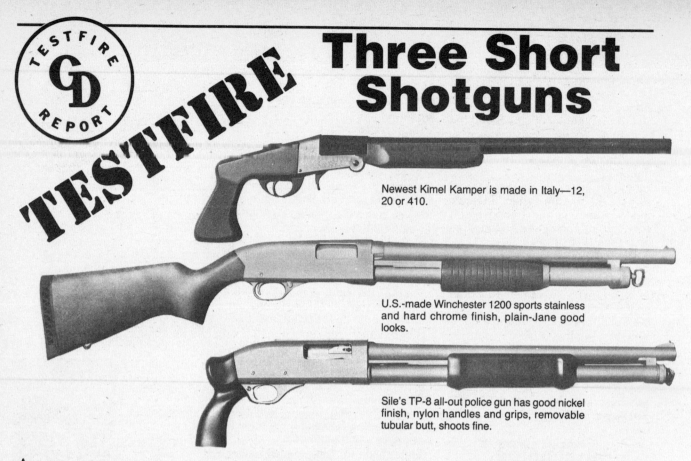

Newest Kimel Kamper is made in Italy—12, 20 or 410.

U.S.-made Winchester 1200 sports stainless and hard chrome finish, plain-Jane good looks.

Sile's TP-8 all-out police gun has good nickel finish, nylon handles and grips, removable tubular butt, shoots fine.

ALMOST TOO late for this issue, several interesting shotguns showed up. They included the familiar Winchester Model 1200 Police—a standard sort of riot gun somewhat dressed up with a stainless sort of finish; the newest version of the Kimel Kamper, a very short version of the Italian folding shotgun long sold by Galef as the Companion; and the TP-8 police and survival pump shotgun sold by Sile Distributors and manufactured in Italy.

A great deal was learned about these guns in a very short time.

The first thing learned was that I believe the standard shotgun configuration is the best for the job. Quick-shooting, whether from hip or shoulder, was really only possible with the conventional Winchester. There is no doubt that a great deal of training would make the TP-8 more familiar, but no amount of training would cure the tremendous blow delivered to the web of the thumb when this gun was fired from the hip, nor would the somewhat sketchy and removable buttstock arrangement provide that lock-on sensation so important to even the snap shot.

Don't get this wrong. This is a robust pump gun with black nylon pistol grip and slide handle and a rough nickel finish. The TP-8 equipped with a buttstock would be an easy to handle fighting shotgun. It loads very easily in conventional style and cheerfully accepts seven or eight cartridges under the barrel. It will accept such cartridges in either 2¾-inch or 3-inch sizes. It is a nice gun, but I don't want to shoot one anymore.

The Kimel Kamper is quite another case. This one has an 18-inch barrel and a pistol grip and is sold as a minimum gun for backpackers and the like, but obviously has other uses. It fulfills all the legal requirements and is a straightforward and rather handsome little gun, somewhat reminiscent of the Handy Guns of the past, which were, in 410 bore, very handy shot pistols.

The Kimel Kamper, of course, has a fully legal 18-inch barrel and it is over 26 inches over-all, so it is in violation of no federal law about short shotguns. (It may violate some state laws—you will have to check for yourself.) Apart from a very handsome light wood stock, a little etching on a bright receiver, and an angular monobloc, the Kamper doesn't look much like a typical sawed-off shotgun, even though that is what it is. It is quite handsome.

The negative points about the Kimel Kamper tested are three: It weighs just 3¾ pounds; it is a 12 gauge; it will fire the 3-inch magnum shells as well as the garden variety 2¾-inch shells. Because of this, the 12 gauge Kimel Kamper is barely manageable and it is hardly any fun at all to shoot. The 20 gauge and 410 bore models are recommended.

Don't get me wrong once again: The

The Kamper fits in small spaces, packs a lot of punch per ounce at both ends.

From 20 yards with Remington's magnum buck loads, any one of the three guns solved the silhouette problem with 14 or more hits.

Kimel Kamper is a reliable firearm and it does exactly what its makers say it will do. Do not plan, however, on any such rapid fire sequence of shots as you might expect from an ordinary single-barrel shotgun, nor for any sort of pin-point pointing with which you might be accustomed with other firearms. It is necessary to grasp it very tightly and to shoot it defensively—that is, so grasped and held as to be sure it won't come back into your face, which on one occasion this one did.

What was I shooting? Well, I was shooting 1-ounce loads of No. 6 shot and I was shooting 3¾-1¼ loads of No. 4s and then I could not resist shooting a 3-inch magnum load of buckshot. Since I was shooting at 20 yards, I held the gun firmly up and forward and aimed it. When I fired, the whole assembly came back and struck me on the jaw.

I have some experience with recoil in rifles and handguns and shotguns. I have felt that my 6¼-pound 308 hunting rifle moved sharply enough to the rear for most purposes; and I must say that I noticed the first few shots I touched off in a very lightweight 357 revolver I once owned; in an iron-sighted Thompson-Center Contender Super 14, 35 Remington factory loads produced noticeable results; and I have fired a variety of genuine elephant guns; and all of these pale into insignificance when compared to a 3¾-pound magnum 12 gauge shooting 24 No. 1 buck pellets. Understand—it does the job and no mistake, but one wants to be prepared.

I'm going to try to master this Kimel Kamper. Probably the main reason for that is that it reminds me of a gun I examined a decade or so ago. That

one was an Italian-made 12-gauge Companion also. It was chopped off to 18 inches and equipped with a recoil pad and a somewhat shorter than normal buttstock and it was an efficient looking gun and for its owner had killed three jaguars, shooting out of tree blinds.

The Kimel Kamper still has some of that flavor for me, but I am going to have to consider matters some before we get much closer acquainted. It may very well be a working gun, the Kamper, but in 12-gauge, it is not really a fun gun.

That is about the size of it with the TP-8 as well. The gun has any number of admirable characteristics and construction details, but the actual shooting with that recoil-sensitive pistol grip creates problems. With a regular buttstock, the TP-8 would be hard to beat in its role.

Looking good, the TP-8 functions well, but slams the hand web in hip-shooting.

To hit at range, it takes this posture with Kimel's Kamper. The little gun jumps.

This gets it done, every time. There is something to be said for familiarity.

Which brings us to the old standby Winchester 1200, a simple little American riot gun with plain barrel, plain buttstock, and, praise be, a nice old-timey round slide handle. The 18-inch barrel is stainless steel, and the remainder of the metal parts of the gun are finished in hard chrome to match. The 1200 Police has a pair of sling swivels and a recoil pad and shooting it is like coming home on a cold day.

Fast repeat shots, whether with magnum or ordinary rounds, are a cinch with the 1200 Police, whether off the shoulder or from the hip. You can get to pumping too hard from the hip, and that means some footwork to stay on target, but you can still hammer those shots in.

The Kimel Kamper at 3¾-pounds is distinctly a lightweight; the Winchester 1200, wood buttstock and slide handle and all, goes 6½ pounds empty; and that is just what the TP-8 weighs, empty. The Kamper would fit, ready to fire, in a 27-inch box and, folded, it would go into a space 20"x6"; the TP-8 with buttstock attached goes just under 40 inches, and just under 30 inches with the buttstock detached; the 1200 Police is an uncompromising 39 inches.

Apart from some convenience while traveling, either by vehicle or afoot, the principal function of short-barreled shotguns is emergency use. You can define emergency fairly broadly, of course, and so encompass situations ranging from a lack of protein or a porcupine gnawing an axe handle to full-scale assault on barricaded armed evil-doers. Any of these guns with ordinary light or express game loads are 30-yard killers on anything from cottontails to Canada geese as would be any cylinder bore 12-bore shotgun.

As for the more exciting potential, I checked into that also: A set of three police pistol silhouette targets was set up at 20 yards and each gun fired once, choosing a separate silhouette for each shot, of course. The ammunition was Remington's 3-inch No. 1 buck; the lowest number of hits on a target was 14, and that was with the Kimel Kamper, because I shot it high. In short, for one shot fired with genuine emergency-type ammunition at genuine emergency-size targets, any of the three short shotguns cut the mustard.

I suppose we all knew that before we started.

And I have about decided that the more a shotgun looks like an Uzi, the less of a shotgun it is.   *KW*

FIE's Super Titan II

The Super Titan II in 380 (top) and 32 auto.

When you can put together a number of good features, keep the quality and dependability right and the price reasonable, you have something. On that basis, Tanfoglio Giuseppe of Italy and Firearms Import/Export of America do, indeed, really have something. It's called the Super Titan II, and over the past few weeks I've been shooting two of them, one in 32 ACP, the other in 380.

The Super Titan II is all-steel, except the wood grips and the heavy plastic magazine floorplate. The floorplate has a Beretta-style extension at the front, and there is ample room on the frontstrap for all three fingers of even the fleshiest hand. The grip panels are hand-checkered European walnut. The stagger-type large-capacity magazine makes the grip a little wider, but it's still comfortable for all but the smallest hands. Magazine capacity is eleven rounds in 380, twelve in 32.

In acknowledgement of today's product liability jungle, F.I.E. has wisely used the entire right slide flat for a warning to read the manual before using the gun. Even the morons who fail to do this, though, will find it difficult to hurt themselves with the Super Titan II. There are four safety systems, and two of these are internal and automatic.

The bottom-rear magazine release is particularly well-designed and easy to operate, being large, deeply serrated, and very similar to the one used on

the Astra A-80 pistol. Both magazines have holes in the back panel at the fully-loaded level, clearly marked "11" on the 380 magazine, and "12" on the one for the 32 pistol. The magazines are not interchangeable. The fit of these magazines, by the way, is superb, and compares well with the fit of my SIG/Sauer P230, a pistol in a much higher price category. This careful magazine fitting no doubt contributed to the fine record of reliability the Super Titan II turned in on the range. In more than 300 rounds fired with both guns, there was not a single malfunction.

This held true even with hollowpoints by Hornady/Frontier and Federal in the 380, and Winchester Silvertip HP's in both guns. A slight digression here, for those who might say "Why bother to make the gun in 32 Auto?" I've always felt and written the performance difference between

---

Specifications

Cartridge: 32 or 380 Auto

Over-all length: 7.38 inches

Height: 5⅛ inches

Barrel length: 3.88 inches

Sight radius: 5 inches

Magazine capacity: 32—12 rounds; 380—11 rounds

Finish: Blue

Suggested retail price: $219.95

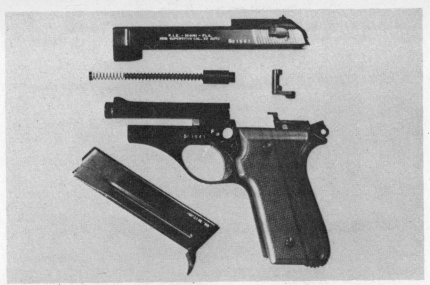

The Super Titan II, field-stripped.

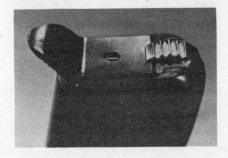

The magazine catch is well-designed and easy to operate.

Short 1100 Magnum

Nobody needs to be told the 1100 works, nor of the joys of the three-inch shell, nor of the uses of the full choke in field shotguns, so there would be no reason at all to provide these test observations except that four inches of missing barrel makes a lot of difference in a duck gun.

That's what sporting Magnum 12s in general are—duck guns, which includes goose and sandhill crane guns and a spot of turkey, too. And that's what an 1100 Magnum 12 with a 26-inch full choke barrel is, but with a difference.

Here's what Remington said: "Shooters will. . .find them a distinct convenience for transporting. . .appreciate having the upland balance and feel in magnum guns." Remington also said the 26-inch full choke models (#6928 to order the 870 slide-action; #5324 to get the 1100 as shown here) are a limited production run, so an early order is a good idea.

A short barrel does not, regardless of the press release, make an 1100 Magnum into a bird gun. The ones I shot—four in all at three different places—weighed eight big pounds. They swung for me better than the 30-inch kind and through two limits of ducks and two of geese the short barrel made only that difference—they swung easier. Four boxes of 8s fired at 16-yard trap were very pleasant and right up to average. But the short barrel makes it, for my money, only into a lot nicer duck gun. I'll never take mine after woodcock. *Ken Warner*

32 and 380 is so small it hardly matters, and that the 32 is actually more accurate. With the 32 Winchester Silvertip, the question becomes almost academic, as this bullet consistently expands to around 50 caliber in ballistic media, even out of a three or four-inch barrel.

The sights on the Super Titan II are European-style, the inverted-V front sight being integral with the barrel. The rear notch is a square-bottomed V, and the sight is dovetail-mounted and laterally adjustable by drifting. On the test guns, the sights were on-center, and required no adjustment. Inherent accuracy was checked by firing from a sandbag rest into paper at 15 yards, and both guns grouped well. I was not surprised when the 32 did best, turning in one neat little 1¼-inch group.

Moving up to 15 feet, both guns were rapid-fired from belt level at combat silhouettes, and all hits were well-grouped in the K area. Again, the lighter recoil of the 32 and its faster recovery resulted in tighter groups. The barrels of these guns are double-pinned in place on the frames, and this sort of rigid mounting always aids accuracy. The solid 28-ounce weight of the pistols also helps.

Trigger pull on both guns was quite stiff at the start, but began to ease up a lot after the first hundred rounds. Slack and over-travel were very slight.

Takedown for cleaning is extremely simple. You must cock the hammer, set the trigger-safety in on-safe position, and remove the magazine. Then, pull the slide all the way back, lift it upward at the rear, and ease it off toward the front. The recoil spring unit and the safety are than easily taken out. This is as far as the non-gunsmith needs to go, and will allow cleaning of all the necessary parts.

The Super Titan II is not a pocket pistol. In size and weight, it would be classified as a medium-frame holster gun. It's not so large, though, that it couldn't be used as a back-up piece for law enforcement. It would be perfect as a pistol for home or personal defense, and in both applications its large-capacity magazine would be a definite advantage.

To sum it up: The Super Titan II is very good quality; it's reliable, and it's accurate. While it doesn't have the exquisite finish of a Beretta, Browning, or Walther, it's still a handsome piece and it costs a lot less. For those who feel no need to impress the peasants with a name, the Super Titan II can be an excellent choice. *J.B. Wood*

Short 1100 Magnum gun with full choke works fine ballistically and practically.

The Beeman/Webley Vulcan

Powerful and accurate spring-piston air rifles were rather scarce until a few short years ago, when the first true modern "magnum" airsporter first appeared. Exceptionally powerful spring-piston rifles were available from time to time, but power and accuracy didn't generally go together.

One of the newest members of this select group is the Beeman/Webley "Vulcan." It takes no back seat to any other rifle in its category, as far as power and accuracy are concerned.

Produced by the long-time famous English gun-making firm of Webley & Scott, Ltd., the Vulcan signifies that company's effort to jump headlong into a field dominated mostly by sizzlers such as the Feinwerkbau 624 and, to a lesser extent, by the Diana-Original 45. Webley's answer to the situation has been to create a really plain-looking barrel-cocker that performs hotly indeed, at a price that is way below that of the competition.

Looking much the same as Webley's now discontinued Hawk Mk. III model, the Vulcan introduces some new and clever features in the powerplant. In order to reach the magical 800 fps mark, which is really the "threshold velocity" that separates true magnum air rifles from other high performance sporters, Webley has increased the size of the cylinder that houses the piston and mainspring assembly. The new piston incorporates a PTFE (polytetrafluoroethylene) seal that in itself is a major breakthrough in spring-piston powerplant technology.

The Vulcan measures 41″ over-all. With a weight of only 7 lbs. and a good balance, the rifle is quite handy and comfortable to carry afield all day. The cocking effort demands approximately 27 lbs., which is also a boon to long shooting sessions. The barrel is 17⅛″ long, with beautiful rifling. There is a smooth breech taper to aid the shooter during the loading procedure.

The Vulcan probably will never win any fancy beauty contests. It has a simple but uncannily rugged elegance that seems to invite shooters to try it out. Once you fire the Vulcan a few times, it becomes quite apparent that most of the fancy stuff went into the *interior* design of this rifle, rather than to jazzing up its looks. A rich, deep blue finish on all metal surfaces is to be expected in a product carrying the Webley name, and the Vulcan cer-

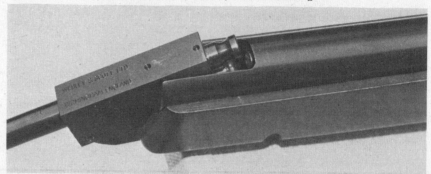

Right side view of the Vulcan shows the out-of-the-box sporter set up with open sights.

The Vulcan's breech seal is located around the transfer port, on the cylinder face, rather than at the rear of the barrel, and the breech has a smooth taper to ease loading.

The Vulcan delivered excellent and *consistent* accuracy with different types of match and sporting pellets.

tainly has that finish. The oil-finished breech stock has a reddish-brown hue that contrasts nicely with the metal surfaces. No checkering anywhere, but that's one luxury we can do without when we consider the price of this gun. There is, however, a gentle cheekpiece *and* a thick rubber recoil pad. Over-all, the stock is very well made and quite functional, having the necessary dimensions to fit most adults, even large adults, comfortably.

The trigger is adjustable by means of an Allen screw located at the top of the cylinder end plug. This screw acts directly on the trigger to control the let-off pressure. The latter can be reduced to approximately 3 lbs. My test sample arrived with a trigger let-off pressure of 5½ lbs., which I quickly

decreased to 3½ lbs. The Vulcan also has a manual trigger safety, located on the left rear side of the receiver above the trigger. It consists of a short lever that can be flicked back after the rifle is cocked, effectively preventing an accidental discharge. My own view on this type of device on a spring-piston airgun is that it should be ignored completely. A spring-piston gun should not be left cocked for any extended period of time and a trigger safety seems like an encouragement to do so. It also provides a false sense of security.

Over a period of four months, I monitored my test Vulcan at different intervals. After some preliminary shake-down sessions during which approximately 500 rounds were fired, I adjusted the rifle, lubricated all cocking linkage friction points, and applied Beeman Spring Cylinder Oil to the mainspring. The initial shakedown sessions had produced some dieseling, but this is to be expected in most high-performance spring-piston rifles when new. Moderate dieseling is a healthy sign that the powerplant is burning off excess oils in the system.

Right out of the box, the Vulcan produced an average MV of 809 fps with H&N Match pellets. Following the aforementioned shake-down firings and lubrication, MV (muzzle velocity) with H&N Match pellets averaged 823 fps. Switching over to the light-weight RWS Hobby pellets, the MV jumped up to an average of 840 fps, while Beeman Laser pellets, which are also quite light, averaged 836 fps. The excellent Silver Sting pointed pellets produced an average MV of 831 fps. Beeman's new heavy Ram Jet silhouette pellets also performed well, developing an average of 812 fps.

The Vulcan also performed very well indeed in the accuracy part of the tests with all of the aforementioned pellets. Not surprisingly, the tightest groups were obtained with H&N Match. The latter averaged .20″ center-to-center at 25 ft. All accuracy tests were conducted with the rifle rested on sandbags. Accuracy tests were conducted using both the rifle's open sights as well as a Tasco 611 VFM telesight. Some preliminary tests were also conducted using a Weaver "Marksman" telesight. Most tests were fired at 25 ft., but tests were also run at 10 M. (33 ft.) and at 50 ft.

The pointed Silver Sting pellets came in second place on group size, averaging .25″ center-to-center at 25 ft. Beeman's new Ram Jet silhouette pellets and RWS Hobby pellets were practically neck and neck on accuracy out of my test Vulcan. Both pellets turned in group averages hovering around .35″ center-to-center, also at 25 ft.

The Vulcan is also available in 22 caliber. Performance data for that caliber, according to Beeman's, list a MV of 610-630 fps and an accuracy average of approximately .32″ center-to-center at 25 ft. It is worth noting that Beeman's claims for the 177-cal. model were generally surpassed by my test rifle. The group size figures did not deviate excessively either way from Beeman's own .28″ center-to-center accuracy rating for the 177-cal. Vulcan.

J. I. Galan

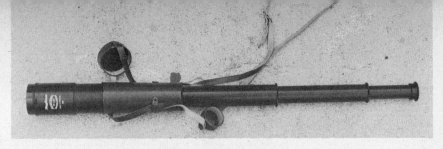

Mayflower Drawtube Scope

Every once in a while it is possible to progress by going just a little bit backward and it is my belief that the Wetzlar optical firm of Schmidt & Bender have done so by creating the 20x50 Mayflower stalking scope, a terrestrial draw tube scope of virtually uncompromising optical clarity. There is a compromise, but it is in a useful direction—when extended and focused at approximate infinity, the Mayflower is about 32 inches long.

That is the retrogression mentioned above. When it is decided that a terrestrial telescope can be 32 inches long, a lot of very complex optical effort becomes unnecessary.

What the hunter or shooter gets, in this case, is a nice little 2-pound package, suitably encased in leather, measuring under eleven inches long. It may be uncased, focused and directed offhand, so to speak, with considerable celerity from a remarkable number of field positions. The focus, being linear, is infinitely variable, very quick, and without any complication whatever of turning and twisting or parts made to do so.

What is the optical quality? Well, genuine optical experts, who examined this particular specimen in their own factory, admitted that it is easily capable of checking on 22-caliber bullet impact at a distance of 300 meters. After they saw that, these experts who market spotting scopes of their own, got quite a bit more serious about this old time style scope.

In fact, it seems to this writer an instrument capable of full spotting scope performance as easy to carry and bring into play as a pair of binoculars. Very few binoculars, of course, will resolve small details at 500 yards the way this glass will. I have hunted with people who carried first class spotting scopes mounted on rifle stocks, or equipped themselves with full-scale tripods, and I've looked through all of those devices, and I

Hunter gets a handy two-pound leather-covered package, easy to tote.

One of several positions from which the Mayflower works and stays steady.

don't recall ever being in a situation that this telescope wouldn't have handled just about as well.

It sells at this writing for under $200; Heckler & Koch imports it. That is probably a pretty expensive draw tube scope, but it is certainly good value for the optical quality obtained.

KW

Sanftl Schuetzen

Deluxe all-out Continental offhand rifle for muzzle-loading targeteers who will stand for it.

For the modern muzzle-loading match shooter, the ultimate refinement of an offhand score is the constant goal, as it once was in the competitive and festive Schuetzen matches in the villages of old Europe, specifically Germany and Switzerland. That good-natured arms race probably reached its muzzle-loading pinnacle around the 1850s.

Schuetzen rifles were characterized by rather heavy barrels, fancy shoulder-and-face-contoured stocks, exquisite double-set triggers, finger-moulded trigger guards, and elaborate sights. They were clearly designed for offhand shooting, where ranges were 100 and 200 yards (later, in the U.S.) at German-styled paper-ring targets.

Dixie Gun Works has now introduced their Sanftl Schuetzen Target Rifle, certainly the most impressive match-grade frontloader I have fired in many a year. Copied from an 1850s percussion Schuetzen made by Sanftl and now in a private collection in Germany, this replica has been reproduced by the famous Italian gunmaking firm of Paulo Bondini.

The 29-inch German barrel has polygroove rifling, with 12 lands and grooves, spiraling 1 turn in 48 inches. The flats of the octagon barrel are ⅞-inch across and the stated caliber is 45. The European walnut stock, buttplate and trigger guard all blend together in a classic Schuetzen profile.

The percussion lock itself is most unusual to the American eye, for it is a true back-action configuration and the hammer faces the shooter. Sanftl's theory was that the backward hammer fall would minimize muzzle movement at the moment of firing. One might surmise that a fast-falling hammer slapping down towards the shooter's sighting eye might be a bit disturbing, but this is not the case, thanks to a metal shield that curves up from the bolster, effectively interrupting both the view of the hammer and black residue. A movable brass shield pivots on the left side of the stock, thereby blocking that eye's vision, so that all concentration is on the target.

Barrel, lock and sights are polished steel, while the adjustable set triggers are blued and can only be fired in the "set" position. The inside of the lock is also polished, which translates into a crisp, smooth action and there is no halfcock on the hammer—just "full" and "fire." That means you only cap the nipple just before you are ready to shoot.

My first trip to the range was a disaster. Believing any 45-caliber rifle ought to take a 440 ball—even though Dixie recommends a 445—that was all I took. Dixie and I were both wrong. Patched or unpatched, those 440s did not even start down the rifled barrel. Rummaging through the shooting box, I eventually found some 435s, but they were difficult to start also.

Another shooter volunteered a few handcast 410s, which I patched with a 20/1000 thick greased muslin, but the fit was too loose to provide the accuracy I felt the rifle could give. Obviously, this exacting rifle required some exacting measurements.

I miked the bore once home and found it came to .443-inch. Obviously, a 10/1000 patch and a 433 round ball was what was needed, not your most popular size. Speer produces swaged 433 round balls, so back to the range I went, armed with a box of those, a package of Ox-Yoke pre-oiled 10/1000 patches, and both FFFg and Pyrodex RS powder, along with some Remington Hot Caps and one of the new Weaver T4 spotting scopes.

The new balls worked just fine, requiring a firm rap on the short-starter to get them past what is obviously a

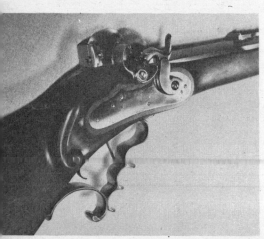

Hammer falls backward, but the big shield takes it out of view, screens off anything else.

Sights, other hardware, on the Sanftl are worked out with distinctly un-American but useful detail.

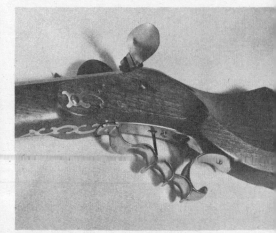

Sanftl offers all the true Schuetzen comforts, to include pillow stock, set triggers, left-eye screen.

slightly choked muzzle. Cleaning the bore after each shot—a time-consuming endeavor but necessary in order to obtain the best load—I was able to get my tightest group by using 50 grains of FFFg, not a heavy-duty charge, but one that still retained sufficient blowback to cock the hammer with each shot. That did cut down time on recapping the nipple, which takes No. 11 caps nicely, but not standard rifle-type nipple wrenches. It requires a musket wrench.

My best group fired that day measured ¾ of an inch for a five-shot string. That includes the fifth and last shot on the wrong target. Fortunately, it was my own target and the bullet hit exactly where the rest of the cluster should have been, only one bull's-eye lower.

This rifle is clearly designed for the target range. The scalloped cheekpiece even has a hollowed out area for the nose to nestle, so that the face and shoulder all tuck nicely and firmly into the stock. And in the true Schuetzen fashion, it is intended for offhand only; firing it from either a prone or sitting position will get you a nice jar in the cheekbone, one even the gun's ten pounds of weight cannot diminish, due to the face-forming contour of the stock. From standing, it is extremely comfortable to shoot, with superb sights, crisp trigger let-off and the ability to enable you to shoot match-winning scores, even when there is a breeze blowing. At $595, Dixie's Sanftl Schuetzen holds the potential of breaking old records wherever adjustable-sight muzzle-loading matches are held.

Rick Hacker

Rossi's Fun Gun

This is the 62SAC, a short—very short—carbine that gobbles 22 Shorts or Longs or Long Rifles as fast as can be.

If it has been too long since you went out to the sandpit and blew away a brick of 22s, get a Rossi 62SAC and see if you're not inspired to return to those good old days. This is fun.

It is also cute. It weighs (mine) 4¾ pounds and it is not 33 inches long. It holds 12 Long Rifles or 18 Shorts. It fires everytime so far except once when I short-shucked on an old 22 Short. And with three different munitions—22 Stinger, standard 22 Long Rifle, and high speed Shorts—it gave me ¾" groups about three inches high at 25 yards right out of the box. That was all the formality there was. Ever since, we have been cleaning up all the stray ammo from the back of the closets.

You see, whatever the purists say about quality, this little item is true to the original design. That means if you hold the trigger back and reciprocate (pump) the slide handle, the little sucker goes off every time your left hand goes forward. You can run 18 shots through there in a whole lot less than 18 seconds. You sure can. Further, you can set up something like maybe five clay targets in the sand bank and step back 15 yards or so and go to shooting from the hip and with just a little bit of practice you'll be busting all five and still have five or six in the tube and only be shooting for maybe six seconds.

It is the pure quill fun gun.

Mind you, if you do get one, you will find some guy who says "It ain't made like the old ones."

He means the Winchesters of at least three model numbers made on this same pattern and he's right, but you ought to say "So what? Are you going to find me a functioning Winchester for $150 I wouldn't be afraid to carry in the rain or out where some purist would steal it? If not, shut up and step aside."

In all detail, this is a sound functioning copy of the 1890-1906 Model 62 slide-action outside hammer 22s. It goes together like they did; it takes down like they did; it is shaped and balanced as they were. It is made in Brazil in the 1980s and it is not so cleanly finished as the Winchesters of three to nine decades ago and it does not have walnut stocks because walnut doesn't grow there. You have to be a better shot than I am to tell if the old ones shoot better than these.

You can buy these with a guarantee. Apart from the one I have, I know three others of these. One is a replacement by the importer, made with no demurr when there was some glitch in the first one.

But that's all detail. The fun is in shooting. Leave the 50-meter 10-ringing to the serious and find joy again.

Ken Warner

Hacker's results speak for themselves and he intends to shoot five more shots some day, using, .433" balls.

This is perhaps how it is the most fun. Every time you pump, it shoots and you can point it very well.

A 9mm Walter Mitty Kit

KG-9, and no doubt KG-99 to follow, are defense guns you carry like cameras. Even the unfamiliar can shoot them for fun and confidence.

The fictional man in Paul Gallico's story, to whom machine guns and high-powered engines said "Ta-pocketa, ta-pocketa," and who said of his injured arm "I'm all right; it's only broken," would have loved this gun. It has everything for Walter, this KG-9 semi-automatic pistol marketed by F.I.E. of Hialeah, Florida, and now, sadly, out of production—to be replaced by the KG-99.

The KG-9 was made in Florida by another firm, named Interdynamics, Inc., and it's the nearly-spitting image of a submachine gun. Unlike most such uncouth automatic weapons, the KG-9 is designed to fire just once per trigger pull and it's quite light and it fits in nearly any briefcase. In all else it is SMG—it fires from an open bolt; the safety is a slot for the bolt handle; there's a 30-round box magazine; it's finished in basic Sneaky Pete black; and if you pull the trigger in the right rhythm, it goes "Ta-pocketa, ta-pocketa."

All in all, Mittiness aside, if there were strange noises at 2 AM out beyond the shed and you felt the need to go see about it and were up to giving it a go, you could do worse than reach the KG-9 down and have at it. One hint: Don't use the safety notch—the gun is far quicker from the empty chamber—bolt forward position and no doubt every bit as safe.

One more thing: The KG-9 is fun to shoot. Those familiar with guns find it very simple. And those unfamiliar with them find it easy and thrilling.

The price is awful. At this writing, just after introduction, it's $400 or so at retail. At the $300 retail first bruited about, there was a lot of action, so much so that like any red-blooded American hot seller, the price went up. The manufacturing costs have nothing to do with this, by the way—if the factory has more than $40 or so in the gun (not *with* magazine) they should fire the engineer. The KG-9 is a reconfigured STEN gun, though it's lots cuter. They say the KG-99 will fire from a closed bolt and be a lot more sophisticated, but not heavier.

As a defense arm either makes more sense than a lot of experts will admit. Such a gun is too big for real concealed carry; it's small enough to take wherever it has to be; it's simple to function, doesn't kick, and it's scary. If it is necessary to shoot a person with one, the gun is accurate enough, but you can forget plinking beer cans—beer kegs you could hit maybe, but not cans. There's no nonsense about holsters or delicate care and feeding: You fill the stick, jam it in, rock back the bolt and pull the trigger or wait for a round to chamber and then pull the trigger, depending on the model.

And you can pull that trigger 30 times before the gun runs dry. The gun doesn't like 32 rounds or 35 rounds in the magazine, but from 30 down to zero it goes bang-bang-bang (or ta-pocketa, ta-pocketa) very reliably. Experts tell me the KG-9 was not made to meet military standards, and I believe it, so that's a hint that its innards may get tired with enough shooting; other experts tell me that out there on the street the boyos were telling each other how easy the KG-9 converts to full auto, so that's a hint of another kind.

In fact, that is why, on January 19, 1982, BATF ruled Interdynamics had to change the model. Among the changes: A fire control system more difficult to alter to full-auto, and a steel number plate in the plastic frame. That—plus some cosmetics—created the KG-99 after 4,039 KG-9s were made.

What you sees is not quite what you gets in the KG-99 or KG-9, but what's left of the dream is still pretty good. For a lot of important purposes in the hands of average folks, a gas-pipe shooter like this beats any National Match 45 or Model 19 Combat Magnum ever minted. Ask the next Israeli National Guard type you see and see what he or she says.   *K.W.*

Lenard M. Brownell
(1922-1982)

THIS MAN was no stranger to these pages over many and many a year. He was an inventive and creative man, a Master Gunsmith, who worked hard at his trade.

He untemperamentally strove with that trade through decades before there was the present burst of enthusiasm and investment in what he made—guns, mostly hunting rifles, to order—which are now called custom guns. And he helped, directly and indirectly, dozens of other craftsmen.

In 1981, in Denver, those other men were able to demonstrate to Lenard Brownell what they thought of him. They did it with a special occasion, and with a plaque—you see it here—and 21 of them signed it as "friends with a common interest."

The plaque says: "In appreciation for leadership and innovation in the art of gunsmithing beautifully exhibited in the Ruger Model 77

and in the Ruger No. 1 as well as in the collections of those fortunate enough to own one of the guns you have customized."

You can see the latest Brownell commercial stock design here, too—the Ruger International Model M-77. It is a remarkable rendition of the principal lines of the Mannlicher-Schoenauer carbines of the first decade of the century.

Lenard Brownell left a host of friends, his wife Catherine, and a going business. Mrs. Brownell, in partnership with Ross Billingsley, will carry on as Billingsley and Brownell, Custom Riflesmiths, and will market the Brownell scope mount and other Brownell-designed accessories.   *K.W.*

ABOUT THAT PLAQUE

It is one of three presented at the Denver NRA meeting. The other two went to Joe Oakley, the wood man, and Monty Kennedy, stockmaker.

Ted Blackburn and Byrd Pearson organized the event, and the well-wishers took the three men to the show, and they and many others honored the trio at a breakfast.

Here's who signed the Brownell and Oakley plaques, not including those honored: Duane Wiebe, Byrd N. Pearson, Bob Emmons, Herman Waldron, Dale W. Goens, Lou Leonard, Al Biesen, Terry Wallace, Jerry Fisher, Roger Biesen, Ted Blackburn, Mark Lee, Robert D. Swartley, Phil Fischer, Maurice D. Ottmar, Reinhart Fajen, Steve Billeb, Hubert Hecht, and Gary Goudy.

NRA meeting, Denver, 1981

The HUNTER SPECIALS

THE MIRACLES of the modern rifle in this country are not the super customs done in painstaking detail by a few dozen craftsmen, though they are certainly the cream of the crop. The miracles are the good, sound and well-made rifles turned out by the millions at unbelievably low cost. When one really considers the labor and materials in that new Ruger or Remington or whatever one has just traded one's hard earned money for, it is nothing short of astounding.

That's the good news, now the less good. In order for the factories to do this, compromises must be made in detail of the shaping, finishing, fit. Individually very small compromises, collectively they make up the difference in *feel* and appearance between "factory" and "custom."

That is where the Hunter Special we make comes in. What we try to do is achieve the feel and at least part of the appearance of the true custom rifle at a price the average hunter can afford and will want to beat the bush with. The key word in this process is *feel* rather than weight. The rifle stock— the Ruger—shown here is the first I weighed before starting. It weighed 2.69 lbs., and when finished 2.05, a reduction of 10 and ¾ oz. The stock was quite dense. Many small changes, we think, result in a neater, trimmer and better handling rifle.

Here's what we do:

After a work order is written up, the gun is disassembled. The barreled action becomes the holder for the stock during shaping and initial sanding. The factory pad and grip cap are removed and the stock is clamped in a Bridgeport and the buttstock bored.

Since this order called for an ebony tip, the forearm was bandsawed off, then mounted in the mill and trued up, as was the block of ebony. The next step was to epoxy the recoil pad, a Len Brownell grip cap and the ebony block on. By the time you get all the assorted pieces covered with Acraglas, lined up and clamped, there is very little around you not covered with Acraglas. Best thing to clean it off and yourself up with is plain household vinegar.

After the epoxy has hardened the recoil pad is ground down on a belt sander. The stock is then set up in a mill again and the barrel channel roughed into the ebony tip, and the forearm milled. For the cuts in the forearm a cutter ground with a radius at the corner is used to remove a maximum amount of wood, but not leave a sharp corner at the bottom. These cuts and bores fore and aft contribute more to the elusive "feel" we're after than just the ounces removed. They shift the center of mass towards the hands.

The inletting of the ebony tip is finished by hand. With the stock assembled to the barreled action, duct tape protects the bluing from marring during reshaping. Entirely by hand, the stock is shaped with various rasps, files and hard-backed coarse sandpaper. This is the next step in developing the "feel"—corners are rounded, straight lines are changed to subtle curves and the stock in most cases is slimmed in varying degree all over. One of the most important changes on most stocks is to set the comb nose back ½- to ¾-inch. With proper flutes, this provides clearance for the hand and feels much better than the issue shape.

Sanding begins with 50 grit garnet paper, and continues through successive steps of 80, 120, 220 and 320 grits. I whisker the stock between each grit, and the last step before applying finish is to *scrub* the stock down with suitable solvent to remove all the sanding dust from the pores.

I use John Bivins Express Oil System to finish. "Express" suggests speed, and "oil" conjures up the poor but dedicated English smith laboring long hours rubbing linseed oil into his gun stock with his hands to generate enough heat to polymerize the oil . . . the Englishman who first told the story is still laughing. Show me a stock saturated with linseed oil and I'll show you a mess. The beautiful old London oil finishes never were oil. They were various natural organic resin varnishes that when exposed to air *hard-*

Elaborated Remington 700 at top of page got a full re-work—forearm tip, extra checkering, etc. At left, team routs out forearms for balance; stock at right has been shaped, needs comb flutes cut.

This team of gunsmiths reworks most factory rifles to get custom feel without the high price.

by LOWELL MANLEY

ened into a film. The Bivins system is a modern polyurethane varnish which gives excellent weather and moisture resistance and when applied in the proper manner will give the feel and appearance of what we have come to call an oil finish.

This finish cures very rapidly and will checker almost immediately, as shown by the pictures nearby. Ted is working here approximately four days after I started the finishing and less than 24 hours after the last wipe on-wipe off. This rifle was done twenty-four lines to the inch, as are most of the Hunter Specials. Ted has used twenty-two lines on a few very soft pieces. Because of the better than average wood in this stock the customer optioned for some extra checkering, going to a full wrap-around forearm pattern and a panel on top of the grip. The standard job consists of a four panel pattern like the Ruger or the Model 70 factory pattern, with approximately 25 percent more coverage.

We have become known as specialists in redoing the 77, but our process lends itself to most mass-produced arms. To date, in addition to the Model 77, we have done the 700 Remington Classic and Standard, also Sakos, including the new Classic, Winchester Model 70's, FN Mausers, Ruger #1's, Savage Anschutz, and Marlin lever actions. Each has its own idiosyncrasies. For instance, the Sako action needs to have the tang reshaped in order for the rest of the work to be worthwhile.

If the factory inletting on a rifle has a lot of gaps I recommend a black glass job. This is just Acraglas pigmented black. When the blued metal is replaced in the finished stock the glass job virtually disappears. I also recommend a glass bead finish prior to hot bluing. It comes close to the appearance of rust bluing, and matches our "oil" finish very well.

(As a writer, Manley has delicately skirted the subject of money. Specifically, what he is talking about here will cost from just under $300 to about $500, depending on patterns and options and additional work. It's about a week's pay for a person with a fair job, more or less, or just about the same as buying a second scoped factory bolt-action rifle. K.W.)

This whole thing sort of came about by accident. A local hunter, Ed Vigrass, wanted some help in reshaping and refinishg a couple of 77 stocks. In talking it over with Ed, I asked him if he was sure he wanted to put this much work into the relatively plain wood in his factory stock.

His answer was very simple: "I just can't afford a custom stock or the fancy wood to make it."

So we went ahead with his project. I think when we were through I had benefited more than Ed had. First and foremost, I learned that a very elegant and beautiful rifle can be built around plain ordinary wood. From the subsequent response, we find a lot of people are looking for that touch of elegance, that hard to define something, that doesn't come out of factory cartons.

And they want it on working rifles, rifles that acquire merit as they acquire that collection of mars and dings common to working guns, marks that bring not pain of lost investments but fond memories of cold mornings, high mountain meadows and bugling elk.

"That mark there on the forearm, I got that scrambling around a rock face trying to get a shot at the best Dall ram I've ever seen, yeah, that one right there on the wall"—that's the point of view our customers have. •

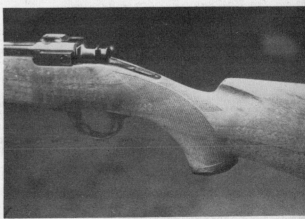

Team gets real custom look as the left side of the M700 shows. Much of the time, Rugers are standard fare. The No. 1 forearm is in European style (at left); the Ruger 77 standard job at right shows off somewhat enlarged checkering coverage.

PETER JOHNSON
This smith for Orvis Co. gets a chance now and again to make a British sidelock sing, new wood and all.

EARL K. MATSUOKA
This Darne 28-gauge was restocked in Honolulu in English walnut, checkered 28 lines to the inch all around the grip.

MIKE YEE
Side-plated Browning with Angelo Bee engraving is stocked in very high grade English walnut.

CUSTOM GUNS

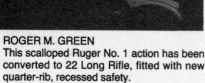

ROGER M. GREEN
This scalloped Ruger No. 1 action has been converted to 22 Long Rifle, fitted with new quarter-rib, recessed safety.

PETERSON-KOCH
Dan Peterson holds KP-33 square bridge 98-type action. He and Al Koch will furnish such Crandell-made actions in three lengths.

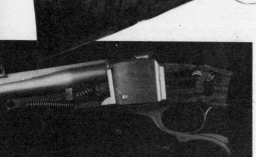

TODD TREFTS
Enthusiastic rework of Mauser rimfire training rifle has everything. With 18-inch barrel, it weighs six pounds.

ROBERT SNAPP
This 1910 Remington was rebarreled to 6mm Remington in full octagon, given short tangs, and all refitted.

J. LYNN CROOK
Handsome Winchester 92 in 218 Bee has Shilen barrel, major metal work, restocked in American walnut.

WARREN HEYDENBERK
This Kimber got English walnut, ebony tip, Biesen butt and cap and Talley swivel bases in its rework.

KARL GUENTHER

G33-40 worked up by old-time G&H worker now free-lancing shows the sound touch and the clean line it takes.

H. L. "PETE" GRISEL

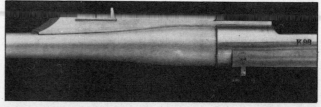

Here's how a Grisel rib and sight look fitted up to a Model 98. This is one of several specialties.

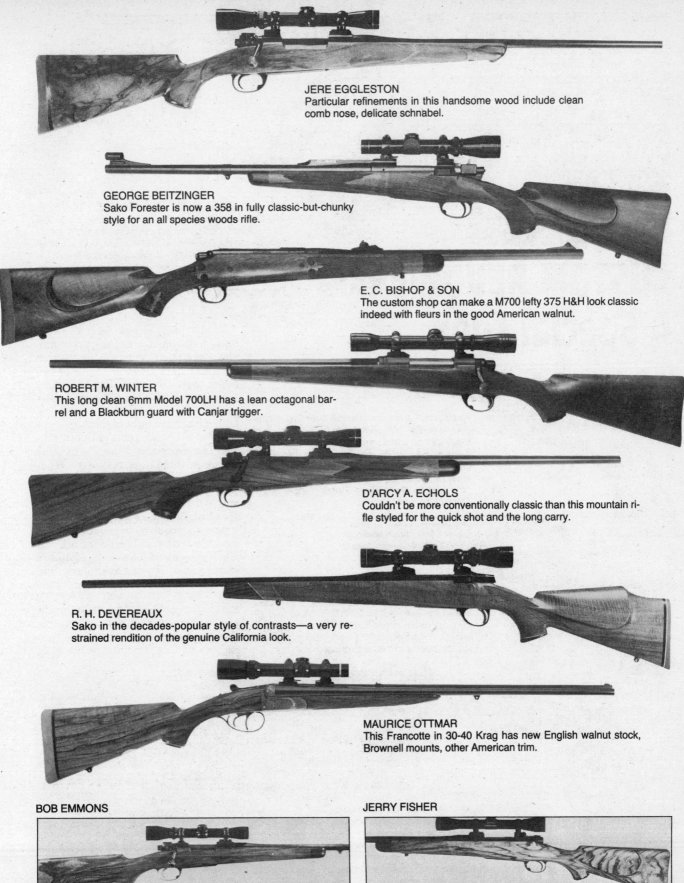

JERE EGGLESTON
Particular refinements in this handsome wood include clean comb nose, delicate schnabel.

GEORGE BEITZINGER
Sako Forester is now a 358 in fully classic-but-chunky style for an all species woods rifle.

E. C. BISHOP & SON
The custom shop can make a M700 lefty 375 H&H look classic indeed with fleurs in the good American walnut.

ROBERT M. WINTER
This long clean 6mm Model 700LH has a lean octagonal barrel and a Blackburn guard with Canjar trigger.

D'ARCY A. ECHOLS
Couldn't be more conventionally classic than this mountain rifle styled for the quick shot and the long carry.

R. H. DEVEREAUX
Sako in the decades-popular style of contrasts—a very restrained rendition of the genuine California look.

MAURICE OTTMAR
This Francotte in 30-40 Krag has new English walnut stock, Brownell mounts, other American trim.

BOB EMMONS

Really striking French walnut graces this square bridge 7x57 which is a genuine seven-pounder.

JERRY FISHER

This most unusual French walnut needs little decoration beyond Burgess metalwork.

This one is a delight. It's an altered 45 Colt S&W 25-5. The barrel is 3.1-inches; the cylinder is a re-fit, a Model 28 cylinder bored out to get optimum holes; the grip is reduced to duplicate the K-frame round butt; full Nite-Sites are in place, as is a smooth trigger and a slick action. Spokhandguns did the work. The only problems: Envy and holsters short enough. Dan Flaherty of Weaver, among others, thinks this is as neat as revolvers get.

CUSTOM REVOLVERS: A Special Look

Alonzo Crull, a Hoosier, worked over Colt single-actions in the '30s; eventually he built some of these 22s on Colt Lightning frames. He altered them to SA, fitted what new parts he could, came up with good-shooting, good-feeling, small rimfire single-actions, built one or two at a time, before there were Ruger Single-Sixes. Think of the work!

OK, it has a slick black chrome finish, and all-steel parts, and really grabby redwood burl grips, but what's unusual about this Bearcat? Would you believe it's a 22 WMR, the factory 22 LR cylinder lengthened and all else arranged to suit? C. S. Lanham did the work; it's a successful job, but one has to work to shoot it well.

In the past, it has been the custom—most often a necessity—to provide only sketchy details on custom guns seen here. Collected on these two pages, however, are a few handguns known to the Editor. They are *not*—except for one or two—his property, but he has fired most of them.

Some are real gems; all function OK. The experience gained with these prompts three observations: What seems like a good idea isn't always; when a good idea works out, it is a real joy; when you can get by with it, the straight factory gun is just fine.

A word about money: Much of the work done at this level—not all, but much—is priced like J. P. Morgan's steam yacht: If you have to ask, you can't afford it. That is, it doesn't take very long to spend $1,000.00, $2,000.00 or even $3,000.00 before you start engraving. You really need a clear understanding with your gunsmith.

K.W.

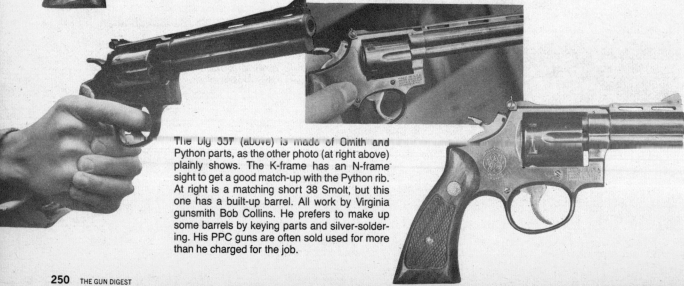

The big 357 (above) is made of Smith and Python parts, as the other photo (at right above) plainly shows. The K-frame has an N-frame sight to get a good match-up with the Python rib. At right is a matching short 38 Smolt, but this one has a built-up barrel. All work by Virginia gunsmith Bob Collins. He prefers to make up some barrels by keying parts and silver-soldering. His PPC guns are often sold used for more than he charged for the job.

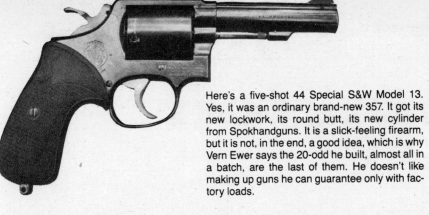

Here's a five-shot 44 Special S&W Model 13. Yes, it was an ordinary brand-new 357. It got its new lockwork, its round butt, its new cylinder from Spokhandguns. It is a slick-feeling firearm, but it is not, in the end, a good idea, which is why Vern Ewer says the 20-odd he built, almost all in a batch, are the last of them. He doesn't like making up guns he can guarantee only with factory loads.

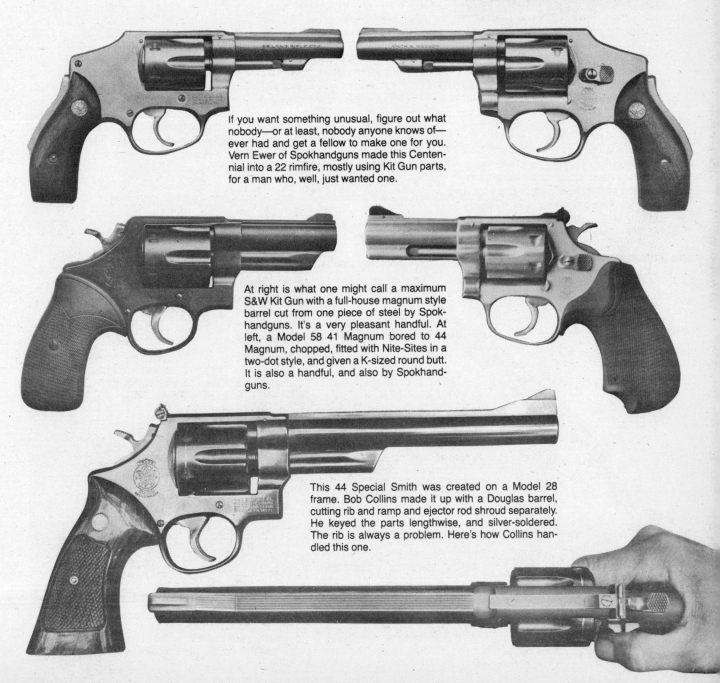

If you want something unusual, figure out what nobody—or at least, nobody anyone knows of—ever had and get a fellow to make one for you. Vern Ewer of Spokhandguns made this Centennial into a 22 rimfire, mostly using Kit Gun parts, for a man who, well, just wanted one.

At right is what one might call a maximum S&W Kit Gun with a full-house magnum style barrel cut from one piece of steel by Spokhandguns. It's a very pleasant handful. At left, a Model 58 41 Magnum bored to 44 Magnum, chopped, fitted with Nite-Sites in a two-dot style, and given a K-sized round butt. It is also a handful, and also by Spokhandguns.

This 44 Special Smith was created on a Model 28 frame. Bob Collins made it up with a Douglas barrel, cutting rib and ramp and ejector rod shroud separately. He keyed the parts lengthwise, and silver-soldered. The rib is always a problem. Here's how Collins handled this one.

Remington
The On-Going Commitment

This was not a big year for new introductions at Remington, nor did the company have any big problem-solving exercise going on. What popped into view were some special models of favorites like the 1100, a useful new 22 rimfire solid, some heavier slugs and the like.

And Hunter's Clays.

This is a new game. Trap is OK and Skeet is still shot, but all the birdwalks and Crazy Quails and the like have just not made it into the big time. So now we'll try Hunter's Clays.

Colleague Bob Brister is very high on the game, and Remington is backing it, and worked very hard at showing the assembled writers and editors just how it worked. Indeed, there was a handicapped competition. Your Editor won nothing, but actually beat some rather good shots, which means there is some ground for suspicion.

It's sure fun, even if it is somewhat complex. The game is designed to duplicate field shots. The targets disappear behind trees at some stations, tower straight up at others, scoot like rabbits some places. In the Remington Farms layout, there was one set of targets hurtling low across a lake and fired on from above which separated the lucky and the rest right away. That is OK because the game is supposed to be tough—no perfect scores at all.

Remington and the National Shooting Sports Foundation hope, naturally, that this game will get all those millions of hunters out there to practice up before the game seasons, burn some powder, see the need for a new gun. . . . whatever. No program that gets people out to shoot can be bad most writers felt.

In the UK and on the Continent, this is called Sporting Clays, and they have competitons, declare champions, and all that. On this side of the water, the Remington folk say, they're going to go slow and make it work.

Happily, there were also more traditional targets, like ducks and geese, and good friends to shoot them, and very good guns as well. See Testfire, p. 239.

Ken Warner

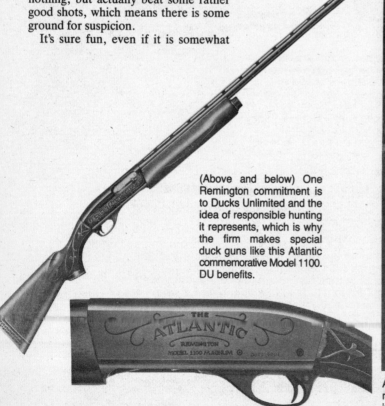

(Above and below) One Remington commitment is to Ducks Unlimited and the idea of responsible hunting it represents, which is why the firm makes special duck guns like this Atlantic commemorative Model 1100. DU benefits.

Another Remington commitment apparently is to individuals it regards as contributors to Remington's eminence in the shooting world—one of those is veteran Les Bowman, 83, who is here anxious to kill just one more goose at Remington's 1981 seminar.

Winchester

Markets, Markets . . . Everywhere

Executing new master marketing plans at a gallop is a specialty in the firearms business and the sales folks of Winchester Group at OLIN demonstrated they were good at it in time for the late-1981 writers' seminar at Nilo Farms in Illinois.

In Winchester Group firearms plans, there are two factors: Winchesters made in Japan are quite acceptable from there right across the Pacific, North America and up to the Iron Curtain; and the folks in Japan are just starting to roll on what sorts of guns they can make.

Thus, it is a line—a whole broad line—of *specialty* guns Winchester is going to turn into money. They'll have Eu-

ropean models and American models and competition models and Winchoked models in over-unders, and side-by-sides tailored to England, and also to the Continent, and also to the 50 States. And for icing, they are moving into the double rifle and combination gun fields.

In ammunition—ah, there they are happy indeed. The Silvertip handgun ammo is a resounding success and so they have added calibers; there's to be one-ounce load in 12-gauge that promises benefits to the wallet and the shoulder alike; and they have 10-gauge steel shot. There are a lot of new things also in train out of East Alton, which is where the new headquarters are.

This Seminar was the occasion when Winchester's longtime ammunition pro, Bill Williams, announced his retirement. Bill had shepherded many programs for Winchester over a long career, and the last of them was the new full-line packaging for Winchester ammunition. All the boxes are the same colors, all with a logo that includes the Pony Express rider.

"It's taken a long time," he reflected, "But there it is—all the same at last."

As for those other Winchesters, the ones made in New Haven, well, they didn't talk much about them at this meeting.

Ken Warner

One would think these writers and editors were saving ducks by using two limits for several sets of photos, but that is not what is happening. Jack Lewis and Ted Wilcox need photos for their particular publications, and colleagues from four other books are . . . well, they're not helping.

One of the benefits of the new packaging is faster filling, no doubt. And another is that the 50-boxes take a firm grip on their contents.

All alike at last, and just in time for Bill Williams' retirement, are the Winchester ammo boxes. Western?? No. they don't use that now.

IT'S AMAZING how different the same sort of gun can be and rarely has such a difference shown up so plainly as in Colt's re-engineering of their Trooper-Lawman medium frame revolvers. They feel and hold and therefore shoot better than the Mark III.

Ordinarily, gun writers at this point have to hem and haw around to try to explain how and why there is an improvement. Colt however has not only improved their guns, but they know how. It goes like this:
- New springs, new angles, new leverage give a DA pull that feels better and is nearly 15% lighter.
- Shorter hammer fall, better positioning of elements gives a perceptible shortening of lock time.
- A backstrap ⅛-inch closer to the trigger and ⅜-inch shorter bottomstrap sets the shooter's hand up better and makes a wide variety of wraparound (as in Pachmayr) grips fit better.

All this was immediately apparent as writers fanned out in a police range in Georgia to entertain themselves with a couple dozen new revolvers, lots of wadcutters and full-hot magnums, silhouette targets and even bowling pins. All the flavors the Trooper Mark V will come in were there. The Lawman comes later.

This writer tried six or eight of the samples, firing 12 to 100 rounds in each. They were as easy to hit with, shooting target loads or the real thing, as medium-frame revolvers get to be. All-around, the six-inchers got the most play, but there were very nice eight-inch guns there. Mostly, in a situation like that, a fellow shoots the longer and heavier pieces and just checks out the louder short barrels. But, regardless, they all shot. And the triggers were so good the writers obviously did not really believe the out-of-box triggers would match them.

A review of the engineering changes, though, makes it look as if there's a good chance the Colt triggers will be that good. Surely there is a physical basis for the improvement.

The two basic models, again, are: Trooper with adjustable white outline rear sight, red insert front sight and vent rib, available in 4, 6 and 8-inch versions; and Lawman, with fixed service sights and solid rib, and choice of 2 or 4-inch barrel. Guns are availble in blue, nickel or Coltguard finishes; first deliveries are planned for mid-1982.

K.W.

colt's new mark v

Complete re-engineering makes a very friendly revolver.

staff report

This duty-bound 357 offers good thickness in the cylinder walls, and recesses the whole cylinder face slightly.

The old bugaboo, the centered cylinder notch, is avoided in the Mark V colt by offsetting the bolt cut.

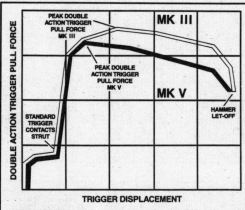

The new trigger action is about the same as the beginining, but it changes a lot for the better thereafter.

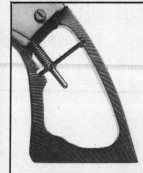

(Left) This set-up on the MK III was virtually a standard pattern, and worked fine.

(Right) The MK V's new length and angle, not to mention the reshaped grip, makes a lot of happy difference.

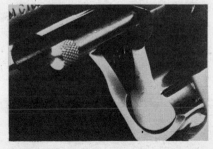

The Mark V is available as the Trooper with target sights and as the Lawman in service sights. Barrel lengths run from two to eight inches, but not all lengths in both models.

At Colt's introductory shoot, friend J. B. Wood burned lots of Colt ammo, but not at that target. That one was the editor's.

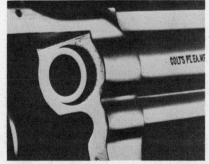

The Mark V engineering permits a large diameter barrel fastened in a frame with meat around its seat.

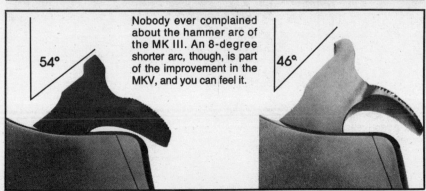

Nobody ever complained about the hammer arc of the MK III. An 8-degree shorter arc, though, is part of the improvement in the MKV, and you can feel it.

54°

46°

The Mark V protects the ejector rod, but lets it float free, while the new crane is plenty sturdy.

Sturm, Ruger, Inc.

New Guts and New Trimmings Make New Guns

Given suitable reason, William B. Ruger Sr. summons writers to the appropriate venue, tells them what is happening, and entertains them baronially, if not royally. In 1981, he had suitable reason, to wit:

- A decision and the hardware to implement a free offer to owners of Old Model Ruger single-action revolvers to fit their personal guns with a Ruger-designed transfer bar mechanism. For details, see facing page.

- Enough 12-bore Red Label shot-guns to show the whole group, let every one shoot them, and see them being made.

- A most handsome International styling for the M-77 short action to be available in—for now—243 and 308.

- A mild sporterizing of the Mini-14.

- A complete rework of the Standard Auto, which means the gun that started the Ruger parade is gone. Its replacement is a close cousin and most handsome; the new features are reported elsewhere, but include a bolt stop, 10-shot magazines, and changes in the safety, trigger and other interior parts.

For news like that, Ruger has a party, this one at his New Hampshire factory. Apart from plant tours, Skeet and trap and range test shooting, those who like a stroll in the woods with a chance at game can have one. And, indeed, whatever all the new models might offer in the future, the International M-77 worked fine at least once on whitetail deer.

Ken Warner

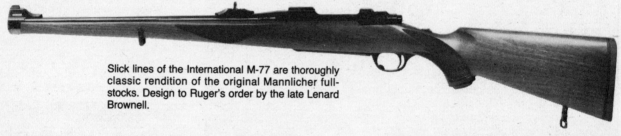

Slick lines of the International M-77 are thoroughly classic rendition of the original Mannlicher full-stocks. Design to Ruger's order by the late Lenard Brownell.

The new buttstock shape is only part of the change in the Mini-14/5-R sporter. See the fold-down rear sight and built-in Ruger mount?

The Red Label 12 is a scaled-up Red Label 20, with the same dead-flat surfaces and geometric curves and shapes. It is somewhat larger, but only somewhat.

(Left) Certainly among the very first International M-77 trophies is this very nice whitetail collected by shotgunner Bob Thruston with a single round in 308. With Thruston, his host, Bill Ruger.

(Right) Last gasp of the original Standard Auto is to be this stainless steel signed version just 5000 units strong. This one is an instant collector special, of course. It may also presage another stainless model in Mark II, and then, it may not.

Most of the external new things can be seen in this view of the Ruger Mark II Standard Auto. There are the scallop cuts in the receiver, the bolt stop release at the top of the grip, subtly changed shapes here and there. Some parts still interchange.

Ruger Official Comments on the Ruger Single Action Conversion Kit

The Ruger Single-Action Conversion Kit has been designed to provide the owners of "old model" Ruger single-action revolvers with the advantages of a modern "transfer-bar" type mechanism by the replacement of a few key parts in the revolver. The seven new parts which comprise the Ruger Single-Action Conversion Kit are the hammer, pawl, transfer-bar, trigger, cylinder latch, cylinder latch spring, and cylinder base pin. A close examination of these parts will reveal some of the truly unique characteristics of this invention: The use of thin spring steel to fabricate the rugged new transfer-bar has made it possible for this part to lie in a shallow recess in the side of the hammer, and the use of hardened alloy steels and spring steels in all of the new parts has resulted in a mechanism which functions perfectly and has tremendous endurance and reliability.

The "transfer-bar" type mechanism of the Ruger Single-Action Conversion Kit prevents the kind of accidental discharge which can occur if the hammer receives a heavy blow while resting over a loaded chamber. With the trigger fully forward, the hammer rests directly on the frame and cannot contact the firing pin. The new transfer-bar is positioned between the hammer and the firing pin to transmit the hammer blow to the firing pin only when the trigger is pulled and held all the way to the rear. This unique new invention provides the owner of an "old model" Ruger single-action revolver with most of the advantages and convenience of the Ruger New Model single-action revolvers (the Conversion Kit does not provide the loading gate/hammer interlock feature of the Ruger New Model revolvers).

While the Ruger "old model" single-action revolvers have always been safe to use when handled properly, Sturm, Ruger & Company nevertheless developed the new Single-Action Conversion Kit to be fitted to any "old model" Ruger single-action revolver. These new parts will protect the shooter from an accidental discharge resulting from a severe blow to the hammer if he has forgotten to load only five cartridges and to keep the hammer down on an empty chamber.

Sturm, Ruger & Co. is now offering to fit any "old model" Ruger Single-Six, Blackhawk, or Super Blackhawk revolver with this new "transfer-bar" type mechanism *at no charge*. The new mechanism can be fitted to any "old model" Single-Six, Blackhawk, or Super Blackhawk revolver without alteration to the revolver, and without changing its outward appearance in any way. Installation of the Ruger Single-Action Conversion Kit parts will not affect the collector value of "old model" Ruger revolvers and the original "old model" parts can be re-installed by the owner for collector purposes at any time.

The new Ruger Single-Action Conversion Kit can help to protect careless shooters from the consequences of their actions, but *all firearms are dangerous weapons,* and the best safety device is a careful shooter. Never rely on *any* mechanical safety device to prevent accidents. Follow the standard safety practice of loading only five cartridges in any older single-action revolver, and always carry the revolver with the hammer resting on an *empty* chamber.

Although the Ruger Single-Action Conversion Kit will be furnished at no charge, *it must be fitted at the factory.* Customers should write to the company at the following address for details: Sturm, Ruger & Co., Inc., Lacey Place, Dept. OM, Southport, CT 06490.

Do not ship your "old model" Ruger revolver until you are contacted by Sturm, Ruger & Co. with shipping instructions.

ROBERT SWARTLEY

HANS OBILTSCHNIG

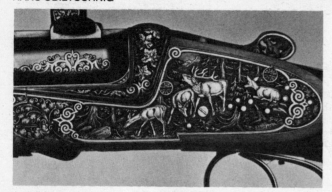

The Art of The Engraver

We selected for this issue the best photos of the best engravings we could get and here try to show each piece to its best advantage.

E. C. PRUDHOMME

ERIC GOLD

ROBERT E. MAKI

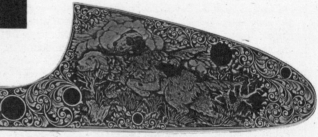

SAM WELCH

JOHN WARREN

RAY VIRAMONTEZ

MARTIN RABENO

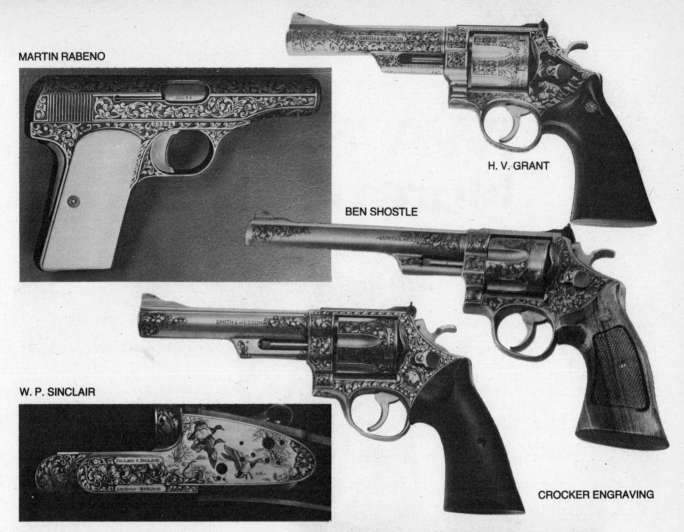

H. V. GRANT

BEN SHOSTLE

CROCKER ENGRAVING

W. P. SINCLAIR

NEIL HERMSEN

Design by F. R. ISOLA
for PERUGINI VISINI/
ARMSPORT

MARCELLO PEDINI

IWA '82: Nuremberg

by Raymond Caranta

Here's how FN makes the Browning Grande Puissance into a target pistol—extended barrel, really adjustable sights.

Tanfoglio of Italy makes this CZ-75ish DA 9mm. A similar gun will be imported here by FIE, they say.

KK Model 2000
Supermatic
electronic

This rather grand free rifle by Feinwerkbau was labelled KK Model 2000. There is no kitchen sink, but there do seem to be archery-style stabilizers and electronic somethings.

NUREMBERG'S IWA 82 had 417 companies represented, among them, 252 from outside Germany. It stands as the major European event for shooting and hunting equipment. Among the foreign exhibitors were 57 Americans, 52 Italians, 35 Austrians, 20 British, 19 Spaniards and 19 Frenchmen. And 26 foreign nations exhibited including Argentina, Brazil, India, Ireland, Israel, Japan, Sweden, Denmark, Soviet Union, Switzerland, Turkey, etc. . . .

There were so many new items we must ignore shotguns and hunting equipment to list hereunder a few pieces:

Webley & Scott—New-cocking lever type compact air "Tracker" rifle. **Dittmar**—Traditional falling block free pistols and single shot hunting rifles. **Erma**—New 32 ACP and 380 pocket pistols, proto-types of a new 22 target pistol and of a 22 WRM hunting pistol. **Heckler and Koch**—New P7 pistol in 22 Long Rifle; new target version of the HK 770, featuring military style diopter sight and stock with a 10-shot magazine. **Valmet**—Target version of the Kalashnikov rifle fitted with a 15-shot magazine. **Delhi Gun House**—Nice replicas of British military muzzleloaders from this previously unknown Indian gunmaker who also makes delicious rosewood cleaning equipment. **Fiocchi**—M. Pardini, the famous Italian shooter and designer, demonstrated the new Pardini-Fiocchi compact air pistol. **Feinwerkbau**—*Short* Model 90 air pistol with a *wonderful* electronic trigger permitting dry-firing without cocking; impressive free rifle for I.S.U. shooting. **Tanfoglio**—New 15-shot pistols chambered in 30 and 9mm Luger, apparently derived from the Czech CZ 75. **F.N. Browning**—A target version of the Browning High Power; a 22 International II target pistol.

Shades of the Standard Modell and the K-43 flicker briefly each time H&K's new rendition of the 770 and 640 is shown.

Benelli's Model 76S is all done up for target-shooting with extended barrel and anatomical—sort of—grips.

This is reported to be the final production version of the Steyr 9mm pistol which saw a brief tour here as the L.E.S. P18.

Hunfishow '82: Monaco

THE TENTH Hunfishow was held in Monte Carlo, quite a reasonable distance from Paris, Brescia, Switzerland, Spain and Austria. There were 190 exhibitors and 3000 visitors at the February, 1982 show.

Among the new developments at Hunfishow '82 was a Press Jury awarding gold medals for the most original new gun and accessory displayed at the Exhibition.

Johann Michelitsch, an Austrian Ferlach craftsman, received his gold medal for his *"Jubilee" three-shot over-under rifle* chambered in three different calibers on request; the accessory prize went to Gaucher/Chapuis of Saint-Etienne, France, for a miniature light projector in the forearm of a single-shot pistol or rifle.

Famars displayed a remarkable brace of "Venus" self-opening sidelock side-by-side shotguns featuring *handmade-at-the-factory absolutely interchangeable detail parts and assemblies* both in the same gun and from one gun to the other. **Colt** showed a special commemorative single action revolver profusely engraved and gold inlaid. **Henri Dumoulin**

showed a special "Jubilee" rifle also richly engraved and gold inlaid.

There were also "real" guns and a whole richness of accessories and ballistic laboratory equipment, such as the **Belgian Delcour** and **Italian Italcaccia** muzzle velocity and pressure measurement equipment. American exhibitors who scored successes included **Sturm, Ruger & Co., Inc., Harrington & Richardson** and **Safariland, Inc.**

The Hunfishow's winner, Johann Michelitsch of Ferlach.

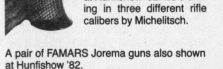

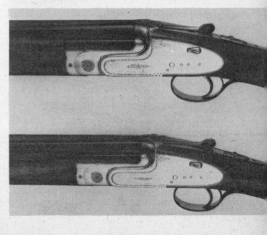

This gun won a gold medal at Hunfishow '82. It's a drilling in three different rifle calibers by Michelitsch.

A pair of FAMARS Jorema guns also shown at Hunfishow '82.

THE SHOWS OF EUROPE

PLOVDIV EXPO '81

This was the third—one each decade—of the 61-nation shows, genuinely a . . . .

by SIDNEY DU BROFF

WORLD HUNTING EXPOSITION

BULGARIA—remote—removed—plundered, fought in, fought over, occupied—and banned to Americans as late as 1960—played host to the Third World Hunting Exposition-Expo '81, staged in the summer of 1981, in the city of Plovdiv. Here East and West come together each ten years to trade and to talk and to show off their achievements.

Considering the devastation much of Europe has known, the show demonstrated the triumph of man's ability to create over man's capacity for destruction. Man's wildlife is safer, more secure, and rapidly increasing, in a milieu that is good for the hunter, who has more game at his disposal, as well as exotic species not hitherto available. Hunting and game and its preservation are taken seriously in all the 61 countries represented here.

Turkey once occupied Bulgaria for 500 years and here returned, represented by Tura Hunting, a private safari firm offering leopard hunting, as well as wild goat, chamois and mountain sheep. Zimbabwe, formerly Rhodesia, was there, with one of the best African displays, showing elephant tusks, and heads, and back in business as far as hunting is concerned. The Algerians were there, too, eager to show the flag, and a falcon tied to a chair. Their game exists, but the set-up: not yet.

There was a band playing, foresters—about 20 of them—from Foigtwagen, in West Germany. The Germans of course have two pavilions—one East; the other West and both very good, each showing their success with game management, and some magnificent guns.

The host nation, Bulgaria, is par-

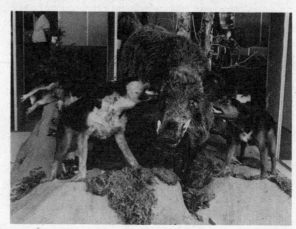

The Bulgarian exhibition included this piece of taxidermic realism, complete with a non-simulated casualty. One wondered whose dogs were used, and how they were chosen for the honor.

ticularly pleased with its moufflon, since before 1967 they had none. Now there are 2000, and they were already harvesting a crop. They also have some Virginia whitetails, and four 1971 European bison from Russia have become 100. Sika deer have also been introduced—fairly big animals that can live in restricted space.

Competitively, with the trophies being judged by an international team of experts, awarding medals in gold, silver and bronze, for wild boar, Bulgaria took 331 in gold, 341 in silver, and 359 in bronze, her best all-around score. Her total, for all species, in all medals went 2914.

Mongolia displayed a magnificent saiga head, the horns of fine sheep and the antlers of impressive deer. Russia recreated a village. The Soviet Union has 3,500,000 hunters, and 134 game preserves, totalling 28,000,000 acres. Twenty-four of their trophies—moose and red deer among them—took Grand Prix awards. Altogether, Russia earned 737 gold medals, well behind Bulgaria's 1239.

The Italian exhibit showed motorcycles for use by game wardens, machines designed for patrol and pursuit on rough roads and mountainous terrain. The Italians also presented 96 game trophies—European ibexes, wild boar, and goat—and took 68 medals.

The Mexicans concentrated on the condor, telling about it, and their other 996 species of birds. Japan had a display of beautifully-mounted game birds, which it breeds with apparent success. Poland had some wolves that appeared to be smiling, obviously much happier here, stuffed, than roaming hungry, in the forest.

Other events included a film festival, in which the United States made a worthwhile contribution. There was a photo competition; a book exhibition; and a gun-dog show.

The exhibition drew people from all over the world. It provided immense satisfaction for all; and the country that hosts Expo '91 will have a hard time matching the quality of Expo '81.

●

This one-of-a-kind was created by John Kopec, using an 1881 Colt Frontier, identical to the guns used by Frank McLaury and Billy Clanton, losers at the O.K. Corral.

O.K. CORRAL
Commemorative Gun

This is not a commemorative model; this is a commemorative gun. There's a difference.

PHOTOS: Tombstone Epitaph

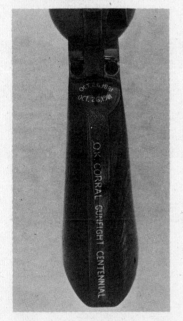

The backstrap of the O.K. Corral gun is engraved with dates and legend only. The letters are filled with gold. Note the nailhole in the bottom of the grip, made from an O.K. Corral fence.

Harold O. Love who now owns the O.K. Corral presents Park Shaw (on left) with the O.K. Corral Gunfight Centennial Commemorative revolver after Shaw's successful bid of $11,000.00.

The gunfight at the O.K. Corral became the most famous and controversial shoot-out in western history. Several motion pictures, two television series and numerous individual programs, and scores of books and uncounted magazine articles have told and retold the story from various perspectives. Thousands visit the Corral and fight site each year. Time has only heightened what is now international interest in the fight and its circumstances.

As the 100th anniversary of the battle was dawning, Harold O. Love, present owner of the O.K. Corral and publisher of the *Tombstone Epitaph*, started thinking of ways to celebrate appropriately. A commemorative gun issue, he felt, might have only a superficial relationship. If there was to be a gun (or guns) he wanted genuine historical interest.

He wound up with an idea of John Kopec's: Why not make a single piece, and use as its base an original antique? As John envisioned it, the gun would be the first commemorative firearm contemporary in age to its event, and it could be identical to the Frontier Six-Shooters in 44-40 used by Frank McLaury and Billy Clanton. In addition it would probably be generally similar to the six-guns used on the Earp side, although Doc Holliday might have used a 41-caliber, double action Colt.

Harold liked the idea of using an antique, and decided to have its new grips made from a piece of the O.K. Corral to make the finished gun a part of the Corral.

Arizona Territory in the 1880s was a hard place. Guns were tools—tools used for killing if and when killing was necessary. Garish decoration didn't make them work any better and most frontiersmen couldn't afford the extra cost anyway—so no engraving on this one, just identification.

John Kopec picked a Colt Frontier, serial number *63619*. It had been shipped to Moore's Sons, the same distributor who had handled Frank McLaury's gun, on June 4th, 1881. It could, in theory, actually have been in Tombstone on the day of the fight.

Four craftsmen did the work, assigned by Kopec:
- Tom Buckley made the new grips.
- Duane Wright engraved the backstrap legend and charcoal blued the hand-polished gun.
- Pete Mazur color case-hardened the frame and hammer.
- Earl Van Curtis made the pine box case of more O.K. Corral wood. Its lining is velvet from a Tombstone saloon.

The O.K. Corral gun was sold at a silent bid auction as part of the O.K. Corral Gunfight Centennial celebration on the afternoon of October 25th, 1981. A hushed crowd waited as a score of bids over the required minimum of $6,000.00 were read. The winner, at $11,000.00, was Park Shaw, a Phoenix insurance executive.

Don Shumar

SHOOTER'S SHOWCASE

Gunskin Really Will Peel

Call'n Inc. has this spray-can product that lets the thinking sport have his fancy guns and hunt them, too. Think of it as thick paint that peels. It comes in colors and it was no trick to create the camo binoculars you see, nor to have a green-brown 12-gauge. And under the Gunskin everything is OK—I checked.
K.W.

Audette Makes All-Purpose Gauge

Recent reporting indicates case walls and squareness directly affect grouping potential in many rifles. The well-known Creighton Audette offers this Case Gauge which will measure five useful case attributes (for one caliber) at $89.50. You'll spend more for more parts, but that gets you started. Audette, a gunsmith and shooter, swears by it.
K.W.

New Sile Rubber Grips

Same idea as Pachmayr, with some differences: The feel is not so "sticky," the surface is a little harder, the shapes—as you can see—a little different. Grip at left in photo is for square-butt Ruger Security Six.
K.W.

Brownell Accessories Still Available

Billingsley and Brownell, Custom Gunsmiths, are going to continue to produce the scope mounts, ribs, bolt handles, Mannlicher stock tips and such created by the late Lenard Brownell. His widow Catherine and long-time associate Ross Billingsley are going to keep the quality up.
K.W.

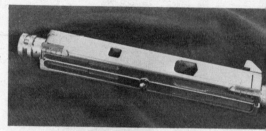

New Universal Charge Bars

Multi-Scale Charge, Ltd., claims their new all-metal adjustable charge bars for popular Mec and Texan reloaders—including the Mec 650 and Grabber—saves the purchase of 32 powder bushings and lots of other stuff. At least, it would if you needed them all. It's about $20 with a five-year guarantee.
K.W.

Clever Holsters Designed by Angell

What you see are the forerunners of a new group of concealment holsters to be designed by ex-Gaylord sidekick and ex-Seventreeser Bob Angell. He'll market them through Sile, where he works now. You see a Star PD, a Walther PP and a Colt Commander, with other-side magazine sheath. The Model 1911 holster will hold most models either hammer down or cocked-and-locked, plus let the gun hang upside-down or horizontally. I've worn 'em all and they work and they're slick.
K.W.

White Still Does Those Fancy Horns

He has to get $3 for the package of photos he sends out, but Thomas F. White is otherwise at the same stand—making first-class decorated powderhorns and accessories. There can be fancy end plugs, choice of hangers, even a screw-on spout. Even at $325 for a medium horn with plain plugs, they're worth a look. Don't forget the $3. *K.W.*

The Screwdriver As Inletting Tool

Having run out of new slots to conquer, Grace Metal Products is somewhat Biblically hammering its screwdrivers into scraping tools. They sell 'em as a set for around $15.
K.W.

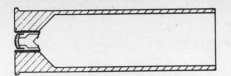

14 Gauge Anyone? How About 24?

GTM Co. manufactures all-brass shotgun shells in 11 different gauges. That means 4, 8, 14, 24 and 32-gauges in addition to the ordinary ones. One of each gauge in a set for collectors is $102; they are lathe-turned, and not cheap, but it sounds like $50 or $70 would get Grampa's 24-gauge going again. What fun.   *K.W.*

Carry A Rifle On Your Belt

This well-made device from Wyman Corp., when threaded on a stout belt, provides a place to rest a rifle or shotgun butt. It's over $25, but some who have tried it sure like it.   *K.W.*

Keep Ammo Up Front

What they really do call "The Great 870 Company" (William A. Harper) makes, among other things, this spare shell band to slide on pump guns or double barrels. Also possible: big head safeties, paramilitary carry handles.   *K.W.*

Get Lawrence In Four Colors

Tired of that old brown ink when you dream of new Lawrence leather? You can now see the stuff in color in Catalog No. 125 for just $2.   *K.W.*

Happiness Is Eyes In The Night

Johnny Stewart, who knows how to do it, has packaged a helmet light for predator and coon hunters. There's two GE 605 bulbs, Lexan light and lens, padded battery pouch, red flip lens, rechargeable battery and charger—it's complete, folks, at about $100.   *K.W.*

Even The Best Can Improve

Brownell's have been passionate for years on the subject of Acraglas, but you should hear them brag about Acraglas Gel. They tested for four years and now they're downright pushy about it, considering they sell a kit for just $6.95.   *K.W.*

A No-Fooling Gun Belt Buckle

Bergamot Brass Works makes seven different bare-buckle pistols like this, from flintlocks to sort-of Colt Pythons. They get about $8 for one, your choice.   *K.W.*

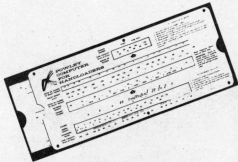

Powley Computing Still Possible

Marian Powley can still furnish the original slide chart for handloaders and a manual for its use for just $7. You sure couldn't make one yourself for that.   *K.W.*

Deluxe Swivel Base For Lever Guns

Lautard gets about $15 for this nicely machined and contoured slide-on Q.D. swivel base. No locking screws; you Loc-Tite it in place.   *K.W.*

This Will Turn Any Neck Around

Marquart will charge you over $40 for it, but this little outfit will turn the outsides of cartridge case necks uniform within .0001", they say. You need new pilots for new calibers, and new holders for new cases.   *K.W.*

Ammunition, Ballistics and Components

The name of this feature section of GUN DIGEST has been changed in order to reflect the coverage given to shotshell ammunition and components. This section has previously been called American Bulleted Cartridges.

by EDWARD A. MATUNAS

AMMUNITION and component manufacturers provide new products to enhance their over-all product line appeal to the consumer and they drop a product when it no longer sells in sufficient volume to maintain a profit. It is the purpose of these pages to keep you abreast of such changes in the product lines of the various ammunition and component manufacturers. In addition, whenever practical, we will conduct tests on the new ammunition or component products.

Keep in mind that as a consumer your desires *can* greatly affect a manufacturer's product line. Want something not currently being offered? Unhappy about a product being changed or discontinued? Then write the prod-

uct manager of the company involved and let your feelings be known. Don't expect much sympathy if you are expressing a desire to have the 22 Savage High Power cartridge reintroduced so that you can shoot a family heirloom 99 Savage once or twice a year. The most important factor involved in ammunition and component availability is volume. No manufacturer can keep a product in his line that does not sell in sufficient volume to maintain a profit.

Federal

Federal Cartridge Corporation has always been an aggressive ammunition company. This year has not been an exception. For their 61st year as a

major supplier of ammunition, Federal has new and/or improved offerings in centerfire metallic, rimfire and shotshell cartridges.

Perhaps the most newsworthy (and long sought-for) items are their new 10-gauge magnum and 12-gauge magnum slug loads. Remington and Winchester both announced new and improved slug loadings during the past few years. Winchester's new loads offered a slight increase in slug weights and a notable improvement in accuracy. Remington went Winchester one better with *their* new slugs by offering a hollow point configuration. Whether or not this hollow point adds any real game stopping capabilities is questionable in my mind,

Federal's new hollow point Super Slugs from left to right: 1¾-ounce, 10 gauge; 1¼-ounce, 12 gauge; 1-ounce, 12 gauge; ⅘-ounce, 16 gauge; ¾-ounce, 20 gauge; ⅕-ounce, 410 gauge.

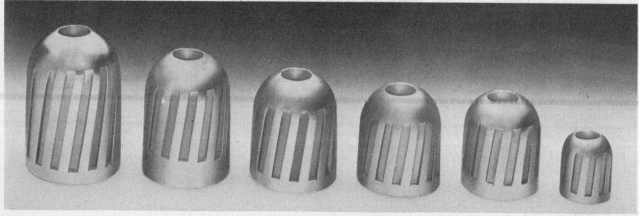

Federal's new 44 Remington Magnum load using a 220-grain metal cased bullet designed for silhouette shooting.

CHART F-1
Super Slug Ballistics

Gauge	Weight Ounces/Grains	Velocity (feet/sec.) Muzzle	50 Yards	Energy (foot pounds) Muzzle	50 Yards
10	1¾ / 766	1280	1080	2785	1980
12	1¼ / 547	1490	1240	2695	1865
12	1 / 437	1580	1310	2425	1665
16	⅘ / 350	1600	1175	1990	1070
20	¾ / 328	1600	1270	1865	1175
410	⅕ / 87	1830	1335	650	345

Federal's new 30-06 load using the 150-grain Sierra Spitzer boat-tail bullet. Federal is claiming an extremely flat trajectory for this load.

but, improvement or not, the hollow point version by Remington had an immediate and warm reception.

Now, Federal has really outdone both major competitors with new slug loads. You may recall Ithaca advertisements showing the Mag-10 as (among other things) a deer gun. Most readers of these ads felt that the ad people had simply gotten carried away, but they were only premature. Federal now offers a 10-gauge slug load.

And what a slug load it is—a full 1¾ ounces of lead at almost 1300 fps (feet per second). That is slower than a standard 12-gauge 1-oz. slug, but it is also 75 percent heavier, and with muzzle energy almost 2800 ft. lbs. (foot pounds), this load dwarfs the standard 12-gauge slug.

Federal calls it a super slug and indeed it is. Even the recoil is super, but recoil for 10-gauge shooters is nothing new. The increased weight, high muzzle energy and large diameter of this slug notably outmatches the already excellent 12-gauge slug.

Federal is, I'm sure, more than aware of the limited 10-gauge market, and has not left out the majority of gunners. They have improved their standard 12-gauge slug by upping its weight to a full ounce and making it a hollow point. Then, in addition, the ballisticians at Federal created Federal's new 12-gauge *Magnum* Super Slug—a full 1¼-oz. slug with almost 2700 ft. lbs. of muzzle energy, loaded

in the standard 2¾" shell.

This certainly should outdate all other 12-gauge slug loads except in guns that shoot the 1-oz. load noticeably better. Which slug is inherently better? I have one 870 that prefers the 1-oz. slug; two other 870 slug guns that perform equally with either; my son's slug barrel definitely prefers the heavy Federal slug.

A ballistics chart (F-1) for Federal's line of "super slugs" is included here.

Federal has two other new shotshell items: The first is a 20-gauge 2¾" magnum (1⅛-oz.) load in a premium shell and copper plated shot in sizes 4 and 6. The second is a 10-gauge 3½" magnum shell loaded with 18 number 00 buckshot. A granulated plastic buffer is used in both of these loads.

Federal also has new metallic cartridge items: The first is the new 44 Magnum metallic silhouette load. This load is readily identified by its nickel plated case, though its 220-gr. metal jacketed Sierra bullet is also quite readily recognized. The jacket and point construction of this bullet will minimize deflection and maximize energy transfer on the steel targets. Chart F-2 lists the exterior ballistics of this load in a 10.5" solid barrel.

CHART F-2
44 Remington Magnum 220-grain Federal load

Range	Velocity (ft./sec.)	Energy (ft. lbs.)
0	1510	1115
50 meters	1360	905
100 meters	1220	725
150 meters	1120	610
200 meters	1050	540

In a 6½" revolver barrel the muzzle velocity for this load is 1390 fps with a corresponding muzzle energy of 945 ft. lbs. This new 220-gr. non-expanding bullet reaches a muzzle velocity of 1850 fps in a 20" rifle barrel.

Federal's new premium 30-06 load with the Sierra 150-gr. spitzer boat-tail and its ballistics coefficient of .449 lets them claim the flattest trajectory among all commercial 30-06 loads. The ballistics for this load as released

CHART F-3

30-06 Federal Cartridge Using A
150-Grain Sierra Boat-Tail Bullet

	New Premium 150-gr. 30-06	Standard 150-gr. 30-06
Muzzle velocity (fps)	2910	2910
100-yard velocity	2690	2620
200-yard velocity	2480	2340
300-yard velocity	2270	2080
400-yard velocity	2070	1840
500-yard velocity	1880	1620
Muzzle energy (ft. lbs.)	2820	2820
100-yard energy	2420	2280
200-yard energy	2040	1830
300-yard energy	1710	1450
400-yard energy	1430	1130
500-yard energy	1180	875

CHART F-4

Trajectory Comparison for a Rifle Sighted in at 200 Yards

	100 yds.	200 yds.	300 yds.	400 yds.	500 yds.
Premium 150-gr.	+1.7"	0	−7.3"	−21.4"	−43.6"
Std. 150-gr.	+2.1"	0	−8.5"	−25.0"	−51.8"

by Federal are as shown in charts F-3 and F-4, and the trajectory and deflection figures seem significant.

A new 7mm Mauser 140-gr. soft point load is really a return of an older Federal loading. It will be offered in addition to the current 175-gr. load, and greatly extends the useful range of the 7mm Mauser. Ballistics for this load are shown in Chart F-5.

Federal has not ignored the rimfire line, either. There are two new 22 Long Rifle cartridges. The first is a silhouette cartridge, which appears to be their normal standard velocity cartridge in a new packaging. I hope to

CHART F-5

140-grain 7mm Mauser

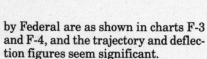

Range	Velocity ft./sec.	Energy ft. lbs.
0	2660	2200
100	2450	1865
200	2260	1585
300	2070	1330
400	1890	1110
500	1730	930

get into comparison testing this new round soon. The other cartridge is a pistol match round.

Things stay pretty much the same in Federal's components. There is the new large pistol magnum primer—designed for the 44 Remington Magnum cartridge and equally at home in the 41 Remington Magnum. It will ignite large quantities of slow burning powders and is sure to become a must for many big pistol fans.

Winchester

Perhaps most notable in the Winchester ammunition line this year is the return of Lubaloy shot. In 1978, Winchester dropped Lubaloy shot from their shotshell ammunition and from the components line. So while Winchester was busy divorcing itself from copper plated shot, Federal was promoting their premium shotshells with copper plated shot and Lawrence shot was coming into the market in a new form as copper plated shot, called "Magnum." Winchester is reintroducing Lubaloy shot, and the gunner interested in a maximum performance shotshell can purchase Winchester Super Double-X loads with either lead or copper plated shot. I suspect

all Super X and Double X loads will eventually use only copper plated shot, which now is offered in four different sizes: 10-gauge offers BB, 2 and 4 shot sizes; 12-gauge will include BB, 2, 4, and 6 sizes; 20-gauge will have 2, 4 and 6 sizes, although I cannot picture a use for #2 shot in charge weights of 1¼ ounces or less.

The success of Winchester's Silvertip hollow point handgun ammunition has been quite impressive. My own tests have shown that the various loadings all produce *positive* expansion with little or no bullet weight loss, even in pocket pistol calibers heretofore known for their total lack of expansion. Winchester is now carrying the concept into cartridges in which bullet expansion has not necessarily been a problem—the 357 Magnum, the 38 Super Auto and the 45 Colt. These three new loads all have the same aluminum jacket construction employed on earlier Silvertip hollow point handgun loads. Aluminum seems to offer the least resistance to bullet/jacket flow.

Another advantage of an aluminum bullet jacket is it generates less pressure at a given level of velocity, so Winchester can have an extra margin

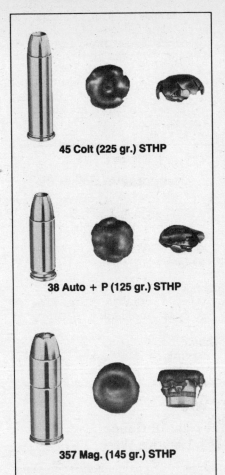

45 Colt (225 gr.) STHP

38 Auto + P (125 gr.) STHP

357 Mag. (145 gr.) STHP

Winchester's three new Silvertip hollow point handgun loads.

Winchester's new 1-ounce 12-gauge wad shown with several other Winchester components.

of safety while maintaining normal velocities. The reduction of bore resistance and the lowered powder charges can add up to a decrease in recoil with a given load.

Winchester is claiming a recoil reduction of 8 percent on the 357 Magnum 145-gr. load when compared to standard 158-gr. loads, and up to 13 percent less recoil with 125-gr. loads. I doubt the average shooter will be aware of the differences. Winchester is using a powder coated with a flash suppressant for the new 357 Magnum Silvertips and the shooter will notice the reduction in muzzle flash.

It has been my experience that Silvertip loads do not group quite as tightly as some other competitive bullets. For instance, in a 9mm S&W Model 59 that I own, most loads will group about 2½" to 3" at 25 yards. The Silvertip hollow points in this 9mm open up to about 4". This trade-off in accuracy is more than repaid in bullet expansion characteristics. I have yet to recover any Silvertip hollow point that wasn't expanded to a very large diameter while retaining almost all of its original weight. For most purposes, positive expansion of handgun bullets is far more important than a 25 percent to 33 percent accuracy loss.

The 38 Super Auto version of this load is at plus-P pressure levels and hence is designed for use only in automatics specifically adaptable to the higher pressure levels. This load has a 125-gr. bullet which looks suspiciously identical to the 125-gr. Silvertip hollow point in the 357 Magnum loading. (See Chart W-1.)

The 45 Colt Silvertip has a 225-gr. bullet. Winchester's tests have shown superb expansion and no fragmentation in both ordnance gelatin and water. Silvertip bullets will offer less fouling than any similar lead bullet load; therefore, Winchester's claim to be fouling free as compared to competitive lead bullet 225-gr. 45 Colt loads is quite valid. The shooter who uses more than a few rounds at a time will appreciate the no-fouling feature.

All of the previous Silvertip hollow point loads have performed well. There is no reason why these three new loads should not continue this tradition. Silvertip hollow point handgun loads are sold for a very small premium over the price of more traditional ammunition.

Winchester has decided to eliminate some unpopular cartridge loads and has discontinued the 87-gr. 257 Roberts, the 125-gr. 284 Winchester and the 22 Xpediter rimfire cartridges. A number of discontinued

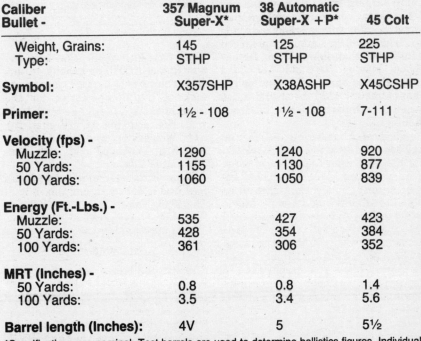

CHART W-1

Ballistics Data for the New (1982) Winchester Silvertip Hollow Point Cartridges

Caliber Bullet -	357 Magnum Super-X*	38 Automatic Super-X +P*	45 Colt
Weight, Grains:	145	125	225
Type:	STHP	STHP	STHP
Symbol:	X357SHP	X38ASHP	X45CSHP
Primer:	1½ - 108	1½ - 108	7-111
Velocity (fps) -			
Muzzle:	1290	1240	920
50 Yards:	1155	1130	877
100 Yards:	1060	1050	839
Energy (Ft.-Lbs.) -			
Muzzle:	535	427	423
50 Yards:	428	354	384
100 Yards:	361	306	352
MRT (Inches) -			
50 Yards:	0.8	0.8	1.4
100 Yards:	3.5	3.4	5.6
Barrel length (Inches):	4V	5	5½

*Specifications are nominal. Test barrels are used to determine ballistics figures. Individual firearms may differ from these test barrel statistics.

CHART W-2

Ball Powder Data for the 12-Gauge
Winchester WAA12F1 1-Ounce Wad
CASE: WINCHESTER COMPRESSION FORMED

Shot Wgt.	Primer	Powder	Charge (Grains)	Wad Column	Velocity (Ft./Sec.)	Pressure (LUP's)
1 oz.	Win. 209	452AA	20.0	WAA12F1	1180	7300
1 oz.	Win. 209	452AA	21.5	WAA12F1	1235	7900
1 oz.	Win. 209	452AA	23.0	WAA12F1	1290	8900
1 oz.	Fed. 209	452AA	20.0	WAA12F1	1180	7300
1 oz.	Fed. 209	452AA	21.5	WAA12F1	1235	7800
1 oz.	Fed. 209	452AA	23.0	WAA12F1	1290	8600
1 oz.	CCI 209	452AA	20.0	WAA12F1	1180	6800
1 oz.	CCI 209	452AA	21.5	WAA12F1	1235	7800
1 oz.	CCI 209	452AA	23.0	WAA12F1	1290	8500
1 oz.	Win. 209	452AA	20.5	WAA12F1	1180	6600
1 oz.	Win. 209	452AA	21.5	WAA12F1	1235	7500
1 oz.	Win. 209	452AA	23.0	WAA12F1	1290	8400
1 oz.	Fed. 209	452AA	20.5	WAA12F1	1180	6700
1 oz.	Fed. 209	452AA	21.5	WAA12F1	1235	7500
1 oz.	Fed. 209	452AA	23.0	WAA12F1	1290	8100

accuracy does not seem to be equal to the standard 22 Long Rifle cartridge. This decrease in accuracy level seems to be standard with all the newer extra velocity loadings that have been offered by the various companies during the past 5 to 10 years. Ballistics for the new cartridge are shown in Chart R-1.

CHART R-1
Comparative Ballistics

	22 LR 40-Gr. Bull.	22 VIPER HV TC 36-Gr. Bull.
Velocity:		
Muzzle	1255 fps	1410 fps
50 Yards	1102 fps	1187 fps
Energy:		
Muzzle	140 ft. lbs.	159 ft. lbs.
50 Yards	108 ft. lbs.	113 ft. lbs.
Drop:		
50 Yards	3.05"	2.46"

loads are still cataloged and no doubt will be until stocks are exhausted.

Late in 1981, Winchester's new 1-oz. 12-gauge target load appeared. It produced a muzzle velocity of 1175 fps in my testing and, due to a slight decrease in cost and a notable decrease in recoil as compared to standard 1⅛-oz. target loads, should prove a favorite of many shooters in the future. The 1-oz. load allows me to break just as many targets as 1⅛-oz. load, and any disadvantage is more theoretical than practical. The only previous factory 1-oz. load (1290 fps) actually produced more recoil than slower 1⅛-oz. factory loads, leaving that old 1-oz. load somewhat as a misfit. The new load at approximately 1175 fps should prove popular with partridge and woodcock hunters.

Winchester has decided to offer the reloader the new AA wad developed for the 1-oz. load. I got a lot of these new wads from Winchester, and recent shooting has shown them to be equal to all previous AA wads. I have been told by Winchester spokesmen that the new wad will be referred to as an AA-plus wad with the designation of WAA12F1. This would make sense, but until I see the designation in printed form I will not guarantee anything. Data for this new wad is shown in Chart W-2.

Happily, Hercules also incorporates a fair amount of data in their new reloading guide for this new wad. The wad will of course have other applications. One such application is in the new Rainel-ACTIV shotshells. In this case the new WAA12F1 seems to make a useful alternative for the sometimes hard-to-find Federal 12S3 wad. Hence in the ACTIV shell the new Winchester wad should work well with 1⅛-ounce loads and some 1¼-ounce loads.

Some of the Hercules data for the new wad is shown in our Chart W-3. The loads shown in Chart W-3 are those that I have personally tried and found quite satisfactory.

Remington

Remington has a new solid bullet version of the Yellow Jacket called the 22 Viper. It sends a 36-gr. Yellow Jacket-shaped bullet from a standard 22 Long Rifle case at a slightly increased velocity over normal 40-gr. high speeds. This increased velocity does give a small gain in energy, but

CHART W-3

Hercules Data for the New 12-Gauge
Winchester WAA12F1 1-Ounce Wad

Case	Shot Wgt.	Primer	Powder	Charge (Grains)	Wad Column	Velocity (Ft./Sec.)	Pressure (LUP's)
Federal Gold Medal	1 oz.	Fed. 209	Red Dot	18.0	WAA12F1 plus 20 ga. .135 card	1200	8400
Peters Blue Magic	1 oz.	Rem. 97	Red Dot	18.0	WAA12F1	1200	8500
Winchester Compression Formed	1 oz.	Win. 209	Red Dot	18.0	WAA12F1	1200	9000

Remington's new Viper 22 Long Rifle extra velocity round.

A close-up view of Remington's new 12-gauge hollow point rifled slug.

CHART R-2
Ballistics Chart
7mm Mauser 140-Grain
Pointed Soft Point

Range (Yards)	Velocity (Ft./Sec.)	Energy (Ft. lbs.)	Trajectory Short Range	Trajectory Long Range
Muzzle	2660	2199	—	—
100	2435	1843	0.0″	2.5″
200	2221	1533	−5.0″	0.0″
300	2018	1266	−17.0″	−9.6″
400	1827	1037	—	−27.7″
500	1648	844	—	−56.3″

Worthy slug has a solid pedestal in the center of the hollow base. The rifling grooves are quite deep in this well-formed slug, which weighs 1 ounce. Accuracy with my samples was excellent and recoil seemed a bit milder than some slug loads I have used. The only possible fault I could find is that the packaging was a bit too light and the boxes began to split after only a modest amount of handling.

All of Remington's new slugs feature a hollow cavity in the nose.

The new Worthy Rifled Slug proved very accurate during the author's testing.

The Worthy shotgun slug and wad column. Note the very deep rifling cuts in the slug and the modified Winchester WAA 12 wad.

We are losing the special match grade ammunition. Remington has announced the discontinuation of all 22 match. They are also discontinuing the 5mm rimfire ammunition and the 30-40 Krag 180-gr. round nose load. In the 300 Savage, the 150-gr. pointed soft point is dropped while the 150-gr. round nose is retained. The 45 ACP 230-gr. Targetmaster load is being dropped.

Despite rumors that Peters Blue Magic target loads would be discontinued, Remington says this line will be retained. Only the 2¾ dram-#8½ shot load will be discontinued from the Blue Magic lineup. Remington is dropping #5 shot from their 16-gauge offerings and they are discontinuing the 12-gauge International target load designated NSP12H8.

Remington has dropped the 12-gauge scatter load, formally cataloged as item RS128. A few shotshell components were also axed, and these included the R16 wad, the SP4103 wad and the RP20 wad. Finally, the 97-4 star primer (410) is no longer with us.

In the plus column, a new 140-gr. pointed soft point Core Lokt 7mm Mauser loading has been added, but it is replacing the 175-gr. soft point.

Remington's shotgun slugs have all undergone improvement projects and the results are now somewhat heavier slugs in 12-, 16- and 20-gauge. This keeps Remington slugs at a competitive weight and with hollow points. Ballistics for the new 7mm are shown in Chart R-2.

Worthy Products Inc.

Who's that, you say? Well, Worthy Products Inc. is a comparatively new ammunition loader. They offer only one product in their ammunition line—a shotgun slug loading using their own slug and the new ACTIV shotshell case. The firm, headed by Worthy H. Brown, recently supplied me with a number of boxes of this load, assembled with the 2¾″ ACTIV shotshell case, Winchester 120 primers, 28 grains of Hercules Green Dot powder and a special wad column developed by Worthy Products. This wad column consists of a specially altered double A wad with the shot cup removed, a soft felt filler wad and a very hard card-like wad.

The slug appears to be conventional, but close examination reveals a radical departure in design. Instead of the usual *hollow* hollow base, the

A bottom and side view of the Worthy slug. Note the unique hollow cavity in the base which incorporates a pedestal.

Omark

The folks at Omark have been quite busy expanding the CCI handgun ammunition line with a completely new approach. Blazer 38 Special ammunition incorporates a "non-reloadable" aluminum cartridge case. This case is "non-reloadable" due to the use of a Berdan-type primer and to the aluminum material from which the case is made. Reloaders may weep over such cases, many consumers will like the advantage—great reduction in the dollars you have to lay out to buy it. Blazer is intended to sell for a full third less than comparable 38 Special ammo. The new cases and primers are manufactured at the CCI plant in Lewiston and bullets for the new loads come from Omark's Speer Bullet plant just down the road. The new 38 Special Blazer line includes a standard 148-gr. hollow base lead wadcutter load, a 158-gr. round nose lead bullet load at usual velocity; and one +P loading of a 125-gr. jacketed hollow point bullet.

These new loads will appeal to anyone who desires to save money on ammunition, but who would rather not reload for one reason or another. A great many police departments will find this high quality line of money-saving ammunition very desirable. The need to reduce shooting costs or to free an officer from a loading room detail will surely cause a lot of interest in the Blazers. It would not surprise me to see reloaders devising ways of decapping the Berdan primer and finding a source for new primers and so on. However, such aspiring reloaders should keep in mind that aluminum does not offer the longevity of brass cases. The reloadable case life of aluminum would be extremely short and hence not worth the bother or risk. Ballistics for the new Blazer ammunition are listed.

Omark's Speer has new 30-cal. match bullets. I tested these 168-gr. boat-tail Gold Match bullets a short while ago. Speer bullets have always impressed me first with their high quality of expansion characteristics, and then with better than required accuracy. Match bullets are not designed for expansion and therefore should not be used on game. My test proved these are extremely accurate. In a featherweight Winchester Model 70 in 30-06 most of my groups were minute-of-angle. I did obtain quite a few groups that measured between 3/4-in. to 7/8-in. These were all ten-shot groups with shots spaced about 45 to 60 seconds apart using an 8x

(Above) The headstamp on Omark's new 38 Special ammunition includes the usual information plus a N.R. designation referring to the non-reloadable characteristics of the shell.

(Right) Omark's new 38 Special Blazer ammunition includes a 125 +P jacketed load, a 158-grain lead round nose and a 148-grain lead wad cutter. Aluminum case is non-reloadable.

scope. This certainly is superb target accuracy. I used CCI Benchrest primers and Dupont IMR-4350 powder in Norma cases.

Also new from Speer are a .243-in. diameter 100-gr. boat-tail bullet and a .257-in. diameter 100-gr. boat-tail. My sample bullets proved very accurate in both diameters. I did my test shooting in 243 Winchester and 257 Roberts rifles. Both of these bullets will improve the down-range effect of the current flat base offerings.

CCI has a new shotshell primer designated 209M. I guess we can consider it a magnum style primer. CCI designed the 209M to allow a reduction in powder charges and thus reduce the reloader's cost to put together a round of ammunition. In many instances such a reduction is possible. However, as with any shotshell component, the primer can and does vary in the way it performs, based on the other components with which it is teamed. There are specific circumstances in which this primer performs colder than its counterpart 209, instead of hotter. In these instances a heavier powder charge is required or lower velocities result with identical powder charges. The best method is, of course, to refer to a reliable data source. At this writing Hercules' newest data book contains quite a number of recipes for this new primer. A selection of these Hercules loads are

Blazer 38 Special Ammunition Specifications

Load	Index Number	Velocity Spec. (Test Barrel)	Pressure Max. Avg.	Accuracy Max. Avg. Extreme Spread at 50 Yards	Avg. Revolver Velocity — 4"	Avg. Revolver Velocity — 6"
38 Spl — 148-Gr. Hollow Base Wadcutter	3517	800 ± 50 fps	18,900 cup	3.0"	700 fps	730 fps
38 Spl — 158-Gr. Round Nose Lead	3522	900 ± 50 fps	18,900 cup	4.0"	770 fps	800 fps
38 Spl +P — 125-Gr. Jacketed Hollow Point	3514	1250 ± 50 fps	22,400 cup	3.0"	1120 fps	1150 fps

TABLE O-1
Some Hercules Data for the New CCI 209M Primer
12 Gauge

Shell (2¾")	Shot Weight (ounces)	Powder Charge (grs.)	Wad	Approx. Velocity F.P.S.	Approx. Pressure P.S.I.
Fed. Pape.	1	21.0 Red Dot	Fed. 12S3	1290	8,700
Fed. Paper	1⅛	20.0 Red Dot	Fed. 12C1	1200	8,700
Fed. Paper	1¼	25.5 Unique	Fed. 12S4	1220	9,700
Fed. Paper	1¼	28.0 Unique	Fed. 12S4	1330	10,700
Fed. Gold Medal	1⅛	18.0 Red Dot	Fed. 12S3	1145	8,600
Fed. Gold Medal	1⅛	19.0 Red Dot	Fed. 12S3	1200	8,900
Fed. Gold Medal	1¼	24.5 Unique	Fed. 12S4	1220	9,500
Peters B.M.	1	20.5 Red Dot	Rem. R12L	1290	9,800
Peters B.M.	1⅛	17.5 Red Dot	Rem. RXP12	1145	9,600
Peters B.M.	1¼	24.5 Herco	Rem. SP12	1220	10,300
Win. AA	1	18.5 Red Dot	Win. WAA12	1290	10,400
Win. AA	1⅛	17.5 Red Dot	Win. WAA12	1145	10,400
Win. AA	1⅛	18.5 Red Dot	Win. WAA12	1200	10,500
Win. AA	1⅛	24.0 Herco	Win. WAA12F114	1220	10,700
		20 GAUGE			
Fed. Paper	⅞	16.0 Unique	Fed. 20S1	1155	8,600

CCI's new 209M primers promise a reduction in powder charge for many loads.

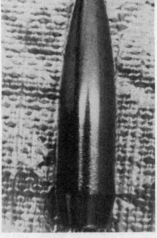

shown in Table O-1 for 12-gauge loads. For additional data, obtain a copy of the new Hercules powder guide from your Hercules powder dealer.

Eclipse

Eclipse Cartridge Corporation started out as the result of Eclipse Target Company's natural interest in shotshells. Eclipse has had years of experience in the manufacture of clay targets and in their distribution.

A one-piece injection molded plastic case is Eclipse's claim to fame. This plain-jane case carries no load identification of any type, except the color of the shell. The color coding employed is:

- Green: 12 ga. 2¾-in., 2¾—1⅛, size 8 (1145fps)
- Orange: 12 ga. 2¾-in, 3—1⅛, Size 8 (1200 fps)
- Red: 12 ga. 2¾-in., 3—1⅛, size 7½ (1200 fps)
- Blue: Blue: 12 ga. 2¾-in., 2¾—1, size 8 (1180 fps)

Color coding is a nice idea if there are not a great many different loads available. For just four loads, colors are easy to remember. If Eclipse broadens the line, color confusion might become a real problem. Eclipse claims savings in low-cost shell production and in not marking cases is passed on to the consumer. This indeed seems to reflect in the selling price of the shell.

Speer is also offering new .243 and .257 diameter 100-grain bullets with boat-tails.

Speer's new and highly accurate 30-caliber 168-grain boat-tail Gold Match bullet.

No attempt to reload the Eclipse shell should be made without the Eclipse wad. The shell has a very heavy case wall taper. This means a reduced diameter requirement for the obturating cup. So use the Eclipse T wad or forget reloading.

I have heard worrisome reports about Eclipse case failures, but Eclipse claims to have solved most of their problems. For a while it was touch and go with respect to the Eclipse plant being for sale. At this writing things appear to be on stream with production in full swing. Only time will tell.

Eclipse did start a very interesting marketing concept for hunting shotshells. They sold a large number of dove loads in 20-round boxes instead of traditional 25-round boxes. The consumer bought a "box" of shells for a very modest cost. The lower price of the shell plus the smaller pack size resulted in an attention-getting price.

Rainel de P.R.

Rainel manufactures a new one-piece plastic case. This case affords excellent reloadability and a very large internal volume. Due to its greater internal capacity it is possible to load shot charges as heavy as 1⅞ ounces in a standard 2¾" case. The owner of a standard 12-gauge gun can give his shotgun magnum capabilities.

Rainel's U.S. effort is being recalculated by the main office in Puerto Rico, however, and just what might happen is uncertain. The shell is a good one, but the story will simply have to await events.

Sierra Bullets

Sierra's Mike Bussard tells of four new bullets and an exciting new concept:

The first is a 55-gr. .224" diameter bullet Blitz construction, designed to be super explosive at velocities under

3000 fps. It is therefore ideally suited to cartridges such as the 222 Remington. The 50-gr. Blitz bullet Sierra has offered for a number of years is still cataloged.

The second is a 140-gr. spitzer boat-tail bullet in .284″ diameter. A number of consumers who wanted a boat-tail bullet in a lighter weight than Sierra's current 160-gr. boat-tail now have it. The flat base 140-gr. bullet will continue as well.

Sierra's third is a 210-gr. jacketed hollow cavity designed for the 44 Magnum. Sierra has offered 240- and 180-gr. bullets of this type for quite some time. The 210-gr. offering will fill in the line nicely.

The fourth new Sierra bullet is a 140-gr. jacketed hollow cavity number designed for the 357 Magnum and the 38 Special. Sierra has had .357″ jacketed bullets in 110-, 125-, 150-, and 158-gr. weights. The new 140-gr. of-

Mike says a very wide range of velocities can be covered with this new bullet concept. He spoke of tests conducted at velocity ranges from 800 to 1600 fps. That range will cover almost all uses in the weights available if at least a 4″ revolver barrel is used.

For the snubbie user, performance of the new bullets is still unknown. In such short barrels velocities of less than 700 fps are common. I can tell you that my experience with the few sample bullets I received indicates excellent results. I used a S&W 38 Special with 6-in. barrel and found a very uniform expansion. And the expansion from one bullet to the next was impressively almost identical. After Sierra has applied this concept to all their handgun bullets, perhaps it can also be applied to rifle bullets.

Norma

The Norma line has been recently

O.S.H. supplied me with a Norma price list and order form. The order form included only loaded ammunition and unprimed brass. This is somewhat contradictory in that there are no listings for powder or component bullets. Obviously some confusion does exist. Additionally, a fair number of loads previously shown on the Norma listing are not on O.S.H. price lists. I was told first that all Norma loads would be retained. Then complete listing of loads to be carried by O.S.H. For this issue we have deleted prices from Norma ammunition listed on our Norma chart and not listed on the O.S.H. price schedule, but we have listed the loads. Hopefully, by next issue, things will be settled down and we will be able to be more positive about the Norma line. As many Norma prices certainly seem to have been reduced as have been increased.

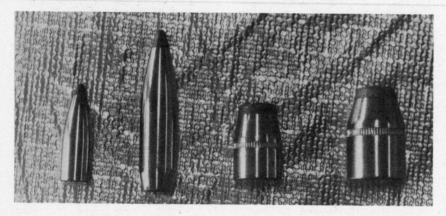

(Above) This photo shows the superb expansion of the new Sierra 125-grain jacketed hollow point with the Power-Jacket feature. An unfired bullet is also shown.

(Left) Sierra's newest bullets are (from right to left): a 55-grain .224″ diameter Blitz: a 140-grain. 284″ diameter boat-tail; a 125-grain .357″ hollow point (with the new Power Jacket); and a 210-grain .430″ diameter hollow point.

fering covers a weight that has proven popular in the Speer bullet line.

The most exciting part of this new bullet is that it incorporates Sierra's new Power Jacket which will be applied to all Sierra handgun jacketed bullets as time goes on. For this year, it appears only in 38/357 hollow cavity bullets in 110-, 125-, 140-, and 150-gr. weights.

This new jacket concept involves six V-notches cut into the nose of the bullet jacket, quite similar to the notches on Winchester's Silvertip hollow point handgun bullets. Mike Bussard assured me that Sierra was not guilty of infringing upon Winchester's patent as their process is unique with respect to manufacturing procedures. Basically what these notches accomplish is a positive and predetermined level of expansion. No longer will the handgun bullet user have to settle for erratic bullet expansion.

taken over by Outdoor Sports Headquarters, a firearms and ammo distributor based in Dayton, Ohio. In a conversation with Bill Willmoth at Outdoor Sports Headquarters I was unable to gain any real insight as to what direction the Norma line will take. The Norma venture is new to O.S.H. It will take some time for things to settle down and for specific marketing plans to be formulated.

I was told the component powder line would be continued. However, O.S.H. had absolutely no inventory of Norma powders. A spokesman indicated that there were outstanding powder orders with Norma but delivery time was impossible to estimate. No one seemed to be sure if Norma bullets would continue to be available. I guess we will simply have to wait and see what direction the Norma components line will take under the O.S.H. firm.

Hornady/Frontier

There are three new items for this year:

The first is a Hornady 45-caliber 200-gr. full metal case bullet being introduced for the combat and target shooting games. It is a .451″ diameter bullet with a semi-wadcutter profile.

Their second new item is a 32-cal. lead semi-wadcutter. This 90-gr. bullet is designed for the users of the 32 S&W guns now finding some popularity as target weapons. Being of .314″ diameter this bullet will of course work nicely in any 32 S&W revolver or semiautomatic target pistol. I would suspect that this bullet is for a very limited audience.

Finally, the 45 ACP bullet mentioned above will be available in Frontier brand ammunition as a loaded round. Retail price is to be $9.50 per box of 20. ●

CENTERFIRE RIFLE CARTRIDGES—BALLISTICS AND PRICES

(R) = REMINGTON; (W) = WINCHESTER-WESTERN); (F) = FEDERAL; (H) = HORNADY-FRONTIER; (PMC) = Patton & Morgan Corp.

Cartridge	— BULLET — Wt. Grs.	Type	Bbl. (in.)	— VELOCITY (fps) — Muzzle	100 yds.	200 yds.	300 yds.	— ENERGY (ft. lbs.) — Muzzle	100 yds.	200 yds.	300 yds.	— BULLET PATH† — 100 yds.	200 yds.	300 yds.	Price Per Box
17 Remington (R)	25	HPPL	24	4040	3284	2644	2086	906	599	388	242	+0.5	–1.5	–8.5	$12.00
22 Hornet (R) (W)	45	PSP	24	2690	2042	1502	1128	723	417	225	127	0.0	–7.7	–31.3	*22.15
22 Hornet (R)	45	HP	24	2690	2042	1502	1128	723	417	225	127	0.0	–7.7	–31.3	*22.15
22 Hornet (W)	46	OPE	24	2690	2042	1502	1128	739	426	230	130	0.0	–7.7	–31.3	*22.15
218 Bee (W)	46	OPE	24	2760	2102	1550	1155	778	451	245	136	0.0	–7.2	–29.4	*32.70
222 Remington (R) (W) (F) (H)	50	PSP, SX	24	3140	2602	2123	1700	1094	752	500	321	+2.2	0.0	–10.0	9.45
222 Remington (R)	50	HPPL	24	3140	2635	2182	1777	1094	771	529	351	+2.1	0.0	–9.5	10.30
222 Remington (R)	55	MC	24	3000	2544	2130	1759	1099	790	554	378	+2.3	0.0	–10.0	9.45
222 Remington (W)	55	FMC	24	3020	2675	2355	2057	1114	874	677	517	+2.0	0.0	–8.3	9.45
222 Remington (F)	55	MC BT	24	3020	2740	2480	2230	1115	915	750	610	+1.9	0.0	–7.7	9.45
222 Remington Magnum (R)	55	PSP	24	3240	2748	2305	1906	1282	922	649	444	+1.9	0.0	–8.5	10.75
222 Remington Magnum (R)	55	HPPL	24	3240	2773	2352	1969	1282	939	675	473	+1.8	0.0	–8.5	11.45
223 Remington (R) (W) (F) (H)	55	PSP	24	3240	2747	2304	1905	1282	921	648	443	+1.9	0.0	–8.5	10.35
223 Remington (R)	55	HPPL	24	3240	2773	2352	1969	1282	939	675	473	+1.8	0.0	–8.2	11.15
223 Remington (R) (H)	55	MC	24	3240	2759	2326	1933	1282	929	660	456	+1.9	0.0	–8.4	10.35
223 Remington (W) (F) (PMC)	55	FMC, MC BT	24	3240	2877	2543	2232	1282	1011	790	608	+1.7	0.0	–7.1	10.35
225 Winchester (W)	55	PSP	24	3570	3066	2616	2208	1556	1148	836	595	+1.2	0.0	–6.2	11.05
22-250 Remington (R) (W) (F) (H)	55	PSP	24	3730	3180	2695	2257	1699	1235	887	622	+1.0	0.0	–5.7	10.35
22-250 Remington (R)	55	HPCL	24	3730	3253	2826	2436	1699	1292	975	725	+0.9	0.0	–5.2	11.15
22-250 Remington (F) — Premium	55	BTHP	24	3730	3330	2960	2630	1700	1350	1070	840	+0.8	0.0	–4.8	11.25
220 Swift (H)	55	SP	24	3630	3176	2755	2370	1609	1229	927	686	+1.0	0.0	–5.6	14.00
220 Swift (H)	60	HP	24	3530	3134	2763	2420	1657	1305	1016	780	+1.1	0.0	–5.7	14.00
243 (W) (R) (F) (H)	80	PSP, HPPL, FMJ	24	3350	2955	2593	2259	1993	1551	1194	906	+1.6	0.0	–7.0	12.90
243 Winchester (F) — Premium	85	BTHP	24	3320	3070	2830	2600	2080	1770	1510	1280	+1.5	0.0	–6.8	13.60
243 Winchester (W) (R) (F) (H)	100	PPSP, PSPCL, SP	24	2960	2697	2449	2215	1945	1615	1332	1089	+1.9	0.0	–7.8	12.90
243 Winchester (F) — Premium	100	BTSP	24	2960	2760	2570	2380	1950	1690	1460	1260	+1.4	0.0	–5.8	13.60
6mm Remington (R) (W) (Also, 244 Rem.)	80	PSP, HPPL	24	3470	3064	2694	2352	2139	1667	1289	982	+1.2	0.0	–6.0	12.90
6mm Remington (R) (W) (F)	100	PSPCL, PPSP	24	3130	2857	2600	2357	2175	1812	1501	1233	+1.7	0.0	–6.8	12.90
25-20 Winchester (W) (R)	86	SP	24	1460	1194	1030	931	407	272	203	165	0.0	–23.5	–79.6	*20.95
256 Winchester (W)	60	OPE	24	2760	2097	1542	1149	1015	586	317	176	0.0	–7.3	–29.6	*26.45
25-35 Winchester (W)	117	SP	24	2230	1866	1545	1282	1292	904	620	427	0.0	–9.2	–33.1	14.35
250 Savage (W)	87	PSP	24	3030	2673	2342	2036	1773	1380	1059	801	+2.0	0.0	–8.4	13.10
250 Savage (W)	100	ST	24	2820	2467	2140	1839	1765	1351	1017	751	+2.4	0.0	–10.1	13.10
250 Savage (R)	100	PSP	24	2820	2504	2210	1936	1765	1392	1084	832	+2.3	0.0	–9.5	13.10
257 Roberts (W)	100	ST	24	2900	2541	2210	1904	1867	1433	1084	805	+2.3	0.0	–9.4	14.45
257 Roberts (W) (R)	117	PPSP, SPCL	24	2650	2291	1961	1663	1824	1363	999	718	+2.9	0.0	–12.0	14.45
25-06 Remington (R)	87	HPPL	24	3440	2995	2591	2222	2286	1733	1297	954	+1.2	0.0	–6.3	14.05
25-06 Remington (W) (F)	90	PEP, HP	24	3440	3043	2680	2344	2364	1850	1435	1098	+1.2	0.0	–6.1	14.05
25-06 Remington (R)	100	PSPCL	24	3230	2893	2580	2287	2316	1858	1478	1161	+1.6	0.0	–6.9	14.05
25-06 Remington (F)	117	SP	24	3060	2790	2530	2280	2430	2020	1660	1360	+1.8	0.0	–7.3	14.05
25-06 Remington (R) (W)	120	PSPCL, PEP	24	3010	2749	2502	2269	2414	2013	1668	1372	+1.9	0.0	–7.4	14.05
6.5mm Remington Magnum (R)	120	PSPCL	24	3210	2905	2621	2353	2745	2248	1830	1475	+1.3	0.0	–6.6	20.90
264 Winchester Magnum (W) (R)	100	PSP, PSPCL	24	3320	2926	2565	2231	2447	1901	1461	1105	+1.3	0.0	–6.7	18.10
264 Winchester Magnum (W) (R)	140	PPSP, PSPCL	24	3030	2782	2548	2326	2854	2406	2018	1682	+1.8	0.0	–7.2	18.10
270 Winchester (W) (R)	100	PSP	24	3480	3067	2690	2343	2689	2088	1606	1219	+1.2	0.0	–6.2	14.05
270 Winchester (W) (R) (F)	130	PPSP, BP, SP	24	3110	2849	2604	2371	2791	2343	1957	1622	+1.7	0.0	–6.8	14.05
270 Winchester (W) (R) (H)	130	ST, PSPCL	24	3110	2823	2554	2300	2791	2300	1883	1527	+1.7	0.0	–7.1	14.05
270 Winchester (F) — Premium	130	BTSP	24	3110	2880	2670	2460	2790	2400	2050	1740	+1.6	0.0	–6.5	14.75
270 Winchester (W) (H)	150	PPSP	24	2900	2632	2380	2142	2801	2307	1886	1528	+2.1	0.0	–8.2	14.05
270 Winchester (F) — Premium	150	BTSP	24	2900	2710	2520	2350	2800	2440	2120	1830	+1.6	0.0	–7.0	14.75
270 Winchester (R) (F)	150	SPCL, SP	24	2900	2550	2225	1926	2801	2165	1649	1235	+2.2	0.0	–9.3	14.05
270 Winchester (F) — Premium	150	NP	24	2900	2630	2380	2140	2800	2310	1890	1530	+2.1	0.0	–8.2	18.10
7mm Mauser (R) (W)	175	SP	24	2440	2137	1857	1603	2313	1774	1340	998	0.0	–6.8	–23.7	14.30
7mm Mauser (F)	175	SP	24	2470	2170	1880	1630	2370	1820	1380	1030	0.0	–6.6	–23.0	14.30
7mm-08 Remington (R)	140	PSPCL	24	2860	2625	2402	2189	2542	2142	1793	1490	+2.1	0.0	–8.1	14.05
7mm Express Remington (R)	150	SPCL	24	2970	2699	2444	2203	2937	2426	1989	1616	+1.9	0.0	–7.8	14.05
280 Remington (R)	165	SPCL	24	2820	2510	2220	1950	2913	2308	1805	1393	+2.3	0.0	–9.4	14.05
284 Winchester (W)	150	PPSP	24	2860	2595	2344	2108	2724	2243	1830	1480	+2.1	0.0	–8.5	16.25
7mm Remington Magnum (W)	125	PPSP	24	3310	2976	2666	2376	3040	2458	1972	1567	+1.2	0.0	–6.5	17.40
7mm Remington Magnum (R) (W) (F)	150	PSPCL, PPSP, SP	24	3110	2830	2568	2320	3221	2667	2196	1792	+1.7	0.0	–7.0	17.40
7mm Remington Magnum (F)	150	BTSP-Prem.	24	3110	2920	2750	2580	3220	2850	2510	2210	+1.6	0.0	–6.2	18.10
7mm Remington Magnum (F)	165	BTSP-Prem.	24	2860	2710	2560	2420	3000	2690	2410	2150	+1.6	0.0	–6.9	18.10
7mm Remington Magnum (R) (W) (F) (H)	175	PSPCL, PPSP	24	2860	2645	2440	2244	3178	2718	2313	1956	+2.0	0.0	–7.9	17.40
7mm Remington Magnum (F)	160	NP	24	2950	2730	2520	2320	3090	2650	2250	1910	+1.8	0.0	–7.7	21.30
30 Carbine (R) (W) (F) (H)	110	SP, HSP, SP, RN	**20**	1990	1567	1236	1035	967	600	373	262	0.0	–13.5	–49.9	*22.50
30 Carbine (W) (F) (H) (PMC)	110	FMC, MC, FMJ, FMC	**20**	1990	1596	1278	1070	967	622	399	280	0.0	–13.0	–47.4	*22.50
30 Remington (R) (W)	170	SPCL, ST	24	2120	1822	1555	1328	1696	1253	913	666	0.0	–9.7	–33.8	14.15
30-30 Accelerator (R)	55	SP	24	3400	2693	2085	1570	1412	886	521	301	+2.0	0.0	–10.2	12.20
30-30 Winchester (F)	125	HP	24	2570	2090	1660	1320	1830	1210	770	480	0.0	–7.3	–28.1	11.00
30-30 Winchester (W) (F)	150	OPE, PPSP, ST, SP	24	2390	2018	1684	1398	1902	1356	944	651	0.0	–7.7	–27.9	11.00
30-30 Winchester (R) (H)	150	SPCL	24	2390	1973	1605	1303	1902	1296	858	565	0.0	–8.2	–30.0	11.00
30-30 Winchester (W) (R) (F)	170	PPSP, ST, SPCL, SP, HPCL	24	2200	1895	1619	1381	1827	1355	989	720	0.0	–8.9	–31.1	11.00
300 Savage (R)	150	SPCL	24	2630	2247	1897	1585	2303	1681	1198	837	0.0	–6.1	–21.9	14.15
300 Savage (W)	150	PPSP	24	2630	2311	2015	1743	2303	1779	1352	1012	+2.8	0.0	–11.5	14.15
300 Savage (W) (F) (R)	150	ST, SP, PSPCL	24	2630	2354	2095	1853	2303	1845	1462	1143	+2.7	0.0	–10.7	14.15
300 Savage (R) (W)	180	SPCL, PPSP	24	2350	2025	1728	1467	2207	1639	1193	860	0.0	–7.7	–27.1	14.15
300 Savage (R) (W)	180	PSPCL, ST	24	2350	2137	1935	1745	2207	1825	1496	1217	0.0	–6.7	–22.8	14.15
30-40 Krag (R) (W)	180	SPCL, PPSP	24	2430	2098	1795	1525	2360	1761	1288	929	0.0	–7.1	–25.0	14.75
30-40 Krag (R) (W)	180	PSPCL, ST	24	2430	2213	2007	1813	2360	1957	1610	1314	0.0	–6.2	–21.1	14.75
303 Savage (W)	190	ST	24	1940	1657	1410	1211	1588	1158	839	619	0.0	–11.9	–41.4	15.85
308 Accelerator (R)	55	PSP	24	3770	3215	2726	2286	1735	1262	907	638	+1.0	0.0	–5.6	15.55
308 Winchester (W)	110	PSP	24	3180	2666	2206	1795	2470	1736	1188	787	+2.0	0.0	–9.3	14.05
308 Winchester (W)	125	PSP	24	3050	2697	2370	2067	2582	2019	1559	1186	+2.0	0.0	–8.2	14.05
308 Winchester (W)	150	PPSP	24	2820	2488	2179	1893	2648	2061	1581	1193	+2.4	0.0	–9.8	14.05
308 Winchester (W) (R) (F) (H) (PMC)	150	ST, PSPCL, SP	24	2820	2533	2263	2009	2648	2137	1705	1344	+2.3	0.0	–9.1	14.05
308 Winchester (PMC)	147	FMC-BT	24	2750	2473	2257	2052	2428	2037	1697	1403	+2.3	0.0	–9.1	8.00
308 Winchester (F) (H)	165	BTSP, SPBT	24	2700	2520	2330	2160	2670	2310	1990	1700	+2.0	0.0	–8.4	14.05
308 Winchester (W) (R)	180	PPSP, SPCL	24	2620	2274	1955	1666	2743	2086	1527	1109	+2.9	0.0	–12.1	14.05
308 Winchester (W) (R) (F) (PMC)	180	ST, PSPCL, SP	24	2620	2393	2178	1974	2743	2288	1896	1557	+2.6	0.0	–9.9	14.05
308 Winchester (W)	200	ST	24	2450	2208	1980	1767	2665	2165	1741	1386	0.0	–6.3	–21.4	14.05
30-06 Springfield (W)	110	PSP	24	3380	2843	2365	1936	2790	1974	1366	915	+1.7	0.0	–8.0	14.05
30-06 Springfield (W) (R) (F)	125	PSP, PSP, SP	24	3140	2780	2447	2138	2736	2145	1662	1269	+1.8	0.0	–7.7	14.05
30-06 Springfield (W)	150	PPSP	24	2920	2580	2265	1972	2839	2217	1708	1295	+2.2	0.0	–9.0	14.05
30-06 Springfield (W) (R) (F) (H) (PMC)	150	ST, PSPCL, SP, SP	24	2910	2617	2342	2083	2820	2281	1827	1445	+2.1	0.0	–8.5	14.05
30-06 Springfield (R)	150	BP	24	2910	2656	2416	2189	2820	2349	1944	1596	+2.0	0.0	–8.0	14.95
30-06 Springfield (PMC)	150	FMC (M-2)	24	2810	2555	2310	2080	2630	2170	1780	1440	+2.2	0.0	–8.8	8.00
30-06 Accelerator	55	PSP	24	4080	3485	2965	2502	2033	1483	1074	764	+1.0	0.0	–5.0	15.55
30-06 Springfield (R)	165	PSPCL	24	2800	2534	2283	2047	2872	2352	1909	1534	+2.3	0.0	–9.0	14.05
30-06 Springfield (F) (H)	165	BTSP	24	2800	2610	2420	2240	2870	2490	2150	1840	+2.1	0.0	–8.0	13.15
30-06 Springfield (R) (W)	180	SPCL, PPSP	24	2700	2348	2023	1727	2913	2203	1635	1192	+2.7	0.0	–11.3	14.05
30-06 Springfield (R) (W) (F) (H) (PMC)	180	PSPCL, ST, NOSLER	24	2700	2469	2250	2042	2913	2436	2023	1666	+2.4	0.0	–9.3	14.05
30-06 Springfield (R)	180	BP	24	2700	2485	2280	2084	2913	2468	2077	1736	+2.4	0.0	–9.1	14.95

Cartridge	Wt. Grs.	— BULLET — Type	Bbl. (in.)	Muzzle	VELOCITY (fps) 100 yds.	200 yds.	300 yds.	Muzzle	ENERGY (ft. lbs.) 100 yds.	200 yds.	300 yds.	BULLET PATH† 100 yds.	200 yds.	300 yds.	Price Per Box
30-06 Springfield (F)	200	BTSP	24	2550	2400	2260	2120	2890	2560	2270	2000	+2.3	0.0	− 9.0	14.05
30-06 Springfield (W) (R)	220	PPSP, SPCL	24	2410	2130	1870	1632	2837	2216	1708	1301	0.0	− 6.8	− 23.6	14.05
30-06 Springfield (W)	220	ST	24	2410	2192	1985	1791	2837	2347	1924	1567	0.0	− 6.4	− 21.6	14.05
300 H & H Magnum (W)	150	ST	24	3130	2822	2534	2264	3262	2652	2138	1707	+1.7	0.0	− 7.2	14.05
300 H & H Magnum (W) (R)	180	ST, PSPCL	24	2880	2640	2412	2196	3315	2785	2325	1927	+2.1	0.0	− 8.0	17.85
300 H & H Magnum (W)	220	ST, PSPCL	24	2580	2341	2114	1901	3251	2677	2183	1765	+2.7	0.0	− 10.5	17.85
300 Winchester Magnum (W) (R)	150	PPSP, PSPCL	24	3290	3051	2826	2242	3605	2900	2314	1827	+1.3	0.0	− 6.6	18.35
300 Winchester Magnum (W) (R) (F) (H)	180	PPSP, PSPCL, SP	24	2960	2745	2540	2344	3501	3011	2578	2196	+1.9	0.0	− 7.3	18.35
300 Winchester Magnum (F) Premium	200	BTSP	24	2830	2680	2530	2380	3560	3180	2830	2520	+1.7	0.0	− 7.1	19.05
303 British (R)	180	SPCL	24	2460	2124	1817	1542	2418	1803	1319	950	0.0	− 6.9	− 24.4	14.40
303 British (W)	180	PPSP	24	2460	2233	2018	1816	2418	1993	1627	1318	0.0	− 6.1	− 20.8	14.40
32-20 Winchester (W) (R)	100	SP	24	1210	1021	913	834	325	231	185	154	0.0	−32.3	−106.3	*21.10
32-20 Winchester (W) (R)	100	L	24	1210	1021	913	834	325	231	185	154	0.0	−32.3	−106.3	*17.05
32 Winchester Special (F) (R)	170	SP	24	2250	1920	1630	1370	1911	1390	1000	710	0.0	− 8.6	− 30.5	11.75
8mm Mauser (R) (W)	170	SPCL, PPSP	24	2360	1969	1622	1333	2102	1463	993	671	0.0	− 8.2	− 29.8	14.45
8mm Mauser (F)	170	SP	24	2510	2110	1740	1430	2380	1670	1140	770	0.0	− 7.0	− 25.7	14.45
8mm Remington Magnum (R)	185	PSPCL	24	3080	2761	2464	2186	3896	3131	2494	1963	+1.8	0.0	− 7.6	21.70
8mm Remington Magnum (R)	220	PSPCL	24	2830	2581	2346	2123	3912	3254	2688	2201	+2.2	0.0	− 8.5	21.70
338 Winchester Magnum (W)	200	PPSP	24	2960	2658	2375	2110	3890	3137	2505	1977	+2.0	0.0	− 8.2	22.00
338 Winchester Magnum (W)	250	ST	24	2660	2395	2145	1910	3927	3184	2554	2025	+2.6	0.0	− 10.2	22.00
348 Winchester (W)	200	ST	24	2520	2215	1931	1672	2820	2178	1656	1241	0.0	− 6.2	− 21.9	25.30
351 Winchester S.L. (W)	180	SP	20	1850	1556	1310	1128	1368	968	686	508	0.0	−13.6	− 47.5	*35.90
35 Remington (R)	150	PSPCL	24	2300	1874	1506	1218	1762	1169	755	494	0.0	− 9.2	− 33.0	12.95
35 Remington (R) (F)	200	SPCL, SP	24	2080	1698	1376	1140	1921	1280	841	577	0.0	−11.3	− 41.2	12.95
35 Remington (W)	200	PPSP, ST	24	2020	1646	1335	1114	1812	1203	791	551	0.0	−12.1	− 43.9	12.95
358 Winchester (W)	200	ST	24	2490	2171	1876	1610	2753	2093	1563	1151	0.0	− 6.5	− 23.0	19.40
350 Remington Magnum (R)	200	PSPCL	20	2710	2410	2130	1870	3261	2579	2014	1553	+2.6	0.0	− 10.3	20.15
375 Winchester (W)	200	PPSP	24	2200	1841	1526	1268	2150	1506	1034	714	0.0	− 9.5	− 33.8	16.70
375 Winchester (W)	250	PPSP	24	1900	1647	1424	1239	2005	1506	1126	852	0.0	−12.0	− 40.9	16.70
38-55 Winchester (W)	255	SP	24	1320	1190	1091	1018	987	802	674	587	0.0	−23.4	− 75.2	15.55
375 H & H Magnum (R) (W)	270	SP, PPSP	24	2690	2420	2166	1928	4337	3510	2812	2228	+2.5	0.0	− 10.0	21.80
375 H & H Magnum (W)	300	ST	24	2530	2268	2022	1793	4263	3426	2723	2141	+2.9	0.0	− 11.5	21.80
375 H & H Magnum (R) (W)	300	FMC, MC	24	2530	2171	1843	1551	4263	3139	2262	1602	0.0	− 6.5	− 23.4	21.80
38-40 Winchester (W)	180	SP	24	1160	999	901	827	538	399	324	273	0.0	−33.9	−110.6	*26.75
44-40 Winchester (W)	200	SP, SP	24	1190	1006	900	822	629	449	360	300	0.0	−33.3	−109.5	*28.25
44 Remington Magnum (R)	240	SP, SJHP	20	1760	1380	1114	970	1650	1015	661	501	0.0	−17.6	− 63.1	10.75
44 Remington Magnum (F) (W)	240	HSP	20	1760	1380	1090	950	1650	1015	640	485	0.0	−18.1	− 65.1	10.75
444 Marlin (R)	240	SP	24	2350	1815	1377	1087	2942	1755	1010	630	0.0	− 9.9	− 38.5	15.60
444 Marlin (R)	265	SP	24	2120	1733	1405	1160	2644	1768	1162	791	0.0	−10.8	− 39.5	15.80
45-70 Government (F)	300	HSP	24	1810	1410	1120	970	2180	1320	840	630	0.0	−17.0	− 61.4	15.95
45-70 Government (W)	300	JHP	24	1880	1559	1294	1105	2355	1619	1116	814	0.0	−13.5	− 47.1	15.95
45-70 Government (W)	405	SP	24	1330	1168	1055	977	1590	1227	1001	858	0.0	−24.6	− 80.3	15.95
458 Winchester Magnum (W) (R)	500	FMC, MC	24	2040	1823	1623	1442	4620	3689	2924	2308	0.0	− 9.6	− 32.5	44.60
458 Winchester Magnum (W) (R)	510	SP, SP	24	2040	1770	1527	1319	4712	3547	2640	1970	0.0	−10.3	− 35.6	29.40

*Price for 50. †Bullet Path based on line-of-sight 0.9″ above center of bore. Bullet type abbreviations: BP—Bronze Point; BT—Boat Tail; CL—Core Lokt; FN—Flat Nose; FMC—Full Metal Case; FMJ—Full Metal Jacket; HP—Hollow Point; HSP—Hollow Soft Point; JHP—Jacketed Hollow Point; L—Lead; Lu—Lubaloy; MAT—Match; MC—Metal Case; NP—Nosler Partition; OPE—Open Point Expanding; PCL—Pointed Core Lokt; PEP—Pointed Expanding Point; PL—Power-Lokt; PP—Power Point; Prem.—Premium; PSP—Pointed Soft Point; SJHP—Semi-Jacketed Hollow Point; SJMP—Semi-Jacketed Metal Point; SP—Soft Point; ST—Silvertip; SX—Super Explosive.

WEATHERBY MAGNUM CARTRIDGES—BALLISTICS AND PRICES

Cartridge	Wt. Grs.	— Bullet — Type	Bbl. (in.)	Muzzle	Velocity (fps) 100 Yds.	200 Yds.	300 Yds.	Muzzle	Energy (ft. lbs.) 100 Yds.	200 Yds.	300 Yds.	Bullet Path† 100 Yds.	200 Yds.	300 Yds.	Price Per Box
224 Weatherby Magnum	55	PE	26	3650	3214	2808	2433	1627	1262	963	723	+2.8	+3.6	0.0	22.95
240 Weatherby Magnum	70	PE	26	3850	3424	3025	2654	2305	1823	1423	1095	+2.2	+3.0	0.0	22.95
240 Weatherby Magnum	87	PE	26	3500	3165	2848	2550	2367	1935	1567	1256	+2.8	+3.6	0.0	22.95
240 Weatherby Magnum	100	PE	26	3395	3115	2848	2594	2560	2155	1802	1495	+2.8	+3.5	0.0	22.95
240 Weatherby Magnum	100	NP	26	3395	3068	2758	2468	2560	2090	1690	1353	+1.1	0.0	− 5.7	30.95
257 Weatherby Magnum	87	PE	26	3825	3470	3135	2818	2827	2327	1900	1535	+2.1	+2.9	0.0	23.95
257 Weatherby Magnum	100	PE	26	3555	3256	2971	2700	2807	2355	1960	1619	+2.5	+3.2	0.0	23.95
257 Weatherby Magnum	100	NP	26	3555	3242	2945	2663	2807	2335	1926	1575	+0.9	0.0	− 4.7	32.95
257 Weatherby Magnum	117	SPE	26	3300	2853	2443	2074	2830	2115	1551	1118	+3.8	+4.9	0.0	23.95
257 Weatherby Magnum	117	NP	26	3300	3027	2767	2520	2830	2381	1990	1650	+1.2	0.0	− 5.9	32.95
270 Weatherby Magnum	100	PE	26	3760	3341	2949	2585	3140	2479	1932	1484	+2.4	+3.2	0.0	23.95
270 Weatherby Magnum	130	PE	26	3375	3110	2856	2615	3289	2793	2355	1974	+2.8	+3.5	0.0	23.95
270 Weatherby Magnum	130	NP	26	3375	3113	2862	2624	3289	2798	2365	1988	+1.0	0.0	− 5.2	32.95
270 Weatherby Magnum	150	PE	26	3245	3012	2789	2575	3508	3022	2592	2209	+3.1	+3.8	0.0	23.95
270 Weatherby Magnum	150	NP	26	3245	3022	2809	2604	3508	3043	2629	2259	+1.2	0.0	− 5.4	23.95
7mm Weatherby Magnum	139	PE	26	3300	3037	2786	2546	3362	2848	2396	2001	+3.0	+3.7	0.0	23.95
7mm Weatherby Magnum	140	NP	26	3300	3047	2806	2575	3386	2887	2448	2062	+1.3	0.0	− 5.4	32.95
7mm Weatherby Magnum	154	PE	26	3160	2928	2706	2494	3415	2932	2504	2127	+3.3	+4.1	0.0	23.95
7mm Weatherby Magnum	160	NP	26	3150	2935	2727	2528	3526	3061	2643	2271	+1.3	0.0	− 5.8	32.95
7mm Weatherby Magnum	175	RN	26	3070	2714	2383	2082	3663	2863	2207	1685	+1.6	0.0	− 7.5	23.95
300 Weatherby Magnum	110	PE	26	3900	3465	3057	2677	3716	2933	2283	1750	+2.2	+3.0	0.0	23.95
300 Weatherby Magnum	150	PE	26	3545	3248	2965	2696	4187	3515	2929	2422	+2.5	+3.2	0.0	23.95
300 Weatherby Magnum	150	NP	26	3545	3191	2857	2544	4187	3392	2719	2156	+1.0	0.0	− 5.3	33.95
300 Weatherby Magnum	180	PE	26	3245	3010	2785	2569	4210	3622	3100	2639	+3.1	+3.8	0.0	23.95
300 Weatherby Magnum	180	NP	26	3245	3064	2696	2444	4210	3512	2906	2388	+1.3	0.0	− 6.0	23.95
300 Weatherby Magnum	220	SPE	26	2905	2578	2276	2000	4123	3248	2531	1955	+1.9	0.0	− 8.6	23.95
340 Weatherby Magnum	200	PE	26	3210	2947	2696	2458	4577	3857	3228	2683	+3.2	+4.0	0.0	25.95
340 Weatherby Magnum	210	NP	26	3180	2927	2686	2457	3996	3365	2816	2347	+1.3	0.0	− 6.2	40.65
340 Weatherby Magnum	250	SPE	26	2850	2516	2209	1929	4510	3515	2710	2066	+2.0	0.0	− 9.2	25.95
340 Weatherby Magnum	250	NP	26	2850	2563	2296	2049	4510	3648	2927	2331	+1.8	0.0	− 8.2	25.95
378 Weatherby Magnum	270	SPE	26	3180	2796	2440	2117	6064	4688	3570	2688	+1.5	0.0	− 7.3	40.95
378 Weatherby Magnum	270	NP	26	3180	2840	2515	2220	6064	4837	3793	2955	+3.9	+4.9	0.0	40.95
378 Weatherby Magnum	300	SPE	26	2925	2564	2234	1935	5700	4380	3325	2495	+1.9	0.0	− 9.0	40.95
378 Weatherby Magnum	300	FMJ	26	2925	2620	2340	2080	5700	4574	3649	2883	+4.9	+6.0	0.0	46.95
460 Weatherby Magnum	500	RN	26	2700	2395	2115	1858	8095	6370	4968	3834	+2.3	0.0	− 10.3	44.95
460 Weatherby Magnum	500	FMJ	26	2700	2416	2154	1912	8095	6482	5153	4060	+2.2	0.0	− 9.8	51.95

†Bullet Path based on line of sight 1.5″ above center of bore. Bullet type abbreviations: FMJ—Full Metal Jacket; NP—Nosler Partition; PE—Pointed Expanding; RN—Round Nose; SPE—Semi-Pointed Expanding.

NORMA C.F. RIFLE CARTRIDGES—BALLISTICS AND PRICES

Cartridge	Wt. Grs.	Bullet Type	Bbl. (in.)	Velocity (fps) Muzzle	100 Yds.	200 Yds.	300 Yds.	Energy (ft. lbs.) Muzzle	100 Yds.	200 Yds.	300 Yds.	Bullet Path† 100 Yds.	200 Yds.	300 Yds.	Price Per Box
222 Remington	50	SP	24	3200	2650	2170	1750	1137	780	520	340	+1.6	0.0	− 8.2	$10.85
222 Remington	50	FJ	24	3200	2610	2080	1630	1137	756	480	295	+1.9	0.0	−10.1	10.85
222 Remington	53	SpPSP	24	3117	2670	2267	1901	1142	838	604	425	+1.7	0.0	− 8.7	10.85
22-250 Remington	53	SpPSP	24	3707	3192	2741	2332	1616	1198	883	639	+1.0	0.0	− 5.7	11.05
220 Swift	50	SP	24	4110	3611	3133	2681	1877	1448	1090	799	+0.6	0.0	− 4.1	15.85
22 Savage Hi-Power (5.6 x 52R)	71	SP	24	2790	2296	1886	1558	1226	831	561	383	+2.4	0.0	−11.4	21.00
22 Savage Hi-Power (5.6 x 52R)	71	FJ	24	2790	2296	1886	1558	1226	831	561	383	+2.4	0.0	−11.4	—
243 Winchester	100	SP, FJ	24	3070	2790	2540	2320	2090	1730	1430	1190	+1.4	0.0	− 6.3	13.60
6.5mm Carcano	139	PPDC	24	2576	2379	2192	2012	2046	1745	1481	1249	+2.3	0.0	− 9.6	21.95
6.5mm Carcano	156	SP	24	2430	2208	2000	1800	2046	1689	1386	1123	+2.9	0.0	−11.7	21.00
6.5mm JAP	139	SPBT	24	2430	2280	2130	1990	1820	1605	1401	1223	+2.7	0.0	−10.8	21.00
6.5mm JAP	156	SP	24	2065	1871	1692	1529	1481	1213	992	810	+4.3	0.0	−16.4	21.00
6.5mm Norma (6.5 x 55)	77	SP	29	2725	2362	2030	1811	1271	956	706	562	+2.4	0.0	−10.9	—
6.5mm Norma (6.5 x 55)	139	PPDC	29	2790	2630	2470	2320	2402	2136	1883	1662	+1.8	0.0	− 7.8	21.95
6.5mm Norma (6.5 x 55)	156	SP	29	2495	2271	2062	1867	2153	1787	1473	1208	+2.6	0.0	−10.9	21.00
270 Winchester	130	SPBT	24	3140	2884	2639	2404	2847	2401	2011	1669	+1.4	0.0	− 6.6	14.75
270 Winchester	150	SPBT	24	2800	2616	2436	2262	2616	2280	1977	1705	+1.8	0.0	− 7.7	14.75
7mm Mauser (7 x 57)	150	SPBT	24	2755	2539	2331	2133	2530	2148	1810	1516	+2.0	0.0	− 8.4	19.45
7 x 57 R	150	SPBT, FJ BT	24	2690	2476	2270	2077	2411	2042	1717	1437	+2.1	0.0	− 8.9	—
7 x 64	150	SPBT	24	2890	2598	2329	2113	2779	2249	1807	1487	+1.7	0.0	− 7.5	18.95
7mm Rem. Express (280 Rem.)	150	SPBT	24	2900	2683	2475	2277	2802	2398	2041	1727	+1.7	0.0	− 7.4	—
7mm Remington Magnum	150	SPBT	26	3250	2960	2638	2440	3519	2919	2318	1983	+1.2	0.0	− 5.8	18.10
30 Carbine U.S.	110	SP	18	1970	1595	1300	1090	948	622	413	290	0.0	−12.4	−45.7	9.50
30-30 Winchester	150	SPFN	20	2410	2075	1790	1550	1934	1433	1066	799	0.0	− 7.0	−26.1	11.00
30-30 Winchester	170	SPFN	20	2220	1890	1630	1410	1860	1350	1000	750	0.0	− 8.1	−29.2	11.00
7.5 x 55 Swiss	180	SPBT	24	2650	2441	2248	2056	2792	2380	2020	1690	+2.1	0.0	− 8.9	22.00
7.62 x 39 Short Russian	125	SP		2385				1580							18.95
7.62 Russian	180	SPBT	24	2625	2415	2222	2030	2749	2326	1970	1644	+2.2	0.0	− 9.1	22.35
308 Winchester	130	SPBT	24	2900	2590	2300	2030	2428	1937	1527	1190	+1.9	0.0	− 8.6	14.75
308 Winchester	150	SPBT	24	2860	2570	2300	2050	2725	2200	1760	1400	+1.9	0.0	− 8.5	14.75
308 Winchester	180	PPDC	24	2610	2400	2210	2020	2725	2303	1952	1631	+2.3	0.0	− 9.4	15.85
30-06	130	SPBT	24	3205	2876	2561	2263	2966	2388	1894	1479	+1.4	0.0	− 6.7	14.75
30-06	150	SPBT	24	2970	2680	2402	2141	2943	2393	1922	1527	+1.7	0.0	− 7.8	—
30-06	180	SP	24	2700	2477	2261	2070	2914	2430	2025	1713	+2.1	0.0	− 8.7	14.75
30-06	180	PPDC	24	2700	2494	2296	2109	2914	2487	2107	1778	+2.0	0.0	− 8.6	16.95
303 British	150	SP	24	2720	2440	2170	1930	2465	1983	1569	1241	+2.2	0.0	− 9.7	15.50
303 British	180	SPBT	24	2540	2340	2147	1965	2579	2189	1843	1544	+2.4	0.0	−10.0	15.50
308 Norma Magnum	180	PPDC	26	3020	2798	2585	2382	3646	3130	2671	2268	+1.3	0.0	− 6.1	27.90
7.65mm Argentine	150	SP	24	2920	2630	2355	2105	2841	2304	1848	1476	+1.7	0.0	− 7.8	21.95
7.7mm JAP	130	SP	24	2950	2635	2340	2065	2513	2004	1581	1231	+1.8	0.0	− 8.2	22.50
7.7mm JAP	180	SPBT	24	2495	2292	2101	1922	2484	2100	1765	1477	+2.6	0.0	−10.4	22.50
8 x 57J (.318)	196	SP	24	2525	2195	1894	1627	2778	2097	1562	1152	+2.9	0.0	−12.7	—
8mm Mauser (8 x 57JS)	196	SP	24	2525	2195	1894	1627	2778	2097	1562	1152	+2.9	0.0	−12.7	19.65
358 Norma Magnum	250	SP	26	2800	2493	2231	2001	4322	3451	2764	2223	+2.0	0.0	− 8.3	—
9.3 x 57mm	286	PPDC	24	2065	1818	1595	1404	2714	2099	1616	1252	0.0	− 9.1	−32.0	—
9.3 x 62mm	286	PPDC	24	2360	2088	1815	1592	3544	2769	2092	1700	+3.3	0.0	−13.7	—

†Bullet Path based on line of sight 1.5″ above center of bore. Bullet type abbreviations: BT—Boat Tail; DC—Dual Core; FJ—Full Jacket; FJBT—Full Jacket Boat Tail; FP—Flat Point; HP—Hollow Point; MC—Metal Case; P—Pointed; PP—Plastic Point; RN—Round Nose; SP—Soft Point; SPFN—Soft Point Flat Nose; SPSBT—Soft Point Semi-Pointed Boat Tail; SPSP—Soft Point Semi-Point; SpPSP—Spire point Soft Point.

RIMFIRE CARTRIDGES—BALLISTICS AND PRICES
Remington-Peters, Winchester-Western, Federal, Omark/CCI
All loads available from all manufacturers except as indicated: R-P (a); W-W (b); Fed. (c); CCI (d). **All prices are approximate.**

CARTRIDGE	WT. GRS.	BULLET TYPE	VELOCITY (fps)/ENERGY (ft. lbs.) 18½″ BARREL MUZZLE	50 YDS.	100 YDS.	VELOCITY (fps)/ENERGY (ft. lbs.) 6½″ BARREL MUZZLE	50 YDS.	MID-RANGE TRAJECTORY 100 YDS.	PRICE PER BOX 50 RDS./100 RDS.
22 CB Short (b,d)	29	L	727/33	667/28	610/23	706/32	—/—	—	$—/4.16
22 CB Long (d)	29	L	727/33	667/28	610/23	706/32	—/—	—	—/4.16
22 Short Std. Vel. (a, b, c)	29	L	1045/70	—/—	872/48	865/48	—/—	4.3	2.05/—
22 Short T22 (b)	29	C, L*	1045/70	—/—	810/42	865/48	—/—	5.6	2.05/—
22 Short Hi-Vel. (c)	29	C, L	1132/83	1004/65	920/54	1065/73	—/—	4.3	2.05/4.10
22 Short Hi-Vel. H.P. (a, b, c)	27	C, L	1164/81	1013/62	904/49	1077/69	—/—	4.2	2.19/4.37
22 Short Match (a)	29	L	830/44	752/36	695/31	786/39	—/—	4.8	—/4.45
22 Long Hi-Vel. (c)	29	C, L	1045/70	—/—	870/49	1045/70	—/—	8.7	2.15/—
22 Long	29	L	1180/90	1038/69	946/57	1031/68	—/—	—	2.19/4.37
22 Long Rifle Std. Vel.	40	L	1138/116	1046/97	975/84	1027/93	925/76	4.0	2.33/4.37 to 4.66
22 Long Rifle T22 (a, b)	40	L*	1145/116	—/—	975/84	950/80	—/—	—	2.33/—
22 Long Rifle Target (a)	40	L	1150/117	—/—	976/85	—/—	—/—	4.0	2.33/4.66
22 Long Rifle Match (Rifle) (a)	40	L	1138/116	1047/97	975/84	1027/93	925/76	—	—/7.39
22 Long Rifle (b)†¹	40	L*	—/—	—/—	—/—	1060/100	—/—	—	5.11/—
22 Long Rifle (d)†²	40	C	1165/121	—/—	980/84	—/—	—/—	4.0	—/4.68
22 Long Rifle Match (Pistol) (a)	40	L	—/—	—/—	—/—	1060/100	950/80	—	3.70/—
22 Stinger (d)	32	C, HP	1687/202	1300/120	1158/95	1430/145	1100/86	−2.61	3.11/—
22 Long Rifle-Viper (a)	36	C	1410/159	1187/113	1015/82	—/—	—/—	—	2.53/—
22 Long Rifle Yellow Jacket (a)	33	HVTCHP	1500/165	1260/116	1075/85	—/—	—/—	2.8	2.92/—
22 Long Rifle Hi-Vel. H.P. (b, d)	36-38	C, L	1370/153	1165/111	1040/96	—/—	—/—	—	2.59/5.18
22 Long Rifle Shot (b, c)		No. 11 or 12 Shot	1047/—	—/—	—/—	950/—	—/—	—	2.42/—
22 LR Mini-Mag. Shotshell (d)		No. 12 Shot	950/—	—/—	—/—	—/—	—/—	—	2.42 (for 20)
22 WMR Shotshell (d)		No. 11 or 12 Shot	1126/—	—/—	—/—	1000/—	—/—	—	3.94/—
22 WMR Mag.	40	JHP, FMC	2025/382	1688/253	1407/175	1339/159	1110/109	1.6	6.43/—
5mm Rem. RFM (a)	38	PLHP	2100/372	—/—	1605/217	—/—	—/—	—	N/A

†Target loads of these ballistics available in: (1) Rem. Match; (2) W-W, Super Match Mark III; (3) Super Match Mark IV Pistol Match; (4) CCI MiniGroup.
C—Copper plated   L—Lead (Wax Coated)   L*—Lead, lubricated   D—Disintegrating   MC—Metal Case   HP—Hollow Point   JHP—Jacket Hollow Point   PLHP—Power-Lokt Hollow Point   HVTCHP—Hyper Velocity Truncated Cone Hollow Point.

CENTERFIRE HANDGUN CARTRIDGES BALLISTICS AND PRICES

Win.-Western, Rem.-Peters, Norma, PMC, and Federal

Most loads are available from W-W and R-P. All available Norma loads are listed. Federal cartridges are marked with an asterisk. Other loads supplied by only one source are indicated by a letter, thus: Norma (a); R-P (b); W-W (c); PMC (d); CCI (e). Prices are approximate.

Cartridge	Bullet Gr.	Bullet Style	Muzzle Velocity	Muzzle Energy	Barrel Inches	Price Per Box
22 Jet (b)	40	SP	2100	390	8⅜	$24.00
221 Fireball (b)	50	SP	2650	780	10½	10.90
25 (6.35mm) Auto*	50	MC	810	73	2	13.70
25 ACP (c)	45	Exp. Pt.	835	70	2	14.40
256 Winchester Magnum (c)	60	HP	2350	735	8½	26.50
30 (7.65mm) Luger Auto	93	MC	1220	307	4½	21.95
32 S&W Blank (b, c)	No bullet		—	—	—	13.05
32 S&W Blank, BP (c)	No bullet		—	—	—	13.05
32 Short Colt	80	Lead	745	100	4	13.10
32 Long Colt IL (c)	82	Lub.	755	104	4	13.70
32 Auto (c)	60	STHP	970	125	4	16.90
32 (7.65mm) Auto*	71	MC	905	129	4	15.95
32 (7.65mm) Auto Pistol (a)	77	MC	900	162	4	15.65
32 S&W	88	Lead	680	90	3	13.20
32 S&W Long	98	Lead	705	115	4	13.70
32-20 Winchester	100	Lead	1030	271	6	17.15
32-20 Winchester	100	SP	1030	271	6	21.20
357 Magnum	110	JHP	1295	410	4	20.55
357 Magnum	110	SJHP	1295	410	4	20.55
357 Magnum	125	JHP	1450	583	4	20.55
357 Magnum (d)	125	JHC	1450	583	4	20.55
357 Magnum (e)	125	JSP	1900	1001	—	20.55
357 Magnum (e)	140	JHP	1775	979	—	20.55
357 Magnum (e)	150	FMJ	1600	852	—	20.55
357 Magnum*	158	SWC	1235	535	4	17.40
357 Magnum (b) (e)	158	JSP	1550	845	8⅜	20.55
357 Magnum	158	MP	1410	695	8⅜	20.55
357 Magnum	158	Lead	1410	696	8⅜	17.40
357 Magnum	158	JHP	1450	735	8⅜	20.55
9mm Luger (c)	95	JSP	1355	387	4	19.45
9mm Luger (c)	115	FMC	1155	341	4	19.45
9mm Luger (c)	115	STHP	1255	383	4	20.40
9mm Luger*	115	JHP	1165	349	4	19.45
9mm Luger*	125	MC	1120	345	4	19.45
9mm Luger (e)	125	JSP	1100	335	—	19.45
38 S&W Blank	No bullet		—	—	—	15.80
38 Smith & Wesson	145	Lead	685	150	4	14.70
38 S&W	146	Lead	730	172	4	14.70
38 Special Blank	No bullet		—	—	—	15.90
38 Special (e)	110	JHP	1200	351	—	18.75
38 Special IL +P (c)	150	Lub.	1060	375	6	16.40
38 Special IL +P (c)	150	MP	1060	375	6	18.75
38 Special	158	Lead	855	256	6	14.80
38 Special	200	Lead	730	236	6	15.80
38 Special	158	MP	855	256	6	18.75
38 Special (b)	125	SJHP	Not available			18.75
38 Special WC (b)	148	Lead	770	195	6	15.40
38 Special Match, IL	148	Lead	770	195	6	15.40
38 Special Match, IL (b)	158	Lead	855	256	6	14.80
38 Special*	158	LRN	755	200	4	14.80
38 Special	158	RN	900	320	6	14.90
38 Special	158	SWC	755	200	4	15.40
38 Special Match*	148	WC	710	166	4	15.40
38 Special +P (c)	95	STHP	1100	255	4	19.70
38 Special +P	95	SJHP	—	—	—	19.70
38 Special +P (b)	110	SJHP	1020	254	4	18.75
38 Special +P	125	JSP	945	248	4	18.75
38 Special +P	158	LRN	915	294	4	14.80
38 Special +P (b)	158	LHP	915	294	4	16.05
38 Special +P*	158	SWC	915	294	4	15.90
38 Special +P*	158	SWCHP	915	294	4	15.90
38 Special +P*	158	LSWC	915	294	4	15.90
38 Special +P (e)	140	JHP	1275	504	—	18.32
38 Special +P (e)	150	FMJ	1175	461	—	18.32
38 Special +P*	110	JHP	1020	254	4	18.75
38 Special +P*	125	JHP	945	248	4	18.75
38 Special Norma +P (a)	110	JHP	1542	580	6	—
38 Short Colt	125	Lead	730	150	6	14.45
38 Short Colt, Greased	130	Lub.	730	155	6	14.45
38 Long Colt	150	Lead	730	175	6	21.70
38 Super Auto +P (b)	130	MC	1280	475	5	16.95
38 Super Auto +P (b)	115	JHP	1300	431	5	19.70
38 Auto, for Colt 38 Super (c)	125	JHP	1280	475	5	19.70
38 Auto	130	MC	1040	312	4½	17.45
38 Auto +P	130	FMC	1280	475	5	17.45
380 Auto (c)	85	STHP	1000	189	3¾	16.75
380 Auto*	95	MC	955	190	3¾	16.00
380 Auto	95	MC	955	192	3¾	16.00
380 Auto	88	JHP	990	191	4	15.63
380 Auto*	90	JHP	1000	200	3¾	16.00
38-40 Winchester	180	SP	975	380	5	26.85
41 Remington Magnum	210	Lead	1050	515	8¾	23.10
41 Remington Magnum	210	SP	1500	1050	8¾	27.05
44 S&W Spec.*	200	LSW	960	410	7½	20.70
44 S&W Special	246	Lead	755	311	6½	20.70
44 Remington Magnum*	180	JHP	1610	1040	4	21.00
44 Remington Magnum (e)	200	JHP	1650	1208	—	13.10
44 Remington Magnum (e)	240	JSP	1625	1406	—	13.10
44 Remington Magnum (b)	240	SP	1470	1150	6½	10.75
44 Remington Magnum	240	Lead	1470	1150	6½	26.25
44 Remington Magnum	240	SJHP	1180	741	4	10.75
44 Remington Magnum (a)	240	JPC	1533	1253	8½	—
44 Auto Mag (a)	240	JPC	1350	976	6½	—
44-40 Winchester	200	SP	975	420	7½	28.35
45 Colt*	225	SWCHP	900	405	5½	17.75
45 Colt	250	Lead	860	410	5½	21.00
45 Colt, IL (c)	255	Lub., L	860	410	5½	21.00
45 Auto (c)	185	STHP	1000	411	5	8.80
45 Auto (e)	200	JHP	1025	466	—	10.83
45 Auto	230	MC	850	369	5	21.40
45 ACP	230	JHP	850	370	5	21.40
45 Auto WC*	185	MC	775	245	5	22.50
45 Auto*	185	JHP	950	370	5	22.50
45 Auto MC	230	MC	850	369	5	21.40
45 Auto Match (c)	185		775	247	5	21.40
45 Winchester Magnum (c)	230	FMC	1400	1001	5	22.95
45 Auto Rim (b)	230	Lead	810	335	5½	22.75

IL—Inside Lub. JSP—Jacketed Soft Point WC—Wad Cutter
RN—Round Nose HP—Hollow Point Lub—Lubricated
MC—Metal Case SP—Soft Point MP—Metal Point
LGC—Lead, Gas Check JHP—Jacketed Hollow Point
SWC—Semi Wad Cutter SJHP—Semi Jacketed Hollow Point
PC—Power Cavity

SHOTSHELL LOADS AND PRICES

Winchester-Western, Remington-Peters, Federal

In certain loadings one manufacturer may offer fewer or more shot sizes than another, but in general all makers offer equivalent loadings. Sources are indicated by letters, thus: W-W (a); R-P (b); Fed. (c). *Prices are approximate, list is a random sampling of offerings.*

GAUGE	Length Shell Ins.	Powder Equiv. Drams	Shot Ozs.	Shot Size	PRICE PER BOX
MAGNUM LOADS					
10 (a)	3½	4½	2¼	BB, 2, 4	$26.95
10 (a¹, b)	3½	Max	2	BB, 2, 4	24.20
12 (a, b, c)	3	Max	1⅞	BB, 2, 4	16.70
12 (a¹, b)	3	4	1⅝	2, 4, 6	14.95
12 (a¹, b)	2¾	Max	1½	2, 4, 5, 6	13.50
16 (a, b, c)	2¾	Max	1¼	2, 4, 6	13.80
20 (a, b, c)	3	Max	1¼	2, 4, 6, 7½	12.95
20 (a¹)	3	3	1¼	4, 6, 7½	14.30
20 (a¹, b, c)	2¾	2¾	1⅛	4, 6, 7½	11.45
LONG RANGE LOADS					
10 (a, b)	2⅞	4¾	1⅝	4	15.50
12 (a¹, b, c)	2¾	3¾	1¼	BB, 2, 4, 5, 6, 7½, 8, 9	10.75
16 (a, b, c)	2¾	3¼	1⅛	4, 5, 6, 7½, 9	10.30
20 (a¹, b, c)	2¾	2¾	1	4, 5, 6, 7½, 9	9.45
28 (a, b)	2¾	2¼	¾	6, 7½, 8	9.55
410 (b)	2½	Max	½	6, 7½	7.55
410 (b)	3	Max	11/16	4, 5, 6, 7½, 8	8.95
FIELD LOADS					
12 (a, b, c)	2¾	3¼	1¼	7½, 8, 9	9.55
12 (a, b, c)	2¾	3¼	1⅛	4, 5, 6, 7½, 8, 9	9.20
12 (a, b, c)	2¾	3¼	1⅛	4, 5, 6, 7½, 8	9.20
12 (a)	3	4	1⅞	BB, 2, 4, 6	17.15
16 (a, b, c)	2¾	2¾	1⅛	4, 5, 6, 7½, 8	9.15
16 (a, b, c)	2¾	2¾	1⅛	4, 6, 7½, 8	9.15
20 (a, b, c)	2¾	2½	1	4, 5, 6, 7½, 8, 9	8.35
20 (a, b, c)	2¾	2½	1	4, 5, 6, 7½, 8, 9	8.35
TARGET LOADS					
12 (a)	2¾	3	1⅛	7½, 8	8.90
12 (a, b, c)	2¾	2¾	1⅛	7½, 8	8.10
20 (a, b, c)	2¾	2½	⅞	9	7.70
28 (a, c)	2¾	2	¾	9	9.30
410 (a, b, c)	2½	Max	½	9	7.55
SKEET & TRAP					
12 (a, b, c)	2¾	3	1⅛	7½, 8	7.95
12 (a, b, c)	2¾	2¾	1⅛	7½, 8, 9	7.95
20 (a, b, c)	2¾	2½	⅞	9	7.70
20 (a)	2¾	2½	⅞	9	8.35
28 (a)	2¾	2	¾	9	9.95
410 (a)	2½	Max	½	9	8.20
BUCKSHOT					
10 (c)	3½	Sup. Mag.	—	4 Buck—54 pellets	5.10
12 (a, b, c)	3 Mag.	4½	—	00 Buck—15 pellets	3.85
12 (a, b, c)	3 Mag.	4½	—	4 Buck—41 pellets	3.85
12 (b)	2¾ Mag.	4	—	1 Buck—20 pellets	3.40
12 (a, b, c)	2¾ Mag.	4	—	00 Buck—12 pellets	3.35
12 (a, b, c)	2¾	Max	—	00 Buck— 9 pellets	3.00
12 (a, b, c)	2¾	3¾	—	0 Buck—12 pellets	3.00
12 (a, b, c)	2¾	Max	—	1 Buck—16 pellets	3.00
12 (a, b, c)	2¾	Max	—	4 Buck—27 pellets	3.00
12 (a)	2¾ Mag.	—	—	000 Buck— 8 pellets	3.05
12 (a)	3 Mag.	—	—	000 Buck—10 pellets	3.90
16 (a, b, c)	2¾	3	—	1 Buck—12 pellets	3.00
20 (a, b, c)	2¾	Max	—	3 Buck—20 pellets	3.00
RIFLED SLUGS					
10	3½″	Mag.	1¾	Slug 5-pack	6.10
12 (a, b, c)	2¾	Max	1	Slug 5-pack	3.50
16 (a, b, c,)	2¾	Max	⅘	Slug	3.50
20 (a, b, c)	2¾	Max	⅝	Slug	3.20
20 (a)	2¾	Max	¾	Slug	3.20
410 (a, b, c)	2½	Max	⅕	Slug	3.00
STEEL SHOT LOADS					
10 (c)	3½	Max	1⅝	BB, 2	22.70
12 (c)	2¾	3¾	1⅛	1, 2, 4	13.50
12 (a, c)	2¾	Max	1¼	BB, 1, 2, 4	16.25
12 (b)	3	Max	1¼	1, 2, 4	17.90
12 (b)	2¾	Max	1⅛	1, 2, 4	14.80
20 (c)	3	3¼	1	4	12.95

W-W 410, 28 and 10-ga. Magnum shells available in paper cases only, as are their scatter and target loads; their Skeet and trap loads come in both plastic and paper.

R-P shells are all of plastic with Power Piston wads except; 12 ga. scatter loads have Post Wad: all 10 ga., 410-3″ and rifled slug loads have standard wad columns.

Federal magnum, range, buckshot, slug and all 410 loads are made in plastic only. Field loads are available in both paper and plastic.

¹—These loads available from W-W with Lubaloy shot at higher price.

The Complete Compact Catalog

This large catalog has been a GUN DIGEST staple since the first edition appeared in 1944. Things were different then, of course. We were embroiled in a world war and firearms weren't generally available. That first GUN DIGEST did, however, publish photos and prices—the Standard Grade Model 70 Winchester was $92.65, the Browning A-5 started at $68.65, and a Colt Single Action Army revolver was $38.50.

In the nearly 40 years hence, things have obviously changed, especially the prices; but GUN DIGEST still showcases everything that's new and available to the American shooter.

For this, our 37th edition, major changes have been added to make this compendium of guns and accessories more useful.

All handguns used in regular competitive events, be they autos, single shots or revolvers, are grouped together to make them easier to find.

Because of the ravenous interest in military-style auto rifles, we have created a separate section for them, rather than bury them with the sporters.

Along these same lines, we have created a grouping of Military and Police shotguns, regardless of action type.

To make it easier for the reader to find the latest specs and prices of his favorite guns, we've also added an index here for the various classifications.

Please remember—if you want more information on any of the products shown here, use the Directory of the Arms Trade, beginning on page 453, for contacting any of the manufacturers, importers or suppliers.

INDEX

Competition Handguns 280
Handguns—Autoloaders, Service & Sport 287
Handguns—Double Action Revolvers, Service & Sport 302
Handguns—Single Action Revolvers 312
Handguns—Miscellaneous 315
Centerfire Rifles—Military Style Autoloaders 317
Centerfire Rifles—Sporting Autoloaders 323
Centerfire Rifles—Lever & Slide Actions 323
Centerfire Rifles—Bolt Actions 327
Centerfire Rifles—Single Shots 339
Drillings, Combination Guns, Double Rifles 340
Rimfire Rifles—Autoloaders 344
Rimfire Rifles—Lever & Slide Actions 348
Rimfire Rifles—Bolt Actions & Single Shots 350
Competition Rifles—Centerfire & Rimfire. 355
Shotguns—Autoloaders 362
Shotguns—Slide Actions 367
Shotguns—Over-Unders. 371
Shotguns—Side-by-Sides 379
Shotguns—Bolt Actions 386
Shotguns—Single shots 387
Shotguns—Military & Police 389
Black Powder Single Shot Pistols—Flint & Percussion 392
Black Powder Revolvers. 397
Black Powder Muskets & Rifles. 401
Black Powder Shotguns 409
Air Guns—Handguns 411
Air Guns—Long Guns. 417

BERNARDELLI MODEL 100 PISTOL
Caliber: 22 LR only, 10-shot magazine.
Barrel: 5.9".
Weight: 37¾ oz. **Length:** 9" over-all.
Stocks: Checkered walnut with thumbrest.
Sights: Fixed front, rear adj. for w. and e.
Features: Target barrel weight included. Heavy sighting rib with interchangeable front sight. Accessories include cleaning equipment and assembly tools, case. Imported from Italy by Interarms.
Price: With case $460.00

Bernardelli Model 100

BERETTA MODEL 76 PISTOL
Caliber: 22 LR, 10-shot magazine.
Barrel: 6".
Weight: 33 ozs. (empty). **Length:** 8.8" over-all.
Stocks: Checkered plastic.
Sights: Interchangeable blade front (3 widths), rear is fully adj. for w. and e.
Features: Built-in, fixed counterweight, raised, matted slide rib, factory adjusted trigger pull from 3 lbs. 5 ozs. to 3 lbs. 12 ozs. Thumb safety. Blue-black finish. Wood grips available at extra cost. Introduced 1977. Imported from Italy by Beretta Arms Co.
Price: With plastic grips $370.00
Price: With wood grips $415.00

Beretta Model 76

BRITARMS 2000 MK.2 TARGET PISTOL
Caliber: 22 LR, 5-shot magazine.
Barrel: 5⅞".
Weight: 48 oz. **Length:** 11" over-all.
Stocks: Stippled walnut, anatomically designed wrap-around type with adjustable palm shelf.
Sights: Target front and rear. Interchangeable front blades of 3.2mm, 3.6mm or 4.0mm; fully adjustable rear.
Features: Offset anatomical and adjustable trigger, top loading magazine. Satin blue-black finish, satin hard chrome frame and trigger. Introduced 1982. Imported from England by Action Arms Ltd.
Price: $1,200.00

Britarms 2000 MK.2

COLT GOLD CUP NAT'L MATCH MK IV Series 70
Caliber: 45 ACP, 7-shot magazine.
Barrel: 5", with new design bushing.
Weight: 38½ oz. **Length:** 8⅜"
Stocks: Checkered walnut, gold plated medallion.
Sights: Ramp-style front, Colt-Elliason rear adj. for w. and e., sight radius 6¾".
Features: Arched or flat housing; wide, grooved trigger with adj. stop; ribbed-top slide, hand fitted, with improved ejection port.
Price: Colt Royal Blue $533.95

Colt Gold Cup

Domino Model SP-602

Domino O.P. 601 Match Pistol
Similar to SP 602 except has different match stocks with adj. palm, shelf, 22 Short only, weighs 40 oz., 5.6" bbl., has gas ports through top of barrel and slide to reduce recoil, slightly different trigger and sear mechanisms.
Price: $1,295.00

DOMINO MODEL SP-602 MATCH PISTOL
Caliber: 22 LR, 5 shot.
Barrel: 5.5".
Weight: 41 oz. **Length:** 11.02" over-all.
Stocks: Full target stocks; adjustable, one-piece. Left hand style avail.
Sights: Match. Blade front, open notch rear fully adj. for w. and e. Sight radius is 8.66".
Features: Line of sight is only ¹¹⁄₃₂" above centerline of bore; magazine is inserted from top; adjustable and removable trigger mechanism; single lever takedown. Full 5 year warranty. Imported from Italy by Mandall Shooting Supplies.
Price: $1,295.00

COMPETITION HANDGUNS

HAMMERLI STANDARD, MODELS 208 & 211
Caliber: 22 LR.
Barrel: 5.9″, 6-groove.
Weight: 37.6 oz. (45 oz. with extra heavy barrel weight). **Length:** 10″.
Stocks: Walnut. Adj. palm rest (208), 211 has thumbrest grip.
Sights: Match sights, fully adj. for w. and e. (click adj.). Interchangeable front and rear blades.
Features: Semi-automatic, recoil operated. 8-shot clip. Slide stop. Fully adj. trigger (2¼ lbs. and 3 lbs.). Extra barrel weight available. Imported from Switzerland by Mandall Shooting Supplies.
Price: Model 208, approx. **$1,295.00**
Price: Model 211 approx. **$1,295.00**
Price: Model 215, approx. **$913.05**

Hammerli Standard Models 208 & 211

Hammerli Model 150 Free Pistol

HAMMERLI MODEL 150 FREE PISTOL
Caliber: 22 LR. Single shot.
Barrel: 11.3″
Weight: 43 ozs. **Length:** 15.35″ over-all.
Stocks: Walnut with adjustable palm shelf.
Sights: Sight radius of 14.6″. Micro rear sight adj. for w. and e.
Features: Single shot Martini action. Cocking lever on left side of action with vertical operation. Set trigger adjustable for length and angle. Trigger pull weight adjustable between 5 and 100 grams. Guaranteed accuracy of .78″, 10 shots from machine rest. Imported from Switzerland by Mandall Shooting Supplies.
Price: About. **$1,500.00**
Price: With electric trigger (Model 152), about **$1,650.00**

Hammerli Model 230 Rapid Fire Pistol

HAMMERLI MODEL 230 RAPID FIRE PISTOL
Caliber: 22 Short.
Barrel: 6.3″, 6-groove.
Weight: 43.8 oz. **Length:** 11.6″.
Stocks: Walnut.
Sights: Match type sights. Sight radius 9.9″. Micro rear, click adj. Interchangeable front sight blade.
Features: Semi-automatic. Recoil-operated, 6-shot clip. Gas escape in front of chamber to eliminate muzzle jump. Fully adj. trigger from 5¼ oz. to 10½ oz. with three different lengths available. Designed for International 25 meter Silhouette Program. Imported from Switzerland by Mandall Shooting Supplies.
Price: Model 230-1 .... **$1,295.00**
Price: Model 232 .... **$1,395.00**

HAMMERLI MODEL 120-1 FREE PISTOL
Caliber: 22 LR.
Barrel: 9.9″.
Weight: 44 oz. **Length:** 14¾″ over-all.
Stocks: Contoured right-hand (only) thumbrest.
Sights: Fully adjustable rear, blade front. Choice of 14.56″ or 9.84″ sight radius.
Features: Trigger adjustable for single- or two-stage pull from 1.8 to 12 oz. Adjustable for length of pull. Guaranteed accuracy of .98″, 10 shots at 50 meters. Imported from Switzerland by Mandall Shooting Supplies.
Price: Model 120-1 .... **$995.00**
Price: Model 120-2 (same as above except has walnut target grips with adjustable palm-rest RH or LH) **$1,195.00**

> Consult our Directory pages for the location of firms mentioned.

High Standard X Series Custom 10-X

HIGH STANDARD X SERIES CUSTOM 10-X
Caliber: 22 LR, 10-shot magazine.
Barrel: 5½″ bull.
Weight: 44½ oz. **Length:** 9¾″ over-all.
Stocks: Checkered walnut.
Sights: Undercut ramp front; frame mounted fully adj. rear.
Features: Completely custom made and fitted for best performance. Fully adjustable target trigger, stippled front- and backstraps, slide lock, non-reflective blue finish. Comes with two extra magazines. Unique service policy. Each gun signed by maker.
Price: **$714.00**

COMPETITION HANDGUNS

HIGH STANDARD SUPERMATIC CITATION MILITARY
Caliber: 22 LR, 10-shot magazine.
Barrel: 5½" bull, 7¼" fluted.
Weight: 46 oz. **Length:** 9¾" (5½" bbl.)
Stocks: Checkered walnut with thumbrest.
Sights: Undercut ramp front; frame mounted rear, click adj.
Features: Adjustable trigger pull; over-travel trigger adjustment; double acting safety; rebounding firing pin; military style grip; stippled front- and back-straps; positive magazine latch.
Price: 5½" barrel $341.00
Price: 7¼" barrel $362.50

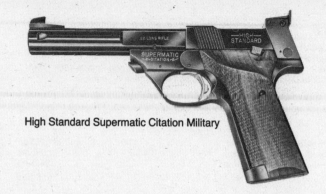

High Standard Supermatic Citation Military

HIGH STANDARD SUPERMATIC TROPHY MILITARY
Caliber: 22 LR, 10-shot magazine.
Barrel: 5½" bull, 7¼" fluted.
Weight: 44½ oz. **Length:** 9¾" (5½" bbl.)
Stocks: Checkered walnut with thumbrest.
Sights: Undercut ramp front; frame mounted rear, click adj.
Features: Grip duplicates feel of military 45; positive action mag. latch; front- and backstraps stippled. Trigger adj. for pull, over-travel
Price: 5½" barrel $362.50
Price: 7¼" barrel $385.00

HIGH STANDARD VICTOR
Caliber: 22 LR, 10-shot magazine.
Barrel: 5½".
Weight: 47 oz. **Length:** 9⅝" over-all.
Stocks: Checkered walnut with thumb rest.
Sights: Undercut ramp front, rib mounted click adj. rear.
Features: Vent. rib, interchangeable barrel, 2 - 2¼ lb. trigger pull, blue finish, back and front straps stippled.
Price: $415.00

M-S SAFARI ARMS MATCHMASTER PISTOL
Caliber: 45 ACP, 7-shot magazine.
Barrel: 5".
Weight: 45 oz. **Length:** 8.7" overall.
Stocks: Combat rubber or checkered walnut.
Sights: Combat adjustable.
Features: Beavertail grip safety, ambidextrous extended safety, extended slide release, combat hammer, threaded barrel bushing; throated, ported, tuned. Finishes: blue, Armaloy, Parkerize, electroless nickel. Also available in a lightweight version (30 oz.) and stainless steel. Made by M-S Safari Arms.
Price: $631.80

M-S Safari Arms Matchmaster Pistol

M-S Safari Arms Model 81NM Pistol
Similar to the Matchmaster except weighs 28 oz., is 8.2" over-all, has Ron Power match sights. Meets all requirements for National Match Service Pistols. Throated, ported, tuned and has threaded barrel bushing. Available in blue, Armaloy, Parkerize, stainless steel and electroless nickel. From M-S Safari Arms.
Price: $818.00

M-S Safari Arms Model 81 Pistol
Similar to Matchmaster except chambered for 45 or 38 Spec. mid-range wadcutter; available with fixed or adjustable walnut target match grips; Aristocrat rib with extended front sight is optional. Other features are the same. From M-S Safari Arms.
Price: $818.00
Price: Model 81L long slide $945.00

M-S Safari Arms Model 81 Pistol

M-S Safari Arms Model 81BP
Similar to the Matchmaster except designed for shooting the bowling pin matches. Extended slide gives 6" sight radius but also fast slide cycle time. Combat adjustable sights, magazine chute, plus same features as Matchmaster.
Price: $906.00
Price: BP Super model has the heavier slide extension with a shorter, lighter slide $995.00

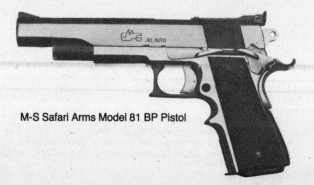

M-S Safari Arms Model 81 BP Pistol

CAUTION: PRICES CHANGE. CHECK AT GUNSHOP.

COMPETITION HANDGUNS

M-S Safari Arms Enforcer

M-S Safari Arms Enforcer Pistol
Shortened version of the Matchmaster. Has 3.8″ barrel, over-all length of 7.7″, and weighs 40 oz. (standard weight), 27 oz. in lightweight version. Other features are the same. From M-S Safari Arms.
Price: **$631.80**

M-S Safari Unlimited Silhouette

M-S SAFARI ARMS UNLIMITED SILHOUETTE PISTOL
Caliber: Any caliber with 308 head size or smaller.
Barrel: 14¹⁵⁄₁₆″ tapered
Weight: 72 oz. **Length:** 21½″ over-all.
Stocks: Fiberglass, custom painted to customer specs.
Sights: Open iron.
Features: Electronic trigger, bolt action single shot. Made by M-S Safari Arms.
Price: **$895.00**
Price: Ultimate model, heavy fluted barrel, shorter action **$895.00**

Navy Grand Prix Silhouette

NAVY GRAND PRIX SILHOUETTE PISTOL
Caliber: 44 Mag., 30-30, 7mm Spacial, 45-70; single shot.
Barrel: 13¾″.
Weight: 4 lbs.
Stocks: Walnut fore-end and thumb-rest grip.
Sights: Adjustable target-type.
Features: Uses rolling block action. Has adjustable aluminum barrel rib; matte blue finish. Made in U.S. by Navy Arms.
Price: **$375.00**

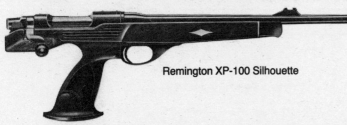

Remington XP-100 Silhouette

REMINGTON XP-100 SILHOUETTE PISTOL
Caliber: 7mm BR Remington, single-shot.
Barrel: 14¾″.
Weight: 4⅛ lbs. **Length:** 21¼″ over-all.
Stocks: Brown nylon, one piece, checkered grip.
Sights: None furnished. Drilled and tapped for scope mounts.
Features: Universal grip fits right or left hand; match-type grooved trigger, two-position thumb safety.
Price: **$359.95**

RUGER MARK II TARGET MODEL AUTO PISTOL
Caliber: 22 LR only, 10-shot magazine.
Barrel: 6⅞″ or 5½″ bull barrel (6-groove, 14″ twist).
Weight: 42 oz. with 6⅞″ bbl. **Length:** 10⅞″ (6⅞″ bbl.)
Stocks: Checkered hard rubber.
Sights: ⅛″ blade front, micro click rear, adjustable for w. and e. Sight radius 9⅜″ (with 6⅞″ bbl.).
Price: Blued, either barrel length............................... **$176.00**

Ruger Mark II Target Model

SEVILLE "SILHOUETTE" SINGLE ACTION
Caliber: 357, 41, 44, 45 Win. Mag.
Barrel: 10½″.
Weight: About 55 oz.
Stocks: Smooth walnut thumbrest, or Pachmayr.
Sights: Undercut Patridge-style front, adjustable rear.
Features: Available only in stainless steel. Six-shot cylinder. From United Sporting Arms of Arizona, Inc.
Price: **$375.00**

SIG/Hammerli P-240

SIG/HAMMERLI P-240 TARGET PISTOL
Caliber: 32 S&W Long.
Barrel: 6".
Weight: 34¼ oz. **Length:** 10" over-all.
Stocks: Walnut, target style, unfinished.
Sights: Match sights; ⅛" undercut front, ⅛" notch micro rear click adj. for w. and e.
Features: Semi-automatic, recoil operated; meets I.S.U. and N.R.A. specs for Center Fire Pistol competition; double pull trigger adj. from 2 lbs., 15 ozs. to 3 lbs., 9 ozs.; trigger stop. Comes with extra magazine, special screwdriver, carrying case. Imported from Switzerland by Mandall Shooting Supplies
Price: About. $1,500.00
Price: 22 cal. conversion unit. $750.00

SMITH & WESSON 22 AUTO PISTOL Model 41
Caliber: 22 LR, 10-shot clip.
Barrel: 7⅜", sight radius 9⁵⁄₁₆".
Weight: 43½ oz. **Length:** 12" over-all.
Stocks: Checkered walnut with thumbrest, usable with either hand.
Sights: Front, ⅛" Patridge undercut; micro click rear adj. for w. and e.
Features: ⅜" wide, grooved trigger with adj. stop; wgts. available to make pistol up to 59 oz.
Price: S&W Bright Blue, satin matted bbl. $348.00

Smith & Wesson Model 41

SMITH & WESSON 22 MATCH HEAVY BARREL M-41
Caliber: 22 LR, 10-shot clip.
Barrel: 5½" heavy. Sight radius, 8".
Weight: 44½ oz. **Length:** 9".
Stocks: Checkered walnut with modified thumbrest, usable with either hand.
Sights: ⅛" Patridge on ramp base. S&W micro click rear, adj. for w. and e.
Features: ⅜" wide, grooved trigger; adj. trigger stop.
Price: S&W Bright Blue, satin matted top area $348.00

SMITH & WESSON K-38 S.A. M-14
Caliber: 38 Spec., 6-shot.
Barrel: 6".
Weight: 38½ oz. **Length:** 11⅛" over-all.
Stocks: Checkered walnut, service type.
Sights: ⅛" Patridge front, micro click rear adj. for w. and e.
Features: Same as Model 14 except single action only, target hammer and trigger.
Price: 6" bbl. . . . . **Special Order only**

Smith & Wesson K-38 S.A. M-14

SMITH & WESSON 38 MASTER Model 52 AUTO
Caliber: 38 Special (for Mid-range W.C. with flush-seated bullet only). 5-shot magazine.
Barrel: 5".
Weight: 41 oz. with empty magazine. **Length:** 8⅝"
Stocks: Checkered walnut.
Sights: ⅛" Patridge front, S&W micro click rear adj. for w. and e.
Features: Top sighting surfaces matte finished. Locked breech, moving barrel system; checked for 10-ring groups at 50 yards. Coin-adj. sight screws. Dry firing permissible if manual safety on.
Price: S&W Bright Blue. $573.50

Smith & Wesson Model 52

SMITH & WESSON 1955 Model 25, 45 TARGET
Caliber: 45 ACP and 45 AR, 6 shot.
Barrel: 6" (heavy target type).
Weight: 45 oz. **Length:** 11⅞".
Stocks: Checkered walnut target.
Sights: ⅛" Patridge front, micro click rear, adjustable for w. and e.
Features: Tangs and trigger grooved; target trigger and hammer standard, checkered target hammer. Swing-out cylinder revolver. Price includes presentation case.
Price: Blued $431.00

COMPETITION HANDGUNS

TAURUS MODEL 86 MASTER REVOLVER
Caliber: 38 Spec., 6-shot.
Barrel: 6″ only.
Weight: 41 oz. **Length:** 11¼″ over-all.
Stocks: Over size target-type, checkered Brazilian walnut.
Sights: Patridge front, micro. click rear adj. for w. and e.
Features: Blue finish with non-reflective finish on barrel. Imported from Brazil by International Distributors.
Price: About **$232.00**
Price: Model 96 Scout Master, same except in 22 cal., about **$232.00**

Taurus Model 86 Master

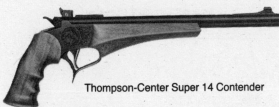

Thompson-Center Super 14 Contender

THOMPSON-CENTER SUPER 14 CONTENDER
Caliber: 222 Rem., 223 Rem., 7mm TCU, 30 Herrett, 357 Herrett, 30-30 Win., 35 Rem., 41 and 44 Mag., 45 Win. Mag. Single shot.
Barrel: 14″.
Weight: 45 oz. **Length:** 17¼″ over-all.
Stocks: Select walnut grip and fore-end.
Sights: Fully adjustable target-type.
Features: Break-open action with auto safety. Interchangeable barrels for both rimfire and centerfire calibers. Introduced 1978.
Price: **$275.00**
Price: Extra barrels **$120.00**

Unique D.E.S. 69

UNIQUE D.E.S. 69 TARGET PISTOL
Caliber: 22 LR.
Barrel: 5.91″.
Weight: Approx. 35 oz. **Length:** 10.63″ over-all.
Stocks: French walnut target style with thumbrest and adjustable shelf; hand checkered panels.
Sights: Ramp front, micro. adj. rear mounted on frame; 8.66″ sight radius.
Features: Meets U.I.T. standards. Comes in a fitted hard case with spare magazine, barrel weight, cleaning rod, tools, proof certificate, test target and two year guarantee. Fully adjustable trigger; dry firing safety device. Imported from France by Solersport.
Price: Right-hand... **$675.00**
Price: Left-hand **$705.00**

Unique D.E.S. VO 79

UNIQUE D.E.S. VO 79 TARGET PISTOL
Caliber: 22 Short.
Barrel: 5.85″, Four gas escape ports, one threaded with plug.
Weight: 44 oz.
Stocks: French walnut, target style with thumbrest and adj. palm shelf. Hand stippled.
Sights: Low, .12″ front, fully adj. rear.
Features: Meets all UIT standards; virtually recoil free. Four-way adj. trigger, dry-firing device, all aluminum frame. Cleaning rod, tools, extra magazine, proof certificate and fitted case. Imported from France by Solersport.
Price: Right hand... **$675.00**
Price: Left hand **$705.00**

Consult our Directory pages for the location of firms mentioned.

WALTHER FREE PISTOL
Caliber: 22 LR, single shot.
Barrel: 11.7″.
Weight: 48 ozs. **Length:** 17.2″ over-all.
Stocks: Walnut, special hand-fitting design.
Sights: Fully adjustable match sights.
Features: Special electronic trigger. Matte finish blue. Introduced 1980. Imported from Germany by Interarms.
Price: **$1,600.00**

WALTHER GSP MATCH PISTOL
Caliber: 22 LR, 32 S&W wadcutter (GSP-C), 5-shot.
Barrel: 5¾".
Weight: 44.8 oz. (22 LR), 49.4 oz. (32). **Length:** 11.8" over-all.
Stocks: Walnut, special hand-fitting design.
Sights: Fixed front, rear adj. for w. & e.
Features: Available with either 2.2 lb. (1000 gm) or 3 lb. (1360 gm) trigger. Spare mag., bbl. weight, tools supplied in Match Pistol Kit. Imported from Germany by Interarms.
Price: GSP.. $1,095.00
Price: GSP-C.. $1,225.00
Price: 22 LR conversion unit for GSP-C $695.00
Price: 22 Short conversion unit for GSP-C $745.00

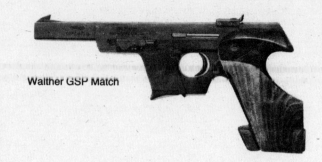

Walther GSP Match

Walther OSP Rapid-Fire Pistol
Similar to Model GSP except 22 Short only, stock has adj. free-style hand rest.
Price: $1,095.00

Consult our Directory pages for the location of firms mentioned.

WICHITA MK-40 SILHOUETTE PISTOL
Caliber: 7mm IHMSA, 308 Win. F.L. Other calibers available on special order. Single shot.
Barrel: 13", non-glare blue; .700" dia. muzzle.
Weight: 4½ lbs. **Length:** 19⅜" over-all.
Stocks: Metallic gray fiberthane glass.
Sights: Wichita Multi-Range sighting system.
Features: Aluminum receiver with steel insert locking lugs, measures 1.360" O.D.; 3 locking lug bolts, 3 gas ports; flat bolt handle; completely adjustable Wichita trigger. Introduced 1981. From Wichita Arms.
Price: $595.00

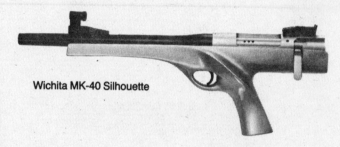

Wichita MK-40 Silhouette

WICHITA SILHOUETTE PISTOL
Caliber: 7mm IHMSA, 308, 7mm x 308. Other calibers available on special order. Single shot.
Barrel: 14¹⁵⁄₁₆" or 10¾".
Weight: 4½ lbs. **Length:** 21⅜" over-all.
Stocks: American walnut with oil finish, or fiberglass (yellow or black). Glass bedded.
Sights: Wichita Multi-Range sight system.
Features: Comes with either right- or left-hand action with right-hand grip. Fluted bolt, flat bolt handle. Action drilled and tapped for Burris scope mounts. Non-glare satin blue finish. Wichita adjustable trigger. Introduced 1979. From Wichita Arms.
Price: Center grip stock $695.00
Price: As above except with Rear Position Stock and target-type Lightpull trigger. (Not illus.) $758.00

Wichita Silhouette Pistol

WICHITA CLASSIC PISTOL
Caliber: Any, up to and including 308 Win.
Barrel: 11¼", octagon.
Weight: About 5 lbs.
Stock: Exhibition grade American black walnut. Checkered 20 lpi. Other woods available on special order.
Sights: Micro open sights standard. Receiver drilled and tapped for scope mount.
Features: Receiver and barrel octagonally shaped, finished in non-glare blue. Bolt has three locking lugs and three gas escape ports. Completely adjustable Wichita trigger. Introduced 1980. From Wichita Arms.
Price: $1,495.00
Price: With fitted case $1,995.00
Price: Engraved, in walnut presentation case $3,250.00

Wichita Classic Pistol

CAUTION: PRICES CHANGE. CHECK AT GUNSHOP.

American Arms TP-70

AMERICAN ARMS TP-70
Caliber: 22 LR, 25 ACP
Barrel: 2.6″
Weight: 12.6 oz. **Length:** 4.72″ over-all.
Stocks: Checkered, composition.
Sights: Open, fixed
Features: Double action, stainless steel. Exposed hammer. Manual and magazine safeties. From M & N Distributors.
Price: About **$199.95**

AMT 45 ACP HARDBALLER LONG SLIDE
Caliber: 45 ACP.
Barrel: 7″.
Length: 10½″ over-all.
Stocks: Checkered walnut.
Sights: Fully adjustable Micro rear sight.
Features: Slide and barrel are 2″ longer than the standard 45, giving less recoil, added velocity, longer sight radius. Has extended combat safety, serrated matte rib, loaded chamber indicator, wide adjustable trigger, custom fitted barrel bushing. From AMT.
Price: **$625.00**

AMT "BACKUP" AUTO PISTOL
Caliber: 22 LR, 8-shot magazine; 380 ACP, 5-shot magazine
Barrel: 2½″
Weight: 17 oz. **Length:** 5″ over-all.
Stocks: Smooth wood.
Sights: Fixed, open, recessed.
Features: Concealed hammer, blowback operation; manual and grip safeties. All stainless steel construction. Smallest domestically-produced pistol in 380. From AMT.
Price: 22 LR **$295.00**
Price: 380 ACP **$250.00**

AMT 45 ACP HARDBALLER
Caliber: 45 ACP.
Barrel: 5″
Weight: 39 oz. **Length:** 8½″ over-all.
Stocks: Checkered walnut.
Sights: Adjustable combat-type.
Features: Extended combat safety, serrated matte slide rib, loaded chamber indicator, long grip safety, beveled magazine well, grooved front and back straps, adjustable target trigger, custom-fitted barrel bushing. All stainless steel. From AMT.
Price: **$550.00**

Consult our Directory pages for the location of firms mentioned.

AMERICAN DERRINGER 25 AUTO
Caliber: 25 ACP or 250 Magnum; 7-shot magazine.
Barrel: 2.1″.
Weight: 15½ oz. **Length:** 4.4″ over-all.
Stocks: Smooth rosewood.
Sights: Fixed.
Features: Stainless or ordnance steel. Magazines have finger extension. Introduced 1982. From American Derringer Corp.
Price: Stainless, 25 ACP **$105.00**
Price: Blue, matte finish, 25 ACP **$89.95**
Price: Blue, high polish, 25 ACP **$97.50**
Price: 250 Mag., stainless **$137.50**
Price: 250 Mag., blued **$110.00**

American Derringer 25 Auto

Arminex Trifire Pistol

ARMINEX TRIFIRE AUTO PISTOL
Caliber: 9mm. Para. (9-shot), 38 Super. (9-shot), 45 ACP (7-shot).
Barrel: 5″.
Weight: 38 oz. **Length:** 8″ over-all.
Stocks: Contoured smooth walnut.
Sights: Interchangeable post front on rib, rear adjustable for windage and elevation.
Features: Single action. Slide mounted firing pin block safety. Specially contoured one-piece backstrap. Convertible by changing barrel, magazine, recoil spring. Introduced 1982. Made in U.S. by Arminex Ltd.
Price: Blue, electroless nickel or stainless steel, about **$400.00**

ASTRA CONSTABLE AUTO PISTOL
Caliber: 22 LR, 10-shot, 380 ACP, 7-shot.
Barrel: 3½″
Weight: 26 oz.
Stocks: Moulded plastic
Sights: Adj. rear.
Features: Double action, quick no-tool takedown, non-glare rib on slide. 380 available in blue or chrome finish. Imported from Spain by Interarms.
Price: Blue, 22 .... $370.00
Price: Chrome, 22 .... $410.00
Price: Blue, 380 .... $355.00
Price: Chrome, 380 .... $395.00

Astra Constable

BAUER AUTOMATIC PISTOL
Caliber: 25 ACP, 6-shot.
Barrel: 2⅛″.
Weight: 10 oz. **Length:** 4″ over-all.
Stocks: Plastic pearl or checkered walnut.
Sights: Recessed, fixed.
Features: Stainless steel construction. Has positive manual safety as well as magazine safety.
Price: Satin stainless steel, 25 ACP $136.40

Bauer Stainless Auto

BERNARDELLI MODEL 80 AUTO PISTOL
Caliber: 22 LR (10-shot); 380 ACP (7-shot).
Barrel: 3½″.
Weight: 26½ oz. **Length:** 6½″ over-all.
Stocks: Checkered plastic with thumbrest.
Sights: Ramp front, white outline rear adj. for w. & e
Features: Hammer block slide safety; loaded chamber indicator; dual recoil buffer springs; serrated trigger; inertia type firing pin. Imported from Italy by Interarms.
Price: Model 80 .... $260.00
Price: Model 90 (22 or 32, 6″ bbl.) $300.00

Bernardelli Model 80

BERETTA JETFIRE AUTO PISTOL
Caliber: 25 ACP
Barrel: 2½″.
Weight: 8 oz. **Length:** 4½″ over-all.
Stocks: Checkered black plastic.
Sights: Fixed.
Features: Thumb safety and half-cock safety; barrel hinged at front to pop up for single loading or cleaning. Made in U.S., available from J. L. Galef.
Price: Blue $189.95

Beretta Minx M2 Auto Pistol
Same basic gun as Jetfire except in 22 Short, weighs 10 oz. 6 shots.
Price: Blue $189.95

Beretta Minx Pistol

BERETTA MODEL 81/84 DA PISTOLS
Caliber: 32 ACP (12 shot magazine), 380 ACP (10 shot magazine).
Barrel: 3¾″
Weight: About 23 oz. **Length:** 6½″ over-all.
Stocks: Smooth black plastic (wood optional at extra cost).
Sights: Fixed front and rear.
Features: Double action, quick take-down, convenient magazine release. Introduced 1977. Imported from Italy by Beretta USA.
Price: M-81 (32 ACP) $408.00
Price: M-84 (380 ACP) $408.00
Price: Either model with wood grips $425.00
Price: M-82B, 32 ACP wood grips, 9-shot mag. $375.00
Price: M-85B, 380 ACP wood grips, 9-shot mag $375.00

Beretta Model 81

BERETTA MODEL 92 SB, 92 SB COMPACT
Caliber: 9mm Parabellum (15-shot magazine, 14-shot on Compact).
Barrel: 4.92″
Weight: 33½ oz. **Length:** 8.54″ over-all.
Stocks: Smooth black plastic; wood optional at extra cost.
Sights: Blade front, rear adj. for w.
Features: Double-action. Extractor acts as chamber loaded indicator, inertia firing pin. Finished in blue-black. Introduced 1977. Imported from Italy by Beretta USA.
Price: $600.00
Price: With wood grips $620.00

Beretta Model 92 SB Compact

BERETTA MODEL 70S PISTOL
Caliber: 22 LR, 380 ACP.
Barrel: 3.5″.
Weight: 23 oz. (Steel) **Length:** 6.5″ over-all.
Stocks: Checkered black plastic.
Sights: Fixed front and rear.
Features: Steel frame in 380, light alloy in 22 (wgt. 18 oz.). Safety lever blocks hammer. Slide lever indicates empty magazine. Magazine capacity is 8 rounds (22). 7 rounds in 380. Introduced 1977. Imported from Italy by Beretta USA.
Price: $274.00

Beretta Model 70S Pistol

BERSA MODEL 644 AUTO PISTOL
Caliber: 22 Long Rifle, 10-shot magazine.
Barrel: 3½″.
Weight: 26½ oz. **Length:** 6½″ over-all.
Stocks: Contoured black nylon.
Sights: Blade front, rear drift-adj. for windage.
Features: Has three safety devices; firing pin safety, hammer safety and magazine safety. Button release magazine with finger rest. Introduced 1980. Imported from Argentina by Interarms.
Price: $165.00
Price: Model 622, 4″ or 6″ bbl. $165.00
Price: Model 97, 380 cal. $205.00

Browning BDA-380 Pistol

BROWNING BDA-380 D/A AUTO PISTOL
Caliber: 380 ACP, 13-shot magazine.
Barrel: 3¹³⁄₁₆″.
Weight: 23 oz. **Length:** 6¾″ over-all.
Stocks: Smooth walnut with inset Browning medallion.
Sights: Blade front, rear drift-adj. for w.
Features: Combination safety and de-cocking lever will automatically lower a cocked hammer to half-cock and can be operated by right or left-hand shooters. Inertia firing pin. Introduced 1978. Imported from Italy by Browning.
Price: Blue. $399.95
Price: Nickel $439.95

Browning Hi-Power Auto

BROWNING HI-POWER 9mm AUTOMATIC PISTOL
Caliber: 9mm Parabellum (Luger), 13-shot magazine.
Barrel: 4²¹⁄₃₂″.
Weight: 32 oz. **Length:** 7¾″ over-all.
Stocks: Walnut, hand checkered.
Sights: ⅛″ blade front; rear screw-adj. for w. and e. Also available with fixed rear (drift-adj for w.).
Features: External hammer with half-cock and thumb safeties. A blow on the hammer cannot discharge a cartridge; cannot be fired with magazine removed. Fixed rear sight model available. Imported from Belgium by Browning.
Price: Fixed sight model $516.95
Price: 9mm with rear sight adj. for w. and e. $569.95
Price: Nickel, fixed sight $589.95
Price: Nickel, adj. sight $634.95
Price: Silver chrome, adj. sight $594.95

Browning Louis XVI Hi-Power

Browning Louis XVI Hi-Power 9mm Auto
Same as Browning Hi-Power 9mm Auto except: fully engraved, silver-gray frame and slide, gold plated trigger, finely checkered walnut grips, with deluxe walnut case
Price: With adj. sights and walnut case **$1,530.00**
Price: With fixed sights **$1,460.00**

High Power 88 Auto Pistol II
Similar to the standard Browning High Power except available only with fixed rear sight, military parkerized finish, black checkered polyamid grips. Comes with extra magazine. Introduced 1982. Imported from Belgium by Howco Distributors, Inc.
Price: With extra magazine **$499.50**

Browning Challenger II Pistol

BROWNING CHALLENGER II AUTO PISTOL
Caliber: 22 LR, 10-shot magazine.
Barrel: 6¾".
Weight: 38 oz. **Length:** 10⅞" over-all.
Stocks: Smooth impregnated hardwood.
Sights: ⅛" blade front on ramp, rear screw adj. for e., drift adj. for w.
Features: All steel, blue finish. Wedge locking system prevents action from loosening. Wide gold-plated trigger; action hold-open. Standard grade only. Made in U.S. From Browning.
Price: **$239.95**

Browning Challenger III Pistol

Browning Challenger III Auto Pistol
Similar to the Challenger II except has a 5½" heavy bull barrel, new lightweight alloy frame and new sights. Over-all length is 9½", weight is 34 oz. Introduced 1982.
Price: **$239.95**

Bushmaster Auto Pistol

BUSHMASTER AUTO PISTOL
Caliber: 223; 30-shot magazine.
Barrel: 11½".
Weight: 5¼ lbs. **Length:** 20½" over-all.
Stocks: Synthetic rotating grip swivel assembly.
Sights: Post front, adjustable open "y" rear
Features: Steel alloy upper receiver with welded barrel assembly, AK-47-type gas system, aluminum lower receiver, one-piece welded steel alloy bolt carrier assembly. From Bushmaster Firearms.
Price: **$439.95**

Charter Explorer S II Pistol

CHARTER EXPLORER S II PISTOL
Caliber: 22 LR, 8-shot magazine.
Barrel: 8".
Weight: 28 oz. **Length:** 15½" over-all.
Stocks: Serrated simulated walnut.
Sights: Blade front, open rear adj. for elevation.
Features: Action adapted from the semi-auto Explorer carbine. Introduced 1980. From Charter Arms.
Price: Satin finish **$99.00**
Price: With extra 6" or 10" bbl., extra magazine **$123.00**

CAUTION: PRICES CHANGE. CHECK AT GUNSHOP.

COLT SERVICE MODEL ACE
Caliber: 22 LR, 10-shot magazine.
Barrel: 5″
Weight: 42 oz. **Length:** 8⅜″ over-all.
Stocks: Checkered walnut.
Sights: Blade front, fully adjustable rear.
Features: The 22-cal. version of the Government Model auto. Based on the Service Model Ace last produced in 1945. Patented floating chamber. Original Ace Markings rolled on left side of slide. Introduced 1978.
Price: Blue only $433.50

Colt Service Model Ace

COLT GOV'T MODEL MK IV/SERIES 70
Caliber: 9mm, 38 Super, 45 ACP, 7-shot.
Barrel: 5″.
Weight: 40 oz. **Length:** 8⅜″ over-all.
Stocks: Sandblasted walnut panels.
Sights: Ramp front, fixed square notch rear.
Features: Grip and thumb safeties, grooved trigger. Accurizor barrel and bushing. Blue finish or nickel in 45 only.
Price: Blue, 45 cal.. . . . . $399.95
Price: Nickel, 45 cal. $426.95
Price: 9mm, blue only $406.95
Price: 38 Super, blue only $413.50
Price: 45, Satin nickel w/blue, Pachmayr grips. $425.50

Colt Conversion Unit
Permits the 45 and 38 Super Automatic pistols to use the economical 22 LR cartridge. No tools needed. Adjustable rear sight; 10-shot magazine. Designed to give recoil effect of the larger calibers. Not adaptable to Commander models. Blue finish.
Price: $234.50
Price: Fixed sight version $224.50

Colt Government Model

COLT COMBAT COMMANDER AUTO PISTOL
Caliber: 45 ACP, 7-shot; 38 Super Auto, 9-shot; 9mm Luger, 9-shot.
Barrel: 4¼″.
Weight: 36 oz. **Length:** 8″ over-all.
Stocks: Sandblasted walnut.
Sights: Fixed, glare-proofed blade front, square notch rear.
Features: Grooved trigger and hammer spur; arched housing; grip and thumb safeties.
Price: Blue, 9mm $406.95
Price: Blue, 45 . . . . $399.95
Price: Blue, 38 super. $399.95
Price: Satin nickel, 45 . . . . $419.50

Colt Combat Commander

Colt Lightweight Commander
Same as Commander except high strength aluminum alloy frame, wood panel grips, weight 27 oz. 45 ACP only.
Price: Blue. $395.50

DETONICS 45 PISTOL
Caliber: 45 ACP, 6-shot clip; 9mm Para., 8-shot clip.
Barrel: 3¼″ (2½″ of which is rifled).
Weight: 29 oz. (empty); MK VII is 26 oz. **Length:** 6¾″ over-all, 4½″ high.
Stocks: Checkered walnut.
Sights: Combat type, fixed; adj. sights avail.
Features: Has a self-adjusting cone barrel centering system, beveled magazine inlet, "full clip" indicator in base of magazine; standard 7-shot (or more) clip can be used in the 45. Throated barrel and polished feed ramp. Mark V, VI, VII available in 9mm. Introduced 1977. From Detonics.
Price: MK. I, matte blue, fixed sights $497.00
Price: MK. IV, polished blue, adj. sights. $539.00
Price: MK. V, matte stainless, fixed sights. $580.00
Price: MK. VI, polished stainless, adj sights $622.00
Price: MK. VII, matte stainless, no sights $622.00

Detonics Auto Pistol

EAGLE 357 MAGNUM PISTOL
Caliber: 357 Magnum, 9-shot clip.
Barrel: 6", 8", 10", 14" interchangeable.
Weight: 52 oz. **Length:** 10¼" over-all (6" bbl.).
Stocks: Wrap-around soft rubber.
Sights: Blade on ramp front, adjustable combat style rear.
Features: Rotating six lug bolt, ambidextrous safety, combat style trigger guard and adjustable trigger. Military epoxy finish. Announced 1982. Imported from Israel by Magnum Research Inc.
Price: 6" barrel **$590.00**
Price: 8" barrel **$595.00**
Price: 10" barrel **$600.00**
Price: 14" barrel **$605.00**
Price: Interchangeable barrels, from **$155.00**

ERMA KGP22 AUTO PISTOL
Caliber: 22 LR, 8-shot magazine.
Barrel: 4".
Weight: 29 oz. **Length:** 7¾" over-all.
Stocks: Checkered plastic.
Sights: Fixed.
Features: Has toggle action similar to original "Luger" pistol. Slide stays open after last shot. Imported from West Germany by Excam. Introduced 1978.
Price: **$250.00**

F.I.E. "SUPER TITAN II" PISTOLS
Caliber: 32 ACP, 380 ACP.
Barrel: 3⅞".
Weight: 28 oz. **Length:** 6¾" over-all.
Stocks: Smooth, polished walnut.
Sights: Adjustable.
Features: Blue finish only. 12 shot (32 ACP), 11 shot (360 ACP). Introduced 1981. From F.I.E. Corp. (32 cal. made in Italy, 380 made in U.S.).
Price: 32 ACP **$189.95**
Price: 380 ACP **$219.95**

F.I.E. "TITAN 25" PISTOL
Caliber: 25 ACP, 6-shot magazine.
Barrel: 2⁷⁄₁₆".
Weight: 12 oz. **Length:** 4⅝" over-all.
Stocks: Checkered nylon; checkered walnut optional.
Sights: Fixed.
Features: External hammer; fast simple takedown. Made in U.S.A. by F.I.E. Corp.
Price: Blued **$64.95**
Price: Chromed **$74.95**

> Consult our Directory pages for
> the location of firms mentioned.

F.I.E. TITAN II PISTOLS
Caliber: 32 ACP, 380 ACP, 6-shot magazine; 22 LR, 10-shot magazine.
Barrel: 3⅞".
Weight: 25¾ oz. **Length:** 6¾" over-all.
Stocks: Checkered nylon, thumbrest-type; checkered walnut optional.
Sights: Adjustable.
Features: Magazine disconnector, firing pin block. Standard slide safety. Available in blue or chrome. Introduced 1978. From F.I.E. Corp. (32 cal. made in Italy, 380 made in U.S.).
Price: 32, blue **$136.95**
Price: 32, chrome **$144.95**
Price: 380, blue **$169.95**
Price: 380, chrome **$179.95**
Price: 22 LR, blue **$129.95**

ERMA KGP32, KGP38 AUTO PISTOLS
Caliber: 32 ACP (6-shot), 380 ACP (5-shot).
Barrel: 4".
Weight: 22½ oz. **Length:** 7⅜" over-all.
Stocks: Checkered plastic. Wood optional.
Sights: Rear adjustable for windage.
Features: Toggle action similar to original "Luger" pistol. Slide stays open after last shot. Has magazine and sear disconnect safety systems. Imported from West Germany by Excam. Introduced 1978.
Price: Plastic grips **$250.00**

Erma KGP22 Pistol

ERMA-EXCAM RX 22 AUTO PISTOL
Caliber: 22 LR, 8-shot magazine.
Barrel: 3¼".
Weight: 21 oz. **Length:** 5.58" over-all.
Stocks: Plastic wrap-around.
Sights: Fixed
Features: Polished blue finish. Double action. Patented ignition safety system. Thumb safety. Assembled in U.S. Introduced 1980. From Excam.
Price: **$159.00**

F.I.E. "THE BEST" A27B PISTOL
Caliber: 25 ACP, 6-shot magazine.
Barrel: 2½".
Weight: 13 oz. **Length:** 4⅜" over-all.
Stocks: Checkered walnut.
Sights: Fixed.
Features: All steel construction. Has thumb and magazine safeties, exposed hammer. Blue finish only. Introduced 1978. Made in U.S. by F.I.E. Corp.
Price: **$154.95**

F.I.E. Titan II Pistol

FTL Auto Nine Pistol

FTL 22 AUTO NINE PISTOL
Caliber: 22 LR, 8-shot magazine.
Barrel: 2¼", 6-groove rifling.
Weight: 8¼ oz. **Length:** 4⅜" over-all.
Stocks: Checkered plastic.
Sights: U-notch in slide.
Features: Alloy frame, rest is ordnance steel. Has barrel support sleeve bush-
ing for better accuracy. Finish is matte hard chrome. Introduced 1978. Made
in U.S. From FTL Marketing.
Price: **$199.95**

Guardian-SS Stainless Pistol

GUARDIAN-SS AUTO PISTOL
Caliber: 380 ACP, 6-shot magazine.
Barrel: 3.25"
Weight: 20 oz. **Length:** 6" over-all.
Stocks: Checkered walnut.
Sights: Ramp front, combat-type rear adjustable for windage.
Features: Double action, made of stainless steel. Custom Guardian has nar-
row polished trigger, Pachmayr grips, blue slide, hand-fitted barrel, polished
feed ramp, funneled magazine well. Introduced 1982. From Michigan Arma-
ment, Inc.
Price: Standard model **$330.00**
Price: Custom Guardian **$395.00**

Heckler & Koch P9S Pistol

HECKLER & KOCH P9S DOUBLE ACTION AUTO
Caliber: 9mm Para., 9-shot magazine; 45 ACP, 7-shot magazine.
Barrel: 4".
Weight: 31 oz. **Length:** 7.6" over-all.
Stocks: Checkered black plastic.
Sights: Open combat type.
Features: Double action; polygonal rifling; sliding roller lock action with station-
ary barrel. Loaded chamber and cocking indicators; un-cocking lever relaxes
springs. Imported from West Germany by Heckler & Koch, Inc.
Price: P-9S Combat Model **$645.00**
Price: P-9S Target Model **$728.00**
Price: Walnut wrap-around competition grips **$135.00**
Price: Sports competition model with 4" and 5½" barrels, 2 slides . **$1,225.00**

HECKLER & KOCH HK-4 DOUBLE ACTION PISTOL
Caliber: 22 LR, 25 ACP, 32 ACP, 380 ACP, 8-shot magazine (7 in 380).
Barrel: 3¹¹⁄₃₂".
Weight: 16½ oz. **Length:** 6³⁄₁₆" over-all.
Stocks: Black checkered plastic.
Sights: Fixed blade front, rear notched drift-adj. for w.
Features: Gun comes with all parts to shoot above four calibers; polygonal
(hexagon) rifling; matte black finish. Imported from West Germany by Heck-
ler & Koch, Inc.
Price: Hk-4 380 with 22 conversion kit **$480.00**
Price: HK-4 in 380 only **$430.00**
Price: HK-4 in four cals. **$590.00**
Price: Conversion units 22, 25 or 32 cal., each **$101.00**

Heckler & Kock P7 (PSP) Pistol

HECKLER & KOCH P7 (PSP) AUTO PISTOL
Caliber: 9mm Parabellum, 8-shot magazine.
Barrel: 4.13".
Weight: 29 oz. **Length:** 6.54" over-all.
Stocks: Stippled black plastic.
Sights: Fixed, combat-type.
Features: Unique "squeeze cocker" in front strap cocks the action. Squared
combat-type trigger guard. Blue finish. Compact size. Imported from West
Germany by Heckler & Koch, Inc.
Price: **$599.00**
Price: Extra magazine **$26.00**

HECKLER & KOCH VP 70Z DOUBLE ACTION AUTO

Caliber: 9mm Para., 18-shot magazine.
Barrel: 4½".
Weight: 32½ oz. **Length:** 8" over-all.
Stocks: Black stippled plastic.
Sights: Ramp front, channeled slide rear.
Features: Recoil operated, double action. Only 4 moving parts. Double column
  magazine. Imported from West Germany by Heckler & Koch, Inc.
Price: $489.00
Price: Extra magazine... $27.00

Heckler & Koch VP 70S Pistol

Helwan Auto Pistol

HELWAN 9mm AUTO PISTOL

Caliber: 9mm Parabellum, 8-shot magazine.
Barrel: 4½".
Weight: 33 oz. **Length:** 8¼" over-all.
Stocks: Grooved black plastic.
Sights: Blade front, rear drift-adjustable for windage.
Features: Updated version of the Beretta Model 951. Made by the Maadi Co.
  for Engineering Industries of Egypt. Introduced to U.S. market 1982. Import-
  ed from Egypt by Steyr Daimler Puch of America.
Price: $345.00

High Standard Sharpshooter

HIGH STANDARD SHARPSHOOTER AUTO PISTOL

Caliber: 22 LR, 10-shot magazine.
Barrel: 5½".
Weight: 42 oz. **Length:** 10¼" over-all.
Stocks: Checkered walnut.
Sights: Ramp front, square notch rear adj. for w. & e.
Features: Military frame. Wide, scored trigger; new hammer-sear design. Slide
  lock, push-button take down.
Price: Blued $300.00

High Standard Survival Pack

Includes the High Standard Sharpshooter pistol finished in electroless nickel,
extra magazine, and a padded canvas carrying case with three interior pockets for carrying the extra magazine, knife, compass, etc. Introduced 1982.
Price: $374.50

HIGH STANDARD SPORT-KING AUTO PISTOL

Caliber: 22 LR, 10-shot.
Barrel: 4½" or 6¾".
Weight: 39 oz. (4½" bbl.). **Length:** 9" over-all (4½" bbl.).
Stocks: Checkered walnut.
Sights: Blade front, fixed rear.
Features: Takedown barrel. Blue only. Military frame.
Price: Either bbl. length, blue finish $259.50

INGRAM M-10, M-11 SEMI-AUTO PISTOLS

Caliber: 9mm, 45 ACP(M-10), 380 ACP (M-11)
Barrel: 5.75" (M-10), 5.06" (M-11).
Weight: 6¼ lbs. (M-10). **Length:** 10.5" over-all (M-10).
Stocks: High impact plastic.
Sights: Protected post front, aperture rear fixed for 100 meters.
Features: Semi-auto versions of the selective-fire submachine guns. 45 and
  380 have 16-round magazines, 9mm is 32 rounds. Made in U.S. by R.P.B.
  Industries.
Price: M-10, 9mm $280.00
Price: M-10, 45 ACP $280.00
Price: M-11, 380 ACP $280.00

Interdynamic KG-9 Pistol

INTERDYNAMIC KG-9 PISTOL

Caliber: 9mm Parabellum; 32 shot magazine.
Barrel: 5".
Weight: 46 oz. **Length:** 12½" over-all.
Stocks: High-impact plastic.
Sights: Blade front; fixed, open rear.
Features: Semi-auto only. Straight blowback action fires from an open bolt.
  Entire frame is high-impact black plastic. Introduced 1982. From F.I.E. Corp.
Price: About $425.00

CAUTION: PRICES CHANGE. CHECK AT GUNSHOP.

JENNINGS J-22 AUTO PISTOL
Caliber: 22 LR, 6-shot magazine.
Barrel: 2½".
Weight: 13 oz. **Length:** 4¹⁵⁄₁₆" over-all.
Stocks: Checkered walnut.
Sights: Fixed.
Features: Satin chrome finish. Introduced 1981. From Jennings Firearms.
Price: About **$99.95**

Jennings J-22 Pistol

IVER JOHNSON MODEL X300 PONY
Caliber: 380 ACP, 6-shot magazine.
Barrel: 3".
Weight: 20 oz. **Length:** 6" over-all.
Stocks: Checkered walnut.
Sights: Blade front, rear adj. for w.
Features: Loaded chamber indicator, all steel construction. Inertia firing pin. Thumb safety locks hammer. No magazine safety. Lanyard ring. Made in U.S., available from Iver Johnson's.
Price: Blue **$279.73**
Price: Military (matte finish) **$279.73**

IVER JOHNSON PP22 AUTO PISTOL
Caliber: 22 LR, 25 ACP.
Barrel: 2.85".
Weight: 14½ oz. **Length:** 5.39" over-all.
Stocks: Black checkered plastic.
Sights: Fixed.
Features: Double action; 7-shot magazine. Introduced 1981. From Iver Johnson's.
Price: Either caliber **$183.24**

IVER JOHNSON PP30 "SUPER ENFORCER" PISTOL
Caliber: 30 U.S. Carbine.
Barrel: 9".
Weight: 4 lbs. **Length:** 17" over-all.
Stocks: American walnut.
Sights: Blade front; click adjustable peep rear.
Features: Shortened version of the M1 Carbine. Uses 15 or 30-shot magazines. From Iver Johnson's.
Price: Blue finish **$299.50**

Llama Omni D.A. Pistol

LLAMA OMNI DOUBLE-ACTION AUTO
Caliber: 9mm (13-shot), 45 ACP (7-shot).
Barrel: 4¼".
Weight: 40 oz. **Length:** 9mm—8", 45–7¾" over-all.
Stocks: Checkered plastic.
Sights: Ramped blade front, rear adjustable for windage and elevation (45), drift-adjustable for windage (9mm).
Features: New DA pistol has ball-bearing action, double sear bars, articulated firing pin, buttressed locking lug and low-friction rifling. Introduced 1982. Imported from Spain by Stoeger Industries.
Price: 9mm or 45 ACP **$599.95**

Llama Large Frame Auto

Llama Small Frame Auto

LLAMA LARGE FRAME AUTO PISTOLS
Caliber: 38 Super, 45 ACP.
Barrel: 5".
Weight: 30 oz. **Length:** 8½" over-all.
Stocks: Checkered walnut.
Sights: Fixed.
Features: Grip and manual safeties, ventilated rib. Engraved, chrome engraved or gold damascened finish available at extra cost. Imported from Spain by Stoeger Industries.
Price: Blue **$366.95**
Price: Satin chrome, 45 only **$424.95**
Price: Blue, engraved, 45 only **$433.95**
Price: Satin chrome, engraved, 45 only **$466.95**

LLAMA SMALL FRAME AUTO PISTOLS
Caliber: 22 LR, 32 ACP and 380.
Barrel: 3¹¹⁄₁₆".
Weight: 23 oz. **Length:** 6½" over-all.
Stocks: Checkered plastic, thumb rest.
Sights: Fixed front, adj. notch rear.
Features: Ventilated rib, manual and grip safeties. Model XV is 22 LR, Model XA is 32 ACP, and Model IIIA is 380. Models XA and IIIA have loaded indicator; IIIA is locked breech. Imported from Spain by Stoeger Industries.
Price: Blue **$283.95**
Price: Satin chrome, 22 & 380 only **$349.95**
Price: Blue, engraved, 380 only **$358.95**
Price: Satin chrome, engraved, 380 . . . . **$366.95**

MAB MODEL P-15 AUTO PISTOL
Caliber: 9mm Para., 15-shot magazine.
Barrel: 4½″.
Weight: 41 oz. **Length:** 8⅛″ over-all.
Stocks: Checkered black plastic.
Sights: Fixed.
Features: Rotating barrel-type locking system; thumb safety, magazine disconnector. Blue finish. Introduced 1982. Imported from France by Howco Distr., Inc.
Price: $375.00

LLAMA 9mm LARGE FRAME AUTO PISTOL
Caliber: 9mm Para.
Barrel: 5″.
Weight: 38 oz. **Length:** 8½″ over-all.
Stocks: Moulded plastic.
Sights: Fixed front, adj. rear.
Features: Also available with engraved, chrome engraved or gold damascened finish at extra cost. Imported from Spain by Stoeger Industries.
Price: Blue only $366.95

MKE AUTO PISTOL
Caliber: 380 ACP; 7-shot magazine.
Barrel: 4″.
Weight: 23 oz. **Length:** 6½″ over-all.
Stocks: Hard rubber.
Sights: Fixed front, rear adjustable for windage.
Features: Double action with exposed hammer; chamber loaded indicator. Imported from Turkey by Mandall Shooting Supplies.
Price: $350.00

Turkish MKE Pistol

N.A.M. 45 WIN MAG+
Caliber: 9mm, Win. Mag. (7-shot magazine.).
Barrel: 5⅜″.
Weight: 51 oz. **Length:** 9¼″ over-all.
Stocks: Checkered rubber combat-type.
Sights: Ramped blade front, rear adjustable for windage and elevation.
Features: Stainless steel slide and frame, non-corrosive alloy steel for other parts. Polished feed ramp, throated barrel. Precision-fitted barrel bushing, hand-honed action. **Announced** 1982. From North American Mfg. Corp.
Price: 45 Win. Mag. with 9mm Win. Mag. conversion unit $595.95
Price: Conversion units for 45 ACP, 9mm P., 38 Super, 9mm Steyr, 38 Spec. W.C. & R.N., 30 Mauser, 30 Luger $99.95

Consult our Directory pages for
the location of firms mentioned.

O.D.I. VIKING D.A. AUTO PISTOL
Caliber: 9mm Para. or 45 ACP.
Barrel: 5″.
Weight: 39 oz.
Stocks: Smooth teakwood standard; other materials available.
Sights: Fixed. Blade front, notched rear.
Features: Made entirely of stainless steel, brushed satin, natural finish. Features the Seecamp double action system. Spur-type hammer. Magazine holds 9 rounds in 9mm, 7 rounds in 45 ACP. Made in U.S.A. From O.D.I.
Price: $489.95

O.D.I. Viking D.A. Pistol

O.D.I. Viking Combat Model D.A. Pistol
Same construction and design as Viking model except has 4¼″ barrel, ring-type hammer, and weighs 36 oz. Made in U.S.A. by O.D.I.
Price: $489.95

RAVEN P-25 AUTO PISTOL
Caliber: 25 ACP, 6-shot magazine.
Barrel: 2⁷⁄₁₆″.
Weight: 15 oz. **Length:** 4¾″ over-all.
Stocks: Smooth walnut.
Sights: Ramped front, fixed rear.
Features: Available in blue, nickel or chrome finish. Made in U.S., available from EMF Co.
Price: $59.95

RG 26 AUTO PISTOL
Caliber: 25 ACP, 6-shot magazine.
Barrel: 2½″.
Weight: 12 oz. **Length:** 4¾″ over-all.
Stocks: Checkered plastic.
Sights: Fixed.
Features: Blue finish. Thumb safety. Imported by RG Industries.
Price: $69.95
Price: Nickel $74.95

Raven P-25 Pistol

Ruger Mark II Auto

RUGER MARK II STANDARD AUTO PISTOL
Caliber: 22 LR, 10-shot magazine.
Barrel: 4¾" or 6".
Weight: 36 oz. (4¾" bbl.). **Length:** 8¾ (4¾" bbl.).
Stocks: Checkered hard rubber.
Sights: Fixed, wide blade front, square notch rear adj. for w.
Features: Updated design of the original Standard Auto. Has new bolt hold-open device, 10-shot magazine, magazine catch, safety, trigger and new receiver contours. Introduced 1982.
Price: Blued **$147.50**

SIG P-210-1 Pistol

SIG P-210-1 AUTO PISTOL
Caliber: 7.65mm or 9mm Para., 8-shot magazine.
Barrel: 4¾".
Weight: 31¾ oz. (9mm) **Length:** 8½" over-all.
Stocks: Checkered walnut.
Sights: Blade front, rear adjustable for windage.
Features: Lanyard loop; polished finish. Conversion unit for 22 LR available. Imported from Switzerland by Mandall Shooting Supplies and Waidmanns Guns International.
Price: P-210-1, about. **$1,500.00**
Price: 22 Cal. Conversion unit. **$750.00**

SIG-Sauer P-220 Pistol

SIG P-210-6 AUTO PISTOL
Caliber: 9mm Para., 8-shot magazine.
Barrel: 4¾".
Weight: 37 oz. **Length:** 8½" over-all.
Stocks: Checkered black plastic.
Sights: Blade front, micro. adj. rear for w. & e.
Features: Adjustable trigger stop; ribbed front stap; sandblasted finish. Conversion unit for 22 LR consists of barrel, recoil spring, slide and magazine. Imported from Switzerland by Mandall Shooting Supplies and Waidmanns Guns International.
Price: P-210-6, about. **$1,500.00**
Price: 22 Cal. Conversion unit. **$750.00**

SIG-SAUER P-220 D.A. AUTO PISTOL
Caliber: 9mm, 38 Super; 45 ACP. (9-shot in 9mm and 38 Super, 7 in 45).
Barrel: 4⅜".
Weight: 28¼ oz. (9mm). **Length:** 7¾" over-all.
Stocks: Checkered walnut.
Sights: Blade front, drift adj. rear for w.
Features: Double action. De-cocking lever permits lowering hammer onto locked firing pin. Squared combat-type trigger guard. Slide stays open after last shot. Imported from West Germany by Interarms.
Price: **$650.00**

SIG-Sauer P-225 Pistol

SIG-SAUER P-225 D.A. AUTO PISTOL
Caliber: 9mm Parabellum, 8-shot magazine.
Barrel: 3.8".
Weight: 26 oz. **Length:** 7⁷⁄₃₂" over-all.
Stocks: Checkered black plastic.
Sights: Blade front, rear adjustable for windage.
Features: Double action; decocking lever permits lowering hammer onto locked firing pin. Squared combat-type trigger guard. Shortened, lightened version of P-220. Imported from West Germany by Interarms.
Price: **$675.00**

HANDGUNS—AUTOLOADERS, SERVICE & SPORT

SIG-Sauer P-230 D.A. Pistol

SILE-SEECAMP II STAINLESS DA AUTO
Caliber: 25 ACP, 8-shot magazine.
Barrel: 2", integral with frame.
Weight: About 10 oz. **Length:** 4⅛" over-all.
Stocks: Black plastic.
Sights: Smooth, no-snag, contoured slide and barrel top.
Features: Aircraft quality 17-4 PH stainless steel. Inertia operated firing pin. Hammer fired double action only. Hammer automatically follows slide down to safety rest position after each shot—no manual safety needed. Magazine safety disconnector. Introduced 1980. From Sile Distributors.
Price: **$199.95**

SILE-BENELLI B76 DA AUTO PISTOL
Caliber: 9mm Para., 8-shot magazine.
Barrel: 4¼", 6-groove. Chrome-lined bore.
Weight: 34 oz. (empty). **Length:** 8¹⁄₁₆" over-all.
Stocks: Walnut with cut checkering and high gloss finish.
Sights: Blade front with white face, rear adjustable for windage with white bars for increased visibility.
Features: Fixed barrel, locked breech. Exposed hammer can be locked in non-firing mode in either single or double action. Stainless steel inertia firing pin and loaded chamber indicator. All external parts blued, internal parts hard-chrome plated. All steel construction. Introduced 1979. From Sile Dist.
Price: **$349.95**

SMITH & WESSON MODEL 59 DOUBLE ACTION
Caliber: 9mm Luger, 14-shot clip.
Barrel: 4".
Weight: 27½ oz., without clip. **Length:** 7⁷⁄₁₆" over-all.
Stocks: Checkered high impact moulded nylon.
Sights: ⅛" serrated ramp front, square notch rear adj. for w.
Features: Double action automatic. Furnished with two magazines. Blue finish.
Price: Blued **$371.50**
Price: Nickel **$405.50**

SMITH & WESSON 9mm MODEL 39 AUTO PISTOL
Caliber: 9mm Luger, 8-shot clip.
Barrel: 4".
Weight: 26½ oz., without magazine. **Length:** 7⁷⁄₁₆" over-all.
Stocks: Checkered walnut.
Sights: ⅛" serrated ramp front, adjustable rear.
Features: Magazine disconnector, positive firing pin lock and hammer-release safety; alloy frame with lanyard loop; locked-breech, short-recoil double action; slide locks open on last shot.
Price: Blued **$310.00**
Price: Nickeled **$341.50**

SMITH & WESSON MODEL 439 DOUBLE ACTION
Caliber: 9mm Luger, 8-shot clip.
Barrel: 4".
Weight: 27 oz. **Length:** 7⁷⁄₁₆" over-all.
Stocks: Checkered walnut.
Sights: ⅛" square serrated ramp front, square notch rear is fully adj. for w. & e.
Features: Rear sight has protective shields on both sides of the sight blade. Frame is alloy. New trigger actuated firing pin lock in addition to the regular rotating safety. Magazine disconnector. New extractor design. Comes with two magazines. Introduced 1980.
Price: Blue **$352.50**
Price: Nickel **$381.00**

SIG-SAUER P-230 D.A. AUTO PISTOL
Caliber: 380 ACP (7 shot).
Barrel: 3¾".
Weight: 16 oz. **Length:** 6½" over-all.
Stocks: One piece black plastic.
Sights: Blade front, rear adj. for w.
Features: Double action. Same basic design as P-220. Blowback operation, stationary barrel. Introduced 1977. Imported from West Germany by Interarms.
Price: **$575.00**

Sile-Benelli Model B76 Pistol

Smith & Wesson Model 59

Smith & Wesson Model 439

SMITH & WESSON MODEL 459 DOUBLE ACTION
Caliber: 9mm Luger, 14-shot clip.
Barrel: 4".
Weight: 28 oz. **Length:** 7⁷⁄₁₆" over-all.
Stocks: Checkered high-impact nylon.
Sights: ⅛" square serrated ramp front, square notch rear is fully adj. for w. & e.
Features: Alloy frame. Rear sight has protective shields on both sides of blade. New trigger actuated firing pin lock in addition to the regular safety. Magazine disconnector; new extractor design. Comes with two magazines. Introduced 1980.
Price: Blue **$417.00**
Price: Nickel **$447.50**

CAUTION: PRICES CHANGE. CHECK AT GUNSHOP.

STAR MODEL PD AUTO PISTOL
Caliber: 45 ACP, 7-shot magazine.
Barrel: 3.94″.
Weight: 28 oz. **Length:** 7⁷⁄₁₆″ over-all.
Stocks: Checkered walnut.
Sights: Ramp front, fully adjustable rear.
Features: Rear sight milled into slide; thumb safety; grooved non-slip front strap; nylon recoil buffer; inertia firing pin; no grip or magazine safeties. Imported from Spain by Interarms.
Price: Blue. **$410.00**

Star Model PD Pistol

STAR BM, BKM AUTO PISTOLS
Caliber: 9mm Para., 8-shot magazine.
Barrel: 3.9″.
Weight: 25 oz.
Stocks: Checkered walnut.
Sights: Fixed.
Features: Blue or chrome finish. Magazine and manual safeties, external hammer. Imported from Spain by Interarms.
Price: Blue, BM and BKM **$340.00**
Price: Chrome, BM only **$365.00**

Star Model BM, BKM Pistol

STERLING MODEL 300
Caliber: 25 ACP, 6-shot.
Barrel: 2½″.
Weight: 13 oz. **Length:** 4½″ over-all.
Stocks: Black Cycolac.
Sights: Fixed.
Features: All steel construction.
Price: Blued **$112.95**
Price: Stainless Steel **$134.95**

STERLING MODEL 302
Caliber: 22 LR, 6-shot.
Barrel: 2½″.
Weight: 13 oz. **Length:** 4½″ over-all.
Stocks: Black Cycolac.
Sights: Fixed.
Features: All steel construction.
Price: Blue. **$112.95**
Price: Stainless steel. **$134.95**

Sterling Model 400 MK. II D.A.

STERLING MODEL 400 MK II DOUBLE ACTION
Caliber: 32, 380 ACP, 7-shot.
Barrel: 3¾″.
Weight: 18 oz. **Length:** 6½″ over-all.
Stocks: Checkered walnut.
Sights: Low profile, adj.
Features: All steel construction. Double action.
Price: Blued **$225.95**
Price: Stainless steel. **$260.95**

Sterling Model 300 Pistol

Steyr GB D.A. Pistol

STEYR GB DOUBLE ACTION AUTO PISTOL
Caliber: 9mm Parabellum; 18-shot magazine.
Barrel: 5.39″.
Weight: 33 oz. **Length:** 8.4″ over-all.
Stocks: Checkered walnut.
Sights: Post front, fixed rear.
Features: Gas-operated, delayed blowback action. Measures 5.7″ high, 1.3″ wide. Introduced 1981. Imported by Steyr Daimler Puch.
Price: **$595.00**

STOEGER LUGER 22 AUTO PISTOL

Caliber: 22 LR, 10-shot.
Barrel: 4½".
Weight: 30 oz. **Length:** 8⅞" over-all.
Stocks: Checkered walnut.
Sights: Fixed.
Features: Action remains open after last shot and as magazine is removed. Grip and balance identical to P-08.
Price: $182.95
Price: Kit includes extra clip, charger, holster $224.95
Price: Combo (includes extra clip, holster, charger and carrying case) $234.95

Stoeger Luger 22 Auto

TARGA MODELS GT32, GT380 AUTO PISTOLS

Caliber: 32 ACP or 380 ACP, 6-shot magazine.
Barrel: 4⅞".
Weight: 26 oz. **Length:** 7⅜" over-all.
Stocks: Checkered nylon with thumb rest. Walnut optional.
Sights: Fixed blade front; rear drift-adj. for w.
Features: Chrome or blue finish; magazine, thumb, and firing pin safeties; external hammer; safety lever take-down. Imported from Italy by Excam, Inc.
Price: 32 cal., blue $133.00
Price: 32 cal., chrome $143.00
Price: 380 cal., blue $159.00
Price: 380 cal., chrome $167.00
Price: 380 cal., chrome, engraved, wooden grips $214.00
Price: 380 cal., blue, engraved, wooden grips $205.00

TARGA GT380XE GT32XE PISTOLS

Caliber: 32 ACP or 380 ACP, 12-shot magazine.
Barrel: 3.88".
Weight: 28 oz. **Length:** 7.38" over-all.
Stocks: Smooth hardwood.
Sights: Adj. for windage.
Features: Blue or satin nickel. Ordnance steel. Magazine disconnector, firing pin and thumb safeties. Introduced 1980. Imported by Excam.
Price: 32 cal., blue $189.00
Price: 380 cal., blue $205.00

TARGA MODEL GT27 AUTO PISTOL

Caliber: 25 ACP, 6-shot magazine.
Barrel: 2⁷/₁₆".
Weight: 12 oz. **Length:** 4⅝" over-all.
Stocks: Checkered nylon.
Sights: Fixed.
Features: Safety lever take-down; external hammer with half-cock. Assembled in U.S. by Excam, Inc.
Price: Blue $58.50
Price: Chrome $64.00

Taurus PT-92 Auto Pistol

TAURUS MODEL PT92 AUTO PISTOL

Caliber: 9mm P., 15-shot magazine.
Barrel: 4.92".
Weight: 34 oz. **Length:** 8.54" over-all.
Stocks: Black plastic.
Sights: Fixed notch rear.
Features: Double action, exposed hammer, chamber loaded indicator. Inertia firing pin. Blue finish.
Price: $363.00
Price: With Brazilian Bolonga wood grips $391.00

THOMPSON 1911A1 AUTOMATIC PISTOL

Caliber: 45 ACP, 7-shot magazine.
Barrel: 5".
Weight: 39 oz. **Length:** 8½" over-all.
Stocks: Checkered plastic with medallion.
Sights: Blade front, rear adj. for windage.
Features: Same specs as 1911A1 military guns—parts interchangeable. Frame and slide blued; each radius has non-glare finish. Made in U.S. by Auto-Ordnance Corp.
Price: Approximately $324.95

Thompson 1911A1 Auto Pistol

Universal Enforcer Model 3000

UNIVERSAL ENFORCER MODEL 3000 AUTO

Caliber: 30 M1 Carbine, 5-shot magazine.
Barrel: 10¼" with 12-groove rifling.
Weight: 4½ lbs. **Length:** 17¾" over-all.
Stocks: American walnut with handguard
Sights: Gold bead ramp front. Peep rear.
Features: Accepts 15 or 30-shot magazines. 4½-6 lb. trigger pull.
Price: Blue finish $279.00
Price: Nickel plated finish (Model 3010N) $329.00
Price: Gold plated finish (Model 3015G) $379.00
Price: Black or olive Teflon-S finish (3020TRB, 3025TCO) $336.00

CAUTION: PRICES CHANGE. CHECK AT GUNSHOP.

VEGA STAINLESS 45 AUTO

Caliber: 45 ACP, 7-shot.
Barrel: 5".
Weight: 40 oz. **Length:** 8⅜" over-all.
Stocks: Checkered walnut, diamond pattern.
Sights: Choice of fixed high combat-type or adjustable rear.
Features: Made completely of stainless steel and matches the original 1911A1 Colt almost exactly. Has both grip and thumb safeties. Slide and frame flats are polished, rest sand blasted. From Pacific International Merchandising Corp.
Price: With fixed sights, about **$349.95**
Price: With Accro-Adjustable sights, about **$379.95**

WALTHER PP AUTO PISTOL

Caliber: 22 LR, 8-shot; 32 ACP, 380 ACP, 7-shot.
Barrel: 3.86".
Weight: 23½ oz. **Length:** 6.7" over-all.
Stocks: Checkered plastic.
Sights: Fixed, white markings.
Features: Double action, manual safety blocks firing pin and drops hammer, chamber loaded indicator on 32 and 380, extra finger rest magazine provided. Imported from Germany by Interarms.
Price: (22 LR) **$615.00**
Price: (32 and 380) **$575.00**
Price: Engraved models . . . . **On Request**

Walther American PPK/S Auto Pistol

Similar to Walther PP except made entirely in the United States. Has 3.27" barrel with 6.1" length over-all.
Price: 380 ACP only **$330.00**

WALTHER P-38 AUTO PISTOL

Caliber: 22 LR, 30 Luger or 9mm Luger, 8-shot.
Barrel: 4¹⁵/₁₆" (9mm and 30), 5¹/₁₆" (22 LR).
Weight: 28 oz. **Length:** 8½" over-all.
Stocks: Checkered plastic.
Sights: Fixed.
Features: Double action, safety blocks firing pin and drops hammer, chamber loaded indicator. Matte finish standard, polished blue, engraving and/or plating available. Imported from Germany by Interarms.
Price: 22 LR **$795.00**
Price: 9mm or 30 Luger **$725.00**
Price: Engraved models . . . . **On Request**

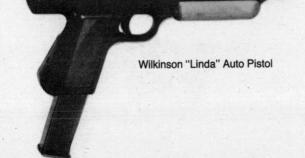

Wilkinson "Linda" Auto Pistol

VIKING SEMI-AUTO MINI PISTOL

Caliber: 9mm Para., 36-shot magazine.
Barrel: 7½".
Weight: About 5½ lbs. **Length:** 14" over-all.
Stocks: Retractable wire. Pistol grip and fore-end of high impact plastic.
Sights: Post front, L-type flip rear for 100 and 200 meters.
Features: Blow-back action, manual and grip safeties. Finished in matte olive green color Introduced in 1982. From W.S.I.
Price: Semi-auto only **$640.00**

Walther PP Auto Pistol

Walther P-38 Auto Pistol

Walther P-38IV Auto Pistol

Same as P-38 except has longer barrel (4½"); over-all length is 8", weight is 29 oz. Sights are non-adjustable. Introduced 1977. Imported by Interarms.
Price: **$695.00**

Walther P-5 Auto Pistol

Latest Walther design that uses the basic P-38 double-action mechanism. Caliber 9mm Luger, barrel length 3½"; weight 28 oz., over-all length 7".
Price: **$925.00**

WILDEY AUTO PISTOL

Caliber: 9mm Win. Mag. (14 shots), 45 Win. Mag. (8 shots).
Barrel: 5", 6", 7", 8", or 10"; vent. rib.
Weight: About 51 oz. (6" bbl.).
Stock: Select hardwood, target style optional.
Sights: Adjustable for windage and elevation; red or white inserts optional.
Features: Patented gas operation; selective single or autoloading capability; 5-lug rotary bolt; fixed barrel; stainless steel construction; double-action trigger mechanism. Has positive hammer block and magazine safety. From Wildey Firearms.
Price: Either caliber, all barrel lengths **$599.95**
Price: Extra magazine **$22.00**

WILKINSON "LINDA" PISTOL

Caliber: 9mm Para., 31-shot magazine.
Barrel: 8⁵/₁₆".
Weight: 4 lbs., 13 oz. **Length:** 12¼" over-all.
Stocks: Checkered black plastic pistol grip, maple fore-end.
Sights: Protected blade front, Williams adjustable rear.
Features: Fires from closed bolt. Semi-auto only. Straight blowback action. Cross-bolt safety. Removable barrel. From Wilkinson Arms.
Price: **$434.18**

ARMINIUS REVOLVERS
Caliber: 38 Special, 357 Mag., 32 S&W (6-shot); 22 Magnum, 22 LR (8-shot).
Barrel: 4″ (38 Spec., 357 Mag., 32 S&W, 22 LR); 6″ (38 Spec., 22 LR/22 Mag., 357 Mag.); 8⅜″ (357 Mag.).
Weight: 35 oz. (6″ bbl.). **Length:** 11″ (6″ bbl. 38).
Stocks: Checkered plastic; walnut optional for $14.95.
Sights: Ramp front, fixed rear on standard models, w. & e. adj. on target models.
Features: Thumb-release, swing-out cylinder. Ventilated rib, solid frame, swing-out cylinder. Interchangeable 22 Mag. cylinder available with 22 cal. versions. Also available in 357 Mag. 3″, 4″, 6″ barrel, adj. sights. Imported from West Germany by F.I.E. Corp.
Price: .... $112.95 to $229.95

> Consult our Directory pages for
> the location of firms mentioned.

CHARTER ARMS BULLDOG
Caliber: 44 Special, 5-shot.
Barrel: 3″.
Weight: 19 oz. **Length:** 7¾″ over-all.
Stocks: Checkered walnut, Bulldog.
Sights: Patridge-type front, square-notch rear.
Features: Wide trigger and hammer; beryllium copper firing pin.
Price: Service Blue $200.00
Price: Stainless steel....................................... $260.00

Charter Arms Bulldog Tracker
Similar to the standard Bulldog except has adjustable rear sight, 4″ or 6″ bull barrel, ramp front sight, square butt checkered walnut grips. Available in blue finish only.
Price: $210.00

CHARTER TARGET BULLDOG
Caliber: 357 Mag., 44 Spec., 5-shot.
Barrel: 4″.
Weight: 20½ oz. **Length:** 8½″ over-all.
Stocks: Checkered American walnut, square butt.
Sights: Full-length ramp front, fully adj., milled channel, square notch rear.
Features: Blue finish only. Enclosed ejector rod, full length ejection of fired cases.
Price: 357 Mag. 4″ $215.50
Price: 44 Spec., 4″... $225.00

CHARTER ARMS POLICE BULLDOG
Caliber: 38 Special, 6-shot.
Barrel: 2″, 4″, 4″ straight taper bull.
Weight: 21 oz. **Length:** 9″ over-all.
Stocks: Hand checkered American walnut; square butt.
Sights: Patridge-type ramp front, notched rear.
Features: Accepts both regular and high velocity ammunition; enclosed ejector rod; full length ejection of fired cases.
Price: Blue only $185.00

CHARTER ARMS UNDERCOVER REVOLVER
Caliber: 38 Special, 5 shot; 32 S & W Long, 6 shot.
Barrel: 2″, 3″.
Weight: 16 oz. (2″). **Length:** 6¼″ (2″).
Stocks: Smooth walnut or checkered square butt.
Sights: Patridge-type ramp front, notched rear.
Features: Wide trigger and hammer spur. Steel frame.
Price: Polished Blue $190.00
Price: 32 S & W Long, blue, 2″ $190.00
Price: Stainless, 38 Spec., 2″................................. $245.00

ASTRA 357 MAGNUM REVOLVER
Caliber: 357 Magnum, 6-shot.
Barrel: 3″, 4″, 6″, 8½″.
Weight: 40 oz. (6″-bbl.). **Length:** 11¼″ (6″ bbl.).
Stocks: Checkered walnut.
Sights: Fixed front, rear adj. for w. and e.
Features: Swing-out cylinder with countersunk chambers, floating firing pin. Target-type hammer and trigger. Imported from Spain by Interarms.
Price: 3″, 4″, 6″ $375.00
Price: 8½″ $390.00

Astra Model 41, 44, 45 Double Action Revolver
Similar to the 357 Mag. except chambered for the 41 Mag., 44 Mag. or 45 Colt. Barrel length of 6″ only, giving over-all length of 11⅜″. Weight is 2¾ lbs. Introduced 1980.
Price: $450.00
Price: 8½″ bbl. (44 Mag. only) $465.00

Charter Arms Bulldog

Charter Arms Target Bulldog

Charter Arms Police Bulldog

Charter Arms Undercover

Charter Arms Pathfinder

Same as Undercover but in 22 LR caliber, and has 3″ or 6″ bbl. Fitted with adjustable rear sight, ramp front. Weight 18½ oz.

Price: 22 LR, blue, 3″ $200.00
Price: 22 LR, square butt, 6″ $215.00
Price: Stainless, 22 LR, 3″ $250.00

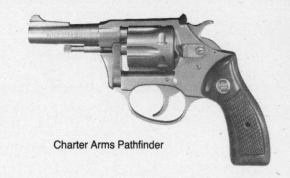

Charter Arms Pathfinder

COLT PYTHON REVOLVER

Caliber: 357 Magnum (handles all 38 Spec.), 6 shot.
Barrel: 2½″, 4″, 6″ or 8″, with ventilated rib.
Weight: 38 oz. (4″ bbl.). **Length:** 9¼″ (4″ bbl.).
Stocks: Checkered walnut, target type.
Sights: ⅛″ ramp front, adj. notch rear.
Features: Ventilated rib; grooved, crisp trigger; swing-out cylinder; target hammer.

Price: Colt Blue, 2½″ $514.50
Price: 4″ $525.50
Price: 6″ $533.50
Price: 8″ $544.95
Price: Nickeled, 4″ $557.95
Price: 6″ $559.95
Price: 8″ $571.50

Colt Python 357

COLT TROOPER MK III REVOLVER

Caliber: 22 LR, 22 WMR, 38 Spec., 357 Magnum, 6-shot.
Barrel: 4″, 6″ or 8″.
Weight: 39 oz. (4″ bbl.), 42 oz., (6″ bbl.). **Length:** 9½″ (4″ bbl.).
Stocks: Checkered walnut, square butt.
Sights: Fixed ramp front with ⅛″ blade, adj. notch rear.

Price: Blued with target hammer and target stocks, 4″, 357 .... $323.95
Price: Nickeled 38/357 Mag. 4″ $343.50
Price: 22 LR, blue, 4″ $323.95
Price: 22 LR, blue, 8″ $330.50
Price: 22 WMR, nickel, 8″ $355.95
Price: 357, blue, 8″ $330.50
Price: 357, Coltguard finish, 8″ $354.95
Price: 22 LR, Coltguard finish, 4″ $342.50

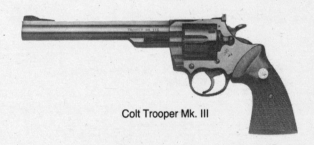

Colt Trooper Mk. III

Colt Lawman/Trooper Mark V Revolvers

Modified versions of the Lawman MK III and Trooper MK III revolvers. Internal lockwork has been redesigned to reduce trigger pull in double action and give faster lock time. Grip has been redesigned for more comfort. MK V Trooper has adjustable rear sight, and red insert front sight, vent rib 4″, 6″, 8″ barrel; MK V Lawman has 2″ or 4″ barrel, fixed sight and solid rib. Introduced 1982.

Price: Lawman, 2″, blue $316.50
Price: As above, Coltguard $335.50
Price: Lawman, 4″, nickel $336.50
Price: Trooper, 4″, blue $372.95
Price: As above, nickel $395.50
Price: As above, 6″, blue $373.95
Price: As above, 8″, Coltguard $408.50

Colt Detective Special

COLT DETECTIVE SPECIAL

Caliber: 38 Special, 6 shot.
Barrel: 2″.
Weight: 22 oz. **Length:** 6⅝″ over-all.
Stocks: Full, checkered walnut, round butt.
Sights: Fixed, ramp front, square notch rear.
Features: Glare-proofed sights, smooth trigger. Nickel finish, hammer shroud available as options.

Price: Blue $335.95
Price: Nickel $369.95

COLT LAWMAN MK III REVOLVER

Caliber: 357 Mag., 6 shot.
Barrel: 2″ or 4″, heavy.
Weight: 33 oz. **Length:** 9⅜″.
Stocks: Checkered walnut, service style.
Sights: Fixed, glare-proofed ramp front, square notch rear.

Price: Blued $274.95
Price: Nickel $292.50
Price: With Coltguard finish $291.50

Colt Lawman Mk. III

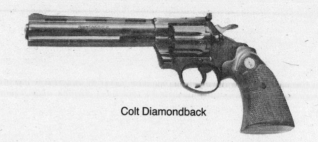

Colt Diamondback

COLT DIAMONDBACK REVOLVER
Caliber: 22 LR or 38 Special, 6 shot.
Barrel: 4" or 6" with ventilated rib.
Weight: 24 oz. (2½" bbl.), 28½ oz. (4" bbl.). **Length:** 9" (4" bbl.)
Stocks: Checkered walnut, target type, square butt.
Sights: Ramp front, adj. notch rear.
Features: Ventilated rib; grooved, crisp trigger; swing out cylinder; wide hammer spur.
Price: Blue, 4" bbl. 38 Spec. or 22 .... $396.50
Price: Blue, 6" bbl., 22 or 38 .... $405.50

F.I.E. MODEL N38 "Titan Tiger" REVOLVER
Caliber: 38 Special.
Barrel: 2" or 4".
Weight: 27 oz. **Length:** 6¼" over-all. (2" bbl.)
Stocks: Checkered plastic, Bulldog style. Walnut optional ($15.95).
Sights: Fixed.
Features: Thumb-release swing-out cylinder, one stroke ejection. Made in U.S.A. by F.I.E. Corp.
Price: Blued, 4" $129.95
Price: Chrome, 4" bbl. $144.95

HARRINGTON & RICHARDSON M686 REVOLVER
Caliber: 22 LR/22 WMRF, 6-shot.
Barrel: 4½", 5½", 7½", 10" or 12".
Weight: 31 oz. (4½"), 41 oz. (12").
Stocks: Two piece, smooth walnut-finished hardwood.
Sights: Western type blade front, adj. rear.
Features: Blue barrel and cylinder, "antique" color case-hardened frame, ejector tube and trigger. Comes with extra cylinder.
Price: 4½", 5½", 7½" bbl. $155.00
Price: 10" or 12" bbl. $175.00

Harrington & Richardson Model 649 Revolver
Similar to model 686 except has 5½" or 7½" barrel, one piece wrap around walnut-finished hardwood grips, western-type blade front sight, adjustable rear. Loads and ejects from side. Weighs 32 oz.
Price: $135.00
Price: Model 650—as above except nickel finish, 5½" only $145.00

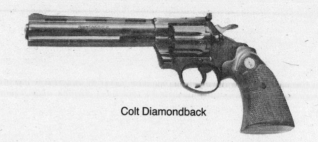

H&R Model 649

HARRINGTON & RICHARDSON M622 REVOLVER
Caliber: 22 S, L or LR, 22 WMR, 6 shot.
Barrel: 2½", 4", round bbl.
Weight: 20 oz. (2½" bbl.).
Stocks: Checkered black Cycolac.
Sights: Fixed, blade front, square notch rear.
Features: Solid steel, Bantamweight frame; patented safety rim cylinder; non-glare finish on frame; coil springs.
Price: Blued, 2½", 4" bbl. $89.00
Price: Model 632 (32 cal.). $89.00
Price: Model 642, 22 WMR $89.00

H&R Model 622

HARRINGTON & RICHARDSON M732
Caliber: 32 S&W or 32 S&W Long, 6 shot.
Barrel: 2½" or 4" round barrel.
Weight: 23½ oz. (2½" bbl.), 26 oz. (4" bbl.).
Stocks: Checkered, black Cycolac or walnut.
Sights: Blade front; adjustable rear on 4" model.
Features: Swing-out cylinder with auto. extractor return. Pat. safety rim cylinder. Grooved trigger.
Price: Blued, 2½" or 4" bbl. $110.00
Price: Nickel, 2½" or 4" bbl. (Model 733) $120.00
Price: Blued, 2½", walnut grips $124.50
Price: Nickled, 2½", walnut grip. $134.50

H&R Model 732

HARRINGTON & RICHARDSON M929
Caliber: 22 S, L or LR, 9 shot.
Barrel: 2½", 4" or 6".
Weight: 26 oz. (4" bbl.).
Stocks: Checkered, black Cycolac or walnut.
Sights: Blade front; adjustable rear on 4" and 6" models.
Features: Swing-out cylinder with auto. extractor return. Pat. safety rim cylinder. Grooved trigger. Round-grip frame.
Price: Blued, 2½", 4" or 6" bbl. $110.00
Price: Nickel (Model 930), 2½" or 4" bbl. $120.00
Price: Blued, 2½", walnut grips $124.50
Price: Nickel, 2½", walnut grips (Model 930) $134.50

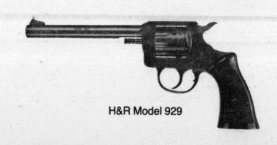

H&R Model 929

CAUTION: PRICES CHANGE. CHECK AT GUNSHOP.

HARRINGTON & RICHARDSON M949
Caliber: 22 S, L or LR, 9 shot.
Barrel: 5½" round with ejector rod.
Weight: 31 oz.
Stocks: One-piece, smooth frontier style wrap-around, walnut-finished hardwood.
Sights: Western-type blade front, rear adj. for w.
Features: Contoured loading gate; wide hammer spur; single and double action. Western type ejector-housing.
Price: H&R Crown Luster Blue $110.00
Price: Nickel (Model 950) $120.00

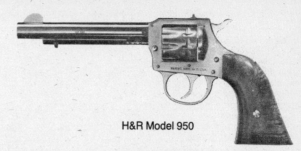

H&R Model 950

H&R SPORTSMAN MODEL 999 REVOLVER
Caliber: 22 S, L or LR, 9 shot.
Barrel: 4", 6" top-break (16" twist), integral fluted vent. rib.
Weight: 34 oz. (6"). **Length:** 10½".
Stocks: Checkered walnut-finished hardwood.
Sights: Front adjustable for elevation, rear for windage.
Features: Simultaneous automatic ejection, trigger guard extension. H&R Crown Lustre Blue.
Price: Blued, 4". $185.00
Price: Blued, 6" engraved. $395.00

H&R Model 999

HARRINGTON & RICHARDSON MODELS 604, 904, 905
Caliber: 22 LR, 9-shot (M904, 905), 22 WMR, 6-shot (M604)
Barrel: 4" (M904 only), 6" target bull.
Weight: 32 oz.
Stocks: Smooth walnut.
Sights: Blade front, fully adjustable "Wind-Elv" rear.
Features: Swing-out cylinder design with coil spring construction. Single stroke ejection. Target-style bull barrel has raised solid rib giving a 7¼" sight radius.
Price: M604 or 904 .... $149.50
Price: M905, 4", H&R "Hard-Guard" finish $155.00

H&R Model 905

Harrington & Richardson Models 603, 903
Similar to 604-904 except has flat-sided barrel.
Price: $149.50

HIGH STANDARD SENTINEL
Caliber: 22 LR and 22 Mag. with extra cylinder.
Barrel: 2" or 4".
Weight: 22 oz. (2" barrel). **Length:** 7⅛" over-all (2" barrel).
Stocks: Checkered walnut.
Sights: ⅛" serrated ramp front, square notched rear.
Features: Double action, dual swing-out cylinders; steel frame; blue finish; combat-style grips. From High Standard.
Price: Model 9390 (fixed sights) $230.00
Price: Model 9392 (adj. sights) $250.00

High Standard Sentinel

HIGH STANDARD DOUBLE-NINE CONVERTIBLE
Caliber: 22 S, L or LR, 9-shot (22 Mag. with extra cylinder).
Barrel: 5½", dummy ejector rod fitted.
Weight: 32 oz. **Length:** 11" over-all.
Stocks: Smooth walnut, frontier style.
Sights: Fixed blade front, rear adj. for w. & e.
Features: Double-action, Western styling, rebounding hammer with auto safety block; spring-loaded ejection. Swing-out cylinder.
Price: Blued $250.00

High Standard Camp Gun

High Standard Long Horn Convertible
Same as the Double-Nine convertible but with a 9½" bbl., adjustable sights, blued only. Weight: 38 oz.
Price: With adjustable sights $255.00

HIGH STANDARD CAMP GUN
Caliber: 22 LR and 22 Mag., 9-shot.
Barrel: 6".
Weight: 28 oz. **Length:** 11⅛" over-all.
Stocks: Checkered walnut.
Sights: ⅛" serrated ramp front, rear adjustable for windage and elevation.
Features: Double-action; comes with two cylinders; blue finish; combat-style wrap around grips. From High Standard.
Price: Model 9393 .... $250.00

HIGH STANDARD CRUSADER COMMEMORATIVE REVOLVER
Caliber: 44 Mag., 45 Long Colt.
Barrel: 6½", 8⅜".
Weight: 48 oz. (6½").
Stocks: Smooth Zebrawood.
Sights: Blade front on ramp, fully adj. rear.
Features: Unique gear-segment mechanism. Smooth, light double-action trigger pull. First production devoted to the commemorative; later guns will be of plain, standard configuration.
Price: .... **N.A.**

LLAMA COMANCHE REVOLVERS
Caliber: 22 LR, 38 Special, 357 Mag.
Barrel: 6", 4" (except 22 LR, 6" only).
Weight: 22 LR 24 oz., 38 Special 31 oz. **Length:** 9¼" (4" bbl.).
Stocks: Checkered walnut.
Sights: Fixed blade front, rear adj. for w. & e.
Features: Ventilated rib, wide spur hammer. Chrome plating, engraved finishes available. Imported from Spain by Stoeger Industries.
Price: Blue finish **$308.95**
Price: Satin chrome, 357 only **$391.95**

Llama Super Comanche Revolver
Similar to the Comanche except; large frame, 357 or 44 Mag., 4", 6" or 8½" barrel only; 6-shot cylinder; smooth, extra wide trigger; wide spur hammer; over-size walnut, target-style grips. Weight is 3 lbs., 2 ozs., over-all length is 11¾". Blue finish only.
Price: 44 Mag. **$481.95**
Price: 357 Mag. **$364.95**

RG 14 REVOLVER
Caliber: 22 LR, 6-shot.
Barrel: 1¾" or 3".
Weight: 15 oz. (1¾" bbl.) **Length:** 5½" over-all.
Stocks: Checkered plastic.
Sights: Fixed.
Features: Blue finish. Cylinder swings out when pin is removed. Imported by RG Industries.
Price: **$56.00**
Price: Model 23 (central ejector, no pin to remove) **$72.95**

> Consult our Directory pages for
> the location of firms mentioned.

RG 31 REVOLVER
Caliber: 32 S & W (6-shot), 38 Spec. (5-shot).
Barrel: 2".
Weight: 24 oz. **Length:** 6¾" over-all.
Stocks: Checkered plastic.
Sights: Fixed.
Features: Cylinder swings out when pin is removed. Blue finish. Imported by RG Industries.
Price: 32 or 38 cal. **$92.95**

RG 40 REVOLVER
Caliber: 38 Spec., 6-shot.
Barrel: 2".
Weight: 29 oz. **Length:** 7¼" over-all.
Stocks: Checkered plastic.
Sights: Fixed.
Features: Swing-out cylinder with spring ejector. Imported by RG Industries.
Price: Plastic grips **$119.95**
Price: Wood grips **$124.95**

HIGH STANDARD HIGH SIERRA DOUBLE ACTION
Caliber: 22 LR and 22 LR/22 Mag., 9-shot.
Barrel: 7" octagonal.
Weight: 36 oz. **Length:** 12½" over-all.
Stocks: Smooth walnut.
Sights: Blade front, adj. rear.
Features: Gold plated backstrap and trigger guard. Swing-out cylinder.
Price: Adj. sights, dual cyl. **$255.00**

Llama Comanche

Llama Super Comanche

RG MODEL 74 REVOLVER
Caliber: 22 LR, 6-shot
Barrel: 3".
Weight: 21½ oz. **Length:** 7¾" over-all.
Stocks: Checkered plastic.
Sights: Fixed.
Features: Swing-out cylinder with spring ejector. Introduced 1980. Imported from Germany by RG Industries.
Price: Blue, plastic grips **$94.95**
Price: Blue, wood grips **$104.95**

RG MODEL 39 REVOLVER
Caliber: 32 S&W, 38 Spec., 6-shot.
Barrel: 2".
Weight: 21 oz. **Length:** 7" over-all.
Stocks: Checkered plastic.
Sights: Fixed.
Features: Swing-out cylinder with spring ejector. Introduced 1980. Imported from Germany by RG Industries.
Price: Blue only **$124.95**

RG 38S REVOLVER
Caliber: 38 Special, 6-shot.
Barrel: 3" and 4".
Weight: 3", 31 oz.; 4", 34 oz. **Length:** 3", 8½", 4", 9¼".
Stocks: Checkered plastic.
Sights: Fixed front, rear adj. for w.
Features: Swing out cylinder with spring ejector. Imported from Germany by RG Industries.
Price: Plastic grips **$124.95**
Price: Wood grips **$139.95**

CAUTION: PRICES CHANGE. CHECK AT GUNSHOP.

Rossi Model 68

ROSSI MODELS 68, 69 & 70 DA REVOLVERS
Caliber: 22 LR (M 70), 32 S & W (M 69), 38 Spec. (M 68).
Barrel: 3".
Weight: 22 oz.
Stocks: Checkered wood.
Sights: Ramp front, low profile adj. rear.
Features: All-steel frame. Thumb latch operated swing-out cylinder. Introduced 1978. Imported from Brazil by Interarms.
Price: 22, 32, or 38, blue $155.00
Price: As above, 38 Spec. only with 4" bbl. as M 31 .... $155.00
Price: Model 51 (6" bbl., 22 cal.) $165.00
Price: M68, M69, M70 in nickel $160.00

Ruger Security-Six

RUGER SECURITY-SIX Model 117
Caliber: 357 Mag. (also fires 38 Spec.), 6-shot.
Barrel: 2¾", 4" or 6", or 4" heavy barrel.
Weight: 33½ oz. (4" bbl.) **Length:** 9¼" (4" bbl.) over-all.
Stocks: Hand checkered American walnut, semi-target style.
Sights: Patridge-type front on ramp, white outline rear adj. for w. and e.
Features: Music wire coil springs throughout. Hardened steel construction. Integral ejector rod shroud and sighting rib. Can be disassembled using only a coin.
Price: 2¾", 6" and 4" heavy barrel $235.00
Price: 4" HB, 6" with Big Grip stocks............................. $253.50

Ruger Police Service-Six

RUGER POLICE SERVICE-SIX Models 107, 108, 109
Caliber: 357 (Model 107), 38 Spec. (Model 108), 9mm (Model 109), 6-shot.
Barrel: 2¾" or 4" and 4" heavy barrel.
Weight: 33½ oz. (4" bbl.). **Length:** 9¼" (4 bbl.) over-all.
Stocks: Checkered American walnut, semi-target style.
Sights: Patridge-type front, square notch rear.
Features: Solid frame with barrel, rib and ejector rod housing combined in one unit. All steel construction Field strips without tools.
Price: Model 107 (357) $207.00
Price: Model 108 (38) $207.00
Price: Model 109 (9mm).. $225.00
Price: Mod. 707 (357), Stainless, 4" & 4" HB $228.00
Price: Mod. 708 (38), Stainless, 4" & 4" HB..................... $228.00

RUGER SPEED-SIX Models 207, 208, 209
Caliber: 357 (Model 207), 38 Spec. (Model 208), 9mm P (Model 209) 6-shot.
Barrel: 2¾" or 4".
Weight: 31 oz. (2¾" bbl.). **Length:** 7¾" over-all (2¾" bbl.).
Stocks: Round butt design, diamond pattern checkered American walnut.
Sights: Patridge-type front, square-notch rear.
Features: Same basic mechanism as Security-Six. Hammer without spur available on special order. All steel construction. Music wire coil springs used throughout.
Price: Model 207 (357 Mag.) $211.00
Price: Model 208 (38 Spec. only) $211.00
Price: Model 209 (9mm P) $229.00
Price: Mod. 737 (357), Stainless................................. $234.50
Price: Mod. 738 (38), Stainless................................. $234.50
Price: Model 739 (9mm P), Stainless............................ $248.50

RUGER STAINLESS SECURITY-SIX Model 717
Caliber: 357 Mag. (also fires 38 Spec.), 6-shot.
Barrel: 2¾", 4" or 6".
Weight: 33 oz. (4 bbl.). **Length:** 9¼" (4" bbl.) over-all.
Stocks: Hand checkered American walnut.
Sights: Patridge-type front, fully adj. rear.
Features: All metal parts except sights made of stainless steel. Sights are black alloy for maximum visibility. Same mechanism and features found in regular Security-Six.
Price: 2¾", 6" and 4" HB....................................... $257.50
Price: 4" HB, 6" with Big Grip stocks............................ $276.00

Ruger Redhawk

RUGER REDHAWK
Caliber: 44 Rem. Mag., 6-shot.
Barrel: 7½".
Weight: About 3¼ lbs. **Length:** 13" over-all.
Stocks: Square butt. American walnut.
Sights: Patridge-type front, rear adj. for w. & e.
Features: Stainless steel, brushed satin finish. Has a 9½" sight radius. Introduced 1979.
Price: $350.00

SMITH & WESSON M&P Model 10 REVOLVER
Caliber: 38 Special, 6 shot.
Barrel: 2″, 4″, 5″ or 6″.
Weight: 30½ oz. (4″ bbl.). **Length:** 9¼″ (4″ bbl.).
Stocks: Checkered walnut, Magna. Round or square butt.
Sights: Fixed, ⅛″ ramp front, square notch rear.
Price: Blued $192.00
Price: Nickeled $207.50

S&W Model 10-H.B.

SMITH & WESSON 38 M&P AIRWEIGHT Model 12
Caliber: 38 Special, 6 shot.
Barrel: 2″ or 4″.
Weight: 18 oz. (2″ bbl.). **Length:** 6⅞″ over-all.
Stocks: Checkered walnut, Magna. Round or square butt.
Sights: Fixed, ⅛″ serrated ramp front, square notch rear.
Price: Blued $240.00
Price: Nickeled $272.00

Smith & Wesson 38 M&P Heavy Barrel Model 10
Same as regular M&P except: 4″ ribbed bbl. with ⅛″ ramp front sight, square rear, square butt, wgt. 34 oz.
Price: Blued $192.00
Price: Nickeled $207.50

S&W Model 13

SMITH & WESSON Model 13 H.B. M&P
Caliber: 357 and 38 Special, 6 shot.
Barrel: 3″ or 4″.
Weight: 34 oz. **Length:** 9¼″ over-all (4″ bbl.).
Stocks: Checkered walnut, service.
Sights: ⅛″ serrated ramp front, fixed square notch rear.
Features: Heavy barrel, K-frame, square butt.
Price: Blue, M-13 .... $190.50
Price: Nickel $208.00
Price: Model 65, as above in stainless steel $220.00

SMITH & WESSON Model 14 K-38 MASTERPIECE
Caliber: 38 Spec., 6-shot.
Barrel: 6″, 8⅜″.
Weight: 38½ oz. (6″ bbl.). **Length:** 11⅛″ over-all (6″ bbl.).
Stocks: Checkered walnut, service.
Sights: ⅛″ Patridge front, micro click rear adj. for w. and e.
Price: 6″ bbl. $267.00
Price: 8⅜″ barrel $280.50
Price: 6″, target hammer, trigger and stocks $306.00
Price: As above, 8⅜″ barrel $319.50

S&W Model 14

SMITH & WESSON MODEL 17 K-22 MASTERPIECE
Caliber: 22 LR, 6-shot.
Barrel: 6″, 8⅜″.
Weight: 38½ oz. (6″ bbl.). **Length:** 11⅛″ over-all.
Stocks: Checkered walnut, service.
Sights: Patridge front, S&W micro. click rear adjustable for windage and elevation.
Features: Grooved tang and trigger. Polished blue finish.
Price: $283.50
Price: Model 48, as above in 22 Mag. $296.50

SMITH & WESSON COMBAT MASTERPIECE
Caliber: 38 Special (M15) or 22 LR (M18), 6 shot.
Barrel: 2″ or 4″ (M15) 4″ (M18).
Weight: Loaded, 22 36½ oz., 38 34 oz. **Length:** 9⅛″ (4″ bbl.).
Stocks: Checkered walnut, Magna. Grooved tangs and trigger.
Sights: Front, ⅛″ Baughman Quick Draw on ramp, micro click rear, adjustable for w. and e.
Price: Blued, M-15, 2″ $216.00
Price: Nickel M-15, 2″ $232.50
Price: Blued, M-18, 4″ (sq. butt, adj. sights) $266.00

S&W Model 19

SMITH & WESSON 357 COMBAT MAGNUM Model 19
Caliber: 357 Magnum and 38 Special, 6 shot.
Barrel: 2½″, 4″, 6″.
Weight: 35 oz. **Length:** 9½″ (4″ bbl.).
Stocks: Checkered Goncalo Alves, target. Grooved tangs and trigger.
Sights: Front, ⅛″ Baughman Quick Draw on 2½″ or 4″ bbl., Patridge on 6″ bbl., micro click rear adjustable for w. and e.
Price: S&W Bright Blue or Nickel, adj. sights $246.50

CAUTION: PRICES CHANGE. CHECK AT GUNSHOP.

SMITH & WESSON HIGHWAY PATROLMAN Model 28
Caliber: 357 Magnum and 38 Special, 6 shot.
Barrel: 4″, 6″.
Weight: 44 oz. (6″ bbl.). **Length:** 11¼″ (6″ bbl.).
Stocks: Checkered walnut, Magna. Grooved tangs and trigger.
Sights: Front, ⅛″ Baughman Quick Draw, on plain ramp, micro click rear, adjustable for w. and e.
Price: S&W Satin Blue, sandblasted frame edging and barrel top ... **$288.00**
Price: With target stocks...................................... **$309.00**

SMITH & WESSON 44 MAGNUM Model 29 REVOLVER
Caliber: 44 Magnum, 44 Special or 44 Russian, 6 shot.
Barrel: 4″, 6″, 8⅜″.
Weight: 47 oz. (6″ bbl.), 43 oz. (4″ bbl.). **Length:** 11⅞″ (6½″ bbl.).
Stocks: Oversize target type, checkered Goncalo Alves. Tangs and target trigger grooved, checkered target hammer.
Sights: ⅛″ red ramp front, micro click rear, adjustable for w. and e.
Features: Includes presentation case.
Price: S&W Bright Blue or Nickel 4″, 6″ **$449.00**
Price: 8⅜″ bbl., blue or nickel **$463.50**
Price: Model 629 (stainless steel), 4″, 6″ **$512.50**
Price: Model 629, 8⅜″ barrel **$528.50**

SMITH & WESSON 32 REGULATION POLICE Model 31
Caliber: 32 S&W Long, 6 shot.
Barrel: 2″, 3″.
Weight: 18¾ oz. (3″ bbl.). **Length:** 7½″ (3″ bbl.).
Stocks: Checkered walnut, Magna.
Sights: Fixed, ⅒″ serrated ramp front, square notch rear.
Features: Blued
Price: **$236.50**

SMITH & WESSON 1953 Model 34, 22/32 KIT GUN
Caliber: 22 LR, 6 shot.
Barrel: 2″, 4″.
Weight: 22½ oz. (4″ bbl.). **Length:** 8″ (4″ bbl. and round butt).
Stocks: Checkered walnut, round or square butt.
Sights: Front, ⅒″ serrated ramp, micro. click rear, adjustable for w. & e.
Price: Blued **$230.00**
Price: Nickeled **$250.00**
Price: Model 63, as above in stainless, 4″ **$265.50**

SMITH & WESSON 38 CHIEFS SPECIAL & AIRWEIGHT
Caliber: 38 Special, 5 shot.
Barrel: 2″, 3″.
Weight: 19 oz. (2″ bbl.); 14 oz. (AIRWEIGHT). **Length:** 6½″ (2″ bbl. and round butt).
Stocks: Checkered walnut, Magna. Round or square butt.
Sights: Fixed, ⅒″ serrated ramp front, square notch rear.
Price: Price: Blued, standard Model 36......................... **$211.50**
Price: As above, nickel **$229.00**
Price: Blued, Airweight Model 37 .... **$235.00**
Price: As above, nickel **$265.00**

Smith & Wesson 60 Chiefs Special Stainless
Same as Model 36 except: 2″ bbl. and round butt only.
Price: Stainless steel...................................... **$255.00**

SMITH & WESSON BODYGUARD MODEL 38
Caliber: 38 Special; 5 shot, double action revolver.
Barrel: 2″.
Weight: 14½ oz. **Length:** 6⅜″.
Stocks: Checkered walnut, Magna.
Sights: Fixed ⅒″ serrated ramp front, square notch rear.
Features: Alloy frame; integral hammer shroud.
Price: Blued **$249.50**
Price: Nickeled **$281.50**

SMITH & WESSON 357 MAGNUM M-27 REVOLVER
Caliber: 357 Magnum and 38 Special, 6 shot.
Barrel: 4″, 6″, 8⅜″.
Weight: 44 oz. (6″ bbl.). **Length:** 11¼″ (6″ bbl.).
Stocks: Checkered walnut, Magna. Grooved tangs and trigger.
Sights: Any S&W target front, micro click rear, adjustable for w. and e.
Price: S&W Bright Blue or Nickel, 4″, 6″......................... **$449.00**
Price: 8⅜″ bbl., sq. butt, target hammer, trigger, stocks............ **$463.50**

S&W Model 29

S&W Model 31

S&W Model 34

S&W Model 38

Smith & Wesson Bodyguard Model 49 Revolver
Same as Model 38 except steel construction, weight 20½ oz.
Price: Blued **$227.50**
Price: Nickeled **$247.50**

SMITH & WESSON 41 MAGNUM Model 57 REVOLVER
Caliber: 41 Magnum, 6 shot.
Barrel: 4", 6" or 8⅜".
Weight: 48 oz. (6" bbl.). **Length:** 11⅜" (6" bbl.).
Stocks: Oversize target type checkered Goncalo Alves.
Sights: ⅛" red ramp front, micro. click rear, adj. for w. and e.
Price: S&W Bright Blue or Nickel 4", 6" $449.00
Price: 8⅜" bbl. $463.50

SMITH & WESSON MODEL 64 STAINLESS M&P
Caliber: 38 Special, 6-shot.
Barrel: 4".
Weight: 30½ oz. **Length:** 9½" over-all.
Stocks: Checkered walnut, service style.
Sights: Fixed, ⅛" serrated ramp front, square notch rear.
Features: Satin finished stainless steel, square butt.
Price: $207.00

SMITH & WESSON MODEL 66 STAINLESS COMBAT MAGNUM
Caliber: 357 Magnum and 38 Special, 6-shot.
Barrel: 2½", 4", 6".
Weight: 35 oz. **Length:** 9½" over-all.
Stocks: Checkered Goncalo Alves target.
Sights: Front, ⅛" Baughman Quick Draw on plain ramp, micro clock rear adj. for w. and e.
Features: Satin finish stainless steel, grooved trigger with adj. stop.
Price: $268.50

SMITH & WESSON MODEL 67 K-38 STAINLESS COMBAT MASTERPIECE
Caliber: 38 Special, 6-shot.
Barrel: 4".
Weight: 34 oz. (loaded). **Length:** 9⅛" over-all.
Stocks: Checkered walnut, service style.
Sights: Front, ⅛" Baughman Quick Draw on ramp, micro click rear adj. for w. and e.
Features: Stainless steel. Square butt frame with grooved tangs, grooved trigger with adj. stop.
Price: $251.50

SMITH & WESSON MODEL 547
Caliber: 9mm Parabellum
Barrel: 3" or 4" heavy.
Weight: 34 oz. (4" barrel). **Length:** 9⅛" over-all (4" barrel).
Stocks: Checkered square butt Magna Service (4"), checkered walnut target, round butt (3").
Sights: ⅛" Serrated ramp front, fixed ⅛" square notch rear.
Features: K-frame revolver uses special extractor system—no clips required. Has ¼" half-spur hammer. Introduced 1981.
Price: Blue only $271.00

SMITH & WESSON MODEL 586 Distinguished Combat Magnum
Caliber: 357 Magnum.
Barrel: 4", 6", both heavy.
Weight: 46 oz. (6"), 42 oz. (4").
Stocks: Goncalo Alves target-type with speed loader cutaway.
Sights: Baughman red ramp front, S&W micrometer click rear (or fixed).
Features: Uses new L-frame, but takes all K-frame grips. Full length ejector rod shroud. Smooth combat-type trigger, semi-target type hammer. Trigger stop on 6" models; 4" models factory fitted with target hammer and trigger will have trigger stop. Also available in stainless as Model 686. Introduced 1981.
Price: Model 586 (blue only) $269.50
Price: Model 586, nickel $269.50
Price: Model 686 (stainless).................................. $294.00
Price: Model 581 (fixed sight, blue), 4"...................... $213.00
Price: Model 581, nickel $233.50
Price: Model 681 (fixed sight, stainless) $246.00

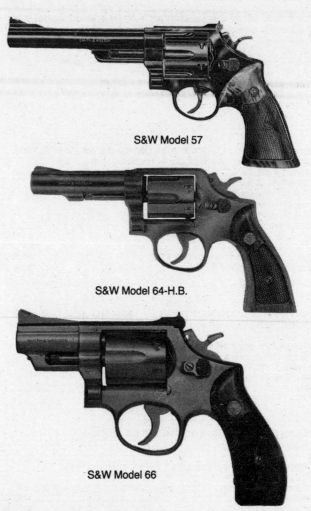

S&W Model 57

S&W Model 64-H.B.

S&W Model 66

Smith & Wesson Accessories
Target hammers with low, broad, deeply-checkered spur, and wide-swaged, grooved target trigger. For all frame sizes, **$10.65** (target hammers not available for small frames). Target stocks: for large-frame guns, N-frame—**$21.20** to **$23.80**; K-frame—**$17.90** to **$21.50**; J-frame— **$15.80** to **$20.80**. These prices applicable only when specified on original order. As separately-ordered parts: target hammer assembly **$21.40** and triggers, **$18.35**; stocks, **$23.30** to **$30.15**. Combat stocks J or K frame, **$31.50**.

S&W Model 586

TAURUS MODEL 83 REVOLVER
Caliber: 38 Spec., 6-shot.
Barrel: 4" only, heavy.
Weight: 34½ oz.
Stocks: Over-size checkered walnut.
Sights: Ramp front, micro. click rear adj. for w. & e.
Features: Blue or nickel finish. Introduced 1977. From International Distributors.
Price: Blue, about $186.00
Price: Satin blue, about..................................... $198.00

CAUTION: PRICES CHANGE. CHECK AT GUNSHOP.

Taurus Model 82

TAURUS MODEL 80 STANDARD REVOLVER
Caliber: 38 Spec., 6-shot.
Barrel: 3″ or 4″.
Weight: 31 oz. (4″ bbl.). **Length:** 9¼″ over-all (4″ bbl.).
Stocks: Checkered Brazilian walnut.
Sights: Serrated ramp front, square notch rear.
Features: Imported from Brazil by International Distributors.
Price: Blue, about $170.00
Price: Satin blue, about..................................... $182.00

TAURUS MODEL 73 SPORT REVOLVER
Caliber: 32 S&W Long, 6-shot.
Barrel: 3″, heavy.
Weight: 22 oz. **Length:** 8¼″ over-all.
Stocks: Oversize target-type, checkered Brazilian walnut.
Sights: Ramp front, notch rear.
Features: Imported from Brazil by International Distributers.
Price: Blue, about $186.00
Price: Satin blue, about..................................... $198.00

DAN WESSON MODEL 9-2, MODEL 15-2 & MODEL 22
Caliber: 22LR, 38 Special (Model 9-2); 357 (Model 15-2), both 6 shot.
Barrel: 2″, 4″, 6″, 8″, 10″, 12″, 15″. "Quickshift" interchangeable barrels.
Weight: 36 oz. (4″ bbl.), 40 oz. (4″ rimfire). **Length:** 9¼″ over-all (4″ bbl.,).
Stocks: "Quickshift" checkered walnut. Interchangeable with eight other styles.
Sights: ⅛″ serrated blade front with red insert (std.), white or yellow insert optional, as is Patridge. White outline rear adj. for w. & e.
Features: Interchangeable barrels; four interchangeable grips; few moving parts, easy disassembly; Bright Blue finish only. Contact Dan Wesson for additional models not listed here. 10″, 12″ and 15″ barrels also available with vent, rib. Rimfire specs. essentially the same as 357 models.
Price: 9-2V, 15-2V (vent. rib) 8″.............................. $324.90
Price: 9-2V, 15-2V, 10″..................................... $344.45
Price: 9-2VH, 15-2VH (heavy vent. shroud) 12″................ $391.30
Price: Pistol Pac, VH..................................... $672.05
Price: 9-2, 15-2 (Std. shroud) 2″............................. $272.50
Price: 9-2, 15-2, 6″...................................... $288.15
Price: 9-2, 15-2, 8″...................................... $297.90
Price: 9-2, 15-2, 15″..................................... $365.25
Price: 9-2, 15-2, Pistol Pac............................... $507.75
Price: 22-cal. same as 357 models.

DAN WESSON MODEL 8-2 & MODEL 14-2
Caliber: 38 Special (Model 8-2); 357 (Model 14-2), both 6 shot.
Barrel: 2″, 4″, 6″, 8″. "Quickshift" interchangeable barrels.
Weight: 34 oz. (4″ bbl.). **Length:** 9¼″ over-all (4″ bbl.).
Stocks: "Quickshift" checkered walnut. Interchangeable with three other styles.
Sights: ⅛″ serrated ramp front, rear fixed.
Features: Interchangeable barrels; 4 interchangeable grips; few moving parts, easy disassembly.
Price: 2″ barrel $234.95
Price: 4″ barrel $241.35
Price: 6″ barrel $248.70
Price: Pistol Pac (cased with all above bbls.) $395.95

TAURUS MODEL 82 HEAVY BARREL REVOLVER
Caliber: 38 Spec., 6-shot.
Barrel: 3″ or 4″, heavy.
Weight: 33 oz. (4″ bbl.). **Length:** 9¼″ over-all (4″ bbl.).
Stocks: Checkered Brazilian walnut.
Sights: Serrated ramp front, square notch rear.
Features: Imported from Brazil by International Distributors.
Price: Blue, about $170.00
Price: Satin blue, about..................................... $182.00

TAURUS MODEL 66 REVOLVER
Caliber: 357 Magnum, 6-shot.
Barrel: 3″, 4″, 6″.
Weight: 35 ozs.
Stocks: Checkered walnut, target-type. Standard stocks on 3″.
Sights: Serrated ramp front, micro click rear adjustable for w. and e.
Features: Wide target-type hammer spur, floating firing pin, heavy barrel with shrouded ejector rod. Introduced 1978. From International Distributors.
Price: Blue, about $226.00
Price: Satin blue, about..................................... $226.00
Price: Model 65 (similar to M66 except has a fixed rear sight and ramp front), blue, about.. $177.00
Price: Model 65, satin blue, about............................ $188.00

TAURUS MODEL 85 REVOLVER
Caliber: 38 Spec., 5-shot.
Barrel: 3″.
Weight: 21 oz.
Stocks: Smooth walnut.
Sights: Ramp front, square notch rear.
Features: Blue or satin blue finish. Introduced 1980. From International Distributors.
Price: Blue, about $188.00
Price: Satin blue, about..................................... $201.00

Dan Wesson 44 Magnum

DAN WESSON 44 MAGNUM REVOLVER
Caliber: 44 Magnum, 6 shots.
Barrel: 4″, 6″, 8″, 10″, interchangeable, with or without "Power Control" gun levelling device.
Weight: 45 oz. (4″ bbl.) **Length:** 12″ (6″ bbl.).
Stocks: Walnut or exotic wood. Two interchangeable styles, Target or Combat.
Sights: Serrated ⅛″ front blade with red insert (yellow and white also available.) White outline rear adj. for w. & e.
Features: Interchangeable barrels, grips, front sight blades. Bright blue finish only. Only 6″ and 8″ guns are shipped from the factory—4″ and 10″ barrel assemblies available separately. Introduced 1981.
Price: 6″, standard weight.................................. $410.65
Price: 8″, standard weight.................................. $424.21
Price: Pistol Pac, standard weight $615.40
Price: 6″ heavy shroud..................................... $432.65
Price: 8″, heavy shroud.................................... $448.20
Price: Pistol Pac, heavy shroud............................. $659.15

Abilene Single Action

ABILENE SINGLE ACTION REVOLVER
Caliber: 357 Mag., 44 Mag., 45 Colt, 6 shot.
Barrel: 4⅝", 6", 7½", 10" (44 Mag. only).
Weight: About 48 oz.
Stocks: Smooth walnut.
Sights: Serrated ramp front, click adj. rear for w. and e.
Features: Wide hammer spur. Blue or Magnaloy finish. From Mossberg.
Price: Blue, 357, 4⅝", 6", 7½" $271.95
Price: Blue, 44 Mag., 7½", ... $274.95
Price: 44 Mag., Magnaloy (hard chrome) $299.95
Price: 10" barrel, 44 Mag., blue only......................... $374.95
Price: 45 LC, blue, 6" only $274.95

Colt Single Action Army

COLT SINGLE ACTION ARMY REVOLVER
Caliber: 357 Magnum, 44 Spec., 44-40, or 45 Colt, 6 shot.
Barrel: 4¾", 5½", 7½" or 12".
Weight: 37 oz. (5½" bbl.). **Length:** 10⅞" (5½" bbl.)
Stocks: Black composite rubber with eagle and shield crest.
Sights: Fixed. Grooved top strap, blade front.
Features: See Colt catalog for variations and prices. Only basic models and prices listed here.
Price: Blued and case hardened 4¾", 5½" bbl., 44 Spec., 45 Colt ... $575.95
Price: Nickel with walnut stocks $657.50
Price: With 7½" bbl., blue, 45 Colt $590.50

Colt New Frontier

Colt Single Action Army—New Frontier
Same specifications as standard Single Action Army except: flat-top frame; high polished finish, blue and case colored; ramp front sight and target rear adj. for windage and elevation; smooth walnut stocks with silver medallion, or composition grips.
Price: 44-40, 4¾", blue... $667.50
Price: Either cal., 7½", blue, 44 Spec., 45 Colt.................. $685.95

COLT NEW FRONTIER 22
Caliber: 22 LR, 6-shot.
Barrel: 4¾", 6", 7½".
Weight: 29½ oz. (4¾" bbl.). **Length:** 9⅝" over-all.
Stocks: Black composite rubber.
Sights: Ramp-style front, fully adjustable rear.
Features: Cross-bolt safety. Color case-hardened frame. Available in blue or Coltguard finishes. Re-introduced 1982.
Price: 4¾", blue $263.50
Price: 4¾", Coltguard $273.95
Price: 6", blue $265.50
Price: 6", Coltguard $275.95
Price: 7½", blue $267.50
Price: 7½", Coltguard $277.95

F.I.E. "LEGEND" SINGLE ACTION REVOLVER
Caliber: 22 LR/22 Mag.
Barrel: 4¾".
Weight: 32 oz.
Stocks: Smooth walnut or black checkered nylon. Walnut optional ($16.95).
Sights: Blade front, fixed rear.
Features: Positive hammer block system. Brass backstrap and trigger guard. Color case hardened steel frame, rest blued. Imported from Italy by F.I.E. Corp.
Price: 22LR.. $104.95
Price: 22 combo with walnut grips $136.95

F.I.E. "HOMBRE" SINGLE ACTION REVOLVER
Caliber: 357 Mag., 44 Mag., 45 LC.
Barrel: 5½" or 7½".
Weight: 45 oz. (5½" bbl.).
Stocks: Smooth walnut with medallion.
Sights: Blade front, grooved topstrap (fixed) rear.
Features: Color case hardened frame. Bright blue finish. Super-smooth action. Introduced 1979. Imported from West Germany by F.I.E. Corp.
Price: 357, 45 Colt... $179.95
Price: 44 Mag. $199.95

F.I.E. E15 BUFFALO SCOUT REVOLVER
Caliber: 22 LR/22 Mag., 6-shot.
Barrel: 4¾", 7", 9".
Weight: 32 oz. **Length:** 10" over-all.
Stocks: Black checkered nylon.
Sights: Blade front, fixed rear.
Features: Slide spring ejector. Blue, chrome or blue with brass backstrap and trigger guard models available.
Price: Blued, 22 LR, 4¾" $64.95
Price: Blue, 22 combo, 4¾" $84.95
Price: Chrome, 22 LR, 4¾" $73.95
Price: Chrome, combo,, 4¾" $89.95
Price: Blue/brass, combo, 4¾" $89.95
Price: Blue, 22 LR, 9" bbl. $79.95
Price: Blue, 22 combo, 9" bbl. $90.95

CAUTION: PRICES CHANGE. CHECK AT GUNSHOP.

HANDGUNS—SINGLE ACTION REVOLVERS

Freedom Arms Mini Revolver

FREEDOM ARMS MINI REVOLVER
Caliber: 22 Short, Long, Long Rifle, 5-shot, 22 Mag., 4-shot.
Barrel: 1″, 1¾″.
Weight: 4 oz. **Length:** 4″ over-all.
Stocks: Black ebonite or simulated ivory.
Sights: Blade front, notch rear.
Features: Made of stainless steel, simple take down; half-cock safety; floating firing pin; cartridge rims recessed in cylinder. Comes in gun rug. Lifetime warranty.
Price: 22 LR, 1″ barrel **$124.75**
Price: 22 LR, 1¾″ barrel **$129.50**
Price: 22 Mag., 1″ barrel **$144.75**
Price: 22 Mag., 1¾″ barrel **$149.50**

Freedom Arms Boot Gun
Similar to the Mini Revolver except has 3″ barrel, weighs 5 oz. and is 5⅞″ over-all. Has over-size grips, floating firing pin. Made of stainless steel. Lifetime warranty. Comes in rectangular gun rug. Introduced 1982. From Freedom Arms.
Price: 22 LR **$147.65**
Price: 22 Mag. **$167.65**

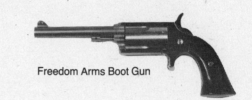

Freedom Arms Boot Gun

MITCHELL SINGLE ACTION REVOLVERS
Caliber: 22 LR/22 Mag., 357 Mag., 44 Mag., 44 Mag./44-40, 45 Colt.
Barrel: 4¾″, 5½″, 6″, 7½″, 10″, 12″, 18″.
Weight: About 36 oz.
Stocks: One-piece walnut.
Sights: Ramp front, rear adj. for w. & e.
Features: Color case-hardened frame, grip frame is polished brass. Hammer block safety. Introduced 1980. From Mitchell Arms Corp.
Price: 22/22 Mag., 357, 44, 45, 4¾″, 5½″, 7½″, fixed sights **$239.00**
Price: As above, adj. sights **$249.00**
Price: 44 Mag., 45 Colt, 10″, 12″, 18″ bbl. **$295.00**
Price: Dual cyl., fixed sights **$259.00**
Price: Dual cyl., adj. sights **$275.00**
Price: Shoulder stock, for 18″ bbl. only **$99.95**

Mitchell Single Action

NAM MINI REVOLVER
Caliber: 22 LR, 22 Mag., 5-shot
Barrel: 1⅛″ (22 Short, LR), 1¼″ (22 Mag.), 1⅝″ (22 LR).
Weight: 4.5 oz. **Length:** 3.8″ over-all.
Stocks: Smooth plastic; walnut on magnum model.
Sights: Blade front only.
Features: Stainless steel, single action only. Spur trugger. From North American Mfg. Corp.
Price: 22 Short **$116.50**
Price: 22 Long Rifle **$117.50**
Price: 22 Long Rifle, 1⅝″ bbl. **$118.50**
Price: 22 Mag. **$134.50**

RUGER NEW MODEL CONVERTIBLE BLACKHAWK
Caliber: 45 Colt or 45 Colt/45 ACP (extra cylinder).
Barrel: 4⅝″ or 7½″ (6-groove, 16″ twist).
Weight: 40 oz. (7½″ bbl.). **Length:** 13⅛″ (7½ bbl.).
Stocks: Smooth American walnut.
Sights: ⅛″ ramp front, micro click rear adj. for w. and e.
Features: Similar to Super Blackhawk, Ruger interlocked mechanism. Convertible furnished with interchangeable cylinder for 45 ACP.
Price: Blued, 45 Colt **$217.50**
Price: Convertilble **$238.00**

RUGER NEW MODEL BLACKHAWK REVOLVER
Caliber: 357 or 41 Mag., 6-shot.
Barrel: 4⅝″ or 6½″, either caliber.
Weight: 42 oz. (6½″ bbl.). **Length:** 12¼″ over-all (6½″ bbl.).
Stocks: American walnut.
Sights: ⅛″ ramp front, micro click rear adj. for w. and e.
Features: New Ruger interlocked mechanism, independent firing pin, hardened chrome-moly steel frame, music wire springs throughout.
Price: Blued **$217.50**
Price: Stainless steel (357) **$260.50**

Ruger New Model Blackhawk

Ruger New Model 30 Carbine Blackhawk
Specifications similar to 45 Blackhawk. Fluted cylinder, round-back trigger guard. Weight 44 oz., length 13⅛″ over-all, 7½″ barrel only.
Price: **$217.50**

Ruger New Model 357/9mm Blackhawk
Same as the 357 Magnum except furnished with interchangeable cylinders for 9mm Parabellum and 357 Magnum cartridges.
Price: **$238.00**

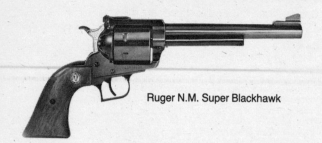

Ruger N.M. Super Blackhawk

Ruger Super Single-Six

RUGER NEW MODEL SUPER BLACKHAWK

Caliber: 44 Magnum, 6-shot. Also fires 44 Spec.
Barrel: 7½" (6-groove, 20" twist), 10½".
Weight: 48 oz. **Length:** 13⅜" over-all (7½" bbl.).
Stocks: Genuine American walnut.
Sights: ⅛" ramp front, micro click rear adj. for w. and e.
Features: New Ruger interlocked mechanism, non-fluted cylinder, steel grip and cylinder frame, square back trigger guard, wide serrated trigger and wide spur hammer. Deep Ruger blue.
Price: **$250.00**

RUGER NEW MODEL SUPER SINGLE-SIX CONVERTIBLE REVOLVER

Caliber: 22 S, L, LR, 6-shot. 22 Mag. in extra cylinder.
Barrel: 4⅝", 5½", 6½" or 9½" (6-groove).
Weight: 34½ oz. (6½" bbl.). **Length:** 11¹³⁄₁₆" over-all (6½" bbl.).
Stocks: Smooth American walnut.
Sights: Improved patridge front on ramp, fully adj. rear protected by integral frame ribs.
Features: New Ruger "interlocked" mechanism, transfer bar ignition, gate-controlled loading, hardened chrome-moly steel frame, wide trigger, music wire springs throughout, independent firing pin.
Price: 4⅝", 5½", 6½", 9½" barrel **$175.00**
Price: 5½", 6½" bbl., stainless steel **$245.00**

SEVILLE SINGLE ACTION REVOLVER

Caliber: 357 Mag., 9mm Win. Mag., 41 Mag., 44 Mag., 45 Colt, 45 Win. Mag.
Barrel: 4⅝", 5½", 6½", 7½".
Weight: 52 oz. (4⅝", loaded)
Stocks: Smooth walnut, thumbrest, or Pachmayr.
Sights: Ramp front with red insert, fully adj. rear.
Features: Available in blue or stainless steel. Six-shot cylinder. From United Sporting Arms of Arizona, Inc.
Price: Blue, 357 Mag. **$252.00**
Price: Blue, 41, 44, 45. .... **$283.50**
Price: Stainless, all cals. **$375.00**
Price: With "Quick Kit" bbl./caliber conversion, blue **$450.00**
Price: As above, stainless **$590.00**

SEVILLE SHERIFF'S MODEL S.A. REVOLVER

Caliber: 44-40, 44 Mag., 45 ACP, 45 Colt.
Barrel: 3½".
Weight: 45 oz. (loaded).
Stocks: Smooth walnut. Square butt or birdshead style.
Sights: Sq. butt—ramp front, adj. rear; birdshead—blade front, fixed rear.
Features: Blue or stainless steel. Six-shot cylinder. Available with square or birdshead grip style. From United Sporting Arms of Arizona, Inc.
Price: Blue. **$300.00**
Price: Stainless steel. **$375.00**
Price: With "Quick Kit" bbl./caliber conversion, blue **$450.00**
Price: As above, stainless **$590.00**

TANARMI S.A. REVOLVER MODEL TA22S LM

Caliber: 22 LR, 22 Mag., 6-shot.
Barrel: 4¾".
Weight: 32 oz. **Length:** 10" over-all.
Stocks: Walnut.
Sights: Blade front, rear adj. for w. & e.
Features: Manual hammer block safety; color hardened steel frame; brass backstrap and trigger guard. Imported from Italy by Excam.
Price: 22 LR., target sights **$105.00**
Price: 22 Mag. **$115.00**

> Consult our Directory pages for the location of firms mentioned.

TANARMI SINGLE ACTION MODEL TA76

Same as TA22 models except blue backstrap and trigger guard.
Price: 22 LR, blue **$67.00**
Price: Combo, blue **$81.00**
Price: 22 LR, chrome. **$75.00**
Price: Combo, chrome **$89.00**

THE VIRGINIAN DRAGOON REVOLVER

Caliber: 357 Mag., 41 Mag., 44 Mag., 45 Colt.
Barrel: 44 Mag., 6", 7½", 8⅜"; 357 Mag. and 45 Colt, 5", 6", 7½".
Weight: 48 oz. (6" barrel). **Length:** 11⅞" over-all (6" barrel).
Stocks: Smooth walnut.
Sights: Ramp-type Patridge front blade, micro. adj. target rear.
Features: Color case-hardened frame, spring-loaded floating firing pin, coil main spring. Firing pin is lock-fitted with a steel bushing. Introduced 1977. Made in the U.S. by Interarms Industries, Inc.
Price: 44 Mag., 6", 7½", 8⅜", blue **$310.00**
Price: 45 Colt, 5", 6", 7½", blue **$310.00**
Price: 357 Mag., 41 Mag., 44 Mag., 45 Colt, 12", blue **$325.00**
Price: 44 Mag., 45 Colt, 6", 7½", 8⅜", stainless **$310.00**
Price: 44 Mag., 10½" Sil. model **$370.00**

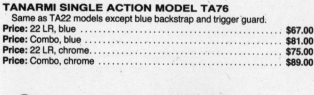

Virginian Dragoon

CAUTION: PRICES CHANGE. CHECK AT GUNSHOP.

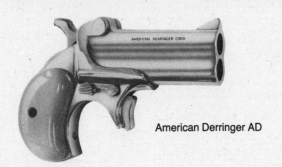

American Derringer AD

C. O. P. 357 MAGNUM

Caliber: 38/357 Mag., 4 shots.
Barrel: 3¼".
Weight: 28 oz. **Length:** 5.5" over-all.
Stocks: Checkered composition.
Sights: Open, fixed.
Features: Double-action, 4 barrels, made of stainless steel. Width is only one inch, height 4.1". From M & N Distributors.
Price: About $250.00
Price: In 22 Mag. $250.00
Price: In 22 LR (blued, aluminum frame) $229.95

Classic Southern Derringer

CLASSIC ARMS TWISTER

Caliber: 22 LR or 9mm Rimfire.
Barrel: 3¼".
Weight: 18 oz.
Stocks: Pearlite.
Sights: None.
Features: Over-under barrels rotate on an axis for two separate shots. Spur trigger. 9mm Rimfire ammunition available. Made in U.S. by Classic Arms Ltd.
Price: Either caliber $79.95

HIGH STANDARD 9194 AND 9306 DERRINGER

Caliber: 22 LR, 22 Mag., 2 shot.
Barrel: 3½", over and under, rifled.
Weight: 11 oz. **Length:** 5" over-all.
Stocks: Smooth plastic.
Sights: Fixed, open.
Features: Hammerless, integral safety hammerblock, all steel unit is encased in a black, anodized alloy housing. Recessed chamber. Dual extraction. Top break, double action.
Price: Blue (M9194) $155.00
Price: Nickel (M9306) $180.00
Price: Blue (M9193), 22 LR $155.00
Price: Electroless nickel (M9420), 22 Mag. $207.00
Price: Electroless nickel (M9421), 22 LR. $207.00

LJUTIC LJ 25 PISTOL

Caliber: 25 ACP.
Barrel: 2¾".
Stocks: Checkered walnut.
Sights: Fixed.
Features: Stainless steel; double action; ventilated rib. Introduced 1981. From Ljutic Industries.
Price: $149.95

AMERICAN DERRINGER MODEL AD

Caliber: 22 LR, 22 Mag., 22 Jet, 223 Rem., 38 Super, 380 ACP, 38 Spec., 9mm Para., 357 Mag., 41 Mag., 44-40 Win., 44 Spec., 44 Mag., 45 Colt, 45 ACP.
Barrel: 3".
Weight: 15½ oz. (38 Spec.). **Length:** 4.82" over-all.
Stocks: Rosewood, Zebra wood, walnut, or plastic ivory.
Sights: Blade front.
Features: Made of stainless steel with high-polish finish. Two shot capacity. Manual hammer block safety. Introduced 1982. From American Derringer Corp.
Price: 22 LR or Mag. $172.50
Price: 223 Rem. or 22 Jet. $275.00
Price: 38 Spec. $197.50
Price: 357 Mag. $212.50
Price: 9mm, 380, 38 Super $212.00
Price: 44 Spec. $250.00
Price: 44-40 Win., 45 ACP, 45 Colt $275.00
Price: 41, 44 Mags. $369.00
Price: Lightweight (7 oz.) model, 38 Spec. only $169.95
Price: 41, 44 Mag. single-shot (wgt. 22 oz.), rosewood grips $250.00

C.O.P. 357 Magnum

CLASSIC ARMS SOUTHERN DERRINGER

Caliber: 22 LR or 41 Rimfire.
Barrel: 2½".
Weight: 12 oz. **Length:** 5" over-all.
Stocks: White plastic.
Sights: Blade front.
Features: Single-shot, spur-trigger derringer. Brass frame, steel barrel. The 41 RF ammunition is available from Navy Arms. Introduced in 1982. Made in U.S. by Classic Arms Ltd.
Price: Either caliber $79.95

F.I.E. MODEL D-38 DERRINGER

Caliber: 38 Special.
Barrel: 3".
Weight: 14 oz.
Stocks: Checkered white nylon, walnut optional.
Sights: Fixed.
Features: Chrome finish. Spur trigger. Tip-up barrel, extractors. Made in U.S. by F.I.E. Corp.
Price: With nylon grips $81.95
Price: With walnut grips $98.95

High Standard Derringer

Mitchell's Derringer

Remington XP-100

MITCHELL'S DERRINGER
Caliber: 38 Spec.
Barrel: 2¾"
Weight: 11 oz. **Length:** 5¼" over-all.
Stocks: Walnut, checkered.
Sights: Fixed, ramp front.
Features: Polished blue finish. All steel. Made in U.S. Introduced 1980. From Mitchell Arms Corp.
Price: .... ₵140.06

REMINGTON MODEL XP-100 Bolt Action Pistol
Caliber: 221 Fireball, single shot.
Barrel: 10½", ventilated rib.
Weight: 60 oz. **Length:** 16¾".
Stock: Brown nylon one-piece, checkered grip with white spacers.
Sights: Fixed front, rear adj. for w. and e. Tapped for scope mount.
Features: Fits left or right hand, is shaped to fit fingers and heel of hand. Grooved trigger. Rotating thumb safety, cavity in fore-end permits insertion of up to five 38 cal., 130-gr. metal jacketed bullets to adjust weight and balance. Included is a black vinyl, zippered case.
Price: Including case $319.95

SEMMERLING LM-4 PISTOL
Caliber: 45 ACP.
Barrel: 3½".
Weight: 24 oz. **Length:** 5.2" over-all.
Stocks: Checkered black plastic.
Sights: Ramp front, fixed rear.
Features: Manually operated repeater. Over-all dimensions are 5.2" x 3.7" x 1". Has a four-shot magazine capacity. Comes with manual, leather carrying case, spare stock screw and wrench. From Semmerling Corp.
Price: Complete $894.00
Price: Thin Version (blue sideplate instead of grips) $894.00

MERRILL SPORTSMAN'S SINGLE SHOT PISTOL
Caliber: 22 LR Sil., 22 Mag., 22 Hornet, 256 Win. Mag., 357 Mag., 357/44 B & D, 30-30 Win., 30 Herrett, 357 Herrett, 41 Mag., 44 Mag., 7mm Merrill, 30 Merrill, 7mm Rocket.
Barrel: 9" or 10¾", semi-octagonal; .450" wide vent. rib, matted to prevent glare; 14" barrel in all except 22 cals.
Weight: About 54 oz. **Length:** 10½" over-all (9" bbl.)
Stocks: Smooth walnut with thumb and heel rest.
Sights: Front .125" blade (.080" blade optional); rear adj. for w. and e.
Features: Polished blue finish, hard chrome optional. Barrel is drilled and tapped for scope mounting. Cocking indicator visible from rear of gun. Has spring-loaded barrel lock, positive thumb safety. Trigger adjustable for weight of pull and over-travel. From Rock Pistol Mfg.
Price: 9" barrel $500.00
Price: 9", 22 Sil. $520.00
Price: 10¾" barrel $500.00
Price: 14" barrel $585.00
Price: Extra barrel, 9", 10¾". $165.00
Price: Extra 14" bbl.. .... $250.00

Sterling X-Caliber

STERLING X-CALIBER SINGLE SHOT
Caliber: 22, 22 Mag., 357 Mag., 44 Mag.
Barrel: 8" or 10", interchangeable.
Weight: 52 oz. (8" bbl.). **Length:** 13" over-all (8" bbl.).
Stocks: Goncolo Alves.
Sights: Patridge front, fully adj. rear.
Features: Barrels are drilled and tapped for scope mounting; hammer is notched for easy cocking with scope mounted. Finger grooved grip.
Price: Any caliber listed $199.95

TANARMI O/U DERRINGER
Caliber: 38 Special.
Barrel: 3".
Weight: 14 oz. **Length:** 4¾" over-all.
Stocks: Checkered white nylon.
Sights: Fixed.
Features: Blue finish; tip-up barrel. Assembled in U.S. by Excam, Inc.
Price: $75.00

Thompson-Center Contender

THOMPSON-CENTER ARMS CONTENDER
Caliber: 221 Rem., 7mm T.C.U., 30-30 Win., 22 S, L, LR, 22 Mag., 22 Hornet, 256 Win., 357 Mag., also 222 Rem., 44 Mag., 45 Long Colt, 45 Win. Mag., single shot.
Barrel: 10", tapered octagon, bull barrel and vent. rib.
Weight: 43 oz. (10" bbl.). **Length:** 13¼" (10" bbl.).
Stocks: Select walnut grip and fore-end, with thumb rest. Right or left hand.
Sights: Under cut blade ramp front, rear adj. for w. & e.
Features: Break open action with auto-safety. Single action only. Interchangeable bbls., both caliber (rim & centerfire), and length. Drilled and tapped for scope. Engraved frame. See T/C catalog for exact barrel/caliber availability.
Price: Blued (rimfire cals.) $255.00
Price: Blued (centerfire cals.). $255.00
Price: Extra bbls. (standard octagon) $105.00
Price: Bushnell Phantom scope base $8.75
Price: 357 and 44 Mag. vent. rib, internal choke bbl. $120.00

AKM Auto Rifle

AKM AUTO RIFLE

Caliber: 7.62x39, 30-shot magazine.
Barrel: 16.33".
Weight: 6.4lbs. **Length:** 34.65" over-all.
Stock: Laminated hardwood. Checkered composition pistol grip.
Sights: Protected post front, U-notch rear adjustable for elevation.
Features: Semi-auto only. Detachable box magazine. Cleaning kit, bayonet and scabbard, and sling available. Introduced to U.S. market 1982. Imported from Egypt by Steyr Daimler Puch.
Price: Standard rifle **$1,250.00**
Price: Paratrooper model **$1,437.00**

Armalite AR-180

ARMALITE AR-180 SPORTER CARBINE

Caliber: 223 semi-automatic, gas operated carbine.
Barrel: 18¼"(12" twist).
Weight: 6½ lbs. **Length:** 38" over-all
Stock: Nylon folding stock, phenolic fiber-glass heat dissipating fore-end.
Sights: Flip-up "L" type sight adj. for w., post front adj. for e.
Features: Safety lever accessible from both sides. Flash hider slotted to prevent muzzle climb.
Price: **$695.00**
Price: 3x (2.75x20mm) scope with quick detachable side-mount. ... **$159.95**
Price: Extra 5-round magazine **$9.95**
Price: Extra 20-shot magazine. **$15.95**
Price: Extra 40-shot magazine. **$29.95**

Auto Ordnance 27 A-1

AUTO-ORDNANCE MODEL 27 A-1

Caliber: 45 ACP, 30-shot magazine.
Barrel: 16".
Weight: 11½ lbs. **Length:** About 39½" over-all (Deluxe).
Stock: Walnut stock and vertical fore-end.
Sights: Blade front, open rear adj. for w.
Features: Re-creation of Thompson Model 1927. Semi-auto only. Deluxe model has finned barrel, adj. rear sight and compensator; Standard model has plain barrel and military sight. From Auto-Ordnance Corp.
Price: Deluxe **$489.95**
Price: Standard **$469.95**
Price: 1927A5 Pistol (M27A1 without stock; wgt. 7 lbs.) **$469.95**
Price: Lightweight model **$469.95**

Auto-Ordnance 1927A-3

A 22 caliber version of the 27A-1. Exact look-alike with alloy receiver. Weight is about 7 lbs., 16" finned barrel, 10-, 30- and 50-shot magazines and drum. Introduced 1977. From Auto-Ordnance Corp.
Price: **$449.65**

Bushmaster Auto Rifle

BUSHMASTER AUTO RIFLE

Caliber: 223; 30-shot magazine
Barrel: 18½".
Weight: 6¼ lbs. **Length:** 37.5" over-all.
Stock: Rock maple
Sights: Protected post front adj. for elevation, protected quick-flip rear peep adj. for windage; short and long range.
Features: Steel alloy upper receiver with welded barrel assembly, AK-47-type gas system, aluminum lower receiver; silent sling and swivels; bayonet lug; one-piece welded steel alloy bolt carrier assembly. From Bushmaster Firearms.
Price: With maple stock **$484.95**
Price: With nylon-coated folding stock **$494.95**

COLT AR-15 SPORTER

Caliber: 223 Rem.
Barrel: 20".
Weight: 7¼ lbs. **Length:** 38⅜" over-all.
Stock: Reinforced polycarbonate with buttstock stowage compartment.
Sights: Post front, rear adj. for w. and e.
Features: 5-round detachable box magazine, recoil pad, flash suppressor, sling swivels.
Price: **$533.50**
Price: With 3x scope **$702.95**

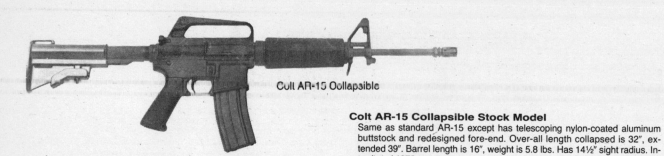

Colt AR-15 Collapsible

Colt AR-15 Collapsible Stock Model

Same as standard AR-15 except has telescoping nylon-coated aluminum buttstock and redesigned fore-end. Over-all length collapsed is 32", extended 39". Barrel length is 16", weight is 5.8 lbs. Has 14½" sight radius. Introduced 1978.

Price: **$584.95**
Price: With 3x scope **$754.50**

COMMANDO ARMS CARBINE

Caliber: 9mm or 45 ACP.
Barrel: 16½".
Weight: 8 lbs. **Length:** 37" over-all.
Stock: Walnut buttstock.
Sights: Blade front, peep rear.
Features: Semi-auto only. Cocking handle on left side. Choice of magazines—5, 15, 30 or 90 shot. From Commando Arms.
Price: Mark 9 or Mark 45, blue **$210.00**
Price: Nickel plated **$240.00**

Demro TAC-1M

DEMRO TAC-1M CARBINE

Caliber: 9mm (32-shot magazine), 45 ACP (30-shot magazine).
Barrel: 16⅞".
Weight: 7¾ lbs. **Length:** 35¾" over-all.
Stock: American walnut, removable.
Sights: Removable blade front, open rear adjustable for w. & e.
Features: Fires from open bolt. Thumb safety, integral muzzle brake. From Demro Products.
Price: **$486.75**
Price: With fitted attache case................................. **$539.00**

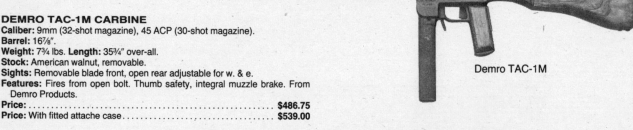

Demro XF-7 Wasp

Demro XF-7 Wasp Carbine

Similar to the TAC-1 Carbine except has collapsible buttstock, high impact synthetic fore-end and pistol grip. Has 5, 15 or 30-shot magazine (45 ACP) or 32-shot magazine (9mm).
Price: **$576.00**
Price: With fitted attache case................................. **$637.50**

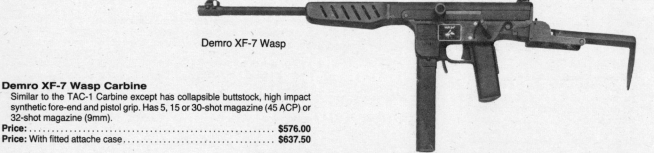

FN-LAR Competition

FN-LAR COMPETITION AUTO

Caliber: 308 Win., 20-shot magazine.
Barrel: 21" (24" with flash hider).
Weight: 9 lbs., 7 oz. **Length:** 44½" over-all.
Stock: Black composition butt, fore-end and pistol grip.
Sights: Post front, aperture rear adj. for elevation, 300 to 600 meters.
Features: Has sling swivels, carrying handle, rubber recoil pad. Consecutively numbered pairs available at additional cost. Imported by Steyr Daimler Puch of America.
Price: **$1,659.00**

FN 308 Model 44

Similar to the FN-LAR except has 18" barrel, skeleton-type folding buttstock, folding cocking handle. Introduced 1982. Imported from Belgium by HOWCO Distr., Inc.
Price: **$1,595.00**

FN-LAR Paratrooper 308 Match

Similar to FN-LAR competition except with folding skeleton stock, shorter barrel, modified rear sight. Imported by Steyr Daimler Puch.
Price: **$1,754.00**

FN-LAR Heavy Barrel 308 Match

Similar to FN-LAR competition except has wooden stock and fore-end, heavy barrel, folding metal bipod. Imported by Steyr Daimler Puch.
Price: With wooden stock.................................... **$2,198.00**
Price: With synthetic stock **$2,030.00**

CAUTION: PRICES CHANGE. CHECK AT GUNSHOP.

CENTERFIRE RIFLES—MILITARY STYLE AUTOLOADERS

FNC Auto Rifle

FNC AUTO RIFLE
Caliber: 223 Rem.
Barrel: 18".
Weight: 9.61 lbs.
Stock: Synthetic stock.
Sights: Post front; flip-over aperture rear adj. for elevation.
Features: Updated version of FN-FAL in shortened carbine form. Has 30-shot box magazine, synthetic pistol grip, fore-end. Introduced 1981. Imported by Steyr Daimler Puch.
Price: Standard model **$1,326.70**
Price: Paratrooper, with folding stock **$1,438.40**

GALIL 308 SEMI-AUTO RIFLE
Caliber: 308 Win., 25-shot magazine.
Barrel: 21".
Weight: 8.7 lbs. **Length:** 41.3" over-all (stock extended).
Stock: Tube-type metal folding stock.
Sights: Post-type front, flip-type "L" rear.
Features: Gas operated, rotating bolt. Cocking handle, safety and magazine catch can be operated from either side. Introduced 1982. Imported from Israel by Magnum Research Inc.
Price: **$1,493.00**
Price: As above in 223 (18.1" bbl., 38.6" o.a.l.) **$1,371.00**

IVER JOHNSON'S PM30G CARBINE
Caliber: 30 U.S. Carbine.
Barrel: 18" four-groove.
Weight: 6½ lbs. **Length:** 35½" over-all.
Stock: Glossy-finished hardwood.
Sights: Click adj. peep rear.
Features: Gas operated semi-auto carbine. 15-shot detachable magazine.
Price: Blue finish **$258.55**
Price: Paratrooper model—with telescoping wire stock, front vertical hand grip, blue finish **$285.03**

FNC-11, 22, 33 Auto Rifles
Similar to the standard FNC except has 16⅛" barrel. Model 11 has folding metal stock; Model 22 has full synthetic stock; Model 33 has full wood stock. Introduced 1982. Imported from Belgium by HOWCO Distr., Inc.
Price: **$1,095.00**

HECKLER & KOCH HK-91 AUTO RIFLE
Caliber: 308 Win., 5- or 20-shot magazine.
Barrel: 19".
Weight: 9½ lbs. **Length:** 40¼" over-all.
Stock: Black high-impact plastic.
Sights: Post front, aperture rear adj. for w. and e.
Features: Delayed roller lock bolt action. Sporting version of West German service rifle. Takes special H&K clamp scope mount. Imported from West Germany by Heckler & Koch, Inc.
Price: HK-91 A-2 with plastic stock **$699.00**
Price: HK-91 A-2 with retractable metal stock **$933.00**

Heckler & Koch HK-93 Auto Rifle
Similar to HK-93 except in 223 cal., 16.13" barrel, over-all length of 35½", weighs 7¾ lbs. Slight differences in stock, fore-end.
Price: HK-93 A-2 with plastic stock **$686.00**
Price: HK-93 A-2 with retractable metal stock **$920.00**

Leader Mk. 5 Rifle

LEADER MARK SERIES AUTO RIFLE
Caliber: 223 Rem.
Barrel: 16.1".
Weight: 7.5 lbs. **Length:** 35.8" over-all.
Stock: Synthetic stock, pistol grip and fore-end.
Sights: Protected post front, revolving aperture rear adj. for windage.
Features: Gas operated, locked breech system based on a fixed piston, mobile cylinder design. Comes with flash suppressor, 10- or 20-round magazine. Introduced 1981. Imported by World Public Safety.
Price: Mk. 5 (synthetic stock) **$537.50**

Ruger Mini-14

RUGER MINI-14 223 CARBINE
Caliber: 223 Rem., 5-shot detachable box magazine.
Barrel: 18½".
Weight: 6.4 lbs. **Length:** 37¼" over-all.
Stock: American hardwood, steel reinforced.
Sights: Ramp front, fully adj. rear.
Features: Fixed piston gas-operated, positive primary extraction. 10 and 20-shot magazines available from Ruger dealers, 30-shot magazine available only to police departments and government agencies.
Price: **$304.00**
Price: As above except in stainless steel **$340.00**
Price: As above with integral dovetails to accept Ruger steel scope rings (illus.) **$345.00**

CENTERFIRE RIFLES—MILITARY STYLE AUTOLOADERS

SIG-AMT Auto Rifle

SIG-AMT AUTO RIFLE
Caliber: 308 Win., 20-shot detachable box magazine.
Barrel: 10¾".
Weight: 9½ lbs. **Length:** 39" over-all.
Stock: Walnut stock and fore-end, composition vertical p.g.
Sights: Adj. post front, adj. aperture rear.
Features: Roller-lock breech, gas-assisted action; right-side cocking handle; loaded chamber indicator; no-tool take-down. Winter trigger (optional) allows firing with mittens. Spare parts, magazine, etc. available. From Mandall Shooting Supplies.
Price: **$2,400.00**

Springfield Armory M1A

SPRINGFIELD ARMORY M1 GARAND RIFLE
Caliber: 30-06, 8-shot clip.
Barrel: 24".
Weight: 9½ lbs. **Length:** 43½" over-all.
Stock: Walnut, military.
Sights: Military square blade front, click adjustable peep rear.
Features: Commercially-made M-1 Garand duplicates the original service rifle. Introduced 1979. From Springfield Armory.
Price: Standard, about **$560.00**
Price: National Match, about **$670.00**
Price: Ultra Match, about **$760.00**

SPRINGFIELD ARMORY M1A RIFLE
Caliber: 7.62mm Nato (308), 5-, 10- or 20-round box magazine.
Barrel: 25¹¹⁄₁₆" with flash suppressor, 22" without suppressor.
Weight: 8¾ lbs. **Length:** 44¼" over-all.
Stock: American walnut or birch with walnut colored heat-resistant fiberglass handguard. Matching walnut handguard available.
Sights: Military, square blade front, full click-adjustable aperture rear.
Features: Commercial equivalent of the U.S. M-14 service rifle with no provision for automatic firing. From Springfield Armory. Military accessories available including 3x-9x2 ART scope and mount.
Price: Standard M1A Rifle, about **$650.00**
Price: Match Grade, about **$775.00**
Price: Super Match (heavy Premium barrel), about **$875.00**
Price: M1A-A1 Assault Rifle, about **$775.00**

Springfield Armory BM-59

SPRINGFIELD ARMORY BM-59
Caliber: 7.62mm NATO (308 Win.); 20-round box magazine.
Barrel: 17.5".
Weight: 9¼ lbs. **Length:** 38.5" over-all.
Stock: Walnut, with trapped rubber butt pad.
Sights: Military square blade front, click adj. peep rear.
Features: Full military-dress Italian service rifle. Available in selective fire or semi-auto only. Refined version of the M-1 Garand. Accessories available include: folding alpine stock, muzzle brake/flash suppressor/grenade launcher combo, bipod, winter trigger, grenade launcher sights, bayonet, oiler. Extremely limited quantities. Introduced 1981.
Price: Standard Italian model, about **$780.00**
Price: Ital-Alpine model, about............................... **$940.00**
Price: Alpine Paratrooper model, about **$1,100.00**
Price: Nigerian Mark IV model, about......................... **$875.00**

Universal 1003 Carbine

UNIVERSAL 1003 AUTOLOADING CARBINE
Caliber: 30 M1, 5-shot magazine.
Barrel: 18".
Weight: 5½ lbs. **Length:** 35½" over-all.
Stock: American hardwood stock inletted for "issue" sling and oiler, blued metal handguard.
Sights: Blade front with protective wings, adj. rear.
Features: Gas operated, cross lock safety. Receiver tapped for scope mounts.
Price: **$224.00**
Price: Model 2560 "Ferret" in 256 Win.................... **$252.00**

CAUTION: PRICES CHANGE. CHECK AT GUNSHOP.

CENTERFIRE RIFLES—MILITARY STYLE AUTOLOADERS

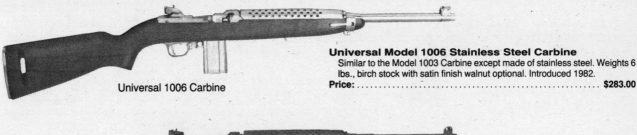

Universal 1006 Carbine

Universal Model 1006 Stainless Steel Carbine

Similar to the Model 1003 Carbine except made of stainless steel. Weights 6 lbs., birch stock with satin finish walnut optional. Introduced 1982.

Price: **$283.00**

Universal 5000PT Carbine

Universal Model 5000PT Carbine

Same as standard Model 1003 except comes with "Schmeisser-type paratrooper" folding stock. Over-all length open 36"; folded 27".

Price: Blue only **$269.00**

Universal Model 1005 SB Carbine

Same as Model 1003 except has "Super-Mirrored" blue finish, walnut Monte Carlo stock, deluxe barrel band. Also available finished in nickel (Model 1010N), 18K gold (Model 1015G), Raven Black Du Pont Teflon-S (Model 1020TB) or Camouflage Olive Teflon-S (Model 1025TCO).

Price: Model 1005SB **$266.50**
Price: Model 1010N... **$299.00**
Price: Model 1015G... **$366.00**
Price: Model 1020TB, 1025TCO .... **$ 299.00**

Universal Commemorative Model 1981 Carbine

Same basic specs as Model 1003 Carbine except comes with 5-, 15- and 30-shot magazines, Weaver scope and mount, bayonet and scabbard, brass belt buckle—all in a foam-fitted case. Stock is of select black walnut with in-letted medallion. Metal parts are Parkerized. Introduced 1981.

Price: Complete **$650.00**

UZI Carbine

UZI CARBINE

Caliber: 9mm Parabellum, 25-round magazine.
Barrel: 16.1".
Weight: 8½ lbs. **Length:** 24.2" (stock folded).
Stock: Folding metal stock.
Sights: Post-type front, "L" flip-type rear adj. for 100 meters and 200 meters.
Features: Adapted by Col. Uzi Gal to meet BATF regulations, this semi-auto has the same qualities as the famous submachine gun. Made by Israel Military Industries. Comes in molded Styrofoam case with sling, magazine and a short "display only" barrel. Exclusively imported from Israel by Action Arms Ltd. Introduced 1980.

Price: **$627.00**

Valmet M76 Bullpup

VALMET M76 BULLPUP CARBINE

Caliber: 223, 15- or 30-shot magazine.
Barrel: 16.5".
Weight: 7¾ lbs. **Length:** 28" over-all.
Stock: High-impact resin composition.
Sights: Post front, peep rear; both sights off-set to the left.
Features: Semi-automatic only. Uses Kalishnikov AK action. Introduced 1982. Imported by Odin International.

Price: **$1,295.00**

Valmet M78 Rifle

VALMET M78 STANDARD RIFLE

Caliber: 7.62 x 39.
Barrel: 24".
Weight: 10.5 lbs. **Length:** 43" over-all.
Stock: Birch buttstock, composition fore-end and pistol grip.
Sights: Hooded post front, open fully adj. rear with "night sight" blade.
Features: Semi-automatic only. Uses basic Kalishnikov action. Introduced 1982. Imported by Odin International.

Price: **$1,495.00**

CENTERFIRE RIFLES—MILITARY STYLE AUTOLOADERS

Valmet M78 LMG

Valmet M78 (NATO) LMG Semi-Auto
Similar to M78 Standard rifle except is chambered for 7.62 x 51 NATO (308 Win.). Has straight 20-round box magazine, rubber recoil pad, folding carrying handle. Introduced 1981. Imported by Odin International. Also available as M78HV chambered for 223. Same price.
Price: **$1,495.00**

VIKING SEMI-AUTO MINI CARBINE
Caliber: 9mm Parabellum, 36-round magazine.
Barrel: 16".
Weight: About 6 lbs. **Length:** 22" over-all (stock closed).
Stock: Retractable wire. Pistol grip and fore-end of high impact plastic.
Sights: Post front, L-type flip for 100 and 200 meters.
Features: Manual and grip safeties; blow-back action. Finished in matte olive green color. Made in U.S.A. Introduced 1982. Available from W.S.I.
Price: About **$650.00**

Wilkinson "Terry"

WILKINSON "TERRY" CARBINE
Caliber: 9mm Para., 30-shot magazine.
Barrel: 16³⁄₁₆".
Weight: 7 lbs. 2 oz. **Length:** 28½" over-all.
Stock: Black P.V.C. plastic stock, grip and fore-end.
Sights: Williams adjustable.
Features: Closed breech, blow-back action. Bolt-type safety and magazine catch. Ejection port has spring operated cover. Receiver dovetailed for scope mount. Semi-auto only. Introduced 1977. From Wilkinson Arms.
Price: **$465.00**

CENTERFIRE RIFLES—SPORTING AUTOLOADERS

Browning Auto Rifle

BROWNING HIGH-POWER AUTO RIFLE
Caliber: 243, 270, 30-06, 308.
Barrel: 22" round tapered.
Weight: 7⅜ lbs. **Length:** 43" over-all.
Stock: French walnut p.g. stock (13⅝"x2"x1⅝") and fore-end, hand checkered.
Sights: Adj. folding-leaf rear, gold bead on hooded ramp front.
Features: Detachable 4-round magazine. Receiver tapped for scope mounts. Trigger pull 3½ lbs. Gold plated trigger on Grade IV. Imported from Belgium by Browning.
Price: Grade I **$564.95**
Price: Grade III **$1,100.00**
Price: Grade IV **$2,090.00**

Browning Magnum Auto Rifle
Same as the standard caliber model, except weighs 8⅜ lbs., 45" over-all, 24" bbl., 3-round mag. Cals. 7mm Mag., 300 Win. Mag.
Price: Grade I **$624.95**
Price: Grade III **$1,160.00**
Price: Grade IV **$2,150.00**

Heckler & Koch 770

HECKLER & KOCH HK770 AUTO RIFLE
Caliber: 308 Win., 3-shot magazine.
Barrel: 19.6".
Weight: 7½ lbs. **Length:** 42.8" over-all.
Stock: European walnut. Checkered p.g. and fore-end.
Sights: Vertically adjustable blade front, open, fold-down rear adj. for w.
Features: Has the delayed roller-locked bolt system and polygonal rifling. Magazine catch located at front of trigger guard. Receiver top is dovetailed to accept clamp-type scope mount. Imported from West Germany by Heckler & Koch, Inc.
Price: **$640.00**
Price: HK630, 223 Rem. **$640.00**
Price: HK940, 30-06 .... **$770.00**
Price: Scope mount with 1" rings **$113.00**

CENTERFIRE RIFLES—SPORTING AUTOLOADERS

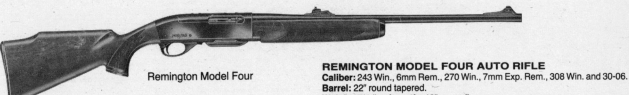

Remington Model Four

REMINGTON MODEL FOUR AUTO RIFLE
Caliber: 243 Win., 6mm Rem., 270 Win., 7mm Exp. Rem., 308 Win. and 30-06.
Barrel: 22" round tapered.
Weight: 7½ lbs. **Length:** 42" over-all.
Stock: Walnut, deluxe cut checkered p.g. and fore-end. Full cheekpiece, Monte Carlo.
Sights: Gold bead front sight on ramp; step rear sight with windage adj.
Features: Redesigned and improved version of the Model 742. Positive cross-bolt safety. Receiver tapped for scope mount. 4-shot clip mag. Has cartridge head medallion denoting caliber on bottom of receiver. Introduced 1981.
Price: $485.95
Price: Extra 4-shot clip magazine $10.95

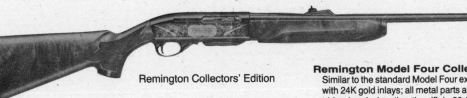

Remington Collectors' Edition

Remington Model Four Collectors' Edition
Similar to the standard Model Four except has an etched scroll-work receiver with 24K gold inlays; all metal parts are polished to a high-lustre finish. A cartridge head, denoting the rifle's 30-06 caliber is imbedded in the receiver. Stock and fore-end are specially matched high-grade walnut; fitted rosewood grip cap, brown butt pad. Serial numbers run from LE-81-001 thru LE-81-1500. Barrel length is 22", blade-ramp front sight, adjustable sliding ramp rear sight. Only 1500 examples will be made. Introduced 1982.
Price: About. $1,500.00

Remington Model 7400 Auto Rifle
Similar to Model Four except does not have full cheekpiece Monte Carlo stock, has slightly different fore-end design, impressed checkering, no cartridge head medallion. Introduced 1981.
Price: $435.95

Ruger 44 Carbine

RUGER 44 AUTOLOADING CARBINE
Caliber: 44 Magnum, 4-shot tubular magazine.
Barrel: 18½" round tapered.
Weight: 5¾ lbs. **Length:** 36¾" over-all.
Stock: One-piece walnut p.g. stock (13⅜"x1⅝"x2¼").
Sights: 1⁄16" front, folding leaf rear sight adj. for e.
Features: Wide, curved trigger. Sliding cross-bolt safety. Receiver tapped for scope mount, unloading button.
Price: $332.00

CENTERFIRE RIFLES—LEVER & SLIDE ACTIONS

Browning B-92

BROWNING B-92 LEVER ACTION
Caliber: 357 Mag., 44 Rem. Mag., 11-shot magazine.
Barrel: 20" round.
Weight: 5 lbs., 8 oz. **Length:** 37½" over-all.
Stock: Straight grip stock and classic fore-end in French walnut with high gloss finish. Steel, modified crescent buttplate. (12¾" x 2" x 2⅞").
Sights: Post front, classic cloverleaf rear with notched elevation ramp. Sight radius 16⅝".
Features: Tubular magazine. Follows design of original Model 92 lever-action. Introduced 1979. Imported from Japan by Browning.
Price: $324.95

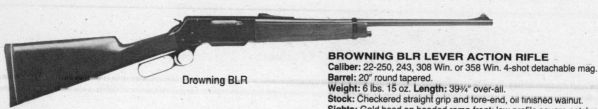

Drowning BLR

BROWNING BLR LEVER ACTION RIFLE
Caliber: 22-250, 243, 308 Win. or 358 Win. 4-shot detachable mag.
Barrel: 20″ round tapered.
Weight: 6 lbs. 15 oz. **Length:** 39¾″ over-all.
Stock: Checkered straight grip and fore-end, oil finished walnut.
Sights: Gold bead on hooded ramp front; low profile square notch adj. rear.
Features: Wide, grooved trigger; half-cock hammer safety. Receiver tapped for scope mount. Recoil pad installed. Imported from Japan by Browning.
Price: **$394.95**

Dixie Model 1873

DIXIE ENGRAVED MODEL 1873 RIFLE
Caliber: 44-40, 11-shot magazine.
Barrel: 20″, round.
Weight: 7¾ lbs. **Length:** 39″ over-all.
Stock: Walnut.
Sights: Blade front, adj. rear.
Features: Engraved and case hardened frame. Duplicate of Winchester 1873. Made in Italy. From Dixie Gun Works.
Price: **$550.00**
Price: Plain, blued carbine **$495.00**

Marlin Model 1894

MARLIN 1894 LEVER ACTION CARBINE
Caliber: 44 Magnum, 10-shot tubular magazine
Barrel: 20″ Micro-Grove®.
Weight: 6 lbs. **Length:** 37½″.
Stock: American black walnut, straight grip and fore-end. Mar-Shield® finish.
Sights: Hooded ramp front, semi-buckhorn folding rear adj. for w. & e.
Features: Receiver tapped for scope mount, offset hammer spur, solid top receiver sand blasted to prevent glare.
Price: **$259.95**

Marlin Model 1895S

MARLIN 1895S LEVER ACTION RIFLE
Caliber: 45-70, 4-shot tubular magazine.
Barrel: 22″ round.
Weight: 7½ lbs. **Length:** 40½″.
Stock: American black walnut, full pistol grip. Mar-Shield® finish; rubber butt-pad; q-d. swivels; leather carrying strap.
Sights: Bead front with Wide-Scan hood, semi-buckhorn folding rear adj. for w. and e.
Features: Solid receiver tapped for scope mounts or receiver sights, offset hammer spur.
Price: **$346.95**

Marlin Model 336C

MARLIN 0060 LEVER ACTION CARBINE
Caliber: 30-30 or 35 Rem., 6-shot tubular magazine
Barrel: 20″ Micro-Grove®.
Weight: 7 lbs. **Length:** 38½″.
Stock: Select American black walnut, capped p.g. with white line spacers. Mar-Shield® finish.
Sights: Ramp front with Wide-Scan™ hood, semi-buckhorn folding rear adj. for w. & e.
Features: Receiver tapped for scope mount, offset hammer spur; top of receiver sand blasted to prevent glare.
Price: Less scope **$246.95**

CAUTION: PRICES CHANGE. CHECK AT GUNSHOP.

CENTERFIRE RIFLES—LEVER & SLIDE ACTIONS

Marlin Model 336T

Marlin 336T Lever Action Carbine
Same as the 336C except: straight stock; cal. 30-30 only. Squared finger lever, 18½″ barrel, weight 6¾ lbs.
Price: $246.95

Marlin 30A Lever Action Carbine
Same as the Marlin 336C except: checkered walnut-finished hardwood p.g. stock, 30-30 only, 6-shot
Price: $230.95

Marlin Model 444S

Marlin 375 Rifle
Similar to 444S except chambered for 375 Win., 5-shot magazine; 20″ barrel; over-all length of 38½″, weight of 6¾ lbs. Comes with adj. leather carrying strap and q.d. swivels
Price: $280.95

MARLIN 444S LEVER ACTION SPORTER
Caliber: 444 Marlin, 4-shot tubular magazine
Barrel: 22″ Micro-Grove®.
Weight: 7½ lbs. **Length:** 40½″.
Stock: American black walnut, capped p.g. with white line spacers, rubber rifle butt pad. Mar-Shield® finish; q.d. swivels, leather carrying strap.
Sights: Hooded ramp front, folding semi-buckhorn rear adj. for w. & e.
Features: Receiver tapped for scope mount, offset hammer spur, leather sling with detachable swivels.
Price: $280.95

NAVY ARMS HENRY CARBINE
Caliber: 44-40 or 44 rimfire.
Barrel: 21″.
Weight: About 9 lbs. **Length:** About 39″ over-all.
Stock: Oil stained American walnut.
Sights: Blade front, rear adj. for e.
Features: Reproduction of the original Henry carbine with brass frame and buttplate, rest blued. Will be produced in limited edition of 1,000 standard models, plus 50 engraved guns. Made in U.S. by Navy Arms.
Price: Standard $500.00
Price: Engraved $1,500.00
Price: Iron frame, standard. $750.00
Price: Iron frame, engraved $1,500.00

MARLIN 1894C CARBINE 357
Caliber: 357 Magnum, 9-shot tube magazine.
Barrel: 18½″ Micro-Groove®.
Weight: 6 lbs. **Length:** 35½″ over-all.
Stock: American black walnut, straight grip and fore-end.
Sights: Bead front, adjustable semi-buckhorn folding rear.
Features: Solid top receiver tapped for scope mount or receiver sight; offset hammer spur. Receiver top sandblasted to prevent glare.
Price: About $259.95

Remington Model Six

ROSSI SADDLE-RING CARBINE
Caliber: 38 Spec. (9 rounds), 357 Mag. (8 rounds).
Barrel: 20″.
Weight: 5¾ lbs. **Length:** 37″ over-all.
Stock: Walnut.
Sights: Blade front, buckhorn rear.
Features: Re-creation of the famous lever-action carbine. Handles 38 and 357 interchangeably. Introduced 1978. Imported by Interarms.
Price: $230.00
Price: Blue, engraved $290.00

REMINGTON MODEL SIX SLIDE ACTION
Caliber: 6mm Rem., 243, 270, 308 Win., 30-06.
Barrel: 22″ round tapered.
Weight: 7½ lbs. **Length:** 42″ over-all.
Stock: Cut-checkered walnut p.g. and fore-end, Monte Carlo with full cheekpiece.
Sights: Gold bead front sight on matted ramp, open step adj. sporting rear.
Features: Redesigned and improved version of the Model 760. Has cartridge head medallion denoting caliber on bottom of receiver. Detachable 4-shot clip. Cross-bolt safety. Receiver tapped for scope mount. Introduced 1981.
Price: $432.95
Price: Extra 4-shot clip $10.25

Remington Model 7600

Remington Model 7600 Slide Action Rifle
Similar to Model Six except does not have Monte Carlo stock or cheekpiece, no cartridge head medallion. Slightly different fore-end design. Impressed checkering. Introduced 1981.
Price: $382.95

Savage Model 99E

SAVAGE 99E LEVER ACTION RIFLE
Caliber: 300 Savage, 243 or 308 Win., 5 shot rotary magazine.
Barrel: 22", chrome-moly steel.
Weight: 7 lbs. **Length:** 39¾" over-all.
Stock: Walnut finished with checkered p.g.
Sights: Ramp front, adjustable ramp rear sight. Tapped for scope mounts.
Features: Grooved trigger, slide safety locks trigger and lever.
Price: $317.50

Savage Model 99A

Savage 99A Lever Action Rifle
Similar to the 99E except: straight-grip walnut stock with schnabel fore-end, top tang safety, no magazine window. Cocking indicator. Drilled and tapped for scope mounting. Available in 250-3000 (250 Savage), 243, 308 Win., or 375 Win.
Price: $349.00

Savage Model 99C

Savage 99C Lever Action Clip Rifle
Similar to M99A except: detachable staggered clip magazine with push-button ejection. Cocking indicator. Drilled and tapped for scope mounting. Cut checkering on Monte Carlo stock and fore-end. Wgt. about 6¾ lbs., 41¾" over-all with 22" bbl. Available in cals. 243, 308, 7mm-08 Rem.
Price: $357.00

Winchester 94 Big Bore

WINCHESTER MODEL 94 BIG BORE XTR
Caliber: 375 Win., 6-shot magazine.
Barrel: 20".
Weight: 6⅛ lbs. **Length:** 37¾" over-all.
Stock: American walnut with fine cut checkering, warm rich color. Satin finish.
Sights: Hooded ramp front, semi-buckhorn rear adjustable for w. & e.
Features: All external metal parts have Winchester's new deep blue high polish finish. Stock measurements are: 13¼" x 1¾" x 2½". Rifling twist 1 in 12". Rubber recoil pad fitted to buttstock. Introduced 1978. Made under license by U.S. Repeating Arms Co.
Price: $320.00

Winchester Model 94

WINCHESTER 94 LEVER ACTION CARBINE
Caliber: 30-30, (12" twist). 6-shot tubular mag.
Barrel: 16", 20".
Weight: 6½ lbs. **Length:** 37¾" over-all.
Stock: Walnut straight grip stock and fore-end (13"x1¾"x2½").
Sights: Bead front sight on ramp with removable cover; open rear. Tapped for receiver sights.
Features: Solid frame, top ejection, half-cock hammer safety. Made under license by U.S. Repeating Arms Co.
Price: $252.00
Price: Trapper model, 16" barrel $252.00

Winchester 94 Antique Carbine
Same as M94 except: color case-hardened and scroll-engraved receiver, brass-plated loading gate and saddle ring. 30-30 only
Price: $270.00

Winchester Model 94XTR Carbine
Same as standard Model 94 except has high-grade finish on stock and fore-end with cut checkering on both. Metal has highly polished deep blue finish.
Price: $275.00

Alpine Custom Grade

ALPINE BOLT ACTION RIFLE
Caliber: 22-250, 243 Win., 264 Win., 270, 30-06, 308, 308 Norma Mag., 7mm Rem Mag., 8mm, 300 Win. Mag., 5-shot magazine (3 for magnum).
Barrel: 23″ (std. cals.), 24″ (mag.).
Weight: 7½ lbs.
Stock: European walnut. Full p.g. and Monte Carlo; checkered p.g. and fore-end; rubber recoil pad; white line spacers; sling swivels.
Sights: Ramp front, open rear adj. for w. and e.
Features: Made by Firearms Co. Ltd. in England. Imported by Mandall Shooting Supplies.
Price: Standard Grade **$375.00**
Price: Custom Grade (illus.)................................. **$395.00**

Anschutz Model 1532D

ANSCHUTZ 1432D/1532D CLASSIC RIFLES
Caliber: 22 Hornet (1432D), 4-shot clip, 222 Rem. (1532D), 3-shot clip.
Barrel: 23½″.
Weight: 7¾ lbs. **Length:** 42½″ over-all.
Stock: Select European walnut with checkered pistol grip and fore-end.
Sights: Hooded ramp front, folding leaf rear.
Features: Adjustable single stage trigger. Receiver drilled and tapped for scope mounting. Introduced 1982. Imported from Germany by Talo Distributors, Inc.
Price: 1432D (22 Hornet) **$612.00**
Price: 1532D (222 Rem.) **$612.00**

ANSCHUTZ 1432D/1532D Custom Rifles
Similar to the Classic models except have roll-over Monte Carlo cheekpiece, slim fore-end with Schnabel tip, Wundhammer palm swell on pistol grip, rosewood grip cap with white diamond insert. Skip-line checkering on grip and fore-end. Introduced 1982. Imported from Germany by Talo Distributors, Inc.
Price: 1432D (22 Hornet) **$662.00**
Price: 1532D (222 Rem.) **$662.00**

BSA CF-2 Rifle

BSA CF-2 BOLT ACTION RIFLE
Caliber: 222 Rem., 22-250, 243, 6.5x55, 7mm Mauser, 7x64, 270, 308, 30-06, 7mm Rem. Mag., 300 Win. Mag.
Barrel: 24″.
Weight: 7¾ lbs. **Length:** 45″ over-all.
Stock: European walnut with roll-over Monte Carlo, palm swell on right side of pistol grip, skip-line checkering. High gloss finish.
Sights: Open adjustable rear, hooded ramp front. Removable.
Features: Adjustable single trigger or optional double-set triggers, side safety, visible cocking indicator. Ventilated rubber recoil pad. North American-style stock has high gloss finish, European has oil. Introduced 1980. From Precision Sports.
Price: Standard calibers, North American style **$600.00**
Price: Magnum calibers, North American style. **$625.00**
Price: Double-set triggers, extra **$65.00**
Price: Heavy barrel, extra **$82.50**
Price: Standard calibers, European style **$650.00**
Price: Magnum calibers, European style **$675.00**

BSA CF-2 Stutzen

BSA CF-2 Stutzen Stock Rifle
Similar to the standard CF-2 except has improved bolt guide rib circlip and precision-ground striker; 20.5″ barrel; full-length Stutzen-style stock with constrasting Schnabel fore-end tip and grip cap. Available in 222, 6.5 x 55, 308 Win., 30-06, 270, 7 x 64. Measures 41.3″ over-all, weighs 7½ lbs. Introduced 1982. From Precision Sports.
Price: **$675.00**
Price: Double set triggers, add **$65.00**

Browning BBR Rifle

BROWNING BBR BOLT ACTION RIFLE

Caliber: 25-06, 270, 30-06, 7mm Rem. Mag., 300 Win. Mag.
Barrel: 24″ medium sporter weight with recessed muzzle.
Weight: 8 lbs. **Length:** 44½″ over-all.
Stock: Select American walnut cut to lines of Monte Carlo sporter; full p.g. and high cheekpiece; 18 l.p.i. checkering. Recoil pad is standard on magnum calibers.
Features: Short throw (60°) bolt with fluted surface, 9 locking lugs, plunger-type ejector, adjustable trigger is grooved and gold plated. Hinged floorplate with detachable box magazine (4 rounds in standard cals, 3 in mags). Convenient slide safety on tang. Special anti-warp aluminum fore-end insert. Low profile swivel studs. Introduced 1978. Imported from Japan by Browning.
Price: $469.95

CHAMPLIN RIFLE

Caliber: All std. chamberings, including 458 Win. and 460 Wea. Many wildcats on request.
Barrel: Any length up to 26″ for octagon. Choice of round, straight taper octagon, or octagon with integral quarter rib, front sight ramp and sling swivel stud.
Weight: About 8 lbs. **Length:** 45″ over-all.
Stock: Hand inletted, shaped and finished. Checkered to customer specs. Select French, Circassian or claro walnut. Steel p.g. cap, trap buttplate or recoil pad.
Sights: Bead on ramp front, 3-leaf folding rear.
Features: Right or left hand Champlin action, tang safety or optional shroud safety, Canjar adj. trigger, hinged floorplate.
Price: From $4,600.00

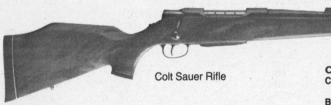

Colt Sauer Rifle

COLT SAUER RIFLE

Caliber: 25-06, 270, 30-06, (std.), 7mm Rem. Mag., 300 Wea. Mag., 300 Win. Mag. (Magnum).
Barrel: 24″, round tapered.
Weight: 8 lbs. (std.). **Length:** 43¾″ over-all.
Stock: American walnut, cast-off M.C. design with cheekpiece. Fore-end tip and p.g. cap rosewood with white spacers. Hand checkering.
Sights: None furnished. Specially designed scope mounts for any popular make scope furnished.
Features: Unique barrel/receiver union, non-rotating bolt wih cam-actuated locking lugs, tang-type safety locks sear. Detachable 3- and 4-shot magazines.
Price: Standard calibers $1,116.95
Price: Magnum calibers..................................... $1,154.95
Price: Grand Alaskan, 375 H&H $1,185.00

COLT SAUER GRAND AFRICAN

Caliber: 458 Win. Mag.
Barrel: 24″, round tapered.
Weight: 10½ lbs. **Length:** 44½″ over-all.
Stock: Solid African bubinga wood, cast-off M.C. with cheekpiece, contrasting rosewood fore-end and p.g. caps with white spacers. Checkered fore-end and p.g.
Sights: Ivory bead hooded ramp front, adj. sliding rear.
Price: $1,242.50

Colt Sauer Short Action Rifle

Same as standard rifle except chambered for 22-250, 243 and 308 Win. 24″ bbl., 43″ over-all. Weighs 7½ lbs. 3-shot magazine
Price: $1,116.95

DuBiel Modern Classic

Du BIEL ARMS BOLT ACTION RIFLES

Caliber: Standard calibers 22-250 thru 458 Win. Mag. Selected wildcat calibers available.
Barrel: Selected weights and lengths. Douglas Premium
Weight: About 7½ lbs.
Stock: Five styles. Walnut, maple, laminates. Hand checkered.
Sights: None furnished. Receiver has integral milled bases.
Features: Basically a custom-made rifle. Left or right-hand models available. Five-lug locking mechanism, 00 degree bolt rotation; adjustable Canjar trigger; oil or epoxy stock finish; Presentation recoil pad; jeweled and chromed bolt body; sling swivel studs; lever latch or button floorplate release. All steel action and parts. Introduced 1978. From Du Biel Arms.
Price: Rollover Model, left or right-hand $2,500.00
Price: Thumbhole, left or right hand $2,500.00
Price: Classic, left or right hand $2,500.00
Price: Modern Classic, left or right hand. $2,500.00
Price: Thumbhole Mannlicher, left or right hand $2,500.00

Consult our Directory pages for the location of firms mentioned.

CAUTION: PRICES CHANGE. CHECK AT GUNSHOP.

H&R Model 340

HARRINGTON & RICHARDSON MODEL 340 RIFLE

Caliber: 243, 7x57, 308, 270, 30-06.
Barrel: 22".
Weight: About 7¼ lbs. **Length:** 43" over-all.
Stock: American walnut, hand checkered pistol grip and fore-end, carved and beaded cheekpiece, metal grip cap, rubber recoil pad.
Sights: None furnished. Drilled and tapped for scope mounts.
Features: Mauser-design action with hinged steel floorplate and trigger guard; adjustable trigger; high lustre blue finish. Introduced 1982. From Harrington & Richardson.
Price: **$350.00**

Heym Model SR-20L

HEYM MODEL SR-20 BOLT ACTION RIFLES

Caliber: 5.6x57, 243, 6.5x57, 270, 7x57, 7x64, 308, 30-06 (SR-20L); 9.3x62 (SR-20N) plus SR-20L cals.; SR-20G—6.5x68, 7mm Rem. Mag., 300 Win. Mag., 8x68S, 375H&H.
Barrel: 20½" (SR-20L), 24" (SR-20N), 26" (SR-20G).
Weight: 7-8 lbs. depending upon model.
Stock: Dark European walnut, hand-checkered p.g. and fore-end. Oil finish. Recoil pad, rosewood grip cap. Monte Carlo-style. SR-20L has full Mannlicher-style stock, others have sporter-style with schnabel tip.
Sights: Silver bead ramp front, adj. folding leaf rear.
Features: Hinged floorplate, 3-position safety,. Receiver drilled and tapped for scope mounts. Adjustable trigger. Options available include double-set triggers, left-hand action and stock, Suhler claw mounts, deluxe engraving and stock carving. Imported from West Germany. Contact Heym for more data.
Price: SR-20L... **$977.00**
Price: SR-20N **$877.00**
Price: SR-20-G.. **$937.00**
Price: Left-hand action and stock, add.......................... **$159.00**

Consult our Directory pages for the location of firms mentioned.

Kimber Hornet Sporter

KIMBER MODEL 82 HORNET SPORTER

Caliber: 22 Hornet, 3-shot magazine.
Barrel: 24".
Weight: About 6½ lbs. **Length:** 41" over-all.
Stock: Select walnut, Classic or Cascade design with hand checkered pistol grip and fore-end.
Sights: Blade front on ramp, open rear adjustable for windage and elevation; also available without sights.
Features: All steel construction. Rocker-type silent safety, checkered steel butt plate, steel grip cap. Receiver grooved for scope mounts. Introduced 1982.
Price: Classic stock, no sights **$505.00**
Price: Classic stock, with sights **$555.00**
Price: Cascade stock, no sights **$515.00**
Price: Cascade stock, with sights **$565.00**
Price: Scope mount and rings **$40.00**

Kleinguenther K-15 Insta-Fire

KLEINGUENTHER K-15 INSTA-FIRE RIFLE

Caliber: 243, 25-06, 270, 30-06, 308 Win., 7x57, 308 Norma Mag., 7mm Rem. Mag., 375 H&H, 257-270-300 Weath. Mag.
Barrel: 24" (Std.), 26" (Mag.).
Weight: 7 lbs., 12 oz. **Length:** 43½" over-all.
Stock: European walnut M.C. with 1" recoil pad. Left or right hand. Rosewood grip cap. Hand checkered. High luster or satin finish.
Sights: None furnished. Drilled and tapped for scope mounts. Iron sights optional.
Features: Ultra-fast lock/ignition time. Clip or feed from top of receiver. Guaranteed ½" 100 yd. groups. Many optional stock features available. Imported from Germany, assembled and accurized by Kleinguenther's.
Price: All calibers... **$975.00**

Krico Model 620L/720L

KRICO MODEL 400L BOLT ACTION RIFLE

Caliber: 22 Hornet, 5-shot magazine.
Barrel: 24".
Weight: 6.6 lbs.
Stock: Select French walnut. Ventilated rubber recoil pad.
Sights: Hooded post front, open rear adj. for windage.
Features: Detachable box magazine; checkered pistol grip and fore-end; sling swivels. Available with single or double set trigger. Imported from West Germany. Contact Krico for more data.
Price: $479.00

Krico Model 400E Bolt Action Rifle

Same as Model 400L except has straight fore-end, walnut-finished beech stock, no fore-end tip, hard rubber butt plate.
Price: With single trigger. $409.00
Price: With set trigger $419.00

Krico Model 620L/720L

Similar to the Model 600/700E except has full Mannlicher-style stock, 21" barrel, weighs 6.8 lbs.
Price: Varmint calibers (M620) $719.00
Price: Standard calibers (M720) $749.00

KRICO MODEL 600/700E BOLT ACTION

Caliber: 17 Rem., 222, 222 Rem. Mag., 223, 243, 308, 7x57, 7x64, 270, 30-06, 7mm Rem. Mag., 300 Win Mag.; 3-shot clip magazine
Barrel: 24" (26" in magnum calibers).
Weight: 7.2 lbs. **Length:** 44" over-all (24" bbl.).
Stock: Hand checkered French walnut, European style with schnabel fore-end. Classic American-style also available.
Sights: Hooded front ramp, fixed rear. Tangent rear sight optional.
Features: Adjustable single or double set trigger, silent safety, double front locking lugs. Action can be disassembled without tools. Custom versions with engraving and stock carving available. Imported from Germany by Krico.
Price: Model 600, varmint calibers $640.00
Price: Model 700E, standard calibers. $690.00
Price: Model 700EM, magnum calibers $730.00

Krico Model 420L Bolt Action Rifle

Same as Model 400L except has full Mannlicher-style stock, 20" barrel, weighs 6.2 lbs. Solid rubber butt pad.
Price: $579.00

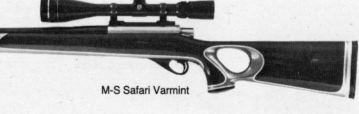

M-S Safari Varmint

M-S SAFARI ARMS VARMINT RIFLE

Caliber: Any standard centerfire; single shot.
Barrel: 24", stainless
Weight: To customer specs.
Stock: Fiberglass, custom painted. Thumbhole or pistol grip style.
Sights: None furnished. Drilled and tapped for scope mounting.
Features: Electronic trigger; high-speed lock time; stainless steel action. Custom built to customer specs. From M-S Safari Arms.
Price: From $1,095.00

Interarms Mark X Alaskan

MARK X CONTINENTAL MANNLICHER STYLE CARBINE

Caliber: 243, 270, 7x57, 308, 30-06.
Barrel: 20".
Weight: 7½ lbs. **Length:** 40" over-all.
Stock: Hand checkered European walnut. Straight European-style comb with sculptured cheekpiece.
Sights: Ramp front with removable hood; open rear adj. for w. and e.
Features: Similar to Marquis except for stock differences noted above, single adjustable or double-set triggers, classic "butter-knife" bolt handle. Button release hinged floorplate. Imported from Czechoslovakia by Interarms.
Price: Double-set triggers, with sights $450.00

MARK X RIFLE

Caliber: 22-250, 243, 270, 308 Win., 30-06, 25-06, 7x57, 7mm Rem. Mag., 300 Win. Mag.
Barrel: 24".
Weight: 7½ lbs. **Length:** 44" over-all.
Stock: Hand checkered walnut, Monte Carlo, white line spacers on p.g. cap, buttplate and fore-end tip.
Sights: Ramp front with removable hood, open rear adj. for w. and e.
Features: Sliding safety, quick detachable sling swivels, hinged floorplate. Also available as actions or bbld. actions. Imported from Czechoslovakia by Interarms.
Price: With adj. trigger and sights, from $350.00
Price: With adj. trigger, no sights, from $335.00

MARK X ALASKAN MAGNUM RIFLE

Caliber: 375 H&H, 458 Win Mag.; 3-shot magazine.
Barrel: 24".
Weight: 8¼ lbs. **Length:** 44¾" over-all.
Stock: Select walnut with crossbolt; hand checkered p.g. and fore-end; Monte Carlo; sling swivels.
Sights: Hooded ramp front; open rear adj. for w. & e.
Features: Hinged floorplate; right-hand thumb (tang) safety; adj. trigger. Imported from Czechoslovakia by Interarms.
Price: $450.00

CAUTION: PRICES CHANGE. CHECK AT GUNSHOP.

Mark X Marquis Carbine

MARK X MARQUIS MANNLICHER-STYLE CARBINE
Caliber: 270, 7x57, 30-06, 308 Win.
Barrel: 20″.
Weight: 7½ lbs. **Length:** 40″ over-all.
Stock: Hand checkered European walnut.
Sights: Ramp front with removable hood; open rear adj. for w. and e.
Features: Quick detachable sling swivels; fully adj. trigger; blue steel fore-end cap; white line spacers at p.g. cap and buttplate. Mark X Mauser action. Imported from Czechoslovakia by Interarms.
Price: With adj. trigger and sights $425.00

MARK X CAVALIER RIFLE
Caliber: 22-250, 243, 25-06, 270, 7x57, 7mm Rem. Mag., 308 Win., 30-06, 300 Win. Mag.
Barrel: 24″.
Weight: 7½ lbs. **Length:** 44″ over-all.
Stock: Checkered walnut with rosewood fore-end tip and pistol grip cap, Monte Carlo cheekpiece and recoil pad.
Sights: Ramp front with removable hood, open rear adjustable for windage and elevation.
Features: Contemporary-styled stock with sculptured accents; roll over cheekpiece and flat bottom fore-end. Adjustable trigger and quick detachable sling swivels, standard. Receiver drilled and tapped for receiver sights and scope mounts. Also available without sights. Imported from Czechoslovakia by Interarms.
Price: With adj. trigger and sights $425.00
Price: Adj. trigger, without sights $410.00
Price: 300 Win. Mag., 7mm Rem. Mag., with sights $425.00
Price: As above, without sights $410.00

MARK X VISCOUNT RIFLE
Caliber: 22-250, 243, 25-06, 270, 7x57, 7mm Rem. Mag., 308 Win., 30-06, 300 Win. Mag.
Barrel: 24″.
Weight: 7½ lbs. **Length:** 44″ over-all.
Stock: Genuine walnut stock, hand checkered with 1″ sling swivels.
Sights: Ramp front with removable hood, open rear sight adjustable for windage and elevation.
Features: One piece trigger guard with hinged floor plate, drilled and tapped for scope mounts and receiver sight, hammer-forged chrome vanadium steel barrel. Imported from Czechoslovakia by Interarms.
Price: With adj. trigger, sights, from $340.00
Price: With adj. trigger, no sights, from $325.00

Mauser Model 66

MAUSER MODEL 66 BOLT ACTION RIFLES
Caliber: 5.6x61, 243, 6.5x57, 270, 7x64, 308 Win., 30-06, 9.3x62.
Barrel: 24″.
Weight: About 7½ lbs. **Length:** 41″ over-all.
Stock: European walnut, oil finish, Pachmayr recoil pad, rosewood fore-end and grip cap, sling swivels.
Sights: Hooded ramp front, Williams open adj. rear.
Features: Interchangeable barrels within caliber groups; silent safety locks bolt and firing pin. Double set or single trigger completely interchangeable. Contact Mauser for more data.
Price: Standard calibers, Model 66S $1,999.00
Price: Standard calibers, full-length stock $2,100.00
Price: Model 66S Ultra (21″ barrel, 7 lbs.) $2,100.00
Price: Model 66SM (single set trigger, special wood and finish) . . . $2,270.00
Price: Interchangeable barrels, from $485.00

Mauser Model 66S Magnum Rifle
Similar to Model 66S except has 26″ barrel, weighs about 8¼ lbs., measures 44″ over-all and comes in 7mm Rem. Mag., 6.5x68, 300 Win. Mag., 7mm SE v.H., 300 Weatherby Mag., 9.3x64, 8x68S.
Price: $2,100.00

Mauser Model 66S Big Game Rifle
Similar to Model 66S except has 26″ barrel, weighs about 9¼ lbs. and is chambered for 375 H&H Mag. and 458 Win. Mag.
Price: $2,300.00

Mauser Model 77

MAUSER MODEL 77 BOLT ACTION RIFLE
Caliber: 243, 6.5x57, 270, 7x64, 308, 30-06.
Barrel: 24″.
Weight: About 7½ lbs. **Length:** 44″ over-all.
Stock: European walnut with oil finish, rosewood fore-end tip and grip cap. Bavarian cheekpiece, recoil pad and palm-swell p.g.
Sights: Ramp front, open rear adj. for w. & e.
Features: Detachable 3-round box magazine; same trigger system as Model 66, single set or double set; patented silent safety. Introduced 1981. Contact Mauser for more data.
Price: Half-stock $1,890.00
Price: Full length stock $1,990.00

Mauser Model 77 DJV Match-Sportsman
Similar to the standard Model 77 except has semi-bull barrel, muzzle brake, sandblasted metal. Full pistol grip, target-type stock with stippled fore-end bottom and pistol grip. Available only in 243 or 308 Win. No open sights furnished.
Price: $2,390.00
Price: With Zeiss 2.5-10 scope, Mauser mounts. $3,400.00

Mauser Model 77 Magnum Rifle
Similar to standard Model 77 except has 26″ barrel, 46″ over-all length, weighs about 7½ lbs. Magnum version chambered for 7mm Rem. Mag., 6.5x68, 300 Win. Mag., 9.3x62, 375 H&H mag., 9.3x64, 8x68S. Big Game version chambered for 375 H&H, 458 Win. Mag.
Price: $1,990.00

CENTERFIRE RIFLES—BOLT ACTIONS

Parker-Hale 1200

PARKER-HALE MIDLAND RIFLE
Caliber: 243, 270, 30-06, 308, 7mm Rem. Mag., 300 Win. Mag.
Barrel: 24″.
Weight: 7 lbs. **Length:** 45″ over-all.
Stock: Walnut; hand-checkered p.g. and fore-end.
Sights: Bead on ramp front, folding adjustable rear.
Features: Uses Springfield action; 4-shot magazine; receiver drilled and tapped and comes with Parker-Hale 1″ mounts and rings. Introduced 1981. Imported from England by Kassnar Imports.
Price: All calibers $289.95

PARKER-HALE SUPER 1200 BOLT ACTION RIFLE
Caliber: 22-250, 243 Win., 6mm Rem., 25-06, 270 Win., 30-06, 308 Win., 7mm Rem. Mag., 300 Win. Mag.
Barrel: 24″.
Weight: 7¼ lbs. **Length:** 45″ over-all.
Stock: 13.5″ x1.8″x2.3″. Hand checkered walnut, rosewood p.g. and fore-end caps, fitted rubber recoil pad with white line spacers.
Sights: Hooded bead front, folding adj. rear. Receiver tapped for scope mounts.
Features: 3-way side safety, single-stage adj. trigger, hinged mag. floorplate. Varmint Model (1200V) has glass-bedded action, free-floating bbl. avail. in 22-250, 6mm Rem., 25-06, 243 Win., without sights. Imported from England by Kassnar.
Price: $369.95
Price: Magnum calibers $374.95
Price: 1200V $374.95

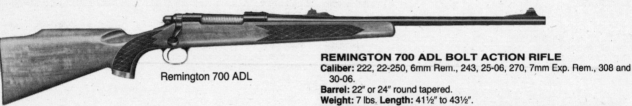

Remington 700 ADL

REMINGTON 700 ADL BOLT ACTION RIFLE
Caliber: 222, 22-250, 6mm Rem., 243, 25-06, 270, 7mm Exp. Rem., 308 and 30-06.
Barrel: 22″ or 24″ round tapered.
Weight: 7 lbs. **Length:** 41½″ to 43½″.
Stock: Walnut, RKW finished p.g. stock with impressed checkering, Monte Carlo (13⅜″x1⅝″x2⅜″).
Sights: Gold bead ramp front; removable, step-adj. rear with windage screw.
Features: Side safety, receiver tapped for scope mounts.
Price: $351.95
Price: 7mm Rem. Mag. $367.95

Remington 700 Classic

Remington 700 C Custom Rifle
Same as the 700 BDL except choice of 20″, 22″, or 24″ bbl. with or without sights. Jewelled bolt, with or without hinged floor plate. Select American walnut stock is hand checkered, rosewood fore-end and grip cap. Hand lapped barrel. 16 weeks for delivery after placing order.
Price: $825.00

REMINGTON 700 "CLASSIC" RIFLE
Caliber: 22-250, 6mm Rem., 243, 270, 30-06, 7mm Rem. Mag.
Barrel: 22″ (6mm, 243, 270, 30-06), 24″ (22-250, 7mm Rem. Mag.).
Weight: About 7 lbs. **Length:** 43½″ over-all (24″ bbl.).
Stock: American walnut, 20 l.p.i. checkering on p.g. and fore-end. Classic styling. Satin finish.
Sights: No sights furnished. Receiver drilled and tapped for scope mounting.
Features: A "classic" version of the M700ADL with straight comb stock. Fitted with rubber butt pad on all but magnum caliber, which has a full recoil pad. Sling swivel studs installed.
Price: All cals. except 7mm Rem. Mag. $381.95
Price: 7mm Rem. Mag. $397.95

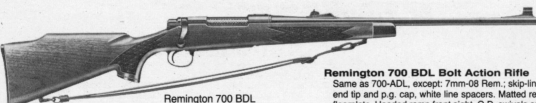

Remington 700 BDL

Remington 700BDL Left Hand
Same as 700 BDL except: mirror-image left-hand action, stock. Available in 270, 30-06 only.
Price: $437.95
Price: 7mm Rem. Mag. $453.95

Remington 700 BDL Varmint
Same as 700 BDL, except: 24″ heavy bbl., 43½″ over-all, wgt. 9 lbs. Cals. 222, 223, 22-250, 6mm Rem., 243, 25-06, 7mm-08 Rem. and 308. No sights.
Price: $441.95

Remington 700 BDL Bolt Action Rifle
Same as 700-ADL, except: 7mm-08 Rem.; skip-line checkering; black fore-end tip and p.g. cap, white line spacers. Matted receiver top, quick release floorplate. Hooded ramp front sight. Q.D. swivels and 1″ sling.
Price: $421.95
Available also in 17 Rem., 7mm Rem. Mag. and 300 Win. Mag., 8mm Rem. Mag., calibers. 44½″ over-all, weight 7½ lbs.
Price: $437.95
Price: Peerless Grade $1,500.00
Price: Premier Grade $3,000.00

Remington 700 Safari
Same as the 700 BDL except 375 H&H or 458 Win. Magnum calibers only. Hand checkered, oil finished stock with recoil pad installed. Delivery time is about five months.
Price: $719.95

Remington Model 788

REMINGTON 788 BOLT ACTION RIFLE

Caliber: 22-250, 222 Rem., 223 Rem., 7mm-08 Rem., 243, and 308 (4-shot).
Barrel: 18½″ round tapered (24″ in 223 and 22-250).
Weight: 7-7½ lbs. **Length:** 41⅝″ over-all.
Stock: Walnut-finished hardwood with Monte Carlo and p.g. (13⅝″x1⅞″x2⅝″).
Sights: Blade ramp front, open rear adj. for w. & e.
Features: Detachable box magazine, thumb safety, receiver tapped for scope mounts.
Price: **$269.95**
Price: Sling strap and swivels, installed **$18.25**
Price: Model 788 with Universal Model UE 4x scope, mounts and rings in cals. 223 Rem., 243 Win., 7mm-08 Rem., 308 and 22-250 .... **$317.95**

Ruger 77 Round Top

RUGER 77 BOLT ACTION RIFLE

Caliber: 22-250, 220 Swift, 243, 6mm, 308, 358 Win. (5-shot).
Barrel: 22″ round tapered (24″ in 220 Swift).
Weight: 6¾ lbs. **Length:** 42″ over-all.
Stock: Hand checkered American walnut (13¾″x1⅝″x2⅛″), p.g. cap, sling swivel studs and recoil pad.
Sights: Optional gold bead ramp front, folding leaf adj. rear, or scope rings.
Features: Integral scope mount bases, diagonal bedding system, hinged floor plate, adj. trigger, tang safety. Scope optional.

Ruger Model 77 Magnum Rifle

Similar to Ruger 77 except: magnum-size action. Calibers 25-06, 270, 280, 7x57, 30-06 (5-shot), 7mm Rem. Mag., 300 Win., Mag., 338 Win. Mag., 458 Win. Mag. (3-shot). 270, 7x57, 280 and 30-06 have 22″ bbl., all others have 24″. Weight and length vary with caliber.
Price: **$374.50**

Price: With Ruger steel scope rings (77R) **$374.50**
Price: With rings and open sights (77RS) **$394.25**
Price: 458 Win. Mag. **$473.00**
Price: Barreled action only all cals. except 458, open sights **$323.00**
Price: Barreled action, all cals. except 458, no sights **$304.00**
Price: Barreled action, 458, with open sights **$413.00**

Ruger International 77

Ruger International Model 77 Rifle

Same as the standard Model 77 except has 18¼″ barrel, full-length Mannlicher-style stock, with steel fore-end cap, loop-type sling swivel. Improved front sight. Available only in 243 or 308. Weighs 6 lbs., 4 oz. and uses the Ruger short action. Length over-all is 38½″.
Price: **$480.00**

Ruger Model 77 Magnum Round Top

Same as Model 77 except: round top receiver, drilled and tapped for standard scope mounts. Open sights are standard equipment. Calibers 25-06, 270, 30-06, 7mm Rem. Mag.
Price: All cals. (Model 77ST) **$374.50**

> Consult our Directory pages for the location of firms mentioned.

Ruger 77 Varmint

RUGER MODEL 77 VARMINT

Caliber: 22-250, 220 Swift, 243, 6mm, 25-06, 280, 308.
Barrel: 24″ heavy straight tapered, 26″ in 220 swift.
Weight: Approx. 9 lbs. **Length:** Approx. 44″ over-all.
Stock: American walnut, similar in style to Magnum Rifle.
Sights: Barrel drilled and tapped for target scope blocks. Integral scope mount bases in receiver.
Features: Ruger diagonal bedding system, Ruger steel 1″ scope rings supplied. Fully adj. trigger. Barreled actions available in any of the standard calibers and barrel lengths.
Price: (Model 77V) **$374.50**

Sako Classic Sporter

SAKO STANDARD SPORTER

Caliber: 17 Rem., 222, 223 (short action); 22-250, 220 Swift, 243, 308 (medium action); 25-06, 270, 30-06, 7mm Rem. Mag., 300 Win. Mag., 338 Win. Mag., 375 H&H Mag. (long action).
Barrel: 23" (222, 223, 243), 24" (other cals.).
Weight: 6¾ lbs. (short); 6¾ lbs. (med.); 8 lbs. (long).
Stock: Hand-checkered European walnut.
Sights: None furnished.
Features: Adj. trigger, hinged floorplate. 222 and 223 have short action, 243 and 22-250 have medium action, others are long action. Imported from Finland by Stoeger.
Price: Short action **$809.00**
Price: Medium action. **$809.00**
Price: Long action **$825.00**
Price: Magnum cals. **$860.00**
Price: 375 H&H **$875.00**

Sako Classic Sporter

Similar to the Standard Sporter except: available in 243 (medium action), 270, 30-06 and 7mm Rem. Mag. (long action) only; straight-comb "classic-style" stock with oil finish; solid rubber recoil pad; recoil lug. No sights furnished—receiver drilled and tapped for scope mounting. Introduced 1980.
Price: 243 . . . . **$975.00**
Price: 270, 30-06 . . . . **$1,020.00**
Price: 7mm Rem. Mag. **$1,035.00**

Sako Safari Grade

Sako Safari Grade Bolt Action

Similar to the Standard Grade Sporter except available in long action, calibers 300 Win. Mag., 338 Win. Mag. or 375 H&H Mag. only. Stocked in French walnut, checkered 20 l.p.i., solid rubber butt pad; grip cap and fore-end tip; quarter-rib "express" rear sight, hooded ramp front. Front sling swivel band-mounted on barrel.
Price: **$1,995.00**

Sako Super Deluxe Sporter

Similar to Deluxe Sporter except has select European Walnut with high gloss finish and deep cut oak leaf carving. Metal has super high polish, deep blue finish.
Price: **$1,995.00**

Sako Carbine

Sako Carbine

Same action as the Standard Sporter except has full "Mannlicher" style stock, 20" barrel, weighs 7½ lbs., chambered for 222 Rem., 243, 270 and 30-06 only. Introduced 1977. From Stoeger.
Price: 243, 270, 30-06 only **$995.00**

Sako Deluxe Sporter

Same action as Standard Sporter except has select wood, rosewood p.g. cap and fore-end tip. Fine checkering on top surfaces of integral dovetail bases, bolt sleeve, bolt handle root and bolt knob. Vent. recoil pad, skip-line checkering, mirror finish bluing.
Price: 222 or 223 cals. **$1,070.00**
Price: 220 Swift, 22-250, 243, 308 . . . . **$1,070.00**
Price: 25-06, 270, 30-06 . . . . **$1,100.00**
Price: 7mm Rem. Mag., 300 Win. Mag., 338 Mag., 375 H&H. **$1,120.00**

Sako Heavy Barrel

Same as std. Super Sporter except has beavertail fore-end; available in 222, 223 (short action), 220 Swift, 22-250, 243, 308 (medium action). Weight from 8¼ to 8½ lbs. 5-shot magazine capacity.
Price: 222, 223 (short action). **$875.00**
Price: 22-250, 243 (medium action) **$875.00**

Savage Model 110C

SAVAGE 110C BOLT ACTION RIFLE

Caliber: 243, 270, 30-06, 4-shot detachable box magazine, 7mm Rem. Mag. (3-shot).
Barrel: 22"; 24" in magnum calibers.
Weight: 7lbs. **Length:** 43" over-all.
Stock: Select walnut with Monte Carlo, skip-line cut checkered p.g. and fore-end. Swivel studs.
Sights: Removable ramp front, open rear adj. for w. & e.
Features: Tapped for scope mounting, free floating barrel, top tang safety, detachable clip magazine, hard rubber buttplate (rubber recoil pad on magnum calibers only). Right hand only in 25-06, 22-250 with 23" barrel.
Price: Right hand 110C. **$317.50**
Price: Left hand 110CL **$319.50**
Price: Right hand, mag. cals. **$327.50**
Price: Left hand, mag. cals. **$329.50**

CAUTION: PRICES CHANGE. CHECK AT GUNSHOP.

CENTERFIRE RIFLES—BOLT ACTIONS

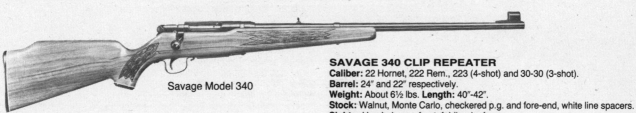

Savage Model 340

SAVAGE 340 CLIP REPEATER
Caliber: 22 Hornet, 222 Rem., 223 (4-shot) and 30-30 (3-shot).
Barrel: 24″ and 22″ respectively.
Weight: About 6½ lbs. **Length:** 40″-42″.
Stock: Walnut, Monte Carlo, checkered p.g. and fore-end, white line spacers.
Sights: Hooded ramp front, folding-leaf rear.
Features: Detachable clip magazine, sliding thumb safety, receiver tapped for scope mounts.
Price: **$223.00**

Stevens Model 110E

STEVENS 110E BOLT ACTION RIFLE
Caliber: 308, 30-06, 243, 4-shot.
Barrel: 22″ round tapered.
Weight: 6¾ lbs. **Length:** 43″ (22″barrel).
Stock: Walnut finished hardwood with Monte Carlo, checkered p.g. and fore-end, hard rubber buttplate.
Sights: Gold bead removable ramp front, step adj. rear.
Features: Top tang safety, receiver tapped for peep or scope sights.
Price: **$232.50**

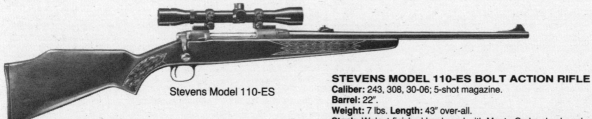

Stevens Model 110-ES

STEVENS MODEL 110-ES BOLT ACTION RIFLE
Caliber: 243, 308, 30-06; 5-shot magazine.
Barrel: 22″.
Weight: 7 lbs. **Length:** 43″ over-all.
Stock: Walnut-finished hardwood with Monte Carlo; checkered p.g. and fore-end.
Sights: Removable ramp front, removable adjustable rear.
Features: Comes with 4x scope and mounts; hard rubber buttplate; top tang safety; free-floating barrel. Introduced 1981. From Savage Arms.
Price: Model 110-ES **$276.00**

SHILEN DGA RIFLES
Caliber: All calibers.
Barrel: 24″ (sporter, #2 Weight), 25″ (Varminter, #5 weight).
Weight: 7½ lbs. (Sporter), 9 lbs., (Varminter).
Stock: Selected Claro walnut. Barrel and action hand bedded to stock with free-floated barrel, bedded action. Swivel studs installed.
Sights: None furnished. Drilled and tapped for scope mounting.
Features: Shilen Model DGA action, fully adjustable trigger with side safety. Stock finish is satin sheen epoxy. Barrel and action non-glare blue-black. From Shilen Rifles, Inc.
Price: Sporter or Varminter rifle............................... **$927.00**

Smith & Wesson Model 1500 Varmint Rifle
Similar to the standard 1500 except has a 22″ heavy barrel and fully adjustable trigger. Chambered for 222, 22-250 and 223. Weighs 9 lbs. 5 oz. Skip-line checkering, q.d. swivels. Introduced 1982.
Price: **$426.95**

S&W Model 1500 Varmint

SMITH & WESSON M1500 BOLT ACTION RIFLE
Caliber: 222, 223, 243, 25-06, 270, 30-06, 7mm Rem. Mag., 300 Win. Mag.
Barrel: 22″ (24″ in 7mm Rem. Mag.).
Weight: 7½-7¾ lbs. **Length:** 42″ over-all (42½″ for 270, 30-06, 7mm).
Stock: American walnut with Monte Carlo comb and cheekpiece; 18-line-per-inch checkering on p.g. and fore-end.
Sights: Hooded ramp gold bead front, open round-notch rear adj. for w. & e. Drilled and tapped for scope mounts.
Features: Trigger guard and magazine box are a single unit with a hinged floorplate. Comes with q.d. swivel studs. Composition non-slip buttplate with white spacer. Magnum models have rubber recoil pad. Introduced 1979.
Price: Standard cals... **$351.95**
Price: Magnum cals... **$367.95**

Smith & Wesson Model 1500 Deluxe Rifle
Similar to Standard model except comes without sights, has engine-turned bolt; floorplate has decorative scroll. Stock has skip-line checkering, pistol grip cap with inset S&W seal, white spacers. Sling, swivels and swivel posts are included. Magnum models have vent, recoil pad.
Price: Deluxe, std. cals. **$401.95**
Price: Deluxe, magnum cals................................... **$417.95**

CENTERFIRE RIFLES—BOLT ACTIONS

Steyr-Mannlicher L

Steyr-Mannlicher Varmint, Models SL and L

Similar to standard SL and L except chambered only for: 222 Rem. (SL), 22-250, 243, 308 and optional 5.6x57 (L). Has 26" heavy barrel, no sights (drilled and tapped for scope mounts). Choice of single or double-set triggers. Five-shot detachable magazine.

Price:	$965.00
Price: Optional caliber, add	$55.00
Price: Spare magazine	$25.00

STEYR-MANNLICHER MODELS SL & L

Caliber: SL—222, 222 Rem. Mag., 223; SL Varmint—222; L—22-250, 6mm, 243, 308 Win., L Varmint—22-250, 243, 308 Win.; L optional cal.—5.6x57.
Barrel: 20" (full stock); 20.6" (half stock).
Weight: 6 lbs. (full stock). **Length:** 38¼" (full stock).
Stock: Hand checkered walnut. Full Mannlicher or standard half-stock with Monte Carlo.
Sights: Ramp front, open U-notch rear.
Features: Choice of interchangeable single or double set triggers. Five-shot detachable "Makrolon" rotary magazine, 6 rear locking lugs. Drilled and tapped for scope mounts. Imported by Steyr Daimler Puch of America.

Price: Full Stock	$958.00
Price: Half-stock	$893.00
Price: Optional caliber, add	$55.00

Steyr-Mannlicher Professional

Steyr-Mannlicher ML79 "Luxus"

Similar to Steyr-Mannlicher models L and M except has single-set trigger and detachable 3-shot steel magazine; 6-shot magazine optional. Same calibers as L and M. Oil finish or high gloss lacquer on stock.

Price: Full stock	$1,172.00
Price: Half stock	$1,097.00
Price: Optional cals., add	$55.00
Price: Extra 3-shot magazine	$41.50
Price: Extra 6-shot magazine	$77.35

STEYR-MANNLICHER MODEL M

Caliber: 7x64, 7x57, 25-06, 270, 30-06. Left-hand action cals.—7x64, 25-06, 270, 30-06. Optional cals.—6.5x57, 8x57JS, 9.3x62, 6.5x55, 7.5x55.
Barrel: 20" (full stock); 23.6" (half stock).
Weight: 6.8 lbs. to 7.5 lbs. **Length:** 39" (full stock); 43" (half stock).
Stock: Hand checkered walnut. Full Mannlicher or std. half stock with M.C. and rubber recoil pad.
Sights: Ramp front, open U-notch rear.
Features: Choice of interchangeable single or double set triggers. Detachable 5-shot rotary magazine. Drilled and tapped for scope mounting. Available as "Professional" model with parkerized finish and synthetic stock (right hand action only). Imported by Steyr Daimler Puch of America.

Price: Full stock	$958.00
Price: Half stock	$893.00
Price: For left hand action add	$127.00
Price: Professional model with iron sights	$737.00

Steyr-Mannlicher S

STEYR-MANNLICHER MODELS S & S/T

Caliber: Model S—300 Win. Mag., 338 Win. Mag., 7mm Rem. Mag., 300 H&H Mag., 375 H&H Mag. (6.5x68, 8x68S, 9.3x64 optional); S/T—375 H&H Mag., 458 Win. Mag. (9.3x64 optional).
Barrel: 25.6".
Weight: 8.4 lbs. (Model S). **Length:** 45" over-all.
Stock: Half stock with M.C. and rubber recoil pad. Hand checkered walnut. Available with optional spare magazine inletted in butt.
Sights: Ramp front, U-notch rear.
Features: Choice of interchangeable single or double set triggers., detachable 4-shot magazine. Drilled and tapped for scope mounts. Imported by Steyr Daimler Puch of America.

Price: Model S or S/T	$962.00
Price: With optional butt magazine (illus.)	$1,012.00
Price: Optional cals., add	$55.00

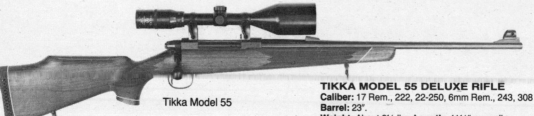

Tikka Model 55

TIKKA MODEL 55 DELUXE RIFLE

Caliber: 17 Rem., 222, 22-250, 6mm Rem., 243, 308.
Barrel: 23".
Weight: About 6½ lbs. **Length:** 41½" over-all.
Stock: Hand checkered walnut with rosewood fore-end tip and grip cap.
Sights: Bead on ramp front, rear adjustable for windage and elevation.
Features: Detachable 3-shot magazine with 5- or 10-shot magazines available. Roll-over cheekpiece, palm swell in pistol grip. Adjustable trigger. Receiver dovetailed for scope mounting. Imported from Finland by Mandall.

Price:	$650.00
Price: QD scope mounts	$89.95

CAUTION: PRICES CHANGE. CHECK AT GUNSHOP.

Tradewinds Husky 5000

TRADEWINDS HUSKY MODEL 5000 BOLT RIFLE
Caliber: 270, 30-06, 308, 243, 22-250.
Barrel: 23¾".
Weight: 6 lbs. 11 oz.
Stock: Hand checkered European walnut, Monte Carlo, white line spacers on p.g. cap, fore-end tip and butt plate.
Sights: Fixed hooded front, adj. rear.
Features: Removable mag., full recessed bolt head, adj. trigger. Imported by Tradewinds.
Price: **$395.00**

Weatherby Vanguard Rifle

Weatherby Mark V Rifle Left Hand
Available in all Weatherby calibers except 224 and 22-250 (and 26" No. 2 contour 300WM). Complete left handed action; stock with cheekpiece on right side. Prices are $10 higher than right hand models except the 378 and 460WM are unchanged.

WEATHERBY VANGUARD BOLT ACTION RIFLE
Caliber: 25-06, 243, 270, and 30-06 (5-shot), 7mm Rem. and 300 Win. Mag. (3-shot).
Barrel: 24" hammer forged.
Weight: 7⅞ lbs. **Length:** 44½" over-all.
Stock: American walnut, p.g. cap and fore-end tip, hand inletted and checkered. 13½" pull.
Sights: Optional, available at extra cost.
Features: Side safety, adj. trigger, hinged floorplate, receiver tapped for scope mounts. Imported from Japan by Weatherby.
Price: **$449.95**

Weatherby Mark V

Weatherby "Lazer Mark" V Rifle
Same as standard Mark V except stock has extensive laser carving on butt, p.g. and fore-end. Introduced 1981.
Price: 22-250, 224 Wea., 24" bbl. **$854.95**
Price: As above, 26" bbl. **$869.95**
Price: 240 Wea. thru 300 Wea., 24" bbl. **$874.95**
Price: As above, 26" bbl. **$894.95**
Price: 340 Wea. **$894.95**
Price: 378 Wea. **$1,049.95**
Price: 460 Wea. **$1,188.95**

WEATHERBY MARK V BOLT ACTION RIFLE
Caliber: All Weatherby cals., 22-250 and 30-06
Barrel: 24" or 26" round tapered.
Weight: 6½-10½ lbs. **Length:** 43¼"-46½".
Stock: Walnut, Monte Carlo with cheekpiece, high luster finish, checkered p.g. and fore-end, recoil pad.
Sights: Optional (extra).
Features: Cocking indicator, adj. trigger, hinged floorplate, thumb safety, quick detachable sling swivels.
Price: Cals. 224 and 22-250, std. bbl. **$729.95**
Price: With 26" semi-target bbl. **$744.95**
Price: Cals. 240, 257, 270, 7mm, 30-06 and 300 (4" bbl.) **$749.95**
Price: With 26" No. 2 contour bbl. **$769.95**
Price: Cal. 340 (26" bbl.). **$769.95**
Price: Cal. 378 (26" bbl.). **$924.95**
Price: Cal. 460 (26" bbl.). **$1,063.95**

Wichita Varmint Rifle

WHITWORTH EXPRESS RIFLE
Caliber: 7mm Rem. Mag., 375 H&H, 458 Win. Mag.
Barrel: 24".
Weight: 7½-8 lbs. **Length:** 44".
Stock: Classic English Express rifle design of hand checkered, select European Walnut.
Sights: Three leaf open sight calibrated for 100, 200, 300 yards on ¼-rib, ramp front with removable hood.
Features: Solid rubber recoil pad, barrel mounted sling swivel, adjustable trigger, hinged floor plate, solid steel recoil cross bolt. Imported by Interarms.
Price: 7mm Rem. Mag. **$575.00**
Price: 375, 458 . . . . **$625.00**

WICHITA VARMINT RIFLE
Caliber: 17 Rem. thru 308 Win., including 22 and 6mm PPC.
Barrel: 20⅛".
Weight: 9 lbs. **Length:** 40⅛" over-all.
Stock: AAA Fancy American walnut. Hand-rubbed finish, hand-checkered, 20 l.p.i. pattern. Hand-inletted, glass bedded steel grip cap, Pachmayr rubber recoil pad.
Sights: None. Drilled and tapped for scope mounts.
Features: Right or left-hand Wichita action with three locking lugs. Available as a single shot or repeater with 3-shot detachable magazine. Checkered bolt handle. Bolt is hand fitted, lapped and jeweled. Side thumb safety. Firing pin fall is ³⁄₁₆". Non-glare blue finish. Shipped in hard Protecto case. From Wichita Arms.
Price: Single shot **$995.00**
Price: With blind box magazine **$1,115.00**

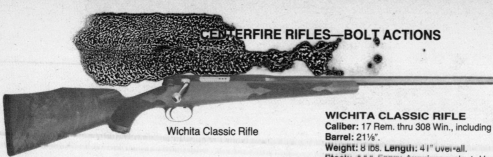

Wichita Classic Rifle

WICHITA MAGNUM STAINLESS RIFLE
Caliber: From 270 Win. through 458 Win. Mag.
Barrel: 22″ or 24″.
Weight: 8½ lbs. **Length:** 44¾″ over-all (24″ barrel).
Stock: AAA fancy walnut; hand inletted; glass bedded; steel grip cap; Pachmayr rubber recoil pad.
Sights: None. Drilled and tapped for Burris scope mounts.
Features: Stainless steel barrel and action, round contour. Target grade barrel. Available as a single shot or with a blind magazine. Fully adj. trigger. Bolt is ⅞″ in diameter with recessed face. Hand rubbed stock finish, checkered 20 l.p.i. Shipped in a hard case. Introduced 1980. From Wichita Arms.
Price: Single shot $1,995.00
Price: With blind box magazine $2,119.00

WICHITA CLASSIC RIFLE
Caliber: 17 Rem. thru 308 Win., including 22 and 6mm PPC.
Barrel: 21⅛″.
Weight: 8 lbs. **Length:** 41″ over-all.
Stock: AAA Fancy American walnut. Hand rubbed and checkered (20 l.p.i). Hand-inletter, glass bedded, steel grip cap. Pachmayr rubber recoil pad.
Sights: None. Drilled and tapped for scope mounting.
Features: Available as single shot or repeater. Octagonal barrel and Wichita action, right or left-hand. Checkered bolt handle. Bolt is hand-fitted, lapped and jewelled. Adjustable Canjar trigger is set at 2 lbs. Side thumb safety. Firing pin fall is ³⁄₁₆″. Non-glare blue finish. Shipped in hard Protecto case. From Wichita Arms.
Price: Single shot $1,595.00
Price: With blind box magazine $1,715.00

Winchester 70 XTR Sporter

Winchester Model 70 XTR Sporter
Same as the Model 70 XTR Sporter Magnum except available only in 270 Win. and 30-06, 5-shot magazine.
Price: $475.00

WINCHESTER 70 XTR SPORTER MAGNUM
Caliber: 264 Win. Mag., 7mm Rem. Mag., 300 Win. Mag., 338 Win. Mag., 3-shot magazine.
Barrel: 24″.
Weight: 7¾ lbs. **Length:** 44½″ over-all.
Stock: American walnut with Monte Carlo cheekpiece. XTR checkering and satin finish.
Sights: Hooded ramp front, adjustable folding leaf rear.
Features: Three-position safety, detachable sling swivels, stainless steel magazine follower, rubber butt pad, epoxy bedded receiver recoil lug. Made under license by U.S. Repeating Arms Co.
Price: $475.00

Winchester 70 XTR Featherweight

Winchester 70 XTR Varmint Rifle
Same as 70 XTR Sporter Magnum except: 22-250 and 243 only, no sights, 24″ heavy bbl., 44½″ over-all, 9¾ lbs. American walnut Monte Carlo stock with cheekpiece, black serrated buttplate, black fore-end tip, high luster finish.
Price: $481.00

Winchester Model 70 XTR Featherweight
Similar to standard Model 70 XTR Sporter Magnum except available only in 243, 257 Roberts, 270, 7x57, 30-06 or 308; 22″ tapered featherweight barrel; classic-style American walnut stock with Schnabel fore-end, wraparound XTR checkering fashioned after early Model 70 custom rifle patterns. Red rubber butt pad with black spacer, detachable sling swivels included. High polish blue metal surfaces, satin finish stock. Optional ramped blade front sight, adjustable folding rear. Weighs 6¾ lbs. Introduced 1981.
Price: $481.00

Winchester 70 XTR Express

Winchester Model 70 Westerner
Same as the Model 70 XTR Sporter except doesn't have the XTR checkering or finish. Available in 243, 270, 30-06 with 22″ barrel, 7mm Rem. Mag. and 300 Win. Mag. with 24″ barrel. Iron sights and 4x scope or iron sights only.
Price: With iron sights $391.00
Price: With iron sights and 4x scope $429.00

WINCHESTER 70 XTR SUPER EXPRESS MAGNUM
Caliber: 375 H&H Mag., 458 Win. Mag., 3-shot magazine.
Barrel: 24″ (375), 22″ (458).
Weight: 8½ lbs.
Stock: American walnut with Monte Carlo cheekpiece. XTR wrap-around checkering and finish.
Sights: Hooded ramp front, open rear.
Features: Two steel crossbolts in stock for added strength. Front sling swivel mounted on barrel. Contoured rubber butt pad. Made under license by U.S. Repeating Arms Co.
Price: 375 H&H $724.00
Price: 458 Win $768.00

CAUTION: PRICES CHANGE. CHECK AT GUNSHOP.

CENTERFIRE RIFLES—SINGLE SHOTS

Browning B-78 Rifle

BROWNING MODEL '78 SINGLE-SHOT RIFLE
Caliber: 25-06, 243, 22-250.
Barrel: 26", tapered octagon or heavy round.
Weight: Oct. bbl. 7¾ lbs. Heavy round bbl. 8½ lbs. **Length:** 42" over-all.
Stock: Select walnut, hand rubbed finish, hand checkered (13⅝"x 1⅝"x2⅛"★). Rubber recoil pad. ★Bore measurement.
Sights: None. Furnished with scope mount and rings.
Features: Closely resembles M1885 High Wall rifle. Falling block action with exposed hammer, auto, ejector. Adj. trigger (3½ to 4½ lbs.), half-cock safety. Imported from Japan by Browning.
Price: **$474.95**

H&R Model 171

HARRINGTON & RICHARDSON Model 171 Cavalry Model Carbine
Caliber: 45-70 single shot.
Barrel: 22".
Weight: 7 lbs. **Length:** 41".
Stock: American walnut with saddle ring and bridle.
Sights: Blade front, barrel mounted leaf rear adj. for e.
Features: Replica of the 1873 Springfield Carbine. Blue-black finish. Deluxe version has engraved breech block, side lock & hammer.
Price: **$349.00**

HARRINGTON & RICHARDSON Model 174.L.B.H. Commemorative Carbine
Caliber: 45-70, single shot.
Barrel: 22".
Weight: 7 lbs., 4 oz. **Length:** 41".
Stock: American walnut with metal grip adapter.
Sights: Blade front, tang mounted aperture rear adj. for w. and e.
Features: Replica of the 1873 Springfield carbine. Engraved breech block, side lock and hammer. Action color case hardened. Each comes with book entitled "In the Valley of the Little Big Horn".
Price: **$349.00**

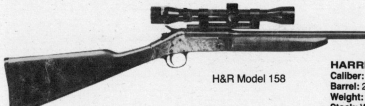

H&R Model 158

HARRINGTON AND RICHARDSON 158 TOPPER FILE
Caliber: 30-30, 22 Hornet, 357 Mag., 44 Mag., single shot.
Barrel: 22" round tapered.
Weight: 6 lbs. **Length:** 37".
Stock: Walnut finished hardwood stock and fore-end.
Sights: Blade front; folding adj. rear.
Features: Side lever break-open action with visible hammer. Easy takedown.
Price: **$94.50**

Harrington & Richardson Model 157 Single Shot Rifle
Same as Model 158 except has pistol grip stock, full length fore-end, and sling swivels. Scope not included; drilled and tapped for mounts. 22 Hornet or 30-30 cals.
Price: **$115.00**

Harrington & Richardson Model 058 Combo Gun
Same as Model 158, except fitted with accessory 20-ga. barrel (26", Mod.).
Price: 22 Hornet, 357 Mag., 44 Mag. or 30-30 Win., plus 20-ga. **$115.00**
Price: Model 258 (as above except nickel finish) **$149.50**

Heym-Ruger HR 30/38

HEYM-RUGER Model HR 30/38 RIFLE
Caliber: 243, 6.5x57R, 7x64, 7x65R, 270, 308, 30-06 (standard); 6.5x68R, 300 Win. Mag., 8x68S, 9.3x74R (magnum).
Barrel: 24" (standard cals.), 26" (magnum cals.).
Weight: 6½ to 7 lbs.
Stock: Dark European walnut, hand checkered p.g. and fore-end. Oil finish, recoil pad. Full Mannlicher-type or sporter-style with schnabel fore-end, Bavarian cheekpiece.
Sights: Bead on ramp front, leaf rear.
Features: Ruger No. 1 action and safety, Canjar single-set trigger, hand-engraved animal motif. Options available include deluxe engraving and stock carving. Imported from West Germany. Contact Heym for more data.
Price: HR-30N, round bbl., sporter stock, std. cals **$1,914.00**
Price: HR-30G, as above except in mag. cals **$1,994.00**
Price: HR-30L, round bbl., full stock, std. cals **$2,053.00**
Price: HR-38N, octagon bbl., sporter stock, std. cals **$2,300.00**
Price: HR-38G, as above, mag. cals **$2,400.00**

CENTERFIRE RIFLES—SINGLE SHOTS

Ruger No. 1 Varminter

RUGER NUMBER ONE SINGLE SHOT
Caliber: 220 Swift, 22-250, 243, 6mm Rem., 25-06, 270, 7x57mm, 30-06, 7mm Rem. Mag., 300 Win., 338 Win. Mag., 45-70, 458 Win. Mag., 375 H&H Mag.
Barrel: 26″ round tapered with quarter-rib (also 22″ and 24″, depending upon model).
Weight: 8 lbs. **Length:** 42″ over-all.
Stock: Walnut, two-piece, checkered p.g. and fore-end (either semi-beavertail or Henry style).
Sights: None, 1″ scope rings supplied for integral mounts. 3 models have open sights.
Features: Under lever, hammerless falling block design has auto ejector, top tang safety. Standard Rifle 1B illus.
Price: **$405.00**
Price: Also available as Light Sporter, Medium Sporter, Special Varminter or Tropical Rifle **$405.00**
Price: Barreled action, blued only **$286.50**

NAVY ARMS ROLLING BLOCK RIFLE
Caliber: 45-70.
Barrel: 26½″.
Stock: Walnut finished.
Sights: Fixed front, adj. rear.
Features: Reproduction of classic rolling block action. Available in Buffalo Rifle (octagonal bbl.) and Creedmore (half round, half octagonal bbl.) models. Made in U.S. by Navy Arms.
Price: 18″, 26″, 30″ full octagon barrel **$355.00**
Price: Creedmore Model, 30″ full octagon **$379.00**
Price: 30″, half-round **$355.00**
Price: 26″, half round **$360.00**
Price: Half-round Creedmore **$379.00**

Ruger No. 3 Carbine

RUGER NO. 3 CARBINE SINGLE SHOT
Caliber: 22 Hornet, 223, 375 Win., 45-70.
Barrel: 22″ round.
Weight: 6 lbs. **Length:** 38½″.
Stock: American walnut, carbine-type.
Sights: Gold bead front, adj. folding leaf rear.
Features: Same action as No. 1 Rifle except different lever. Has auto ejector, top tang safety, adj. trigger.
Price: **$284.00**

SHARPS "OLD RELIABLE" RIFLE
Caliber: 45-70, 45-120-3¼″ Sharps.
Barrel: 28″, full octagon, polished blue.
Weight: 9½ lbs. **Length:** 45″ over-all.
Stock: Walnut with deluxe checkering at p.g. and fore-end.
Sights: Sporting blade front, folding leaf rear. Globe front, vernier rear optional at extra cost.
Features: Falling block, lever action. Color case-hardened hammer, buttplate and action with automatic safety. Available with engraved action for $97.25 extra. From Shore.
Price: Old Reliable **$377.50**
Price: Sporter Rifle **$362.50**
Price: Military Carbine **$345.00**
Price: Sporter Carbine **$362.50**

Navy Creedmoor Target Rifle
Similar to standard Rolling Block rifle except has checkered pistol grip stock and fore-end and cheek rest. Full octagon barrel. Available in 45-70 and 45-90. Has a vernier peep sight on buttstock. From Navy Arms.
Price: **$600.00**

DRILLINGS, COMBINATION GUNS, DOUBLE RIFLES

ARMSPORT "EMPEROR" 4000 DOUBLE RIFLE
Caliber: 243, 270, 284, 7.65, 308, 30-06, 7mm Rem. Mag., 9.3, 300 H&H, 375 H&H; Shotgun barrels in 12, 16 or 20-ga.
Barrel: Shotgun barrel length and chokes to customer specs.
Stock: Dimensions to customer specs. Stock and fore-end of root walnut.
Sights: Rifle barrels have blade front with bead, leaf rear adj. for w.
Features: Receiver and sideplates engraved. Gun comes with extra set of barrels fitted to action. Packaged in a hand-made, fitted luggage-type leather case lined with Scotch loden cloth. Introduced 1978. From Armsport.
Price: Complete **$16,300.00**

ARMSPORT "EMPEROR" 4010 DOUBLE RIFLE
Side-by-side version of the Model 4000 over-under rifle. Available in 243, 270, 284, 7.65, 308, 30-06, 7mm Rem. Mag., 9.3, 300 H&H, 338 Win. and 375 H&H. Shotgun barrels in 16 or 20 ga., choice of length and choke. Comes in fitted luggage-type case.
Price: **$12,750.00**

Bauer Rabbit

BAUER RABBIT
Caliber/Gauge: 22 LR over 410 (3″).
Barrel: 20″.
Weight: 4¾ lbs. **Length:** 38½″; disassembled 20″.
Stock: Metal skeleton.
Sights: Fixed.
Features: Takes down quickly into two pieces. Single selective trigger. Rust resistant finish on stock, barrel and receiver.
Price: **$89.60**

CAUTION: PRICES CHANGE. CHECK AT GUNSHOP.

DRILLINGS, COMBINATION GUNS, DOUBLE RIFLES

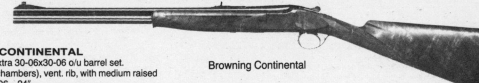

Browning Continental

BROWNING SUPERPOSED CONTINENTAL
Caliber/Gauge: 20 ga. x 20 ga. with extra 30-06x30-06 o/u barrel set.
Barrel: 20 ga.—26½″ (Mod. & Full, 3″ chambers), vent. rib, with medium raised German nickel silver sight bead. 30-06—24″.
Weight: 6 lbs. 14 oz. (rifle barrels) 5 lbs. 14 oz. (shotgun barrels)
Stock: Select high grade American walnut with oil finish. Straight grip stock and schnabel fore-end with 26 l.p.i. hand checkering.
Sights: Rifle barrels have flat face gold bead front on matted ramp, folding leaf rear.
Features: Action is based on a specially engineered Superposed 20-ga. frame. Single selective trigger works on inertia; let-off is about 4½ lbs. Automatic selective ejectors. Manual top tang safety incorporated with barrel selector. Furnished with fitted luggage-type case. Introduced 1979. Imported from Belgium by Browning.
Price: **$5,720.00**

CHAPUIS EXPRESS RIFLE
Caliber: 7x57R, 7x65R, 30-06, 9.3x74R, 444 Marlin, 45-70, 375 H&H. Set of extra 20-ga. barrels optional.
Barrel: 23.6″ for rifle except 444 and 45-70 which are 21½″; 26½″ or 27½″ for shotgun.
Weight: 7¼ to 8½ lbs. **Length:** 44″ over-all (std. cals.).
Stock: Select French or American walnut, oil finish. Fine checkering on p.g. and fore-end. Right or left-hand stock. Deluxe wood, accessories optional.
Sights: Express sights; blade on ramp front, fixed shallow-V rear. Optional rear sight with folding leaves available.
Features: Single joining rib between barrels. Auto ejectors standard. Game motif and scroll engraving on receiver and sideplates. Rifle comes with regulation target for 75 meters. Available in three models: RG boxlock; R Deluxe false sideplates, and President with blued sideplates and receiver with gold inlays. Imported from France by R. Painter Co.
Price: RG boxlock. **$2,803.00**
Price: R Deluxe. **$3,329.00**
Price: President. **$3,860.00**
Price: Extra set of 20-ga. barrels with fitted leather case **$868.89**
Price: Extra set of rifle barrels . . . . **P.O.R.**

Colt Sauer Drilling

COLT SAUER DRILLING
Caliber/Gauge: 12 ga., over 30-06, 12 ga. over 243.
Action: Top lever, cross bolt, box lock.
Barrel: 25″ (Mod. & Full).
Weight: 8 lbs. **Length:** 41¾″ over-all.
Stock: American walnut, oil finish. Checkered p.g. and fore-end. Black p.g. cap, recoil pad. 14¼″x2″x1½″.
Sights: Blade front with brass bead, folding leaf rear.
Features: Cocking indicators, tang barrel selector, automatic sight positioner, set rifle trigger, side safety. Blue finish with bright receiver engraved with animal motifs and European-style scrollwork. Imported from West Germany by Colt.
Price: **$3,757.95**

Ferlach Custom Drilling

FERLACH CUSTOM DRILLING (FRANZ SODIA)
Caliber/Gauge: Any desired.
Action: Blitz, with Greener cross-bolt.
Barrel: Any length, to customer specs.
Weight: To customer specs. **Length:** To customer specs.
Stock: Custom or standard dimensions; best wood on request.
Sights: Any style, to customer specs.
Features: Options include highly figured wood, magnum chambering, scope, fancy side plates, cartridge trap, set trigger, etc. Imported from Austria by Ferlach (Austria) of North America.
Price: **$3,950.00**

Ferlach Double Rifle

FERLACH CUSTOM DOUBLE RIFLE (FRANZ SODIA)
Caliber: Any caliber desired; metric, English or American.
Action: Boxlock or sidelock, side-by-side or over-under, with or without ejectors.
Barrel: Any length desired.
Weight: To customer specs. **Length:** To customer specs.
Stock: Best walnut; fine checkering.
Sights: Silver bead front, with folding night sight if specified. Sourdough rear with vertical inlay and 200 yd. folding leaf. Scope with claw mount available.
Features: Any desired including highly figured wood, auto ejection, set trigger, folding sights, extra barrel sets, night sights. Imported from Austria by Ferlach (Austria) of North America.
Price: Base, boxlock action. **$5,750.00**
Price: Base, sidelock action **$9,500.00**

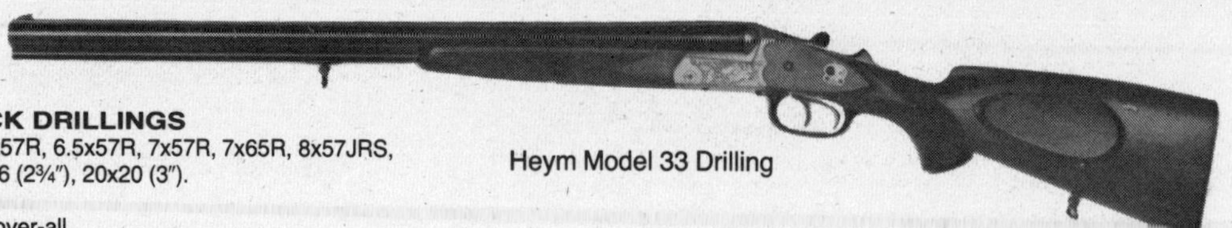

DRILLINGS, COMBINATION GUNS, DOUBLE RIFLES

Heym Model 33 Drilling

HEYM MODEL 33 BOXLOCK DRILLINGS
Caliber/Gauge: 5.6x50R Mag., 5.6x57R, 6.5x57R, 7x57R, 7x65R, 8x57JRS, 9.3x74R, 243, 270, 308, 30-06; 16x16 (2¾"), 20x20 (3").
Barrel: 25" (Full & Mod.).
Weight: About 6½ lbs. **Length:** 42" over-all.
Stock: Dark European walnut, checkered p.g. and fore-end; oil finish.
Sights: Silver bead front, folding leaf rear. Automatic sight positioner. Available with scope and Suhler claw mounts.
Features: Greener-type crossbolt and safety, double under-lugs. Double set triggers. Plastic or steel trigger guard. Engraving coverage varies with model. Imported from West Germany. Contact Heym for more data.
Price: Model 33, from. $3,979.00

Heym Model 88B Double

HEYM MODEL 88B SIDE-BY-SIDE DOUBLE RIFLE
Caliber: 5.6x50R, 222 Rem., 5.6x57R, 243, 6.5x57R, 7x57R, 7x65R, 308, 30-06, 8x57JRS, 9.3x74R, 375 H&H.
Barrel: 25".
Weight: 7½ lbs. (std. cals.), 8½ lbs. (mag.) **Length:** 42" over-all.
Stock: Fancy French walnut, classic North American design.
Sights: Silver bead post on ramp front, fixed or 3-leaf express rear.
Features: Action has complete coverage hunting scene engraving. Comes with fitted leather case. Available as boxlock or with q.d. sidelocks. Imported from West Germany. Contact Heym for more data.
Price: Boxlock, from. $5,500.00
Price: Sidelock, Model 88B-SS, from $7,000.00

Heym Model 37 Side Lock Drilling
Similar to Model 37 Double Rifle Drilling except has 12x12, 16x16 or 20x20 over 5.6x50R Mag., 5.6x57R, 6.5x57R, 7x57R, 7x65R, 8x57JRS, 9.3x74R, 243, 270, 308 or 30-06. Rifle barrel is manually cocked and uncocked.
Price: Model 37 with border engraving. $5,269.00
Price: As above with engraved hunting scenes. $6,269.00

HEYM MODEL 37 DOUBLE RIFLE DRILLING
Caliber/Gauge: 7x65R, 30-06, 8x57JRS, 9.3x74R; 20 gag. (3").
Barrel: 25" (shotgun barrel choked Full or Mod.).
Weight: About 8½ lbs. **Length:** 42" over-all.
Stock: Dark European walnut, hand-checkered p.g. and fore-end. Oil finish.
Sights: Silver bead front, folding leaf rear. Available with scope and Suhler claw mounts.
Features: Full side-lock construction. Greener-type crossbolt, double under lugs, cocking indicators. Imported from West Germany. Contact Heym for more data.
Price: Model 37 double rifle drilling $7,159.00
Price: Model 37 Deluxe (hunting scene engraving) from, ... $8,169.00

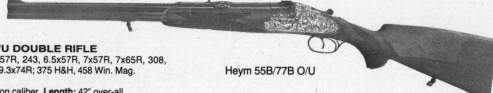

Heym 55B/77B O/U

HEYM MODEL 55B/77B O/U DOUBLE RIFLE
Caliber: 5.6x50R, 222 Rem., 5.6x57R, 243, 6.5x57R, 7x57R, 7x65R, 308, 30-06, 8x57JRS, 300 Win. Mag., 9.3x74R; 375 H&H, 458 Win. Mag.
Barrel: 25"
Weight: About 8 lbs., depending upon caliber. **Length:** 42" over-all.
Stock: Dark European walnut, hand-checkered p.g. and fore-end. Oil finish.
Sights: Silver bead ramp front, open V-type rear.
Features: Boxlock or full sidelock; Kersten double crossbolt, cocking indicators; hand-engraved hunting scenes. Options available include interchangeable barrels, Zeiss scopes in claw mounts, deluxe engravings and stock carving, etc. Imported from West Germany. Contact Heym for more data.
Price: Model 55B boxlock $4,159.00
Price: Model 55BSS sidelock $6,388.00
Price: Interchangeable shotgun barrels $1,839.00

Heym Model 55BF/77BF O/U Combo Gun
Similar to Model 77B/55B o/u rifle except chambered for 12, 16 or 20 ga. (2¾" or 3") over 5.6x50R, 222 Rem., 5.6x57R, 243, 6.5x57R, 270, 7x57R, 7x65R, 308, 30-06, 8x57JRS, 9.3x74R, or 375 H&H. Has solid rib barrel. Available as boxlock or sidelock, with interchangeable shotgun and rifle barrels.
Price: Model 55BF boxlock $3,329.00
Price: Model 55BFSS sidelock $5,558.00

HEYM MODEL 22S SAFETY COMBO GUN
Caliber/Gauge: 16 or 20 ga. (2¾", 3") over 22 Hornet, 22 WMR, 222 Rem., 222 Rem. Mag., 223, 22-250, 243 Win., 5.6x50R, 6.5x57R, 7x57R.
Barrel: 24", solid rib.
Weight: About 5½ lbs.
Stock: Dark European walnut, hand-checkered p.g. and fore-end. Oil finish.
Sights: Silver bead ramp front, folding leaf rear.
Features: Tang mounted cocking slide, separate barrel selector, single set trigger. Base supplied for quick-detachable scope mounts. Patented rocker-weight system automatically uncocks gun if accidentally dropped or bumped hard. Imported from West Germany. Contact Heym for more data.
Price: Model 22S $1,459.00
Price: Cals. 6.5x57R, 243, and 7x57R $1,659.00
Price: Factory fitted scope mounts, add. $123.00

KRIEGHOFF RIFLE-SHOTGUN COMBO
Caliber/Gauge: Top—12, 16, 20 (2¾"), 20 ga. 3"; lower—all popular U.S. and metric cartridges, rimless and rimmed.
Action: Sidelock—Ulm; Boxlock—Teck.
Barrel: 25", solid rib.
Weight: 6¼ lbs. **Length:** 41" over-all.
Stock: 14¼"x1¼"x2¼", European walnut.
Sights: Sourdough front, express rear.
Features: Interchangeable rifle barrels in 22 Hornet, 222 Rem., 222 Rem. Mag. priced at $250.00. Scope optional. Imported from West Germany by Creighton & Warren.
Price: . . . . **Prices on request**

Savage Model 24-C

SAVAGE MODEL 24-C O/U
Caliber/Gauge: Top bbl. 22 S, L, LR; bottom bbl. 20 gauge cyl. bore.
Action: Take-down, low rebounding visible hammer. Single trigger, barrel selector spur on hammer.
Barrel: 20″ separated barrels.
Weight: 5¾ lbs. **Length:** 35″ (taken down 20″).
Stock: Walnut finished hardwood, straight grip.
Sights: Ramp front, rear open adj. for e.
Features: Trap door butt holds one shotshell and ten 22 cartridges, comes with special carrying case. Measures 7″x22″ when in case.
Price: **$171.00**

Savage Model 24-F.G. O/U
Same as Model 24-D except: color case hardened frame, stock is walnut finished hardwood, no checkering or M.C.
Price: **$154.50**

Savage Model 24-D

Savage Model 24-D O/U
Caliber/Gauge: Top bbl. 22 S, L, LR or 22 Mag.; bottom bbl. 20 or 410 gauge.
Action: Bottom opening lever, low rebounding visible hammer, single trigger, barrel selector spur on hammer, separate extractors, color case-hardened frame.
Barrel: 24″, separated barrels.
Weight: 6¾ lbs. **Length:** 40″.
Stock: Walnut, checkered p.g. and fore-end (14″x1½″x2½″).
Sights: Ramp front, rear open adj. for e.
Features: Receiver grooved for scope mounting.
Price: **$199.95**

Savage Model 24-V
Similar to Model 24-D except: 22 Hornet, 222 Rem or 30-30 and 20 ga., 223 or 357 and 20 ga.; stronger receiver; color case-hardened frame; folding leaf rear sight; receiver tapped for scope.
Price: **$233.00**

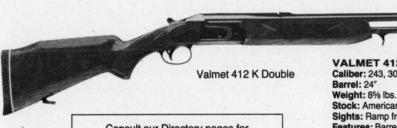

Valmet 412 K Double

VALMET 412K DOUBLE RIFLE
Caliber: 243, 308, 30-06, 375 win.
Barrel: 24″
Weight: 8⅝ lbs.
Stock: American walnut with Monte Carlo style.
Sights: Ramp front, adjustable open rear.
Features: Barrel selector mounted in trigger. Cocking indicators in tang. Recoil pad. Valmet scope mounts available. Interchangeable barrels. Introduced 1980. Imported from Finland by Valmet.
Price: Either caliber **$999.00**
Price: With ejectors **$1,069.00**

Consult our Directory pages for the location of firms mentioned.

VALMET 412KE COMBINATION GUN
Caliber/Gauge: 12 over 222, 223, 243, 308, 30-06.
Barrel: 24″ (Imp. & Mod.).
Weight: 7⅝ lbs.
Stock: American walnut, with recoil pad. Monte Carlo style. Standard measurements 14″x1⅜″x2″x2⅜″.
Sights: Blade front, flip-up-type open rear.
Features: Barrel selector on trigger. Hand checkered stock and fore-end. Barrels are screw-adjustable to change bullet point of impact. Barrels are interchangeable. Introduced 1980. Imported from Finland by Valmet.
Price: **$779.00**

WINCHESTER DOUBLE XPRESS O/U RIFLE
Caliber: 30-06/30-06.
Barrel: 23½″.
Weight: 8½ lbs. **Length:** 39⅝″ over-all.
Stock: 2½″x1¹¹⁄₁₆″x14⅜″. Walnut with hand checkered pistol grip and fore-end, solid rubber butt pad.
Sights: Bead on ramp front, folding leaf rear on quarter-rib.
Features: Integral scope bases; q.d. sling swivels. Uses Model 101 action; receiver silvered and engraved, barrels blued. Introduced 1982. Imported from Japan by Winchester Group, Olin Corp.
Price: **$2,500.00**

A. ZOLI RIFLE-SHOTGUN O/U COMBO
Caliber/Gauge: 12 ga./308 Win., 12 ga./222, 12 ga./30-06.
Barrel: Combo—24″; shotgun—28″ (Mod. & Full).
Weight: About 8 lbs. **Length:** 41″ over-all (24″ bbl.).
Stock: European walnut.
Sights: Blade front, flip-up rear.
Features: Available with German claw scope mounts on rifle/shotgun barrels. Comes with set of 12/12 (Mod. & Full) barrels. Imported from Italy by Mandall Shooting Supplies.
Price: With two barrel sets, without claw mounts **$1,395.00**
Price: With two barrel sets, with claw mounts **$1,495.00**

WINCHESTER SUPER GRADE O/U COMBO
Caliber/Gauge: 12 ga. over 30-06.
Barrel: 25″. Shot barrel uses Winchoke system.
Weight: 8½ lbs. **Length:** 41¼″ over-all.
Stock: 2½″x1¾″x14″. Walnut with hand checkered pistol grip and fore-end; ventilated rubber recoil pad.
Sights: Bead front, folding leaf rear.
Features: Full length top barrel rib with integral scope bases. Uses Model 101 frame. Silvered and engraved receiver, blued barrels. Other calibers available on special order. Imported from Japan by Winchester Group, Olin Corp.
Price: **$2,000.00**

AM-180 Auto Carbine

AM-180 AUTO CARBINE
Caliber: 22 LR, 177-round magazine.
Barrel: 16½".
Weight: 5¾ lbs. (empty), 10 lbs. (loaded). **Length:** 36" over-all.
Stock: High impact plastic stock and fore-end.
Sights: Blade front, peep rear adj. for w. and e.
Features: Available in selective fire version for law enforcement or semi-auto only for civilians. Imported from Austria by Christopher & Assoc.
Price: $595.00
Price: Laser sight system, about $795.00
Price: Extra drum magazine $80.00
Price: Winding mechanism $47.00

AP-74 AUTO RIFLE
Caliber: 22 LR, 32 ACP, 15 shot magazine.
Barrel: 20" including flash reducer.
Weight: 6½ lbs. **Length:** 38½" over-all.
Stock: Black plastic.
Sights: Ramp front, adj. peep rear.
Features: Pivotal take-down, easy disassembly. AR-15 look-alike. Sling and sling swivels included. Imported by EMF.
Price: $198.00
Price: With walnut stock and fore-end $220.00
Price: 32 ACP $210.00
Price: With wood stock and fore-end $230.00

Anschutz Model 520/61

ANSCHUTZ DELUXE MODEL 520/61 AUTO
Caliber: 22 LR, 10-shot clip.
Barrel: 24".
Weight: 6½ lbs. **Length:** 43" over-all.
Stock: European hardwood; checkered pistol grip, Monte Carlo comb, beaver-tail fore-end.
Sights: Hooded ramp front, folding leaf rear.
Features: Rotary safety, empty shell deflector, single stage trigger. Receiver grooved for scope mounting. Introduced 1982. Imported from Germany by Talo Distributors, Inc.
Price: $249.50

Auto-Ordnance 1927A-3

AUTO-ORDNANCE MODEL 1927A-3
Caliber: 22 LR, 10, 30 or 50-shot magazine.
Barrel: 16", finned.
Weight: About 7 lbs.
Stock: Walnut stock and fore-end.
Sights: Blade front, open rear adjustable for windage and elevation.
Features: Re-creation of the Thompson Model 1927, only in 22 Long Rifle. Alloy receiver, finned barrel.
Price: $449.65

Browning Auto Rifle

BROWING AUTOLOADING RIFLE
Caliber: 22 LR, 11-shot.
Barrel: 19¼"
Weight: 4¾ lbs. **Length:** 37" over-all.
Stock: Checkered select walnut (13¾"x1¹³⁄₁₆"x2⅝") with p.g. and semi-beavertail fore-end.
Sights: Gold bead front, folding leaf rear.
Features: Engraved receiver is grooved for tip-off scope mount; cross-bolt safety; tubular magazine in buttstock; easy take down for carrying or storage. Imported from Japan by Browning.
Price: Grade I $259.95
Price: Grade II $380.00
Price: Grade III $815.00
Price: Also available in Grade I, 22 S (16-shot) $259.95

Browning BAR-22 Auto

BROWNING BAR-22 AUTO RIFLE
Caliber: 22 LR only, 15-shot tube magazine.
Barrel: 20¼".
Weight: About 6¼ lbs. **Length:** 38¼" over-all.
Stock: French walnut. Cut checkering at p.g. and fore-end.
Sights: Gold bead front, folding leaf rear. Receiver grooved for scope mounting.
Features: Magazine tube latch locks closed from any position. Cross bolt safety in rear of trigger guard. Trigger pull about 5 lbs. Introduced 1977. Imported from Japan by Browning.
Price: Grade I **$229.95**
Price: Grade II **$329.95**

Charter AR-7 Explorer

CHARTER AR-7 EXPLORER CARBINE
Caliber: 22 LR, 8-shot clip.
Barrel: 16" alloy (steel-lined).
Weight: 2½ lbs. **Length:** 34½"/16½" stowed.
Stock: Moulded grey Cycloac, snap-on rubber butt pad.
Sights: Square blade front, aperture rear adj. for e.
Features: Take-down design stores bbl. and action in hollow stock. Light enough to float.
Price: Black **$98.00**
Price: Satin chrome **$101.00**

ERMA ESG22 GAS-OPERATED CARBINE
Caliber: 22 Mag., 12-shot magazine, 22 LR, 15-shot magazine.
Barrel: 18".
Weight: 6 lbs. **Length:** 35½" over-all.
Stock: Walnut-stained beech.
Sights: Military post front, peep rear adj. for w. & e.
Features: Locked breech, gas-operated action. Styled after M-1 Carbine. Also available as standard blowback action. Receiver grooved for scope mounting. Introduced 1978. From Excam.
Price: Gas. 22 Mag. **$329.00**
Price: Blowback, 22 LR (EM-1) **$221.00**

H&R Model 700 Auto

HARRINGTON & RICHARDSON Model 700 Auto Rifle
Caliber: 22 Mag., 5-shot clip.
Barrel: 22".
Weight: 6½ lbs. **Length:** 43¼" over-all.
Stock: Walnut, Monte Carlo, full p.g., composition buttplate.
Sights: Blade front, folding leaf rear.
Features: Drilled and tapped for scope mounting. 10-shot clip available. Made in U.S. by H&R.
Price: **$185.00**

H&R Model 700 Deluxe Rifle
Same as Model 700 except has select walnut stock with cheekpiece, checkered grip and fore-end, rubber rifle recoil pad. No iron sights; comes with H&R Model 432 4x, 1" tube scope, with base and rings.
Price: **$295.00**

H&K Model 270 Auto

HECKLER & KOCH HK270 AUTO RIFLE
Caliber: 22 LR, 5-shot magazine.
Barrel: 19¾".
Weight: 5.5 lbs. **Length:** 38.2" over-all.
Stock: European walnut with Monte Carlo cheek rest.
Sights: Post front adj. for elevation, diopter rear adjustable for windage and elevation.
Features: Straight blow-back action; 3½ lb. trigger pull. Extra 20-shot magazine available. Receiver grooved for scope mount. Introduced 1978. Imported from West Germany by Heckler & Koch.
Price: **$360.00**
Price: Scope mount, rings **$65.10**
Price: 20-shot magazine **$24.00**

HECKLER & KOCH MODEL 300 AUTO RIFLE
Caliber: 22 Mag., 5-shot box mag.
Barrel: 19¾".
Weight: 5¾ lbs. **Length:** 39½" over-all.
Stock: European walnut, Monte Carlo with cheek rest; checkered p.g. and Schnabol fore-end.
Sights: Post front adj. for elevation, V-notch rear adj. for windage.
Features: Hexagon (polygonal) rifling, comes with sling swivels; straight blow-back inertia bolt action; single-stage trigger (3½-lb. pull). HK-05 clamp scope mount with 1" rings available at extra cost. Imported from West Germany by Heckler & Koch, Inc.
Price: HK300 . . . . **$420.00**
Price: Scope mount with 1" rings **$113.00**

Marlin Model 990

MARLIN MODEL 990 SEMI-AUTO RIFLE
Caliber: 22 LR, 18-shot tubular magazine.
Barrel: 22" Micro-Groove®.
Weight: About 5½ lbs. **Length:** 40¾" over-all.
Stock: American black walnut, Monte Carlo style with fluted comb and full pistol grip; checkered p.g. and fore-end.
Sights: Ramp bead front with Wide-Scan™ hood, adjustable folding semi-buckhorn rear.
Features: Receiver grooved for tip-off mount; bolt hold-open device; cross-bolt safety. Introduced 1979.
Price: $124.95

Marlin Model 995

MARLIN MODEL 995 SEMI-AUTO RIFLE
Caliber: 22 LR, 7-shot clip magazine
Barrel: 18" Micro-Grove®.
Weight: 5½ lbs. **Length:** 36¾" over-all.
Stock: American black walnut, Monte Carlo-style, with full pistol grip. Checkered p.g. and fore-end.
Sights: Ramp bead front with Wide-Scan hood; adjustable folding semi-buckhorn rear.
Features: Receiver grooved for tip-off scope mount; bolt hold-open device; cross-bolt safety. Introduced 1979.
Price: $115.95

Marlin Model 60

MARLIN 60 SEMI-AUTO RIFLE
Caliber: 22 LR, 18-shot tubular mag.
Barrel: 22" round tapered.
Weight: About 5½ lbs. **Length:** 41" over-all.
Stock: Walnut finished Monte Carlo.
Sights: Ramp front, open adj. rear.
Features: Matted receiver is grooved for tip-off mounts. Has new tube magazine closure system.
Price: Less scope.. $96.95

MARLIN 70 AUTO
Caliber: 22 LR, 7-shot clip magazine.
Barrel: 18" (16-groove rifling).
Weight: 4½ lbs. **Length:** 36½" over-all.
Stock: Walnut-finished hardwood with Monte Carlo, full p.g., checkered p.g.
Sights: Ramp front, adj. open rear. Receiver grooved for scope mount.
Features: Receiver top has serrated, non-glare finish; chrome plated trigger; cross-bolt safety; bolt hold-open; chrome plated magazine.
Price: Less scope.. $96.95

MARLIN MODEL 75C SEMI-AUTO RIFLE
Caliber: 22 LR, 14-shot magazine.
Barrel: 18".
Weight: 5 lbs. **Length:** 36¾" over-all.
Stock: Walnut-finished hardwood; Monte Carlo with full p.g.
Sights: Ramp front, adj. open rear.
Features: Bolt hold-open device; cross-bolt safety; receiver grooved for scope mounting.
Price: $96.95

Mossberg 377 Plinkster

MOSSBERG 377 PLINKSTER AUTO RIFLE
Caliber: 22 LR, 15-shot tube magazine
Barrel: 20" AC-KRO-GRUV.
Weight: 6¼ lbs. **Length:** 40" over-all.
Stock: Straight line, moulded one-piece thumbhole.
Sights: No iron sights. Comes with 4x scope.
Features: Walnut texture stock finish, checkered fore-end. Tube magazine loads through port in buttstock. Has bolt hold-open.
Price: With 4x scope $119.95

MOSSBERG MODEL 380 AUTO RIFLE
Caliber: 22 LR, 15-shot tube magazine.
Barrel: 20", tapered, with AC-KRO-GRUV.
Weight: About 5½ lbs. with scope.
Stock: Walnut-finished hardwood, with black non-slip buttplate.
Sights: Bead front, adj. open rear.
Features: Receiver grooved for scope mounting. Available with optional 4x scope, mount. Magazine feeds through buttstock. Introduced 1981.
Price: With open sights, about .... NA
Price: With 4x scope, about .... NA

Mossberg Model 353

MOSSBERG MODEL 353 AUTO LOADING RIFLE
Caliber: 22 LR, 7-shot clip.
Barrel: 18" AC-KRO-GRUV.
Weight: 5 lbs. **Length:** 38" over-all.
Stock: Walnut, checkered at p.g. and fore-end. Black Tenite two-position fold-down fore-end.
Sights: Open step adj. U-notch rear, bead front on ramp.
Features: Sling swivels and web strap on left of stock, extension fore-end folds down for steady firing from prone position. Receiver grooved for scope mounting.
Price: $124.95

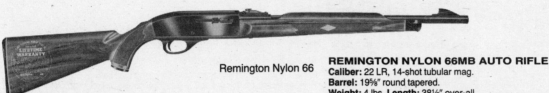

Remington Nylon 66

Remington Nylon 66BD Auto Rifle
Same as the Model 66AB except has black stock, barrel, and receiver cover. Black diamond-shape inlay in fore-end. Introduced 1978.
Price: $124.95
Price: Model 66 BD with 4x scope $139.95

Remington Nylon 66AB Auto Rifle
Same as the Model 66MB except: Apache Black Nylon stock, chrome plated receiver.
Price: $133.95

REMINGTON NYLON 66MB AUTO RIFLE
Caliber: 22 LR, 14-shot tubular mag.
Barrel: 19⅝" round tapered.
Weight: 4 lbs. **Length:** 38½" over-all.
Stock: Moulded Mohawk Brown Nylon, checkered p.g. and fore-end.
Sights: Blade ramp front, adj. open rear.
Features: Top tang safety, double extractors, receiver grooved for tip-off mounts.
Price: $124.95
Price: Model 66MB With Universal UA 4x scope $139.95

Remington Model 552A

Remington Model 552BDL Auto Rifle
Same as Model 552A except: Du Pont RKW finished walnut stock, checkered fore-end and capped p.g. stock. Blade ramp front and fully adj. rear sights.
Price: $188.95

REMINGTON 552A AUTOLOADING RIFLE
Caliber: 22 S (20), L (17) or LR (15) tubular mag.
Barrel: 21" round tapered.
Weight: About 5¾ lbs. **Length:** 40" over-all.
Stock: Full-size, walnut-finished hardwood.
Sights: Bead front, step open rear adj. for w. & e.
Features: Positive cross-bolt safety, receiver grooved for tip-off mount.
Price: $167.95

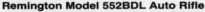

Ruger 10/22 Sporter

Ruger 10/22 Auto Sporter
Same as 10/22 Carbine except: Walnut stock with hand checkered p.g. and fore-end with straight buttplate, no bbl. band, has sling swivels.
Price: Model 10/22 DSP $155.00

RUGER 10/22 AUTOLOADING CARBINE
Caliber: 22 LR, 10-shot rotary mag.
Barrel: 18½" round tapered.
Weight: 5 lbs., 12 oz. **Length:** 36¾" over-all.
Stock: Birch with p.g. and bbl. band.
Sights: Gold bead front, folding leaf rear adj. for e.
Features: Detachable rotary magazine fits flush into stock, cross-bolt safety, receiver tapped and grooved for scope blocks or tip-off mount. Scope base adapter furnished with each rifle.
Price: Model 10/22 RB $128.00

Savage Model 980-DL

SAVAGE MODEL 980-DL AUTO RIFLE
Caliber: 22 LR, 15-shot tube magazine.
Barrel: 20".
Weight: 6 lbs. **Length:** 40½" over-all.
Stock: Select walnut with Monte Carlo, checkered p.g. and fore-end.
Sights: Hooded ramp front, folding leaf rear.
Features: Receiver grooved for scope mounting; top tang safety; white line spacer at buttplate. Introduced 1981.
Price: $151.00

RIMFIRE RIFLES—AUTOLOADERS

SQUIRES BINGHAM M20D SEMI AUTO RIFLE
Caliber: 22 LR, 15-shot clip.
Barrel: 19½".
Weight: 6 lbs. **Length:** 40½" over-all.
Stock: Pulong Dalaga wood with contrasting fore-end tip.
Sights: Blade front, V-notch rear adj. for e.
Features: Positive sliding thumb safety. Receiver grooved for tip-off scope mount. Imported from the Philippines by Kassnar Imports.
Price: $89.95
Price: Model 2000 Deluxe $99.95

SQUIRES BINGHAM M16 SEMI AUTO RIFLE
Caliber: 22 LR, 15-shot clip.
Barrel: 16½".
Weight: 6 lbs. **Length:** 38½" over-all.
Stock: Black painted mahogany.
Sights: Post front, rear adj. for e.
Features: Box magazine, muzzle brake/flash suppressor. Imported from the Philippines by Kassnar Imports.
Price: $129.95

Tradewinds Model 260-A

TRADEWINDS MODEL 260-A AUTO RIFLE
Caliber: 22 LR, 5-shot (10-shot mag. avail.).
Barrel: 22½".
Weight: 5¾ lbs. **Length:** 41½".
Stock: Walnut, with hand checkered p.g. and fore-end.
Sights: Ramp front with hood, 3-leaf folding rear, receiver grooved for scope mount.
Features: Double extractors, sliding safety. Imported by Tradewinds.
Price: $250.00

UNIVERSAL 2200 LEATHERNECK CARBINE
Caliber: 22 LR, 10-shot.
Barrel: 18".
Weight: 5½ lbs. **Length:** 35¾" over-all.
Stock: Birch hardwood with lacquer finish.
Sights: Blade front, peep rear adj. for w. & e.
Features: Look-alike to the G.I. Carbine except in rimfire. Recoil operated. Metal parts satin-polish blue. Flip-type safety. Optional 30-shot magazine available. Receiver drilled and tapped for scope mounting. Introduced 1979. From Universal Firearms.
Price: $246.00

Consult our Directory pages for the location of firms mentioned.

Weatherby Mark XXII

WEATHERBY MARK XXII AUTO RIFLE, CLIP MODEL
Caliber: 22 LR only, 5- or 10-shot clip.
Barrel: 24" round contoured.
Weight: 6 lbs. **Length:** 42¼" over-all.
Stock: Walnut, Monte Carlo comb and cheekpiece, rosewood p.g. cap and fore-end tip. Skip-line checkering.
Sights: Gold bead ramp front, 3-leaf folding rear.
Features: Thumb operated side safety also acts as single shot selector. Receiver grooved for tip-off scope mount. Single pin release for quick take-down.
Price: $279.95
Price: Extra 5-shot clip $6.95
Price: Extra 10-shot clip $7.95

Weatherby Mark XXII Tubular Model
Same as Mark XXII Clip Model except: 15-shot tubular magazine.
Price: $289.95

RIMFIRE RIFLES—LEVER & SLIDE ACTIONS

Browning BL-22

BROWNING BL-22 LEVER ACTION RIFLE
Caliber: 22 S(22), L(17) or LR(15). Tubular mag.
Barrel: 20" round tapered.
Weight: 5 lbs. **Length:** 36¾" over-all.
Stock: Walnut, 2-piece straight grip Western style.
Sights: Bead post front, folding-leaf rear.
Features: Short throw lever, ½-cock safety, receiver grooved for tip-off scope mounts. Imported from Japan by Browning.
Price: Grade I $239.95
Price: Grade II, engraved receiver, checkered grip and fore-end $274.95

CAUTION: PRICES CHANGE. CHECK AT GUNSHOP.

RIMFIRE RIFLES—LEVER & SLIDE ACTIONS

Browning BPR-22 Pump

BROWNING BPR-22 PUMP RIFLE
Caliber: 22 Mag., 11-shot magazine.
Barrel: 20¼".
Weight: About 6¼ lbs. **Length:** 38¼" over-all.
Stock: French walnut. Cut checkered p.g. and fore-end.
Sights: Gold bead front, folding leaf rear. Receiver grooved for scope mount.
Features: Short, positive pump stroke, side ejection. Magazine tube latches from any position. Cross bolt safety in rear of trigger guard. Introduced 1977. Imported from Japan by Browning.
Price: 22 Magnum, Grade I **$269.95**
Price: 22 Magnum, Grade II **$379.95**

Erma Lever Action Carbines
Model EG712. Similar to Magnum model except chambered for 22 S, L, LR with magazine capacity of 21, 17 and 15 respectively. Barrel length is 18½", weight is 5½ lbs. Introduced 1978.
Price: **$226.00**
Model EG712 L. As above except has European walnut stock, engraved nickel silver receiver, heavy octagonal barrel. Imported by Excam. Introduced 1978.
Price: **$339.00**

ERMA EG73 LEVER ACTION CARBINE
Caliber: 22 Mag., 12-shot magazine.
Barrel: 19¼".
Weight: 6 lbs. **Length:** 37⅜" over-all.
Stock: Walnut-staned beech.
Sights: Hooded ramp front, buckhorn rear. Receiver grooved for scope mounting.
Features: Tubular magazine, side ejection. Introduced 1978. Imported by Excam.
Price: **$259.00**

Marlin Model 39A

MARLIN GOLDEN 39A LEVER ACTION RIFLE
Caliber: 22 S(26), L(21), LR(19), tubular magazine.
Barrel: 24" Micro-Groove®.
Weight: 6½ lbs. **Length:** 40" over-all.
Stock: American black walnut with white line spacers at p.g. cap and buttplate.
Sights: Bead ramp front with detachable "Wide-Scan"™ hood, folding rear semi-buckhorn adj. for w. and e.
Features: Take-down action, receiver tapped for scope mount (supplied), sling swivels, offset hammer spur. Mar-Shield® stock finish.
Price: **$240.95**

Marlin Model 39M

MARLIN GOLDEN 39M CARBINE
Caliber: 22 S(21), L(16), LR(15), tubular magazine.
Barrel: 20" Micro-Grove®.
Weight: 6 lbs. **Length:** 36" over-all.
Stock: American black walnut, straight grip, white line buttplate spacer. Mar-Shield® finish.
Sights: "Wide-Scan"™ ramp front with hood, folding rear semi-buckhorn adj. for w. and e.
Features: Squared finger lever. Receiver tapped for scope mount (supplied) or receiver sight, offset hammer spur, sling swivels, take-down action.
Price: **$240.95**

Remington Model 572

REMINGTON 572 FIELDMASTER PUMP RIFLE
Caliber: 22 S(20), L(17) or LR(14). Tubular mag.
Barrel: 21" round tapored.
Weight: 5½ lbs. **Length:** 42" over-all.
Stock: Walnut-finished hardwood with p.g. and grooved slide handle.
Sights: Blade ramp front; sliding ramp rear adj. for w. & e.
Features: Cross-bolt safety, removing inner mag. tube converts rifle to single shot, receiver grooved for tip-off scope mount.
Price: **$174.95**
Price: Sling and swivels installed **$17.00**

Remington Model 572 BDL Deluxe
Same as the 572 except: p.g. cap, walnut stock with RKW finish, checkered grip and fore-end, ramp front and fully adj. rear sights.
Price: **$195.95**
Price: Sling and swivels installed **$17.00**

CAUTION: PRICES CHANGE. CHECK AT GUNSHOP.

Rossi 62 SAC Carbine

Same as standard model except has 16¼″ barrel. Magazine holds slightly fewer cartridges.
Price: Blue. $165.00
Price: Nickel $185.00

ROSSI 62 SA PUMP RIFLE

Caliber: 22 S, L or LR.
Barrel: 23″.
Weight: 5¾ lbs. **Length:** 39¼″ over-all.
Stock: Walnut, straight grip, grooved fore-end.
Sights: Fixed front, adj. rear.
Features: Capacity 20 Short, 16 Long or 14 Long Rifle. Quick takedown. Imported from Brazil by Interarms.
Price: Blue. $165.00
Price: Nickel $185.00

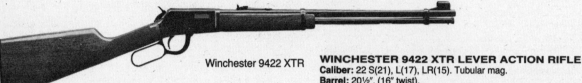

Winchester 9422 XTR

WINCHESTER 9422 XTR LEVER ACTION RIFLE

Caliber: 22 S(21), L(17), LR(15). Tubular mag.
Barrel: 20½″. (16″ twist).
Weight: 6½ lbs. **Length:** 37⅛″ over-all.
Stock: American walnut, 2-piece, straight grip (no p.g.).
Sights: Hooded ramp front, adj. semi-buckhorn rear.
Features: Side ejection, receiver grooved fro scope mounting, takedown action. Has XTR wood and metal finish. Made under license by U.S. Repeating Arms Co.
Price: $307.00

Winchester 9422M XTR Lever Action Rifle

Same as the 9422 except chambered for 22 Mag. cartridge, has 11-round mag. capacity.
Price: $315.00

RIMFIRE RIFLES—BOLT ACTIONS & SINGLE SHOTS

Anschutz 1416/1516

ANSCHUTZ DELUXE 1416/1516 RIFLES

Caliber: 22 LR (1416D), 5-shot clip, 22 Mag. (1516D), 4-shot clip.
Barrel: 22½″.
Weight: 6 lbs. **Length:** 41″ over-all.
Stock: European walnut; Monte Carlo with cheekpiece, schnabel fore-end, checkered pistol grip and fore-end.
Sights: Hooded ramp front, folding leaf rear.
Features: Uses Model 1403 target rifle action. Adjustable single stage trigger. Receiver grooved for scope mounting. Imported from Germany by Talo Distributors, Inc.
Price: 1416D, 22 LR $346.00
Price: 1516D, 22 Mag. $360.00

Anschutz 1418D/1518D Deluxe Rifles

Similar to the 1416D/1516D rifles except has full length Mannlicher-style stock, shorter 19¾″ barrel. Weighs 5½ lbs. Stock has buffalo horn schnabel tip. Double set trigger available on special order. Model 1418D chambered for 22 LR, 1518D for 22 Mag. Imported from Germany by Talo Distributors, Inc.
Price: 1418D. $521.50
Price: 1518D. $533.50

Anschutz 1422/1522

ANSCHUTZ 1422D/1522D CLASSIC RIFLES

Caliber: 22 LR (1422D), 5-shot clip, 22 Mag. (1522D), 4-shot clip.
Barrel: 24″.
Weight: 7¼ lbs. **Length:** 43″ overall.
Stock: Select European walnut; checkered pistol grip and fore-end.
Sights: Hooded ramp front, folding leaf rear.
Features: Uses Match 54 action. Adjustable single stage trigger. Receiver drilled and tapped for scope mounting. Introduced 1982. Imported from Germany by Talo Distributors, Inc.
Price: 1422D (22 LR) $580.00
Price: 1522D (22 Mag.) $593.00

Anschutz 1422D/1522D Custom Rifles

Similar to the Classic models except have roll-over Monte Carlo cheekpiece, slim fore-end with schnabel tip, Wundhammer palm swell on pistol grip, rosewood grip cap with white diamond insert. Skip-line checkering on grip and fore-end. Introduced 1982. Imported from Germany by Talo Industries.
Price: 1422D. $615.00
Price: 1522D. $627.00

RIMFIRE RIFLES—BOLT ACTIONS & SINGLE SHOTS

Chipmunk Single Shot

CHIPMUNK SINGLE SHOT RIFLE

Caliber: 22, S, L, LR, single shot.
Barrel: 16⅛″.
Weight: About 2½ lbs. **Length:** 30″ over-all.
Stock: American walnut.
Sights: Post on ramp front, peep rear adj. for windage and elevation.
Features: Drilled and tapped for scope mounting using special Chipmunk base (about $9.95). Made in U.S.A. Introduced 1982. From Chipmunk Mfg.
Price: $119.95

H&R Model 865

HARRINGTON & RICHARDSON 865 PLAINSMAN RIFLE

Caliber: 22 S, L or LR. 5-shot clip mag.
Barrel: 22″ round tapered.
Weight: 5 lbs. **Length:** 39″ over-all.
Stock: Walnut finished hardwood with Monte Carlo and p.g.
Sights: Blade front, step adj. open rear.
Features: Cocking indicator, sliding side safety, receiver grooved for tip-off scope mounts.
Price: $84.50

HARRINGTON & RICHARDSON MODEL 750 PIONEER

Caliber: 22 S, L or LR, single shot.
Barrel: 22″ round tapered.
Weight: 5 lbs. **Length:** 39″ over-all.
Stock: Walnut finished hardwood with Monte Carlo comb and p.g.
Sights: Blade front, step adj. open rear.
Features: Double extractors, feed platform, cocking indicator, sliding side safety, receiver grooved for tip-off scope mount.
Price: $74.50

H&R 5200 Sporter

HARRINGTON & RICHARDSON MODEL 5200 SPORTER

Caliber: 22 LR, 5-shot magazine.
Barrel: 24″, with recessed muzzle.
Weight: 6½ lbs. **Length:** 42″ over-all.
Stock: Classic-style American walnut with hand-cut checkering, rubber butt pad.
Sights: Hooded ramp front, Lyman peep rear fully adjustable for w. & e.
Features: Adjustable tirgger, recessed magazine release, high polish blue finish. Drilled and tapped for scope mounting. Introduced 1982. From Harrington & Richardson.
Price: $375.00

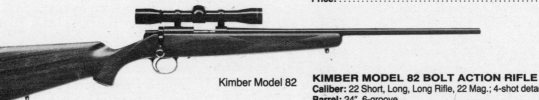

Kimber Model 82

KIMBER MODEL 82 BOLT ACTION RIFLE

Caliber: 22 Short, Long, Long Rifle, 22 Mag.; 4-shot detachable magazine.
Barrel: 24″, 6-groove.
Weight: About 6¼ lbs. **Length:** 41″ over-all.
Stock: Select walnut. "Classic" style stock. Checkered p.g. and fore-end.
Sights: Blade front on ramp, open rear adj. for w. & e.
Features: High quality adult-sized bolt action rifle. All steel construction. Rocker-type silent safety. All metal parts finished in high polish blue. Available with or without sights. Barreled actions available. Made in U.S.A. Introduced 1980. From Kimber of Oregon.
Price: Classic stock without sights $495.00
Price: Classic stock with sights $545.00
Price: Scope mounts and rings $40.00
Price: Cascade sporter stock, no sights $505.00
Price: Cascade sporter stock, with sights $555.00
Price: Classic stock, no sights, 22 Mag. $505.00
Price: Classic stock, with sights, 22 Mag. $555.00
Price: Cascade sporter stock, no sights, 22 Mag. $515.00
Price: Cascade sporter stock, with sights, 22 Mag. $565.00
Price: Extra 4-shot magazine $8.50
Price: Extra 10-shot magazine $10.00

> Consult our Directory pages for the location of firms mentioned.

RIMFIRE RIFLES—BOLT ACTIONS & SINGLE SHOTS

Krico Model 304 Bolt Action Rifle
Same as Model 302 except has 20″ barrel, weighs 6.2 lbs., has full-length Mannlicher-style stock.
Price: Model 304 (22 LR) $439.00
Price: Model 354 (22 Mag.) $449.00

Krico Model 302E/352E
Same as Model 302 but has straight fore-end, stock of walnut-finished hardwood, no white line spacers.
Price: With single trigger, (22 LR) $269.00
Price: As above, (22 Mag.). $279.00

KRICO MODEL 302 BOLT ACTION RIFLE
Caliber: 22 LR.
Barrel: 24″.
Weight: 6½ lbs.
Stock: Select walnut with checkered pistol grip and fore-end.
Sights: Post front with hood, rear adj. for windage.
Features: High quality bolt action rifle available with 5- or 10-shot magazine, single or double-set trigger. Imported from West Germany. Contact Krico for more data.
Price: Model 302 (22 LR) $309.00
Price: Model 352 (22 Mag.) $319.00
Price: Model 302 with double-set trigger $329.00

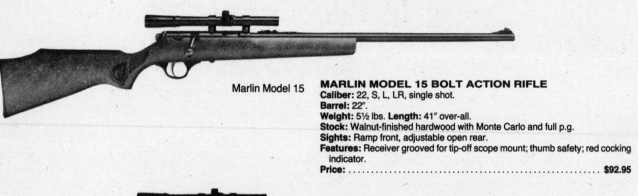

Marlin Model 15

MARLIN MODEL 15 BOLT ACTION RIFLE
Caliber: 22, S, L, LR, single shot.
Barrel: 22″.
Weight: 5½ lbs. **Length:** 41″ over-all.
Stock: Walnut-finished hardwood with Monte Carlo and full p.g.
Sights: Ramp front, adjustable open rear.
Features: Receiver grooved for tip-off scope mount; thumb safety; red cocking indicator.
Price: $92.95

Marlin Model 780

MARLIN 780 BOLT ACTION RIFLE
Caliber: 22 S, L, or LR; 7-shot clip magazine.
Barrel: 22″ Micro-Groove.
Weight: 5½ lbs. **Length:** 41″.
Stock: Monte Carlo American black walnut with checkered p.g. and fore-end. White line spacer at buttplate. Mar-Shield® finish.
Sights: "Wide-Scan"™ ramp front, folding semi-buckhorn rear adj. for w. & e.
Features: Gold plated trigger, receiver anti-glare serrated and grooved for tip-off scope mount.
Price: $118.95

> Consult our Directory pages for the location of firms mentioned.

Marlin 781 Bolt Action Rifle
Same as the Marlin 780 except: tubular magazine holds 25 Shorts, 19 Longs or 17 Long Rifle cartirdges. Weight 6 lbs.
Price: $123.95

Marlin Model 782

Marlin 782 Bolt Action Rifle
Same as the Marlin 783 except: 22 Rimfire Magnum cal. only, weight about 6 lbs. Sling and swivels attached
Price: $131.95

Marlin Model 783

Marlin 783 Bolt Action Rifle
Same as Marlin 782 except: Tubular magazine holds 12 rounds of 22 Rimfire Magnum ammunition.
Price: $136.95

CAUTION: PRICES CHANGE. CHECK AT GUNSHOP.

RIMFIRE RIFLES—BOLT ACTIONS & SINGLE SHOTS

Marlin Model 25

Marlin 25 Bolt Action Repeater
Similar to Marlin 780, except: walnut finished p.g. stock, adjustable open rear sight, ramp front.
Price: **$101.95**

Mossberg Model 341

MOSSBERG MODEL 341 RIFLE
Caliber: 22 S, L, LR, 7-shot clip.
Barrel: 24″ AC-KRO-GRUV.
Weight: 6½ lbs. **Length:** 43½″ over-all.
Stock: Walnut, checkered p.g. and fore-end, Monte Carlo and cheekpiece. Buttplate with white line spacer.
Sights: Bead front, U-notch rear adj. for w. and e.
Features: Sliding side safety, 8 groove rifling.
Price: **$114.95**

Mossberg 640K Chuckster

MOSSBERG MODEL 640K CHUCKSTER
Caliber: 22 Mag. 5-shot clip mag.
Barrel: 24″ AC-KRO-GRUV.
Weight: 6¼ lbs. **Length:** 44¾″ over-all.
Stock: Walnut, checkered p.g. and fore-end, Monte Carlo comb and cheekpiece.
Sights: Ramp front with bead, fully adj. leaf rear.
Features: Grooved trigger, sliding side safety, double extractors, receiver grooved for tip-off scope mounts and tapped for aperture rear sight.
Price: **$124.95**

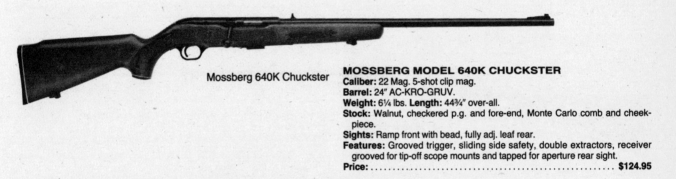

Remington 541-S Custom

REMINGTON MODEL 541-S
Caliber: 22 S, L, LR; 5-shot clip.
Barrel: 24″.
Weight: 5½ lbs. **Length:** 42⅝″ over-all.
Stock: Walnut, checkered p.g. and fore end.
Sights: None. Drilled and tapped for scope mounts or receiver sights.
Features: Clip repeater. Thumb safety. Receiver and trigger guard scroll engraved.
Price: **$359.95**
Price: Extra 10-shot clip **$6.50**

Remington Model 582 Rifle
Same as M581 except: tubular magazine under bbl. holds 20 S, 15 L or 14 LR cartridges. Wgt. 5½ lbs.
Price: **$165.95**

Remington Model 581

REMINGTON MODEL 581 RIFLE
Caliber: 22 S, L or LR. 5-shot clip mag.
Barrel: 24″ round.
Weight: 4¾ lbs. **Length:** 42⅝″ over-all.
Stock: Walnut finished Monte Carlo with p.g.
Sights: Bead post front, screw adj. open rear.
Features: Sliding side safety, wide trigger, receiver grooved for tip-off scope mounts. Comes with single-shot adapter.
Price: **$141.95**
Price: Left hand action and stock **$146.95**

Springfield Armory M6

SPRINGFIELD ARMORY M6 SURVIVAL RIFLE
Caliber: 22 LR over 410 shotgun.
Barrel: 18".
Weight: 3½ lbs. **Length:** 31½" over-all.
Stock: Steel, folding, with magazine for nine 22 LR, four 410 cartridges.
Sights: Blade front, military aperture for 22; V-notch for 410.
Features: All metal construction. Designed for quick disassembly and minimum maintenance. Folds for compact storage. Introduced 1982. Made in U.S. by Springfield Armory.
Price: About $129.00

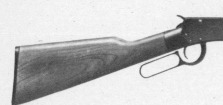

Stevens Model 89

SAVAGE-STEVENS MODEL 89
Caliber: 22 LR, single shot.
Barrel: 18½".
Weight: 5 lbs. **Length:** 35" over-all.
Stock: Walnut finished hardwood.
Sights: Blade front, step adj. rear.
Features: Single-shot Martini-type breech block. Hammer must be cocked by hand independent of lever prior to firing. Automatic ejection. Satin black frame finish.
Price: $76.50

Stevens Model 72

SAVAGE STEVENS MODEL 72 CRACKSHOT
Caliber: 22 S, L, LR, single shot.
Barrel: 22" octagonal.
Weight: 4½ lbs. **Length:** 37" over-all.
Stock: Walnut, straight grip and fore-end.
Sights: Blade front, step adj. rear.
Features: Falling block action, color case hardened frame.
Price: $118.50

STEVENS MODEL 125 BOLT ACTION RIFLE
Caliber: 22 LR, single shot.
Barrel: 22".
Weight: 5 lbs. **Length:** 38" over-all.
Stock: Walnut-finished hardwood.
Sights: Sporting front, open rear with elevator.
Features: Manual cocking with rebounding safety lock. Blue finish. Receiver grooved for scope mounting. From Savage Arms.
Price: $66.75

Stevens Model 35

STEVENS MODEL 35 BOLT ACTION RIFLE
Caliber: 22 LR or 22 Mag. (Model 35-M); detachable 5-shot clip.
Barrel: 22".
Weight: 4¾ lbs. **Length:** 41" over-all.
Stock: Walnut-finished hardwood.
Sights: Ramp front, step-adjustable open rear.
Features: Checkered pistol grip and fore-end. Receiver grooved for scope mounting. Introduced 1982. From Savage Arms.
Price: Model 35 .... $85.00
Price: Model 35-M $108.00

TRADEWINDS MODEL 311-A BOLT ACTION RIFLE
Caliber: 22 LR, 5-shot (10-shot mag. avail.).
Barrel: 22½".
Weight: 6 lbs. **Length:** 41¼".
Stock: Walnut, Monte Carlo with hand checkered p.g. and fore-end.
Sights: Ramp front with hood, folding leaf rear, receiver grooved for scope mt.
Features: Sliding safety locks trigger and bolt handle. Imported by Tradewinds.
Price: $185.00

COMPETITION RIFLES—CENTERFIRE & RIMFIRE

Anschutz 1427B Biathlon

ANSCHUTZ 1427B BIATHLON RIFLE
Caliber: 22 LR, 5-shot magazine.
Barrel: 21½".
Weight: 9 lbs. with sights. **Length:** 42½" over-all.
Stock: Walnut-finished hardwood; cheekpiece, stippled pistol grip and fore-end.
Sights: Globe front specially designed for Biathlon shooting, micrometer rear with hinged snow cap.
Features: Uses Match 54 action and adjustable trigger; adjustable wooden buttplate, Biathlon butt hook, adjustable hand stop rail. **Special Order Only.** Introduced 1982. Imported from Germany by Talo Distributors, Inc.
Price: Right-hand $969.00
Price: Left-hand $1,014.00

ANSCHUTZ 1811 MATCH RIFLE
Caliber: 22 LR. Single Shot.
Barrel: 27¼" round (1" dia.)
Weight: 11 lbs. **Length:** 46" over-all.
Stock: French walnut, American prone style with Monte Carlo, cast-off cheekpiece, checkered p.g., beavertail fore-end with swivel rail and adj. swivel, adj. rubber buttplate.
Sights: None. Receiver grooved for Anschutz sights (extra). Scope blocks.
Features: Single stage adj. trigger, wing safety, short firing pin travel. Imported from West Germany by Talo Distributors, Inc.
Price: Right hand, no sights $774.00
Price: M1811-L (true left-hand action and stock) $850.00
Price: Anschutz Int'l. sight set $156.00

Anschutz 1813 Super Match

Anschutz 1813 Super Match Rifle
Same as the model 1811 except: International-type stock with adj. cheekpiece, adj. aluminum hook buttplate, weight 15½ lbs., 50" over-all. Imported from West Germany by Talo Distributers, Inc.
Price: Right hand, no sights $1,125.00
Price: M1813-L (left-hand action and stock) $1,231.00

Anschutz Model 1810 Super Match II
Similar to the Super Match 1813 rifle except has a stock of European hardwood with tapered fore-end and deep receiver area. Hand and palm rests not included. Uses Match 54 action. Adjustable hook buttplate and cheekpiece. Sights not included. Introduced 1982. Imported from Germany by Talo Distributors, Inc.
Price: Right-hand $999.50
Price: Left-hand $1,099.50
Price: International sight set $156.00
Price: Match sight set $113.00

Anschutz 1807 Match Rifle
Same as the model 1811 except: 26" bbl. (⅞" dia.), weight 10 lbs. 44½" over-all to conform to ISU requirements and also suitable for NRA matches.
Price: Right hand, no sights $706.00
Price: M1807-L (true left-hand action and stock) $775.00
Price: Int'l sight set $156.00
Price: Match sight set $113.00

Anschutz 54.18 MS

Anschutz Model 54.18 MS Silhouette Rifle
Same basic features as Anschutz 1813 Super Match but with special metallic silhouette stock and two-stage trigger.
Price: $682.00

Anschutz 1403B Biathlon

Anschutz Model 1403B Biathlon Rifle
Similar to the 1427B except weighs 8¼ lbs., over-all length is 39¾", uses Match 64 action. Has Biathlon-style butt, walnut-finished stock with stippled pistol grip. Two-stage trigger **Special Order Only.** Introduced 1982. Imported from Germany by Talo Distributors, Inc.
Price: With sights, right-hand only $667.00
Price: Biathlon shooting sling, clamp and hand stop $55.00
Price: Biathlon carrying sling $77.10

Anschutz 1808ED

ANSCHUTZ 1808ED SUPER RUNNING TARGET
Caliber: 22 LR, single shot.
Barrel: 23½″; ⅞″ diameter.
Weight: 9¼ lbs. **Length:** 42″ over-all.
Stock: European hardwood. Heavy beavertail fore-end, adjustable cheek-piece, buttplate, stippled pistol grip and fore-end.
Sights: None furnished. Receiver grooved for scope mounting.
Features: Uses Super Match 54 action. Adjustable trigger from 14 oz. to 3.5 lbs. Removable sectioned barrel weights. **Special Order Only.** Introduced 1982. Imported from Germany by Talo Distributors, Inc.
Price: Right-hand **$790.00**
Price: Left-hand, 1808EDL **$868.00**

Anschutz Mark 2000

ANSCHUTZ MARK 2000 TARGET RIFLE
Caliber: 22 LR, single-shot.
Barrel: 26″, heavy. ⅞″ diameter.
Weight: 8 lbs. **Length:** 43″ over-all.
Stock: Walnut finished hardwood.
Sights: Globe front (insert-type), micro-click peep rear.
Features: Action similar to the Anschutz Model 1403D. Stock has thumb groove, Wundhammer swell p.g., adjustable hand stop and sling swivel.
Price: **$198.00**

Consult our Directory pages for
the location of firms mentioned.

ANSCHUTZ MODEL 64-MS
Caliber: 22 LR, single shot.
Barrel: 21¾″, medium heavy, ⅞″ diameter.
Weight: 8 lbs. 1 oz. **Length:** 39½″ over-all.
Stock: Walnut-finished hardwood, silhouette-type.
Sights: None furnished. Receiver drilled and tapped for scope mounting.
Features: Designed for metallic silhouette competition. Stock has stippled checkering, contoured thumb groove with Wundhammer swell. Two-stage trigger is adj. for weight of pull, take-up, and over-travel. Slide safety locks sear and bolt. Introduced 1980. Imported from West Germany by Talo Distributors, Inc.
Price: **$365.00**

ANSCHUTZ MODEL 1403D MATCH RIFLE
Caliber: 22 LR only. Single shot.
Barrel: 26″ round (1¹/₁₆″ dia.)
Weight: 7¾ lbs. **Length:** 44″ over-all.
Stock: Walnut finished hardwood, cheekpiece, checkered p.g., beavertail fore-end, adj. buttplate.
Sights: None (extra). Scope blocks.
Features: Sliding side safety, adj. single stage trigger, receiver grooved for Anschutz sights. Imported from West Germany by Talo Distributors, Inc.
Price: **$374.50**
Price: 1403DL (left hand) **$398.00**
Price: Match sight set **$113.00**

BSA Martini Match

BSA MARTINI ISU MATCH RIFLE
Caliber: 22 LR, single shot.
Barrel: 28″.
Weight: 10¾ lbs. **Length:** 43-44″ over-all.
Stock: Match type French walnut butt and fore-end, flat cheekpiece, full p.g.; spacers are fitted to allow length adjustment to suit each shooting position; adj. buttplate.
Sights: Modified PH-1 Parker-Hale tunnel front, PH-25 aperture rear with aperture variations from .080″ to .030″.
Features: Fastest lock time of any commercial target rifle; designed to meet I.S.U. specs. for the Standard Rifle. Fully adjustable trigger (less than ½ lb. to 3½ lbs.). Mark V has heavier barrel, weighs 12¼ lbs. Imported from England by Freelands Scope Stands.
Price: I.S.U., Standard weight **$950.00**
Price: Mark V heavy bbl. **$1,000.00**

BEEMAN/WEIHRAUCH HW60 TARGET RIFLE
Caliber: 22 LR, single shot.
Barrel: 26.8″.
Weight: 10.8 lbs. **Length:** 45.7″ over-all.
Stock: Walnut with adjustable buttplate. Stippled p.g. and fore-end. Rail with adjustable swivel.
Sights: Hooded ramp front, match-type aperture rear.
Features: Adj. match trigger with push-button safety. Left-hand version also available. Introduced 1981. Imported from West Germany by Beeman's, Inc.
Price: Right-hand **$495.00**
Price: Left-hand **$545.00**

CAUTION: PRICES CHANGE. CHECK AT GUNSHOP.

Beeman Mini-Match 2000

BEEMAN/FEINWERKBAU 2000 TARGET RIFLE
Caliber: 22 LR.
Barrel: 26¼"; 22" for Mini-Match.
Weight: 9 lbs. 12 oz. **Length:** 43¾" over-all (26¼" bbl.).
Stock: Standard match. Walnut with stippled p.g. and fore-end; walnut-stained birch for the Mini-Match.
Sights: Globe front with interchangeable inserts; micrometer match aperture rear.
Features: Meets ISU standard rifle specifications. Extremely short lock time. Trigger fully adjustable for weight, release point, length, lateral position, etc. Available in Standard and Mini-Match models. Introduced 1979. Imported from West Germany by Beeman's Inc.
Price: Right-hand...$795.00
Price: Left-hand..$855.00
Price: Mini-Match, right-hand...............................$765.00
Price: Mini-Match, left-hand................................$798.00

FINNISH LION STANDARD TARGET RIFLE
Caliber: 22 LR, single-shot.
Barrel: 27⅝".
Weight: 10½ lbs. **Length:** 44⁹⁄₁₆" over-all.
Stock: French walnut, target style.
Sights: None furnished. Globe front, International micrometer rear available.
Features: Optional accessories: palm rest, hook buttplate, fore-end stop and swivel assembly, buttplate extension, 5 front sight aperture inserts, 3 rear sight apertures, allen wrench. Adjustable trigger. Imported from Finland by Mandall Shooting Supplies.
Price: $500.00
Price: Thumbhole stock model $695.00
Price: Heavy barrel model (either stock) $535.00
Price: Sight set (front and rear) $100.00

H&R 5200 Match

HARRINGTON & RICHARDSON MODEL 5200 RIFLE
Caliber: 22 LR, single shot.
Barrel: 28" target-weight with recessed muzzle.
Weight: 11 lbs. **Length:** 46" over-all.
Stock: American walnut; target-style with full length accessory rail, rubber butt pad. Comes with palm stop.
Sights: None supplied. Receiver drilled and tapped for receiver sight, barrel for front sight.
Features: Fully adj. trigger (1.1 to 3.5 lbs.), heavy free-floating target weight barrel, "Fluid-Feed" loading platform, dual extractors. Polished blue-black metal finish. Introduced 1981. From Harrington & Richardson.
Price: $325.00

Kimber Model 82 M/S

KIMBER MODEL 82 M/S
Caliber: 22 LR, single shot.
Barrel: 20½"
Weight: 8½ lbs. **Length:** 38½" over-all.
Stock: Claro walnut, offhand style. Length of pull 13½", drop at comb ½", drop at heel ½". Hand checkered panels on p.g. and underside of fore-end.
Sights: None furnished. Receiver grooved for Kimber scope mounts and other mounts for ⅜" receiver grooves.
Features: Target quality heavy barrel, free-floated. Adjustable, target-type trigger. Redesigned action has extra-fast lock time. Aluminum trigger guard. Meets NRA official MS rules. Introduced 1982. From Kimber of Oregon.
Price: Model 82 M/S $650.00
Price: Barreled action only....................................$389.00

KRICO MODEL 650 S/2 BENCHRESTER
Caliber: 223, 243, 6mm, 308.
Barrel: 23.6" bull.
Weight: 11.5 lbs.
Stock: Special benchrest stock of French walnut with adjustable recoil pad.
Sights: Metallic sights on request; drilled and tapped for scope mounts.
Features: Bolt action single shot. Stippled pistol grip area. Standard trigger is 8 oz. single stage, available with double set or pure match trigger. Imported from West Germany. Contact Krico for more data.
Price: $1,049.00

KRICO MODEL 430S MATCH RIFLE
Caliber: 22 Hornet.
Barrel: 24".
Weight: 8.6 lbs.
Stock: Walnut. Target style with stippled p.g. and fore-end.
Sights: None furnished. Drilled and tapped for scope mounts.
Features: Comes with either double set or match trigger. Has 11mm dovetail rail for scope mounting. Imported from West Germany. Contact Krico for more data.
Price: Single shot, set trigger.................................$499.00
Price: Repeater, set trigger $559.00

COMPETITION RIFLES—CENTERFIRE & RIMFIRE

Krico Model 650S Sniper

KRICO MODEL 650S SNIPER RIFLE
Caliber: 222, 223, 243, 308.
Barrel: 26". Specially designed match bull barrel, matte blue finish, with muzzle brake/flash hider.
Weight: 10.6 lbs. **Length:** 46" over-all.
Stock: Select walnut with oil finish. Spring-loaded, adj. cheekpiece, adjustable recoil pad.
Sights: None furnished. Drilled and tapped for scope mounts.
Features: Match trigger with 10mm wide shoe; single standard or double set trigger available. All metal has matte blue finish. Bolt knob has ¾" diameter. Scope mounts available for special night-sight devices. Imported from West Germany. Contact Krico for more data.
Price: Without scope, mount **$1,139.00**
Price: With Nickel 3-12x56 scope and mount **$1,908.00**
Price: With Schmidt & Bender 1.5-6x42 or 2.5-10x56 sniper scope **$2,090.00**

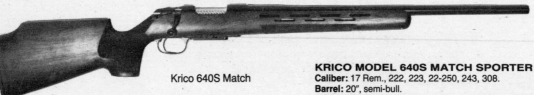

Krico 640S Match

KRICO MODEL 640S MATCH SPORTER
Caliber: 17 Rem., 222, 223, 22-250, 243, 308.
Barrel: 20", semi-bull.
Weight: 7.5 lbs.
Stock: French walnut with ventilated fore-end.
Sights: None furnished.
Features: Five-shot repeater with detachable box magazine. Available with single or double-set trigger. Imported from West Germany. Contact Krico for more data.
Price: 17 Rem., 222, 223 cals **$739.00**
Price: 22-250, 243, 308 cals **$759.00**
Price: Silhouette 340S, 22 LR **$579.00**
Price: Model 440S, 22 Hornet **$559.00**

Krico Model 330S Match

KRICO MODEL 330S MATCH RIFLE
Caliber: 22 LR, single shot.
Barrel: 25.6", heavy.
Weight: 9.9 lbs.
Stock: Special match stock of walnut finished beech; built-in hand-stop; adjustable recoil pad.
Sights: Hooded front with interchangeable inserts; diopter match rear with rubber eye-cup.
Features: Match trigger set at factory for 4 oz. pull. Stippled pistol grip area. Imported from West Germany. Contact Krico for more data.
Price: **$559.00**

M-S Silhouette Rifle

M-S SAFARI ARMS SILHOUETTE RIFLE
Caliber: 22 LR or any standard centerfire cartridge; single shot.
Barrel: 23" (rimfire); 24" (centerfire). Fluted or smooth.
Weight: 10 lbs., 2 oz. (with scope).
Stock: Fiberglass, silhouette-design; custom painted.
Sights: None furnished. Drilled and tapped for scope mounting.
Features: Electronic trigger, stainless steel action, high-speed lock time. Custom built to customer specs. From M-S Safari Arms.
Price: 22 LR **$1,095.00**
Price: Centerfire, from **$1,095.00**

CAUTION: PRICES CHANGE. CHECK AT GUNSHOP.

COMPETITION RIFLES—CENTERFIRE & RIMFIRE

M-S SAFARI ARMS 1000 YARD MATCH RIFLE
Caliber: 30-338, 300 Win. Mag.; single shot.
Barrel: 28″, heavy.
Weight: 18½ lbs. with scope.
Stock: Fiberglass, custom painted to customer specs.
Sights: None furnished. Drilled and tapped for scope mounting.
Features: Sleeved stainless steel action, high-speed lock time. Fully adjustable prone stock. Electronic trigger. From M-S Safari Arms.
Price: **$1,995.00**

M-S Safari Match

Mauser Model 66SP

MOSSBERG MODEL 144 TARGET RIFLE
Caliber: 22 LR only. 7-shot clip.
Barrel: 27″ round (1⁵⁄₁₆″ dia.)
Weight: About 8 lbs. **Length:** 43″ over-all.
Stock: Target-style walnut with high thick comb, cheekpiece, p.g., beavertail fore-end, adj. handstop and sling swivels.
Sights: Lyman 17A hooded front with inserts, Mossberg S331 receiver peep with ¼-minute clicks.
Features: Wide grooved trigger adj. for wgt. of pull, thumb safety, receiver grooved for scope mounting.
Price: **$184.95**

MAUSER MODEL 66 SP MATCH RIFLE
Caliber: 308 Win.
Barrel: 27.5″ with muzzle brake.
Weight: 12 lbs. (without scope).
Stock: Special walnut match design with broad fore-end, thumbhole pistol grip, spring-loaded cheekpiece, Morgan adj. recoil pad.
Features: Uses the Mauser telescopic short action. Other calibers available upon request. Has 3-shot magazine, match trigger adjustable for pull and travel. Contact Mauser for more data.
Price: .... **P.O.R.**

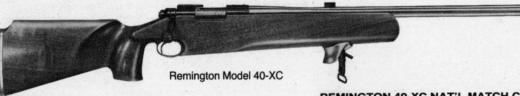

Remington Model 40-XC

REMINGTON 40-XC NAT'L MATCH COURSE RIFLE
Caliber: 7.62 NATO, 5-shot.
Barrel: 23¼″, stainless steel.
Weight: 10 lbs. without sights. **Length:** 42½″ over-all.
Stock: Walnut, position-style, with palm swell.
Sights: None furnished.
Features: Designed to meet the needs of competitive shooters firing the national match courses. Position-style stock, top loading clip slot magazine, anti-bind bolt and receiver, bright stainless steel barrel. Meets all I.S.U. Army Rifle specifications. Adjustable buttplate, adjustable trigger.
Price: **$864.95**

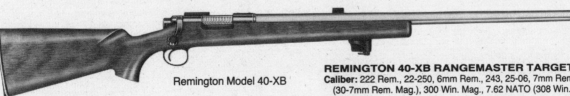

Remington Model 40-XB

REMINGTON 40-XB RANGEMASTER TARGET Centerfire
Caliber: 222 Rem., 22-250, 6mm Rem., 243, 25-06, 7mm Rem. Mag., 30-338 (30-7mm Rem. Mag.), 300 Win. Mag., 7.62 NATO (308 Win.), 30-06. Single shot.
Barrel: 27¼″ round (Stand. dia.—¾″, Hvy. dia.—⅞″)
Weight: Std —9¼ lbs., Hvy.—11¼ lbs. **Length:** 47″.
Stock: American walnut with high comb and beavertail fore-end stop. Rubber non-slip buttplate.
Sights: None. Scope blocks installed.
Features: Adjustable trigger pull. Receiver drilled and tapped for sights.
Price: Standard s.s., stainless steel barrel **$799.95**
Price: Repeating model **$852.90**
Price: Extra for 2 oz. trigger **$88.95**

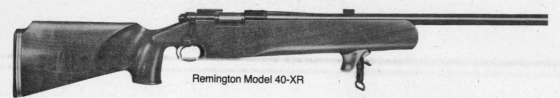

Remington Model 40-XR

REMINGTON 40-XR RIMFIRE POSITION RIFLE
Caliber: 22 LR, single-shot.
Barrel: 24", heavy target.
Weight: 10 lbs. **Length:** 43" over-all.
Stock: Position-style with front swivel block on fore-end guide rail.
Sights: Drilled and tapped. Furnished with scope blocks.
Features: Meets all I.S.U. specifications. Deep fore-end, buttplate vertically adjustable, wide adjustable trigger.
Price: $626.95

Remington Model 40XB-BR

REMINGTON MODEL 40XB-BR
Caliber: 22 BR Rem., 222 Rem., 223, 6mm x47, 6mm BR Rem., 7.62 NATO (308 Win.).
Barrel: 20" (light varmint class), 26" (heavy varmint class).
Weight: Light varmint class, 7¼ lbs., Heavy varmint class, 12 lbs. **Length:** 38" (20" bbl.), 44" (26" bbl).
Stock: Select walnut.
Sights: None. Supplied with scope blocks.
Features: Unblued stainless steel barrel, trigger adj. from 1½ lbs. to 3½ lbs. Special 2 oz. trigger at extra cost. Scope and mounts extra.
Price: $842.95

REMINGTON 540-XR RIMFIRE POSITION RIFLE
Caliber: 22 LR, single-shot.
Barrel: 26" medium weight target. Countersunk at muzzle.
Weight: 8 lbs., 13 oz. **Length:** Adj. from 43½" to 46¾".
Stock: Position-style with Monte Carlo, cheekpiece and thumb groove. 5-way adj. buttplate and full length guide rail.
Sights: None furnished. Drilled and tapped for target scope blocks. Fitted with front sight base.
Features: Extra-fast lock time. Specially designed p.g. to eliminate wrist twisting. Adj. match trigger. Match-style sling with adj. swivel block ($15.50) and sight set ($59.95) available.
Price: $338.95

Remington 540-XRJR Junior Rimfire Position Rifle
Same as 540-XR except fitted with 1¾" shorter stock to fit the junior shooter. Over-all length adjustable from 41¾" to 45". Length of pull adjustable from 11" to 14¼".
Price: $338.95

Savage 110S Silhouette

SAVAGE 110S, SILHOUETTE RIFLE
Caliber: 308 Win., 7mm-08 Rem., 5-shot.
Barrel: 22", heavy tapered.
Weight: 8 lbs., 10 oz. **Length:** 43" over-all.
Stock: Special Silhouette stock of select walnut. High fluted comb, Wundhammer swell, stippled p.g. and fore-end. Rubber recoil pad.
Sights: None. Receiver drilled and tapped for scope mounting.
Features: Receiver has satin blue finish to reduce glare. Barrel is free-floating. Top tang safety, internal magazine. Available in right-hand only. Introduced 1978.
Price: $319.50

SHILEN DGA SILHOUETTE RIFLE
Caliber: 308 Win., 7x308 recommended. Others available. Single shot or magazine.
Barrel: 25", #5 contour.
Weight: 8 lbs., 11 oz.
Stock: Select walnut. Competition-developed pattern for Silhouette shooting. Free-floated barrel, bedded action. Recoil pad installed with 13¾" pull.
Sights: None furnished. Drilled and tapped for scope mounting.
Features: Shilen DGA action. Fully adjustable trigger with side safety. Available with left-hand cheekpiece. Chrome-moly steel barrel; bore and chamber held to target tolerances. Available with Benchrest trigger (2.6 oz., $40.00) or Electric trigger ($150.00). Base and ring options same as Shilen Sporter and Varminter.
Price: Silhouette rifle $883.00

SHILEN DGA BENCHREST SINGLE SHOT RIFLE
Caliber: 22, 22-250, 6x47, 308.
Barrel: Select/Match grade stainless. Choice of caliber, twist, chambering, contour or length shown in Shilen's catalog.
Weight: To customer specs.
Stock: Fiberglass. Choice of Classic or thumbhole pattern.
Sights: None furnished. Specify intended scope and mount.
Features: Fiberglass stocks are spray painted with acrylic enamel in choice of basic color. Comes with Benchrest trigger. Basically a custom-made rifle. From Shilen Rifles, Inc.
Price: DGA Benchrest Rifle $1,060.00

CAUTION: PRICES CHANGE. CHECK AT GUNSHOP.

COMPETITION RIFLES—CENTERFIRE & RIMFIRE

Steyr SSG Marksman

STEYR-MANNLICHER SSG MARKSMAN
Caliber: 308 Win.
Barrel: 25.6".
Weight: 8.6 lbs. **Length:** 44.5" over-all.
Stock: Choice of ABS "Cycolac" synthetic half stock or walnut. Removable spacers in butt adjusts length of pull from 12¾" to 14".
Sights: Hooded blade front, folding leaf rear.
Features: Parkerized finish. Choice of interchangeable single or double set triggers. Detachable 5-shot rotary magazine (10-shot optional). Drilled and tapped for scope mounts. Imported from Austria by Steyr Daimler Puch of America.
Price: Synthetic half stock **$765.35**
Price: Walnut half stock **$887.30**
Price: Synthetic half stock with Kahles ZF69 scope **$1,482.00**
Price: Optional 10-shot magazine **$66.00**

Steyr-Mannlicher SSG Match
Same as Model SSG Marsksman except has heavy barrel, match bolt, Walther target peep sights and adj. rail in fore-end to adj. sling travel. Weight is 11 lbs.
Price: Synthetic half stock **$996.00**
Price: Walnut half stock **$1,106.00**

Swiss K-31 Target

SWISS K-31 TARGET RIFLE
Caliber: 308 Win., 6-shot magazine.
Barrel: 26".
Weight: 9½ lbs. **Length:** 44" over-all.
Stock: Walnut.
Sights: Protected blade front, ladder-type adjustable rear.
Features: Refined version of the Schmidt-Rubin straight-pull rifle. Comes with sling and muzzle cap. Imported from Switzerland by Mandall Shooting Supplies.
Price: **$1,000.00**

Tikka Wild Boar

TIKKA MODEL 65 WILD BOAR RIFLE
Caliber: 7x64, 308, 30-06, 7mm Rem. Mag., 300 Win. Mag.; 5-shot detachable clip.
Barrel: 20½".
Weight: About 7½ lbs. **Length:** 41" over-all.
Stock: Hand checkered walnut; vent. rubber recoil pad.
Sights: Bead on post front, special ramp-type open rear.
Features: Adjustable trigger; palm swell in pistol grip. Sight system developed for low-light conditions. Imported from Finland by Mandall Shooting Supplies.
Price: **$650.00**

UNIQUE T-66 MATCH RIFLE
Caliber: 22 LR, single shot.
Barrel: 25.6".
Weight: 11 lbs., 6 oz. **Length:** 43.5" over-all.
Stock: Straight grained French walnut, fore-end and p.g. hand stippled.
Sights: Interchangeable globe front; fully adj. Micro-Match rear; 8 inserts for front sight.
Features: Meets both NRA and U.I.T. standards. Extremely fast lock time. Comes with proof certificate, two year guarantee, test target of 10-shot 50 meter group. True left hand model available. Imported from France by Solersport.
Price: Right hand **$575.00**
Price: Left hand **$605.00**

Walther GX-1 Match Rifle
Same general specs as U.I.T. except has 25½" barrel, over-all length of 44½", weight of 15½ lbs. Stock is designed to provide every conceivable adjustment for individual preference and anatomical compatibility. Left-hand stock available on special order. Imported from Germany by Interarms.
Price: **$1,395.00**

Walther U.I.T. Match
Same specifications and features as standard U.I.T. Super rifle but has scope mount bases. Fore-end had new tapered profile, fully stippled. Imported from Germany by Interarms.
Price: **$995.00**

WALTHER U.I.T. SUPER
Caliber: 22 LR, single shot.
Barrel: 25½".
Weight: 10 lbs., 3 oz. **Length:** 44¾".
Stock: Walnut, adj. for length and drop; fore-end guide rail for sling or palm rest.
Sights: Globe-type front, fully adj. aperture rear.
Features: Conforms to both NRA and U.I.T. requirements. Fully adj. trigger. Left hand stock available on special order. Imported from Germany by Interarms.
Price: **$925.00**

WALTHER RUNNING BOAR MATCH RIFLE
Caliber: 22 LR, single shot.
Barrel: 23.6".
Weight: 8 lbs. 5 oz. **Length:** 42" over-all.
Stock: Walnut thumb-hole typo. Foro ond and p.g. stippled.
Features: Especially designed for running boar competition. Receiver grooved to accept dovetail scope mounts. Adjustable cheekpiece and butt plate. 1.1 lb. trigger pull. Left hand stock available on special order. Imported from Germany by Interarms.
Price: **$895.00**

Benelli SL 123V

BENELLI AUTOLOADING SHOTGUN
Gauge: 12 ga. (5-shot, 3-shot plug furnished).
Barrel: 26″ (Skeet, Imp. Cyl., Mod.); 28″ (Spec., Full, Imp. Mod., Mod.). Vent. rib.
Weight: 6¾ lbs.
Stock: European walnut. 14″x1½″x2½″. Hand checkered p.g. and fore-end.
Sights: Metal bead front.
Features: Quick interchangeable barrels. Cross-bolt safety. Hand engraved receiver on higher grades. Imported from Italy by Heckler & Koch, Inc.
Price: Standard model, SL 121V **$449.00**
Price: Engraved, SL 123V **$525.00**
Price: Slug gun, 121V **$492.00**
Price: Model SL 201, 20 ga. **$453.00**
Price: Extra barrels **$236.00**

Beretta Model A-302

BERETTA A-301 AUTO SHOTGUN
Gauge: 12 or 20.
Action: Gas operated.
Barrel: 12 ga.—22″ (slug); 26″ (Imp. Cyl.); 28″ (Mod., Full); 30″ (Full, 3″ chamber); 20 ga.—28″ (Full, Mod.); 26″ (Imp. Cyl.). Vent. rib except slug gun.
Weight: 6 lbs., 5 oz. (20 ga., 28″).
Stock: 14⅛″x1⅜″x2⅜″, European walnut. Magnum guns have recoil pad.
Features: All gas system parts are of stainless steel. Alloy receiver decorated with scroll pattern engraving. Push button safety in trigger guard. Introduced 1977. Imported by Beretta U.S.A. Co.

Beretta A-301 Skeet and Trap
Same as standard A-301 except: Trap has M.C. stock (14¼″x1⅜″ x1⁹⁄₁₆″x1⅝″) with recoil pad, gold plated trigger, trap choke 30″ bbl. Skeet gun has Skeet choke, gold plated trigger, Skeet stock (14¼″x1⅜″x2⅜″x2⁹⁄₁₆″) and 26″ barrel. Introduced 1977. Imported by Beretta U.S.A. Co.
Price: Skeet, 12 or 20 ga. **$485.00**
Price: Trap, 12 ga. only **$500.00**
Price: Extra barrels **$186.00**

Price: 12 or 20, 2¾″ **$485.00**
Price: 12 or 20 ga., 3″ Magnum **$530.00**
Price: Slug gun **$485.00**
Price: Extra barrels, from **$170.00**
Price: 12 ga. with four interchangeable choke tubes **$590.00**

Beretta A-302 Mag-Action Auto Shotgun
Same basic gun as the A-301 except has improved gas system and requires change of barrel for 2¾″ or 3″ shells. Has lever-operated magazine cut-off. Introduced 1981.
Price: From **$565.00**

Browning Auto-5

BROWNING AUTO-5 LIGHT 12 and 20
Gauge: 12, 20; 5-shot; 3-shot plug furnished; 2¾″ chamber.
Action: Recoil operated autoloader; takedown.
Barrel: 26″ (Skeet boring in 12 & 20 ga., Cyl., Imp. Cyl., Mod in 20 ga.); 28″ (Skeet in 12 ga., Mod., Full); 30″ (Full in 12 ga.).
Weight: 12 ga. 7¼ lbs., 20 ga. 6⅜ lbs.
Stock: French walnut, hand checkered half-p.g. and fore-end. 14¼″ x 1⅝″ x 2½″.
Features: Receiver hand engraved with scroll designs and border. Double extractors, extra bbls. interchangeable without factory fitting; mag. cut-off; cross-bolt safety. Imported from Japan by Browning.
Price: Vent. rib only **$559.95**
Price: Extra barrels, vent. rib only **$175.00**

Browning Auto-5 Magnum 12
Same as Std. Auto-5 except: chambered for 3″ magnum shells (also handles 2¾″ magnum and 2¾″ HV loads). 28″ Mod., Full; 30″ and 32″ (Full) bbls. 14″x1⅝″x2½″ stock. Recoil pad. Wgt. 8¾ lbs.
Price: Vent. rib only **$569.95**

Browning Auto-5 Light Skeet
Same as Light Standard except: 12 and 20 ga. only, 26″ or 28″ bbl. (Skeet). With vent. rib. Wgt. 6⅜-7½ lbs.
Price: **$559.95**

Browning Auto-5 Magnum 20
Same as Magnum 12 except barrels 28″ Full or Mod., or 26″ Full, Mod. or Imp. Cyl. With ventilated rib, 7½ lbs.
Price: **$569.96**

CAUTION: PRICES CHANGE. CHECK AT GUNSHOP.

SHOTGUNS—AUTOLOADERS

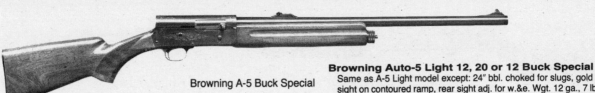

Browning A-5 Buck Special

Browning Auto-5 Light 12, 20 or 12 Buck Special

Same as A-5 Light model except: 24″ bbl. choked for slugs, gold bead front sight on contoured ramp, rear sight adj. for w.&e. Wgt. 12 ga., 7 lbs.; 20 ga., 6 lbs. 2 oz.; 3″ Mag. 12, 8¼ lbs.

Price: **$569.95**

Price: 12 or 20 ga. Magnum **$584.95**

All Buck Specials are available with carrying sling, detachable swivels and swivel attachments for **$20.00** extra.

Browning B-80 Auto

BROWNING B-80 AUTO SHOTGUN

Gauge: 12 (2¾″ & 3″), 20 (2¾″ & 3″)

Barrel: 22″ (Slug), 26″ (Imp. Cyl., Cyl., Skeet, Full, Mod.), 28″ (Full, Mod.), 30″ (Full), 32″ (Full).

Weight: About 6½ lbs.

Stock: 14¼″ x 1⅝″ x 2½″. Hand checkered French walnut. Solid black recoil pad.

Features: Vent. rib barrels have non-reflective rib; steel receiver with high-polish blue; cross-bolt safety; interchangeable barrels. Introduced 1981. Imported from Belgium by Browning.

Price: 12 or 20 ga., 2¾″ or 3″, vent, rib **$529.95**

Price: Buck Special, 12 or 20 ga., 2¾″ or 3″ **$529.95**

Price: Buck Special, with accessories (carrying strap, swivels)...... **$549.95**

Price: Extra barrels **$171.50**

Fox Model FA-1

FOX FA-1 AUTO SHOTGUN

Gauge: 12 only, 2¾″.

Barrel: 28″ (Mod.), 30″ (Full); vent. rib.

Weight: 7½ lbs. **Length:** 47¾″ over-all (28″ bbl.)

Stock: Walnut (14″x1½″x2½″).

Sights: Metal bead front.

Features: Gas system is self-compensating for different loads. Chrome moly steel barrel, highly polished receiver. Cross-bolt safety. Rosewood grip cap with inlay. Imported from Japan by Savage Arms. Introduced 1981.

Price: **$380.00**

FRANCHI STANDARD AUTO SHOTGUN

Gauge: 12 or 20, 5-shot. 2¾″ or 3″ chamber.

Action: Recoil-operated automatic.

Barrel: 24″ (Imp. Cyl. or Cyl.); 26″ (Imp. Cyl. or Mod); 28″ (Skeet, Mod. or Full); 30″, 32″ (Full). Interchangeable barrels.

Weight: 12 ga. 6¼ lbs., 20 ga. 5 lbs. 2 oz.

Stock: Epoxy-finished walnut, with cut-checkered pistol grip and fore-end.

Features: Chrome-lined bbl., easy takedown, 3-round plug provided. Ventilated rib barrel. Imported from Italy by F.I.E.

Price: Vent. rib 12, 20 .... **$394.95**

Price: Hunter model (engraved) **$419.95**

Price: 12 ga. Magnum **$419.95**

Franchi Slug Gun

Same as Standard automatic except 22″ Cylinder bored plain barrel, adj. rifle-type sights, sling swivels.

Price: 12 or 20 ga., standard **$394.95**

Price: As above, Hunter grade **$419.95**

Ithaca Model 51

ITHACA MODEL 51 FEATHERLIGHT AUTOMATIC

Gauge: 12 or 20 ga., 2¾″ chamber.

Action: Gas-operated, rotary bolt has three locking lugs. Takedown. Self-compensating for high or low base loads.

Barrel: Roto-Forged, 30″ (Full), 28″ (Full, Mod., or Skeet), 26″ (Imp. Cyl. or Skeet). Extra barrels available. Raybar front sight.

Weight: About 7½ lbs.

Stock: 14″x1⅝″x2½″. Hand checkered walnut, white spacers on p.g. and under recoil pad.

Features: Hand fitted, engraved receiver, 3 shot capacity, safety is reversible for left hand shooter.

Price: With vent, rib **$477.00**

Price: Presentation Series **$1,425.00**

Ithaca Model 51 Magnum

Same Standard Model 51 except has 3″ chamber.

Price: With vent rib **$525.00**

Ithaca Model 51 Trap

Ithaca Model 51 Featherlight Deluxe Trap

Same gun as standard Model 51 with fancy American walnut trap stock, 30" (Full or Imp. Cyl.) or 28" (Full or Imp. Mod.) barrel.
Price: **$585.00**
Price: With Monte Carlo stock **$620.00**

Ithaca Model 51 Featherlight Deluxe Skeet

Same gun as Model 51 Skeet with fancy American walnut stock, 28" or 29" (Skeet) barrel.
Price: **$575.00**

ITHACA MODEL 51 DEERSLAYER

Gauge: 12 or 20 ga., 2¾" chamber.
Action: Gas-operated, semi-automatic.
Barrel: 24", special bore.
Weight: 7½ lbs. (12 ga.), 7¼ lbs. (20 ga.).
Stock: 14"x1½"x2¼", American walnut. Checkered p.g. and fore-end.
Sights: Raybar front, open rear adj. for w. and e.
Features: Sight base grooved for scope mounts. Easy takedown, reversible safety. Scope optional.
Price: **$475.00**

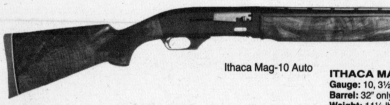

Ithaca Mag-10 Auto

KASSNAR FOX AUTO SHOTGUN

Gauge: 12 only (2¾" or 3").
Barrel: 26" (Imp. Cyl., Mod., Skeet), 28" (Full, Mod.), 30" (Full). Vent rib.
Weight: 7¼ lbs.
Stock: American walnut.
Sights: Metal bead front.
Features: Cross bolt safety, interchangeable barrels. From Kassnar Imports.
Price: **$329.95**

ITHACA MAG-10 GAS OPERATED SHOTGUN

Gauge: 10, 3½" chamber, 3-shot.
Barrel: 32" only. Full choke.
Weight: 11¼ lbs.
Stock: American walnut, checkered p.g. and fore-end (14⅛"x2⅜"x1½"), p.g. cap, rubber recoil pad.
Sights: White Bradley.
Features: "Countercoil" gas system. Piston, cylinder, bolt, charging lever, action release and carrier made of stainless steel. ⅜" vent. rib. Reversible cross-bolt safety. Low recoil force. Deluxe model has full fancy claro American black walnut.
Price: Standard, plain barrel **$670.00**
Price: Deluxe, vent. rib **$860.00**
Price: Standard, vent. rib **$730.00**
Price: Supreme, vent. rib **$980.00**
Price: Presentation Series **$1,645.00**

Ithaca Mag-10 Deerslayer

Ithaca Mag-10 Deerslayer

Similar to the standard Mag-10 except has 22" barrel, rifle sights.
Price: Std., vent. rib, Parkerized finish **$730.00**
Price: Deluxe, blue finsih **$860.00**
Price: Supreme grade **$980.00**

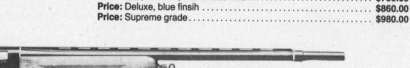

K.F.C. Model 250

KAWAGUCHIYA K.F.C. M-250 AUTO SHOTGUN

Gauge: 12, 2¾".
Barrel: 24½" (Imp. Cyl. Mod., Full, interchangeable choke tubes); or 26" (Imp. Cyl.), 28" (Mod.), 30" (Full) for standard choke models.
Weight: 7 lbs. 6 oz. **Length:** 48" over-all (28" barrel).
Stock: 14⅛"x1½"x2½". American walnut, hand checkered p.g. and fore-end.
Features: Gas-operated, ventilated barrel rib. Has only 79 parts. Cross-bolt safety is reversible for left-handed shooters. Introduced 1980. Imported from Japan by La Paloma Marketing.
Price: Standard Grade **$485.00**
Price: Deluxe Grade (silvered, etched receiver).................. **$520.00**
Price: With choke tubes, Standard Grade **$565.00**
Price: As above, Deluxe Grade................................ **$599.00**

CAUTION: PRICES CHANGE. CHECK AT GUNSHOP.

SHOTGUNS—AUTOLOADERS

Remington Model 1100

REMINGTON MODEL 1100 AUTO
Gauge: 12, 3-shot plug furnished.
Action: Gas-operated autoloader.
Barrel: 26″ (Imp. Cyl.), 28″ (Mod., Full), 30″ Full in 12 ga. only.
Weight: 12 ga. 7½ lbs.
Stock: 14″x1½″x2½″ American Walnut, checkered p.g. and fore-end.
Features: Quickly interchangeable barrels within gauge. Matted receiver top with scroll work on both sides of receiver. Crossbolt safety.
Price: $427.95
Price: With vent. rib $469.95
Price: Left hand model with vent. rib $498.95

Remington 1100 Magnum
   Same as 1100 except: chambered for 3″ magnum loads. Available in 12 ga. (30″) or 20 ga. (28″) Mod. or Full, 14″x1½″x2½″ stock with recoil pad, Wgt. 7¾ lbs.
Price: $469.95
Price: With vent. rib $511.95
Price: Left hand model with vent. rib $540.95
Price: Ducks Unlimited Commemorative Edition
   (32″, Full choke, vent. rib) $551.95

Remington 1100 Small Gauge
   Same as 1100 except: 28 ga. 2¾″ (5-shot) or 410, 3″ (except Skeet, 2½″ 4-shot). 45½″ over-all. Available in 25″ bbl. (Full, Mod., or Imp. Cyl.) only.
Price: With vent. rib $480.95

Remington 1100D Tournament Auto
   Same as 1100 Standard except: vent, rib, better wood, more extensive engraving.
Price: $1,850.00

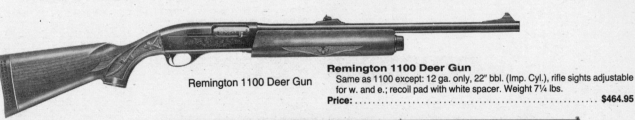

Remington 1100 LT-20

Remington 1100 LT-20
   Basically the same design as Model 1100, but with special weight-saving features that retain strength and dependability of the standard Model 1100.
Barrel: 28″ (Full, Mod.), 26″ (Imp. Cyl.).
Weight: 6½ lbs.
Price: $427.95
Price: With vent. rib $469.95
Price: LT-20 magnum (28″ Full) $469.95
Price: With vent. rib $511.95
Price: LT-20 Deer Gun (20″ bbl.) $469.95
Price: LT-20 Ltd. has 23″ (Mod. or Imp. Cyl.) bbl., 1″ shorter stock... $469.95

Remington 1100F Premier Auto
   Same as 1100D except: select wood, better engraving
Price: $3,700.00
Price: With gold inlay $5,500.00

Remington 1100 Extra bbls. 12 and 20 ga.: Plain **$97.95** (20, 28 & 410, **$106.95**). Vent., rib 12 and 20 **$139.95** (20, 28 & 410, **$148.95**). Vent. rib Skeet **$149.95**. Vent. rib Trap **$149.95**. Deer bbl. **$115.95**. Available in the same gauges and chokes as shown on guns. **Prices are approximate.**

Remington 1100 SA Skeet
   Same as the 1100 except: 26″ bbl., special Skeet boring, vent. rib (high rib on LT-20), ivory bead front and metal bead middle sights. 14″x1½″x2½″ stock. 12, 20, 28, 410 ga. Wgt. 7½ lbs., cut checkering, walnut, new receiver scroll.
Price: 12 ga., Skeet SA $484.95
Price: 12 ga. Left hand model with vent. rib $513.95
Price: 28 & 410 ga., 25″ bbl. $495.95
Price: 20 ga. LT-20 Skeet SA $484.95
Price: Tournament Skeet (28, 410) $585.95
Price: Tournament Skeet (12 or 20) $474.95

Remington 1100 Deer Gun

Remington 1100 Deer Gun
   Same as 1100 except: 12 ga. only, 22″ bbl. (Imp. Cyl.), rifle sights adjustable for w. and e.; recoil pad with white spacer. Weight 7¼ lbs.
Price: $464.95

Remington 1100 TA Trap

Remington 1100 TA Trap
   Same as the standard 1100 except: recoil pad. 14⅜″x1⅜″x1¾″ stock. Right- or left-hand models. Wgt. 8¼ lbs. 12 ga. only. 30″ (Mod. Trap, Full) vent. rib bbl. Ivory bead front and white metal middle sight.
Price: $494.95
Price: With Monte Carlo stock $504.95
Price: 1100TA Trap, left hand $523.95
Price: With Monte Carlo stock $533.95
Price: Tournament Trap $584.95
Price: Tournament Trap with M.C. stock, better grade wood, different checkering, cut checkering $594.95

S & W Model 1000 Auto

SMITH & WESSON MODEL 1000 AUTO
Gauge: 12, 2¾" or 3" chamber, 4-shot.
Action: Gas-operated autoloader.
Barrel: 26" (Skeet, Imp. Cyl.), 28" (Mod. Full). Also available with screw-in Multi-Choke tubes.
Weight: 7½ lbs. (28" bbl.). **Length:** 48" over-all (28" bbl.).
Stock: 14"x1½"x2⅜", American walnut.
Features: Interchangeable crossbolt safety, vent. rib with front and middle beads, engraved alloy receiver, pressure compensator and floating piston for light recoil.
Price: **$469.95**
Price: Extra barrels (as listed above) **$139.95**
Price: Extra 22" barrel (Cyl. bore) with rifle sights **$115.95**
Price: With 3" chamber, 30" (Mod., Full) barrel. **$511.95**
Price: With Multi-Choke system **$496.95**
Price: Extra Multi-Choke barrel **$166.95**

Smith & Wesson Model 1000 20 Gauge & 20 Magnum
Similar to 12 ga. model except slimmed down to weigh only 6½ lbs. Has self-cleaning gas system. Choice of four interchangeable barrels (26", Imp. Cyl. or Skeet, 28" Mod., Full).
Price: **$469.95**
Price: Extra barrels **$139.95**
Price: With 3" chamber, (Mod., Full). **$511.95**

S & W Model 1000 S

Smith & Wesson Model 1000S Super Skeet Shotgun
Similar to Model 1000 except has "recessed-type" Skeet choke with a compensator system to soften recoil and reduce muzzle jump. Stock has right-hand palm swell. Trigger is contoured (rounded) on right side; pull is 2½ to 3 lbs. Vent. rib has double sighting beads with a "Bright Point" fluorescent red front bead. Fore-end cap weights (included) of 1 and 2 oz. can be used to change balance. Select-grade walnut with oil finish. Barrel length is 25", weight 8¼ lbs., over-all length 45.7". Stock measures 14"x1½"x2½" with .08" cast-off at butt, .16" at toe.
Price: **$709.95**
Price: Super Skeet interchangeable barrel **$229.95**

Smith & Wesson Model 1000 Waterfowler Auto
Similar to the standard Model 1000 except all exterior metal is Parkerized to reduce glare, bolt is black oxidized, stock has a dull oil finish. Comes with q.d. swivels and a padded, camouflaged sling. Available with 30" (Full) barrel with 3" chamber. Introduced 1982.
Price: **$538.95**

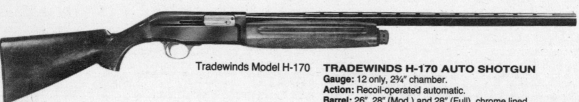

Tradewinds Model H-170

TRADEWINDS H-170 AUTO SHOTGUN
Gauge: 12 only, 2¾" chamber.
Action: Recoil-operated automatic.
Barrel: 26", 28" (Mod.) and 28" (Full), chrome lined.
Weight: 7 lbs.
Stock: Select European walnut stock, p.g. and fore-end hand checkered.
Features: Light alloy receiver, 5-shot tubular magazine, ventilated rib. Imported from Japan by Tradewinds.
Price: **$395.00**

Weatherby Eighty-Two Auto

WEATHERBY EIGHTY-TWO AUTO
Gauge: 12 only, 2¾" and 3" chamber.
Action: Gas operated autoloader with "Floating Piston."
Barrel: 26" (Mod., Imp. Cyl., Skeet), 28" (Full, Mod.), 30" (Full, Full Trap, Full 3" Mag.). Vent. Rib. Also available with Multi choke interchangeable choke tubes.
Weight: About 7½ lbs. **Length:** 48¼" (28").
Stock: Walnut, hand checkered p.g. and fore-end, rubber recoil pad with white line spacer.
Features: Cross bolt safety, fluted bolt, gold plated trigger. Imported from Japan by Weatherby. Introduced 1982.
Price: Field or Skeet grade. **$439.95**
Price: Trap Grade **$469.95**
Price: Extra interchangeable barrels, from **$164.95**
Price: Multi-Choke models. **$459.95**

WESTERN FIELD 650 AUTOLOADING SHOTGUN
Gauge: 12 only.
Barrel: 28" (Full, Mod., Imp. Cyl. choke tubes).
Weight: About 7¾ lbs.
Stock: Walnut finished hardwood.
Sights: Metal bead front.
Features: Interchangeable barrel and Accu-Choke tubes; vent. rib; top safety. From Montgomery Ward.
Price: Ward's catalog #10650. . . . . **$249.99**

SHOTGUNS—AUTOLOADERS

Winchester 1500 XTR

WINCHESTER 1500 XTR AUTO SHOTGUN
Gauge: 12 and 20, 2¾" chamber, 2-shot magazine.
Barrel: 28" plain or vent. rib Winchoke with Full, Mod., Imp. Cyl. tubes.
Weight: 7 to 7¼ lbs. **Length:** 50⅝" over-all.
Stock: American walnut, cut-checkered p.g. and fore-end.
Sights: Metal bead front.
Features: Winchester XTR fit and finish. Gas-operated action; front locking, rotating bolt. Interchangeable barrels. Engine turned bolt, nickel plated carrier, cross-bolt safety. Introduced 1978. Made under license by U.S. Repeating Arms Co.
Price: Plain barrel with Winchoke $423.00
Price: Vent. rib barrel with Winchoke $461.00
Price: Extra barrel, plain field. $108.95
Price: As above, with Winchoke $125.95
Price: Extra barrel, vent. rib $139.95
Price: As above, with Winchoke $156.95

> Consult our Directory pages for the location of firms mentioned.

SHOTGUNS—SLIDE ACTIONS

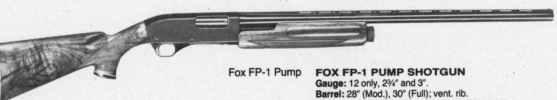

Browning BPS Pump

BROWNING BPS PUMP SHOTGUN
Gauge: 12 only, 3" chamber (2¾" in target guns), 5-shot magazine.
Barrel: 26", 28", 30" (Imp. Cyl., Mod. or Full).
Weight: 7 lbs. 12 oz. (28" barrel). **Length:** 48¾" over-all (28" barrel).
Stock: 14¼"x1½"x2½". Select walnut, semi-beavertail fore-end, full p.g. stock.
Features: Bottom feeding and ejection, receiver top safety, high post vent. rib. Double action bars eliminate binding. Vent. rib barrels only. Introduced 1977. Imported from Japan by Browning.
Price: Grade I, Hunting $364.95
Price: Grade I, Trap. $384.95
Price: Extra Trap barrel. $130.50
Price: Extra hunting barrel $122.50
Price: Buck Special (no accessories) $389.95
Price: Buck Special with accessories $409.95

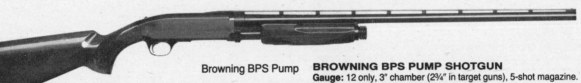

Fox FP-1 Pump

FOX FP-1 PUMP SHOTGUN
Gauge: 12 only, 2¾" and 3".
Barrel: 28" (Mod.), 30" (Full); vent. rib.
Weight: 7¼ lbs. **Length:** 47¾" over-all (28" bbl.)
Stock: Walnut, checkered p.g. and fore-end; (14"x1½"x 2½").
Sights: Metal bead front.
Features: Dual action bars for smooth functioning; handy action release and cross-bolt safety. Rosewood p.g. cap with inlay. Imported from Japan by Savage Arms. Introduced 1981.
Price: $347.50

Ithaca 37 Basic

ITHACA 37 BASIC FEATHERLITE
Gauge: 12 ga; 2¾" chamber or 3"
Barrel: 26" (Imp. Cyl.), 28" (Mod.) or 30" (Full).
Weight: 6¾ lbs.
Stock: Walnut, uncheckered and finished with tung oil.
Features: All metal surfaces vapor blasted to a non-glare matte finish. Fore-end is the traditional "Ring tail" style. Plain or vent. rib. Introduced 1980.
Price: Plain barrel $328.00
Price: Vent Rib $377.00
Price: Magnum, Full choke $402.00

Ithaca Model 37

ITHACA MODEL 37 FEATHERLIGHT

Gauge: 12, 20 (5-shot; 3-shot plug furnished).
Action: Slide; takedown; bottom ejection.
Barrel: 26", 28", 30" in 12 ga. 26" or 28" in 20 ga. (Full, Mod. or Imp. Cyl.)
Weight: 12 ga. 6½ lbs., 20 ga. 5¾ lbs.
Stock: 14"x1⅝"x2⅝". Checkered walnut p.g. stock and fore-end.
Features: Ithaca Raybar front sight; decorated receiver, crossbolt safety; action release for removing shells.
Price: Standard **$345.00**
Price: Standard Vent Rib **$396.00**
Price: 2500 Series **$875.00**
Price: Presentation Series **$1,425.00**

Ithaca Model 37 Supreme

Same as Model 37 except: hand checkered beavertail fore-end and p.g. stock, Ithaca recoil pad and vent, rib
Price: **$620.00**
Model 37 Supreme also with Skeet (14"x1½"x2¼") or Trap (14½"x1½"x1⅞") stocks available at no extra charge. Other options available at extra charge.

Ithaca 37 English Ultra

Ithaca Model 37 English Ultra

Similar to the standard Model 37 Featherlight except vent. rib barrel has straight-grip stock with better wood, cut-checkered pump handle, grip area and butt, oil finished wood. Introduced 1981.
Price: **$496.00**

Ithaca Model 37 Ultra-Featherlight

Weighs five pounds. Same as standard Model 37 except in 20 ga. only, comes only with 25" vent. rib barrel choked Full, Mod. or Imp. Cyl. Has recoil pad, gold plated trigger, Sid Bell-designed grip cap. Also available as Ultra-Deerslayer with 20" barrel.
Price: **$435.00**
Price: Deerslayer model **$414.00**

Ithaca Model 37 De Luxe Featherlight

Same as Model 37 except: checkered stock with p.g. cap; beavertail fore-end; vent. rib; recoil pad. Wgt. 12 ga. 6¾ lbs.
Price: With vent. rib **$414.00**

Ithaca 37 Deerslayer

Ithaca Model 37 Deerslayer

Same as Model 37 except: 26" or 20" bbl. designed for rifled slugs; sporting rear sight, Raybar front sight: rear sight ramp grooved for Redfield long eye relief scope mount. 12, or 20 gauge. With checkered stock, beavertail fore-end and recoil pad.
Price: **$385.00**
Price: Super Deluxe model **$435.00**

Ithaca Model 37 Magnum

Same as standard Model 37 except chambered for 3" shells with resulting longer receiver. Stock dimensions are 14"x1⅞"x1½". Grip cap has a Sid Bell-designed flying mallard on it. Has a recoil pad, vent. rib barrel with Raybar front sight. Available in 12 or 20 ga. with 30" (Full) or 28" (Mod.) barrel. Weight about 7¼ lbs. Introduced 1978.
Price: **$435.00**

Marlin Model 120

MARLIN 120 MAGNUM PUMP GUN

Gauge: 12 ga. (2¾" or 3" chamber) 5-shot; 3-shot plug furnished.
Action: Hammerless, side ejecting, slide action.
Barrel: 20" slug, 26" (Imp. Cyl.), 28" (Mod.) 30" (Full), with vent. rib. or 38" MXR plain.
Weight: About 8¼ lbs. **Length:** 50½" over-all (30" bbl.).
Stock: 14"x1½"x2⅜". Hand-checkered walnut, capped p.g., semi-beavertail fore-end. Mar-Shield® finish.
Features: Interchangeable bbls., slide lock release; large button cross-bolt safety.
Price: **$351.95**
Price: Extra barrels, about **$102.95**

MARLIN GLENFIELD 778 PUMP GUN

Gauge: 12 (2¾" or 3" chamber). 5-shot, 3-shot plug furnished.
Barrel: 20" slug (with sights), 26" (Imp. Cyl.), 28" (Mod.) 30" (Full), all with or without rib; 38" MXR (Full), no rib.
Weight: 7¾ lbs. **Length:** 48½" over-all.
Stock: Walnut-finished hardwood. Semi-beavertail fore-end, vent. recoil pad.
Features: Machined steel receiver, double action bars, engine-turned bolt, shell carrier and bolt slide. Interchangeable barrel. Introduced 1978.
Price: Plain barrel **$242.95**
Price: Vent. rib barrel **$274.95**

Mossberg Model 500

MOSSBERG MODEL 500 ALDR, CLDR
Gauge: 12, 20, 3".
Action: Takedown.
Barrel: 28" ACCU-CHOKE (interchangeable tubes for Imp. Cyl., Mod., Full). Vent. rib only.
Weight: 6¾ lbs. (20-ga.), 7¼ lbs. (12-ga.) **Length:** 48" over-all.
Stock: Walnut-finished hardwood; checkered p.g. and fore-end; recoil pad. (14"x1½"x2½").
Features: Side ejection; top tang safety; trigger disconnector prevents doubles. Easily interchangeable barrels within gauge.
Price: Vent rib, either gauge **$279.95**
Price: Extra barrels, from **$71.95**

New Haven Model 600AST Slugster
Same as standard Mossberg Model 500 except has Slugster barrel with ramp front sight, open adj. folding-leaf rear, running deer scene etched on receiver. 12 ga.—18½", 24", 20-ga.—24" bbl.
Price: . . . . **N.A.**

Mossberg 500 AHT/AHTD

Mossberg Model 500AHT/AHTD
Same as Model 500 except 12 ga. only with extra-high Simmons Olympic-style free floating rib and built-up Monte Carlo trap-style stock. 30" barrel (Full), 28" ACCU-CHOKE with 3 interchangeable choke tubes (Mod., Imp. Mod., Full).
Price: With 30" barrel, fixed choke **$479.95**
Price: With ACCU-CHOKE barrel, 28" or 30" **$489.95**

New Haven Model 600ETV
Similar to Mossberg Model 500 except: 410 bore only, 26" bbl. (Full); 2½", 3" shells; holds six 2¾" or five 3" shells. Walnut-finished stock with checkered p.g. and fore-end, fluted comb and recoil pad (14"x1¼"x2½"). Weight about 6 lbs., length over-all 45¾".
Price: With vent. rib barrel . . . . **N.A.**

Remington Model 870

REMINGTON 870 WINGMASTER PUMP GUN
Gauge: 12, 20, (5-shot; 3-shot wood plug).
Action: Takedown, slide action
Barrel: 12, 20, ga., 26" (Imp. Cyl.); 28" (Mod. or Full); 12 ga., 30" (Full).
Weight: 7 lbs., 12 ga. (7¾ lbs. with Vari-Weight plug); 6½ lbs., 20 ga.
Length: 48½" over-all (28" bbl.).
Stock: 14"x1⅝"x2½". Checkered walnut, p.g.; fluted extension fore-end; fitted rubber recoil pad.
Features: Double action bars, crossbolt safety. Receiver machined from solid steel. Hand fitted action.
Price: Plain bbl. **$326.95**
Price: With vent. rib **$368.95**
Price: Left hand, vent. rib., 12 and 20 ga. **$392.95**
Price: Lt. Wt. Limited, 23" vent. rib, Imp. Cyl., Mod **$368.95**

Remington 870 Magnum
Same as the M870 except 3" chamber, 12 ga. 30" bbl. (Mod. or Full), 20 ga. 28" bbl. (Mod. or Full). Recoil pad installed. Wgt., 12 ga. 8 lbs., 20 ga. 7½ lbs.
Price: Plain bbl. **$351.95**
Price: With vent. rib **$393.95**
Price: Left hand model, vent. rib. bbl. **$417.95**

Remington 870 Extra Barrels
Plain **$83.95**. Vent. rib **$125.95**. Vent. rib Skeet **$135.95**. Vent. rib Trap **$135.95**. 34" Trap **$151.95**. With rifle sights **$102.95**. Available in the same gauges and chokes as shown on guns. **Prices are approximate.**

Remington 870 Small Gauges
Exact copies of the large ga. Model 870, except that guns are offered in 28 and 410 ga. 25" barrel (Full, Mod., Imp. Cyl.). D and F grade prices same as large ga. M870 prices.
Price: With vent. rib barrel **$379.95**
Price: Lightweight Magnum, 20 ga. plain bbl. (5¾ lbs.) **$351.95**
Price: Lightweight Magnum, 20 ga., vent. rib bbl. **$393.95**

Remington 870F Premier
Same as M870, except select walnut, better engraving
Price: **$3,700.00**
Price: With gold inlay **$5,500.00**

Remington 870 TA Trap

Remington 870 TA Trap
Same as the M870 except: 12 ga. only, 30" (Mod., Full) vent. rib. bbl., ivory front and white metal middle beads. Special sear, hammer and trigger assy. 14⅜"x1½"x1⅞" stock with recoil pad. Hand fitted action and parts. Wgt. 8 lbs.
Price: Model 870TA Trap **$377.95**
Price: TA Trap with Monte Carlo stock **$387.95**

SHOTGUNS—SLIDE ACTIONS

Remington 870 Lightweight

Remington Model 870 Competition Trap
Same as standard 870 except single shot, gas reduction system, select wood. Has 30" (Full choke) vent. rib barrel
Price: $589.95

Remington Model 870 20 Ga. Lt. Wt.
Same as standard Model 870 except weighs 6 lbs.; 26" (Imp. Cyl.), 28" (Full, Mod.), 30" (Full).
Price: Plain barrel $020.95
Price: Vent. rib barrel $060.95

Remington 870 Deer Gun

Remington Model 870 Brushmaster Deluxe
Carbine version of the M870 with 20" bbl. (Imp. Cyl.) for rifled slugs. 40½" over-all, wgt. 6½ lbs. Recoil pad. Adj. rear, ramp front sights, 12 or 20 ga. Deluxe.
Price: $347.95

Remington 870D Tournament
Same as 870 except: better walnut, hand checkering. Engraved receiver and bbl. Vent. rib. Stock dimensions to order.
Price: $1,850.00

S & W Model 3000

Smith & Wesson Model 3000 Waterfowler Pump
Similar to the standard Model 3000 except all exterior metal is Parkerized to reduce glare, bolt is black oxidized, stock has a dull oil finish. Comes with q.d. swivels and a padded, camouflaged sling. Available with 30" (Full) barrel with 3" chamber. Introduced 1982.
Price: $405.95

SMITH & WESSON MODEL 3000 PUMP
Gauge: 12 or 20 ga., 3" chamber.
Barrel: 22" (Cyl.) with rifle sights, 26" (Imp. Cyl.), 28" (Mod.), 30" (Full), vent. rib or plain. Also available with Multi-Choke system.
Weight: About 7½ lbs. **Length:** 48½" over-all (28" bbl.).
Stock: 14"x1⅜"x2¼". American walnut
Features: Dual action bars for smooth functioning. Rubber recoil pad, steel receiver, chrome plated bolt. Cross-bolt safety reversible for left-handed shooters. Introduced 1980.
Price: With vent. rib barrel $378.95
Price: Extra vent. rib barrel.................................... $125.95
Price: Slug barrel with rifle sights $102.95
Price: With Multi-Choke system $405.95
Price: Extra Multi-Choke barrel $152.95

Stevens Model 67

STEVENS MODEL 67 PUMP SHOTGUN
Gauge: 12, 20 (2¾" & 3"), 410 (2½" & 3").
Barrel: 26" (Full, 410 ga.), 28" (Mod., Full), 30" (Full, 12 ga.).
Weight: 7 lbs. **Length:** 49½" over-all (30" bbl.).
Stock: Walnut-finished hardwood; checkered p.g. and slide handle. 14"x1½"x2½".
Sights: Metal bead front.
Features: Tapered slide handle, top tang safety, steel receiver. From Savage Arms. Introduced 1981.
Price: Model 67 .... $168.00
Price: Model 67VR (vent. rib)................................. $184.50
Price: Model 67 Slug Gun (21" barrel, rifle sights) $168.00

Stevens Model 79-VR

STEVENS MODEL 79-VR PUMP SHOTGUN
Gauge: 12, 20 (2¾" & 3"), 410 (2½" & 3").
Barrel: 26" (Full 410 ga.), 28" (Mod. 12 & 20 ga.), 28" (Full), 30" (Full, 12 ga.), vent. rib.
Weight: 7 lbs. **Length:** 49½" over-all (30" bbl.).
Stock: Walnut-finished hardwood, checkered p.g. and slide handle. 14"x1½"x2½".
Sights: Metal bead front.
Features: Top tang safety, tapered slide handle, interchangeable barrels. Introduced 1981. From Savage Arms.
Price: Model 79-VR $201.00

CAUTION: PRICES CHANGE. CHECK AT GUNSHOP.

SHOTGUNS—SLIDE ACTIONS

Weatherby Ninety-Two

WESTERN FIELD 550 PUMP SHOTGUN
Gauge: 12 and 20.
Action: Slide action, takedown; top tang safety.
Barrel: 12 ga. 26″ (Variable); 28″ (Mod.); 30″ (Full); 20 ga. 26″ (Variable); 28″ (Mod., Full).
Weight: 8½ lbs.
Stock: Walnut finished p.g. stock, moulded buttplate, serrated fore-end.
Features: Straight-line feed, interchangeable bbls., trigger disconnector prevents doubling.
Price: $169.99
Price: As above, but with variable choke in 12 or 20 ga.............. $179.99
Price: Slug gun with 24″ bbl. without choke...................... $199.99
Price: Deluxe Vent. rib models available with ACCU-CHOKE....... $249.99
Price: Vent rib models with variable choke $189.99

Winchester 1300 XTR Deer Gun
Similar to the 1300 XTR except available only in 12 gauge with 24⅛″ barrel (Cyl.) and rifle-type sights. Weight is 6½ lbs.
Price: $359.00

Winchester 1300 XTR Waterfowl Pump Gun
Similar to the 1300 XTR except available only in 12 ga. with 30″ vent rib barrel and Winchoke.
Price: $379.00

WEATHERBY NINETY-TWO PUMP
Gauge: 12 only, 3″ chamber.
Action: Short stroke slide action.
Barrel: 26″ (Mod., Imp. Cyl., Skeet), 28″ (Full, Mod.), 30″ (Full, Full Trap, 3″ Mag. Full). Vent. Rib; or Multi-Choke barrel with interchangeable tubes.
Weight: About 7½ lbs. **Length:** 48⅛″ (28″ bbl.)
Stock: Walnut, hand checkered p.g. and fore-end, white line spacers at p.g. cap and recoil pad.
Features: Short stroke action, crossbolt safety. Introduced 1982. Imported from Japan by Weatherby.
Price: Field or Skeet grade, fixed chokes $399.95
Price: Trap grade $429.95
Price: Extra interchangeable bbls. $164.95
Price: Multi-Choke models $419.95

WINCHESTER 1300 XTR PUMP GUN
Gauge: 12 and 20, 3″ chamber, 4-shot.
Barrel: 28″, plain or vent. rib with Full, Mod., Imp. Cyl. Winchoke tubes.
Weight: 7¼ lbs. **Length:** 48⅝″ over-all.
Stock: American walnut, cut-checkered p.g. and fore-end. XTR finish.
Sights: Metal bead front.
Features: Winchester XTR fit and finish. Has twin action bars, cross-bolt safety, alloy receiver and trigger guard. Front-locking, rotating bolt, engine-turned bolt. Introduced 1978. Made under license by U.S. Repeating Arms Co.
Price: Plain barrel with Winchoke $341.00
Price: Vent. rib with Winchoke................................ $379.00
Price: Extra field barrel, plain................................ $104.95
Price: As above with Winchoke................................ $120.95
Price: Extra field barrel with vent. rib $135.95
Price: As above with Winchoke................................ $151.95
Price: 1300 Deer Slug barrel $118.95

Winchester Ranger

WINCHESTER RANGER PUMP GUN
Gauge: 12 or 20, 3″ chamber, 4-shot magazine.
Barrel: 28″ vent rib or plain with Full, Mod., Imp. Cyl. Winchoke tubes, or 30″ plain.
Weight: 7¼ to 7½ lbs. **Length:** 48⅝″ to 50⅝″ over-all.
Stock: Walnut finished hardwood with ribbed fore-end.
Sights: Metal bead front.
Features: Cross-bolt safety, black rubber butt pad, twin action slide bars, front-locking rotating bolt. Made under license by U.S. Repeating Arms Co.
Price: Plain barrel $222.00
Price: Vent rib barrel $264.00

SHOTGUNS—OVER-UNDERS

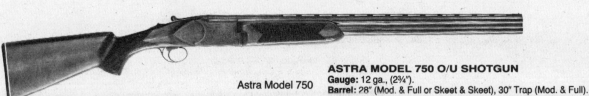

Astra Model 750

ASTRA MODEL 750 O/U SHOTGUN
Gauge: 12 ga., (2¾″).
Barrel: 28″ (Mod. & Full or Skeet & Skeet), 30″ Trap (Mod. & Full).
Weight: 6½ lbs.
Stock: European walnut, hand-checkered p.g. and fore-end.
Features: Single selective trigger, scroll-engraved receiver, selective auto ejectors, vent. rib. Introduced 1980. From L. Joseph Rahn, Inc.
Price: $733.00
Price: With extractors only $600.00
Price: Trap or Skeet (M.C. stock and recoil pad.)............... $850.00

Astra Model 650 O/U Shotgun
Same as Model 750 except has double triggers.
Price: With extractors $493.00
Price: With ejectors $630.00

BAIKAL MC-5-105 O/U
Gauge: 20 ga., 2¾" chambers.
Barrel: 26" (Imp. Cyl. & Mod., Skeet & Skeet).
Weight: 5¾ lbs.
Stock: Fancy hand checkered walnut. Choice of p.g. or straight stock, with or without cheekpiece. Fore-end permanently attached to barrels.
Features: Fully engraved receiver. Double triggers, extractors. Chrome barrels, chambers and internal parts. Hand-fitted solid rib. Hammer interceptors. Comes with case. Imported from Russia by Baikal International.
Price: MC-5-105 . . . . **$1,495.00**

BAIKAL MC-8-0 O/U
Gauge: 12 ga., 2¾" chambers.
Barrel: 26" special parabolic Skeet, 28" (Mod. & Full). Available in 2 bbl. sets.
Weight: 7¾ lbs.
Stock: Fancy walnut. Beavertail fore-end permanently attached to barrels. Hand checkered p.g. and fore-end. Monte Carlo.
Features: Hand-made competition shotgun. Blued, hand-engraved receiver. Single trigger, extractors. Chrome barrels, chambers and internal parts. Hand fitted vent. rib. Comes with case. Imported from Russia by Baikal International.
Price: MC-8-0 Skeet **$2,895.00**
Price: MC-8-01 Trap **$2,895.00**
Price: MC-8-03 with 2-barrel set **$3,850.00**

BAIKAL IJ-27E1C O/U
Gauge: 12 ga., 2¾" chambers, 20 ga., 3" chambers.
Barrel: 26" (Skeet & Skeet), 28" (Mod. & Full).
Weight: 7¾ lbs.
Stock: Hand checkered walnut, rubber recoil pad. Ventilated fore-end. White spacers at p.g. and recoil pad.
Features: Single selective trigger. Chrome barrels, chambers internal parts. Hand fitted vent. rib. Hand engraved receiver. Selective extractors/ejectors. Imported from Russia by Baikal International.
Price: **$485.00**
Price: Skeet or Trap versions **$485.00**
Price: With silver receiver inlays **$599.00**
Price: Skeet or Trap versions **$485.00**

ARMSPORT MODEL 2500 O/U
Gauge: 12 or 20 ga.
Barrel: 26" (Imp. Cyl. & Mod.); 28" (Mod. & Full); vent. rib.
Weight: 8 lbs.
Stock: European walnut, hand checkered p.g. and fore-end.
Features: Single selective trigger, automatic ejectors, engraved receiver. Imported by Armsport.
Price: **$695.00**
Price: With extractors only **$595.00**

BAIKAL MC-7 O/U
Gauge: 12 or 20 ga., 2¾" chambers.
Barrel: 12 ga. 28" (Mod. & Full), 20 ga. 26" (Imp. Cyl. & Mod.).
Weight: 7 lbs. (12 ga.), 6¾ lbs. (20 ga.)
Stock: Fancy walnut. Hand checkered, with or without p.g. and cheekpiece. Beavertail fore-end.
Features: Fully chiseled and engraved receiver. Chrome barrels, chambers and internal parts. Double trigger, selective ejectors. Solid raised rib. Single selective trigger available. Comes with case. Imported from Russia by Baikal International.
Price: **$2,995.00**

BAIKAL MC-109 O/U
Gauge: 12 ga., 2¾" chambers.
Barrel: 28" (Mod. & Full).
Weight: 7¼ lbs.
Stock: Fancy walnut. Choice of p.g. or straight stock, with or without cheekpiece. Beavertail fore-end. Hand carved and checkered to customer's specs.
Features: Hand-made sidelock shotgun. Removable sideplates. Chrome barrels, chambers and internal parts. Single selective trigger, selective ejectors, cocking indicators, hammer interceptors. Hand chiseled scenes on receiver to customer specs. Inlays to customer specs. Comes with case. Imported from Russia by Baikal International.
Price: Special order only **$5,495.00**

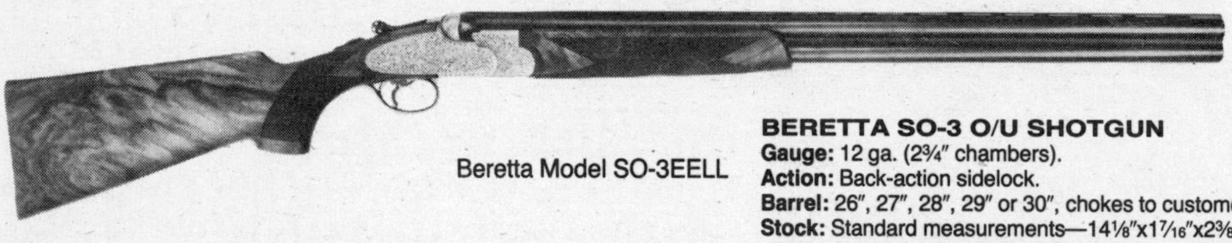

Beretta Model SO-3EELL

BAIKAL TOZ-34E SOUVENIR O/U
Gauge: 12 or 28 ga., 2¾".
Barrel: 12 ga.—28" (Mod. & Full), 28 ga.—26" (Mod. & Full).
Weight: 12 ga.—7¾ lbs.; 28 ga.—6¾ lbs.
Stock: Hand checkered fancy European walnut. Permanently attached fore-end. Rubber recoil pad.
Features: Double triggers, chrome lined barrels and chambers, cocking indicators. Hand engraved receiver. Hammer interceptors. Extractors only. Silvered, hand-engraved receiver. Imported from Russia by Baikal International.
Price: **$725.00**

BERETTA SO-3 O/U SHOTGUN
Gauge: 12 ga. (2¾" chambers).
Action: Back-action sidelock.
Barrel: 26", 27", 28", 29" or 30", chokes to customer specs.
Stock: Standard measurements—14⅛"x1⁷⁄₁₆"x2⅜". Straight "English" or p.g.-style. Hand checkered European walnut.
Features: SO-3—"English scroll" floral engraving on action body, sideplates and trigger guard. Stocked in select walnut. SO-3EL—as above, with full engraving coverage. Hand-detachable sideplates. SO-3EELL—as above with deluxe finish and finest full coverage engraving. Internal parts gold plated. Top lever is pierced and carved in relief with gold inlaid crown. Introduced 1977. Imported from Italy by Beretta U.S.A. Corp.
Price: SO-3 . . . . **$6,245.00**
Price: SO-3EL **$7,440.00**
Price: SO-3EELL **$10,000.00**

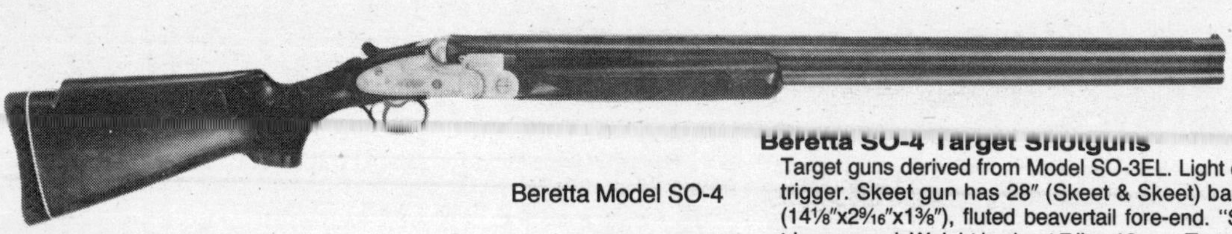

Beretta Model SO-4

Beretta SO-4 Target Shotguns
Target guns derived from Model SO-3EL. Light engraving coverage. Single trigger. Skeet gun has 28" (Skeet & Skeet) barrels, 10mm rib, p.g. stock (14⅛"x2⁹⁄₁₆"x1⅜"), fluted beavertail fore-end. "Skeet" is inlaid in gold into trigger guard. Weight is about 7 lbs. 10 ozs. Trap guns have 30" (Imp. Mod. & Full or Mod. & Full) barrels, trap stock dimensions, fitted recoil pad, fluted beavertail fore-end. Weight is about 7 lbs. 12 ozs. "Trap" is inlaid in gold into trigger guard. Special dimensions and features, within limits, may be ordered. Introduced 1977.
Price: Skeet **$7,285.00**
Price: Trap **$7,285.00**

CAUTION: PRICES CHANGE. CHECK AT GUNSHOP.

Beretta Model 686

BERETTA SERIES 680 OVER-UNDER
Gauge: 12 (2¾").
Barrel: 29½" (Imp. Mod. & Full, Trap), 28" (Skeet & Skeet).
Weight: About 8 lbs.
Stock: Trap—14⅜"x1¼"x2⅛"; Skeet—14⅜"x1⅜"x2⁷⁄₁₆". European walnut with hand checkering.
Sights: Luminous front sight and center bead.
Features: Trap Monte Carlo stock has deluxe trap recoil pad, Skeet has smooth pad. Imported from Italy by Beretta U.S.A. Corp.
Price: Skeet or Trap gun **$1,580.00**
Price: As above with fitted case **$1,580.00**
Price: M686 Field gun (illus.) **$980.00**
Price: M685 Field gun **$820.00**
Price: M687EL, Field **$2,212.00**
Price: M680 Single bbl. Trap, 32" or 34" **$1,580.00**
Price: M680 Combo Trap O/U, with single bbl. **$2,100.00**

> Consult our Directory pages for the location of firms mentioned.

Browning Citori Field

BROWNING CITORI O/U SHOTGUN
Gauge: 12, 20, 28 and 410.
Barrel: 26", 28" (Mod. & Full, Imp. Cyl. & Mod.), in all gauges, 30" (Mod. & Full, Full & Full) in 12 ga. only.
Weight: 6 lbs. 8 oz. (26" 410) to 7 lbs. 13 oz. (30" 12-ga.).
Length: 43" over-all (26" bbl.).
Stock: Dense walnut, hand checkered, full p.g., beavertail fore-end. Field-type recoil pad on 12 ga. field guns and trap and Skeet models.
Sights: Medium raised beads, German nickel silver.
Features: Barrel selector integral with safety, auto ejectors, three-piece take-down. Imported from Japan by Browning.
Price: Grade I, 12 and 20 . . . . **$749.95**
Price: Grade I, 28 and 410 . . . . **$784.95**
Price: Grade II, 12 and 20 . . . . **$1,300.00**
Price: Grade V, 12 and 20 . . . . **$1,960.00**
Price: Grade II, 28 and 410 . . . . **$1,345.00**
Price: Grade V, 28 and 410 . . . . **$2,010.00**

Browning Citori O/U Sporter
Similar to standard Citori except; comes with 26" (Mod. & Full, Imp. Cyl. & Mod.) only; straight grip stock with schnabel fore-end; satin oil finish.
Price: Grade I, 12 and 20 . . . . **$749.95**
Price: Grade I, 28 and 410 . . . . **$784.95**
Price: Grade II, 12 and 20 . . . . **$1,300.00**
Price: Grade V, 12 and 20 . . . . **$1,960.00**
Price: Grade II, 28 and 410 . . . . **$1,345.00**
Price: Grade V, 28 and 410 . . . . **$2,010.00**

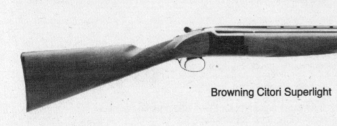

Browning Citori Superlight

Browning Superlight Citori Over-Under
Similar to the standard Citori except availiable in 12 or 20 gauge (3" chambers) with 26" barrels choked Imp. Cyl. & Mod. or 28" choked Mod. & Full. Has straight grip stock, schnabel fore-end tip. Superlight 12 weighs 6 lbs., 9 oz. (26" barrels); Superlight 20, 5 lbs., 12 oz. (26" barrels). Introduced 1982.
Price: Grade I only, 12 or 20 . . . . **$774.95**

Browning Citori Sideplate

Browning Citori Sideplate 20 Gauge
Same as the Citori Sporter except available only in 20 gauge with 26" barrels (Imp. Cyl. & Mod. or Mod. & Full). The satin steel sideplates, receiver and long trigger guard tang have etched upland game scenes. Wood and checkering of Grade V style.
Price: **$1,960.00**

Browning Citori O/U Trap Models
Similar to standard Citori except: 12 gauge only; 30", 32" (Full & Full, Imp. Mod. & Full, Mod. & Full), 34" single barrel in Combo Set (Full, Imp. Mod., Mod.); Monte Carlo cheekpiece (14⅜"x1⅜"x1⅜"x2"); fitted with trap-style recoil pad; conventional target rib and high post target rib.
Price: Grade I, (high post rib) **$839.95**
Price: Grade II (high post rib) **$1,410.00**
Price: Grade V (high post rib) **$2,095.00**
Price: Grade I Combo (32" O/U & 34" single bbl., high post ribs) incl. luggage case **$1,410.00**

Browning Citori O/U Skeet Models
Similar to standard Citori except: 26", 28" (Skeet & Skeet) only; stock dimensions of 14⅜"x1½"x2", fitted with Skeet-style recoil pad; conventional target rib and high post target rib.
Price: Grade I, 12 & 20 (high post rib) **$839.95**
Price: Grade I, 28 & 410 (high post rib) **$869.95**
Price: Grade II, all gauges (high post rib) **$1,410.00**
Price: Grade V, all gauges (high post rib) **$2,095.00**

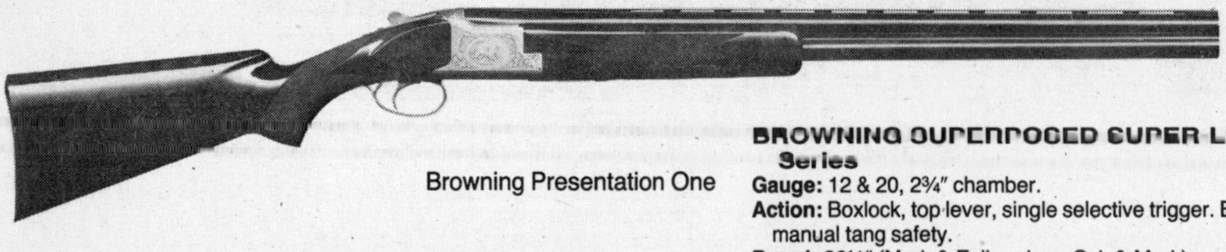

Browning Presentation One

Browning Limited Edition Waterfowl Superposed
Same specs as the Lightning Superposed. Available in 12 ga. only, 28″ (Mod. & Full). Limited to 500 guns, the edition number of each gun is inscribed in gold on the bottom of the receiver with "American Mallard" and its scientific name. Sides of receiver have two gold inlayed Mallards, bottom has three. Receiver is completely engraved and grayed. Stock and fore-end are highly figured dark French walnut with 24 lpi checkering, hand-oiled finish, checkered butt. Comes with form fitted, velvet-lined, black walnut case. Introduced 1981.
Price: **$7,700.00**

Browning Presentation Superposed Magnum 12
Browning Superposed 3″ chambers; 30″ (Full & Full or Full & Mod.) barrels. Stock, 14¼″x1⅝″x2½″ with factory fitted recoil pad. Weight 8 lbs.
Price: From **$4,500.00**

Browning Presentation Superposed Lightning Trap 12
Same as Browning Lightning Superposed except: semi-beavertail fore-end and ivory sights; stock, 14⅜″x1⁷⁄₁₆″x1⅝″. 7¾ lbs. 30″ (Full & Full, Full & Imp. Mod. or Full & Mod.)
Price: From **$4,570.00**

Browning Presentation Superposed Combinations
Standard and Lightning models are available with these factory fitted extra barrels: 12 and 20 ga., same gauge bbls.; 12 ga., 20 ga. bbls.; 20 ga., extra sets 28 and/or 410 gauge; 28 ga., extra 410 bbls. Extra barrels may be had in Lightning weights with Standard models and vice versa. Prices range from **$6,275.00** (12, 20 ga., one set extra bbls. same gauge) for the Presentation I Standard to about **$18,800.00** for the Presentation 4 grade in a 4-barrel matched set (12, 20, 28 and 410 gauges).

BROWNING SUPERPOSED SUPER-LIGHT Presentation Series
Gauge: 12 & 20, 2¾″ chamber.
Action: Boxlock, top lever, single selective trigger. Bbl. selector combined with manual tang safety.
Barrel: 26½″ (Mod. & Full, or Imp. Cyl. & Mod.)
Weight: 6⅜ lbs., average
Stock: Straight grip (14¼″x1⅝″x2½″) hand checkered (fore-end and grip) select walnut.
Features: The Presentation Series is available in four grades and covers the Superposed line. Basically this gives the buyer a wide choice of engraving styles and designs and mechanical options which would place the gun in a "custom" bracket. Options are too numerous to list here and the reader is urged to obtain a copy of the latest Browning catalog for the complete listing. Series introduced 1977. Imported from Belgium by Browning.
Price: From **$4,560.00**

Browning Presentation Superposed Lightning Skeet
Same as Standard Superposed except: Special Skeet stock, fore-end; center and front ivory bead sights. Wgt. 6½-7¾ lbs.
Price: All gauges, from **$4,570.00**

Superposed Presentation Broadway Trap 12
Same as Browning Lightning Superposed except: ⅝″ wide vent. rib; stock, 14⅜″x1⁷⁄₁₆″x1⅝″. 30″ or 32″ (Imp. Mod, Full; Mod., Full; Full, Full). 8 lbs. with 32″ bbls.
Price: From **$4,680.00**

Browning Presentation Superposed All-Gauge Skeet Set
Consists of four matched sets of barrels in 12, 20, 28 and 410 ga. Available in either 26½″ or 28″ length. Each bbl. set has a ¼″ wide vent. rib with two ivory sight beads. Grade I receiver is hand engraved and stock and fore-end are checkered. Weight 7 lbs., 10 oz. (26½″ bbls.), 7 lbs., 12 oz. (28″ bbls.). **Contact Browning for prices.**

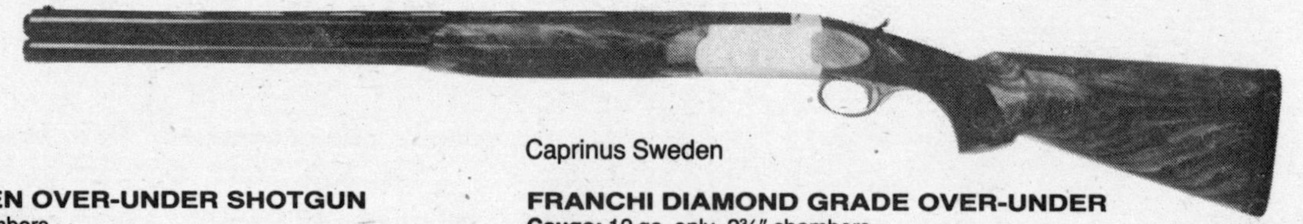

Caprinus Sweden

CAPRINUS SWEDEN OVER-UNDER SHOTGUN
Gauge: 12 only, 2¾″ chambers
Barrel: 28″, 30″ (interchangeable choke tubes—Cyl., Skeet, Imp. Cyl., Mod., Imp. Mod. and Full)
Weight: 6.8 lbs. (Game model).
Stock: 14″x1¾″x2⅛″ (Game model). High-grade walnut with rubber pad or checkered butt. Monte Carlo optional. Tru-oil or linseed oil finish.
Features: Made completely of stainless steel. Single selective trigger; barrel selector in front of the trigger; gas pressure activated auto. ejectors; firing pins set by top lever action; double safety system. Six standard choke tubes, plus optional tubes to change point of impact. Imported from Sweden by Caprinus U.S.A. Introduced 1982.
Price: Skeet Special, from. **$5,500.00**
Price: Skeet Game, from. **$5,800.00**
Price: Game, from **$5,800.00**
Price: Trap, from. **$5,840.00**

ERA "THE FULL LIMIT" O/U SHOTGUN
Gauge: 12 or 20 ga., 2¾″.
Barrel: 28″ (Mod. & Full); vent. top and middle ribs.
Weight: 7¾ lbs.
Stock: Walnut-finished hardwood, hand checkered.
Features: Auto. safety; extractors; double triggers; engraved receiver. Imported from Brazil by F.I.E.
Price: **$299.95**

FRANCHI DIAMOND GRADE OVER-UNDER
Gauge: 12 ga. only, 2¾″ chambers.
Barrel: 28″ (Mod. & Full).
Weight: 6 lbs. 13 oz.
Stock: French walnut with cut checkered pistol grip and fore-end.
Features: Top tang safety, automatic ejectors, single selective trigger. Chrome plated bores. Decorative scroll on silvered receiver. Introduced 1982. Imported from Italy by F.I.E. Corp.
Price: Diamond Grade **$850.00**

Franchi Falconet Super
Similar to the Diamond Grade except has a lightweight alloy receiver, single selective mechanical trigger with the barrel selector button on the trigger, and a rubber butt pad. Higher quality hand engraved receiver. Available in 12 ga. only, 27″ (Imp. Cyl. & Mod.) or 28″ (Mod. & Full) barrels. Translucent front sight bead. Introduced 1982.
Price: Falconet Super **$1,015.00**

Franchi Alcione Super Deluxe
Similar to the Falconet Super except has best quality hand engraved, silvered receiver, 24K gold plated trigger, elephant ivory bead front sight. Comes with luggage-type fitted case. Has 14K gold inlay on receiver. Same barrel and chokes as on Falconet Super. Introduced 1982.
Price: Alcione Super Deluxe. **$1,595.00**

 CAUTION: PRICES CHANGE. CHECK AT GUNSHOP.

SHOTGUNS—OVER-UNDERS

Beretta Model 686

Consult our Directory pages for the location of firms mentioned.

BERETTA SERIES 680 OVER-UNDER
Gauge: 12 (2¾").
Barrel: 29½" (Imp. Mod. & Full, Trap), 28" (Skeet & Skeet).
Weight: About 8 lbs.
Stock: Trap—14⅜"x1¼"x2⅛"; Skeet—14⅜"x1⅜"x2⁷⁄₁₆". European walnut with hand checkering.
Sights: Luminous front sight and center bead.
Features: Trap Monte Carlo stock has deluxe trap recoil pad, Skeet has smooth pad. Imported from Italy by Beretta U.S.A. Corp.
Price: Skeet or Trap gun $1,580.00
Price: As above with fitted case $1,580.00
Price: M686 Field gun (illus.) $980.00
Price: M685 Field gun $820.00
Price: M687EL, Field $2,212.00
Price: M680 Single bbl. Trap, 32" or 34" $1,580.00
Price: M680 Combo Trap O/U, with single bbl. $2,100.00

Browning Citori Field

BROWNING CITORI O/U SHOTGUN
Gauge: 12, 20, 28 and 410.
Barrel: 26", 28" (Mod. & Full, Imp. Cyl. & Mod.), in all gauges, 30" (Mod. & Full, Full & Full) in 12 ga. only.
Weight: 6 lbs. 8 oz. (26" 410) to 7 lbs. 13 oz. (30" 12-ga.).
Length: 43" over-all (26" bbl.).
Stock: Dense walnut, hand checkered, full p.g., beavertail fore-end. Field-type recoil pad on 12 ga. field guns and trap and Skeet models.
Sights: Medium raised beads, German nickel silver.
Features: Barrel selector integral with safety, auto ejectors, three-piece take-down. Imported from Japan by Browning.

Browning Citori O/U Sporter
Similar to standard Citori except; comes with 26" (Mod. & Full, Imp. Cyl. & Mod.) only; straight grip stock with schnabel fore-end; satin oil finish.
Price: Grade I, 12 and 20 . . . . $749.95
Price: Grade I, 28 and 410 . . . . $784.95
Price: Grade II, 12 and 20 . . . . $1,300.00
Price: Grade V, 12 and 20 . . . . $1,960.00
Price: Grade II, 28 and 410 . . . . $1,345.00
Price: Grade V, 28 and 410 . . . . $2,010.00

Price: Grade I, 12 and 20 . . . . $749.95
Price: Grade I, 28 and 410 . . . . $784.95
Price: Grade II, 12 and 20 . . . . $1,300.00
Price: Grade V, 12 and 20 . . . . $1,960.00
Price: Grade II, 28 and 410 . . . . $1,345.00
Price: Grade V, 28 and 410 . . . . $2,010.00

Browning Citori Superlight

Browning Superlight Citori Over-Under
Similar to the standard Citori except availiable in 12 or 20 gauge (3" chambers) with 26" barrels choked Imp. Cyl. & Mod. or 28" choked Mod. & Full. Has straight grip stock, schnabel fore-end tip. Superlight 12 weighs 6 lbs., 9 oz. (26" barrels); Superlight 20, 5 lbs., 12 oz. (26" barrels). Introduced 1982.
Price: Grade I only, 12 or 20 . . . . $774.95

Browning Citori Sideplate

Browning Citori Sideplate 20 Gauge
Same as the Citori Sporter except available only in 20 gauge with 26" barrels (Imp. Cyl. & Mod. or Mod. & Full). The satin steel sideplates, receiver and long trigger guard tang have etched upland game scenes. Wood and checkering of Grade V style.
Price: $1,960.00

Browning Citori O/U Trap Models
Similar to standard Citori except: 12 gauge only; 30", 32" (Full & Full, Imp. Mod. & Full, Mod. & Full), 34" single barrel in Combo Set (Full, Imp. Mod., Mod.); Monte Carlo cheekpiece (14⅜"x1⅜"x1⅜"x2"); fitted with trap-style recoil pad; conventional target rib and high post target rib.
Price: Grade I, (high post rib) $839.95
Price: Grade II (high post rib) $1,410.00
Price: Grade V (high post rib) $2,095.00
Price: Grade I Combo (32" O/U & 34" single bbl., high post ribs) incl. luggage case $1,410.00

Browning Citori O/U Skeet Models
Similar to standard Citori except: 26", 28" (Skeet & Skeet) only; stock dimensions of 14⅜"x1½"x2", fitted with Skeet-style recoil pad; conventional target rib and high post target rib.
Price: Grade I, 12 & 20 (high post rib) $839.95
Price: Grade I, 28 & 410 (high post rib) $869.95
Price: Grade II, all gauges (high post rib) $1,410.00
Price: Grade V, all gauges (high post rib) $2,095.00

Browning Presentation One

Browning Limited Edition Waterfowl Superposed

Same specs as the Lightning Superposed. Available in 12 ga. only, 28″ (Mod. & Full). Limited to 500 guns, the edition number of each gun is inscribed in gold on the bottom of the receiver with "American Mallard" and its scientific name. Sides of receiver have two gold inlayed Mallards, bottom has three. Receiver is completely engraved and grayed. Stock and fore-end are highly figured dark French walnut with 24 lpi checkering, hand-oiled finish, checkered butt. Comes with form fitted, velvet-lined, black walnut case. Introduced 1981.
Price: **$7,700.00**

Browning Presentation Superposed Magnum 12

Browning Superposed 3″ chambers; 30″ (Full & Full or Full & Mod.) barrels. Stock, 14¼″x1⅝″x2½″ with factory fitted recoil pad. Weight 8 lbs.
Price: From **$4,500.00**

Browning Presentation Superposed Lightning Trap 12

Same as Browning Lightning Superposed except: semi-beavertail fore-end and ivory sights; stock, 14⅜″x1⁷⁄₁₆″x1⅝″. 7¾ lbs. 30″ (Full & Full, Full & Imp. Mod. or Full & Mod.)
Price: From **$4,570.00**

Browning Presentation Superposed Combinations

Standard and Lightning models are available with these factory fitted extra barrels: 12 and 20 ga., same gauge bbls.; 12 ga., 20 ga. bbls.; 20 ga., extra sets 28 and/or 410 gauge; 28 ga., extra 410 gauge. Extra barrels may be had in Lightning weights with Standard models and vice versa. Prices range from **$6,275.00** (12, 20 ga., one set extra bbls. same gauge) for the Presentation I Standard to about **$18,800.00** for the Presentation 4 grade in a 4-barrel matched set (12, 20, 28 and 410 gauges).

BROWNING SUPERPOSED SUPER-LIGHT Presentation Series

Gauge: 12 & 20, 2¾″ chamber.
Action: Boxlock, top lever, single selective trigger. Bbl. selector combined with manual tang safety.
Barrel: 26½″ (Mod. & Full, or Imp. Cyl. & Mod.)
Weight: 6⅜ lbs., average
Stock: Straight grip (14¼″x1⅝″x2½″) hand checkered (fore-end and grip) select walnut.
Features: The Presentation Series is available in four grades and covers the Superposed line. Basically this gives the buyer a wide choice of engraving styles and designs and mechanical options which would place the gun in a "custom" bracket. Options are too numerous to list here and the reader is urged to obtain a copy of the latest Browning catalog for the complete listing. Series introduced 1977. Imported from Belgium by Browning.
Price: From **$4,560.00**

Browning Presentation Superposed Lightning Skeet

Same as Standard Superposed except: Special Skeet stock, fore-end; center and front ivory bead sights. Wgt. 6½-7¾ lbs.
Price: All gauges, from **$4,570.00**

Superposed Presentation Broadway Trap 12

Same as Browning Lightning Superposed except: ⅝″ wide vent. rib; stock, 14⅜″x1⁷⁄₁₆″x1⅝″. 30″ or 32″ (Imp. Mod, Full; Mod., Full; Full, Full). 8 lbs. with 32″ bbls.
Price: From **$4,680.00**

Browning Presentation Superposed All-Gauge Skeet Set

Consists of four matched sets of barrels in 12, 20, 28 and 410 ga. Available in either 26½″ or 28″ length. Each bbl. set has a ¼″ wide vent. rib with two ivory sight beads. Grade I receiver is hand engraved and stock and fore-end are checkered. Weight 7 lbs., 10 oz. (26½″ bbls.), 7 lbs., 12 oz. (28″ bbls.). **Contact Browning for prices.**

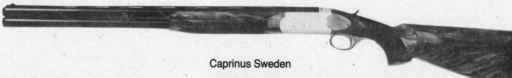

Caprinus Sweden

CAPRINUS SWEDEN OVER-UNDER SHOTGUN

Gauge: 12 only, 2¾″ chambers
Barrel: 28″, 30″ (interchangeable choke tubes—Cyl., Skeet, Imp. Cyl., Mod., Imp. Mod. and Full)
Weight: 6.8 lbs. (Game model).
Stock: 14″x1¾″x2⅛″ (Game model). High-grade walnut with rubber pad or checkered butt. Monte Carlo optional. Tru-oil or linseed oil finish.
Features: Made completely of stainless steel. Single selective trigger; barrel selector in front of the trigger; gas pressure activated auto. ejectors; firing pins set by top lever action; double safety system. Six standard choke tubes, plus optional tubes to change point of impact. Imported from Sweden by Caprinus U.S.A. Introduced 1982.
Price: Skeet Special, from **$5,500.00**
Price: Skeet Game, from **$5,800.00**
Price: Game, from **$5,800.00**
Price: Trap, from **$5,840.00**

ERA "THE FULL LIMIT" O/U SHOTGUN

Gauge: 12 or 20 ga., 2¾″.
Barrel: 28″ (Mod. & Full); vent. top and middle ribs.
Weight: 7¾ lbs.
Stock: Walnut-finished hardwood, hand checkered.
Features: Auto. safety; extractors; double triggers; engraved receiver. Imported from Brazil by F.I.E.
Price: **$299.95**

FRANCHI DIAMOND GRADE OVER-UNDER

Gauge: 12 ga. only, 2¾″ chambers.
Barrel: 28″ (Mod. & Full).
Weight: 6 lbs. 13 oz.
Stock: French walnut with cut checkered pistol grip and fore-end.
Features: Top tang safety, automatic ejectors, single selective trigger. Chrome plated bores. Decorative scroll on silvered receiver. Introduced 1982. Imported from Italy by F.I.E. Corp.
Price: Diamond Grade **$850.00**

Franchi Falconet Super

Similar to the Diamond Grade except has a lightweight alloy receiver, single selective mechanical trigger with the barrel selector button on the trigger, and a rubber butt pad. Higher quality hand engraved receiver. Available in 12 ga. only, 27″ (Imp. Cyl. & Mod.) or 28″ (Mod. & Full) barrels. Translucent front sight bead. Introduced 1982.
Price: Falconet Super **$1,015.00**

Franchi Alcione Super Deluxe

Similar to the Falconet Super except has best quality hand engraved, silvered receiver, 24K gold plated trigger, elephant ivory bead front sight. Comes with luggage-type fitted case. Has 14K gold inlay on receiver. Same barrel and chokes as on Falconet Super. Introduced 1982.
Price: Alcione Super Deluxe **$1,595.00**

CAUTION: PRICES CHANGE. CHECK AT GUNSHOP.

K.F.C. "FG" Standard

HEYM MODEL 55/77 O/U SHOTGUN
Gauge: 12, 16, 20 ga. (2¾″ or 3″).
Barrel: 28″ (Full & Mod.) standard; other lengths and chokes to customer specs.
Weight: 6¾-7½ lbs.
Stock: European walnut, hand-checkered p.g. and fore-end.
Features: Boxlock or full sidelock action; Kersten double cross bolt, double under lugs; cocking indicators. Arabesque or hunting engraving. Options include interchangeable barrels, front trigger that functions as a single non-selective trigger, deluxe engraving and stock carving. Imported from West Germany. Contact Heym for more data.
Price: Model 55F or 77F boxlock **$3,329.00**
Price: Model 55FSS or 77FSS sidelock **$5,558.00**
Price: Interchangeable o/u rifle barrels **$2,719.00**
Price: Interchangeable rifle-shotgun barrels **$1,839.00**

K.F.C. "FG" OVER-UNDER SHOTGUN
Gauge: 12 only (2¾″).
Barrel: 26″, 28″ (Imp. Cyl. & Imp. Mod.); vent. rib.
Weight: About 6.8 lbs.
Stock: 14″x1½″x2⅜″. High grade French walnut.
Sights: Sterling silver front bead.
Features: Selective single trigger, selective auto ejectors, non-automatic safety; chrome lined bores, chrome trigger. Introduced 1981. Imported from Japan by La Paloma Marketing.
Price: **$748.00**

K.F.C. OT-Skeet Shotguns
Skeet versions of FG model. Model E-1 has 26″ or 28″ (Skeet & Skeet) barrels with 13mm vent. rib, middle and front bead sights, gold colored wide trigger. Stock dimensions are 14″x1½″x2½″. Plastic buttplate, push-button fore-end release. Weight is about 7½ lbs.
Price: E-1 . . . . **$1,070.00**
Price: E-2 . . . . **$1,660.00**

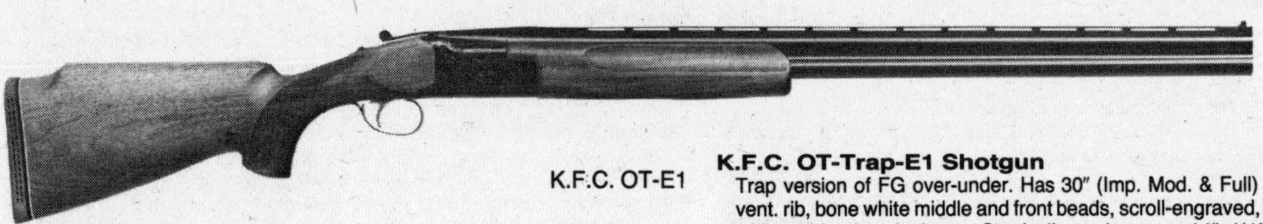

K.F.C. OT-E1

K.F.C. OT-Trap-E2 Shotgun
Same as E-1 model except chromed receiver has high grade scroll engraving, super deluxe French walnut stock and fore-end.
Price: **$1,660.00**

K.F.C. OT-Trap-E1 Shotgun
Trap version of FG over-under. Has 30″ (Imp. Mod. & Full) barrels, 13mm vent. rib, bone white middle and front beads, scroll-engraved, blued receiver, wide gold-colored trigger. Stock dimensions are 14″x1¼″x1¼″x2″; high grade French walnut; rubber recoil pad; oil finish. Weight is about 7.9 lbs. Introduced 1981. From La Paloma Marketing.
Price: **$1,070.00**

KASSNAR/FIAS SK-1 O/U SHOTGUN
Gauge: 12 or 20 ga. (3″ chambers).
Action: Top lever break open, boxlock, Greener cross bolt.
Barrel: 26″ (Imp. Cyl. & Mod.), 28″ (Mod. & Full), 30″ (Mod. & Full), 32″ (Full & Full).
Weight: 6-6½ lbs.
Stock: Select European walnut. 14″x2¼″x1¼″.
Features: Double triggers and non-automatic extractors. Checkered p.g. and fore-end. Imported by Kassnar Imports.
Price: **$429.95**

Kassnar/Fias SK-3 O/U Shotgun
Same as SK-1 except has single selective trigger.
Price: **$449.95**

Kassnar/Fias SK-4D O/U Shotgun
Same as SK-4 except has deluxe receiver engraving, sideplates, better wood.
Price: **$499.95**

LJUTIC BI GUN O/U SHOTGUN
Gauge: 12 ga only.
Barrel: 28″ or 33″, choked to customer specs.
Weight: To customers specs.
Stock: To customer specs. Oil finish, hand checkered.
Features: Custom-made gun. Hollow-milled rib, choice of pull or release trigger, pushbutton opener in front of trigger guard. From Ljutic Industries.
Price: **$6,000.00**
Price: Combo (interchangeable single bbl., top or un-single bbl.) . . **$2,000.00**
Price: Extra barrels with screw-in chokes **$2,500.00**

Ljutic Four Barrel Skeet Set
Similar to Bi Gun except comes with matched set of four 28″ barrels in 12, 20, 28 and 410. Ljutic Paternator chokes and barrel are integral. Stock is to customer specs, of American or French walnut with fancy checkering.
Price: Four barrel set **$16,000.00**

MERKEL 201E O/U
Gauge: 12, 16, 20, 28, 3″ chambers on request.
Action: Kersten double crossbolt.
Barrel: 26″ (Mod. & Imp. Cyl., Cyl. & Imp. Cyl.)
Weight: 6¾ lbs.
Stock: Walnut with p.g. or English style. 14¼″x1½″x2¼″.
Features: Double, single or single selective trigger. Cocking indicators. Fine hunting scene engraving. Imported from East Germany by Jenkins Imports.
Price: With single selective trigger **$4,468.00**

MERKEL MODEL 203E O/U
Gauge: 12, 16, 20, 28, 3″ chambers on request.
Action: Merkel H&H hand-detachable side locks with double sears. Double crossbolt breech.
Barrel: 26″ (Mod. & Imp. Cyl.).
Weight: 7 lbs.
Stock: Deluxe walnut with p.g. or English style. 14¼″x1½″x2¼″.
Features: Double, single or single selective trigger. Cocking indicators. Choice of arabesque or fine hunting scene engraving. Genuine high-speed lock time sidelock action. Imported from East Germany by Jenkins Imports.
Price: With single selective trigger **$7,995.00**

Gamba Edinburgh Trap

RENATO GAMBA EDINBURGH O/U SHOTGUNS
Gauge: 12 only, 2¾" chambers.
Barrel: Skeet—26.5" (Skeet); Trap—30", 32" (trap chokes); Mono Trap—32", 34" (trap choke).
Weight: 7¼ to 7¾ lbs.
Stock: Trap—14½"x1½"x2"; Skeet—14"x1¼"x2"xN.A. Select walnut with M.C. trap stock. Hand checkered, rubbed European oil finish. Skeet comes with high gloss lacquer finish and Skeet pad.
Features: Chrome lined barrels, double vent. ribs, shaped single trigger (selective available), auto ejectors, silvered receiver with light border scroll engraving. Made by Renato Gamba. Imported from Italy by Steyr Daimler Puch of America.
Price: Trap o-u $1,995.00
Price: Skeet o-u $1,995.00
Price: Mono Trap $1,995.00

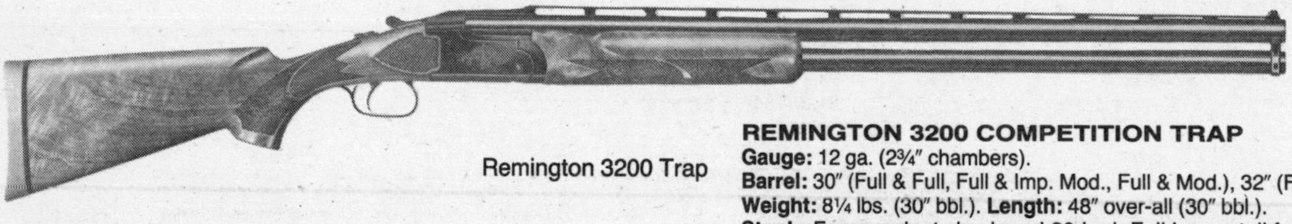

Remington 3200 Trap

REMINGTON 3200 COMPETITION TRAP
Gauge: 12 ga. (2¾" chambers).
Barrel: 30" (Full & Full, Full & Imp. Mod., Full & Mod.), 32" (Full & Imp. Mod.).
Weight: 8¼ lbs. (30" bbl.). **Length:** 48" over-all (30" bbl.).
Stock: Fancy walnut checkered 20 l.p.i. Full beavertail fore-end. Satin finish.14⅜"x2"x1½". Optional 1⅜" or 1½" drop on Monte Carlo stocks.
Features: Super-fast lock time, separated barrels, engraved receiver. Combination manual safety and barrel selector on top tang. Single selective trigger. Ivory bead front sight, white-metal middle.
Price: Competition Trap with or without M.C. stock $1,750.00
Price: Pigeon (28", Imp. Mod. & Full) $1,750.00

REMINGTON 3200 COMPETITION SKEET
Same as Trap except: 26" or 28" (Skeet & Skeet) barrels, stock measures 14"x2⅛"x1½". Over-all length is 43" with 26" barrels, weight is 7¾ lbs.
Price: Competition Skeet $1,750.00
Price: Competition Skeet 4-bbl. set (with bbls. for 12, 20, 28 and 410 in luggage case........................... $6,250.00

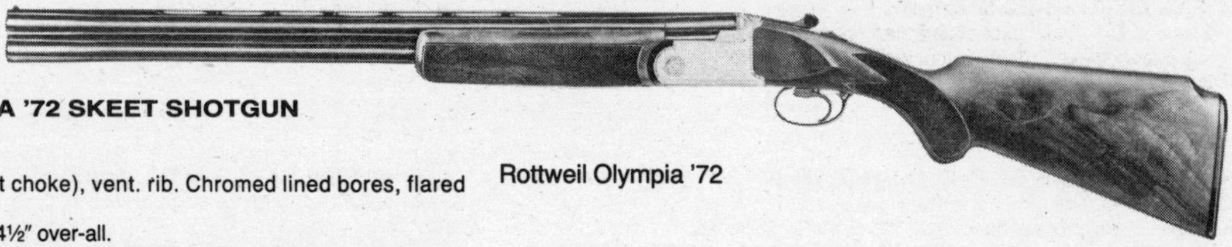

Rottweil Olympia '72

ROTTWEIL OLYMPIA '72 SKEET SHOTGUN
Gauge: 12 ga. only.
Action: Boxlock.
Barrel: 27" (special Skeet choke), vent. rib. Chromed lined bores, flared chokes.
Weight: 7¼ lbs. **Length:** 44½" over-all.
Stock: French walnut, hand checkered, modified beavertail fore-end. Oil finish.
Sights: Metal bead front.
Features: Inertia-type trigger, interchangeable for any system. Frame and lock milled from steel block. Retracting firing pins are spring mounted. All coil springs. Selective single trigger. Action engraved. Extra barrels are available. Introduced 1976. Imported from West Germany by Dynamit Nobel.
Price: $2,395.00
Price: Trap model (Montreal) is similar to above except has 30" (Imp. Mod. & Full) bbl., weighs 8 lbs., 48½" over-all....................... $2,395.00

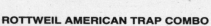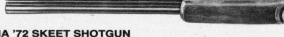

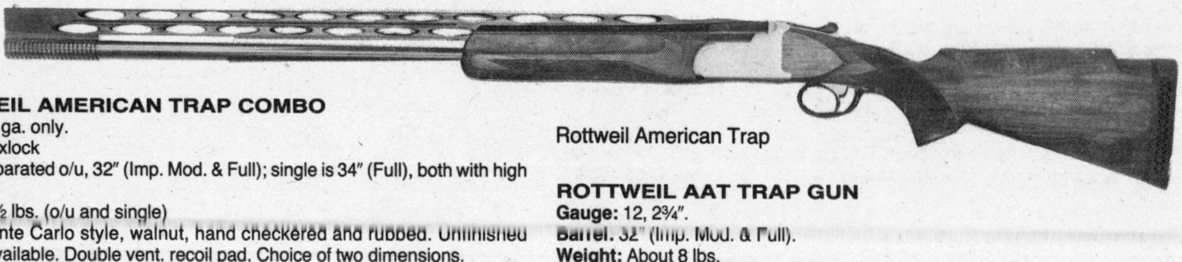

Rottweil American Trap

ROTTWEIL AMERICAN TRAP COMBO
Gauge: 12 ga. only.
Action: Boxlock
Barrel: Separated o/u, 32" (Imp. Mod. & Full); single is 34" (Full), both with high vent. rib.
Weight: 8½ lbs. (o/u and single)
Stock: Monte Carlo style, walnut, hand checkered and rubbed. Unfinished stocks available. Double vent. recoil pad. Choice of two dimensions.
Sights: Plastic front in metal sleeve, center bead.
Features: Interchangeable inertia-type trigger groups. Trigger groups available: single selective; double triggers;, release/pull; release/release selective. Receiver milled from block steel. Chokes are hand honed, test fired and reworked for flawless patterns. All coil springs, engraved action. Introduced 1977. Imported from West Germany by Dynamit Nobel.
Price: $3,655.00
Price: American Trap O/U (as above except only with o/u bbls.) ... $2,395.00
Price: American Skeet O/U $2,395.00

ROTTWEIL AAT TRAP GUN
Gauge: 12, 2¾".
Barrel: 32" (Imp. Mod. & Full).
Weight: About 8 lbs.
Stock: 14½"x1⅜"x1⅜"x1⅞". Monte Carlo style of selected French walnut with oil finish. Checkered fore-end and p.g.
Features: Has infinitely variable point of impact via special muzzle collar. Extra single lower barrels available—32" (Imp. Mod.) or 34" (Full). Special trigger groups—release/release or release/pull—also available. Introduced 1979. From Dynamit Nobel.
Price: With single lower barrel $2,655.00
Price: Combo (single and o/u barrels) $3,655.00
Price: Interchangeable trap trigger group $345.00

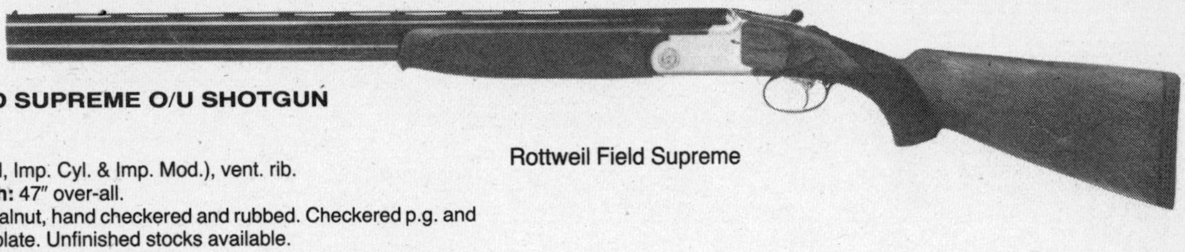

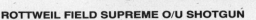

Rottweil Field Supreme

ROTTWEIL FIELD SUPREME O/U SHOTGUN

Gauge: 12 only.
Action: Boxlock.
Barrel: 28″ (Mod. & Full, Imp. Cyl. & Imp. Mod.), vent. rib.
Weight: 7¼ lbs. **Length:** 47″ over-all.
Stock: Select French walnut, hand checkered and rubbed. Checkered p.g. and fore-end, plastic buttplate. Unfinished stocks available.
Sights: Metal bead front.
Features: Removable single trigger assembly with button selector (same trigger options as on American Trap Combo); retracting spring mounted firing pins; engraved action. Extra barrels available. Imported from West Germany by Dynamit Nobel.
Price: **$2,395.00**
Price: Live Pigeon (28″ Mod. & Full) **$2,395.00**

Ruger Red Label

RUGER "RED LABEL" O/U SHOTGUN

Gauge: 20, 3″ chambers, 12, 2¾″ chambers.
Barrel: 26″, (Skeet & Skeet, Imp. Cyl. & Mod., Full & Mod.) 12 and 20 ga.; 28″ (20 ga. only, Skeet & Skeet, Imp. Cyl. & Mod., Full & Mod.).
Weight: About 7 lbs. **Length:** 43″ (26″ barrels).
Stock: 14″x1½″x2½″. Straight grain American walnut. Checkered p.g. and fore-end, rubber recoil pad.
Features: Automatic safety/barrel selector, stainless steel trigger. Patented barrel side spacers may be removed if desired. 20 ga. introduced 1977; 12 ga. introduced 1982.
Price: About **$798.00**

Valmet 412KE Target Series

Trap and Skeet versions of 412 gun. Auto. ejectors only; 12 ga., 2¾″, 3″ chambers, 30″ barrels (Imp. & Full.—Trap, Skeet & Skeet—Skeet). 20 ga., 3″ chambers. Trap stock measures $14\frac{3}{10}$″x1⅖″x1⅗″x2½″; Skeet stock measures $13\frac{9}{10}$″x1⅘″x2⅘″x1⅘″. Trap weight 7⅝ lbs.: Skeet weight 7½ lbs. Non-automatic safety. Introduced 1980. Imported from Finland by Valmet.
Price: Trap **$709.00**
Price: Skeet **$704.00**

Francisco Sarriugarte Model 400 Trap, 501E Special

True sidelock over-under. Barrel length and chokes to order. Stock dimensions, engraving to customer specifications. Introduced 1982.
Price: From **$1,975.00**
Price: Model 501E Special **$1,660.00**
Price: Model 501E Special "Niger" **$2,116.00**
Price: Model 501E Special "Excelsior" **$2,215.00**

Francisco Sarriugarte Model 200 Trap

Similar to the Model 101E except has 30″ (Full & Full) barrels, weighs 8 lbs., Monte Carlo stock. Automatic ejectors, single trigger, ventilated middle rib. Introduced 1982.
Price: **$872.00**

VALMET MODEL 412K OVER-UNDER

Gauge: 12 or 20 ga. (2¾″ or 3″).
Barrel: 26″ (Imp. Cyl. & Mod.), 28″ (Mod. & Full), 30″ (Mod. & Full); vent. rib.
Weight: About 7½ lbs.
Stock: American walnut. Standard dimensions-$13\frac{9}{10}$″x1½″x2⅖″. Checkered p.g. and fore-end.
Features: Model 412K is extractor (basic) model. Free interchangeability of barrels, stocks and fore-ends into KE (auto. ejector) model, double rifle model, combination gun, etc. Barrel selector in trigger; auto. top tang safety; barrel cocking indicators. Double triggers optional. Introduced 1980. Imported from Finland by Valmet.
Price: Model 412K (extractors), from **$669.00**
Price: Model 412 KE (ejectors) **$699.00**

FRANCISCO SARRIUGARTE MODEL 101E O/U

Gauge: 12, 2¾″ chambers.
Barrel: 26″ (Imp. Cyl. & Mod.), 28″ (Mod. & Full).
Weight: About 7 lbs. **Length:** 43″ over-all (26″ barrels).
Stock: Hand checkered European walnut with full pistol grip.
Sights: Medium bead front.
Features: Single trigger, automatic ejectors. Receiver has border engraving. Introduced 1982. Imported from Spain by Toledo Armas.
Price: Model 101E **$585.00**
Price: Model 101E DS (selective trigger) **$623.00**
Price: Model 101 DS (selective trigger and extractors) **$495.00**

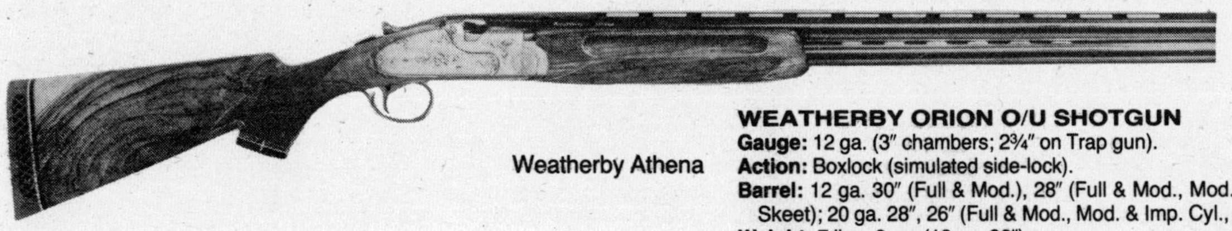

Weatherby Athena

WEATHERBY ORION O/U SHOTGUN

Gauge: 12 ga. (3″ chambers; 2¾″ on Trap gun).
Action: Boxlock (simulated side-lock).
Barrel: 12 ga. 30″ (Full & Mod.), 28″ (Full & Mod., Mod. & Imp. Cyl., Skeet & Skeet); 20 ga. 28″, 26″ (Full & Mod., Mod. & Imp. Cyl., Skeet & Skeet).
Weight: 7 lbs., 8 oz. (12 ga. 26″).
Stock: American walnut, checkered p.g. and fore-end. Rubber recoil pad. Dimensions for field and Skeet models, 20 ga. 14″x1½″x2½″.
Features: Selective auto ejectors, single selective mechanical trigger. Top tang safety, Greener cross-bolt. Introduced 1982. Imported from Japan by Weatherby.
Price: 12 ga. Field **$749.95**
Price: Skeet **$789.95**
Price: 12 ga. Trap **$799.95**

Weatherby Orion

WEATHERBY ATHENA O/U SHOTGUN

Gauge: 12 or 20 ga. (3" chambers; 2¾" on Trap gun).
Action: Boxlock (simulated side-lock) top lever break-open. Selective auto ejectors, single selective trigger (selector inside trigger guard).
Barrel: 28" with vent rib and bead front sight, Full & Mod., Mod. & Imp. Cyl. or Skeet & Skeet.
Weight: 12 ga. 7⅜ lbs., 20 ga. 6⅞ lbs.
Stock: American walnut, checkered p.g. and fore-end (14¼"x1½"x2½").
Features: Mechanically operated trigger. Top tang safety, Greener cross-bolt, fully engraved receiver, recoil pad installed.
Price: 12 or 20 ga. Field **$1,079.95**
Price: Skeet **$1,089,95**
Price: 12 ga. Trap Model **$1,099.95**

Winchester Model 501

WINCHESTER MODEL 501 GRAND EUROPEAN O-U

Gauge: 12 only, 2¾" chambers.
Barrel: 27" (Skeet & Skeet), 30" (Imp. Mod. & Full), 32" (Imp. Mod. & Full).
Weight: 7½ lbs. (Skeet), 8½ lbs. (Trap) **Length:** 47⅛" over-all (30" barrel).
Stock: 14⅛"x1½"x2½" (Skeet). Full fancy walnut, hand-rubbed oil finish.
Features: Silvered, engraved receiver; engine-turned breech interior. Slide-button selector/safety, selective auto. ejectors. Chrome bores, tapered vent. rib. Trap gun has Monte Carlo or regular stock, recoil pad; Skeet gun has rosewood buttplate. Introduced 1981. Imported from Japan by Winchester Group, Olin Corp.
Price: Trap or Skeet **$1,800.00**

Winchester 101 Lightweight

WINCHESTER 101 XTR O/U FIELD GUN

Gauge: 12, 2¾"; 20, 3" chambers.
Action: Top lever, break open. Manual safety combined with bbl. selector at top of receiver tang.
Barrel: 27", 32" (Waterfowl), Winchoke interchangeable choke tubes.
Weight: 12 ga. 7¾ lbs. Others 6¼ lbs. **Length:** 44¾" over-all (28" bbls.).
Stock: 14"x1½"x2½". Checkered walnut p.g. and fore-end; fluted comb.
Features: Single selective trigger, auto ejectors. Hand engraved receiver. Comes with trunk-style gun case. Imported from Japan by Winchester Group, Olin Corp.
Price: Lightweight, 12 or 20, Winchoke system **$1,150.00**
Price: Lightweight, 12 ga., 28" (Mod. & Full) **$1,400.00**
Price: Lightweight-Winchoke, 12 or 20 ga., 27" **$1,450.00**

Winchester 101 Diamond Grade Target Guns

Similar to the Model 101 XTR except designed for trap and Skeet competition, with tapered and elevated rib, anatomically contoured trigger and internationally-dimensioned stock. Receiver has deep-etched diamond-pattern engraving. Skeet guns available in 12, 20, 28 and 410 with ventilated muzzles to reduce recoil. Trap guns in 12 ga. only; over-under, combination and single-barrel configurations in a variety of barrel lengths with Winchoke system. Straight or Monte Carlo stocks available. Introduced 1982. Imported from Japan by Winchester Group, Olin Corp.
Price: Trap, o/u, standard and Monte Carlo, 30", 32" **$1,500.00**
Price: Trap, single barrel, 34" **$1,550.00**
Price: Trap, o/u-single bbl. combo sets **$2,250.00**
Price: Skeet, 12 and 20 . . . . **$1,400.00**
Price: Skeet, 28 and 410 . . . . **$1,450.00**

Winchester Model 101 XTR Waterfowl Winchoke

Same as Model 101 Field Grade except in 12 ga. only, 3" chambers, 32" barrels. Comes with four Winchoke tubes: Mod., Imp. Mod., Full, Extra-Full. Introduced 1981. Imported from Japan by Winchester Group, Olin Corp.
Price: **$1,150.00**

Winchester 101 Pigeon Grade

Winchester Model 101 Pigeon Grade

Same as Model 101 Field with vent. rib with bead front and middle sights, hand-engraved satin finish receiver, knurled, non-slip trigger. Stock and fore-end of fancy French walnut, hand checkered p.g. and fore-end. 12 or 20, 2¾" chambers. Barrels 25½", 27" or 28" with a full range of chokes. Weighs 8¼ lbs. Imported from Japan by Winchester Group, Olin Corp.
Price: XTR Featherweight, 12 or 20, 25½" (Imp. Cyl. & Mod.) **$1,400.00**

CAUTION: PRICES CHANGE. CHECK AT GUNSHOP.

SHOTGUNS—OVER-UNDERS

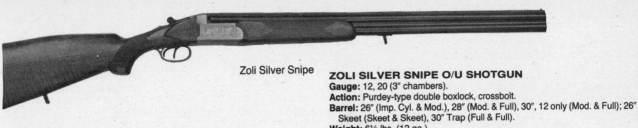

Zoli Silver Snipe

A. ZOLI DELFINO S.P. O/U
Gauge: 12 or 20 (3″ chambers).
Barrel: 28″ (Mod. & Full); vent. rib.
Weight: 5½ lbs.
Stock: Walnut. Hand checkered p.g. and fore-end; cheekpiece.
Features: Color case hardened receiver with light engraving; chrome lined barrels; automatic sliding safety; double triggers; ejectors. From Mandall Shooting Supplies.
Price: $695.00

ZOLI SILVER SNIPE O/U SHOTGUN
Gauge: 12, 20 (3″ chambers).
Action: Purdey-type double boxlock, crossbolt.
Barrel: 26″ (Imp. Cyl. & Mod.), 28″ (Mod. & Full), 30″, 12 only (Mod. & Full); 26″ Skeet (Skeet & Skeet), 30″ Trap (Full & Full).
Weight: 6½ lbs. (12 ga.).
Stock: Hand checkered p.g. and fore-end, European walnut.
Features: Auto. safety (exc. Trap and Skeet), vent rib, single trigger, chrome bores. Imported from Italy by Mandall Shooting Supplies.
Price: Field $695.00

Zoli Golden Snipe O/U Shotgun
Same as Silver Snipe except selective auto. ejectors.
Price: Field $775.00

SHOTGUNS—SIDE-BY-SIDES

Union Armera Winner

ARMSPORT WESTERN DOUBLE
Gauge: 12 only (3″ chambers).
Barrel: 20″.
Weight: 6½ lbs.
Stock: European walnut, checkered p.g. and beavertail fore-end.
Sights: Metal front bead on matted solid rib.
Features: Exposed hammers. Imported by Armsport.
Price: $500.00

UNION ARMERA "WINNER" DOUBLE
Gauge: 12 and 20 ga., 2¾″ chambers.
Barrel: Length and choking to customer specs.
Weight: To customer specs.
Stock: Ultra deluxe European walnut; dimensions to customer specs.
Features: Hand engraved action, automatic ejectors. All options available. Introduced 1982. Imported from Spain by Toledo Armas.
Price: Winner, from $3,055.00
Price: Luxe, from $5,622.00

ARMSPORT GOOSEGUN SIDE-BY-SIDE
Gauge: 10 ga. (3½″ chambers).
Barrel: 32″ (Full & Full). Solid matted rib.
Weight: 11 lbs.
Stock: European walnut, checkered p.g. and fore-end.
Features: Double triggers, vent. rubber recoil pad with white spacer. Imported by Armsport.
Price: $595.00

AyA Model No. 2

AYA No. 1 Side-by-Side
Similar to the No. 2 except barrel lengths to customer specifications. Barrels are of chrome-nickel steel. Imported from Spain by Wm. Larkin Moore & Co. and Precision Sports, Inc.
Price: 12, 16, 20 ga., from.................................. $3,800.00
Price: 28 ga., from $4,000.00
Price: 410 ga., from $4,100.00

AYA Model 56 Side-By-Side
Similar to the No. 1 except in 12, 16 or 20 ga. only, available with raised, level or vent rib. Does not have hand-detachable locks. Imported from Spain by Wm. Larkin Moore & Co. and Precision Sports, Inc.
Price: About... $4,000.00

AYA No. 2 SIDE-BY-SIDE
Gauge: 12, 16, 20, 28, 410.
Barrel: 26″, 27″, 28″, choked to customer specs.
Weight: 5 lbs. 15 oz. to 7½ lbs.
Stock: 14½″x2¼″x1½″. European walnut. Straight grip stock, checkered butt, classic fore-end. Can be made to custom dimensions.
Features: Sidelock action with auto. ejectors, double triggers standard, single trigger optional. Hand-detachable locks. Color case-hardened action. Imported from Spain by Wm. Larkin Moore & Co. and Precision Sports, Inc.
Price: 12, 16, 20 ga., from.................................. $1,700.00
Price: 28 ga., from $1,800.00
Price: 410 ga., from $1,850.00

AYA MODEL 117 DOUBLE BARREL SHOTGUN
Gauge: 12 (2¾″), 20 (3″).
Action: Holland & Holland sidelock, Purdey treble bolting.
Barrel: 26″ (Imp. Cyl. & Mod.) 28″ (Mod. & Full).
Stock: 14½″x2⅜″x1½″. Select European walnut, hand checkered p.g. and beavertail fore-end.
Features: Single selective trigger, automatic ejectors, cocking indicators; concave barrel rib; hand-detachable lockplates; hand engraved action. Imported from Spain by Precision Sports, Inc.
Price: $1,500.00

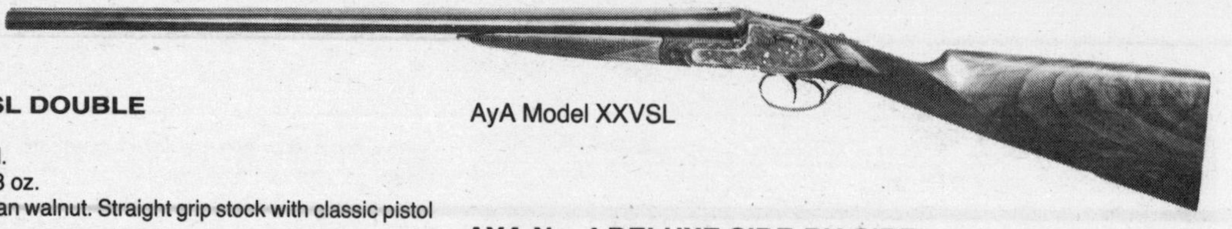

SHOTGUNS—SIDE-BY-SIDES

AYA MODEL XXV BL, SL DOUBLE
Gauge: 12, 16, 20.
Barrel: 25", chokes as specified.
Weight: 5 lbs., 15 oz. to 7 lbs., 8 oz.
Stock: 14½"x2¼"x1½". European walnut. Straight grip stock with classic pistol grip, checkered butt.
Features: Boxlock (Model BL), sidelock (Model SL). Churchill rib, auto ejectors, double triggers (single available), color case-hardened action (coin-finish available). Imported from Spain by Wm. Larkin Moore & Co. and Precision Sports, Inc.
Price: BL, 12 ga., about..$1,600.00
Price: BL, 20 ga., about..$1,650.00
Price: SL, 12 ga., about..$2,450.00
Price: SL, 20 ga., about..$2,500.00

BAIKAL LMC-111 SIDE-BY-SIDE
Gauge: 12 ga., 2¾" chambers.
Barrel: To customer's specifications, choice of chokes.
Weight: 7 lbs.
Stock: Fancy walnut. Choice of p.g. or straight stock. Gold and silver inlays in butt. Semi-beavertail fore-end. Monte Carlo. To customer's specifications.
Features: Handmade sidelock shotgun. Removable sideplates. Chrome barrels, chambers and internal parts. Selective ejectors, single selective trigger, hammer interceptors, cocking indicators. Hand chiseled animal and bird scenes on receiver. Comes with case. Imported from Russia by Baikal International.
Price: Special order only..$5,850.00

BERNARDELLI XXVSL DOUBLE
Gauge: 12.
Action: Holland & Holland-style sidelock with double sears.
Barrel: Demi-block (chopper lump), 25", choice of choke.
Weight: About 6½ lbs. **Length:** To customer specs.
Stock: Best walnut with dimensions to customer specs.
Features: Firing pins removable from face of standing breech; manual or auto safety; selective auto ejectors; classic or beavertail fore-end. Imported from Italy by Knight & Knight.
Price: With fitted luggage case............................$1,865.00

AyA Model XXVSL

AYA No. 1 DELUXE SIDE BY SIDE
Gauge: 12, 16, 20, 28 & 410.
Barrel: 26", 27", 28" (Imp. Cyl. & Mod. or Mod. & Full).
Weight: 5 lbs. 2 oz. to 6½ lbs.
Stock: 14½"x2¼"x1½". European walnut. Straight grip with checkered butt, classic fore-end.
Features: Boxlock action, color case-hardened, automatic ejectors, double triggers (single trigger available). Imported from Spain by William Larkin Moore & Co. and Precision Sports, Inc.
Price: 12, 16 ga., about..$1,600.00
Price: 20, 28 ga., about..$1,650.00
Price: 410 ga., about..$1,700.00

BAIKAL IJ-58MAE SIDE-BY-SIDE
Gauge: 12 ga., 2¾" chambers, 20 ga., 3" chambers.
Barrel: 26" (Imp. Cyl. & Mod.), 28" (Mod. & Full).
Weight: 6¾ lbs.
Stock: Walnut. Hand checkered p.g. and beavertail fore-end.
Features: Hinged front double trigger. Chrome barrels and chambers. Hammer interceptors. Fore-end center latch. Hand engraved receiver. Selective ejection or extraction. Imported from Russia by Baikal International.
Price: About..$299.95

BAIKAL MC-110 SIDE-BY-SIDE
Gauge: 12 or 20 ga., 2¾" chambers.
Barrel: 12 ga. 28" (Mod. & Full), 20 ga. 26" (Imp. Cyl. & Mod.).
Weight: 6 lbs. (20 ga.), 6¾ lbs. (12 ga.).
Stock: Fancy walnut. Hand checkered p.g. and fore-end. Choice of full p.g. or straight stock. Semi-beavertail fore-end.
Features: Fully engraved receiver with animal and bird scenes. Engraved trigger guard and tang. Double trigger. Chrome barrels, chambers and internal parts. Raised solid rib. Extractors, hammer interceptors. Auto, safety. Comes with case. Imported from Russia by Baikal International.
Price: $3,400.00

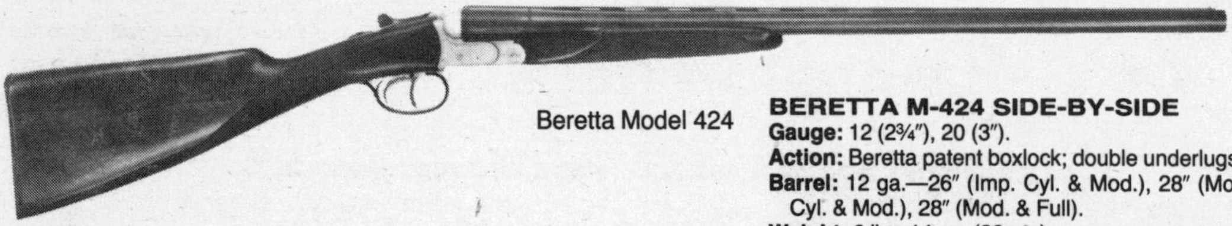

Beretta Model 424

BERETTA M-424 SIDE-BY-SIDE
Gauge: 12 (2¾"), 20 (3").
Action: Beretta patent boxlock; double underlugs and bolts.
Barrel: 12 ga.—26" (Imp. Cyl. & Mod.), 28" (Mod. & Full); 20 ga.—26" (Imp. Cyl. & Mod.), 28" (Mod. & Full).
Weight: 6 lbs. 14 oz. (20 ga.).
Stock: 14⅛"x1⁹⁄₁₆"x2⁹⁄₁₆". "English" straight-type, hand checkered European walnut.
Features: Coil springs throughout action; double triggers (front is hinged); automatic safety; extractors. Concave matted barrel rib. Introduced 1977. Imported by Beretta U.S.A. Corp.
Price: $900.00

Beretta M-426 Side-By-Side
Same as M-424 except action body is engraved; pistol grip stock; a silver pigeon is inlaid into top lever; single selective trigger; selective automatic ejectors. Introduced 1977. Imported by Beretta U.S.A. Corp.
Price: $1,115.00

Browning B-SS

BROWNING B-SS
Gauge: 12 (2¾"), 20 (3").
Action: Top lever break-open action, top tang safety, single trigger.
Barrel: 26" (Mod. and Full or Imp. Cyl. and Mod.), 28" (Mod. and Full), 30" (Full & Full or Mod. & Full).
Weight: 6¾ lbs. (26" bbl., 20 ga.); 7½ lbs. (30" bbl., 12 ga.).
Stock: 14¼"x1⅝"x2½". French walnut, hand checkered. Full p.g., full beavertail fore-end.
Features: Automatic safety, automatic ejectors. Hand engraved receiver, mechanical single selective trigger with barrel selector in rear of trigger guard. Imported from Japan by Browning.
Price: Grade I, 12 or 20 ga. $724.95
Price: Grade II, 12 or 20 ga. $1,285.00

Browning B-SS Sporter
Similar to standard B-SS except has straight-grip stock and full beavertail fore-end with traditional oil finish. Introduced 1977.
Price: Grade I, 12 or 20 ga. $724.95
Price: Grade II, 12 or 20 ga. $1,285.00

CAUTION: PRICES CHANGE. CHECK AT GUNSHOP.

Hermanos Model 150

CHAPUIS PROGRESS RBV, R-20 SIDE-BY-SIDE
Gauge: 12 ga. (2¾″), 20 ga. (3″).
Barrel: 26½″ or 27½″ depending on choke (any choke available). Chrome-moly steel with chrome plated bores.
Weight: About 6¼ lbs.
Stock: Select French or American walnut, oil finish. Fine checkering on p.g. and fore-end. Right or left-hand stock available as options.
Features: Single barrel joining rib. Auto ejectors are standard. Double triggers. Scroll engraving on frame and sideplates. Extra barrel set available. Introduced 1979. Imported from France by R. Painter Co.
Price: **$1,415.00**
Price: Extra barrel set **$390.24**
Price: Model Progress-RG (boxlock) **$832.00**
Price: Progress-Hobby (same as RBV/R-20 except profuse engraving, presentation French walnut stock, bbls. browned) .... **P.O.R.**
Price: Progress-Slug (boxlock-style with right barrel rifled for slugs) **$954.00**

CRUCELEGUI HERMANOS MODEL 150 DOUBLE
Gauge: 12 or 20 (2¾″ chambers).
Action: Greener triple crossbolt.
Barrel: 20″, 26″, 28″, 30″, 32″ (Cyl. & Cyl., Full & Full, Mod. & Full, Mod. & Imp. Cyl., Imp. Cyl. & Full, Mod. & Mod.).
Weight: 5 to 7¼ lbs.
Stock: Hand checkered walnut, beavertail fore-end.
Features: Exposed hammers; double triggers; color casehardened receiver; sling swivels; chrome lined bores. Imported from Spain by Mandall Shooting Supplies.
Price: **$299.50**
Price: Model 225 (hammerless version) **$295.00**

> Consult our Directory pages for the location of firms mentioned.

Danok Red Prince

INDUSTRIAS DANOK "RED PRINCE" DOUBLE
Gauge: 12 only, 2¾″ chambers.
Barrel: 28″ (Mod. & Full).
Weight: About 7 lbs. **Length:** 45″ over-all.
Stock: Hand checkered European walnut; straight grip stock.
Sights: Medium bead front.
Features: Automatic ejectors, double triggers, hand engraved action. Introduced 1982. Imported from Spain by Toledo Armas.
Price: **$896.00**

Erbi Model 76

ERBI MODEL 76 DOUBLE
Gauge: 10, 12, 20, 28.
Barrel: 28″ (Mod. & Full); 28-ga. in 26″ only.
Weight: About 7 lbs. **Length:** 45″ over-all.
Stock: Hand checkered European walnut.
Sights: Medium bead front.
Features: Straight grip stock, silvered, engraved receiver, double triggers. Introduced 1982. Imported from Spain by Toledo Armas.
Price: Model 76ST (extractors) **$590.00**
Price: Model 76AJ (auto. ejectors) **$668.00**
Price: Model 80 (sidelock) **$1,003.00**

F.I.E. "THE BRUTE" DOUBLE BARREL
Gauge: 12, 16, 20 (2¾″ chambers), 410 (3″ chambers).
Action: Boxlock.
Barrel: 18″ (Cyl.), 28″ (Mod. & Full).
Weight: 5 lbs. 2 oz. **Length:** 30″ over-all.
Stock: Hand checkered walnut with full beavertail fore-end.
Features: The smallest, lightest double barrel shotgun available. Introduced 1979. Imported from Brazil by F.I.E. Corp.
Price: With 28″ barrels **$229.95**
Price: "Riot" model with 18″ barrels **$242.95**
Price: "Brute" model with 18″ barrels **$259.95**

GIB Magnum

GIB 10 GAUGE MAGNUM SHOTGUN
Gauge: 10 ga. (3½″ chambers).
Action: Boxlock.
Barrel: 32″ (Full).
Weight: 10 lbs.
Stock: 14½″x1½″x2⅝″. European walnut, checkered at p.g. and fore-end.
Features: Double triggers; color hardened action, rest blued. Front and center metal beads on matted rib; ventilated rubber recoil pad. Fore-end release has positive Purdey-type mechanism. Imported from Spain by Mandall Shooting Supplies.
Price: **$500.00**

Gamba Principessa

RENATO GAMBA PRINCIPESSA SHOTGUN
Gauge: 28 ga., 2¾".
Barrel: 26" (Imp. Cyl. & Mod.), 28" (Mod. & Full).
Weight: About 5½ lbs.
Stock: 14½" x 1¼" x 2". Select European walnut, straight English grip and slim English style fore-end.
Features: Chrome-lined demi-block barrels; single or double trigger; boxlock action only. Beavertail fore-end available. Fitted with rubber recoil pad. Engraved, color case-hardened receiver. Introduced 1981. Imported from Italy by Steyr Daimler Puch.
Price: With double triggers **$1,566.00**
Price: With single trigger **$1,695.00**

Gamba Oxford Double

RENATO GAMBA OXFORD DOUBLE
Gauge: 12 (2¾"); 20 (2¾" or 3").
Barrel: 26" (Imp. Cyl. & Mod.), 28" (Mod. & Full).
Weight: 5¾ to 6½ lbs.
Stock: 14½"x1½"x2½". Select European walnut, hand checkered straight grip. Checkered butt. Hand rubbed European oil finish.
Features: Boxlock action based on the Anson & Deeley system. Auto ejectors, chrome lined barrels. Single or double trigger (double with articulated front trigger). Made by Renato Gamba, imported from Italy by Steyr Daimler Puch of America.
Price: Double trigger, either gauge **$1,768.00**
Price: Single trigger, either gauge **$1,919.40**
Price: Optional leather case **$197.00**

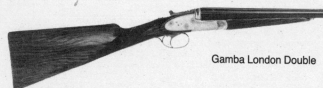

Gamba London Double

RENATO GAMBA LONDON DOUBLE
Gauge: 12 or 20 ga., 2¾" chambers.
Barrel: 26" (Imp. Cyl. & Mod.), 28" (Mod. & Full).
Weight: 5¾ to 6½ lbs.
Stock: 14½"x1½"x2½". Select European walnut with finely cut hand checkered straight grip. Checkered butt. Hand rubbed European oil finish.
Features: Sidelock action based on the Holland & Holland system with double safety and three-lug Purdey locking system. Chrome lined barrels, auto ejectors, single or double triggers. Made by Renato Gamba, imported from Italy by Steyr Daimler Puch of America.
Price: Double trigger, either gauge **$3,806.00**
Price: Single trigger, either gauge **$3,978.00**

GALEF'S DOUBLE BARREL SHOTGUN
Gauge: 10 (3½"); 12, 20, 410 (3"); 16, 20 (2¾").
Action: Modified Anson & Deeley boxlock, case hardened.
Barrel: 32" 10, 12 only (Full & Full); 30" 12 only (Mod. & Full); 28" all exc. 410 (Mod. & Full); 26" 12, 20, 28 (I.C. & Mod.); 26" 410 only (Mod. & Full); 22" 12 only (I.C. & I.C.).
Weight: 10½ lbs. (10), 7¾ lbs. (12) to 6 lbs. (410).
Stock: Hand checkered European walnut, p.g., beavertail fore-end, rubber recoil pad. Dimensions vary with gauge.
Features: Auto safety, plain extractors. Imported from Spain by Galef.
Price: 10 ga. **$439.00**
Price: 12 - 410 . . . . **$298.90**

GARBI MODEL 51 SIDE-BY-SIDE
Gauge: 12, 16, 20 (2¾" chambers).
Barrel: 28" (Mod. & Full).
Weight: 5½ to 6½ lbs.
Stock: Walnut, to customer specs.
Features: Boxlock action; hand-engraved receiver; hand-checkered stock and fore-end; double triggers; extractors. Introduced 1980. Imported from Spain by L. Joseph Rahn, Inc.
Price: **$515.00**

Garbi Model 00

GARBI MODEL 60 SIDE-BY-SIDE
Gauge: 12, 16, 20 (2¾" chambers).
Barrel: 26", 28", 30"; choked to customers specs.
Weight: 5½ to 6½ lbs.
Stock: Select walnut. Dimensions to customer specs.
Features: Sidelock action. Scroll engraving on receiver. Hand checkered stock. Double triggers. Extractors. Imported from Spain by L. Joseph Rahn, Inc.
Price: **$830.00**
Price: With demi-bloc barrels and ejectors. **$1,139.00**

Garbi Model 62
Similar to Model 60 except choked Mod. & Full, plain receiver with engraved border, demi-bloc barrels, gas exhaust valves, jointed triggers, extractors. Imported from Spain by L. Joseph Rahn.
Price: **$830.00**
Price: With ejectors **$1,115.00**

Garbi Model 71

Garbi Model 101 Side-by-Side

Similar to the Garbi Model 71 except is available with optional level, file-cut, Churchill or ventilated top rib, and in a 12-ga. pigeon or wildfowl gun. Has Continental-style floral and scroll engraving, select walnut stock. Better overall quality than the Model 71. Imported from Spain by Wm. Larkin Moore.
Price: **$2,800.00**

Garbi Model 103A, B Side-by-Side

Similar to the Garbi Model 71 except has Purdey-type fine scroll and rosette engraving. Better over-all quality than the Model 101. Model 103B has nickel-chrome steel barrels, H&H-type easy opening mechanism; other mechanical details remain the same. Imported from Spain by Wm. Larkin Moore.
Price: Model 103A **$2,800.00**
Price: Model 103B **$3,800.00**

GARBI MODEL 102 SHOTGUN

Gauge: 12, 16, 20.
Barrel: 12 ga.-25″ to 30″; 16 & 20 ga.-25″ to 28″. Chokes as specified.
Weight: 20 ga.-5 lbs., 15 oz. to 6 lbs., 4 oz.
Stock: 14½″x2¼″x1½″; select walnut.
Features: Holland pattern sidelock ejector with chopper lump barrels, Holland-type large scroll engraving. Double triggers (hinged front) std., non-selective single trigger available. Many options available. Imported from Spain by Wm. Larkin Moore.
Price: From **$2,800.00**

GARBI MODEL 71 DOUBLE

Gauge: 12, 16, 20.
Barrel: 26″, 28″, choked to customer specs.
Weight: 5 lbs., 15 oz., (20 ga.).
Stock: 14½″x2¼″x1½″. European walnut. Straight grip, checkered butt, classic fore-end.
Features: Sidelock action, automatic ejectors, double triggers standard. Color case-hardened action, coin finish optional. Five other models are available. Imported from Spain by Wm. Larkin Moore.
Price: Model 71, from **$1,675.00**

Garbi Model 200 Side-by-Side

Similar to the Garbi Model 71 except has barrels of nickel-chrome steel, heavy duty locks, magnum proofed. Very fine continental-style floral and scroll engraving, well figured walnut stock. Other mechanical features remain the same. Imported from Spain by Wm. Larkin Moore.
Price: **$4,300.00**

Garbi Model Special Side-by-Side

Similar to the Garbi Model 71 except has best quality wood and metal work. Special game scene engraving with or without gold inlays, fancy figured walnut stock. Imported from Spain by Wm. Larkin Moore.
Price: **$4,400.00**

Garbi Model 110 Double

True sidelock available in 12, 20 and 28 ga. with barrel length, chokes and stock dimensions made to customer specifications. Introduced 1982. Imported from Spain by Toledo Armas.
Price: Model 110 .... **$2,433.00**
Price: Model 300 .... **$5,980.00**

KASSNAR-ZABALA DOUBLE BARREL SHOTGUN

Gauge: 10 (3½″), 12, 20, 410.
Action: Anson & Deeley-type boxlock with double underlocking lugs.
Barrel: 26″ (Imp. Cyl. & Mod.), 28″, 30″ (Mod. & Full), 32″ (Full & Full). Raised, matted solid rib.
Weight: About 7 lbs. (12 ga.).
Stock: French walnut with plastic finish. Hand checkered p.g. and beavertail fore-end. 14¼″x1⅝″x2¼″.
Features: Hand engraved action, blue finish. Double triggers; front trigger hinged. Metal bead front sight. Imported from Spain by Kassnar Imports.
Price: 12, 20 or 410 ga. **$329.95**
Price: 10 gauge **$349.95**

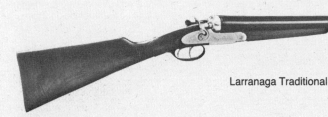

Larranaga Traditional

MIGUEL LARRANAGA "THE TRADITIONAL" DOUBLE

Gauge: 12 or 20 ga., 2¾″ chambers.
Barrel: 28″ (Mod. & Full).
Weight: About 6½ lbs. **Length:** 45″ over-all.
Stock: Hand engraved European walnut, straight grip.
Sights: Medium bead front.
Features: Exposed hammers, hand engraved locks, checkered butt. Introduced 1982. Imported from Spain by Toledo Armas.
Price: **$497.00**

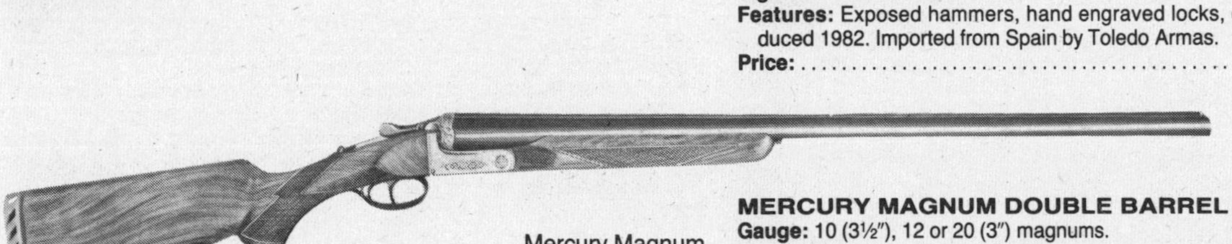

Mercury Magnum

MERCURY MAGNUM DOUBLE BARREL SHOTGUN

Gauge: 10 (3½″), 12 or 20 (3″) magnums.
Action: Triple-lock Anson & Deeley type.
Barrel: 28″ (Full & Mod.), 12 and 20 ga.; 32″ (Full & Full), 10 ga.
Weight: 7¼ lbs. (12 ga.); 6½ lbs. (20 ga.); 10⅛ lbs. (10 ga.). **Length:** 45″ (28″ bbls.).
Stock: 14″x1⅝″x2¼″ walnut, checkered p.g. stock and beavertail fore-end, recoil pad.
Features: Double triggers, front hinged, auto safety, extractors; safety gas ports, engraved frame. Imported from Spain by Tradewinds.
Price: (12, 20 ga.) **$295.00**
Price: (10 ga.) **$480.00**

MERKEL 147E SIDE-BY-SIDE
Gauge: 12, 16, 20, 3″ chambers on request.
Action: Anson-Deeley with double hook bolting and Greener breech.
Barrel: 26″ (Mod. & Imp. Cyl., Cyl. & Imp. Cyl.).
Weight: 6¼ to 6½ lbs.
Stock: Walnut. English style or p.g., 14¼″x1½″x2¼″.
Features: Hunting scene engraving. Double triggers. Imported from East Germany by Jenkins Imports.
Price: Double trigger only **$2,018.00**
Price: Model 47E (as above except has scroll engraving) **$1,762.00**

MERKEL 147S SIDE-BY-SIDE
Gauge: 12, 16, 20 ga. with 3″ chambers on request.
Action: Sidelock with double hook bolting and Greener breech. Trigger catch bar.
Barrel: 26″ (Mod. & Imp. Cyl., Cyl. & Imp. Cyl.).
Weight: 6½ to 6¾ lbs.
Stock: Walnut, oil finish. English style or p.g., 14¼″x1½″x2¼″.
Features: 30% faster trigger than conventional lock design. Hunting scene engraving. Highest grade side-by-side Merkel. Double triggers. Imported from East Germany by Jenkins Imports.
Price: **$4,382.00**

Parquemy Model 48E

Piotti Model Monte Carlo Side-by-Side
Similar to the Piotti King No. 1 except has Purdey-style scroll and rosette engraving, no gold inlays, over-all workmanship not as finely detailed. Other mechanical specifications remain the same. Imported from Italy by Wm. Larkin Moore.
Price: **$9,200.00**

PARQUEMY MODEL 48E DOUBLE
Gauge: 12, 20, 28 (2¾″ chambers), 410 (3″).
Barrel: 28″ (Mod. & Full).
Weight: 5½ to 7 lbs. **Length:** 45″ over-all.
Stock: Hand checkered European walnut, straight grip.
Sights: Medium bead front.
Features: Automatic ejectors, hand engraved locks, double triggers, checkered butt. Introduced 1982. Imported from Spain by Toledo Armas.
Price: Model 41 (410 ga.) **$336.00**
Price: Model 45E (boxlock) **$507.00**
Price: Model 48 (410 ga., extractors) **$608.00**
Price: Model 48E **$718.00**
Price: Model 50 . . . . **$858.00**

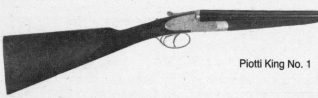

Piotti King No. 1

PIOTTI MODEL PIUMA SIDE-BY-SIDE
Gauge: 12, 16, 20, 28, 410.
Barrel: 25″ to 30″ (12 ga.), 25″ to 28″ (16, 20, 28, 410).
Weight: 5½ to 6¼ lbs. (20 ga.).
Stock: Dimensions to customer specs. Straight grip stock with checkered butt, classic splinter fore-end, hand rubbed oil finish are standard; pistol grip, beavertail fore-end, satin luster finish optional.
Features: Anson & Deeley boxlock ejector double with chopper lump barrels. Level, file-cut rib, light scroll and rosette engraving, scalloped frame. Double triggers with hinged front standard, single non-selective optional. Coin finish standard, color case hardened optional. Imported from Italy by Wm. Larkin Moore.
Price: **$4,700.00**

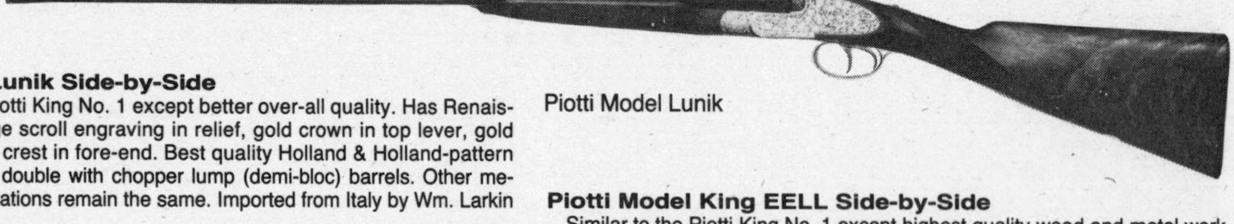

PIOTTI KING NO. 1 SIDE-BY-SIDE
Gauge: 12, 16, 20, 28, 410.
Barrel: 25″ to 30″ (12 ga.), 25″ to 28″ (16, 20, 28, 410). To customer specs. Chokes as specified.
Weight: 6½ lbs. to 8 lbs. (12 ga., to customer specs.)
Stock: Dimensions to customer specs. Finely figured walnut; straight grip with checkered butt with classic splinter fore-end and hand-rubbed oil finish standard. Pistol grip, beavertail fore-end, satin luster finish optional.
Features: Holland & Holland pattern sidelock action, auto. ejectors. Double trigger with front trigger hinged standard; non-selective single trigger optional. Coin finish standard; color case-hardened optional. Top rib: level, file cut standard; concave, ventilated optional. Very fine, full coverage scroll engraving with small floral bouquets, gold crown in top lever, name in gold, and gold crest in fore-end. Imported from Italy by Wm. Larkin Moore.
Price: **$11,000.00**

Piotti Model Lunik

Piotti Model Lunik Side-by-Side
Similar to the Piotti King No. 1 except better over-all quality. Has Renaissance-style large scroll engraving in relief, gold crown in top lever, gold name, and gold crest in fore-end. Best quality Holland & Holland-pattern sidelock ejector double with chopper lump (demi-bloc) barrels. Other mechanical specifications remain the same. Imported from Italy by Wm. Larkin Moore.
Price: **$11,500.00**

Piotti Model King EELL Side-by-Side
Similar to the Piotti King No. 1 except highest quality wood and metal work. Choice of either bulino game scene engraving or game scene engraving with gold inlays. Engraved and signed by a master engraver. Exhibition grade wood. Other mechanical specifications remain the same. Imported from Italy by Wm. Larkin Moore.
Price: **$16,000.00**

ROSSI "SQUIRE" DOUBLE BARREL
Gauge: 12, 20, 410 (3″ chambers).
Barrel: 12 ga.—26″ (Imp. Cyl. & Mod.), 28″ (Mod. & Full); 20 ga.—28″ (Mod. & Full); 410—26″ (Full & Full).
Weight: About 7½ lbs.
Stock: Walnut finished hardwood.
Features: Double triggers, raised matted rib, beavertail fore-end. Massive twin underlugs mesh with synchronized sliding bolts. Introduced 1978. Imported by Interarms.
Price: 12 ga., 20 ga. **$315.00**
Price: 410 . . . . **$330.00**

ROSSI OVERLAND DOUBLE BARREL
Gauge: 12, 20, 410 (3″ chambers).
Action: Sidelock with external hammers; Greener crossbolt.
Barrel: 12 ga., 20″ (Imp. Cyl., Mod.) 28″ (Mod. & Full), 20 ga., 20″ (Mod., Full), 410 ga., 26″ (Full & Full).
Weight: 6½ to 7 lbs.
Stock: Walnut p.g. with beavertail fore-end.
Features: Solid raised matted rib. Exposed hammers. Imported by Interarms.
Price: 12 or 20 . . . . **$300.00**

Sarasqueta Model 119E

J. J. SARASQUETA MODEL 119E DOUBLE
Gauge: 12 ga., 2¾″ chambers.
Barrel: 28″ (Mod. & Full, Imp. Cyl. & Mod.).
Weight: About 7 lbs. **Length:** 45″ over-all.
Stock: Hand checkered European walnut, straight grip.
Sights: Medium bead front.
Features: Automatic ejectors, hand engraved locks, double triggers. Introduced 1982. Imported from Spain by Toledo Armas.
Price: Model 119E $732.00
Price: Model 130 (made to order only) $1,445.00

Savage Fox B-SE

SAVAGE FOX MODEL B-SE DOUBLE
Gauge: 12, 20, 410 (20, 2¾″ and 3″; 410, 2½″ and 3″ shells).
Action: Hammerless, takedown; non-selective single trigger; auto. safety. Automatic ejectors.
Barrel: 12, 20 ga., 26″ (Imp. Cyl., Mod.); 12 ga. (Mod., Full); 410, 26″ (Full, Full). Vent. rib on all.
Weight: 12 ga. 7 lbs., 16 ga. 6¾ lbs., 20 ga. 6½ lbs., 410 ga. 6¼ lbs.
Stock: 14″x1½″x2½″. Walnut, checkered p.g. and beavertail fore-end.
Features: Decorated, case-hardened frame; white bead front and middle sights.
Price: $362.50
Price: Also available with double triggers, case hardened frame, without white line spacers and auto. ejectors as Model B $317.00

SAVAGE-STEVENS MODEL 311 DOUBLE
Gauge: 12, 16, 20, 410 (12, 20 and 410, 3″ chambers).
Action: Top lever, hammerless; double triggers, auto. top tang safety.
Barrel: 12, 16, 20 ga. 26″ (Imp. Cyl., Mod.); 12 ga. 28″ (Mod., Full); 12 ga. 30″ (Mod., Full); 410 ga. 26″ (Full, Full).
Weight: 7-8 lbs. (30″ bbl.). **Length:** 45¾″ over-all.
Stock: 14″x1½″x2½″. Walnut finish, p.g., fluted comb.
Features: Box type frame, case-hardened finish.
Price: $299.50

Toledo Armas Velasquez

TOLEDO ARMAS "VALEZQUEZ" DOUBLE
Gauge: 12 ga., 2¾″ chambers.
Barrel: Length and choking to customer specs.
Weight: To customer specs.
Stock: Exhibition grade European walnut; dimensions to customer specs.
Features: Hand engraved action. Automatic ejectors. All options available. Introduced 1982. Imported from Spain by Toledo Armas.
Price: From $3,275.00

Urbiola Model 160E

URBIOLA MODEL 160E DOUBLE
Gauge: 12 and 20 ga., 2¾″ chambers.
Barrel: 12 ga.—28″ (Mod. & Full), 20 ga.—26″ (Imp. Cyl. & Full).
Weight: About 7 lbs. **Length:** 45″ over-all (28″ barrels).
Stock: Hand checkered European walnut, straight grip, checkered butt.
Sights: Medium bead front.
Features: Hand engraved locks, automatic ejectors, double triggers. Introduced 1982. Imported from Spain by Toledo Armas.
Price: Model 160E $727.00
Price: Model 165 . . . . $825.00

VENTURA 66 "ELITE"/66 "ELITE" XXV-SL DOUBLES
Gauge: 12 ga. (2¾″), 20 ga. (3″), 28 ga. (2¾″).
Action: H&H sidelock with double underbolts.
Barrel: 25″, 27½″, 30″ (12 ga. only).
Weight: 12 ga.—6½ lbs.; 20 ga.—5¾ lbs.
Stock: Highly figured French walnut, hand checkered. Straight English or pistol grip stock, slender beavertail fore-end.
Features: Single selective or double triggers, auto. ejectors, cocking indicators, gas escape valves, and intercepting safeties. Extensive hand engraving and finishing with perforated top lever. Can be made to customer specs. Accessories also available. Imported from Spain by Ventura Imports.
Price: From . . . . $1,572.00 to 1,840.00

VENTURA 62/62 XXV-SL DOUBLES
Gauge: 12 ga. (2¾″), 20 ga. (3″), 28 ga. (2¾″).
Action: H&H sidelock with double underbolts.
Barrel: 25″, 27½″, and 30″ (12 ga. only).
Weight: 12 ga.—6½ lbs.; 20 ga.—5¾ lbs.
Stock: Figured French walnut, hand checkered. Straight English or pistol grip, with slender beavertail fore-end.
Features: Single selective or double triggers, auto ejectors, Purdey engraving, gas escape valves, and intercepting safeties. Accessories also available. Imported from Spain by Ventura Imports.
Price: From . . . . $1,120.00 to 1,380.00

SHOTGUNS—SIDE-BY-SIDES

VENTURA 53/53XXV-BL DOUBLES
Gauge: 12 ga. (2¾″), 20 ga. (3″), 28 ga. (2¾″), 410 (3″).
Action: Anson & Deeley with double underlugs.
Barrel: 25″, 27½″, 30″ (12 ga. only).
Weight: 12 ga.—6½ lbs.; 20 ga.—5¾ lbs.
Stock: Figured French walnut, hand checkered. Straight English or pistol grip stock with slender beavertail fore-end.
Features: Single selective or double triggers, auto ejectors, hand engraved scalloped frames. Accessories also available. Imported from Spain by Ventura Imports.
Price: From .... **$748.00 to 972.00**

WINCHESTER MODEL 23 PIGEON GRADE DOUBLE
Gauge: 12, 20, 3″ chambers.
Barrel: 26″, 28″, 30″ (Imp. Cyl. & Mod., Mod. & Full, Full & Full). Vent. rib.
Weight: 7 lbs. (12 ga.); 6½ lbs. (20 ga.). **Length:** 46¾″ over-all (30″ bbls.).
Stock: High grade American walnut, beavertail fore-end. Deep cut checkering, new warm, rich color, high-lustre finish. 14″x1½″x2½″.
Features: Mechanical trigger; ventilated tapered rib; selective ejectors. Receiver, top lever and trigger guard have silver gray satin finish and fine line scroll engraving. Introduced 1978. Imported from Japan by Winchester Group, Olin Corp.
Price: **$1,175.00**

VENTURA MODEL 51 DOUBLE
Gauge: 12 ga. (2¾″), 20 ga. (3″).
Action: Anson & Deeley with double underlugs.
Barrel: 27½″, 30″ (12 ga. only) with chokes according to use.
Weight: 6¼ to 6¾ lbs.
Stock: Select French walnut, hand checkered pistol grip stock with slender beavertail fore-end.
Features: Single selective trigger, auto ejectors, hand-engraved action. Leather trunk cases, wood cleaning rods and brass snap caps available. Imported from Spain by Ventura Imports.
Price: From **$696.00**

Winchester Model 23 XTR Lightweight
Similar to standard Pigeon Grade except has 25½″ barrel, English-style straight grip stock, thinner semi-beavertail fore-end. Available in 12 or 20 gauge (Imp. Cyl. & Imp. Mod.). Silver-gray frame has engraved bird scenes. Introduced 1981. Imported from Japan by Winchester Group, Olin Corp.
Price: **$1,200.00**

SHOTGUNS—BOLT ACTIONS

Marlin Model 55

MARLIN SUPERGOOSE 10 M5510
Gauge: 10, 3½″ Magnum or 2⅞″ regular, 2-shot clip.
Barrel: 34″ (Full), bead front sight, U-groove rear sight.
Weight: About 10½ lbs. **Length:** 55½″ over-all.
Stock: Extra long American black walnut with p.g., Pachmayr vent. pad., white butt spacer.
Features: Bolt action, removable 2-shot clip magazine. Positive thumb safety, red cocking indicator. Comes with quick-detachable swivels and leather carrying strap.
Price: **$262.95**

MARLIN MODEL 55 GOOSE GUN BOLT ACTION
Gauge: 12 only, (3″ mag. or 2¾″).
Action: Bolt action, thumb safety, detachable 2-shot clip. Red cocking indicator.
Barrel: 36″, Full choke.
Weight: 8 lbs. **Length:** 57″ over-all.
Stock: Walnut-finished hardwood, p.g., ventilated recoil pad, leather strap & swivels. Mar-Shield® finish.
Features: Tapped for receiver sights. Swivels and leather carrying strap. Brass bead front sight, U-groove rear sight.
Price: **$159.95**

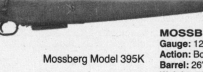

Mossberg Model 395K

MOSSBERG MODEL 395K BOLT ACTION
Gauge: 12, 3-shot (3″ chamber).
Action: Bolt; takedown; detachable clip.
Barrel: 26″ with C-Lect-Choke.
Weight: 7½ lbs. **Length:** 45¾″ over-all.
Stock: Walnut finish, p.g. Monte Carlo comb; recoil pad.
Features: Streamlined action; top safety; grooved rear sight.
Price: **$132.95**
Price: 20 ga., 3″ chamber, 28″ bbl., 6¼ lbs., as M 385K **$132.95**
Price: 12 ga., 38″ bbl., Full choke (Model 395 SPL) **$152.50**

MOSSBERG MODEL 183K BOLT ACTION
Gauge: 410, 3-shot (3″ chamber).
Action: Bolt; top-loading mag.; thumb safety.
Barrel: 25″ with C-Lect-Choke.
Weight: 5¾ lbs. **Length:** 45¼″ over-all.
Stock: Walnut finish, p.g., Monte Carlo comb., rubber recoil pad w/spacer.
Features: Moulded trigger guard with finger grooves, gold bead front sight.
Price: **$121.95**

WESTERN FIELD BOLT ACTION SHOTGUN
Gauge: 12, 20 or 410 (3″ chamber).
Action: Self cocking, bolt action. Thumb safety. 3-shot magazine.
Barrel: 24″ (Full) 410, 26″ (20 ga.), 28″ (12 ga.).
Weight: 5½ lbs. **Length:** 44½″ over-all (410 ga.).
Stock: Hardwood, Monte Carlo design.
Features: Top safety, grooved rear sight.
Price: 410 ga. **$99.99**
Price: 20 ga. **$99.99**
Price: 12 ga. **$109.99**

Beretta Model 680

BERETTA 680 MONO SINGLE BARREL
Gauge: 12 only (2¾").
Barrel: 32", 34" (Full).
Weight: About 8 lbs.
Stock: 14⅜"x1⅜"x1⅝". Premium walnut with Monte Carlo, checkered p.g. and fore-end.
Features: Low profile boxlock action, auto ejector, manual safety. High rib, two sight beads, chrome lined bores. Ventilated recoil pad. Comes with fitted case. Imported from Italy by Beretta U.S.A. Corp.
Price: **$1,580.00**

BAIKAL IJ-18 SINGLE BARREL
Gauge: 12 or 20 ga., 2¾" chamber; 410 ga., 3" chamber.
Barrel: 12 ga. 28" (Mod.), 30" (Full), 20 ga. 26" (Mod.), 410 ga. 26" (Full).
Weight: 5¾ lbs.
Stock: Walnut-finished hardwood. Hand checkered p.g. White spacers on butt-plate.
Features: Chrome barrel and chamber. Cross-bolt safety in trigger guard. Cocking indicator. Extractor only. Imported from Russia by Baikal International.
Price: **$81.50**

Browning BT-99

BROWNING BT-99 COMPETITION TRAP SPECIAL
Gauge: 12 gauge only (2¾").
Action: Top lever break-open, hammerless.
Barrel: 32" or 34" (Mod., Imp. Mod. or Full) with ¹¹⁄₃₂" wide high post floating vent. rib.
Weight: 8 lbs. (32" bbl.).
Stock: French walnut; hand checkered, full pistol grip, full beavertail fore-end; recoil pad. Trap dimensions with M.C. 14⅜"x1⅜"x1⅜"x2".
Sights: Ivory front and middle beads.
Features: Gold plated trigger with 3½-lb. pull, deluxe trap-style recoil pad, auto ejector, no safety. Also available in engraved Pigeon Grade. Imported from Japan by Browning.
Price: Grade I Competition **$724.95**
Price: Grade I Competition with extra bbl. **$1,030.00**
Price: Pigeon Grade Competition **$1,650.00**

FIE "S.O.B." SINGLE BARREL
Gauge: 12, 20 (2¾"), 410 (3").
Action: Button-break on trigger guard.
Barrel: 12 & 20 ga. 18½" (Cyl.), 28" (Full); 410 ga. 26" (Full).
Weight: 6½ lbs.
Stock: Walnut finished hardwood, full beavertail fore-end.
Sights: Metal bead front.
Features: Exposed hammer. Automatic ejector. Imported from Brazil by F.I.E. Corp.
Price: **$69.95**
Price: With 18½" bbl., short stock **$89.95**

ERA "THE WINNER" SINGLE BARREL SHOTGUN
Gauge: 12, 16, 20 (2¾"), 410 (3").
Barrel: 12 ga. & 20 ga. 28" (Full); 410 ga. (Full).
Weight: 6½ lbs.
Stock: Walnut stained hardwood, beavertail fore-end.
Sights: Metal bead front.
Features: Trigger guard is pulled to open action. Exposed hammer, auto extractor. Imported from Brazil by F.I.E. Corp.
Price: **$68.95**
Price: 20 and 410 ga. Youth Model **$69.95**

GALEF COMPANION SINGLE BARREL SHOTGUN
Gauge: 12, 20, 410 (3"); 16, 28 (2¾").
Action: Folding boxlock.
Barrel: 28" exc. 12 (30") and 410 (26"), all Full.
Weight: 5½ lbs. (12) to 4½ lbs. (410).
Stock: 14"x1½"x2⅝" hand checkered walnut, p.g.
Features: Non-auto safety, folds. Imported from Italy by Galef.
Price: Plain bbl. **$138.00**
Price: Vent. rib **$167.20**

H&R Model 099

HARRINGTON & RICHARDSON MODEL 099 DELUXE
Gauge: 12, 20, 410 (3" chamber); 16 (2¾").
Barrel: 12 ga. 28" (Full, Mod.); 16 ga. 28" (Mod.); 20 ga. 26" (Full, Mod.); 410 ga. 25" (Full).
Weight: About 5½ lbs. **Length:** 43" over-all (28" barrel).
Stock: Semi-pistol grip walnut finished hardwood; semi-beavertail fore-end. 13¾"x1½"x2½".
Sights: Bead front.
Features: All metal finished with H & R's "Hard-Guard" electroless matte nickel. Introduced 1982. From Harrington & Richardson.
Price: **$89.50**

H & R Topper Buck Model 162
Same as the 099 except 12 or 20 ga., 24" Cyl. bored bbl., adj. folding leaf rear sight, blade front, 5½ lbs.; over-all 40". Cross bolt safety; push-button action release.
Price: **$94.50**

H & R Model 088
Same features as Model 099 except has semi-pistol grip stock. Available in most popular gauge and choke combinations, including 12 ga. with 30" or 32" (Full) barrel. Junior model also available (does not have recoil pad).
Price: **$75.50**
Price: 12 ga., 30", 32" (Full) **$77.50**
Price: 12 ga., 36" (Full) **$79.50**

H & R Topper Jr. Model 490
Like the 099 except ideally proportioned stock for the smaller shooter. Can be cheaply changed to full size. 20 ga. (Mod.), 28 ga. (Mod.) or 410 (Full) 26" bbl. Weight 5 lbs., 40½" over-all.
Price: **$79.50**

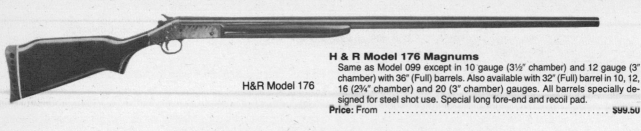

H&R Model 176

H & R Model 176 Magnums
Same as Model 099 except in 10 gauge (3½″ chamber) and 12 gauge (3″ chamber) with 36″ (Full) barrels. Also available with 32″ (Full) barrel in 10, 12, 16 (2¾″ chamber) and 20 (3″ chamber) gauges. All barrels specially designed for steel shot use. Special long fore-end and recoil pad.
Price: From **$99.50**

H&R 176 Slug Gun

H & R Model 176 10 Ga. Slug Gun
Similar to standard Model 176 magnums except chambered for 10 ga. slugs. Ramp front sight, adjustable folding leaf rear sight, recoil pad, sling swivels. Has 28″ barrel (Cyl.), 3½″ chamber. Extra length magnum-type fore-end. Weighs 9¼ lbs. Introduced 1982.
Price: **$115.00**

H&R 490 Greenwing

H & R Model 490 Greenwing
Same as Model 490 except specially polished blue finish with gold-finish trigger and gold-filled inscription on frame.
Price: **$89.50**

ITHACA 5E GRADE SINGLE BARREL TRAP GUN
Gauge: 12 only.
Action: Top lever break open hammerless, dual locking lugs.
Barrel: 30″ or 32″, rampless vent. rib.
Stock: (14½″x1½″x1⅞″). Select walnut, checkered p.g. and beavertail fore-end, p.g. cap, recoil pad, Monte Carlo comb, cheekpiece. Cast-on, cast-off or extreme deviation from standard stock dimensions $100 extra. Reasonable deviation allowed without extra charge.
Features: Frame, top lever and trigger guard extensively engraved and gold inlaid. Gold name plate in stock.
Price: Custom made **$7,000.00**
Price: Dollar Grade........................... **$9,700.00**

Ljutic Adjustable Barrel Mono Gun
Similar to standard Mono except has micrometer-adjustable choke (allows shooter to adj. the pattern from flat to an elevation of 4 feet), choice of Olympic, step-style or standard rib. Custom stock measurements, fancy wood, etc.
Price: **$3,595.00**

LJUTIC SPACE GUN SHOTGUN
Gauge: 12 only, 2¾″ chamber.
Barrel: 30″ (Full).
Weight: 8½ lbs.
Stock: 14½″ to 15″ pull length; universal comb; medium or large p.g.
Sights: Choice of front sight or vent. rib.
Features: Choice of pull or release button trigger; anti-recoil mechanism. Revolutionary new design. Introduced 1981. From Ljutic Industries.
Price: From **$2,995.00**

LJUTIC MONO GUN SINGLE BARREL
Gauge: 12 ga. only.
Barrel: 34″, choked to customer specs; hollow-milled rib, 35½″ sight plane.
Weight: Approx. 9 lbs.
Stock: To customer specs. Oil finish, hand checkered.
Features: Pull or release trigger; removable trigger guard contains trigger and hammer mechanism; Ljutic pushbutton opener on front of trigger guard. From Ljutic Industries.
Price: **$3,295.00**
Price: With Olympic Rib, custom 32″ barrel, 2 screw-in chokes.... **$3,450.00**
Price: As above with screw-in chokes......................... **$3,695.00**

Ljutic Dyna Trap II Shotgun
Similar to the Mono Gun Single Barrel except has 33″ single barrel, choice of Monte Carlo or straight stock.
Price: Pull or release trigger................................. **$1,895.00**

MONTE CARLO SINGLE BARREL SHOTGUN
Gauge: 12 (2¾″ chamber).
Action: Monte Carlo, bottom release.
Barrel: 32″ (Trap).
Weight: 8¼ lbs.
Stock: 14½″x1⅛″x1⅝″ hand checkered walnut, p.g., beavertail fore-end, recoil pad.
Features: Auto ejector, slide safety, gold plated trigger. Imported from Italy by Galef.
Price: **$317.00**

Stevens Model 94-C

Stevens M94-Y Youth's Gun
Same as Model 94-C except: 26″ bbl., 20 ga. Mod. or 410 Full, 12½″ stock with recoil pad. Wgt. about 5½ lbs. 40½″ over-all.
Price: **$98.00**

SAVAGE-STEVENS MODEL 94-C Single Barrel Gun
Gauge: 12, 16, 20, 410 (12, 20 and 410, 3″ chambers).
Action: Top lever break open; hammer; auto. ejector.
Barrel: 12 ga. 28″, 30″, 32″, 36″; 16, 20 ga. 28″; 410 ga. 26″. Full choke only.
Weight: About 6 lbs. **Length:** 42″ over-all (26″ bbl.).
Stock: 14″x1½″x2½″. Walnut finish, checkered p.g. and fore-end.
Features: Color case-hardened frame, low rebounding hammer.
Price: 26″ to 32″ bbls. **$87.50**
Price: With 36″ bbl. **$89.50**

SHOTGUNS—SINGLE SHOTS

Stevens Model 9478

STEVENS "Super Value" 9478 SINGLE BARREL

Gauge: 10, 12, 20 or 410.
Barrel: 26" (Full, Mod.), 28" (Full), 30" (Full), 32" (Full), 36" (Full).
Weight: 6¼ lbs. (9½ lbs. for 10 ga.) **Length:** 42" to 52" over-all.
Stock: Walnut finished hardwood. 14"x1½"x2½".
Features: Bottom opening action "lever", manually cocked hammer, auto.
ejection. Color case-hardened frame. Youth Model available in 20 or 410,
26" (Mod.) barrel, 12½" pull stock, weighs 5½ lbs.

Price: 9478	**$75.60**
Price: 9478-Y (Youth Model)	**$75.60**
Price: 12 ga., 36" (Full)	**$83.00**
Price: 10 ga., 36" (Full)	**$102.00**

"SNAKE CHARMER" SHOTGUN

Gauge: 410, 3" chamber.
Barrel: 18⅛" (Cyl.).
Weight: 3½ lbs. **Length:** 28⅛" over-all.
Stock: Moulded plastic, thumbhole type.
Sights: None.
Features: Measures 19" when taken apart. All stainless steel construction.
Storage compartment in buttstock holds four spare rounds of 410. Introduced 1978. From H. Koon, Inc.

Price:	**$110.00**
Price: Vinyl carrying case	**$7.00**
Price: Leather scabbard	**$32.00**

SHOTGUNS—MILITARY & POLICE

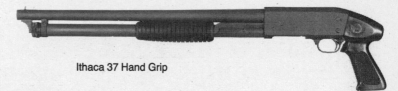

Benelli Model 121-M1

BENELLI MODEL 121-MI POLICE SHOTGUN

Gauge: 12, 2¾" chamber.
Barrel: 20" (Cyl.).
Weight: About 7½ lbs.
Stock: Oil-finished Beech.
Sights: Post front, buckhorn-type rear.
Features: All metal parts black Parkerized, including bolt; smooth, non-checkered stock, swivel stud on butt.

Price:	**$499.00**

Ithaca 37 Hand Grip

ITHACA MODEL 37 M & P SHOTGUN

Gauge: 12, 2¾" chamber, 5-shot magazine.
Barrel: 18" (Cyl.), 20" (Cyl. or Full).
Weight: 6½ lbs.
Stock: Oil-finished walnut with grooved walnut pump handle.
Sights: Bead front.
Features: Metal parts are Parkerized or matte chrome. Available with vertical hand grip instead of full butt.

Price: 5-shot, Parkerized	**$328.70**
Price: 8-shot, Parkerized	**$343.50**
Price: 8-shot, chrome	**$383.50**
Price: Hand Grip stock, 5-shot	**$351.75**
Price: Hand Grip stock, 8-shot	**$366.75**

Ithaca 37 DSPS

Ithaca Model 37 DSPS Shotgun

Law enforcement version of the Model 37 Deerslayer. Designed primarily for shooting rifled slugs but equally effective with buckshot. Available in either 5- or 8-shot models in blue, Parkerized or matte chrome finishes. Has 20" barrel with Full choke, oil-finished stock, adjustable rifle-type sights.

Price: Parkerized, 5-shot	**$363.50**
Price: Blue, 5-shot	**$363.50**
Price: Matte chrome, 8-shot	**$418.50**
Price: Parkerized or blue, 8-shot	**$378.50**

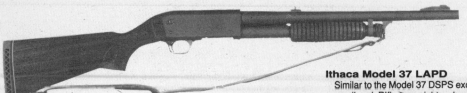

Ithaca 37 LAPD

Ithaca Model 37 LAPD
Similar to the Model 37 DSPS except comes with sling swivels, sling, rubber recoil pad. Rifle-type sights, checkered pistol grip stock, 5-shot magazine.
Price: **$405.00**

Ithaca Mag-10 Roadblocker

ITHACA MAG-10 ROADBLOCKER
Gauge: 10, 3½" chamber.
Barrel: 22" (Cyl.).
Weight: 10¾ lbs.
Stock: Walnut stock and fore-end, oil finish.
Sights: Bead front.
Features: Non-glare finish on metal parts. Uses Ithaca's Countercoil gas system. Rubber recoil pad. Vent. rib or plain barrel.
Price: Plain barrel **$696.75**
Price: Vent rib barrel **$725.50**

Mossberg 500 Security

MOSSBERG MODEL 500 SECURITY SHOTGUNS
Gauge: 12, 20 (2¾"), 410 (3").
Barrel: 18½", 20" (Cyl.).
Weight: 5½ lbs. (410), 7 lbs. (12 ga.).
Stock: Walnut-finished hardwood.
Sights: Rifle-type front and rear or metal bead front.
Features: Available in 6- or 8-shot models. Top-mounted safety, double action slide bars, sling swivels, rubber recoil pad. Blue, Parkerized or electroless nickel finishes. Price list not complete—contact Mossberg for full list.
Price: 12 ga., 6-shot, 18½", blue, bead sight **$227.95**
Price: As above, Parkerized. **$247.95**
Price: As above, nickel **$276.50**
Price: 12 ga., 8-shot, 20" Parkerized, rifle sights **$270.95**
Price: 20 ga., 6-shot, 18½", blue, bead sight **$219.95**

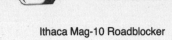

Mossberg Cruiser Persuader

Mossberg Cruiser Persuader Shotgun
Similar to the Model 500 Security guns except fitted with the "Cruiser" pistol grip. Grip and fore-end are solid black. Available in either blue or electroless nickel; 12 gauge only with 18½" (6-shot) or 20" (8-shot) barrel. Comes with extra long black web sling. Weight is 5¾ lb. (18½"), 6 lb. (20"). Over-all length is 28" with 18½" barrel.
Price: 6-shot, 18½", blue **$227.95**
Price: As above, nickel **$276.50**
Price: 8-shot, 20", blue **$240.95**
Price: As above, nickel **$289.50**

Sile Model TP-8

SILE TP8 POLICE/SURVIVAL SHOTGUN
Gauge: 12, 2¾" chamber, 7-shot magazine.
Barrel: 19¾".
Weight: 6¾ lbs. **Length:** 39½" over-all with stock, 29½" without.
Stock: Hollow, plastic coated, steel tube, plastic fore-end.
Sights: Bead on ramp front, open bar rear.
Features: Dual action bars, non-reflective electroless nickel finish. Stock holds spare ammunition or survival equipment. Rotating sling swivels. Hard chrome lined barrel. Introduced 1982. Imported from Italy by Sile.
Price: **$255.00**

Remington 870 Police

REMINGTON MODEL 870P POLICE SHOTGUN
Gauge: 12, 2¾″ chamber.
Barrel: 18″, 20″ (Police Cyl.), 20″ (Imp. Cyl.).
Weight: About 7 lbs.
Stock: Lacquer-finished hardwood or folding stock.
Sights: Metal bead front or rifle sights.
Features: Solid steel receiver, double-action slide bars.
Price: Wood stock, 18″ or 20″, bead sight **$304.95**
Price: Wood stock, 20″, rifle sights **$328.95**
Price: Folding stock, 18″ or 20″, bead sight **$374.95**

Stevens Model 69-RXL

STEVENS MODEL 69-RXL PUMP SHOTGUN
Gauge: 12 only, 3″ chamber.
Barrel: 18¼″ (Cyl.).
Weight: 6½ lbs. **Length:** 38″ over-all.
Stock: Walnut-finished hardwood.
Sights: Bead front.
Features: Top tang safety, 7-shot capacity. Stock has fluted comb and full pistol grip, ventilated rubber pad. QD swivel studs. Introduced 1982.
Price: **$189.50**

Stevens 311-R Guard Gun

STEVENS MODEL 311-R GUARD GUN DOUBLE
Gauge: 12 only, 3″ chambers.
Barrel: 18¼″ (Cyl. & Cyl.).
Weight: 6¾ lbs. **Length:** 35¼″ over-all.
Stock: Walnut-finished hardwood.
Sights: Bead front.
Features: Top tang safety, double triggers, color case-hardened frame, blue barrels. Ventilated rubber recoil pad. Introduced 1982.
Price: **$238.50**

Winchester 1200 Defender

WINCHESTER 1200 DEFENDER PUMP GUN
Gauge: 12, 3″ chamber, 7-shot capacity.
Barrel: 18″ (Cyl.).
Weight: 7 lbs. **Length:** 38⅝″ over-all.
Stock: Walnut finished hardwood stock and ribbed fore-end.
Sights: Metal bead front.
Features: Cross-bolt safety, front-locking rotating bolt, twin action slide bars. Black rubber butt pad. Made under license by U.S. Repeating Arms Co.
Price: **$249.00**

Winchester 1200 Police

Winchester 1200 "Stainless" Pump Gun
Same as the 1200 Defender except has bright chrome finish, rifle-type sights only. Has special fore-end cap for easy cleaning and inspection.
Price: **$375.00**

Winchester 1200 Police Pump Gun
Same as the 1200 Defender except has satin chrome finish, 6-shot capacity, detachable sling swivels. Metal bead front sight or rifle-type front and rear sights.
Price: With bead front sight **$394.00**
Price: With rifle-type sights **$409.00**

The following pages catalog the black powder arms currently available to U.S. shooters. These range from quite precise replicas of historically significant arms to totally new designs created expressly to give the black powder shooter the benefits of modern technology.

Most of the replicas are imported, and many are available from more than one source. Thus examples of a given model such as the 1860 Army revolver or Zouave rifle purchased from different importers may vary in price, finish and fitting. Most of them bear proof marks, indicating that they have been test fired in the proof house of their country of origin.

A list of the importers and the retail price range are included with the description for each model. Many local dealers handle more than one importer's products, giving the prospective buyer an opportunity to make his own judgment in selecting a black powder gun. Most importers have catalogs available free or at nominal cost, and some

are well worth having for the useful information on black powder shooting they provide in addition to their detailed descriptions and specifications of the guns.

A number of special accessories are also available for the black powder shooter. These include replica powder flasks, bullet moulds, cappers and tools, as well as more modern devices to facilitate black powder cleaning and maintenance. Ornate presentation cases and even detachable shoulder stocks are also available for some black powder pistols from their importers. Again, dealers or the importers will have catalogs.

The black powder guns are arranged in four sections: Single Shot Pistols, Revolvers, Muskets & Rifles, and Shotguns. The guns within each section are arranged by date of the original, with the oldest first. Thus the 1847 Walker replica leads off the revolver section, and flintlocks precede percussion arms in the other sections.

BLACK POWDER SINGLE SHOT PISTOLS—FLINT & PERCUSSION

Dixie Charleville

CHARLEVILLE FLINTLOCK PISTOL
Caliber: 69, (.680" round ball).
Barrel: 7½".
Weight: 48 oz. **Length:** 13½" over-all.
Stock: Walnut.
Sights: None.
Features: Brass frame, polished steel barrel, iron belt hook, brass buttcap and backstrap. Replica of original 1777 pistol. Imported by Dixie.
Price: $135.00

Scottish Black Watch

BLACK WATCH SCOTCH PISTOL
Caliber: 577 (.550" round ball).
Barrel: 7", smoothbore.
Weight: 1½ lbs. **Length:** 12" over-all.
Stock: Brass.
Sights: None.
Features: Faithful reproduction of this military flintlock. From Dixie.
Price: $99.95

CVA TOWER PISTOL
Caliber: 45.
Barrel: 9", octagon, rifled.
Weight: 36 oz. **Length:** 15¼" over-all.
Stocks: Selected hardwood.
Sights: Brass front, dovetail open fixed rear.
Features: Color case-hardened and engraved lock plate; early-style brass trigger; brass trigger guard, nose cap, thimbles, grip cap; blued barrel and ramrod. Introduced 1981.
Price: Complete, percussion $99.95
Price: Kit form, percussion $69.95
Price: Kit form, flintlock $79.95

TOWER FLINTLOCK PISTOL
Caliber: 45, 69.
Barrel: 8¼".
Weight: 40 oz. **Length:** 14" over-all.
Stock: Walnut.
Sights: Fixed.
Features: Engraved lock, brass furniture. Specifications, including caliber, weight and length may vary with importers. Available as flint or percussion. Imported by F.I.E., Toledo Armas.
Price: $59.95

Harper's Ferry 1806

HARPER'S FERRY 1806 PISTOL
Caliber: 54.
Barrel: 10".
Weight: 40 oz. **Length:** 16" over-all.
Stock: Walnut.
Sights: Fixed.
Features: Case hardened lock, brass mounted browned bbl. Replica of the first U.S. Gov't.-made flintlock pistol. Imported by Navy Arms.
Price: $150.00

BLACK POWDER SINGLE SHOT PISTOLS—FLINT & PERCUSSION

H & A English Flint

H & A ENGLISH FLINTLOCK TARGET PISTOL
Caliber: 45.
Barrel: 10″.
Weight: 2 lbs. 4 oz. **Length:** 15″ over-all.
Stock: English walnut with checkered grip.
Sights: Fixed.
Features: Engraved lock in white, browned barrel, German silver furniture. Special roller bearing frizzen spring. Also available in percussion lock. From Hopkins & Allen.
Price: $254.30

Dixie Pennsylvania Pistol

DIXIE PENNSYLVANIA PISTOL
Caliber: 44 (.430″ round ball).
Barrel: 10″ (⅞″ octagon).
Weight: 2½ lbs.
Stocks: Walnut-stained hardwood.
Sights: Blade front, open rear drift-adj. for windage; brass.
Features: Available in flint or percussion. Brass trigger guard, thimbles, nose-cap, wedgeplates; high-lustre blue barrel. Imported from Italy by Dixie Gun Works.
Price: Flint, finished................................ $119.95
Price: Percussion, finished.......................... $105.00
Price: Flint, kit................................... $85.00
Price: Percussion, kit.............................. $72.50

Lyman Plains Pistol

LYMAN PLAINS PISTOL
Caliber: 50 or 54.
Barrel: 8″, 1-in-66″ twist.
Weight: 50 oz. **Length:** 15″ over-all.
Stock: Walnut half-stock.
Sights: Blade front, V-notch rear adj. for windage.
Features: Polished brass trigger guard and ramrod tip, color case-hardened lock, spring-loaded target hammer, blackened iron furniture. Hooked patent breech, detachable belt hook. Introduced 1981. From Lyman Products.
Price: Finished.................................... $159.95
Price: Kit.. $119.95

KENTUCKY FLINTLOCK PISTOL
Caliber: 44, 45.
Barrel: 10⅛″.
Weight: 32 oz. **Length:** 15½″ over-all.
Stock: Walnut.
Sights: Fixed.
Features: Specifications, including caliber, weight and length may vary with importer. Case hardened lock, blued bbl.; availble also as brass bbl. flint Model 1821 ($110.00, Navy). Imported by Navy Arms, The Armoury, CVA (kit only), Hopkins & Allen, Sile.
Price: .... $40.95 to $142.00
Price: In kit form, from................... $90.00 to $112.00
Price: Brass barrel (Navy Arms).................. $140.00
Price: Single cased set (Navy Arms)............... $191.00
Price: Brass bbl., single cased set (Navy Arms)..... $206.00

Kentucky Percussion Pistol
Similar to flint version but percussion lock. Imported by The Armoury, Navy Arms, F.I.E., CVA, Dixie, Armsport, Sile, Hopkins & Allen, Toledo Armas.
Price: About...................................... $110.00
Price: Brass barrel................................ $132.00
Price: In kit form...................... $35.95 to $102.00
Price: Single cased set (Navy Arms)............... $176.00
Price: Brass bbl. single cased set (Navy Arms)....... $191.00

J & S Hawken Pistol

SILE NORTH & CHENEY PISTOL
Caliber: 69.
Barrel: 7″, round tapered, smoothbore.
Weight: 46 oz. **Length:** 13½″ over-all.
Stock: Smooth walnut.
Sights: None.
Features: Polished brass furniture; color case-hardened hammer, trigger and frizzen, browned barrel and ramrod. Imported by Sile.
Price: $97.75

CVA MOUNTAIN PISTOL
Caliber: 45 or 50 cal.
Barrel: 9″, octagon. ¹⁵⁄₁₆″ across flats.
Weight: 40 oz. **Length:** 14″ over-all.
Stocks: Select hardwood.
Sights: German silver blade front, fixed primitive rear.
Features: Engraved color case-hardened lock. Adjustable sear engagement. Fly and bridle. Hooked breech. Browned steel on finished pistol. German silver wedge plates. Stainless steel nipples. Hardwood ramrod. Belt hook optional. Introduced 1978. From CVA.
Price: $124.95
Price: Kit form....................................... $109.95

J&S HAWKEN PERCUSSION PISTOL
Caliber: 50, uses 50-cal. mini; 54, uses 54-cal. mini.
Barrel: 9″.
Weight: 41 oz. **Length:** 14″ over-all.
Stock: European walnut with checkered grip.
Sights: Fixed.
Features: Blued steel barrel with swivel-type rammer, three-quarter stocked, adj. single set trigger, German silver furniture, scroll engraved lock. From Navy Arms.
Price: Finished, either cal............................ $200.00

BLACK POWDER SINGLE SHOT PISTOLS—FLINT & PERCUSSION

Dixie Overcoat Pistol

DIXIE OVERCOAT PISTOL
Caliber: 39.
Barrel: 4″, smoothbore.
Weight: 13 oz. **Length:** 8″ over-all.
Stock: Walnut-finished hardwood. Checkered p.g.
Sights: Dead front.
Features: Shoots .380″ balls. Breech plug and engraved lock are burnished steel finish; barrel and trigger guard blued.
Price: Engraved model $34.50

CVA COLONIAL PISTOL
Caliber: 45 (.451″ bore).
Barrel: 6¾″, octagonal, rifled.
Length: 12¾″ over-all.
Stocks: Selected hardwood.
Features: Case hardened lock, brass furniture, fixed sights. Steel ramrod. Available in either flint or percussion. Imported by CVA.
Price: Percussion.. $69.95
Also available in kit form, either flint or percussion. Stock 95% inletted.
Price: Flint... $54.95
Price: Percussion.. $49.95

PHILADELPHIA DERRINGER PERCUSSION PISTOL
Caliber: 45.
Barrel: 3⅛″.
Weight: 14 oz. **Length:** 7″ over-all.
Stock: Walnut, checkered grip.
Sights: Fixed.
Features: Engraved wedge holder and bbl. Also available in flintlock version (Armoury, $29.95). Imported by Sile (45-cal. only), CVA (45-cal. percussion only), Navy Arms, Toledo Armas.
Price: .... $18.37 to $120.00
Price: Kit form (CVA, Navy Arms) $90.00

Dixie Lincoln Derringer

DIXIE LINCOLN DERRINGER
Caliber: 41.
Barrel: 2″, 8 lands, 8 grooves.
Weight: 7 oz. **Length:** 5½″ over-all.
Stock: Walnut finish, checkered.
Sights: Fixed.
Features: Authentic copy of the "Lincoln Derringer." Shoots .400″ patched ball. German silver furniture includes trigger guard with pineapple finial, wedge plates, nose, wrist, side and teardrop inlays. All furniture, lockplate, hammer, and breech plug engraved. Imported from Italy by Dixie Gun Works.
Price: With wooden case $159.95
Price: Kit (not engraved) $59.95

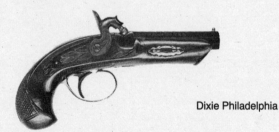

Dixie Philadelphia

DIXIE PHILADELPHIA DERRINGER
Caliber: 41.
Barrel: 3½″, octagon.
Weight: 8 oz. **Length:** 5½″ over-all.
Stock: Walnut, checkered p.g.
Sights: Fixed.
Features: Barrel and lock are blued; brass furniture. From Dixie Gun Works.
Price: $45.00

Dixie Brass Frame

DIXIE BRASS FRAME DERRINGER
Caliber: 41.
Barrel: 2½″.
Weight: 7 oz. **Length:** 5½″ over-all.
Stocks: Walnut.
Features: Brass frame, color case hardened hammer and trigger. Shoots .395″ round ball. Engraved model available. From Dixie Gun Works.
Price: Plain model $49.95
Price: Engraved model $59.95
Price: Kit form, plain model $37.50

CLASSIC ARMS SOUTHERN DERRINGER
Caliber: 44.
Barrel: 2½″.
Weight: 12 oz. **Length:** 5″ over-all.
Stock: White plastic.
Sights: Blade front.
Features: Percussion, uses .440″ round ball. Brass frame, steel barrel. Introduced 1982. Made in U.S. by Classic Arms Ltd.
Price: $79.95

NAVY ARMS LE PAGE DUELING PISTOL
Caliber: 44.
Barrel: 9″, octagon.
Weight: 34 oz. **Length:** 15″ over-all.
Stock: European walnut.
Sights: Adjustable rear.
Features: Single set trigger. Silvered metal finish. From Navy Arms.
Price: $300.00
Price: Single cased set $400.00
Price: Double cased set $700.00

CAUTION: PRICES CHANGE. CHECK AT GUNSHOP.

BLACK POWDER SINGLE SHOT PISTOLS—FLINT & PERCUSSION

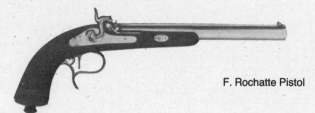

F. Rochatte Pistol

F. ROCHATTE PERCUSSION PISTOL
Caliber: 45, uses .440″ round ball.
Barrel: 10″.
Weight: 32 oz. **Length:** 16½″ over-all.
Stock: European walnut.
Sights: Dovetailed front and rear, adj. for windage.
Features: Single adj. trigger, highly polished lock and round barrel with top flat; all steel furniture. French-style finial on butt. From Navy Arms.
Price: Finished gun $250.00

John Manton Pistol

JOHN MANTON MATCH PISTOL
Caliber: 45, uses .440″ round ball.
Barrel: 10″, rifled.
Weight: 36 oz. **Length:** 15½″ over-all.
Stock: European walnut; checkered grip.
Sights: Bead front.
Features: Highly polished steel barrel and lock, brass furniture. From Navy Arms.
Price: Finished gun $225.00

W. Parker Pistol

W. PARKER PERCUSSION PISTOL
Caliber: 45, uses .440″ round ball.
Barrel: 10″, rifled.
Weight: 40 oz. **Length:** 16″ over-all.
Stock: European walnut; checkered grip.
Sights: Dovetailed front and rear, adj.for windage.
Features: Fully adj. double set triggers, German silver furniture; lock engraved "London." From Navy Arms.
Price: Finished gun $250.00
Price: As above from Dixie, 11″ bbl. $250.00

MOORE & PATRICK FLINT DUELING PISTOL
Caliber: 45.
Barrel: 10″, rifled.
Weight: 32 oz. **Length:** 14½″ over-all.
Stock: European walnut, checkered.
Sights: Fixed.
Features: Engraved, silvered lock plate, blue barrel. German silver furniture. Imported from Italy by Dixie and Navy Arms.
Price: . . . . $200.00 to $225.00

BRITISH DRAGOON FLINT PISTOL
Caliber: .615″.
Barrel: 12″, polished steel.
Weight: 3 lbs., 2 oz. **Length:** 19″ over-all.
Stock: Walnut, with brass furniture.
Features: Lockplate marked "Willets 1761." Brass trigger guard and butt cap. Made in U.S. by Navy Arms.
Price: $350.00
Price: $295.00

Napolean Le Page

NAPOLEAN LE PAGE PERCUSSION PISTOL
Caliber: 45, uses .440″ round ball.
Barrel: 10″.
Weight: 39 oz. **Length:** 15″ over-all.
Stock: European walnut.
Sights: Fixed.
Features: Percussion. Fully adjustable double-set trigger, spur-type trigger guard, fluted grip, scroll-engraved lock. From Navy Arms.
Price: Finished gun $175.00
Price: As above, from Dixie as Le Page Duelling Pistol $155.00

H & A 1810 Dueller

H&A 1810 ENGLISH DUELING PISTOL
Caliber: 45.
Barrel: 11″.
Weight: 2 lbs., 5 oz. **Length:** 15″ over-all.
Stock: European walnut, checkered, with German silver inlays.
Sights: Fixed.
Features: Double set triggers, precision "match" barrel, silver plated furniture, browned barrel. Percussion lock only. From Hopkins & Allen.
Price: $265.30

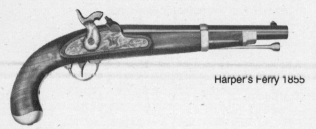

Harper's Ferry 1855

HARPER'S FERRY MODEL 1855 PERCUSSION PISTOL
Caliber: 58.
Barrel: 11¾", rifled.
Weight: 56 oz. **Length:** 18" over-all.
Stock: Walnut.
Sights: Fixed.
Features: Case hardened lock and hammer; brass furniture; blued bbl. Shoulder stock available, priced at $35.00. Imported by Navy Arms.
Price: $200.00
Price: With detachable shoulder stock $245.00

LE PAGE PERCUSSION PISTOL
Caliber: 45, uses .440" round ball.
Barrel: 9", rifled.
Weight: 34 oz. **Length:** 15" over-all.
Stock: European walnut.
Sights: Dovetailed front adjustable for windage, rear adjustable for elevation.
Features: Tapered octagonal barrel, adj. single set trigger. Engraved over-all with traditional scrollwork. From Navy Arms.
Price: Finished gun $250.00
Price: French fitted, single cased set $400.00
Price: As above, double set $700.00

Consult our Directory pages for the location of firms mentioned.

Dixie Screw Barrel

DIXIE SCREW BARREL PISTOL
Caliber: .445".
Barrel: 2½".
Weight: 8 oz. **Length:** 6½" over-all.
Stock: Walnut.
Features: Trigger folds down when hammer is cocked. Close copy of the originals once made in Belgium. Uses No. 11 percussion caps.
Price: $79.95

Dixie Abilene

DIXIE ABILENE DERRINGER
Caliber: 41.
Barrel: 2½", 6-groove rifling.
Weight: 8 oz. **Length:** 6½" over-all.
Stocks: Walnut.
Features: All steel version of Dixie's brass-framed derringers. Blued barrel, color case hardened frame and hammer. Shoots .395" patched ball. Comes with wood presentation case.
Price: $54.95
Price: Kit form $45.00

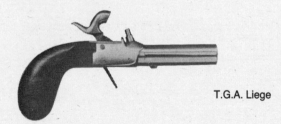

T.G.A. Liege

T.G.A. LIEGE DERRINGER
Caliber: 451".
Barrel: 2⅜".
Weight: 7 oz. **Length:** 6½" over-all.
Stock: Walnut.
Sights: None.
Features: Removable round, rifled barrel. All metal parts case-hardened. Folding trigger. Introduced 1980. From Trail Guns Armory.
Price: Deluxe engraved model with case and flask $99.00

CLASSIC ARMS ELGIN CUTLASS PISTOL
Caliber: 44 (.440").
Barrel: 4¼".
Weight: 21 oz. **Length:** 12" over-all.
Stock: Walnut.
Sights: None.
Features: Replica of the pistol used by the U.S. Navy as a boarding weapon. Smoothbore barrel. Available as a kit or finished. Made in U.S. by Navy Arms.
Price: Kit $75.00
Price: Finished $99.95

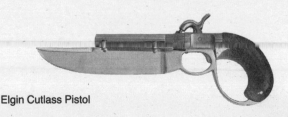

Elgin Cutlass Pistol

CAUTION: PRICES CHANGE. CHECK AT GUNSHOP.

BLACK POWDER SINGLE SHOT PISTOLS—FLINT & PERCUSSION

H & A Target Boot

HOPKINS & ALLEN BOOT PISTOL
Caliber: 36 or 45.
Barrel: 6".
Weight: 42 oz. **Length:** 13" over-all.
Stock: Walnut.
Sights: Silver blade front; rear adj. for e.
Features: Under-hammer design. From Hopkins & Allen.
Price: $71.50
Price: Kit form $55.20
Price: Target version with wood fore-end, ramrod, hood front sight, elevator
        rear $89.80

BUCCANEER DOUBLE BARREL PISTOL
Caliber: 44.
Barrel: 9½".
Weight: 40 oz. **Length:** 15½" over-all.
Stock: Walnut, one piece.
Sights: Fixed.
Features: Case hardened and engraved lockplate, solid brass fittings. Percussion or flintlock. Imported by The Armoury. Available as the "Corsair" from Armsport, Sile.
Price: Complete $73.95
Price: Kit form $61.96
Price: Corsair, complete .... $99.00 Kit $86.00

THOMPSON/CENTER PATRIOT PERCUSSION PISTOL
Caliber: 45.
Barrel: 9¼".
Weight: 36 oz. **Length:** 16" over-all.
Stock: Walnut.
Sights: Patridge-type. Rear adj. for w. and e.
Features: Hook breech system; double set triggers; coil mainspring. From Thompson/Center Arms.
Price: $185.00

BLACK POWDER REVOLVERS

Colt 1847 Walker

COLT 1847 WALKER PERCUSSION REVOLVER
Caliber: 44.
Barrel: 9", 7 groove, RH twist.
Weight: 73 oz.
Stocks: One-piece walnut.
Sights: German silver front sight, hammer notch rear.
Features: Made in U.S. by Colt. Faithful reproduction of the original gun, including markings. Color cased frame, hammer, loading lever and plunger. Blue steel backstrap, brass square-back trigger guard. Blue barrel, cylinder, trigger and wedge. Accessories available. Re-introduced 1979.
Price: $561.50

WALKER 1847 PERCUSSION REVOLVER
Caliber: 44, 6-shot.
Barrel: 9".
Weight: 72 oz. **Length:** 15½" over-all.
Stocks: Walnut.
Sights: Fixed.
Features: Case hardened frame, loading lever and hammer; iron backstrap; brass trigger guard; engraved cylinder. Imported by Sile, Navy Arms, Dixie, Armsport.
Price: .... $125.00 to $185.00
Price: Single cased set (Navy Arms) $264.00

Walker 1847

Colt First Dragoon

COLT 1st MODEL DRAGOON
Caliber: 44.
Barrel: 7½", part round, part octagon.
Weight: 66 oz.
Stocks: One piece walnut.
Sights: German silver blade front, hammer notch rear.
Features: First model has oval bolt cuts in cylinder, square-back flared trigger guard, V-type mainspring, short trigger. Ranger and Indian scene on cylinder. Color cased frame, loading lever, plunger and hammer; blue barrel, cylinder, trigger and wedge. Polished brass backstrap and trigger guard. Re-introduced in 1979. From Colt.
Price: $447.95

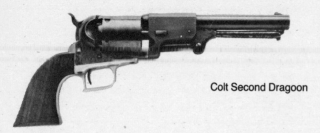

Colt Second Dragoon

Colt 2nd Model Dragoon Revolver
Similar to the 1st Model except this model is distinguished by its rectangular bolt cuts in the cylinder, straight square-back trigger guard, short trigger and flat mainspring with roller in hammer.
Price: **$447.95**

Colt 3rd Model Dragoon Revolver
Similar to the 1st Model except has oval trigger guard, long trigger, flat mainspring and rectangular bolt cuts.
Price: **$447.95**

Dixie Third Dragoon

DIXIE THIRD MODEL DRAGOON
Caliber: 44 ((.454″ round ball).
Barrel: 7⅜″.
Weight: 4 lbs., 2½ oz.
Stocks: One-piece walnut.
Sights: Brass pin front, hammer notch rear.
Features: Cylinder engraved with Indian fight scene; steel backstrap with polished brass backstrap; color case-hardened steel frame, blue-black barrel. Imported by Dixie Gun Works.
Price: **$140.00**

Dixie Baby Dragoon

BABY DRAGOON 1848 PERCUSSION REVOLVER
Caliber: 31, 5-shot.
Barrel: 4″, 5″, 6″.
Weight: 24 oz. (6″ bbl.). **Length:** 10½″ (6″ bbl.).
Stocks: Walnut.
Sights: Fixed.
Features: Case hardened frame; safety notches on hammer and safety pin in cylinder; engraved cylinder scene; octagonal bbl. Imported by Sile, F.I.E., Dixie.
Price: .... **$59.95 to $125.00**
Price: Fully engraved (F.I.E. Corp.) **$69.95**

NAVY MODEL 1851 PERCUSSION REVOLVER
Caliber: 36 or 44, 6-shot.
Barrel: 7½″.
Weight: 44 oz. **Length:** 13″ over-all.
Stocks: Walnut finish.
Sights: Post front, hammer notch rear.
Features: Brass backstrap and trigger guard; some have engraved cylinder with navy battle scene; case hardened frame, hammer, loading lever. Imported by Shore, (36 cal. only), The Armoury, Navy Arms, Valor, F.I.E., Dixie, (illus.) Richland, Euroarms of America, Sile, Armsport, Hopkins & Allen, CVA.
Price: Brass frame .... **$31.50 to $119.95**
Price: Steel frame .... **$40.95 to $140.95**
Price: Kit form .... **$30.95 to $87.95**
Price: Engraved model (Dixie) **$97.50**
Price: Also as "Hartford Pistol," Kit (Richard) ...... **$59.95** Complete **$79.95**
Price: Also as "Hartford Dragoon Buntline" (Hopkins & Allen) **$166.95**
Price: Navy-Civilian model (Navy Arms) **$118.00**
Price: Single cased set, steel frame (Navy Arms) **$180.00**
Price: As above, civilian model (Navy Arms) **$185.00**
Price: Shoulder stock (Navy Arms) **$45.00**

Dixie 1851 Navy

ARMY 1851 PERCUSSION REVOLVER
Caliber: 44, 6-shot.
Barrel: 7½″.
Weight: 45 oz. **Length:** 13″ over-all.
Stocks: Walnut finish.
Sights: Fixed.
Features: 44 caliber version of the 1851 Navy. Imported by Sile, Valor, The Armoury.
Price: .... **$33.50 to $138.00**

COLT BABY DRAGOON REVOLVER
Caliber: 31.
Barrel: 4″, 7 groove, RH twist.
Weight: About 21 oz.
Stocks: Varnished walnut.
Sights: Brass pin front, hammer notch rear.
Features: Unfluted cylinder with Ranger and Indian scene; cupped cylinder pin; no grease grooves; one safety pin on cylinder and slot in hammer face; straight (flat) mainspring. Silver backstrap and trigger guard. Re-introduced in 1979. From Colt.
Price: **$404.95**

CAUTION: PRICES CHANGE. CHECK AT GUNSHOP.

BLACK POWDER REVOLVERS

Colt 1861 Navy

1851 NAVY-SHERIFF
Same as 1851 Sheriff model except: 4" barrel, fluted cylinder, belt ring in butt. Imported by Richland, Sile, Euroarms of America.
Price: .... $50.00 to $114.95

Colt 1851 Navy

Dixie New Model Army

Colt 1860 Army

LYMAN 44 NEW MODEL ARMY REVOLVER
Caliber: 44, 6-shot.
Barrel: 8".
Weight: 40 oz. **Length:** 13½" over-all.
Stocks: Walnut.
Sights: Fixed.
Features: Replica of 1858 Remington. Brass trigger guard and backstrap, case hardened hammer and trigger. Solid frame with top strap. Heavy duty nipples. From Lyman Products.
Price: $169.95
Price: Kit form. $134.95

Colt 1861 Navy Percussion Revolver
Similar to 1851 Navy except has round 7½" barrel, rounded trigger guard, German silver blade front sight, "creeping" loading lever.
Price: $419.50
Price: As above in stainless steel $472.50

1851 SHERIFF MODEL PERCUSSION REVOLVER
Caliber: 36, 44, 6-shot.
Barrel: 5".
Weight: 40 oz. **Length:** 10½" over-all.
Stocks: Walnut.
Sights: Fixed.
Features: Brass backstrap and trigger guard; engraved navy scene; case hardened frame, hammer, loading lever. Available with brass frame from some importers at slightly lower prices. Imported by Sile, The Armoury.
Price: Steel frame .... $41.95 to $110.00
Price: Brass frame .... $34.95 to $102.00
Price: Kit, brass or steel frame (Sile) $66.15

COLT 1851 NAVY PERCUSSION REVOLVER
Caliber: 36.
Barrel: 7½", octagonal, 7 groove, LH twist.
Weight: 42 oz.
Stocks: One-piece varnished walnut.
Sights: Brass pin front, hammer notch rear.
Features: Made in U.S. by Colt. Faithful reproduction of the original gun. Color cased frame, loading lever, plunger, hammer and latch. Blue cylinder, trigger, barrel, screws, wedge. Silver plated brass backstrap and square-back trigger guard. Accessories available. Re-introduced in 1979.
Price: $419.50
Price: As above in stainless steel $472.50

Lyman 1851 Squareback Navy 36
Same as standard Colt model except 36 cal. only, has square-back trigger guard, nickel plated backstrap, color case hardened frame.
Price: $154.95
Price: Kit form. $119.95

NEW MODEL 1858 ARMY PERCUSSION REVOLVER
Caliber: 36 or 44, 6-shot.
Barrel: 6½" or 8".
Weight: 40 oz. **Length:** 13½" over-all.
Stocks: Walnut.
Sights: Blade front, groove-in-frame rear.
Features: Replica of Remington Model 1858. Also available from some importers as Army Model Belt Revolver in 36 cal., shortened and lightened version of the 44. Target Model (Iver Johnson, Navy) has fully adj. target rear sight, target front, 36 or 44 ($74.95-$152.45). Imported by CVA, Dixie, Navy Arms, F.I.E., Iver Johnson, The Armoury, Shore (44 cal., 8" bbl. only), Richland, Euroarms of America (engraved and plain), Armsport, Sile.
Price: .... $49.95 to $163.95
Price: Kit form. .... $66.95 to $123.95
Price: Nickel finish (Navy Arms) $145.00
Price: Stainless steel (Euroarms, Navy Arms, Sile) ...... $140.00 to $200.00
Price: Target model (Sile, Euroarms, Navy Arms) .... $95.95 to $185.00

COLT 1860 ARMY PERCUSSION REVOLVER
Caliber: 44.
Barrel: 8", 7 grooves, LH twist.
Weight: 42 oz.
Stocks: One-piece walnut.
Sights: German silver front sight, hammer notch rear.
Features: Made in U.S. by Colt. Steel backstrap cut for shoulder stock; brass trigger guard. Cylinder has Navy scene. Color case hardened frame, hammer, loading lever. Basically a continuation of production with all original markings, etc. Original-type accessories available. Re-introduced 1979.
Price: Unfluted cylinder $430.50
Price: As above in stainless steel $484.50
Price: Fluted cylinder model. $455.50

BLACK POWDER REVOLVERS

Dixie 1860 Army

CVA 1861 ARMY REVOLVER
Caliber: 44, 6-shot.
Barrel: 8″ round.
Weight: 44 oz. **Length:** 13½″ over-all.
Stocks: One-piece walnut.
Sights: Blade front, hammer-notch rear.
Features: Engraved cylinder, creeping-style loading lever, solid brass trigger guard, blued barrel. Introduced 1982. From CVA.
Price: Finished $157.95
Price: Kit $121.95

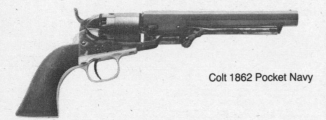

Colt 1862 Pocket Navy

Colt 1862 Pocket Police Revolver
Similar to 1862 Pocket Navy except has 5½″ round barrel, fluted cylinder, different markings and loading lever. Faithful reproduction of the original gun.
Price: $393.95
Price: As above in stainless steel $437.50

NAVY ARMS 1862 LEECH & RIGDON REVOLVER
Caliber: 375″.
Barrel: 7½″.
Weight: 2 lbs., 10 oz. **Length:** 13½″ over-all.
Stocks: Smooth walnut.
Sights: Fixed.
Features: Modern version of the famous Civil War revolver. Brass backstrap and trigger guard. Color case hardened frame. Copy of the Colt Navy but with round barrel. From Navy Arms.
Price: $125.00

GRISWOLD & GUNNISON PERCUSSION REVOLVER
Caliber: 36, 44, 6-shot.
Barrel: 7½″.
Weight: 44 oz. (36 cal.). **Length:** 13″ over-all.
Stocks: Walnut.
Sights: Fixed.
Features: Replica of famous Confederate pistol. Brass frame, backstrap and trigger guard; case hardened loading lever; rebated cylinder (44 cal. only). Imported by Navy Arms, Sile.
Price: $125.00
Price: As above from Sile (1851 Confederate) $75.90
Price: Kit (Navy Arms) $73.00
Price: Single cased set (Navy Arms) $150.50
Price: Shoulder stock (Navy Arms) $45.00

1860 ARMY PERCUSSION REVOLVER
Caliber: 44, 6-shot.
Barrel: 8″.
Weight: 40 oz. **Length:** 13⅝″ over-all.
Stocks: Walnut.
Sights: Fixed.
Features: Engraved navy scene on cylinder; brass trigger guard; case hardened frame, loading lever and hammer. Some importers supply pistol cut for detachable shoulder stock, have accessory stock available. Imported by Navy Arms, Shore, The Armoury, Dixie (half-fluted cylinder, not roll engraved), Lyman, Iver Johnson, Richland, Euroarms of America (engraved, burnished steel model), Armsport, Sile, Hopkins & Allen.
Price: .... $44.95 to $178.00
Price: Single cased set (Navy Arms) $194.00
Price: 1861 Navy: Same as Army except 36 cal., 7½″ bbl., wt. 41 oz., cut for stock; round cylinder (fluted avail.), from Navy $135.00
Price: Kit (Lyman) $134.95

1861 NAVY MODEL REVOLVER
Caliber: 36, 6-shot.
Barrel: 7½″.
Weight: 2½ lbs. **Length:** 13″ over-all.
Stocks: One piece smooth walnut.
Sights: Blade front, hammer notch rear.
Features: Shoots .380″ ball. Case hardened frame, loading lever and hammer. Cut for shoulder stock. Non-fluted cylinder. From CVA, Navy Arms, Armsport, Euroarms of America.
Price: .... $100.00 to $155.95
Price: With full fluted cyl. .... $100.00 to $135.00
Price: Single cased set (Navy Arms) $201.00
Price: Kit form (CVA) $114.95

COLT 1862 POCKET NAVY PERCUSSION REVOLVER
Caliber: 36.
Barrel: 5½″, octagonal, 7 groove, LH twist.
Weight: 27 oz.
Stocks: One piece varnished walnut.
Sights: Brass pin front, hammer notch rear.
Features: Made in U.S. by Colt. Rebated cylinder, hinged loading lever, silver plated backstrap and trigger guard, color cased frame, hammer, loading lever, plunger and latch, rest blued. Has original-type markings. Re-introduced 1979.
Price: $393.95
Price: As above in stainless steel $437.50

1862 POLICE MODEL PERCUSSION REVOLVER
Caliber: 36, 5-shot.
Barrel: 4½″, 5½″, 6½″.
Weight: 26 oz. **Length:** 12″ (6½″ bbl.).
Stocks: Walnut.
Sights: Fixed.
Features: Half-fluted and rebated cylinder; case hardened frame, loading lever and hammer; brass trigger guard and backstrap. Imported by Navy Arms (5½″ only), Euroarms of America.
Price: .... $125.00 to $165.00
Price: Cased with accessories (Navy Arms) $165.00

ROGERS & SPENCER PERCUSSION REVOLVER
Caliber: 44.
Barrel: 7½″.
Weight: 47 oz. **Length:** 10¾″ over-all.
Stocks: Walnut.
Sights: Cone front, integral groove in frame for rear.
Features: Accurate reproduction of a Civil War design. Solid frame; extra large nipple cut-out on rear of cylinder; loading lever and cylinder easily removed for cleaning. Comes with six spare nipples and wrench/screwdriver. From Euroarms of America, Navy Arms, Dixie, Sile.
Price: .... $120.00 to $160.00
Price: Nickel plated $120.00
Price: Kit version $95.00
Price: Target version $200.00

BLACK POWDER REVOLVERS

Dixie Spiller & Burr

SPILLER & BURR REVOLVER
Caliber: 36 (.375″ round ball).
Barrel: 7″, octagon.
Weight: 2½ lbs. **Length:** 12½″ over-all.
Stocks: Two-piece walnut.
Sights: Fixed.
Features: Reproduction of the C.S.A. revolver. Brass frame and trigger guard. Also available as a kit. From Dixie, Navy Arms.
Price: .... $69.95 to $100.00
Price: Kit form .... $39.95 to $65.00

Dixie "Wyatt Earp"

DIXIE "WYATT EARP" REVOLVER
Caliber: 44.
Barrel: 12″ octagon.
Weight: 46 oz. **Length:** 18″ over-all.
Stocks: Two piece walnut.
Sights: Fixed.
Features: Highly polished brass frame, backstrap and trigger guard; blued barrel and cylinder; case hardened hammer, trigger and loading lever. Navy-size shoulder stock ($45.00) will fit with minor fitting. From Dixie Gun Works.
Price: $99.95

Ruger Old Army

RUGER 44 OLD ARMY PERCUSSION REVOLVER
Caliber: 44, 6-shot. Uses .457″ dia. lead bullets.
Barrel: 7½″ (6-groove, 16″ twist).
Weight: 46 oz. **Length:** 13½″ over-all.
Stocks: Smooth walnut.
Sights: Ramp front, rear adj. for w. and e.
Features: Stainless steel standard size nipples, chrome-moly steel cylinder and frame, same lockwork as in original Super Blackhawk. Also available in stainless steel in very limited quantities. Made in USA. From Sturm, Ruger & Co.
Price: Stainless steel (Model KBP-7) $285.00
Price: Blued steel (Model BP-7) $216.50

BLACK POWDER MUSKETS & RIFLES

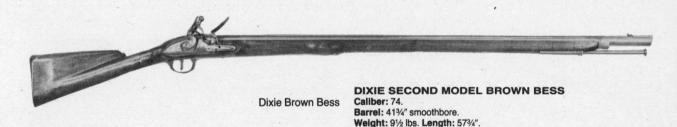

Dixie Brown Bess

DIXIE SECOND MODEL BROWN BESS
Caliber: 74.
Barrel: 41¾″ smoothbore.
Weight: 9½ lbs. **Length:** 57¾″.
Stock: Walnut-finished hardwood.
Sights: Fixed.
Features: All metal finished bright. Brass furniture. Lock marked "Tower" and has a crown with "GR" underneath. From Dixie Gun Works.
Price: $275.00
Price: Kit form $245.00

NAVY ARMS BROWN BESS MUSKET
Caliber: 75, uses .735″ round ball.
Barrel: 42″, smoothbore.
Weight: 9½ lbs. **Length:** 59″ over-all.
Stock: Walnut.
Sights: Fixed.
Features: Polished barrel and lock with brass trigger guard and buttplate. From Navy Arms.
Price: Finished $400.00
Price: Kit $325.00
Price: Finished gun with maple stock $275.00

CVA Big Bore Mountain Rifle
Similar to the standard Mountain Rifle except comes in 54 or 58 cal. only. Barrel flats measure 1″ across. Stock does not have a patch box. Introduced 1980.
Price: 54 cal., percussion, complete rifle $294.95
Price: 54 cal., percussion, kit $209.95
Price: 58 cal. percussion, 1-72″ twist, kit only $209.95

CVA MOUNTAIN RIFLE
Caliber: 50.
Barrel: 32″, octagon; ¹⁵⁄₁₆″ across flats; 1-66″ twist.
Weight: 8 lbs. **Length:** 48″ over-all.
Stock: Select hardwood with cheekpiece.
Sights: German silver blade front, screw-adj. rear.
Features: Available in percussion or flintlock. Engraved lock with adj. sear engagement; hooked breech with two barrel tenons; rifled 1-in-66″; double set triggers; German silver patch box, tenon plates, pewter-type nosecap; browned iron furniture. From CVA.
Price: Kit, percussion $189.95
Price: Kit, flintlock $199.95
Price: Finished rifle, percussion $284.95
Price: Finished rifle, flintlock $294.95

BLACK POWDER MUSKETS & RIFLES

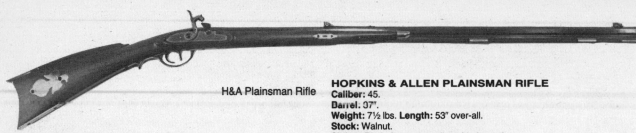

H&A Plainsman Rifle

HOPKINS & ALLEN PLAINSMAN RIFLE
Caliber: 45.
Barrel: 37".
Weight: 7½ lbs. **Length:** 53" over-all.
Stock: Walnut.
Sights: Blade front, rear adjustable for w. & e.
Features: Double set triggers, blued barrel has $^{13}/_{16}$" flats, solid brass barrel rib, engraved percussion lockplate. From Hopkins & Allen.
Price: $292.60

CVA KENTUCKY RIFLE
Caliber: 45 (.451" bore).
Barrel: 32", rifled, octagon (⅞" flats).
Length: 48" over-all.
Stock: Select hardwood.
Sights: Brass Kentucky blade type front, dovetail open rear.
Features: Available in either flint or percussion. Stainless steel nipple included. From CVA.
Price: Percussion... $184.95
Price: Flint... $194.95
Price: Percussion Kit.. $109.95
Price: Flint Kit.. $117.95

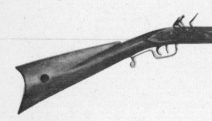

Dixie Tennessee Rifle

DIXIE TENNESSEE MOUNTAIN RIFLE
Caliber: 32 or 50.
Barrel: 41½", 6-groove rifling, brown finish.
Length: 56" over-all.
Stock: Walnut, oil finish; Kentucky-style.
Sights: Silver blade front, open buckhorn rear.
Features: Re-creation of the original mountain rifles. Early Schultz lock, interchangeable flint or percussion with vent plug or drum and nipple. Tumbler has fly. Double-set triggers. All metal parts browned. From Dixie.
Price: Flint or Percussion, finished rifle, 50 cal. $225.00
Price: Kit, 50 cal. $175.00
Price: Left-hand model, flint or perc.......................... $245.00
Price: Left-hand kit, flint or perc., 50 cal. $225.00
Price: Squirrel Rifle (as above except in 32 cal. with $^{13}/_{16}$" barrel), flint or percussion $295.00
Price: Kit, 32 cal., flint or percussion $255.00

TRYON RIFLE
Caliber: 50, 54 cal.
Barrel: 34", octagon; 1-63" twist.
Weight: 9 lbs. **Length:** 49" over-all.
Stock: European walnut with steel furniture.
Sights: Blade front, fixed rear.
Features: Reproduction of an American plains rifle with double set triggers and back-action lock. Imported from Italy by Trail Guns Armory.
Price: Percussion only $350.00

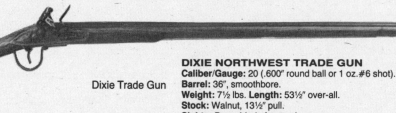

Dixie Trade Gun

DIXIE NORTHWEST TRADE GUN
Caliber/Gauge: 20 (.600" round ball or 1 oz.#6 shot).
Barrel: 36", smoothbore.
Weight: 7½ lbs. **Length:** 53½" over-all.
Stock: Walnut, 13½" pull.
Sights: Brass blade front only.
Features: Flintlock. Brass buttplate, serpentine sideplate; browned barrel, Wheeler flint lock, triggerguard; hickory ramrod with brass tip. From Dixie Gun Works.
Price: $399.95

Lyman Trade Rifle

LYMAN TRADE RIFLE
Caliber: 50 or 54.
Barrel: 28" octagon, 1-48" twist.
Weight: 8¾ lbs. **Length:** 45" over-all.
Stock: European walnut.
Sights: Blade front, open rear adj. for w.
Features: Polished brass furniture with blue steel parts. Hook breech, single trigger, coil spring percussion lock. Steel barrel rib and ramrod ferrules. Introduced 1979. From Lyman.
Price: Percussion... $269.95
Price: Kit, percussion $199.95
Price: Flintlock $279.95
Price: Kit, flintlock $214.95

BLACK POWDER MUSKETS & RIFLES

Lyman Great Plains

LYMAN GREAT PLAINS RIFLE
Caliber: 50 or 54 cal.
Barrel: 32", 1-66" twist.
Weight: 9 lbs.
Stock: Walnut.
Sights: Steel blade front, buckhorn rear adj. for w. & e.
Features: Browned steel furniture. Coil spring lock, Hawken-style trigger guard and double set triggers. Round thimbles recessed and sweated into rib. Steel wedge plates and toe plates. Introduced 1980. From Lyman.
Price: Percussion... $354.95
Price: Flintlock $369.95
Price: Percussion Kit... $249.95

CVA FRONTIER RIFLE
Caliber: 50.
Barrel: 28", octagon; ¹⁵/₁₆" flats, 1-66" twist.
Weight: 6 lbs., 14 oz. **Length:** 44" over-all.
Stock: American hardwood.
Sights: Brass blade front, fully adjustable hunting-style rear.
Features: Available in flint or percussion. Solid brass nosecap, trigger guard, buttplate, thimbles and wedge plates; blued barrel; color case-hardened lock and hammer. Double set triggers, patented breech plug bolster, V-type main-spring. Hooked breech. Introduced 1980.
Price: 50 cal., percussion, complete rifle......................... $204.95
Price: 50-Cal. flint, complete rifle $214.95
Price: 50 cal., percussion, kit.................................. $149.95
Price: 50 cal. flint, kit....................................... $159.95

PENNSYLVANIA HALF-STOCK PLAINS RIFLE
Caliber: 45 or 50.
Barrel: 32" rifled, ¹⁵/₁₆" dia.
Weight: 8½ lbs.
Stock: Walnut.
Sights: Fixed.
Features: Available in flint or percussion. Blued lock and barrel, brass furniture. Offered complete or in kit form. From The Armory.
Price: Flint... $235.00
Price: Percussion... $210.00

H & A Buggy Rifle

HOPKINS & ALLEN BUGGY RIFLE
Caliber: 45.
Barrel: 20", 25" or 32", octagonal.
Weight: 6½ lbs. **Length:** 37" over-all.
Stock: American walnut.
Features: A short under-hammer rifle. Blued barrel and receiver, black plastic buttplate.
Price: 20" or 25" bbl.. $189.50
Price: 32" bbl.. $204.42

ALAMO LONG RIFLE
Caliber: 38, 45, 50 cal.
Barrel: 35".
Weight: 7½ lbs. **Length:** 51" over-all.
Stock: European walnut.
Sights: Blade front, fixed rear.
Features: Double set trigger. Blued octagon barrel, bright lock, brass trigger guard, patch box, buttplate, thimbles. Has Alamo battle scene engraved on patch box. Imported from Italy by Trail Guns Armory.
Price: Percussion... $265.00
Price: Flintlock $275.00

Kentucky Percussion Rifle
Similar to flintlock except percussion lock. Finish and features vary with importer. Imported by Navy Arms, F.I.E. Corp., The Armoury, CVA, Hopkins & Allen, Armsport (rifle-shotgun combo), Shore, Sile.
Price:... $54.95 to 250.00
Price: Kit form (F.I.E., Sile).................................. $169.95
Price: Armsport combo $295.00
Price: Deluxe model (Navy Arms).............................. $375.00
Price: 50 cal. (Navy Arms)................................... $235.00

KENTUCKY FLINTLOCK RIFLE
Caliber: 44 or 45.
Barrel: 35".
Weight: 7lbs. **Length:** 50" over-all.
Stock: Walnut stained, brass fittings.
Sights: Fixed.
Features: Available in Carbine model also, 28" bbl. Some variations in detail, finish. Kits also available from some importers. Imported by Navy Arms, The Armoury, Challenger, F.I.E., CVA, Armsport, Hopkins & Allen, Sile, Shore (45-cal. only).
Price:... $59.95 to $250.00
Price: Kit form (CVA, Numrich, F.I.E., Sile).............. $72.95 to 189.95
Price: Deluxe model, flint or percussion (Navy Arms, Sile), about ... $400.00
Price: As above, 50-cal. (Navy Arms) $260.00

Kentuckian Rifle

KENTUCKIAN RIFLE & CARBINE
Caliber: 44.
Barrel: 35" (Rifle), 27½" (Carbine).
Weight: 7 lbs. (Rifle), 5½ lbs. (Carbine). **Length:** 51" (Rifle) over-all, Carbine 43".
Stock: Walnut stain.
Sights: Brass blade front, steel V-Ramp rear.
Features: Octagon bbl., case hardened and engraved lock plate. Brass furniture. Imported by Dixie.
Price: Rifle or carbine, flint.................................. $185.00
Price: As above, percussion $175.00

BLACK POWDER MUSKETS & RIFLES

Dixie York County

YORK COUNTY RIFLE
Caliber: 45 (.445″ round ball)
Barrel: 36″, rifled, ⅞″ octagon, blue
Weight: 7½ lbs. **Length:** 51½″ over-all.
Stock: Maple, one piece.
Sights: Blade front, V-notch rear, brass.
Features: Adjustable double-set triggers. Brass trigger guard, patchbox, butt-plate, nosecap and sideplate. Case-hardened lockplate. From Dixie Gun Works.
Price: Percussion. **$165.00**
Price: Flint. **$179.95**
Price: Percussion Kit. **$139.95**
Price: Flint Kit. **$149.95**

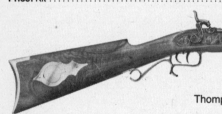

Mowrey Squirrel Rifle

MOWREY ETHAN ALLEN SQUIRREL RIFLE
Caliber: 32, 36, or 45.
Barrel: 28″, 8-groove rifling, octagon, 1:60 twist.
Weight: 7½ lbs. **Length:** 43″ over-all.
Stock: Curly maple.
Sights: Open, fully adj.
Features: Box-lock action, cut-rifled barrel, hand-rubbed oil finish. Available with either brass or steel furniture, action. Made in U.S.
Price: Complete. **$328.00**
Price: Kit. **$237.00**

Mowrey Ethan Allen Plains Rifle
Similar to Squirrel Rifle except in 50 or 54 caliber, 32″ barrel, weighs 9½ lbs.
Price: Complete. **$328.00**
Price: Kit. **$237.00**

Thompson/Center Hawken

THOMPSON/CENTER HAWKEN RIFLE
Caliber: 45, 50 or 54.
Barrel: 28″ octagon, hooked breech.
Stock: American walnut.
Sights: Blade front, rear adj. for w. & e.
Features: Solid brass furniture, double set triggers, button rifled barrel, coil-type main spring. From Thompson/Center Arms.
Price: Percussion Model (45, 50 or 54 cal.) **$270.00**
Price: Flintlock model (45, 50, or 54 cal.) **$282.50**
Price: Percussion kit. **$185.00**
Price: Flintlock kit. **$197.50**

T/C Hawken Cougar

Thompson/Center Hawken Cougar
Similar to the standard T/C Hawken except stock is of highly figured walnut; all furniture—lock plate, hammer, triggers, trigger plate, trigger guard, fore-end cap, thimbles escutcheons, etc. are of stainless steel with matte finish. Replacing the patch box is a stainless steel medallion cast in deep relief depicting a crouching cougar. Internal parts, breech plug, tang, barrel, sights and under rib are ordnance steel. Barrel, sights and under rib are blued. Butt-plate is solid brass, hard chromed to match the stainless parts. Limited production. Introduced 1982. From Thompson/Center Arms.
Price: **$550.00**

THOMPSON/CENTER RENEGADE RIFLE
Caliber: 50 and 54 plus 56 cal., smoothbore.
Barrel: 26″, 1″ across the flats.
Weight: 8 lbs.
Stock: American walnut.
Sights: Open hunting (Patridge) style, fully adjustable for w. and e.
Features: Coil spring lock, double set triggers, blued steel trim.
Price: Percussion model. **$205.00**
Price: Flintlock model, 50 and 54 cal. only **$217.50**
Price: Percussion kit. **$165.00**
Price: Flintlock kit. **$177.50**

THOMPSON/CENTER SENECA RIFLE
Caliber: 36, 45.
Barrel: 27″.
Weight: 6½ lbs.
Stock: American walnut.
Sights: Open hunting style, square notch rear fully adj. for w. and e.
Features: Coil spring lock, octagon bbl. measures ¹³/₁₆″ across flats, brass stock furniture.
Price: **$270.00**

BLACK POWDER MUSKETS & RIFLES

Buffalo Hunter Rifle

ARMOURY R140 HAWKIN RIFLE
Caliber: 45, 50 or 54.
Barrel: 29″.
Weight: 8¾ to 9 lbs. **Length:** 45¾″ over-all.
Stock: Walnut, with cheekpiece.
Sights: Dovetail front, fully adjustable rear.
Features: Octagon barrel, removable breech plug; double set triggers; blued barrel, brass stock fittings, color case hardened percussion lock. From Armsport, The Armoury, Sile.
Price: .... $175.00 to $282.00
Price: Kit .... $205.70 to $210.00

BUFFALO HUNTER PERCUSSION RIFLE
Caliber: 58.
Barrel: 25½″.
Weight: 8 lbs. **Length:** 41½″ over-all.
Stock: Walnut finished, hand checkered, brass furniture.
Sights: Fixed.
Features: Designed for primitive weapons hunting. 20 ga. shotgun bbl. also available $90.00. Imported by Navy Arms, Dixie.
Price: .... $215.00 to $250.00

SILE HAWKEN HUNTER CARBINE
Caliber: 45, 50, 54.
Barrel: 22″, full octagon with hooked breech and hard chrome smooth bore.
Weight: 7 lbs. **Length:** 38″ over-all.
Stock: Walnut with checkered p.g. and fore-end, rubber recoil pad.
Sights: Blade front, fully adjustable open rear.
Features: Black oxidized brass hardware, engraved case hardened lock plate, sear fly and coil spring mechanism. Stainless steel nipple. Adjustable double set triggers. From Sile Dist.
Price: Percussion, rifle or carbine $261.00
Price: Flintlock $271.80

Navy Hawken Mark I

DELUXE HAWKEN RIFLE
Caliber: 50.
Barrel: 28″.
Weight: 7 lbs. **Length:** 43½″ over-all.
Stock: Dark polished walnut.
Sights: Blade front, open rear adj. for w.
Features: Brass patchbox, trigger guard, buttplate and furniture; color case hardened lock, rest blued. From F.I.E. Corp., Toledo Armas.
Price: $174.95
Price: Kit form $159.95
Price: Finished flintlock model $239.95

NAVY ARMS MARK I HAWKEN RIFLE
Caliber: 50 and 54.
Barrel: 26″.
Weight: 9 lbs. **Length:** 43″ over-all.
Stock: American walnut with cheek rest.
Sights: Blade front, adjustable Williams rear.
Features: Designed specifically for maxi-ball shooting. Double set triggers, blued barrel, polished brass furniture. Stainless steel chamber insert. Flint or percussion. Made in U.S. by Navy Arms.
Price: Finished, percussion, 50 or 54 .... $249.00
Price: As above, kit $166.95
Price: Finished, flintlock, 50 or 54 .... $259.00
Price: As above, kit $176.95

Dixie Hawken Rifle

CVA HAWKEN RIFLE
Caliber: 50 or 54.
Barrel: 28″, octagon; 1″ across flats; 1-66″ twist.
Weight: 7 lbs. 15 oz. **Length:** 44″ over-all.
Stock: Select walnut.
Sights: Beaded blade front, fully adj. open rear.
Features: Fully adj. double set triggers; brass patch box, wedge plates, nose cap, thimbles, trigger guard and buttplate; blued barrel; color case-hardened, engraved lockplate. Percussion or flintlock. Hooked breech. Introduced 1981.
Price: Finished rifle, percussion $249.95
Price: Finished rifle, flintlock $259.95
Price: Kit, percussion $167.95
Price: Kit, flintlock $177.95

HAWKEN RIFLE
Caliber: 45, 50, 54 or 58.
Barrel: 28″, blued, 6-groove rifling.
Weight: 8¾ lbs. **Length:** 44″ over-all.
Stock: Walnut with cheekpiece.
Sights: Blade front, fully adj. rear.
Features: Coil mainspring, double set triggers, polished brass furniture. Also available with chrome plated bore or in flintlock model from Sile. Introduced 1977. From Kassnar, Sile, Dixie (45 or 50 only, walnut stock), Armsport, Toledo Armas, Shore and Hopkins & Allen, 50-cal. only.
Price: .... $175.00 to $252.95
Price: Hard chrome bore, Sile, about $238.95
Price: True left-hand rifle, flint and percussion (Kassnar) $299.95

Armsport Hawken Rifle-Shotgun Combo
Similar to Hawken above except 50-cal. only, with 20 gauge shotgun barrel. From Armsport.
Price: $250.00

Dixie Wesson Rifle

RICHLAND PERCUSSION WESSON RIFLE
Caliber: 50.
Barrel: 28″; 1⅛″ octagon.
Length: 45″ over-all.
Stock: Walnut.
Sights: Blade front, rear adj. for e.
Features: Adjustable double set triggers, color case hardened frame. Introduced 1977. From Richland Arms.
Price: With false muzzle $295.00
Price: Engraved version $412.00

Dixie Wesson Rifle
Similar to the Richland version except barrel is fitted with a false muzzle, hand checkered stock and fore-end. Comes with loading rod and loading accessories. From Dixie Gun Works.
Price: $325.00

Jonathan Browning Rifle

JONATHAN BROWNING PERCUSSION MOUNTAIN RIFLE
Caliber: 45, 50 or 54.
Barrel: 30″, 1″ across flats.
Stock: Traditional half-stock with semi-cheekpiece.
Sights: Blade front, buckhorn rear screw-adj. for e.
Features: Single set trigger; hooked breech. 45-cal. rifled 1 in 56″, 50-cal. rifled 1 in 62″, 54-cal. rifled 1 in 66″ twist. Offered in choice of browned steel or brass finish on buttplate, trigger guard and complimentary furniture. Hickory ramrod with brass ends. Spare nipple and cleaning jag included. Introduced 1977. Made in U.S. by Browning.
Price: Brass or browned furniture, 45, 50 or 54 cal. $449.95

ITHACA-NAVY HAWKEN RIFLE
Caliber: 50 and 54.
Barrel: 32″ octagonal, 1-inch dia.
Weight: About 9 lbs.
Stock: Black walnut.
Sights: Blade front, rear adj. for w.
Features: Completely made in U.S. Hooked breech, 1⅞″ throw percussion lock. Attached twin thimbles and under-rib. German silver barrel key inlays, Hawken-style toe and buttplates, lock bolt inlays, barrel wedges, entry thimble, trigger guard, ramrod and cleaning jag, nipple and nipple wrench. American made. Introduced 1977. Made in U.S. by Navy Arms.
Price: Complete, percussion $395.00
Price: Kit, percussion $275.00
Price: Complete, flint $425.00
Price: Kit, flint $300.00

Consult our Directory pages for
the location of firms mentioned.

Parker-Hale Whitworth

PARKER-HALE WHITWORTH MILITARY TARGET RIFLE
Caliber: 45.
Barrel: 36″.
Weight: 9¼ lbs. **Length:** 52½″ over-all.
Stock: Walnut. Checkered at wrist and fore-end.
Sights: Hooded post front, open step-adjustable rear.
Features: Faithful reproduction of the Whitworth rifle, only bored for 45-cal. Trigger has a detented lock, capable of being adjusted very finely without risk of the sear nose catching on the half-cock bent and damaging both parts. Introduced 1978. Imported from England by Navy Arms.
Price: $575.00

Parker-Hale 1861

PARKER-HALE ENFIELD 1861 CARBINE
Caliber: 577.
Barrel: 24″.
Weight: 7½ lbs. **Length:** 40¼″ over-all.
Stock: Walnut.
Sights: Fixed front, adj. rear.
Features: Percussion muzzle loader, made to original 1861 English patterns. Imported from England by Navy Arms.
Price: $300.00
Price: As made by Navy Arms, finished or kit $175.00

CAUTION: PRICES CHANGE. CHECK AT GUNSHOP.

BLACK POWDER MUSKETS & RIFLES

Parker-Hale Volunteer

PARKER-HALE VOLUNTEER RIFLE
Caliber: .451″.
Barrel: 32″.
Weight: 9½ lbs. **Length:** 49″ over-all.
Stock: Walnut, checkered wrist and fore-end.
Sights: Globe front, adjustable ladder-type rear.
Features: Recreation of the type of gun issued to volunteer regiments during the 1860's. Rigby-pattern rifling, patent breech, detented lock. Stock is glass bedded for accuracy. Comes with comprehensive accessory/shooting kit. From Navy Arms.
Price: **$575.00**

PARKER-HALE ENFIELD PATTERN 1858 NAVAL RIFLE
Caliber: .577″.
Barrel: 33″.
Weight: 8½ lbs. **Length:** 48½″ over-all.
Stock: European walnut.
Sights: Blade front, step adj. rear.
Features: Two-band Enfield percussion rifle with heavy barrel. 5-groove progressive depth rifling, solid brass furniture. All parts made exactly to original patterns. Imported from England by Navy Arms.
Price: **$370.00**

Parker-Hale 1853

PARKER-HALE ENFIELD 1853 MUSKET
Caliber: .577″.
Barrel: 39″, 3-groove cold-forged rifling.
Weight: About 9 lbs. **Length:** 55″ over-all.
Stock: Seasoned walnut.
Sights: Fixed front, rear step adj. for elevation.
Features: Three band musket made to original specs from original gauges. Solid brass stock furniture, color hardened lock plate, hammer; blued barrel, trigger. Imported from England by Navy Arms.
Price: **$400.00**

Parker-Hale 1858

London Armory Co. 3-Band Musket
Re-creation of the famed London Armory Company Pattern 1862 Enfield Musket. One-piece walnut stock, brass buttplate, trigger guard and nosecap. Lockplate marked "London Armoury Co." and with a British crown. Blued Baddeley barrel bands. From Dixie, Euroarms of America.
Price: **$285.00**
Price: **$280.00**

NAVY ARMS 2-BAND ENFIELD 1858
Caliber: .577 Minie, .575 round ball.
Barrel: 33″.
Weight: 10 lbs. **Length:** 49″ over-all.
Stock: Walnut.
Sights: Folding leaf rear adjustable for elevation.
Features: Blued barrel, color case-hardened lock and hammer, polished brass buttplate, trigger guard, nose cap. From Navy Arms.
Price: **$290.00**

Navy 3-Band Enfield

NAVY ARMS 3-BAND 1853 ENFIELD
Caliber: 58 (577 Minie, 575 round ball, 580 maxi ball).
Barrel: 39″.
Weight: 9½ lbs. **Length:** 54″ over-all.
Stock: European walnut.
Sights: Inverted "V" front, traditional Enfield folding ladder rear.
Features: Faithful reproduction of the Confederate-used rifle. Blued barrel, brass buttplate, trigger guard, nose cap. From Navy Arms.
Price: **$300.00**

ERMA-EXCAM GALLAGER CARBINE
Caliber: 54 (.540″ ball).
Barrel: 22⅓″.
Weight: 7¼ lbs. **Length:** 39″ over-all.
Stock: European walnut.
Sights: Post front, rear adjustable for w. & e.
Features: Faithful reproduction of the 1860 breech-loading carbine. Made in West Germany. Imported by Excam. Introduced 1978.
Price: **$373.00**

F.I.E. PERCUSSION BERDAN RIFLE
Caliber: 45.
Barrel: 25″, rifled, octagon.
Weight: 7 lbs. **Length:** 42¾″ over-all.
Stock: Walnut-finished hardwood.
Sights: Brass blade front, adj. open rear.
Features: Double-set triggers; brass trigger guard, patch box and buttplate. From F.I.E. Corp.
Price: **$87.95**

BLACK POWDER MUSKETS & RIFLES

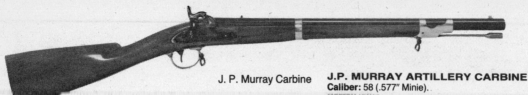

J. P. Murray Carbine

U.S. M-1862 REMINGTON CONTRACT RIFLE
Caliber: 58.
Barrel: 33".
Weight: 9½ lbs. **Length:** 48½" over-all.
Stock: Walnut, brass furniture.
Sights: Blade front, folding 3-leaf rear.
Features: Re-creation of the 1862 military rifle. Each rifle furnished with two stainless steel nipples. From Euroarms of America.
Price: About $200.00

Shiloh New Model 1863 Sharps Carbine
Shortened, carbine version of the 1863 rifle. Caliber 54. Has 22" barrel, black walnut stock without patch box, single barrel band. Weighs 8 lbs., 12 oz., over-all length is 39⅛". Made in U.S. by Shiloh Rifle Co. Available from C. Sharps Arms Co.
Price: $445.00

J.P. MURRAY ARTILLERY CARBINE
Caliber: 58 (.577" Minie).
Barrel: 23½".
Weight: 7 lbs., 9 oz. **Length:** 39" over-all.
Stock: Walnut.
Sights: Blade front, rear drift adj. for windage.
Features: Browned barrel, color case-hardened lock, blued swivel and band springs, polished brass buttplate, trigger guard, barrel bands. From Navy Arms.
Price: $250.00

COOK & BROTHER CONFEDERATE CARBINE
Caliber: 58.
Barrel: 24".
Weight: 7½ lbs. **Length:** 40½" over-all.
Stock: Select walnut.
Features: Re-creation of the 1861 New Orleans-made artillery carbine. Color case-hardened lock, browned barrel. Buttplate, trigger guard, barrel bands, sling swivels and nosecap of polished brass. From Euroarms of America.
Price: $190.00

Dixie Sharps Rifle

Dixie Sharps Rifle
Similar to the Shiloh Sharps except has 28½" barrel, checkered half-stock fore-end and stock wrist, flat lockplate. Carbine-style case hardened buttplate. Imported from Italy by Dixie Gun Works.
Price: $300.00
Price: Military Carbine (22" barrel) $250.00

SHILOH NEW MODEL 1863 SHARPS RIFLE
Caliber: 54.
Barrel: 30", 1-in 48".
Weight: 8¾ lbs. **Length:** 47" over-all.
Stock: Black walnut, oil finish.
Sights: Blade front, rear leaf adj. for e.
Features: Duplicate of original percussion rifle. Receiver, sideplate, hammer, buttplate, patch box color hardened; barrel is blue-black. Twelve different models of the Sharps now available in many original chamberings. Made in U.S. by Shiloh Rifle Co. Available from C. Sharps Arms Co.
Price: $575.00

Dixie 1863 Musket

SHARPS MILITARY CARBINE
Caliber: 54 Sharps.
Barrel: 22", round, polished blue.
Weight: 7¾ lbs. **Length:** 39" over-all.
Stock: Walnut.
Sights: Blade front, rear adj. for w. and e.
Features: Faithful reproduction of the original 1863 carbine. Receiver, sideplate, hammer and buttplate are color case hardened. Rifle model has 28" barrel, checkered p.g. and fore-end. Six different models of the Sharps are now available. Introduced 1977. From Shore.
Price: Carbine, about $283.95
Price: Rifle, about $300.00

NAVY ARMS 1863 SPRINGFIELD
Caliber: 58, uses .575" mini-ball.
Barrel: 40", rifled.
Weight: 9½ lbs. **Length:** 56" over-all.
Stock: Walnut.
Sights: Open rear adj. for elevation.
Features: Full-size 3-band musket. Polished bright metal, including lock. From Navy Arms.
Price: Finished rifle $350.00
Price: Kit $295.00

DIXIE 1863 SPRINGFIELD MUSKET
Caliber: 58 (.570" patched ball or .575 Minie).
Barrel: 50", rifled.
Stock: Walnut stained.
Sights: Blade front, adjustable ladder-type rear.
Features: Bright-finish lock, barrel, furniture. Reproduction of the last of the regulation muzzle loaders. Imported from Japan by Dixie Gun Works.
Price: Finished $265.00
Price: Kit $225.00

SHILOH SHARPS 1874 MILITARY RIFLE
Caliber: 45-70, 50-70.
Barrel: 30", Round.
Weight: 8¾ lbs.
Stock: American walnut.
Sights: Blade front, Lawrence-style open rear.
Features: Military-style fore-end with three barrel bands and 1¼" sling swivels. Color case-hardened receiver, buttplate and barrel bands, blued barrel. Re-creation of the original Sharps rifles. Five other models in many original chamberings available. From C. Sharps Arms Co.
Price: 1874 Military Rifle $575.00
Price: 1874 Carbine $445.00
Price: 1874 Business Rifle $535.00
Price: 1874 Sporting Rifle No. 1 . . . . $649.00
Price: 1874 Sporting Rifle No. 3 . . . . $579.00
Price: 1874 Long Range Express Sporting Rifle $699.00

BLACK POWDER MUSKETS & RIFLES

Dixie Zouave Rifle

ZOUAVE PERCUSSION RIFLE
Caliber: 58, 59.
Barrel: 32½".
Weight: 9½ lbs. **Length:** 48½" over-all.
Stock: Walnut finish, brass patch box and buttplate.
Sights: Fixed front, rear adj. for e.
Features: Some small details may vary with importers. Also available from Navy Arms as carbine, with 22" bbl. Extra 20 ga. shotgun bbl. $45.00. Imported by Navy Arms, Shore (58-cal. only), F.I.E., Dixie.
Price: .... $87.95 to $265.00
Price: Kit form (Sile) $165.00
Price: Deluxe Model (Navy Arms).......................... $325.00

Mississippi Model 1841 Percussion Rifle
Similar to Zouave Rifle but patterned after U.S. Model 1841. Imported by Navy Arms, Dixie.
Price: .... $225.00 to $275.00.

Consult our Directory pages for
the location of firms mentioned.

KODIAK DOUBLE RIFLE
Caliber: 58x58, 50x50 and 58-cal./12 ga. optional.
Barrel: 28", 5 grooves, 1-in-48" twist.
Weight: 9½ lbs. **Length:** 43¼" over-all.
Stock: Czechoslovakian walnut, hand checkered.
Sights: Adjustable bead front, adjustable open rear.
Features: Hooked breech allows interchangeability of barrels. Comes with sling and swivels, adjustable powder measure, bullet mould and bullet starter. Engraved lock plates, top tang and trigger guard. Locks and top tang polished, rest blued. Imported from Italy by Trail Guns Armory, Inc.
Price: 58 cal. SxS $495.00
Price: 50 cal. SxS $495.00
Price: 50 cal. x 12 ga., 58x12. .... $495.00
Price: Spare barrels, 58 cal. SxS, 50 cal. SxS $294.25
Price: Spare barrels, 58x12 ga. $294.25
Price: Spare barrels, 12 ga. x 12 ga. $160.00

MORSE/NAVY RIFLE
Caliber: 45, 50 or 58.
Barrel: 26", octagonal.
Weight: 6 lbs. (45 cal.). **Length:** 41½" over-all.
Stock: American walnut, full p.g.
Sights: Blade front, open fixed rear.
Features: Brass action, trigger guard, ramrod pipes. Made in U.S. by Navy Arms.
Price: $149.95
Price: Kit $100.00

Sanftl Schuetzen Rifle

SANFTL SCHUETZEN PERCUSSION TARGET RIFLE
Caliber: 45 (.445" round ball).
Barrel: 29", ⅞" octagon.
Weight: 9 lbs. **Length:** 43" over-all.
Stock: Walnut, Schuetzen-style.
Sights: Open tunnel front post, peep rear adjustable for windage & elevation.
Features: True back-action lock with "backward" hammer; screw-in breech plug; buttplate, trigger guard and stock inlays are polished brass. Imported from Italy by Dixie Gun Works.
Price: $595.00

BLACK POWDER SHOTGUNS

Beretta O/U Shotgun

BERETTA MODEL 1000 MUZZLE LOADING O-U SHOTGUN
Gauge: 12 only.
Barrel: 30".
Weight: About 7 lbs. **Length:** 46½" over-all.
Stock: Walnut; English-style with checkpiece.
Features: Special limited production replica of an early Beretta over-under. Silvered, engraved lockplates, trigger guard, hammers, barrel bands. Ramrod fits on right side of blued barrels. Introduced 1981. Imported from Italy by Beretta U.S.A. Corp.
Price: $840.00

BLACK POWDER SHOTGUNS

Mowrey A & T Shotgun

MOWREY A. & T. 12 GAUGE SHOTGUN
Gauge: 12 ga. only.
Barrel: 32", octagon.
Weight: 8 lbs. **Length:** 48" over-all.
Stock: Curly maple, oil finish, brass furniture.
Sights: Bead front.
Features: Available in percussion only. Steel or brass action. Uses standard 12 ga. wadding. Made by Mowrey.
Price: Complete $328.00
Price: Kit form. $237.00

TRAIL GUNS KODIAK 10 GAUGE DOUBLE
Gauge: 10.
Barrel: 20", 30¾" (Cyl. bore).
Weight: About 9 lbs. **Length:** 47⅛" over-all.
Stock: Walnut, with cheek rest. Checkered wrist and fore-end.
Features: Chrome plated bores; engraved lockplates, brass bead front and middle sights; sling swivels. Introduced 1980. Imported from Italy by Trail Guns Armory.
Price: $379.95

Navy Classic Double

NAVY CLASSIC DOUBLE BARREL SHOTGUN
Gauge: 10, 12.
Barrel: 28".
Weight: 7 lbs., 12 ozs. **Length:** 45" over-all.
Stock: Walnut.
Features: Color case-hardened lock plates and hammers; hand checkered stock. Imported by Navy Arms.
Price: 10 or 12 ga. $325.00
Price: Kit, 12 ga. $250.00
Price: Kit, 10 ga. $260.00
Price: As "Texas Ranger," 12 ga., 14" bbls. $325.00

"THE GALLYON" FOWLING PIECE
Gauge: 12.
Barrel: 32" (open choked).
Weight: 7½ lbs.
Stock: European walnut, English style. Hand checkered satin oil finish.
Sights: Bead front.
Features: Faithful reproduction of an old English fowling piece. Fine scroll engraving on lock, barrel and trigger guard. Steel buttplate. Introduced 1979. From F.I.E. Corp., Sile.
Price: $209.95
Price: As the "Gallion" (Sile) $299.00

SILE DELUXE DOUBLE BARREL SHOTGUN
Gauge: 12.
Barrel: 28" (Cyl. & Cyl.); hooked breech, hard chrome lining.
Weight: 6 lbs. **Length:** 44½" over-all.
Stock: Walnut, with checkered grip.
Features: Engraved, polished blue and color case-hardened hardware; locks are color case-hardened and engraved. Steel buttplate; brass bead front sight. From Sile.
Price: Percussion only $299.00
Price: Confederate Cavalry Model (shortened version of above model with 14" bbl. 30½" o.a.l., checkered stock, swivels, brass ramrod) $299.00

Morse Single Barrel

MORSE/NAVY SINGLE BARREL SHOTGUN
Gauge: 12 ga.
Barrel: 26".
Weight: 5 lbs. **Length:** 41½" over-all.
Stock: American walnut, full p.g.
Sights: Front bead
Features: Brass receiver, black buttplate. Made in U.S. by Navy Arms.
Price: $149.95
Price: Kit $100.00

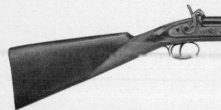

Dixie Double Barrel

DOUBLE BARREL PERCUSSION SHOTGUN
Gauge: 12.
Barrel: 30" (I.C.&Mod.).
Weight: 6¼ lbs. **Length:** 45" over-all.
Stock: Hand checkered walnut, 14" pull.
Features: Double triggers, light hand engraving. Details vary with importer. Imported by The Armoury, Dixie, Euroarms of America, Toledo Armas, Hopkins & Allen.
Price: Upland . . . . $125.00 to $299.85
Price: 12 ga. kit (Dixie) $235.00
Price: 10 ga. (Dixie) $330.00
Price: 10 ga. kit (Dixie) $275.00

CAUTION: PRICES CHANGE. CHECK AT GUNSHOP.

AIR GUNS—HANDGUNS

Guns in this section are powered by: A) disposable CO$_2$ cylinders, B) hand-pumped compressed air released by trigger action, C) air compressed by a spring-powered piston released by trigger action. Calibers are generally 177 (BB or pellet) and 22 (ball or pellet); a few guns are made in 20 or 25 caliber. Pellet guns are usually rifled, those made for BB's only are smoothbore.

BSA SCORPION AIR PISTOL
Caliber: 177 or 22, single shot.
Barrel: 7⅞", rifled.
Weight: 3.6 lbs. **Length:** 15¾" over-all.
Power: Spring-air, barrel cocking.
Stock: Moulded black plastic contoured with thumbrest.
Sights: Interchangeable bead or blade front with hood, open rear adjustable for w. & e.
Features: Muzzle velocity of 510 fps (177) and 380 fps (22). Comes with pellets, oil, targets and steel target holder. Scope and mount optional. Introduced 1980. Imported from England by Precision Sports.
Price: 177 or 22 cal. **$124.95**
Price: 1.5x15 scope and mount **$54.95**

BSA Scorpion

BEEMAN 800 TARGET/SPORT PISTOL
Caliber: 177, single shot.
Barrel: 7", rifled steel.
Weight: 3.2 lbs. **Length:** 16" over-all.
Power: Spring piston.
Stocks: Exotic wood; ambidextrous grip.
Sights: Hooded front with interchangeable inserts, micro click rear with 4 rotating notches.
Features: Velocity 400 fps MV. Advanced recoilless action. Shoulder stock and scope mount available. Imported by Beeman's.
Price: **$195.00**

Beeman Model 800

BEEMAN MODEL 850 AIR PISTOL
Caliber: 177, single shot.
Barrel: 7", rifled steel.
Weight: 3.2 lbs. **Length:** 16" over-all.
Power: Spring, barrel cocking.
Stocks: Exotic wood; ambidextrous grip.
Sights: Infinite width rotating post front 2.5 to 4mm, micro click rear with 4 rotating notches.
Features: Velocity 490 fps. Advanced recoilless action. Rotating barrel housing for easier cocking. Optional muzzle weight available. Scope mount and shoulder stock available. Introduced 1979. Imported by Beeman.
Price: Right-hand. **$225.00**

Beeman Model 850

BEEMAN/FEINWERKBAU MODEL 80 MATCH PISTOL
Caliber: 177, single shot.
Barrel: 7.5"; 12 groove rifling.
Weight: 2.8 to 3.2 lbs. (varies with weight selection). **Length:** 16.4" over-all.
Power: Spring piston, single-stroke sidelever cocking.
Stocks: Stippled walnut with adjustable palm shelf.
Sights: Interchangeable-blade front, rear notch micro. adj. for w. and e.
Features: Four-way adjustable match trigger. Recoilless operation. Metal piston ring and dual mainsprings. Interchangeable weights attach to frame, not barrel. Weights may be arranged to suit balance preference. Cocking effort 16 lbs. Muzzle velocity 475-525 fps. Introduced 1978. Imported by Beeman.
Price: Right-hand. **$595.00**
Price: Left-hand **$625.00**

FWB Model 80

BEEMAN/WISCHO S-20 STANDARD
Caliber: 177, single shot.
Barrel: 7".
Weight: 2 lbs., 2 oz.
Power: Spring piston.
Stocks: Walnut.
Sights: Hooded front, open rear adj. for elevation.
Features: Stocks suitable for right or left-handed shooters; 450 fps; 24 oz. trigger pull. Introduced 1980. Imported by Beeman.
Price: **$115.00**

BEEMAN/WEBLEY TEMPEST AIR PISTOL
Caliber: 177 or 22, single shot.
Barrel: 6.75", rifled ordnance steel.
Weight: 32 oz. **Length:** 9" over-all.
Power: Spring piston.
Stocks: Checkered black epoxy with thumbrest.
Sights: Post front; rear has sliding leaf adjustable for w. and e.
Features: Adjustable trigger pull, manual safety. Velocity 470 fps (177 cal.). Steel piston in steel liner for maximum performance and durability. Unique rearward spring simulates firearm recoil. Shoulder stock available. Introduced 1979. Imported from England by Beeman.
Price: **$89.95**

Beeman/Webley Tempest

BEEMAN/WEBLEY HURRICANE PISTOL
Caliber: 177 or 22, single shot.
Barrel: 8", rifled.
Weight: 2.4 lbs. **Length:** 11½" over-all.
Power: Spring piston.
Stocks: Thumbrest, checkered plastic.
Sights: Hooded front, micro-click rear adj. for w. and e.
Features: Velocity of 470 fps (177-cal.). Single stroke cocking, adjustable trigger pull, manual safety. Rearward recoil like a firearm pistol. Steel piston and cylinder. Scope base included; 1.5x scope **$39.95** extra. Shoulder stock available. Introduced 1977. Imported from England by Beeman's.
Price: **$125.00**

Beeman/Webley Hurricane

BEEMAN/WISCHO BSF S-20 MATCH PISTOL
Caliber: 177, single shot.
Barrel: 7" rifled.
Weight: 45 oz. **Length:** 15.8" over-all.
Power: Spring piston barrel cocking.
Stocks: Walnut with thumbrest.
Sights: Bead front, rear adj. for e.
Features: Cocking effort of 17 lbs.; M.V. 450 f.p.s.; adj. trigger. Optional scope and mount available. Detachable aluminum stock. Available from Beeman.
Price: **$145.00**

Beeman/Wischo S-20

BENJAMIN SUPER S. S. TARGET PISTOL SERIES 130
Caliber: BB, 22 and 177; single shot.
Barrel: 8"; BB smoothbore; 22 and 177, rifled.
Weight: 2 lbs. **Length:** 11" over-all.
Power: Hand pumped.
Features: Bolt action; fingertip safety; adj. power.
Price: M130, BB **$78.10**
Price: M132, 22 .... **$78.10**
Price: M137, 177 .... **$78.10**

Crosman 1861 Shiloh

Consult our Directory pages for the location of firms mentioned.

CROSMAN MODEL 1861 SHILOH REVOLVER
Caliber: 177 pellets or BBs, 6-shot.
Barrel: 6" rifled.
Weight: 1 lb., 14 oz. **Length:** 12¾" over-all.
Power: CO_2 Powerlet.
Stocks: Wood-grained plastic.
Sights: Fixed.
Features: Modeled after the 1861 Remington revolver. Averages 42 shots per CO_2 Powerlet. Velocity of 330 to 350 fps with pellets. Introduced 1981.
Price: About **$28.00**

Crosman 1322/1377

CROSMAN MODEL 1322 AIR PISTOL
Caliber: 22, single shot.
Barrel: 8", button rifled.
Weight: 37 oz. **Length:** 13⅝".
Power: Hand pumped.
Sights: Blade front, rear adj. for w. and e.
Features: Moulded plastic grip, hand size pump forearm. Cross bolt safety. Also available in 177 Cal. as **Model 1377** (same price).
Price: About **$45.00**

CAUTION: PRICES CHANGE. CHECK AT GUNSHOP.

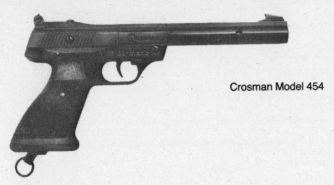

Crosman Model 454

CROSMAN 454 BB PISTOL
Caliber: BB, 16-shot.
Weight: 30 oz. **Length:** 11″ over-all.
Power: Standard CO₂.
Stocks: Contoured with thumbrest.
Sights: Patridge-type front, fully adj. rear.
Features: Gives about 80 shots per powerlet, slide-action safety, steel barrel, die-cast receiver. Lanyard ring for easy piercing of CO₂ cylinder.
Price: About $33.00

Crosman Model 1600 Air Pistol
Same specifications as Model 454 except has fixed sights, black plastic grips, no lanyard ring.
Price: About $27.00

Crosman Mark I

CROSMAN MARK I TARGET PISTOL
Caliber: 22, single shot.
Barrel: 7¼″, button rifled.
Weight: 42 oz. **Length:** 11″.
Power: Crosman Powerlet CO₂ cylinder.
Features: New system provides same shot-to-shot velocity of 370-420 fps. Checkered thumbrest grips, right or left. Patridge front sight, rear adj. for w. & e. Adj. trigger.
Price: About $49.00

Crosman Mark II Target Pistol
Same as Mark I except 177 cal.
Price: About $49.00

Crosman Model 38T

CROSMAN 38T TARGET REVOLVER
Caliber: 177, 6-shot.
Barrel: 6″, rifled.
Weight: 40 oz. **Length:** 11″ over-all.
Power: CO₂ Powerlet cylinder.
Features: Double action, revolving cylinder. Adj. rear sight.
Price: About $44.00

Crosman 38C Combat Revolver
Same as 38 Target except 3½″ bbl., 36 oz.
Price: About $44.00

Daisy Model 179

DAISY 179 SIX GUN
Caliber: BB, 12-shot.
Barrel: Steel lined, smoothbore.
Weight: NA **Length:** 11½″ over-all.
Power: Spring.
Features: Forced feed from under-barrel magazine. Single action, molded wood grained grips.
Price: About $21.00

Daisy Model 188

DAISY MODEL 188 BB/PELLET PISTOL
Caliber: 177.
Barrel: 9.9″.
Weight: 1.67 lbs. **Length:** 12″ over-all.
Stocks: Die-cast metal; checkered with thumbrest.
Sights: Blade and ramp front, notched rear.
Features: Single shot for pellets, 24-shot for BBs. Spring action with under-barrel cocking lever. Grip and receiver of die-cast metal. Introduced 1979.
Price: About $21.00

AIR GUNS—HANDGUNS

FEINWERKBAU FWB-65 MKI AIR PISTOL
Caliber: 177, single shot.
Barrel: 7½"; fixed bbl. wgt. avail.
Weight: 42 oz. **Length:** 14½" over-all.
Power: Spring, sidelever cocking.
Stocks: Walnut, stippled thumbrest.
Sights: Front, interchangeable post element system, open rear, click adj. for w. & e. and for sighting notch width. Scope mount avail.
Features: Cocking effort 9 lbs. 2-stage trigger, 4 adjustments. Quiet firing, 525 fps. Programs instantly for recoil or recoilless operation. Permanently lubricated. Steel piston ring. Special switch converts trigger from 17.6 oz. pull to 42 oz. let-off. Available from Beeman.
Price: Right-hand... $485.00
Price: Left-hand... $499.50

FWB-65 Mk. I

Feinwerkbau Model 65 International Match Pistol
Same as FWB 65 MKI pistol except: new adj. wood grips to meet international regulations, optional 3 oz. barrel sleeve weight. Available from Beeman.
Price: Right-hand... $545.00
Price: Left-hand... $575.00

GAMO CENTER AIR PISTOL
Caliber: 177, single shot.
Barrel: 7", rifled.
Weight: 46 oz. **Length:** 13.8" over-all.
Power: Underlever spring air.
Sights: Hooded front, micro-adjustable rear.
Features: Velocity of 400 to 435 fps on single stroke of the lever. Sight radius of 13". Adjustable trigger. Blued metal finish. Introduced 1981. Imported from Spain by Stoeger Industries.
Price: $110.00
Price: With ambidextrous grip and safety, non-adj. trigger........... $90.00

Gamo Center

HAMMERLI "MASTER" CO₂ TARGET PISTOL
Caliber: 177, single shot.
Barrel: 6.4", 12-groove.
Weight: 38.4 oz. **Length:** 16" over-all.
Power: 12 gram cylinder.
Stocks: Plastic with thumbrest and checkering.
Sights: Ramp front, micro rear, click adj. Adj. sight radius from 11.1" to 13.0".
Features: Single shot, manual loading. Residual gas vented automatically. 5-way adj. trigger. Available from Mandall Shooting Supplies.
Price: $495.00

HEALTHWAYS TOPSCORE 9100 AIR PISTOL
Caliber: 177, BB, 50-shot magazine.
Barrel: 6½".
Weight: 28 oz.
Power: Spring.
Stocks: Checkered, integral with frame.
Sights: Open, fixed.
Features: Quick, top-load magazine mass loads 50 BBs at a time. Cock by releasing a locking lever on left side of frame and lifting barrel.
Price: $22.95

MARKSMAN PLAINSMAN 1049 CO₂ PISTOL
Caliber: BB, 100-shot repeater.
Barrel: 5⅞", smooth.
Weight: 28 oz. **Length:** 9½" over-all.
Stocks: Simulated walnut with thumbrest.
Power: 8.5 or 12.5 gram CO₂ cylinders.
Features: 3 position power switch. Auto. ammunition feed. Positive safety.
Price: $32.95

MARKSMAN #1010 REPEATER PISTOL
Caliber: 177, 20-shot repeater.
Barrel: 2½", smoothbore.
Weight: 24 oz. **Length:** 8¼".
Power: Spring
Features: Thumb safety. Uses BBs, darts or pellets. Repeats with BBs only.
Price: Black finish... $14.95

Power Line 777

POWER LINE MATCH 777 PELLET PISTOL
Caliber: 177, single shot.
Barrel: 9.61" rifled steel.
Weight: 49 oz. **Length:** 13½" over-all.
Power: Sidelever, single pump pneumatic.
Stocks: Smooth hardwood, fully contoured; right or left hand.
Sights: Blade and ramp front, match-grade open rear with adj. width notch, micro. click adjustments.
Features: Adjustable trigger; manual cross-bolt safety. MV of 360 fps. Comes in foam-filled carrying case and complete cleaning kit, adjustment tool and pellets.
Price: About... $230.00

Power Line 780/790

POWER LINE MODELS 780 & 790
Caliber: 22 cal. pellet (780), 177 cal. pellet (790), single-shot.
Barrel: 8½", rifled steel.
Weight: 42 oz.
Power: 12 gram CO₂ cartridge.
Stocks: Simulated walnut, checkered. Thumbrest. Left or right hand.
Sights: Patridge front, fully adj. rear with micro. click windage adjustment.
Features: Pull-bolt action, crossbolt safety. High-low power adjustment.
Price: $68.00

CAUTION: PRICES CHANGE. CHECK AT GUNSHOP.

POWER LINE 717/722 PELLET PISTOLS
Caliber: 177 (Model 717), 22 (Model 722), single shot.
Barrel: 9.61".
Weight: 48 oz. **Length:** 13½" over-all.
Stocks: Molded wood-grain plastic, with thumbrest.
Sights: Blade and ramp front, micro. adjustable notch rear.
Features: Single pump pneumatic pistol. Rifled brass barrel. Cross-bolt trigger block. Muzzle velocity 360 fps (177 cal.), 290 fps (22 cal.). From Daisy. Introduced 1979.
Price: Either model, about **$68.00**

Power Line 717/722

POWER LINE CO₂ 1200 CUSTOM TARGET PISTOL
Caliber: BB, 177.
Barrel: 10½", smooth.
Weight: 30 oz. **Length:** 11¼" over-all.
Power: Daisy CO₂ cylinder.
Stocks: Contoured, checkered moulded wood-grain plastic.
Sights: Blade ramp front, fully adj. square notch rear.
Features: 60-shot BB reservoir, gravity feed. Cross bolt safety. Velocity of 420-450 fps for more than 100 shots.
Price: About **$34.00**

Power Line 1200

PRECISE/RO-72 BULLSEYE AIR PISTOL
Caliber: 177, single shot.
Barrel: 7¼", rifled.
Weight: 35 oz.
Power: Spring air, barrel cocking.
Stock: Molded plastic with thumbrest.
Sights: Hooded front, micro. adj. open rear for w. and e.
Features: Four interchangeable front sights—triangle, bead, narrow post, wide post. Rear sight rotates to give four distinct sight pictures. Muzzle velocity 325 fps. Precise International, importer.
Price: **$39.95**

Precise RO-72

RWS MODEL 5G AIR PISTOL
Caliber: 177, single shot.
Barrel: 7".
Weight: 2¾ lbs. **Length:** 16" over-all.
Power: Spring air, barrel cocking.
Stocks: Plastic, thumbrest design.
Sights: Tunnel front, micro click open rear.
Features: Velocity of 410 fps. Two-stage trigger with automatic safety. Imported from West Germany by Dynamit Nobel of America.
Price: **$122.00**

RWS Model 5G

RWS MODEL 6G AIR PISTOL
Caliber: 177, single shot.
Barrel: 7".
Weight: 3 lbs. **Length:** 16" over-all.
Power: Spring air, barrel cocking.
Stocks: Plastic, thumbrest design.
Sights: Tunnel front with interchangeable inserts, micro click open rear.
Features: Velocity of 410 fps. Recoilless double piston system, two-stage adjustable trigger. Comes with sight inserts. Imported from West Germany by Dynamit Nobel of America.
Price: **$191.00**

RWS MODEL 6M MATCH AIR PISTOL
Caliber: 177, single shot.
Barrel: 7".
Weight: 3 lbs. **Length:** 16" over-all.
Power: Spring air, barrel cocking.
Stocks: Walnut-finished hardwood with thumbrest.
Sights: Adjustable front, micro click open rear.
Features: Velocity of 410 fps. Recoilless double piston system, moveable barrel shroud to protect front sight during cocking. Imported from West Germany by Dynamit Nobel of America.
Price: **$225.00**

RWS Model 6M

RWS Model 10

RWS Model 10 Match Air Pistol

Refined version of the Model 6M. Has special adjustable match trigger, oil finished and stippled match grips, barrel weight. Also available in left-hand version, and with fitted case.

Price: Model 10 .... $445.00
Price: Model 10, left hand. $490.00
Price: Model 10, with case $490.00
Price: Model 10, left hand, with case $525.00

Sheridan Model HB

SHERIDAN MODEL HB PNEUMATIC PISTOL

Caliber: 5mm; single shot.
Barrel: 9⅜″, rifled.
Weight: 36 oz. **Length:** 12″ over-all.
Power: Underlever pneumatic pump.
Stocks: Checkered simulated walnut; forend is walnut.
Sights: Blade front, fully adjustable rear.
Features: "Controller-Power" feature allows velocity and range control by varying the number of pumps—3 to 10. Maximum velocity of 400 fps. Introduced 1982. From Sheridan Products.
Price: $80.40

Sheridan Model EB

SHERIDAN MODEL EB CO₂ PISTOL

Caliber: 20 (5mm).
Barrel: 6½″, rifled, rust proof.
Weight: 27 oz. **Length:** 9″ over-all.
Power: 12 gram CO₂ cylinder.
Stocks: Checkered simulated walnut. Left- or right-handed.
Sights: Blade front, fully adjustable rear.
Features: Turn-bolt single-shot action. Gives about 40 shots at 400 fps per CO₂ cylinder.
Price: $60.35

WALTHER MODEL LP-3

Caliber: 177, single shot.
Barrel: 9⅜″, rifled.
Weight: 45½ oz. **Length:** 13³⁄₁₆″ over-all.
Power: Compressed air, lever cocking.
Features: Recoiless operation, cocking in grip frame. Micro-click rear sight, adj. for w. & e., 4-way adj. trigger. Plastic thumbrest grips. Imported by Interarms.
Price: $425.00

Walther Model LP-3 Match Pistol

Same specifications as LP-3 except for grips, frame shape and weight. Has adjustable walnut grips to meet international shooting regulations. Imported by Interarms.
Price: $515.00

> Consult our Directory pages for the location of firms mentioned.

WALTHER MODEL LP-53 PISTOL

Caliber: 177, single shot.
Barrel: 9⅜″.
Weight: 40.5 oz. **Length:** 12⅜″ over-all.
Power: Spring air.
Features: Micrometer rear sight. Interchangeable rear sight blades. Target grips. Bbl. weight availble at extra cost. Inported from West Germany by Interarms.
Price: $235.00

Weihrauch HW-70

WEIHRAUCH HW-70 AIR PISTOL

Caliber: 177, single shot.
Barrel: 6¼″, rifled.
Weight: 38 oz. **Length:** 12¾″ over-all.
Power: Spring, barrel cocking.
Stocks: Plastic, with thumbrest.
Sights: Hooded post front, square notch rear adj. for w. and e.
Features: Adj. trigger. 24-lb. cocking effort, 410 f.p.s. M.V.; automatic barrel safety. Available from Beeman.
Price: $98.50

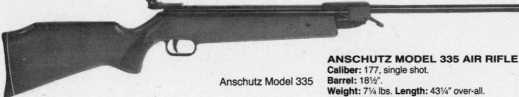

Anschutz Model 335

ANSCHUTZ MODEL 335 AIR RIFLE
Caliber: 177, single shot.
Barrel: 18½".
Weight: 7¼ lbs. **Length:** 43¼" over-all.
Power: Spring piston; barrel cocking.
Stock: European hardwood; checkered pistol grip.
Sights: None furnished. Receiver grooved for Williams peep rear, Anschutz globe front.
Features: Specially designed for 10 meter "novice-expert" shooters. Adjustable two-stage trigger. Introduced 1982. Imported from Germany by Talo Distributors, Inc.
Price: **$165.00**

Anschutz Model 380

ANSCHUTZ MODEL 380 AIR RIFLE
Caliber: 177, single shot.
Barrel: 20¼".
Weight: 10.8 lbs. (including sights). **Length:** 42⅛" over-all.
Power: Spring piston; sidelever cocking.
Stock: Walnut with stippled pistol grip and fore-end. Adjustable cheekpiece and rubber buttpad.
Sights: Globe front; match aperture rear.
Features: Recoilless and vibration free. Two-stage adjustable match trigger. Introduced 1982. Imported from Germany by Talo Distributors, Inc.
Price: With sights... **$864.00**
Price: Left-hand, with sights.................................... **$905.00**

BSA AIRSPORTER-S AIR RIFLE
Caliber: 177 or 22.
Barrel: 19.5", rifled.
Weight: 8 lbs. **Length:** 44.7" over-all.
Power: Spring air, underlever action.
Stock: Oil-finished walnut, high comb Monte Carlo cheekpiece.
Sights: Ramp front with interchangeable bead and blade, adjustable for height; tangent-type rear adj. for w. & e.
Features: Muzzle velocity of 825 fps (177) and 635 fps (22). Fully adj. trigger. Cylinder is a large diameter, one-piece impact extrusion. Scope and mount optional. Introduced 1980. Imported from England by Precision Sports.
Price: 177 or 22 cal. **$369.95**
Price: Standard Airsporter **$299.95**
Price: 4x20 scope and mount **$54.95**

BSA Airsporter-S

BSA MERCURY AIR RIFLE
Caliber: 177 or 22, single shot.
Barrel: 18.5", rifled.
Weight: 7 lbs. **Length:** 43.5" over-all.
Power: Spring-air, barrel cocking.
Stock: European hardwood, Monte Carlo cheekpiece, ventilated butt pad.
Sights: Adjustable bead/blade front, tangent rear adj. for w. & e.
Features: Muzzle velocity of 700 fps (177) and 550 fps (22). Reversible "V" and "U" notch rear sight blade. Single stage match-type trigger, adj. for weight of pull and sear engagement. Scope and mount optional. Introduced 1980. Imported from England by Precision Sports.
Price: 177 or 22 cal. **$209.95**
Price: 4x20 scope and mount **$54.95**

BSA Mercury-S

BSA Mercury-S Air Rifle
Similar to the standard Mercury model except weighs 7¼ lbs., has European walnut stock with oil finish, checkered fore-end and pistol grip. Introduced 1982. From Precision Sports.
Price: **$269.95**

BSA METEOR/METEOR SUPER AIR RIFLES
Caliber: 177 or 22, single shot.
Barrel: 18.5″, rifled.
Weight: 6 lbs. **Length:** 42″ over-all.
Power: Spring air, barrel cocking.
Stock: European hardwood.
Sights: Adj. bead/blade front, adj. tangent rear with reversible "U" and "V" notch blade.
Features: Muzzle velocity of 650 fps (177) and 500 fps (22). Aperture rear sight element supplied. Cylinder is dovetailed for scope mounting. Adjustable trigger mechanism. Meteor Super has M.C. cheekpiece, vent. rubber recoil pad. Introduced 1980. Imported from England by Precision Sports.
Price: Meteor $124.95
Price: Meteor Super $139.95

BSA Meteor Super

BSA BUCCANEER AIR RIFLE
Caliber: 177 or 22, single shot.
Barrel: 18.5″, rifled.
Weight: 6 lbs. **Length:** 35.5″ over-all.
Power: Spring-air, barrel cocking.
Stock: High impact polyurethane, thumbhole design.
Sights: Interchangeable bead or blade front, aperture rear adjustable for windage and elevation.
Features: Adjustable trigger; non-automatic safety; checkered p.g. and fore-end. Comes with targets and steel target holder, oil, pellets. Scope and mounts optional. Introduced 1980. Imported from England by Precision Sports.
Price: 177 or 22 cal. $139.50
Price: 5x15 scope and mount $39.50

BSA Buccaneer

BEEMAN/FEINWERKBAU 124/127 MAGNUM
Caliber: 177 (FWB-124); 22 (FWB-127); single shot.
Barrel: 18.3″, 12-groove rifling.
Weight: 6.8 lbs. **Length:** 43½″ over-all.
Power: Spring piston air; single stroke barrel cocking.
Stock: Walnut finished hardwood.
Sights: Tunnel front; click-adj. rear for w., slide-adj. for e.
Features: Velocity 680-820 fps, cocking effort of 18 lbs. Forged steel receiver; nylon non-drying piston and breech seals. Auto. safety, adj. trigger. Standard model has no checkering, cheekpiece, or swivels. Deluxe has hand-checkerd p.g. and fore-end, high comb cheekpiece, ⅞″ sling swivels and buttplate with white spacer. Imported by Beeman.
Price: Standard model $230.00
Price: Deluxe model (illus.) $280.00

Beeman FWB 124/127

Beeman/Webley Vulcan

BEEMAN/WEBLEY VULCAN MARK II AIR RIFLE
Caliber: 177 or 22, single shot.
Barrel: 17″, rifled steel.
Weight: 6.8 lbs. **Length:** 41″ over-all.
Power: Spring piston air, barrel cocking.
Stock: Beech with cheekpiece and rubber buttplate.
Sights: Hooded front; micro click rear adj. for w. & e.
Features: Receiver grooved for scope mounting. Manual safety. Trigger adjustable down to about 2 lbs. Velocity 800 fps (177), 600 fps (22). Imported by Beeman.
Price: $179.95

BEEMAN/NORICA AIR RIFLE KIT
Caliber: 177, single shot.
Barrel: 17.9″, rifled.
Weight: 4.9 lbs. **Length:** 40″ over-all.
Power: Spring-piston, barrel cocking.
Stock: Beech, unfinished.
Sights: Hooded ramp front, adjustable rear.
Features: Velocity 600 fps. World's only air rifle kit. Metal parts are factory blued. Stock may be finished to individual taste. Imported by Beeman.
Price: $79.95

CAUTION: PRICES CHANGE. CHECK AT GUNSHOP.

Beeman Carbine C1

BEEMAN CARBINE MODEL C1
Caliber: 177, single shot.
Barrel: 14″, 12-groove rifling.
Weight: 6¼ lbs. **Length:** 38″ over-all.
Power: Spring-piston, barrel cocking.
Stock: Walnut-stained beechwood with rubber butt pad.
Sights: Blade front, rear click-adjustable for windage and elevation.
Features: Velocity 830 fps. Adjustable trigger. Receiver grooved for scope mounting. Imported by Beeman.
Price: $149.95

Beeman Falcon 1

BEEMAN FALCON 1 AIR RIFLE
Caliber: 177, single shot.
Barrel: 18″, rifled.
Weight: 6.6 lbs. **Length:** 43″ over-all.
Power: Spring-piston, barrel cocking.
Stock: Walnut-stained hardwood.
Sights: Tunnel front with interchangeable inserts; rear with rotating disc to give four sighting notches.
Features: Velocity 680 fps. Match-type adjustable trigger. Receiver grooved for scope mounting. Imported by Beeman.
Price: $129.95

Beeman Falcon 2 Air Rifle
Similar to the Falcon 1 except weighs 5.8 lbs., 41″ over-all; front sight is hooded post on ramp, rear sight has two-way click adjustments. Adjustable trigger. Imported by Beeman.
Price: $99.95

Beeman Model R9

BEEMAN R9 AIR RIFLE
Caliber: 177, single shot.
Barrel: 18.3″.
Weight: 7.2 lbs. **Length:** 43.1″ over-all.
Power: Barrel cocking, spring-piston.
Stock: Walnut with Monte Carlo cheekpiece; checkered pistol grip.
Sights: Globe front, fully adjustable rear; interchangeable inserts.
Features: Velocity of 715 fps. Nylon piston and breech seals. Adjustable match-grade, two-stage, grooved metal trigger. Rubber butt pad. Imported by Beeman.
Price: $220.00

Beeman R7 Air Rifle
Similar to the R9 model except has double-jointed cocking lever, match grade trigger block; velocity of 660 fps; barrel length 17″; weights 5.8 lbs. Imported by Beeman.
Price: $170.00

BENJAMIN SERIES 3100 SUPER REPEATER RIFLES
Caliber: BB, 100-shot; 22, 85-shot.
Barrel: 23″, rifled or smoothbore.
Weight: 6¼ lbs. **Length:** 35″ over-all.
Power: Hand pumped.
Features: Bolt action. Piggy back full view magazine. Bar V adj. rear sight. Walnut stock and pump handle.
Price: M3100, BB $92.60
Price: M3120, 22 rifled $92.60

BEEMAN R1 AIR RIFLE
Caliber: 177 or 22, single shot.
Barrel: 19.6″, 12-groove rifling.
Weight: 8.5 lbs. **Length:** 45.2″ over-all.
Power: Spring-piston, barrel cocking.
Stock: Walnut-stained beech; cut checkered pistol grip Monte Carlo comb and cheekpiece; rubber butt pad.
Sights: Tunnel front with interchangeable inserts, open rear click adjustable for windage and elevation. Grooved for scope mounting.
Features: Velocity of 940 fps (177), 800 fps (22). Non-drying nylon piston and breech seals. Adjustable metal trigger. Right or left hand stock. Imported by Beeman.
Price: Right hand, 177 .... $289.50
Price: Left hand, 177 .... $315.00
Price: Right hand, 22 .... $294.00
Price: Left hand, 22 .... $320.00

BENJAMIN SERIES 340 AIR RIFLE
Caliber: 22 or 177, pellets or BB; single shot.
Barrel: 23″, rifled and smoothbore.
Weight: 6 lbs. **Length:** 35″ over-all.
Power: Hand pumped.
Features: Bolt action, walnut Monte Carlo stock and pump handle. Ramp-type front sight, adj. stepped leaf type rear. Push-pull safety.
Price: M340, BB $96.20
Price: M343, 22 .... $96.20
Price: M347, 177 .... $96.20

Crosman Model 73

CROSMAN MODEL 73 SADDLE PAL CO₂
Caliber: 177 pellets or BBs, 16-shot magazine.
Barrel: 18″, steel.
Weight: 3 lbs., 3 oz. **Length:** 34¾″ over-all.
Stock: Simulated wood.
Sights: Ramp front, rear adj. for e.
Features: Positive lever safety. Velocity is 475 fps (pellets), 525 fps (BBs). 100 shots per CO₂ cartridge.
Price: About $28.00

Crosman 2200 Magnum

CROSMAN MODEL 1 RIFLE

Caliber: 22, single shot.
Barrel: 19", rifled brass.
Weight: 5 lbs., 1 oz. **Length:** 39" over-all.
Power: Pneumatic, variable power.
Stock: Walnut stained American hardwood.
Sights: Blade front, Williams rear with micrometer click settings.
Features: Precision trigger mechanism for light, clean pull. Metal receiver grooved for scope mounting. Bolt action with cross-bolt safety. Muzzle velocities range from 365 fps (three pumps) to 625 fps (10 pumps). Introduced 1981.
Price: About **$79.00**

CROSMAN MODEL 2200 MAGNUM AIR RIFLE

Caliber: 22, single-shot.
Barrel: 19", rifled steel.
Weight: 4 lbs., 13 oz. **Length:** 39¾" over-all.
Stock: Full-size, wood-grained plastic with checkered p.g. and fore-end.
Sights: Ramp front, open step-adjustable rear.
Features: Variable pump power—3 pumps give 395 fps, 6 pumps 530 fps, 10 pumps 620 fps (average). Full-size adult air rifle. Has white line spacers at pistol grip and buttplate. Introduced 1978.
Price: About **$54.00**

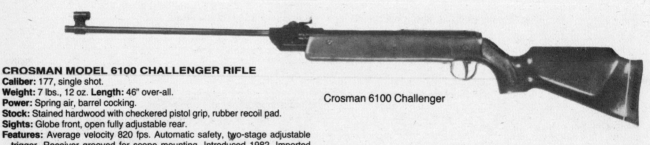

Crosman 6100 Challenger

CROSMAN MODEL 6100 CHALLENGER RIFLE

Caliber: 177, single shot.
Weight: 7 lbs., 12 oz. **Length:** 46" over-all.
Power: Spring air, barrel cocking.
Stock: Stained hardwood with checkered pistol grip, rubber recoil pad.
Sights: Globe front, open fully adjustable rear.
Features: Average velocity 820 fps. Automatic safety, two-stage adjustable trigger. Receiver grooved for scope mounting. Introduced 1982. Imported from West Germany by Crosman Air Guns.
Price: About **$202.25**

Crosman Model 788

CROSMAN MODEL 788 BB SCOUT RIFLE

Caliber: 177, BB.
Barrel: 14", steel.
Weight: 2 lbs. 7 oz. **Length:** 31" over-all.
Stock: Wood-grained ABS plastic.
Sights: Blade on ramp front, open adj. rear.
Features: Variable pump power—3 pumps give MV of 330 fps, 6 pumps 437 fps, 10 pumps 470 fps (BBs, average). Steel barrel, cross-bolt safety. Introduced 1978.
Price: About **$26.00**

Crosman Classic 766

CROSMAN AMERICAN CLASSIC 766 AIR RIFLE

Caliber: 177 pellets or BBs, 15-shot magazine.
Barrel: 19", rifled.
Weight: 4 lbs., 4 oz. **Length:** 39½" over-all.
Power: Pump-up, pneumatic.
Stock: Wood-grained checkered ABS plastic.
Features: Three pumps gives about 450 fps, 10 pumps about 700 fps. Cross-bolt safety; concealed reservoir holds over 180 BBs.
Price: About **$49.00**

Crosman Model 760

CROSMAN MODEL 760 POWERMASTER

Caliber: 177 pellets or BB, 200 shot.
Barrel: 19½", rifled steel.
Weight: 4 lbs., 3 oz. **Length:** 35" over-all.
Power: Pneumatic, hand pump.
Features: Short stroke, power determined by number of strokes. Walnut finished plastic checkered stock and fore-end. Post front sight and adjustable rear sight. Cross-bolt safety.
Price: About **$39.00**

Daisy Model 850

DAISY MODEL 850/851 PNEUMATIC RIFLE

Caliber: BB or 177, 100-shot BB reservoir.
Barrel: 20.8", rifled steel.
Weight: 4.3 lbs. **Length:** 33⅜" over-all.
Power: Single pump pneumatic.
Stock: Moulded plastic with woodgrain finish.
Sights: Ramp front, fully adjustable open rear.
Features: Shoots either BB's or pellets at 520 fps (BB) and 480 fps (pellet). Manual cross-bolt trigger block safety. Introduced 1981.
Price: About **$61.50**
Price: Model 851 (as above with wood stock and fore-end) **$86.00**

Daisy Model 1894

DAISY 1894 SPITTIN' IMAGE CARBINE

Caliber: BB, 40-shot.
Barrel: 17½", smoothbore.
Length: 38⅜" over-all.
Power: Spring.
Features: Cocks halfway on forward stroke of lever, halfway on return.
Price: About **$42.50**

Daisy Model 845

DAISY MODEL 840

Caliber: 177 pellet (single-shot) or BB (350-shot).
Barrel: 19", smoothbore, steel.
Weight: 3¼ lbs. **Length:** 37⅛" over-all.
Stock: Moulded wood-grain stock and fore-end.
Sights: Ramp front, open, adj. rear.
Features: Single pump pneumatic rifle. Muzzle velocity 325 fps (BB), 300 fps (pellet). Steel buttplate; straight pull bolt action; cross-bolt safety. Fore-end forms pump lever. Introduced 1978.
Price: About **$34.00**

Daisy Model 845 Target Gun

Special target version of the Model 840. Same as the 840 except comes with globe front sight and No. 5845 Daisy Receiver Sight.
Price: About **$39.50**

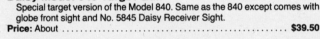

Daisy Model 499

DAISY 499 MATCH TARGET

Caliber: BB, single shot.
Barrel: 18", smoothbore.
Weight: About 4 lbs. **Length:** 36¼" over-all.
Stock: Stained hardwood, Monte Carlo-style. Fore-end has provision for adding extra weight.
Sights: Globe front, peep rear (Daisy No. 5845, fully adj.).
Features: Official model of the NRA-sanctioned Daisy/U.S. Jaycees Shooting Education Program. Introduced 1980.
Price: About **$49.00**

Daisy Model 105

DAISY RIFLES

Model:	95	111	105
Caliber:	BB	BB	BB
Barrel:	18"	18"	13½"
Length:	35"	35"	30½"
Power:	Spring	Spring	Spring
Capacity:	700	700	450
Price: About	$32.75	$27.75	$22.50

Features: 95 stock is wood, fore-end plastic; 105 and 111 have plastic stocks.

DAISY 1938 RED RYDER COMMEMORATIVE

Caliber: BB, 650-shot repeating action.
Barrel: Sturdy steel, under-barrel loading port.
Weight: 3½ lbs. **Length:** 35" over-all.
Stock: Wood stock burned with Red Ryder lariat signature.
Sights: Post front, adjustable V-slot rear.
Features: Wood fore-end. Saddle ring with leather thong. Lever cocking. Gravity feed. Controlled velocity. Commemorates one of Daisy's most popular guns, the Red Ryder of the 1940s and 1950s.
Price: About **$39.95**

Erma ELG 10

ERMA ELG 10 AIR RIFLE
Caliber: 177, single shot.
Barrel: 17.7", rifled.
Weight: 6.4 lbs. **Length:** 38.2".
Power: Spring-piston, lever-action cocking.
Stock: Walnut-stained beechwood.
Sights: Hooded ramp post front, open rear adjustable for windage and elevation.
Features: Velocity to 550 fps. Sliding manual safety. Dummy magazine tube under barrel contains a brass cleaning rod. Imported by Beeman.
Price: $279.50

FEINWERKBAU 300-S SERIES MATCH RIFLE
Caliber: 177, single shot.
Barrel: 19.9", fixed solid with receiver.
Weight: Approx. 10 lbs. with optional bbl. sleeve. **Length:** 42.8" over-all.
Power: Single stroke sidelever, spring piston.
Stock: Match model—walnut, deep fore-end, adj. buttplate.
Sights: Globe front with interchangeable inserts. Click micro. adj. match aperture rear.
Features: Recoilless, vibration free. Five-way adjustable match trigger. Grooved for scope mounts. Permanent lubrication, steel piston ring. Cocking effort 9 lbs. Optional 10 oz. bbl. sleeve. Available from Beeman.
Price: Right hand $675.00
Price: Left hand $728.50

FEINWERKBAU F300-S RUNNING BOAR (TH)
Caliber: 177, single shot.
Barrel: 19.9", rifled.
Weight: 10.9 lbs. **Length:** 43" over-all.
Power: Single stroke sidelever, spring piston.
Stock: Walnut with adjustable buttplate, grip cap and comb. Designed for fixed and moving target use.
Sights: None furnished; grooved for optional scope.
Features: Recoilless, vibration free. Permanent lubrication and seals. Barrel stabilizer weight included. Crisp single-stage trigger. Available from Beeman.
Price: Right-hand $698.00
Price: Left-hand $760.00

FWB 300-S Universal

FEINWERKBAU 300-S "UNIVERSAL" MATCH
Caliber: 177, single shot.
Barrel: 19.9".
Weight: 10.2 lbs. (without barrel sleeve). **Length:** 43.3" over-all.
Power: Spring piston, single stroke sidelever.
Stock: Walnut, stippled p.g. and fore-end. Detachable cheekpieces (one std., high for scope use.) Adjustable buttplate, accessory rail. Buttplate and grip cap spacers included.
Sights: Two globe fronts with interchangeable inserts. Rear is match aperture with rubber eyecup and sight viser.
Features: Recoilless, vibration free. Grooved for scope mounts. Steel piston ring. Cocking effort about 9½ lbs. Barrel sleeve optional. Left-hand model available. Introduced 1978. Imported by Beeman.
Price: Right-hand $801.00

FWB 300-S

FEINWERKBAU 300-S MINI-MATCH
Caliber: 177, single shot.
Barrel: 17⅛".
Weight: 8.8 lbs. **Length:** 40" over-all.
Power: Spring piston, single stroke sidelever cocking.
Stock: Walnut. Stippled grip, adjustable buttplate. Scaled-down for youthful or slightly built shooters.
Sights: Globe front with interchangeable inserts, micro. adjustable rear.
Features: Recoilless, vibration free. Grooved for scope mounts. Steel piston ring. Cocking effort about 9½ lbs. Barrel sleeve optional. Left-hand model available. Introduced 1978. Imported by Beeman.
Price: Right-hand $598.50
Price: Left-hand $655.00

GAMO GAMATIC AIR RIFLE
Caliber: 177, repeater.
Weight: 6.5 lbs. **Length:** 38" over-all.
Power: Barrel cocking spring type.
Stock: Aluminum buttstock with polymer fore-end.
Sights: Hooded front, micro-adj. rear.
Features: Velocity over 660 fps. Blued metal finish. Introduced 1981. Imported from Spain by Stoeger Industries.
Price: $178.00

GAMO 68 AIR RIFLE
Caliber: 177, 22, single shot.
Weight: 6.5 lbs. **Length:** 38" over-all.
Power: Barrel cocking spring type.
Stock: Aluminum buttstock with polymer fore-end.
Sights: Hooded front, micro-adj. rear.
Features: Velocity of 600 fps. Blued metal finish. Introduced 1981. Imported from Spain by Stoeger Industries.
Price: $144.00

Gamo Cadet

GAMO CADET AIR RIFLE
Caliber: 177 only.
Weight: 5 lbs. **Length:** 37″ over-all.
Power: Barrel cocking spring type.
Stock: Lacquered beechwood.
Sights: Hooded front, micro-adj. open rear.
Features: Velocity of 570 fps. Blued metal finish. Receiver grooved for scope mounting. Introduced 1981. Imported from Spain by Stoeger Industries.
Price: **$94.00**

Gamo Expomatic

GAMO EXPOMATIC AIR RIFLE
Caliber: 177 only, repeater.
Weight: 5.5 lbs. **Length:** 42″ over-all.
Power: Barrel cocking spring type.
Stock: Lacquered beechwood.
Sights: Hooded front, micro-adj. rear.
Features: Velocity of 600 fps. Blued metal finish. Introduced 1981. Imported from Spain by Stoeger Industries.
Price: **$144.00**

GAMO EXPO AIR RIFLE
Caliber: 177, 22.
Weight: 5.5 lbs. **Length:** 42″ over-all.
Power: Barrel cocking spring type.
Stock: Lacquered beechwood.
Sights: Hooded front, open micro-adj. rear.
Features: Velocity of 600 fps. Blued metal finish. Introduced 1981. Imported from Spain by Stoeger Industries.
Price: **$110.00**

GAMO MODEL 600 AIR RIFLE
Caliber: 177, 22, single shot.
Weight: 7 lbs. **Length:** 44″ over-all.
Power: Barrel cocking spring type.
Stock: Lacquered beechwood.
Sights: Hooded front, micro-adj. open rear.
Features: Velocity over 660 fps. Blued metal finish. Introduced 1981. Imported from Spain by Stoeger Industries.
Price: **$144.00**

GAMO MODEL 300 AIR RIFLE
Caliber: 22 only, single shot.
Weight: 7 lbs. **Length:** 44″ over-all.
Power: Barrel cocking spring type.
Stock: Lacquered beechwood.
Sights: Hooded front, micro-adj. rear.
Features: Velocity of 600 fps. Blued metal finish. Introduced 1981. Imported from Spain by Stoeger Industries.
Price: **$104.00**

MARKSMAN 1741 AIR RIFLE
Caliber: 177, 100-shot.
Barrel: 15½″, smoothbore.
Weight: 4 lbs., 2 oz. **Length:** 36½″ over-all.
Power: Spring, barrel cocking.
Stock: Moulded high-impact ABS plastic.
Sights: Ramp front, open rear adj. for e.
Features: Automatic safety; fixed front, adj. rear sight; shoots 177 cal. BB's pellets and darts. Velocity about 450 fps.
Price: **$29.50**

Power Line 880

POWER LINE 880 PUMP-UP AIR GUN
Caliber: 177 pellets, BB.
Barrel: Smooth bore, steel.
Weight: 6 lbs. **Length:** 37¾″ over-all.
Power: Spring air.
Stock: Wood grain moulded plastic.
Sights: Ramp front, open rear adj. for e.
Features: Crafted by Daisy. Variable power (velocity and range) increase with pump strokes. 10 strokes for maximum power. 100-shot BB magazine. Cross-bolt trigger safety. Positive cocking valve.
Price: About **$50.75**

POWER LINE 881 PUMP-UP AIR GUN
Caliber: 177 pellets, BB.
Barrel: Decagon rifled.
Weight: 6 lbs. **Length:** 37¾″ over-all.
Power: Spring air.
Stock: Wood grain moulded plastic with Monte Carlo cheekpiece.
Sights: Ramp front, step-adj. rear for e.
Features: Crafted by Daisy. Accurized version of Model 880. Checkered fore-end and p.g.
Price: About **$61.50**

Power Line 917/922

Power Line 977 Target Rifle
Similar to Model 917/922 except has engraved black finish receiver; hooded front sight with aperture inserts, fully adj. precision rear with micrometer calibrations. Has 5-shot clip, moulded Monte Carlo stock.
Price: About **$82.75**

POWER LINE MODEL 917/922
Caliber: 177 or 22 pellets, 5-shot clip.
Barrel: 20.8″. Decagon rifled brass barrel.
Weight: 5 lbs. **Length:** 37¾″ over-all.
Stock: Moulded wood-grained plastic with checkered p.g. and fore-end.
Sights: Ramp front, full adj. open rear.
Features: Muzzle velocity from 285 fps (two pumps) to 555 fps. (ten pumps). Straight pull bolt action. Separate buttplate and grip cap with white spacers. Introduced 1978.
Price: About **$67.95**

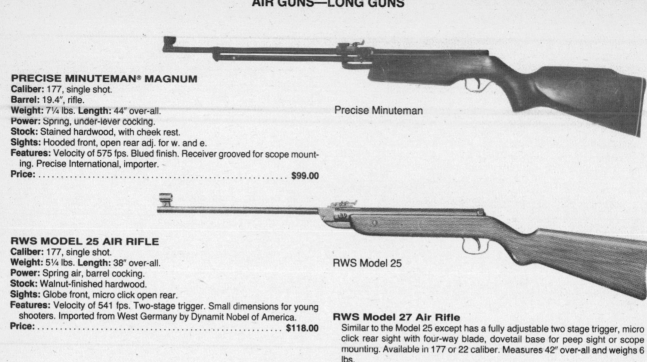

Precise Minuteman

PRECISE MINUTEMAN® MAGNUM
Caliber: 177, single shot.
Barrel: 19.4″, rifle.
Weight: 7¼ lbs. **Length:** 44″ over-all.
Power: Spring, under-lever cocking.
Stock: Stained hardwood, with cheek rest.
Sights: Hooded front, open rear adj. for w. and e.
Features: Velocity of 575 fps. Blued finish. Receiver grooved for scope mount-
ing. Precise International, importer.
Price: **$99.00**

RWS Model 25

RWS MODEL 25 AIR RIFLE
Caliber: 177, single shot.
Weight: 5¼ lbs. **Length:** 38″ over-all.
Power: Spring air, barrel cocking.
Stock: Walnut-finished hardwood.
Sights: Globe front, micro click open rear.
Features: Velocity of 541 fps. Two-stage trigger. Small dimensions for young
shooters. Imported from West Germany by Dynamit Nobel of America.
Price: **$118.00**

RWS Model 27 Air Rifle
Similar to the Model 25 except has a fully adjustable two stage trigger, micro
click rear sight with four-way blade, dovetail base for peep sight or scope
mounting. Available in 177 or 22 caliber. Measures 42″ over-all and weighs 6
lbs.
Price: 177 or 22 .... **$160.00**

RWS Model 35

RWS Model 35 Air Rifle
Similar to the Model 27 except slightly heavier and needs less cocking effort.
Has hardwood stock with cheekpiece, checkered pistol grip, rubber butt pad.
Globe front sight uses optional interchangeable inserts. Available in 177 or
22 caliber. Weighs 6½ lbs.
Price: **$199.00**

RWS Model 90

RWS MODEL 50 AIR RIFLE
Caliber: 177, single shot.
Weight: 8 lbs. **Length:** 45″ over-all.
Power: Spring air, underlever cocking.
Stock: Walnut-finished hardwood with cheekpiece, checkered grip, rubber butt
pad.
Sights: Globe front, micro click open rear.
Features: Velocity of 750 fps. Automatic safety. Dovetail base for scope or
peep sight mounting. Imported from West Germany by Dynamit Nobel of
America.
Price: **$275.00**

RWS Model 75

RWS MODEL 75 MATCH AIR RIFLE
Caliber: 177, single shot.
Barrel: 19″.
Weight: 11 lbs. **Length:** 43.7″ over-all.
Power: Spring air, side-lever cocking.
Stock: Oil finished walnut with stippled grip, adjustable buttplate, accessory
rail, Conforms to I.S.U. rules.
Sights: Globe front with 5 inserts, fully adjustable match peep rear.
Features: Velocity of 574 fps. Fully adjustable trigger. Model 75 HV has stip-
pled fore-end, adjustable cheekpiece. Uses double opposing piston system
for recoilless operation. Imported from West Germany by Dynamit Nobel of
America.
Price: Model 75 .... **$615.00**
Price: Model 75 HV **$720.00**
Price: Model 75 left hand **$650.00**
Price: Model 75 HV left hand **$765.00**

Consult our Directory pages for
the location of firms mentioned.

CAUTION: PRICES CHANGE. CHECK AT GUNSHOP.

RWS MODEL 45 AIR RIFLE

Caliber: 177 or 22, single shot.
Weight: 7¾ lbs. **Length:** 46″ over-all.
Power: Spring air, barrel cocking.
Stock: Walnut-finished hardwood with rubber recoil pad.
Sights: Globe front with interchangeable inserts, micro click open rear with four-way blade.
Features: Velocity of 820 fps (177 cal.), 689 fps (22 cal.). Dovetail base for either micrometer peep sight or scope mounting. Automatic safety. Imported from West Germany by Dynamit Nobel of America.
Price: 177 or 22 . . . . **$217.00**
Price: With deluxe walnut stock. **$240.00**

RWS Model 45

SIG-Hammerli 420

SIG-HAMMERLI MILITARY LOOK 420

Caliber: 177 or 22, single shot.
Barrel: 19″, rifled.
Weight: About 7 lbs. **Length:** 44¼″ over-all.
Stock: Synthetic stock and handguard.
Sights: Open, fully adj.
Features: Side lever cocking; adjustable trigger; rifled steel barrel. Introduced 1977. Imported by Mandall Shooting Supplies.
Price: **$295.00**

SIG-Hammerli 403

SIG-HAMMERLI MODELS 401 & 403 AIR RIFLES

Caliber: 177, single shot.
Weight: 7.8 lbs. **Length:** 44″ over-all.
Power: Spring air, sidelever cocking.
Stock: Beechwood.
Sights: Globe front accepts interchangeable inserts; fully adj. open rear (Model 401) or match aperture rear (Model 403).
Features: Sidelever cocking effort of 20 lbs. Automatic safety. Model 403 has a 2-lb. barrel sleeve and adj. buttplate. Fully adj. trigger. Introduced 1980. Imported by Mandall Shooting Supplies.
Price: Model 401 . . . . **$279.95**
Price: Model 403 . . . . **$299.95**

Sheridan CO₂

SHERIDAN CO₂ AIR RIFLES

Caliber: 5mm (20 cal.), single shot.
Barrel: 18½″, rifled.
Weight: 6 lbs. **Length:** 37″ over-all.
Power: Walnut sporter.
Stock: Standard 12.5 gram CO₂ cylinder.
Sights: Open, adj. for w. and e. Optional Sheridan-Williams 5D-SH receiver sight or Weaver D4 scope.
Features: Bolt action single shot, CO₂ powered. Velocity approx. 514 fps., manual thumb safety. Blue or Silver finish. Left-hand models avail. at same prices.
Price: CO₂ Blue Streak **$101.55**
Price: CO₂ Silver Streak **$105.40**
Price: CO₂ Blue Streak with receiver sight **$118.15**
Price: CO₂ Blue Streak with scope **$134.15**

Sheridan accessories: Intermount, a base for ⅜″ Tip-Off scope mounts, **$12.65;** Sheridan-Williams 5DSH receiver sight, **$12.40;** Sheridan Pelle-trap, **$19.00;** Sheridan 5mm pellets, **$5.80** for 500. Weaver 4 x scope and Intermount installed **$30.60 (extra).**

Sheridan Blue Streak

SHERIDAN BLUE AND SILVER STREAK RIFLES

Caliber: 5mm (20 cal.), single shot.
Barrel: 18½″, rifled.
Weight: 5 lbs. **Length:** 37″ over-all.
Power: Hand pumped (swinging fore-end).
Features: Rustproof barrel and piston tube. Takedown. Thumb safety. Mannlicher type walnut stock. Left-hand models same price.
Price: Blue Streak **$101.55**
Price: Silver Streak **$105.40**

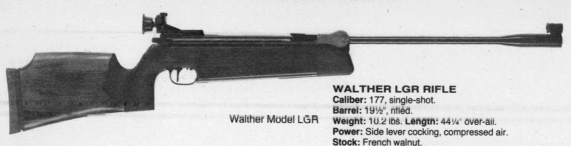

Walther Model LGR

WALTHER LGR RIFLE
Caliber: 177, single-shot.
Barrel: 19½", rifled.
Weight: 10.2 lbs. **Length:** 44¼" over-all.
Power: Side lever cocking, compressed air.
Stock: French walnut.
Sights: Replaceable insert hooded front, Walther micro. adjustable rear.
Features: Recoilless operation. Trigger adj. for weight, pull and position. High comb stock with broad stippled fore-end and p.g. Imported from Germany by Interarms.
Price: $695.00

Walther LGV Special

WALTHER LGV SPECIAL
Caliber: 177, single shot.
Barrel: 16", rifled.
Weight: 10¼ lbs. **Length:** 41⅜" over-all.
Power: Spring air (barrel cocking).
Features: Micro. click adj. aperture receiver sight; Adj. trigger. Walnut match stock, adj. buttplate. Double piston provides vibration-free shooting. Easily operated bbl. latch. Removable heavy bbl. sleeve. 5-way adj. trigger. Imported from Germany by Interarms:
Price: $595.00

Walther LGR Match Air Rifle
Same basic specifications as standard LGR except has a high comb stock, sights are mounted on riser blocks. Introduced 1977.
Price: $795.00

Weihrauch Model 55T

WEIHRAUCH 35L/35EB SPORTER RIFLES
Caliber: 177 (35L), 177 or 22 (35EB), single shot.
Barrel: 19½".
Weight: 8 lbs. **Length:** 43½" over-all (35L).
Power: Spring, barrel cocking.
Stock: Walnut finish with high comb, full pistol grip.
Sights: Globe front with five inserts, target micrometer rear with rubber eye-cup.
Features: Fully adjustable trigger, manual safety. Thumb-release barrel latch. Model 35L has Bavarian cheekpiece stock, 35EB has walnut, American-style stock with cheekpiece, sling swivels, white spacers. Imported by Beeman.
Price: Model 35L $249.95
Price: Model 35EB $269.95

Weihrauch Model 35EB

WEIHRAUCH 55 TARGET RIFLES

Model:	55SM	55MM	55T
Caliber:	177	177	177
Barrel:	19¼"	19¼"	19¼"
Length:	43½"	43½"	43½"
Wgt. lbs.:	7.8	7.8	7.8
Rear sight:	All aperture		
Front sight:	All with globe and 4 interchangeable inserts.		
Power:	All spring (barrel cocking). 660-700 fps.		
Price:	$350.00	$387.50	$437.50

Features: Trigger fully adj. and removable. Micrometer rear sight adj. for w. and e. on all. Pistol grip high comb stock with beavertail fore-end, walnut finish stock on 55SM. Walnut stock on 55MM, Tyrolean stock on 55T. Available from Beeman.

> Consult our Directory pages for the location of firms mentioned.

Chokes & Brakes

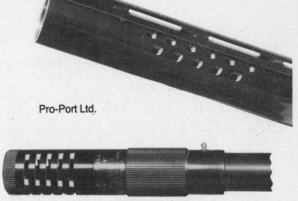

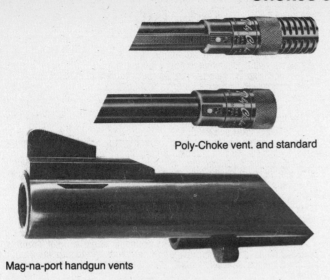

Poly-Choke vent. and standard

Pro-Port Ltd.

Mag-na-port handgun vents

Emsco choke

Choke-Matic
Cutts Compensator

The Cutts Compensator is one of the oldest variable choke devices available. Manufactured by Lyman Gunsight Corporation, it is available with a steel body. A series of vents allows gas to escape upward and downward. For the 12-ga. Comp body, six fixed-choke tubes are available: the Spreader—popular with Skeet shooters; Improved Cylinder; Modified; Full; Superfull, and Magnum Full. Full, Modified and Spreader tubes are available for 12, or 20, and an Adjustable Tube, giving Full through Improved Cylinder chokes, is offered in 12, or 20 gauges. Cutts Compensator, complete with wrench, adaptor and any single tube **$63.35;** with adjustable tube **$80.80.** All single choke tubes **$17.50** each. No factory installation available.

Dahl Muzzle Blast Controller

Only 1⅞″ long by ¾″ in diameter, this device is claimed to reduce recoil up to 30%. An outer sleeve, threaded onto the gun muzzle, is threaded on the inside to accept a machined plug which is bored through for bullet passage. Gas behind the bullet is bled off through slots in the plug, swirled through a number of tiny passages while contained by the sleeve, and then vented upward, this final action offsetting muzzle jump without discomfort to the shooter or bystanders. Price is **$50.00,** installed.

Emsco Choke

E. M. Schacht of Waseca, Minn., offers the Emsco, a small diameter choke which features a precision curve rather than a taper behind the 1½″ choking area. 9 settings are available in this 5 oz. attachment. Its removable recoil sleeve can be furnished in dural if desired. Choice of three sight heights. For 12, 16 or 20 gauge. Price installed, **$27.95.** Not installed, **$18.50.**

Jet-Away Choke

Arms Ingenuity Corp., makers of the Jet-Away, say that this device controls patterns through partial venting of the powder gases which normally enlarge patterns. The Jet-Away has a series of three slots in the top of the tube and a sliding control sleeve. When the sleeve is in its rearward position, all slots are uncovered, the maximum of gas is vented and patterns are densest. To obtain more open patterns, the sleeve is moved to cover one or more slots. Jet-Away is the only adjustable choke made in 10 gauge.

In 10, 12, 16 or 20 gauge only, the Jet-Away is made of aluminum and weighs 3 ozs. Prices (installed), 10 and 12 gauge **$80.00;** 16 and 20 gauge **$60.00.**

Lyman CHOKE

The Lyman CHOKE is similar to the Cutts Comp in that it comes with fixed-choke tubes or an adjustable tube, with or without recoil chamber. The adjustable tube version sells for **$34.95** with recoil chamber, in 12 or 20 gauge. Lyman also offers Single-Choke tubes at **$17.50.** This device may be used with or without a recoil-reduction chamber; cost of the latter is **$7.95** extra. Available in 12 or 20 gauge only, no factory installation offered.

Mag-Na-Port

Electrical Discharge Machining works on any firearm except those having shrouded barrels. EDM is a metal erosion technique using carbon electrodes that control the area to be processed. The Mag-na-port venting process utilizes small trapezoidal openings to direct powder gases upward and outward to reduce recoil.

No effect is had on bluing or nickeling outside the Magna-port area so no refinishing is needed. Cost for the Magna-port treatment is **$49.00** for handguns, **$65.00** for rifles, plus transportation both ways, and **$2.00** for handling.

Poly-Choke

The Poly-Choke Co., manufacturers of the original adjustable shotgun choke, now offers two models in 12, 16, 20 and 28 gauge, the Deluxe Ventilated and the Deluxe Standard. Each provides 9 choke settings including Xtra-Full and Slug. The Ventilated model reduces 20% of a shotgun's recoil, the company claims, and is priced at **$47.50.** The Standard model is **$45.00,** postage not included.

Pro-Port

A compound ellipsoid muzzle venting process similar to Mag-na-porting, only exclusively applied to shotguns. Like Mag-na-porting, this system reduces felt recoil, muzzle jump, and shooter fatigue. Very helpful for Trap doubles shooters. Pro-Port is a patented process and installation is available in both the U.S. and Canada. Cost for the Pro-Port process is **$110.00** for over-unders (both barrels); **$80.00** for only the bottom barrel; and **$65.00** for single barrel shotguns. Prices do not include shipping and handling.

Micrometer Receiver Sights

B-SQUARE SMLE (LEE-ENFIELD)
For No. 4 and Jungle carbine. No drilling or tapping required. ³⁄₃₂″ disc furnished. Price...**$5.95**

BUEHLER
"Little Blue Peep" auxiliary rear sight used with Buehler scope mounts. Price..**$3.75**

FREELAND TUBE SIGHT
Uses Unertl 1″ micrometer mounts. For 22-cal. target rifles, inc. 52 Win., 37, 40X Rem. and DCA Martini. Price..................**$123.00**

REDFIELD "PALMA" TARGET SIGHT
Windage and elevation adjustments are ¼-MOA and can be adjusted for "hard" or "soft" feel. Repeatability error limited to .001″ per click. Windage latitude 36 MOA, elevation 60 MOA. Mounting arm has three positions, providing ample positioning latitude for other sighting aids such as variable diopter correction, adjustable filters. An insert in the sighting disc block accepts either the standard American sighting disc thread or the European 9.5mm × 1 metric thread. Elevation staff and the sighting disc block have dovetail construction for precise travel. Price..................**$199.90**

WILLIAMS FP
Internal click adjustments. Positive locks. For virtually all rifles, T/C Contender, plus Win., Rem. and Ithaca shotguns. Price.............**$32.67**
With Twilight Aperture.............................**$33.60**
With Target Knobs................................**$38.85**
With Target Knobs & Twilight Aperture.................**$39.80**
With Square Notched Blade.........................**$34.35**
With Target Knobs & Square Notched Blade.............**$40.60**

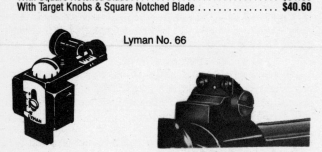

Lyman No. 66

Buehler "Little Blue Peep"

Williams FP-TK

LYMAN No. 57
¼-min. clicks. Target or Stayset knobs. Quick release slide, adjustable zero scales. Made for almost all modern rifles. Price............**$43.95**

LYMAN No. 66
Fits close to the rear of flat-sided receivers, furnished with target or Stayset knobs. Quick release slide, ¼-min. adj. For most lever or slide action or flat-sided automatic rifles. Price..........................**$43.95**

WILLIAMS 5-D SIGHT
Low cost sight for shotguns, 22's and the more popular big game rifles. Adjustment for w. and e. Fits most guns without drilling or tapping. Also for Br. SMLE. Price...............................**$18.55**
With Twilight Aperture.............................**$19.50**
Extra Shotgun Aperture............................**$4.90**

WILLIAMS GUIDE
Receiver sight for .30 M1 Car., M1903A3 Springfield, Savage 24's, Savage-Anschutz rifles and Wby. XXII. Utilizes military dovetail; no drilling. Double-dovetail W. adj., sliding dovetail adj. for e. Price............**$17.75**
With Twilight Aperture.............................**$18.70**
With Open Sight Blade.............................**$16.35**

Sporting Leaf and Tang Sights

BINGHAM SPORTING RIFLE SIGHTS
All-steel sights are imported from Europe. Many styles of both front and rear sights available; random sampling listed here.
European express gold bead for European express ramp.......**$4.25**
European express ramp.............................**$7.50**
Semi-buckhorn rear, with elevator....................**$6.50**
Rocky Mountain front, blue or bright..................**$3.95**
European 2-leaf folding express rear (V and U notch)........**$12.50**

BINGHAM CLASSIC SIGHTS
All-steel sights for "classic" rifles. Rear sights only. This listing not complete; contact Bingham for full list.
Model 66 folding ladder-type........................**$19.95**
Model Saddle Ring Carbine (73, 92, 94, etc.).............**$14.95**
Elevator, Winchester-type, early series (1876-WW II).........**$4.95**

BURRIS SPORTING REAR SIGHT
Made of spring steel, supplied with multi-step elevator for coarse adjustments and notch plate with lock screw for finer adjustments. Price **$10.95**

LYMAN No. 16
Middle sight for barrel dovetail slot mounting. Folds flat when scope or peep sight is used. Sight notch plate adjustable for e. White triangle for quick aiming. 3 heights: A—.400″ to .500″, B—.345″ to .445″, C—.500″ to .600″. Price...**$9.95**

MARBLE FALSE BASE
New screw-on base for most rifles replaces factory base. ⅜″ dovetail slot permits installation of any Marble rear sight. Can be had in sweat-on models also. Price...**$3.60**

MARBLE CONTOUR RAMP
For late model Rem. 725, 740, 760, 742 rear sight mounting. ⁹⁄₁₆″ between mounting screws. Price.............................**$8.00**

Wichita Multi Range System

MARBLE FOLDING LEAF
Flat-top or semi-buckhorn style. Folds down when scope or peep sights are used. Reversible plate gives choice of "U" or "V" notch. Adjustable for elevation. Price.................................**$7.20**
Also available with both w. and e. adjustment.............**$8.40**

MARBLE SPORTING REAR
With white enamel diamond, gives choice of two "U" and two "V" notches of different sizes. Adjustment in height by means of double step elevator and sliding notch piece. For all rifles; screw or dovetail installation. Price......................................**$7.40-$8.40**

WICHITA MULTI RANGE SIGHT SYSTEM
Designed for silhouette shooting. System allows you to adjust the rear sight to four repeatable range settings, once it is pre-set. Sight clicks to any of the settings by turning a serrated wheel. Front sight is adjustable for weather and light conditions with one adjustment. Specify gun when ordering.
Price: Rear sight...............................**$69.95**
Front sight...............................**$39.95**

WILLIAMS DOVETAIL OPEN SIGHT
Open rear sight with w. and e. adjustment. Furnished with "U" notch or choice of blades. Slips into dovetail and locks with gib lock. Heights from .281″ to .531″. Price with blade......................**$10.15**
Less Blade......................................**$6.65**
Extra Blades....................................**$3.50**

WILLIAMS GUIDE OPEN SIGHT
Open rear sight with w. and e. adjustment. Bases to fit most military and commercial barrels. Choice of square "U" or "V" notch blade, ³⁄₁₆″, ¼″, ⁵⁄₁₆″, or ⅜″ high. Price.................................**$12.25**
Extra blades, each................................**$3.50**
Price, less blade.................................**$8.75**

Front Sights

BURRIS FRONT SIGHTS
Two styles: Patridge, gold bead. Widths are .250″, .340″, .500″ and Mauser .310″. Price from . . . . $5.45 to $5.95

LYMAN BLADE & DOVETAIL SIGHTS
Made with gold or ivory beads ¹⁄₁₆″ to ³⁄₃₂″ wide and in varying heights for most military and commercial rifles. Price $6.95

MARBLE STANDARD
Ivory, red, or gold bead. For all American made rifles, ¹⁄₁₆″ wide bead with semi-flat face which does not reflect light. Specify type of rifle when ordering. Price. $4.25

Marble's Standard Blade, Sheard, Contour, Standard

MARBLE-SHEARD "GOLD"
Shows up well even in darkest timber. Shows same color on different colored objects; sturdily built. Medium bead. Various models for different makes of rifles so specify type of rifle when ordering. Price. $5.25

MARBLE CONTOURED
Same contour and shape as Marble-Sheard but uses standard ¹⁄₁₆″ or ³⁄₃₂″ bead, ivory, red or gold. Specify rifle type. Price $4.80

WILLIAMS GUIDE BEAD SIGHT
Fits all shotguns, ⅛″ ivory, red or gold bead. Screws into existing sight hole. Various thread sizes and shank lengths. Price $3.45

Globe Target Front Sights

FREELAND SUPERIOR
Furnished with six 1″ plastic apertures. Available in 4½″-6½″ lengths. Made for any target rifle. Price. $33.75
Price with 6 metal insert apertures $35.95
Price, front base $8.00

Lyman No. 17A   Freeland Military

FREELAND TWIN SET
Two Freeland Superior or Junior Globe Front Sights, long or short, allow switching from 50 yd. to 100 yd. ranges and back again without changing rear sight adjustment. Sight adjustment compensation is built into the set; just interchange and you're "on" at either range. Set includes 6 plastic apertures. Price, Twin set (long or short) $51.00
Price with 6 metal apertures $54.50

FREELAND MILITARY
Short model for use with high-powered rifles where sight must not extend beyond muzzle. Screw-on base; six plastic apertures. Price . . $32.75
Price with 6 metal apertures $35.90
Price, front base $8.00

LYMAN No. 17A
7 interchangeable inserts which include 4 apertures, one transparent amber and two posts .50″ and .100″ in width. Price $18.95

REDFIELD Nos. 63 and 64
For rifles specially stocked for scopes where metallic sights must be same height as scopes. Instantly detachable to permit use of scope. Two styles and heights of bases. Interchangeable inserts. No. 64 is ¼″ higher. Price with base, ... $33.70
No. 64 . . . . $39.70

REDFIELD No. 65
1″ long, ⅝″ diameter. Standard dovetail base with 7 aperture or post inserts which are not reversible. For any rifle having standard barrel slot. ¹³⁄₃₂″ height from bottom of base to center of aperture. No. 65NB ($26.30) same as above with narrow base for Win. 64 N.R.A., 70, and Savage 40, 45, and 99 with ramp front sight base. Price $27.50

REDFIELD No. 66
Replaces entire removable front sight stud, locked in place by screw in front of barrel band. ¾″ from bottom of base to center of aperture. For Spgfld. 1903. Price. $30.10

REDFIELD No. 68
For Win. 52, heavy barrel, Sav. 19 and 33, and other rifles requiring high front sight. ¹⁷⁄₃₂″ from bottom of base to center of aperture. Standard dovetail size only. Price. $25.50

REDFIELD OLYMPIC FRONT
Detachable. 10 inserts—5 steel, sizes .090″, .110″, .120″, .140″, .150″; one post insert, size .100″; four celluloid, sizes .090″, .110″, .120″, .140″. Celluloid inserts in clear, green, or amber, with or without cross hairs. For practically all rifles and with any type rear sight. Fits all standard Redfield, Lyman, or Fecker scope blocks. Price with base. $50.10

REDFIELD INTERNATIONAL SMALLBORE FRONT
Similar to Olympic. Drop-in insertion of eared inserts. Outer sleeve prevents light leakage. Comes complete with 6 clear inserts and 6 skeleton inserts. Price $53.50

REDFIELD INTERNATIONAL MILITARY BIG BORE
Same as International Match except tube only 2¼″ long. For 30 cal. use. Price $53.50

Ramp Sights

LYMAN SCREW-ON RAMP AND SIGHT
Used with 8-40 screws but may also be brazed on. Heights from .10″ to .350″. Ramp without sight $10.95

MARBLE FRONT RAMPS
Available in either screw-on or sweat-on style. 5 heights; ³⁄₁₆″, ⁵⁄₁₆″, ⅜″, ⁷⁄₁₆″, ⁹⁄₁₆″. Standard ⅜″ dovetail slot. Price $7.50
Hoods for above ramps $1.65

WILLIAMS SHORTY RAMP
Companion to "Streamlined" ramp, about ½″ shorter. Screw-on or sweat-on. It is furnished in ⅛″, ³⁄₁₆″, ⁹⁄₃₂″, and ⅜″ heights without hood only. Price $8.75

WILLIAMS STREAMLINED RAMP
Hooded style in screw-on or sweat-on models. Furnished in ⁹⁄₁₆″, ⁷⁄₁₆″, ⅜″, ⁵⁄₁₆″, ³⁄₁₆″ heights. Price with hood $13.80
Price without hood $11.45

WILLIAMS SHOTGUN RAMP
Designed to elevate the front bead for slug shooting or for guns that shoot high. Diameters to fit most 12, 16, 20 ga. guns. Fastens by screw-clamp, no drilling required. Price, with Williams gold bead $8.50
Price, without bead $6.25
Price, with Guide Bead $9.70

Handgun Sights

BINGHAM PISTOL SIGHTS
All-steel sights of various designs for Colt Government Model and Browning Hi-Power. Low profile "battle sights" (front and rear) for either Colt G.M. or Browning HP. Price. $16.95
Combat sight set, low profile, white outline for Colt G.M., front and rear $21.95
National Match front sight, Colt G.M. $3.75
Camp Perry front sight, Colt G.M. $4.95

BO-MAR DE LUXE
Gives ⅜″ w. and e. adjustment at 50 yards on Colt Gov't 45, sight radius under 7″. For GM and Commander models only. Uses existing dovetail slot. Has shield-type rear blade. Price $38.00

BO-MAR LOW PROFILE RIB
Streamlined rib with front and rear sights; 7⅛″ sight radius. Brings sight line closer to the bore than standard or extended sight and ramp. Weighs 4 oz. Made for Ruger Mark I Bull Barrel, Colt Gov't 45, Super 38, and Gold Cup 45 and 38. Price. $50.00
With extended sight and ramp, 8⅛″ radius, 5¾ oz. $57.00
Rib & Tuner—inserted in Low Profile Rib—accuracy tuner. Adjustable for barrel positioning $59.00

BO-MAR COMBAT RIB
For S&W Model 19 revolver with 4″ barrel. Sight radius 5¾″; weight 5½ oz. Price $50.00

BO-MAR FAST DRAW RIB
Streamlined full length rib with integral Bo-Mar micrometer sight and serrated fast draw sight. For Browning 9mm, S&W 39, Colt Commander 45, Super Auto and 9mm. Price $50.00

BO-MAR WINGED RIB
For S&W 4" and 6" length barrels—K-38, M10, HB 14 and 19. Weight for the 6" model is about 7¼ oz. Price. $58.00

BO-MAR COVER-UP RIB
Adj. rear sight, winged front guards. Fits right over revolver's original front sight. For S&W 4" M-10HB, M-13, M-58, M-64 & 65, Ruger 4" models SDA-34, SDA-84, SS-34, SS-84, GF-34, GF-84. Price. $56.00

MICRO
Click adjustable w. and e. rear with plain or undercut front sight in ⅛" widths. Standard model available for 45, Super 38 or Commander autos. Low model for above pistols plus Colt Service Ace. Also for Ruger with 4¾" or 6" barrel. Price for sets. $28.50
Price with ramp front sight $35.00
Adjustable rear sight only $24.00
Front ramp only, with blade $14.00

MICRO
All-steel replacement for Ruger single-action and double-action revolvers. Two styles: MR-44 for square front end of sight leaf. Price. . . . $18.00

MMC "BAR CROSS" SIGHT SYSTEM
Provides a quick, clear sight picture in a variety of lighting conditions. Black oxide finish is non-reflective. Front sight has a horizontal white bar with vertical white bar, gives illusion of cross hair in poor light. Fixed rear comes with or without white outline. Various front blades available.
White outline rear sight $17.30
Plain rear $13.50
Ramp Bar Cross front $12.40

MMC COMBAT DESIGN
Available specifically for Colt M1911 and descendants, High Standard autos, Ruger standard autos. Adaptable to other pistols. Some gunsmithing required. Not necessary to replace front sight. Contact MMC for complete details.
Price, less leaf. $26.15
Plain leaf. $7.75
White outline leaf $11.40
Extra for satin nickel finish (base only) $8.50
With reflector beads, add $2.25

MILLETT SERIES 100 SIGHTS
Replacement sights for revolvers and auto pistols. Positive click adjustments for windage and elevation. Designed for accuracy and ruggedness. Made to fit S&W, Colt, High Standard, Ruger, Dan Wesson, Browning, AMT Hardballer and Abilene handguns. Rear blades are available in white outline or positive black target. All steel construction and easy to install.
Price . . . . $39.95 to $56.95

MILLETT MARK SERIES PISTOL SIGHTS
Mark I and Mark II replacement combat sights for government-type auto pistols. Mark I is high profile, Mark II low profile. Both have horizontal light deflectors.
Mark I, front and rear. $27.95
Mark II, front and rear $39.95

OMEGA OUTLINE SIGHT BLADES
Replacement rear sight blades for Colt and Ruger single action guns and the Interarms Virginian Dragoon. Standard Outline available in gold or white notch outline on blue metal. Price $5.95

OMEGA MAVERICK SIGHT BLADES
Replacement "peep-sight" blades for Colt, Ruger SAs, Virginian Dragoon. Three models available—No. 1, Plain, No. 2, Single Bar, No. 3 Double Bar Rangefinder. Price, each $6.95

Wichita 45 System

Millett Series 100

WICHITA SIGHT SYSTEMS
For 45 auto pistols. Target and Combat styles available. Designed by Ron Power. All-steel construction, click adjustable. Each sight has two traverse pins, a large hinge pin and two elevation return springs. Sight blade is serrated and mounted on an angle to deflect light. Patridge front for target, ramp front for combat. Both are legal for ISPC and NRA competitons.
Rear sight, target or combat $49.50
Front sight, patridge or ramp $8.95

Sight Attachments

FREELAND LENS ADAPTER
Fits 1⅛" O.D. presciption ground lens to all standard tube and receiver sights for shooting without glasses. Price without lens $44.00
Clear lens ground to prescription $21.00
Yellow or green prescription lens $21.00

MERIT ADAPTER FOR GLOBE FRONT SIGHTS
An Iris Shutter Disc with a special adapter for mounting in Lyman or Redfield globe front sights. Price $42.00

MERIT IRIS SHUTTER DISC
Eleven clicks gives 12 different apertures. No. 3 and Master, primarily target types, 0.22" to .125"; No. 4, ½" dia. hunting type, .025" to .155". Available for all popular sights. The Master Disc, with flexible rubber light shield, is particularly adapted to extension, scope height, and tang sights. All Merit Deluxe models have internal click springs; are hand fitted to minimum tolerance.
Std. Master $45.00
Master Deluxe $54.30
No. 4 Hunting Disc $37.50

MERIT LENS DISC
Similar to Merit Iris Shutter (Model 3 or Master) but incorporates provision for mounting prescription lens integrally. Lens may be obtained locally, or prescription sent to Merit. Sight disc is ⁷⁄₁₆" wide (Mod. 3), or ¾" wide (Master). Lens, ground to prescription, $19.00 Standard tints, $23.50 Model 3 Deluxe. Price. $57.75
Master Deluxe $67.50

MERIT OPTICAL ATTACHMENT
For revolver and pistol shooters, instantly attached by rubber suction cup to regular or shooting glasses. Any aperture .020" to .156". Price, Deluxe (swings aside). $54.75

REDFIELD SURE-X SIGHTING DISC
Eight hole selective aperture. Fits any Redfield target sight. Each click changes aperture .004". Price $21.10

REDFIELD SIGHTING DISCS
Fit all Redfield receiver sights. .046" to .093" aperture. ⅜", ½" and ⅞" O.D. Price, each $4.70

WILLIAMS APERTURES
Standard thread, fits most sights. Regular series ⅜" to ½" O.D., .050" to .125" hole. "Twilight" series has white reflector ring. .093" to .125" inner hole. Price, regular series . . . $3.00. Twilight series $3.15
New wide open ⁵⁄₁₆" aperture for shotguns fits 5-D and Foolproof sights.
Price $4.30

Shotgun Sights

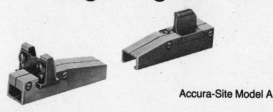

Accura-Site Model A

ACCURA-SITE
For shooting shotgun slugs. Three models to fit most shotguns—"A" for vent. rib barrels, "B" for solid ribs, "C" for plain barrels. Rear sight has windage and elevation provisions. Easily removed and replaced. Includes front and rear sights. Price . . . . $14.95 to $18.95

FOR DOUBLE BARREL SHOTGUNS (PRESS FIT)
Marble 214—Ivory front bead, ¹¹⁄₆₄" . . $2.40; 215—same with .080" rear bead and reamers . . $8.15. Marble 220—Bi-color (gold and ivory) front bead, ¹¹⁄₆₄" and .080" rear bead, with reamers . . $9.25; Marble 221—front bead only . . . $3.50. Marble 223—Ivory rear .080" . . . $2.20. Marble 224—Front sight reamer for 214-221 beads . . . $2.25; Marble 226—Rear sight reamer for 223. Price $1.75

FOR SINGLE OR DB SHOTGUNS (SCREW-ON FIT)
Marble 217—Ivory front bead ¹¹⁄₆₄" . . . $2.65; Marble 216 . . $5.50; Marble 218—Bi-color front, ¹¹⁄₆₄" . . $3.85; Marble 219 . . $6.70 Marble 223T—Ivory rear .080" Price. $3.65
Marble Bradley type sights 223BT—⅛", ⁵⁄₆₄" and ¹¹⁄₆₄" long. Gold, Ivory or Red bead. $2.50

SLUG SITE
A combination V-notch rear and bead front sight made of adhesive-backed formed metal approx. 7" over-all. May be mounted, removed and remounted as necessary, using new adhesive from the pack supplied.
Price $10.00

Maker and Model	Magn.	Field at 100 Yds (feet)	Relative Brightness	Eye Relief (in.)	Length (in.)	Tube Diam. (in.)	W&E Adjustments	Weight (ozs.)	Price	Other Data
American Import Co.										[1]Complete with mount for 22-cal. RF rifles. [2]Standard crosshair reticle, coated lenses. [3]Anodized finish. [4]Wide angle. [5]Super wide angle. [6]Post and crosshair, 3 post,, tapered post, crosshair and 4-post crosshair all available as options. 2, 3, 6 apply to all models.
Dickson 200[1]	4	19	13.7	3.5	11.5	¾	Int.	6	$ 13.95	
Dickson 218 32mm	2½	32	164	3.7	12	1	Int.	9.3	47.95	
Dickson 220 32mm[2]	4	29	64	3.6	12	1	Int.	9.1	46.95	
Dickson 226 40mm[3]	6	20	44.7	3.7	13	1	Int.	10	54.95	
Dickson 228 32mm[4]	4	37	64	3.3	12	1	Int.	10.5	65.95	
Dickson 230 40mm[4]	4	37	100	3.8	12.4	1	Int.	12	70.95	
Dickson 233 20mm[5]	4	42	25	3	9.8	1	Int.	10.2	66.95	
Dickson 240 32mm	3-9	37-12.3	112-13	3	12.8	1	Int.	13.8	64.95	
Dickson 242 40mm	3.9	37-12.3	177-19.4	3	12.8	1	Int.	15.2	70.95	
Beeman										[1]Pistol scope. All glass, coated lenses, 5-pt. reticle. Milled mounts included. [2]Pistol scope. Silhouette knobs, all glass, coated lenses, 5-pt. reticle. [3]Rubber armor coating. Built-in double adj. mount, parallax-free setting, 5-pt. reticle. All glass, coated lenses. [4]Same as Model 45R. [5]Objective focus, 5-pt. reticle. Milled mounts included. Coated glass lenses. [6]Milled mounts included, 5-pt. reticle. Coated glass lenses. [7]Objective focus, silhouette knobs, 5-pt. reticle. Coated glass lenses. [8]Objective focus, 5-pt. reticle. Coated glass lenses. Imported from Japan by Beeman.
Blue Ribbon 20[1]	1.5	14	—	11-16	8.3	¾	Int.	3.6	44.95	
Blue Ribbon 25[2]	2	19	—	10-24	9¹/₁₆	1	Int.	7.4	124.50	
Beeman SS-1[3]	2.5	30	—	3¼	5½	1	Int.	7	99.95	
Model 50R[4]	2.5	33	164	3½	12	1	Int.	11.8	87.50	
Model 35R[5]	3	25	45	2½	11¼	¾	Int.	5.1	39.95	
Model 30[6]	4	21	—	2	10.2	¾	Int.	4.5	19.98	
Blue Ribbon 66[7]	2-7	58-16	—	3	11.4	1	Int.	13.1	159.50	
Model 45R[8]	3-7	26.2-12	45-8	2.5	10⁵/₈	¾	Int.	6	62.95	
Burris										Dot reticle $10 extra. Target knobs $15 extra. ½-minute dot $10 extra. LER = Long Eye Relief—ideal for forward mounting on handguns. Plex or crosshair only. Matte "Safari" finish avail. on 4x, 6x, 2-7x, 3-9x with Plex reticle, $10 extra, [1]3" dot $10 extra. [2]1"-3" dot $10 extra. [3]1"-3" dot $10 extra. [4]With parallax adjustment $135.95. [5]With parallax adjustment $142.95. [6]With parallax adjustment $151.95. [7]With parallax adjustment $158.95. Parallax adjustment adds 5 oz. to weight.
4x Fullfield[1]	3.8	37	49	3¼	11¼	1	Int.	11	159.95	
2x-7x Fullfield[2] HiLume	2.5-6.8	50-19	81-22	3¼	11⅞	1	Int.	14	213.95	
3x-9x Fullfield[3] HiLume	3.3-8.6	40-15	72-17.6	3¼	12¾	1	Int.	15	229.95	
2¾ Fullfield	2.7	53	49	3¼	10½	1	Int.	9	150.95	
6x Fullfield	5.8	24	36	3¼	13	1	Int.	12	172.95	
1¾-5x Fullfield HiLume	2.5-6.8	70-27	121-25	3¼	10¾	1	Int.	13	188.95	
4x-12x Fullfield	4.4-11.8	28-10½	—	3-3¼	15	1	Int.	18	263.95	
■ 6x-18x Fullfield	6.5-17.6	17-7.5	—	3-3¾	15.8	12	Int.	18.5	267.95	
■ 10x Fullfield	9.8	12½	—	3¼	15	1	Int.	15	224.95	
■ 12x Fullfield	11.8	11	—	3¼	15	1	Int.	15	231.95	
2x LER	1.7	21	—	10-24	8¾	1	Int.	6.8	117.95	
3x LER	2.7	17	—	10-20	8⅞	1	Int.	6.8	124.95	
4x LER[6]	3.7	11	—	10-22	9⅝	1	Int.	8.5	133.95	
5x LER[7]	4.5	8.7	—	12-22	10⅞	1	Int.	9.5	140.95	
2x-7x Mini	2.5-6.9	32-14	—	3¾	9⅜	1	Int.	10.5	159.95	
4x Mini	3.6	24	—	3¾	8¼	1	Int.	7.8	116.95	
6x Mini	5.5	17	—	3¾	9	1	Int.	7.8	124.95	
3x-9x Mini	3.6-8.8	25-11	—	3¾	9⅞	1	Int.	11.5	168.95	
Bushnell										All ScopeChief, Banner and Custom models come with Multi-X reticle, with or without BDC (bullet drop compensator) that eliminates holdover. Prismatic Rangefinder (PRF) on some models. Contact Bushnell for data on full line. Prices include BDC—deduct $5 if not wanted. Add $30 for PRF. BDC feature available in all Banner models, except 2.5x. [1]Wide angle. [2]Complete with mount rings. [3]Equipped with Wind Drift Compensator and Parallax-free adjustment. [4]Parallax focus adjustment. [5]Wide angle. [6]Wide angle. [7]Parallax focus adjustment. [8]Phantoms intended for handgun use. [9]Mount separate.
Scope Chief VI	4	37.3	150	3	12.3	1	Int.	12	159.95	
Scope Chief VI	4	29	96	3½	12	1	Int.	9.3	119.95	
Scope Chief VI	3-9	35-12.6	267-30	3½-3⅓	12.6	1	Int.	14.3	191.95	
Scope Chief VI	3-9	43-14.6	241-26.5	3	12.1	1	Int.	15.4	239.95	
Scope Chief VI	2½-8	45-14	247-96	3.7-3.3	11.2	1	Int.	12.1	169.95	
Scope Chief VI	1½-4½	73.7-24.5	267-30	3.5-3.5	9.6	1	Int.	9.5	159.95	
Scope Chief VI	4-12	29-10	150-17	3.2	13.5	1	Int.	17	234.95	
Custom 22	4	28.4	—	2½	10⁵/₁₆	⅞	Int.	5¼	41.95	
Custom 22	3-7	29-13.6	28-5	2¼-2½	10	⅞	Int.	6½	51.95	
Banner	2½	45	96	3½	10.9	1	Int.	8	86.95	
Banner 32mm	4	29	96	3½	12	1	Int.	10	100.95	
Banner 40mm	4	37⅓	150	3	12⅓	1	Int.	12	131.95	
Banner 40mm	6	19.5	67	3	13.5	1	Int.	11.5	109.95	
Banner[1]	6	19½	42	3	13½	1	Int.	10½	109.95	
Banner 22[2]	4	27.5	37.5	3	11⅝	1	Int.	8	64.95	
■ Banner Silhouette[3]	10	12	24	3	14½	1	Int.	14.6	167.95	
■ Banner	10	12	24	3	14½	1	Int.	14.6	167.95	
Banner[4]	1½-4	63-28	294-41	3½	10½	1	Int.	10.3	123.95	
Banner[5]	1¾-4½	71-27	216-33	3	10.2	1	Int.	11½	143.95	
Banner 32mm	3-9	39-13	171-19	3½	11.5	1	Int.	11	137.95	
Banner 38mm[6]	3-9	43-14.6	241-26½	3	12	1	Int.	14	160.95	
Banner 40mm	3-9	35-12.6	267-30	3½	13	1	Int.	13	180.95	
Banner[7]	4-12	29-10	150-17	3.2	13½	1	Int.	15½	163.95	
Magnum Phantom[8]	1.3	17	441	7-21	7.8	15/16	Int.	5½	71.95	
Magnum Phantom[9]	2½	9	100	8-21	9.7	15/16	Int.	6½	79.95	
Sportview	3-9	41.5-13.6	241-26.5	3	12.5	1	Int.	14	N.A.	
Sportview	4	34.5	135	3	12.5	1	Int.	11.5	N.A.	
Sportview 22	3-7	26-12	67.4-12.6	2.5	11.5	1	Int.	5.5	N.A.	
Davis Optical										Focus by moving non-rotating obj. lens unit. Ext. mounts included. Recoil spring $4.50 extra.
Spot Shot 1½"	10,12 15,20 25,30	10-4	—	2	25	.75	Ext.	—	116.00	
Spot Shot 1¼"	10,12, 15,20	10.6	—	2	25	.75	Ext.		90.00	
Fontaine										Non-waterproof also available. Scopes listed have Jennison TCS with Optima system. Extra TCS drums $5.50 ea. Scopes with TCS also avail. (continued)
4x32 Wide Angle	4	38	64	3.0	11.8	1	Int.	10.0	104.45	
4 x 40 Wide Angle	4	38	100	3.0	12.0	1	Int.	11.6	115.45	
3-9 x 32 Wide Angle	3-9	43.5-15	114-12.8	3.3-3.0	12.2	1	Int.	12.0	156.20	

CAUTION: PRICES CHANGE. CHECK AT GUNSHOP.

Maker and Model	Magn.	Field at 100 Yds (feet)	Relative Bright-ness	Eye Relief (in.)	Length (in.)	Tube Diam. (in.)	W&E Adjust-ments	Weight (ozs.)	Price	Other Data
Fontaine (cont'd.)										
3-9 x 40 Wide Angle	3-9	43.5-15	177.3-19.6	3.3-3.0	12.2	1	Int.	12.5	159.45	
4 x 32 Standard	4	29	64	3.3	11.7	1	Int.	10.2	87.95	
4 x 40 Standard	4	29	100	3.3	13.0	1	Int.	23.0	93.45	
3-9 x 32 Standard	3.9	35.3-13.2	114-12.8	3.3-3.0	12.0	1	Int.	11.3	126.45	
3-9 x 40 Standard	3-9	35.3-13.2	177.3-19.6	3.3-3.0	12.0	1	Int.	12.7	134.15	
Hertel & Heuss										
3-10 x 40 Exclusiv[1]	3 10	32-14	160-21 2	2-3	12.7	26	Int.	18.7	519.00	Other models available. Imported by Krico. [1]Alu-minum tube with mounting rail(s). [2]Aluminum tube with mounting rails on middle and objective tubes. [3]Highest luminosity of the H&R scopes. [4]With mounts. [5]Very high luminosity. [6]Focus with right turret. [7]Focus with right turret.
6 x 46 Exclusiv[2]	6	22	59	3-3¼	12.7	26	Int.	14.8	379.00	
Macro-Variables[3]										
2¾-10 x 46	2¾	35-14	150-21.2	3.4	12.7	26	Int.	14.1	509.00	
2-7 x 36	2-7	53-18	150-27	3-4	11.3	26	Int.	12.3	439.00	
Fixed Power[4] 4 x KK 22	4	29	23	2½-3½	11.2	22	Int.	7.4	129.00	
4 x 36[5]	4	36	81	3¼-4½	11.3	26	Int.	10.2	319.00	
6 x 46[6]	6	24	60	3¼-4½	12.7	26	Int.	12.3	359.00	
8 x 46[7]	8	20	34	3¼-4½	12.7	26	Int.	12.3	359.00	
Jason										
860	4	29	64	3	11.8	1	Int.	9.2	50.00	Constantly centered reticles, ballbearing click stops, nitrogen filled tubes, coated lenses. 4-Post crosshair about $3.50 extra on models 860, 861, 864, 865.
861	3-9	35-13	112-12	3	12.7	1	Int.	10.9	76.00	
862	4	19	14	2	11	¾	Int.	5.5	13.50	
863C	3-7	23-10	43-8	3	11	¾	Int.	8.4	44.00	
Jason										
865	3-9	35-13	177-19	3	13	1	Int.	12.2	80.00	
869	4	19	25	2	11.4	¾	Int.	6	23.00	
873	4	29	100	3	12.7	1	Int.	11.1	75.00	
875	3-9	35-13	177-19	3	13	1	Int.	12.2	80.00	
877	4	37	100	3	11.6	1	Int.	11.6	85.00	
878	3-9	42.5-13.6	112-12	2.7	12.7	1	Int.	12.7	110.00	
Kahles										
Helia Super 2/S[1]	2.5	57.2	64	3.15	9.6	1" or 26mm	Int.	11.3	279.00	[1]L Model (Alloy) weighs 10.5 oz. [2]L Model—11 oz. [3]L Model—12.9 oz. [4]L Model—17.8 oz. [5]L Model—10 oz. [6]L Model—10 oz. [7]L Model—12.25 oz. Alloy only. All models except ZF69 avail. in alloy or steel tube. All scopes have con-stantly centered reticles. Imported by Del-Sports, Inc.
Helia Super 4/S[2]	4	32.9	60	3.15	11	1" or 26mm	Int.	12.9	319.00	
Helia Super 6/S[3]	6	22.5	49	3.15	12.2	1" or 26mm	Int.	15.7	349.00	
Helia Super 8/S[4]	8	17.4	49	3.15	14	1" or 26mm	Int.	20.6	389.00	
Helia Super 15/S[5]	1.5-4.5	89.6-30	176-19.6	3.15	10	1" or 26mm	Int.	12.2	369.00	
Helia Super 27/S[6]	2.3-7	45.7-21	182-19.5	3.15	11.4	1" or 26mm	Int.	13.3	469.00	
Helia Super 39/S[7]	3-9	36.5-16.4	196-22	3.15	12.6	1" or 26mm	Int.	16.2	489.00	
ZF 69	6	22.5	49	3.15	12.2	26mm	Int.	16.8	579.00	
Kassnar										
2x-7x Wide Angle	2-7	49-19	258-21	3-2.7	11	1	Int.	12.8	94.95	Other models avail., including ¾" and ⅞" tubes for 22-cal. rifles. Contact Kassnar for details. [1]Also in 3x-9x40—$109.95 [2]Also in 4x40—$79.95. [3]Also in 3x-9x40—$89.95.
3x-9x Wide Angle[1]	3-9	42-15	112-13	3-2.7	12.2	1	Int.	13	99.95	
4x32 Wide Angle[2]	4	36	64	3.5	12	1	Int.	9.2	69.95	
6x40 Wide Angle	6	24	44	3	12.8	1	Int.	12	84.95	
1.5-4x Std.	1.5-4	52-27	177-25	4.4-3	10	1	Int.	9.5	79.95	
2x-7x Std.	2-7	42-16	256-21	3.1-3	11	1	Int.	12.5	84.95	
3x-9x Std.[3]	3-9	36-13	112-13	3.1-3	12.2	1	Int.	13.5	87.95	
4x-12x40 Std.	4-12	27-9.6	100-11	3-2.7	13.5	1	Int.	16	159.95	
2.5x32 Std.	2.5	36	164	3.6	12	1	Int.	9.3	64.95	
Leupold										
M8-2X EER[1]	1.8	22.0	—	12-24	8.1	1	Int.	6.8	146.15	Constantly centered reticles, choice of Duplex, tapered CPC, Leupold Dot, Crosshair and Dot. CPC and Dot reticles extra. [1]2x and 4x scope have from 12"-24" of eye relief and are suitable for handguns, top ejection arms and muzzle-loaders. [2]8x, 12x, 3x9, 3.5x10 and 6.5x20 come with Adjustable Objective. [3]Silhouette/Target scopes have 1-min divisions with ¼ min clicks, and Adjustable Objectives. 50-ft. Focus Adaptor available for indoor target ranges, $37.50. Sun-shade available for all Adjustable Objective scopes, $10.35.
M8-2X EER Silver[1]	1.8	22.0	—	12-24	8.1	1	Int.	6.8	160.45	
M8-4X EER[1]	3.5	9.5	—	12-24	8.4	1	Int.	7.6	178.40	
M8-4X EER Silhouette[1]	3.5	9.5	—	12-24	8.4	1	Int.	8.5	194.45	
M8-2.5X Compact	2.3	42	—	4.3	8.5	1	Int.	7.4	156.20	
M8-4X Compact	3.6	26.5	—	4.1	10.3	1	Int.	8.5	178.40	
M8-4X	4.1	28	—	4.4	11.4	1	Int.	8.8	178.40	
M8-6X	5.9	18.0	—	4.3	11.4	1	Int.	9.9	189.55	
M8-8X[2]	7.8	14.5	—	4.0	12.5	1	Int.	13.0	254.00	
M8-12X[2]	11.6	9.2	—	4.2	13.0	1	Int.	13.5	257.40	
M8-12X Silhouette[3]	11.6	9.2	—	4.2	13.0	1	Int.	14.5	289.55	
M8-24X[3]	24.0	4.7	—	3.2	13.6	1	Int.	14.5	358.55	
M8-36X[3]	36.0	3.2	—	3.4	13.9	1	Int.	15.5	358.55	
Vari-X-II 1X4	1.6-4.2	70.5-28.5	—	4.3-3.8	9.2	1	Int.	9.0	218.50	
Vari-X-II 2X7	2.5-6.6	44.0-19.0	—	4.1-3.7	10.7	1	Int.	10.4	238.55	
Vari-X-II 3X9	3.5-9.0	32.0-13.5	—	4.1-3.7	12.3	1	Int.	13.1	256.25	
Vari-X-II 3X9[2]	3.5-9.0	32.0-13.5	—	4.1-3.7	12.3	1	Int.	14.5	288.55	
Vari-X-III 1.5X5	1.5-4.6	66.0-24.0	—	4.7-3.5	9.4	1	Int.	9.3	259.55	
Vari-X-III 2.5X8	2.7-7.9	38.0-14.0	—	4.2-3.4	11.3	1	Int.	11.0	292.95	
Vari-X-III 3.5X10	3.4-9.9	29.5-10.5	—	4.6-3.6	12.4	1	Int.	13.0	306.25	
Vari-X-III 3.5X10[2]	3.4-9.9	29.5-10.5	—	4.6-3.6	12.4	1	Int.	14.4	336.35	
Vari-X-III 6.5X20[2]	6.5-19.2	14.8- 5.7	—	5.3-3.7	14.2	1	Int.	16	362.70	
Lyman										
Lyman 4x	4	30	—	3¼	12	1	Int.	10	149.95	Choice of standard CH, tapered post, or tapered post and CH reticles. All-weather reticle caps. All Lyman scopes have Perma-Center reticle which remains in optical center regardless of changes in w&e. Adj. for parallax. ⅛ or ¼ MOA clicks. [2]Non-rotating objective lens focusing. ¼ MOA click ad-justments. 5 different dot reticles, $12.50 extra. [3]Standard crosswire, 4 Center-Range reticles.
Variable	1¾-5	47-18	—	3	12¼	1	Int.	12¼	159.95	
■ 20x LWBR[1]	20	5.5	—	2¼	17⅛	1	Int.	15¼	339.95	
■ All-American[2]	3-9	39-13	—	3¾-3¼	10½	1	Int.	14	179.95	
2x-7x Var.	1.9-6.8	49-19	—	3¼	11⅝	1	Int.	10½	169.95	
■ 25x LWBR	25	4.8	—	3	17	1	Int.	19	369.95	
■ 35x LWBR	35	3.8	—	3	17	1	Int.	19	399.95	

(continued)

CAUTION: PRICES CHANGE. CHECK AT GUNSHOP.

HUNTING, TARGET ■ & VARMINT ■ SCOPES

Maker and Model	Magn.	Field at 100 Yds (feet)	Relative Bright-ness	Eye Relief (in.)	Length (in.)	Tube Diam. (in.)	W&E Adjust-ments	Weight (ozs.)	Price	Other Data
Lyman (cont'd.)										[4]Std. Fine, Extra Fine, 1 Min. Dot, ½-Min. Dot reticles. External adjustment knobs; hand lapped zero repeat w. and e. systems. Choice of 4 reticles.
Metallic Silhouette[3] 6x-SL	6.2	20	—	3¼	13⅞	1	Int.	14¼	249.95	
Metallic Silhouette[4] 8x-SL	8.1	14	—	3¼	14⅝	1	Int.	15¼	259.95	
Metallic Silhouette 10x-SL	10	12	—	3¼	15⅜	1	Int.	15¼	269.95	
Nickel										[1]Steel or aluminum tube, with or without rail mount. [2]Aluminum tube with rail mount. [3]Steel tube, w/o rail. [4]Aluminum tube with rail. Other models available. Imported by Krico.
Fixed										
1x12 Supralyt[1]	1	118	114	4	10.6	26mm	Int.	11.3	269.00	
2.5 x 20 Supralyt	2.5	49	64	4	10.6	26mm	Int.	11.3	269.00	
4 x 20 Supralyt	4	36	25	4	10.6	26mm	Int.	11.3	269.00	
4 x 36 Supra	4	23	36	4	11.4	26mm	Int.	13.4	309.00	
6 x 36 Supra	6	23	36	4	11.4	26mm	Int.	13.4	309.00	
Variables										
1.5-6 x 36 Supra[2]	1.5-6	66-25	176-36	4	12.2	30mm	Int.	15.5	489.00	
3-10 x 42 Supra[3]	3-10	35-14	81-16	4	12.6	26mm	Int.	18.3	479.00	
3-12 x 50 Supra[4]	3-12	31-11	276-17.6	4	14.9	30mm	Int.	21.5	589.00	
RWS										Air gun scopes. All have Dyna-Plex reticle. Imported from Japan by Dynamit Nobel of America.
100 4x32	4	20	—	—	10⅞	¾	Int.	6	26.60	
200 3-7x-20	3-7	24-17	—	—	11¼	¾	Int.	6	42.60	
300 4x32	4	28	—	—	12¾	1	Int.	11	66.60	
400 2-7x32	2-7	56-17	—	—	12¾	1	Int.	12	105.00	
800 1.5x20	1.5	19	—	—	8¾	1	Int.	6½	69.95	
Redfield										*Accutrac feature avail. on these scopes at extra cost. Traditionals have round lenses. 4-Plex reticle is standard. [1]"Magnum Proof." Specially designed for magnum and auto pistols. Uses "Double Dovetail" mounts. [2]Mounts solidly on receiver. CH or dot. 20x—$308.20, 24x—$317.65.
Illuminator Trad. 3-9x	2.9-8.7	33-11	—	3½	12¾	1	Int.	17	330.30	
Illuminator Widefield 3-9x*	2.9-8.7	38-13	—	3½	12¾	1	Int.	17	366.05	
Tracker 4x	3.9	28.9	—	3½	11.02	1	Int.	9.8	89.20	
Tracker 2-7x	2.3-6.9	36.6-12.2	—	3½	12.20	1	Int.	11.6	133.85	
Tracker 3-9x	3.0-9.0	34.4-11.3	—	3½	14.96	1	Int.	13.4	151.70	
Traditional 4x¾"	4	24½	27	3½	9⅜	¾	Int.	—	98.15	
Traditional 2½x	2½	43	64	3½	10¼	1	Int.	8½	135.65	
Traditional 4x	4	28½	56	3½	11⅜	1	Int.	9¾	153.50	
Traditional 6x	6	19	—	3½	12½	1	Int.	11½	178.50	
Traditional 3x-9x* Royal	3-9	34-11	—	3½-4¼	12½	1	Int.	13	267.86	
Traditional 2x-7x*	2-7	42-14	207-23	3½	11¼	1	Int.	12	210.65	
Traditional 3x-9x*	3-9	34-11	163-18	3½	12½	1	Int.	13	232.10	
Redfield										
Traditional 8xMS	8	16.6	—	3-3¾	14⅛	1	Int.	17⅕	244.60	
Traditional 10xMS	10	12.6	—	3-3¾	14⅛	1	Int.	17½	255.30	
Traditional 12xMS	12.4	8.1	—	3-3¾	14⅛	1	Int.	17½	267.80	
Pistol Scopes										
1½xMP[1]	1.5	14	—	19-32	9¹³⁄₁₆	1	Int.	10.5	128.50	
2½xMP	2.5	9	—	14-24	9¹³⁄₁₆	1	Int.	10.5	135.65	
4xMP	3.6	9	—	12-22	9¹¹⁄₁₆	1	Int.	11.1	160.80	
Traditional 4x-12x*	4-12	26-9	112-14	3½	13⅞	1	Int.	14	321.40	
Traditional 6x-18x*	6-18	18-6	50-6	3½	13¹⁵⁄₁₆	1	Int.	18	357.10	
Low Profile Scopes										
Widefield 2¾xLP	2¾	55½	69	3½	10½	1	Int.	8	169.60	
Widefield 4xLP	3.6	37½	84	3½	11½	1	Int.	10	189.40	
Widefield 6xLP	5.5	23	—	3½	12¾	1	Int.	11	207.25	
Widefield 1¾x5xLP	1¾-5	70-27	136-21	3½	10¾	1	Int.	11½	223.15	
Widefield 2x7xLP*	2-7	49-19	144-21	3½	11¾	1	Int.	13	243.00	
Widefield 3x-9xLP*	3-9	39-15	112-18	3½	12½	1	Int.	14	269.95	
■ 6400 Target[4]	16, 20, 24	6½, 5, 4½	5¾, 3½, 2½	3	17	1	Int.	18	298.70	
Sanders										Alum. alloy tubes, ¼" adj. coated lenses. Five other scopes are offered; 6x45 at $68.50, 8x45 at $70.50, 2½x7x at $69.50, 3-9x33 at $72.50 and 3-9x40 at $78.50. Rubber lens covers (clear plastic) are $3.50. Write to Sanders for details. Choice of reticles in CH, PCH, 3-post.
Bisley 2½x20	2½	42	64	3	10¾	1	Int.	8¼	48.50	
Bisley 4x33	4	28	64	3	12	1	Int.	9	52.50	
Bisley 6x40	6	19	45	3	12½	1	Int.	9½	56.50	
Bisley 8x40	8	18	25	3¼	12½	1	Int.	9½	62.50	
Bisley 10x40	10	12½	16	2½	12½	1	Int.	10¼	64.50	
Bisley 5-13x40	5-13	29-10	64-9	3	14	1	Int.	14	86.50	
Schmidt u. Bender										[1]With or without rail mount. [2]With or without rail. [3]Rail. [4]Rail. [5]Rail. Imported from West Germany.
Vari M 1½-6x42[1]	1½-6	65½-21⅓	—	3.1	12½	30mm	Int.	17½	481.75	
Vari M 2½-10x56[2]	2½-10	41-13⅛	—	3.1	14⅕	30mm	Int.	21.8	530.70	
Light Metal M 4x36[3]	4	33	—	3.1	11⅖	26mm	Int.	13	286.10	
Light Metal M 6x42[4]	6	23	—	3.1	12½	26mm	Int.	15½	311.10	
Light Metal M 8x56[5]	8	18	—	3.1	14⅕	26mm	Int.	20½	382.80	
Steel M 1¼x15	1¼	105	—	3.1	10	26mm	Int.	11	252.40	
Steel M 4x36	4	32⅘	—	3.1	11¼	26mm	Int.	13	286.10	
Steel M 6x42	6	23	—	3.1	12⅖	26mm	Int.	17¼	311.10	
Steel M 8x56	8	18	—	3.1	14⅕	26mm	Int.	22¼	382.80	
Swarovski Habicht										All models steel except LD model light alloy. All-weather scopes. 4x & 6x scopes have centered reticles—7 different designs. NOVA has eyepiece recoil mechanism and rubber ring shield to protect face. Five Year warranty. For spirit Level, add $47. Importer-distributor: Strieter Corp.
1.5x20 DV SD	1.5	69	—	3⅛	10	26mm	Int.	12.0	290.00	
Nova 4x32 DV LD	4	30	—	3⅛	11	26mm	Int.	15.9	330.00	
Nova 4x32 DV SD	4	30	—	3⅛	11	26mm	Int.	16.6	330.00	
Nova 6x42 DV SD	6	20	—	3¼	11	26mm	Int.	18.7	350.00	
Swift										All Swift Mark I scopes, with the exception of the 4x15, have Quadraplex reticles and are fog-proof and waterproof. The 4x15 has crosshair reticle and is non-waterproof. (continued)
Mark I 4x15	4	16.2	—	2.4	11	¾	Int.	4.7	22.00	
Mark I 4x32	4	29	—	3½	12	1	Int.	9	68.00	
Mark I 4x32 WA	4	37	—	3½	11¾	1	Int.	10½	74.00	
Mark I 4x40 WA	4	35½	—	3¾	12¼	1	Int.	12	86.00	
Mark I 3-9x32	3-9	35¾-12¾	—	3	12¾	1	Int.	13¾	89.50	

HUNTING, TARGET ■ & VARMINT ■ SCOPES

Maker and Model	Magn.	Field at 100 Yds (feet)	Relative Brightness	Eye Relief (in.)	Length (in.)	Tube Diam. (in.)	W&E Adjustments	Weight (ozs.)	Price	Other Data
Swift (cont'd.)										
Mark I 3-9x40 WA	3-9	42½-13½	—	2¾	12¾	1	Int.	14	**99.50**	
Mark I 6x40	6	18	—	3¾	13	1	Int.	10	**76.00**	
Mark I 1½-4½x32	1½-4½	55-22	—	3½	12	1	Int.	13	**94.50**	
Tasco										
611V Wide Angle	2-6	66-25	100-16	2¾	10	1	Int.	9.5	**114.95**	Lens covers furnished. Constantly centered reticles. Write the importer, Tasco, for data on complete line. [1]Brass tube for Hawkins, Plaines, Pa. ½ steel, FIE Zouave and Ky. [2]For Savage #72 and Gallagher.
627W	3-9	35-14	177-19	3½	12⅛	1	Int.	13	**99.95**	
628V Wide Angle	3-9	43.5-15	177-10	3½	12	1	Int.	12¼	**149.95**	
1860 Tube sight[1]	4	12½	14	3	32½	¾	Ext.	25	**124.95**	
1903 Tube Sight[2]	4	14	14	3¾	18½	¾	Ext.	17½	**104.95**	
Unertl										
■ 1" Target	6,8,10	16-10	17.6-6.25	2	21½	¾	Ext.	21	**155.00**	[1]Dural ¼ MOA click mounts. Hard coated lenses. Non-rotating objective lens focusing. [2]¼ MOA click mounts. [3]With target mounts. [4]With calibrated head. [5]Same as 1" Target but without objective lens focusing. [6]Price with ¼ MOA click mounts. [7]With new Posa mounts. [8]Range focus until near rear of tube. Price is with Posa mounts. Magnum clamp. With standard mounts and clamp ring **$266.00.**
■ 1¼" Target[1]	8,10,12,14	12-16	15.2-5	2	25	¾	Ext.	21	**203.00**	
■ 1½" Target	8,10,12,14 16,18,20	11.5-3.2	—	2¼	25½	¾	Ext.	31	**230.00**	
■ 2" Target[2]	8,10,12, 14,16,18, 24,30,36	8	22.6-2.5	2¼	26¼	1	Ext.	44	**310.00**	
■ Varmint, 1¼"[3]	6,8,10,12	1-7	28-7.1	2½	19½	⅞	Ext.	26	**204.00**	
■ Ultra Varmint, 2"[4]	8,10 12,15	12.6-7	39.7-11	2½	24	1	Ext.	34	**291.00**	
■ Small Game[5]	4,6	25-17	19.4-8.4	2¼	18	¾	Ext.	16	**120.00**	
■ Vulture[6]	8 10	11.2 10.9	29 18½	3-4 —	15⅝ 16⅛	1	Ext.	15½	**226.00**	
■ Programmer 200[7]	8,10,12 14,16,18, 20,24,30,36	11.3-4	39-1.9	—	26½	1	Ext.	45	**385.00**	
■ BV-20[8]	20	8	4.4	4.4	17⅞	1	Ext.	21¼	**278.00**	
Weatherby										
Mark XXII[1]	4	25	50	2½-3½	11¾	⅞	Int.	9¼	**85.35**	[1]Focusing in top turret. [2]Centered, non-magnifying reticles. Binocular focusing. Lumi-Plex $10 extra.
Premier Standard	2¾	45	212	3½	11¾	1	Int.	12¼	**149.95**	
Premier Standard[2]	4	31	100	3½	12¾	1	Int.	12¼	**154.95**	
Premier Standard	3-9	43½-14½	177-19	3	12	1	Int.	14¾	**164.95**	
Premier Wide Angle	4	35¾	100	3	11¾	1	Int.	14	**179.95**	
Premier Wide Angle	3-9	43½-14¾	177-19	3	12	1	Int.	14¾	**199.95**	
Weaver										
K1.5[1]	1½	55	—	5¼	9⅜	1	Int.	9¾	**110.00**	Steel-Lite II (lighter weight, glossy finish) in K, V and Wider View scopes. Crosshair and Dual-X reticle optional on all K and V scopes (except no RF on K1.5, K2.5, K3 and K3W; no post in K8, 10, 12; no post or RF in T models). Dot, post and RF $18 extra in T models. [1]Avail. with mount for Rem. 1100 or 870, Dual-X reticle. K1.5—$147, K2.5—$147. [2]Stainless (K4S) $190. K4M (matte finish) $167. [3]56mm objective gives big 7mm exit pupil. Excellent for low light conditions. German post reticle $18 extra. [4]Micro-Trac standard on all K and V models. ¼" Graduated adjustments .V9M has matte finish, $224. [5]¼-minute adj. [6]¼-minute adj. [7]¼" click stops. Crosshair and Dual-X Standard on T models. [8]Features both range determination and trajectory compensation in fixed power. [9]Range determination and trajectory compensation are toally independent of variable magnification function. [10]$2.50 extra for Dual-X on V22, D4 or D6. D model prices include N or Tip-Off mount. [11]Projects red dot aiming point. [12]KT models have fast focus front ends, SL-II finish, smaller, covered knobs. [13]Stainless steel. Dual-X only. [14]AR models intended for airguns.
K2.5[1]	2.6	38	—	4½	10⅜	1	Int.	10¼	**110.00**	
K3	3.2	34	—	4	10⅝	1	Int.	10¼	**119.00**	
K4[2]	4.1	27	—	4	11¾	1	Int.	12	**124.00**	
K6	5.9	19	—	3⅞	13½	1	Int.	13½	**153.00**	
K-856[3]	7.7	15	—	3½	15	1	Int.	18.7	**239.00**	
K3-W	2.9	48	—	3½	11	1	Int.	11	**147.00**	
K4-W	3.7	38	—	3⅝	11[13/16]	1	Int.	13	**161.00**	
K6-W	6	24	—	3½	13¼	1	Int.	14½	**190.00**	
KT6[12]	6	17	—	3.7	13¾	1	Int.	16.5	**229.00**	
KT10	10	11	—	3.1	14.3	1	Int.	17	**247.00**	
KT 16	16	6.4	—	3.5	15	1	Int.	17½	**267.00**	
P2S[13]	1.9	14	—	10-24	10	1	Int.	—	**157.00**	
V4.5-W	1.6-4.2	74-27	—	4¼-3¾	10⅜	1	Int.	14¼	**200.00**	
V7-W	2.6-6.9	43-17	—	3⅝-3¾	12⅜	1	Int.	15¼	**210.00**	
V9-W	3.3-9	35-13	—	3⅝	14⅛	1	Int.	18¼	**219.00**	
V9-WF[5]	3.3-9	35-13	—	3⅝	14	1	Int.	18¼	**239.00**	
V4.5	1.6-4.3	63-24	—	4⅜-3⅞	10⅜	1	Int.	13½	**161.00**	
V7	2.5-6.7	40-15	—	4-3⅞	12⅜	1	Int.	14½	**171.00**	
V9	3.3-8.8	31-12	—	3¾	14⅛	1	Int.	17½	**181.00**	
V9F[4]	3.3-8.8	31-12	—	3¾	14	1	Int.	17½	**200.00**	
V12F	4.4-11.8	23-9	—	3⅞-4¼	14	1	Int.	17½	**210.00**	
T6[7]	6	19	—	3½	14¼	1	Int.	17¾	**267.00**	
T10	10	11	—	3½	15	1	Int.	18	**286.00**	
T16	16	7	—	3⅝	15¾	1	Int.	18¾	**309.00**	
T25[5]	25	4.2	—	3¾	19⅛	1	Int.	20	**353.00**	
Auto-Comp[8] FX-4	4	27	—	4	11.8	1	Int.	13	**229.00**	
Auto-Comp[9] VX-9	3.3-8.8	31-12	—	3.8	14.2	1	Int.	18	**286.00**	
V22[10]	3-5.8	31-16	—	1⅝-2¼	12⅜	⅞	Int.	7¾	**45.00**	
D4	4.2	29	—	2¼	11⅞	⅞	Int.	6½	**34.50**	
D6	6.2	20	—	2¼	12[5/16]	⅞	Int.	6¾	**38.00**	
V22-AR[14]	3.0-5.8	31-16	—	1.7-2.3	12.4	⅞	Int.	7.7	**45.00**	
D4-AR[14]	4.2	29	—	2.3	11.9	⅞	Int.	6.5	**34.50**	
Quik-Point[11]	1	—	—	6	—	—	Int.	8	**86.00**	
Williams										
Twilight Crosshair	2½	32	64	3¾	11¼	1	Int.	8½	**101.75**	TNT models
Twilight Crosshair	4	29	64	3½	11¾	1	Int.	9½	**111.40**	
Twilight Crosshair	2-6	45-17	256-28	3	11½	1	Int.	11½	**151.50**	
Twilight Crosshair	3-9	36-13	161-18	3	12¾	1	Int.	13½	**159.00**	
Zeiss										
Diatal C 4x32	4	30	—	3.5	10.6	1	Int.	11.3	**295.00**	All scopes have ¼-minute click-stop adjustments. Choice of Z-Plex or fine crosshair reticles. Rubber armored objective bell, rubber eyepiece ring. Lenses have T-Star coating for highest light transmission. Imported from West Germany by Carl Zeiss, Inc.
Diatal C 6x32	6	20	—	3.5	10.6	1	Int.	11.3	**325.00**	
Diatal C 10x36	10	12	—	3.5	12.7	1	Int.	14.1	**375.00**	
Diavari C 3-9x36	3-9	36-13	—	3.5	11.2	1	Int.	15.2	**495.00**	

■ Signifies target and/or varmint scope. Hunting scopes in general are furnished with a choice of reticle—crosshairs, post with crosshairs, tapered or blunt post, or dot crosshairs, etc. The great majority of target and varmint scopes have medium or fine crosshairs but post or dot reticles may be ordered. W—Windage E—Elevation MOA—Minute of angle or 1" (approx.) at 100 yards, etc.

CAUTION: PRICES CHANGE. CHECK AT GUNSHOP.

SCOPE MOUNTS

Maker, Model, Type	Adjust.	Scopes	Price	Suitable for
B-Square				
Dovetail Rings[1]	No.	1" scopes.	$19.95	[1]All dovetail receivers such as Nylon 66. No drilling or tapping. [2]M-94 Winchester. No drilling or tappering. Clamps on barrel. [3]M-94 Winchester. No drilling or tapping. [4]Instant on and off (with large thumb screw). [5]Ruger Mini-14. Mounts on top of receiver. Gunsmith Drill Jig avail. for guns not drilled—$39.95. [6]Ruger Mini-14. Attaches by replacing bolt stop cover. No gunsmithing and no sight removal. [7]Most popular rifles. [8]Remington 40X, 700 Models. [9]All standard target blocks. [10]Ruger Blackhawk (has bolted rings). [11]T-C Contender, all calibers. Heavy Recoil model. [12]No gunsmithing. Clamps on vent rib barrel. [13]No gunsmithing. Clamps on vent rib barrel. [14]Slides onto receiver. No gunsmithing. Thumb screw clamps. Use with iron sights.
M-94 Mono-Mount[2]	No	1", long eye relief such as Leupold M8-2X. Mounts ahead of action.	39.95	
M-94 Side Mount[3]	W&E	All 1" scopes.	39.95	
AR-15 Mount[4]	W&E	All 1" scopes.	49.95	
Mini-14 Mount[5] (180 Series)	W&E	all 1" scopes.	39.95	
Mini-14 Mount[6] (181 & 182 Series)	W&E	all 1" scopes.	Blue—49.95 Stainless—59.95	
One Piece Base Mounts[7] (Includes B-Square Dovetail Rings)	No	1" scopes.	29.95	
Target Mounts[8]	W&E	1" scopes.	39.95	
Target Block Mount[9]	W&E	1" scopes.	39.95	
Ruger Blackhawk Pistol[10]	No	1" scopes.	39.95	
T-C Contender Pistol[11]	No	1" scopes.	39.95	
Dan Wesson Pistol[12]	W&E	1" scopes.	39.95	
Colt Python Pistol[13]	W&E	1" scopes.	39.95	
Heckler & Koch M91/M93[14]	No	1" scopes.	149.95	
Buehler				
One Piece (T)[1]	W only	1" split rings, 3 heights. / 1" split rings, 3 heights, engraved 26mm, 2 heights	Complete—54.50 Rings only—76.50 Rings only—39.50	[1]Most popular models. [2]Most popular models. [3]Most popular models. [4]Sako dovetail receivers. [5]15 models. [6]No drilling & tapping.
One Piece Micro Dial (T)[2]	W&E	1" split rings.	Complete—67.50	
Two Piece (T)[3]	W only	1" split rings.	Complete—54.50	
Two Piece Dovetail (T)[4]	W only	1" split rings.	Complete—67.50	
One Piece Pistol (T)[5]	W only	1" split rings.	Complete—54.50	
One Piece Ruger Mini 14 (T)[6]	W only	1" split rings.	Complete—67.50	
Burris				
Supreme One Piece (T)[1]	W only	1" split rings, 3 heights.	25.95 1 piece-base—18.95	[1]Most popular rifles. Universal, rings, mounts fit Burris. Universal, Redfield, Leupold and Browning bases. Comparable prices. [2]Browning Standard 22 Auto rifle. [3]Most popular rifles. [4]Grooved receivers. [5]Universal dovetail; accept Burris, Universal, Redfield, Leupold rings. For Dan Wesson, S&W, Virginian, Ruger Blackhawk, Win. 94. [6]Medium standard front, extension rear, per pair. Low standard front, extension rear, per pair.
Trumount Two Piece (T)	W only	1" split rings, 3 heights.	16.95 2 piece base—14.95	
Browning Auto Mount[2]	No	¾", 1" split rings.	14.95	
Sight-Thru Mount[3]	No	1" Split rings.	16.95	
Rings Mounts[4]	No	¾", 1" split rings.	¾" rings—12.95 1" rings—12.95	
L.E.R. Mount Bases[5]	No	1" split rings.	16.95	
Extension Rings[6]	No	1" scopes.	29.95	
Bushnell				
Detachable (T) mounts only[1]	W only	1" split rings, uses Weaver base.	Rings—19.95	[1]Most popular rifles. Includes windage adj. [2]V-block bottoms lock to chrome-moly studs seated into two 6-48 holes. Rem. XP-100. [3]Heavy loads in Colt, S&W, Ruger revolvers. Ruger Hawkeye. [4]M94 Win., center dovetail.
22 mount	No	1" only.	Rings—19.95	
All Purpose[2]	No	Phantom.	19.95	
Rigid[3]	No	Phantom.	19.95	
94 Win.[4]	No	Phantom.	19.95	
Clearview				
Universal Rings (T)[1]	No	1" split rings.	19.95	[1]All popular rifles including Sav. 99. Uses Weaver bases. [2]Rings have wide oval effect for use of open sights. [3]For 22 rimfire rifles, with grooved receivers or bases. [4]Remington 14, 141, Sears 54, 100, Win. 94, 94-375.
Mod 101, & 336[2]	No	1" split rings.	19.95	
Model 104[3]	No	1" split rings.	11.95	
SM-94[4]	No	1" split rings.	19.95	
Conetrol				
Hunter[1]	W only	1", 26mm, 26.5mm solid or split rings, 3 heights.	48.93	[1]All popular rifles, including metric-drilled foreign guns. Price shown for base, two rings. Matte finish. [2]Gunnur grade has mirror-finished rings, satin-finish base. Price shown for base, two rings. [3]Custom grade has mirror-finished rings and mirror-finished, contoured base. Price shown for base, 2 rings. [4]Win. 94, Krag, older split-bridge Mannlicher-Schoenauer, Mini-14, M-1 Garand, etc. Prices same as above. [5]For all popular guns with integral mounting provision, including Sako, BSA, Ithacagun, Ruger, H&K and many others. Also for grooved-receiver rimfires and air rifles. Prices same as above. [6]For XP-100, T/C Contender, Colt SAA, Ruger Blackhawk, S&W.
Gunnur[2]	W only	1", 26mm, 26.5mm solid or split rings, 3 heights.	59.91	
Custum[3]	W only	1", 26mm, 26.5mm solid or split rings, 3 heights.	74.91	
One Piece Side Mount[4]	W only	1", 26mm, 26.5mm solid or split rings, 3 heights.		
Daptar Bases[5]	W only	1", 26mm, 26.5mm solid or split rings, 3 heights.		
Pistol Bases[6]	W only	1" scopes.		
Pistol Bases, 3-Ring[7]	W only	1" scopes.		
EAW				
Pivot Mount	W&E	1" or 26mm.	125.00-135.00	Most popular magazine rifles. Imported by Del Sports, Inc. (Kahles of America).
Griffin & Howe				
Standard Double Lever (S).	No	1" or 26mm split rings.	110.00	All popular models (Garand $110; Win. 94 $110). All rings $45.
Holden				
Wide Ironsighter®	No	1" Split rings.	18.95	[1]Most popular rifles including Ruger Mini-14, H&R M700, Win. 94BB and muzzleloaders. Rings have oval holes to permit use of iron sights. [2]For 1" dia. scopes. [3]For ¾" or ⅞" dia. scopes. [4]For 1" dia. extended eye relief scopes. [5]Fits Redfield and Weaver bases.
Ironsighter Center Fire[1]	No	1" Split rings.	18.95	
Ironsighter 22 cal. rimfire Model #500[2]	No	1" Split rings.	9.95	
Model #600[3]	No	⅞" Split rings also fits ¾".	9.95	
Ironsighter Handguns[4]	No	1" Split rings.	20.95	
Holden "Straight Shooter"[5] Bullet Drop Compensating Scope Mount	Yes	1" Split rings.	44.95	
Jaeger				
QD, with windage (S)	W only	1", 3 heights.	125.00	All popular models
Jaguar				
QD Dovetail (T)	No	1", 26mm and 26½mm rings.	23.30	For BSA Monarch rifle (Galef, importer.
Kesselring				
Standard QD (T)	W only	¾", ⅞", 1", 26mm split rings.	29.95	All popular rifles, one or two piece bases. Rem. 760, 740, Win. 100, 88, Marlin 336, Steyr 22, Sako, BRNO, Krico.
See-Em-Under (T)	W only	Same.	35.00	
Dovetail (T)	W only	1", 26mm.	35.00	

SCOPE MOUNTS

Maker, Model, Type	Adjust.	Scopes	Price	Suitable for
Kris Mounts				
Side-Saddle[1]	No	1″, 26mm split rings.	11.98	[1]One-piece mount for Win. 94. [2]Most popular rifles
Two Piece (T)[2]	No	1″, 26mm split rings.	7.98	and Ruger. [3]Blackhawk revolver. Mounts have oval
One Piece (T)[3]	No	1″, 26mm split rings.	11.98	hole to permit use of iron sights.
Kwik-Site				
KS-See-Thru[1]	No	1″	18.95	[1]Most rifles. Allows use of iron sights. [2]22-cal. rifles
KS-22 See-Thru[2]	No	1″	15.95	with grooved receivers. Allows use of iron sights.
K3-W94[3]	Yes	1″	32.95	[3]Model 94, 94 Big Bore. No drilling or tapping. [4]Most
KSM Imperial[4]	No	1″	25.95	rifles. One-piece solid construction. Use on Weaver
KS-WEV	No	1″	19.95	bases. 32mm obj. lens or larger.
KS-WEV-HIGH	No	1″	19.95	
Leupold				
STD Bases (T)[1]	W only	One piece base (dovetail front, windage rear)	Base—18.70	[1]Most popular rifles. [2]Ruger revolvers, Thompson/ Center Contender, S&W K&N Frame revolvers and Colt .45 "Gold Cup" N.M. [3]Reversible extended
STD Handgun mounts[2] Base and two rings[2]	No	1″	47.80	front; regular rear rings, in two heights.
STD Rings		1″ & 26mm, 3 ring heights interchangeable with other mounts of similar design.	1″ rings—27.00 26mm rings—29.50	
Extension-Ring Sets[3]		1″	37.40	
Marlin				
One Piece QD (T)	No	1″ split rings.	12.10	Most Marlin and Glenfield lever actions.
Millett				
Diamond-Facet		1″ Low, medium, high Engraved Black Onyx	26.95 39.95	Rem. 40X, 700, 722, 725, Ruger 77 (round top) Weatherby, etc. FN Mauser, FN Brownings, Colt 57,
Universal Two Piece Bases				Interarms MKX, Parker-Hale, Sako (round receiver),
700 Series	W only	Two-piece bases	20.95	many others.
FN Series	W only	Two-piece bases	20.95	
T/C Contender	W only	One-piece base	21.95	
XP-100 Base	W only	Two-piece base	20.95	
Numrich				
Side Mount	No	1″ split rings.	7.95	M-1 carbine.
Pachmayr				[1]All popular rifles, including Ruger Mini-14, Browning
Lo-Swing (S)[1]	Yes	¾″, ⅞″, 1″, 26mm solid or split loops.	65.00	BBR, Scope swings aside for instant use of iron sights. [2]Adjustable base. Win. 70, 88; Rem. 721, 722, 725, 740, 760; Mar. 336; Sav. 99, New Model
Lo-Swing (T)[2]	Yes	¾″, ⅞″, 1″, 26mm split rings.	65.00	for Colt Sauer.
Parker-Hale				
Roll-Off	No	1″ and 26mm.	15.55	Most popular rifles.
Redfield				
JR-SR(T)[1]	W only	¾″, 1″, 26mm.	JR—18.90-22.20 SR—21.90-25.70	[1]Low, med. & high, split rings. Reversible extension front rings for 1″. 2-piece bases for Sako. Colt Sauer bases $63.90. [2]Split rings for grooved 22's. See-thru
Ring (T)[2]	No	¾″ and 1″.		mounts $23.30. [3]Used with MP scopes for: S&W K or
Double Dovetail MP[3]	No	1″, split rings.	51.50	N frame. XP-100, Colt J or I frame. T/C Contender, Colt autos, black powder rifles.
S&K				[1]1903, A3, M1 Carbine, Lee Enfield #3, #4, #5, P14, M1917, M98 Mauser, FN Auto, AR-15, AR-180, M-
Insta-Mount (T) base only[1]	No	Most take S&K or Weaver rings.	15.00-36.00	14, M-1. Bases—M94, 64. [2]Most popular rifles. For
Conventional rings and bases[2]	No	1″ split rings.	30.00	"see through underneath" risers, add $4.15.
Sako				Sako, or any rifle using Sako action, 3 heights avail-
QD Dovetail	W only	1″ only.	82.00	able, Stoeger, importer.
Tasco				
790 and 792 series[1]	Yes	1″ split rings, regular or high.	9.95	[1]Many popular rifles. [2]For 22s with grooved receiv-
794[2]	No	Split rings.	9.95	ers. [3]Most popular rifles. [4]Most popular rifles.
795 Quick Peep[3]	No	1″ only.	11.95	
800L Series (with base)[4]	No	1″ only.	13.95	
Unerti				
Posa (T)[1]	Yes	¾″, ⅞, 1″ scopes.	Per set 63.00	[1]Unerti target or varmint scopes. [2]Any with regular
¼ Click (T)[2]	Yes	¾″, 1″ target scopes.	Per set 59.00	dovetail scope bases.
Weaver				
Detachable Mount (T & S)[1]	No	¾″, ⅞″, 1″, 26mm.	20.00	[1]Nearly all modern rifles. Extension rings, 1″ $20.95.
Pivot Mount (T)[2]	No	1″	25.75	[2]Most modern big bore rifles. [3]22s with grooved re-
Tip-Off (T)[3]	No	¾″, ⅞″.	11.15	ceivers. [4]Same. Adapter for Lee Enfield—$9.65.
Tip-Off (T)[4]	No	1″, two-piece.	20.00	5⅞″—$11.95. 1″ See-Thru extension—$23.45. [6]Colt
See-Thru Mount[5]	No	1″ Split rings and ⅞″-tip-off. Fits all top mounts.	17.95	Officer's Model, Python, Ruger B'hawk, Super B'hawk, Security Six, 22 Autos, Mini-14. No drilling or tapping.
Mount Base System[6]	No	1″	44.95	
Williams				
Offset (S)[1]	No	¾″, ⅞″, 1″ 26mm solid, split or extension rings.	47.05	[1]Most rifles, Br. S.M.L.E. (round rec) $3.85 extra. [2]Same. [3]Most rifles. [4]Most rifles. [5]Many modern ri-
QC (T)[2]	No	Same.	38.60	fles. [6]Most popular rifles.
QC (S)[3]	No	Same.	38.60	
Low Sight-Thru[4]	No	1″, ⅞″, sleeves $1.80.	17.75	
Sight-Thru[5]	No	1″, ⅞″, sleeves $1.80.	17.75	
Streamline[6]	No	1″ (bases form rings).	17.75	

(S)—Side Mount (T)Top Mount 22mm—.866″ 25.4mm = 1″1.024″ 26.5mm = 1.045″ 30mm = 1.81″

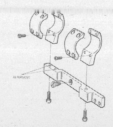

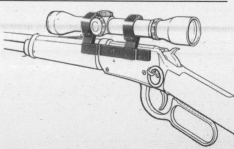

Holden Ironsighter Model S-94 is a side mount for the Model 94 Winchester. It fits factory drilled and tapped holes in the side of the receiver on rifles serially numbered above 1,400,000.

CAUTION: PRICES CHANGE. CHECK AT GUNSHOP.

SPOTTING SCOPES

BAUSCH & LOMB DISCOVERER—15X to 60X zoom, 60mm objective. Constant focus throughout range. Field at 1000 yds. 40 ft (60X), 156 ft. (15X). Comes with lens caps. Length 17½", wgt. 48½ oz.
Price: **$399.95**

BUSHNELL SPACEMASTER—60MM objective. Field at 1000 yds., 158' to 37'. Relative brightness, 5.76. Wgt., 36 oz. Length closed, 11⅝". prism focusing, without eyepiece.
Price: **$254.95**
15X, 20X, 40X and 60X eyepieces, each **$49.95**
22X wide angle eyepiece **$54.95**

BUSHNELL SPACEMASTER 45°—Same as above except: Wgt., 43 oz., length closed 13". Eyepiece at 45°, without eyepiece.
Price: **$319.95**

BUSHNELL ZOOM SPACEMASTER—20X-45X zoom. 60mm objective. Field at 1000 yards 120'-72'. Relative brightness 9-1.7. Wgt. 36 oz., length 11⅝".
Price: **$379.95**

BUSHNELL SENTRY®—50mm objective. Field at 1000 yards 120'-45'. Relative brightness 6.25. Wgt., 25½ oz., length 12⅝", without eyepiece.
Price: **$139.95**
20X, 32X and 48X eyepieces, each **$44.95**

BUSHNELL ZOOM SPOTTER—40mm objective. 9X-30X var. power.
Price: **$99.95**

BUSHNELL COMPETITOR—40mm objective. Prismatic. Field at 1000 yards 140'. Minimum focus 33'. Length 12½", weight 18½ oz.
Price: **$94.95**

BUSHNELL TROPHY—16X-36X zoom. Rubber armored, prismatic. 50mm objective. Field at 1000 yards 131' to 90'. Minimum focus 20'. Length with caps 13⅝", weight 38 oz.
Price: **$319.95**
With interchangeable eyepieces—20x, 32x, 48x............. **$244.95**

BUSHNELL—10x30mm hand telescope. Field 183 ft. at 1000 yards. Weight 11 ozs.; 10" long. Tripod mount
Price: **$34.95**

DICKSON 270—20x to 60x variable, 60mm objective, achromatic coated objective lens, complete with metal table tripod with 5' vertical and horizontal adjustments. Turret type, 20x, 30x, 40x 60x
Price: **$239.95**

DICKSON 274A—20x to 60x variable zoom. 60mm achromatic coated objective lens, complete with adjustable metal table tripod.
Price: **$150.00**

DICKSON 274B—As above but with addition of 4 × 16 Finder Scope.
Price: **$161.95**

HUTSON CHROMATAR 60—63.4mm objective. 22.5X eyepiece at 45°. Wgt. 24 oz., 8" over-all. 10½ foot field at 100 yards.
Price: **$119.00**
15X or 45X eyepieces, each................................... **$22.00**

OPTEX MODEL 420—15x-60x-60 Zoom; 18" overall; weighs 4 lbs. with folding tripod (included). From Southern Precision Instrument
Price: **$135.00**

OPTEX MODEL 421—15x-45x-50 Zoom; 18" over-all; weighs 4 lbs. with folding tripod (included). From Southern Precision Instrument
Price: **$110.00**

OPTEX MODEL 422—8x-25x-30 Zoom. Armour coated; 18" over-all; weighs 3 lbs. with tripod (included). From Southern Precision Instrument
Price: **$100.00**

OPTEX MODEL 423—Same as Model 422 except 12x-40x-40
Price: **$120.00**

REDFIELD 30x SPOTTER—60mm objective, 30x. Field of view 9.5 ft. at 100 yds. Uses catadioptric lens system. Length over-all is 7.5", weight is 11.5 oz. Eye relief 0.5".
Price: **$390.40**

SWAROVSKI HABICHT HAWK 30x75 IRALIN TELESCOPE—75mm objective, 30X. Field at 1,000 yds. 90ft. Minimum, focusing distance 90 ft. Length: closed 13 in., extended 20½". Weight: 47 oz. Precise recognition of smallest details even at dusk. Leather or rubber covered, with caps and carrying case.
Price: **$895.00**
Same as above with short range supplement. Minimum focusing distance 24 to 30 ft. **$935.00**

SWIFT TELEMASTER M841—60mm objective. 15X to 60X variable power. Field at 1000 yards 160 feet (15X) to 40 feet (60X). Wgt. 3.4 lbs. 17.6" over-all.
Price: **$415.00**
Tripod for above. **$79.95**
Photo adapter... **$19.00**
Case for above **$57.50**

SWIFT TELEMASTER JR. M842—25-50mm zoom spotting scope. Smaller version of M841 with same features. 14.9" over-all, wgt. 2.2 lbs.
Price: **$255.00**

SWIFT M844 COMMANDO PRISMATIC SPOTTING SCOPE, MK.II—60mm objective. Comes with 20X eyepiece; 15X, 30X, 40X, 50X, 60X available. Built-in sunshade. Field at 1000 yards. with 20X, 120 ft. Length 13.7", wgt. 2.1 lbs.
Price: **$245.00**

SWIFT M847 SCANNER—50mm objective. Comes with 25x eyepiece; 20x, 30x, 35x eyepieces available. Field of view at 1000 yds. is 112 ft. (25x). Length 13.6", weight 23 oz.
Price: **$147.50**
Each additional eyepiece..................................... **$25.50**
Tubular case.. **$25.00**
Tripod **$79.95**

SWIFT M700 SCOUT—9X-30X, 30mm spotting scope. Length 15½", weighs 2.1 lbs. Field of 204 ft. (9X), 60 ft. (30X).
Price: **$96.00**

TASCO 18T ZOOM—60mm objective. 20X to 60X variable power. Field at 100 yards 9 feet (20X) to 3 feet (60X). Wgt. 4 lbs. 16" overall
Price: **$199.95**

UNERTL RIGHT ANGLE—63.5mm objective, 24X. Field at 100 yds., 7 ft. Relative brightness, 6.96. Eye relief, ½". Wgt., 41 oz. Length closed, 19". Push-pull and screw-focus eyepiece. 16X and 32X eyepieces **$35.00** each.
Price: **$242.00**

UNERTL STRAIGHT PRISMATIC—Same as Unertl Right Angle except: straight eyepiece and wgt. of 40 oz.
Price: **$205.00**

UNERTL 20X STRAIGHT PRISMATIC—54mm objective. 20X. Field at 100 yds., 8.5 ft. Relative brightness, 6.1. Eye relief, ½". Wgt. 36 oz. Length closed, 13½". Complete with lens covers.
Price: **$172.00**

UNERTL TEAM SCOPE—100mm objective. 15X, 24X, 32X eyepieces. Field at 100 yds. 13 to 7.5 ft. Relative brightness, 39.06 to 9.79. Eye relief, 2" to 1½". Weight 13 lbs. 29⅞" overall. Metal tripod, yoke and wood carrying case furnished (total weight, 67 lbs.)
Price: **$900.00**

WEATHERBY—60mm objective, 20X-45X zoom
Price: **$323.95**
Tripod for above.. **$69.95**

WEAVER TS4 SPOTTING SCOPE—50mm objective. Power determined by choice of eyepiece—12x, 16x, 20x, 32x. Field of view (20x) 117 ft. at 1000 yds. Uses 45° sighting angle. Length 12.6", weight 37.4 oz.
Price:Body only... **$225.00**
12x eyepiece **$65.00**
16x eyepiece **$75.00**
20x eyepiece **$75.00**
32x eyepiece **$80.00**

WEAVER TS6 SPOTTING SCOPE—60mm objective. Power determined by choice of eyepiece—15x, 20x, 25x, 40x. Field of view (15x) of 150 ft. at 1000 yds. Straight-through sighting. Length 12.4", weight 37.4" oz.
Price:Body only... **$20.00**
15x eyepiece **$65.00**
20x eyepiece **$75.00**
25x eyepiece **$75.00**
40x eyepiece **$80.00**

SCOPE ATTACHMENTS

BUTLER CREEK LENS COVERS—Waterproof, dustproof. Springs open at a touch. Work in all weather. Sizes to fit all scopes.
Price:Per pair **$10.95**

DAVIS TARGETEER—Objective lens/tube units that attach to front of low power scopes, increase magnification to 8X. 1¼" lens.
Price: .... **$ 27.50**
1½" lens... **$32.50**

HERMANN LONGHORN DUST CAPS—All leather. Connected leather straps, hand made, natural color. For all popular scopes.
Price: **$10.50**

LEE TACKHOLE DOTS—Various size dots for most scopes.
Price: .... **$16.00—$25.00**

W.H. SIEBERT—Converts Lyman, Leupold and Unertl varmint scopes to 15X-36X
Price: **$40.00**

STORM KING LENS COVER—Parallel watch crystal optics provide instant "shoot thru." Sizes available for all scopes. From Anderson Mfg.
Price:Per pair... **$7.95**
With Haze Cutter **$8.50**

SUPREME LENS COVERS—Hinged protectors for most scope models, front and rear lenses shielded. Butler Creek Corp. Per pair, postpaid
Price: **$7.95**

SPOTTING SCOPE STANDS

FREELAND REGAL BIPOD—Choice of saddle or zoom head. All adjustment knobs are oversize for easy adjusting. Large "ball" carrying knob. Gray finish.
Price: **$70.50**
As above with stability weight **$94.00**

FREELAND GALLERY SPECIAL BIPOD—For all shooting positions. Zoom or saddle head. Adjustable for elevation. Comes with bipod base, gallery special head assembly and 12" extension.
Price:Gray finish, saddle head **$57.60**
As above with 18" extension................................. **$60.00**

ARMS ASSOCIATIONS IN AMERICA AND ABROAD

UNITED STATES

ALABAMA

Alabama Gun Collectors Assn.
Dick Boyd, Secy., P.O. Box 5548, Tuscaloosa, AL 35405

ALASKA

Alaska Gun Collectors Assn.
Gene Coppedge, P.O. Box 4-1898, Anchorage, AK 99509

ARIZONA

Arizona Arms Assn.,
Clay Fobes, Secy., P.O. Box 17061, Tucson, AZ 85731

CALIFORNIA

Calif. Hunters & Gun Owners Assoc.
V.H. Wacker, 2309 Cipriani Blvd., Belmont, CA 94002
Greater Calif. Arms & Collectors Assn.
Donald L. Bullock, 8291 Carburton St., Long Beach, CA 90808
Los Angeles Gun & Ctg. Collectors Assn.
F.H. Ruffra, 20810 Amie Ave., Torrance, CA 90503

COLORADO

Pikes Peak Gun Collectors Guild
Charles Cell, 406 E. Uintah St., Colorado Springs, CO 80903

CONNECTICUT

Ye Conn. Gun Guild, Inc.
Robert L. Harris, P.O. Box 8, Cornwall Bridge, CT 06754

FLORIDA

Florida Gun Collectors Assn., Inc.
John D. Hammer, 5700 Mariner Dr., 304-W, Tampa, FL 33609

Unified Sportsmen of Florida
P.O. Box 6565, Tallahassee, FL 32301

GEORGIA

Georgia Arms Collectors
Cecil W. Anderson, P.O. Box 218, Conley, GA 30027

HAWAII

Hawaii Historic Arms Assn.
John N. Butchart, P.O. Box 1733, Honolulu, HI 96806

IDAHO

Idaho State Rife and Pistol Assn.
Tom Price, 3631 Pineridge Dr., Coeur d'Alene, ID 83814

ILLINOIS

Central Illinois Gun Collectors Assn., Inc.
Joe Richardson, R.R. 3, Jacksonville, IL 62650
Fox Valley Arms Fellowship, Inc.
P.O. Box 301, Palatine, IL 60067
Illinois State Rifle Assn.
224 S. Michigan Ave., Room 200, Chicago, IL 60604

Illinois Gun Collectors Assn.
P.O. Box 1694, Kankakee, IL 60901
Little Fort Gun Collectors Assn.
Ernie Robinson, P.O. Box 194, Gurnee, IL 60031
Mississippi Valley Gun & Cartridge Coll. Assn.
Lawrence Maynard, R.R. 2, Aledo, IL 61231
Sauk Trail Gun Collectors
Gordell M. Matson, 3817-22 Ave., Moline, IL 61265
Wabash Valley Gun Collectors Assn., Inc.
Mrs. Betty Baer, 1659 N. Franklin St., Danville, IL 61832

INDIANA

Indiana Sportsmen's Council-Legislative
Maurice Latimer, P.O. Box 93, Bloomington, IN 47402
Indiana State Rifle & Pistol Assn.
Thos. Glancy, P.O. Box 552, Chesterton, IN 46304
Southern Indiana Gun Collectors Assn., Inc.
Harold M. McClary, 509 N. 3rd St., Boonville, IN 47601

IOWA

Central States Gun Collectors Assn.
Avery Giles, 1104 S. 1st Ave. Marshtown, IA 50158

KANSAS

Four State Collectors Assn.
M.G. Wilkinson, 915 E. 10th, Pittsburg, KS 66762
Kansas Cartridge Coll. Assn.
Bob Linder, Box 84, Plainville, KS 67663
Missouri Valley Arms Collectors Assn.
Chas. F. Samuel, Jr., Box 8204, Shawnee Mission, KS 66208

KENTUCKY

Kentuckiana Arms Coll. Assn.
Tony Wilson, Pres., Box 1776, Louisville, KY 40201
Kentucky Gun Collectors Assn., Inc.
J.A. Smith, Box 64, Owensboro, KY 42302
Kentucky Rifle Assn.
Ronald Gabel, 158 W. Unionville, RD 1, Schnecksville, PA 18078

LOUISIANA

Ft. Miro Muzzleloaders
Sandra Rushing, P.O. Box 256, Main St., Grayson, LA 71435

MARYLAND

Baltimore Antique Arms Assn.
Stanley I. Kellert, E-30, 2600 Insulator Dr., Baltimore, MD 21230

MASSACHUSETTS

Bay Colony Weapons Collectors, Inc.
Ronald B. Santurjian, 47 Homer Rd., Belmont, MA 02178
Massachusetts Arms Collectors
John J. Callan, Jr., P.O. Box 1001, Worcester, MA 01613

MICHIGAN

Royal Oak Historical Arms Collectors, Inc.
Dee Hamal, P.O. Box 202, Royal Oak, MI 48067

MINNESOTA

Minnesota Weapons Coll. Assn., Inc.
Box 662, Hopkins, MN 55343

MISSISSIPPI

Mississippi Gun Collectors Assn.
Mrs. Jack E. Swinney, P.O. Box 1332, Hattiesburg, MS 39401

MISSOURI

Mineral Belt Gun Coll. Assn.
D.F. Saunders, 1110 Cleveland Ave., Monett, MO 65708

MONTANA

Montana Arms Collectors Assn.
Lewis E. Yearout, 308 Riverview Dr. East, Great Falls, MT 59404
The Winchester Arms Coll. Assn.
Lewis E. Yearout, 308 Riverview Dr. East, Great Falls, MT 59404

NEW HAMPSHIRE

New Hampshire Arms Collectors, Inc.
Frank H. Galeucia, Rte. 28, Box 44, Windham, NH 03087

NEW JERSEY

Englishtown Benchrest Shooters Assn.
Tony Hidalgo, 6 Capp St., Carteret, NJ 07008
Experimental Ballistics Associates
Ed Yard, 110 Kensington, Trenton, NJ 08618
Jersey Shore Antique Arms Collectors
Joe Sisia, P.O. Box 100, Bayville, NJ 08721
New Jersey Arms Collectors Club, Inc.
Angus Laidlaw, 230 Valley Rd., Montclair, NJ 07042

NEW YORK

Hudson-Mohawk Arms Collectors Assn., Inc.
Bennie S. Pisarz, 6 Lamberson St., Dolgeville, NY 13329
Iroquois Arms Collectors Assn.
Dennis Freeman, 12144 McNeeley Rd., Akron, NY 14001
Mid-State Arms Coll. & Shooters Club
Jack Ackerman, 24 S. Mountain Terr., Binghamton, NY 13903
Westchester Arms Collectors Club, Inc.
F.E. Falkenbury, Secy., 79 Hillcrest Rd., Hartsdale, NY 10530

NORTH CAROLINA

Carolina Gun Collectors Assn.
David Blalock, Jr., Rt. 1, Linden, NC 28356

OHIO

Central Ohio Gun and Indian Relic Coll. Assn.
Coyt Stookey, 134 E. Ohio Ave., Washington C.H., OH 43160
Maumee Valley Gun Collectors Assn.
A. Kowalka, 3203 Woodville Rd., Northwood, OH 43619
Ohio Gun Collectors, Assn., Inc.
Drawer 24F, Cincinnati, OH 45224
The Stark Gun Collectors, Inc.
Russ McNary, 147 Miles Ave., N.W., Canton, OH 44708

OKLAHOMA

Indian Territory Gun Collectors Assn.
P.O. Box 4491, Tulsa, OK 74104

OREGON

Oregon Cartridge Coll. Assn.
Richard King, 3228 N.W. 60th, Corvallis, OR 97330
Oregon Arms Coll. Assn., Inc.
Ted Dowd, P.O. box 25103, Portland, OR 97225

PENNSYLVANIA

Presque Isle Gun Coll. Assn.
James Welch, 156 E. 37 St., Erie, PA 16504

SOUTH CAROLINA

Belton Gun Club, Inc.
J.K. Phillips, Route 1, Belton, SC 29627
South Carolina Arms Coll. Assn.
J.W. McNelley, 3215 Lincoln St., Columbia, SC 29201

SOUTH DAKOTA

Dakota Territory Gun Coll. Assn., Inc.
Curt Carter, Castlewood, SD 57223

TENNESSEE

Memphis Antique Weapons Assn.
Jan Clement, 1886 Lyndale #1, Memphis TN 38107
Smoky Mountain Gun Coll. Assn., Inc.
M.C. Wiest, P.O. Box 8880, Knoxville, TN 37916
Tennessee Gun Collectors Assn., Inc.
M.H. Parks, 3556 Pleasant Valley Rd., Nashville, TN 37204

TEXAS

Houston Gun Collectors Assn.
P.O. Box 37369, Houston, TX 77237
Texas State Rifle Assn.
P.O. Drawer 340809, Dallas, TX 75234

UTAH

Utah Gun Collectors Assn.
Nick Davis, 5676 So. Meadow Lane #4, Ogden, UT 84403

VIRGINIA

Virginia Arms Collectors & Assn.
Clinton E. Jones, P.O. Box 333, Mechanicsville, VA 23111

WASHINGTON

Washington Arms Collectors, Inc.
J. Dennis Cook, P.O. Box 7335, Tacoma, WA 98407

WISCONSIN

Great Lakes Arms Coll. Assn., Inc.
E. Warnke, 1811 N. 73rd St. Wauwatosa, WI 53213
Wisconsin Gun Collectors Assn., Inc.
Rob. Zellmer, P.O. Box 181, Sussex, WI 53089

WYOMING

Wyoming Gun Collectors
Bob Funk, Box 1805, Riverton, WY 82501

NATIONAL ORGANIZATIONS

Amateur Trap Shooting Assn.
P.O. Box 458, Vandalia, OH 45377
American Association of Shotgunning
P.O. Box 3351, Reno, NV 89505
American Defense Preparedness Assn.
Rosslyn Center, Suite 900, 1700 N. Moore St., Arlington, VA 22209
American Police Pistol & Rifle Assn.
1100 N.E. 125th St., No. Miami, FL 33161
American Single Shot Rifle Assn.
L.B. Thompson, 987 Jefferson Ave., Salem, OH 44460
American Society of Arms Collectors, Inc.
Robt. F. Rubendunst, 6550 Baywood Lane, Cincinnati, OH 45224

Armor & Arms Club
J.K. Watson, Jr., c/o Lord, Day & Lord, 25 Broadway, New York, NY 10004
Association of Firearm and Toolmark Examiners
Eugenia A. Bell, Secy., 7857 Esterel Dr., LaJolla, CA 92037
Boone & Crockett Club
205 South Patrick, Alexandria, VA 22314
Cast Bullet Assn., Inc.
Ralland J. Fortier, 14193 Van Dorn Rd., Manassas, VA 22111
Citizens Committee for the Right to Keep and Bear Arms
Natl. Hq.: Bellefield Office Park, 1601 114, S.E., Suite 151, Bellevue, WA 98004
Deer Unlimited of America, Inc.
P.O. Box 509, Clemson, SC 29631
Ducks Unlimited, Inc.
P.O. Box 66300, Chicago, IL 60666
Experimental Ballistics Associates
Ed Yard, 110 Kensington, Trenton, NJ 08618
Handgun Hunters International
J. D. Jones, Dir., P. O. Box 357 MAG, Bloomingdale, OH 43910
International Benchrest Shooters
Evelyn Richards, 411 N. Wilbur Ave. Sayre, PA 18840
International Cartridge Coll. Assn., Inc.
Victor v. B. Engel, 1211 Walnut St., Williamsport, PA 17701
International Handgun Metallic Silhouette Assoc.
Box 1609, Idaho Falls, ID 83401
Marlin Firearms Coll. Assn., Ltd.
Dick Paterson, Secy., 407 Lincoln Bldg., 44 Main St., Champaign, IL 61820
Miniature Arms Collectors/Makers Society Ltd.
Joseph J. Macewicz, 104 White Sand Lane, Racine, WI 53402
National Assn. of Federally Licd. Firearms Dealers
Andrew Molchan, 2801 E. Oakland Park Blvd., Ft. Lauderdale, Fl 33306
National Automatic Pistol Collectors Assn.
Tom Knox, P.O. Box 15738, Tower Grove Station, St. Louis, MO 63163
National Bench Rest Shooters Assn., Inc.
Stella Buchtel, 5735 Sherwood Forest Dr., Akron, OH 44139
National Deer Hunter Assn.
1415 Fifth St. So., Hopkins, MN 55343
National Muzzle Loading Rifle Assn.
Box 67, Friendship, IN 47021
National Police Officers Assn. of America
Frank J. Schira, Ex. Dir., 609 West Main St., Louisville, KY 40202
National Reloading Mfrs. Assn., Inc.
4905 S.W. Griffith Dr., Suite 101, Beaverton, OR 97005
National Rifle Assn.
1600 Rhode Island Ave., N.W., Washington, DC 20036
National Shooting Sports Fdtn., Inc.
Arnold H. Rohlfing, Exec. Director, 1075 Post Rd., Riverside, Ct 06878
National Skeet Shooting Assn.
Ann Myers, P.O. Box 28188, San Antonio, TX 78228
National Wild Turkey Federation, Inc.
P.O. Box 530, Edgefield, SC 29824
North American Edged Weapon Collectors Assn.
John Cox, 2224 Wyandoge Dr., Oakville, Ont. L6L 2T5, Canada
North-South Skirmish Assn., Inc.
T.E. Johnson, Jr., 9700 Royerton Dr., Richmond, VA 23228
Remington Society of America
Fritz Baehr, 3125 Fremont Ave., Boulder, CO 80302
Ruger Collector's Assn., Inc.
Nancy J. Padua, P.O. Box 211, Trumbull, CT 06611
SAAMI, Sporting Arms and Ammunition Mfrs. Inst., Inc.
P.O. Box 218, Wallingford, CT 06492
Safari Club International
Holt Bodinson, 5151 E. Broadway, Suite 1680, Tucson, AZ 85711
Second Amendment Foundation
James Madison Building, 12500 N.E. 10th Pl., Bellevue, WA 98005
Southern California Schuetzen Society
Thomas Trevor, 13621 Sherman Way, Van Nuys, CA 91405
U.S. Revolver Assn.
Stanley A. Sprague, 59 Alvin St., Springfield, MA 01104

Winchester Arms Collectors Assoc.
Lewis E. Yearout, 308 Riverview Dr., E., Great Falls, MT 59404
World Fast Draw Assn.
1026 Llagas Rd., Morgan Hill, CA 95037

AUSTRALIA

Sporting Shooters' Assn. of Australia Inc.
Mr. K. MacLaine, P.O. Box 210, Belgrave, Vict. 3160, Australia

CANADA

Alberta

Canadian Historical Arms Society
P.O. Box 901, Edmonton, Alb., Canada T5J 2L8

BRITISH COLUMBIA

B.C. Historical Arms Collectors
Ron Tyson, Box 80583, Burnaby, B.C. Canada V5H 3X9

NEW BRUNSWICK

Canadian Black Powder Federation
Mrs. Janet McConnell, P.O. Box 2876, Moncton, N.B. E1C 8T8, Can.

ONTARIO

Ajax Antique Arms Assn.
Monica A. Wright, P.O. Box 145, Millgrove, Ont., L0R 1VO, Canada
Oshawa Antique Gun Coll. Inc.
Monica A. Wright, P.O. Box 145, Millgrove, Ont., L0R 1VO, Canada

EUROPE

ENGLAND

Arms and Armour Society of London
Joseph G. Rosa, 17 Woodville Gardens, Ruislip, Middlesex HA4 7NB
British Cartridge Collectors Club
Peter F. McGowan, 15 Sandhurst Dr., Ruddington, Nottingham
Historical Breechloading Smallarms Assn.
D.J. Penn, M.A., Imperial War Museum, Lambeth Rd., London SE1 6HZ, England.Journal and newsletter are $8 a yr. seamail; surcharge for airmail
Muzzle Loaders's Assn. of Great Britain
Membership Records, 12 Frances Rd., Baginton, Coventry, England
National Rifle Assn. (British)
Bisley Camp, Brookwood, Woking, Surrey, GU24 OPB, England

FRANCE

Syndicat National de l'Arquebuserie du Commerce de l'Arme Historique
B.P. No 3, 78110 Le Vesient, France

GERMANY (WEST)

Deutscher Schützenbund
Lahnstrasse, 6200 Wiesbaden-Klarenthal, West Germany

NEW ZEALAND

New Zealand Deerstalkers Assn.
Mr. Shelby Grant, P.O. Box 6514, Wellington, New Zealand

SOUTH AFRICA

Historical Firearms Soc. of South Africa
P.O. Box 145, 7725 Newlands, Republic of South Africa
South African Reloaders Assn.
Box 27128, Sunnyside, Pretoria 0132, South Africa

The Arms Library for

COLLECTOR · HUNTER · SHOOTER · OUTDOORSMAN

A selection of books—old, new and forthcoming—for everyone in the arms field, with a brief description by . . . JOE RILING

NEW BOOKS

(Alphabetically, no categories)

After Your Deer is Down, by Josef Fischl and Leonard Lee Rue, III, Winchester Press, Tulsa, OK, 1981. 160 pp., illus. Paper covers. $9.95.

The care and handling of big game, with a bonus of venison recipes.

The AK-47 Assault Rifle, Desert Publications, Cornville, AZ, 1981. 150 pp., illus. Paper covers. $5.95

Complete and practical technical information on the only weapon in history to be produced in an estimated 30,000,000 units.

All About Airguns, by Robert J. Traister, TAB Books, Blue Ridge, Summit, PA, 1981. 304 pp., illus. $14.95.

A complete guide to airguns as a hobby, with special information and easy-to-follow directions on how to use them.

American Handguns & their Makers, compiled by J.B. Roberts, Jr. and Ted Bryant, NRA Books, Wash., D.C., 1981. 248pp., illus. Paper covers. $11.95.

First in a series of manuals on gun collecting and the history of firearms manufacturing.

American Tools of Intrigue, by John Minnery & Joe Ramos, Desert Publications, Cornville, AZ, 1981. 128 pp., illus. Paper covers. $8.95.

Clandestine weapons which the Allies supplied to resistance fighters.

"...And Now Stainless", by Dave Ecker with Bob Zwirz, Charter Arms Corp., Bridgeport, CT, 1981. 165 pp., illus. $15.00.

The Charter Arms story. Covers all models to date.

The Art of Bullet Casting from Handloader & Rifle Magazines 1966-1981, compiled by Dave Wolfe, Wolfe Publishing Co., Prescott, AZ, 1981. 258 pp., illus. Paper covers. $12.95. Deluxe hardbound. $19.50.

Articles from "Handloader" and "Rifle" magazines by authors such as Jim Carmichel, John Wootters, and the late George Nonte.

Basic Handloading, by George C. Nonte., Jr., Outdoor Life Books, New York, NY, 1982. 192 pp., illus. Paper covers. $4.50.

How to produce high-quality ammunition using the safest, most efficient methods known.

Basic Manual of Military Small Arms, by W.H.B. Smith, Stackpole Books, Harrisburg, Pa., 1980. 216 pp., illus. $22.95.

Reprinting of the scarce 1943 original edition. An extensive source representing the small arms of 14 countries.

The Best of Sheep Hunting, by John Batten, Amwell Press, Clinton, NJ, 1981. 500 pp., illus. In slipcase. $40.00.

An anthology of the finest stories on sheep ever assembled under one cover.

The Best Shotguns Ever Made in America, by Michael McIntosh, Charles Scribner's Sons, New York, NY 1981. 185 pp., illus. $17.95.

Seven vintage doubles to shoot and to treasure.

Black Powder Gun Digest, 3rd Edition, edited by Jack Lewis, DBI Books, Inc., Northfield, IL, 1982. 256 pp., illus. Paper covers. $9.95.

All new articles, expressly written for the black powder gun buff.

Blue Book of Gun Values, 1982 Edition, Vol. 2, No. 1, compiled by Barry Fain, Investment Rarities, Inc., Minneapolis, MN, 1982. 341 pp. Paper covers. $12.95.

Analysis of the prices for which collectible firearms have been actually selling.

The Bobwhite Quail Book, compiled by Lamar Underwood, Amwell Press, Clinton, NJ, 1981. 442 pp., illus. $25.00.

An anthology of the finest stories on Bobwhite quail ever assembled under one cover.

The Book of the Wild Turkey, by Lovett E. Williams, Jr., Winchester Press, Tulsa, OK, 1981. 204 pp., illus. $15.95.

A definitive reference work on the wild turkey for hunter, game manager, conservationist, or amateur naturalist.

The British Service Lee, Lee-Metford, and Lee-Enfield, by Ian Skennerton, Arms & Armour Press, London, England, 1982. 380 pp., illus. $35.00.

A comprehensive and authoritative book on these famous military arms.

The British Shotgun, Vol. One, 1850-1870, by I.M. Crudgington and D.J. Baker, Barrie & Jenkins, London, England, 1979. 256 pp., illus. $27.50.

The evolution of the shotgun during its formative years in Great Britain.

Carbines of the Civil War, by John D. McAulay, Pioneer Press, Union City, TN, 1981. 123 pp., illus. Paper covers. $7.95.

A guide to the student and collector on the colorful arms used by the Federal cavalry.

The Cartridge Guide, by Ian V. Hogg, Stackpole Books, Harrisburg, PA., 1982. 160 pp., illus. $19.95.

The small arms ammunition identification manual.

A Collector's Guide to Air Rifles, by Dennis E. Hiller, D.E. Hiller, London, England, 1980. 170 pp., illus. Paper covers. $15.00.

Valuations, exploded diagrams and many other details of air rifles old and new.

Colonial Frontier Guns, by T.M. Hamilton, The Fur Press, Chadron, NE, 1980. 176 pp., illus. Paper covers. $12.00.

French, Dutch, and English trade guns before 1780.

Colt Engraving, by R. L. Wilson, The Gun Room Press, Highland Park, NJ, 1982. Over 400 pp., illus. $69.95.

New and completely revised edition of the author's original work on finely engraved Colt firearms.

Colt Pistols 1836-1976, by R. L. Wilson in association with R.E. Hable, Jackson Arms, Dallas, TX, 1976. 380 pp., illus. $100.00.

A magnificently illustrated book in full-color featuring Colt firearms from the famous Hable collection.

Combat Loads for the Sniper Rifle, by Ralph Avery, Desert Publications, Cornville, AZ, 1982. 156 pp., illus. Paper covers. $6.95.

Commercial hunting and military armor piercing loads, plus some of the author's own AP bullet designs and loading data.

The Commercial Mauser '98 Sporting Rifle, by Lester Womack, Womack Associates, Publishers, Prescott, AZ, 1980. 69 pp., illus. $20.00.

The first work on the sporting rifles made by the original Mauser plant in Oberndorf.

The Complete Book of Hunting, Robert Elman, Winchester Press, Tulsa, OK, 1982. 320 pp., illus. $49.95.

A compendium of world's game birds and animals, handloading, international hunting, etc.

The Complete Book of Thompson Patents, compiled by Don Thomas, Desert Publications, Cornville, AZ, 1981. 482 pp., illus. Paper covers. $19.95.

From John Blish's breech closure patented in 1915 to Charles W. Robin's automatic sear release of 1947. Includes all other firearm patents granted to the developers of the famed "Tommy Gun."

The Complete Book of Trick & Fancy Shooting, by Ernie Lund, The Citadel Press, Secaucus, NJ, 1977. 159 pp., illus. Paper covers. $6.00.

Step-by-step instructions for aquiring the whole range of shooting skills with rifle, pistol and shotgun.

Contemporary Makers of Muzzleloading Firearms, by Robert Weil, Screenland Press, Burbank, CA, 1981. 300 pp., illus. $39.95.

Illustrates the work of over thirty different contemporary makers.

Coveys and Singles: The Handbook of Quail Hunting, by Robert Gooch, A.S. Barnes, San Diego, CA, 1981. 196 pp., illus. $11.95.

The story of the quail in North America.

The Defensive Use of the Handgun for the Novice, by Mason Williams, Charles C. Thomas, Publisher, Springfield, IL, 1980. 226 pp., illus. $15.00.

This book was developed for the home owner, housewife, elderly couple, and the woman who lives alone. Basic instruction for purchasing, loading and firing pistols and revolvers.

Discover Swaging, by David Corbin, Stackpole Books, Harrisburg, PA, 1980. 288 pp., illus. $16.95.

A book for the serious rifle and handgun reloading enthusiast.

The Elephant Hunters of the Lado, by Major W. Robert Foran, Amwell Press, Clinton, NJ, 1981. 311 pp., illus. Limited, numbered, and signed edition, in slipcase. $40.00.

From a previously unpublished manuscript by a famous "white hunter".

Famous Guns & Gunners, by George E. Virgines, Leather Stocking Press, West Allis, WI, 1980. 113 pp., illus. $12.95.

Intriguing and fascinating tales of men of the West and their guns.

First Book of Gunsmithing, by John E. Traister, Stackpole Books, Harrisburg, Pa., 1981. 192 pp., illus. $14.95.

Beginner's guide to gun care, repair, and modification.

F.N. F.A.L. Auto Rifles, Desert Publications, Cornville, AZ, 1981. 130pp., illus. Paper covers. $6.95.

A definitive study of one of the Free World's finest combat rifles.

Frankonia Jagd Catalogue, 1980-81, Waffen-Frankonia, Wurzburg, Germany, 1980. 372 pp., illus. Paper covers. $9.50.

Latest catalogue from this famous German sporting goods supplier. Rifles, shotguns, handguns, and accessories.

The Game-Trophies of the World, edited and compiled by G. Kenneth Whitehead, Paul Parey, Hamburg, W. Germany, 215 pp., illus. Paper covers. $29.00.

Covers all the game trophies of the world using the Boone & Crockett method of scoring. Text in English, French and German.

The German Sniper, 1914-1945, by Peter R. Senich, Paladin Press, Boulder, CO, 1982. 468 pp., illus. $49.95.

The development and application of Germany's sniping weapon systems and tactics is traced from World War I through World War II.

The Grizzly Book, edited by Jack Samson, Amwell Press, Clinton, NJ, 1981. 301 pp., illus. Limited, numbered, and signed edition. $50.00.

An anthology of stories about grizzlies by men such as O'Connor, Keith, Fitz, Pope, and others.

Grizzlies Don't Come Easy, by Ralph W. Young, Winchester Press, Tulsa, OK, 1981. 200 pp., illus. $13.95.

The life story of a great woodsman who guided such famous hunters as Jack O'Connor and Warren Page.

Great Sporting Posters, by Sid Latham, Stackpole Books, Harrisburg, Pa., 1980. 48 pp., illus. Paper covers. $14.95.

23 full color reproductions of beautiful hunting and fishing poster art, mostly of the early 1900s.

Gun Collector's Digest, 3rd Edition, edited by Joseph J. Schroeder, DBI Books, Inc., Northfield, IL., 1981. 256 pp., illus. Paper covers. $9.95.

Excellent reading by some of the world's finest collector/writers. The best book on general gun collecting available.

Gun Digest, 1983, 37th Edition, edited by Ken Warner, DBI Books, Inc., Northfield, Il., 1982. 472 pp., illus. Paper covers. $12.95.

The world's greatest gun book in its 37th annual edition.

The Gun Digest Book of Firearms Assembly/Disassembly Part VI: Law Enforcement Weapons, by J.B. Wood, DBI Books, Inc., Northfield, IL, 1981. 288 pp., illus. Paper covers. $9.95.

A professional presentation on the assembly and disassembly of weapons used by law enforcement agencies.

Gun Digest Book of Knives, 2nd Edition, by Jack Lewis and Roger Combs, DBI Books, Inc., Northfield, IL, 1982. 288 pp., illus. Paper covers. $9.95.

Covers the complete spectrum of the fascinating world of knives.

Guns & Ammo, 1983 Annual, edited by Craig Boddington, Petersen Publishing Co., Los Angeles, CA 1982. 288 pp., illus. Paper covers. $6.95.

Annual catalog of sporting firearms and accessories along with articles for the gun enthusiast.

Guns of the Gunfighters, by the editors of Guns & Ammo, Crown Publishing Co., New York, NY 1982. 50 pp., illus. $6.98.

A must for Western buffs and gun collectors alike.

Guns Illustrated, 1983, 15th Edition, edited by Harold A. Murtz, D8I Books, Inc., Northfield, IL, 1982. 344 pp., illus. Paper covers. $10.95.

Technical articles for gun enthusiasts plus a complete illustrated catalog of all current guns, ammo, and accessories including specifications and prices. A must for the modern gun buff.

Guns & Shooting: A Selected Bibliography, by Ray Riling, Ray Riling Arms Books Co., Phila., PA, 1982. 434 pp., illus. Limited, numbered memorial edition. $75.00.

A limited edition of this superb bibliographical work, the only modern listing of books devoted to guns and shooting.

The Gunsmith's Manual, by J.P. Stelle and Wm. B. Harrison, The Gun Room Press, Highland Park, NJ, 1982. $12.95.

For the gunsmith in all branches of the trade.

Gunstock Finishing and Care, by A. Donald Newell, Stackpole Books, Harrisburg, PA., 1982. 512 pp., illus. $22.95.

The most complete resource imaginable for finishing and refinishing gun wood.

The Hand Cannons of Imperial Japan, 1543-1945, by Harry Derby, Harry Derby, 1982. 300 pp., illus. $37.00.

A superb, comprehensive and definitive study of Japanese handguns beginning with the introduction of the matchlock in Japan and continuing into the post WW II period.

Handguns of the World, by Edward C. Ezell, Stackpole Books, Harrisburg, PA., 1981. 704 pp., illus. $39.95.

Encyclopedia for identification and historical reference that will be appreciated by gun enthusiasts, collectors, hobbyists or professionals.

Handloaders Digest, 9th Edition, edited by Ken Warner, DBI Books, Inc., Northfield, IL, 1982. 320 pp., illus. Paper covers. $9.95.

Latest edition of the book no handloader should be without.

The Hawken Rifle; Its Place in History, by Charles E. Hanson, Jr., The Fur Press, Chadron, NE, 1979. 104 pp., illus. Paper covers. $6.00.

A definitive work on this famous rifle.

High Standard Automatic Pistols, 1932-1950, by Charles E. Petty, American Ordnance Publications, Charlotte, NC, 1976. 124 pp., illus. $12.95.

Describes and illustrates the early history of the company and many details of the various popular pistols. Includes dates and serial numbers.

The History and Development of Small Arms Ammunition, Vol. 1, by George A. Hoyem, Armory Publications, Tacoma, WA, 1981. 230 pp., illus. $27.50.

Describes and illustrates cartridges from military long arms—flintlock through rimfire.

The History of Wildfowling, by John Marchington, Adam and Charles Black, London, England, 1980. 288 pp., illus. $27.50.

Covers decoys, punting, and punt guns.

Home Guide to Muzzle Loaders, by George C. Nonte, Jr., Stackpole Books, Harrisburg, Pa., 1982. 224 pp., illus. Paper covers. $14.95.

From the basics of muzzle loading, to the differences between the modern and replica muzzle loader, plus how to make one.

How to Hunt, by Dave Bowring, Winchester Press, Tulsa, OK, 1982. 208 pp. illus. Cloth. $15.00. Paper covers. $10.95.

A basic guide to hunting big game, small game, upland birds, and waterfowl.

The Hunter's Shooting Guide, by Jack O'Connor, Outdoor Life Books, New York, NY 1982. 176 pp., illus. Paper covers. $4.50.

A classic; covers rifles, cartridges, shooting techniques for shotguns/rifles/handguns.

Hunting in Africa, by Bill Morkel, Howard Timmins, Publishers, Capetown, South Africa, 1980. 252 pp., illus. $25.00.

An invaluable guide for the inexperienced hunter contemplating a possible safari.

Hunting America's Mule Deer, by Jim Zumbo, Winchester Press, Tulsa, OK, 1981. 272 pp., illus. $14.95.

The best ways to hunt mule deer. The how, when, and where to hunt all seven subspecies.

Hunting the Big Cats, two volume set, edited by Jim Rikhoff, Amwell Press, Clinton, NJ, 1981. Total of 808 pp., illustrated by Bob Kuhn. Limited, numbered, and signed edition. In slipcase. $150.00.

The most definitive work on hunting the world's largest wild cats ever compiled. A collection of 70 articles on hunting in Africa, Asia, North and South America.

The Illustrated Encyclopedia of 19th Century Firearms, by Major Frederick Myatt, Crescent Books, New York, NY, 1980. 216 pp., illus. $12.95.

An illustrated history of the development of the world's military firearms during the 19th century.

The Illustrated Encyclopedia of Pistols & Revolvers, by Major Frederick Myatt, Crescent Books, New York, NY, 1980. 208 pp., illus. $14.98.

An illustrated history of hand guns from the 16th century to the present day.

The Illustrated Book of Pistols, by Frederick Wilkinson, Hamlyn Publishing Group, Ltd., London, England, 1979. 192 pp., illus. $10.98.

A carefully researched study of the pistol's evolution and use in war and peace.

An Illustrated Guide to Rifles and Automatic Weapons, by Major Frederick Myatt, Arco Publishing Co., Inc., New York, NY, 1981. 160 pp., illus. $8.95.

Stories of gun designs, combat efficiency, production records, etc.

Ivory, by Tony Sanchez-Arino, Amwell Press, Clinton, NJ, 1981. 252 pp., illustrations by Bob Kuhn. Limited, numbered, and signed edition. In slipcase. $45.00.

A definitive work on elephants and elephant hunting covering the whole African Continent.

Knives '83, edited by Ken Warner, DBI Books, Inc., Northfield, IL, 1982. 224 pp., illus. Paper covers. $8.95.

The third edition of the world's greatest knife book.

Know Your Ruger Single Action Revolvers 1953-1963, by John C. Dougan, edited by John T. Amber, Blacksmith Corp., Southport, CT, 1981. 199 pp., illus. $35.00.

A definitive reference work for the Ruger revolvers produced in the period 1953-1963.

The Law Enforcement Book of Weapons, Ammunition and Training Procedures, Handguns, Rifles and Shotguns, by Mason Williams, Charles C. Thomas, Publisher, Springfield, IL, 1977. 496 pp., illus. $35.00.

Data on firearms, firearm training, and ballistics.

Lyman Muzzleloader's Handbook, 2nd Edition, edited by C. Kenneth Ramage, Lyman Publications, Middlefield, CT, 1982. 248 pp., illus. Paper covers. $11.95.

Hunting with rifles and shotguns, plus muzzle loading products.

Lyman Reloading Handbook No. 46, edited by C. Kenneth Ramage, Lyman Publications, Middlefield, CT, 1982. 300 pp., illus. $16.95.

A large and comprehensive book on reloading. Extensive list of loads for jacketed and cast bullets.

Manual of Pistol and Revolver Cartridges, Volume 2, Centerfire U.S. and British Calibers, by Hans A. Erlmeier and Jakob H. Brandt, Journal-Verlag, Weisbaden, Germany, 1981. 270 pp., illus. $9.95.

Catalog system allows cartridges to be traced either by caliber or alphabetically.

The Metric FAL, by R. Blake Stevens and Jean E. Van Rutten, Collector Grade Publications, Toronto, Canada, 1981. 372 pp., illus. Paper covers. $50.00.

Volume three of the FAL series. The free world's right arm.

Military Small Arms of the 20th Century, 4th Edition, by Ian V. Hogg and John Weeks, DBI Books, Inc., Northfield, IL., 1981. 288 pp., illus. Paper covers. $10.95.

A comprehensive illustrated encyclopedia of the world's small-caliber firearms.

Mixed Bag, by Jim Rikhoff, National Rifle Association of America, Wash., D.C., 1981. 284 pp., illus. Paper covers. $9.95.

Remiscences of a master raconteur.

Modern Airweapon Shooting, by Bob Churchill & Granville Davis, David & Charles, London, England, 1981. 196 pp., illus. $18.95.

A comprehensive, illustrated study of all the relevant topics, from beginnings to World Championship shooting.

Modern American Centerfire Handguns, by Stanley W. Trzoniec, Winchester Press, Tulsa, OK, 1981. 260 pp., illus. $24.95.

The most comprehensive reference on handguns in print.

Modern Gun Values, 3rd Edition, by Jack Lewis, edited by Harold A. Murtz, DBI Books, Inc., Northfield, IL, 1981. 384 pp., illus. $9.95.

New expanded edition. Used values, full specifications, discontinuation dates—for all domestic and imported handguns, rifle, shotguns, and commemoratives manufactured between 1900 and 1978.

Modern Pheasant Hunting, by Steve Grooms, Stackpole Books, Harrisburg, Pa., 1982. 224 pp., illus. $14.95.

New look at pheasants and hunters from an experienced hunter who repects this splendid gamebird.

Modern Wildfowling, by Eric Begbie, Saiga Publishing Co. Ltd., Surrey, England, 1980. 171 pp., illus. $27.50.

History of wildfowling, guns and equipment, etc.

The Muzzleloading Hunter, by Rick Hacker, Winchester Press, Tulsa, OK, 1981. 283 pp., illus. $14.95.

A comprehensive guide for the black powder sportsman.

The Nash Buckingham Library, compiled by Douglas C. Mauldin, Delta Arms Sporting Goods, Indianola, MS, 1980. 7 volume set in slipcase. $150.00.

Seven outdoor hunting classics by Nash Buckingham, the 20th century's greatest sporting writer.

The New Handbook of Handgunning, by Paul B. Weston, Charles C. Thomas, Publisher, Springfield, IL, 1980. 102 pp., illus. $15.00.

A step-by-step, how-to manual of handgun shooting.

North American Big Game Hunting, by Byron W. Dalrymple, Winchester Press, New York, NY, 1974. 384 pp., illus. $15.00.

A comprehensive, practical guide, with individual chapters devoted to all native species.

North American Elk; Ecology and Management, edited by Jack Ward Thomas and Dale E. Toweill, Stackpole Books, Harrisburg, Pa., 1982. 576 pp., illus. $39.95.

The definitive, exhaustive, classic work on the North American Elk.

North American FALs, by R. Blake Stevens, Collector Grade Publications, Toronto, Canada, 1979. 166 pp., illus. Paper covers. $20.00.

NATO's search for a standard rifle.

The Official 1981 Price Guide to Antique and Modern Firearms, edited by Thomas E. Hudgeons, House of Collectibles, Inc., Orlando, FL, 1981. 450 pp., illus. Paper covers. $9.95.

Over 10,000 current collectors values for over 650 manufacturers of American and foreign made firearms.

Old Time Posters from the Great Sporting Days, Stackpole Books, Harrisburg, Pa., 1982. 48 pp., illus. Paper covers. $19.95.

Quality reproductions of 22 fine sporting posters in full color. 11" x 16".

Pinnell and Talifson:Last of the Great Brown Bear Men, by Marvin H. Clark, Jr., Great Northwest Publishing and Distributing Co., Spokane, WA, 1980. 224 pp., illus. $20.00.

The story of these famous Alaskan guides and some of the record bears taken by them.

Pistols of the World, Revised Edition, by Ian V. Hogg and John Weeks, DBI Books, Inc., Northfield, IL, 1982. 304 pp., illus. $12.95.

A valuable reference for collectors and everyone interested in guns.

Plans and Specifications of the L.C. Smith Shotgun, by Lt. Col. William S. Brophy, USAR Ret., F. Brownell & Son, Montezuma, IA, 1982. 247 pp., illus. $19.95.

The only collection ever assembled of all the drawings and engineering specifications on the incomparable and very collectable L.C. Smith.

Practical Handgun Ballistics, by Mason Williams, Charles C. Thomas, Publisher, Springfield, IL, 1980. 215 pp., illus. $19.50.

Factual information on the practical aspects of ammunition performance in revolvers and pistols.

The Practical Wildfowler, by John Marchington, Adam and Charles Black, London, England, 1977. 143 pp., illus. $21.95.

Advice on both the practical and ethical aspects of the sport.

Predator Caller's Companion, by Gerry Blair, Winchester Press, Tulsa, OK, 1981. 280 pp., illus. $13.95.

Predator calling techniques and equipment for the hunter and trapper.

The Post-War Colt Single-Action Revolver, by Don Wilkerson, Don Wilkerson, St. Paul, MN, second edition, 1980. 284 pp., illus. $39.95.

The most complete, up-to-date, and impressive work on Colt's post-war single-action revolvers. Covers all models, plus commemoratives.

Rifle Shooting as a Sport, by Bernd Klingner, A.S. Barnes & Co., Inc., San Diego, CA, 1980. 186 pp., illus. Paper covers. $15.00.

All factors for correct and incorrect shooting methods explained by an international expert marksman.

The Recollections of an Elephant Hunter 1864-1875, by William Finaughty, Books of Zimbabwe, Bulawayo, Zimbabwe, 1980. 244 pp., illus. $40.00.

Reprinting of the very scarce 1916 edition from the journals of this famous elephant hunter.

Recollections of a Shooting Guest, by George Bird Evans, Amwell Press, Clinton, NJ, 1978. 186 pp., illus. Limited, numbered, and signed edition. In slipcase. $45.00.

Including an unfinished manuscript of Charles C. Norris, author of "Eastern Upland Shooting".

Records of North American Big Game, edited by Wm. H. Nesbitt and Philip L. Wright, The Boone and Crockett Club, Alexandria, VA, 8th edition, 1981. 409 pp., illus. $29.50.

Tabulations of outstanding North American big game trophies, compiled from data in the club's big game records archives.

Remington Rolling Block Pistols, by Jerry Landskorn, Rolling Block Press, Buena Park, CA, 1981. 296 pp., illus. $34.95.

Describes all rolling block pistol models and variations as well as many rolling block rifles and carbines.

The Samurai Sword, by Gary D. Murtha, Gary D. Murtha, 1980. 126 pp., illus. $23.95.

An American perspective on the Samurai sword.

Shooter's Bible No. 74, 1983 Edition, ed. by R.F. Scott, Stoeger Publishing Co., So. Hackensack, NJ, 1982. 575 PP., illus. Paper covers. $11.95.

Annually published guide to firearms, ammunition and accessories.

Shooting Facts & Fancies, by Gough Thomas, Adam & Charles Black, London, England, 1978. 280 pp., illus. $27.50.

A new version of the author's second gun book.

Shootout: Modern Gunfighting, by Tony Lesce, Desert Publications, Cornville, AZ, 1981. 80 pp., illus. Paper covers. $4.95.

A book on combat and defensive shooting.

Shootout II, by Tony Lesce, Desert Publications, Cornville, AZ, 1981. 286 pp., illus. Paper covers. $7.95.

A thorough compilation of combat shooting data for handguns, rifles and shotguns.

The Shotgun, by Macdonald Hastings, David & Charles, London, England, 1981. 240 pp., illus. $29.95.

The story of shotgun development from the muzzleloaders to the present day shotguns.

Shots Fired in Anger, by Lt. Col. John B. George, NRA Books, Wash, D.C., 1981. 350 pp., illus. $18.00.

A new and enlarged edition of a classic work on an American sniper in the war against Japan.

Simonov SKS-45 Type Carbines, compiled and edited by Wyant Lamont and Stephen Fuller, Military Arms Research Service, San Jose, CA 1981. 218 pp., illus. Paper covers. $19.95.

Fully covers this milestone military weapon.

Single-Shot Rifles, by James Grant, The Gun Room Press, Highland Park, NJ, 1982. 385 pp., illus. $25.00.

A definitive study of the old single shot target gun.

Small Arms of the World, 11th Edition, by W.H.B. Smith, revised by Edward C. Ezell, Stackpole Books, Harrisburg, PA, 1980. 672 pp., illus. $29.95.

The standard bible for gun enthusiasts and collectors of small arms.

The Sporting Shotgun, by Robin Marshall-Ball, Saiga Publishing Co., Ltd., Surrey, England, 1981. 162 pp., illus. Paper covers. $27.50.

The history and uses of sporting shotguns.

The Sporting Use of the Handgun, by Mason Williams, Charles C. Thomas, Publisher, Springfield, IL, 1979. 272 pp., illus. $16.50.

An in-depth examination of the sporting use of the handgun for recreation, relaxation, competition and hunting.

Survival Shooting, by Tom Givens, Desert Publications, Cornville, AZ, 1981. 183 pp., illus. Paper covers. $6.95.

An illustrated guide to the defensive use of firearms and shotguns.

Survival Shooting for Women, by Tom Givens, Paladin Press, Boulder, Co., 1982. 106 pp., illus. Paper covers. $4.95.

The author takes a close look at the attitude and mental conditioning necessary to prepare a woman to fire in self-defense.

Survivalist Weapons and Ammunition Reloading, by Miles Stair, Paladin Press, Boulder, CO, 1982. 206 pp., illus. Paper covers. $14.00.

Guns and ammunition for everyone.

The Sword and the Centuries, by Alfred Hutton, Charles E. Tuttle Co., Rutland, VT, 1981. 367 pp., illus. $14.50.

A description of the various swords used in civilized Europe during the last five centuries.

The Sword in the Age of Chivalry, by R. Ewart Oakeshott, Arms & Armour Press, London, England, 1981. 160 pp., illus. $32.50.

A study of the medieval sword.

Swords of the British Army, by Brian Robson, Arms and Armour Press, London, England, 1975. 208 pp., illus. $45.00.

The regulation patterns of British swords, 1788-1914.

Tables of Bullet Performance, by Philip Mannes, Wolfe Publishing Co., Inc., Prescott, AZ, 1980. 407 pp. Paper covers. $17.50.

Tables for the advanced experimenter and ballistician for determining remaining velocity and energy, without calculations.

Thompson Guns Models 1921-1923, Americana Archives Publishing, Topsfield, MA, n.d. 24 pp., illus. Paper covers. $5.00.

Facsimile reprint of material on Thompson guns manufactured by Colt's Patent Fire Arms Mfg. Co.

Thompson Submachine Guns, Desert Publications, Cornville, AZ, 1980. 218 pp., illus. Paper covers. $7.95.

Facsimile reprinting of five complete manuals on the Thompson submachine gun.

Training the Gunfighter, by Capt. Timothy John Mulen, Paladin Press, Boulder, CO, 1981. 280 pp., illus. $21.95.

An encyclopedic, collector's volume on the combat application of firearms.

The Tsuba, by Gary D. Murtha, Gary D. Murtha, 1981. 50 pp., illus. Paper covers. $10.00.

Covers lives, schools, families, working styles, and periods of the artists. Almost 500 artists are listed alphabetically.

The Turkey Hunter's Book, by John M. McDaniel, Amwell Press, Clinton, NJ, 1980. 147 pp., illus. Paper covers. $7.95.

Hunting techniques, natural history and woods lore.

U.K. & Commonwealth FALs, by R. Blake Stevens, Collector Grade Publications, Toronto, Canada, 1981. 266 pp., illus. Paper covers. $30.00.

Covers British, Australian, and Indian models.

Walther, Volume III, 1908-1980, by James L. Rankin, J.L. Rankin, Coral Gables, FL, 1981. 226 pp., illus. $24.50.

Covers all models of Walther handguns from 1908 to date, includes holsters, grips and magazines.

The Wanderings of an Elephant Hunter, by W.D.M. Bell, Neville Spearman, Suffolk, England, 1981. 187 pp., illus. $27.50.

The greatest of elephant books by perhaps the greatest of elephant hunters, 'Karamojo' Bell.

The Whispering Wings of Autumn, by Gene Hill and Steve Smith, Amwell Press, Clinton, NJ, 1982. 192 pp., illus. $17.50.

A collection of both fact and fiction on two of North America's most famous game birds, the Ruffed Grouse and the Woodcock.

The Wild Turkey Book, edited and with special commentary by J. Wayne Fears, Amwell Press, Clinton, NJ, 1982. 303 pp., illus. $22.50.

An anthology of the finest stories on wild turkey ever assembled under one cover.

Winchester, Dates of Manufacture, by George Madis, Art & Reference House, Lancaster, TX, 1982. 51 pp. $4.95.

Dates, serial numbers and number of each model made.

The Winchester Handbook, by George Madis, Art & Reference House, Lancaster, TX, 1982. 287 pp., illus. $19.95.

The complete line of Winchester guns with dates of manufacture, serial numbers, etc.

ballistics *and* handloading

ABC's of Reloading, 2nd Edition, by Dean A. Grennell, DBI Books, Inc., Northfield, IL, 1980. 288 pp., illus. Paper covers. $9.95.

A natural, logical, thorough set of directions on how to prepare shotgun shells, rifle and pistol cases prior to reloading.

American Ammunition and Ballistics, by Edward A. Matunas, Winchester Press, New York, NY, 1979. 288 pp., illus. $13.95.

A complete reference book covering all presently manufactured and much discontinued American rimfire, centerfire, and shotshell ammunitiion.

Ballistic Science for the Law Enforcement Officer, by Charles G. Wilber, Ph.D., Charles C. Thomas, Springfield, IL, 1977. 309 pp., illus. $33.00.

A scientific study of the ballistics of civilian firearms.

The Bullet's Flight, by Franklin Mann, Wolfe Publishing Co., Inc., Prescott, AZ, 1980. 391 pp., illus. $22.00.

The ballistics of small arms. A reproduction of Harry Pope's personal copy of this classic with his marginal notes.

Cartridges of the World 4th Edition, by Frank C. Barnes, DBI Books, Inc., Northfield, IL. 352 pp., illus. Paper covers. $10.95.

Gives the history, dimensions, performance and physical characteristics for more than 1,000 different cartridges.

Cast Bullets, by Col. E. H. Harrison, A publication of the National Rifle Association of America, Washington, DC, 1979. 144 pp., illus. Paper covers. $8.95.

An authoritative guide to bullet casting techniques and ballistics.

The Complete Book of Practical Handloading, by John Wooters, Winchester Press, NY, 1976. 320 pp., illus. $13.95.

An up-to-the-minute guide for the rifleman and shotgunner.

Computer for Handloaders, by Homer Powley. A Slide rule plus 12 page instruction book for use in finding charge, most efficient powder and velocity for any modern centerfire rifle. $6.95.

Firearms Identification, by Dr. J. H. Mathews, Charles C. Thomas, Springfield, IL, 1973 3 vol set. A massive, carefully researched, authoritative work published as:

Vol. I **The Laboratory Examination of Small Arms.** 400 pp., illus. $56.75.

Vol. II **Original Photographs and Other Illustrations of Handguns** 492 pp., illus. $56.75.

Vol. III **Data on Rifling Characteristics of Handguns and Rifles** 730 pp., illus. $88.00.

Firearms Investigation, Identification and Evidence, by J. S. Hatcher, Frank J. Jury and Jac Weller. Stackpole Books, Harrisburg, PA, 1977. 536 pp., illus. $24.95.

Reprint of the 1957 printing of this classic book on forensic ballistics. Indispensable for those interested in firearms identification and criminology.

Game Loads and Practical Ballistics for The American Hunter, by Bob Hagel, Alfred A. Knopf, NY, NY, 1978. 315 pp., illus., hardbound. $13.95.

Everything a hunter needs to know about ballistics and performance of commercial hunting loads.

Handbook for Shooters and Reloaders, by P.O. Ackley, Salt Lake City, UT, 1970, *Vol. I,* 567 pp., illus. $9.75. *Vol. II,* a new printing with specific new material. 495 pp., illus. $9.75. Both volumes. Paper covers. $19.50.

Handbook of Metallic Cartridge Reloading, by Edward Matunas, Winchester Press, Tulsa, OK, 1981. 272 pp., illus. $14.95.

Up-to-date, comprehensive loading tables prepared by the four major powder manufacturers.

Handloader's Digest Bullet and Powder Update, edited by Ken Warner, DBI Books, Inc., Northfield, IL. 1980. 128 pp., illus. Paper covers $4.95.

An update on the 8th ed. of "Handloader's Digest." Included is a round-up piece on new bullets, another on new primers and powders plus five shooters' reports on the various types of bullets.

Handloading, by Bill Davis, Jr., NRA Books, Wash., D.C., 1980. 400 pp., illus. Paper covers. $12.95.

A complete update and expansion of the NRA Handloader's Guide.

Handloading for Handgunners, by Geo. C. Nonte, DBI Books, Inc., Northfield, IL, 1978. 288 pp., illus. Paper covers. $9.95.

An expert tells the ins and outs of this specialized facet of reloading.

Handloading for Hunters, by Don Zutz, Winchester Press, NY, 1977. 288 pp., illus. Paper covers $9.95.

Precise mixes and loads for different types of game and for various hunting situations with rifle and shotgun.

Hodgon "New" Data Manual No. 23, Hodgdon Powder Co., Shawnee Mission, KS, 1977. 192 pp., illus. $4.95.

New data on Pyrodex and black powder. New section on how to reload for beginners. Information on rifle, pistol, shotgun and lead bullet loads.

The Home Guide to Cartridge Conversions, by Maj. George C. Nonte Jr., The Gun Room Press, Highland Park, NJ, 1976. 404 pp., illus. $15.00.

Revised and updated version of Nonte's definitive work on the alteration of cartridge cases for use in guns for which they were not intended.

Hornady Handbook of Cartridge Reloading, Hornady Mfg. Co., Grand Island, NE, 1981. 650 pp., illus. $9.95.

New edition of this famous reloading handbook. Latest loads, ballistic information, etc.

Lyman Cast Bullet Handbook, 3rd Edition, edited by C. Kenneth Ramage, Lyman Publications, Middlefield, CT, 1980. 416 pp., illus. Paper covers. $16.95.

Information on more than 5,000 tested cast bullet loads and 19 pages of trajectory and wind drift tables for cast bullets.

Lyman Centennial Journal 1878-1978, edited by C. Kenneth Ramage and Edward R. Bryant, Lyman Publications, Middlefield, CT, 1980. 222 pp., illus. Paper covers. $10.95.

The history of the Lyman company and its products in both words and pictures.

Lyman Black Powder Handbook, ed. by C. Kenneth Ramage, Lyman Products for Shooters, Middlefield, CT, 1975. 239 pp., illus. Paper covers $11.95.

The most comprehensive load information ever published for the modern black powder shooter.

Lyman Pistol & Revolver Handbook, edited by C. Kenneth Ramage, Lyman Publications, Middlefield, CT, 1978. 280 pp., illus. Paper covers. $11.95.

An extensive reference of load and trajectory data for the handgun.

Lyman Shotshell Handbook, 2nd ed., edited by C. Kenneth Ramage, Lyman Gunsight Corp., Middlefield, CT, 1976. 288 pp., illus., paper covers. $11.95.

Devoted exclusively to shotshell reloading, this book considers: gauge, shell length, brand, case, loads, buckshot, etc. plus an excellent reference section. Some color illus.

Metallic Cartridge Reloading, edited by Robert S.L. Anderson, DBI Books, Inc., Northfield, IL, 1982. 320 pp., illus. Paper covers. $10.95.

A true reloading manual with a wealth of invaluable technical data provided by outstanding reloading experts. A must for any reloader. Extensive load tables.

Metallic Reloading Basics, edited by C. Kenneth Ramage, Lyman Publications, Middlefield, CT, 1976. 60 pp., illus. Paper covers. $1.95.

Provides the beginner with loading data on popular bullet weights within the most popular calibers.

Modern Handloading, by Maj. Geo. C. Nonte, Winchester Press, NY, 1972. 416 pp., illus. $15.00.

Covers all aspects of metallic and shotshell ammunition loading, plus more loads than any book in print; state and Federal laws, reloading tools, glossary.

Pet Loads, by Ken Waters, Wolfe Publ. Co., Inc., Prescott, AZ, 1979. Unpaginated. In looseleaf form. $29.50.

A collection of the last 13 years' articles on more than 70 metallic cartridges. Most calibers featured with updated material.

Pocket Manual for Shooters and Reloaders, by P.O. Ackley, publ. by author, Salt Lake City, UT, 1964. 176 pp., illus., spiral bound. $4.95.

Good coverage on standard and wildcat cartridges and related firearms in popular calibers.

Reloading for Shotgunners, edited by Robert S.L. Anderson, DBI Books, Inc., Northfield, IL, 1981. 224 pp., illus. Paper covers. $8.95.

Articles on wildcatting, slug reloading, patterning, skeet and trap loads, etc., as well as extensive reloading tables.

Sierra Bullets Reloading Manual, Second Edition, by Robert Hayden et al, The Leisure Group, Inc., Santa Fe Springs, CA, 1978. 700 pp., illus. Looseleaf binder. $11.95.

Includes all material in the original manual and its supplement updated, plus a new section on loads for competitive shooting.

Small-Caliber Ammunition Identification Guide Volume I:Small Arms Cartridges up to 15mm, by R.T. Huntington, Military Arms Research Service, San Jose, CA, 1978. 204 pp., illus. Paper covers. $9.95.

Covers center-fire military cartridges from 25 ACP to 15mm Besa. Historical employment, weapons used, and a comprehensive section on headstamps.

Small-Caliber Ammunition Identification Guide Volume II: Small Arms Cartridges 20mm to 40mm, by R. T. Huntington, Military Arms Research Service, San Jose, CA, 1978. 165 pp., illus. Paper covers. $9.95.

Identifies the large infantry and aircraft cartridges giving full coverage to Soviet and East Bloc ammunition.

Speer Reloading Manual Number 10 , Omark Industries, Inc., Lewiston, ID, 1979, 560 pp., illus. Paper covers. $10.00.

Expanded version with facts, charts, photos, tables, loads and tips.

Why Not Load Your Own? by Col. T. Whelen, A. S. Barnes, New York, 1957, 4th ed., rev. 237 pp., illus, $7.95.

A basic reference on handloading, describing each step, materials and equipment. Loads for popular cartridges are given.

Yours Truly, Harvey Donaldson, by Harvey Donaldson, Wolfe Publ. Co., Inc., Prescott, AZ, 1980. 288 pp., illus. $19.50.

Reprint of the famous columns by Harvey Donaldson which appeared in "Handloader" from May 1966 through December 1972.

COLLECTORS

American Boys' Rifles 1890-1945, by Jim Perkins, RTP Publishers, Pittsburg, PA, 1976. 245 pp., illus. $17.50.

The history and products of the arms companies who made rifles for the American boy, 1890-1945.

American, British & Continental Pepperbox Firearms, by Jack Dunlap. H.J. Dunlap, Los Altos, CA, 1964. 279 pp., 665 illus. $19.95.

Comprehensive history of production pepperboxes from early 18th cent. through the cartridge pepperbox. Variations are covered, with much data of value to the collector.

The American Cartridge, by Charles R. Suydam, Borden Publ. Co., Alhambra, CA, rev. ed., 1973. 184 pp., illus. $8.50.

An illus. study of the rimfire cartridge in the U.S.

Arms Makers of Maryland, by Daniel D. Hartzler, George Shumway, York, PA, 1975. 200 pp., illus. $35.00.

A thorough study of the gunsmiths of Maryland who worked during the late 18th and early 19th centuries.

Ballard Rifles in the H.J. Nunnemacher Coll., by Eldon G. Wolff. Milwaukee Public Museum, Wisc., 2nd ed., 1961. Paper, 77 p. plus 4pp. of carts and 27 plates. $3.50.

A thoroughly authoritative work on all phases of the famous rifles, their parts, patent and manufacturing history.

Basic Documents on U.S. Marital Arms, commentary by Col. B. R. Lewis, reissue by Ray Riling, Phila., PA., 1956 and 1960. *Rifle Musket Model 1855.* The first issue rifle of musket caliber, a muzzle loader equipped with the Maynard Primer, 32 pp. $2.50. *Rifle Musket Model 1863.* The Typical Union muzzle-loader of the Civil War, 26 pp. $1.75. *Breech-Loading Rifle Musket Model 1866.* The first of our 50 caliber breechloading rifles, 12 pp. $1.75. *Remington Navy Rifle Model 1870.* A commercial type breech-loader made at Springfield, 16 pp. $1.75 *Lee Straight Pull Navy Rifle Model 1895.* A magazine cartridge arm of 6mm caliber. 23 pp. $3.00. *Breech-Loading Arms* (five models)-27pp. $2.75. *Ward-Burton Rifle Musket 1871*-16 pp. $2.50. *U.S. Magazine Rifle and Carbine (cal. 30) Model 1892*(the Krag Rifle) 36 pp. $3.00.

The Breech-Loader in the Service, 1816-1917, by Claud E. Fuller, N. Flayderman, New Milford, Conn., 1965. 381 pp., illus. $14.50.

Revised ed. of a 1933 historical reference on U.S. Standard and experimental military shoulder arms. Much patent data, drawings, and photographs of the arms.

A voluminous work that covers handloading-and other things-in great detail. Replete with data for all cartridge forms.

British Military Pistols 1603-1888, by R. E. Brooker, Jr., Le Magazine Royal Press, Coral Gables, FL, 1978. 139 pp., illus. $20.00.

Covers flintlock and percussion pistols plus cartridge revolvers up to the smokeless powder period.

California Gunsmiths 1846-1900, by Lawrence P. Sheldon, Far Far West Publ., Fair Oaks, CA, 1977. 289 pp., illus. $29.65.

A study of early California gunsmiths and the firearms they made.

Cartology Savalog, by Gerald Bernstein, Gerald Bernstein, St. Louis, MO, 1976. 177 pp., illus. Paper covers. $8.95.

An infinite variations catalog of small arms ammunition stamps.

Civil War Carbines, by A.F. Lustyik. World Wide Gun Report, Inc., Aledo, Ill, 1962. 63 pp., illus. Paper covers. $2.00.

Accurate, interesting summary of most carbines of the Civil War period, in booklet form, with numerous good illus.

Civil War Guns, by William B. Edwards, Castle Books, NY, 1976. 438 pp., illus. $15.00.

Describes and records the exciting and sometimes romantic history of forging weapons for war and heroism of the men who used them.

The Collector's Handbook of U.S. Cartridge Revolvers, 1856 to 1899, by W. Barlow Fors, Adams Press, Chicago, IL, 1973. 96 pp., illus. $10.95.

Concise coverage of brand names, patent listings, makers' history, and essentials of collecting.

Colt Firearms from 1836, by James E. Serven, new 8th edition, Stackpole Books, Harrisburg, PA, 1979. 398 pp., illus. $29.95. Deluxe ed. $49.95.

Excellent survey of the Colt company and its products. Updated with new SAA production chart and commemorative list.

The Colt Heritage, by R.L. Wilson, Simon & Schuster, 1979. 358 pp., illus. $50.00.

The official history of Colt firearms 1836 to the present.

Colt Peacemaker Dictionary & Encyclopedia Illustrated, by Keith A. Cochran, Colt Collectors Press, Rapid City, SD, 1976, 300 pp., illus. Paper covers. $25.00.

Over 1300 entries pertaining to everything there is to know about the Colt Peacemaker.

Colt's SAA Post War Models, by George Garton, Beinfield Publishing, Inc., No. Hollywood, CA, 1978. 176 pp., illus. $17.95.

Complete story on these arms including charts, tables and production information.

Colt's Variations of the Old Model Pocket Pistol, 1848 to 1872, by P.L. Shumaker, Borden Publishing, Co., Alhambra, CA, 1966, a reprint of the1957 edition. 150 pp., illus. $8.95.

A useful tool for the Colt specialist and a welcome return of a popular source of information that had been long out-of-print.

Confederate Longarms and Pistols, "A Pictorial Study", by Richard Taylor Hill and Edward W. Anthony, Taylor Publishing Co., Dallas, TX, 1978. $29.95.

A reference work identifying over 175 Confederate arms through detailed photography, and a listing of information.

Digest of Patents Relating to Breech-Loading and Magazine Small Arms (1836-1873), by V. D. Stockbridge, WA, 1874. Reprinted 1963 by E.N. Flayderman, Greenwich, Conn. $25.00.

An exhaustive compendium of patent documents on firearms, indexed and classified by breech mechanism types, valuable reference for students and collectors.

Early Indian Trade Guns:1625-1775, by T.M. Hamilton, Museum of the Great Plains, Lawton, OK, 1968. 34 pp., illus. Paper covers. $7.95.

Detailed descriptions of subject arms, compiled from early records and from the study of remnants found in Indian country.

Fifteen Years in the Hawken Lode, by John D. Baird, The Gun Room Press, Highland Park, NJ, 1976. 120 pp., illus. $15.00.

A collection of thoughts and observations gained from many years of intensive study of the guns from the shop of the Hawken brothers.

'51 Colt Navies, by N.L. Swayze, Gun Hill Publ. Co., Yazoo City, MS, 1967. 243 pp., well illus. $15.00.

The first major effort devoting its entire space to the 1851 Colt Navy revolver. There are 198 photos of models, sub-models, variations, parts, markings, documentary material, etc. Fully indexed.

Firearms in Colonial America: The Impact on History and Technology 1492-1792, by M.L. Brown, Smithsonian Institution Press, Wash., D.C., 1980. 449 pp., illus. $45.00.

An in-depth coverage of the history and technology of firearms in Colonial North America.

Firearms of the Confederacy, by Claud R. Fuller & Richard D. Steuart, Quarterman Publ., Inc., Lawrence, MA, 1977. 333 pp., illus. $25.00.

The shoulder arms, pistols and revolvers of the Confederate soldier, including the regular United States Models, the imported arms and those manufactured within the Confederacy.

The Firearms Price Guide, 2nd Edition, by D. Byron, Crown Publishers, New York, NY, 1981. 448 pp., illus. Paper covers. $9.95.

An essential guide for every collector and dealer.

Flayderman's Guide to Antique American Firearms...and Their Values, 2nd Edition, by Norm Flayderman, DBI Books, Inc., Northfield, IL, 1980. 608 pp., illus. Paper covers. $15.95.

All values in this new second edition have been completely brought up-to-date and a number of guns not covered in the first edition have been included.

The .45-70 Springfield, by Albert J. Frasca and Robert H. Hall, Springfield Publishing Co., Northridge, CA, 1980. 380 pp., illus. $39.95.

A carefully researched book on the trapdoor Springfield, including all experimental and very rare models.

The 45/70 Trapdoor Springfield Dixie Collection, compiled by Walter Crutcher and Paul Oglesby, Pioneer Press, Union City, TN, 1975. 600 pp.

An illustrated listing of the 45-70 Springfields in the Dixie Gun Works Collection. Little known details and technical information is given, plus current values.

The Gun Collector's Handbook of Values 1980-81, by C. E. Chapel, Coward, McCann & Geoghegan, Inc., New York, NY, 1980. 462 pp., illus. $17.95.

Thirteenth rev. ed. of the best-known price reference for collectors.

Gun Digest Book of Modern Gun Values, 3rd Edition, by Jack Lewis, edited by Harold A. Murtz, DBI Books, Inc., Northfield, IL, 1981. 384 pp., illus. Paper covers. $9.95.

Expanded to include all commercial guns introduced in the U.S. between 1900 and 1978.

Gunmarks, by David Byron, Crown Publishers, Inc., New York, NY, 1979. 185 pp., illus. $11.95.

Trade names, codemarks, and proofs from 1870 to the present.

Gun Traders Guide, 9th Edition, by Paul Wahl, Stoeger Publ. Co., S. Hackensack, NJ, 1978. 256 pp., illus. Paper covers. $9.95.

A fully illustrated and authoritative guide to identification of modern firearms with current market values.

Gunsmiths of Ohio—18th & 19th Centuries: Vol. I, Biographical Data, by Donald A. Hutslar, George Shumway, York, PA, 1973. 444 pp., illus. $35.00.

An important source book, full of information about the old-time gunsmiths of Ohio.

Hawken Rifles, The Mountan Man's Choice, by John D. Baird, The Gun Room Press, Highland Park, NJ, 1976. 95 pp., illus. $15.00.

Covers the rifles developed for the Western fur trade. Numerous specimens are described and shown in photographs.

Historical Hartford Hardware, by William W. Dalrymple, Colt Collector Press, Rapid City, SD, 1976. 42 pp., illus. Paper covers. $5.50.

Historically associated Colt revolvers.

A History of the Colt Revolver, by Charles T. Haven and Frank A. Belden, Outlet Books, New York, NY, 1978. 711 pp., illus. $10.95.

A giant of a book packed with information and pictures about the most cherished American revolver.

History of Modern U.S. Military Small Arms Ammunition, Vol. 2, 1940-1945, by F.W. Hackley, W.M. Woodin and E.L. Scranton, The Gun Room Press, Highland Park, NJ, 1976. 300 pp., illus. $25.00.

A unique book covering the entire field of small arms ammunition developed during the critical World War II years.

The History of Weapons of the American Revolution, by George C. Neuman, Outlet Books, NY, 1976. 373 pp., illus. $15.00.

A new printing of this important and timely work. Traces the history of Revolutionary War weapons of all types.

The History of Winchester Firearms 1866-1980, edited by Duncan Barnes, et al, Winchester Press, Tulsa, OK, 1980. 237 pp., illus. $21.95.

Specifications on all Winchester firearms. Background information on design, manufacture and use.

The Kentucky Rifle, by Merrill Lindsay, Arma Press, NY/the Historical Society of York County, York, PA, 1972. 100 pp., 81 large colored illustrations. $17.95.

Presents in precise detail and exact color 77 of the finest Kentucky rifles ever assembled in one place. Also describes the conditions which led to the development of this uniquely American arm.

Kentucky Rifle Patchboxes & Barrel Marks, by Roy F. Chandler, Valley View Offset, Duncannon, PA, 1971. 400 pp., $20.00.

Reference work illustrating hundreds of patchboxes, together with the mark or signature of the maker.

Kentucky Rifles and Pistols 1756-1850, compiled by members of the Kentucky Rifle Association, Wash., DC, Golden Age Arms Co., Delaware, OH, 1976. 275 pp., illus. $29.50.

Profusely illustrated with more than 300 examples of rifles and pistols never before published.

The Krag Rifle Story, by Franklin B. Mallory and Ludwig Olson, Springfield Research Service, Silver Spring, MD, 1979. 224 pp., illus. $20.00.

Covers both U.S. and European Krags. Gives a detailed description of U.S. Krag rifles and carbines and extensive data on sights, bayonets, serial numbers, etc.

Krag Rifles, by William S. Brophy, Beinfeld Pub. Inc., No. Hollywood, CA, 1980. 200 pp., illus. $24.95.

The first comprehensive work detailing the evolution and various models, both military and civilian.

The Krieghoff Parabellum, by Randall Gibson, Randall Gibson, Midland, TX, 1980. 280 pp., illus. $30.00.

A definitive work on the most desirable model Luger pistol.

Lever Action Magazine Rifles Derived from the Patents of Andrew Burgess by Samuel L. Maxwell Sr., Samuel L. Maxwell, Bellevue, WA, 1976. 368 pp., illus. $29.95.

The complete story of a group of lever action magazine rifles collectively referred to as the Burgess/Morse, the Kennedy or the Whitney.

Mauser Bolt Rifles, by Ludwig Olson, F. Brownell & Son, Inc., Montezuma, IA, 1976. 364 pp., illus. $29.95.

The most complete, detailed, authoritative and comprehensive work ever done on Mauser bolt rifles.

Military Small Arms Ammunition of the World, 1945-1980, by Peter Labbett, Presidio Press, San Rafael, CA, 1980. 129 pp., illus. $18.95.

An up-to-date international guide to the correct identification of ammunition by caliber, type, and origin.

M1 Carbine, Design, Development and Production, by Larry Ruth, Desert Publications, Cornville, AZ. 300 pp., illus. Paper covers. $14.95.

The complete history of one of the world's most famous and largest produced firearms.

Modern Guns Identification and Values, 3rd Edition, edited by Russell and Steve Quertermous, Collector Books, Paducah, KY, 1981. 432 pp., illus. Paper covers. $11.95.

A catalog of well over 20,000 guns with important identifying information and facts.

More Single Shot Rifles, by James C. Grant, The Gun Room Press, Highland Park, NJ, 1976. 324 pp., illus. $15.00.

Details the guns made by Frank Wesson, Milt Farrow, Holden, Borchardt, Stevens, Remington, Winchester, Ballard and Peabody-Martini.

The Muzzle-Loading Cap Lock Rifle, by Ned H. Roberts, George Shumway Publisher, York, PA and Track of the Wolf Co., Osseo, MN, 1978. 308 pp., illus. $24.50.

Reprint of the revised and enlarged privately printed edition of this general survey of its subject and of the makers of the rifles.

The New England Gun, by Merrill Lindsay, David McKay Co., NY, 1976. 155 pp., illus. Paper covers. $12.50. Cloth, $20.00.

A study of more than 250 New England guns, powder horns, swords and polearms in an exhibition by the New Haven Colony Historical Society.

Simeon North: First Official Pistol Maker of the United States, by S. North and R. North, Rutgers Book Center, Highland Park, NJ, 1972. 207 pp., illus. $9.95.

Exact reprint of the original. Includes chapters on New England pioneer manufacturers and on various arms.

The Northwest Gun, by Charles E. Hanson, Jr., Nebraska State Historical Society, Lincoln, NB, 1976. 88 pp., illus., paper covers. $6.

Number 2 in the Society's "Publications in Anthropology." Historical survey of rifles which figured in the fur trade and settlement of the Northwest.

Paterson Colt Pistol Variations, by R.L. Wilson and R. Phillips, Jackson Arms Co., Dallas, TX, 1979. 250 pp., illus. $35.00.

A tremendous book about the different models and barrel lengths in the Paterson Colt story.

Peacemaker Evolutions & Variations, by Keith A. Cochran, Colt Collectors Press, Rapid City, SD, 1975. 47 pp., illus. Paper covers. $7.50.

Corrects many inaccuracies found in other books on the Peacemaker and gives much new information regarding this famous arm.

The Pennsylvania-Kentucky Rifle, by Henry J. Kauffman, Crown Publishers, New York, NY 1981. 293 pp., illus. $9.98.

A colorful account of the history and gunsmiths who produced the first American rifle superior to those brought from the Old Country.

Pennsylvania Longrifles of Note, by George Shumway, George Shumway, Publisher, York, PA, 1977. 63 pp., illus. Paper covers. $6.95.

Illustrates and describes samples of guns from a number of Pennsylvania rifle-making schools.

The Plains Rifle, by Charles E. Hanson, Jr., The Gun Room Press, Highland Park, NJ, 1977. 171 pp., illus. $15.00.

Historical survey of popular civilian arms used on the American frontiers, their makers, and their owners.

The Rare and Valuable Antique Arms, by James E. Serven, Pioneer Press, Union City, TN, 1976. 106 pp., illus. Paper covers. $4.95.

A guide to the collector in deciding which direction his collecting should go, investment value, historic interest, mechanical ingenuity, high art or personal preference.

Rifles in Colonial America, Vol. I, by George Shumway, George Shumway, Publisher, York, PA, 1980. 353 pp., illus. $49.50.

An extensive photographic study of American longrifles made in the late Colonial, Revolutionary, and post-Revolutionary periods.

Rifles in Colonial America, Vol. II, by George Shumway, George Shumway, Publisher, York, PA, 1980. 302 pp., illus. $49.50.

Final volume of this study of the early evolution of the rifle in America.

Ruger Rimfire Revolvers, 1953-1973, by J.C. Munnell, McKeesport, PA, 1978. 48 pp., illus. Paper covers. $7.95.

A definitive work on the most neglected facet of Ruger pistol collecting.

Samuel Colt's New Model Pocket Pistols; The Story of the 1855 Root Model Revolver, by S. Gerald Keogh, S.G. Keogh, Ogden, UT, 1974. 31 pp., illus., paper covers. $5.00.

Collector's reference on various types of the titled arms, with descriptions, illustrations, and historical data.

Savage Automatic Pistols, by James R. Carr. Publ. by the author, St. Charles, Ill., 1967. A reprint. 129 pp., illus. with numerous photos. $10.00.

Collector's guide to Savage pistols, models 1907-1922, with features, production data, and pictures of each.

Small Arms of the Sea Services, by Robert H. Rankin. N. Flayderman & Co., New Milford, CT, 1972. 227 pp., illus. $14.50.

Encyclopedic reference to small arms of the U.S. Navy, Marines and Coast Guard. Covers edged weapons, handguns, long arms and others, from the beginnings.

Southern Derringers of the Mississippi Valley, by Turner Kirkland. Pioneer Press, Tenn., 1971. 80 pp., illus., paper covers. $2.00.

A guide for the collector, and a much-needed study.

The Standard Directory of Proof-Marks, ed. by R.A. Steindler, The John Olson Company, Paramus, NJ, 1976. 144 pp., illus. Paper covers. $5.95.

A comprehensive directory of the proof-marks of the world.

Still More Single Shot Rifles, by James J. Grant, Pioneer Press, Union City, TN, 1979. 211 pp., illus. $17.50.

A sequel to the author's classic works on single shot rifles.

The Story of Allen & Wheelock Firearms, by H.H. Thomas, C.J. Krehbiel Co., Cincinnati, OH, 1965. 125 pp., illus. $10.95.

A comprehensive study of the firearms made by the firm of Allen & Wheelock.

The 36 Calibers of the Colt Single Action Army, by David M. Brown. Publ. by the author at Albuquerque, NM, new reprint 1971. 222 pp., well-illus. $15.00.

Edited by Bev Mann of *Guns Magazine.* This is an unusual approach to the many details of the Colt S.A. Army revolver. Halftone and line drawings of the same models make this of especial interest.

The Trapdoor Springfield, by M.D. Waite and B.D. Ernst, Beinfeld Publ. Co., Inc., No. Hollywood, CA, 1979. 250 pp., illus. $29.95.

The first comprehensive book on the famous standard military rifle of the 1873-92 period.

Underhammer Guns, by H.C. Logan. Stackpole Books, Harrisburg, PA, 1965. 250 pp., illus. $10.00.

A full account of an unusual form of firearm dating back to flintlock days. Both American and foreign specimens are included.

U.S. Cartridges and Their Handguns, by Charles R. Suydam, Beinfeld Publ., Inc., No. Hollywood, CA, 1977. 200 pp., illus. Paper covers. $9.95.

The first book ever showing which gun used what cartridge. A must for the gun and cartridge collector.

The Virginia Manufactory of Arms, by Giles Cromwell, University Press of Virginia, Charlottesville, VA, 1975. 205 pp., illus. $29.95.

The only complete history of the Virginia Manufactory of Arms which produced muskets, pistols, swords, and cannon for the state's militia from 1802 through 1821.

Walther Models PP and PPK, 1929-1945, by James L. Rankin, assisted by Gary Green, James L. Rankin, Coral Gables, FL, 1974. 142 pp., illus. $15.00.

Complete coverage on the subject as to finish, proof marks and Nazi party inscriptions.

Walther Volume II, Engraved, Presentation and Standard Models, by James L. Rankin, J.L. Rankin, Coral Gables, FL, 1977. 112 pp., illus. $17.50.

The new Walther book on embellished versions and standard models. Has 88 photographs, including many color plates.

The Whitney Firearms, by Claud Fuller. Standard Publications, Huntington, W. Va., 1946. 334 pp., many plates and drawings. $30.00.

An authoritative history of all Whitney arms and their maker. Highly recommended. An exclusive with Ray Riling Arms Books Co.

The William M. Locke Collection, compiled by Robert B. Berryman, et al, The Antique Armory, Inc., East Point, GA, 1973. 541 pp., illus. $40.00.

A magnificently produced book illustrated with hundreds of photographs of guns from one of the finest collection of American firearms ever assembled.

The Winchester Book, by George Madis, Art & Reference House, Lancaster, TX, 1980. 638 pp., illus. $39.50.

A greatly enlarged edition of this most informative book on these prized American arms.

Winchester—The Gun That Won the West, by H.F. Williamson. Combat Forces Press, Washington, D.C., 1952. Later eds. by Barnes, NY. 494 pp., profusely illus., paper covers. $14.95.

A scholarly and essential economic history of an honored arms company, but the early and modern arms introduced will satisfy all but the exacting collector.

EDGED WEAPONS

The Robert Abels Collection of Bowie Type Knives of American Interest, by Robert Abels, Robert Abels, Hopewell Junction, NY, 1974. 20 pp., illus. Paper covers. $1.95.

A selection of American Bowie-type knives from the collection of Robert Abels.

American Axes, by Henry Kauffman, The Stephen Green Press, Brattleboro, VT, 1972. 200 pp., illus. $25.00.

A definitive work on the subject. Contains a roster of American axe makers, glossary and notes on the care and use of axes.

The American Bayonet 1776-1964, by Albert N. Hardin, Jr., Albert N. Hardin, Jr., Pennsauken, NJ, 1977. 234 pp., illus. $30.00.

Describes and illustrates over two hundred separate and distinct types of American bayonets from Colonial times to the present day.

American Knives; The First History and Collector's Guide, by Harold L. Peterson, The Gun Room Press, Highland Park, NJ, 1980. 178 pp., illus. $15.00.

A reprint of this 1958 classic. Covers all types of American knives.

American Polearms 1526-1865, by Rodney Hilton Brown, H. Flayderman & Co., New Milford, CT, 1967. 198 pp., illus. $14.50.

The lance, halbred, spontoon, pike and naval boarding weapons used in the American military forces through the Civil War.

The American Sword, 1775-1945, by Harold L. Peterson, Ray Riling Arms Books, Co., Phila., PA, 1980. 286 pp. plus 60 pp. of illus. $25.00.

1977 reprint of a survey of swords worn by U.S. uniformed forces, plus the rare "American Silver Mounted Swords, (1700-1815)."

The Art of Blacksmithing, by Alex W. Bealer, Funk & Wagnalls, New York, NY, revised edition, 1976. 438 pp., illus. $16.95.

Required reading for anyone who makes knives or is seriously interested in the history of cutlery.

Basic Manual of Knife Fighting, by William L. Cassidy, Paladin Press, Boulder, CO, 1978. 41 pp., illus. Paper covers. $4.

A manual presenting the best techniques developed by the experts from 1930 to date.

The Best of Knife World, Volume I, edited by Knife World Publ., Knoxville, TN, 1980. 92 pp., illus. Pater covers. $3.95.

A collection of articles about knives. Reprinted from monthly issues of Knife World.

Blacksmithing for the Home Craftsman, by Joe Pehoski, Joe Pehoski, Washington, TX, 1973. 44 pp., illus. Paper covers. $3.50.

This informative book is chock-full of drawings and explains how to make your own forge.

Blades and Barrels, by H. Gordon Frost, Wallon Press, El Paso, TX, 1972. 298 pp., illus. $16.95.

The first full scale study about man's attempts to combine an edged weapon with a firearm.

Bowie Knives, by Robert Abels, Robert Abels, NY, 1960. 48 pp., illus. Paper covers. $3.00.

A booklet showing knives, tomahawks, related trade cards and advertisements.

British Cut and Thrust Weapons, by John Wilkinson Latham, Charles E. Tuttle Co., VT, 1971. 112 pp., illus. $7.50.

Well illustrated study tracing the development of edged weapons and their adoption by the British armed forces.

Classic Bowie Knives, by Robert Abels, The Gun Room Press, Highland Park, NJ, 1980. 96 pp., illus. $15.00.

A reprint of the classic work on these American knives.

Custom Knife...II, by John Davis Bates, Jr., and James Henry Schippers, Jr., Custom Knife Press, Memphis, TN, 1974. 112 pp., illus. $20.00.

The book of pocket knives and folding hunters. A guide to the 20th century makers' art.

The Cutlery Story: From Stone Age to Steel Age, by Lewis D. Bement, Custom Cutlery Co., Dalton, GA, 1972. 36 pp., illus. Paper covers. $3.50.

A classic booklet about the history, romance, and manufacture of cutlery from the earliest times to modern methods of manufacture.

A Directory of Sheffield: Including the Manufacturers of the Adjacent Villages, a facsimile reprint of the 1707 London edition, Da Capo Press, Inc., NY, 1969. Illus. $11.50.

With the several marks of the cutlers, scissor and edge-tool makers.

Edge of the Anvil, by Jack Andrews, Rodale Press, Emmaus, PA, 1978. 224 pp., illus. $11.95.

A basic blacksmith book.

The Fighting Knife, by W.D. Randall, Jr. and Col.Rex Applegate, W.D. Randall, Orlando, FL, 1975. 60 pp., illus. Paper covers. $2.75.

Manual for the use of Randall-made fighting knives and similar types.

Fighting Knives, by Frederick J. Stephens, Arco Publishing Co., Inc., New York, NY, 1980. 127 pp., illus. $14.95.

An illustrated guide to fighting knives and military survival weapons of the world.

For Knife Lovers Only, by Harry K. McEvoy, Knife World Publ., Knoxville, TN, 1979. 67 pp., illus. Paper covers. $4.95.

A fascinating and unusual approach to the story of knives.

A Guide to Handmade Knives, edited by Mel Tappan, The Janus Press, Inc., Los Angeles, CA, 1977. No paper covers. Deluxe hardbound. $19.50.

The official directory of the Knifemakers Guild.

Gun Digest Book of Folding Knives, by Jack Lewis and B.R. Hughes, DBI Books, Inc. Northfield, IL, 1977. 288 pp., illus. Paper covers. $7.95.

A cut above any other volume published on pocket or folding knives.

The History of the John Russell Cutlery Company, 1833-1936, by Robert L. Merriam et al, The Bete Press, Greenfield, MA, 1976. 120 pp., illus. $12.95.

A complete history of the people, places and events behind legendary American knives such as the Barlow, Green River Knife, Dadley and others.

How to Make Knives, by Richard W. Barney & Robert W. Loveless, Beinfield Publ., Inc., No. Hollywood, CA, 1977. 178 pp., illus. $13.95.

A book filled with drawings, illustrations, diagrams, and 500 how-to-do-it photos.

How to Make Your Own Knives, by Jim Mayes, Everest House, New York, NY, 1978. 191 pp., illus. $7.95.

An illustrated step-by-step guide for the sportsman and home hobbyist.

Kentucky Knife Traders Manual No. 6, by R.B. Ritchie, Hindman, KY, 1980. 217 pp., illus. Paper covers. $10.00.

Guide for dealers, collectors and traders listing pocket knives and razor values.

The Knife Album Price Guide 1976 Edition, by Robert Mayes, Robert Mayes, Middlesboro, KY, 1976. 174 pp. Paper covers. $6.00.

The only book on identification and accurate pricing.

Knife Digest, First Annual Edition, edited by William L. Cassidy, Knife Digest Publ. Co., Berkeley, CA, 1974. 285 pp., illus. $15.00.

The first annual publication ever produced for the knife and edged weapon enthusiast and collector.

Knife Digest, Second Annual Edition, edited by William L. Cassidy, Knife Digest Publ. Co., Berkeley, CA, 1976. 178 pp., illus. $15.00.

The second annual edition of the internationally known book on blades.

Knife Throwing, Sport...Survival...Defense, by Blackie Collins, Knife World Publ., Knoxville, TN, 1979. 31 pp., illus. Paper covers. $3.00.

How to select a knife, how to make targets, how to determine range and how to survive with a knife.

Knife Throwing a Practical Guide, by Harry K. McEvoy, Charles E. Tuttle Co., Rutland, VT, 1973. 108 pp., illus. Paper covers. $3.95.

If you want to learn to throw a knife this is the "bible".

Knifecraft: A Comprehensive Step-by-Step Guide to the Art of Knifemaking, by Sid Latham, Stackpole Books, Harrisburg, PA, 1978. 224 pp., illus. $24.95.

An exhaustive volume taking both amateur and accomplished knifecrafter through all the steps in creating a knife.

Knifemakers of Old San Francisco, by Bernard R. Levine, Badger Books, San Francisco, CA, 1978. 240 pp., illus. $12.95.

The story about the knifemakers of San Francisco, the leading cutlers of the old West.

The Knife Makers Who Went West, by Harvey Platts, Longspeak Press, Longmont, CO, 1978. 200 pp., illus. $19.95.

Factual story of an important segment of the American cutlery industry. Primarily about Western knives and the Platts knife makers.

Knives and Knifemakers, by Sid Latham, Winchester Press, NY, 1973. 152 pp., illus. $17.50.

Lists makers and suppliers of knife-making material and equipment.

Light But Efficient, by Albert N. Hardin, Jr. and Robert W. Hedden, Albert N. Hardin, Jr., Pennsauken, NJ, 1973. 103 pp., illus. $7.95.

A study of the M1880 Hunting and M1890 intrenching knives and scabbards.

Marble Knives and Axes, by Konrad F. Schreier, Jr., Beinfeld Publ., Inc., No. Hollywood, CA, 1978. 80 pp., illus. Paper covers. $5.95.

The first work ever on the knives and axes made by this famous old, still-in-business, manufacturer.

The Modern Blacksmith, by Alexander G. Weygers, Van Nostrand Reinhold Co., NY, 1977. 96 pp., illus. $10.95.

Shows how to forge objects out of steel. Use of basic techniques and tools.

Nathan Starr Arms Maker 1776-1845, by James E. Hicks, The Restoration Press, Phoenix, AZ, 1976. 166 pp., illus. $12.95.

Survey of the work of Nathan Starr of Middletown, CT, in producing edged weapons and pole arms for the U.S., 1799-1840, also some firearms.

Naval Swords, by P.G.W. Annis, Stackpole Books, Harrisburg, PA, 1970. 80 pp., illus. $5.50.

British and American naval edged weapons 1660-1815.

The Official 1981 Price Guide to Collector Knives, by James F. Parker and J. Bruce Voyles, House of Collectibles, Orlando, FL, 1981. 533 pp., illus. Paper covers. $9.95.

Buying and selling prices on collector pocket and sheath knives.

A Photographic Supplement of Confederate Swords with Addendum, by William A. Albaugh III, Moss Publications, Orange, VA, 1979. 259 pp., illus. $20.00.

A new updated edition of the classic work on Confederate edged weapons.

Pocket Knife Book 1 & 2—Price Guide, by Roy Ehrhardt, Heart of America Press, Kansas City, MO, 1974. 96 pp., illus. Spiral bound stiff paper covers. $6.95.

Reprints from the pocket knife sections of early manufacturers and sporting goods catalogs.

Pocket Knife Book 3—Price Guide, by Roy and Larry Ehrhardt, Heart of America Press, Kansas City, MO, 1974. Spiral bound stiff paper covers. $6.95.

Compiled from sections of various product sales catalogs of both Winchester and Marble Co. dating from the '20s and '30s.

The Pocketknife Manual, by Blackie Collins, Blackie Collins, Rock Hill, SC, 1976. 102 pp., illus. Paper covers. $5.50.

Building, repairing and refinishing pocketknives.

Practical Blacksmithing, edited by J. Richardson, Outlet Books, NY, 1978. four volumes in one, illus. $7.98.

A reprint of the extremely rare, bible of the blacksmith. Covers every aspect of working with iron and steel, from ancient uses to modern.

The Practical Book of Knives, by Ken Warner, Winchester Press, New York, NY, 1976. 224 pp., illus. $12.95.

All about knives for sport and utility.

Rice's Trowel Bayonet, reprinted by Ray Riling Arms Books, Co., Phila., PA, 1968. 8 pp., illus. Paper covers. $3.00.

A facsimile reprint of a rare circular originally published by the U.S. Government in 1875 for the information of U.S. Troops.

The Samurai Sword, by John M. Yumoto, Charles E. Tuttle Co., Rutland, VT, 1958. 191 pp., illus. $11.00.

A must for anyone interested in Japanese blades, and the first book on this subject written in English.

Scottish Swords from the Battlefield at Culloden, by Lord Archibald Campbell, The Mowbray Co., Providence, RI, 1973. 63 pp., illus. $5.00.

A modern reprint of an exceedingly rare 1894 privately printed edition.

Secrets of Modern Knife Fighting, by David E. Steele, Phoenix Press, Arvada, CO, 1974. 149 pp., illus. $17.50.

Details every facet of employing the knife in combat, including underwater fighting.

Step-by-Step Knifemaking, by Davis Boye, Rodale Press, Emmous, PA, 1978. 288 pp., illus. $12.95.

Gives the fundamentals of knifemaking and shows how to make knives either as a hobby or as a business.

Swords and Other Edged Weapons, by Robert Wilkinson-Latham, Arco Publishing Co., New York, NY, 1978. 227 pp., illus. $8.95.

Traces the history of the "Queen of Weapons" from its earliest forms in the stone age to the military swords of the Twentieth century.

Tomahawks Illustrated, by Robert Kuck, Robert Kuck, New Knoxville, OH, 1977. 112 pp., illus. Paper covers. $8.50.

A pictorial record to provide a reference in selecting and evaluating tomahawks.

U.S. Military Knives, Bayonets and Machetes, Book III, by M. H. Cole, M.H. Cole, Birmingham, AL, 1979. 219 pp., illus. $23.00.

The most complete text ever written on U.S. military knives, bayonets, machetes and bolos.

GENERAL

The Airgun Book, by John Walter, Stackpole Books, Harrisburg, PA, 1981. 320 pp., illus. $21.95.

Provides the airgun enthusiast with a much-needed basic book on his subject.

Air Gun Digest, by Robert Beeman & Jack Lewis, D8I Books, Inc., Northfield, IL, 1977. 224 pp., illus. Paper covers. $7.95.

Traces the first air, spring air, CO2 and other types from prototype to current models.

Bannerman Catalogue of Military Goods—1927, replica edition, DBI Books, Inc., Northfield, IL 1981. 384 pp., illus. Paper covers. $12.95.

Fascinating insights into one of the more colorful American arms merchants.

Beginner's Guide to Guns and Shooting, by Clair F. Rees, DBI Books, Inc., Northfield, IL, 1978. 224 pp., illus. Paper covers. $7.95.

Indispensible to the beginner, and an enlightening review for the seasoned sportsman.

The Book of Shooting for Sport and Skill, edited by Frederick Wilkinson, Crown Publishers, Inc., New York, NY, 1980. 348 pp., illus. $19.95.

A comprehensive and practical encyclopedia of gunmanship by a squad of over twenty experts from both sides of the Atlantic.

Carbine; The Story of David Marshall "Carbine" Williams, by Ross E. Beard, Jr., The Sandlapper Store, Inc., Lexington, SC, 1977. 315 pp., illus. Deluxe limited edition, numbered and signed by the author and "Carbine". $25.

The story of the man who invented the M1 Carbine and holds 52 other firearms patents.

Carbine Handbook, by Paul Wahl. Arco Publ. Co., N.Y.C., 1964. 80 pp., illus. Paperbound, $4.95.

A manual and guide to the U.S. Carbine, cal. .30, M1, with data on its history, operation, repair, ammunition, and shooting.

Colonial Riflemen in the American Revolution, by Joe D. Huddleston, George Shumway Publisher, York, PA, 1978. 70 pp., illus. $18.00.

This study traces the use of the longrifle in the Revolution for the purpose of evaluating what effects it had on the outcome.

The Complete Black Powder Handbook, by Sam Fadala, DBI Books, Inc., Northfield, IL, 1979. 288 pp., illus. Paper covers. $9.95.

Everything you want to know about black powder firearms and their shooting.

Dead Aim, by Lee Echols, Acme Printing Co., San Diego, CA, a reprint, 1972. 116 pp., illus. $9.95.

Nostalgic antics of hell-raising pistol shooters of the 1930's.

Eli Whitney and the Whitney Armory, by Merrill Lindsay, Arma Press, North Branford, CT, 1979. 95 pp., illus. Paper covers. $4.95. Cloth $9.95.

History of the Whitney Armory 1767-1862, with notes on how to identify Whitney flintlocks.

The Encyclopedia of Infantry Weapons of World War II, by Ian V. Hogg, Harper & Row, New York, NY, 1977. 192 pp., illus. $15.95.

A fully comprehensive and illustrated reference work including every major type of weapon used by every army in the world during World War II.

Encyclopedia of Modern Firearms, Vol. 1, compiled and publ. by Bob Brownell, Montezuma, IA, 1959. 1057 pp. plus index, illus. $50.00. Dist. by Bob Brownell, Montezuma, IA 50171.

Massive accumulation of basic information of nearly all modern arms pertaining to "parts and assembly". Replete with arms photographs, exploded drawings, manufacturers' lists of parts, etc.

The FP-45 Liberator Pistol, 1942-1945, by R.W. Koch, Research, Arcadia, CA, 1976. 116 pp., illus. $15.00.

A definitive work on this unique clandestine weapon.

Gun Digest Book of Metallic Silhouette Shooting, by Elgin Gates, DBI Books, Inc., Northfield, IL, 1979. 256 pp., illus. Paper covers. $7.95.

Examines all aspects of this fast growing sport including history, rules and meets.

Gun Digest Book of Gun Accessories, by Joseph Schroeder and the editors of Gun Digest, DBI Books, Inc., Northfield, IL, 1980. 288 pp., illus. Paper covers. $8.95.

The first single source reference for gun related items ever published.

Gun Talk, edited by Dave Moreton. Winchester Press, NY, 1973. 256 pp., illus. $9.95.

A treasury of original writing by the top gun writers and editors in America. Practical advice about every aspect of the shooting sports.

The Gun That Made the Twenties Roar, by Wm. J. Helmer, rev. and enlarged by George C. Nonte, Jr., The Gun Room Press, Highland Park, NJ, 1977. Over 300 pp., illus. $16.95.

Historical account of John T. Thompson and his invention, the infamous "Tommy Gun."

The Gunfighter, Man or Myth? by Joseph G. Rosa, Oklahoma Press, Norman, OK, 1969. 229 pp., illus. (including weapons). $9.95.

A well-documented work on gunfights and gunfighters of the West and elsewhere. Great treat for all gunfighter buffs.

The Gunfighters, by Dale T. Schoenberger, The Caxton Printers, Ltd., Caldwell, ID, 1971. 207 pp., illus. $12.95.

Startling expose of our foremost Western folk heroes.

The Guns of Harpers Ferry, by S.E. Brown Jr. Virginia Book Co., Berryville, VA, 1968. 157 pp., illus. $20.00.

Catalog of all known firearms produced at the U.S. armory at Harpers Ferry, 1798-1861, with descriptions, illustrations and a history of the operations there.

The Gunsmith in Colonial Virginia, by Harold B. Gill, Jr., University Press of Virginia, Charlottesville, VA, 1975. 200 pp., illus. $11.95.

The role of the gunsmith in colonial Virginia from the first landing at Jamestown through the Revolution is examined, with special attention to those who lived and worked in Williamsburg.

Guns, Pistols, Revolvers, by Heinrich Muller, St. Martin's Press, New York, NY, 1980. 224 pp., illus. $29.95.

A comprehensive overview of the various types of hand and small arms in use from the 14th to the 19th century.

Hatcher's Notebook, by Maj. Gen. J. S. Hatcher. Stackpole Books, Harrisburg, Pa., 1952. 2nd ed. with four new chapters, 1957. 629 pp., illus. $19.95.

A dependable source of information for gunsmiths, ballisticians, historians, hunters, and collectors.

The Identification and Registration of Firearms, by Vaclav "Jack" Krcma, C. C. Thomas, Springfield, IL, 1971. 173 pp., illus. $21.50.

Analysis of problems and improved techniques of recording firearms data accurately.

Kill or Get Killed, by Col. Rex Applegate, new rev. and enlarged ed. Paladin Press, Boulder, CO, 1976. 421 pp., illus. $17.95.

For police and military forces. Last word on mob control.

Law Enforcement Handgun Digest, 3rd Edition, by Jack Lewis, DBI Books, Inc., Northfield, IL, 1980. 288 pp., illus. Paper covers. $9.95.

Covers such subjects as the philosophy of a firefight, SWAT, weapons, training, combat shooting, etc.

Medicolegal Investigation of Gunshot Wounds, by Abdullah Fatteh, J.B. Lippincott Co., Phila., PA, 1977. 272 pp., illus. $23.75.

A much-needed work, clearly written and easily understood, dealing with all aspects of medicolegal investigation of gunshot wounds and deaths.

No Second Place Winner, by Wm. H. Jordan, publ. by the author, Shreveport, LA (Box 4072), 1962. 114 pp., illus. $10.00.

Guns and gear of the peace officer, ably discussed by a U.S. Border Patrolman for over 30 years, and a first-class shooter with handgun, rifle, etc.

Olympic Shooting, by Colonel Jim Crossman, NRA, Washington, DC, 1978. 136 pp., illus. $12.95.

The complete, authoritative history of U.S. participation in the Olympic shooting events from 1896 until the present.

Outdoor Life Gun Data Book, by F. Philip Rice, Harper & Row Publ., Inc., NY, 1975. 480 pp., illus. $12.95.

Packed with formulas, data, and tips essential to the modern hunter, target shooter, gun collector, and all others interested in guns.

The Practical Book of Guns, by Ken Warner, Winchester Press, New York, NY, 1978. 261 pp., illus. $14.95.

A book that delves into the important things about firearms and their use.

E.C. Prudhomme, Master Gun Engraver, A Retrospective Exhibition: 1946-1973, intro. by John T. Amber, The R.W. Norton Art Gallery, Shreveport, LA, 1973. 32 pp., illus., paper covers. $5.00.

Examples of master gun engraving by Jack Prudhomme.

The Quiet Killers II: Silencer Update, by J. David Truby, Paladin Press, Boulder, CO, 1979. 92 pp., illus. Paper covers. $8.00.

A unique and up-to-date addition to your silencer bookshelf.

Sam Colt: Genius, by Robt. F. Hudson, American Archives Publ. Co., Topsfield, MA, 1971. 160 pp., illus. Plastic spiral bound. $6.50.

Historical review of Colt's inventions, including facsimiles of patent papers and other Colt information.

The Shooter's Workbench, by John A. Mosher, Winchester Press, NY, 1977. 256 pp., illus. $12.95.

Accessories the shooting sportsman can build for the range, for the shop, for transport and the field, and for the handloading bench.

Small Arms of the World, 11th Edition, a complete revision of W.H.B. Smith's firearms classic by Edward Clinton Ezell, Stackpole Books, Harrisburg, PA, 1977. 667 pp., illus. $29.95.

A complete revision of this firearms classic now brings all arms enthusiasts up to date on global weapons production and use.

Sporting Arms of the World, by Ray Bearse, Outdoor Life/Harper & Row, N.Y., 1977. 500 pp., illus. $15.95.

A mammoth, up-to-the-minute guide to the sporting world's favorite rifles, shotguns, handguns.

Survival Guns, by Mel Tappan, The Janus Press, Inc., Los Angeles, CA, 1976. 458 pp., illus. Paper covers. $9.95.

A guide to the selection, modification and use of firearms and related devices for defense, food gathering, etc. under survival conditions.

Triggernometry, by Eugene Cunningham. Caxton Printers Lt., Caldwell, ID, 1970. 441 pp., illus. $9.95.

A classic study of famous outlaws and lawmen of the West—their stature as human beings, their exploits and skills in handling firearms. A reprint.

Weapons of the American Revolution, and Accoutrements, by Warren Moore. A & W Books, NY, 1974. 225 pp., fine illus. $15.

Revolutionary era shoulder arms, pistols, edged weapons, and equipment are described and shown in fine drawings and photographs, some in color.

Gunsmithing

American Engravers, by C. Roger Bleile, Beinfeld Publishing Inc., North Hollywood, CA, 1980. 191 pp., illus. $29.95.

A comprehensive overview of those men (and women) who are working in the gun and knife engraving field.

The Art of Engraving, by James B. Meek, F. Brownell & Son, Montezuma, IA, 1973. 196 pp., illus. $19.95.

A complete, authoritative, imaginative and detailed study in training for gun engraving. The first book of its kind—and a great one.

Artistry in Arms, The R.W. Norton Gallery, Shreveport, LA., 1970. 42 pp., illus. Paper, $5.00.

The art of gunsmithing and engraving.

Black Powder Gunsmithing, by Ralph T. Walker, DBI Books, Inc., Northfield, IL, 1978. 288 pp., illus. Paper covers. $8.95.

An overview of the entire subject from replica building to the advanced, intricate art of restoration.

Building the Kentucky Pistol, by James R. Johnston, Golden Age Arms Co., Worthington, OH, 1974. 36 pp., illus. Paper covers. $4.00.

A step-by-step guide for building the Kentucky pistol. Illus. with full page line drawings.

Building the Kentucky Rifle, by J.R. Johnston. Golden Age Arms Co., Worthington, OH, 1972. 44 pp., illus. Paper covers. $5.00.

How to go about it, with text and drawings.

Checkering and Carving of Gun Stocks, by Monte Kennedy. Stackpole Books, Harrisburg, PA, 1962. 175 pp., illus. $24.95.

Rev., enlarged clothbound ed. of a much sought-after, dependable work.

Clyde Baker's Modern Gunsmithing, revised by John E. Traister, Stackpole Books, Harrisburg, PA, 1981. 530 pp., illus. $24.95.

A revision of the classic work on gunsmithing.

The Complete Rehabilitation of the Flintlock Rifle and Other Works, by T.B. Tryon. Limbo Library, Taos, NM, 1972. 112 pp., illus. Paper covers. $6.95.

A series of articles which first appeared in various issues of the *American Rifleman* in the 1930s.

Do-It-Yourself Gunsmithing, by Jim Carmichel, Outdoor Life-Harper & Row, New York, NY, 1977. 371 pp., illus. $16.95.

The author proves that home gunsmithing is relatively easy and highly satisfying.

Firearms Assembly 3: The NRA Guide to Rifle and Shotguns, NRA Books, Wash., D.C., 1980. 264 pp., illus. Paper covers. $8.95.

Text and illustrations explaining the takedown of 125 rifles and shotguns, domestic and foreign.

Firearms Assembly 4: The NRA Guide to Pistols and Revolvers, NRA Books, Wash., D.C., 1980. 253 pp., illus. Paper covers. $8.95.

Text and illustrations explaining the takedown of 124 pistol and revolver models, domestic and foreign.

Firearms Blueing and Browning, by R.H. Angier. Stackpole Books, Harrisburg, PA, 151 pp., illus. $12.95.

A useful, concise text on chemical coloring methods for the gunsmith and mechanic.

Gun Care and Repair, by Monte Burch, Winchester Press, NY, 1978. 256 pp., illus. $14.95.

Everything the gun owner needs to know about home gunsmithing and firearms maintenance.

Gun Digest Book of Firearms Assembly/Disassembly Part I: Automatic Pistols, by J.B. Wood, DBI Books, Inc., Northfield, IL, 1979. 320 pp., illus. Paper covers. $9.95.

A thoroughly professional presentation on the art of pistol disassembly and reassembly. Covers most modern guns, popular older models, and some of the most complex pistols ever produced.

Gun Digest Book of Firearms Assembly/Disassembly Part II: Revolvers, by J. B. Wood, DBI Books, Inc., Northfield, IL, 1979. 320 pp., illus. Paper covers. $9.95.

How to properly dismantle and reassemble both the revolvers of today and of the past.

The Gun Digest Book of Firearms Assembly/Disassembly Part III: Rimfire Rifles, by J. B. Wood, DBI Books, Inc., Northfield, IL, 1980. 288 pp., illus. Paper covers. $9.95.

A most comprehensive, uniform, and professional presentation available for disassembling and reassembling most rimfire rifles.

The Gun Digest Book of Firearms Assembly/Disassembly Part IV: Centerfire Rifles, by J. B. Wood, DBI Books, Inc., Northfield, IL, 1980. 288 pp., illus. Paper covers. $9.95.

A professional presentation on the assembly and reassembly of centerfire rifles.

The Gun Digest Book of Firearms Assembly/Disassembly, Part V: Shotguns, by J.B. Wood, DBI Books, Inc., Northfield, IL, 1980. 288 pp., illus. Paper covers. $9.95.

A professional presentation on the complete disassembly and assembly of 26 of the most popular shotguns, new and old.

The Gun Digest Book of Firearms Assembly/Disassembly Part VI: Law Enforcement Weapons, by J.B. Wood, DBI Books, Inc., Northfield, IL, 1981. 288 pp., illus. Paper covers. $9.95.

Step-by-step instructions on how to completely dismantle and reassemble the most commonly used firearms found in law enforcement arsenals.

Gun Digest Book of Gunsmithing Tools and Their Uses, by John E. Traister, DBI Books, Inc., Northfield, IL, 1980. 256 pp., illus. Paper covers. $8.95.

The how, when and why of tools for amateur and professional gunsmiths and gun tinkerers.

The Gun Digest Book of Pistolsmithing, by Jack Mitchell, DBI Books, Inc., Northfield, IL, 1980. 288 pp., illus. Paper covers. $9.95.

An expert's guide to the operation of each of the handgun actions with all the major functions of pistolsmithing explained.

Gun Digest Review of Custom Guns, edited by Ken Warner, DBI Books, Inc., Northfield, IL, 1980. 256 pp., illus. Paper covers. $9.95.

An extensive look at the art of custom gun making. This book is a must for anyone considering the purchase of a custom firearm.

Gun Owner's Book of Care, Repair & Improvement, by Roy Dunlap, Outdoor Life-Harper & Row, NY, 1974. 336 pp., illus. $12.95.

A basic guide to repair and maintenance of guns, written for the average firearms owner.

Gunsmith Kinks, by F.R. (Bob) Brownell. F. Brownell & Son, Montezuma, I. 1st ed., 1969. 496 pp., well illus. $12.95.

A widely useful accumulation of shop kinks, short cuts, techniques and pertinent comments by practicing gunsmiths from all over the world.

Gunsmithing, by Roy F. Dunlap. Stackpole Books, Harrisburg, PA, 714 pp., illus. $24.95.

Comprehensive work on conventional techniques, incl. recent advances in the field. Valuable to rifle owners, shooters, and practicing gunsmiths.

Gunsmiths and Gunmakers of Vermont, by Warren R. Horn, The Horn Co., Burlington, VT, 1976. 76 pp., illus. Paper covers. $5.00.

A checklist for collectors, of over 200 craftsmen who lived and worked in Vermont up to and including 1900.

Hobby Gunsmithing, by Ralph Walker, DBI Books, Inc., Northfield, IL, 1972, 320 pp., illus. Paper. $8.95.

Kitchen table gunsmithing for the budding hobbyist.

Home Gun Care & Repair, by P.O. Ackley, Stackpole Books, Harrisburg, PA, 1969. 191 pp., illus. Paper covers. $6.95.

Basic reference for safe tinkering, fixing, and converting rifles, shotguns, handguns.

Home Gunsmithing Digest, 2nd ed., by Robt. Steindler, DBI Books, Inc., Northfield, IL, 1978. 288 pp., very well illus. within stiff decorated paper covers. $8.95.

An unusually beneficial assist for gun owners doing their own repairs, maintenance, etc. Many chapters on tools, techniques and theories.

How to Build Your Own Wheellock Rifle or Pistol, by George Lauber, The John Olson Co., Paramus, NJ, 1976. Paper covers. $6.95.

Complete instructions on building these arms.

How to Build Your Own Flintlock Rifle or Pistol, by Georg Lauber, The John Olson Co., Paramus, NJ, 1976. Paper covers. $6.95.

The second in Mr. Lauber's three-volume series on the art and science of building muzzle-loading black powder firearms.

"How to Build Your Own Percussion Rifle or Pistol", by Georg Lauber, The John Olson Co., Paramus, NJ, 1976. Paper covers, $6.95.

The third and final volume of Lauber's set of books on the building of muzzle-loaders.

Learn Gunsmithing, by John Traister, Winchester Press, Tulsa, OK, 1980. 202 pp., illus. $12.95.

The troubleshooting method of gunsmithing for the home gunsmith and professional alike.

Lock, Stock and Barrel, by R.H. McCrory. Publ. by author at Bellmore, NY, 1966. Paper covers. 122 pp., illus. $6.00.

A handy and useful work for the collector or the professional with many helpful procedures shown and described on antique gun repair.

The Modern Kentucky Rifle, How to Build Your Own, by R.H. McCrory. McCrory, Wantagh, NY, 1961. 68 pp., illus., paper bound. $6.00.

A workshop manual on how to fabricate a flintlock rifle. Also some information on pistols and percussion locks.

The NRA Gunsmithing Guide, National Rifle Association, Wash., D.C., 1971. 336 pp., illus. Paper. $9.95.

Information of the past 15 years from the "American Rifleman", ranging from 03A3 Springfields to Model 92 Winchesters.

Pistolsmithing, by George C. Nonte, Jr., Stackpole Books, Harrisburg, PA, 1974. 560 pp., illus. $19.95.

A single source reference to handgun maintainence, repair, and modification at home, unequaled in value.

Professional Gunsmithing, by W.J. Howe, Stackpole Books, Harrisburg, PA, 1968 reprinting. 526 pp., illus. $24.95.

Textbook on repair and alteration of firearms, with detailed notes on equipment and commercial gunshop operation.

Respectfully Yours H.M. Pope, compiled and edited by G.O. Kelver, Brighton, CO, 1976. 266 pp., illus. $16.50.

A compilation of letters from the files of the famous barrelmaker, Harry M. Pope.

The Trade Gun Sketchbook, by Charles E. Hanson, The Fur Press, Chadron, NB, 1979. 48 pp., illus. Paper covers. $4.00.

Complete full-size plans to build seven different trade guns from the Revolution to the Indian Wars and a two-thirds size for your son.

The Trade Rifle Sketchbook, by Charles E. Hanson, The Fur Press, Chadron, NB, 1979. 48 pp., illus. Paper covers. $4.00.

Includes full scale plans for ten rifles made for Indian and mountain men; from 1790 to 1860, plus plans for building three pistols.

Troubleshooting Your Handgun, by J.B. Wood, DBI Books, Inc., Northfield, IL, 1978. 192 pp., illus. Paper covers. $6.95.

A masterful guide on how to avoid trouble and how to operate guns with care.

Troubleshooting Your Rifle and Shotgun, by J.B. Wood, DBI Books, Inc., Northfield, IL, 1978. 192 pp., illus. Paper covers. $6.95.

A gunsmiths advice on how to keep your long guns shooting.

handguns

American Pistol and Revolver Design and Performance, by L.R. Wallack, Winchester Press, NY, 1978. 224 pp., illus. $15.95.

How different types and models of pistols and revolvers work, from trigger pull to bullet impact.

American Police Handgun Training, by Charles R. Skillen and Mason Williams, Charles C. Thomas, Springfield, IL, 1980. 216 pp., illus. $17.50.

Deals comprehensively with all phases of current handgun training procedures in America.

Askins on Pistols and Revolvers, by Col. Charles Askins, NRA Books, Wash., D.C., 1980. 144 pp., illus. Paper covers. $8.95.

A book full of practical advice, shooting tips, technical analysis and stories of guns in action.

The Black Powder by Sam Fadala, DBI Books, Inc., Northfield, IL, 1981. 288 pp., illus. Paper covers. $9.95.

The author covers this oldtimer in all its forms: pistols and six-shooters in both small and large bore, target and hunting.

Blue Steel and Gun Leather, by John Bianchi, Beinfeld Publishing, Inc., No. Hollywood, CA, 1978. 200 pp., illus. $12.00.

A complete and comprehensive review of holster uses plus an examination of available products on today's market.

Colt Automatic Pistols, by Donald B. Bady, Borden Publ. Co., Alhambra, CA, 1974. 368 pp., illus. $15.

The rev. and enlarged ed. of a key work on a fascinating subject. Complete information on every automatic marked with Colt's name.

The Colt .45 Auto Pistol, compiled from U.S. War Dept. Technical Manuals, and reprinted by Desert Publications, Cornville, AZ, 1978. 80 pp., illus. Paper covers. $4.95.

Covers every facet of this famous pistol from mechanical training, manual of arms, disassembly, repair and replacement of parts.

Combat Handgun Shooting, by James D. Mason, Charles C. Thomas, Springfield, IL, 1976. 256 pp., illus. $27.50.

Discusses in detail the human as well as the mechanical aspects of shooting.

Combat Handguns, edited by Edward C. Ezell, Stackpole Books, Harrisburg, PA, 1980. 288 pp., illus. $19.95.

George Nonte's last great work, edited by Edward C. Ezell. A comprehensive reference volume offering full coverage of automatic handguns vs. revolvers, custom handguns, combat autoloaders and revolvers—domestic and foreign, and combat testing.

Combat Shooting for Police, by Paul B. Weston. Charles C. Thomas, Springfield, IL, 1967. A reprint. 194 pp., illus. $13.95.

First publ. in 1960 this popular self-teaching manual gives basic concepts of defensive fire in every position.

Defensive Handgun Effectiveness, by Carroll E. Peters, Carroll E. Peters, Manchester, TN, 1977. 198 pp., charts and graphs. $10.00.

A systematic approach to the design, evaluation and selection of ammunition for the defensive handgun.

Flattops & Super Blackhawks, by H.W. Ross, Jr., H.W. Ross, Jr., Bridgeville, PA, 1979. 93 pp., illus. Paper covers. $9.75.

An expanded version of the author's book "Ruger Blackhawks" with an extra chapter on Super Blackhawks and the Mag-Na-Ports with serial numbers and approximate production dates.

Hallock's .45 Auto Handbook, by Ken Hallock, The Mihan Co., Oklahoma City, OK, 1981. 178 pp., illus. Paper covers. $11.95.

For gunsmiths, dealers, collectors and serious hobbyists.

A Handbook on the Primary Identification of Revolvers & Semi-automatic Pistols, by John T. Millard, Charles C. Thomas, Springfield, IL, 1974. 156 pp., illus. $15.00.

A practical outline on the simple, basic phases of primary firearm identification with particular reference to revolvers and semi-automatic pistols.

Handgun Competition, by Maj. Geo. C. Nonte, Jr., Winchester Press, NY, 1978. 288 pp., illus. $14.95.

A comprehensive source-book covering all aspects of modern competitive pistol and revolver shooting.

High Standard Automatic Pistols 1932-1950, by Charles E. Petty, American Ordnance Publ., Charlotte, NC, 1976. 124 pp., illus. $12.95.

A definitive source of information for the collector of High Standard pistols.

Japanese Hand Guns, by F.E. Leithe, Borden Publ. Co., Alhambra, CA, 1968. Unpaginated, well illus. $9.95.

Identification guide, covering models produced since the late 19th century. Brief text material gives history, descriptions, and markings.

Jeff Cooper on Handguns, by Jeff Cooper, Petersen Publishing Co., Los Angeles, CA, 1979. 96 pp., illus. Paper covers. $2.50.

An expert's guide to handgunning. Technical tips on actions, sights, loads, grips, and holsters.

Know Your 45 Auto Pistols—Models 1911 & A1, by E.J. Hoffschmidt, Blacksmith Corp., Southport, CT, 1974. 58 pp., illus. Paper covers. $5.95.

A concise history of the gun with a wide variety of types and copies.

Know Your Walther P.38 Pistols, by E.J. Hoffschmidt, Blacksmith Corp., Southport, CT, 1974. 77 pp., illus. Paper covers. $5.95. variations.

Covers the Walther models Armee, M.P., H.P., P.38—history and variations.

Know Your Walther P.P. & P.P.K. Pistols, by E.J. Hoffschmidt, Blacksmith Corp., Southport, CT, 1975. 87 pp., illus. Paper covers. $5.95.

A concise history of the guns with a guide to the variety and types.

The Luger Pistol (Pistole Parabellum), by F.A. Datig. Borden Publ. Co., Alhambra, CA, 1962. 328 pp., well illus. $9.50.

An enlarged, rev. ed. of an important reference on the arm, its history and development from 1893 to 1945.

Luger Variations, by Harry E. Jones, Harry E. Jones, Torrance, CA, 1975. 328 pp., 160 full page illus., many in color. $30.00.

A rev. ed. of the book known as "The Luger Collector's Bible".

Lugers at Random, by Charles Kenyon, Jr. Handgun Press, Chicago, IL. 1st ed., 1970. 416 pp., profusely illus. $20.00.

An impressive large side-opening book carrying throughout alternate facing-pages of descriptive text and clear photographs. A new boon to the Luger collector and/or shooter.

Mauser Pocket Pistols 1910-1946, by Roy G. Pender, Collectors Press, Houston, TX, 1971. 307 pp. $14.50.

Comprehensive work covering over 100 variations, including factory boxes and manuals. Over 300 photos. Limited, numbered ed.

The Mauser Self-Loading Pistol, by Belford & Dunlap, Borden Publ. Co., Alhambra, CA. Over 200 pp., illus., large format. $13.50.

The long-awaited book on the "Broom Handles", covering their inception in 1894 to the end of production. Complete and in detail: pocket pistols, Chinese and Spanish copies, etc.

The Pistol Guide, by George C. Nonte, Stoeger Publ. Co., So. Hackensack, NJ, 1980. 256 pp., illus. Paper covers. $8.95.

A unique and detailed examination of a very specialized type of gun: the autoloading pistol.

Pistol & Revolver Guide, 3rd Ed., by George C. Nonte, Stoeger Publ. Co., So. Hackensack, NJ, 1975. 224 pp., illus. Paper covers. $6.95.

The standard reference work on military and sporting handguns.

Quick or Dead, by William L. Cassidy, Paladin Press, Boulder, CO, 1978. 178 pp., illus. $12.95.

Close-quarter combat firing, with particular reference to prominent twentieth-century British and American methods of instruction.

Report of Board on Tests of Revolvers and Automatic Pistols. From the *Annual Report* of the Chief of Ordnance, 1907. Reprinted by J.C. Tillinghast Marlow, NH, 1969. 34 pp., 7 plates, paper covers. $5.00.

A comparison of handguns, including Luger, Savage, Colt, Webley-Fosbery and other makes.

Revolver Guide, by George C. Nonte, Jr., Stoeger Publishing Co., So. Hackensack, NJ, 1980. 288 pp., illus. Paper covers. $8.95.

Fully illustrated guide to selecting, shooting, caring for and collecting revolvers of all types.

System Mauser, a Pictorial History of the Model 1896 Self-Loading Pistol, by J.W. Breathed, Jr., and J.J. Schroeder, Jr. Handgun Press, Chicago, IL, 1967. 273 pp., well illus., 1st limited ed. hardbound. $17.50.

10 Shots Quick, by Daniel K. Stern, Globe Printing Co., San Jose, CA, 1967. 153 pp., photos. $12.50.

History of Savage-made automatic pistols, models of 1903-1917, with descriptive data for shooters and collectors.

U.S. Test Trials 1900 Luger, by Michael Reese II, Pioneer Press, Union City, TN, 1976. 130 pp., illus. Paper covers. $4.95.

Revised edition containing much additional material on the notable American Eagle test pieces. Rare illustrations.

The Walther P-38 Pistol, by Maj. Geo. C. Nonte, Paladin Press, Boulder, CO, 1975. 90 pp., illus. Paper covers. $5.00.

Covers all facets of the gun—development, history, variations, technical data, practical use, rebuilding, repair and conversion.

The Walther Pistols 1930-1945, by Warren H. Buxton, Warren H. Buxton, Los Alamos, NM, 1978. 350 pp., illus. $29.95.

Volume I of a projected 4 volume series "The P.38 Pistol". The histories, evolutions, and variations of the Walther P.38 and its predecessors.

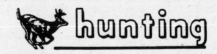

hunting

NORTH AMERICA

All About Deer in America, ed. by Robert Elman, Winchester Press, NY, 1976. 256 pp., illus. $13.95.

Twenty of America's great hunters share the secrets of their hunting success.

All Season Hunting, by Bob Gilsvik, Winchester Press, NY, 1976. 256 pp., illus. $12.95.

A guide to early-season, late-season and winter hunting in America.

All About Small-Game Hunting in America, ed. by Russell Tinsley, Winchester Press, NY, 1976. 308 pp., illus. $11.95.

Collected advice by the finest small-game experts in the country.

All About Wildfowling in America, by Jerome Knap, Winchester Press, NY, 1977. 256 pp., illus. $11.95.

More than a dozen top writers provide new and controversial ideas on how-to and where-to hunt wildfowl successfully.

The Art of Hunting Big Game in North America, by Jack O'Connor, Random House, NY, 1978. 418 pp., illus. $17.95.

A revised and updated edition on technique, planning, skill, outfitting, etc.

The Best of Nash Buckingham, by Nash Buckingham, selected, edited and annotated by George Bird Evans. Winchester Press, NY, 1973. 320 pp., $14.50.

Thirty pieces that represent the very cream of Nash's output on his whole range of outdoor interests—upland shooting, duck hunting, even fishing.

Big Game Hunter's Digest, by Tom Brakefield, DBI Books, Inc., Northfield, IL, 1977. 288 pp., illus. Paper covers. $7.95.

A truly complete reference to North American big game hunting.

Bird Hunting Know-How, by D.M. Duffey. Van Nostrand, Princeton, NJ, 1968. 192 pp., illus. $9.95.

Game-getting techniques and sound advice on all aspects of upland bird hunting, plus data on guns and loads.

Black Powder Hunting, by Sam Fadala, Stackpole Books, Harrisburg, PA, 1978. 192 pp., illus. $10.95.

The author demonstrates successful hunting methods using percussion firearms for both small and big game.

Bobwhite Quail Hunting, by Charley Dickey, printed for Stoeger Publ. Co., So. Hackensack, NH, 1974. 112 pp., illus., paper covers. $2.95.

Habits and habitats, techniques, gear, guns and dogs.

The Bobwhite Quail, Its Life and Management, by Walter Rosene. Rutgers University Press, New Brunswick, NJ. 1st ed., 1969. 418 pp., photographs, maps and color plates. $50.00.

An exhaustive study of an important species which has dimished under the impact of changing agricultural and forestry practices.

The Complete Book of Deer Hunting, by Byron W. Dalrymple, Winchester Press, NY, 1973. 247 pp., illus. $12.95.

Practical "how-to" information. Covers the 20 odd North-American sub-species of deer.

The Complete Book of the Wild Turkey, by Roger M. Latham, Stackpole Books, Harrisburg, Pa., 1978. 228 pp., illus. $12.95.

A new revised edition of the classic on American wild turkey hunting.

The Complete Guide to Bird Dog Training, by John R. Falk, Winchester Press, NY, 1976. 256 pp., illus. $12.95.

How to choose, raise, train, and care for a bird dog.

The Complete Guide to Game Care and Cookery, by Sam Fadala, DBI Books, Inc., Northfield, IL., 1981. 288 pp., illus. Paper covers. $8.95.

How to dress, preserve and prepare all kinds of game animals and birds.

Death in the Silent Places, by Peter Hathaway Capstick, St. Martin's Press, New York, NY, 1981. 243 pp., illus. $13.95.

The author recalls the extraordinary careers of legendary hunters such as Corbett, Karamojo Bell, Stigand and others.

Deer Hunting, by R. Smith, Stackpole Books, Harrisburg, PA, 1978. 224 pp., illus. Paper covers. $9.95.

A professional guide leads the hunt for North America's most popular big game animal.

The Desert Bighorn, edited by Gale Monson and Lowell Sumner, University of Arizona Press, Tucson, AZ, 1980. 392 pp., illus. $27.50.

Life history, ecology and management of the Desert Bighorn.

The Dove Shooter's Handbook, by Dan M. Russell, Winchester Press, NY, 1974. 256 pp., illus. $9.95.

A complete guide to America's top game bird—natural history, hunting methods, equipment, conservation and future prospects.

Dove Hunting, by Charley Dickey, Galahad Books, NY, 1976. 112 pp., illus. $6.00.

This indispensable guide for hunters deals with equipment, techniques, types of dove shooting, hunting dogs, etc.

Drummer in the Woods, by Burton L. Spiller, Stackpole Books, Harrisburg, PA, 1980. 240 pp., illus. $13.95.

Twenty-one wonderful stories on grouse shooting by "the Poet Laureate of Grouse".

The Duck Hunter's Handbook, by Bob Hinman, Winchester Press, NY, 1974. 252 pp., illus. $12.95.

Down-to-earth, practical advice on bagging ducks and geese.

The Duck-Huntingest Gentlemen, by Keith C. Russell et al, Winchester Press, Tulsa, OK, 1980. 284 pp., illus. $14.95.

A collection of stories on waterfowl hunting.

Ducks of the Mississippi Flyway, ed. by John McKane, North Star Press, St. Cloud, MN, 1969. 54 pp., illus. Paper covers. $4.50.

A duck hunter's reference. Full color paintings of some 30 species, plus descriptive text.

Expert Advice on Gun Dog Training, ed. by David M. Duffey, Winchester Press, NY, 1977. 256 pp., illus. $11.95.

Eleven top pros talk shop, revealing the techniques and philosophies that account for their consistent success.

The Gallant Grouse, by Cecil E. and Dorothy Heacox, David McKay Co., Inc., New York, NY, 1981. 171 pp., illus. $14.95.

All about the hunting and natural history of "old Ruff".

A Gallery of Waterfowl and Upland Birds, by Gene Hill, with illustrations by David Maass, Pedersen Prints, Los Angeles, CA, 1978. 132 pp., illus. $39.95. Deluxe bound, signed edition, in slipcase. $250.

Gene Hill at his best. Liberally illustrated with fifty-one full-color reproductions of David Maass' finest paintings.

Getting the Most out of Modern Waterfowling, by John O. Cartier, St. Martin's Press, NY, 1974. 396 pp., illus. $10.95.

The most comprehensive, up-to-date book on waterfowling imaginable.

Goose Hunting, by Charles L. Cadieux, Stackpole Books, Harrisburg, PA, 1979. 197 pp., illus. $16.95.

Personal stories of goose hunting from Quebec to Mexico.

The Great Arc of the Wild Sheep, by J.L. Clark, Univ. of Oklahoma Press, Norman, Okla., 1978. 247 pp., illus. Paper covers. $8.95.

Every classified variety of wild sheep is discussed, as found in North America, Asia & Europe. Numerous hunting stories by experts.

Grizzly Country, by Andy Russell. A.A. Knopf, NYC, 1973, 302 pp., illus. $10.95.

Many-sided view of the grizzly bear and his world, by a noted guide, hunter and naturalist.

Grouse and Woodcock, An Upland Hunter's Book, by Nick Sisley, Stackpole Books, Harrisburg, PA, 1980. 192 pp., illus. $11.95.

Latest field techniques for effective grouse and woodcock hunting.

Hal Swiggett on North American Deer, by Hal Swiggett, Jolex, Inc., Oakland, NJ, 1980. 272 pp., illus. Paper covers. $8.95.

Where and how to hunt all species of North American deer.

Handgun Hunting, by Maj. George C. Nonte, Jr. and Lee E. Jurras, Winchester Press, NY, 1975. 245 pp., illus. $10.95.

A book with emphasis on the hunting of readily available game in the U.S. with the handgun.

Hard Hunting, by Patrick Shaughnessy and Diane Swingle, Winchester Press, New York, NY, 1978. $11.95.

A couple explores a no-frills, low-cost, highly successful, adventurous approach to wilderness hunting.

Horns in the High Country, by Andy Russell, Alfred A. Knopf, NY, 1973. 259 pp., illus. $10.95.

A many-sided view of wild sheep and their natural world.

Hunter's Digest, 2nd Edition, edited by Erwin A. Bauer, DBI Books, Inc., Northfield, IL, 1980. 288 pp., illus. Paper covers. $8.95.

The best ways, times and places to hunt the most popular species of large and small game animals of North America.

A Hunter's Fireside Book, by Gene Hill Winchester Press, NY, 1972. 192 pp., illus. $12.95.

An outdoor book that will appeal to every person who spends time in the field—or who wishes he could.

Hunting the American Wild Turkey, by Dave Harbour, Stackpole Books, Harrisburg, PA, 1975. 256 pp., illus. $14.95.

The techniques and tactics of hunting North America's largest, and most popular, woodland game bird.

Hunting America's Game Animals and Birds, by Robert Elman and George Peper, Winchester Press, NY, 1975. 368 pp., illus. $14.95.

A how-to, where-to, when-to guide—by 40 top experts—covering the continent's big, small, upland game and waterfowl.

Hunting Big-Game Trophies; A North America Guide, by Tom Brakefield, E.P. Dutton & Co., Inc., NY, 1976. 446 pp., illus. $10.95.

Where to go, when to go, camp savvy, animal lore, the hunt, etc.

Hunting Dog Know-How, by D.M. Duffey, Van Nostrand, Princeton, NJ, 1965. 177 pp., illus. $9.95.

Covers selection, breeds, and training of hunting dogs, problems in hunting and field trials.

Hunting Moments of Truth, by Eric Peper and Jim Rikhoff, Winchester Press, NY, 1973. 208 pp., illus. $12.95.

The world's most experienced hunters recount 22 most memorable occasions.

Hunting with Bow and Arrow, by George Laycock and Erwin Bauer. Arco Publ. Co., Inc., NYC, 1966. $3.95.

A practical guide to archery as a present-day sport. Mentions equipment needed and how to select it. Illus. instructions on how to shoot with ease and accuracy.

Hunting Trophy Deer, by John Wootters, Winchester Press, NY, 1977. 288 pp., illus. $14.95.

One of America's most experienced and respected hunting writers provides all the specialized advice you need to succeed at bagging trophy deer.

Hunting Upland Birds, by Chas. F. Waterman. Winchester Press, NY, 1972. 320 pp., illus. $10.95.

Excellent treatment of game habits and habitat, hunting methods, and management techniques for each of the 18 major North American game-bird species.

Hunting the Uplands with Rifle and Shotgun, by Luther A. Anderson, Winchester Press, NY, 1977. 224 pp., illus. $12.95.

Solid practical know-how to help make hunting deer and every major species of upland game bird easier and more satisfying.

Hunting Whitetail Deer, by Robert E. Donovan, Winchester Press, NY, 1978. 256 pp., illus. $12.50.

For beginners and experts alike, this book is the key to successful whitetail hunting.

Hunting the Whitetail Deer, by Norm Nelson, David McKay Co., Inc., New York, NY, 1980. 212 pp., illus. $12.95.

How to bring home North America's No. 1 big-game animal.

Hunting the Woodlands for Small and Big Game, by Luther A. Anderson, A. S. Barnes & Co., New York, NY, 1980. 256 pp., illus. $12.00.

A comprehensive guide to hunting in the United States. Chapters on firearms, game itself, marksmanship, clothing and equipment.

In Search of the Wild Turkey, by Bob Gooch, Greatlakes Living Press, Ltd., Waukegan, IL, 1978. 182 pp., illus. $9.95.

A state-by-state guide to wild turkey hot spots, with tips on gear and methods for bagging your bird.

The Market Hunter, by David and Jim Kimball, Dillon Press Inc., Minneapolis, MN, 1968. 132 pp., illus. $6.95.

The market hunter, one of the "missing chapters" in American history, is brought to life in this book.

Modern Hunting with Indian Secrets, by Allan A. Macfarlan. Stackpole Books, Harrisburg, PA, 1971. 222 pp., $10.00.

How to acquire the new-old skills of the Redman, how to apply them to modern hunting.

Modern Turkey Hunting, by James F. Brady, Crown Publ., N.Y.C., NY, 1973. 160 pp., illus. $9.95.

A thorough guide to the habits, habitat, and methods of hunting America's largest game bird.

More Grouse Feathers, by Burton L. Spiller. Crown Publ., NY, 1972. 238 pp., illus. $15.00.

Facsimile of the original Derrydale Press issue of 1938. Guns and dogs, the habits and shooting of grouse, woodcook, ducks, etc. Illus by Lynn Bogue Hunt.

Mostly Tailfeathers, by Gene Hill, Winchester Press, NY, 1975. 192 pp., illus. $12.95.

An interesting, general book about bird hunting.

The North American Waterfowler, by Paul S. Bernsen, Superior Publ. Co., Seattle, WA, 1972. 206 pp., Paper covers. $4.95.

The complete inside and outside story of duck and goose shooting. Big and colorful, illus. by Les Kouba.

1001 Hunting Tips, by Robert Elman, Winchester Press, N.Y.,NY, 1978. 256 pp., illus. $16.95.

A post-graduate course in big-game hunting, small-game hunting, wild-fowling, and hunting upland birds.

The Old Man's Boy Grows Older, by Robert Ruark, Holt, Rinehart and Winston, New York, NY, 1961. 302 pp., illus. $35.00.

A classic by a big-game hunter and world traveler.

One Man's Wilderness, by Warren Page, Holt, Rinehart and Winston, NY, 1973. 256 pp., illus. $15.00.

A world-known writer and veteran sportsman recounts the joys of a lifetime of global hunting.

The Outlaw Gunner, by Harry M. Walsh, Tidewater Publishers, Cambridge, MD, 1973. 178 pp., illus. $12.50.

A colorful story of market gunning in both its legal and illegal phases.

The Practical Hunter's Dog Book, by John R. Falk, Winchester Press, NY, 1971. 314 pp., illus. $10.95.

Helps to choose, train and enjoy your gun dog.

The Practical Hunter's Handbook, by Anthony J. Acerrano, Winchester Press, New York, NY, 1978. 224 pp., illus. Paper covers. $9.95.

How the time-pressed hunter can take advantage of every edge his hunting situation affords him.

Ranch Life and the Hunting Trail, by Theodore Roosevelt, Readex Microprint Corp., Dearborn, MI. 1966 186 pp. With drawings by Frederic Remington. $15.00.

A facsimile reprint of the original 1899 Century Co., edition. One of the most fascinating books of the West of that day.

Ringneck! Pheasants & Pheasant Hunting, by Ted Janes, Crown Publ., NY, 1975. 120 pp., illus. $8.95.

A thorough study of one of our more popular game birds.

Sheep and Sheep Hunting, by Jack O'Connor, Winchester Press, Tulsa, OK, 1980. 308 pp., illus. $12.95.

Memorial edition of the definitive book on wild sheep.

Shooting Pictures, by A.B. Frost, with 24 pp. of text by Chas. D. Lanier. Winchester Press, NY, 1972. 12 color plates. Enclosed in a board portfolio. Ed. limited to 750 numbered copies. $100.00.

Frost's twelve superb 12" by 16" pictures have often been called the finest sporting prints published in the U.S. A facsimile of the 1895-6 edition printed on fine paper with superb color fidelity.

Shots at Mule Deer, by Rollo S. Robinson, Winchester Press, New York, NY, 1970. 209 pp., illus. $15.

Description, strategies for bagging it, the correct rifle and cartridge to use.

Small Game Hunting, by Tom Brakefield, J.B. Lippincott Co., Phila., PA, 1978. 244 pp., illus. $10.

Describes where, when, and how to hunt all major small game species from coast to coast.

The Sportsman's Companion, by Lee Wulff. Harper & Row, N.Y.C., 1968, 413 pp., illus. $11.95.

Compendium of writings by various experts on hunting and fishing for American game. A useful reference for the outdoorsman.

Squirrels and Squirrel Hunting, by Bob Gooch. Tidewater Publ., Cambridge, MD, 1973. 148 pp., illus. $6.

A complete book for the squirrel hunter, beginner or old hand. Details methods of hunting, squirrel habitat, management, proper clothing, care of the kill, cleaning and cooking.

Successful Waterfowling, by Zack Taylor, Crown, Publ., NY, 1974. 276 pp., illus. Paper covers. $15.95.

The definitive guide to new ways of hunting ducks and geese.

Timberdoodle, by Frank Woolner, Crown Publ., Inc., NY, 1974. 168 pp., illus. $10.95.

A thorough, practical guide to the American woodcock and to woodcock hunting.

Topflight; A Speed Index to Waterfowl, by J.A. Ruthven & Wm. Zimmerman, Moebius Prtg. Co., Milwaukee, WI, 1968. 112 pp. $7.50.

Rapid reference for specie identification. Marginal color band of book directs reader to proper section. 263 full color illustrations of body and feather configurations.

The Trophy Hunter, by Col. Allison, Stackpole Books, Harrisburg, 1981. 240 pp., illus. $24.95.

Action-packed tales of hunting big game trophies around the world— 1860 to today.

Trouble With Bird Dogs...and What to do About Them, by George Bird Evans, Winchester Press, NY, 1976. 288 pp., illus. $13.95.

How to custom-train your dog for specific kinds of hunting.

Turkey Hunting with Charlie Elliot, by Charles Elliot, David McKay Co., Inc., New York, NY 1979. 275 pp., illus. $14.95.

The old professor tells all about America's big-game bird.

Turkey Hunter's Guide, by Byron W. Dalrymple, et al, a publication of The National Rifle Association, Washington, DC, 1979. 96 pp., illus. Paper covers. $4.95.

Expert advice on turkey hunting hotspots, guns, guides, and calls.

Upland Bird & Waterfowl Hunting, ed. by Dave Petzal, Simon & Schuster, NY, 1976. 315 pp., illus. $9.95.

A collection of stories by an outstanding panel of knowledgeable experts on the subject.

The Whitetail Deer Hunter's Handbook, by John Weiss, Winchester Press, New York, NY, 1979. 256 pp., illus. Paper covers. $9.95.

Wherever you live, whatever you level of experience, this brand-new handbook will make you a better deer hunter.

Whitetail: Fundamentals and Fine Points for the Hunter, by George Mattis, World Publ. Co. New York, NY, 1976. 273 pp., illus. $9.95.

A manual of shooting and trailing and an education in the private world of the deer.

The Wings of Dawn, by George Reiger, Stein and Day, New York, NY, 1980. 320 pp., illus. $29.95.

The complete book of North American waterfowling.

20 Great Trophy Hunts, by John O. Cartier, David McKay Co., Inc., New York, NY, 1981. 320 pp., illus. $22.50.

The cream of outstanding true-life hunting stories.

AFRICA/ASIA

African Rifles & Cartridges, by John Taylor. The Gun Room Press, Highland Park, NJ, 1977. 431 pp., illus. $16.95.

Experiences and opinions of a professional ivory hunter in Africa describing his knowledge of numerous arms and cartridges for big game. A reprint.

Big Game Hunting Around the World, by Bert Klineburger and Vernon W. Hurst, Exposition Press, Jericho, NY, 1969. 376 pp., illus. $25.00.

The first book that takes you on a safari all over the world.

Death in the Long Grass, by Peter Hathaway Capstick, St. Martin's Press, New York, NY, 1977. 297 pp., illus. $11.95.

A big game hunter's adventures in the African bush.

Great Game Animals of the World, by Russell B. Aitken. Winchester Press, N.Y., 1969. 192 pp., profusely illus. in monochrome and color. $40.00.

Accounts of man's pursuit of big game in all parts of the world, told in many fine pictures.

Green Hills of Africa, by Ernest Hemingway. Charles Scribner's Sons, NY, 1963. 285 pp., illus. Paper covers. $4.95.

A famous narrative of African big-game hunting, first published in 1935.

Horned Death, by John F. Burger. Standard Publications, Huntington, WV, 1947. 340 pp., illus. $60.00.

Hunting the African cape buffalo.

Uganda Safaris, by Brian Herne, Winchester Press, Tulsa, OK, 1979. 236 pp., illus. $12.95.

The chronicle of a professional hunter's adventures in Africa.

RIFLES

The Accurate Rifle, by Warren Page. Winchester Press, NY, 1973. 256 pp., illus. $11.95.

A masterly discussion. A must for the competitive shooter hoping to win, and highly useful to the practical hunter.

American Rifle Design and Performance, by L.R. Wallack, Winchester Press, NY, 1977. 288 pp., illus. $14.95.

An authoritative, comprehensive guide to how and why every kind of sporting rifle works.

The Bolt Action: A Design Analysis, by Stuart Otteson, ed. by Ken Warner, Winchester Press, NY, 1976. 320 pp., illus. $12.95.

Precise and in-depth descriptions, illustrations and comparisons of 16 bolt actions. A new approach.

The Book of the Garand, by Maj.-Gen. J.S. Hatcher, The Gun Room Press, Highland Park, NJ, 1977. 292 pp., illus. $15.00.

A new printing of the standard reference work on the U.S. Army M1 rifle.

Carbines Cal. .30 M1, M1A1, M2 and M3, by D.B. McLean, Normount Armament Co., Wickenburg, AZ, 1964. 221 pp., well illus., paperbound. $6.95.

U.S. field manual reprints on these weapons, edited and reorganized.

The Deer Rifle, by L.R. Wallack, Winchester Press, New York, NY, 1978. 256 pp., illus. $12.95.

Everything the deer hunter needs to know to select and use the arms and ammunition appropriate to his needs.

Description and Instructions for the Management of the Gallery-Practice Rifle Caliber .22—Model of 1903. Inco., 1972. 12 pp., 1 plate. Paper, $2.50.

Reprint of 1907 War Dept. pamphlet No. 1925.

Description of Telescopic Musket Sights, Inco, 1972. 10 pp. 4 plates. Paper, $2.50.

Reprint of 1917 War Dept. pamphlet No. 1957, first publ. in 1908.

The First Winchester, by John E. Parsons. Winchester Press, New York, NY, 1977. 207 pp., well illus. $24.95.

This new printing of *The Story of the 1866 Repeating Rifle* (1st publ. 1955) is revised, and additional illustrations included.

A Forgotten Heritage; The Story of a People and the Early American Rifle, by Harry P. Davis, The Gun Room Press, Highland Park, NJ, 1976. 199 pp., illus. $9.95.

Reprint of a very scarce history, originally published in 1941, the Kentucky rifle and the people who used it.

Garand Rifles M1, M1C, M1D, by Donald B. McLean, Normount Armament Co., Wickenburg, AZ, 1968. Over 160 pp., 175 illus., paper wrappers. $6.95.

Covers all facets of the arm: battlefield use, disassembly and maintenance, all details to complete lock-stock-and-barrel repair, plus variations, grenades, ammo., and accessories; plus a section on 7.62mm NATO conventions.

The Golden Age of Single-Shot Rifles, by Edsall James, Pioneer Press, Union City, TN, 1975. 33 pp., illus. Paper covers. $2.75.

A detailed look at all of the fine, high quality sporting single-shot rifles that were once the favorite of target shooters.

The Gun Digest Book of the .22 Rimfire, by John Lachuk, DBI Books, Northfield, IL, 1978. 224 pp., illus. Paper covers. $7.95.

Everything you want to know about the .22 rimfire and the arms that use it.

The Hunting Rifle, by Jack O'Connor. Winchester Press, NY, 1970. 352 pp., illus. $13.95.

An analysis, with wit and wisdom, of contemporary rifles, cartridges, accessories and hunting techniques.

Know Your M1 Garand, by E. J. Hoffschmidt, Blacksmith Corp., Southport, CT, 1975, 84 pp., illus. Paper covers. $5.95.

Facts about America's most famous infantry weapon. Covers test and experimental models, Japanese and Italian copies, National Match models.

The Model 70 Winchester 1937-1964, by Dean H. Whitaker, Taylor Publishing Co., Dallas, TX, 1978. 210 pp., illus. $24.95.

An authoritative reference book on this model. Gives production history, changes, dimensions, specifications on special-order guns, etc.

The M-14 Rifle, facsimile reprint of FM 23-8, Desert Publications, Cornville, AZ, 50 pp., illus. Paper $4.95.

In this well illustrated and informative reprint, the M-14 and M-14E2 are covered thoroughly.

The Modern Rifle, by Jim Carmichel, Winchester Press, NY, 1975. 320 pp., illus. $12.95.

The most comprehensive, thorough, up-to-date book ever published on today's rifled sporting arms.

100 Years of Shooters and Gunmakers of Single Shot Rifles, by Gerald O. Kelver, Brighton, CO, 1975. 212 pp., illus. Paper covers $10.00.

The Schuetzen rifle, targets and shooters, primers, match rifles, original loadings and much more. With chapters on famous gunsmiths like Harry Pope, Morgan L. Rood and others.

The '03 Springfields, by Clark S. Campbell, Ray Riling Arms Books Co., Phila., PA, 1978. 320 pp., illus. $25.00.

The most authoritative and definitive work on this famous U.S. rifle, the 1903 Springfield and its 30-06 cartridge.

The Pennsylvania Rifle, by Samuel E. Dyke, Sutter House, Lititz, PA, 1975. 61 pp., illus. Paper covers. $5.00.

History and development, from the hunting rifle of the Germans who settled the area. Contains a full listing of all known Lancaster, PA, gunsmiths from 1729 through 1815.

Position Rifle Shooting, by Bill Pullum and F.T. Hanenkrat. Winchester Press, NY, 1973. 256 pp., illus. Paper covers, $5.95.

The single most complete statement of rifle shooting principles and techniques, and the means of learning, teaching and using them, ever to appear in print.

The Revolving Rifles, by Edsall James, Pioneer Press, Union City, TN, 1975. 23 pp., illus. Paper covers. $2.50.

Valuable information on revolving cylinder rifles, from the earliest matchlock forms to the latest models of Colt and Remington.

The Rifle Book, by Jack O'Connor, Random House, NY, 1978. 337 pp., illus. Paper covers. $10.95.

The complete book of small game, varmint and big game rifles.

Rifle Guide, by Robert A. Steindler, Stoeger Publishing Co., South Hackensack, NJ, 1978. 304 pp., illus. Paper covers. $7.95.

Complete, fully illustrated guide to selecting, shooting, caring for, and collecting rifles of all types.

Rifles AR15, M16, and M16A1, 5.56 mm, by D.B. McLean. Normount Armament Co., Wickenburg, AZ, 1968. Unpaginated, illus., paper covers. $6.95.

Descriptions, specifications and operation of subject models are set forth in text and picture.

Schuetzen Rifles, History and Loading, by Gerald O. Kelver, Gerald O. Kelver, Publisher, Brighton, CO, 1972. Illus. $7.50.

Reference work on these rifles, their bullets, loading, telescopic sights, accuracy, etc. A limited, numbered ed.

Single Shot Rifles and Actions, by Frank de Haas, ed. by John T. Amber, DBI Books, Northfield, IL, 1969. 352 pp., illus. $9.95.

The definitive book on over 60 single shot rifles and actions. Covers history, parts photos, design and construction, etc.

The Sporting Rifle and its Projectiles, by Lieut. James O Forsyth, The Buckskin Press, Big Timber, MT, 1978. 132 pp., illus. $9.50.

Facsimile reprint of the 1863 edition, one of the most authoritative books ever written on the muzzle-loading round ball sporting rifle.

The .22 Rifle, by Dave Petzal. Winchester Press, NY, 1972. 244 pp., illus. $9.95.

All about the mechanics of the .22 rifle. How to choose the right one, how to choose a place to shoot, what makes a good shot, the basics of small-game hunting.

The American Shotgun, by David F. Butler, Lyman Publ., Middlefield, CT, 1973. 256 pp. illus. Paper covers. $11.95.

A comprehensive history of the American smoothbore's evolution from Colonial times to the present day.

American Shotgun Design and Performance, by L.R. Wallack, Winchester Press, NY 1977. 184 pp., illus. $14.95.

An expert lucidly recounts the history and development of American shotguns and explains how they work.

The Double Shotgun, by Don Zutz, Winchester Press, New York, NY 1978. 288 pp., illus. $15.95.

The history and development of the most classic of all sporting arms.

How to be a Winner Shooting Skeet & Trap, by Tom Morton, Tom Morton, Knoxville, MD, 1974. 144 pp., illus. Paper covers. $8.95.

The author explains why championship shooting is more than a physical process.

The Mysteries of Shotgun Patterns, by Geo. G. Oberfell and Chas. E. Thompson, Oklahoma State University Press, Stillwater, OK, Xerox edition, 1978. 328 pp. Paper covers $50.00.

Shotgun ballistics for the hunter in non-technical language, with information on improving effectiveness in the field.

New England Grouse Shooting, by W.H. Foster, Chas. Scribner's, NY, 193 pp. illus. $25.00.

Many interesting and hepful points on how to hunt grouse.

The Parker Gun, by Larry L. Baer, Beinfeld Publ., Inc., No. Hollywood, CA, 1980. 240 pp., illus. $24.95.

Originally published as two separate volumes. This is the only comprehensive work on the subject of America's most famous shotgun. Incuded are new material and new photographs.

The Police Shotgun Manual, by Robert H. Robinson, Charles C. Thomas, Springfield, IL 1973. 153 pp., illus. $17.50.

A complete study and analysis of the most versatile and effective weapon in the police arsenal.

Score Better at Skeet, by Fred Missildine, with Nick Karas. Winchester Press, NY 1972. 160 pp., illus. In paper covers, $5.95; cloth, $10.00.

The long-awaited companion volume to *Score Better at Trap.*

75 Years with the Shotgun, by C.T. (Buck) Buckman, Valley Publ., Fresno, CA, 1974. 141 pp., illus. $7.50.

An expert hunter and trapshooter shares experiences of a lifetime.

The Shotgun Book, by Jack O'Connor, Alfred A. Knopf, New York, NY, 1978. 341 pp., illus. $16.95.

An indispensable book for every shotgunner containing up-to-the-minute authoritative information on every phase of the shotgun.

The Shotgun in Combat, by Tony Lesce, Desert Publications, Cornville, AZ, 1979. 148 pp., illus. Paper covers. $5.95.

A history of the shotgun and its use in combat.

Shotgun Digest, 2nd Edition, edited by Jack Lewis and Jack Mitchell, DBI Books, Inc., Northfield, IL 1980. 288 pp., illus. Paper covers. $9.95.

All-new look at shotguns by a double-barreled team of writers.

Shotgunners Guide, by Monte Burch, Winchester Press, New York, NY, 1980. 208 pp., illus. $12.95.

A basic book for the young and old who want to try shotgunning or who want to improve their skill.

Shotgunning: The Art and the Science, by Bob Brister, Winchester Press, NY 1976. 321 pp., illus. $14.95.

Hundreds of specific tips and truly novel techniques to improve the field and target shooting of every shotgunner.

Shotguns & Shooting, by E.S. McCawley, Jr., Van Nostrand Reinhold Co., NY 1965. 146 pp., illus. Paper covers. $5.95.

Covers the history and development, types of shotguns and ammunition, shotgun shooting, etc.

Sure-Hit Shotgun Ways, by Francis E. Sell, Stackpole Books, Harrisburg, PA, 1967. 160 pp., illus. $15.00.

On guns, ballistics and quick skill methods.

Skeet Shooting with D. Lee Braun, edited by R. Campbell, Grosset & Dunlap, NY, 1967. 160 pp., illus. Paper covers $3.95.

Thorough instructions on the fine points of Skeet shooting.

Trapshooting with D. Lee Braun and the Remington Pros., ed. by R. Campbell. Remington Arms Co., Bridgeport, CT. 1969. 157 pp., well illus., Paper covers. $3.95.

America's masters of the scattergun give the secrets of professional marksmanship.

Wing & Shot, by R.G. Wehle, Country Press, 167. 190 pp., illus. $12.

Step-by-step account on how to train a fine shooting dog.

The World's Fighting Shotguns, by Thomas F. Swearengen, T. B. N. Enterprises, Alexandria, VA 1979. 500 pp., illus. $29.95.

The complete military and police reference work from the shotgun's inception to date, with up-to-date developments.

You and the Target, by Kay Ohye, Kay Ohye Enterprises, No. Brunswick, NJ, 1978. 83 pp., illus. Paper cover. $9.95.

All new trapshooting handbook to better scores.

Directory of the Arms Trade

AMMUNITION (Commercial)

Alcan Shells, (See Smith & Wesson Ammunition Co.)
Bingham Ltd., 1775-C Wilwat Dr., Norcross, GA 30093
Cascade Cartridge Inc., (See Omark)
DWM, (See RWS)
Dynamit Nobel of America, Inc., 105 Stonehurst Court, Northvale, NJ 07647/201-767-1660(RWS)
Eclipse Cartridge, Inc., 26407 Golden Valley Rd., Saugus, CA 91350/805-251-6610
Eley-Kynoch, ICI-America, Wilmington, DE 19897/302-575-3000
Federal Cartridge Co., 2700 Foshay Tower, Minneapolis, MN 55402/612-333-8255
Frontier Cartridge Division-Hornady Mfg. Co., Box 1848, Grand Island, NE 68801/308-382-1390
ICI-America, Wilmington, DE 19897/302-575-3000(Eley-Kynoch)
Midway Arms, Inc., R. R. #5, Box 298, 7450 Old Hwy. 40 West, Columbia, MO 65201/314-445-3030
Omark Industries, Box 856, Lewiston, ID 83501
Precision Prods. of Wash., Inc., N. 311 Walnut Rd., Spokane, WA 99206/509-928-0604 (Exammo)
RWS, (See Dynamit Nobel of America)
Remington Arms Co., 939 Barnum Ave., P. O. Box #1939, Bridgeport, CT 06601
Service Armament, 689 Bergen Blvd., Ridgefield, NJ 07657
Super Vel, Hamilton Rd., Rt. 2, P. O. Box 1398, Fond du Lac, WI 54935/414-921-2652
Weatherby's, 2781 E. Firestone Blvd., South Gate, CA 90280
Winchester, Shamrock St.. East Alton. IL 62024

AMMUNITION (Custom)

American Pistol Bullet, 133 Blue Bell Rd., Greensboro, NC 27406/919-272-6151
Bill Ballard, 830 Miles Ave., Billings, MT 59101 (ctlg. 50¢)
Ballistek, Weapons Systems Div., 3450 Antelope Dr., Lake Havasu City, AZ 86403/602-855-0997
Beal's Bullets, 170 W. Marshall Rd., Lansdowne, PA 19050 (Auto Mag Specialists)
Bell's Gun & Sport Shop, 3309-19 Mannheim Rd., Franklin Park, IL 60131
Brass Extrusion Labs. Ltd., 800 W. Maple Lane, Bensenville, IL 60106
C.W. Cartridge Co., 71 Hackensack St., Wood-Ridge, NJ 07075
Russell Campbell Custom Loaded Ammo, 219 Leisure Dr., San Antonio, TX 78201/512-735-1183
Crown City Arms, P.O. Box 1126, Cortland, NY 13045/607-753-8238
Cumberland Arms Rt. 1, Shafer Rd., Blantons Chapel, Manchester, TN 37355
E.W. Ellis Sport Shop, RFD 1, Box 315, Corinth, NY 12822
Ellwood Epps Northern Ltd., 210 Worthington St. W., North Bay, Ont. PIB 3B4, Canada
Ramon B. Gonzalez, P.O. Box 370, Monticello, NY 12701
Gussert Bullet & Cartridge Co., Inc., P.O. Box 3945, Green Bay, WI 54303
Jensen's Custom Ammunition, 5146 E. Pima, Tucson, AZ 85716
R.H. Keeler, 817 "N" St., Port Angeles, WA 98362/206-457-4702
KTW Inc., 710 Foster Park Rd., Lorain, OH 44053 (bullets)
Dean Lincoln, P.O. Box 1886, Farmington, NM 87401
Lindsley Arms Cartridge Co., Inc., P.O. Box 1287, 408 N.E. 3rd St., Boynton Beach, FL 33435/305-737-8562 (inq. S.A.S.E.)
Lomont Precision Bullets, 4421 S. Wayne Ave., Ft. Wayne, IN 46807/219-694-6792 (custom cast bullets only)
Numrich Arms Corp., 203 Broadway, W. Hurley, NY 12491
Pearl Armory, Revenden Springs, AR 72460
Robert Pomeroy, Morison Ave., Corinth, ME 04427/207-285-7721 (custom shells)
Precision Prods. of Wash., Inc., N. 311 Walnut Rd., Spokane, WA 99206/509-928-0604 (Exammo)
Anthony F. Sailer-Ammunition, 707 W. Third St., P. O. Box L, Owen, WI 54460/715-229-2516
Sanders Cust. Gun Serv., 2358 Tyler Lane, Louisville, KY 40205
Senica Run, Inc., P.O. Box 3032, Greeley, CO 80633
Geo. Spence, 202 Main St., Steele, MO 63877/314-695-4926 (boxer-primed cartridges)
The 3-D Company, Box 142, Doniphan, NB 68832 (reloaded police ammo)

AMMUNITION (Foreign)

K.J. David & Company, P.O. Box 12595, Lake Park, FL 33043
Dynamit Nobel of America, Inc., 105 Stonehurst Court, Northvale, NJ 07647/210-767-1660(RWS, Gooo, Rottwoil)
Quilio Fiocchi S.p.A., P.O. Box 236, 22053 Lecco-Belledo, Italy
Norma, (See Outdoor Sports Headquarters, Inc.)
Hirtenberger Patronen-, Zündhütchen- & Metallwarenfabrik, A.G., Leobersdorfer Str. 33, A2552 Hirtenberg, Austria
Patton and Morgan Corp., 405 Park Ave., New York, NY 10022/212-370-0777 (PMC ammo)
Paul Jaeger Inc., 211 Leedom St., Jenkintown, PA 19046/215-884-6920
RWS (Rheinische-Westfälische Sprengstoff) [See Dynamit Nobel of America]

AMMUNITION COMPONENTS—BULLETS, POWDER, PRIMERS

Accurate Arms Co., Inc., (Propellents Div.), Rt. 1, Box 167, McEwen, TN, 37101/615-729-5301 (powders)
The Alberts Corp., P.O. Box 157, Franklin Lakes, NJ 07417/201-337-5848 (Taurus Bullets)
Ammo-O-Mart Ltd., P.O. Box 125, Hawkesbury, Ont., Canada K6A 2R8 (Curry Bullets)
Austin Powder Co. (See Red Diamond Dist. Co.)
Ballistic Prods., Inc., Box 488, 2105 Shaughnessy Circle, Long Lake, MN 55356
Ballistic Research Industries (BRI), 6000 B Soquel Ave., Santa Cruz, CA 95062/408-476-7981 (12-ga. shotgun slug)
Barnes Bullets, P.O. Box 215, American Fork, UT 84003/801-756-4222
Bell's Gun & Sport Shop, 3309-19 Mannheim Rd., Franklin Pk., IL 60131
Bitterroot Bullet Co., Box 412, Lewiston, ID 83501/208-743-5635 (Coin or stamps) f.50¢ U.S.; 75¢ Can. & Mex.; intl. $3.00 and #10 SASE for lit.
B.E.L.L., Brass Extrusion Laboratories, Ltd., 800 W. Maple Lane, Bensenville, IL 60106
CCI, (See: Omark Industries)
Kenneth E. Clark, 18738 Highway 99, Madera, CA 93637 (Bullets)
Division Lead, 7742 W. 61 Pl., Summit, IL 60502
DuPont, Explosives Dept., Wilmington, DE 19898
Dynamit Nobel of America, Inc., 105 Stonehurst Court, Northvale, NJ 07647/201-767-1660 (RWS percussion caps)
Elk Mountain Shooters Supply Co., 1719 Marie, Pasco, WA 99301 (Alaskan bullets)
Farmer Bros., 1616-15th St., Eldora, IA 50627/515-858-3651 (Lage wad)
Federal Cartridge Co., 2700 Foshay Tower, Minneapolis, MN 55402/612-333-8255 (nickel cases)
Forty Five Ranch Enterprises, 119 S. Main, Miami, OK 74354/918-542-9307
Godfrey Reloading Supply, Hi-Way 67-111, Brighton, IL 62012 (cast bullets)
Lynn Godfrey, (See: Elk Mtn. Shooters Supply)
Green Bay Bullets, 233 No. Ashland, Green Bay, WI 54303 (lead)
GTM Co., George T. Mahaney, 15915B E. Main St., La Puente, CA 91744 (all brass shotshells)
Gussert Bullet & Cartridge Co., Inc., P.O. Box 3945, Green Bay, WI 54303
Hardin Specialty Distr., P. O. Box 338, Radcliff, KY 40160/502-351-6649 (empty, primed cases)
Hepplers Gun Shop, 6000 B Soquel Ave., Santa Cruz, CA 95062/408-475-1235 (BRI 12-ga. slug)
Hercules Powder Co., 910 Market St.,Wilmington, DE 19899
Hodgdon Powder Co. Inc., 7710 W. 63rd St., Shawnee Mission, KS 66202/913-362-5410
Hornady Mfg. Co., Box 1848, Grand Island, NE 68801/308-382-1390
NORMA (See Outdoor Sports Headquarters, Inc.)
N.E. House Co., 195 West High St., R.R. 4, Box 68, E. Hampton, CT 06424/203-267-2133 (zinc bases only)
Jaro Bullet Co., P.O. Box 6125, Pasadena, TX 77506/713-472-6141
L.L.F. Die Shop, 1281 Highway 99 North, Eugene, OR 97402/503-688-5753
Lage Uniwad Co., 1102 Washington St., Eldora, IA 50627
Ljutic Ind., Inc. Box 2117,Yakima, WA 98902 (Mono-wads)
Lomont Precision Bullets, 4421 S. Wayne Ave., Ft. Wayne, IN 46807/219-694-6792 (custom cast bullets)
Lyman Products Corp., Rte. 147, Middlefield, CT 06455
Michael's Antiques, Box 233, Copiague, L.I., NY 11726 (Balle Blondeau)
Miller Trading Co., 20 S. Front St., Wilmington, NC 28401/919-762-7107 (bullets)
Nosler Bullets, P.O. Box 688, Beaverton, OR 97005
Omark Industries, Box 856, Lewiston, ID 83501/208-746-2351
The Oster Group, 50 Sims Ave., Providence, RI 02909 (alloys f. casting bull.)
Outdoor Sports Headquarters, Inc., 2290 Arbor Blvd., Dayton, OH 45439/513-294-2811
Pyrodex, Inc., 7710 W. 63rd St., Shawnee Mission, KS 66202 (black powder substitute)
Robert Pomeroy, Morison Ave., East Corinth, ME 04427
Red Diamond Distributing Co., 1304 Snowdon Dr., Knoxville, TN 37912 (black powder)
Remington-Peters, 939 Barnum Ave., P.O. Box #1939, Bridgeport, CT 06601
Sierra Bullets Inc., 10532 So. Painter Ave., Santa Fe Springs, CA 90670
Speer Products, Box 856, Lewiston, ID 83501
C.H. Stocking, Rte. 3, Box 195, Hutchinson, MN 55350 (17 cal. bullet jackets)
Taracorp Industries, 16th & Cleveland Blvd., Granite City, IL 62040/618-451-4524 (Lawrence Brand lead shot)
Taurus Bullets, (See Alberts Corp.)
Taylor Bullets, P.O. Box 21254, San Antonio, TX 78221 (cast)
United Cartridge Co., P.O. Box 604, Valley Industrial Park, Casa Grande, AR 85222/002-836-2510 (P.C. wads)
Vitt & Boos, 2178 Nichols Ave., Stratford, CT 06497/203-375-6859 (Aerodynamic shotgun slug, 12-ga. only)
Winchester, Shamrock St., East Alton, IL 62024
Worthy Products, Inc., R.D. #7, Box 60, Fulton, NY 13069/315-593-1858 (slug loads)
Xelex Ltd., P.O. Box 543, Renfrow, Ont. K7V 4B1, Canada (powder, Curry bullets)
Zero Bullet Co., P.O. Box 1188, Cullman, AL 35055

ANTIQUE ARMS DEALERS

Robert Abels, 2881 N.E. 33 Ct., Ft. Lauderdale, FL 33306/305-564-6985 (Catalog $1.00)
Beeman Precision Airguns, Inc., 47 Paul Dr., San Rafael, CA 94903/415-472-7121 (airguns only)
Wm. Boggs, 1243 Grandview Ave., Columbus, OH 43212
Ed's Gun House, Rte. 1, Minnesota City, MN 55959/507-689-2925
Ellwood Epps Northern Ltd., 210 Worthington St. W., North Bay, Ont. PIB 3B4 Canada
William Fagan, 126 Belleview, Mount Clemens, MI 48043/313-465-4637
N. Flayderman & Co., Squash Hollow, New Milford, CT 06776
Fulmer's Antique Firearms, Chet Fulmer, P.O. Box 792, Detroit Lakes, MN 56501/218 847 7712
Garcia National Gun Traders, Inc., 225 S.W. 22nd Ave., Miami, FL 33135
Herb Glass, Bullville, NY 10915/914-361-3021
James Goergen, Rte. 2, Box 182BB, Austin, MN 55912/507-433-9280
Goodman's for Guns, 1002 Olive St., St. Louis, MO 63101/314-421-5300
Griffin's Guns & Antiques, R.R. 4, Peterborough, Ont., Canada K9J 6X5/705-748-3220
The Gun Shop, 6497 Pearl Rd., Cleveland, OH 44130/216-884-7476
Hansen & Company, 244 Old Post Rd., Southport, CT 06490
Holbrook Antique Militaria, 4050 S.W. 98th Ave., Miami, FL 33165/305-223-6500
Jackson Arms, 6209 Hillcrest Ave., Dallas, TX 75205
Lever Arms Serv. Ltd., 572 Howe St., Vancouver, B.C., Canada V6C 2E3/604-685-6913
Lone Pine Trading Post, Jct. Highways 61 and 248, Minnesota City, MN 55959/507-689-2922
Charles W. Moore, R.D. 2, Box 276, Schenevus, NY 12155/607-278-5721
Museum of Historical Arms, 1038 Alton Rd., Miami Beach, FL 33139/305-672-7480 (ctlg $5)
New Orleans Arms Co., 5001 Treasure St., New Orleans, LA 70186/504-944-3371
O.K. Hardware, Westgate Shopping Center, Great Falls, MT 59404
Old West Gun Room, Old Western Scrounger, 3509 Carlson Blvd., El Cerrito, CA 94530/415-527-3872 (write for list)
Pioneer Guns, 5228 Montgomery, (Cincinnati) Norwood, OH 45212/513-631-4871
Pony Express Sport Shop, Inc., 17460 Ventura Blvd., Encino, CA 91316/213-788-0123
Martin B. Retting, Inc., 11029 Washington, Culver City, CA 90230/213-837-6111
Ridge Guncraft, Inc., 125 E. Tyrone Rd., Oak Ridge, TN 37830/615-483-4024
San Francisco Gun Exch., 124 Second St., San Francisco, CA 94105/415-982-6097
Santa Ana Gunroom, P.O. Box 1777, Santa Ana, CA 92701
Ward & Van Valkenburg, 114-32nd Ave. N., Fargo, ND 58102
M.C. Wiest, 125 E. Tyrone Rd., Oak Ridge, TN 37830/615-483-4024
J. David Yale, Ltd., 2618 Conowingo Rd., Bel Air, MD 21014/301-838-9479
Lewis Yearout, 308 Riverview Dr. E., Great Falls, MT 59404

BOOKS (ARMS), Publishers and Dealers

Arms & Armour Press, 2-6 Hampstead High Street, London NW3 1QQ, England
Beinfeld Publishing, Inc., 12767 Saticoy St., No. Hollywood, CA 91605/213-982-3700
Blacksmith Corp., P.O. Box 424, Southport, CT 06490/203-367-4041
Blacktail Mountain Books, 42 First Ave. West, Kalispell, MT 59901/406-257-5573
DBI Books, Inc., One Northfield Plaza, Northfield, IL 60093/312-441-7010
Dove Press, P.O. Box 3882, Enid, OK 73701/405-234-4347
EPCO Publ. Co., 62-19 Cooper Ave., Glendale, NY 11385/212-497-1100
Empire Co.,P.O. Box 2902, Santa Fe, NM 87501/505-983-2381
Fairfield Book Co., Inc., P.O. Box 289, Brookfield Center, Ct. 06805/800-243-1318; 203-775-0053
Fortress Publications Inc., P.O. Box 241, Stoney Creek, Ont. L8G 3X9, Canada/416-662-3505
Guncraft Books, Div. of Ridge Guncraft, Inc., 125 E. Tyrone Rd., Oak Ridge, TN 37830/615-483-4024
Gunnerman Books, P.O. Box 4292, Auburn Heights, MI 48057/313-879-2779
Handgun Press, 5832 S. Green, Chicago, IL 60621
Jackson Arms, 6209 Hillcrest Ave., Dallas, TX 75205
Jolex Inc., 294 W. Oakland, Oakland, NJ 07436/201-337-3356
Lyman, Route 147, Middlefield, CT 06455
John Olson Co., 294 W. Oakland Ave., Oakland, NJ 07436
Pachmayr Gun Works, Inc., 1220 S. Grand Ave., Los Angeles, CA 90015/213-748-7271
Personal Firearms Record Book Co., P.O. Box 2800, Santa Fe, NM 87501/505-983-2381
Gerald Pettinger Arms Books, Route 2, Russell, IA 50238/515-535-2239
Ray Riling Arms Books Co., 114 Greenwood Ave., Box 135, Wyncote, PA 19095/215-438-2456
Rutgers Book Center, Mark Aziz, 127 Raritan Ave., Highland Park, NJ 08904
Stackpole Books, Cameron & Keiker Sts., Telegraph Press Bldg., Harrisburg, PA 17105
Stoeger Publishing Co., 55 Ruta Court, South Hackensack, NJ 07606
James C. Tillinghast, Box 405, Hancock, NH 03449/603-525-6615
Ken Trotman, 2-6 Hampstead High St., London, NW3, 1QQ, England
Winchester Press, 1421 S. Sheridan Rd., P.O. Box 1260, Tulsa, OK 74101/918-835-3161
Wolfe Publishing Co., Inc., Box 30-30, Prescott, AZ 86302/602-445-7810

BULLET & CASE LUBRICANTS

Chopie Mfg. Inc., 700 Copeland Ave., La Crosse, WI 54601/608-784-0926 (Black-Solve)
Cooper-Woodward, Box 972, Riverside, CA 92502/714-683-5952 (Perfect Lube)
Corbin Mfg. & Supply Inc., P.O. Box 758, Phoenix, OR 97535/503-826-5211
Green Bay Bullets, 233 N. Ashland, Green Bay, WI 54303 (EZE-size case lube)
Gussert Bullet & Cartridge Co., Inc., P.O. Box 3945, Green Bay, WI 54303 (Super Lube)
Hodgdon Powder Co., Inc., 7710 W. 63rd St., Shawnee Mission, KS 66202/913-362-5410
Javelina Products, Box 337, San Bernardino, CA 92402/714-882-5847 (Alox beeswax)
Jet-Aer Corp., 100 Sixth Ave., Paterson, NJ 07524
LeClear Industries, P.O. Box 484, 1126 Donald Ave., Royal Oak, MI 48068/313-588-1025
Lenz Prod. Co., Box 1226, Sta. C, Canton, OH 44708 (Clenzoil)
Lyman Products Corp., Rte. 147, Middlefield, CT. 06455 (Size-Ezy)
Marmel Prods., P.O. Box 97, Utica, MI 48087/313-731-8029 (Marvellube, Marvelux)
Micro Ammunition Co., P.O. Box 117, Mesilla Park, NM 88047/505-522-2674 (Micro-Lube)
Mirror Lube, P.O. Box 693, San Juan Capistrano, CA 92675
M&N Bullet Lube, Box 495, Jefferson St., Madras, OR 97741/503-475-2992
Northeast Industrial, Inc., 2516 Wyoming, El Paso, TX 79903/915-532-8344 (Ten X-Lube; NEI mold prep)
Pacific Tool Co., P.O. Box 2048, Ordnance Plant Rd., Grand Island, NE 68801/308-384-2308
RCBS, Inc., Box 1919, Oroville, CA 95965
SAECO Rel. Inc., 525 Maple Ave., Carpinteria, CA 93103/805-684-6925
Shooters Accessory Supply (SAS) (See Corbin Mfg. & Supply)
Tamarack Prods., Inc., Box 224, Barrington, IL 60010 (Bullet lube)
Testing Systems, Inc., 220 Pegasus Ave., Northvale, NJ 07647/201-767- 7300

BULLET SWAGE DIES AND TOOLS

C-H Tool & Die Corp., 106 N. Harding St., Owen, WI 54461/715-229-2146
Lester Coats, 416 Simpson St., North Bend, OR 97459/503-756-6995 (lead wire core cutter)
Corbin Mfg. & Supply Inc., P.O. Box 758, Phoenix, OR 97535/503-826-5211
Hollywood, Whitney Sales Inc., P.O. Box 875, Reseda, CA 91335
Huntington's Die Specialties, P.O. Box 991, Oroville, CA 95965
Independent Machine & Gun Shop, 1416 N. Hayes, Pocatello, ID 83201 (TNT bullet dies)
L.L.F. Die Shop, 1281 Highway 99 North, Eugene, OR 97402/503-688-5753
Rorschach Precision Products, P.O. Box 1613, Irving, TX 75060/214-254-2762
SAS Dies, (See Corbin Mfg. & Supply)
Sport Flite Mfg., Inc., 2520 Industrial Row, Troy, MI 48084/313-280-0648
TNT (See Ind. Mach. & Gun Shop)

CARTRIDGES FOR COLLECTORS

AD Hominem, R.R. 3, Orillia, Ont., Canada L3V 6H3
Antique Arsenal, 365 S. Moore, Lakewood, CO 80226
Cameron's, 16690 W. 11th Ave., Golden CO 80401/303-279-7365
Centrefire Sports Dunedin, P.O. Box 1293, 41 Dowling St., Dunedin, New Zealand
Chas. E. Duffy, Williams Lane, West Hurley, NY 12419
Tom M. Dunn, 1342 So. Poplar, Casper, WY 82601
Ellwood Epps (Orillia) Ltd., Hwy. 11 North, Orillia, Ont. L3V 6H3, Canada/705-689-5333
"Gramps" Antique Cartridges, Box 341, Washago, Ont., Canada L0K 2B0
Idaho Ammunition Service, 410 21st Ave., Lewiston, ID 83501
San Francisco Gun Exchange, 124 Second St., San Francisco, CA 94105/415-982-6097
Ernest Tichy, 365 So. Moore, Lakewood, CO 80226
James C. Tillinghast, Box 405, Hancock, NH 03449/603-525-6615 (list 50¢)
Lewis Yearout, 308 Riverview Dr. E., Great Falls, MT 59404

CASES, CABINETS AND RACKS—GUN

Action Co., P.O. Box 528, McKinney, TX 75069
Alco Carrying Cases, 601 W. 26th St., New York, NY 10001/212-675-5820
Bob Allen Sportswear, 214 S.W. Jackson, Des Moines, IA 50315/515-283-1988 (carrying)
Allen Co., Inc., 640 Compton St., Broomfield, CO 80020/303-469-1857
Art Jewel Enterprises,Box 819, Berkeley, IL 60163/312-941-1110
Morton Booth Co., Box 123, Joplin, MO 64801
Boyt Co., Div. of Welsh Sportg. Gds., Box 1108, Iowa Falls, IA 50126
Brenik, Inc., 925 W. Chicago Ave., Chicago, IL 60622
Browning, Rt. 4, Box 624-B, Arnold, MO 63010
Cap-Lex Gun Cases, Capitol Plastics of Ohio, Inc., 333 Van Camp Rd., Bowling Green, OH 43402
Dara-Nes Inc., P.O. Box 119, East Hampton, CT 06424/203-267-4175 (firearms security chests)
East Tenn Mills, Inc., 2900 Buffalo Rd., Johnson City, Tn 37601 (gun socks)
Ellwood Epps (Orillia) Ltd., R.R. 3, Hwy. 11 North, Orillia, Ont. L3V 6H3, Canada/705-689-5333 (custom gun cases)
Norbert Ertel, Box 1150, Des Plaines, IL 60018 (cust. gun cases)
Flambeau Plastics Corp., 801 Lynn, Baraboo, WI 53913
Gun-Ho Case Mfg. Co., 110 East 10th St., St. Paul, MN 55101
Harbor House Gun Cabinets, 12508 Center St., South Gate, CA 90280
Marvin Huey Gun Cases, Box 98, Reed's Spring, MO 65737/417-538-4233 (handbuilt leather cases)
Jumbo Sports Prods., P.O. Box 280-Airport Rd., Frederick, MD 21701
Kalispel Metal Prods. (KMP), Box 267, Cusick, WA 99119 (aluminum boxes)
Kolpin Mfg., Inc., Box 231, Berlin, WI 54923/414-361-0400
Marble Arms Corp., 420 Industrial Park, Gladstone, MI 49837/906-428-3710

Bill McGuire, 1600 No. Eastmont Ave., East Wenatchee, WA 98801 (custom cases)
Merchandise Brokers, P.O. Box 491, Lilburn, GA 30247/404-923-0015 (GunSlinger portable rack)
W.A. Miller Co., Inc., (Wamco), Mingo Loop, Oguossoc, ME 04964 (wooden handgun cases)
Nortex Industrial Fan Co., 2821 Main St., Dallas TX 75226/214-748-1157 (automobile gun rack)
Paul-Reed, Inc., P.O. Box 227, Charlevoix, MI 49720
Penguin Industries, Inc., Airport Industrial Mall, Coatesville, PA 19320/215-384-6000
Precise, 3 Chestnut, Suffern, NY 10901
Protecto Plastics, Inc., 201 Alpha Rd., Wind Gap, PA 18091/215-863-6997 (carrying cases)
Provo Steel & Supply Co., P.O. Box 977, Provo, UT 84601 (steel gun cases)
Red Head Brand Corp., 4949 Joseph Hardin Dr., Dallas, TX 75236/214-333-4141
Richland Arms Co., 321 W. Adrian, Blissfield, MI 49228
Saf-T-Case Mfg. Co., Inc., P.O. Box 5472, Irving, TX 75062
San Angelo Co. Inc., Box 984, San Angelo, TX 76901
Buddy Schoellkopf, 4949 Joseph Hardin Dr., Dallas, TX 75236/214-333-2121
Se-Cur-All Cabinet Co., K-Prods., P.O. Box 2052, Michigan City, IN 46360/219-872-7957
Security Gun Chest, (See Tread Corp.)
Spitz & Blauvelt, Inc., P.O. Box 643/1100 W. South, Hastings, NE 68901/402-462-4178 (cases)
Stearns Mfg. Co., P.O. Box 1498, St. Cloud, MN 56301
Stowline Inc., 811 So. 1st Kent, WA 98031/206-852-9200 (vaults)
Tread Corp., P.O. Box 13207, 1734 Granby St. N.E., Roanoke, VA 24012 (security gun chest)
Trik Truk, P.O. Box 3760, Kent, WA 98301 (P.U. truck cases)
Weather Shield Sports Equipm. Inc., Rte. #3, Petoskey Rd., Charlevoix, MI 49720
Woodstream Corp., Box 327, Lititz, PA 17543
Yield House, Inc., RFD, No. Conway, NH 03860

CHOKE DEVICES, RECOIL ABSORBERS & RECOIL PADS

Arms Ingenuity Co., Box 1; 51 Canal St., Weatogue, CT 06089/203-658-5624 (Jet-Away)
Stan Baker, 5303 Roosevelt Way NE, Seattle, WA 98105/206-522-4575 (shotgun)
C&H Research, 115 Sunnyside Dr., Lewis, KS 67552/316-324-5445 (Mercury recoil suppressor)
Vito Cellini, P. O. Box 17792, San Antonio, TX 78217/512-826-2584
Dahl's Gun Shop, 6947 King Ave., Route 4, Billings, MT 59102/406-656-6132
Diverter Arms, Inc., P.O. Box 22084, Houston, TX 77027 (shotgun diverter)
Edwards Recoil Reducer, 269 Herbert St., Alton, IL 62002/618-462-3257
Emsco Variable Shotgun Chokes, 101 Second Ave., S.E., Waseca, MN 56093/507-835-1481
Griggs Recreational Prods. Inc., P.O. Box 324, Twin Bridges, MT 59754/406-684-5202 (recoil director)
Lyman Products Corp., Rte. 147, Middlefield, CT. 06455 (Cutts Comp.)
Mag-Na-Port Arms, Inc., 30016 S. River Rd., Mt. Clemens, MI 48043 (muzzle-brake system)
Mag-Na-Port of Canada, 1861 Burrows Ave., Winnipeg, Manitoba R2X 2V6, Canada
Poly-Choke Co., Inc., 150 Park Ave., Hartford, CT. 06108/203-289-2743
Pro-Port Canada, 1861 Burrows Ave., Winnipeg, Manitoba R2X 2V6, Canada
Pro-Port U.S.A., 30016 South River Rd., Mt. Clemens, MI 48045/313-469-7323

CHRONOGRAPHS AND PRESSURE TOOLS

B-Square Co., Box 11281, Ft. Worth, TX 76110
Custom Chronograph Co., Box 1601, Brewster, WA 98812/509-689-2004
Diverter Arms, Inc., P.O. Box 22084, Houston, TX 77027 (press. tool)
Oehler Research, P.O. Box 9135, Austin, TX 78756
Telepacific Electronics Co., Inc., P.O. Box 1329, San Marcos, CA 92069/714-744-4415
Tepeco, P.O. Box 502, Moss Point, MS 601-475-7645 (Tepeco Speed-Meter)
M. York, 5508 Griffith Rd., Gaithersburg, MD 20760/301-253-4217 (press. tool)

CLEANING & REFINISHING SUPPLIES

A 'n A Co., Box 571, King of Prussia, PA 19406 (Valet shotgun cleaner)
Armite Labs., 1845 Randolph St., Los Angeles, CA 90001/213-587-7744 (pen oiler)
Armoloy Co. of Ft. Worth, 204 E. Daggett St., Ft Worth, TX 76104/817-461-0051
Belltown, Ltd., 33 Belltown Rd., Stamford, CT 06905/203-348-0911 (gun clg. cloth kit)
Birchwood-Casey, 7900 Fuller Rd., Eden Prairie, MN 55344/612-927-7933
Bisonite Co., Inc., P.O. Box 84, Kenmore Station, Buffalo, NY 14217
Blue and Gray Prods., Inc., R.D. #6, Box 348, Wellsboro, PA 16901/717-724-1383
Break-Free, a Div. of San/Bar Corp., 9999 Muirlands Blvd., Irvine, CA 92714/714-855-9911
Jim Brobst, 299 Poplar St., Hamburg, PA 19526/215-562-2103 (J-B Bore Cleaning Compound)
GB Prods. Dept., H & R, Inc., Industrial Rowe, Gardner, MA 01440
Browning Arms, Rt. 4, Box 624-B, Arnold, MO 63010
J.M. Bucheimer Co., P.O. Box 280, Airport Rd., Frederick, MD 21701/301-662-5101
Burnishine Prod. Co., 8140 N. Ridgeway, Skokie, IL 60076 (Stock Glaze)
Call 'N, Inc., 1615 Bartlett Rd., Memphis, TN 38134/901-372-1682 (Gunskin)
Chem-Pak, Inc., Winchester, VA 22601/703-667-1341 (Gun-Savr.protect. & lubricant)

Chopie Mfg. Inc., 700 Copeland Ave., La Crosse, WI 54601/608-784-0926 (Black-Solve)
Clenzoil Co., Box 1226, Sta. C, Canton, OH 44708/216-833-9758
Clover Mfg. Co., 139 Woodward Ave., Norwalk, Ct. 06856/800-243-6492 (Clover compound)
J. Dewey Mfg. Co., 186 Skyview Dr., Southbury, CT 06488/203-264-3064 (one-piece gun clg. rod)
Diah Engineering Co., 5177 Haskell St., La Canada, CA 91011/213-625-2184 (barrel lubricant)
Dri-Slide, Inc.,Industrial Park, 1210 Locust St., Fremont, MI 49412
Forty-Five Ranch Enterpr., 119 S. Main St., Miami, OK 74354/918-542-9307
Gun-All Products, Box 244, Dowagiac, MI 49047
Frank C. Hoppe Div., Penguin Ind., Inc., Airport Industrial Mall, Coatesville, PA 19320/215-384-6000
Jet-Aer Corp., 100 Sixth Ave., Paterson, NJ 07524 (blues & oils)
Kellog's Professional Prods., Inc., P.O. Box 1201, Sandusky, OH 44870
K.W. Kleinendorst, R.D. #1, Box 113B, Hop Bottom, PA 18824/717-289-4687 (rifle clg. cables)
LPS Chemical Prods., Holt Lloyd Corp., 4647 Hugh Howell Rd., Tucker, GA 30048/404-934-7800
LEM Gun Spec., Box 31, College Park, GA 30337/404-761-9054 (Lewis Lead Remover)
Liquid Wrench, Box 10628, Charlotte, NC 28201 (pen. oil)
Lynx Line Gun Prods. Div., Protective Coatings, Inc., 20626 Fenkell Ave., Detroit, MI 48223/313-255-6032
Marble Arms Co., 420 Industrial Park, Gladstone, MI 49837/906-428-3710
Micro Sight Co., 242 Harbor Blvd., Belmont; CA 94002/415-591-0769 (bedding)
Mirror-Lube, P.O. Box 693, San Juan Capistrano, CA 92675
New Method Mfg. Co., Box 175, Bradford, PA 16701/814-262-6611 (gun blue; Minute Man gun care)
Northern Instruments, Inc., 6680 North Highway 49, Lino Lake, MN 55014 (Stor-Safe rust preventer)
Numrich Arms Co., West Hurley, NY 12491 (44-40 gun blue)
Old World Oil Products, 3827 Queen Ave. No., Minneapolis, MN 55412
Original Mink Oil, Inc., P.O. Box 20191, 10652 N.E. Holman, Portland, OR 97220/503-255-2814
Outers Laboratories, Route 2, Onalaska, WI 54650/608-783-1515 (Gunslick kits)
Radiator Spec. Co., 1400 Independence Blvd., Charlotte, NC 28201 (liquid wrench)
Reardon Prod., 103 W. Market St., Morrison, IL 61270 (Dry-Lube)
Rice Protective Gun Coatings, 235-30th St., West Palm Beach, FL 33407/305-845-2383
Rig Products, P.O. Box 1990, Sparks, NV 89432/703-331-5666
Rusteprufe Labs., Rte. 5, Sparta, WI 54656/608-269-4144
San/Bar Corp., Break-Free Div., 9999 Muirlands Blvd, Irvine, CA 92714/714-855-9911
Saunders Sptg. Gds., 338 Somerset, No. Plainfield, NJ 07060 (Sav-Bore)
Schultea's Gun String 67 Burress, Houston, TX 77022 (pocket-size rifle cleaning kit)
Schwab Industries, Inc., P.O. Box 5705, Santa Monica, CA 90405/213-395-6997 (Rust Guardit)
Service Armament, 689 Bergen Blvd., Ridgefield, NJ 07657 (Parker-Hale)
Silicote Corp., Box 359, Oshkosh, WI 54901 (Silicone cloths)
Silver Dollar Guns, P.O. Box 475, 10 Frances St., Franklin, NH 03235/603-934-3292 (Silicone oil)
Sportsmen's Labs., Inc., Box 732, Anoka, MN 55303 (Gun Life lube)
Taylor & Robbins, Box 164, Rixford, PA 16745 (Throat Saver)
Testing Systems, Inc., 220 Pegasus Ave., Northgale, NJ 07647/201-767-7300 (gun lube)
Texas Platers Supply Co., 2453 W. Five Mile Parkway, Dallas, TX 75233 (plating kit)
Totally Dependable Prods., Inc., (TDP Ind.), P.O. Box 277, Zieglerville, PA 19492/215-287-7851
Treso Inc., 120 N. Pagosa Blvd,. Pagosa Springs, CO 81147/303-264-2295 (mfg. Durango Gun Rod)
C. S. Van Gorden, 120 Tenth Ave., Eau Claire, WI 54701 (Instant Blue)
WD-40 Co., 1061 Cudahy Pl., San Diego, CA 92110
West Coast Secoa, 3915 U S Hwy 98S, Lakeland, FL 33801 (Teflon coatings)
Williams Gun Sight, 7389 Lapeer Rd., Davison, MI 48423 (finish kit)
Winslow Arms Inc., P.O. Box 783, Camden, SC 29020 (refinishing kit)
Wisconsin Platers Supply Co., (See Texas Platers Supply Co.)
Woodstream Corp., P.O. Box 327, Lititz, PA 17543 (Mask)
Zip Aerosol Prods., 21320 Deering Court, Canoga Park, CA 91304

CUSTOM GUNSMITHS

Ahlman's Inc., R.R. 1, Box 20, Morristown, MN 55052/507-685-4244
Don Allen Inc., R.R. 4, Northfield, MN 55057/507-645-9216
Amrine's Gun Shop, 937 Luna Ave., Ojai, CA 93023
Andy's Gun Shop, A. Fleury, Burke, NY 12917
Antique Arms Co., D. F. Saunders, 1110 Cleveland Ave., Monett, MO 65708/417-235-6501 (Hawken copies)
R. J. Anton, 874 Olympic Dr., Waterloo, IA 50701/319-233-3666
John & Mary Armbrust, John's Gun Shop, 823 S. Union St., Mishawaka, IN 46544/219-255-0973
Armurier Hiptmayer, P.O. Box 136, Eastman, Que. JOE 1P0, Canada/514-297-2492
Armuriers Liegeois-Artisans Reunis "ALAR," rue Masset 27, 4300 Ans, Belgium
Atkinson Gun Co., P.O. Box 512, Prescott, AZ 86301
E. von Atzigen, The Custom Shop, 890 Cochrane Crescent, Peterborough, Ont., K9H 5N3 Canada/705-742-6693
Creighton Audette, RFD 1, Box 55, Highland Circle, Springfield, VT 05156/802-885-2331
Richard W. Baber, 28 Dudley Ave., Colorado Springs, CO 80909

Bain and Davis Sptg. Gds., 599 W. Las Tunas Dr., San Gabriel, CA 91776/213-284-2264

Stan Baker, 5303 Roosevelt Way NE, Seattle, WA 98105/206-522-4575 (shotgun specialist)

Joe J. Balickie, Rte. 2, Box 56-G, Apex, NC 27502

Barta's Gunsmithing, 10231 USH, #10, Cato, WI 54206/414-732-4472

Roy L. Bauer, c/o C-D Miller Guns, St. Onge, SD 57779

George Beitzinger, Ltd., 116-20 Atlantic Ave., Richmond Hill, NY 11419/212-846-2753

Bell's Custom Shop, David Norin, 3319 Mannheim Rd., Franklin Park, IL 60131/312-678-1900 (handguns)

Bennett Gun Works, 561 Delaware Ave., Delmar, NY 12054/518-439-1862

Gordon Bess, 708 River St., Canon City, CO 81212/303-275-1073

Al Biesen, 5021 Rosewood, Spokane, WA 99208/509-328-9340

Roger Biesen, W. 2039 Sinto Ave., Spokane, WA 99201

Billingsley & Brownell, Box 25, Wyarna, WY 82845/307-737-2468 (cust. rifles)

John Bivins, Jr., 200 Wicklow Rd., Winston-Salem, NC 27106

Bob's Gun & Tackle Shop, 746 Granby St., Norfolk, VA 23510/804-627-8311

Boone Mountain Trading Post, 118 Sunrise Rd., Saint Marys, PA 15857/814-834-4879

Victor Bortugno, Atlantic & Pacific Arms Co., 4859 Virginia Beach Blvd., Virginia Beach, VA 23462

Art Bourne, (See Guncraft)

Breckheimers, Rte. 69-A, Parish, NY 13131

L. H. Brown, Brown's Rifle Ranch, 1820 Airport Rd., Kalispell, MT 59901

Lenard M. Brownell, (See Billingsley & Brownell)

E. J. Bryant, 3154 Glen St., Eureka, CA 95501

Ted Buckland, 361 Flagler Rd., Nordland, WA 98358/206-385-2142 (ML)

David Budin, Main St., Margaretville, NY 12455/914-568-4103

George Bunch, 7735 Garrison Rd., Hyattsville, MD 20784

Samuel W. Burgess, Sam's Gun Shop, 25 Squam Rd., Rockport, MA 01966/617-546-6839 (bluing repairs)

Leo Bustani, P.O. Box 8125, W. Palm Beach, FL 33407

Cache La Poudre Rifleworks, 168 No. College Ave., Ft. Collins, CO 80524/303-482-6913 (cust. ML)

Cameron's Guns, 16690 W. 11th Ave., Golden, CO 80401

Lou Camilli, 4700 Oahu Dr. N.E., Albuquerque, NM 87111/505-293-5259 (ML)

Ralph L. Carter, Carter's Gun Shop, 225 G St., Penrose, CO 81240/303-372-6240

R. MacDonald Champlin, P.O. Box 693, Manchester, NH 03105/603-622-1420 (ML rifles and pistols)

Mark Chanlynn, Bighorn Trading Co., 1704-14th St., Boulder, CO 80302

Classic Arms Corp., P.O. Box 8, Palo Alto, CA 94302/415-321-7243

Kenneth E. Clark, 18738 Highway 99, Madera, CA 93637

Combat Weapons, 1265 Balsam St., Lakewood, CO 80215 (shotgun/riot)

John Corry, P.O. Box 109, Deerfield, IL 60015/312-541-6250 (U.S. agent for Frank E. Malin & Son)

The Country Gun Shoppe Ltd., 251 N. Front St., Monument, CO 80132

Raymond A. Cover, Rt. 1, Box 101A, Mineral Point, MO 63660/314-749-3783

Crest Carving Co., 14849 Dillow St., Westminster, CA 92683

Crocker, 1510 - 42nd St., Los Alamos, NM 87544 (rifles)

J. Lynn Crook, Rt. 7, Box 119-A, Lebanon, TN 37087/615-449-1930

Philip R. Crouthamel, 513 E. Baltimore, E. Lansdowne, PA 19050/215-623-5685

Curt Crum, c/o Dave Miller, 3131 E. Greenlee Rd., Tucson, AZ 85716/602-326-3117

Jim Cuthbert, 715 S. 5th St., Coos Bay, OR 97420

Dahl's Custom Stocks, Rt. 4, Box 558, Schofield Rd., Lake Geneva, WI 53147/414-248-2464

Dahl's Gunshop, 6947 King Ave., Route 4, Billings, MT 59102/406-656-6132

Homer L. Dangler, Box 254, Addison, MI 49220/517-547-6745 (Kentucky rifles)

Jack Dever, 8520 N.W. 90, Oklahoma City, OK 73132/405-721-6393

R. H. Devereaux, The Custom Gunsmith, 475 Trucky St., St. Igance, MI 49781/906-643-8625

Dominic DiStefano, 4303 Friar Lane, Colorado Springs, CO 80907

Dixon Muzzleloading Shop, Inc., RD #1, Box 175, Kempton, PA 19529/215-756-6271 (ML)

William Dixon, 230 S. Canyon Rd., Rapid City, SD 57701/605-341-4428

Bill Dowtin, P.O. Box 72, Celina, TX 75009

Charles Duffy, Williams Lane, W. Hurley, NY 12491

David R. Dunlop, Rte. 1, Box 199, Rolla, ND 58367

D. W. Firearms, D. Wayne Schlumbaum, 1821 - 200th S.W., Alderwood Manor, WA 98036

John H. Eaton, 8516 James St., Upper Marlboro, MD 20870

Jere Eggleston, P.O. Box 50238, Columbia, SC 29250/803-799-3402

Elko Arms, Dr. L. Kortz, 28 rue Ecole Moderne, B-7400 Soignies, H.T., Belgium

Bob Emmons, 238 Robson Rd., Grafton, OH 44044/216-458-5890

Bill English, 4411 S.W. 100th, Seattle, WA 98146/206-932-7345

Armas ERBI, S. coop., Avda. Eulogio Estarta, Elgoibar (Guipuzcoa), Spain

Ken Eyster, Heritage Gunsmiths Inc., 6441 Bishop Rd., Centerburg, OH 43011/614-625-6131

N. B. Fashingbauer, P.O. Box 366, Lac Du Flambeau, WI 54538/715-588-7116

Andy Fautheree, P.O. Box 863, Pagosa Springs, CO 81147/303-264-2295 (cust. ML)

Ted Fellowes, Beaver Lodge, 9245-16th Ave., S.W., Seattle, WA 98106/206-763-1698 (muzzleloaders)

Jack First Distributors Inc., 44633 Sierra Highway, Lancaster, CA 93534/805-945-6981

Fischer Sports Center, 221 E. Washington, Ann Arbor, MI 48104/313-769-4166

Marshall F. Fish, Rt. 22 North, Westport, NY 12993

Jerry A. Fisher, 1244-4th Ave. West, Kalispell, MT 59901/406-755-7093

Flynn's Cust. Guns, P.O. Box 7461, Alexandria, LA 71306/318-445-7130

John Fordham, Box 9 Dial Star Rt., P.O. Box 1093, Blue Ridge, GA 30513/404-632-3602

Larry L. Forster, Box 212, Gwinner, ND 58040/701-678-2475

Jay Frazier, S.R. Box 8644, Bird Creek, AK 99540/903-653-8302

Freeland's Scope Stands, 3737—14th Ave., Rock Island, IL 61201/309-788-7449

Fredrick Gun Shop, 10 Elson Drive, Riverside, RI 02915/401-433-2805

R. L. Freshour, P.O. Box 2837, Texas City, TX 77590

Frontier Arms, Inc., 420 E. Riding Club Rd., Cheyenne, WY 82001

Frontier Shop & Gallery, The Depot, Main St., (Box 1805), Riverton, WY 82501/307-856-4498

Fuller Gunshop, Cooper Landing, AK 99572

Karl J. Furr, 76 East 350 No., Orem, UT 84057/801-225-2603

Garcia Natl. Gun Traders, Inc., 225 S.W. 22nd Ave., Miami, FL 33135

Gentry's, The Bozeman Gunsmith, 218 No. 7th, Bozeman, MT 59715/406-586-1405 (cust. Montana Mtn. Rifle)

Gentry's Gun Shop, 314 N. Hoffman, Belgarde, MT 59715

Edwin Gillman, R.R. 6, Box 195, Hanover, PA 17331/717-632-1662

Dale Goens, Box 224, Cedar Crest, NM 87008

A. R. Goode, 12845 Catoctin Furnace Rd., Thurmont, MD 21788/301-271-2228

Goodling's Gunsmithing, R.D. #1, Box 1097, Spring Grove, PA 17362/717-225-3350

Gordie's Gun Shop, Gordon Mulholland, 1401 Fulton St., Streator, IL 61364/815-672-7202

Charles E. Grace, 10144 Elk Lake Rd., Williamsburg, MI 49690/616-264-9483

Roger M. Green, 315 S. 2nd St., P.O. Box 984, Glenrock, WY 82637/307-436-9804

Griffin & Howe, 589 Broadway, New York, NY 10012

H. L. "Pete" Grisel, 61912 Skyline View Dr., Bend, OR 97701/503-389-2649 (rifles)

Karl Guenther, 43-32 160th St., Flushing, NY 11372/212-461-7325

Gun City, 504 Main Ave., Bismarck, ND 58501

Guncraft, Inc., 117 W. Pipeline, Hurst, TX 76053/817-268-2887

Guncraft (Kamloops) Ltd., 127 Victoria St., Kamloops, B.C. V2C 1Z4, Canada/604-374-2151

Guncraft (Kelowna) Ltd., 1771 Harvey Ave., Kelowna, B.C. V1Y 6G4, Canada/604-860-8977

The Gunshop, R.D. Wallace, 320 Overland Rd., Prescott, AZ 86301

H & R Custom Gun Serv., 68 Passaic Dr., Hewitt, NJ 07421

H-S Precision, Inc., 112 N. Summit, Prescott, AZ 85302/602-445-0607

Paul Haberly, 2364 N. Neva, Chicago, IL 60635/312-889-1114

Martin Hagn, Herzogstandweg 41, 8113 Kochel a. See, W. Germany (s.s. actions & rifles)

Chas. E. Hammans, Box 788, Stuttgart, AR 72160

Harkrader's Cust. Gun Shop, 825 Radford St., Christiansburg, VA 24073

Harp's Gun Repair Shop, 3349 Pio-Nono Circle, Macon, GA 31206 (cust. rifles)

Rob't W. Hart & Son Inc., 401 Montgomery St., Nescopeck, PA 18635/717-752-3481 (actions, stocks)

Hal Hartley, 147 Blairs Fork Rd., Lenoir, NC 28645

Hartmann & Weiss KG, Rahlstedter Str. 139, 2000 Hamburg 73, W. Germany

Hubert J. Hecht, Waffen-Hecht, 724-K St., Sacramento, CA 95814/916-448-1177

Edw. O. Hefti, 300 Fairview, College Station, TX 77840/715-846-4959

Iver Henriksen, 1211 So. 2nd St. W., Missoula, MT 59801

Wm. Hobaugh, Box M, Philipsburg, MT 59858/406-859-3515

Richard Hodgson, 5589 Arapahoe, Unit 104, Boulder, CO 80301

George Hoenig, 6521 Morton Dr., Boise, ID 83705/208-375-1116

Dick Holland, 422 N.E. 6th St., Newport, OR 97365/503-265-7556

Hollingsworth's Guns, Route 1, Box 55B, Alvaton, KY 42122/502-842-3580

Hollis Gun Shop, 917 Rex St., Carlsbad, NM 88220/505-835-3782

Bill Holmes, Rt. 2, Box 242, Fayetteville, AR 72701/501-521-8958

Huntington's, P.O. Box 991, Oroville, CA 95965

Hyper-Single Precision SS Rifles, 520 E. Beaver, Jenks, OK 74037/918-299-2391

Independent Machine & Gun Shop, 1416 N. Hayes, Pocatello, ID 83201

Paul Jaeger, Inc. 211 Leedom St., Jenkintown, PA 19046/215-884-6920

J. J. Jenkins Ent. Inc., 375 Pine Ave. No. 25, Goleta, CA 93017/805-967-1366

Jerry's Gun Shop, 9220 Ogden Ave., Brookfield, IL 60513/312-485-5200

Neal G. Johnson, 111 Marvin Dr., Hampton, VA 23666/804-838-8091

Peter S. Johnson, The Orvis Co., Inc., Manchester, VT 05254/802-362-3622

Bruce Jones, 389 Calla Ave., Imperial Beach, CA 92032

Joseph & Associates, 4810 Riverbend Rd., Boulder, CO 80301/303-332-6720

Jos. Jurjevic, Gunshop, 605 Main St., Marble Falls, TX 78654/512-693-3012

John Kaufield Small Arms Eng. Co., 7698 Garden Prairie Rd., Garden Prairie, IL 61038/815-597-3981 (restorations)

Ken's Gun Specialties, K. Hunnell, Box 241, Lakeview, AR 72642/501-431-5606

Kennedy Gun Shop, Rte. 12, Box 21, Clarksville, TN 37040/615-647-6043

Monty Kennedy, P.O. Box 214, Kalispell, MT 59901/406-857-3596

Kennon's Custom Rifles, 5408 Biffle, Stone Mtn., GA 30083/404-469-9339

Stanley Kenvin, 5 Lakeville Lane, Plainview, NY 11803/516-931-0321

Kesselring Gun Shop, 400 Pacific Hiway No., Burlington, WA 98233/206-724-3113

Don Klein Custom Guns, P.O. Box 277, Camp Douglas, WI 54618/608-427-6948

K. W. Kleinendorst, R.D. #1, Box 113B, Hop Bottom, PA 18824/717-289-4687

Terry K. Kopp, Highway 13, Lexington, MO 64067/816-259-2636

J. Korzinek, R.D. #2, Box 73, Canton, PA 17724/717-673-8512 (riflesmith) (broch. $1.50)

L & W Casting Co., 5014 Freeman Rd. E., Puyallup, WA 98371

Sam Lair, 520 E. Beaver, Jenks, OK 74037/918-299-2391 (single shots)

Maynard Lambert, Kamas, UT 84036

Harry Lawson Co., 3328 N. Richey Blvd., Tucson, AZ 85716/602-326-1117

John G. Lawson, (The Sight Shop), 1802 E. Columbia, Tacoma, WA 98404/206-474-5465

Mark Lee, 2333 Emerson Ave., N., Minneapolis, MN 55411/612-938-4540

Bill Leeper, (See Guncraft)

Art LeFeuvre, 1003 Hazel Ave., Deerfield, IL 60015/312-945-0073

LeFever Arms Co. Inc., R.D. #1, Box 31, Lee Center, NY 13363/315-337-6722

Leland Firearms Co., 13 Mountain Ave., Llewellyn Park, West Orange, NJ 07052/201-964-7500 (shotguns)

Lenz Firearms Co., 310 River Rd., Eugene, OR 97404/503-689-6900

Al Lind, 7821—76th Ave. S.W., Tacoma, WA 98498/206-584-6363

Max J. Lindauer, R.R. 2, Box 27, Washington, MO 63090

Robt. L. Lindsay, J & B Enterprises, 9416 Emory Grove Rd., Gaithersburg, MD 20760/301-948-2941 (services only)

Ljutic Ind., Box 2117, Yakima, WA 98904 (shotguns)

Llanerch Gun Shop, 2800 Township Line, Upper Darby, PA 19082/215-789-5462

James W. Lofland, 2275 Larkin Rd., Boothwyn, PA 19061/215-485-0391 (SS rifles)

London Guns, 1528—20th St., Santa Monica, CA 90404/213-828-8486

McCann's Muzzle-Gun Works, Tom McCann, 200 Federal City Rd., Pennington, NJ 08354/609-737-1070 (ML)

McCormick's Gun Bluing Service, 609 N.E. 104th Ave., Vancouver, WA 98664/206-256-0579

Bill McGuire, 1600 N. Eastmont Ave., East Wenatchee, WA 98801

R. J. Maberry, 511 So. K, Midland, TX 79701

Harold E. MacFarland, Route #4, Box 1249, Cottonwood, AZ 86326/602-634-5320

Frank E. Malin & Son (See John Corry)

Monte Mandarino, 136 Fifth Ave. West, Kalispell, MT 59901/406-257-6208 (Penn. rifles)

Lowell Manley, 3684 Pine St., Deckerville, MI 48427/313-376-3665

Dale Marfell, 107 N. State St., Litchfield, IL 62056/217-327-3832

Marquart Precision Co., P.O. Box 1740, Prescott, AZ 86302/602-445-5646

Marsh Al's, Rt. #3, Box 729, Preston, ID 83263/208-852-2437

Elwyn H. Martin, Martin's Gun Shop, 937 S. Sheridan Blvd., Lakewood, CO 80226/303-922-2184

Mashburn Arms Co., 1218 N. Pennsylvania, Oklahoma City, OK 73107/405-236-5151 (special orders only)

Seely Masker, Custom Rifles, 261 Washington Ave., Pleasantville, NY 10570/914-769-2627

Geo. E. Matthews & Son Inc., 10224 S. Paramount Blvd., Downey, CA 90241

Maurer Manchester Arms, Inc., 6858 Manchester Rd., Clinton, OH 44216/216-882-3133 (muzzleloaders)

John E. Maxson, Box 332, Dumas, TX 79029/806-935-5990 (high grade rifles)

Eric Meitzner, c/o Don Allen, Inc., Rt. 1, Timberlane, Northfield, MN 55057/507-645-9216

Miller Custom Rifles, 655 Dutton Ave., San Leandro, CA 94577/415-568-2447

Miller Gun Works, S. A. Miller, P.O. Box 7326, Tamuning, Guam 96911

C-D Miller Guns, Purl St., Box 260, St. Onge, SD 57779/605-578-1790

David Miller Co., 3131 E. Greenlee Rd., Tucson, AZ 85716/602-326-3117 (classic rifles)

Earl Milliron, 1249 N.E. 166th Ave., Portland, OR 97230/503-252-3725

Wm. Larkin Moore & Co., 31360 Via Colinas, Suite 109, Westlake Village, CA 91360/213-889-4160

Mountain Bear Rifle Works, Inc., Wm. Scott Bickett, 100-B Ruritan Rd., Sterling, VA 22170/703-430-0420

Larry Mrock, R.F.D. 3, Box 207, Woodhill-Hooksett Rd., Bow, NH 03301/603-224-4096 (broch. $3)

Clayton N. Nelson, R.R. #3, Box 119, Enid, OK 73701

Newman Gunshop, 119 Miller Rd., Agency, IA 52530/515-937-5775

Ted Nicklas, 5504 Hegel Rd., Goodrich, MI 48438/313-797-4493

William J. Nittler, 290 More Drive, Boulder Creek, CA 95006/408-338-3376 (shotgun repairs)

Jim Norman, Custom Gunstocks, 11230 Calenda Rd., San Diego, CA 92127/714-487-4173

Nu-Line Guns, 1053 Caulkshill Rd., Harvester, MO 63303/314-441-4500

O'Brien Rifle Co., 324 Tropicana No. 128, Las Vegas, NV 89109/702-736-6082 (17-cal. Rifles)

Vic Olson, 5002 Countryside Dr., Imperial, MO 63052/314-296-8086

The Orvis Co., Inc., Peter S. Johnson, Manchester, VT 05254/802-362-3622

Maurice Ottmar, Box 657, 113 East Fir, Coulee City, WA 99115/509-632-5717

Pachmayr Gun Works, 1220 S. Grand Ave., Los Angeles, CA 90015

Paterson Gunsmithing, 438 Main St., Paterson, NJ 07501/201-345-4100

C. R. Pedersen & Son, 2717 S. Pere Marquette, Ludington, MI 49431/616-843-2061

John Pell, 410 College Ave., Trinidad, CO 81082

A. W. Peterson Gun Shop, 1693 Old Hwy. 441, Mt. Dora, FL 32757 (ML rifles, also)

Eugene T. Plante, Gene's Custom Guns, 3890 Hill Ave., P.O. Box 8534, White Bear Lake, MN 55110/612-429-5105

R. Neal Rice, 5152 Newton, Denver, CO 80221

Ridge Guncraft, Inc., 125 E. Tyrone Rd., Oak Ridge, TN 37830/615-483-4024

Rifle Ranch, Jim Wilkinson, Rte. 5, Prescott, AZ 86301/602-445-5640

Rifle Shop, Box M, Philipsburg, MT 59858

Wm. A. Roberts II, Rte. 4, Box 34, Athens, AL 35611 (ML)

Carl Roth, 4728 Pine Ridge Ave., Cheyenne, WY 82001/307-634-3958 (rust bluing)

Royal Arms, 1210 Bert Acosta, El Cajon, CA 92020/714-448-5466

R.P.S. Gunshop, 11 So. Haskell, Central Point, OR 97502/503-664-5010

Murray F. Ruffino, c/o Neal G. Johnson, 111 Marvin Dr., Hampton, VA 23666/804-838-8091

Rush's Old Colonial Forge, 106 Wiltshire Rd., Baltimore, MD 21221 (Ky.-Pa. rifles)

Russell's Rifle Shop, Route 5, Box 92, Georgetown, TX 78626/512-778-5338 (gunsmith services)

Lewis B. Sanchez, Cumberland Knife & Gun Works, 5661 Bragg Blvd., Fayetteville, NC 28303

Sanders Custom Gun Serv., 2358 Tyler Lane, Louisville, KY 40205

Sandy's Custom Gunshop, Rte. #1, Box 20, Rockport, IL 62370/217-437-4241

Saratoga Arms Co., 1752 N. Pleasantview Rd., Pottstown, PA 19464/215-323-8326

Roy V. Schaefer, 965 W. Hilliard Lane, Eugene, OR 97404/503-688-4333

N. H. Schiffman Cust. Gun Serv., 963 Malibu, Pocatello, ID 83201

SGW, Inc. (formerly Schuetzen Gun Works), 624 Old Pacific Hwy. S.E., Olympia, WA 98503/206-456-3471

Schumaker's Gun Shop, Rte. 4, Box 500, Colville, WA 99114/509-684-4848

Schwartz Custom Guns, 9621 Coleman Rd., Haslett, MI 48840/517-339-8939

Schwarz's Gun Shop, 41-15th St., Wellsburg, WV 26070/304-737-0533

Shane's Gunsmithing, 321 Hwy. 51 So., Minocqua, WI 54548/715-356-9631

Shaw's, Finest in Guns, 9447 W. Lilac Rd., Escondito, CA 92025/714-728-7070

Shell Shack, 113 E. Main, Laurel, MT 59044

George H. Sheldon, P.O. Box 489, Franklin, NH 03235 (45 autos & M-1 carbines only)

Lynn Shelton Custom Rifles, P.O. Box 681, Elk City, OK 73644

Shilen Rifles, Inc., 205 Metropark Blvd., Ennis, TX 75119/214-875-5318

Harold H. Shockley, 204 E. Farmington Rd., Hanna City, IL 61536/309-565-4524 (hot bluing & plating)

Shootin' Shop, Inc., 1169 Harlow Rd., Springfield, OR 97477/503-747-0175

Walter Shultz, 1752 N. Pleasantview Rd., Pottstown, PA 19464

Silver Dollar Guns, P.O. Box 475, 10 Frances St., Franklin, NH 03235/603-934-3292 (45 autos & M-1 carbines only)

Simmons Gun Spec., 700 Rogers Rd., Olathe, KS 66061

Simms Hardware Co., 2801 J St., Sacramento, CA 95816/916-442-3800

Sklany's Shop, 566 Birch Grove Dr., Kalispell, MT 59901/406-755-4527 (Ferguson rifle)

Markus Skosples, c/o Ziffren Sptg. Gds., 124 E. Third St., Davenport, IA 52801

Jerome F. Slezak, 1290 Marlowe, Lakewood (Cleveland), OH 44107/216-221-1668

Small Arms Eng., 7698 Garden Prairie Rd., Garden Prairie, IL 61038/815-597-3981 (restorations)

John Smith, 912 Lincoln, Carpentersville, IL 60110

Snapp's Gunshop, 6911 E. Washington Rd., Clare, MI 48617/517-386-9226

Southern Penna. Sporting Goods Center, R.D. No. 1, Spring Grove, PA 17362/717-225-5908

Fred D. Speiser, 2229 Dearborn, Missoula, MT 59801/406-549-8133

Sport Service Center, 2364 N. Neva, Chicago, IL 60635

Sportsman's Bailiwick, 5306 Broadway, San Santonio, TX 78209/512-824-9649

Sportsmen's Equip. Co., 915 W. Washington, San Diego, CA 92103/714-296-1501

Sportsmen's Exchange & Western Gun Traders, Inc., P.O. Box 111, 560 S. "C" St., Oxnard, CA 93030/805-483-1917

Jess L. Stark, 12051 Stroud, Houston, TX 77072

Ken Starnes, Rt. 1, Box 89-C, Scorggins, TX 75480/214-365-2566

Keith Stegall, Box 696, Gunnison, CO 81230

Victor W. Strawbridge, 6 Pineview Dr., Dover Point, Dover, NH 03820/603-742-0013

W. C. Strutz, Rifle Barrels, Inc., P.O. Box 611, Eagle River, WI 54521/715-479-4766

Suter's House of Guns, 332 N. Tejon, Colorado Springs, CO 80902

A. D. Swenson's 45 Shop, P.O. Box 606, Fallbrook, CA 92028

T-P Shop, 212 E. Houghton, West Branch, MI 48661

Tag Gun Works, 236 Main, Springfield, OR 97477/503-741-4118 (ML)

Talmage Ent., 43197 E. Whittier, Hemet, CA 92343

Taylor & Robbins, Box 164, Rixford, PA 16745

James A. Tertin, c/o Gander Mountain, P.O. Box 128 - Hwy. W, Wilmot, WI 53152/414-862-2331

Larry R. Thompson, Larry's Gun Shop, 440 E. Lake Ave., Watsonville, CA 95076/408-724-5328

Gordon A. Tibbitts, 1378 Lakewood Circle, Salt Lake City, UT 84117/801-272-4126

Daniel Titus, 872 Penn St., Bryn Mawr, PA 19010/215-525-8829

Tom's Gunshop, 4435 Central, Hot Springs, AR 71901

Todd Trefts, 1290 Story Mill Rd., Bozeman, MT 59715/406-586-6003

Trinko's Gun Serv., 1406 E. Main, Watertown, WI 53094

Herb G. Troester's Accurizing Serv., 2292 W. 1000 North, Vernal, UT 84078/801-789-2158

Dennis A. "Doc" Ulrich, 2511 S. 57th Ave., Cicero, IL 60650

Brent Umberger, Sportsman's Haven, R.R. 4, Cambridge, OH 43725

Upper Missouri Trading Co., Inc., Box 181, Crofton, MO 68730

Chas. VanDyke Gunsmith Service, 201 Gatewood Cir. W., Burleson, TX 76028/817-295-7373 (shotgun & recoil pad specialist)

Milton Van Epps, Rt. 69-A, Parish, NY 13131/313-625-7498

J. W. Van Patten, Box 145, Foster Hill, Milford, PA 18337

Vic's Gun Refinishing, 6 Pineview Dr., Dover, NH 03820/603-742-0013

Walker Arms Co., Rt. 2, Box 73, Selma, AL 36701

Walker Arms Co., 127 N. Main St., Joplin, MO 64801

R. D. Wallace, 320 Overland Rd., Prescott, AZ 86301/602-445-0568

R. A. Wardrop, Box 245, 409 E. Marble St., Mechanicsburg, PA 17055

Weatherby's, 2781 Firestone Blvd., South Gate, CA 90280/213-569-7186

Weaver Arms Co., P.O. Box 8, Dexter, MO 63841/314-624-3218 (ambidextrous bolt action)

Terry Werth, 1203 Woodlawn Rd., Lincoln, IL 62656/217-732-3870

Jerry Wetherbee, 63470 Hamehook Rd., Bend, OR 97701/503-389-6080 (ML)

Cecil Weems, Box 657, Mineral Wells, TX 76067

Wells Sport Store, 110 N. Summit St., Prescott, AZ 86301

R. A. Wells, 3452 N. 1st, Racine, WI 53402

Robert G. West, 27211 Huey Lane, Eugene, OR 97402/503-689-6610

Western Gunstocks Mfg. Co., 550 Valencia School Rd., Aptos, CA 95003

Duane Wiebe, P.O. Box 497 Lotus, CA 95651/916-626-6240

M. Wiest & Son, 125 E. Tyrone Rd., Oak Ridge, TN 37830/615-483-4024

Dave Wills, 2776 Brevard Ave., Montgomery, AL 36109/205-272-8446

Williams Gun Sight Co., 7389 Lapeer Rd., Davison, MI 48423

Bob Williams, P.O. Box 143, Boonsboro, MD 21713

Williamson-Pate Gunsmith Service, 117 W. Pipeline, Hurst, TX 76053/817-268-2887

Thomas E. Wilson, 644 Spruce St., Boulder, CO 80302 (restorations)

Robert M. Winter, Box 484, Menno, SD 57045

Stan Wright, Billings Gunsmiths Inc., 421 St. Johns Ave., Billings, MT 59101/406-245-3337

J. David Yale, Ltd., 2618 Conowingo Rd., Bel Air, MD 21014/301-838-9479 (ML work)

Mike Yee, 4700-46th Ave. S.W., Seattle, WA 98116/206-935-3682
York County Gun Works, RR 4, Tottenham, Ont., LOG 1WO Canada (muzzle-loaders)
Russ Zeeryp, 1601 Foard Dr., Lynn Ross Manor, Morristown, TN 37814
John G. Zimmerman, 60273 N.W. 31st Ave., Ft. Lauderdale, FL 33309

CUSTOM METALSMITHS

Ted Blackburn, 85 E., 700 South, Springville, UT 84663/801-489-7341 (precision metalwork; steel trigger guard)
Gregg Boeke, 1812 Coolidge Ct., Northfield, MN 55057/507-645-6346
Tom Burgess, 180 McMannamy Draw, Kalispell, MT 59901/406-755-4110
Dave Cook, c/o Marble Arms Corp., 420 Industrial Park, Gladstone, MI 49837/906-425-2841
John H. Eaton, 8516 James St., Upper Marlboro, MD 20870
Phil Fischer, 2625 N.E. Multnomah, Portland, OR 97232/503-282-7151
Geo. M. Fullmer, 2499 Mavis St., Oakland, CA 94601/415-533-4193 (precise chambering—300 cals.)
Harkrader's Custom Gun Shop, 825 Radford St., Christiansburg, VA 24073
Huntington's, P.O. Box 991, Oroville, CA 95965
Paul Jaeger, Inc., 211 Leedom St., Jenkintown, PA 19046/215-884-6920
Ken Jantz, Rt. 1, Sulphur, OK 73086/405-622-3790
Terry K. Kopp, Highway 13, Lexington, MO 64067/816-259-2083
R. H. Lampert, Rt. 1, Box 61, Guthrie, MN 56451/218-854-7345
Mark Lee, 2333 Emerson Ave., N., Minneapolis, MN 55411/612-938-4540
Dave Talley, Rte. 10, Box 249-B, Easley, SC 29640/803-295-2012
John Vest, 6715 Shasta Way, Klamath Falls, OR 97601/503-884-5585
Herman Waldron, Box 475, Pomeroy, WA 99347
Edward S. Welty, R.D. 2, Box 25, Cheswick, PA 15024
Terry Werth, 1203 Woodlawn Rd., Lincoln, IL 62656/217-732-3870
Dick Willis, 141 Shady Creek Rd., Rochester, NY 14623

DECOYS

Carry-Lite, Inc., 5203 W. Clinton Ave., Milwaukee, WI 53223
Custom Purveyors, P.O. Box 886, Fort Lee, NJ 07024
Deeks, Inc., P.O. Box 2309, Salt Lake City, UT 84114
Flambeau Plastics Corp., P.O. Box 97, Middlefield, OH 44062/216-632-1631
G & H Decoy Mfg. Co., P.O. Box 937, Henryetta, OK 74437
Penn's Woods Products, Inc., 19 W. Pittsburgh St., Delmont, PA 15626/412-468-8311
Sports Haven Inc., P.O. Box 88231, Seattle, WA 98188
Tex Wirtz Ent., Inc., 1925 Hubbard St., Chicago, IL 60622
Woodstream Corp., P.O. Box 327, Lititz, PA 17543

ENGRAVERS, ENGRAVING TOOLS

Abominable Engineering, P.O. Box 1904, Flagstaff, AZ 86002/602-779-3025
John J. Adams, 47 Brown Ave., Mansfield, MA 02048/617-339-4613
Aurum Etchings, P.O. Box 401059, Garland, TX 75040/214-276-8551 (acid engraving)
Paolo Barbetti, c/o Stan's Gunshop, 53103 Roosevelt Way N.E., Seattle, WA 98105/206-522-4575
Billy R. Bates, 2905 Lynnwood Circle, Decatur, AL 35603/205-355-3690
Joseph C. Bayer, 439 Sunset Ave., Sunset Hill Griggstown, RD 1, Princeton, NJ 08540/201-359-7283
Angelo Bee, 10703 Irondale Ave., Chatsworth, CA 91311/213-882-1567
Sid Bell Originals, R.D. 2, Tully, NY 13159
Weldon Bledsoe, 6812 Park Place Dr., Fort Worth, TX 76118/817-589-1704
Carl Bleile, Box 11285, Cincinnati, OH 45211/513-662-0802
C. Roger Bleile, Box 5112, Cincinnati, OH 45205/513-251-0249
Erich Boessler, Am Vogeltal 3, 8732 Münnerstadt, W. Germany
Henry "Hank" Bonham, 218 Franklin Ave., Seaside Heights, NJ 08751
D. Boone Trading Co., 7218 S. Alaska, Tacoma, WA 98408/206-474-5046 (ivory, scrimshaw tools)
Bryan Bridges, 6350 E. Paseo San Andres, Tucson, AZ 85710
Burgess Vibrocrafters (BVI), Rt. 83, Grayslake, IL 60030
Byron Burgess, 1941 Nancy, Los Osos, CA 93402/805-528-3349
Winston Churchill, Twenty Mile Stream Rd., RFD Box 29B, Proctorsville, VT 05153/802-226-7772
Crocker Engraving, 1510 - 42nd St., Los Alamos, NM 87544
W. Daniel Cullity, 209 Old County Rd., East Sandwich, MA 02537/617-888-1147
Art A. Darakis, RD #2, Box 165D, Fredericksburg, OH 44627/216-695-4271
Tim Davis, 230 S. Main St., Eldorado, OH 45321
James R. DeMunck, 3012 English Rd., Rochester, NY 14616
Gerald R. Desquesnes, P.O. Box 884, Paris, TX 75460
M. W. Dubber, 3107 E. Mulberry, Evansville, IN 47714/812-476-4036
Ernest Dumoulin-Deleye, 8 rue Florent Boclinville, 4410 Herstal (Vottem), Belgium
Henri Dumoulin & Fils, rue du Tilleul 16, B-4411 Liege, Belgium
Ken Eyster, Heritage Gunsmiths Inc., 6441 Bishop Rd., Centerburg, OH 43011/614-625-6131
John Fanzoi, P.O. Box 25, Ferlach, Austria 9170
Jacqueline Favre, 3111 So. Valley View Blvd., Suite B-214, Las Vegas, NV 89102/702-876-6278
Armi FERLIB, 46 Via Costa, 25063 Gardone V.T. (Brescia), Italy
L. R. Fliger, 3616 78th Ave. N., Brooklyn Park, MN 55443/612-566-3808
Heinrich H. Frank, 210 Meadow Rd., Whitefish, MT 59937/406-862-2681
Leonard Francolini, P.O. Box 32, West Granby, CT 06090/203-651-9422
J. R. French, 2633 Quail Valley, Irving TX 75060
GRS Corp., P.O. Box 748, Emporia, KS 66801/316-343-1084 (Gravermeister tool)
Donald Glaser, 1520 West St., Emporia, KS 66801
Eric Gold, Box 1904, Flagstaff, AZ 86002

Daniel Goodwin, P.O. Box 1619, Kalispell, MT 59901/406-752-1116
Howard V. Grant, P.O. Box 396, Lac Du Flambeau, WI 54538
Griffin & Howe, 589 Broadway, New York, NY 10012
The Gunshop, R. D. Wallace, 320 Overland Rd., Prescott, AZ 86301/602-445-0568
F. R. Gurney Engraving Method Ltd., #2301, 9925 Jasper Ave., Edmonton, Alberta, Canada T5J 2X4/403-426-7474
Bryson J. Gwinnell, 32 Lincoln St., Hartford, CT 06106/203-278-9879
Hand Engravers Supply Co., P.O. Box 3001, Overlook Branch, Dayton, OH 45431/513-426-6762
Frank E. Hendricks, Inc., Rt. 2, Box 189J, San Antonio, TX 78229/512-696-2876
Neil Hermsen, 505 Pepperidge Rd., Lewisville, NC 27023/919-945-9304
Heidemarie Hiptmayer, R.R. 112, #760, P.O. Box 136, Eastman, Que. J0E 1P0, Canada/514-297-2492
Ken Hunt, c/o Hunting World, Inc., 16 E. 53rd St., New York, NY 10022/212-755-3400
Ken Hurst/Firearms Engraving Co., Suite 200, Krise Building, Lynchburg, VA 24504/804-847-0636
Ralph W. Ingle, #4 Missing Link, Rossville, GA 30741/404-866-5589 (color broch. $3)
Paul Jaeger, Inc., 211 Leedom, Jenkintown, PA 19046/215-884-6920
Bill Johns, 1113 Nightingale, McAllen, TX 78501/512-682-2971
Ann C. Jordan, 733 Santa Lucia, Los Osos, CA 93402/805-528-7398 (scrimshaw)
Steven Kamyk, 19 Wilder Ter., West Springfield, MA 01089/413-788-6200
T. J. Kaye, P.O. Box 4, Telegraph, TX 76883
Lance Kelly, 1824 Royal Palm Dr., Edgewater, FL 32032/904-423-4933
Jim Kelso, Rt. 1, Box 950, Worcester, VT 05682/802-229-4254
Kleinguenther's, P.O. Box 1261, Seguin, TX 78155
E. J. Koevenig, Engraving Service, P.O. Box 55, Hill City, SD 57745/605-574-2239
John Kudlas, 622-14th St. S.E., Rochester, MN 55901/507-288-5579
Ben Lane, Jr., 2118 Lipscomb St., Amarillo, TX 79109/806-372-3771
Beth Lane, Pontiac Gun Co., 815 N. Ladd, Pontiac, IL 61764/815-842-2402
Herb Larsen, 35276 Rockwell Dr., Abbotsford, B.C. V2S 4N4, Canada/604-853-5151
Terry Lazette, R.D. 5, Box 142, Millersburg, OH 44654/216-893-2181
W. Neal Lewis, 9 Bowers Dr., Newnan, GA 30263/404-251-3045
Frank Lindsay, 1326 Tenth Ave., Holdrege, NE 68949/308-995-4623
Steve Lindsay, P.O. Box 1413, Kearney, NE 68847/308-236-7885
London Guns, 1528-20th St., Santa Monica, CA 90404/213-828-8486
Ed. J. Machu, Jr., Sportsman's Bailiwick, 5306 Broadway, San Antonio, TX 78209
Lynton S.M. McKenzie, 6940 N. Alvernon Way, Tucson, AZ 85718/602-299-5090
Wm. H. Mains, 3111 S. Valley View Blvd., Suite B-214, Las Vegas, NV 89102/702-876-6278
Robert E. Maki, P.O. Box 947, Northbrook, IL 60062/312-724-8238
Rudy Marek, Rt. 1, Box 1A, Banks, OR 97106
S. A. Miller, Miller Gun Works, P.O. Box 7326, Tamuning, Guam 96911
Frank Mittermeier, 3577 E. Tremont Ave., New York, NY 10465
Gary K. Nelson, 975 Terrace Dr., Oakdale, CA 95361/209-847-4590
NgraveR Co., 879 Raymond Hill Rd., Oakdale, CT 06370/203-848-8031 (engr. tool)
New Orleans Jewelers Supply, 206 Chartres St., New Orleans, LA 70130/504-523-3839 (engr. tool)
Hans Obiltschnig, 12. November St. 7, 9170 Ferlach, Austria
Oker's Engraving, 365 Bell Rd., Bellfort Mtn. Hts., P.O. Box 126, Shawnee, CO 80475/303-838-6042
Gale Overbey, 612 Azalea Ave., Richmond, VA 23227
Pachmayr Gun Works, Inc., 1220 S. Grand Ave., Los Angeles, CA 90015/213-748-7271
Rex Pedersen, C. R. Pedersen & Son, 2717 S. Pere Marquette, Ludington, MI 49431/616-843-2061
Marcello Pedini, 5 No. Jefferson Ave., Catskill, NY 12414/518-943-5257
Arthur Pitetti, Hawk Hollow Rd., Denver, NY 12421
Jeremy W. Potts, 912 Poplar St., Denver, CO 80220/303-355-5462
Wayne E. Potts, 912 Poplar St., Denver, CO 80220/303-355-5462
Ed Pranger, 1414-7th St., Anacortes, WA 98221/206-293-3488
E. C. Prudhomme, 513 Ricou-Brewster Bldg., Shreveport, LA 71101/318-425-8421
Puccinelli Design, 114 Gazania Ct., Novato, CA 94947/415-892-7977
Martin Rabeno, Spook Hollow Trading Co., Box 37F, RD #1, Ellenville, NY 12428/914-647-4567
Wayne Reno, c/o Blackhawk Mtn., P.O. Box 1983, Englewood, CO 80150
Jim Riggs, 206 Azalea, Boerne, TX 78006/512-249-8567 (handguns)
Hans Rohner, Box 224, Niwot, CO 80544/303-652-2659
John R. Rohner, Sunshine Canyon, Boulder, CO 80302/303-444-3841
Joe Rundell, 6198 Frances Rd., Clio, MI 48420/313-687-0559
Robert P. Runge, 94 Grove St., Ilion, NY 13357/315-894-3036
Shaw-Leibowitz, Rt. 1, Box 421, New Cumberland, WV 26047/304-564-3108 (etchers)
George Sherwood, Box 735, Winchester, OR 97495/503-672-3159
Ben Shostle, The Gun Room, 1201 Burlington Dr., Muncie, IN 47302/317-282-9073
Don Simmons, c/o Paul Jaeger, Inc., 211 Leedom St., Jenkintown, PA 19046
W. P. Sinclair, 36 South St., Warminster, Wiltsh. BA12 8DZ, England
Ron Skaggs, 508 W. Central, Princeton, IL 61536/815-872-1661
Russell J. Smith, 231 Springdale Rd., Westfield, MA 01085/413-568-5476
R. Spinale, 3415 Oakdale Ave., Lorain, OH 44055/216-246-5344
Robt. Swartley, 2800 Pine St., Napa, CA 94559
George W. Thiewes, 1846 Allen Lane, St. Charles, IL 60174/312-584-1383
Anthony Tuscano, 1473 Felton Rd., South Euclid, OH 44121
Robert Valade, Rte. 1, Box 30-A, Cove, OR 97824
John Vest, 6715 Shasta Way, Klamath Falls, OR 97601
Ray Viramontez, 4348 Newberry Ct., Dayton, OH 45432/513-426-6762

Louis Vrancken, 30-rue sur le bois, 4531 Argenteau (Liege), Belgium
Vernon G. Wagoner, 2340 East Fox, Mesa, AZ 85203/602-835-1307
R. D. Wallace/The Gun Shop, 320 Overland Rd., Prescott, AZ 86301/602-445-0568
Terry Wallace, 385 San Marino, Vallejo, CA 94590
Floyd E. Warren, 1273 St. Rt. 305 N.E. Rt. #3, Cortland, OH 44410
John E. Warren, P.O. Box 72, Eastham, MA 02642
David W. Weber Custom Engraving, 420 E. 57th, #125, Loveland, CO 80537/303-663-1183
Rachel Wells, 110 N. Summit St., Prescott, AZ 86301
Sam Welch, Box 2152, Kodiak, AK 99615/907-486-5085
Claus Willig, c/o Paul Jaeger, Inc., 211 Leedom St., Jenkintown, PA 19046
Mel Wood, Star Route, Box 364, Elgin, AZ 85611/602-455-5541

GAME CALLS

Black Duck, 1737 Davis Ave., Whiting, IN 46394/219-659-2997
Burnham Bros., Box 669, 912 Main St., Marble Falls, TX 78654/512-693-3112
Call'N, Inc., 1615 Bartlett Rd., Memphis, TN 38134/901-372-1682
Faulk's, 616 18th St., Lake Charles, LA 70601
Lohman Mfg. Co., P.O. Box 220, Neosho, MO 64850/417-451-4438
Mallardtone Game Calls, 2901 16th St., Moline, IL 61265/309-762-8089
Phil. S. Olt Co., Box 550, Pekin, IL 61554/309-348-3633
Penn's Woods Products, Inc., 19 W. Pittsburgh St., Delmont, PA 15626
Scotch Game Call Co., Inc., 60 Main St., Oakfield, NY 14125
Johnny Stewart Game Calls, Box 7954, Waco, TX 76710/817-772-3261
Sure-Shot Game Calls, Inc., P.O. Box 816, Groves, TX 77619
Thomas Game Calls, P.O. Box 336, Winnsboro, TX 75494
Weems Wild Calls, P.O. Box 7261, Ft. Worth, TX 76111/817-531-1051
Tex Wirtz Ent., Inc., 1925 W. Hubbard St., Chicago, IL 60622

GUNMAKERS, FERLACH, AUSTRIA

Ludwig Borovnik, Dollichgasse 14, A-9170
Johann Fanzoj, Griesgasse 1, A-9170
Wilfried Glanznig, Werkstr. 9, A-9170
Josef Hambrusch, Gartengasse 2, A-9170
Karl Hauptmann, Bahnhofstr. 5, A-9170
Gottfried Juch, Pfarrhofgasse 2, A-9170
Josef Just, Hauptplatz 18, A-9170
Jakob Koschat, 12.-November-Str. 2, A-9170
Johaqn Michelitsch, 12.-November-Str. 2, A-9170
Josef Orasche, Lastenstr. 5, A-9170
Komm.-Rat A. Sch. Outschar, Josef-Orgis-Gasse 23, A-9170
Valentin Rosenzopf's Erbe, Griesgasse 2, A-9170
Helmut Scheiring-Düsel, 10.-Oktober-Str. 8, A-9170
R. Franz Schmid, Freibacherstr. 10, A-9170
Anton Sodia, Unterferlach 39, A-9170
Vinzenz Urbas, Neubaugasse 6, A-9170
Benedikt Winkler, Postgasse 1, A-9170
Josef Winkler, Neubaugasse 1, A-9170

GUN PARTS, U.S. AND FOREIGN

Badger Shooter's Supply, Box 397, Owen, WI 54460
Behlert Custom Guns, Inc., 725 Lehigh Ave., Union, NJ 07083 (handgun parts)
Philip R. Crouthamel, 513 E. Baltimore, E. Lansdowne, PA 19050/215-623-5685
Charles E. Duffy, Williams Lane, West Hurley, NY 12491
Christian Magazines, P.O. Box 184, Avoca, PA 18641
Federal Ordnance Inc., 1443 Potrero Ave., So. El Monte, CA 91733/213-350-4161
Jack First Distributors Inc., 44633 Sierra Highway, Lancaster, CA 93534/805-945-6981
Gun City, 504 Main, Bismarck, ND 58501/701-223-2304 (magazines, gun parts)
Gun-Tec, P.O. Box 8125, W. Palm Beach, FL 33407 (Win. mag. tubing; Win. 92 conversion parts)
Hunter's Haven, Zero Prince St., Alexandria, VA 22314
Walter H. Lodewick, 2816 N.E. Halsey, Portland, OR 97232/503-284-2554 (Winchester parts)
Marsh Al's, Rte. #3, Box 729, Preston, ID 83263/208-852-2437 (Contender rifle)
Morgan Arms Co., Inc., 1770-C Industrial Rd., Las Vegas, NV 89102 (MK-I kit)
Numrich Arms Co., West Hurley, NY 12491
Pacific Intl. Merch. Corp., 2215 "J" St., Sacramento, CA 95816/916-446-2737 (Vega 45 Colt mag.)
Potomac Arms Corp. (See Hunter's Haven)
Pre-64 Winchester Parts Co., P.O. Box 8125, West Palm Beach, FL 33407 (send stamped env. w. requ. list)
Martin B. Retting, Inc., 11029 Washington Blvd., Culver City, CA 90230/213-837-6111
Sarco, Inc., 323 Union St., Stirling, NJ 07980
Sherwood Intl. Export Corp., 18714 Parthenia St., Northridge, CA 91324
Simms, 2801 J St., Sacramento, CA 95816/916-442-3800
Clifford L. Smires, R.D. 1, Box 100, Columbus, NJ 08022/609-298-3158 (Mauser rifles)
Springfield Sporters Inc., R.D. 1, Penn Run, PA 15765/412-254-2626
Tomark Industries, 12043 S. Paramount Blvd., Downey, CA 90242 (Cherokee gun accessories)
Triple-K Mfg. Co., 568-6th Ave., San Diego, CA 92101 (magazines, gun parts)

GUNS (Foreign)

Abercrombie & Fitch, 2302 Maxwell Lane, Houston, TX 77023 (Ferlib)
Alpha Arms, Inc., 1602 Stemmons, Suite "D," Carrollton, TX 75006/214-245-3115
American Arms International, P.O. Box 11717, Salt Lake City, UT 84147/801-531-0180
Anschutz (See Talo Distributors, Inc.)
Action Arms, 4567 Bermuda, Philadelphia, PA 19124/215-744-3400
AYA (Aguirre y Aranzabal) See IGI Domino or Wm. L. Moore (Spanish shotguns)
Armoury Inc., Rte. 202, New Preston, CT 06777
Armsport, Inc., 3590 N.W. 49th St., Miami, FL 33142/305-592-7850
Armurier Liegeois-Artisans Reunis (A.L.A.R.), 27, rue Lambert Masset, 4300 Ans, Belgium
Baikal International, 12 Fairview Terrace, Paramus, NJ 07652/201-845-8710 (Russian shotguns)
Pedro Arrizabalaga, Eibar, Spain
Beeman, Inc., 47 Paul Dr., San Rafael, CA 94903/415-472-7121 (FWB, Weihrauch firearms)
Benelli Armi, S.p.A., via della Staziona 50, 61029 Urbino, Italy
Beretta U.S.A., 17601 Indian Head Highway, Accokeek, MD 20607/301-283-2191
M. Braun, 32, rue Notre-Dame, 2240 Luxemburg, Luxemburg (all types)
Britarms Gunmakers Ltd., Unit 1, Raban's Close, Raban's Lane Industrial Estate, Aylesbury, Bucks, England
Bretton, 21 Rue Clement Forissier, 42-St. Etienne, France
Browning (Gen. Offices), Rt. 1, Morgan, UT 84050/801-876-2711
Browning, (parts & service), Rt. 4, Box 624-B, Arnold, MO 63010/314-287-6800
Caprinus U.S.A., Inc., 100 Prospect St., Stamford, CT 06901/203-359-3773 (stainl. steel shotguns)
Carlo Casartelli, 25062 Concesio (Brescia), Italy
Century Arms Co., 3-5 Federal St., St. Albans, VT 05478
Champlin Firearms, Inc., Box 3191, Enid, OK 73701
Ets. Chapuis, 42380 St. Bonnet-le-Chateau, France (See R. Painter)
Christopher & Associates, 5636 San Fernando Rd., Glendale, CA 91202/312-245-3135 (SAM 180 rifle)
Connecticut Valley Arms Co., Saybrook Rd., Haddam, CT 06438 (CVA)
Walter Craig, Inc., Box 927-A, Selma, AL 36701
Creighton & Warren, P.O. Box 15723, Nashville, TN 37215 (Krieghoff combination guns)
Morton Cundy & Son, Ltd., P.O. Box 315, Lakeside, MT 59922
Charles Daly (See Outdoor Sports HQ)
Dikar s. Coop. (See Connecticut Valley Arms Co.)
Dixie Gun Works, Inc., Hwy 51, South, Union City, TN 38261/901-885-0561 ("Kentucky" rifles)
Henri Dumoulin & Fils, rue du Tilleul 16, B-4411 Liege, Belgium
Dynamit Nobel of America, Inc., 105 Stonehurst Court, Northvale, NJ 07647/201-767-1660 (Rottweil)
E.M.F. Co. Inc. (Early & Modern Firearms), 1900 E. Warner Ave. 1-D, Santa Ana, CA 92705/714-966-0202
Ernest Dumoulin-Deleye, 8 rue Florent Boclinville, 4410 Herstal (Vottem), Belgium
Peter Dyson Ltd., 29-31 Church St., Honley, Huddersfield, Yorkshire HD7 2AH, England (accessories f. antique gun collectors)
Elko Arms, 28 rue Ecole Moderne, 7400 Soignes, Belgium
Euroarms of American, Inc., P.O. Box 3277, 1501 Lenoir Dr., Winchester, VA 22601/703-661-1863 (ML)
Excam Inc., 4480 E. 11 Ave., P.O. Box 3483, Hialeah, FL 33013
Famars, Abbiatico & Salvinelli, Via Cinelli 29, Gardone V.T. (Brescia) Italy 25063
J. Fanzoj, P.O. Box 25, Ferlach, Austria 9170
Armi FERLIB, 46 Via Costa, 25063 Gardone V.T. (Brescia), Italy
Ferlach (Austria) of North America, 2320 S.W. 57th Ave., Miami, FL 33155/305-266-3030
Firearms Center Inc. (FCI), 308 Leisure Lane, Victoria, TX 77901
Firearms Imp. & Exp. Corp., (F.I.E.), P.O. Box 4866, Hialeah Lakes, Hialeah, FL 33014/305-685-5966
Flaig's Inc., Babcock Blvd. & Thompson Rd., Millvale, PA 15209/412-821-1717
Auguste Francotte & Cie, S.A., 61 Mont St. Martin, 4000 Liege, Belgium
Freeland's Scope Stands, Inc., 3737 14th Ave., Rock Island, IL 61201/309-788-7449
J. L. Galef & Son, Inc., 85 Chambers, New York, NY 10007
Renato Gamba, S.p.A., Gardone V.T. (Brescia), Italy (See Steyr Daimler Puch of America Corp.)
Armas Garbi, Urki #12, Eibar (Guipuzcoa) Spain (shotguns, See W. L. Moore)
Gastinne Renette, 39 Ave. F.D. Roosevelt, 75008 Paris, France
George Granger, 66 Cours Fauriel, 42 St. Etienne, France
Griffin & Howe, Inc., 589 Broadway, 4th Fl., New York, NY 10012/212-966-5323
Healthways, Box 45055, Los Angeles, CA 90061
Gil Hebard Guns, Box 1, Knoxville, IL 61448 (Hammerli)
Heckler & Koch Inc., 933 N. Kenmore St., Suite 218, Arlington, VA 22201/703-243-3700
A. D. Heller, Inc., Box 66, 2322 Grand Ave., Baldwin, NY 11510/516-868-6300
Heym, Friedr. Wilh., K.G., Coburgerstr. 8, 8732 Münnerstadt, West Germany
HOWCO Dist. Inc., 122 Lafayette Ave., Laurel, MD 20707/301-953-3301
Hunting World, 16 E. 53rd St., New York, NY 10022
IGI Domino Corp., 200 Madison Ave., New York, NY 10016/212-889-4889 (Breda)
Incor, Inc., P.O. Box 132, Addison, TX 75001/214-931-3500 (Cosmi auto shotg.)
Interarmco, See Interarms (Walther)

Interarms Ltd., 10 Prince St., Alexandria, VA 22313 (Mauser, Valmet M-62/S)
International Distr., Inc., 7290 S.W. 42nd St., Miami, FL 33155 (Taurus rev.)
Italguns, Via Voltabo, 20090 Cusago (Milano), Italy
Paul Jaeger Inc., 211 Leedom St., Jenkintown, PA 19046/215-884-6920
Jana Intl. Co., Box 1107, Denver, CO 80201 (Parker-Hale)
Jenkins Imports Corp., 462 Stanford Pl., Santa Barbara, CA 93111/805-967-5092 (Gebrüder Merkel)
Kassnar Imports, 5480 Linglestown Rd., Harrisburg, PA 17110
Kawaguchiya Firearms, c/o La Paloma Marketing, 4500 E. Speedway Blvd., Suite 93, Tucson, AZ 85712/602-881-4750
Kleinguenther's, P.O. Box 1261, Seguin, TX 78155
Knight & Knight, 5930 S.W. 48 St., Miami, FL 33155 (made-to-order only)
Krico, P.O. Box 266, Bolton, Ont. LOP 1AO, Canada/416-857-6444
L. A. Distributors, 4 Centre Market Pl., New York, NY 10010
Lanber Arms of America, Inc., 377 Logan St., Adrian, MI 49221/518-263-7444 (Spanish o-u shotguns)
La Paloma Marketing, 4500 E. Speedway Blvd., Suite 93, Tucson, AZ 85712/602-881-4750 (K.F.C. shotguns)
Leland Firearms Co., 13 Mountain Ave., Llewellyn Park, West Orange, NJ 07052/201-325-3379 (Spanish shotguns)
Lever Arms Serv. Ltd., 572 Howe St., Vancouver, B.C., Canada V6C 2E3/604-685-6913
Liberty Arms Organization, Box 306, Montrose, CA 91020/213-248-0618
Llama (See Stoeger)
Magnum Research, Inc., 2825 Anthony Lane So., Minneapolis, MN 55418/612-781-3446 (Israeli Galil)
Mandall Shtg. Suppl. 7150 East 4th St., Scottsdale, AZ 85252/602-945-2553
Mannlicher (See Steyr Daimler Puch of Amer.)
Manu-Arm, B.P. No. 8, Veauche 42340, France
Manufrance, 100-Cours Fauriel, 42 St. Etienne, France
Mauser-Werke Oberndorf, P. O. Box 1349, 7238 Oberndorf/Neckar, West Germany
Mendi s. coop. (See Connecticut Valley Arms Co.)
Merkuria, FTC, Argentinska 38, 17005 Prague 7, Czechoslovakia (BRNO)
Mitchell Arms Corp., 116 East 16th St., Costa Mesa, CA 92627/714-548-7701 (Uberti pistols)
Moore Supply Co., 3000 So. Main, Salt Lake City, UT 84115/801-487-1671 (Nikko)
Wm. Larkin Moore & Co., 31360 Via Colinas, Suite 109, Westlake Village, CA 91360/213-889-4160 (AYA, Garbi, Ferlib, Piotti, Lightwood)
Navy Arms Co., 689 Bergen Blvd., Ridgefield, NJ 07657
NIKKO (See Moore Supply)
Odin International, Ltd. 818 Slaters Lane, Alexandria, VA 22314/703-549-2508 (Valmet/military types; Zastava)
Outdoor Sports Headquarters, Inc., 2290 Arbor Blvd., Dayton, OH 45439/513-294-2811 (Charles Daly shotguns)
P.M. Air Services, Ltd., P.O. Box 1573, Costa Mesa, CA 92626
Pachmayr Gun Works, 1220 S. Grand Ave., Los Angeles, CA 90015
Pacific Intl. Merch. Corp., 2215 "J" St., Sacramento, CA 95816/916-446-2737
Rob. Painter, 2901 Oakhurst Ave., Austin, TX 78703 (Chapuis)
Parker Arms of Texas, 520 Lemmon Ave., Dallas, TX 75209/214-522-5871 (Sterling)
Parker-Hale, Bisleyworks, Golden Hillock Rd., Sparbrook, Birmingham B11 2PZ, England
Perazzi U.S.A. Inc., 206 S. George St., Rome, NY 13440/315-337-8566
Picard-Fayolle, 42-rue du Vernay, 42100 Saint Etienne, France
Precise, 3 Chestnut, Suffern, NY 10901
Precision Sports, 798 Cascadilla St., Ithaca, NY 14850/607-273-2993 (BSA Stutzen CF rifle; AYA side-by-side shotgun)
Puccinelli Co., 114 Gazania Ct., Novato, CA 94947/415-892-7977 (I.A.B., Rizzini, Bernardelli shotguns of Italy)
Quantetics Corp., Imp.-Exp. Div., 582 Somerset St. W., Ottawa, Ont. K1R 5K2 Canada/613-237-0242 (Unique pistols-Can. only)
RG Industries, Inc., 2485 N.W. 20th St., Miami, FL 33142 (Erma)
L. Joseph Rahn, Inc., 3940 Trade Center Dr., Ann Arbor, MI 48104/313-971-1195 (Garbi, Astra shotguns)
Ravizza Caccia Pesca Sport, s.p.a., Via Volta 60, 20090 Cusago, Italy
Richland Arms Co., 321 W. Adrian St., Blissfield, MI 49228
F. lli Rizzini, 25060 Magno di Gardone V.T., (Bs.) Italy
Rottweil, (See Dynamit Nobel of America)
Victor Sarasqueta, S.A., V. Pzal. Box 25, 3 Victor Sarasqueta St., Eibar, Spain
Sarco, Inc., 323 Union St., Stirling, NJ 07980/201-647-3800
Savage Arms Corp., Westfield, MA 01085/413-562-2361
W. C. Scott & Co. (British shotguns), (See Griffin & Howe)
Security Arms Co., (See Heckler & Koch)
Service Armament, 689 Bergen Blvd., Ridgefield, NJ 07657 (Greener Harpoon Gun)
Sherwood Intl. Export Corp., 18714 Parthenia St., Northridge, CA 91324
Shore Galleries, Inc., 3318 W. Devon Ave., Chicago, IL 60645
Shotguns of Ulm, P.O. Box 253, Millitown, NJ 08850/201-297-0573
Sile Distributors, 7 Centre Market Pl., New York, NY 10013/212-925-4111
Simmons Spec., Inc., 700 Rogers Rd., Olathe, KS 66061
Sloan's Sprtg. Goods, Inc., 10 South St., Ridgefield, CT 06877
Franz Sodia Jagdgewehrfabrik, Schulhausgasse 14, 9170 Ferlach, (Kärnten) Austria
Solersport, 23629 7th Ave. West, Bothell, WA 98011/206-483-9607 (Unique)
Steyr-Daimler-Puch of America Corp., 85 Metro Way, Secaucus, NJ 07094/201-865-4330
Stoeger Industries, 55 Ruta Ct., S. Hackensack, NJ 07606/201-440-2700
Talo Distributors, Inc., P.O. Box 177, Westfield, MA 01086/800-343-1111 (Anschutz)
Toledo Armas, S.A., P.O. Box 430535, So. Miami, FL 33143
Tradewinds, Inc., P.O. Box 1191, Tacoma, WA 98401
Uberti, Aldo & Co., Via G. Carducci 41 or 39, Ponte Zanano (Brescia), Italy
Ignacio Ugartechea, Apartado 21, Eibar, Spain
Valmet Sporting Arms Div., 7 Westchester Plaza, Elmsford, NY 10523/914-347-4440 (sporting types)

Valor Imp. Corp., 5555 N.W. 36th Ave., Miami, FL 33142/212-765-4660 (Valmet)
Ventura Imports, P.O. Box 2782, Seal Beach, CA 90740 (European shotguns)
Verney-Carron, B.P. 88, 17 Cours Fauriel, 42010 St. Etienne Cedex, France
Perugini Visini & Co. s.r.l., Via Camprelle, 126, 25080 Nuvolera (Bs.), Italy
Waffen-Frankonia, Box 6780, 87 Wurzburg 1, W. Germany
Weatherby's, 2781 Firestone Blvd., So. Gate, CA 90280/213-569-7186
Winchester, Olin Corp., 120 Long Ridge Rd., Stamford, CT 06904
World Public Safety, 5855 Green Valley Circle, Suite 103, Culver City, CA 90230/213-670-4693 (Leader auto rifle)
Fabio Zanotti di Stefano, Via XXV Aprile 1, 25063 Gardone V.T. (Brescia) Italy
Zavodi Crvena Zastava, 29 Novembra St., No. 12, Belgrade, Yugosl.
Antonio Zoli & Co., 39 Via Zanardelli, 25063 Gardone V.T., Brescia, Italy

GUNS & GUN PARTS, REPLICA AND ANTIQUE

Antique Gun Parts, Inc., 1118 S. Braddock Ave., Pittsburgh, PA 15218/412-241-1811 (ML)
Armoury Inc., Rte. 202, New Preston, CT 06777
Artistic Arms, Inc., Box 23, Hoagland, IN 46745 (Sharps-Borchardt replica)
Bob's Place, Box 283J, Clinton, IA 52732 (obsolete Winchester parts only)
Dixie Gun Works, Inc., Hwy 51, South, Union City, TN 38261/901-885-0561
Federal Ordnance Inc., 1443 Portrero Ave., So. El Monte, CA 91733/213-350-4161
Fred Goodwin, Goodwin's Gun Shop, Sherman Mills, ME 04776/207-365-4451 (antique guns & parts)
Terry I. Kopp, Highway 13, Lexington, MO 64067/816-259-2636 (restoration & pts. 1890 & 1906 Winch.)
The House of Muskets, Inc., 120 N. Pagosa Blvd., Pagosa Springs, CO 81147/303-264-2295 (ML guns)
Log Cabin Sport Shop, 8010 Lafayette Rd., Lodi, OH 44254/216-948-1082 (ctlg. $30)
Edw. E. Lucas, 32 Garfield Ave., East Brunswick, NJ 08816/201-251-5526 (45/70 Springfield parts)
Lyman Products Corp., Middlefield, CT 06455
Tommy Munsch Gunsmithing, Rt. 2, Box 248, Little Falls, MN 56345/612-632-5835 (parts list $1.50; oth. inq. SASE)
Numrich Arms Co., West Hurley, NY 12491
Replica Models, Inc., 610 Franklin St., Alexandria, VA 22314
S&S Firearms, 88-21 Aubrey Ave., Glendale, NY 11385/212-497-1100
Sarco, Inc., 323 Union St., Stirling, NJ 07980/201-647-3800
C. H. Stoppler, 1426 Walton Ave., New York, NY 10452 (miniature guns)
Upper Missouri Trading Co., 3rd & Harold Sts., Crofton, NB 68730
C. H. Weisz, Box 311, Arlington, VA 22210
W. H. Wescombe, P.O. Box 488, Glencoe, CA 95232 (Rem. R.B. parts)

GUNS (Pellet)

Beeman Precision Airguns, 47 Paul Dr., San Rafael, CA 94903/415-472-7121
Benjamin Air Rifle Co., 1525 So. 8th St., Louis, MO 63104
Crosman Airguns, 980 Turk Hill Rd., Fairport, NY 14450/716-223-6000
Daisy Mfg. Co., Rogers, AR 72756 (also Feinwerkbau)
K. J. David & Co., P.O. Box 12595, Lake Park, FL 33403/305-844-5124
Dynamit Nobel of America, Inc., 105 Stonehurst Ct., Northvale, NJ 07647/201-767-1660 (Dianawerk)
J. L. Galef & Son, Inc., 85 Chambers St., New York, NY 10007 (B.S.A.)
Great Lakes Airguns, 6175 So. Park Ave., Hamburg, NY 14075/716-648-6666
Harrington & Richardson Arms Co., Industrial Rowe, Gardner, MA 01440 (Webley)
Healthways, Box 45055, Los Angeles, CA 90061
Gil Hebard Guns, Box 1, Knoxville, IL 61448
Interarms, 10 Prince, Alexandria, VA 22313 (Walther)
Marksman Products, P.O. Box 2983, Torrance, CA 90509
Phoenix Arms Co., Little London Rd., Horam, Heathfield, East Sussex TN21 OBJ, England (Jackal)
Power Line (See Daisy Mfg. Co.)
Precise, 3 Chestnut, Suffern, NY 10901
Precision Sports, 798 Cascadilla St., Ithaca, NY 14850/607-273-2993 (B.S.A.)
Service Armament, 689 Bergen Blvd., Ridgefield, NJ 07657 (Webley)
Sheridan Products, Inc., 3205 Sheridan, Racine, WI 53403
Smith & Wesson, 2100 Roosevelt Ave., Springfield, MA 01104
Target Airgun Supply, 11552 Knott St., Suite 3, Garden Grove, CA 92641

GUNS, SURPLUS—PARTS AND AMMUNITION

Can Am Enterprises, Canfield, Ont. NOA 1CO, Canada/416-772-3633 (Enfield rifles)
Century Arms, Inc., 3-5 Federal St., St. Albans, VT 05478
Walter Craig, Inc., Box 927-A, Selma, AL 36701
Eastern Firearms Co., 790 S. Arroyo Pkwy., Pasadena, CA 91105
Garcia National Gun Traders, 225 S.W. 22nd, Miami, FL 33135
Lever Arms Serv. Ltd., 572 Howe St., Vancouver, B.C., Canada V6C 2E3/604-685-6913
Sarco, Inc., 323 Union St., Stirling, NJ 07980/201-647-3800
Service Armament Co., 689 Bergen Blvd., Ridgefield, NJ 07657
Sherwood Intl. Export Corp., 18714 Parthenia St., Northridge, CA 91324
Springfield Sporters Inc., R.D. 1, Penn Run, PA 15765/412-254-2626

GUNS, U.S.-made

AMT (Arcadia Machine & Tool), 536 N. Vincent Ave., Covina, CA 91722/213-915-7803

Accuracy Systems, Inc., 2105 S. Hardy Dr., Tempe, AZ 85282

Alpha Arms (See H. Koon, Inc.)

American Derringer Corp., P.O. Box 8983, Waco, TX 76710/817-662-6187

ArmaLite, 118 E. 16th St., Costa Mesa, CA 92627

Armament Systems and Procedures, Inc., Box 356, Appleton, WI 54912/414-731-8893 (ASP pistol)

Arminex, 7882 E. Gray Rd., Scottsdale Airpark, Scottsdale, AZ 85260/602-998-5774 (Excalibur s.a. pistol)

Arnett Guns (See Gary DelSignore Weaponry)

Artistic Arms, Inc.,Box 23, Hoagland, IN 46745 (Sharps-Borchardt)

Artistic Firearms Corp., John Otteman, 4005 Hecker Pass Hwy., Gilroy, CA 95020/408-842-4278 (A.F.C. Comm. Rife 1881-1981)

Auto-Ordnance Corp., Box ZG, West Hurley, NY 12491

Bauer Firearms, 34750 Klein Ave., Fraser, MI 48026

Bogun Corp., 7350 E. Compton Blvd., P.O. Box 949, Paramount, CA 90973/213-531-4000 (conv. rifle/shotgun)

Brown Precision Co., P.O. Box 270W; 7786 Molinos Ave., Los Molinos, CA 96055/916-384-2506 (High Country rifle)

Browning (Gen. Offices), Rt. 1, Morgan, UT 84050/801-876-2711

Browning (Parts & Service), Rt. 4, Box 624-B, Arnold, MO 63010/314-287-6800

Buffalo Arms Inc., 10 Tonawanda St., Tonawanda, NY 14150/716-693-7970

Bushmaster Firearms Co., 309 Cumberland Ave., Portland ME 04101/207-775-3339 (police handgun)

Butler Manufacturing, P.O. Box 8207, New Haven, CT 06530/203-562-5608

CB Arms, Inc., 65 Hathaway Court, Pittsburgh, PA 15235/412-795-4621 (Double Deuce h'gun)

Challanger Mfg. Corp., 118 Pearl St., Mt. Vernon, NY 10550 (Hopkins & Allen)

Champlin Firearms, Inc., Box 3191, Enid, OK 73701

Charter Arms Corp., 430 Sniffens Ln., Stratford, CT 06497

Chipmunk Manufacturing Inc., 114 E. Jackson, Medford, OR 97501/503-826-7329 (22 S.S. rifle)

Colt Firearms, P.O. Box 1868, Hartford, CT 06102/203-236-6311

Commando Arms, Inc., Box 10214, Knoxville, TN 37919

Coonan Arms, Inc., 570 S. Fairview, St. Paul, MN 55116/612-699-5639 (357 Mag. Autom.)

Crown City Arms, P.O. Box 1126, Cortland, NY 13045/607-753-8238 (45 auto handgun)

Cumberland Arms, Rt. 1, Shafer Rd., Blanton Chapel, Manchester, TN 37355

Day Arms Corp., 2412 S.W. Loop 410, San Antonio, TX 78227

Leonard Day & Co., P.O. Box 723, East Hampton, MA 01027/413-527-7990 (ML)

Gary DelSignore Weaponry, 3675 Cottonwood, Cedar City, UT 84720/801-586-2505 (Arnett Guns)

Demro Products Inc., 345 Progress Dr., Manchester, CT. 06040/203-649-4444 (wasp, Tac guns)

Detonics 45 Associates, 2500 Seattle Tower, Seattle, WA 98101 (auto pistol)

Deutsch Waffen und Maschine Fabriken, Inc., 113 N. 2nd St., Whitewater, WI 53190/414-473-4848 (Ugly gun)

Dornaus & Dixon Enterprises, Inc., 16718 Judy Way, Cerritos, CA 90701/213-926-7004 (Bren-Ten)

DuBiel Arms Co., 1724 Baker Rd., Sherman, TX 75090/214-893-7313

El Dorado Arms, 35 Gilpin Ave., Happauge, NY 11787/516-234-0212

Excalibur (See Arminex)

FTL Marketing Corp., 12521-3 Oxnard St., No. Hollywood, CA 91601/213-985-2939

Falling Block Works, P.O. Box 3087, Fairfax, VA 22038

Firearms Imp. & Exp. Corp., P.O. Box 4866, Hialeah Lakes, Hialeah, FL 33014/305-685-5966 (FIE)

Freedom Arms Co., Freedom, WY 83120 (mini revolver, Casull rev.)

Golden Age Arms Co., 14 W. Winter St., Delaware, OH 43015

Franklin C. Green, 530 W. Oak Grove Rd., Montrose, CO 81401/303-249-7003 (Green Free Pistol)

Harrington & Richardson, Industrial Rowe, Gardner, MA 01440

Hawken Armory, P.O. Box 2604, Hot Springs, AR 71901/501-268-8296 (ML)

A.D. Heller, Inc., Box 268, Grand Ave., Baldwin, NY 11510

High Standard Sporting Firearms, 31 Prestige Park Circle, East Hartford, CT 06108

Holmes Firearms Corp., Rte. 6, Box 242, Fayetteville, AR 72701

Hopkins & Allen Arms, 3 Ethel Ave., P.O. Box 217, Hawthorne, NJ 07507/201-427-1165 (ML)

Hyper-Single Precision SS Rifles, 520 E. Beaver, Jenks, OK 74037/918-299-2391

Ithaca Gun Co., Ithaca, NY 14850

Iver Johnson Arms Inc., P.O. Box 251, Middlesex, NJ 08846

Paul Jaeger, Inc., 211 Leedom St., Jenkintown, Pa 19046

Jennings Firearms, 4510 Carter Ct., Chino, CA 91710/714-591-3921

Kimber of Oregon, Inc., 9039 S.E. Jannsen Rd., Clackamas, OR 97015/503-656-1704

H. Koon, Inc., 12523 Valley Branch, Dallas, TX 75234/214-243-8124

Krupp KK Arms Co., Star Route, Box 671, Kerrville, TX 78028/512-257-4718 (handguns)

Ljutic Ind., Inc., P.O. Box 2117, 918 N. 5th Ave., Yakima, WA 98902/509-248-0476 (Mono-Gun)

M & N Distributors, 23535 Telo St., Torrance, CA 90505/213-530-9000 (Budischowsky)

MS Safari Arms, P.O. Box 23370, Phoenix, AZ 85062/602-269-7283

Marlin Firearms Co., 100 Kenna Drive, New Haven, CT 06473

Matteson Firearms Inc., Otsego Rd., Canajoharie, NY 13317/607-264-3744 (SS rifles)

Merrill Co., 704 E. Commonwealth, Fullerton, CA 92631/714-879-8922

Michigan Armament, Inc., P.O. Box 9, Walled Lake, MI 48088/313-624-5635 (pistols)

Mitchell Arms Corp., 116 East 16th St., Costa Mesa, CA 92627/714-548-7701

O.F. Mossberg & Sons, Inc., 7 Grasso St., No. Haven, CT 06473

Mowrey Gun Works, Box 38, Iowa Park, TX 76367

Navy Arms Co., 689 Bergen Blvd., Ridgefield, NJ 07657

North American Arms, 310 West 700 S., Provo, UT 84601/801-375-8074

Numrich Arms Corp., W. Hurley, NY 12491

ODI, Inc., 124A Greenwood Ave., Midland Park, NJ 07432/201-444-4557

R G Industries, 2485 N.W. 20th St., SE., Miami, FL 33142

Raven Arms, 1300 Bixby Dr., Industry, CA 91745/213-961-2511 (P-25 pistols)

Remington Arms Co., 939 Barnum Ave., P.O. Box #1939, Bridgeport, CT 06601

Rock Pistol Mfg., Inc., 704 E. Commonwealth, Fullerton, CA 92631/714-870-8530 (Merrill pistol, etc.)

Ruger (See Sturm, Ruger & Co.)

Savage Arms Corp., Westfield, MA 01085

Sceptre, Inc., P.O. Box 1282, Marietta, GA 30061/404-428-5513

Sears, Roebuck & Co., 825 S. St. Louis, Chicago, IL 60607

Semmerling Corp., P.O. Box 400, Newton, MA 02160

Sharps Rifle Co., 3428 Shakertown Rd., Dayton, OH 45430

Shiloh Products, 37 Potter St., Farmingdale, NY 11735 (Sharps)

Six Enterprises, 6564 Hidden Creek Dr., Dan Jose, CA 95120/408-268-8296 (Timberliner rifle)

Smith & Wesson, Inc., 2100 Roosevelt Ave., Springfield, MA 01101

Springfield Armory, 111 E. Exchange St., Geneseo, IL 61254

SSK Industries, Rt. 1, Della Dr., Bloomingdale, OH 43910/614-264-0176

Sterling Arms Corp., 211 Grand St., Lockport, NY 14094/716-434-6631

Sturm, Ruger & Co., Southport, CT 06490

Tennessee Valley Arms, P.O. Box 2022, Union City, TN 38261/901-885-4456

Texas Gun & Machine Co., P.O. Box 2837, Texas City, TX 77590/713-945-0070 (Texas rifles)

Thompson-Center Arms, Box 2405, Rochester, NH 03867

Trail Guns Armory, 1634 E. Main St., League City, TX 77573 (muzzleloaders)

Trapper Gun, Inc., 18717 E. 14 Mile Rd., Fraser, MI 48026/313-792-0133 (handguns)

United Sporting Arms of Arizona, Inc, 2021 E. 14th St., Tucson, AZ 85719/602-632-4001 (handguns)

U.S. Repeating Arms Co., P.O. Box 30-300, New Haven, CT 06511/203-789-5000

Universal Firearms, 3740 E. 10th Ct., Hialeah, FL 33013

Ward's, 619 W. Chicago, Chicago, IL 60607 (Western Field brand)

Weatherby's, 2781 E. Firestone Blvd., South Gate, CA 90280

WSI, P.O. Box 66, Youngstown, OH 44501/216-743-9666 (9mm Viking)

Dan Wesson Arms, 293 So. Main St., Monson, MA 01057

Western Arms/Allen Arms, 1107 Pen Rd., Santa Fe, NM 87501/505-982-3399 (ML)

Wichita Arms, 333 Lulu, Wichita, KS 67211/316-265-0661

Wildey Firearms Co., Inc., P.O. Box 4264, New Windsor, NY 12250/203-272-7215

Wilkinson Arms, Rte. #2, Box 2166, Parma, ID 83660/208-722-6771

Winchester, (See U.S. Repeating Arms)

GUNSMITHS, CUSTOM (see Custom Gunsmiths)

GUNSMITHS, HANDGUN (see Pistolsmiths)

GUNSMITH SCHOOLS

Colorado School of Trades, 1575 Hoyt, Lakewood, CO 80215/303-233-4697

Lassen Community College, P.O. Box 3000, Susanville, CA 96130

Modern Gun Repair School, 2538 No. 8th St., Phoenix, AZ 85006/602-990-8346 (home study)

Modern Schools of America, Inc., 2538 No. 8th St., Phoenix, AZ 85006 (outdoor camping, sporting goods course; home study)

Montgomery Technical Institute, P.O. Drawer 487, Troy, NC 27371/919-572-3691

Murray State College, Gunsmithing Program, Tishomingo, OK 73460/405-371-2371

North American School of Firearms, 4401 Birch St., Newport Beach, CA 92663/714-546-7360 (correspondence)

Oregon Institute of Technology, Small Arms Dept., Klamath Falls, OR 97601

Penn. Gunsmith School, 812 Ohio River Blvd., Avalon, Pittsburgh, PA 15202

Pine Technical Institute, 100 Fourth St., Pine City, MN 55063/612-629-6764

Police Sciences Institute, 4401 Birch St., Newport Beach, CA 92660/714-546-7360 (General Law Enforcement Course)

Southeastern Community College, Gunsmithing Dept., Drawer F, West Burlington, IA 52655/319-752-2731

Trinidad State Junior College, 600 Prospect, Trinidad, CO 81082/303-846-5631

Yavapai College, 1100 East Sheldon St., Prescott, AZ 86301/602-445-7300

GUNSMITH SUPPLIES, TOOLS, SERVICES

Albright Prod. Co., P. O. Box 1144, Portola, CA 96122 (trap buttplates)

Alley Supply Co., Carson Valley Industrial Park, P.O. Box 848, Gardnerville, NV 89410/702-782-3800 (JET line lathes, mills, etc.)

Ametek, Hunter Spring Div., One Spring Ave., Hatfield, PA 10440/215-822-2971 (triggor gaugo)

Anderson Mfg. Co., Union Gap Sta., P.O. Box 3120, Yakima, WA 98903/509-453-2349 (tang safe)

Armite Labs., 1845 Randolph St., Los Angeles, CA 90001/213-587-7744 (pen oiler)

B-Square Co., Box 11281, Ft. Worth, TX 76110

Jim Baiar, 490 Halfmoon Rd., Columbia Falls, MT 59912 (hex screws)

Behlert Custom Guns, Inc., 725 Lehigh Ave., Union, NJ 07083

Dennis M. Bellm Gunsmithing, Inc., dba P.O. Ackley Rifle Barrels, 2376 S. Redwood Rd., Salt Lake City, UT 84119/801-974-0697 (rifles only)

Al Biesen, W. 2039 Sinto Ave., Spokane, WA 99201 (grip caps, buttplates)

Billingsley & Brownell, Box 25, Wyarno, WY 82845/307-737-2468 (cust. grip caps, bolt handle, etc.)

Blue Ridge Machine and Tool, 165 Midland Trail, Hurricane, WV 25526/304-562-3538 (machinery, tools, shop suppl.)

Bonanza Sports Mfg. Co., 412 Western Ave., Faribault, MN 55021/507-332-7153

Briganti Custom Gun-Smithing, P.O. Box 56, 475-Route 32, Highland Mills, NY 10930/914-928-9816 (cold rust bluing, hand polishing, metal work)

Brookstone Co., 125 Vose Farm Rd., Peterborough, NH 03458

Bob Brownell's, Main & Third, Montezuma, IA 50171/515-623-5401

Lenard M. Brownell (See Billingsley & Brownell)

W.E. Brownell, 1852 Alessandro Trail, Vista, CA 92083 (checkering tools)

Burgess Vibrocrafters, Inc. (BVI), Rte. 83, Grayslake, IL 60030

M.H. Canjar, 500 E. 45th Denver, CO 80216/303-623-5777 (triggers, etc.)

Chapman Mfg. Co., Rte. 17 at Saw Mill Rd., Durham, CT 06422

Chase Chemical Corp., 3527 Smallman St., Pittsburgh, PA 15201/412-681-6544 (Chubb Multigauge for shotguns)

Chubb (See Chase Chem. Co.)

Chicago Wheel & Mfg. Co., 1101 W. Monroe St., Chicago, IL 60607/312-226-8155 (Handee grinders)

Christy Gun Works, 875-57th St., Sacramento, CA 95819

Classic Arms Corp., P.O. Box 8, Palo Alto, CA 94302/415-321-7243 (floorplates, grip caps)

Clover Mfg. Co., 139 Woodward Ave., Norwalk, CT 06856/800-243 6492 (Clover compound)

Clymer Mfg. Co., Inc., 14241 W. 11 Mile Rd., Oak Park, MI 48237/313-541-5533 (reamers)

Dave Cook, 720 Hancock Ave., Hancock, MI 49930 (metalsmithing only)

Dayton-Traister Co., 9322-900th West, P.O. Box 593, Oak Harbor, WA 98277/206-675-5375 (triggers)

Delta Arms Sporting Goods, Highway 82 West, Indianola, MS 38751/601-887-5566 (Lightwood/England)

Dem-Bart Checkering Tools, Inc., 6807 Hiway #2, Snohomish, WA 98290/206-568-7536

Dremel Mfg. Co., 4915-21st St., Racine, WI 53406 (grinders)

Chas. E. Duffy, Williams Lane, West Hurley, NY 12491

Peter Dyson Ltd., 29-31 Church St., Honley, Huddersfield, Yorksh. HD7 2AH, England (accessories f. antique gun coll.)

E-Z Tool Co., P.O. Box 3186, 25 N.W. 44th Ave., Des Moines, IA 50313 (lathe taper attachment)

Edmund Scientific Co., 101 E. Glouster Pike, Barrington, NJ 08007

Emco-Lux, 2050 Fairwood Ave., P.O. Box 07861, Columbus, OH 43207/614-445-8328

Forster Products, Inc., 82 E. Lanark Ave., Lanark, IL 61046/815-493-6360

Francis Tool Co., (f'ly Keith Francis Inc.), 1020 W. Catching Slough Rd., Coos Bay, OR 97420/593-269-2021 (reamers)

G. R. S. Corp., P.O. Box 748, Emporia, KS 66801/316-343-1084 (Grarermeister)

Gilmore Pattern Works, P.O. Box 50084, Tulsa, OK 74150/918-245-9627 (Wagner safe-T-planer)

Glendo Corp., P.O. Box 1153, Emporia, KS 66801/316-343-1084 (Accu-Finish tool)

Gold Lode, Inc., 1305 Remington Rd., Suite A, Schaumburg, IL 60195 (gold inlay kit)

Gopher Shooter's Supply, Box 278, Faribault, MN 55021 (screwdrivers, etc.)

Grace Metal Prod., 115 Ames St., Elk Rapids, MI 49629 (screw drivers, drifts)

Gunline Tools, Box 478, Placentia, CA 92670/714-528-5252

Gun-Tec, P.O. Box 8125, W. Palm Beach, Fl 33407

Half Moon Rifle Shop, 490 Halfmoon Rd., Columbia Falls, MT 59912/406-892-4409 (hex screws)

Henriksen Tool Co., Inc., P.O. Box 668, Phoenix, OR 97535/503-535-2309 (reamers)

Huey Gun Cases (Marvin Huey), Box 98, Reed's Spring, MO 65737/417-538-4233 (high grade English ebony tools)

Paul Jaeger Inc., 211 Leedom St., Jenkintown, PA 19046

Jeffredo Gunsight Co., 1629 Via Monserate, Fallbrook, CA 92028 (trap buttplate)

John's Rifle Shop, 25 NW 44th Ave., Des Moines, IA 50313/515-288-8680

K&D Grinding Co., P.O. Box 1766, Alexandria, LA 71301/318-487-0823 (cust. tools f. pistolsmiths)

Kasenit Co., Inc., 3 King St., Mahwah, NJ 07430/201-529-3663 (surface hrdng. comp.)

Terry K. Kopp, Highway 13, Lexington, MO 64067/816-359-2636 (stock rubbing compound)

J. Korzinek, RD#2, Box 73, Canton, PA 17724/717-673-8512 (stainl. steel bluing; broch. $1.50)

John G. Lawson, (The Sight Shop) 1802 E. Columbia Ave., Tacoma, WA 98404/206-474-5465

Lea Mfg. Co., 237 E. Aurora St., Waterbury, CT 06720/203-753-5116

Lightwood (Fieldsport) Ltd., Britannia Rd., Banbury, Oxfordsh. OX16 8TD, England

Leek's Phila. Gun Exch., 6700 Rowland Ave., Philadelphia, PA 19149/215-332-6225

John McClure, 4549 Alamo Dr., San Diego, CA 92115 (electric checkering tool)

McIntrye Tools, P.O. Box 491/State Road #1144, Troy, NC 27371/919-572-2603 (shotgun bbl. facing tool)

Michaels of Oregon Co., P.O. Box 13010, Portland, OR 97213/503-255-6890

Viggo Miller, P.O. Box 4181, Omaha, NE 68104 (trigger attachment)

Miller Single Trigger Mfg. Co., R.D. 1, Box 99, Millersburg, PA 17061/717-692-3704

Frank Mittermeier, 3577 E. Tremont, New York, NY 10465

Moderntools, 1671 W. McNab Rd., Ft. Lauderdale, FL 33309/305-979-3900

N&J Sales, Lime Kiln Rd., Northford, CT 06472/203-484-0247 (screwdrivers)

Karl A. Neise, Inc., 1671 W. McNab Rd., Ft. Lauderdale, FL 33309/305-979-3900

Palmgren Prods., Chicago Tool & Eng. Co., 8383 South Chicago Ave., Chicago, IL 60167/312-721-9675 (vises, etc.)

Panavise Prods., Inc., 2850 E. 29th St., Long Beach, CA 90806/213-595-7621

C.R. Pedersen & Son, 2717 S. Pere Marquette, Ludington, MI 49431/616-843-2061

Pilkington Gun Co., P.O. Box 1296, Mukogee, OK 74401/918-683-9418 (Q.D. scope mt.)

Richland Arms Co., 321 W. Adrian St., Blissfield, MI 49228

Riley's Supply Co., 116 No. Main St., Avilla, IN 46710/219-897-2351 (Niedner buttplates, grip caps)

A.G. Russell, 1705 Hiway 71N, Springdale, AR 72764 (Arkansas oilstones)

Schaffner Mfg. Co., Emsworth, Pittsburgh, PA 15202 (polishing kits)

SGW, Inc. (formerly Schuetzen Gun Works), 624 Old Pacific Hwy., S.E. Olympia, WA 98503/206-456-3471

Shaw's, 9447 W. Lilac Rd., Escondido, CA 92025/714-728-7070

Shooters Specialty Shop, 5146 E. Pima, Tucson, AZ 85712/602-325-3346

L.S. Starrett Co., 121 Crescent St., Athol, MA 01331/617-249-3551

Texas Platers Supply Co., 2453 W. Five Mile Parkway, Dallas, TX 75233 (plating kit)

Timney Mfg. Inc., 3106 W. Thomas Rd., Phoenix, AZ 85017/602-269-6937

Stan de Treville, Box 33021, San Diego, CA 92103/714-298-3393 (checkering patterns)

Turner Co., Div. Cleanweld Prods., Inc., 821 Park Ave., Sycamore, IL 60178/815-895-4545

Twin City Steel Treating Co., Inc. 1114 S. 3rd, Minneapolis, MN 55415 (heat treating)

Will-Burt Co., 169 So. Main, Orrville, OH 44667 (vises)

Williams Gun Sight Co., 7389 Lapeer Rd., Davison, MI 48423

Wilson Arms Co., 63 Leetes Island Rd., Branford, CT 06405

Wisconsin Platers Supply Co. (See Texas Platers)

W.C. Wolff Co., Box 232, Ardmore, PA 19003 (springs)

Woodcraft Supply Corp., 313 Montvale, Woburn, MA 01801

HANDGUN ACCESSORIES

Baramie Corp., 6250 E. 7 Mile Rd., Detroit, MI 48234 (Hip-Grip)

Bar-Sto Precision Machine, 13377 Sullivan Rd., Twentynine Palms, CA 92277/714-367-2747

Behlert Custom Guns, 725 Lehigh Ave., Union, NJ 07083

Belt Slide, Inc, 1301 Brush Bend Dr., Round Rock, TX 78664/512-255-1805

Bingham Ltd., 1775-C Wilwat Dr., Norcross, GA 30093 (magazines)

C'Arco, P.O. Box 308, Highland, CA 92346 (Ransom Rest)

Central Specialties Co., 6030 Northwest Hwy., Chicago, IL 60631/312-774-5000 (trigger lock)

D&E Magazines Mfg., P.O. Box 4876, Sylmar, CA 91342 (clips)

Essex Arms, Box 345, Phaerring St., Island Pond, VT 05846 (45 Auto frames)

R. S. Frielich, 211 East 21st St., New York, NY 10010/212-777-4477 (cases)

Laka Tool Co., 62 Kinkel St., Westbury, L.I., NY 11590/516-334-4620 (stainless steel 45 Auto parts)

Lee's Red Ramps, 7252 E. Ave. U-3, Littlerock, CA 93543 (illuminated sights)

Lee Precision Inc., 4275 Hwy. U, Hartford, WI 53027 (pistol rest holders)

Kent Lomont, 4421 So. Wayne Ave., Ft. Wayne, In 46807/219-694-6792 (Auto Mag only)

Los Gatos Grip & Specialty Co., P.O. Box 1850, Los Gatos, CA 95030 (custom-made)

Mascot rib sight (See Travis R. Strahan)

Mellmark Mfg. Co., P.O. Box 139, Turlock, CA 95380 (pistol safe)

W. A. Miller Co., Inc., Mingo Loop, Oguossoc, ME 04964 (cases)

No-Sho Mfg. Co., 10727 Glenfield Ct., Houston, TX 77096/713-723-0966

Harry Owen (See Sport Specialties)

Pachmayr, 1220 S. Grand, Los Angeles, CA 90015 (cases)

Pacific Intl. Mchdsg. Corp., 2215 "J" St., Sacramento, CA 95818/916-446-2737 (Vega 45 Colt comb. mag.)

Sile Distributors, 7 Centre Market Pl., New York, NY 10013

Sport Specialties, (Harry Owen), Box 5337, Hacienda Hts., CA 91745/213-968-5806 (.22 rimfire adapters; insert bbls. f. T-C Cont.)

Sportsmen's Equipment Co., 415 W. Washington, San Diego, CA 92103/714-296-1501

Travis R. Strahan, Rt. 7, Townsend Circle, Ringgold, GA 30736/404-937-4495 (Mascot rib sights)

M. Tyler, 1326 W. Britton, Oklahoma City, OK 73114 (grip adaptor)

Whitney Sales, Inc., P.O. Box 875, Reseda, CA 91335

HANDGUN GRIPS

Ajax Custom Grips, Inc., 12229 Cox Lane, Dallas, TX 75234/214-241-6302

Art Jewel Enterprises, Box 819, Berkeley, IL 60163/312-941-1110

Beeman Precision Airguns, 47 Paul Dr., San Rafael, CA 94903/415-472-7121 (airguns only)

Bingham Ltd., 1775-C Wilwat Dr., Norcross, GA 30093

Fitz Pistol Grip Co., P.O. Box 55, Grizzly Gulch, Whiskeytown, CA 96055/916-778-3136

Gateway Shooters' Supply, Inc., 10145-103rd St., Jacksonville, FL 32210 (Rogers grips)

The Gunshop, R.D. Wallace, 320 Overland Rd., Prescott, AZ 86301

Herrett's, Box 741, Twin Falls, ID 83301

Hogue Combat Grips, P.O. Box 2036, Atascadero, CA 93423/805-466-6266 (Monogrip)

Paul Jones Munitions Systems, (See Fitz Co.)

Russ Maloni, 40 Sigman Lane, Elma, NY 14059/716-652-7131

Millett Industries, 16131 Gothard St., Huntington Beach, CA 92647/714-842-5575 (custom)

Monogrip, (See Hogue)
Monte Kristo Pistol Grip Co., P.O. Box 55 Grizzly Gulch, Whiskeytown, CA 96095/916-778-3136
Mustang Custom Pistol Grips, 27616 Tyler, Romoland, CA 92380/714-657-0006
Pachmayr Gun Works, Inc., 1220 S. Grand Ave., Los Angeles, CA 90015/213-748-7271
Robert H. Newell, 55 Coyote, Los Alamos, NM 87544/505-662-7135 (custom)
Rogers Grips (See Gateway Shooters' Supply)
A. Jack Rosenberg & Sons, 12229 Cox Lane, Dallas, TX 75234/214-241-6302 (Ajax)
Russwood Custom Pistol Grips, 40 Sigma Lane, Elma, NY 14059/716-652-7131 (cust. exotic woods)
Jean St. Henri, 6525 Dume Dr., Malibu, CA 90265 (custom)
Schiermeier Custom Handgun Stocks, 306 No. 1st St., Kent, WA 98031/206-854-5358
Jay Scott, Inc., 81 Sherman Place, Garfield, NJ 07026/201-340-0550
Sile Dist., 7 Centre Market Pl., New York, NY 10013/212-925-4111
Southern Gun Exchange, Inc., 4311 Northeast Expressway, Atlanta (Doraville), GA 30340 (Outrider brand)
Sports Inc., P.O. Box 683, Park Ridge, IL 60068/312-825-8952 (Franzite)
Bob Allen Sportswear, 214 S.W. Jackson, Des Moines, IA 50315/515-283-1988

HEARING PROTECTORS

AO Safety Prods., Div. of American Optical Corp., 14 Mechanic St., Southbridge, MA 01550/617-765-9711 (ear valves, ear muffs)
Bausch & Lomb, 635 St. Paul St., Rochester, NY 14602
David Clark Co., Inc., 360 Franklin St., Worcester, MA 01604
Norton Co., Safety Prods. Div., 16624 Edwards Rd., Cerritos, CA 90701/213-926-0545 (Lee-Sonic ear valve)
Safety Direct, 23 Snider Way, Sparks, NV 89431 (Silencio)
Smith & Wesson, 2100 Roosevelt Ave., Springfield, MA 01101
Willson Safety Prods. Div., P.O. Box 622, Reading, PA 19603 (Ray-O-Vac)

HOLSTERS & LEATHER GOODS

Alessi Custom Concealment Holsters, 2465 Niagara Falls Blvd., Tonawanda, NY 14150/716-691-5615
American Sales & Mfg. Co., P.O. Box 677, Laredo, TX 78040/512-723-6893
Andy Anderson, P.O. Box 225, North Hollywood, CA 91603/213-877-2401 (Gunfighter Custom Holsters)
Armament Systems & Procedures, Inc., P.O. Box 356, Appleton, WI 54912/414-731-8893 (ASP)
Beeman Precision Airguns, 47 Paul Dr., San Rafael, CA 94903/415-472-7121 (airguns only)
Belt Slide, Inc., 1301 Brushy Bend, Round Rock, TX 78664/512-255-1805
Bianchi Holster Co., 100 Calle Cortez, Temecula, CA 92390
Ted Blocker's Custom Holsters, Box 821, Rosemead, CA 91770/213-442-5772 (shop: 4945 Santa Anita Ave., Temple City, CA 91780)
Edward H. Bohlin, 931 N. Highland Ave., Hollywood, CA 90038/213-463-4888
Bo-Mar Tool & Mfg. Co., P.O. Box 168, Carthage, TX 75633/214-693-5220
Boyt, Div. of Welch Sptg., Box 1108, Iowa Falls, IA 51026
Brauer Bros. Mfg. Co., 2012 Washington Ave., St. Louis, MO 63103/314-231-2864
Browning, Rt. 4, Box 624-B, Arnold, MO 63010
J.M. Bucheimer Co., P.O. Box 280, Airport Rd., Frederick, MD 21701/301-662-5101
Cathey Enterprises, Inc., 9516 Neils Thompson Dr., Suite 116, Austin, TX 78758/512-837-7150
Chace Leather Prods., Longhorn Div., 507 Alden St., Fall River, MA 02722/617-678-7556
Cobra Ltd., 1865 New Highway, Farmingdale, NY 11735/516-752-8544
Colt, P.O. Box 1868, Hartford, CT. 06102/203-236-6311
Daisy Mfg. Co., Rogers, AR 72756
Davis Leather Co., G. Wm. Davis, P.O. Box 446, Arcadia, CA 91006/213-445-3872
Eugene DeMayo & Sons, Inc., 2795 Third Ave., Bronx, NY 10455
Ellwood Epps Northern Ltd., 210 Worthington St. W., North Bay, Ont. P1B 3B4, Canada (custom made)
The Eutaw Co., Box 608, U.S. Highway 176W, Holly Hill, SC 29059
Gunfighter (See Anderson)
Hoyt Holster Co., P.O. Box 69, Coupeville, WA 98239/206-678-6640
Don Hume, Box 351, Miami, OK 74354/918-542-6604
The Hunter Corp., 3300 W. 71st Ave., Westminster, CO 80030/303-427-4626
Jackass Leather Co., 7383 N. Rogers Ave., Chicago, IL 60626/312-338-2800
John's Custom Leather, 525 S. Liberty St., Blairsville, PA 15717/412-459-6802
Jumbo Sports Prods., P.O. Box 280, Airport Rd., Frederick, MD 21701
Kirkpatrick Leather, Box 3150, Laredo, TX 89041/512-723-6631
Kolpin Mfg. Inc., P.O. Box 231, Berlin, WI 54923/414-361-0400
Morris Lawing, 150 Garland Ct., Charlotte, NC 28202/704-375-1740
Lawman Leather, Inc., P.O. Box 4772, Scottsdale, AZ 85258
George Lawrence Co., 306 S. W. First Ave., Portland, OR 97204
Liberty Organization Inc., P.O. Box 306, Montrose, CA 91020/213-248-0618
Mixson Leathercraft Inc., 1950 W. 84th St., Hialeah, FL 33014/305-820-5190
Nordac Mfg. Corp., Rt 12, Box 124, Fredericksburg, VA 22401/703-752-2552
Kenneth L. Null-Custom Concealment Holsters, R.D. #5, Box 197, Hanover, PA 17331 (See Seventrees)
Arvo Ojala, 3960 S.E. 1st, Gresham, OR 97030
Old West Inc. Leather Prods., P.O. Box 2030, Chula Vista, CA 92012/714-429-8050
Pioneer Products, 1033 W. Amity Rd., Boise, ID 83075/208-345-2003

Pony Express Sport Shop Inc., 17460 Ventura Blvd., Encino, CA 91316/213-788-0123
Red Head Brand Corp., 4949 Joseph Hardin Dr., Dallas, TX 75236/214-333-4141
Rogers Holsters, 1736 St. Johns Bluff Rd., Jacksonville, FL 32216/904-641-9434
Roy's Custom Leather Goods, Hwy, 1325 & Rawhide Rd., P.O. Box G, Magnolia, AR 71753/501-234-1566
Safariland Leather Products, 1941 So. Walker Ave., Monrovia, CA 91016/213-357-7902
Safety Speed Holster, Inc., 910 So. Vail, Montebello, CA 90640/213-723-4140
Buddy Schoellkopf Products, Inc., 4949 Joseph Hardin Dr., TX 75236/214-333-2121
Seventrees Systems Ltd., R.D. 5, Box 197, Hanover, PA 17331/717-632-6873 (See Null)
Sile Distr., 7 Centre Market Pl., New York NY 10013/212-925-4111
Smith & Wesson, 2100 Roosevelt Ave., Springfield, MA 01101
Milt Sparks, Box 7, Idaho City, ID 83631
Robert A. Strong Co., 105 Maplewood Ave., Gloucester, MA 01930/617-281-3300
Torel, Inc., 1053 N. South St., Yoakum, TX 77995 (gun slings)
Triple-K Mfg. Co., 568 Sixth Ave., San Diego, CA 92101
Universal Leathergoods, Inc., 6573 E. 21st Pl., Tulsa, OK 74124
Viking Leathercraft, P.O. Box 203, Chula Vista, CA 92012/714-423-8991
Whitco, Box 1712, Brownsville, TX 78520 (Hide-A-Way)
Wyman Corp., P.O. Box 8644, Salt Lake City, UT 84104/801-359-0368 (Cannon Packer f. rifle, shotgun)

HUNTING AND CAMP GEAR, CLOTHING, ETC.

Bob Allen Sportswear, P.O. Box 477, Des Moines, IA 50302
Eddie Bauer, 15010 NE 36th St., Redmond, WA 98052
L. L. Bean, Freeport, ME 04032
Bear Archery, R.R. 4, 4600 Southwest 41st Blvd., Gainesville, FL 32601/904-376-2327 (Himalayan backpack)
Bernzomatic Corp., 740 Driving Pk. Ave., Rochester, NY 14613 (stoves & lanterns)
Big Beam, Teledyne Co., 290 E. Prairie St., Crystal Lake, IL 60014 (lamp)
Browning, Rte. 1, Morgan, UT 84050
Camp Trails, P.O. Box 23155, Phoenix, AZ 85063/602-272-9401 (packs only)
Camp-Ways, 12915 S. Spring St., Los Angeles, CA 90061/213-532-0910
Challanger Mfg. Co., Box 550, Jamaica, NY 11431 (glow safe)
Chippewa Shoe Co., 925 First Ave., Chippewa Falls, WI 54729/715-723-5571 (boots)
Cobra, Box 167, Brady, TX 76825 (Cobra 3-in-1 light)
Coleman Co., Inc., 250 N. St. Francis, Wichita, KS 67201
Converse Rubber Co., 55 Fordham Rd., Wilmington, MA 01887 (boots)
Dana Safety Heater, J. L. Galef & Son, Inc., 85 Chamber St., New York, NY 10007
Danner Shoe Mfg. Co., 5188 S.E. International Way, Milwaukie, OR 97222/503-653-2920 (boots)
DEER-ME Prod. Co., Box 345, Anoka, MN 55303 (tree steps)
Dunham Co., P.O. Box 813, Brattleboro, VT 05301/802-254-2316 (boots)
Durango Boot Div., U.S. Industry, 1810 Columbia Ave., Franklin, TN 37064/615-794-1556
Freeman Ind., Inc., 100 Marblehead Rd., Tuckahoe, NY 10707 (Trak-Kit)
French Dressing Inc., 15 Palmer Heights, Burlington, VT 05401/802-658-1434 (boots)
Game-Winner, Inc., 2690 Cumberland Parkway, Suite 440, Atlanta, GA 30339/404-588-0401 (camouflage suits)
Gander Mountain, Inc., Box 248, Wilmot, WI 53192/414-862-2331
Georgia Boot Div., U.S. Industry, 1810 Columbia Ave., Franklin, TN 37064/615-794-1556
Gokey, 94 E. 4th St., St. Paul, MN 55101
Gun Club Sportswear, Box 477, Des Moines, IA 50302
Gun-Ho Case Mfg. Co., 110 E. 10th St., St. Paul, MN 55101
Joseph M. Herman Shoe Co., Inc., 114 Union St., Millis, MA 02054/617-376-2601 (boots)
Himalayan Industries, Inc., P.O. Box 7465, Pine Bluff, AR 71611/501-534-6411
Bob Hinman Outfitters, 1217 W. Glen, Peoria, IL 61614
Hunting World, 16 E. 53rd St., New York, NY 10022
Jung Shoe Mfg. Co., 620 S. 8th St., Sheboygan, WI 53081/414-458-3483 (boots)
Kelty Pack, Inc., 9281 Borden Ave., Sun Valley, CA 91352/213-768-1922
La Crosse Rubber Mills Co., P.O. Box 1328, La Crosse, WI 54601/608-782-3020 (boots)
Peter Limmer & Sons Inc., Box 66, Intervale, NH 03845 (boots)
Marathon Rubber Prods. Co. Inc., 510 Sherman St., Wausau, WI 54401 (rain gear)
Marble Arms Corp., 420 Industrial Park, Gladstone, MI 49837
Nimrod & Wayfarer Trailers, 500 Ford Blvd., Hamilton, OH 45011
The Orvis Co., Manchester, VT 05254/802-362-3622 (fishing gear; clothing)
PGB Assoc., 310 E. 46th St., Suite 3E, New York, NY 10017/212-867-9560
Prime Leather Finishes Co., 205 S. Second St., Milwaukee, WI 53204 (leath. waterproofer; Boot n' Saddle Soap)
Quabaug Rubber Co./Vibram U.S.A., 17 School St. N. Brookfield, MA 01535/617-867-7731 (boots)
Quoddy Moccasins, Div. R. G. Barry Corp., 67 Minot Ave., Auburn, ME 04210/207-784-3555
Ranger Mfg. Co., Inc., P.O. Box 3676, Augusta, GA 30904
Ranger Rubber Co., 1100 E. Main St., Endicott, NY 13760/607-757-4260 (boots)
Red Ball, c/o Uniroyal Inc., World Hq., Middlebury, CT 06749 (boots)
Red Head Brand Corp., 4949 Joseph Hardin Dr., Dallas, TX 75236/214-333-4141
Red Wing Shoe Co., Rte 2, Red Wing, MN 55066

Refrigiwear, Inc., 71 Inip Dr., Inwood, Long Island, NY 11696
Reliance Prod. Ltd., 1830 Dublin Ave., Winnipeg 21, Man. R3H 0H3 Can. (tent peg)
W. R. Russell Moccasin Co., 285 S.W. Franklin, Berlin, WI 54923
Buddy Schoellkopf Prods Inc., 4949 Joseph Hardin Dr., Dallas, TX 75236/214-333-2121
Servus Rubber Co., 1136 2nd St., Rock Island, IL 61201 (footwear)
The Ski Hut-Trailwise, 1615 University Ave., P.O. Box 309, Berkeley, CA 94710
Stearns Mfg. Co., P.O. Box 1498, St. Cloud, MN 56301
Sterno Inc., 300 Park Ave., New York, NY 10022 (camp stoves)
Teledyne Co., Big Beam, 290 E. Prairie St., Crystal Lake, IL 60014
10-X Mfg. Co., 316 So. Lexington Ave., Cheyenne, WY 82001/307-635-9192
Thermos Div., KST Co., Norwich, CT 06361 (Pop Tent)
Norm Thompson, 1805 N.W. Thurman St., Portland, OR 97209
Utica Duxbak Corp., 1745 S. Acoma St., Denver, CO 80223/303-778-0324
Waffen-Frankonia, Box 6780, 87 Wurzburg 1, W. Germany
Weinbrenner Shoe Corp., Polk St., Merrill, WI 54452
Wenzel Co., 1280 Research Blvd., St. Louis, MO 63132
Wolverine Boots & Shoes Div., Wolverine World Wide, 9341 Courtland Dr., Rockford, MI 49351/616-866-1561 (footwear)
Woods Bag & Canvas Co., Ltd., 90 River St., P.O. Box 407, Ogdensburg, NY 13669/315-393-3520
Woodstream Corp., Box 327, Lititz, PA 17543 (Hunter Seat)
Woolrich Woolen Mills, Woolrich, PA 17779
Yankee Mechanics, RFD No. 1, Concord, NH 03301/603-225-3181 (hand winches)

KNIVES AND KNIFEMAKER'S SUPPLIES—FACTORY and MAIL ORDER

Alcas Cutlery Corp., Olean, NY 14760/716-372-3111 (Cutco)
Atlanta Cutlery, Box 839, Conyers, GA 30207/404-922-3700 (mail order, supplies)
Bali-Song Inc., 3039 Roswell St., Los Angeles, CA 90085/213-258-7021
L. L. Bean, 386 Main St., Freeport, ME 04032/207-865-3111 (mail order)
Benchmark Knives, P.O. Box 998, Gastonia, NC 28052/704-867-1307
Crosman Blades™, The Coleman Co., 250 N. St. Francis, Wichita, KS 67201
Bladesmith, P.O. Box 743, Orange, CA 92666 (supplies)
Boker, The Cooper Group, P.O. Box 728, Apex, NC 27502/919-362-7510
Bowen Knife Co., P.O. Drawer 590, Blackshear, GA 31516/912-449-4794
Browne and Pharr Inc., 1775-I Wilwat Dr., Norcross, GA 30091/404-447-9285
Browning, Rt. 1, Morgan, UT 84050/801-876-2711
Buck Knives, Inc., P.O. Box 1267; 1900 Weld Blvd., El Cajon, CA 92022/714-449-1100 or 800-854-2557
Camillus Cutlery Co., Main St., Camillus, NY 13031/315-672-8111 (Sword Brand)
W. R. Case & Sons Cutlery Co., 20 Russell Blvd., Bradford, PA 16701/814-368-4123
Charter Arms Corp., 430 Sniffens Lane, Stratford, CT 06497/203-377-8080 (Skatchet)
Chicago Cutlery Co., 441 Bonner Rd., Wauconda, IL 60084/312-526-2144
E. Christopher Firearms, State Rte. 123 and Ferry Rd., Miamitown, OH 45041/513-353-1321 (supplies)
Collins Brothers Div. (belt-buckle knife), See Bowen Knife Co.
Colonial Knife Co., P.O. Box 3327, Providence, RI 02909/401-421-1600 (Master Brand)
Custom Purveyors, (Ted Devlet), P.O. Box 886, Fort Lee, NJ 07024/201-886-0196 (mail order)
Dixie Gun Works, Inc., P.O. Box 130, Union City, TN 38261/901-885-0700 (supplies)
Eze-Lap Diamond Prods., Box 2229, 15164 Weststate St., Westminster, CA 92683/714-847-1555 (knife sharpeners)
Gerber Legendary Blades, 14200 S.W. 72nd St., Portland, OR 99223/503-639-6161
Golden Age Arms Co., 14 W. Winter St., Delaware, OH 43015/614-369-6513 (supplies)
Gutmann Cutlery Co., Inc., 900 S. Columbus Ave., Mt. Vernon, NY 10550/914-699-4044
H & B Forge Co., Rte. 2, Box 24, Shiloh, OH 44878/419-896-3435 (throwing knives, tomahawks)
Russell Harrington Cutlery, Inc., Subs. of Hyde Mfg. Co., 44 River St., Southbridge, MA 01550/617-764-4371 (Dexter, Green River Works)
J. A. Henckels Zwillingswerk, Inc., 1 Westchester Plaza, Elmsford, NY 10523/914-592-7370
Imperial Knife Associated Companies, 1776 Broadway, New York, NY 10019/212-757-1814
Indian Ridge Traders, Box 869, Royal Oak, MI 48068/313-399-6034 (mostly blades)
Jet-Aer Corp., 100 Sixth Ave., Paterson, NJ 07524/201-278-8300
KA-BAR Cutlery Inc., 5777 Grant Ave., Cleveland, OH 44105/216-271-4000
KA-BAR Knives, Collectors Division, 434 No. 9th St., Olean, NY 14760/716-372-5811
Keene Corp., Cutting Serv. Div., 1569 Tower Grove Ave., St. Louis, MO 63110/314-771-1550
Kershaw Cutlery Co., 6024 Jean Rd., Suite D, Lake Oswego, OR 97034/503-636-0111
Knife and Gun Supplies, P.O. Box 13522, Arlington, TX 76013/817-261-0569
Koval Knives, P.O. Box 14130, Columbus, OH 43214/614-888-6486 (supplies)
Lakota Corp., 30916 Agoura Rd., Suite 311, Westlake Village, CA 91361/213-889-7177
Lamson & Goodnow Mfg. Co., Shelburne Falls, MA 03170/413-625-6331
Al Mar Knives, Inc., 5861 S.W. Benfield Ct., Lake Oswego, OR 97034/503-639-8554
Marble Arms Corp., 420 Industrial Park, Gladstone, MI 49837/906-425-3710

Marttiini Knives, Box 38866, Chicago, IL 60648/312-470-0233
Matthews Cutlery, P.O. Box 33095, Decatur, GA 30033/404-636-7923 (mail order)
R. Murphy Co., Inc., 13 Groton-Harvard Rd., Ayer, MA 01432/617-772-3481 (StaySharp)
Nordic Knives, 1643-C-Z Copenhagen Dr., Solvang, CA 93463 (mail order)
Normark Corp., 1710 E. 78th St., Minneapolis, MN 55423/612-869-3291
Olsen Knife Co., Inc., 7 Joy St., Howard City, MI 49329/616-937-4373
Ontario Knife Co., Subs. of Servotronics, Inc., P.O. Box 145, Franklinville, NY 14737/716-676-5527 (Old Hickory)
Parker Cutlery, 6928 Lee Highway, Chattanooga, TN 37415/615-894-1782
Plaza Cutlery Inc., 3333 Bristol, #161, Costa Mesa, CA 92626/714-549-3932 (mail order)
Queen Cutlery Co., P.O. Box 500, Franklinville, NY 14737/617 676 5540
R & C Knives and Such, P.O. Box 32631, San Jose, CA 95152/408-923-5728 (mail order)
Randall-Made Knives, Box 1988, Orlando, FL 32802/305-855-8075 (ctlg. $1)
Rigid Knives, P.O. Box 816, Hwy. 290E, Lake Hamilton, AR 71951/501-525-1377
A. G. Russell, 1705 Hiwy. 71 N., Springdale, AR 72764/501-751-7341
Bob Sanders, 2358 Tyler Lane, Louisville, KY 40205 (Bahco steel)
San Diego Knives, 2785 Kurtz No. 8, San Diego, CA 92110/714-297-4530 (mail order)
Schrade Cutlery Corp., 1776 Broadway, New York, NY 10019/212-757-1814
Bob Schrimsher, Custom Knifemaker's Supply, P.O. Box 308, Emory, TX 75440/214-328-2453
Paul Sheffield, P.O. Box 141, Deland, FL 32720/904-736-9356 (supplies)
Smith & Wesson, 2100 Roosevelt Ave., Springfield, MA 01101/413-781-8300
Jesse W. Smith Saddlery, E. 3024 Sprague, Spokane, WA 99201 (sheathmakers)
Swiss Army Knives, Inc., P.O. Box 846, Shelton, CT 06484/203-929-6391 (Victorinox; folding)
Tekna, 3549 Haven Ave., Menlo Park, CA 94025/415-365-5112
Thompson/Center, P.O. Box 2405, Rochester, NH 03867/603-332-2394
Tommer-Bordein Corp., 220 N. River St., Delano, MN 55328/612-972-3901
Tru-Balance Knife Co., 2115 Tremond Blvd., Grand Rapids, MI 49504/616-453-3679
Utica Cutlery Co., 820 Noyes St., Utica, NY 13503/315-733-4663 (Kutmaster)
Valor Corp., 5555 N.W. 36th Ave., Miami, FL 33142
Washington Forge, Inc., Englishtown, NJ 07727/201-446-7777 (Carriage House)
Wenoka Cutlery, 85 North Ave., Natick, MA 01760/617-453-3679
Western Cutlery Co., 1800 Pike Rd., Longmont, CO 80501/303-772-5900 (Westmark)
Walt Whinnery, Walts Cust. Leather, 1947 Meadow Creek Dr., Louisville, KY 40281/502-458-4351 (sheathmaker)
Wilkinson Sword, 1316 W. Main St., Richmond, VA 23220/804-353-1812
J. Wolfe's Knife Works, Box 1056, Larkspur, CA 94939 (supplies)
Wyoming Knife Co., 3700 E. 20th, Casper, WY 82601/307-265-7437

LABELS, BOXES, CARTRIDGE HOLDERS

Milton Brynin, 214 E. Third St., Mount Vernon, NY 10710/914-667-6549 (cartridge box labels)
E-Z Loader, Del Rey Products, P.O. Box 91561, Los Angeles, CA 90009
Peterson Label Co., P.O. Box 186, 23 Sullivan Dr., Redding Ridge, CT 06876/203-938-2349 (cartridge box labels; Targ-Dots)
N. H. Schiffman, 963 Malibu, Pocatello, ID 83201 (cartridge carrier)

LOAD TESTING and PRODUCT TESTING, (CHRONOGRAPHING, BALLISTIC STUDIES)

Hutton Rifle Ranch, 1802 S. Oak Park Dr., Rolling Hills, Tucson, AZ 85710
Kent Lomont, 4421 S. Wayne Ave., Ft. Wayne, IN 46807/219-694-6792 (handguns, handgun ammunition)
Plum City Ballistics Range, Norman E. Johnson, Rte. 1, Box 29A, Plum City, WI 54761/715-647-2539
Russell's Rifle Shop, Rte. 5, Box 92, Georgetown, TX 78626/512-778-5338 (load testing and chronographing to 300 yds.)
John M. Tovey, 4710 - 104th Lane NE, Circle Pines, MN 55014
H. P. White Laboratory, Inc., 3114 Scarboro Rd., Street, MD 21154/301-838-6550

MISCELLANEOUS

Accurizing Service, Herbert G. Troester, 2292 W. 1000 North, Vernal, UT 84078/801-789-2158
Action, Mauser-style only, Crandell Tool & Machine Co., 1540 N. Mitchell St., Cadillac, MI 49601/616-775-5562
Activator, B.M.F. Activator, Inc., 3705 Broadway, Houston, TX 77017/713-645-6726
Adapters, Sage Industries, P.O. Box 2248, Hemet, CA 92343/714-925-1006 (12-ga. shotgun; 38 S&W blank)
Adhesive Flannel, Forest City Prod., 722 Bolivar, Cleveland, OH 44115
Adjusta-Targ, Inc., 1817 Thackeray N.W., Massillon, OH 44646
Archery, Bear, R.R. 4, 4600 Southwest 41st Blvd., Gainesville, FL 32601/904-376-2327
Arms Restoration, J. J. Jenkins Ent. Inc., 375 Pine Ave. No. 25, Goleta, CA 93017/805-967-1366
Barrel Band Swivels, Phil Judd, 83 E. Park St., Butte, MT 59701
Bedding Kit, Bisonite Co., P.O. Box 84, Kenmore Station, Buffalo, NY 14217

Bedding Kit, Fenwal, Inc., Resins Systems Div., 400 Main St., Ashland, MA 01721

Belt Buckles, Adina Silversmiths Corp., P.O. Box 348, 3195 Tucker Rd., Cornwell Heights, PA 19020/215-639-7246

Belt Buckles, Bergamot Brass Works, 820 Wisconsin St., Delavan, WI 53115/414-728-5572

Belt Buckles, Just Brass Inc., 21 Filmore Place, Freeport, NY 11520 (ctlg. $2)

Belt Buckles, Sports Style Associates, 148 Hendrickson Ave., Lynbrook, NY 11563/516-599-5080

Belt Buckles, Pilgrim Pewter Inc., R.D. 2, Tully, NY 13159/607-842-6431

Benchrest & Accuracy Shooters Equipment, Bob Pease Accuracy, P.O. Box 787, Zipp Road, New Braunfels, TX 78130/512-625-1342

Blowgun, PAC Outfitters, P.O. Box 56, Mulvane, KS 67110/316-777-4909

Bootdryers, Baekgaard Ltd., 1855 Janke Dr., Northbrook, IL 60062

Breech Plug Wrench, Swaine Machine, 195 O'Connell, Providence, RI 02905

Cannons, A & K Mfg. Co., Inc., 1651 N. Nancy Rose Ave., Tucson, AZ 85712 (replicas)

Cannons, South Bend Replicas Ind., 61650 Oak Rd., S. Bend, IN 44614/219-289-4500 (ctlg. $5)

Cartridge Adapters, Sport Specialties, Harry Owen, Box 5337, Hacienda Hts., CA 91745/213-968-5806

Case Gauge, Plum City Ballistics Range, Rte. 1, Box 29A, Plum City, WI 54761/715-647-2539

Cased, high-grade English tools, Marvin Huey Gun Cases, Box 98, Reed's Spring, MO 65737/417-538-4233 (ebony, horn, ivory handles)

Clips, D&E Magazines Mfg., P.O. Box 4876, Sylmar, CA 91342 (handgun and rifle)

CO2 Cartridges, Nittan U.S.A. Inc., 4901 Morena Blvd., Suite 307, San Diego, CA 92117/714-272-6113

Deer Drag, D&H Prods. Co., Inc., P.O. Box 22, Glenshaw, PA 15116/412-443-2190

Defendor, Ralide, Inc., P.O. Box 131, Athens, TN 37303/615-745-3525

Dryer, Thermo-Electric, Golden-Rod, Buenger Enterprises, Box 5286, Oxnard, CA 93030/805-985-9596

E-Z Loader, Del Rey Prod., P.O. Box 91561, Los Angeles, CA 90009

Ear-Valve, Norton Co. Safety Prods. Div., 16624 Edwards Rd., Cerritos, CA 90701/213-926-0545 (Lee-Sonic)

Flares, Colt Industries, P.O. Box 1868, Hartford, CT 06102

Flares, Smith & Wesson Chemical Co., 2399 Forman Rd., Rock Creek, OH 44084

Game Hoist, Cam Gear Ind., P.O. Box 1002, Kalispell, MT 59901 (Sportsmaster 500 pocket hoist)

Game Hoist, Precise, 3 Chestnut, Suffern, NY 10901

Game Scent, Buck Stop Lure Co., Inc., 3015 Grow Rd. N.W., Stanton, MI 48888/517-762-5091

Game Scent, Pete Rickard, Box 1250, Cobleskill, NY 12043/518-234-2731 (Indian Buck lure)

Gas Pistol, Penguin Ind., Inc., Airport Industrial Mall, Coatesville, PA 19320/215-384-6000

Grip Caps, Classic Arms Corp., P.O. Box 8, Palo Alto, CA 94301/415-321-7243

Grip Caps, Knickerbocker Enterprises, 16199 S. Maple Ln. Rd., Oregon City, OR 97045

Grip Caps, Philip D. Letiecq, AQ 18 Wagon Box Rd., P.O. Box 251, Story, WY 82842/307-683-2817

Gun Bedding Kit, Fenwal, Inc., Resins System Div., 400 Main St., Ashland, MA 01721/617-881-2000

Gun Jewelry, Sid Bell Originals, R.D. 2, Tully, NY 13159/607-842-6431

Gun Jewelry, Pilgrim Pewter Inc., R.D. 2, Tully, NY 13159/607-842-6431

Gun Jewelry, Al Popper, 6l4 Turnpike St., Stoughton, MA 02072/617-344-2036

Gun Jewelry, Sports Style Assoc., 148 Hendricks Ave., Lynbrook, NY 11563

Gun photographer, Mustafa Bilal, 727 Belleview Ave. East, Suite 103, Seattle, WA 98102/206-322-5449

Gun photographer, Art Carter, 818 Baffin Bay Rd., Columbia, SC 29210/803-772-2148

Gun photographer, Jim Weyer, 224½ Huron St., Toledo, OH 43604/419-241-5454

Gun Record Book, B. J. Co., Bridge St., Bluffton, SC 29910

Gun Sling, Kwikfire, Wayne Prods. Co., P.O. Box 247, Camp Hill, PA 17011

Gun Slings, Torel, Inc., 1053 N. South St., Yoakum, TX 77995

Hugger Hooks, Roman Products, 4363 Loveland St., Golden, CO 80403/303-279-6959

Insect Repellent, Armor, Div. of Buck Stop, Inc., 3015 Grow Rd., Stanton, MI 48888

Insert Barrels, Sport Specialties, H. Owen, Box 5337, Hacienda Hts., CA 91745/213-968-5806

Light Load, Jacob & Tiffin Inc., P.O. Box 547, Clanton, AL 35045

Locks, Gun, Bor-Lok Prods., 105 5th St., Arbuckle, CA 95912

Locks, Gun, Master Lock Co., 2600 N. 32nd St., Milwaukee, WI 53245

Miniature Cannons, A & K Mfg. Co., 5146 E. Pima, Tucson, AZ 85712/602-327-9275 (ctlg. $1)

Miniature Cannons, Karl J. Furr, 76 East, 350 North, Orem, UT 84057/801-225-2603 (replicas)

Miniature Guns, Charles H. Stoppler, 5 Minerva Place, New York, NY 10468

Monte Carlo Pad, Frank A. Hoppe Div., Penguin Ind., Airport Industrial Mall, Coatesville, PA 19320/215-384-6000

Muzzle Rest, Meadow Industries, P.O. Box 50, Forest, VA 24551/804-525-2567

Muzzle-Top, Allen Assoc., 7502 Limekiln, Philadelphia, PA 19150 (plastic gun muzzle cap)

Patterning Data, Whits Shooting Stuff, P.O. Box 1340, Cody, WY 82414

Pell Remover, A. Edw. Terpening, 838 E. Darlington Rd., Tarpon Springs, FL 33589

Powderhorns, Kirk Olson, Ft. Woolsey Guns, P.O. Box 2122, Prescott, AZ 86302/602-778-3035

Powderhorns, Thomas F. White, 5801 Westchester Ct., Worthington, OH 43085/614-888-0128

Practice Ammunition, Hoffman New Ideas Inc., 821 Northmoor Rd., Lake Forest, IL 60045/312-234-4075

Pressure Testg. Machine, M. York, 5508 Griffith Rd., Gaithersburg, MD 20760/301-253-4217

Ram-Line accessories, Chesco, Inc., 2323 W. 2nd Ave., Denver, CO 80223/303-698-1333

Ransom Handgun Rests, C'Arco, P.O. Box 308, Highland, CA 92346

Retriev-R-Trainer, Scientific Prods. Corp., 426 Swann Ave., Alexandria, VA 22301

Rifle Magazines, Butler Creek Corp., Box GG, Jackson Hole, WY 83001/307-733-3599 (30-rd. Mini-14)

Rifle Slings, Bianchi Leather Prods., 100 Calle Cortez, Temecula, CA 92390/714-676-5621

Rifle Slings, Chace Leather Prods., Longhorn Div., 507 Alden St., Fall River, MA 02722/617-678-7556

Rifle Slings, John's Cust. Leather, 525 S. Liberty St., Blairsville, PA 15717/412-459-6802

Rifle Slings, Kirkpatrick Leather Co., Box 3150, Laredo, TX 78041/512-723-6631

RIG, NRA Scoring Plug, Rig Products, P.O. Box 1990, Sparks, NV 89432/702-331-5666

Rubber Cheekpiece, W. H. Lodewick, 2816 N.E. Halsey, Portland, OR 97232/503-284-2554

Saddle Rings, Studs, Fred Goodwin, Sherman Mills, ME 04776

Safeties, William E. Harper, The Great 870 Co., P.O. Box 6309. El Monte, CA 91734/213-579-3077 (f. Rem. 870P)

Safeties, Williams Gun Sight Co., 7389 Lapeer Rd., Davison, MI 48423

Salute Cannons, Naval Co., R.D. 2, 4747 Cold Spring Creamery Rd., Doylestown, PA 18901

Sav-Bore, Saunders Sptg. Gds., 338 Somerset St., N. Plainfield, NJ 07060

Scrimshaw Engraving, C. Milton Barringer, 217-2nd Isle N., Port Richey, FL 33568/813-868-3777

Sharpening Stones, Russell's Arkansas Oilstones, 1705 Hiway 71N., Springdale, AR 72764

Shell Shrinker Mfg. Co., P.O. Box 462, Fillmore, CA 93015

Shooter's Porta Bench, Centrum Industries, Inc., 443 Century, S.W., Grand Rapids, MI 49503/616-454-9424

Shooters Rubber Stamps, Craft Haven, 828 N. 70th, Lincoln, NE 68505/402-466-5739

Shooting Coats, 10-X Mfg. Co., 316 So. Lexington Ave., Cheyenne, WY 82001/307-635-9192

Shooting Glasses, Willson Safety Prods. Division, P.O. Box 622, Reading, PA 19603

Shotgun/riot, Combat Weapons, 1265 Balsam St., Lakewood, CO 80215

Shotgun Sight, bi-ocular, Trius Prod., Box 25, Cleves, OH 45002

Shotshell Adapter, PC Co., 5942 Secor Rd., Toledo, OH 43623/419-472-6222 (Plummer 410 converter)

Single Shot Action, John Foote, Foote-Shephard Inc., P.O. Box 6473, Marietta, GA 30065

Snap Caps, Edwards Recoil Reducer, 269 Herbert St., Alton, IL 62002/618-462-3257

Sportsman's Chair, Custom Purveyors, P.O. Box 886, Fort Lee, NJ 07024

Springfield Safety Pin, B-Square Co., P.O. Box 11281, Ft. Worth, TX 76110

Springs, W. Wolff Co., Box 232, Ardmore, PA 19003

Stock pad, variable, Meadow Industries, P.O. Box 50, Forest, VA 24551/804-525-2567

Supersound, Edmund Scientific Co., 101 E. Gloucester Pike, Barrington, NJ 08007 (safety device)

Swivel base (f. lever actions), Lautard Tool Works, 2570 Rosebery Ave., W. Vancouver, B.C., Canada V7V 2Z9/604-926-7150

Swivels, Michaels, P.O. Box 13010, Portland, OR 97213/503-255-6890

Swivels, Sile Dist., 7 Centre Market Pl., New York, NY 10013/212-925-4111

Swivels, Williams Gun Sight Co., 7389 Lapeer Rd., Davison, MI 48423

Tree Stand, Advanced Hunting Equipment Inc., P.O. Box 1277, Cumming, GA 30130/404-887-1171 (tree lounge)

Tree Stand, Climbing, Amacker Prods., P.O. Box 1432; 1011 Beech St., Tallulah, LA 71282/318-574-4907

Trophies, Blackinton & Co., 140 Commonwealth, Attleboro Falls, MA 02763

Trophies, F. H. Noble & Co., 888 Tower Rd., Mundelein, IL 60060

W&E target tang sight, Lautard Tool Works, 2570 Rosebery Ave., W. Vancouver, B.C., Canada V7V 2Z9/604-926-7150

World Hunting Info., Jack Atcheson & Sons, Inc., 3210 Ottawa St., Butte, MT 59701

World Hunting Info., J/b adventures & Safaris, Inc., 800 E. Girard, Suite 603, Denver, CO 80231/303-696-0261

World Hunting Info. Klineburger, 12 & East Pine, Seattle, WA 98122/206-329-1600

World Hunting Info., Wayne Preston, Inc., 3444 Northhaven Rd., Dallas, TX 75229/214-358-4477

MUZZLE-LOADING GUNS, BARRELS or EQUIPMENT

A&K Mfg. C., Inc., 1651 N. Nancy Rose Ave., Tucson, AZ 85712/602-327-9275 (ctlg. $1)

Luther Adkins, Box 281, Shelbyville, IN 47176/317-392-3795 (breech plugs)

Anderson Mfg. Co., Union Gap Sta. P.O. Box 3120, Yakima, WA 98903/509-453-2349

Armoury, Inc., Rte. 202, New Preston, CT 06777

Beaver Lodge, 9245 16th Ave. S.W., Seattle, WA 98106/206-763-1698

John Bivins, Jr., 200 Wicklow Rd., Winston-Salem, NC 27106

Blackhawk East, C2274 POB, Loves Park, IL 61131/815-633-7784

Blackhawk Mtn., 1337 Delmar Parkway, Aurora, CO 80010

Blackhawk West, Box 285, Hiawatha, KS 66434

Blue and Gray Prods., Inc. RD #6, Box 348, Wellsboro, PA 16901/717-724-1383

Jim Brobst, 299 Poplar St., Hamburg, PA 19526/215-562-2103 (ML rifle bbls.)

Ted Buckland, 361 Flagler Rd., Nordland, WA 98358/206-385-2142 (custom only)

G. S. Bunch, 7735 Garrison, Hyattsville, MD 20784 (flask repair)
Butler Creek Corp., Box GG, Jackson Hole, WY 83001/307-733-3599 (poly & maxi patch)
Butler Mfg., P.O. Box 8207, New Haven, CT 06530/203-562-5608 (22 & 31-cal. derringers)
Cache La Poudre Rifleworks, 168 N. College, Ft. Collins, CO 80521/303-482-6913 (custom muzzleloaders)
Challanger Mfg. Co., 118 Pearl St., Mt. Vernon, NY 10550
R. MacDonald Champlin, P.O. Box 693, Manchester, NH 03105/603-622-1420 (custom muzzleloaders)
Chopie Mfg. Inc., 700 Copeland Ave., LaCrosse, WI 54601/608-784-0926 (nipple wrenches)
Connecticut Valley Arms Co. (CVA), Saybrook Rd., Haddam, CT 06438 (kits also)
Earl T. Cureton, Rte. 2, Box 388, Willoughby Rd., Bulls Gap, TN 37711/615-235-2854 (powder horns)
Leonard Day & Co., P.O. Box 723, East Hampton, MA 01027/413-527-7990
Dixie Gun Works, Inc., P.O. Box 130, Union City, TN 38261
Dixon Muzzleloading Shop, Inc., RD #1, Box 175, Kempton, PA 19529/215-756-6271
EMF Co., Inc., 1900 E. Warner Ave. 1-D, Santa Ana, CA 92705/714-966-0202
Euroarms of America, Inc., P.O. Box 3277, 1501 Lenoir Dr., Winchester, VA 22601/703-662-1863
The Eutaw Co., Box 608, U.S. Highway 176W, Holly Hill, SC 29059 (accessories)
Excam, Inc., 4480 E. 11th Ave., Hialeah, FL 33012
Andy Fautheree, P.O. Box 863, Pagosa Springs, CO 81147/303-264-2295 (cust. ML)
Ted Fellowes, Beaver Lodge, 9245 16th Ave. S.W., Seattle, WA 98106/206-763-1698
Firearms Imp. & Exp. Corp., (F.I.E.), P.O. Box 4866, Hialeah Lakes, Hialeah, FL 33014/305-685-5966
Marshall F. Fish, Rt. 22 N., Westport, NY 12993 (antique ML repairs)
Flamingo Co., 29 Tiburon Lane, Lake Havasu City, AZ 86403/602-855-4856 (Flame-N-Go fusil)
The Flintlock Muzzle Loading Gun Shop, 1238 "G" So. Beach Blvd., Anaheim, CA 92804/714-821-6655
C. R. & D. E. Getz, Box 88, Beavertown, PA 17813 (barrels)
Golden Age Arms Co., 14 W. Winter St., Delaware, OH 43015 (ctlg. $2.50)
A. R. Goode, 12845 Catoctin Furnace Rd., Thurmont, MD 21788/301-271-2228 (ML rifle bbls.)
Green Mountain Rifle Barrel, RFD 1, Box 184, Center Ossipee, NH 03814
Guncraft Inc., 117 W. Pipeline, Hurst, TX 76053/817-268-2887
Hawken Armory, P.O. Box 2604, Hot Springs, AR 71901/501-268-8296
Hopkins & Allen, 3 Ethel Ave., P.O. Box 217, Hawthorne, NJ 07507/201-427-1165
The House of Muskets, Inc., 120 N. Pagosa Blvd., Pagosa Springs, CO 81147/303-264-2295 (ML bbls. & supplies)
International Arms, 23239 Doremus St., St. Clair Shores, MI 48080
JJJJ Ranch, Wm. Large, Rte. 1, State Route 243, Ironton, OH 45638/614-532-5298
Jerry's Gun Shop, 9220 Odgen Ave., Brookfield, IL 60513/312-485-5200
Kern's Gun Shop, 319 E. Main St., Ligonier, PA 15658/412-238-7651 (ctlg. $1.50)
Art LeFeuvre, 1003 Hazel Ave., Deerfield, IL 60015/312-945-0073 (antique gun restoring)
Les' Gun Shop (Les Bauska), 105-9th West, P.O. Box 511, Kalispell, MT 59901/406-755-2635
Lever Arms Serv. Ltd., 572 Howe St., Vancouver, BC V6C 2E3, Canada
Log Cabin Sport Shop, 8010 Lafayette Rd., Lodi, OH 44254/216-948-1082 (ctlg. $3)
Lyman Products Corp., Rte. 147, Middlefield, CT 06455
McCann's Muzzle-Gun Works, 200 Federal City Rd., Pennington, NJ 08354/609-737-1707
McKenzie River Arms, P.O. Box 766, Springfield, OR 97477
McKeown's Sporting Arms, R.R. 4, Pekin, IL 61554/309-347-3559 (E-Z load rev. stand)
Maurer Manchester Arms Inc., 6858 Manchester Rd., Clinton, OH 44216/216-882-3133 (cust. muzzleloaders)
Michigan Arms Corp., 479 W. 14 Mile Rd., Clawson, MI 48017/313-435-0160
Mountain State Muzzleloading Supplies, Box 154-1, Williamstown, WV 26187/304-375-7842
Mowrey Gun Works, FM 368, Box 28, Iowa Park, TX 76367/817-592-2331
Muzzleloaders Etc., Inc., Jim Westberg, 9901 Lyndale Ave. S., Bloomington, MN 55420/612-884-1161
Numrich Corp., W. Hurley, NY 12491 (powder flasks)
Kirk Olson, Ft. Woolsey Guns, P.O. Box 2122, Prescott, AZ 86302/602-778-3035 (powderhorns)
Ox-Yoke Originals, 130 Griffin Rd., West Suffield, CT 06093/203-668-5110 (dry lubr. patches)
Orrin L. Parsons, Jr., Central Maine Muzzle-Loading & Gunsmithing, RFD #1, Box 787, Madison, ME 04950
Ozark Mountain Arms Inc., S.R. 4, Box 4000-W, Branson, MO 65616/417-334-6971
A. W. Peterson Gun Shop, 1060 Old Hwy. 441 N., Mt. Dora, FL 32757 (ML guns)
Richland Arms, 321 W. Adrian St., Blissfield, MI 49228
Rush's Old Colonial Forge, 106 Wiltshire Rd., Baltimore, MD 21221
Salish House, Inc., P.O. Box 383, Lakeside, MT 55922/406-844-3625
H. M. Schoeller, 569 So. Braddock Ave., Pittsburgh, PA 15221
Sharon Rifle Barrel Co., P.O. Box 106, Kalispell, MT 59901
Shiloh Products, 37 Potter St., Farmingdale, NY 11735 (4-cavity mould)
Shore Galleries, Inc., 3318 W. Devon Ave., Chicago, IL 60645/312-676-2900
Sile Distributors, 7 Centre Market Pl., New York, NY 10013/213-925-4111
C. E. Siler Locks, Rt. 6, Box 5, Candler, NC 28715/704-667-2376 (flint locks)
Ken Steggles, 17 Bell Lane, Byfield, Near Daventry, Northants NN11 6US, England (accessories)

The Swampfire Shop, 1693 Old Hwy. 441 N., Mt. Dora, FL 32757/904-383-0595
Tag Gun Works, 236 Main, Springfield, OR 97477/503-741-4118 (supplies)
Tennessee Valley Arms, P.O. Box 2022, Union City, TN 38261/901-885-4456
Ten-Ring Precision, Inc., 1449 Blue Crest Lane, San Antonio, TX 78232/512-494-3063
Treso Inc., 120 N. Pagosa Blvd., Pagosa Springs, CO 81147 (accessories)
Upper Missouri Trading Co., 3rd and Harold Sts., Crofton, NB 68730
R. Watts, 826 Springdale Rd., Atlanta, GA 30306 (ML rifles)
Western Arms/Allen Arms, 1107 Pen Rd., Santa Fe, NM 87501/505-982-3399 (guns)
W. H. Wescomb, P.O. Box 488, Glencoe, CA 95232 (parts)
Thos. F. White, 5801 Westchester Ct., Worthington OH 43085/614-888-0128 (powder horn)
Williamson-Pate Gunsmith Serv., 117 W. Pipeline, Hurst, TX 76053/817-268-2887
York County Gun Works, R.R. #4, Tottenham, Ont. LOG 1WO, Canada (locks)

PISTOLSMITHS

Allen Assoc., 7502 Limekiln Pike, Philadelphia, PA 19150 (speed-cock lever for 45 ACP)
Bain and Davis Sptg. Gds., 559 W. Las Tunas Dr., San Gabriel, CA 91776/213-284-2264
Lee Baker, 7252 East Ave. U-3, Littlerock, CA 93543/805-944-4487
Bar-Sto Precision Machine, 73377 Sullivan Rd., Twentynine Palms, CA 92277/714-367-2747(S.S. bbls. f. 45 ACP)
Behlert Custom Guns, Inc., 725 Lehigh Ave., Union, NJ 07083 (short actions)
F. Bob Chow, Gun Shop, Inc., 3185 Mission, San Francisco, CA 94110/415-282-8358
Brown Custom Guns, Inc., Steven N. Brown, 8810 Rocky Ridge Rd., Indianapolis, IN 46217/317-881-2771 aft. 5 PM
Dick Campbell, 365 W. Oxford Ave., Englewood, CO 80110/303-781-2470 (PPC guns)
J. E. Clark, Rte. 2, Box 22A, Keithville, LA 71047
Custom Gun Shop, 725 Lehigh Ave., Union, NJ 07083
Davis Co., 2793 Del Monte St., West Sacramento, CA 95691/916-372-6789
Day Arms Corp., 2412 S.W. Loop 410, San Antonio, TX 78227
Dominic DiStefano, 4303 Friar Lane, Colorado Springs, CO 80907/303-599-3366 (accurizing)
Dan Dwyer, 915 W. Washington, San Diego, CA 92103
Ken Eversull Gunsmith, Inc., P.O. Box 1766, Alexandria, LA 71301/318-487-0823
Giles' 45 Shop, 8614 Tarpon Springs Rd., Odessa, FL 33556/813-920-5366
The Gunshop, R. D. Wallace, 320 Overland Rd., Prescott, AZ 86301
Gil Hebard Guns, Box 1, Knoxville, IL 61448
Paul Jaeger, Inc., 211 Leedom St., Jenkintown, PA 19046/215-884-6920
J. D. Jones, Rt. 1, Della Dr., Bloomingdale, OH 43910/614-264-0176
Lee E. Jurras & Assoc., Inc., P.O. Drawer F, Hagerman, NM 88232
Kart Sptg. Arms Corp., 1190 Old Country Rd., Riverhead, NY 11901/516-727-2719 (handgun conversions)
Terry K. Kopp, Highway 13, Lexington, MO 64067/816-259-2636 (rebblg., conversions)
John G. Lawson, The Sight Shop, 1802 E. Columbia Ave., Tacoma, WA 98404/206-474-5465
Lenz Firearms Co., 310 River Rd., Eugene, OR 97404/503-689-6900
Kent Lomont, 4421 So. Wayne Ave., Ft. Wayne, IN 46807/219-694-6792 (Auto Mag only)
Mag-Na-Port Arms, Inc., 30016 S. River Rd., Mt. Clemens, MI 48043/313-469-6727
Robert A. McGrew, 3315 Michigan Ave., Colorado Springs, CO 80910/303-636-1940
Rudolf Marent, 9711 Tiltree, Houston, TX 77075/713-946-7028 (Hammerli)
Nu-Line Guns, 1053 Caulks Hill Rd., Harvester, MO 63303/314-441-4501
Pachmayr Gun Works, 1220 S. Grand Ave., Los Angeles, CA 90015
SSK Industries (See: J. D. Jones)
L. W. Seecamp Co., Inc., Box 255, New Haven, CT 06502/203-877-3429 (DA Colt auto conversions)
Silver Dollar Guns, P.O. Box 475, 10 Frances St., Franklin, NH 03235/603-934-3292 (45 ACP)
Spokhandguns Inc., Vern D. Ewer, East 1911 Sprague Ave., Spokane, WA 99202/509-534-4112
Sportsmens Equipmt. Co., 915 W. Washington, San Diego, CA 92103/714-296-1501
Irving O. Stone, Jr., 73377 Sullivan Rd., Twentynine Palms, CA 92277/714-367-2747
Victor W. Strawbridge, 6 Pineview Dr., Dover Pt., Dover, NH 03820
A. D. Swenson's 45 Shop, P.O. Box 606, Fallbrook, CA 92028
Trapper Gun, 18717 East 14 Mile Rd., Fraser, MI 48026/313-792-0134
Dennis A. "Doc" Ulrich, 2511 S. 57th Ave., Cicero, IL 60650
Vic's Gun Refinishing, 6 Pineview Dr., Dover, NH 03820
Walters Industries, 6226 Park Lane, Dallas, TX 75225

REBORING AND RERIFLING

P.O. Ackley (See Dennis M. Bellm Gunsmithing, Inc.)
Atkinson Gun Co., P.O. Box 512, Prescott, AZ 86301
Dennis M. Bellm Gunsmithing Inc., 2376 So. Redwood Rd., Salt Lake City, UT 84119/801-974-0697; price list $3 (rifle only)
H-S Precision, Inc., 112 N. Summit, Prescott, AZ 85302/602-445-0607
Bruce Jones, 389 Calla Ave., Imperial Beach, CA 92032
Terry K. Kopp, Highway 13, Lexington, MO 64067/816-259-2636 (relining)

Les' Gun Shop, (Les Bauska), 105-9th West, P.O. Box 511, Kalispell, MT 59901/406-755-2635
Morgan's Cust. Reboring, 707 Union Ave., Grants Pass, OR 97526
Nu-Line Guns, 1053 Caulks Hill Rd., Harvester, MO 63303/314-441-4500 (handguns)
Redman's Gun Shop, 3015 So. Illinois, Caldwell, ID 83605/208-454-9435
SGW, Inc. (formerly Schuetzen Gun Works), 624 Old Pacific Hwy. S.E., Olympia, WA 98503/206-456-3471
Sharon Gun Specialties, 14587 Peaceful Valley Rd., Sonora, CA 95370
Siegrist Gun Shop, 2689 McLean Rd., Whittemore, MI 48770/517-873-3929
Snapp's Gunshop, 6911 E. Washington Rd., Clare, MI 48617
J. W. Van Patten, Box 145, Foster Hill, Milford, PA 18337
Robt. G. West, 27211 Huey Lane, Eugene, OR 97402

RELOADING TOOLS AND ACCESSORIES

Advance Car Mover Co., Inc., P.O. Box 1181, Appleton, WI 54911/414-734-1878 (bottom pour lead casting ladles)
American Wad Co., P&P Tool, 125 W. Market St., Morrison, IL 61270/815-772-7618 (12-ga. shot wad)
Anderson Mfg. Co., R.R.1, Royal, IA 51357/712-933-5542 (Shotshell Trimmers)
C'Arco, P.O. Box 308, Highland, CA 92346/714-862-8311 (Ransom "Grand Master" progr. loader)
Aurands, 229 E. 3rd St., Lewistown, PA 17044
B-Square Eng. Co., Box 11281, Ft. Worth, TX 76110
Bill Ballard, 830 Miles Ave., Billings, MT 59101 (ctlg. 50¢)
Ballistic Prods., P.O. Box 488, 2105 Shaughnessy Circle, Long Lake, MN 55356/612-473-1550
Bear Machine Co., 2110 1st Natl. Tower, Akron, OH 44308/216-253-4039
Belding & Mull, P.O. Box 428, 100 N. 4th St., Philipsburg, PA 16866/814-342-0607
Berdon Machine Co., Box 483, Hobart, WA 98025/206-392-1866 (metallic press)
Blackhawk East, Dowman Greene, C2274 POB, Loves Park, IL 61131/815-633-7784
Blackhawk Mtn., Richard Miller, 1337 Delmar Parkway, Aurora, CO 80010/303-366-3659
Blackhawk West, Box 285, Hiawatha, KS 66434
Bonanza Sports, Inc., 412 Western Ave., Faribault, MN 55021/507-332-7158
Gene Bowlin, Rt. 1, Box 890, Snyder, TX 79549/915-573-2323 (arbor press)
Brown Precision Co., 5869 Indian Ave., San Jose, CA 95123 (Little Wiggler)
C-H Tool & Die Corp., 106 N. Harding St., Owen, WI 54461/715-229-2146
Camdex, Inc., 2228 Fourteen Mile Rd., Warren, MI 48092/313-977-1620
Carbide Die & Mfg. Co., Box 226, Covina, CA 91724
Carter Gun Works, 2211 Jefferson Pk. Ave., Charlottesville, VA 22903
Cascade Cartridge, Inc., (See: Omark)
Cascade Shooters, 60916 McMullin Dr., Bend, OR 97702/503-389-5872 (bull. seating depth gauge)
Central Products f. Shooters, 435 Route 18, East Brunswick, NJ 08816 (neck turning tool)
Chevron Case Master, R.R. 1, Ottawa, IL 61350
Lester Coats, 416 Simpson St., No. Bend, OR 97459/503-756-6995 (core cutter)
Container Development Corp., 424 Montgomery St., Watertown, WI 53094
Continental Kite & Key Co., Box 40, Broomall, PA 19008 (primer pocket cleaner)
Cooper-Woodward, Box 972, Riverside, CA 92502/714-683-5952 (Perfect Lube)
Corbin Mfg. & Supply Inc., P.O. Box 758, Phoenix, OR 97535/503-826-5211
Custom Products, 686 Baldwin St., Meadville, PA 16335/814-724-7045 (decapping tool, dies, etc.)
J. Dewey Mfg. Co., 186 Skyview Dr., Southbury, CT 06488/203-264-3064
Dillon Precision Prods., Inc., 7755 E. Gelding Dr., Suite 106, Scottsdale, AZ 85260/602-948-8009
Diverter Arms, Inc., P.O. Box 22084, Houston, TX 77027 (bullet puller)
Division Lead Co., 7742 W. 61st Pl., Summit, IL 60502
Eagle Products Co., 1520 Adelia Ave., So. El Monte, CA 91733
Edmisten Co. Inc., P.O. Box 1293, Hwy 105, Boone, NC 28607/704-264-1490
Efemes Enterprises, P.O. Box 122M, Bay Shore, NY 11706 (Berdan decapper)
W. H. English, 4411 S. W. 100th, Seattle, WA 98146 (Paktool)
Farmer Bros., 1616-15th St., Eldora, IA 50627 (Lage)
Fitz, P.O. Box 55, Grizzly Gulch, Whiskey Town, CA 96095/916-778-3136 (Fitz Flipper)
Flambeau Plastics Corp., P.O. Box 97 Middlefield, OH 44062/216-632-1631
Forster Products, P.O. Box A, Lanark IL 61046/815-493-6360
Geo. M. Fullmer, 2499 Mavis St., Oakland, CA 94601 (seating die)
Gene's Gun Shop, Rt. 1, Box 890, Snyder, TX 79549/915-573-2323 (arbor press)
Gopher Shooter's Supply, Box 278, Faribault, MN 55021
The Gun Clinic, 81 Kale St., Mahtomedi, MN 55115
Hart Products, Rob W. Hart & Son Inc., 401 Montgomery St., Nescopeck, PA 18635
Hensley & Gibbs, Box 10, Murphy, OR 97533
Richard Hoch, The Gun Shop, 62778 Spring Creek Rd., Montrose, CO 81401/303-249-3625 (custom Schuetzen bullet moulds)
Hoffman New Ideas Inc., 821 Northmoor Rd., Lake Forest, IL 60045/312-234-4075 (spl. gallery load press)
Hollywood Reloading, (See Whitney Sales, Inc.)
Hornady (See Pacific)
Hulme Firearm Serv., Box 83, Millbrae, CA 94030 (Star case feeder)
Independent Mach. & Gun Shop, 1416 N. Hayes, Pocatello, ID 83201
Ivy Armament, P.O. Box 10, Greendale, WI 53129
Javelina Products, Box 337, San Bernardino, CA 92402 (Alox beeswax)
Neil Jones, 686 Baldwin St., Meadville, PA 16335 (decapping tool, dies)

Paul Jones Munitions Systems (See Fitz Co.)
Kexplore, P.O. Box 22084, Houston, TX 77027/713-789-6943
Kuharsky Bros. (See Modern Industries)
Lac-Cum Bullet Puller, Star Route, Box 240, Apollo, PA 15613/412-478-1794
Lage Uniwad Co., 1102 N. Washington St., Eldora, IA 50627 (Universal Shotshell Wad)
Lee Custom Engineering, Inc. (See Mequon Reloading Corp.)
Lee Precision, Inc., 4275 Hwy. U, Hartford, WI 53027/414-673-3075
Lewisystems, Menasha Corp., 426 Montgomery St., Watertown, WI 53094
L. L. F. Die Shop, 1281 Highway 99 N., Eugene, OR 97402/503-688-5753
Dean Lincoln, P.O. Box 1886, Farmington, NM 87401 (mould)
Ljutic Industries, 918 N. 5th Ave., Yakima, WA 98902
Lock's Phila. Gun Exch., 6700 Rowland, Philadelphia, PA 19149/215-332-6225
Lyman Products Corp., Rte. 147, Middlefield, CT 06455
McKillen & Heyer Inc., 37603 Arlington Dr., Box 627, Willoughby, OH 44094/216-942-2491 (case gauge)
Paul McLean, 2670 Lakeshore Blvd., W., Toronto, Ont. M8V 1G8 Canada/416-259-3060 (Universal Cartridge Holder)
MEC, Inc. (See Mayville Eng. Co.)
MTM Molded Prod., 5680 Webster St., P.O. Box 1438, Dayton, OH 45414/513-890-7461
Magma Eng. Co., P.O. Box 881, Chandler, AZ 85224
Marmel Prods., P.O. Box 97, Utica, MI 48087/313-731-8029 (Marvelube, Marvelux)
Marquart Precision Co., P.O. Box 1740, Prescott, AZ 86302/602-445-5646 (precision case-neck turning tool)
Marshall Enterprises, P.O. Box 83, Millbrae, CA 94030/415-365-1230 (Hulme autom. case feeder f. Star rel.)
Mayville Eng. Co., 715 South St., Mayville, WI 53050/414-387-4500 (shotshell loader)
Mequon Reloading Corp., P.O. Box 253, Mequon, WI 53092/414-673-3060
Merit Gun Slight Co., P.O. Box 995, Sequim, WA 98382
Multi-Scale Charge Ltd., 3269 Niagara Falls Blvd., North Tonawanda, NY 14120/416-967-5305
Normington Co., Box 6, Rathdrum, ID 83858 (powder baffles)
NorthEast Industrial Inc., 2516 Wyoming, El Paso, TX 79903/915-532-8344 (bullet mould)
Ohaus Scale, (See RCBS)
Omark Industries, Box 856, Lewiston, ID 83501/208-746-2351
P&P Tool Co., 125 W. Market St., Morrison, IL 61270/815-772-7618 (12-ga. shot wad)
Pacific Tool Co., P.O. Box 2048, Ordnance Plant Rd., Grand Island, NE 68801/308-384-2308
Pak-Tool Co., 4411 S.W. 100th, Seattle, WA 98146
Pem's Manufacturing Co., 5063 Waterloo Rd., Atwater, OH 44201/216-947-2202 (pedestal cranks, primer pocket cleaner)
Plum City Ballistics Range, Rte. 1, Box 29A, Plum City, WI 54761
Ponsness-Warren, Inc., P.O. Box 8, Rathdrum, ID 83858/208-687-1331
Marian Powley, Petra Lane, R.R.1, Eldridge, IA 52748/319-285-9214
Precise Alloys Inc., 406 Hillside Ave., New Hyde Park, NY 11040/516-354-8860 (chilled lead shot; bullet wire)
Quinetics Corp., P.O. Box 29007, San Antonio, TX 78229/516-684-8561 (kinetic bullet puller)
RCBS, Inc., Box 1919, Oroville, CA 95965/916-533-5191
Redding Inc., 114 Starr Rd., Cortland, NY 13045
Reloaders Equipment Co., 4680 High St., Ecorse, MI 48229 (bullet puller)
Rifle Ranch, Rte. 5, Prescott, AZ 86301
Rochester Lead Works, 76 Anderson Ave., Rochester, NY 14607/716-442-8500 (leadwire)
Rorschach Precision Prods., P.O. Box 1613, Irving, TX 75060/214-254-9762 (carboloy bull. dies)
Rotex Mfg. Co. (See Texan)
SAECO Rel. 525 Maple Ave., Carpinteria, CA 93013/805-684-6925
SSK Industries, Rt. 1, Della Drive, Bloomingdale, OH 43910/614-264-0176 (primer tool)
Sandia Die & Cartridge Co., Rte. 5, Box 5400, Albuquerque, NM 87123/505-298-5729
Shassere, Box 35865, Houston, TX 77096/713-780-7041 (cartridge case caddy/loading block)
Shiloh Products, 37 Potter St., Farmingdale, NY 11735 (4-cavity bullet mould)
Shooters Accessory Supply, (See Corbin Mfg. & Supply)
Sil's Gun Prod., 490 Sylvan Dr., Washington, PA 15301 (K-spinner)
Jerry Simmons, 715 Middlebury St., Goshen, IN 46526/219-533-8546 (Pope de- & recapper)
J. A. Somers Co., P.O. Box 49751, Los Angeles, CA 90049 (Jasco)
Sport Flite Mfg., Inc., 2520 Industrial Row, Troy, MI 48084/313-280-0648 (swaging dies)
Star Machine Works, 418 10th Ave., San Diego, CA 92101/714-232-3216
TEK Ind., Inc., 2320 Robinson St., Colorado Springs, CO 80904/303-630-1295 (Vibra Tek Brass Polisher & Medium, Vibra Brite Rouge)
T&T Products, Inc., 6330 Hwy. 14 East, Rochester, MN 55901 (Meyer shotgun slugs)
Texan Reloaders, Inc., 444 Cip St., Watseka, IL 60970/815-432-5065
Trico Plastics, 590 S. Vincent Ave., Azusa, CA 91702
WAMADET, Silver Springs, Goodleigh, Barnstaple, Devon, England
Walker Mfg. Inc., 8296 So. Channel, Harsen's Island, MI 48028 (Berdan decapper)
Wammes Guns Inc., 236 N. Hayes St., Bellefontaine, OH 43311 (Jim's powder baffles)
Weatherby, Inc., 2781 Firestone Blvd., South Gate, CA 90280/213-569-7186
Webster Scale Mfg. Co., Box 188, Sebring, FL 33870
Whits Shooting Stuff, P.O. Box 1340, Cody, WY 82414
Whitney Sales, Inc., P.O. Box 875, Reseda, CA 91335 (Hollywood)
L. E. Wilson, Inc. P.O. Box 324, 404 Pioneer Ave., Cashmere, WA 98815
Xelex, Ltd., P.O. Box 543, Renfrow K7V 4B1, Canada (powder)
Zenith Enterprises, 361 Flagler Rd., Nordland, WA 98358

RESTS—BENCH, PORTABLE, ETC.

A&A Design & Manufacturing, 361 SW "K" St., Grants Pass, OR 97526/503-474-1026 (Tour de Force bench rest)

B-Square Co., P.O. Box 11281, Ft. Worth, TX 76109/817-923-0964 (handgun)

Bausch & Lomb, 635 St. Paul St., Rochester, NY 14602 (rifle rest)

Jim Brobst, 299 Poplar St., Hamburg, PA 19526/215-562-2103 (bench rest pedestal)

C'Arco, P.O. Box 2043, San Bernardino, CA 92401 (Ransom handgun rest)

Cravener's Gun Shop, 1627 - 5th Ave., Ford City, PA 16226/412-763-8312 (portable)

Decker Shooting Products, 1729 Laguna Ave., Schofield, WI 54476 (rifle rests)

The Gun Case, 11035 Maplefield, El Monte, CA 91733

Harris Engineering, Inc., Barlow, KY 42024/502-334-3633 (bipods)

Rob. W. Hart & Son, 401 Montgomery St., Nescopeck, PA 18635

Tony Hidalgo, 6 Capp St., Carteret, NJ 07008/201-541-5894 (shooters stools)

North Star Devices, Inc., P.O. Box 2095, North St. Paul, MN 55109 (Gun Slinger)

Progressive Prods., Inc., P.O. Box 67, Holmen, WI 54636/608-526-3345 (Sandbagger rifle rest)

Rec. Prods., Res., Inc., 158 Franklin Ave., Ridgewood, NJ 07450 (Butts Bipod)

Suter's, 332 Tejon, Colorado Springs, CO 80902

Tuller & Co., Basil Tuller 29 Germania, Galeton, PA 16922/814-435-2442 (Protector sandbags)

Turkey Creek Enterprises, Rt. 1, Box 10, Red Oak, CA 74563/918-754-2884 (portable shooting rest)

Wichita Arms, 333 Lulu, Wichita, KS 67211

RIFLE BARREL MAKERS

P.O. Ackley Rifle Barrels (See David M. Bellm Gunsmithing Inc.)

Luther Adkins, P.O. Box 281, Shelbyville, IN 46176/317-392-3795

Atkinson Gun Co., P.O. Box 512, Prescott, AZ 86301

Jim Baiar, 490 Halfmoon Rd., Columbia Falls, MT 59912/406-892-4409

Bauska Rifle Barrels, Inc., 105-9th Ave. West, Kalispell, MT 59901/406-755-2635

Dennis M. Bellm Gunsmithing Inc., 2376 So. Redwood Rd., Salt Lake City, UT 84119/801-974-0697; price list $3 (new rifle bbls., incl. special & obsolete)

Leo Bustani, P.O. Box 8125, West Palm Beach, FL 33407/305-622-2710 (Win.92 take-down; Trapper 357-44 mag. bbls.)

Ralph L. Carter, Carter's Gun Shop, 225 G St., Penrose, CO 81240/303-372-6240

Christy Gun Works, 875 57th St., Sacramento, CA 95819

Clerke Prods., 2219 Main St., Santa Monica, CA 90405

Cuthbert Gun Shop, 715 So. 5th Coos Bay, OR 97420

Charles P. Donnelly & Son, Siskiyou Gun Works, 405 Kubli Rd., Grants Pass, OR 97526/503-846-6604

Douglas Barrels, Inc., 5504 Big Tyler Rd., Charleston, WV 25312/304-776-1341

Douglas Jackalope Gun & Sport Shop, Inc., 1048 S. 5th St., Douglas, WY 82633/307-358-3854

Federal Firearms Co., Inc., Box 145, 145 Thomas Run Rd., Oakdale, PA 15071/412-221-0300

C. R. & D. E. Getz, Box 88, Beavertown, PA 17813

A. R. Goode, 12845 Catoctin Furnace Rd., Thurmont, MD 21788/301-271-2228

Half Moon Rifle Shop, 490 Halfmoon Rd., Columbia Falls, MT 59912/406-892-4409

H-S Precision, Inc., 112 N. Summit, Prescott, AZ 85302/602-445-0607

Hart Rifle Barrels, Inc., RD 2, Lafayette, NY 13084/315-677-9841

H&H Barrels Works, Inc., 1520 S.W. 5th Ave., Ocala, FL 32674/904-351-4200

Wm. H. Hobaugh, Box M, Philipsburg, MT 59858/406-859-3515

Huntington Precision Arms Inc., David R. Huntington, 670 So. 300 West, Heber City, UT 84032/801-654-2953

Kogot, John Pell, 410 College Ave., Trinidad, CO 81082/303-846-9006 (custom octagon)

Terry K. Kopp, Highway 13, Lexington, MO 64067/816-259-2636 (22-cal. blanks)

Les' Gun Shop, (Les Bauska), 105-9th West, P.O. Box 511, Kalispell, MT 59901/406-755-2635

Marquart Precision Co., P.O. Box 1740, Prescott, AZ 86302/602-445-5646

Nu-Line Guns, 1053 Caulkshill Rd., Harvester, MO 63303/314-441-4500

Numrich Arms, W. Hurley, NY 12491

Sanders Cust. Gun Serv., 2358 Tyler Lane, Louisville, KY 40205

SGW, Inc., D. A. Schuetz, 624 Old Pacific Hwy. S.E., Olympia, WA 98503/206-456-3471

Sharon Gun Specialties, 14587 Peaceful Valley Rd., Sonora, CA 95370/209-532-4139

E. R. Shaw, Inc., Prestley & Thomas Run Rd., Bridgeville, PA 15017/412-221-3636

Shilen Rifles, Inc., 205 Metropark Blvd., Ennis, TX 75119/214-875-5318

W. C. Strutz, Rifle Barrels, Inc., P.O. Box 611, Eagle River, WI 54521/715-479-4766

Titus Barrel & Gun Co., R.F.D. #1, Box 23, Herber City, UT 84032

Bob Williams, P.O. Box 143, Boonsboro, MD 21713

Wilson Arms, 63 Leetes Island Rd., Branford, CT 06405

SCOPES, MOUNTS, ACCESSORIES, OPTICAL EQUIPMENT

Aimpoint U.S.A., 201 Elden St., Suite 103, Herndon, VA 22070/703-471-6828 (electronic sight)

The American Import Co., 1167 Mission, San Francisco, CA 94103/415-863-1506

Anderson Mfg. Co., Union Gap Sta. P.O. Box 3120, Yakima, WA 98903/509-453-2349 (lens cap)

Armsport, Inc., 3590 N.W. 49th St., Miami, FL 33122/305-592-7850

Armson O.E.G. (See Leadership Keys, Inc.)

B-Square Co., Box 11281, Ft. Worth, TX 76109 (Mini-14 mount)

Bausch & Lomb Inc., 1400 Goodman St., Rochester, NY 14602/716-338-6000

Beeman Precision Airguns, 47 Paul Dr., San Rafael, CA 94903/415-472-7121

Bennett, 561 Delaware, Delmar, NY 12054/518-439-1862 (mounting wrench)

Billingsley & Brownell, Box 25, Wyarno, WY 82845/307-737-2468 (cust. mounts)

Lenard M. Brownell (See Billingsley & Brownell)

Browning Arms, Rt. 4, Box 624-B, Arnold, MO 63010

Maynard P. Buehler, Inc., 17 Orinda Highway, Orinda, CA 94563/415-254-3201 (mounts)

Burris Co. Inc., 331 E. 8th St., Box 1747, Greeley, CO 80631/303-356-1670

Bushnell Optical Co., 2828 E. Foothill Blvd., Pasadena, CA 91107

Butler Creek Corp., Box GG, Jackson Hole, WY 83001 (lens caps)

Kenneth Clark, 18738 Highway 99, Madera, CA 93637

Clearview Mfg. Co., Inc. 20821 Grand River Ave., Detroit, MI 48219 (mounts)

Colt Firearms, P.O. Box 1868, Hartford CT 06102/203-236-6311

Compass Instr. & Optical Co., Inc., 104 E. 25th St., New York, NY 10010

Conetrol Scope Mounts, Hwy 123 South, Seguin, TX 78155

D&H Prods. Co., Inc., P. O. Box 22, Glenshaw, PA 15116/412-443-2190 (lens covers)

Davis Optical Co., P.O. Box 6, Winchester, IN 47934

Del-Sports Inc., Main St., Margaretville, NY 12455/914-586-4103 (Kahles)

Eder Instrument Co., 5115 N. Ravenswood, Chicago, IL 60640 (borescope)

Flaig's, Babcock Blvd., Millvale, PA 15209

Fontaine Ind., Inc., 11552 Knott St., Suite 2, Garden Grove, CA 92641/714-892-4473

Freeland's Scope Stands, Inc., 3737 14th, Rock Island, IL 61201/309-788-7449

Griffin & Howe, Inc., 589 Broadway, New York, NY 10012

H&H Assoc., P.O. Box 447, Strathmore, CA 93267 (target adj. knobs)

Heckler & Koch, Inc., 933 N. Kenmore St., Suite 218, Arlington, VA 22201/703-243-3700

H.J. Hermann Leather Co., Rt. 1, Skiatook, OK 74070 (lens caps)

Friedr. Wilh. Heym, Box 266, Bolton, Ont. Canada I0P 1AO (Nickel; Hertel & Reuss scopes)

J.B. Holden Co., 295 W. Pearl, Plymouth, MI 48170/313-455- 4850

The Hutson Corp., 105 Century Dr., No., Mansfield, TX 76063/817-477-3421

Import Scope Repair Co., P.O. Box 2633, Durango, CO 81301/303-247-1422

Interarms, 10 Prince St., Alexandria, VA 22313

Paul Jaeger, Inc., 211 Leedom St., Jenkintown, PA 19046/215-884-6920

Jana Intl. Co., Box 1107, Denver, CO 80201

Jason Empire Inc., 9200 Cody, P.O. Box 12370, Overland Park, KS 66212/913-888-0220

Jennison TCS (See Fontaine Ind., Inc.)

Kahles of America, Div. of Del-Sports, Inc., Main St., Margaretville, NY 12455/914-586-4103

Kesselring Gun Shop, 400 Pacific Hiway No., Burlington, WA 98283/206-724-3113

Krico, P.O. Box 266, Bolton, Ont. L0P 1A0, Canada/416-857-6444 (Nickel; Hertel & Reuss)

Kris Mounts, 108 Lehigh St., Johnstown, PA 15905

Kuharsky Bros. (See Mondern Industries)

Kwik-Site, 5555 Treadwell, Wayne, MI 48185/313-326-1500 (rings, mounts only)

S.E. Laszlo House of Imports, 200 Tillary St., Brooklyn, NY 11201

Leadership Keys, Inc., P.O. Box 2130, Farmington Hills, MI 48018/313-478-2577 (Armson O.E.G.)

Leatherwood Enterprises, P.O. Box 111, Stephenville, TX 76401/817-968-2719

T.K. Lee, 2830 S. 19th St., Off. #4, Birmingham, AL 35209/205-871-6065 (reticles)

E. Leitz, Inc., Rockleigh, NJ 07647

Leupold & Stevens Inc., P.O. Box 688, Beaverton, OR 97075/503-646-9171

Jake Levin and Son, Inc., 9200 Cody, Overland Park, KS 66214

W.H. Lodewick, 2816 N.E. Halsey, Portland, OR 97232/503-284-2554 (scope safeties)

Lyman Products Corp., Route 147, Middlefield, CT. 06455

Mandall Shooting Supplies, 7150 E. 4th St., Scottsdale, AZ 85252

Marble Arms Co., 420 Industrial Park, Gladstone, MI 49837/906-428-3710

Marlin Firearms Co., 100 Kenna Dr., New Haven, CT 06473

Robert Medaris, P.O. Box 309, Mira Loma, CA 91752/714-685-5666 (side mount f. H&K 91 & 93)

Millet Industries, 16131 Gothard St., Huntington Beach, CA 92647/714-842-5575 (mounts)

O.F. Mossberg & Sons, Inc., 7 Grasso Ave., North Haven, CT 06473

Orchard Park Enterprise, P.O. Box 563, Orchard Park, NY 14127 (Saddleproof mount)

Nite-Site, Inc., P.O. Box O, Rosemount, MN 55068/612-890-7631

Numrich Arms, West Hurley, NY 12491

Nydar, (See Swain Nelson Co.)

PEM's Mfg. Co., 5063 Waterloo Rd., Atwater, OH 44201/216-947-2202 (rings, mounts)

Pachmayr Gun Works, 1220 S. Grand Ave., Los Angeles, CA 90015/213-748-7271

Remington Gun Co., P.O. Box 1200, Muskogee, OK 74401/918-683-9418 (O.D. mt.)

Precise, 3 Chestnut, Suffern, NY 10901

Ranging, Inc., 90 Lincoln Rd. North, East Rochester, NY 14445/716-385-1250

Ray-O-Vac, Willson Prod. Div., P.O. Box 622, Reading, PA 19603 (shooting glasses)

Redfield Gun Sight Co., 5800 E. Jewell Ave., Denver, CO 80222/303-757-6411

S & K Mfg. Co., Box 247, Pittsfield, PA 16340 (Insta-Mount)

SSK Industries, Rt. 1, Della Dr., Bloomingdale, OH 43910/614-264-0176 (bases)

Sanders Cust. Gun Serv., 2358 Tyler Lane, Louisville, KY 40205 (MSW)

Savage Arms, Westfield, MA 01085

Sears, Roebuck & Co., 825 S. St. Louis, Chicago, IL 60607

Sherwood Intl. Export Corp., 18714 Parthenia St., Northridge, CA 91324 (mounts)

W.H. Siebert, 22720 S.E. 56th Pl., Issaquah, WA 98027

Singlepoint (See Normark)

Southern Precision Inst. Co., 3419 E. Commerce St., San Antonio, TX 78219

Spacetron Inc., Box 84, Broadview, IL 60155(bore lamp)

Stoeger Industries, 55 Ruta Ct., S. Hackensack, NJ 07606/201-440-2700

Strieter Corp., 2100-18th Ave., Rock Island, IL 61201/309-794-9800 (Swarovski)

Supreme Lens Covers, Box GG, Jackson Hole, WY 83001 (lens caps)

Swain Nelson Co., Box 45, 92 Park Dr., Glenview, IL 60025 (shotgun sight)

Swift Instruments, Inc., 952 Dorchester Ave., Boston, MA 02125

Tasco, 7600 N.W. 26th St., Miami, FL 33122/305-591-3670

Ted's Sight Aligner, Box 1073, Scottsdale, AZ 85252

Thompson-Center Arms, P.O. Box 2405, Rochester, NH 03867 (handgun scope)

Tradewinds, Inc., Box 1191, Tacoma, WA 98401

John Unertl Optical Co., 3551-5 East St., Pittsburgh, PA 15214

United Binocular Co., 9043 S. Western Ave., Chicago, IL 60620

Verano Corp., Box 270, Glendora, CA 91740

Vissing (See Supreme Lens Covers)

Wasp Shooting Systems, Box 241, Lakeview, AR 72642/501-431-5606 (mtg. system f. Ruger Mini-14 only)

Weatherby's, 2781 Firestone, South Gate, CA 90280/213-569-7186

W.R. Weaver Co., 7125 Industrial Ave., El Paso, TX 79915

Wide View Scope Mount Corp., 26110 Michigan Ave., Inkster, MI 48141

Williams Gun Sight Co., 7389 Lapeer Rd., Davison, MI 48423

Boyd Williams Inc., 8701-14 Mile Rd. (M-57),Cedar Springs, MI 49319 (BR)

Willrich Precision Instrument Co., 95 Cenar Lane, Englewood, NJ 07631/201-567-1411 (borescope)

Carl Zeiss Inc.,Consumer Prods. Div., Box 2010, 1015 Commerce St., Petersburg, VA 23803/804-861-0033

SIGHTS, METALLIC

Accura-Site Co., Inc., Box 114, Neenah, WI 54956/414-722-0039

B-Square Eng. Co., Box 11281, Ft. Worth, TX 76110

Beeman Precision Airguns, 47 Paul Dr., San Fafael, CA 94903/415-472-7121 (airguns only)

Behlert Custom Sights, Inc., 725 Lehigh Ave., Union, NJ 07083

Bingham Ltd., 1775-C Wilwat Dr., Norcross, GA 30093/404-448-1440

Bo-Mar Tool & Mfg. Co., Box 168, Carthage, TX 75633

Maynard P. Buehler, Inc., 17 Orinda Highway, Orinda, CA 94563/415-254-3201

Christy Gun Works, 875 57th St., Sacramento, CA 95819

Freeland's Scope Stands, Inc., 3734-14th Ave., Rock Island, IL 61201/309-788-7449

Paul T. Haberly, 2364 N. Neva, Chicago, IL 60635

Paul Jaeger, Inc., 211 Leedom St., Jenkintown, PA 19046/215-884-6920

Lautard Tool Works, 2570 Rosebery Ave., W. Vancouver, B.C., Canada V7V 2Z9/604-926-7150 (W&E adj. target tang sight)

Lee's Red Ramps, 7252 E. Ave. U-3, Littlerock, CA 93543/805-944-4487 (illuminated sights)

James W. Lofland, 2275 Larkin Rd., Boothwyn, PA 19061/215-485-0391

Lyman Products Corp., Rte. 147, Middlefield, CT 06455

Marble Arms Corp., 420 Industrial Park, Gladstone, MI 49837/906-428-3710

Merit Gunsight Co., P.O. Box 995, Sequim, WA 98382

Micro Sight Co., 242 Harbor Blvd., Belmont, CA 94002/415-591-0769

Millet Industries, 16131 Gothard St., Huntington Beach, CA 92647/714-842-5575

Miniature Machine Co., 210 E. Poplar, Deming, NM 88030/505-546-2151

C.R. Pedersen & Son, 2717 S. Pere Marquette, Ludington, MI 49431/616-843-2061

PEM's Manufacturing Co., 5063 Waterloo Rd., Atwater, OH 44201/216-947-2202

Poly Choke Co., Inc., 150 Park Ave., Hartford CT 06108/203-289-2743

Redfield Gun Sight Co., 5800 E. Jewell St., Denver, CO 80222

S&M Tang Sights, P.O. Box 1338, West Babylon, NY 11704

Schwarz's Gun Shop, 41-15th St., Wellsburg, WV 26070

Simmons Gun Specialties, Inc., 700 Rodgers Rd., Olathe, KS 66061

Slug Site Co., Whitetail Wilds, Lake Hubert, MN 56469/218-963-4617

Sport Service Center, 2364 N. Neva, Chicago, IL 60635/312-889-1114

Tradewinds, Inc., Box 1191, Tacoma, WA 98401

Wichita Arms, 333 Lulu, Wichita, KS 67211/316-265-0661

Williams Gun Sight Co., 7389 Lapeer Rd., Davison, MI 48423

STOCKS (Commercial and Custom)

Adams Custom Gun Stocks, 13461 Quito Rd., Saratoga, CA 95070

Ahlman's Inc., R.R. 1, Box 20, Morristown, MN 55052

Don Allen Inc., R.R. 4, Northfield, MN 55057/507-645-9216 (blanks)

R.J. Anton, 874 Olympic Dr., Waterloo, IA 50701/319-233-3666

Creighton Audette, RFD 1, Box 55, Highland Circle, Springfield, VT 05156/802-885-2331 (custom)

Jim Baiar, 490 Halfmoon Rd., Columba Falls, MT 599123

Joe J. Balickie, Custom Stocks, Rte. 2, Box 56-G, Apex, NC 27502

Bartas Gunsmithing, 10231 U.S.H.#10, Cato, WI 54206/414-732-4472

Donald Bartlett, 16111 S.E. 229th Pl., Kent, WA 98031/206-630-2190 (cust.)

Beeman Precision Airguns, 47 Paul Dr., San Rafael, CA 94903/415-472-7121 (airguns only)

Al Biesen, West 2039 Sinto Ave., Spokane, WA 99201

Stephen L. Billeb, Box 219, Philipsburg, MT 59858/406-859-3919

Billingsley & Brownell, Box 25, Wyarno, WY 82845/307-737-2468 (cust.)

E.C. Bishop & Son Inc., 119 Main St., Box 7, Warsaw MO 65355/816-438-5121

Gregg Boeke, 1812 Coolidge Ct., Northfield, MN 55057/507-645-6346 (custom)

John M. Boltin, 2008 Havens Dr., North Myrtle Beach, SC 29582/803-272-6581

Border Gun Shop, Gary Simmons, 2760 Tucson Hiway, Nogales, AZ 85621/602-281-0045 (spl. silueta stocks, complete rifles)

Garnet D. Brawley, P.O. Box 668, Prescott, AZ 86301/602-445-4768 (cust.)

Brown Precision Co., P.O. Box 270W; 7786 Molinos Ave., Los Molinos, CA 96055/916-384-2506

Lenard M. Brownell, (See Billingsley & Brownell)

E.J. Bryant, 3154 Glen St., Eureka, CA 95501

Jack Burres, 10333 San Fernando Road, Pacoima, CA 91331 (English, Claro, Bastogne Paradox walnut blanks only)

Calico Hardwoods, Inc., 1648 Airport Blvd., Windsor, CA 95492/707-546-4045 (blanks)

Dick Campbell, 365 W. Oxford Ave., Englewood, CO 80110/303-781-2470

Shane Caywood, 321 Hwy. 51 So., Minocqua, WI 54548/715-356-9631 (cust.)

Winston Churchill, Twenty Mile Stream Rd., Rt. 1, Box 29B, Proctorsville, VT 05153

Crane Creek Gun Stock Co., 25 Shephard Terr., Madison, WI 53705

Reggie Cubriel, 15502 Purple Sage, San Antonio, TX 78255/512-695-8401 (cust. stockm.)

Bill Curtis, 4919 S. Spade, Murray, UT 84107/801-262-8413

Dahl's Custom Stocks, Rt. 4, Box 558, Schofield Rd., Lake Geneva, WI 53147/414-248-2464 (Martin Dahl)

Sterling Davenport, 9611 E. Walnut Tree Dr., Tucson, AZ 85715/602-749-5590 (custom)

Jack Dever, 8520 N.W. 90, Oklahoma City, OK 73132/405-721-6393

Charles De Veto, 1087 Irene Rd., Lyndhurst, OH 44124/216-442-3188

Bill Dowtin, 3919 E. Thrush Lane, Flagstaff, AZ 86001/602-526-5355 (Calif. Engl., black walnut *blanks* only)

Gary Duncan, 1118 Canterbury, Enid, OK 73701 (blanks only)

David R. Dunlop, Rte. 1, Box 199, Rolla, ND 58367

D'Arcy A. Echols, P.O. Box 532, Broomfield, OH 80020/303-466-7788 (custom)

Jere Eggleston, P.O. Box 50238, Columbia, SC 29250/803-799-3402 (cust.)

Bob Emmons, 238 Robson Road, Grafton, OH 44044 (custom)

Ken Eyster Heritage Gunsmiths Inc., 6441 Bishop Rd., Centerburg, OH 43011/614-625-6131 (cust.)

Reinhart Fajen, Box 338, Warsaw, MO 65355/816-438-5111

N.B. Fashingbauer, P.O. Box 366, Lac Du Flambeau, WI 54538/715-588-7116

Ted Fellowes, Beaver Lodge, 9245 16th Ave. S.W., Seattle WA 98106/206-763-1698

Phil Fischer, 2625 N.E. Multnomah, Portland, OR 97232/503-282-7151 (cust.)

Clyde E. Ficher, Rt. 1, Box 170-M, Victoria, TX 77901

Jerry A. Fisher, 1244-4th Ave. W., Kalispell, MT 59901/406-755-7093

Flaig's Lodge, Millvale, PA 15209

Donald E. Folks. 205 W. Lincoln St., Pontiac, IL 61764/815-844-7901 (custom trap, Skeet, livebird stocks)

Larry L Forster, Box 212, Gwinner, ND 58040/701-678-2475

Freeland's Scope Stands, Inc., 3737 14th Ave., Rock Island, IL 61201/309-788-7449

Dale Goens, Box 224, Cedar Crest, NM 87008

Gordie's Gun Shop, Gordon Mulholland, 1401 Fulton St., Streator, IL 61364/815-672-7202 (cust.)

Gary Goudy, 263 Hedge Rd., Menlo Park, CA 94025/415-322-1338 (cust.)

Gould's Myrtlewood, 1692 N. Dogwood, Coquille, OR 97423 (gun blanks)

Charles E. Grace, 10144 Elk Lake Rd., Williamsburg, MI 49690/616-264-9483

Rolf R. Gruning, 315 Busby Dr., San Antonio, TX 78209

Karl Guenther, 43-32 160th St., Flushing, NY 11372/212-461-7325

Guncraft, Inc., 117 W. Pipeline, Hurst, TX 76053/817-268-2887

The Gunshop, R.D. Wallace, 320 Overland Rd., Prescott, AZ 86301 (custom)

Half Moon Rifle Shop, 490 Halfmoon Rd., Columbia Falls, MT 59912

Harper's Custom Stocks, 928 Lombrano St., San Antonio, TX 78207

Hal Hartley, 147 Blairsfork Rd., Lenoir, NC 28645

Hayes Gunstock Service Co., 914 E. Turner St., Clearwater, FL 33516

Hubert J. Hecht, Waffen-Hecht, 724-K St., Sacramento, CA 95814/916-448-1177

Edward O. Hefti, 300 Fairview, College Station, TX 77840/715-846-4959

Warren Heydenberk, 187 W. Sawmill Rd., Rt. 4, Quakertown, PA 18951/215-536-0798 (custom)

Klaus Hiptmayer, P.O. Box 136, Eastman, Que., J0E 1P0 Canada/514-297-2492

Richard Hodgson, 5589 Arapahoe, Unit 104, Boulder, CO 80301

Hoenig & Rodman, 6521 Morton Dr., Boise, ID 83705/208-375-1116 (stock duplicating machine)

George Hoenig, 6521 Morton Dr., Boise, ID 83705/208-375-1116

Hollis Gun Shop, 917 Rex St., Carlsbad, NM 88220

Paul Jaeger, Inc., 211 Leedom St., Jenkintown, PA 19046/215-884-6920

Johnson Wood Products, I.D. Johnson & Sons, Rte. #1, Strawberry Point, IA 52076/319-933-4930 (blanks)

Monty Kennedy, P.O. Box 214, Kalispell, MT59901/406-857-3596

Don Klein, P.O. Box 277, Camp Douglas, WI 54618/608-427-6948

LeFever Arms Co., Inc., R.D.#1, Box 31, Lee Center-Stokes Rd., Lee Center, NY 13363/315-337-6422

Lenz Firearms Co., 310 River Rd., Eugene, OR 97404/503-689-6900

Stanley Kenvin, 5 Lakeville Lane, Plainview, NY 11803/516-931-0321 (custom)

Philip D. Letiecq, AQ, 18 Wagon Box Rd., P.O. Box 251, Story, WY 82842/307-683-2817

Al Lind, 7821 76th Ave. S. W., Tacoma, WA 98498/206-584-6361 (cust. stockm.)

Earl K. Matsuoka, 2801 Kinohou Pl., Honolulu, HI 96822/808-988-3008 (cust.)

Bill McGuire, 1600 N. Eastmont Ave., East Wenatchee, WA 98801

Gale McMillan, 28638 N. 42 St., Box 7870-Cave Creek Stage, Phoenix, AZ 85020/602-585-4684

Maurer Manchester Arms Inc., 6858 Manchester Rd., Clinton, OH 44216/216-882-3133

John E. Maxson, Box 332, Dumas, TX 79029/806-935-5990 (custom)

Leonard Mews, Spring Rd., Box 242, Hortonville, WI 54944

Robt. U. Milhoan & Son, Rt. 3, Elizabeth, WV 26143

C-D Miller Guns, Purl St., Box 260, St. Onge, SD 57779/605-578-1790

Earl Milliron Custom Guns & Stocks, 1249 N.E. 166th Ave., Portland, OR 97230/503-252-3725

Ted Nicklas, 5504 Hegel Rd., Goodrich, MI 48438/313-797-4493 (custom)

Nelsen's Gun Shop, 501 S. Wilson, Olympia, WA 98501

Oakley and Merkley, Box 2446, Sacramento, CA 95811 (blanks)

Jim Norman, Custom Gunstocks, 11230 Calenda Road, San Diego, CA 92127/714-487-4173

Maurice Ottmar, Box 657, 113 E. Fir, Coulee City, WA 99115/509-632-5717 (cust.)

Pachmayr Gun Works, 1220 S. Grand Ave., Los Angeles, CA 90015 (blanks and custom jobs)

Paulsen Gunstocks, Rte. 71, Box 11, Chinook, MT 59523/406-357-3403 (blanks)

Peterson Mach. Carving, Box 1065, Sun Valley, CA 91352

R. Neal Rice, 5152 Newton, Denver, CO 80221

Richards Micro-Fit Stocks, P.O. Box 1066, Sun Valley, CA 91352 (thumbhole)

Carl Roth, Jr., 4728 Pineridge Ave., Cheyenne, WY 82001/309-634-3958

Matt Row, Lock, Stock 'N Barrel, 8972 East Huntington Dr., San Gabriel, CA 91775/213-287-0051

Royal Arms, 1210 Bert Acosta, El Cajon, CA 92020/714-448-5466

Sanders Cust. Gun Serv., 2358 Tyler Lane, Louisville, KY 40205 (blanks)

Saratoga Arms Co., 1752 N. Pleasantview RD., Pottstown, PA 19464/215-323-8386

Roy Schaefer, 965 W. Hilliard Lane, Eugene, OR 97404/503-688-43333 (blanks)

Schwartz Custom Guns, 9621 Coleman Rd., Haslett, MI 48840/517-339-8939

Shaw's, The Finest in Guns, 9447 W. Lilac Rd., Escondido, CA 92025/714-728-7070

Hank Shows, The Best,1078 Alice Ave., Ukiah, CA 95482/707-462-9060

Walter Shultz, 1752 N. Pleasantview Rd., Pottstown, PA 19464

Sile Dist., 7 Centre Market Pl., New York, NY 10013/213-925-4111 (shotgun stocks)

Six Enterprises, 6564 Hidden Creek Dr., San Jose, CA 95120/408-268-8296 (fiberglass)

Ed Sowers, 8331 DeCelis Pl., Sepulveda, CA 91343 (hydro-coil gunstocks)

Fred D. Speiser, 2229 Dearborn, Missoula, MT 59801/406-549-8133

Sport Service Center, 2364 N. Neva, Chicago, IL 60635/312-889-1114 (custom)

Sportsmen's Equip. Co., 915 W. Washington, San Diego, CA 92103/714-296-1501 (carbine conversions)

Keith Stegall, Box 696, Gunnison, CO 81230

Stinhour Rifles, Box 84, Cragsmoor, NY 12420/914-647-4163

Surf N' Sea, Inc., 62-595 Kam Hwy., Box 268, Haleiwa, HI 96712 (custom gunstocks blanks)

Talmage Enterpr., 43197 E. Whittier, Hemet, CA 92343

Brent L. Umberger, Sportsman's Haven, R.R. 4, Cambridge, OH 43725

Milton van Epps, Rt. 69-A, Parish, NY 13131

John Vest, 6715 Shasta Way, Klamath Falls, OR 97601/503-884-5585 (classic rifles)

Weatherby's, 2781 Firestone, South Gate, CA 90280/213-569-7186

Cecil Weems, Box 657, Mineral Wells, TX 76067

Frank R. Wells, 4025 N. Sabino Canyon Rd., Tucson, AZ 85715/602-887-3559 (custom stocks)

Western Gunstocks Mfg. Co., 550 Valencia School Rd., Aptos, CA 95003

Duane Wiebe, P.O. Box 497, Lotus, CA 95651

Bob Williams, P.O. Box 143, Boonsboro, MD 21713

Williamson-Pate Gunsmith Service, 117 W. Pipeline, Hurst, TX 76053/817-268-2887

Jim Windish, 2510 Dawn Dr., Alexandria, VA 22306/703-765-1994 (walnut blanks)

Robert M. Winter, Box 484, Menno, SD 57045

Mike Yee, 4700-46th Ave. S.W., WA 98116/206-935-3682

Russell R. Zeryp, 1601 Foard Dr., Lynn Ross Manor, Morristown, TN 37814

TARGETS, BULLET & CLAYBIRD TRAPS

Beeman Precision Airguns, 47 Paul Dr., San Rafael, CA 94903/415-472-7121 (airgun targets, silhouettes and traps)

Bulletboard Target Systems Laminations Corp., Box 469, Neenah, WI 54956/414-725-8368

Caswell Equipment Co., Inc., 1221 Marshall St. N.E., Minneapolis, MN 55413/612-379-2000 (target carriers; commercial shooting ranges)

Data-Targ, (See Rocky Mountain Target Co.)

Detroit Bullet Trap Co., 2233 N. Palmer Dr., Schaumburg, IL 60195/312-397-4070

Electro Ballistic Lab., 616 Junipero Serva Blvd., Stanford, CA 94305 (Electronic Trap Boy)

Ellwood Epps Northern Ltd., 210 Worthington St., W.; North Bay, Ont. P1B 3B4, Canada (hand traps)

Gopher Shooter's Supply, Box 278, Faribault, MN 55021 (Lok-A-Leg target holders)

Laminations Corp. ("Bullettrap"), Box 469, Neenah, WI 54956/414-725-8368

Laporte S.A., B.P. 212, 06603 Antibes, France (claybird traps)

Laporte Equipment Inc., 70 rue Martin St., Granby, Queb. J2G 8B3, Canada (claybird traps)

MCM (Mathalienne de Construction Mecanique), P.O. Box 18, 17160 Matha, France (claybird traps)

Millard F. Lerch, Box 163, 10842 Front St., Mokena, IL 60448 (bullet target)

National Target Co., 4960 Wyaconda Rd., Rockville, MD 20852

Outers Laboratories, Inc., Rte. 2, Onalaska, WI 54650/608-783-1515 (claybird traps)

Peterson Label Co., P.O. Box 186, 23 Sullivan Dr., Redding Ridge, CT 06876/203-938-2349 (paste-ons; Targ-Dots)

Professional Tape Co., 355 E. Burlington Rd., Riverside, IL 60546 (Time Labels)

Recreation Prods. Res. Inc., 158 Franklin Ave., Ridgewood, NJ 07450 (Butts Bullet trap)

Remington Arms Co., Bridgeport, CT 06602 (claybird traps)

Reproductions West, Box 6765, Burbank, CA 91510 (silhouette targets)

Rocky Mountain Target Co., P.O. Box 700, Black Hawk, SD 57718/605-787-5946 (Data-Targ)

Scientific Prod. Corp., 426 Swann Ave., Alexandria, VA 22301 (Targeteer)

Sheridan Products, Inc., 3205 Sheridan, Racine, WI 54303 (traps)

South West Metallic Silhouettes, P.O. Box 476, Uvalde, TX 78801

Time Products Co., (See Prof. Tape Co.)

Trius Prod., Box 25, Cleves, OH 45002 (claybird, can thrower)

U.S. Repeating Arms Co., P.O. Box 30-300, New Haven, CT 06511/203-789-5000 (claybird traps)

Winchester, Olin Corp., 120 Long Ridge Rd., Stamford, CT 06904

TAXIDERMY

Jack Atcheson & Sons, Inc., 3210 Ottawa St., Butte, MT 59701

Dough's Taxidermy Studio, Doug Domedion, 2027 Lockport-Olcott Rd., Burt, NY 14028/716-625-8377 (deer head specialist)

Jonas Bros., Inc., 1037 Broadway, Denver, CO 80203 (catlg. $2)

Kulis Freeze-Dry Taxidermy, 725 Broadway Ave., Bedford, OH 44146

Mark D. Parker, 1233 Sherman Dr., Longmont, CO 80501/303-772-0214

TRAP & SKEET SHOOTERS EQUIP.

D&H Prods. Co., Inc., P.O. Box 22, Glenshaw, PA 15116/412-443-2190 (snap shell)

Griggs Recreational Prods. Inc., 200 S. Main, Twin Bridges, MT 59754/406-684-5202 (recoil redirector)

Ken Eyster Heritage Gunsmiths, Inc., 6441 Bishop Rd., Centerburg, OH 43011/614-625-6131 (shotgun competition choking)

LaPorte S.A., B.P. 212, Pont de la Brague, 06603 Antibes, France (traps, claybird)

LaPorte Equipment Inc., 70 Rue Martin St., Granby, Queb. J2G 8B3, Canada (claybird traps)

MCM (Mathalienne de Construction de Mecanique), P.O. Box 18, 17160 Matha, France (claybird traps)

Wm. J. Mittler, 290 Moore Dr., Boulder Creek, CA 95006 (shotgun choke specialist)

Multi-Gauge Enterprises, 433 W. Foothill Blvd., Monrovia, CA 91061/213-358-4549; 357-6117 (shotgun specialists)

William J. Mittler, 290 Moore Dr., Boulder Creek, CA 95006/408-338-3376 (shotgun repairs)

Outers Laboratories, Inc., Route 2, Onalaska, WI 54650/608-783-1515 (trap, claybird)

Purbaugh & Sons (See Multi-Gauge) (shotgun barrel inserts)

Remington Arms Co., P.O. Box 1939, Bridgeport, Ct. 06601 (trap, claybird)

Super Pigeon Corp., P.O. Box 428, Princeton, MN 55371 (claybird target)

Daniel Titus, 872 Penn St., Bryn Mawr, PA 19010 (hullbag)

Trius Products, Box 25, Cleves, OH 45002 (can thrower; trap, claybird)

Winchester-Western, New Haven, CT 06504 (trap, claybird)

TRIGGERS, RELATED EQUIP.

Ametek, Hunter Spring Div., One Spring Ave., Hatfield, PA 19440/215-822-2971 (trigger gauge)

NOC, Cadillac Industrial Park, 1610 Corwin St., Cadillac, MI 49601/616-775-3425 (triggers)

M.H. Canjar Co., 500 E. 45th Ave., Denver, CO 80216/303-623-5777 (triggers)

Central Specialties Co., 6030 Northwest Hwy., Chicago,IL 60631/312-774-5000 (trigger lock)

Custom Products, 686 Baldwin St., Meadville, PA 16335/814-724-7045 (trigger guard)

Dayton-Traister Co., 9322-900th West, P.O. Box 593, Oak Harbor, WA 98277/206-675-5375 (triggers)

Electronic Trigger Systems, 4124 Thrushwood Lane, Minnetonka MN 55343/612-935-7829

Flaig's, Babcock Blvd. & Thompson Run Rd., Millvale, PA 15209 (trigger shoes)

Franklin C. Green, (See Electronic Trigg. System)

Bill Holmes, Rt. 2, Box 242, Fayetteville, AR 72701/501-521-8958 (trigger release)

Michaels of Oregon Co., P.O. Box 13010, Portland, OR 97213/503-255-6890 (trigger guards)

Miller Single Trigger Mfg. Co., R.D. 1, Box 99, Millersburg, PA 17061/717-692-3704

Viggo Miller, P.O. Box 4181, Omaha, NB 68104 (trigger attachment)

Ohaus Corp., 29 Hanover Rd., Florham Park, NJ 07932 (trigger pull gauge)

Pachmayr Gun Works, 1220 S. Grand Ave., Los Angeles, CA 90015 (trigger shoe)

Pacific Tool Co., P.O. Box 2048, Ordnance Plant Rd., Grand Island, NE 68801 (trigger shoe)

Richland Arms Co., 321 W. Adrian St., Blissfield, MI 49228 (trigger pull gauge)

Sport Service Center, 2364 N. Neva, Chicago, IL 60635 (release triggers)

Timney Mfg. Co., 3106 W. Thomas Rd., Suite 1104, Phoenix, AZ 85017/602-269-6937 (triggers)

Melvin Tyler, 1326 W. Britton Ave., Oklahoma City, OK 73114 (trigger shoe)

Williams Gun Sight Co., 7389 Lapeer Rd., Davison, MI 48423 (trigger shoe)

SPECIAL OFFER FOR BOOK CLUB MEMBERS

Save $10 on these versatile Stellar 7 X 35 Binoculars

They're ideal all-purpose binoculars — good for a wide range of outdoor activities from football games to bird watching.

Look at these features:

☐ **Fully coated optics.** Both lenses and prisms are coated to give them maximum light-gathering power and to insure bright, clear, sharp images.

☐ **Quick, accurate focusing.** A right-eye adjustment compensates for differences in vision of the two eyes. A center focusing wheel permits fast adjustment.

☐ **Magnification.** "7 X" refers to the magnifying power of the binoculars. It means an object 700 feet away will appear to be only 100 feet away. "35" refers to the diameter in millimeters of the objective lenses, which determines the amount of light admitted. The larger the lenses, the greater the amount of light and the later in the evening you can use the binoculars.

☐ **Field of View.** The Stellar Binoculars provide a 393-foot field of view at 1000 yards.

☐ **Weight.** 21½ ounces.

The binoculars come in a soft vinyl case with carrying strap. You also get a shoulder strap and four lens covers.

Suggested Retail Price $49.95. Your Club Price only

$39.95
plus delivery and handling

Stellar 7 X 35 Binoculars are fully guaranteed against any defects in workmanship.

TO GET YOUR BINOCULARS, JUST SEND YOUR ORDER TO: BOOK CLUB P.O. BOX 2044, LATHAM, N.Y. 12111

Ask for STELLAR BINOCULARS, NO. 7000, and enclose your check or money order for $39.95 plus $3.10 for delivery and handling and we'll send you your binoculars right away.